ENCYCLOPEDIA OF THE RENAISSANCE

Michelangelo. *Last Judgment.* Michelangelo painted the *Last Judgment* in the Sistine Chapel in the Vatican from 1536 to 1541. [See the entry on Michelangelo in this volume.] VATICAN MUSEUMS AND GALLERIES, VATICAN CITY/THE BRIDGEMAN ART LIBRARY

ENCYCLOPEDIA OF THE

RENAISSANCE

Paul F. Grendler

Editor in Chief

PUBLISHED IN ASSOCIATION WITH
THE RENAISSANCE SOCIETY OF AMERICA

VOLUME 4

Machiavelli – Petrarchism

CHARLES SCRIBNER'S SONS

An Imprint of The Gale Group

NEW YORK

Charles Scribner's Sons
1633 Broadway
New York, New York 10019

1 3 5 7 9 11 13 15 17 19   20 18 16 14 12 10 8 6 4 2

PRINTED IN THE UNITED STATES OF AMERICA

Library of Congress Cataloging-in-Publication Data
Encyclopedia of the Renaissance / Paul F. Grendler, editor in chief.
      p. cm.
      Includes bibliographical references and index.
      ISBN 0-684-80514-6 (set) — ISBN 0-684-80508-1 (v. 1) — ISBN 0-684-80509-X (v. 2)
      — ISBN 0-684-80510-3 (v. 3) — ISBN 0-684-80511-1 (v. 4) — ISBN 0-684-80512-X (v.
      5) — ISBN 0-684-80513-8 (v. 6)
      1. Renaissance—Encyclopedias.   I. Grendler, Paul F.   II. Renaissance Society of
      America.
      CB361.E52   1999
      940.2′3′03—dc21   99-048290

The paper used in this publication meets the requirements of ANSI/NISO Z39.48-1992
(Permanence of Paper).

The typeface used in this book is ITC Garamond, a version of a typeface attributed to the
French publisher and type founder Claude Garamond (c. 1480–1561).

CONTENTS OF OTHER VOLUMES

COMMON ABBREVIATIONS
USED IN THIS WORK

A.D.	*Anno Domini,* in the year of the Lord
A.H.	*Anno Hegirae,* in the year of the Hegira
b.	born
B.C.	before Christ
B.C.E.	before the common era (= B.C.)
c.	*circa,* about, approximately
C.E.	common era (= A.D.)
cf.	*confer,* compare
chap.	chapter
d.	died
D.	Dom, Portuguese honorific
diss.	dissertation
ed.	editor (pl., eds.), edition
e.g.	*exempli gratia,* for example
et al.	*et alii,* and others
etc.	*et cetera,* and so forth
f.	and following (pl., ff.)
fl.	*floruit,* flourished
HRE	Holy Roman Empire, Holy Roman Emperor
ibid.	*ibidem,* in the same place (as the one immediately preceding)
i.e.	*id est,* that is
MS.	manuscript (pl. MSS.)
n.	note
n.d.	no date
no.	number (pl., nos.)
n.p.	no place
n.s.	new series
N.S.	new style, according to the Gregorian calendar
O.F.M.	*Ordo Fratrum Minorum,* Order of Friars Minor; Franciscan
O.P.	*Ordo Predicatorum,* Order of Preachers; Dominican
O.S.	old style, according to the Julian calendar
p.	page (pl., pp.)
pt.	part
rev.	revised
S.	*san, sanctus, santo,* male saint
ser.	series

S.J.	*Societas Jesu,* Society of Jesus; Jesuit
SS.	*sancti, sanctae,* saints; *sanctissima, santissima,* most holy
Sta.	*sancta, santa,* female saint
supp.	supplement
vol.	volume
?	uncertain, possibly, perhaps

ENCYCLOPEDIA OF THE RENAISSANCE

MACHIAVELLI, NICCOLÒ (1469–1527), Florentine statesman and political theorist. [This entry includes four subentries:

The Life of Machiavelli

Born on 3 May 1469 to the lawyer Bernardo Machiavelli and Bartolomea de' Nelli, Niccolò Machiavelli grew up in the Florence of Lorenzo de' Medici and received a humanist education in the Latin authors. His father's friendship with the chancellor Bartolomeo Scala may have provided the young Niccolò with an introduction into the city's humanistic and literary circles. But very little is known of his life before 1498, especially during the dramatic events of the French invasion of Italy and Tuscany, the expulsion of the Medici, and the creation of a broadly based republican government urged on the Florentines by the charismatic Dominican friar Girolamo Savonarola. The few known facts of Machiavelli's early life include his friendship with Lorenzo de' Medici's youngest son, Giuliano, to whom he addressed some poetry and in whom he would later invest many hopes; and his transcription of a humanist edition of Lucretius's *De rerum natura*.

Machiavelli began his political career in June 1498, just after Savonarola's trial and execution. As head of the second chancery, he coordinated Florence's relations with its subject territories, visiting the cities and towns of the dominion and advising the government on particular problems. In July 1498 he also became secretary to the foreign policy magistracy of the Ten, who frequently sent him as an envoy (although never as ambassador, a post reserved for the members of Florence's social elite) to the princes and governments of Italy and Europe. He spent much of the next fourteen years traveling to negotiate agreements, convey messages, gather information, and report anything and everything he heard and saw. Still, he found time for literature (he wrote his two historical poems, the *Decennali,* in 1504 and 1509) and for family life. He was married in 1501 to Marietta Corsini, with whom he had seven children over more than twenty years.

The most important of his early legations and commissions took him frequently to the crisis points of the Florentine dominion: to Pisa, which had rebelled against Florentine rule in 1494, and to the rulers of the unstable Romagna region of north-central Italy, most notably, to Caterina Sforza in Forlì in 1499, and twice in 1502 to Cesare Borgia in Imola and Cesena. As his later writings make clear, the encounters with Borgia made a particularly vivid impression on Machiavelli. Subsequently, he was sent to the papal court of Julius II (in 1503 and 1506), that of Louis XII of France (in 1500, 1504, and 1510), and to the imperial court of Maximilian (in 1507–1508 and again in 1509). Machiavelli's reports to his government sometimes caused controversy because, instead of confining himself to gathering information as some thought he should, he did not hesitate to express unconventional opinions, including his advocacy of an alliance with Borgia and his harsh criticism of the republic's lack of a homegrown military force. But he gained the confidence of Piero Soderini, elected *gonfalonier*-for-life in 1502, with whose support—and over the objections of the upper-class families—he planned, recruited from the dominion, and trained a militia that played an important role in the reconquest of Pisa in 1509. Showered with compliments for his part in the victory, Machiavelli was at the peak of his political career.

But when the French, Florence's most important allies, were chased out of Italy by Swiss intervention on the side of Julius II's anti-French league in 1512, the republic was at the mercy of the pope and Ferdinand of Spain, who sent an army in August to force the removal of the Soderini government. Machiavelli's militia was no match for the mostly Spanish troops who attacked and sacked neighboring Prato, a disaster that resulted in Soderini's resignation, the return of the Medici in September, and the dismantling of the republic's institutions, including the militia. Machiavelli's decade-long collaboration with Soderini put him in a precarious position, and on 7 November he was dismissed from his posts, assessed a heavy fine, and forbidden to travel outside the Florentine dominion for a year. The worst came in February 1513, when he was arrested for suspected complicity in a plot against the Medici. Although there is no evidence that he was involved, he was tortured in an effort to extract information. He begged for help from Giuliano de' Medici in a pair of sonnets, but his release in March was actually part of a general amnesty in celebration of the election of Giuliano's brother Giovanni as Pope Leo X.

With his political career finished, Machiavelli spent much of the next few years at the family's country home at Sant'Andrea in Percussina, a few miles south of Florence. His major contact with the outside world was Francesco Vettori, a longtime friend and Florentine diplomat who had been appointed ambassador to the papal court. From their correspondence in 1513 emerged many of the themes of *Il principe* (trans. *The Prince*), which Machiavelli wrote in the second half of that year (although some scholars believe the text was significantly altered and expanded in either 1515–1516 or 1518). In 1513 and 1514 he hoped that *The Prince* (first "addressed" to Giuliano and later dedicated to Giuliano's nephew, the younger Lorenzo, who assumed command of the regime in Florence in August 1513) might find favor with the Medici and pave the way for his return to political service. But early in 1515 the Medici made it clear that they had no intention of employing him.

Niccolò Machiavelli. Portrait by Santi di Tito in the Palazzo Vecchio, Florence. ALINARI/ART RESOURCE

Machiavelli then turned his energies to a series of major writing projects in a remarkable decade of literary and theoretical productivity. He joined the political discussions in the Rucellai Gardens, and from these talks and his immersion in Roman history emerged the *Discorsi sopra la prima deca di Tito Livio* (Discourses on the first ten books of Livy), most likely written between 1515 and 1517 (although some believe the book was begun in 1513 before *The Prince*). Then came the satirical poem *Asino* (1517); the great comedy *Mandragola* (The Mandrake Root; c. 1518); *Dell'Arte della guerra* (The art of war; 1519–1520); the *Vita di Castruccio Castracani* (Life of Castruccio Castracani; 1520); the *Istorie fiorentine* (Florentine histories; 1520–1524); another comedy, *Clizia* (1525); the novella *Belfagor* (of uncertain date); some poetry; and many shorter political works, including the *Discursus florentinarum rerum post mortem iunioris Laurentii Medices* (Discourse on Florentine affairs after the death of the younger Lorenzo; 1519–1520).

Machiavelli wrote the *Florentine Histories* under a contract from the University of Florence that was approved by Cardinal Giulio de' Medici, soon to be

Pope Clement VII, to whom he dedicated and presented the work in 1525. This partial reconciliation with the Medici opened the door to other opportunities for occasional employment and minor public service, and to the publication in 1521 of the *Art of War*. In these years Machiavelli and Francesco Guicciardini, the historian and governor of papal territories under the Medici, became friends and exchanged some memorable letters. In 1526 Clement asked Machiavelli's advice about Florentine fortifications, and the discussions led to the creation of a magistracy with Machiavelli as its secretary. Once again, as in the old days, he traveled around central Italy inspecting fortifications and troops. In the spring of 1527 the Florentines drove out the Medici one last time and restored the republican constitution of 1494–1512. Ironically, Machiavelli's recent reconciliation with the Medici now made him suspect to the republicans, even though his writings were and remain the greatest theoretical treatment of republicanism in the Renaissance. But fate left him little time to ponder such ironies. He fell ill and died on 21 June 1527.

BIBLIOGRAPHY

Primary Works

Machiavelli and His Friends: Their Personal Correspondence. Translated and edited by James B. Atkinson and David Sices. DeKalb, Ill., 1996. Excellent translations of the letters by and to Machiavelli, set in a rich biographical framework.

Machiavelli, Niccolò. *Legazioni, commissarie, scritti di governo.* 4 vols. Edited by Fredi Chiappelli and Jean-Jacques Marchand. Bari, Italy, 1971–1985. Definitive editions of the chancery documents by and to Machiavelli, to 1505.

Secondary Works

De Grazia, Sebastian. *Machiavelli in Hell.* Princeton, N.J., 1989. A provocative portrait of Machiavelli as a Christian moralist.

Hale, J. R. *Machiavelli and Renaissance Italy.* London, 1961. Still an excellent introduction, especially to the political and diplomatic context.

Najemy, John M. *Between Friends: Discourses of Power and Desire in the Machiavelli-Vettori Letters of 1513–1515.* Princeton, N.J., 1993. A study of the famous correspondence in the two years of Machiavelli's crisis and its role in his emergence as a writer and political thinker.

Ridolfi, Roberto. *The Life of Niccolò Machiavelli.* Translated by Cecil Grayson. Chicago, 1963. A translation of the second edition of the standard biography, which Ridolfi kept revising through a seventh Italian edition (Florence, 1978).

JOHN M. NAJEMY

The Political Theorist

In the years of his diplomatic and chancery work for the Florentine republic (1498–1512), Niccolò Machiavelli occasionally displayed his interest in a number of theoretical questions: the sometimes unfath-omable relationship in politics between means and ends; the problem of fortune, free will, and the possibilities and limits of effective human action; and the necessity for any government to possess and control its own armed forces. Just before he entered the chancery in 1498, Machiavelli sardonically described the skill with which the Dominican preacher Girolamo Savonarola, deftly exploiting the religious sensibilities of his listeners, adjusted his message in response to quickly changing political circumstances. The spectacle of Cesare Borgia's meteoric rise and fall provided an early occasion for pondering the dangers of excessive dependence on fortune.

The equation of fortune with lack of autonomy, in particular with dangerous dependence on military strength that is not one's own, became a basic presupposition of Machiavelli's early thought. Watching Pope Julius II march into Perugia in 1506 without an adequate armed force, and in the face of well-armed enemies who chose not to stop him, Machiavelli was moved to wonder whether any meaningful correlation could be postulated between means and outcomes. The pope's risky action ought to have failed, and Machiavelli confessed his puzzlement about why "opposing methods sometimes yield the same result." He adduced the contrasting examples of Hannibal and Scipio, both great generals who kept their armies united, the one with cruelty and treachery, the other with compassion and loyalty. Machiavelli ventured the opinion that nature provides each person with a different temperament and imagination, which never change, whereas times and circumstances constantly vary. If one's way of proceeding matches the times, the result is success and good fortune; failure results when one's way of proceeding does not correspond to what the times require. In these years, Machiavelli frequently presupposed the immobility of individual natures and figured fortune as the inevitable but unpredictable mutability of the times.

Despite the unresolved problem of fortune, Machiavelli never ceased preaching the need for arms to the governors of the republic, which had depended on mercenaries for more than a century. Arguing that "without arms cities come either to ruin or to servitude," he urged the government to recruit and train its own armed force, to regard as a potential enemy anyone against whom it could not defend the city, and not to expect the inhabitants of the subject territories to be loyal to a government incapable of either punishing or defending them. He cited the exemplary severity of the Romans as the model to be imitated—a conviction that would dominate his major works and which implicitly rejected the then fashionable praise of Venice.

The Prince.   The frequent recurrence of these themes in Machiavelli's dispatches, letters, memoranda, and poems provides glimpses of the theoretical, historical, and even philosophical levels of his thinking in the years of political service. But there is no persuasive evidence of any attempt to organize his occasional reflections in systematic fashion before 1513. But only with the enforced leisure that followed the collapse of the republic, the return of the Medici, and Machiavelli's removal from his posts did he have the opportunity and perhaps the incentive to write more systematically about politics. Although motivated in part by the wish to find favor with the Medici and thereby to return to active political work, at a deeper level Machiavelli's turn to political theory was spurred by his grief over Italy's ongoing catastrophe and by the need to find a solution grounded in a new understanding of politics. In the famous correspondence of 1513 with Francesco Vettori, Machiavelli's thought assumed the form that led to _Il principe_ (_The Prince;_ written in the second half of 1513 and first published in 1532).

Against Vettori's skepticism, which asserted the bewildering mutability of politics (in terms that were actually closer to Machiavelli's own early ideas), Machiavelli defended the intelligibility of politics: princes could know their own minds and achieve their purposes. Machiavelli even asserted (in one of these letters) that successful princes were those who kept observers and subjects baffled with the unpredictability of their actions—an idea he worked into chapter 21 of _The Prince._ For a clever prince even apparent incoherence could be part of an intelligible strategy. In other letters of the same year Machiavelli compared the disunity and military weakness of Italy with the recent military successes of the Swiss. He reiterated his view that the best armies are those of self-armed peoples like the Swiss, whom he briefly imagined as the new Romans, but he also began to speculate about the kind of military leader, or prince, who could infuse the necessary "spirit and discipline" into peoples who lacked arms. This ability he now associated with _virtù._ Machiavelli was ready to invent his prince as the personification of _virtù,_ whose charisma, craftiness, and military skill could redeem a lacerated and beaten Italy.

In _The Prince,_ Machiavelli elaborated the concept of _virtù_ in the context of the innovatory political action of "new princes" who achieve power without traditional forms of legitimation. From the very first chapter, utilizing the rhetorical technique of binary oppositions, Machiavelli argues that a new prince can acquire power with his own arms (_virtù_) or with those of others (_fortuna_). After distinguishing hereditary principalities from new ones (chap. 2), he reviews the different kinds of new principalities (chaps. 3–11). In chapter 6 he argues that the greatest examples of "new princes" are the founders of states—he names Moses, Cyrus, Romulus, and Theseus—who depended less on fortune and more on their own _virtù_ and thus on their own arms. This allowed them to secure their rule and to accomplish the most difficult and dangerous of all things any ruler can attempt, the introduction of new institutions ("new methods and orders"). Machiavelli compares these ancient and mythical exemplars of _virtù_ with Girolamo Savonarola, the republican reformer who "failed in his new orders" because he lacked the force—the arms—he needed to "keep firm" the loyalties of his followers.

Chapter 7 applies this argument to an analysis of the career of Cesare Borgia (c. 1476–1507), who relied excessively on the power of his father, Pope Alexander VI, and thus on fortune. Within these limits, Machiavelli asserts, Borgia in fact did everything he could to consolidate his power and win the support of the people of the Romagna: he brought peace to a lawless region; successfully shifted the blame for the necessary severity of his rule to his lieutenant, whom he even had killed; and ruthlessly eliminated former allies who were about to betray him. But, Machiavelli argues, despite all these well-calculated and skillfully executed actions, Borgia nonetheless failed because of his reliance on the power and money of his father. Borgia is thus not the hero of _The Prince_ or its model new prince: his story functions as a cautionary tale of how even the greatest skill and shrewdness will fall short of success in the absence of military power controlled by the prince himself. Indeed, the heart of _The Prince_ (chaps. 12–14) is devoted to the indispensable military foundation of a successful prince's power. Here Machiavelli reiterates his long-standing polemic against mercenaries and auxiliaries as the chief cause of Italy's ruin. Strong states, whether republics or principalities, must have their own arms, and successful princes must devote all their attention and energies to the art of war and to the organization and training of their forces.

Chapters 15 to 23 of _The Prince_ deal with the ways in which a prince should conduct himself vis-à-vis his subjects, advisers, and other princes. These are the work's most controversial chapters because their central argument is that a successful prince should, whenever necessary, be willing to disregard conventional norms of behavior and morality in order to maintain his power. Declaring his intention to discuss the "effectual truth of things" in place of things "imagined," Machiavelli asserts (chap. 15) that a prince "must learn to be able not to be good and must use or not use such knowledge as necessity demands." The prince should ignore the traditional virtue of liberality in order not to have to tax his subjects excessively (chap. 16). He must exercise cruelty whenever compassion and leniency would only make problems worse. Thus he should base his power more on the fear than on the love of his subjects (chap. 17). It will sometimes be necessary to break agreements, and, in general, while it is useful for a prince to appear to have all the traditional virtues recommended for rulers (compassion, good faith, integrity, humanity, and respect for religion), he must decide when it will serve his purposes to adhere to these norms and when to ignore them (chap. 18). Above all, a prince must avoid bringing on himself the contempt and hatred of his subjects (chap. 19). In these chapters Machiavelli hypothesizes a prince who understands the effective connections between words and deeds better than his subjects, better even than his advisers, whom he must carefully control. Whereas most people remain trapped by the mere appearances of things or by the conventions of moral and political rhetoric, Machiavelli's prince somehow knows the real results of different modes of conduct and policy, and both uses language and sees causes and effects beyond ordinary human capacity. Machiavelli's constant impulse in *The Prince* is to remove the prince's dependence on the subjects he rules and to imagine a prince who is secure in the possession of his state.

The conclusion of *The Prince* is a call to action. Chapter 24 declares that the princes of Italy have lost their states and power because they lacked the *virtù* to arm themselves and their people and thus let themselves become contemptible. Chapter 25 argues against the opinion that fortune inevitably controls all human endeavors—a view that Machiavelli admits he once shared—but strangely returns to the notion of immutable individual natures and the impossibility of adjusting to changing times. With no apparent rational exit from the dilemma of fortune, Machiavelli concludes this chapter with the dramatic personification of fortune as a woman, who, because she is a woman and a friend of the young, will let herself be contained by those whose mode of action is more impetuous than cautious.

The last chapter grounds the possibility for effective action (and thus the intelligibility of politics) in the providentialistic reading of history adumbrated in chapter 6. Machiavelli proclaims that the historical moment is indeed propitious for the appearance of a "new prince" and for the "redemption" of Italy, because Italy's condition had reached the worst that could be imagined: complete degradation is always the precondition for the appearance of a "redeemer." The echo of the language and structure of the Christian story of salvation at the end of a book that rejects or ignores the traditional moral and religious framework of politics is striking. So is the faith that Machiavelli is willing to place in the Medici. Italy's redeemer, he claims, can emerge from their family and furnish the required *virtù* to achieve military reform, introduce new institutions, expel the barbarous foreigners occupying the peninsula, and win the love of all Italians by carrying out this great redemptive project. The passionate appeal to the Medici to become the princes redeeming a suffering Italy is an indication of the desperation Machiavelli felt in this bleakest year of his life.

Discourses on the First Ten Books of Livy. Sometime between 1514 and 1515, Machiavelli turned to different problems in a very different kind of book, in which he set aside the dreams of political redemption in favor of a more historical inquiry into the factors behind the strengths and weaknesses of states. In *Discorsi sopra la prima deca di Tito Livio* (first published 1531; trans. *Discourses on the First Ten Books of Livy*) he focuses largely on republics, and in particular the Roman republic, which he upheld as a model and source of lessons and insights for modern states. But the *Discourses* also revisit many of the themes of *The Prince* in ways that suggest that Machiavelli was quite deliberately distancing himself from some of the central assumptions of the earlier work. For example, near the beginning of the *Discourses* (1.2) he undermines the very notion of the stability of categories and terms and his earlier use of binary oppositions by asserting that the traditional types of government and their paired opposites (principality/tyranny; rule of the best/rule of the few; popular rule/anarchy) do not represent stable alternatives, because "each of them is so similar to the one that is closest to it that they easily jump from the one to the other." Thus no constitution can last for very long because there is "no remedy to prevent it from slipping into its contrary, on account of the similarity of the virtue [the good kind of a government] and the vice [the bad kind] in such cases." This is a universe of permanent instability in the meanings of terms, in the forms of governments, and in the results of political action. The source of this instability is history itself, the inexorable effect of time on all things. Machiavelli was now drawn to historians (Livy, Sallust, Plutarch, and others), to theories of cyclical change (above all the cycle of constitutions, or anacyclosis, that he encountered in Polybius), and to poets (in particular Ovid and Lucretius) who helped him ponder the mysteries of time and change.

In similar fashion Machiavelli deconstructs the myth of the prince-redeemer. Although at first he declares that a well-organized state is almost always the work of one man, he quickly qualifies this by adding that the preservation of such a state must be the work of many (1.9) and that "States that depend exclusively on the *virtù* of a single man do not last very long, because his *virtù* dies with him. . . . Thus, the health of a republic or a kingdom does not consist in having a prince who prudently governs it during his lifetime, but rather in having one who organizes it in such a way that it maintains itself once he dies." Returning to the central hypothesis of *The Prince*—the possibility of redemptive action by one man who uses violence and arms because lawful methods no longer suffice—Machiavelli now claims (1.18) that this is nearly impossible because a "good man" rarely brings himself to use violent methods to gain power, whereas a "bad man" who has no such hesitations about gaining power with violence would seldom think of employing his power for the good end of reforming the state. The prince-redeemer was now a psychological improbability for Machiavelli.

Within this transformed perspective, Machiavelli approaches the early history of Rome and asks how and why this greatest of all republics became so powerful. His answers in the *Discourses* gradually diminish the role of solitary founders and innovators and bring into focus the political, religious, and military institutions, or, in Machiavelli's language, the *ordini*, on which the life and vigor of states depend. He now emphasizes the multiplicity of lawgivers that Rome had, including Romulus, who made Rome a constitutional monarchy by giving it a senate; Numa, who gave Rome its religious institutions; Brutus, who transformed Rome into a republic to which he was so devoted that he agreed to the execution of his own sons when they plotted to restore the monarchy; and many others who intervened at decisive moments to reform or defend the republic and to expand its power. Machiavelli appropriated these mostly legendary figures as emblems of the principles he saw as fundamental to a healthy republic: the sanctity of the laws, religious observance, severity in punishing domestic enemies, and military valor against foreign enemies. But it was the *ordini* themselves that were the real foundation of Rome's *virtù*, a term that now acquires the sense of collective power, strength, and liberty.

In his most revolutionary break with the whole tradition of political thought that preceded him, Machiavelli argued that the chief cause of Roman strength and freedom lay in the conflicts between the city's social classes. In every state, he wrote, the nobles (*grandi*) and the plebeians or people (*plebe, popolo*) are natural enemies: the former seek to rule while the latter only seek not to be oppressed. Early in Rome's history, the people gained a share of power in the office of the tribunes, which "impeded the insolence of the nobles" (1.3). The competition between the two classes was thus channeled through constitutional structures and gave rise to debates and laws that prevented the hegemony of either class. The people's share of power also extended to military organization: the conquering armies of the early republic came from the ever growing ranks of its own armed citizens. For Machiavelli, Rome was the model republic above all because it was organized for expansion, and protected its liberty, through the prominent role given to the plebs. Venice, by contrast, he saw as a republic unfit for expansion because it excluded the people from both political power and the army (1.4–6).

In well-organized republics and kingdoms, according to the *Discourses*, citizens live in freedom protected by laws, by open and public debates in which they do not fear to speak their opinions, and by procedures that allow for bringing charges against citizens who violate these foundations of civic life (1.7). Authority, whether civil or military, must remain public, and the state must always have the power to prosecute individuals, including military commanders, who transgress their mandates or abuse their power. Machiavelli argues that Rome's religion was crucial to the strength of its laws and arms because the sanctity of oaths, reverence for auguries, and fearsome rituals of sacrifice instilled respect for laws among citizens and obedience to military commanders. Roman religion was in his view invented and interpreted by an elite for the purposes of strengthening the allegiance of citizens to the state and increasing their willingness to make sacrifices for the republic and its expansion (1.11–15). This understanding of the political importance of Roman religion led Machiavelli to contrast it with the deleterious effects of Christianity and the Roman Church, which he held responsible for weakening modern states by glorifying humility and contemplation rather than civic honor and military glory, thus depriving the modern Christian world of the kind of religion that can make states strong and free (1.12 and 2.2).

A healthy republic's military *ordini* are no less important than its political and religious institutions. Machiavelli's most consistently argued conviction (*Discourses* 1.21; 2.10; 2.18; and many other chapters, as well as in *The Prince* and the *Art of War*) was that mercenaries were a disaster for Italy. He insisted that good soldiers must be citizens (not professional or career soldiers) and conversely that good citizens had to be soldiers. Machiavelli elaborated these views at greater length in his dialogue *Arte della guerra* (written c. 1519–1520; trans. *Art of War*), in which, paradoxically and perhaps ironically, the professional soldier Fabrizio Colonna argues for the superiority of the Roman approach to war, even if modern conditions no longer permit the exact imitation of Roman methods. In the *Discourses* Machiavelli praises the early Roman command structure and the great degree of freedom that the consuls enjoyed (2.33). But he also sees the apparently inevitable prolongation of military commands that came with the expansion of consular authority as one of the main causes of the later professionalization of Rome's military force and thus of its ultimate decline (3.24). Paradoxically, Rome's great expansion was the beginning of its downfall.

The great evil, according to Machiavelli, that states should do everything to avoid is the degeneration of civic life into private feuding and factionalism, in which men feel greater loyalty to individuals—whether party bosses or military commanders—than to the state or republic. Rome preserved the health of its *ordini* until the Gracchi led the plebeians astray by encouraging them to pursue land reforms that would have upset the tense equilibrium between the classes (1.37). The nobles preferred civil war to any compromise on this issue, and the result was the growth of private armies, networks of favor and influence, and the rise of powerful individuals who acquired more power than the public magistrates. This is the condition that Machiavelli calls "corruption," or "disorder" (*disordine*)—literally, the disintegration of the *ordini* and of public authority (1.17–18). In Rome it led to factional wars and ultimately to the emergence of the strongest of the factional leaders as tyrants and emperors. From the same political competition between classes and

the same military might that made Rome powerful came the seeds of its undoing and the causes of its decline. As he wrote at the beginning of the work, nothing can prevent things from "slipping into their contraries."

The *Florentine Histories*. In many pages of the *Discourses* and in *Istorie fiorentine* (1520–1524; trans. *Florentine Histories*) Machiavelli applies the analytical framework of *ordini* and social conflict to the experience of modern republics, and most saliently to Florence. He saw much *virtù* in thirteenth-century Florence, when as an armed people the Florentines successfully combined republican liberty with military might and expanding power in Tuscany. But he argues that by the early fifteenth century factionalism had infested and corrupted Florentine political life and paved the way for the rise of powerful private individuals not unlike those who ruined Rome (*Discourses* 1.33; *Histories* 7.1). He was harshly critical of the Florentine republic for its endemic factionalism, for its reliance on mercenaries, for the hegemonic ambitions of its elite of great families, and for the exaggerated reaction of the mercantile middle class, which deprived the upper class of much of its political power and all of its military function (*Histories* 3.1). Fearful of putting arms in the hands of either the elite or the masses, the middle class turned Florence into an unarmed republic. In some carefully written pages in which he stopped short of openly calling them tyrants, Machiavelli made clear his view of the rise of the Medici family as evidence of the weakening of Florentine *ordini* and of the republic's fatal dependence on their money and patronage (*Histories* 4.27). Dependence on the alleged *virtù* of skillful political leaders like the Medici (and he did not deny their skills) now became for Machiavelli the surest sign of political corruption and degeneration (*Histories* 4.1). Having once seen them as potential redeemers of Italy, he now viewed the Medici as party bosses whose power was a measure of the corruption of republican institutions.

The dreams of political redemption associated with charismatic princely leadership gradually gave way in Machiavelli's thought to an emphasis on the need for political structures and collective attitudes capable of protecting the health of public institutions, laws, liberty, and citizen participation in politics and the military. At the same time the framework of his political theorizing became progressively more historical and more accepting of the irony that all forms of government contain the seeds of their endlessly cyclical metamorphosis.

See also **Virtù.**

BIBLIOGRAPHY

Primary Works

Atkinson, James B. *Niccolò Machiavelli: The Prince.* Indianapolis, Ind., 1976. Excellent translation and valuable notes.

Gilbert, Allan, trans. *Niccolò Machiavelli: The Chief Works and Others.* 3 vols. Durham, N.C., 1965. Reprint, 1989. There is no adequately annotated English translation of either the *Art of War* or the *Florentine Histories,* but the translations in these volumes are serviceable.

Martelli, Mario, ed. *Niccolò Machiavelli: Tutte le opere.* Florence, 1971. The best single-volume edition of the original texts.

Walker, Leslie J. *The Discourses of Niccolò Machiavelli.* Introduction and appendices by Cecil H. Clough. 2 vols. London, 1975. The second volume is especially valuable for its extensive notes and analysis of sources.

Secondary Works

Baron, Hans. *In Search of Florentine Civic Humanism: Essays on the Transition from Medieval to Modern Thought.* 2 vols. Princeton, N.J., 1988. See "Machiavelli the Republican Citizen and Author of *The Prince,*" vol. 2, pages 101–151. A fundamental clarification of the major issues in Machiavelli scholarship in the nineteenth and first half of the twentieth centuries; first published in the *English Historical Review* in 1961.

Bock, Gisela, Quentin Skinner, and Maurizio Viroli, eds. *Machiavelli and Republicanism.* Cambridge, U.K., 1990. Essays on the republican dimension of Machiavelli's thought in the context of contemporary republican experience.

Gilbert, Felix. *Machiavelli and Guicciardini: Politics and History in Sixteenth-Century Florence.* Princeton, N.J., 1965. A summary of several decades of pioneering work on Machiavelli's texts and times.

Mansfield, Harvey C. *Machiavelli's Virtue.* Chicago, 1996. Essays by Leo Strauss's most important intellectual heir among modern students of Machiavelli.

Najemy, John M. *Between Friends: Discourses of Power and Desire in the Machiavelli-Vettori Letters of 1513–1515.* Princeton, N.J., 1993. A close reading of the correspondence that led Machiavelli to—and away from—*The Prince.*

Najemy, John M. "Machiavelli and the Medici: The Lessons of Florentine History." *Renaissance Quarterly* 35 (1982): 551–576. The development of Machiavelli's ideas about Florence's leading family.

Pitkin, Hanna Fenichel. *Fortune Is a Woman: Gender and Politics in the Thought of Niccolò Machiavelli.* Berkeley, Calif., 1984. The first serious feminist interpretation of Machiavelli's images of women and the role of gender in his writings.

Pocock, J. G. A. *The Machiavellian Moment: Florentine Political Thought and the Atlantic Republican Tradition.* Princeton, N.J., 1975. A magisterial analysis, centered on the problem of the search for the significance of republican values and experience in secular time.

Sasso, Gennaro. *Machiavelli e gli antichi e altri saggi* (Machiavelli and the ancients and other essays). 3 vols. Milan, 1987–1988. Brilliant, indispensable studies of Machiavelli's dialogue with antiquity, and many other topics.

Sasso, Gennaro. *Niccolò Machiavelli: Storia del suo pensiero politico* (Niccolò Machiavelli: The history of his political thought). 2d ed. Bologna, Italy, 1980. The most learned and philosophically rigorous reading of Machiavelli's oeuvre in modern times. See also the second volume, *La storiografia* (Historiography). Bologna, Italy, 1993.

Skinner, Quentin. *Machiavelli.* Oxford, 1981. The best short introduction in English.

Whitfield, J. H. *Discourses on Machiavelli.* Cambridge, U.K., 1969. An acute reader's lively essays, at least one of which ("On Machiavelli's Use of *Ordini*") is indispensable.

JOHN M. NAJEMY

The Literary Figure

The status of the literary in the study of Niccolò Machiavelli evolved considerably in the last thirty years of the twentieth century. Traditional accounts of Machiavelli's oeuvre, rooted in nineteenth- and twentieth-century separations of subject matter by discipline, tended to divide it into three sharply distinct areas: the practical diplomatic and political writings, dating from his service as head of the Second Chancellery of the revitalized Florentine republic between 1498 and 1512; his major political, historical, and military writings, composed between the fall of the republic, and the return of the Medici, in 1512 and his death in 1527; and the literary works, which also date, in large part, from 1512 forward. Somewhat less easy to categorize are the ample and fascinating collection of surviving letters from throughout Machiavelli's career and *Discorso o dialogo intorno alla nostra lingua* (Discourse or dialogue concerning our language), whose attribution to Machiavelli has been long debated. In contrast with the traditional scheme of rigidly categorizing Machiavelli's works, late-twentieth-century scholarship emphasized the conceptual and thematic interrelatedness of literary and nonliterary works.

The Literary Works. Machiavelli's formation as a writer and thinker was influenced both by the Latin humanist tradition, which tended to give equal emphasis to the study of classical historical, poetic, and other authors under the general rubric of epideictic rhetoric, and by the powerful Florentine tradition of vernacular literature. Machiavelli wrote extensively in several of the principal literary modes and genres available to him: verse and prose; lyric, dramatic, and narrative forms. Like his other writings, and despite his strong links to classicizing humanism, these literary works were all composed in a colloquially flavored Florentine Italian. The best known are two classically influenced comedies, *Mandragola* (The mandrake root; c. 1517) and *Clizia* (c. 1525), and the prose novella *Belfagor* (dating uncertain), but there are also several poems, finished and unfinished, longer and shorter, mostly in Dantean terza rima, in particular the two *Decennali* (c. 1504 and 1513) and the incomplete *Asino* (The golden ass; c. 1516).

Machiavelli's literary debut (leaving aside some short poetic compositions whose dating is uncertain) was the first *Decennale,* which reviews ten years (1494–1504) of significant events in Florentine political and military history. Written in Dantean terza rima and addressed, with a characteristic mixture of affection and irony, to Florence itself, the *Decennale* offers a tantalizing synthesis of poetic and historical discourse. A second *Decennale,* which would presumably have covered the period 1504–1514, breaks off in 1509 at line 216, after reporting the battle of Agnadello and other events of consequence for the peninsula in the conflict between Venice and the emperor Maximilian I. The *Decennali* give proof of Machiavelli's strong roots in a Florentine vernacular tradition, which includes not only Dante but also fifteenth-century versified chronicles on historical and political topics.

Very different in kind is the unfinished allegorical and satirical dream vision known as *Asino* or *Asino d'oro,* which reflects Machiavelli's knowledge and appropriation of fifteenth-century Latin humanism. The surviving version of *Asino* is composed of eight chapters of between 121 and 151 lines each, again in terza rima, mixing its basic conceit of Apuleian metamorphosis with elements from Dante's *Inferno,* the Circe episode from Homer's *Odyssey,* Plutarch's *Grillus,* and Pliny's *Historia naturalis* (Natural history). This poem combines tantalizing autobiographical references and obscure topical political allegory (particularly the bestiary of chapter 7) and appropriates and transforms moral and spiritual satire and allegory for decidedly nontraditional purposes. To judge by a letter to Luigi Alamanni of 17 December 1517, Machiavelli at one time thought of *Asino* as a major literary endeavor, comparable in some respects to Ludovico Ariosto's just-published *Orlando furioso.* The letter also confirms that the poem dates from relatively early in Machiavelli's period of exclusion from politics.

Historically, *Asino* and the *Decennali* have ceded pride of place to Machiavelli's theatrical compositions, above all *Mandragola.* Early sixteenth-century Italy, anticipating later developments in England, Spain, and France, fostered an explosive revival of comic drama modeled on the Latin classics, especially Plautus and Terence, in the works of Ariosto, Il Bibiena, and others. Machiavelli, too, clearly took the Romans as his point of departure: of his three surviving plays, *Andria* (dating uncertain, though probably early) is a relatively straightforward translation of Terence's comedy of the same name into idiomatic Tuscan, and *Clizia,* written and produced a year or two before Machiavelli's death in 1527, is more loosely adapted from Plautus's *Casina. Mandragola* is another matter. Though elements of the plot conform to the classical model and many of the characters have close affinities to the stock figures of Roman comedy (Ligurio and Siro as parasites, for instance), the most evident models for the play are, on the one hand, Livy's telling of the Lucretia story in *Ab urbe condita* (the subject of Machiavelli's extended commentary in *Discorsi*) and, on the other hand, various Boccaccian novelle (notably *Decameron* 2.9 and 7.7).

Mandragola recounts the tale of Callimaco, who falls in love by hearsay with the beautiful and chaste Lucrezia, the wife of the foolish old braggart Messer Nicia. Aided and abetted by his servant, Siro, the trickster, Ligurio, Lucrezia's corrupt confessor, Fra Timoteo, and even Lucrezia's mother, Sostrata, Callimaco manages to enter Lucrezia's bed with Nicia's full approval. This feat is accomplished by convincing the impotent Nicia that his wife will conceive a child and heir if she takes a potion derived from the mandrake plant but that, since the first one to have sex with her after she takes it will die poisoned, a scapegoat must be found to undergo this sacrifice. The play concludes not with marriage or the reconstitution of an original order, as more typically occurs in *commedia erudita,* but rather with the founding of a new community in which Lucrezia abandons her chastity to a long-term affair with Callimaco, who, with Ligurio, Siro, and the others, becomes a permanent parasitic fixture in the household of the unwitting Nicia.

Mandragola was composed in the late 1510s, contemporaneously with, or just subsequent to, the great political and historical works of Machiavelli's early exile. The author's prologue presents it as a second best not only to active employment in the political realm but also to writing of a more significant kind, which, however, has failed to gain him employment or other rewards. In several respects, this play deploys the themes and problems of Machiavelli's nonliterary works: it stages in a positive light the alternative political morality embodied in *Il principe* (The Prince; 1513); it works out certain categories—virtue and fortune, transformation and adaptation—basic to his political thought; and it satirizes the degraded politics and morals of Florence by comparing them with the ideal virtue of Livy's republican Rome. The comedy is indicative of Machiavelli's programmatic fusion of humanist classicism with the vernacular literary tradition of Florence and his transformative appropriation and adaptation of materials from both of these traditions to the special circumstances of the Italian and Florentine crisis of the early sixteenth century.

Clizia, also an adaptation and transposition of a classical comedy, though not without Boccaccian elements, has typically been judged a far weaker effort than *Mandragola.* It depicts the grotesque rivalry of an aging father, Nicomaco, with his son, Cleandro, for the love of a beautiful young ward of the household, Clizia, and the violent and obscene trick that Nicomaco's long-suffering wife, Sofronia (whose name makes her a quasi-allegorical embodiment of the virtue of temperance), employs to restore Nicomaco to his former, virtuous self. It has long been recognized that there is a strong, and strongly elegiac, autobiographical element embedded in Nicomaco, whose name echoes his author's.

Machiavelli's links to the tradition of the novella are clear in the plays but they have their fullest embodiment in the satirical prose of *Belfagor arcidiavolo, o, Il demonio che prese moglie* (Belfagor the arch-demon, or, the devil who took a wife). *Belfagor* derives from a central text of the antifeminist tradition, Jehan Le Fèvre's *Les lamentations de Matheolus* (The lamentations of Matheolus). Attempting to determine if it is true that wives cause more suffering to men than hell itself, the titular arch-demon goes to earth, to Florence in fact, to marry, assuming the name Roderigo di Castiglia (with possible allusion to Roderigo Borgia, Pope Alexander VI). His bride, Madonna Onesta dei Donati (the family name of Dante's wife, Gemma), proves "prouder than Lucifer himself," and Belfagor soon resorts to the power of a peasant trickster, Gianmatteo del Brica, to escape from her. Roderigo then rewards Gianmatteo by allowing him to cure the daughters of rich and powerful men of a demonic possession that he himself has effected but simultaneously lays a trap for his rescuer's destruction. The cunning Florentine peasant, however, proves wilier than the devil, frightening him back into hell under threat of reconsignment to his abandoned wife. *Belfagor,* in addition to its explicit antiwoman polemic, presents a series of typical Machiavellian themes: the improvisational abilities and astuteness of the Florentines; the inversion of traditional cosmic order, in which the world above becomes more hellish than hell itself; and the underlying current of satirical political and literary allegory.

Machiavelli's literary production in a strict sense is rounded out by a series of *capitoli* (chapters) on topics central to his thought (fortune, ambition, ingratitude), by a series of carnival songs in the fifteenth-century tradition, and by a number of shorter poems, most notably the two plaintive tailed sonnets written to Giuliano de' Medici when Machiavelli was temporarily incarcerated, and subjected to torture, in 1513 after the Medici restoration.

Boundary Works. Two other works by Machiavelli fall partially under the heading of the literary: the collected letters, which cover a variety of topics, personal, social, and political; and the dialogue on language. The letters, like so many other works of Machiavelli's, bear a clear but idiosyncratic relationship to the classical and humanist epistolary tradition, exemplified most notably by Cicero and Seneca among the Romans and refounded in the fourteenth century by Petrarch in his two collections of letters, *Rerum familiarium libri* (Letters on familiar matters) and *Rerum senilium libri* (Letters of old age). While Machiavelli did not organize his letters into the same kind of crafted collection as Petrarch did, they *were* carefully preserved and display artistry, for example in their careful mirroring of the letters to which they respond, the complex sequences formed among them (especially in the series of missives addressed to Francesco Vettori and Francesco Guicciardini), their elaborate internal structures, and their powerful use of allusion to classical and vernacular poetry.

Discorso o dialogo intorno alla nostra lingua participates (again idiosyncratically) in the "questione della lingua," the debate over the proper form of the Italian language to be used by literary writers. Among the crucial events in the debate were Gian Giorgio Trissino's rediscovery and divulgation (1513) of Dante's unfinished treatise *De vulgari eloquentia* (On eloquence in the vernacular), which had not circulated since its composition in the early fourteenth century, and Pietro Bembo's *Prose della volgar lingua* (Prose writings on the vulgar tongue; 1525). Machiavelli's dialogue takes the form of a polemical introduction followed by a conversation between N. (Niccolò) and D. (Dante), in which N. fiercely attacks the Dantean concept of an illustrious vernacular tied to no specific place in the Italian peninsula but common to all, asserting instead that Dante himself clearly writes in Florentine dialect and defending the value of a locally based linguistic and literary tradition. The dialogue, with its insistence on using the language that is actually spoken in Florence, also constitutes an implicit alternative to Bembo's (hugely successful) advocacy of a classical Florentine, modeled on the works of Petrarch and Boccaccio, as a solution for Italian literary culture. The authenticity of the dialogue has been frequently and hotly contested. Even if it is not by Machiavelli, however, its use of him as a character indicates his status as a major representative of a specifically Florentine linguistic and literary tradition, one that would become increasingly marginalized in the sixteenth century with the rise of a peninsula-wide court system and the effective loss of local political and cultural autonomy throughout Italy.

Literary Elements of the Nonliterary Works. Late twentieth-century interdisciplinary studies emphasized the relations among the various categories of Machiavelli's writing, questioning, though by no means eradicating, the boundaries between the literary works and other emanations of his creative personality. Against this trend, one may note that Machiavelli himself at times designated his literary work as a debased and degrading substitute for his true vocation as a political operative and student of politics and history (as in the prologue to *Mandragola*), and separated the world of imagination and rhetorical ornament from that of the unembellished "effectual truth of things" presented in his political treatises (for example, in the dedicatory letter and chapter 15 of *The Prince*). It is nonetheless true that there are numerous continuities of theme and problem that link the literary works to Machiavelli's principal vocations and that the political and historical works are shot through with rhetorical stratagems, figurative language, mythic and fabulous narrative, and literary allusions that link them to the world of rhetoric and of literature.

In its most extreme version, the homogenizing approach leads to a reading of *The Prince* as the Italian instantiation of tragic drama. It has, even more crucially, sponsored important rhetorical readings of *The Prince* and other nonliterary works, as well as several recent studies that have emphasized the complex intertextuality that links Machiavelli's works to classical and Italian precursors (above all, Dante). Finally, some critics have argued that Machiavelli's oeuvre as a whole represents an interesting and important step in the historical process by which the humanist linkage of literature, history, and politics under the general rubric of epideictic rhetoric was eroded and replaced by an increasingly rigid distinction between literary and scientific modes of discourse.

BIBLIOGRAPHY

Primary Works

Machiavelli, Niccolò. *Machiavelli: The Chief Works and Others.* 3 vols. Translated by Allan Gilbert. 1965. Reprint, Durham, N.C., 1989.

Sices, David, and James B. Atkinson, eds. and trans. *The Comedies of Machiavelli.* Hanover, N.H., 1985.

Secondary Works

Aquilecchia, Giovanni. "La favola *Mandragola* si chiama." In *Collected Essays on Italian Language and Literature Presented to Kathleen Speight.* Edited by Giovanni Aquilecchia, Stephen N. Cristea, and Sheila Ralphs. New York, 1971. Pages 74–100.

Ascoli, Albert Russell. "Pyrrhus' Rules: Playing with Power from Boccaccio to Machiavelli." *Modern Language Notes* (winter 1999), forthcoming.

Ascoli, Albert Russell, and Victoria Kahn, eds. *Machiavelli and the Discourse of Literature.* Ithaca, N.Y., 1993.

Barberi Squarotti, Giorgio. *La forma tragica del "Principe" e altri saggi sul Machiavelli.* Florence, 1966.

Chiappelli, Fredi. *Nuovi studi sul linguaggio del Machiavelli.* Florence, 1969.

Chiappelli, Fredi. *Studi sul linguaggio del Machiavelli.* Florence, 1952.

Dionisotti, Carlo. *Machiavellerie.* Turin, Italy, 1980.

Ferroni, Giulio. *Mutazione e riscontro nel teatro di Machiavelli e altri saggi sulla commedia del Cinquecento,* Rome, 1972.

Greene, Thomas M. "The End of Discourse in Machiavelli's *Prince.*" In *Literary Theory/Renaissance Texts.* Edited by Patricia Parker and David Quint. Baltimore, 1986. Pages 63–77.

Kahn, Victoria. *Machiavellian Rhetoric: From the Counter-Reformation to Milton.* Princeton, N.J., 1994.

Martinez, Ronald L. "The Pharmacy of Machiavelli: Roman Lucretia in *Mandragola.*" *Renaissance Drama* 14 (1983): 1–43.

Mattingly, Garrett. "Machiavelli's *Prince:* Political Science or Political Satire?" *The American Scholar* 27 (1958): 482–491.

Najemy, John M. *Between Friends: Discourses of Power and Desire in the Machiavelli-Vettori Letters of 1513–1515.* Princeton, N.J., 1993.

Perocco, Daria. "Rassegna di Studi sulle Opere Letterarie di Machiavelli (1969–1986)." *Lettere Italiane* 39 (1987): 544–579.

Pitkin, Hanna Fenichel. *Fortune Is a Woman: Gender and Politics in the Thought of Niccolò Machiavelli.* Berkeley, Calif., 1984.

Raimondi, Ezio. *Politica e commedia: Dal Beroaldo al Machiavelli.* Bologna, Italy, 1972.

Rebhorn, Wayne. *Foxes and Lions: Machiavelli's Confidence Men.* Ithaca, N.Y., 1988.

ALBERT RUSSELL ASCOLI

Machiavelli's Influence

Machiavelli ranks as one of the most influential political writers in the Western tradition. He was not a systematic thinker, however, and his ideas have been open to varying, even contradictory, interpretations. Especially in the early modern period, writers concealed his influence on them because of his unsavory reputation. Three principal currents of his thought stand out; they overlap and are not always consistent among themselves.

Overview. Machiavelli's long-lived notoriety stems from the first of these currents. Precisely as the form of the modern state began to emerge in the sixteenth century, Machiavelli raised anew in a highly provocative fashion the issue of the relationship between politics on the one hand, and on the other religion and morality, where morality was usually rooted in natural law. Thus he revived a debate with origins in classical times that persists to the present day. This he did in two ways. First, he advanced the secularization of politics by withdrawing it from a hierarchy of Christian values that assumed humankind's fulfillment in the knowledge and love of God ultimately in heaven: the goal of politics became increasingly the development and maintenance of a powerful state; politics was about power. Second, he asserted that it was not possible for a man of politics to be successful without forsaking traditional Christian and moral principles, for the good (*honestum*) and the useful (*utile*) inevitably diverged. In order to succeed in politics, one had to learn to abandon goodness, at least at times. The only conclusion the sincere Christian could draw from this assertion was to reject the world of politics; thus, this first current of thought prompted a vigorous anti-Machiavellian response.

The second current of Machiavelli's thought contributed to a conception of politics that, as an analytical or descriptive rather than a normative science, dealt with statecraft or the acquisition and uses of power. The third main current advanced republican government, based on the classical model of Rome, as most favorable to both the liberty of the citizens and the preservation and expansion of the state. Ironically, Machiavelli, who so lauded the political life as lived in a free republic, contributed to the pejorative connotation that came often to be associated with the term "politician."

Machiavelli's most influential works were *Il Principe* (*The Prince*) and the *Discorsi* (*Discourses*), and to a lesser extent *Arte della guerra* (*The Art of War;* 1521) and *Storie fiorentine* (*The History of Florence;* 1532). Controversy swirled about *The Prince* even before its publication along with the *Discourses* in the winter of 1531–1532, with the permission of Pope Clement VII. Approximately fifteen editions of *The Prince* and nineteen of the *Discourses,* along with French translations of each, were in circulation when both were placed on the Index of Paul IV in

1559. This measure nearly stopped their publication in Catholic areas outside of France, where translations appeared with regularity into the mid-1600s. The first Latin version of *The Prince* appeared at Basel in 1560 followed by eleven more, along with fewer editions of the *Discourses,* all published at Leiden or in Protestant areas of the Holy Roman Empire. Only one English version of each appeared before 1660, two in Dutch, and none in German. Both books circulated widely, even in Catholic areas, and the reaction was not all negative. Yet the response was overwhelmingly anti-Machiavellian. Already in the time of Christopher Marlowe and Shakespeare the word "Machiavellian" had assumed for the Elizabethan stage the sinister connotations that it retains today. Machiavelli intended to shock, and he did.

Politics, Religion, and Morality. "Machiavelli's theory was a sword which was plunged into the flank of the body politic of Western humanity, causing it to shriek and rear up. This was bound to happen; for not only had genuine moral feeling been seriously wounded, but death had also been threatened to the Christian views of all churches and sects." So in 1924 wrote Friedrich Meinecke, the historian of the concept "reason of state," in a classic passage (*Machiavellism,* p. 49). The sword was the alleged irreconcilability of political success with traditional morality, Christian or otherwise. Not that the position was by any means unique. Socrates, according to Plato's *Apology,* had said as much. Thomas More's fictional Raphael Hythlodaeus repeated it in *Utopia* (1516), and later Michel de Montaigne (1533–1592) clearly inclined to the same view. But Machiavelli's aggressive assertion touched a raw nerve. By the end of the sixteenth century, the relationship between politics, religion, and morality was a dominant issue often discussed around the term "reason of state" (*ragione di stato, raison d'état*), which did not originate with Machiavelli, but was popularly associated with him. Reason of state became a popular topic even for fishmongers, according to the Italian satirist Traiano Boccalini in a letter of 1616, and Gabriel Naudé, Richelieu's librarian, remarked in 1627 that politics and morality occupied the majority of the best and most vigorous writers.

Beginning with the *Apologia ad Carolum Quintum Caesarem* (Apology for Emperor Charles V) written in the late 1530s by the English cardinal Reginald Pole, numerous critics castigated Machiavelli for divorcing politics from any transcendent goal. Others objected to certain features of his thought, such as his reduction of religion to a tool for the strengthening of the state. The French Huguenot Innocent Gentillet published at Geneva in 1576 his *Discours contre Machiavel* (Discourse against Machiavelli). It was the first systematic attempt to refute Machiavelli, and it influenced subsequent Catholic and Protestant writers, going through twenty-four editions before 1655.

Of particular significance was a school of writers who were anti-Machiavellian in a specific sense; they prescinded from or assumed the theological and philosophical arguments against Machiavelli and aimed to meet him on his grounds of political effectiveness. They were influenced also by the second current of his thought in that they frequently recognized him as an astute observer of statecraft and accepted his view that the goal of politics was the foundation and maintenance of a powerful state. But they contended that the immoral means to which he often resorted were ineffective and even counterproductive. They then produced their own program of state building that combined the good and the useful. In doing so, they attempted to demonstrate that a Christian could indeed be a successful politician, thus supporting the conviction of both Catholics and Protestants that a full Christian life could be lived in the world, even the world of politics. Founders of this tradition were the Flemish humanist Justus Lipsius, whose *Politicorum libri sex* (Six books on politics) appeared in 1589, and the Italian cleric Giovanni Botero, whose *Della ragione di stato* (*Reason of State*) was published the same year. Both books were best-sellers in the first half of the seventeenth century.

Botero popularized the term "reason of state" and assigned three meanings to it. All of them reveal the influence of Machiavelli, and the first two represent most fully what historically came to be known as "Machiavellism." Reason of state denoted first, according to Botero, a manner of government hostile to conscience and the law of God; this derived from Machiavelli and from the ancient Roman historian Tacitus, who was considered less distasteful than Machiavelli. For Traiano Boccalini in his *Ragguagli di Parnaso* (Reports from Parnassus; 1612), reason of state was much the same, a law useful to states but contrary to the law of God and men. The second meaning Botero presented indicated recourse in extreme circumstances, for the sake of the common good, to violations of customary or positive law (but not usually natural or divine law), or in other words, that the end justified the means. The third meaning was Botero's own: "knowledge of the means to es-

tablish, preserve, and expand a state," or a Christian program of state building, a Christian reason of state. Later writers came to assign to different forms of government and then to individual states a particular reason of state, or "interest," which indicated and justified their policies. Different states came to defend and to pursue their interests in the international competition for power.

The Spanish Jesuit anti-Machiavellian Pedro de Ribadeneira, in his *Tratado de la religión y virtudes que deve tener el príncipe christiano* (Christian prince) of 1595, first designated Machiavelli a politician (*político*). The term had already taken on a negative connotation because of its association with the French *politiques,* who allegedly subordinated religion to the needs of the state. The designation stuck, and "politician" and Machiavelli were frequently associated. The English Catholic writer Thomas Fitzherbert in 1606 lamented the transformation of the term from one "who practices that part of human prudence which concerns state . . . to those who framing a policy after their own fancy, no less repugnant to reason than to conscience and religion, change all the course of true wisdom and prudence" (*The First Part of a Treatise concerning Policy and Religion,* 2d ed., 1615; reprint, 1974, preface). Other writers pointed to a Christian politics and outlined the profile of the Christian politician, thus rescuing the term to a degree. In doing so they groped toward an ethics of power.

Political Science.   Besides the anti-Machiavellians, many others valued Machiavelli as an observer and analyst of politics. This was the case with Jean Bodin (initially at least in 1566), the German maverick and Catholic convert Kaspar Schoppe (1622), and Francis Bacon (1623). Some saw a connection between Machiavelli and Aristotle in a common desire to describe political activity as it really was, and not as it ought to be. This was the position of the German savant Hermann Conring in his edition of *The Prince* (1660), though he also condemned Machiavelli for recommending the tyrannical measures that Aristotle only described, thus illustrating the frequent ambivalence of those who admired Machiavelli's analytical skills. Associated with the recognition of Machiavelli as an observer of politics was the turn to history as the source of political wisdom. For Bacon, Machiavelli used history not as a source of examples in the humanist fashion but as the foundation of his argument.

With both friend and foe Machiavelli's influence was felt in the topics and language of the discussion.

Issues such as the uses of deceit; the relative importance for a ruler to be loved or feared, the distinction between virtue and *virtù,* which combined political virtuosity and moral virtue; the value of the military, and the relative merits of mercenary or native soldiers; the role of religion in the state; the place of fortune or providence, necessity, and occasion in history; the contrast between the French monarchy and the government of the Turks; and the difference between a republic for conquest or one for preservation—all bore Machiavelli's imprint or were directly taken over from him. Prussia's Frederick (II) the Great, in his eighteenth-century *Anti-Machiavel* (1767), composed with the help of Voltaire, discussed each of *The Prince*'s twenty-six chapters. Machiavelli also set part of the agenda for the growing casuistry that attempted to adapt moral principles to the changing world of the sixteenth century. Most anti-Machiavellian writers realized the need for forms of secrecy or deception in politics—Lipsius distinguished deception from deceit—but what precisely was permitted? Opponents of Machiavelli who decried his reduction of religion to an instrument of the state so emphasized the utility of Christianity for government, which he denied, that they seemed to fall into his position.

Republicanism. The influence of the third main current of Machiavelli's thought, his republican legacy, was chiefly felt first in England during the civil war and interregnum and then across the Atlantic. This current was carried by the *Discourses,* an English translation of which by Edward Dacres appeared in 1636. Here *The Prince* was often taken as a satire warning against the ills of princely government, an interpretation dating from the 1530s and espoused in England by the Italian exile Alberico Gentili (1584).

Machiavelli was in fact a significant bearer of the Aristotelian tradition of the importance and dignity of the political life and an influential mediator of classical republicanism. At the heart of this republicanism lay the value of personal liberty for the citizens, which only a self-governing, independent state could provide. It emerged in England when the country was in crisis and alert to new forms of government. There *The Prince* was considered a protest against one-man rule with a view to Charles I (ruled 1625–1649), Oliver Cromwell (virtual ruler 1649–1660), and later even Charles II (ruled 1660–1685). Both the republican and the stereotypical Machiavelli appeared in the political treatises of John Milton (1608–1674).

Most important were the writings of James Harrington, perhaps "the greatest and most astute interpreter of Machiavelli" (Procacci, p. 235), especially his *Oceana* of 1656, which attempted to close the gap between republicanism and constitutionalism. For Harrington as for Machiavelli citizenship was characterized by civic virtue and the bearing of arms, to which Harrington added, on the basis of an original analysis of the relations between forms of government and land tenure, ownership of a freehold. Republicanism remained a modest force during the seventeenth-century English Restoration, especially in the work of Algernon Sidney. In turn, it played a part in the thought of the Founding Fathers of the United States. The republican Machiavelli appeared on the Continent as well in the eighteenth century, in Pierre Bayle's *Dictionnaire historique et critique* (Historical and critical dictionary; 1697), where it combined with the other two currents, and in Jean-Jacques Rousseau's *Du contrat social* (*Social Contract;* 1762) and the *Encyclopédie* (1765), where the republican current predominated.

All three currents of Machiavelli's thought have continued to have an impact up to the present day, especially in champions of the autonomy of politics in the pursuit of national interests; in practitioners of politics as a social science; and to a lesser degree, in republican political theorists like Quentin Skinner. In the early nineteenth century a new, relatively short-lived current appeared when the German philosophers Georg Wilhelm Friedrich Hegel and Johann Fichte discovered Machiavelli as a forerunner of the unitary national state and then, on the basis of the final chapter of *The Prince,* when leaders of the nineteenth-century *Risorgimento* (Resurgence) found in him a prophet of Italian unification. The term "*Machiavellian*" retains today its nefarious connotation.

See also **Republicanism; Virtù;** *and biographies of figures mentioned in this entry.*

BIBLIOGRAPHY

Berlin, Isaiah. "The Originality of Machiavelli." In *Studies on Machiavelli.* Edited by Myron P. Gilmore. Pages 147–206. Florence, 1972. Printed in condensed form as "The Question of Machiavelli" in *New York Review of Books,* 4 November 1971, 20–32. Discusses a wide range of the many interpretations of Machiavelli.

Bireley, Robert. *The Counter-Reformation Prince: Anti-Machiavellianism or Catholic Statecraft in Early Modern Europe.* Chapel Hill, N.C., 1990. Traces an anti-Machiavellian tradition and its relationship to the Counter-Reformation and baroque culture.

Burns, J. H., with the assistance of Mark Goldie, ed. *The Cambridge History of Political Thought, 1450–1700.* Cambridge, U.K., 1991. A reliable, standard reference work.

Gilbert, Felix. "Machiavellism." In *History: Choice and Commitment.* Cambridge, Mass., 1977. Pages 155–176. Originally in the *Dictionary of the History of Ideas,* vol. 3. New York, 1971–1972. Pages 116–126. An overview of forms of "Machiavellism" that developed out of Machiavelli's thought.

Kahn, Victoria. *Machiavellian Rhetoric from the Counter-Reformation to Milton.* Princeton, N.J., 1994. A difficult book that argues for the intersection in the reception of Machiavelli of the republican interpretation and the tradition of the nefarious "Machiavel."

Meinecke, Friedrich. *Machiavellism: The Doctrine of Raison d'État and Its Place in Modern History.* Translated by Douglas Scott. New Haven, Conn., 1957. Reprint, New York, 1965. Translation of *Die Idee der Staatsräson* (1924). A classic if somewhat outdated history of reason of state, which is closely associated with Machiavellism.

Pocock, J. G. A. *The Machiavellian Moment: Florentine Political Thought and the Atlantic Republican Tradition.* Princeton, N.J., 1975. A magnificent, sweeping, and controversial interpretation of the impact of Machiavelli's republican thought in Florence, England, and among the American Founding Fathers.

Procacci, Giuliano. *Machiavelli nella cultura europea dell'età moderna.* Bari, Italy, 1995. A study of the impact of Machiavelli's thought through the middle of the nineteenth century, which however prescinds largely from Machiavellism understood as reason of state and from anti-Machiavellianism.

Raab, Felix. *The English Face of Machiavelli: A Changing Interpretation, 1500–1700.* London and Toronto, 1964. Still a valuable overview.

Viroli, Maurizio. *From Politics to Reason of State: The Acquisition and Transformation of the Language of Politics, 1250–1600.* Cambridge, U.K., 1992. Important especially for the impact of Machiavelli in Italy.

ROBERT BIRELEY

MADRID. Before Philip II (ruled 1556–1598) chose it as the capital of the Spanish empire in 1561, Madrid was a small, walled market town in the center of the Iberian Peninsula, inconspicuous in the flourishing urban network of sixteenth-century Castile. Its cultural evolution mirrored that of Castile as a whole, where the Renaissance appeared late and proved artistically peripheral. As in Castile, the Renaissance in Madrid centered on the Christianization of classical motifs and found its principal support in the monarchy. Lacking major aristocratic or clerical patrons, Madrid's monuments from the early sixteenth century—the San Jerónimo monastery and the hospital of La Latina, named after the Latinist Beatriz Galindo—were recognizably Gothic. The so-called Bishop's Chapel (c. 1535) in the church of San Andrés was the first example of plateresque, or early Renaissance architecture.

The monarchy left its imprint throughout the city. Population grew with the court (from 20,000 inhabitants around 1560 to 90,000 in 1600) and fell by half when Philip III (ruled 1598–1621) temporarily moved to Valladolid in 1601–1605. Thereafter, it peaked at 130,000 in 1630. Most of the populace worked as servants or suppliers for the minority of nobles, clergy, and public officials who lived off rents from the rest of the empire. The court, housed in the Alcázar, the castle-palace of medieval origin that would be completely rebuilt after the 1734 fire, was the unrivaled center of intellectual life. Direct monarchical patronage of architecture, theater, music (including late sixteenth-century composer Tomás Luis de Victoria) culminated with the diverse royal collections—remarkably, the more than 1,500 paintings Philip II assembled, with works by Flemish and Italian masters, especially Titian. Indirectly, the court attracted the few other cultural patrons in town, such as Philip III's favorite, the duke of Lerma, and religious orders (forty-two new convents and monasteries added between 1561 and 1650). Prospects of patronage drew painters, poets, and playwrights. The first printing press was installed in 1566, and by 1600 Madrid led the publishing business in Spain (Miguel de Cervantes's *Don Quixote* was printed there in 1605). The kings' preference for building palaces and hunting parks in the nearby countryside over reforming urban public spaces helped account for the lack of monumental ceremonial spaces, excepting the huge Plaza Mayor (completed in 1619).

Madrid was therefore less a Renaissance town than a baroque court. Golden age drama, written by playwrights like Félix Lope de Vega and Pedro Calderón de la Barca for a popular, national theater, was born on the stages of La Cruz (built 1579) and Príncipe (1582). Baroque spectacle dominated civic life, from the Inquisition *autos de fé* to Corpus Christi pageants, bullfights, and other celebrations, all held in the palace square or in the Plaza Mayor. Educational institutions demonstrated the same Counter-Reformation leanings; the old municipal school, where local humanist Juan López de Hoyos taught from 1568 to 1583, languished until 1619, eclipsed by the school founded in 1567 by the Jesuits, which would later be known as the Imperial School.

All that remains of Renaissance Madrid are the paintings of the royal collections now in the Prado museum, the Bishop's Chapel, and the facade of the monastery of the Descalzas Reales. However, forty miles northwest stands the monastery of El Escorial, the most revealing monument to the strengths and limitations of Philip II's classicism.

See also **Spain**, *subentry on* **Art in Spain and Portugal.**

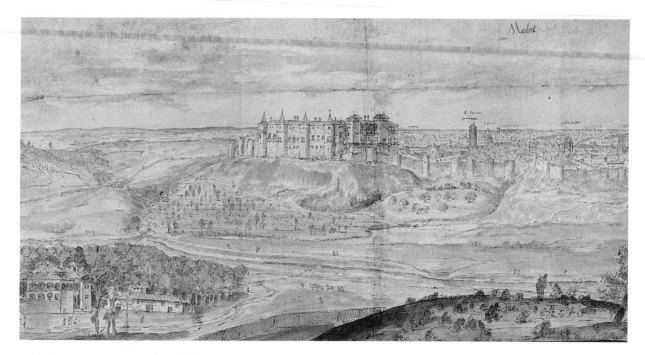

Madrid. Panoramic view of Madrid by Anton van Wyngaerde, c. 1560. BIBLIOTECA NACIONAL, MADRID/ORONOZ

BIBLIOGRAPHY

Brown, Jonathan. *The Golden Age of Painting in Spain*. London, 1989.

Castillo Oreja, Miguel Angel, ed. *Madrid en el Renacimiento*. Madrid, 1986. Exhibition catalog focusing on the city and its surroundings.

Checa, Fernando, ed. *El Real Alcázar de Madrid: Dos Siglos de Arquitectura y Coleccionismo en la Corte de los Reyes de España*. Madrid, 1994. Exhibition catalog on the royal palace and its artistic treasures.

Lopez Garcia, José Miguel, and Santos Madrazo. "A Capital City in the Feudal Order: Madrid from the Sixteenth to the Eighteenth Century." In Peter Clark and Bernard Lepitit, eds. *Capital Cities and Their Hinterlands in Early Modern Europe*. Aldershot, U.K., 1996. Pp. 119–142.

McKendrick, Melveena. *Theatre in Spain, 1490–1700*. London, 1990.

Pinto Crespo, Virgilio, and Santos Madrazo, eds. *Madrid: Atlas histórico de la ciudad, Siglos 9–19*. Madrid, 1995. Thoroughly researched and well-illustrated historical atlas.

Sieber, Claudia W. "The Invention of a Capital: Phillip II and the First Reform of Madrid." Ph.D. dissertation, Johns Hopkins University, 1986.

MAURO HERNÁNDEZ

MADRIGAL. *See* **Music,** *subentry on* **Secular Vocal Music.**

MAGELLAN, FERDINAND (c. 1480–1521), Portuguese navigator. Magellan was the first European to sail through the South American straits that bear his name. He discovered the Marianas and the Phil-ippines for Spain, and is considered by many to be the greatest navigator of the era of discoveries.

The exact date and place of Magellan's birth are not known, although it is clear that he was born in northern Portugal of the lower nobility. He sailed to Asia in 1505 on the armada of Dom Francisco de Almeida, first viceroy of India. In 1509 he accompanied Diogo Lopes de Sequeira on an unsuccessful effort to capture Malacca. While in Malacca he heard of the Spice Islands (the Moluccas). There is no firm evidence, as some claim, that Magellan accompanied António de Abreu's 1511–1512 voyage of discovery to the western Pacific. In 1513 Magellan was back in Portugal in time to participate in the capture and occupation of the Moroccan outpost of Azemmour.

Dissatisfied in King Manuel's (ruled 1495–1521) service, Magellan left court and began preparing a voyage to the Spice Islands by sailing westward. Evidence for the voyage's feasibility was supplied by his friend, mathematician and astrologer Rui Faleiro. Arriving in Seville on 20 October of that year, Magellan won the support of powerful men at the Spanish court, including Juan Rodríguez de Fonseca, bishop of Burgos and vice president of the Council of the Indies, and signed a contract with Charles I (the future Charles V, Holy Roman emperor), on 22 March 1518. As a sign of the monarch's esteem, Magellan was made a knight and commander in the Spanish Order of Santiago. Faleiro and Magellan were initially named joint captains-general of the expedition, but Faleiro was replaced by the Spaniard Juan de Cartagena several weeks before the fleet left Seville for San Lúcar de Barrameda on 10 August 1519.

The five ships—*Trinidad* (the flagship), *Victoria, San Antonio, Concepción,* and *Santiago*—were all relatively small. About 240 men, including a substantial number of Portuguese and other foreigners, manned the fleet. On board was the Italian-born Antonio Pigafetta, whose account is the major source for the voyage. After stopping briefly at the Canary Islands, the expedition sailed between the Cape Verde Islands and the African coast before turning west toward Brazil. In early December 1519 Magellan arrived in the area of Rio de Janeiro and then spent nearly a year searching for a westward passage through or around South America. Five months were spent wintering at Puerto San Julián, during which time a serious mutiny was put down and one ship, the *Santiago,* ran aground and was destroyed, although few lives or provisions were lost. On 21 October 1520, Magellan's expedition sighted what they called Cabo Vírgenes at 52° 20′ south latitude, which proved to be the opening of the strait that now bears his name. By 28 November 1520 Magellan had carefully explored and sailed through the treacherous 334 nautical-mile-long passage into the Pacific Ocean. During the voyage through the strait, the *San Antonio* abandoned the rest of the expedition and returned to Spain.

After an epic voyage of almost one hundred days on the high seas, during which the crew endured terrible hardships, Magellan's expedition finally landed on one of the Mariana islands, probably Guam, on 6 March 1521. By mid-March the island of Samar in the Philippines was sighted. Shortly after landing on the island of Cebú, Magellan became involved in a local war and was killed on the neighboring island of Mactan on 27 April 1521. Subsequently, more than several dozen other members of the expedition were enslaved or massacred, and the *Concepción* was burned. The remnants of the expedition, after exploring, plundering, and arranging treaties, reached Tidore in the Moluccas on 8 November 1521. After loading the two remaining ships with a fortune in cloves, the *Victoria* under the leadership of the Basque Juan Sebastian de Elcano and fifty-nine men (including Pigafetta) set sail for Spain on 21 December 1521 via the Cape of Good Hope. The *Trinidad,* which planned to return the way it had come, was captured by the Portuguese. On 6 September 1522 the *Victoria* with Elcano, seventeen other Europeans, and three East Indians arrived at

Ferdinand Magellan. Portrait by Antonio Giovanni di Varese in the Sala del Mappamondo (hall of the world map) of the Palazzo Farnese, Caprarola (near Viterbo), Italy. GIRAUDON/ART RESOURCE, NY

Sanlúcar, a little less than three years after the voyage had begun. To this day, controversy continues about whether Magellan initially planned to circumnavigate the world and risk capture by the Portuguese or to return the way he came, across the Pacific Ocean.

BIBLIOGRAPHY

Primary Work
Most valuable for both its introduction and reprinting of the major sixteenth-century accounts is Charles E. Nowell, ed., *Magellan's Voyage around the World* (Evanston, Ill., 1962).

Secondary Works
Essential reading is Martin Torodash, "Magellan Historiography" in *Hispanic American Historical Review* 51 (1971): 313–335, and its update by the same author, "Magellanic Historiography: Some Twenty Years Later," in Francis A. Dutra and João Camilo dos Santos, eds., *The Portuguese and the Pacific* (Santa Barbara, Calif., 1995), pp. 11–16. The best account in English is still Francis Henry Hill Guillemard, *Life of Ferdinand Magellan* (London, 1890; reprint, New York, 1971), although Samuel Eliot Morison, *The European Discovery of America: The Southern Voyages,* A.D. *1492–1616* (New York, 1974), pp. 313–374, and Tim Joyner, *Magellan* (Camden, Maine, 1992), also deserve high marks. An

older biography that has withstood the test of time is Jean Denucé, *Magellan, la question des Moluques et la première circumnavigation du globe* (Brussels, 1911). Two important Portuguese sources are Visconde de Lagôa, *Fernão de Magalhâis (A sua vida a sua viagem)*, 2 vols. (Lisbon, 1938), and Avelino Teixeira da Mota, ed., *A viagem de Fernão de Magalhães e a questão das Molucas* (Lisbon, 1975).

FRANCIS A. DUTRA

MAGIC AND ASTROLOGY.

[This entry includes three subentries:

Magic and Astrology (an overview)
Jewish Astrology and the Occult
Jewish Magic and Divination]

Magic and Astrology

What Europeans in the Renaissance called "magic" (*magia*) had been known by forms of that name since the fifth century B.C.E. The broader term "occultism," coined in the nineteenth century, puts magic, astrology, alchemy, Kabbalah, demonology, divination, spiritualism, theosophy, witchcraft, and related items in a single, loose category. Renaissance thinkers also saw a family resemblance among a similar set of beliefs and practices. Magic, both theory and practice, is the most general term in question: the theory tries to explain phenomena so unusual as to be incredible; the practice aims to cause or prevent such effects. The magus—an expert who understands the theory—can predict future effects by studying astrological causes, attract celestial powers by manipulating terrestrial objects, summon good angels by composing incantations, or drive off demons by designing talismans. But knowledge, ritual, and invocation seen from one point of view as religious may be treated as magical from another perspective; thus some Renaissance Protestants attacked the Catholic sacraments as so much hocus-pocus and the cult of saints as idolatrous superstition. In academic debates of more recent times, magic, religion, and science have been treated as fields to be delimited or derived from one another, sometimes by arranging them as evolutionary stages. But no transcultural or metahistorical theory of magic applies well to the Renaissance, when magic reached its apex in Europe's learned culture.

Astrology, Magic, and Magicians. Renaissance magic, especially the learned kind, almost always involved astrology; in fact, magic was often defined as a way of making higher heavenly causes active in producing lower earthly effects. Since the prevailing physics and metaphysics treated stars and planets above as material (though unusual) objects, it was thought that other material objects below could be manipulated to stimulate celestial activity by techniques of concentration, assimilation, separation, and so on. Thus the magus would arrange stones, plants, animals, vapors, odors, sounds, and other such objects according to qualities—color, shape, texture, taste, smell, tone—that were to be blended or dispersed in order to attract or repel similar features of heavenly bodies. Except for the magician, all the objects involved were material and none was a person; hence the magic was natural by definition, since all its means and ends were nonpersonal material objects—stones, stars, and anything else of a natural, impersonal kind that might be found between earth and heaven and used to bind them together.

Heavenly bodies, however, were not just the bodies of celestial physics; metaphysically, they were also minds or intelligences and in this way conformable to the personal agents in ancient astral mythologies, whose star-gods suffered demotion to star-demons when pagan religions succumbed to Christianity. The old gods lost their Olympian standing in late antiquity, just as magic was reaching another cultural peak. After Plotinus (205–270 C.E.), the later Neoplatonists from Porphyry (c. 234–c. 305) to Proclus (410–485) took magic even more seriously than their founder and worked out philosophical theories of magical causation and moral justifications of magical practice. Synesius (370–413), for example, presented ritual initiation as a final step toward ecstatic union with the One and philosophy as a curricular preparation for theurgy—the magical invocation of divinities or demons. Iamblichus (245–325) and Proclus, who saw theurgy in the same way, explained how forms of natural objects used in magical rites were akin to forms of planets, stars, and other higher, intelligent entities. Because of this kinship, magical use of a natural object—even a stone or a plant—would automatically attract higher personal powers, including planetary and stellar demons, despite the magician's desires.

Augustine, a contemporary of the Neoplatonists, knew that the magician's best intentions paved the way to the demons, so he gave no credit to the notion of a natural, nondemonic magic. But William of Auvergne, Albertus Magnus, Thomas Aquinas, and other medieval Christians extended the saving grace of this conception to the magus and equipped him with subtle scholastic reasoning to support it. A major motive for isolating licit *natural* magic from illicit *demonic* magic was that medicine depended routinely on unexplained properties of natural objects, mainly plants but also mineral and animal substances, regarded as occult because they fell outside the normal taxonomy of manifest (hot, cold, wet, and dry) qualities of the four elements (fire, earth, water, and air). Established by the physician Galen in the second century C.E. and elaborated by the Muslim philosophers Alkindi, Averroes, and Avicenna in the Middle Ages, the theory of occult qualities eventually looked to the heavens, whence substantial forms and their qualitative effects were thought to be produced in natural objects. Along with Galenic and Muslim medicine, scholastic metaphysics, physics, and astrology provided the foundations of a theory of magic for the Middle Ages.

Ficino. Marsilio Ficino (1433–1499), a physician as well as a philosopher, inherited the scholastic theory of magic and in large part preserved it. His great innovation was to recover Neoplatonic philosophizing about magic that the Middle Ages had forgotten. Like others before and after him, Ficino put forward three kinds of evidence for magic: not only theoretical but also empirical and genealogical proofs. His empirical reasons for believing in magic were the hundreds and hundreds of phenomena—the heliotrope, magnet, remora, and electric ray, the lion that fears the cock, the peony root that cures epilepsy, and many other wonders—recorded since antiquity and long reputed to be magical.

These literary data made concrete the theory that Ficino filled out from Plotinus, Proclus, and other Neoplatonists and published in his 1489 treatise *De vita libri tres* (Three books on life). The third book of this work, *De vita coelitus comparanda* (On regulating life by the heavens) was the most original and influential Renaissance statement of a philosophical theory of magic. Its sophisticated metaphysics of forms establishes a cosmic and hypercosmic context for magical influence moving downward from mind through soul to matter and thus to the natural objects that the magician can use. One of the more dangerous of these objects for Ficino was the talisman, a gem decorated with an astrological image. The stone is a natural object, but the astral figure is artificial, a sign that may attract a demon. A major point of Ficino's theory was to make the talisman safe—natural rather than demonic—by using its figure not to communicate by signs with higher persons but to open an ontological channel to higher forms.

Ficino usually began his genealogy of magical wisdom with Zoroaster, less often with Hermes Trismegistus; the ensuing line of ancient sages culmi-

Astrological Sign. The sun portrayed as a ruler with the sign of Leo below him presides over the exercise field. BIBLIOTECA ESTENSE, MODENA

nates in Plato and then extends through Plotinus and his successors. Plato's *Symposium,* with its organic cosmos of erotic sympathies and demonic (in the good sense) energies, gave Ficino one of his key texts, while another came from Plotinus in a passage that raises the question of magically ensouled statues, a graver problem than talismans. Having translated the Greek Hermetic texts, Ficino knew that they have little to say about magic, and he made no great use of them in *De vita.* In the finale of that work, however, he cited passages of the Latin *Asclepius* about god-making—the magical animation of statues—only to condemn this Egyptian demonolatry, as he had to in a work meant to support natural magic and to extend its protection to the difficult case of talismans.

Pico della Mirandola. Giovanni Pico della Mirandola (1463–1494) opened his famous *De hominis dignitate oratio* (Oration on the dignity of man; 1486) with an allusion to *Asclepius,* but not to the god-making passages, and Hermes appears nowhere among the many authorities used toward the end of that work, where Pico sketches a theory of natural magic like Ficino's. Neither Pico's philosophy of magic nor Ficino's is "Hermetic," if that term refers to the Greek *Hermetica* that Ficino translated; if it refers to the Latin *Asclepius,* Ficino's position was anti-Hermetic in rejecting the demonic statue-magic of that work. Like the author of *Asclepius,* but more artfully, Pico combined moments of world-affirming engagement—most famously in praising human liberty and choice at the start of the *Oration*—with a pervasive, world-denying supernaturalism. The choice recommended by the *Oration* is to choose the disembodied life of the highest angels, to rise toward a sublime and sublimated freedom through philosophical study and ascetic discipline—in the manner of the Neoplatonists—and to reach ecstatic union with the One through a mystical, theurgic vision, a divinization that transcends rational theologizing.

The intended commerce with angels, as Pico knew, ran the risk of calling up demons instead. To ward off this risk of theurgy was one purpose of his major innovation in magic, blending Kabbalah with the scholastic and Neoplatonic ingredients of Ficino's theory. In his *Conclusiones nongentae in omni genere scientiarum* (Nine hundred conclusions in every kind of science; 1486), Pico speculates cryptically about Kabbalah as a countermagic against evil demons, whom he planned to defeat by invoking good angels. He also presents the holy letters of the Hebrew alphabet as forces in themselves, shapes with powers independent of the meanings of the words that they spell. Used formally or figurally rather than semantically, the letters in the sacred names of God tap the divine energies without opening dark passages to the demon world. They can mark talismans addressed only to the triune God who used them in the very words of creation. This was another goal of Pico's: to construct a new natural magic fortified by Kabbalah and secure against the perils of demonic magic. As of 1487, two years before Ficino published his *Three Books on Life* but long after he had explored its basis in earlier works, Pico advertised himself as a magus and as founder of the new mysticism of Christian Kabbalah. A few years later, before he died in 1494, he began (but never completed) a long book entitled *Disputationes adverus astrologos* (Disputations against divinatory astrology; published 1513).

Pomponazzi.   Pico's approach to magic and astrology stands in stark contrast to the views of Pietro Pomponazzi (1462–1525), a naturalist Aristotelian influenced by the newly available Neoplatonists. While Pico and Ficino had both developed theories

of natural magic meant to avoid the demons that they feared, Pomponazzi settled the issue by eliminating demons altogether from natural philosophy (but not theology) and therefore from any magic based on such a philosophy. He finished his study *De naturalium effectuum causis sive de incantationibus* (Of the causes of natural effects and of incantations; published 1556) in 1520. In thorough scholastic style, he found many reasons to exclude demons from the natural world: they cannot know concrete particulars; they cannot act on bodies directly; any magical effect they might cause is redundant because humans can do the same. The magus, now liberated from demonic terrors, operates on metaphysical, psychological, and cosmological principles of natural philosophy. Without much argument, Pomponazzi simply asserts the usual metaphysics of celestially produced substantial forms and occult qualities. His psychology of magic depends on a faculty of imagination intermediate between mind and body and on a versatile substance, *spiritus,* able to mediate even between subject and object. Reflecting the human microcosm, the greater cosmos is also a hierarchy of mediations, from the intelligences on high through stars and planets to embodied persons and natural objects on earth below. Astrology is the engine of Pomponazzi's world system, which kept no trace of the demonic but was not yet disenchanted.

Other Views of the Occult.   Although Heinrich Cornelius Agrippa von Nettesheim (1486–1535), Giordano Bruno (1548–1600), Giambattista Della Porta (1535?–1615), Tommaso Campanella (1568–1639), and other Renaissance thinkers developed new kinds of occultism, almost all depended either on the Neoplatonic and Kabbalist inventions of Ficino and Pico or on an Aristotelian approach like Pomponazzi's (whose direct influence was delayed for a time) or on both. The most extravagant exception was Theophrast Bombast von Hohenheim, who named himself Paracelsus (1493–1541). Paracelsus made creative use of the teachings of Pico and Ficino, but his idiosyncratic genius also fed on alchemical, theological, and craft traditions independent of conventional Platonism or Aristotelianism. Although Ficino's and Pico's ideas stimulated positive interest in magic and astrology throughout the sixteenth century, their influence weakened in the seventeenth century, when the occult philosophy lost its philosophical authority, though it never lost popular appeal.

Occultism always had enemies, even in antiquity, but this ancient belief system lost its standing among educated Europeans only after Francis Bacon (1561–1626) and Marin Mersenne (1588–1648) gave the seventeenth century a new choice: to reform the occultist tradition or to repudiate it. Bacon preferred the former option. His reform of learning began by detaching from classical authority—from Plato, Aristotle, Pliny, Plotinus, and all the other sages whose ancient wisdom made magic venerable and credible. Efforts to reconstruct occultism on some new scientific basis continue to this day but have never won the confidence of the educated establishment. Hence it was Mersenne and the critics of occultism rather than Bacon and the reformers who fixed the place of the occult philosophy in modern learned culture—where it has no place at all.

BIBLIOGRAPHY

Allen, Michael J. B. "Summoning Plotinus: Ficino, Smoke, and the Strangled Chickens." In *Reconsidering the Renaissance*. Edited by Mario A. Di Cesare. Binghamton, N.Y., 1992. Pages 63–88.

Copenhaver, Brian P. "Astrology and Magic." In *The Cambridge History of Renaissance Philosophy*. Edited by Charles B. Schmitt et al. Cambridge, U.K., and New York, 1988. Pages 264–300.

Copenhaver, Brian P. "Did Science Have a Renaissance?" *Isis* 83 (1992): 387–407.

Copenhaver, Brian P. "Hermes Trismegistus, Proclus, and the Question of a Philosophy of Magic in the Renaissance." In *Hermeticism and the Renaissance: Intellectual History and the Occult in Early Modern Europe*. Edited by Ingrid Merkel and Allen G. Debus. Washington, D.C., 1988. Pages 79–110.

Copenhaver, Brian P. "Natural Magic, Hermetism, and Occultism in Early Modern Science." In *Reappraisals of the Scientific Revolution*. Edited by David C. Lindberg and Robert S. Westman. Cambridge, U.K., and New York, 1990. Pages 261–301.

Copenhaver, Brian P. "Scholastic Philosophy and Renaissance Magic in the *De vita* of Marsilio Ficino." *Renaissance Quarterly* 37 (1984): 523–554.

Copenhaver, Brian P. "The Occultist Tradition and Its Critics." In *The Cambridge History of Seventeenth-Century Philosophy*. Edited by Daniel Garber and Michael Ayers. Cambridge, U.K., and New York, 1998. Volume 1, pages 454–512.

Garin, Eugenio. *Astrology in the Renaissance: The Zodiac of Life*. Translated by Carolyn Jackson, June Allen, and Clare Robertson. London and Boston, 1983.

Walker, D. P. *Spiritual and Demonic Magic from Ficino to Campanella*. London, 1958.

Webster, Charles. *From Paracelsus to Newton: Magic and the Making of Modern Science*. Cambridge, U.K., and New York, 1982.

Zambelli, Paola. *L'ambigua natura della magia: Filosofi, streghe, riti nel Rinascimento*. Milan, 1991.

BRIAN P. COPENHAVER

Jewish Astrology and the Occult

Astrology flourished in the Jewish communities in the Renaissance, especially in Italy. A variety of manuscript traditions attest to this fact: notebooks containing astrological information, often together with a mixture of medicinal, magical, and other formulas; copies of medieval treatises; original writings of Renaissance Jews; and numerous jottings on the endleaves of books of all sorts. Geomancy and magic also seem to have been widely accepted, though they were perhaps more controversial. On the other hand, there is little evidence for widespread interest in alchemy.

One outstanding feature of the late fourteenth century was the surge of interest in the writings of Abraham ibn Ezra, the most famous Jewish astrologer of all time. This activity was centered in the Iberian Peninsula, but Jews throughout the Mediterranean basin participated; there was a particularly active group working in the Byzantine cultural sphere. The literary medium for this school was usually the supercommentary to Ibn Ezra's Bible commentary. In general, these exegetes developed some sort of amalgamation of Moses Maimonides's rational approach to religion with Ibn Ezra's theories of astral governance.

Several members of the Calonymous family, working in southern Italy during the second half of the fifteenth century, were particularly active in astrology. David ben Jacob Meir Calonymous has left us two short treatises. The first is a messianic apocalypse for the years 1464–1468, presented to Ferdinand I of Naples; like so many other ventures of this sort, its theoretical basis is a cyclical conjunction of Jupiter with Saturn. The second is a defense of this type of astrological prognostication. A number of codices preserves sets of short writings by members of the same family. These include disquisitions on the writings of earlier figures, such as Abraham bar Hiyya and Emmanuel ben Jacob, some translations from the Latin, and a number of tables, prognostications, and horoscopes. To the last category belong some Hebrew treatises by Calonymous ben David, otherwise known as Maestro Calo. Calonymous refers to the comet of 1491 (said to be a harbinger of war), and he prepared detailed forecasts for the years 1494 and 1495, devoting separate chapters to the fortunes of the different faiths, kingdoms, professions, and so forth.

Calonymous is only one of several Jewish astrologers known to have served at the court of Naples. However, there was no shortage of patrons, and, moreover, some astrologers worked independently. Bonet (Jacob) de Lattes, like many Provençal Jews, found refuge in Italy. During the last decade of the fifteenth century he published a series of annual prognostications, dedicated to scions of the Borgia family. His most famous prediction is that of the coming of the Messiah in the year 1505. Abraham Zakkut was born in Portugal but was forced to move eastward, eventually settling in Jerusalem. Several of his forecasts for the early decades of the sixteenth century survive in Hebrew. A different individual bearing the same family name published annual prognostications in Ferrara between the years 1525 and 1535.

Of singular interest is *Gey hizzayon* (A valley of vision), a comprehensive astrological treatise written by a certain Eliezer, which survives in a single manuscript. Little is known about the author; he probably flourished at the end of the sixteenth century, and he may be the author of additional writings on astrology and geomancy. *Gey hizzayon* contains detailed excursions into astrological theory as well as analyses of the horoscopes of famous Renaissance personalities. For example, Eliezer discusses the aspects of the moon and Mercury which determine intelligence. He then describes the configurations which indicate proficiency in astronomy and delves into the horoscopes of Nicolaus Copernicus, the German astronomer Erasmus Rheinhold, and others.

Judging by the manuscript evidence, geomancy (divination by means of lines or geographic features) was widely practiced. Mordecai Finzi of Mantua wrote an original treatise in fourteen chapters. The first chapter sketches the history of the art and offers a spirited defense; the closing chapter exposes some frauds which have given the practice a bad name. Many Italian Jews in particular were attracted to magic. Some of the outstanding intellectuals of the period, such as Yohanan Alemanno, Gedalyah ibn Yahya, Abraham Yagel, Leone Modena, and Joseph Hamiz, are known to have taken a serious interest in that art. Several important codices of magical texts, comprising *Picatrix* (the Latin version of an Arabic astrological compendium), Pseudo-Plato, and other key magical texts in Hebrew translation, are written in Italian hands of the period.

Alchemy seems to have been much less in vogue. However, a pseudepigraphon attributed to Moses Maimonides, in which the great master purportedly reveals the secrets of the art in order to relieve his favorite student of any financial worry, seems to have been written in the fifteenth century. This book survives in about half a dozen copies, making it by far the most popular Hebrew alchemical treatise. Finally, it should be noted that some or all of these arts were part and parcel of the physician's repertoire, where they found their place along with the academic tradition (e.g., Galen or Avicenna) and various folk remedies. The distinctions were not always clear in the eyes of either patients or practitioners. The physician Samuel Castiglioni of Mantua, who practiced around the turn of the sixteenth century, notes with some amusement that one of his cures was so successful that people thought he had employed magic. Yet he does on other occasions provide recipes for various sorts of "philosopher's oils."

BIBLIOGRAPHY

Langermann, Y. Tzvi. "The Scientific Writings of Mordekhai Finzi." *Italia* 7 (1988): 7–44.

Langermann, Y. Tzvi. "Some New Medical Manuscripts from Moscow." *Korot* 10 (1993–1994): 54–73.

Patai, Raphael. *The Jewish Alchemists*. Princeton, N.J., 1994.

Roth, Cecil. *The Jews in the Renaissance*. New York, 1965.

Twersky, Isadore, and Jay M. Harris. *Rabbi Abraham ibn Ezra: Studies in the Writings of a Twelfth-Century Jewish Polymath*. Cambridge, Mass., 1993.

Y. TZVI LANGERMANN

Jewish Magic and Divination

Magic played a significant role in Jewish culture during the Renaissance. Jewish intellectual figures in Renaissance Italy left a sizable body of literature that allows for a nuanced evaluation of the elite preoccupation with magic and its relation to the well-known reassessment of magic by Christian figures such as Marcilio Ficino and Giovanni Pico della Mirandola, who construed it as the highest actualization of human potential. Indeed, the premier Jewish and Christian exponents of this view had close personal contact with one another. Giovanni's "tutor" in Kabbalah was Rabbi Yohanan Alemanno (c. 1435–c. 1504), who argued that the study and mastery of magic was to be regarded as the final stage of one's intellectual and spiritual education. This contact, initiated as a result of Christian interest in plumbing the ancient wisdom found in Jewish mystical sources, resulted in unprecedented bidirectional influence between Jewish and Christian Renaissance thought.

Esoteric Magic. Alemanno, who met Pico in Florence in 1488, was immersed in the magical and Neoplatonic studies that flourished there in the late fifteenth century. While magical and hermetic thought, apparently Arabic in origin, appears in the works of such twelfth-century Spanish rabbis as Abraham ibn Ezra and Judah ha-Levi, the reawakening of interest in these ideas among Jewish figures in Renaissance Italy seems to have been encouraged by their close contact with interested Christian intellectuals. It should be noted that while Christian Renaissance figures who engaged in magical theorizing (not to mention practice) did so under the watchful eye of a church hostile to such activity, the Jewish interest in magic found expression at the highest echelons of rabbinic authority. This structural difference allowed Jewish thinkers to frame even more radical magical interpretations of Judaism than was possible for their Christian counterparts, whose writing was far more restricted by antimagical persecution. Moreover, with its emphasis on the ritual performance of commandments, Judaism was perhaps better suited to magical exegesis than Christianity. Indeed, many Jewish thinkers, including Alemanno, proposed Neoplatonic, hermetical, and astrological interpretations of Jewish rituals. Thus, according to Alemanno, the ancient Tabernacle and its vessels that served the Israelites in the wilderness of Sinai was a giant talisman for attracting the divine effulgence.

By the end of the Renaissance, Italian Jewish thinkers had fully absorbed the prevailing Christian view of permissible magic as *magia naturalis,* or natural magic. The physician, Kabbalist, and naturalist Abraham Yagel (1553–c. 1623) was deeply influenced by Heinrich Agrippa of Nettesheim's *De occulta philosophia* (c. 1510) and its tripartite division of magic into the categories of elementary, celestial, and intellectual. Yagel regarded it as the proper task of a physician to work with natural materials, fully exploiting their apparent and occult properties as a natural magus of the elementary world. By employing talismanic amulets, Yagel also made celestial magic the province of the physician. Finally, like Agrippa, Pico, and Alemanno, Yagel regarded the Kabbalah as interrelated, if not identified, with intellectual magic.

While Italian Jewish thinkers displayed intense theoretical interest in magic, it appears that aside from interpreting performative Jewish traditions as magical acts themselves and the Kabbalah as magical philosophy, there was no involvement in anomian (non-Jewish legal) magical activities of the type that flourished in Spain before the expulsion of the Jews and in various Spanish-influenced centers thereafter. While the proliferation of magical interest and activity among the Spanish Jewish elite occurred during the same period as the Italian developments, the former did so in a manner that was extremely mythical, antinatural, and antiphilosophical. The Italian Jewish magus applied a magical hermeneutics of a universalistic and syncretistic hue to Jewish texts and ceremonies. The Spanish Jewish magus, of a more mythic, ethnocentric mind, engaged in magical acts independent of Jewish texts and ceremonies, though these were intended to have redemptive—that is to say, national—consequences.

Popular Magic. Turning to popular Jewish magic, we find little evidence to suggest that it underwent any sort of transformation in the Renaissance; most Jews seem to have simply perpetuated folk magic practices that had been common among them for centuries. Contemporary Christians regarded the Jews, perhaps not entirely gratuitously, as expert magicians—an appraisal in which respect and fear were intertwined. This reputation is reflected in the use of a Castilian Jewish protagonist in Ludovico Ariosto's 1535 comedy, *The Sorcerer,* as well as in the justification proffered by Pope Pius V in the bull *Hebraeorum gens* of 1569 calling for the expulsion of the Jews from the Papal States, in part due to their sorcerous activity. The imputed magical prowess of Jewish women led to their employment as diviners and potion makers, as well to their death at the stake. Thus, in 1600, the aged Judith Franchetti was burned in Mantua for the crime of sorcery.

In addition to forms of wisdom divination (divining from impersonal signatures of reality) such as astrology, chiromancy (palm reading), and lecanomancy (reading water in a bowl) that were practiced at all levels of Jewish society in this period, the sixteenth century also witnessed the rise of possession divination (communication of spirits through humans) among Jews, including the first documented cases of demonic or dybbuk possession in Jewish culture for over a millennium. Gedalyah ibn Yahya (1515–1587), an Italian Jewish loan banker, historian, and Talmudist, discusses a 1575 case in Ferrara at length in his historical work, *The Chain of Tradition* (Venice, 1586), as well as another case in Ancona of multiple possession. Leon Modena (1571–1648), a Venetian rabbi, and Jean Bodin (1530–1596) also mention possession episodes in Italy involving Jews (recent apostates, in the case of Bodin). Exorcism techniques were deployed by rabbi-Kabbalists that drew primarily upon magical techniques with ancient pedigrees, though new techniques in the sixteenth and particularly the seventeenth century were influenced by the Kabbalah of Isaac Luria, as well as by Catholic ritual paradigms. Notwithstanding biblical prohibitions, rabbis of this period found ingenious ways of allowing Jews to consult sorcerers, including Gentiles, where health was concerned—particularly if it was believed that an illness was brought on by witchcraft. In this, as in all areas related to magical activity, rabbis demonstrated a tendency to tolerate most forms of magic.

BIBLIOGRAPHY

Chajes, J. H. "Judgements Sweetened: Possession and Exorcism in Early Modern Jewish Culture." *Journal of Early Modern History* 1, no. 2 (1997): 124–169.

Idel, Moshe. "Jewish Magic from the Renaissance Period to Early Hasidism." In *Religion, Science, and Magic, in Concert and in Conflict*. Edited by Jacob Neusner, Ernest S. Frerichs, and Paul Virgil McCracken Flesher. New York, 1989. Pages 82–117.

Idel, Moshe. "The Magical and Neoplatonic Interpretations of the Kabbalah in the Renaissance." In *Jewish Thought in the Sixteenth Century*. Edited by Bernard Dov Cooperman. Cambridge, Mass., and London, 1983. Pages 186–242.

Ruderman, David B. *Kabbalah, Magic, and Science: The Cultural Universe of a Sixteenth-Century Jewish Physician*. Cambridge, Mass., 1988.

Trachtenberg, Joshua. *Jewish Magic and Superstition: A Study in Folk Religion*. New York, 1939.

J. H. CHAJES

MAHARAL OF PRAGUE

MAHARAL OF PRAGUE (Judah Loew ben Bezalel; c. 1525–1609), rabbi, academy head, homilist, commentator, community leader, educational reformer. Maharal of Prague was probably born in Posnan, Poland. His ancestry included renowned fifteenth-century rabbis, such as the Prague chief rabbi Avigdor Kara (d. 1439). Like Maharal, his three brothers (Hayyim, Sinai, and Samson ben Bezalel) all became renowned scholars and religious leaders. ("Maharal" is a Hebrew acronym designating "Our teacher, Rabbi Loew.")

From 1553 to 1573 Maharal served as *Landesrabbiner* (chief rabbi) of Moravian Jewry. In 1573 he moved to Prague and founded an advanced rabbinical academy. Maharal became chief rabbi of Posnan in 1584, but he returned to Prague in 1587. In 1592 he was summoned to meet with Emperor Rudolf II; a witness recorded that they discussed "mysteries." Soon thereafter, Maharal quit Prague to reassume his position in Posnan. In 1597 he once again returned to Prague, and two years later he was elected chief rabbi. In 1602 he was imprisoned in Bürglitz castle after two local Jews denounced him. He was soon released and restored to his post, which he held until he died.

Maharal wrote prolifically. His writings include commentaries and supercommentaries on the Bible and Talmud, homilies, polemics, legal rulings, and excursus into philosophy, natural philosophy, and Kabbalah. In these works Maharal advocated educational reforms, such as revision of the elementary curriculum and banning *pilpul,* or casuistry, in advanced academies. He also advocated political re-

Maharal of Prague. Statue by Ladislas Saloun at the town hall, Prague. FROM THE LIBRARY OF THE JEWISH THEOLOGICAL SEMINARY OF AMERICA

forms guaranteeing that lay leaders rule only with popular consent and safeguarding the independence of rabbis, and he wrote and preached against the putative moral laxity of his contemporaries.

Maharal's outlook was eclectic and is not easily characterized. One important theme was the radical distinction between the physical and metaphysical. As the historian David Ruderman has observed, this distinction warranted philosophical study of nature, which in principle never conflicted with matters of spirit. Maharal himself was familiar with Copernicanism and other recent developments in natural philosophy. Still, he insisted that the realm of the spirit greatly surpasses the physical realm in importance.

His attitudes toward matter and spirit reflected profound kabbalistic and Neoplatonic influences.

Maharal wrote extensively about the relationship between the Jews and gentiles. He asserted that the Jewish diaspora contravened the world's natural order and would be reversed. Arguing that gentiles are primarily physical beings, while Jews are largely metaphysical, he took this fundamental difference to have far-reaching implications.

Scholars disagree about Maharal's impact. His books were not reprinted in his lifetime, which may betoken limited interest in them. His complex outlook was never fully adopted by colleagues or students, and his pedagogic reforms failed. Still, there are indications that his influence was enduring. Portions of his views were adopted by influential contemporaries like Efraim Lenczycz, David Gans, and Yom Tov Lippmann Heller. His attitudes toward the study of nature found purchase well into the nineteenth century. His writing greatly influenced leaders of the Hasidic movement, which began in the eighteenth century. Today, owing to his emphases on the uniqueness of Jews and the inevitability of their return to the Holy Land, Maharal's thought enjoys renewed popularity among many orthodox Israelis.

Since the nineteenth century, storybooks, plays and films have related that Maharal built an artificial man, called a *golem,* and used kabbalistic incantations to endow him with life. In many versions of this story, Maharal instructed his *golem* to protect Prague Jews from malevolent Christians. It is difficult to determine why these later legends became associated with Maharal. Ironically, Maharal is better remembered in popular lore for this legendary feat than he is for his important, actual achievements.

BIBLIOGRAPHY

Primary Works
Judah Loew ben Bezalel. *The Book of Divine Power.* Translated by Shlomo Mallin. Jerusalem and New York, 1975.
Judah Loew ben Bezalel. *The Mizvah Candle.* Translated and edited by Shlomo Mallin. Jerusalem and Spring Valley, N.Y., 1993.
Judah Loew ben Bezalel. *Nesivos Olam, Nesiv ha-Torah: An Appreciation of Torah Study.* Translated and adapted by Eliakim Willner. Brooklyn, N.Y., 1994.

Secondary Works
Bokser, Ben Zion. *From the World of the Cabbalah: The Philosophy of Rabbi Judah Loew of Prague.* New York, 1954.
Ruderman, David B. *Jewish Thought and Scientific Discovery in Early Modern Europe.* New Haven, Conn., 1995. See chapter 2, "The Legitimation of Scientific Activity among Central and Eastern European Jews," pp. 54–99.
Sherwin, Byron L. *Mystical Theology and Social Dissent: The Life and Works of Judah Loew of Prague.* London and Rutherford, N.J., 1982.

NOAH J. EFRON

MAJOR, JOHN (Mair; 1469–1550), philosopher, theologian, political theorist, and historian; head of a school that rejuvenated Scholasticism at the University of Paris in the beginning of the sixteenth century. Born at Glenhornie, near Haddington, Scotland, Major received his early education there and at Cambridge (1491–1492). Later in life he returned to teach philosophy and theology at the University of Glasgow (1518–1522) and theology at the University of Saint Andrews (1522–1525; 1531–1550). The better part of Major's career was spent in Paris, where he studied at the Colleges of Santa Barbara and Montaigu (1492–1495). Known there as Jean Mair, he taught philosophy and theology at both institutions, and, from about 1501, at the College of Navarre. His students, and their students in turn, unified the "learning of the Schools" on the continent and exerted an influence there that was unparalleled in its time.

Major himself had a diversified training, having been taught at Paris by the nominalist Thomas Bricot (d. 1516), the logician Jeronimo Pardo (d. 1505), and the Scotist Peter Tartaret (d. c. 1522). Generally eclectic, he professed a large number of nominalist theses while remaining open to consideration of their realist alternatives. To his eclecticism Major brought a great concern for positive sources, researching and editing with his students many terminist and Aristotelian treatises of the High and Late Middle Ages. A distinctive historical contribution was his *Historia Majoris Brittaniae, tam Angliae quam Scotiae* (History of Great Britain, both England and Scotland; Paris, 1521), the first critical history of the Scots, in which Major favors the union of the two kingdoms. He edited the works of his disciple Jacques Almain (c. 1480–1515) as well as those of his countryman John Duns Scotus (c. 1266–1308). Among his theological writings were commentaries on the *Sentences* of Peter Lombard (c. 1095–1160), which are notable for their nominalist stress on the individual in moral matters and their treatment of scientific problems in a theological context. They were used and cited, generally favorably, until the end of the sixteenth century. Major taught theology to John Knox (1513–1572), George Buchanan (1506/07–1592), and John Calvin (1509–1564) but was unsympathetic to the Reformers, remaining faithful to Rome until his death.

In philosophy Major produced many logical treatises—monographs, such as his *Insolubilia* (Insolubles; Paris, 1500) and commentaries on Peter of Spain and Aristotle, including the latter's *Posterior Analytics*. He also composed questions on all of Aristotle's physical works and his *Metaphysics* (Paris, 1526), giving a balanced exposition of positions then being taught "in the way of the nominalists and the realists." In so doing Major became an important conduit through which the writings of fourteenth-century Mertonians exerted an influence in the schools of the sixteenth century, including those in Scotland, Belgium, Spain, and Italy. Major's most original work was his *Propositum de infinito* (Treatise on the infinite; edited and translated into French by Hubert Élie; Paris, 1938). This work treats three questions: whether actual infinities exist; whether God could create an actual infinite; and whether, given an infinite body, such a body could move. Major argued in favor of actual infinities, using techniques that anticipate modern mathematical treatments of infinity; held that God could produce infinities of particular types; and argued that God could move a body infinite in all directions both rectilinearly and circularly.

Among Major's students were the Spaniards Gaspar Lax (1487–1560), important for his work in mathematics; Luis Nuñez Coronel (d. 1531); and Coronel's younger brother Antonio (fl. 1509–1518), who was Major's favorite; and the Flemings Peter Crockaert of Brussels (c. 1470–1540) and John Dullaert of Ghent (c. 1470–1513). Lax and Dullaert in turn taught Juan Luis Vives (1492–1540), who recorded their regret for time earlier wasted on logical subtleties, and the Valencian Juan de Celaya (c. 1490–1558), who composed commentaries on many of Aristotle's works "in the threefold way of St. Thomas, the realists, and the nominalists." Celaya's influence is clear in the works of Francisco de Vitoria (d. 1546) and Domingo de Soto (1494/95–1560).

The circle surrounding Major included, apart from logicians, the mathematicians Pedro Ciruelo (1470–1554), who published numerous editions of earlier works on astronomy and mathematics, and the Portuguese Alvaro Thomaz (fl. 1509–1513), whose *Liber de triplici motu* (Book on the three kinds of movement; Paris, 1509) manifests a sophisticated knowledge of fourteenth-century calculatory techniques. The merging of their ideas with those of the nominalist, Scotist, Thomist, and Augustinian Aristotelians of Major's school became a catalyst for serious discussion of problems of motion. It provided a foundation on which later sixteenth- and early seventeenth-century thinkers would erect the edifice of modern science.

BIBLIOGRAPHY

Broadie, Alexander. *The Circle of John Mair: Logic and Logicians in Pre-Reformation Scotland*. Oxford and New York, 1985.

Élie, Hubert, ed. *Le traité "De l'infini" de Jean Mair*. Paris, 1938.

Villoslada, Ricardo García. *La Universidad de Paris durante los estudios de Francisco de Vitoria (1507–1522)*. Rome, 1938.

Wallace, William A. *Prelude to Galileo: Essays on Medieval and Sixteenth-Century Sources of Galileo's Thought*. Dordrecht, Netherlands; Boston; and London; 1981.

WILLIAM A. WALLACE

MAKIN, BATHSUA (c. 1600–c. 1674), English educator. Makin was born in London. Her father, Henry Reginald, was a schoolmaster, and her sister, Ithamaria, married the mathematician John Pell. As a young woman she worked in her father's school helping to instruct adolescent boys. Her early knowledge of languages is displayed in her *Musa Virginea*. Written when she was sixteen, it includes poems and passages in Latin, Greek, French, and Hebrew dedicated to various members of the Stuart family. She was tutor to Princess Elizabeth, daughter of King Charles I, and established a school in London to teach advanced subjects to girls at the secondary level. The school built upon her concern that women were denied learning in classical languages and advanced training in mathematics, sciences, literature, and history.

Makin is known primarily for *An Essay to Revive the Antient Education of Gentlewomen* (1673). In this work Makin disguises her identity as a woman, directing the work to her "fellow" men. She encouraged her male audience to support women's education because it would allow them to have better-educated and more competent companions. She also castigated their claims of superiority over women and questioned the manhood of those who "trample upon those that are down" and "scoff at Women kept ignorant on purpose to be made slaves."

Makin included learned women in her treatise and had a close correspondence with the Dutch scholar Anna Maria van Schurman, in Latin as well as Greek. She discussed women intellectuals from the past and present, noting of Margaret Cavendish, "by her own Genius, rather than any timely Instruction, [she] over-tops many grave 'Gown-Men.'" The link among learned women was further confirmed by Mary Astell's use of Makin's *Essay* in her own proposal for a women's college near the end of the seventeenth century.

See also Education.

BIBLIOGRAPHY
Brink, Jean R. "Bathsua Reginald Makin: 'Most Learned Matron.'" *Huntington Library Quarterly* 54 (fall 1991): 313–326.
Teague, Frances. *Bathsua Makin, Woman of Learning.* Lewisburg, Pa., 1998.

HILDA SMITH

MALDONADO, JUAN (c. 1485–c. 1554), Castilian humanist. Juan Maldonado, one of the few Castilian intellectuals with whom Erasmus corresponded, wrote a number of interesting but little-studied Latin works. Although born in a small town in the diocese of Cuenca and educated in Salamanca, where his scholarly interests were shaped by the Italian-trained grammarian Elio Antonio de Nebrija (1444–1522) and the Flemish humanist Christophe de Longueil (1488–1522), most of Maldonado's publications date from his years as the diocese of Burgos's examiner of candidates for ordination. Many modern scholars have written that he eventually became vicar general, but surviving documents do not support this assertion.

Maldonado has been a writer more used than studied, and because his surviving work relates to two different scholarly controversies, no real sense of his intellectual program or activities has emerged. He has been understood in relation to his writing on political conflict or his conformity to Erasmus's educational and religious positions.

Only a few years after the *comunidades,* or revolt of the comuneros (1520–1521), Maldonado reflected on these events in a long dialogue, *De motu Hispaniae* (The movement of Spain; written 1524–1525), in which the protagonists discussed the course and significance of these events, some of which the author had witnessed. Although never printed in Maldonado's lifetime, in 1840 the Escorial monastery's librarian published a Castilian translation in response to the interest in the *comunidades* among educated readers as a result of the successful implantation in Spain of the liberal constitutionalist movement.

In his masterwork on Spanish humanism, *Erasmus and Spain* (1937), Marcel Bataillon provided the first systematic discussion of many of the works the Burgos humanist had printed. Bataillon used Maldonado as an example of an intellectual whose early enthusiasm for Erasmus's religious reform program was dampened by fear of the Inquisition's repressive activities. Although he did nothing with the insight, Bataillon did identify as a major part of Maldonado's writing his attention to the dialogue form and indicated the great importance of such experi-

mentation: within a generation of Maldonado's death, Castilian writers would begin publishing vernacular novels of high quality.

Translations of several of Maldonado's books have been published by various scholars, and Heliodoro García García has clarified greatly our understanding of his work by tying together the two scholarly streams. Moreover, from this new work on Maldonado, it is becoming clear that the Iberian impact of Renaissance humanism has been both undervalued and misunderstood. As a humanities teacher Maldonado was a leader of a group of reform writers who advocated leadership by activist bishops, municipal patricians, and monarchs educated in eloquence and Christian piety as the foundation of good government and civic responsibility. He opposed violence, injustices against the poor, and factionalism; Maldonado saw Erasmus's blanket attacks on the mendicant orders as a form of factionalism that strengthened heresy. Maldonado is an important figure for any serious study of Castilian humanism and Latin letters, including that dealing with later developments like Jesuit educational and religious reform.

BIBLIOGRAPHY
There is nothing significant on Maldonado in English, and there is no modern edition of many of his most important publications, including *Pastor bonus* (Good pastor; Burgos, c. 1531). There are recent editions of Castilian translations.

García García, Heliodoro. *El pensamiento comunero y erasmista de Juan Maldonado.* Madrid, 1983. Contains selections from several of his books (Latin originals and Castilian translations) and Castilian translations of Maldonado's two letters to Erasmus and the latter's replies.
Maldonado, Juan. *De motu Hispaniae. El levantamiento de España.* Edited by María Angeles Durán Ramas. Madrid, 1991. Latin text (originally written 1524–1525) and Castilian translation of the manuscript in the National Library in Madrid.
Rivera, Milagros, and Peter G. Bietenholz, eds. "Juan Maldonado." In *Contemporaries of Erasmus: A Biographical Register of the Renaissance and Reformation.* Vol. 2, *F–M.* Toronto; Buffalo, N.Y.; and London; 1996. Pages 370–371. Concerns Maldonado's relations with Erasmus.

J. B. OWENS

MALHERBE, FRANÇOIS DE (1555–1628), French poet and literary theorist. The son of a Protestant magistrate, Malherbe was born at Caen in Normandy and studied law in Germany. In 1577 he became secretary to Henri d'Angoulême, natural son of Charles IX and governor of Provence, and spent twenty years in that province. In 1605, upon the recommendation of Cardinal Du Perron, he became official court poet under Henry IV, a position he retained during the regency and the early years of Louis XIII's personal reign. He was known mainly as a legislator of French poetry, in spite of not having written or published much verse. He demoted the status of the poet from that of prophet-seer upheld by Pierre de Ronsard; he is reported to have said that "a good poet is of no more use to his country than a good skittle-player." He became a purist in style, concerned with conciseness in diction, a pure French grammar and vocabulary, and an intellectual poetry lauding primarily the achievements of wealthy patrons. He condemned hiatus and run-on lines and created exacting rules governing meter and rhyme; he prohibited Latinisms, neologisms, archaisms, and regionalisms from poetic expression; he insisted on a natural word order and excluded mythological erudition. He sought a simplified, classical form. Honorat de Racan and François Maynard were among his disciples. His theoretical opinions can be gathered from Racan's biography of him, from his marginal comments on Philippe Desportes's poetry, and from his letters to his friend Nicolas Peiresc.

BIBLIOGRAPHY

Primary Works

Malherbe, François de. *Oeuvres.* Edited by Antoine Adam. Paris, 1971.
Malherbe, François de. *Oeuvres poétiques.* Edited by René Fromilhague and Raymond Lebègue. 2 vols. Paris, 1968.

Secondary Works

Baustert, Raymond. *L'univers moral de Malherbe: Étude de la pensée dans l'oeuvre poétique.* Bern, Switzerland, and New York, 1997.
Henry, Gilles. *François de Malherbe: Gentilhomme et poète, 1555–1628.* Mondeville, France, 1984. Standard biography.

ANNE R. LARSEN

MANNERISM. Mannerism is the term commonly used to define the art and architecture of Italy and other parts of Europe between the phases of the high Renaissance and the baroque (c. 1520–c. 1600). Mannerist artists rejected the classical principles of the high Renaissance in favor of a more subjective and highly expressive approach to their work.

The meanings of the term are rooted in the Italian word *maniera,* which, in the sixteenth century, Giorgio Vasari used in the sense of "style" or "stylishness." In the following century, Giovanni Pietro Bellori applied the same word to the work of Vasari and other sixteenth-century artists; their art was criticized for displaying a certain artificiality and for presenting a distorted view of nature. Until the 1920s,

A Mannerist Painting. *Moses Defending the Daughters of Jethro* by Rosso Fiorentino (1494–1540). The painting illustrates the passage in Exodus 2:16–20 (where Jethro is named Reuel). GALLERIA DEGLI UFFIZI, FLORENCE/ALINARI/ ART RESOURCE, NY

the term was used in a pejorative sense because mannerism was seen to have brought about a decline from the ideals of the high Renaissance. However, since the 1920s, as sixteenth-century art has returned to favor, the term has lost its negative connotations. The art of the period has come to be prized for its bizarre effects, emotionalism, elegant forms, vivid colors, sense of movement, and subjective expression.

In painting, the style evolved in Rome from Raphael's late phase and from the work of Michelangelo's middle career. Subsequently, it spread to various Italian centers. Parmigianino (1503–1540), who visited Rome in the 1520s, was strongly influenced by Raphael, as the facial types and studied gracefulness of the *Madonna of the Long Neck* (c. 1535; Florence, Uffizi) indicate. Considered to be an important work in the development of mannerist painting, the *Madonna* displays elongated anatomical forms and curious inconsistencies in the scale of the figures and architectural features. These aspects of Parmigianino's work contrast with the harmonious ideals and lucid compositions of the high Renaissance. Michelangelo's influence is discernible in the work of Rosso Fiorentino (1495–1540), whose picture of *Moses Defending the Daughters of Jethro* (1523; Florence, Uffizi) is filled with a violent power. The mass of tumbling bodies in the composition creates a profound emotional impact, which is further strengthened by the expressive distortion of the bodies. Jacopo da Pontormo (1494–1556), Rosso's friend in Florence, was another remarkable painter of the period, and his *Deposition* (c. 1528; Florence, Santa Felicità) is typically mannerist in the suggested movement of the figures, the spiritual intensity of the scene, the elongated limbs, and the dramatic use of color.

In sculpture, the style is characterized, most importantly, by a shift from high Renaissance frontality to an approach where multiple views were favored. The spectator, in the process, can move around the statue, which appears to be in constant movement. The term *figura serpentinata* (serpentine line) expresses this idea and can be used to describe, for example, the marble *Rape of a Sabine* (1582; Florence, Loggia dei Lanzi) by Giambologna (1529–1608), with its multiple viewpoints and highly dramatic movement. Giambologna's bronze *Mercury* (1580; Florence, Bargello) displays the mannerist hallmarks of elongation of the body and a conscious courtly elegance, as does the gold salt cellar (1540–1544; Vienna, Kunsthistorisches Museum), by Benvenuto Cellini (1500–1571), with its intellectually complex iconography.

Mannerist architecture defies the rules of the classical orders and is frequently characterized by a curious treatment of space, surface, and decorative motifs. These features could easily describe Michelangelo's designs for the New Sacristy (1519–1533) of San Lorenzo and the vestibule of the Laurenziana Library (from 1524), both in Florence. In each project, the inner walls are treated as sculptural elements and have become inward-turning facades. In the case of the library vestibule, pairs of columns are set into the wall, while panels at either side project beyond the level of the columns. In his designs for the Palazzo del Tè (from 1526; Mantua), Giulio Romano (c. 1499–1546) also included deliberately ambiguous forms and treated the wall surface in an irrational way. Like Michelangelo, Giulio Romano moved away from the balanced proportions and clarity of form of high Renaissance architecture and developed an idiosyncratic style.

Mannerism spread to other parts of Europe. In France it was developed at the court of Francis I at Fontainebleau, where Rosso and Francesco Primaticcio (1504/05–1570) worked on the Galerie François I (1533–1540), and Cellini executed a bronze relief of a *Nymph* (1542–1544; Paris, Louvre). The style was also adopted by native artists, such as Jean Goujon (c. 1510–1568) and Germain Pilon (c. 1525–1590). In the Low Countries, Maerten van Heemskerck (1498–1574) and Marten de Vos (1532–1603), who had visited Italy, created an influential mannerist style back in their homeland. Other notable centers of the style were the courts of Rudolf II in Prague and Albert V in Munich.

See also **Florence**, *subentry on* **Art in the Sixteenth Century**; *and biographies of figures mentioned in this entry.*

BIBLIOGRAPHY

Briganti, Giuliano. *Italian Mannerism.* Translated by Margaret Kunzle. Princeton, N.J., 1962.

Freedberg, Sydney J. *Painting in Italy, 1500–1600.* 3d ed. New Haven, Conn., 1993.

Pope-Hennessy, John. *Italian High Renaissance and Baroque Sculpture.* 3 vols. 3d ed. Oxford, 1986.

Shearman, John. *Mannerism.* Harmondsworth, U.K., 1967.

Wundram, Manfred. *Renaissance und Manierismus.* Stuttgart, Germany, and Zurich, Switzerland, 1985.

FLAVIO BOGGI

MANTEGNA, ANDREA (1430/31–1506), north Italian painter. Born to a humble carpenter in a village near Padua, Andrea Mantegna was apprenticed at age eleven to the Paduan painter Francesco Squarcione, who became his adoptive father and with whom he later had a falling out.

Mantegna in Padua. Squarcione was no great painter, but in his *studium* apprentices were exposed to Renaissance artistic ideals and practices, such as copying after classical sculpture. Mantegna was therefore trained in the atmosphere of academic antiquarianism that was particular to mid-fifteenth-century Padua, and with which he was temperamentally entirely in sympathy. This shows clearly in his first major works, his contributions to the fresco decoration (largely destroyed in 1944) of the Ovetari Chapel in the Church of the Eremitani. In *St. James before Herod Agrippa* (1450–1451) Mantegna incorporated classical motifs and details gleaned from Roman triumphal arches and tombs known to him in north Italy, placing these within a perspectival setting that indicates his knowledge of Leon Battista Alberti's treatise *Della pittura* (1436).

Andrea Mantegna. *St. Sebastian.* According to legend, Sebastian was a Christian soldier sentenced to be executed by being shot with arrows during the persecution under the emperor Maximinus between 304 and 311. Oil on poplar wood; c. 1460; 68 × 30 cm (26.75 × 12 in.). [For other depictions of St. Sebastian, see the entries on Correggio and Hans Holbein.] KUNSTHISTORISCHES MUSEUM, GEMÄLDEGALERIE, VIENNA/ERICH LESSING/ART RESOURCE

His Paduan works also show his strong response to the sculpture of the Florentine Donatello, who worked in Padua from 1443 to 1453. The combined influences of classical statuary and Donatello's Paduan bronzes led Mantegna to develop an exceptionally sculptural treatment of the human figure. This provided the foundation for the severe, statuesque figure style to be seen in mature paintings like the *St. Sebastian* (Paris, Louvre), probably painted in the early 1480s.

Mantegna in Mantua. In 1459 Mantegna completed the high altarpiece for San Zeno in Verona, one of the most influential north Italian altarpieces of the fifteenth century and still in situ. He left Padua in January 1460 to enter the service of Lodovico Gonzaga, marquess of Mantua from 1444 to 1478, as his court painter. Mantegna's early works in Mantua were all small paintings on panel, some of which were made during the 1460s for the decoration of the chapel in the Mantuan castle. Although he never adopted a Netherlandish oil-painting technique, Mantegna was indebted to northern painting, as the intricate surfaces of these paintings demonstrate. The *Circumcision* (Florence, Uffizi) perhaps best shows his brilliant, miniaturist painting of fine details. Using crystal-clear lighting and an evolved sense of the colors and surface textures (especially of minerals), Mantegna here showed a subtle feeling for the variety of expression required in narrative presentation.

The principal surviving work done for Lodovico Gonzaga is the fresco decoration of the Camera Picta (also known as the Camera degli Sposi), started in 1465 and completed in 1474 [see the color plates in this volume]. Using fictive classicizing architecture and elaborate illusionistic devices, Mantegna depicted the Gonzaga family within their court environment. On the west wall, set against an extensive landscape dotted with the ruins of classical buildings, Lodovico greets his second son Francesco, perhaps on his return from Rome after his investiture as a cardinal in December 1461. In contrast to the flat, tonally high-key treatment of these figures, Mantegna portrayed the assembled Gonzaga family on the north wall with rounded forms and a rich tonality, as though to suggest their physical presence within the space of the room. Especially ingenious and witty is the painted oculus at the crown of the vault through which, silhouetted against the open sky, a group of women and sharply foreshortened putti peer down at the family group.

After Lodovico Gonzaga's death in 1478, Mantegna's next major patron was Lodovico's grandson Francesco, marquess of Mantua from 1484 to 1519, for whom probably Mantegna painted the nine canvases of the *Triumphs of Caesar* (Hampton Court Palace, Royal Collection). Already under way in 1486, work on these huge canvases was interrupted by Mantegna's stay in Rome between 1488 and 1490, where for Pope Innocent VIII he decorated a chapel (destroyed in 1780) in the Villa Belvedere. The *Triumphs* are an inventive reconstruction of a triumphal procession of Julius Caesar, who is shown in the last canvas enthroned on his chariot. The procession includes sacrificial animals and enemy captives, the weaponry of classical warfare, and miscellaneous booty won in conflict, all represented with unprecedented archaeological accuracy.

Work for Isabella d'Este. The last phase of Mantegna's career was dominated by painting for Francesco Gonzaga's wife, Isabella d'Este. Soon after her marriage in 1490 she constructed a *studiolo* (a small room embellished with paintings and other objects of art) in her new apartments in the castle of Mantua. For this room Mantegna supplied the first two (and started a third) of a series of elaborate allegorizing paintings, in which Isabella sought to make visually evident her moral and intellectual qualities. Mantegna's own intellectual skills and profound knowledge of the antique world allowed him to match the complex allegorical programs of the *Parnassus* (installed in 1497) and the *Pallas Expelling the Vices from the Garden of Virtue* (completed 1502; both in Paris, Louvre) with great pictorial inventiveness and brilliant surface treatment. The decoration of Isabella d'Este's *studiolo* also included two works painted to imitate bronze. These and other late paintings that imitate sculptural reliefs offer further indications of Mantegna's interest both in depicting minerals and in establishing visually the representational superiority of painting over sculpture. The final tribute both to Mantegna's intellectual learning and to his renown as a creative artist was the establishment of his funerary chapel in Alberti's great church of S. Andrea in Mantua. Mantegna's *all'antica* (in a classical style) bronze self-portrait bust, probably cast some twenty years before his death, was later installed at the entrance to his chapel.

Influence. In 1453 Mantegna married Nicolosia, daughter of the Venetian painter Jacopo Bellini and sister to Gentile and Giovanni Bellini. The latter in particular was powerfully affected in his early work by his brother-in-law's style and pictorial skills. In the later fifteenth century Mantegna's influence was felt, in part through his activities as a printmaker, throughout north Italy and beyond—by, for example, the German painter Albrecht Dürer (1471–1528). But the severity of Mantegna's style did not chime in well with new artistic directions at the start of the sixteenth century, and after his death his influence rapidly diminished.

BIBLIOGRAPHY

Kristeller, Paul. *Andrea Mantegna*. London, 1901. The great early monograph and still an indispensable analysis of Mantegna's life and work.

Lightbown, Ronald. *Mantegna*. Oxford, 1986. The most recent important monograph and catalogue raisonné, and a major contribution to the study of Mantegna within his historical context.

Martindale, Andrew. *The Triumphs of Caesar*. London, 1979. A volume in the series of catalogs of the Royal Collection, in which the *Triumphs* are set within the broader context of Mantegna's art.

Martineau, Jane, ed. *Andrea Mantegna*. Exhibition catalog (London, Royal Academy of Arts). London, 1992. With important contributions on Mantegna's techniques, graphic works, portraiture, and other themes.

FRANCIS AMES-LEWIS

MANTUA. The seat of an important Lombard state in the Renaissance, Mantua sits on the banks of the Mincio River approximately ten miles upstream from the Po River. The city is surrounded by the Mincio on three sides. Additional fortifications and a canal on the fourth side made it impregnable to attack throughout the Renaissance. Its population in the Renaissance probably rose somewhat above thirty thousand.

In 1328 Luigi Gonzaga (c. 1267–1360) seized control of the government and transformed the territory into a hereditary lordship. The Gonzaga ruled there until 1707. In 1433 Emperor Sigismund (1433–1437) made the Mantuan state a marquisate and a fief of the Holy Roman Empire. During the fourteenth and fifteenth centuries, Mantua struggled to maintain its independence in the face of the ambitions of its larger neighbors, Venice and Milan. The Gonzaga achieved this both by timely alliances with one or the other of these two states and by acting as their condottieri, or mercenary captains. Ludovico II (1412/14–1478) in particular succeeded at this policy.

During the late fifteenth and sixteenth centuries Mantua became involved in the struggle between the Habsburgs and the Valois for control of northern Italy. In 1495 Francesco II Gonzaga (1466–1519) played an important role in the expulsion of the

French king, Charles VIII (1470–1498) from Italy. Under Federico II (1500–1540), who was already Capitano Generale della Chiesa, or commander of papal forces, Mantua established a close alliance with the Habsburgs. This determined Mantuan foreign policy for the remainder of the Renaissance.

During the Renaissance Mantua was the scene of important cultural developments. In 1423 Gianfrancesco Gonzaga (1395–1444) invited the humanist Vittorino da Feltre (1378–1446) to establish a school of the humanities for the education of his children and those of other notable families of the area. This boarding school became the model for many subsequent humanist schools.

In order to embellish their court the Gonzaga also invited many artists to Mantua. Gianfrancesco Gonzaga brought Antonio Pisanello (c. 1395–1455) to decorate his palace with frescoes depicting the Arthurian legends. Ludovico II and his wife, Barbara of Brandenburg (1422–1481), employed the painter Andrea Mantegna (1431–1506) for many years. His frescoes in the Camera degli Sposi in the Ducal Palace are among the greatest works of fifteenth-century Italian painting [see the color plates in this volume]. Ludovico and Barbara also had Leonbattista Alberti (1404–1472) design the new Basilica of Sant' Andrea and the church of San Sebastiano. In the sixteenth century Francesco Gonzaga and his wife, Isabella d'Este (1474–1539), supported a splendid court. Isabella in particular maintained a large correspondence with numerous artists and literary figures. Giulio Romano (c. 1499–1546) held the post of chief architect of Mantua under Duke Federico II and his brother Cardinal Ercole Gonzaga (1505–1563). His works there include the Palazzo del Tè on the outskirts of the city, the remodeled interior of the Cathedral of San Pietro, and the monastery church of San Benedetto in Polirone.

Mantua held a significant place in Renaissance religious history as well. Pope Pius II (1458–1464) convened the Diet of Mantua in 1459 as a part of his failed attempt to organize a crusade against the Turks. The younger sons of the Gonzaga family played an important role in church politics as bishops of Mantua and cardinals. Starting with Cardinal Francesco Gonzaga (1461–1483) a series of ten Gonzaga held the post of cardinal and brought the interests of the ruling family to bear on the policies of the Holy See. During the sixteenth century Protestantism made inroads for a time among merchants, peasants, and clerics. A Mantuan, Benedetto da Mantova (fl. 1534–1541) authored *Il Beneficio di Cristo* (The benefit of Christ's death; 1543), the most significant

product of Italian Reform thought. The Gonzaga's family's commitment to Roman Catholicism prevented this from taking root, however. Cardinal Ercole Gonzaga acted as president and papal legate at the Council of Trent from 1562–1563.

The death in 1627 of Vincenzo II, the last of the original line, led to the decline of the duchy. There ensued a war of succession, the Mantuan War (1627–1630) that became a part of the Thirty Years' War (1618–1648). France supported Carlo I (1580–1637), a representative of a French branch of the family, the Gonzaga-Nevers. He succeeded in winning the duchy for himself but not before imperial forces that had been supporting his rival sacked the city. Mantua never fully recovered from this destruction. In 1707 the last Gonzaga duke of Mantua, the dissolute Ferdinando Carlo (1652–1708), was exiled by the Habsburgs for supporting Louis XIV in the War of the Spanish Succession (1701–1713). The duchy, an imperial fief, then reverted to the Habsburgs.

See also **Gonzaga, House of.**

BIBLIOGRAPHY

Coniglio, Giuseppe. *I Gonzaga.* Milan, 1967.

Mazzoldi, Leonardo, ed. *Mantova: La Storia.* Mantua, Italy, 1958, 1963.

Mozzarelli, Cesare. *Mantova e i Gonzaga: dal 1382 al 1707.* Turin, Italy, 1987.

Simon, Kate. *A Renaissance Tapestry: The Gonzaga of Mantua.* New York, 1988.

PAUL V. MURPHY

MANUSCRIPTS. From the Latin *manu scriptum,* the word "manuscript" means any text written by hand. Until the advent of movable-type printing in Renaissance Europe, manuscript books were the primary means for transmission of literary and documentary material, and although printing radically changed the literary landscape of early modern Europe, manuscripts continued to be crucially important cultural phenomena. To understand manuscripts fully, one must imagine oneself in a very different world, a world where the book was a repository of texts (much as it is today) but also where the book was an artifact, every one distinct, quite unlike most present-day books, in composition, layout, and value.

Late Ancient and Medieval Background. The late ancient world witnessed an important transition from the papyrus roll to the book, or codex. Because of their transportability and the relative ease of reference they provided, codices became the preferred mode of textual transmission. With the ad-

Manuscript of Ficino. Opening page of Marsilio Ficino's Latin translation of *Pimander* (the opening treatise of the *Corpus hermeticum*). Early printed typefaces and page design imitated the look of manuscripts. BIBLIOTECA MEDICEO-LAURENZIANA, FLORENCE, MS. 21, 8, FOL. 3R

vance of cenobitic monasticism and the provision in St. Benedict's Rule that monks engage in manual labor, the stage was set for the large-scale Western transmission of texts, both sacred and secular. The copying of books was interpreted to "count" as manual labor and the monastic *scriptorium* became the central place for this enterprise. This continued throughout the early Middle Ages.

Physically, manuscripts were composed of animal skins, usually of sheep or calves, which were soaked in lye, scraped, and dried. The product is known as parchment, sometimes "vellum" parchment. (*Vellum* is related to the Latin verb *vello*, which means "pluck," and thus refers to the manner in which the skin was prepared.) Sheets of parchment were sewn together into quires, which were themselves bound into book form.

The twelfth-century revival of learning and the subsequent rise of universities both increased the scope of manuscript production and changed its parameters. Manuscripts were produced using the *pecia* (or "piece") system. University officials would deposit a standardized copy of a certain text with an official custodian, known as a *stationarius* (literally, "stationer"). The *stationarius* would loan out "pieces," or *peciae,* of the book to professional scribes, who would then copy them, creating the opportunity for production and distribution on a scale hitherto unknown. The wide-scale introduction of paper into western Europe in the thirteenth and fourteenth centuries combined with the "piece system" to contribute to the availability and affordability of manuscript books. Later, the shop of the *stationarius* would evolve into a full-scale manuscript copy shop, and would become an important feature on the cultural landscape of the Renaissance.

Before arriving at the Renaissance, there is another piece of the manuscript puzzle worth considering: the art of manuscript illumination and the book as commodity. In the courts of kings and queens, in the libraries of well-endowed monasteries, in mendicant houses, in both Latin and in the evolving European vernacular tongues, manuscripts were objets d'art. Commissioning a finely illuminated manuscript would allow one to engage in that complicated process of give-and-take, patronage; owning one might demonstrate one's impeccable taste; worshiping with the aid of a precious literary artifact such as the eighth-century *Book of Kells* or the early-fifteenth-century *Très riches heures* (Very rich hours) of the duc de Berry brought one that much closer to God. Economically, such books were significant investments. Until the introduction of paper in the West in the late thirteenth and fourteenth centuries, a finely produced Bible might require the skins of five hundred sheep. Indeed, throughout the Middle Ages and Renaissance, de luxe parchment manuscripts continued to be showpieces for the virtuosity of artisanal book producers.

Renaissance Developments. These aspects of the medieval manuscript tradition continued but were transformed by new Renaissance social and intellectual conditions. The impulse to investigate the ancient world was accompanied by a renewed attention to familiar texts and a desire to rediscover ancient texts which existed in medieval copies, but which had in practice fallen out of circulation. Petrarch's 1345 "discovery" of Cicero's *Letters to Atticus* in Verona, Poggio Bracciolini's discovery of Lucretius's *De rerum natura* (On the nature of things) in 1417, and similar Latin manuscript "discoveries" had significant effects on the cultural world of the Renaissance; they fueled and were fueled by the desire to revive ancient culture.

As the Latin past began to unfold more clearly, questions naturally arose concerning the Greek past, which no one interested in the ancient world could ignore. So in the early years of the fifteenth century, scholars such as Francesco Filelfo and Giovanni Aurispa made protracted trips to the Byzantine world, often returning laden with Greek manuscripts acquired by purchase or by less upstanding means. Upon their arrival in the West the manuscripts were eagerly traded, copied, and translated and their texts disseminated. But for a generation still learning Greek, it is clear that these manuscripts must have served more than simply a text-storage function; they were seen as repositories of ancient wisdom and symbols of a deeper antiquity. Petrarch's famous Greek manuscript of Plato, which in the late fourteenth century he was proud to own but unable to read, is the archetype of the manner in which a book could be more than a book. Manuscripts could serve a purely but powerfully symbolic function.

They could also be objects of scholarly quests. Intellectual communities are heavily invested in things which offer novel contributions to a selected field of study. So it is not without a note of frustration that we hear Poggio Bracciolini complain at Cardinal Giordano Orsini's reticence to loan a newly discovered Plautus manuscript: "I asked the cardinal before he left to release the book. He didn't want to do it. I don't understand the man" (Celenza, "The Will of Cardinal Giordano Orsini," p. 259). A sentiment of this sort points us toward a clearly discernible early Renaissance impulse: the move toward public libraries.

Manuscripts and the Evolution of Libraries.

Obtaining books was a problem in an era in which institutional libraries, such as those of universities, hardly existed. The private scholar had even more difficulty. As humanism evolved, however, one encounters a group of thinkers, humanists, who practiced their literary trade largely outside of an institutional context and were interested in what were then uncommon texts. The literary interests of these skilled rhetoricians were often indulged apart from their place of employment. Thus, they had to content themselves with a catch-as-catch-can approach to

Manuscript of Book of Hours. David proclaiming the glory of God by Jean Colombe from *Très riches heures du duc de Berry,* fifteenth century. MUSÉE CONDÉ, CHANTILLY, FRANCE/GIRAUDON/ART RESOURCE, NY

seeing the books which piqued their interest. Two connected developments are linked to the progression of Renaissance humanism and the desire for texts not linked to traditional professional canons: first, the evolution of libraries of figures connected in some way to curial culture, and second, the development of public libraries.

"Curial" culture is connected not only to the papal court but also refers to a "culture that, although not entirely foreign to the university, was largely formed outside of it—a culture created by laymen, notaries, judges, and chancellors" (Petrucci, *Writers and Readers,* p. 211). As the intensity of late medieval Italy's business culture increased and the star of ancient Latinity was in the ascendant, professional rhetoricians of all stripes (who might find themselves working in the courts of princes, as chancellors of republics, as secretaries to cardinals and popes) became more and more interested in adorning their prose with citations from and allusions to classical literature. The development of humanism thus directly encouraged many of the better off of these figures to develop their own libraries.

However, as the cultural appeal of humanism grew, it is unsurprising that we hear a call for public libraries, since not all had the means to maintain their own. Petrarch actually used the phrase *bibliotheca publica* when discussing the fate of his own library (which he would have left to the republic of Venice had he not felt slighted by the Venetians). Coluccio Salutati (1331–1406), in his *De fato* (2.6, 102–104), wrote: "Let there be founded public libraries into which a copy of all books would be collected." The church politician, bibliophile, and patron of humanism, Cardinal Giordano Orsini, desired in his 1434 testament to leave his manuscript library to the Church of San Biagio in Rome. He wanted to have a library created there and to have that church unified to the Basilica of Saint Peter; "both," he said, "so that divine worship in both of the mentioned churches increase, and so that in the aforesaid church of Saint Peter, as well as in the city of Rome, the number of learned and knowledgeable men increases, in so far as will be possible" (Celenza, "The Will," sec. 14, pp. 277–278).

It is clear that by the early fifteenth century there was a definable will among scholars and patrons to have manuscripts collected into fairly centralized places. Two early libraries are notable. First, there is the library of the monastery of San Marco in Florence: the first public library in western Europe, it was in operation by 1444. Funded by Cosimo (the Elder) de' Medici, at its core were the books left behind by the great antiquarian Niccolò Niccoli. Second, the Vatican library was founded notionally by Pope Nicholas V (reigned 1447–1455) and formally by Sixtus IV in 1475. At that time it contained 2,527 manuscripts. It would grow into one of the greatest repositories of Western manuscripts and was unique among libraries of its day in including a large number of Greek texts.

The Impact of Printing.

By the years of Sixtus IV, printing with movable type was being diffused throughout European culture. Nevertheless, manuscripts continued to pervade the intellectual landscape of Renaissance Europe. We can distinguish three reasons for this: intellectual conservatism; the use of manuscripts to circulate dangerous texts, or materials still in draft; and the use of manuscripts as personal copybooks.

Conservatism. One need look only so far as the earliest printed books to understand the impact of intellectual conservatism: they looked like manuscripts and used the conventions of manuscript writing. Probably influenced by a correctly perceived audience expectation, early printers laid out the printed page in a manner consistent with the way manuscripts were formatted. They even went so far as to create elaborate fonts for certain abbreviations when it would have been more economical simply to print all words out. When printing arrived in Italy, printing firms such as Sweynheym and Pannartz in Rome in the 1460s were quick to adopt in their font-making the calligraphic innovations which had been part of the humanist cultural revival. Also, the manuscript retained its status as an individual product of high craftsmanship: both as text and as objet d'art. [See illustration of the opening page of Marsilio Ficino's translations from the *Corpus hermeticum*.] Many preferred the manuscript to the printed book and expected their most valued tomes to be individually produced, finely illustrated, and extravagantly bound works of art.

Dangerous or incomplete works. Only at the end of the Renaissance do we see the birth of the scientific "academy," the Renaissance equivalent of the professional academic society. There, among other things, scholars could "test out" their ideas among interested colleagues before formally publishing them. So it is no surprise that, before the widespread existence of these societies, intellectuals would circulate their ideas in manuscript before permanently instantiating them in print. One might have been justifiably concerned, say, about the religious orthodoxy of one's ideas but still desirous of communicating them to colleagues. The case of Henry Cornelius Agrippa (1486–1535) comes to mind. He completed in manuscript form his *De occulta philosophia* (On occult philosophy) by 1510. But he waited until 1533, well after the print publication of his *De vanitate scientiarum* (On the vanity of the sciences)—a clearly orthodox work—in 1530 before having the former, more dangerous work printed. One might also think of Copernicus (1473–1543), who feared the ridicule of his peers and thus waited until the last year of his life before agreeing to have his *De revolutionibus orbium caelestium* (On the revolutions of the celestial orbs) printed, even though the ideas contained therein had been circulating in manuscript form and in printed abridgements long before, some since 1512.

Personal copybook. A final reason for the continued importance of manuscripts well into the printing era has to do with the personal copybook. Often these were *florilegia,* anthology-like compilations of a thinker's favorite passages from his favorite works. These are invaluable to historians today, for they demonstrate the literary tastes of Renaissance thinkers. They help us answer the question: Which texts did Renaissance thinkers in practice judge most important? In addition, despite the fact that many ancient authors were edited and printed in the Renaissance, a number were not. Therefore, well into the eighteenth century, manuscripts remained necessary vehicles for the transmission of texts. Printing did not obviate manuscripts; rather, the two media existed side by side and influenced each other in varied ways.

See also **Calligraphy**; **Libraries**.

BIBLIOGRAPHY

Primary Work

Salutati, Coluccio. *De fato et fortuna*. Edited by Concetta Bianca. Florence, 1985.

Secondary Works

Bischoff, Bernhard. *Latin Palaeography: Antiquity and the Middle Ages*. Translated by Dáibhí Ó Cróinín and David Ganz. Cambridge, U.K., 1990. Invaluable survey by a master in the field, covering not only the development of script types but manuscript production as well.

Celenza, Christopher S. "The Will of Cardinal Giordano Orsini (ob. 1438)." *Traditio* 51 (1996): 257–286.

D'Amico, John. "Manuscripts." In *The Cambridge History of Renaissance Philosophy*. Edited by Charles B. Schmitt. Cambridge, U.K., 1988. Pages 11–24. An essential starting point.

Davies, Martin. "Humanism in Script and Print in the Fifteenth Century." In *The Cambridge Companion to Renaissance Humanism*. Edited by Jill Kraye. Cambridge, U.K., 1996. Pages 47–62. A lucidly written, informative recent survey.

De La Mare, Albinia. *The Handwriting of the Italian Humanists*. Oxford, 1973. Invaluable on the interaction of certain humanists with manuscript culture.

Grafton, Anthony, ed. *Rome Reborn: The Vatican Library and Renaissance Culture*. Washington, D.C., and New Haven, Conn., 1993. Excellent on the Vatican Library and its manuscripts, with contributions by leading scholars.

Laistner, Max L. W. *Thought and Letters in Western Europe, A.D. 500 to 900*. Rev. ed. Ithaca, N.Y., 1957. Standard intellectual history of the period in the title. See ch. 9, "Libraries and Manuscripts," for manuscript production centers in the early Middle Ages.

Petrucci, Armando. *Writers and Readers in Medieval Italy: Studies in the History of Written Culture*. Edited and translated by Charles M. Radding. New Haven, Conn., 1995. A highly learned collection of essays that touch in various ways on what the author calls "written culture," and illuminate well many aspects of the world of the manuscript in the Middle Ages and Renaissance.

Roberts, Colin H., and T. C. Skeat. *The Birth of the Codex*. London, 1983.

Ullman, Berthold L., and Philip A. Stadter. *The Public Library of Renaissance Florence*. Padua, Italy, 1972. Tells in a well-documented fashion the story of the founding of the library of San Marco.

Walker, Daniel P. *Spiritual and Demonic Magic from Ficino to Campanella*. London, 1959.

CHRISTOPHER S. CELENZA

MANUTIUS, ALDUS. *See* **Aldine Press.**

MAPS. *See* **Geography and Cartography.**

MARGARET OF AUSTRIA (1480–1530), Habsburg ruler. Daughter of the Habsburg prince and Holy Roman Emperor Maximilian I and Mary of Burgundy, Margaret was destined like many high-ranking women to be used as a pawn in the political machinations of her powerful kin. By age twenty-four she had outlived three arranged marriages. Refusing to remarry, she spent the rest of her life as regent for her nephew, Charles, and effective ruler of the Netherlands.

Her first marriage, to the future French king Charles VIII, was made when Margaret was only two. As a condition of the Treaty of Arras, which stipulated this alliance among its terms, she moved to the French court to be raised by the regent, her husband's older sister Anne de Beaujeu. The marriage was annulled in 1491, when Charles repudiated Margaret in favor of a more advantageous marriage partner. In 1493, Margaret returned to her father's household, where plans for a second marriage began.

The second marriage was meant to unite the Habsburgs with Spain. Margaret was wed to Juan (by proxy in 1495, solemnized 1497), while her brother Philip was married to Juana; both were the children of Ferdinand of Aragon and Isabella of Castile. When Juan died in 1497 and their daughter, born posthumously, did not long survive, Margaret returned to Flanders. At this point, Margaret became godmother to her brother's first son, Charles, the future Emperor Charles V.

Soon she was dispatched again, to become in 1501 the unwilling wife of Philibert, duc de Savoy, who had been her childhood companion at the French court. As duchess, Margaret took over much of the management of the realm (with which Philibert concerned himself little) and developed her cultural interests through contacts with the nearby city of Lyon, a major intellectual center. She also arranged for the building of the church and monastery, an exemplar of late Gothic architecture, in which she would be buried with her husband more than two decades after his death, which occurred following a swift illness in 1504.

After Philibert's death Margaret declined to marry again. In 1506, her brother Philip having died, Margaret was appointed regent for her nephew in the Netherlands (which included today's Netherlands as well as Belgium and part of France), a small but crucial corner of the Habsburg realm. Establishing her court at Malines (between Brussels and Antwerp), she saw to the rearing of Charles, then seven, and his three sisters. Margaret was an effective ruler who assiduously pursued Habsburg interests and sought peaceful solutions to political crises. Her administrative work is recorded in several volumes of letters directed to her father, her nephew, her ambassadors, and her agents everywhere. The culmination of her political achievement was the negotiation of the Treaty of Cambrai (or Ladies' Peace) with the French regent, Louise of Savoy. Signed on 3 August 1529, the treaty put an end, for the moment, to the hostilities between Charles V and Francis I, king of France.

Not all of Margaret's time was given to political work. Her education had begun at the French court, and her career of artistic patronage with the construction of the church and monastery at Brou. Now she presided over a vital court, employing artists and musicians, assembling a library and art collection, and offering patronage to leading intellectual figures; at one point, she lent Erasmus an eleventh-century manuscript of the Gospels for his New Testament edition. Margaret also wrote poetry, a volume of which was published in the nineteenth century as *Albums et oeuvres poétiques de Marguerite d'Autriche* (Poetic works of Margaret of Austria; 1849).

A woman whose aristocratic ancestry put her at risk of being no more than an instrument of the political ambitions of her male kin, Margaret of Austria became a capable ruler and a significant force in the development of the northern Renaissance civilization.

BIBLIOGRAPHY

Iongh, Jane de. *Margaret of Austria, Regent of the Netherlands.* Translated by M. D. Herter Norton. New York, 1953.

Strelka, Josef. *Der burgundische Renaissancehof Margarethes von Österreich und seine literarhistorische Bedeutung.* Vienna, 1957.

Tobriner, Alice, and Ilse Guenther. "Margaret of Austria." In *Contemporaries of Erasmus: A Biographical Register of the Renaissance and Reformation.* Edited by Peter G. Bietenholz; Thomas B. Deutscher, associate editor. 3 vols. Toronto and Buffalo, N.Y., 1985–1987. Vol. 2, pp. 388–389.

MARGARET L. KING

MARGARET OF NAVARRE (Margaret of Angoulême; 1492–1549), French writer. Duchess of Angoulême, daughter of Louise of Savoy and Charles of Angoulême, sister of Francis I (1494–1547), and

queen of Navarre, Margaret became an important political and social figure when Francis became king in 1515. Two years after the death of her first husband, Charles d'Alençon, following the Battle of Pavia on 24 February 1525, she married Henri d'Albret, king of Navarre. Interested in philosophical and religious matters ranging from Neoplatonism to church reform, Margaret was familiar with the works of Dante and Petrarch as well as with the Bible. She set the intellectual and cultural tone at court, especially in the 1530s and early 1540s. An early supporter of reform in the Gallican church, she remained outwardly obedient to Rome. At the same time, however, she protected leading evangelical reformers such as Guillaume Briçonnet and Jacques Lefèvre d'Étaples, who were suspected of Lutheran leanings.

A prolific writer, Margaret wrote a vast body of work, little of which was published in her lifetime. In 1531 she published *Le miroir de l'âme pécheresse* (Mirror of the sinful soul), a long poem that, when it was reprinted in 1533 along with the *Dialogue en forme de vision nocturne* (Dialogue in the form of a nocturnal vision), was condemned by the Sorbonne because of its reformist views concerning grace, faith, and free will. In 1547 she published a collection of her poetry under the title of *Les marguerites de la marguerite des princesses* (Pearls from the pearl of princesses ["marguerite" means both "daisy" and "pearl"]). Many of her major works were not published until the end of the nineteenth century or the twentieth century. Her poems and plays are mainly allegories of the Christian life, fraught with temptation but always moving toward salvation. Judged by early critics to be poorly constructed and prolix, they are now appreciated for their expression of an intensely religious spirit that is often tormented but seeks to find joy in Christ.

Margaret's most famous work, incomplete at her death, is the *Heptameron,* a collection of novellas modeled after Boccaccio's *Decameron.* Ten aristocrats, five men and five women, stranded by a flood, tell stories while waiting for a bridge to be built. After each story, they comment on the tale just told, drawing from it moral lessons that are usually contradictory and inconclusive. Complex relationships are established among the speakers, who focus on the difficulties of reconciling the demands of a worldly life with those of a life lived in accord with the Christian message of charity. Because of its frank and stark depiction of sexual desire, the work perplexed many early readers, who often saw in it a collection of scabrous tales. Late-twentieth-century critics have dwelled on the work's narrative complexity, its subtle and ambiguous moral insights, and the prominence of women in the text. The *Heptameron* is now almost universally ranked alongside the books of Rabelais and Montaigne as one of the greatest works of prose narrative in the French Renaissance.

BIBLIOGRAPHY

Primary Works

Marguerite, Queen, consort of Henry II, king of Navarre. *The Heptameron*. Translated by Paul Chilton. New York, 1984. Translation of French edition of *L'heptaméron* (1943).

Marguerite, Queen, consort of Henry II, king of Navarre. *Le miroir de l'âme pécheresse*. Edited by Joseph L. Allaire. Munich, 1972.

Martineau, Christine, Michel Vessière, and Henry Heller, eds. *Guillaume Briçonnet–Marguerite d'Angoulême correspondence (1521–1524)*. Paris, 1975–1979.

Secondary Works

Cottrell, Robert D. *The Grammar of Silence: A Reading of Marguerite de Navarre's Poetry*. Washington, D.C., 1986.

Lyons, John D., and Mary B. McKinley, eds. *Critical Tales: New Studies of the Heptameron and Early Modern Culture*. Philadelphia, 1993.

ROBERT D. COTTRELL

MARGARET OF PARMA (1522–1586), duchess of Parma and Piacenza and regent of the Low Countries. The illegitimate daughter of the Habsburg emperor Charles V and a servant, Johanna van der Gheenst, Margaret was born in Oudenaarde, Flanders. Reared at the Habsburg court in Mechelen by the successive regents Margaret of Austria and Mary of Hungary, who ruled the Low Countries in the absence of Charles V, she is often described as sharing the strong manners of her two successful predecessors.

In 1536 Margaret entered the treachery of Renaissance patronage politics when she became the wife of Alessandro de' Medici, duke of Florence. After he was murdered in his sleep in 1537, she became the wife of Ottavio Farnese (1525–1586) in 1538. Ironically, they became duke and duchess of Parma and Piacenza in 1550 as a result of a war mounted against his father, Pierluigi, by allies of Charles V; the war resulted in Pierluigi's death and the loss of Piacenza to Charles V. With French help Ottavio was able to hold onto Parma. Relations with the French soured as Margaret struggled to claim the inheritance of her first husband from Catherine de Médicis, queen mother of France, at a time when their French subsidy shrank. In 1556 Ottavio and Margaret returned to the Habsburg fold by reaching a settlement with Margaret's half-brother, Philip II, for the return of Piacenza. He had received the Habsburg titles in Spain, the Low Countries, and Italy from their father in 1555.

Philip tapped Margaret to become regent of the Low Countries in 1559. Margaret left Italy to confront the most dramatic events of her life at the court of her birth. Several factors contributed to a period of growing unrest in the Low Countries: Philip's plan for radical reform of the bishoprics; the presence of Spanish troops; the struggle for power between Antoine Perrenot, Cardinal Granvelle (a leading adviser to Philip), and the local magnates William of Nassau (prince of Orange), Philippe de Montmorency (count of Hornes), and Lamoral (count of Egmont); and Philip's insistence on the enforcement of the laws against Protestant heresy in the face of a growing Calvinist presence. On 5 April 1566 Margaret was confronted by a group of lesser nobles who requested the temporary suspension of these laws. She followed a policy of moderation and compromise while she awaited instructions from Philip.

That summer fierce Protestant iconoclastic riots erupted, followed by an armed rebellion of lesser nobles. Margaret moved to suppress the rebels and punish the leaders without direction from Philip and with limited cooperation from the local authorities. Some historians have seen her actions as preparation for the severe repression that was to follow, while others have viewed her correspondence with Philip as proof of her inexperience and ineptness, which seemed to necessitate that Philip send an army under the captain general Fernando Alvárez de Toledo, duke of Alba. He arrived in 1567 with secret instructions from Philip to install an inquisition, the Council of Troubles, which came to be called the Council of Blood by the locals. Despite her pleas for greater clemency, Margaret soon saw that Alba was ignoring her requests and was pursuing a broader policy of repression. She asked to be relieved of her post and returned to Italy in 1567.

In 1580 Margaret returned as regent of the Low Countries with her son, Alessandro Farnese, whom Philip had selected as his new captain general in yet another phase of the Dutch revolt. Mother and son were unable to cooperate, and Margaret returned to Italy in 1583. She died at Ortona in 1586.

BIBLIOGRAPHY

Primary Work

Thiessen, J. S., and H. A. Enno Van Gelder, eds. *Correspondance française de Marguerite d'Autriche, duchesse de Parme, avec Philippe II*. 3 vols. Utrecht, Netherlands, 1925–1942.

Secondary Works

Iongh, J. de. *Madama: Margaretha van Oostenrijk, hertogin van Parma en Piacenza, 1522–1586*. 3d ed. Amsterdam, 1981.

Probably the best of several non-English biographies. Two others with virtually identical titles are by Anne Puaux in French (1987) and Renato Lefèvre in Italian (1986).

Parker, Geoffrey. *The Dutch Revolt*. Ithaca, N.Y., 1977. The best account in English.

Rodriguez-Salgado, M. J. *The Changing Face of Empire: Charles V, Philip II, and Habsburg Authority, 1551–1559.* Cambridge, U.K., and New York, 1988. Untangles the web of Habsburg politics.

F. E. BEEMON

MARGARET OF VALOIS

MARGARET OF VALOIS (1553–1615), daughter of Henry II of France and Catherine de Médicis, queen consort of Navarre upon her marriage in 1572 to the Protestant Henry of Bourbon, king of Navarre. That wedding, intended to reduce violence between Catholics and Huguenots in the Wars of Religion (1562–1598), instead set the stage for the Saint Bartholomew's Day massacre (24/25 August 1572). In the ensuing struggle for power as her brother King Charles IX was dying, Margaret remained loyal to her new husband and aligned herself with her brother François, duke of Alençon, against their brother Henry, duke of Anjou, and their mother. Anjou became King Henry III when Charles died in 1574. Margaret, Henry of Navarre, and the duke of Alençon were sequestered at the Louvre. Both men eventually escaped, but Henry III and Catherine detained Margaret until 1578, when she rejoined her husband in Gascony. For several years she was involved in efforts to maintain the fragile peace between the moderate Catholics supporting the French royal family and the Huguenots, led by Navarre. At the same time, her sympathies lay with François, who became duke of Anjou in 1574, in his opposition to the crown. After François died in 1584, her situation at her husband's court became increasingly difficult; she left Nérac and retired to Agen in 1585. The same year, a resurgence of conservative Catholic factions and former followers of François joined under the leadership of Henry, third duke of Guise, to proclaim the Holy League. Margaret supported the League, but she had become financially and politically powerless, severed from both her brother and her husband. In 1586 she was captured on Henry III's orders by the marquis of Canillac and imprisoned for several months at Usson in Auvergne. That remote place became her home in self-imposed exile for the next nineteen years. After Henry III was assassinated in 1589, Henry of Navarre became Henry IV of France, and in 1593 he converted to Catholicism. At his initiative, his marriage to Margaret was annulled in 1599.

While at the royal court, Margaret read extensively and became a student of Neoplatonic philosophy, an interest that she further developed in Gascony and Auvergne. In 1574 she wrote and addressed to Catherine the *Mémoire justificatif pour Henri de Bourbon* (Defense of Henry of Bourbon). She wrote poetry and letters, often on Neoplatonist themes. She knew Montaigne, who addressed part of his "Apology for Raymond Sebond" to her. In 1594 she began writing her *Mémoires*. In 1605 Margaret returned to Paris and eventually settled in her palace on the rue de Seine. Reconciled with Henry IV, she enjoyed an amiable relationship with him, his second wife Marie de Médicis, and the young dauphin, the future Louis XIII. Her home became a lively center of intellectual life where she supported writers such as Philippe Desportes, Honoré d'Urfé, and Marie de Gournay. In 1614 she wrote a defense of women, the "Learned and Subtle Discourse." Writers from the sixteenth to the twentieth centuries created about Margaret a legend of disrepute that more recent historians have sought to rectify.

See also **Valois Dynasty**.

BIBLIOGRAPHY

Primary Works

Correspondance, 1569–1614: Marguerite de Valois. Critical edition by Eliane Viennot. Paris, 1998.

Memoirs of Marguerite de Valois. Translated by Liselotte Dieckmann. Paris, 1984. Translation of *Les memoires de la roine Marguerite* (1628).

Mémoires et lettres de Marguerite de Valois. Edited by François Guessard. Paris, 1842. Reprint, New York, 1966.

Secondary Works

Sealy, Robert J. *The Myth of the Reine Margot: Toward the Elimination of a Legend.* New York, 1994.

Viennot, Eliane. *Marguerite de Valois: Histoire d'une femme, histoire d'un mythe.* Paris, 1993.

MARY B. MCKINLEY

MARIANA, JUAN DE

MARIANA, JUAN DE (1535/36–1624), Castilian humanist and Jesuit. After teaching at Italian and French schools of the Society of Jesus, Mariana moved in 1574 to Toledo in Castile. His writing there was marked by the Jesuit instructional technique of presenting the favorite ancient authors of the Renaissance humanist curriculum, to which he added medieval and recent historical examples, within the context of a scholastic deductive framework.

Until the mid-nineteenth century, Mariana's reputation was closely associated with his *Historiae de rebus Hispaniae* (*The General History of Spain;* Latin, 1592; Castilian, 1601). He shaped material from published vernacular chronicles into a Latin account with a Jesuit humanist didactic thrust stressing leaders' eloquent discourse, the moral precepts for evaluating events, and the Roman church's guidance for an understanding of the divine plan. Although Mariana revised and expanded both versions, it was the vernacular translation that was often republished after his death. He showed his continued interest in historical problems in several treatises published in 1609 as *Tractatus VII* (Seven treatises).

Mariana is now more discussed as a standard point of reference for debates about the nature and course of Renaissance political theory and public policy, especially as expressed in his plan of instruction for the future Philip III (ruled 1598–1621) (*De rege et regis institutione* [*The King and the Education of the King*]; 1598) and his treatise on the debasement of coinage (*De monetae mutatione* [On alterations in the value of currency]; 1609). This tendency began in the mid-nineteenth century as Castilian translations of the book on the monarch's education were published to display the domestic roots of liberal constitutionalism. Because the predominant historiographical position was that Mariana's "medieval" views had been superseded by "absolutism" after the defeat of the revolt of the comuneros of 1520–1521, he has often been seen as an isolated voice for defeated ideas. Other scholars have placed Mariana within the development of the theory of the state or have tied him to Netherlander Justus Lipsius's (1547–1606) promotion of the Roman historian Cornelius Tacitus (c. A.D. 55–c. 120) as a political guide. Much recent research on the kingdom's representative institution, the Cortes, has demonstrated that many of his views were commonplace among Castilian political leaders. Mariana defended tyrannicide and became especially identified with the doctrine when French officials ordered the royal educational treatise burned after the assassination of their king Henry IV in 1610.

In the third and final book of *De rege et regis institutione*, Mariana discussed how rulers should handle a number of contemporary problems. He inserted in the second edition of 1605 a chapter on the debasement of coinage and was sufficiently attracted by this abuse of royal authority to expand his comments in one of the *Tractatus VII*. Because of allusions to royal ministers, Mariana was subjected to a hearing in Madrid and confined for about a year. He was subsequently rehabilitated and later honored by Philip IV (reigned 1621–1665). His concern for public-policy issues makes Mariana a link

between Renaissance humanist educators and the seventeenth-century *arbitristas*, who published reform projects.

Too little effort has been made to understand Mariana's work within the context of Toledo's printing industry, of the city's intellectuals and politicians dissatisfied with royal government, and of disputes among Jesuits and between them and other orders.

See also **Political Thought**.

BIBLIOGRAPHY

Primary Works

Mariana, Juan de. *The General History of Spain.* . . . Edited by John Stevens. London, 1699. A translation probably based on one of the seventeenth-century republications of the author's final Castilian version, *Historia general de España* (1623). The relevant Latin publications are *Historiae de rebus Hispaniae. Libri XXX* (1605) and *Summarium ad Historiam Hispaniae eorum quae acciderunt annis sequentibus* (1619).

Mariana, Juan de. *The King and the Education of the King.* Edited by George A. Moore. Washington, D.C., 1948. Translation of *De rege et regis institutione. Libri III* (1599). Publication delays kept the work from appearing until the prince for whom it was intended had become king. The most faithful to the original of any translation.

Secondary Works

Laures, John. *The Political Economy of Juan de Mariana.* New York, 1928. Valuable for its detailed description of *De monetae mutatione* and the Latin text, published in 1609 in *Tractatus VII*.

Lewy, Guenter. *Constitutionalism and Statecraft during the Golden Age of Spain: A Study of the Political Philosophy of Juan de Mariana, S.J.* Geneva, 1960. Although dated by more recent work on Castilian government, it remains a clear presentation of Mariana's political ideas.

Soons, Alan. *Juan de Mariana.* Boston, 1982. Excellent, brief account of his life and almost all of his work.

J. B. OWENS

MARIE DE MÉDICIS (1573–1642), queen and regent of France, patron of artists. Marie was born in Florence to Francesco de' Medici, grand duke of Tuscany, and Joanna, an Austrian archduchess. In 1600 she became queen in France by marriage to Henry IV, and between 1601 and 1608 she gave birth to five children: Louis XIII; Gaston, duke of Orléans; Elizabeth, queen of Spain; Christine, duchess of Savoy; and Henriette, queen of England. Marie was crowned queen on 13 May 1610 and designated regent; she acted as regent following Henry IV's assassination the following day, on 14 May 1610.

Political Activity. Defamed by some of her contemporaries and later histories as obstinate, ambitious, passionate, and stupid, Marie actually maneuvered shrewdly in the political arena, where jurists, now bereft of the alleged Salic law purportedly excluding women from rule (proved fraudulent), were attempting to establish the unique male right to rule and to deny the political authority of queen regents. Some writers held that female rule (gynecocracy) was unnatural and illegal in France, others that French queens had the constitutional right to exercise regental office and government administration. The day after Henry IV's death, 15 May 1610, Marie boldly convoked an unprecedented inaugural *lit de justice* assembly in the Parlement of Paris at which the minor king, Louis XIII, was enthroned beside the queen regent, preempting the traditional program of inauguration (royal funeral and coronation). Countering efforts to undermine regental authority, she publicly exercised the office and also commissioned artistic images lauding the role. Sustaining regental claims made by Louise of Savoy (1527) and Catherine de Médicis (1563, 1574), Marie commemorated the important inaugural event. François Quesnel's engraving (1610) depicted the crowned child-king, Louis XIII, scepter at hand, with the crowned regent Marie at his side; Guillaume Dupré's medal (1611) paired Marie (as Minerva) with Louis (the rising Sun). As regent, Marie supported many of Henry IV's policies, negotiated royal marriages, and sought peace in Europe.

Using the Estates General (1614–1615) and the Parlement of Paris, Marie successfully held at bay noble faction and rebellion. When Louis XIII, pushed by dissidents, wrested power from her in 1617, she was exiled to Blois but escaped and led a revolt that concluded with a peace treaty in 1620. She returned to Paris, where she served on the Royal Council, worked with Cardinal Richelieu (admitted to the council in 1624), and was designated regent in 1629 during the king's absence.

Patronage of the Arts.   Attuned to the persuasive power of art, Marie provided patronage for probably half the French and European artists in the Louvre. Throughout the 1620s she patronized such talented artists as Peter Paul Rubens, Philippe de Champaigne, Guido Reni, Frans Pourbus, and Salomon de Brosse. Marie commissioned many notable works and often specified to the artist what the work or its contents should be. The equestrian statue of Henry IV (on the Pont Neuf) is one of her commissions; she also was responsible for the creation of medals, bronze busts, tapestries, and portrait paintings. She decorated the Carmelite convent in Paris, donated major artworks to many Parisian churches, and completed work on the Luxembourg Palace.

The artworks she commissioned for the Luxembourg overtly expressed her belief in strong female rule; they included eight statues of famous women from history, as well as ceiling murals such as the *Apotheosis of Marie de Médicis* and *Marie de Médicis and the Unity of the State.* The most innovative project, the *Life of Marie de Médicis,* was contracted in 1622 with Rubens, who translated Marie's bold political themes on active female rule into twenty-four large paintings that hung on the walls of the Luxembourg Palace by 1625 (now in the Louvre). These life-cycle paintings were a consciously constructed autobiographical narrative. In them, the artist portrayed Marie's acts of good government, portrayed her as the embodiment of France and Justice, and chronicled her embattled and heroic role as ruler, as depicted in *Queen Triumphant,* the *Felicity of the Regency,* and the *Escape from Blois,* the third representing her return to power. [See the frontispiece to volume 5 for Rubens's depiction of the reception of Marie in Marseille in 1600.]

Final Years.   Marie's triumph was not to last. Her political coup against Richelieu's rising power failed in 1630, and in 1631 she fled from France with her entourage. She made triumphal entries into cities in Flanders, went to Holland in 1638, and that same year moved to England and resided with her daughter Queen Henriette and her son-in-law King Charles I. This stay lasted until 1641, when internal politics forced her to move to Cologne. Shortly before her death in 1642, Marie requested royal burial at Saint-Denis, gravesite of the French monarchy. Her request was granted in 1643.

See also biographies of Louis XIII and Rubens.

BIBLIOGRAPHY

Carmona, Michel. *Marie de Médicis.* Paris, 1981.

Hanley, Sarah. "Identity Politics and Rulership in France: Female Political Place and the Fraudulent Salic Law in Christine de Pizan and Jean de Montreuil." In *Changing Identities in Early Modern France.* Edited by Michael Wolfe. Durham, N.C., 1996. Pages 78–94.

Hanley, Sarah. *The Lit de Justice of the Kings of France: Constitutional Ideology in Legend, Ritual, and Discourse.* Princeton, N.J., 1983. French edition, Aubier, 1991.

Marrow, Deborah. *The Art Patronage of Maria de' Medici.* Ann Arbor, Mich., 1982.

Millen, Ronald Forsythe, and Robert Erich Wolf. *Heroic Deeds and Mystic Figures: A New Reading of Rubens's Life of Maria de' Medici.* Princeton, N.J., 1989.

SARAH HANLEY

MARINELLA, LUCREZIA (1571–1653), Venetian lyric and narrative poet, polemicist. Marinella was born in Venice, where she lived all her life. Her father, Giovanni Marinelli, was a noted physician who wrote on gynecology and on women's health and beauty. She married a physician, Girolamo Vacca, and bore two children by him. Little else is known about her private life. But together with her brother Curzio, these men provided Marinella with the conditions in which her education could flourish; in particular, she had access to Giovanni's vast library of the classics and Italian literature, works she made ample use of in her own writings.

Marinella's production oscillates between sacred genres and secular, allegorizing ones. She wrote several lives of the saints in verse (usually ottava rima)—St. Columba, St. Justine, St. Catherine of Siena, St. Clare, St. Francis—and a virtuoso double life of the Virgin Mary published as a single volume, the first part in prose and the second in verse. She also excelled in writing learned commentaries on poems, and even her own pastoral drama in verse, *Felice arcadia* (Happy Arcadia; 1605) or *Amore innamorato e impazzato* (Cupid in love and driven mad; 1598). The latter was in a long Italian tradition of allegorical-philosophical commentaries on a love poem, in this case the soul's conflict between sensual and divine love.

Her greatest poetic achievement was an epic, consciously rivaling Torquato Tasso's *Gerusalemme liberata* (Jerusalem delivered; 1581) and *Gerusalemme conquistata* (Jerusalem conquered; 1593), *L'Enrico, overo Bisantio acquistato* (Enrico, or Byzantium gained; 1635). In this poem a Venetian military leader of the twelfth century, Enrico Dandolo, "liberates" Byzantium from Orthodox Greeks and places the fabled city in the hands of Venetians. Like Tasso, Marinella combines heroic exploits with the Christian marvelous: benign magic, prophecies, visionary dreams, and the like.

In her epic Marinella alters significantly the representation of women. Her virgin Amazons never abandon their professional independence, remaining unbeaten by male counterparts. The sibyl-like Erina is a wise prophetess versed in natural philosophy with a palace dominated by an observatory. Typically, Marinella's women have no need of men and no need of erotic liaisons or even marriage. The rapport they value is friendship, which allows them to be morally and intellectually men's equals. The women of her religious poetry have also sublimated passion, living in the world like St. Catherine of Siena but in the service of a divine, just, and compassionate Lord.

Although belonging to a long Renaissance tradition contributed to by Baldassare Castiglione, Ludovico Ariosto, Lodovico Domenichi, Tommaso Garzoni, and Moderata Fonte, Marinella's *La nobiltà et l'eccellenza delle donne, co' diffettie mancamenti de gli huomini* (The nobility and excellence of women, with the defects and vices of men; 1600) was occasioned, Marinella makes clear, by the publication of Giuseppe Passi's *I donneschi diffetti* (The defects of women) of 1599, a lengthy, virulently misogynistic attack on women's nature as inherently depraved and incapable of reform. The one merit of Passi's work is that it inspired this powerful and learned defense of women's moral and intellectual equality with—and, in some respects, superiority to—men from Marinella. Not only did she show by examples, quotations from authorities, and arguments that women are more virtuous than men; she then attacked men, revealing that they were far more culpable of the vices Passi accused women of. She made her case with vigor and indignation, as well as learning, and defeated Passi—and the Aristotelian school she believed nourished him—resoundingly.

In an enlarged, second edition of 1601, Marinella strengthened her argument with an analysis and refutation of modern Italian tracts. Giovanni Boccaccio's *Il corbaccio,* known as *Laberinto d'amore* (The labyrinth of love), composed in 1355 and printed frequently in the Renaissance, Marinella judges a bundle of insults, against which one cannot reason. Sperone Speroni's *Della dignità delle donne* (On the dignity of women; 1542) appears to be an urbane discussion of women's nature but introduces a female character who takes the side of women's inferiority; Marinella is not fooled by the underhanded strategy. She also exposes two pieces by the Tasso family. Torquato Tasso, a friend of Speroni and a sympathizer with the neo-Aristotelian currents at Padua, wrote what amounted to a gender-based ethics in *Discorso della virtù feminile e donnesca* (Oration on virtue for women and ladies; 1582), according to which intellectual virtues and the ones needed to rule—prudence, justice, fortitude—are appropriate only for men, and temperance, or the restraining of mainly the sexual instincts, is appropriate for women. Ercole Tasso, a younger relative, wrote a treatise titled *Dello ammogliarsi* (On taking a wife; 1594) in which he argued that the disadvantages of taking a wife far outweighed the advantages and denied that wives could be bound in friendship with their husbands. For Marinella both men would deny women equal nobility and excellence with men.

In old age Marinella devoted herself to spiritual writings and, weary of life, regretted her youthful polemics, advocating instead traditional domestic tasks for women. Her contemporaries admired her; Cristofano Bronzini thought that, along with Fonte, Marinella had finally succeeded in overturning the misogynists.

BIBLIOGRAPHY

Primary Works

Conti Odorisio, Ginevra. *Donna e società nel Seicento.* Rome, 1979. Contains extracts of Marinella's writings in Italian.

Conti Odorisio, Ginevra. *Le Stanze ritrovate: Antologia di scrittrici venete dal Quattrocento al Novecento.* Edited by Antonia Arslan, Adriana Chemello, and Gilberto Pizzamiglio. Venice, 1991. Pages 95–108. Contains extracts of Marinella's writings in Italian.

Marinella, Lucrezia. *Arcadia felice (1605).* Edited by Françoise Lavocat. Florence, 1998.

Marinella, Lucrezia. *The Nobility and Excellence of Women and the Defects and Vices of Men.* Edited and translated by Anne Dunhill. Chicago, 2000. Includes an introductory essay by Letizia Panizza with Anne Dunhill.

Secondary Works

Chemello, Adriana. "La donna, il modello, l'immaginario: Moderata Fonte e Lucrezia Marinella." In *Nel cerchio della luna.* Edited by Marina Zancan. Venice, 1983. Pages 95–170.

Cox, Virginia. "The Single Self: Feminist Thought and the Marriage Market in Early Modern Venice." *Renaissance Quarterly* 48, no. 3 (1995): 513–581.

King, Margaret L. *Women of the Renaissance.* Chicago, 1991.

Labalme, Patricia. "Venetian Women on Women: Three Early Modern Feminists." *Archivio veneto,* 5th series, no. 197 (1981): 81–109.

Price, Paola Malpezzi. "Lucrezia Marinella." In *Italian Women Writers.* Edited by Rinaldina Russell. Westport, Conn., 1994. Pages 234–242.

LETIZIA PANIZZA

MARINO, GIAMBATTISTA (1569–1625), Italian poet. Born in Naples, Marino was the son of a lawyer who disowned him when he refused to pursue a legal career in favor of the arts. At the age of nineteen he became a member of the Accademia degli Svegliati, and his poems won him the protection of Giambattista Manzo and a post as secretary to Matteo di Capua, prince of Conca. Matteo's rich collection of paintings and large library were at the disposition of the young poet. While in Naples he was imprisoned twice, once for sodomy and a second time for forgery. He escaped to Rome with the financial assistance of Prince Matteo and entered the service of Melchiorre Crescenzio, an official in the pontifical court.

Giambattista Marino. Anonymous portrait. Oil on canvas; first half of the seventeenth century; 68 × 55 cm (27 × 22 in.). MUSÉE DES BEAUX-ARTS DE LYON

Marino's life in Rome was a happy and productive one, allowing him to complete a collection of lyric poems begun in Naples. He traveled to Venice to oversee the printing of his first collection of poems, *Rime* (1602), divided by theme, which the poet boasted of as a "rustico ma nuoya ordine" (a rustic but new order). This volume enjoyed enormous success and he was invited to enter the service of Cardinal Pietro Aldobrandini, a wealthy patron of the arts and nephew of Pope Clement VIII. In Rome he became a member of the Accademia degli Umoristi and enjoyed the favors of the academy's leader, Battista Guarini, whom Marino considered one of the major poets of the period. When Cardinal Aldobrandini's episcopal seat was transferred to Ravenna, Marino followed his patron and established his fame in northern cities such as Bologna, Parma, Venice, and Turin.

In Turin he was appointed personal secretary to the duke of Savoy, Carl Emmanuel I, and given the title of *cavaliere dei SS. Maurizio e Lazzaro,* in recognition of a flattering poetic portrait of the duke entitled *Ritratto* (Portrait). However, in 1611 Marino was imprisoned due to the machinations of a rival for the duke's favors and was set free more than a year later through the intervention of friends. The following years were productive ones for the poet. In 1614 he published three long eulogies in prose, *Dicerie sacre* (Sacred sayings), which reveal both his theological erudition and his rhetorical skills. In the same year he published a second collection of poems, *Lira,* ostensibly the third part of the earlier collection of 1602. The poems in the *Lira* are thematically similar to those of the earlier collection but reveal a growing subtlety of his use of metaphor. The love poems in the collection are heavily Petrarchist in their use of ambiguity and metaphor, although he aimed for novelty in new erotic connotations. Marino's style might well be described as "hyper-Petrarchist." His symbolism is based on well-established Petrarchist metaphors, which he rejuvenates by widening their original referential spectrum and recasting them in very elaborate syntactical phrasing. This is particularly evident in the ornate stanzas of *L'Adone* (Adonis), in which Marino makes a systematic use of all the canonical Petrarchist attributes of the woman, although he does so in describing the appearance of the male protagonist of the poem.

Uncomfortable in Turin, Marino decided to go to France, where he successfully gained entry into the circle of the regent queen, Marie de Médicis, widow of Henry IV. During his years in France (1615–1623) he focused his attention on *L'Adone* after completing other minor works, including *Epitalami* (Epithilamia; 1616), a series of nuptial poems in honor of the noblest families of the period. Three years later he published *Galeria* (The art gallery), a collection of several hundred poems testifying to his lifelong passion for the visual arts. (His original intention of a volume with illustrations of images commented on by his poems was abandoned.) In 1620 *La sampogna* (The syrinx) was published, a work containing twelve idylls— eight mythological poems and four pastoral poems. It is now considered one of the best examples of post-Petrarchist lyric style.

It took Marino three more years to complete *L'Adone,* which was published in 1623. It includes over five thousand stanzas in twenty cantos, the longest poem in Italian literature. Printed in large folio and subsidized by the king of France, it was dedicated to the king and his mother. The success of the poem was immediate and enormous. Marino then returned to Italy, where his masterpiece was reprinted in several editions. He was hailed as the greatest living poet of the time, with aristocrats and academicians vying for his attention.

Unfortunately, the new pope, Urban VIII, a poet himself, disliked Marino's works due to their overt eroticism, and *L'Adone* soon came under ecclesiastical scrutiny for obscenity. Marino's health rapidly declined as, embittered, he worked on revisions of the poem. He also worked on revisions of his *Strage degl'Innocenti* (Slaughter of the Innocents) and on the organization of his correspondence. The latter works were published posthumously.

Marino had numerous followers in Italy, among them Girolamo Preti, Claudio Achillini, Antonio Bruni, Giuseppe Artale, and Giacomo Lubrano. Marino's influence in Italian literature, however, extends well beyond the seventeenth century; Pietro Metastasio, for instance, in the eighteenth century, was an avid reader of Marino's works, as was Vittorio Alfieri. Marino's poems, and in particular *L'Adone,* were widely admired and imitated throughout Europe. Philippe Desportes translated into French Marino's early lyrics, *Rime,* and Richard Crashaw translated into English a substantial portion of *Strage degl'Innocenti,* which was also translated into Russian. For well over a century after Marino's death, *L'Adone* was considered not only the most refined expression of Italian poetry, but also of the Italian language. An Italian grammar produced in France in 1667 for the general public uses *L'Adone* as a basic linguistic model. In the nineteenth century, and for at least half of the twentieth, Marino's work was often referred to as an example of literary decadence or bad taste; but later critical studies corrected this perception by showing how similar in baroque greatness to Caravaggio's paintings or Monteverdi's madrigals Marino's poems are.

BIBLIOGRAPHY

Primary Works

Marino, Giambattista. *L'Adone.* Edited by Giovanni Pozzi. Milan, 1976.

Marino, Giambattista. *Dicerie sacre; e la "Strage de gl'Innocenti."* Edited by Giovanni Pozzi. Turin, Italy, 1960.

Marino, Giambattista. *Lettere.* Edited by Marziano Guglielminetti. Turin, Italy, 1966.

Marino, Giambattista. *Rime amorose.* Edited by Ottavio Besomi and Alessandro Martini. Ferrare, Italy, 1987.

Marino, Giambattista. *Rime boscherecce.* Edited by Janina Hauser-Jakubowicz. Ferrara, Italy, 1991.

Marino, Giambattista. *Rime marittime.* Edited by Ottavio Besomi, Costanzo Marchi, and Alessandro Martini. Modena, Italy, 1988.

Marino, Giambattista. *La sampogna.* Edited by Vania De Maldé. Parma, Italy, 1993.

Marino, Giambattista. *La sferza e il tempio.* Edited by Gian Piero Maragoni. Rome, 1995.

Marino, Giambattista. *Selections from L'Adone.* Translated by Harold Martin Priest. Ithaca, N.Y., 1967.

Secondary Works

Borzelli, Angelo. *Il Cavalier Giovan Battista Marino* (1569–1625). 2d ed. Naples, 1906.

Fulco, Giorgio. "Giovan Battista Marino." In *Storia della letteratura italiana.* Edited by Enrico Malato. Vol. 5, *La fine del Cinquecento e il Seicento.* Rome, 1997. Pages 597–652.

Guardiani, Francesco. *La meravigliosa retorica dell' Adone di G. B. Marino.* Florence, 1989.

Guardiani, Francesco, ed. *Lectura Marini:* L'Adone *letto e commentato.* Ottawa, Canada, 1989.

Guardiani, Francesco, ed. *The Sense of Marino: Literature, Fine Arts, and Music of the Italian Baroque.* New York and Ottawa, Canada, 1994.

Martini, Alessandro. "Giovan Battista Marino. Opere." In *Dizionario delle opere della letteratura italiana.* Edited by Alberto Asor Rosa. Turin, Italy, 1998. Pages 777–797.

Mirollo, James V. *The Poet of the Marvelous: Giambattista Marino.* New York, 1963.

Peters, Susan N. "The Anatomical Machine: A Representation of the Microcosm in the *Adone* of G. B. Marino." *Modern Language Notes* 88 (1973): 95–110.

Slawinski, Maurice. "The Poet's Senses: G. B. Marino's Epic Poem *L'Adone* and the New Science." *Comparative Criticism* 13 (1991): 51–81.

FRANCESCO GUARDIANI

MARLOWE, CHRISTOPHER

MARLOWE, CHRISTOPHER (1564–1593), English playwright, poet. Christopher Marlowe flourished during the last decades of the sixteenth century, at the moment when English playwrights began to produce Renaissance drama of lasting importance.

Family Background and Education. Marlowe's father, John Marley, was a migrant worker who became a citizen and shoemaker in the cathedral city of Canterbury. Marley married Katherine Arthur in 1561; she gave birth to their first son, Christopher, in 1564. Shortly before his fifteenth birthday, Marlowe obtained a scholarship at the King's School, a royal foundation attached to the cathedral. The school provided places for "fifty poor boys," whom it taught to speak and write in classical Latin. Marlowe later won an endowed scholarship to Corpus Christi College, Cambridge, where he took up residence in December 1580. His scholarship was tenable for four years, but candidates who intended to enter holy orders could extend it, as Marlowe did, for an additional three years after the bachelor's and proceed to the master's degree.

Although degrees in the arts certified graduates for careers in the church, the Elizabethan university curriculum emphasized classical studies. Marlowe's education at Cambridge involved extensive work in Ciceronian dialectic and rhetoric, ancient literature and history, Aristotelian philosophy, Ptolemaic astronomy, geography, and cosmography. Like many of his classmates, Marlowe was frequently absent from college during his final three years there. The last time his name appears in the Corpus Christi account books is February 1587. On 29 June 1587 William Cecil and other Privy Councillors in his faction instructed the university authorities to discount a rumor that Marlowe had defected to the Roman Catholic seminary in Reims. They said that Marlowe had served Queen Elizabeth well and deserved to be rewarded for his loyal endeavors on her behalf. The council ordered the university to award Marlowe his master's degree at the commencement ceremony in July.

Translations and Early Plays. Marlowe's translation of Ovid's *Amores* into English pentameter couplets probably belongs to his undergraduate years. His rendition of Ovid is always lively, intermittently opaque, and has occasional flashes of brilliance. Since the *Amores* had not previously appeared in a modern European language, Marlowe's translation of them, published under the title *Elegies* (1599?), introduced English readers to Ovid's lurid account of his adulterous love affair with Corinna and helped bring about the turn from Petrarchan to Ovidian love poetry that occurred during the 1590s. Marlowe's line-for-line translation of the first book of Lucan's *Pharsalia* into English blank (unrhymed) verse is a more accomplished work and may date from a later period in his life. In contrast to the work of earlier translators, the blank-verse line in *Lucan His First Book* has considerable metrical variety and enabled Marlowe to emulate the strongly marked rhythms and Latinate constructions of Lucan's declamatory style. Lucan's portrayal of Roman civil wars provided a classic model for the delegitimized, egregiously violent world of Marlowe's tragedies.

Dido, Queen of Carthage, which was jointly attributed to Marlowe and Thomas Nashe and performed by the Children of the Chapel Royal (c. 1587), participated in the same humanistic traditions of translation, declamation, and imitation that underlay *Ovid's Elegies* and *Lucan His First Book.* In rewriting Virgil's narrative of Dido and Aeneas, Marlowe and Nashe emphasized the ineluctable force of erotic desire. A pederastic Jove woos his boy lover, Ganymede, in phrases that echo, or anticipate, Marlowe's sole surviving lyric, "The Passionate Shepherd to His Love" (1599). Dido expresses her love for Aeneas in the extravagant terms employed by her counterpart in Ovid's *Heroides.* Although the hero dutifully obeys Jove's command to abandon Dido and sail for Italy, the play questions the renunciatory ethic that Aeneas espouses. At a moment when Sir

Philip Sidney and Edmund Spenser, the dominant literary voices of the 1580s, held up Virgil as the model poet, Marlowe's affinities lay with Ovid and Lucan.

By the spring of 1588, the Lord Admiral's Men had begun giving performances of Marlowe's *Tamburlaine the Great* on public stages in the city of London. Marlowe's early masterpiece decisively demonstrated the rhythmic powers of English blank verse written in iambic pentameter. The author encodes his own genius for prosody within the structure of his fable. Tamburlaine is an extemporaneous oral poet who, as the title page to the 1590 quarto puts it, "from a Scythian Shephearde . . . became a most puissant and mightye monarque." The hero's verses energize his followers and so provide the impetus for his astonishing rise to eminence. Marlowe's blaspheming peasant hero proved enormously popular with the common spectators who thronged to the new London playhouses. Marlowe capitalized on this enthusiastic reception with a sequel, *Tamburlaine, Part Two,* in which the hero sickens and dies but remains obdurate and unvanquished to the end.

Marlowe's focus on the fall of princes locates his two-part play within the medieval tradition of homiletic tragedy depicting the mutability of fortune; but he modifies the traditional form with a new emphasis on subaltern violence. Before Marlowe's intervention, in the mystery cycles and in homespun tragedies like Thomas Preston's *Cambises, King of Persia* (1569), violence runs from the top down or circulates among equals; in *Tamburlaine,* and in many of the tragedies that follow, the killing comes from the bottom up as well. Tamburlaine's seizure of rule brings out a central contradiction in the Protestant political theory of the state. Romans 13:1 prohibits rebellion on the grounds that "every soul [is] subject unto the higher powers"; but since "the powers that be are ordained of God," St. Paul's logic tacitly enfranchises a successful usurper. The homiletic stereotype of the "scourge of God" attempts to resolve this contradiction by reducing the usurper to a doomed and unthinking instrument of God's justice. But Tamburlaine invokes the orthodox doctrine of obedience in a sophisticated defense of his own right to disobey. Since he is termed the scourge of God and terror to the world, Tamburlaine argues that he must fulfill that role and destroy everyone who resists the divine will embodied in him.

Tamburlaine inspired a flurry of imitations and became the most frequently cited play in Renaissance England. Over the long run of the English Renaissance, Marlowe's initiative succeeded brilliantly: iambic pentameter blank verse provided the metrical basis for a new canon of vernacular classics written by William Shakespeare, Ben Jonson, and John Milton. During the brief span of Marlowe's life, however, his popular success exposed him to derision.

Subsequent Plays and Criminal Record. In September 1589 Marlowe and the poet Thomas Watson became embroiled in a murderous feud between John Alleyn, probably the actor-manager of the Lord Admiral's Men, and a yeoman named William Bradley. Marlowe spent two weeks in Newgate prison, where, according to the informant Richard Baines, he became acquainted with a prisoner named John Poole, who taught him the rudiments of counterfeiting. Poole maintained extensive contacts in the Roman Catholic underground and was related to Ferdinando Stanley (Lord Strange), whom Roman Catholic conspirators saw as a prospective successor to Queen Elizabeth I.

Marlowe prepared scripts for Stanley's acting company. The playwright Thomas Kyd (1558–1594), who appears to have been Stanley's servant, recalled that he and Marlowe were "writing in one chamber" in 1591. Strange's Men gave the first recorded performance of Marlowe's *The Jew of Malta* early in the following year. The play contains verbal echoes of Kyd's masterly *Spanish Tragedie* (c. 1587) and bears family resemblances to Kyd's intricate revenge plot. Mingling tragedy and farce, Marlowe portrays a decadent Christian republic governed by a Machiavellian politician. Barabas, the Jew of the title and a type of Antichrist, epitomizes the city's amoral proclivity for nascent Mediterranean capitalism. Over the course of the play, he exacts his revenge on the urban elite with a Turkish bondsman purchased in a Christian slave market, only to be entrapped in a device of his own contriving. With its sharp operators, confidence games, and lyric celebration of wealth, *The Jew of Malta* inspired Jonson's *Volpone* (1605) and became a prototype for city comedy in Jacobean England.

The provenance of Marlowe's *Doctor Faustus,* which could have been written at any time between 1588 and 1592, has long been in doubt. By the late twentieth century most scholars believed that the earliest quarto of this work, published in 1604, derived from an authorial manuscript jointly composed by Marlowe and a collaborator who wrote the comic scenes. The 1616 quarto, in contrast, contains numerous additions and revisions by other writers. *Doctor Faustus* considers the Calvinist doctrines of reprobation and predestination from the standpoint of a defiant human agent. Convinced that he is condemned to an everlasting death, Marlowe's protagonist deeds his soul to the devil in exchange for twenty-four years of carnal pleasure. In rejecting God's sovereignty, Faustus condemns himself to hell for eternity; but since, according to Calvinist doctrine, the reprobate are already guilty, what difference could his choice possibly make? Damnation is at once the consequence and the cause of his voluptuously sinful life.

In *Doctor Faustus* Marlowe used the homiletic form of the morality play to interrogate divine justice. He retained the traditional configuration of a protagonist flanked by good and bad angels but positioned these figures behind Doctor Faustus, so that they appear to voice the hero's spontaneous impulses. Such moments inscribe a post-Reformation drama of being chosen within a pre-Reformation fable of moral choice and stage the predicament of willful agents in a predestined universe. *Doctor Faustus* established the modern form of Christian tragedy that Shakespeare developed in *Hamlet* and *Macbeth*. The 1616 quarto further testifies to the power of Marlowe's conception: the reviser consistently remakes Doctor Faustus into a rational agent who exercises his own free will and can decide to repent and be saved. With the waning of Calvinism in the later seventeenth century, *Doctor Faustus* literally degenerated into farce; but the play achieved classic status during the nineteenth century, when its hero reemerged as a mythic embodiment of modern individualism.

Marlowe completed *Edward II* in 1591 or early 1592. The play was performed by the Earl of Pembroke's Men, whose repertory also included an early version of Shakespeare's *2 Henry VI*. In writing *Edward II*, Marlowe borrowed passages from *2* and *3 Henry VI* and adopted the basic plot formula of Shakespeare's early trilogy, in which a contentious nobility and a strong-willed queen destroy a weak king. Marlowe's extraordinary variation on this theme was to place the homoerotic attachment between King Edward and his baseborn favorites Piers Gaveston and Hugh Spencer at the center of the action. When the king invites his lowly favorites to share the kingdom, he detaches the social custom of male friendship from the maintenance of class privilege. What drives Edward's peers to armed rebellion is not the crime of sodomy (the mightiest kings have had their minions) but the elevation of the king's subaltern lovers into the aristocracy.

With the aid of Spencer's father, who leads a citizen militia of foot soldiers, the king improbably de-

Christopher Marlowe. REPRODUCED BY COURTESY OF THE DIRECTOR AND UNIVERSITY LIBRARIAN, THE JOHN RYLANDS UNIVERSITY LIBRARY OF MANCHESTER

feats the combined armies of his peers and institutes a new order grounded in the royal will. *Edward II* successfully destabilizes the Renaissance regime of heterosexual gender relations but does not offer an alternative to it. Edward's sodomitic government unleashes a tragic cycle of adultery, wanton violence, regicide, and belated retribution. This is the bleakest of Marlowe's tragedies; its influence on other works, apart from Shakespeare's *Richard II,* is elusive.

During the winter of 1592, Marlowe was living in Flushing, in the Netherlands, where he found lodgings with Baines and a goldsmith named Gifford Gilbert. Prompted by his companions, Gilbert counterfeited Dutch and English money. After a fake Dutch shilling went into circulation, Baines informed on Marlowe and Gilbert to the English governor, Sir Robert Sidney. Under interrogation, Marlowe confessed that he had joined in this venture but tried to shift the blame back onto Baines. The two men accused each other of intending to defect to Rome or to Spain. Marlowe described himself as a scholar and told Sidney that he was on close terms with Henry Percy, the earl of Northumberland, and Ferdinando Stanley (Lord Strange), the leading Roman Catholic heirs apparent to the English crown. These facts lend credence to Baines's charge that Marlowe intended to go over to the enemy—as a defector, a double agent, or both. Sidney placed Marlowe and Gilbert under arrest and sent all three men back to William Cecil to dispose of as he saw fit. Marlowe was on the streets by 9 May 1592, when a London constable cited him for disturbing the peace. Strange's Men subsequently performed *The Massacre at Paris,* which appears to be the last of Marlowe's works for the stage.

Marlowe's Last Year. In a dedication addressed to Pembroke's wife, Lady Mary Sidney, in the autumn of 1592, Christopher Marlowe, writing as C. M., sought admission to the circle of poets who enjoyed the countess's patronage. Like Shakespeare, Marlowe turned to nondramatic verse during a period when the playhouses were closed on account of the plague. In *Hero and Leander* he imitated a Hellenistic narrative poem about amorous pursuit and conquest, interlacing it with ingenious variations on the theme of erotic desire. While the young lovers exhibit the spontaneous attraction of naive sexuality, the witty narrator views them from the urbane perspective of Ovid's *Amores*. The poem represents Leander as both masculine and feminine: he is at once the subject of heterosexual desire for Hero and the object of homosexual desire for Neptune. Where the Greek source concludes with Leander drowning in the Hellespont, Marlowe's comedy ends at the moment of sexual consummation. The dramatic tension in *Hero and Leander* arises not from Leander's impending doom but from the erotic appropriation of Hero. Although the Elizabethan writer and translator George Chapman published a continuation of *Hero and Leander,* Marlowe's poem is fully coherent as it stands. *Hero and Leander* went through ten editions between 1598 and 1637, was the most widely read of Marlowe's works, and inspired numerous imitations, including the puppet show at the conclusion of Jonson's *Bartholomew Fair* (1614).

During the autumn of 1592, Robert Greene's *Groatsworth of Wit, Bought with a Million of Repentance* leveled a thinly veiled and eerily prescient public warning at the "famous gracer of tragedians," Christopher Marlowe. Portraying himself as one who had denied, with the tragedian, the existence of God, Marlowe's acquaintance warned him to repent before it was too late. Greene's admonition took on fresh urgency in the spring of 1593, when Queen Elizabeth launched the first major heresy hunt since the reign of her sister Mary. On 5 May 1592, in the midst of this investigation, an anonymous rhymester who styled himself "Tamberlaine" posted a seditious ultimatum on the wall of the Dutch Church in London. This incendiary placard contained numerous allusions to Marlowe's plays. The queen ordered her agents to interrogate all persons who could be suspected of taking part in this incident. One day later, royal commissioners arrested Marlowe's former chambermate Kyd and ransacked his lodgings, where they found a transcript of Arian writings. Kyd, who was severely tortured, affirmed that this document had originally belonged to Marlowe. The queen's Privy Council sought more information about Marlowe's alleged blasphemies from his nemesis Baines.

In addition, the council procured a spy's report linking Marlowe to a mutinous agitator named Richard Cholmley. This communication revealed that Cholmley led a gang of sixty armed followers and intended to kill Queen Elizabeth. An endorsement on the back of the report included the names of John and James Tippings and Henry Young, Roman Catholic dissidents who were involved in conspiracies to assassinate the queen. Cholmley himself did not profess Roman Catholicism but claimed that Marlowe made better arguments for atheism than any cleric in England could offer on behalf of God. In exhorting his followers to become atheists, Cholmley made ribald jokes about the Bible. His witticisms closely resemble Kyd's allegations about Marlowe's jests against scripture. On 18 May 1593 the council arrested Marlowe and brought him to the court at Greenwich. After posting bail on 20 May, Marlowe was commanded to report to the council on a daily basis. Baines's note on Marlowe's blasphemies arrived at court around 27 May and contained yet another, more elaborate collection of anti-scriptural jokes, arranged in a logical sequence, like the articles of a creed. Baines depicted Marlowe as a proselytizing atheist who claimed that he had as good a right to coin money as the queen of England. According to Thomas Drury, the government agent who seems to have obtained this intelligence from Baines, the articles of atheism were delivered to Queen Elizabeth, who ordered her servants to prosecute Marlowe to the maximum extent.

Marlowe died of a puncture wound through the eye on 30 May 1593. The killing took place at the home of Eleanor Bull, a notional cousin of Queen Elizabeth's lady-in-waiting Blanche Parry and a personal acquaintance of her chief councillor William Cecil. Although Marlowe's biographers routinely describe Bull's house as a tavern, its status remains unclear. The ranking official at the scene of the crime was the queen's man Robert Poley, a government agent who specialized in protecting her from would-be assassins. Since Eleanor Bull's residence lay within the verge of the court, a vicinity that extended twelve miles in every direction from the person of the sovereign, William Danby, the queen's coroner, conducted the formal inquest on 1 June 1593. Danby determined that Marlowe's killer, Ingram Frizer, had acted in self-defense during a quarrel over money, but many scholars have refused to accept this verdict. The archival records that bear on the last weeks of Marlowe's life describe a quarrel between Marlowe and the court. This dispute came to a climax when Baines's note arrived at Greenwich and ended with the death of Marlowe a few days later. The court bureaucracy that summoned Marlowe into the verge cannot be relied on to divulge the truth about what happened there.

Importance and Subsequent Reputation.
In the aftermath of Marlowe's death, his fellow poets praised his genius for prosody and his orphic powers of invention while Protestant divines denounced him for atheism and immorality. His admirers were right, and his detractors had a valid point: Marlowe's stunning representations of epicurean and underclass values decisively enlarged the moral and ideological range of English drama. The blaspheming peasant hero of *Tamburlaine the Great* founds an idolatrous cult dedicated to violent appropriation. The Jew of Malta gleefully poisons an entire nunnery (the scene always evokes raucous laughter in the playhouse) and reduces all forms of organized religion to mockery. The epicurean monarch in *Edward II* elevates his lover, Gaveston, above the claims of the church, the nobility, and his wife. The reprobate protagonist of *Doctor Faustus* proclaims hell a fable and decides that his mortal soul is worth a lifetime of carnal delight. Protracted critical debate about the morally correct response to these villain-heroes misses the thrust of Marlowe's achievement, which was to make such figures conceivable to a theatergoing public.

Marlowe sank into oblivion during the Restoration and most of the eighteenth century. His fortunes began to rise in 1781, when Joseph Warton informed readers of his canon-forming *History of English Poetry* that Marlowe deserved to be ranked among the foremost tragic poets of his age. A year later, the antiquarian Joseph Ritson again assailed Marlowe for atheism and published Baines's note. Marlowe's nineteenth-century admirers conceived of him in the likeness of romantic and Victorian poets: he entered the canon of English literature as a visionary rebel like Percy Bysshe Shelley and Lord Byron or as an honest doubter like Matthew Arnold. Since Marlowe left behind no first-person statements, apart from the fawning Latin dedication to Lady Pembroke, this perception of him was mainly derived from interpretations of his plays.

The nineteenth-century version of Marlowe persisted well into the twentieth century but eventually fell into disrepute. The romantic individualist who freely organized his life and inscribed his beliefs in his works was largely discarded by critics and scholars who focused on the social and discursive framework that could produce a figure like Christopher Marlowe.

BIBLIOGRAPHY

Primary Work
Marlowe, Christopher. Editions of individual works published in The Revels Plays. Manchester and New York, 1962–. The authoritative modern edition of Marlowe's works.

Secondary Works
Bakeless, John. *The Tragicall History of Christopher Marlowe.* Cambridge, Mass., 1942. Standard biography of Marlowe. Though out-of-date, it is the most extensive compilation of materials relating to Marlowe's life and works.
Bartels, Emily. *Spectacles of Strangeness: Imperialism, Alienation, and Marlowe.* Philadelphia, 1993. Describes and explains Marlowe's ongoing fascination with exotic, marginal, and subversive figures.
Bartels, Emily, ed. *Critical Essays on Christopher Marlowe.* New York, 1997. Anthology of modern critical and scholarly writings about Marlowe. Select bibliography.
Chan, Lois. *Marlowe Criticism: A Bibliography.* Boston, 1978. Thorough bibliography of criticism and scholarship. The annual bibliographies in the *Publications of the Modern Language Association* provide listings from 1975 to the present.
Cheney, Patrick. *Marlowe's Counterfeit Profession: Ovid, Spenser, Counter-Nationhood.* Toronto, Canada, 1997. In-depth account of Marlowe's literary career and relationship to classical authors.
Goldberg, Jonathan. "The Transvestite Stage: More on the Case of Christopher Marlowe." In *Sodometries: Renaissance Texts, Modern Sexualities.* Stanford, Calif., 1992. Pages 105–143. Polemical and illuminating interpretation of Marlowe from the perspective of gay and lesbian studies.
Greenblatt, Stephen. "Marlowe and the Will to Absolute Play." In *Renaissance Self-Fashioning: From More to Shakespeare.* Chicago, 1980. Pages 193–221. An incisive and influential essay on Marlowe's place in Elizabethan culture.
Levin, Harry. *The Overreacher.* Cambridge, Mass., 1952. Classic study of Marlowe in relation to Renaissance humanism.
MacLure, Millar. *Marlowe, the Critical Heritage, 1588–1896.* London, 1979. Annotated anthology of materials relating to Marlowe's reception and reputation.
Nicholl, Charles. *The Reckoning: The Murder of Christopher Marlowe.* London, 1992. Original, lively, and well-documented study covering the last seven years of Marlowe's life. The bibliography includes all the major biographical findings that have come to light since Bakeless.

Urry, William. *Christopher Marlowe and Canterbury.* London, 1988. Definitive account of Marlowe's early years, with pertinent observations about his later life.

Wraight, A. D. *In Search of Christopher Marlowe: A Pictorial Biography.* New York, 1965. Useful for transcripts and photo facsimiles of essential life records.

DAVID RIGGS

MAROT, CLÉMENT (1496–1544), French poet. Clément Marot, son of the *rhétoriqueur* poet Jean Marot, was born in Cahors in Quercy. Introduced early to court, he became in 1519 the *valet de chambre* of Margaret of Alençon, future queen of Navarre, and soon entered as well the service of Francis I. In 1526, however, he was imprisoned at the Châtelet in Paris, supposedly for having broken the Lenten fast. He became suspect with the authorities eager to suppress any adherence to Lutheranism. He reported on his imprisonment in his satirical poem *L'enfer* (Hell; 1532). He was imprisoned again in October 1527. Released by the king, he defended his religious beliefs and concerns, which bore a strong resemblance to those of his "évangélique" protectress, Margaret of Navarre. His defense appeared in his famous *Deploration de Florimond Robertet,* written on the death of the treasurer of France and published in the 1532 *Adolescence clémentine* (Early verse). He began translating the Psalms into metrical verse at the probable request of Margaret of Navarre. The year 1527 was a watershed year in that Marot abandoned medieval poetic forms such as the rondeau, the ballade, and the chant royal for a new lighthearted, elegant, and witty spirit, the "badinage élégant" of Nicolas Boileau's description. He included in his *Adolescence* poems of circumstance such as epitaphs, epistles, and *blasons* (short descriptive poems).

In early 1535 he went into exile. Following the 1534 Affair of the Placards against the Mass in half a dozen cities during the night of 17 October, he sought safety in Navarre, then at the court of the Lutheran sympathizer Renée of France at Ferrara. There he composed his "Blason du beau tetin" (*Blason* on the breast), which he sent to France as a challenge to other poets. Soon he received ten poems, all in response to his, and Renée of France awarded first place to Maurice Scève. Two volumes, *Blasons anatomiques des parties du corps féminin* (Anatomical *blasons* on parts of the female body; 1536) and a further volume including *contreblasons* (1543), were published by François Juste at Lyon. Marot also composed what many consider the first French sonnet during his exile in Italy, where he came under the increasing influence of Petrarch, Pietro Bembo, and Aquilano Serafino. He was allowed to return to France in 1536 upon abjuration of his errors.

In 1538 Marot published his *Oeuvres* (Works) and in 1539 the first edition of his translation of several psalms set to music. In 1541 he added eighteen psalms to the collection, and by the end of the year he dedicated thirty psalms to the king. By early 1543, three editions of the *Cinquante Psaumes de David mis en rimes françaises* (Fifty Psalms of David, put into French verse) were condemned by the Faculty of Theology at the University of Paris. These poetic adaptations became so successful that they were sung at court, and then also adopted by the Protestants. More than five hundred editions appeared throughout the sixteenth century. At the end of 1542, Marot fled the country for the last time for reasons that may relate to the publication of his poem *L'enfer* by Etienne Dolet. After two years in Geneva, he moved on to Savoy, and died suddenly in Turin in September 1544.

Marot's influence on French verse was considerable; he influenced English sixteenth-century poets as well. He was the first French poet to create a collection of verse organized by genre: besides the elegies and epistles (mostly in decasyllabic couplets) that he helped to develop, he added epitaphs and shorter verse that he called epigrams (of which he composed some three hundred). He also published in 1526 an edition of the *Roman de la rose* by the thirteenth-century poet Guillaume de Lorris and in 1533 an edition of François Villon. He influenced the meters of French verse and increased the range of tones and moods, from the light and frivolous to the serious and weighty. He is remembered for the special way in which he allied technical ease with subjects of a more personal nature.

BIBLIOGRAPHY

Primary Works

Marot, Clément. *Oeuvres complètes.* Edited by C. A. Mayer. 6 vols. Paris, 1978.

Marot, Clément. *Oeuvres poétiques complètes.* Edited by Gérard Defaux. Paris, 1990–.

Secondary Works

Defaux, Gérard, ed. *La génération Marot: Poètes français et néolatins (1515–1550).* Paris, 1997.

Dejean, Jean-Luc. *Clément Marot.* Paris, 1990. Complete biography.

Mayer, C. A. *La religion de Clément Marot.* Geneva, 1960.

Screech, M. A. *Clément Marot: A Renaissance Poet Discovers the Gospel: Lutheranism, Fabrism, and Calvinism in the Royal Courts of France and of Navarre and in the Ducal Court of Ferrara.* Leiden, Netherlands, and New York, 1994.

ANNE R. LARSEN

MARRIAGE. In Renaissance society marriage was the foundation of the household and of kinship, which in turn were the foundations of society and the state. In most parts of Europe starting a household and starting married life were practically synonymous. Kin were acutely aware of their connections by blood and by marriage, which was an instrument for extending and strengthening kinship. Marriage alliances between ruling families sealed peace treaties and sometimes created empires.

All religions agreed on the value of marriage as "a remedy for fornication," and endowed marriage with spiritual values as well. In 1439 it was officially proclaimed a sacrament of the Roman Catholic Church. Alone among the sacraments, marriage was a sacrament that the couple conferred on each other. Protestants regarded marriage as a relationship singularly blessed by God and one that fostered piety. In defiant opposition to Catholicism, Protestant churches encouraged marriage for ministers. Until the Reformation ecclesiastical courts had legal jurisdiction over marriage.

Getting Married. Although a fairly large number of people never married, marriage was considered the normal lot of ordinary people. In addition to religious celibates, the unmarried included those whose economic circumstances made marriage undesirable or unlikely, ranging from scions of wealthy families to paupers without the means to start households.

The pool of potential marriage partners for most people consisted of those from like backgrounds who were either neighbors or who worked nearby. Courtship developed from the contacts of daily life in rural villages and urban neighborhoods. Young people of higher status were more closely supervised, and the marriage pool for them had to be wider if they were to be appropriately matched. Members of the highest nobility married people from other regions or even other countries. For them courtship took place only after a mate had already been selected by parents or other kin. The right to veto a selection existed in principle, but was not often exercised. In the lower classes the choices made by young people themselves were subject to parental veto, which was also rarely exercised, although occasionally conflicts found their way into the ecclesiastical courts. Choosing a mate beyond one's own social or occupational group posed the much-feared danger of misalliance, especially for the nobility, who were faced with the temptation of alliances with newly rich merchant families. A mate was not supposed to be too close to one's kinship group, although there was a common inclination to marry distant relatives. Most Protestant churches reduced the number of forbidden degrees of consanguinity and affinity in this period. The Catholic Church retained them all but continued to grant dispensations for couples who were not within the closest degrees.

Marriage negotiations between families might extend over weeks or months and were more complicated for families higher on the social scale. The commonest concerns were the dowry contributed by the bride's side and the distribution of possessions after death, in particular the provision for a surviving wife, which might include a contribution—called the dower in England—from the husband's side. The details were spelled out in a contract.

Although premarital sexual intimacy was generally disapproved of, a considerable number of lower-class women were pregnant at the time of their weddings. Village youth groups, which had some control over marital choices, discouraged what they considered inappropriate matches, for example those in which there was great disparity of ages or where one of the parties was an outsider, but tolerated copulation if the parties were well matched and seriously intended to marry. Bridal pregnancy was very rare in the upper classes, where rituals of courtship were sometimes highly stylized. Traditional gifts were exchanged and the man was expected to assume the role of subservient suitor. He was the "servant," she the "mistress."

Betrothal. Courtship culminated in betrothal, an important stage in the process of getting married that began to lose its central place only toward the end of the seventeenth century. It was often a formal ceremony, which might be performed in front of a priest at the church door. Betrothal bound the couple in a relationship that could be broken only by mutual consent, which was supposed to be as public as the betrothal itself. The legal difference between a betrothal and a wedding was not easy to understand, and canon lawyers had wrestled with it for a long time.

In most cases, betrothal led directly to marriage after an interval of a month or two. However, betrothals might last for years, one of the parties in an informal betrothal might go back on his or her word, one party in a formal betrothal would refuse to break it at the request of the other, or a pregnant woman would insist that she was actually married since she was betrothed to the man with whom she had had sexual intercourse. Perhaps the hardest kind of case was one in which a woman sued a seducer who, she claimed, had promised to marry her, thus creating both a betrothal (the promise) and a de facto marriage (the copulation). The ecclesiastical courts had to decide if a betrothal and marriage existed.

These cases, often lumped under the term "clandestine marriage," took up a lot of time in the church courts and were notorious for the perjury they caused. After the confessional split in the sixteenth century both Catholics and Protestants sought to eliminate them by abolishing betrothal as a separate step, concentrating instead on the public exchange of consent at the wedding. Betrothal was still widely practiced, however.

Weddings. Wedding ceremonies varied widely. Some took place in church or, more often, at the church door. Some took place in private houses. In much of Italy, the "wedding" consisted of so many steps that it is hard to know which was decisive. It may have been the appearance before a notary, who recorded what he witnessed. Every regional variation included its own version of the words that were to be spoken, as the couple agreed to have each other and, in many versions, the bride's father gave his daughter into the keeping of the bridegroom. There were common symbols like the ring and common gestures like the kiss. One common gesture was the clasping of hands, which was a synonym for a wedding (or a betrothal) in many places.

The legal requirements of a marriage were a confusing hodgepodge of canon law, diocesan regulations, and local civil rules until the middle and late sixteenth century. Then the church became a legal part of the marriage ceremony. Most Protestant towns and governments adopted ordinances requiring a wedding to take place in a recognized church in the presence of a minister. In the Catholic world, the Council of Trent in 1563 defined a valid marriage as one in which consent was exchanged in front of a priest and other witnesses. It may be that of all the religious changes of the period, those that most affected ordinary people were in marriage practices.

Many wedding customs and celebrations remained unchanged. The signing of the marriage contract, when there was one, preceded or closely followed the exchange of vows. There were processions to or from the church, there were communal meals with traditional foods, there were dances, music, and songs. All of this often took place out of doors with many participants. On higher social levels there was a trend to more private and more re-

strained weddings. Church authorities were generally in favor of eliminating all vestiges of paganism and superstition in wedding celebrations, and Protestant authorities in particular attempted to ban noise, music, and dancing. Yet the Roman Catholic Church had long disapproved of weddings that were too private, and discouraged such aristocratic practices as midnight ceremonies in private chapels. Class differences persisted, but the popular practices that were most offensive to religion gradually disappeared.

A small number of couples eloped, usually because of parental disapproval. Since the Roman Catholic Church never required parental consent, an elopement could be perfectly regular in the religious and legal sense while being irregular in the social and customary sense. Many Protestant ordinances required parental consent, especially for people under a certain age. No matter how strict regulations became there were always ingenious eloping couples who managed to elude them.

Married Life. The conventional view of married life saw the husband as superior to the wife in authority and judgment. The subservient suitor was transformed into the master of the household, whom the bride promised to obey. Everything in law and religion reinforced this inequality. No matter how large a dowry a wife brought into the marriage, it was the husband who assumed control of it. Generally speaking, wives could not act for themselves either in law or in commerce.

Scholars generally agree that behind the rigid conventional view were moderating realities. The husband's authority carried with it important obligations—to support and protect his wife, to treat her kindly, and to provide for her in case of his death. In addition, the circumstances of individual marriages created a variety of relationships. Disparity of ages, especially if the wife was very young, reinforced inequality. Such disparity appeared on all social levels. In the lower classes there was likely to be less of an age gap, and husband and wife often had similar premarital working experiences as servants. In practice many marriages were economic partnerships, with rural wives in particular doing work in the household and on the land that complemented the work of husbands. Popular sayings about assertive wives suggest that couples did not always fit the conventional roles and that men relied on their wives' ability and judgment more than they might admit. Some literate upper-class men expressed ad-

Marriage. *Marriage of the Young Women* by Domenico di Bartolo (c. 1360–1428) in the Spedale di S. Maria della Scala, Siena, Italy. ALINARI/ART RESOURCE

miration for their wives and confessed to being at a loss in practical affairs after their wives died. Husbands' wills not infrequently conferred considerable power on their widows.

The distrust of love as a proper basis for marriage did not extend to the feelings that developed between the pair as they lived together and shared responsibilities. Many were companions in work, as parents, and as bedfellows. Sexual pleasure was one of the most important things they shared, but sexuality in marriage was regarded with ambivalence. The common view was that it was a necessary and valuable part of marriage. It promoted companionability and prevented fornication, but it had to be kept within bounds. While husbands and wives were not supposed to succumb to sensuality, they were expected to satisfy each other. This was the so-called conjugal debt, and sometimes cases were brought in

ecclesiastical courts by spouses who complained that it was not being paid.

Religious writers warned that overindulgence in marital sex was no better than adultery, a sin singled out for special condemnation. In theory, both husbands and wives might commit adultery. Some ecclesiastical courts attempted to prosecute faithless husbands, but the prevalent attitude, expressed in many secular laws, was that the adultery of wives was the greater evil. The double standard became even more firmly entrenched in this period. The adulteries of husbands were expected to be endured by their wives as long as they were not too blatant or scandalous. Husbands who allowed themselves to be betrayed by their wives, however, earned both condemnation and contempt. One of the worst social insults was to call a man a cuckold. From every indication, wives were rarely unfaithful, and the few who were found guilty were severely punished. This did not prevent male jealousy from being one of the most common themes in Renaissance literature.

Most marriages did not end until one of the partners died. Yet marriages rarely lasted long because the death rate was high. It was not uncommon for men who married in their late twenties to die in their forties. Furthermore, women who died in childbirth usually did so after only a few years of marriage.

Some couples separated before death. Divorce was not available as a real option, even though some Protestant jurisdictions allowed it. The Catholic Church allowed legal separation (*divortium*), and most Protestant authorities preferred separation to outright divorce, in which remarriage was permitted. The usual ground for separation was adultery, and few believed that a person who had committed adultery should remarry. Other grounds included impotence and abuse, but it was no easy matter for ordinary people to be granted permanent separations.

People in power had more options. Especially when policy seemed to require a new marriage alliance, a ruler might ask for an annulment, which stated that a legal (that is, real or legally valid) marriage had never existed. This claim was usually based on the lack of proper consent on the part of one or the other of the couple, lack of consummation of the marriage, lack of the freedom to marry in the first place because of something like consanguinity, or some other reason. But an annulment after a marriage had existed for several years and had produced children was always a problem. The most famous annulment of the period was the so-called divorce of Henry VIII and Catherine of Aragon. When the pope would not grant it, Henry brought about the English church's break from Rome. Some marriages of lesser folk were annulled fairly easily, usually ones that had never been consummated.

Unhappy marriages were usually endured, but some people chose the most direct route to "divorce," desertion. It was usually men who deserted. A wife was left in the painful position of one who had lost a husband but was still married and thus unable to remarry. The poor communication of the time made it possible for a deserting husband to go somewhere else and remarry. If such a bigamy was discovered it was automatically annulled and severely punished.

Remarriage. Although the normal way of looking at marriage was that it was a union of young people who had never been married before, a large proportion of people, perhaps 25 percent, were mar-

rying for the second or third time because death had dissolved a previous marriage. A widower was likely to marry again after a fairly short interval. Widows were somewhat less likely to remarry, but much depended on age and circumstances. Families were often eager to use young widows to form desirable new alliances, but some widows of maturer years clung to an autonomy they had never enjoyed before in their lives. There was considerable ambivalence about remarriage, in spite of its routine frequency. Weddings in second marriages tended to be less festive and even omitted some religious solemnities. Mocking popular demonstrations, like the French charivari, which often targeted marital irregularities, were frequently directed against second marriages.

See also **Family and Kinship; Women.**

BIBLIOGRAPHY

Cressy, David. *Birth, Marriage, and Death: Ritual, Religion and the Life-Cycle in Tudor and Stuart England.* Oxford, 1997.

Esmein, A. *Le mariage en droit canonique.* Edited by R. Génestal and Jean Dauvillier. 2d ed. 2 vols. Paris, 1935. Discussion in vol. 2, pp. 157–235, of the debate at the Council of Trent.

Harrington, Joel. *Reordering Marriage and Society in Reformation Germany.* Cambridge, U.K., 1995.

Houlbrooke, Ralph A. *The English Family 1450–1700.* London and New York, 1984.

Howell, Martha. *The Marriage Exchange: Property, Social Place, and Gender in Cities of the Low Countries, 1300–1550.* Chicago, 1998. Based on the study of marriage contracts.

Klapisch-Zuber, Christiane. *Women, Family, and Ritual in Renaissance Italy.* Translated by Lydia Cochrane. Chicago, 1985.

Molho, Anthony. *Marriage Alliance in Late Medieval Florence.* Cambridge, Mass., and London, 1994.

Ozment, Steven. *When Fathers Ruled: Family Life in Reformation Europe.* Cambridge, Mass., and London, 1983.

Thomas, Keith. "The Double Standard." *Journal of the History of Ideas* 20 (1959): 195–216.

Wheaton, Robert, and Tamara K. Hareven, eds. *Family and Sexuality in French History.* Philadelphia, 1980. See especially the introduction by Wheaton and essays by André Burguière, Jean-Louis Flandrin, and Beatrice Gottlieb.

BEATRICE GOTTLIEB

MARTINI, SIMONE. *See* **Siena,** *subentry on* **Art in Siena.**

MARVELL, ANDREW (1621–1678), English metaphysical poet. The author of many celebrated short lyrics, including "To His Coy Mistress" and "The Garden," Marvell is regarded as one of the wittiest, most accomplished, and most elusive writers of his age. A typical Marvell lyric offers not one but several— sometimes many—intricately wrought perspectives. Verbal compression came easy to him; so did a sense of irony, as Marvell combined a Donnean interest in startling conceits (like the famous image of "vegetable love" in "To His Coy Mistress"), characteristic of metaphysical poetry generally, with a Jonsonian, or neoclassical, emphasis on surface polish and epigrammatic neatness. Marvell had a special fondness for the eight-syllable line, which he liked to craft into stanzas of eight lines each—the length, in effect, mirroring the breadth and signaling a desire for balance in even the smallest things.

Marvell's favorite themes revolve around the clash between innocence and experience and the alternating attractions of the contemplative versus the active life—subjects appropriate to his complex pastoral vision and to an England deeply divided by civil war. This most reticent of poets (only a few of his poems were published in his lifetime) could also deliver a waspish sting to timeservers and "barbed censurers" alike (see "Tom May's Death" and "To His Noble Friend, Richard Lovelace upon His Poems"). In the Restoration, he was the feared and admired satirist of "The Last Instructions to a Painter" and *The Rehearsal Transpros'd* (1672–1673). Lampooned in the latter work, John Dryden took a special dislike to Marvell; John Milton was among his closest friends—their overlapping interests and substantial differences in part indicated in the commendatory poem Marvell wrote for the second edition of Milton's *Paradise Lost* (1674). Most of Marvell's poetry did not appear in print until after his death; his *Miscellaneous Poems* was first published in 1681. He never married, although his housekeeper ("Mary Marvell") claimed to be his wife in an attempt to gain a portion of his estate.

The few biographical facts known about Marvell shed little light on the poetry, which in most cases can be only approximately dated. The son of a clergyman with strong Calvinist leanings, Marvell attended Hull Grammar School, then Trinity College, Cambridge (1633–1639). Reputed to have converted briefly to Catholicism around 1640, Marvell traveled on the Continent for some four years and returned to England in 1647. After indicating Royalist sympathies in several early poems, he came out, in 1650, on the side of the fledgling English Republic in "An Horatian Ode upon Cromwell's Return from Ireland." Marvell spent the early 1650s, however, as a tutor: first to Mary Fairfax, daughter of Sir Thomas Fairfax, the lord general of the Parliamentary army who, rather than invading Scotland, retired to his Yorkshire estate at Nun Appleton (described by Marvell in "Upon Appleton House"); then to William Dutton, later Cromwell's ward, in the home of John

Andrew Marvell. Portrait engraving, seventeenth century.
PRIVATE COLLECTION/THE BRIDGEMAN ART LIBRARY

Oxenbridge at Eton College. In 1657 Marvell was appointed Latin secretary to the Council of State under Cromwell, having failed in an earlier attempt to procure the position. The following year he was elected to Parliament representing Hull, and served in this capacity until his death in 1678. A defender of religious nonconformity in his later years, Marvell's politics are as complicated as the age in which he lived and are the subject of ongoing critical debate.

BIBLIOGRAPHY

Primary Work
Marvell, Andrew. *The Poems and Letters of Andrew Marvell.* Edited by H. M. Margoliouth. 3d ed., rev. by Pierre Legouis and E. E. Duncan-Jones. 2 vols. Oxford, 1971.

Secondary Works
Colie, Rosalie L. *"My Ecchoing Song": Andrew Marvell's Poetry of Criticism.* Princeton, N.J., 1970.
Legouis, Pierre. *Andrew Marvell: Poet, Puritan, Patriot.* Oxford, 1968.
Patterson, Annabel M. *Marvell and the Civil Crown.* Princeton, N.J., 1978.

JONATHAN F. S. POST

MARY I (1516–1558), queen of England (1553–1558). Mary was born at Greenwich on 18 February 1516, the second child of Henry VIII and Catherine of Aragon to be born alive. Her brother Henry, born in 1511, had lived only a few weeks, and Catherine had endured several stillbirths and miscarriages; so Mary, who lived and flourished, was known as the "token of hope." The hope, of course, was for a son, and it remained unfulfilled. Mary was provided with a lavish household in 1525 and dispatched to Ludlow as the nominal head of the council in the Marches of Wales, but she was never created princess of Wales, which was the title of an acknowledged heir.

Princess Mary. So exercised had the king become about his lack of a son that he became determined to annul his marriage, Catherine now being past the childbearing age. He endeavored to persuade the pope that his union was, and always had been, contrary to the law of God. Having failed in this endeavor, and being fully convinced of the rightness of his own cause, he acted unilaterally and persuaded Parliament to declare that the pope had no authority in England. On 23 May 1533 Archbishop Thomas Cranmer declared the king's marriage null and void on his own authority, and it was revealed that Henry had already secretly taken another wife. Mary was now seventeen and had been carefully and thoroughly educated in the humanist tradition, mostly on the initiative of her mother, to whom she remained very close.

Bastardized by Cranmer's decision and outraged by her father's behavior, Mary was placed under virtual house arrest in the household created for her infant half sister, Elizabeth, who was born in September 1533 to Anne Boleyn, Catherine's supplanter. Under extreme nervous stress, she made herself as objectionable as possible to her father's servants and was frequently ill. The experience permanently undermined her health, and all talk of her marrying was abandoned. After her mother died in January 1536, Mary became the chief hope of those who wished to create opposition to her father's policies, and her political position became exposed and dangerous.

In May 1536 Anne Boleyn spectacularly fell from grace and was beheaded. Mary, deceived by the evidence of her own popularity, believed that the status quo ante would be restored, but Henry still had no son and was unwilling to surrender the political gains of the last three years. He forced his daughter to accept her illegitimacy and, having done so, received her back into favor. The birth of Prince Edward (to Henry's third wife, Jane Seymour) in 1537

Princess Mary. Portrait by John Master, 1544. Mary became queen of England in 1553. BY COURTESY OF THE NATIONAL PORTRAIT GALLERY, LONDON

relieved the pressure on Mary, and she occupied an honored, if not particularly important, place at court for the rest of her father's reign.

When her father died in 1547 and she was finally accorded an independent patrimony worth over three thousand pounds a year, she was thirty-one and her unmarried state was anomalous. In the eyes of Catholic Europe she was already the true queen of England, since her brother had been born while the church was in schism, but she made no move to claim that status. As Edward's reign progressed, Mary emerged increasingly as an opponent of the religious policies carried out in her brother's name but, at the same time, as a defender of her father's settlement. If she retained any residual allegiance to the papacy, she concealed it. Apart from a high-profile campaign in defense of traditional religious practices, Mary carefully avoided political involvement. During the summer of 1549 her servants were accused of fomenting traditionalist religious protests in Devon and Cornwall, but no accusation was made against Mary herself. When the council wished to remove the lord protector, the duke of Somerset, in October

1549, she declined to become involved and turned down an offer of the regency.

Her relations with Edward's second regent, the earl of Northumberland, were extremely strained. She did everything in her power to obstruct his religious policy, and he harried her and her servants, imprisoning a number of them. When Edward was in the throes of his last illness, in the summer of 1553, he did his best to exclude Mary from the succession. However, after his death on 6 July, Mary claimed the crown, as she was entitled to do both by her father's will and by his last succession act. She was supported by the majority of the political nation and duly succeeded after a bloodless campaign lasting less than two weeks.

Mary the Queen. As queen, Mary wasted no time in declaring her priorities. To no one's surprise she asserted her commitment to traditional religion, but her announced intention of destroying her father's settlement and returning to the papal allegiance was much less well received. Heavily influenced by her cousin, the emperor Charles V, for whom she had always had a daughterly regard, she listened to the political advice of his ambassador, Simon Renard, and decided to marry Charles's son Philip, the prince of Spain. This highly controversial course provoked much opposition.

Mary's difficulties were greatly increased by the fact that inexperience, compounded by the circumstances of her accession, had caused her to form a large and heterogeneous council, many of whom had also served her father and brother. The men whom she most trusted had little political ability, and her ablest servants, such as her chancellor, Stephen Gardiner, were always kept at arm's length. Nevertheless her position was at first extremely strong, and she used it to get her own way, both over her marriage and over the return to Rome.

She successfully overcame Sir Thomas Wyatt's disorganized rebellion in February 1554; the arrival of Philip in July provoked none of the dire consequences that pessimists had been forecasting—not even an irretrievable breakdown in relations with France. Philip eliminated the unhelpful influence of Renard and persuaded the pope to negotiate a reconciliation on terms acceptable to the English aristocracy, which meant that they were able to keep the former ecclesiastical land they had purchased. Apart from that mediation, Philip played little part in the government of England, a situation that his own servants found intolerable and that he himself disliked. By the autumn of 1554 Mary was declared pregnant, and the following months were the most successful of the reign. The reconciliation was completed in January 1555, and Mary's kinsman Reginald Pole was able to assume his responsibilities as cardinal legate. Although the council remained disunited, it functioned well as an executive instrument; Philip's advice to some extent made up for Mary's inexperience.

Disintegration of the Reign. The failure of the queen's supposed pregnancy in the summer of 1555 altered the whole climate of the regime. Although Mary herself would not acknowledge the fact, most people, including Philip, realized that such a disaster at the age of thirty-nine almost certainly signaled the end of her hopes of childbearing. This meant not only that the advantageous dynastic provisions of the marriage treaty were a dead letter but also that Elizabeth, whom the queen so disliked and distrusted, would be very likely to succeed her.

Philip departed for the Low Countries in August 1555 and turned his attention to taking over his father's many responsibilities as Charles V gradually retired from public life. Stephen Gardiner died in November and the quality of government began to decline as less able men were appointed. Mary and Pole, who was now her chief prop and confidante, concentrated their energy on enforcing religious conformity. The resulting persecution of Protestants, which had started with high hopes in February 1555, became increasingly mechanical and fruitless. Mary's health, never very robust, took a long time to recover from the trauma of her false pregnancy, and she remained sickly and depressed for most of the following autumn and winter.

The year 1556 saw little change. Philip remained away and tried to claim a higher-profile role in England as the price of his return. In March, Thomas Cranmer, the architect of English Protestantism, went to the stake at Oxford with quite unexpected defiance. Pole labored to create a Catholic church out of the somewhat demoralized remnants of conformity and enjoyed some success at the pastoral level. The harvests of both 1555 and 1556 were poor, and hunger was followed by an influenza epidemic that was to last for about eighteen months. On the other hand, tight controls by the council began to discharge the queen's debt, and diligent attention to security prevented any serious outbreaks of disorder. In autumn Philip was forced into war with the belligerent Pope Paul IV, and although England was not at once involved, relations with the Holy See deteriorated; the

French speedily entered the conflict on the papal side.

In 1557 Mary's fortunes continued to decline. Philip returned briefly, but only to support his wife in drawing England into the war, a move that most of her own council (including Pole) resisted. However, the decision to enter a war was a prerogative of the crown, and formal hostilities commenced in June. At the same time, although Pope Paul IV had withdrawn from the conflict, he canceled Pole's legatine status and ordered him back to Rome. Mary refused to allow him to go, and Anglo-Roman relations remained in uneasy deadlock. In January 1558 England's last continental possession, Calais, fell to a surprise French attack. The queen's health began to deteriorate alarmingly. By October she was clearly dying, and at the eleventh hour, with the greatest reluctance, she acknowledged Elizabeth as her heir. She died on 17 November, and Cardinal Pole followed her to the grave a few hours later.

Mary had the pride and obstinacy of both her parents, and her conscience was an inflexible tyrant. However, she also had the capacity to inspire intense loyalty and affection, particularly among those who served her. As a woman she found neither love nor fulfillment, but as a queen she did her duty with unflinching rectitude and ruled the country as effectively as any other Tudor. If she had not died at the lowest ebb of her fortunes and been succeeded by a woman who cordially hated her, she might have been more favorably remembered by a country to which she was genuinely devoted.

See also **Tudor Dynasty.**

BIBLIOGRAPHY

Loades, David. *Mary Tudor: A Life*. Oxford, 1989.

MacCulloch, Diarmaid. "The *Vitae Mariae Reginae* of Robert Wingfield of Branthum." *Camden Miscellany* 29 (1984): 181–301. Eyewitness account of the succession crisis of July 1553 by one of Mary's supporters.

Nichols, J. G., ed. *The Chronicle of Queen Jane and of the First Two Years of Mary*. London, 1850. An eyewitness account of Northumberland's conspiracy and the high rebellion by a resident of the Tower of London.

Strype, John. *Ecclesiastical Memorials*. Oxford, 1721. Has large appendices of documents.

DAVID LOADES

MARY STUART (1542–1587), queen of Scots. Born 8 December 1542 to Mary of Guise and James V of Scotland (ruled 1513–1542), Mary Stuart was crowned queen on 9 September 1543, nine months after her father's death. As her paternal grandmother was Margaret Tudor, the elder sister of Henry VIII

Mary Stuart, Queen of Scots. Anonymous portrait, 1578. SCOTTISH NATIONAL PORTRAIT GALLERY

(ruled 1509–1547), she had a strong claim to the English throne. Her marriage to Henry's son, who succeeded as Edward VI (b. 1537; ruled 1547–1553), was arranged, but as many Scots opposed this match, she was secretly sent to France in July 1548.

Educated with the royal children of France, Mary retained the Scots tongue but French became her first language. She also studied Latin, Italian, Spanish, and perhaps some Greek, and learned to write, draw, sing, dance, and play the lute. On 24 April 1558, she wed Francis of Valois (b. 1544; ruled 1559–1560), the heir of Henry II (ruled 1547–1559) of France. As Henry VIII's daughter Elizabeth (ruled 1558–1603) had been declared illegitimate by statutory law, on the death of Mary I, Mary was proclaimed queen of England by her father-in-law, Henry II, and made to assume the English royal arms to indicate that according to him she possessed the best claim to that throne. In 1559, her husband became king of France but died prematurely the next year.

In Scotland. In 1561 Mary sailed to Scotland, where she presided over a brilliant court that was interested in French, Italian, and Latin, as well as Scots, literature. An influential patron and book collector, she had a special love for poetry, and had encouraged Pierre de Châtelard and Seigneur de Brantôme to return home with her. The Presbyterian Reformation in which John Knox had played a major role dominated religious life. Willing to worship privately as a Catholic, she tolerated the reformers but ultimately attempted to persuade the nobility to convert to her faith. Ambitious for the English crown, she refused to ratify the Treaty of Edinburgh with Elizabeth or to abandon the English royal arms. On 29 July 1565, she wed Henry Stewart, Lord Darnley (1545–1567), a lukewarm Catholic with a claim to the English throne, as he was a grandson of Margaret Tudor by her second husband, Archibald Douglas, earl of Angus.

As king of Scotland, Darnley had disagreements with Mary about the nature of his powers. With the support of several lords, some of whom were Protestant, he led an attack on David Riccio, her personal secretary, who was rumored to be her lover. At Holyrood Palace on 9 March 1566, Riccio was stabbed to death outside her presence chamber. Then pregnant with Darnley's son and fearing for her life, Mary rewon her husband's confidence and escaped with him from the palace. On 19 June 1566, their son James (ruled 1567–1625) was born, and on 9 February 1567, she left her convalescent husband at Kirk o'Field House, which was blown up. He escaped the explosion only to be strangled in the garden.

Mary protected James Hepburn, earl of Bothwell, a leading conspirator who was acquitted of Darnley's murder at a farcical trial in Edinburgh. Bothwell gained control of Mary and, on 15 May 1567, after he was divorced from his wife, Lady Jean Gordon, they were wed by Protestant rites. Widespread outrage led to a Scottish revolt against them: he fled and she surrendered to the rebel forces. She suffered an imprisonment of about one year during which time she had a miscarriage and abdicated her crown to her son. Then she escaped to England.

In England. From 1568, Mary was the prisoner of Elizabeth, whom she never met. A conference was begun at York and continued at Westminster in which the "casket letters" were introduced by Mary's illegitimate brother, James Stewart, earl of Moray, to prove her guilty of Darnley's murder. Although enough doubt about their authenticity existed for the inquiry to end without a verdict of guilty, Mary remained an English prisoner. She considered marrying Thomas Howard, fourth duke of Norfolk, whom she never met, even though Bothwell remained alive in the Danish cell in which he was imprisoned until 1578. Rumors about the Norfolk match served to rally Catholic resistance to Elizabeth in the Northern Rising of 1569 and the Ridolfi Plot of 1571. Letters that Mary seems to have written sup-

Mary Stuart's Monogram. Mary passed the time with embroidery when she was imprisoned at Oxburgh Hall, Norfolk. VICTORIA & ALBERT MUSEUM, LONDON/ART RESOURCE, NY

porting the latter plot were used as evidence in the treason trial of the duke of Norfolk, who was executed in 1572.

George Talbot, earl of Shrewsbury, who became Mary's jailer in January 1569, at first made her imprisoned life as pleasant as possible. She headed a household of forty, went horseback riding, and attended the Buxton baths to ease her chronic ill health, which has led to modern speculation that she suffered from porphyria, a metabolic disorder. Apologists, like John Leslie, bishop of Ross, Nicholas Sanders, and Adam Blackwood, published tracts abroad defending her actions. She embroidered tapestries with her jailer's wife, Bess of Hardwicke, and composed an essay and verses that referred to sad memories and unfaithful friends.

After Bess of Hardwicke accused her husband of committing improper acts with Mary, her life became more confined. Sir Amias Paulet, a devout Protestant who replaced Shrewsbury as her jailer in 1585, stopped all her correspondence except that with the French ambassador, which he read before it was delivered to her. Equally responsible for the increased severity of her captivity had been the Throckmorton Plot in 1583 that led to the parliamentary enactment of the Bond of Association, which made it legal to arrest and try a person on whose behalf a plot against Elizabeth was initiated.

Conspiracy and Death. In 1586, Sir Francis Walsingham, the royal secretary, enabled Mary to resume correspondence, which she thought was secret, with various sympathizers, including Sir Anthony Babington. Walsingham read all the messages going in and out of Chartley, where she had been transferred, and by July 1587 he was in possession of a letter in her hand that approved of Babington's plot to assassinate Elizabeth. In October, twenty-four peers and privy councillors assembled at Fotheringhay to put her on trial. At first she denied the court's legality but ultimately decided to appear before it to declare her innocence. It reconvened at Westminster and convicted her.

Elizabeth delayed signing Mary's death warrant until 5 February, all the while hoping that Paulet would take the suggestion to murder Mary privately and spare her the trouble of the execution. On 8 February, dressed in red, the liturgical color of martyrdom, Mary faced her death with courage. It took two blows of the axe and the sawing of a sinew to complete the beheading. She was buried at Peterborough, but her body was transferred to Westminster Abbey by her son, whose succession as king of England in 1603 vindicated her life-long dynastic ambitions.

BIBLIOGRAPHY

Donaldson, Gordon. *Mary Queen of Scots.* London, 1974.
Fraser, Antonia. *Mary Queen of Scots.* New York, 1969.
Lynch, Michael, ed. *Mary Stewart: Queen in Three Kingdoms.* Oxford, 1988.
Swain, Margaret. *The Needlework of Mary, Queen of Scots.* New York, 1973.
Wormald, Jenny. *Mary Queen of Scots: A Study in Failure.* London, 1988.

RETHA M. WARNICKE

MASACCIO (Tommaso di Giovanni di Simone Cassai; 1401–c. 1428), Italian painter considered the founder of fifteenth-century Italian painting. Masaccio's style is characterized by volumetric and muscular figures placed in compositions organized according to the system of linear perspective. The directional light illuminating his scenes imparts to them further depth and three-dimensionality and makes the figures appear to inhabit measurable spaces.

Masaccio was born in San Giovanni Valdarno. His brief professional life was centered in Florence. He is first documented as a painter there on 14 October 1418; on 7 January 1422 he enrolled in the Florentine painters' guild; in 1424 he joined the Compagnia di San Luca, the professional organization of painters.

Masaccio's earliest extant work may be the *San Giovenale Triptych,* depicting the Virgin and Child flanked by angels and saints (dated 23 April 1422, Regello, San Giovenale di Cascia). It is attributed to the painter on stylistic grounds, and thus subject to debate.

The altarpiece of the *Virgin and Child with St. Anne* (c. 1424–1425, Florence, Uffizi) was attributed to Masaccio by Giorgio Vasari (1511–1574), although cleaning and close examination revealed involvement of additional artists, including Masolino (Tommaso di Cristoforo Fini; 1383–c. 1444/47), with whom Masaccio collaborated on numerous commissions.

Vasari also ascribed to Masaccio a now dismantled and scattered triptych originally in the Carnesecchi Chapel of Santa Maria Maggiore in Florence (c. 1423?); it depicted the Virgin and Child framed by SS. Catherine and Julian, and scenes from the lives of these saints in the predella below. Today the authorship of the panels is again in question, and Masolino's participation in this work is suggested as well.

Better documented is Masaccio's *Pisa Altarpiece,* commissioned in 1426 by the Pisan notary Ser Giu-

Masaccio. *Expulsion from Paradise.* Fresco in the Bran-cacci Chapel, church of S. Maria del Carmine, Florence. SANTA MARIA DEL CARMINE, FLORENCE/CANALI PHOTOBANK, MILAN/SUPERSTOCK

liano di Colino degli Scarsi da San Giusto for his chapel in the Carmine in Pisa. Following the remodeling of the church in the late sixteenth century, the altarpiece was dispersed; its original form is reconstructed from Vasari's description. It focused on the enthroned Virgin and Child entertained by musical angels and flanked by SS. Peter, John the Baptist, Julian, and Nicholas. The predella narrated episodes from the lives of these saints, while the upper story of the polyptych contained a crucifixion and additional saints. Today parts of the altarpiece belong to multiple museums: the *Virgin and Child* is in London, in the National Gallery; the predella scenes and four small saints are in Berlin, in the Gemäldegalerie; and other pieces are further dispersed.

Still in its original location is Masaccio's *Trinity* fresco (1425–1427?, Florence, Santa Maria Novella; see the color plates in this volume), thought to have been ordered by a member of the Lenzi family because the tombstone of Domenico Lenzi (d. 1427)

and his family, dated 1426, was once in front of the fresco, and Domenico's relative Benedetto served as a prior of Santa Maria Novella in 1426–1428 and could thus have supervised the memorial. Masaccio's fresco depicts Christ on the cross upheld by God the Father and flanked by the Virgin and St. John. This group is set in an illusionistic classicizing chapel crowned by a coffered barrel vault. Kneeling in front and outside the chapel are presumably its donors. Below them is painted a skeleton reposing on a catafalque that bears an inscription: "IO FU G[I]A QUEL CHE VOI S[I]ETE E QUEL CHI SON[O] VOI A[N]CO[RA] SARETE" ("I was once that which you are and that which I am you will also be").

Masaccio's most celebrated work is a series of frescoes in the Brancacci Chapel in the Church of Santa Maria del Carmine, Florence (the commission and its execution are not documented but dated c. 1425–1427). The chapel was founded by Pietro Brancacci (d. 1367); his son Antonio left a further bequest for it in his will (dated 16 August 1383); Pietro's nephew Felice owned the chapel from 1422 to 1434. In 1434, when Felice was exiled from Florence to Siena, the frescoing had not been finished; it was finally completed by Filippino Lippi in the early 1480s. The initial painting campaign was carried out by Masaccio jointly with Masolino (the chronology of the work is uncertain). The cycle is devoted to the life and ministry of St. Peter; the entrance piers also feature the *Temptation of Adam and Eve* by Masolino, and the *Expulsion from Paradise* by Masaccio. The *Expulsion* vividly conveys the profound remorse and anguish of the first sinners through their body language and the facial expression. Similar psychological complexity characterizes other scenes of the cycle painted by Masaccio. The most famous episode, the *Tribute Money,* gathers the apostles in an intimate circle around Christ, who commands Peter to fetch the tribute money out of a fish's mouth and deliver it to a Roman official. [See the color plates in this volume.] The expressive interlocking arrangement and communication of the characters creates a tangible drama in front of the beholder. But here, too, as in other works associated with Masaccio, Masolino's hand has been discerned.

In 1423–1425 or 1428 Masaccio and Masolino seem to have collaborated on the double-sided *Altarpiece of Santa Maria Maggiore* in Rome, likely commissioned by Pope Martin V (reigned 1417–1431). The front of the altarpiece depicted the *Assumption of the Virgin,* flanked by four saints; the rear, the *Foundation of Santa Maria Maggiore,* with saints in the wings. Today the altarpiece, like so

Masaccio and Masolino. *Virgin, Child, and St. Anne.*
Painting by Masaccio and Tommaso di Cristoforo Fini,
called Masolino da Pancale (1383–c. 1447). GALERIA DEGLI
UFFIZI, FLORENCE/ALINARI/ART RESOURCE

his notebooks, praised Masaccio for taking lessons
from nature and thus attaining perfection. Vasari eulogized Masaccio in his *Lives* (1568) as the founder
of the second period of Italian painting and reported
that twenty-five Florentine artists (including Michelangelo and Raphael) studied and copied the Brancacci Chapel paintings.

See also **Florence**, *subentry on* **Art of the Fifteenth
Century; Optics; Space and Perspective.**

BIBLIOGRAPHY

Primary Works

Alberti, Leon Battista. *On Painting*. Edited by Martin Kemp.
Translated by Cecil Grayson. London, 1991.

Landino, Cristoforo. *Commento di Cristoforo Landino fiorentino
sopra Comedia di Dante* (Commentary on the divine comedy of Dante). Florence, 1481. Edited by R. Cardini. In *Scritti
critici e teorici* (Critical and theoretical writings). Rome,
1974.

Vasari, Georgio. *Lives of the Painters, Sculptors, and Architects*.
Translated by Gaston du C. de Vere. New York, 1996. The
translation was made from *Vite de' più eccelenti pittori scultori, ed architettori*. Edited by G. Milanesi. 9 vols. Florence,
1877–1885.

Secondary Works

Beck, James H. *Masaccio, the Documents*. Locust Valley, N.Y.,
1978.

Berti, Luciano. *Masaccio*. Florence, 1988.

Borsook, Eve. *The Mural Painters of Tuscany*. Rev. ed. Oxford,
1980.

Cole, Bruce. *Masaccio and the Art of Early Renaissance Florence*. Bloomington, Ind., 1980.

Joannides, Paul. *Masaccio and Masolino: A Complete Catalogue*.
London and New York, 1993.

MARINA BELOZERSKAYA

MASQUE. *See* **Drama, English,** *subentry on*
Jacobean Court Masque.

MASSINGER, PHILIP. *See* **Drama, English,**
subentry on **Jacobean Drama.**

MATERIAL CULTURE. The Renaissance was an
age that experienced unprecedented changes in the
acquisition of material objects, as consumption habits and cultural values led individuals into an entirely
new relationship with their possessions. Buildings,
paintings, tapestries, Turkish carpets, leather-bound
books, glass and porcelein objects, jewelry and
clothes, scientific instruments and specimens—all
crowded a new world of conspicuous abundance.
Behind these objects, however, existed myriad economic, political, and social realities characteristic of
the period that changed not only the motives behind
ownership but the nature of the objects themselves.

many others, is scattered among European and
American museums.

Masaccio's career ended tragically early, and
many works attributed to him by Vasari and other
authors do not survive. He was, however, admired
and emulated by Florentines shortly after his death.
Leon Battista Alberti in *Della pittura* (1436) lauded
Masaccio, along with Brunelleschi, Donatello, Ghiberti, and Luca della Robbia, as in no way inferior to
the ancient masters. Cristoforo Landino, in the *Commentary on the Divine Comedy* (1481), praised Masaccio for his ability to convey the true appearance
of objects in nature, his volumetric construction of
figures and spaces with the aid of perspective, and
his technical mastery. Leonardo da Vinci, in one of

As a consequence, while people increasingly began to seek out new possessions, those possessions came to define them in turn, shaping not only their identities as consumers, patrons, or scientists, but also impelling them to make more profound changes on the world to come.

The Italian city-states provided the model in the demand for both secular and religious objects, having been at the forefront of economic growth, international trade, and commercial innovations since the eleventh century. Interrupted by the devastation wrought by the bubonic plague after 1348, Italy emerged at the end of the fourteenth century with a new abundance of disposable wealth, resulting in the release of a long pent-up urge to obtain luxury goods of various kinds. Traditional explanations have attributed this new "consumerist" impulse to the idea that the effects of the plague led the rich away from long-term business investments and toward an increasing and hedonistic propensity to spend. More recent explanations, however, argue in favor of overall wealth outpacing investment opportunities from the fourteenth through the seventeenth centuries, due to vibrant export activity in goods and services, the money released by wars and invasions, and developments in the industrial and agricultural sectors. The distribution and structure of this wealth were also important factors in creating demand for commodities, as urban centers ensured that Italy would retain its market dominance (especially in luxury goods), backed by an elaborate system of patronage on the part of a newly enriched class of urban elites. Indeed, so secure was Italy in its wealth that not until the seventeenth century would northern Europe overtake economic predominance, a shift due to factors such as demographic stagnation and the decline of the Mediterranean as a center of trade.

Spending and the Urge Toward Display. Over time, a new class of elites, different from the more rural-based and "feudal" elites of the past, benefited from this wealth, attaining a degree of stability and financial expertise and the means with which to set standards of taste. Many (but by no means all) humanists supported this new embracing of things—or rather, they didn't stand in the way. By the Renaissance attitudes toward wealth in general had in fact undergone enough of a shift that the old suspicions of money fell away as a new spirit of material acquisitiveness took over—much to the consternation of preachers such as Girolamo Savonarola, who heaped everything from false hair to cosmetics and gowns into the flames. Among the "five virtues" listed by the Neapolitan humanist and philosopher Giovanni Pontano, writing about 1500, "magnificence" and "splendour" involved some kind of expenditure, on architecture or personal possessions, to prove one's own civic or ethical worth. Although such notions had existed in the Middle Ages in regard to Thomas Aquinas's ideas about the virtuous uses of money, by the Renaissance they were adapted to a new and more worldly urban context.

This meant that elites were now free, even in a philosophically sanctioned sense, to project their authority and diplomatic power through unprecedented levels of free spending. In personal and civic celebrations, material objects were extended to their decorative and creative limits. Children appeared gilded from head to foot; machines (including those constructed by Leonardo da Vinci) represented moving and colossal heavenly bodies; chariots were drawn by concealed horses; and a calvacade of camels paraded through the streets, bearing masks representing captured Turkish warriors. Venice especially reached a heightened level of show, revealing the accoutrements of a kind of state liturgy, as vessels coursed through the water bearing fluttering banners, garlands, strapping girls, winged boys, and representations of more constellations. Moreover, in Venice ducal coronations were no longer simple, penitential affairs as they had been in the Middle Ages, but elaborate ceremonies involving days of highly coordinated processions culminating in nights illuminated by banquet tables, golden chandeliers, and hundreds of red candles.

Architecture. The physical landscape of the cities where these public displays took place underwent perhaps the most important material transformation, especially in Italy where the largest expenditures were directed toward architecture, resulting in a building boom that lasted throughout the Renaissance. Forces of greater institutionalization and organizational developments, long in place since the Middle Ages, brought about an increasing number of churches. With the creation or enlargement of liturgical space came an increasing number of material and pictorial objects to fill it, in the form of murals, altarpieces, and paintings. These objects, while not new to the Renaissance, nevertheless generated in turn an internal demand based on factors of competitiveness, taste, and ecclesiastical patronage.

In general, the material culture of the church experienced a quantitative rather than qualitative change over the course of the Renaissance, as it simply increased and artistically elaborated the number of buildings, accessories, utensils, and furnishings that had long existed.

In the secular realm, however, expenditures underwent a more drastic change that reflected demand generated by new economic and urban realities. Urban monuments were commissioned by Italy's competitive city-states to solidify their new role as cultural and political centers, resulting in a new kind of aesthetic found in civic halls, public buildings, symmetrical and centrally planned streets, public squares, and public sculptures. Equally significant were the private residences created by an elite now secure enough in its wealth and standing to forge structures of permanence around new kinds of public identities. For such families as the Medici and Strozzi, private palaces were intended to project dynasty and family across space and time, from one generation to another. Borrowing heavily from ancient Roman models, they served as visible advertisements of social dominance and authority, going so far, as in the case of Cosimo de' Medici's Florentine town palace, to work in the family coat of arms onto the facade—an act that further distinguished such architecture from the more anonymous structures where the rich dwelled in the Middle Ages.

The interior spaces of these castles also were transformed, with internal, arcaded courtyards and vaulted double-ramp internal staircases constituting innovative developments during this period. While houses of the poor often continued to be single-room, single-bed communal dwellings, domestic interiors among the better off became increasingly privatized and gender-segregated. Walled gardens lay enclosed behind espaliered fruit trees (trees trained on a latticework or stakes) and rose trellises, becoming sites of courtship and intimacy, as other features—the bed chamber, the alcove, the ruelle—became secret places where one could stash personal papers or objects of private devotion such as hair shirts. For Leon Bastista Alberti, one of the most important rooms was the study, a retreat for the master of the house where letters, papers, and accounts were kept away from women and others of the house by sturdy bolts and locks. Originally a place of monkish simplicity, the study had, by the Renaissance, become a sanctified male space and an essential contribution in the development of privacy. [For a photograph of such a study, the *studiolo* of Urbino, see the color plates in volume 6.]

Art and Domestic Furnishings. Buildings, in turn, generated a demand for domestic furnishings, which increased dramatically in quantities accumulated by the later fifteenth century and constituted a larger percentage of overall household expenditure than before, according to domestic account inventories. Studies contained men's most precious treasures, with silver, tapestries, jewels, and account books locked away, alongside the requisite bed, chests, and benches. By the sixteenth century, household accounts reveal further increases in gilded leather and luxury stuffs, elaborate armoires, credenzas, and chests, as well as decorative objects such as terra-cotta sculpture and ceramics. Art belonged firmly within the context of these furnishings. With developments in oil painting, artists could produce larger pictures in less time and at lower prices for an enormous market. Indeed, art became part of this world of consumption, and behind every painting existed a complicated business relationship forged between patron and client to produce a negotiated work of homage as well as an aesthetically pleasing object.

The material culture of domestic furnishings also called forth changes in behavior and manners. At the table, northern Europeans such as Montaigne commented on the Italians' use of the fork, which came into use by the sixteenth century. Whereas medieval people had shared from the same bowl and cup, by the seventeenth century, across Europe, each person had his or her own plate, napkin, fork, spoon, and knife—with the latter utensils often bearing significant colors, such as ebony for use in the penitential Lenton season, and handles that were half black and half white to express the "half-sad, half-happy nature" of Whitsunday. Prescriptions of etiquette—at least as they were directed to the elites—were created to ensure the proper handling of such objects, as manuals enjoined the reader to eat most foods with a fork, but to use a spoon for olives and eat green walnuts with the fingers. Such behaviors were necessary at court, and it was absolutely imperative for the rising courtier to be able to negotiate his or her way through the material culture that he or she faced. Standards of taste and civility were set by elites such as Cardinal Francesco Gonzaga (1444–1483), who was known to travel in eighty-horse entourages to homes filled with gems, opulent tapestries of silk and gold, tables crowded with elaborate candlesticks and goblets, closets filled with velvet and ermine robes, collections of illuminated manuscripts, and various other finely cultivated objects d'art. The cost of all this display, however, was great; After Gonzaga's death, he was revealed to be deeply in debt—a common phenomenon of the time, and one made more prevalent by new mechanisms of credit.

Book and Scientific Collections. The urge to collect became a hallmark of the Renaissance, as even a contemplative humanist such as Petrarch was possessed by a desire to acquire manuscripts and create a library—a desire that would be carried further by bibliophiles such as Pope Nicholas V (1447–1455). Such people continued to collect ornately bound and illuminated manuscripts—especially those that arrived from the east, in the wake of Constantinople's collapse in 1453—but the development of print technology in the mid-fifteenth century brought on the printed book as one of the newest and most central objects in this material culture. Collectors such as Isabella d'Este and Federigo da Montefeltro amassed, if sometimes reluctantly, printed editions along with the more cherished handwritten copies, often commissioning elaborate bindings on the printed copies to meld the collection into a consistent visual piece. At the same time, the mass manufacture of printed books generated a thirst among the larger literate public for private devotional or dedicated books as well as best-sellers such as Castiglione's *The Book of the Courtier* and Erasmus's various treatises.

Joining household furnishings, generally in the private studies of men, distinct objects of desire also began to emerge that reflected the broadening tastes in a new culture of scientific inquiry. In Italy and the northern European countries, every self-respecting collector owned some kind of scientific instrument such as the telescope or microscope, along with key scientific texts made newly available through the printing press, including works of Ptolemy, Pliny, Archimedes, and the Arab commentators. Maps also enjoyed particular favor among collectors and were often jealously guarded, not only in their capacity as objects of intrinsic beauty but also as sources of important cartographical and business-related information pertaining to emerging overseas exploration.

A distinct part of this scientific material culture consisted of the cabinet of curiosity, or *Kunstkammer,* an encyclopedic collection of normal and abnormal objects from nature, indiscriminately brought together to form what has been called a "microcosm of the world." Objects included everything from plant and fish specimens, lizards and anteaters from the New World, skeletons, religious relics, and paintings representing the elements and parts of the year. Out of these collections emerged new kinds of empirical (and occult) understandings; they led, too, to

the first museums of natural history. For the first time, collectors became self-consciously aware of themselves as collectors and used their accumulations of oddities and specimens to further their prestige, knowledge, patronage, and—in the case of courts—princely majesty. The most important collection in this sense belonged to Rudolf II of Prague, whose seventeenth-century world was a magic universe of stables, aviaries, gardens, ponds, workshops, libraries, laboratories, and rooms crammed with one of the most impressive gatherings of paintings and oddities of the day.

The Reformation and Material Culture. With the Catholic or Counter-Reformation of the sixteenth century, material proliferations only increased, as spirituality generated materiality and the church was able to market its presence to a world of ready wealth and demand. With the Reformation in the northern countries, however, this kind of material culture became a significant part of the challenges made by Protestants, as even the most central material object of all—the communion host—became a source of contention and discord. In many respects pamphlets propelled these debates, and on the streets—especially in French towns such as Lyon—violence could erupt between people who distinguished themselves and their beliefs by pointedly wearing garments such as white hats and stitched-on crosses that distinguished them as Protestants or Catholics. Iconoclasm among Calvinists also made it a religious imperative to destroy all objects that evoked what they saw as idolatry and false worship; in sixteenth-century England the smashing, effacing, scratching, burning, or melting of liturgical objects became something approaching a ritual. For Protestants, the authority of scripture rendered the Bible as the central and sometimes sole material artifact of faith; nevertheless, even living in a supposedly tight-fisted Calvinist country such as the Dutch Republic did not preclude people from having a distinct and very real attachment to things. In cities such as Amsterdam—which overtook Italy as the scene of economic dominance in the later seventeenth century—foreign travelers commented on the sheer abundance of country mansions, extravagant gardens, and numerous specialized shops bursting with wares. Indeed, so attached were the Dutch to their decorative objects—their Venetian mirrors and Persian silks—that their desire approached the level of a fetish, culminating in the tulip craze of the seventeenth century.

Tulips, along with most other possessions in the Renaissance, remained luxury items. Not until the eighteenth century did real markets emerge to channel mass production of objects to a large public that now had access to them. Advertisements and fashion magazines would play to this larger public, which could tap into an ever-expanding network of shops and other commercial outlets. At the same time, while goods themselves had once been unique and produced to last lifetimes, by the eighteenth century new products were either affordable or plentiful enough to be bought over and over. In the Renaissance, the feverish pursuit of worldly goods was thus a new development, but the actual ability to attain the objects of desire remained restricted to a very privileged few and should thus not be seen as a completely modern phenomenon. Nevertheless, museums today attest to the profusion of goods in the Renaissance, which speak of consumption habits and the vicissitudes of desire as much as they speak of the objects themselves.

See also **Architecture; Clothing; Decorative Arts; Food and Drink; Jewelry; Parades, Processions, and Pageants; Ritual, Civic; Scientific Instruments; Social Status; Sumptuary Laws.**

BIBLIOGRAPHY

Findlen, Paula. *Possessing Nature: Museums, Collecting, and Scientific Culture in Early Modern Italy.* Berkeley, Calif., 1994.

Goldthwaite, Richard. *Wealth and the Demand for Art in Italy, 1300–1600.* Baltimore, 1993.

Jardine, Lisa. *Worldly Goods: A New History of the Renaissance.* New York, 1996.

Schama, Simon. *The Embarrassment of Riches: An Interpretation of Dutch Culture in the Golden Age.* New York, 1987.

SARAH COVINGTON

MATHEMATICS. The flowering of mathematics in the Renaissance was stimulated both by the social and economic changes of the time and by the recovery of Greek mathematical works. There were major breakthroughs in algebra, a subject that continued a largely Islamic tradition. Renaissance algebraists succeeded in solving both the general cubic and fourth-degree equations. The use of letters, which characterizes algebra to us, is also a Renaissance creation. Renaissance mathematicians adopted the Hindu-Arabic notation for base-10 arithmetic. More important, they applied and advanced trigonometry, used Euclidean geometry to perfect perspective in painting, and invented logarithms.

Mathematicians were connected with humanists through networks of personal friendships and patronage. Renaissance intensification of interest in

Platonic and Neoplatonic doctrine helped encourage the view that mathematics was the key to understanding nature. Universities established professorships of mathematics and its applications. New courses in mathematics and mathematical books aimed at accountants, artisans, engineers, and navigators abounded. This boom in mathematical awareness and sophistication set the stage for the scientific revolution of the seventeenth century.

The Abacists and the Rise of Algebra. In the early fourteenth century, a new class of professional mathematicians produced a set of practical mathematical texts largely based on Islamic algebraic work. These "abacists" taught merchants how to use the Hindu-Arabic system, introduced some abbreviations and symbols for operations, and applied algebra to solve problems arising from commerce, banking, and weights and measures. They lectured in the language people actually spoke and wrote accessible books which contained not theoretical discussions but worked-out examples and "do this, then do that" instructions.

Many of these works solved particular cubic equations. For instance, the algebra (c. 1344) by Master Dardi of Pisa solved an equation (in modern notation, $x^3 + 60x^2 + 1200x = 4000$) by observing that if one adds 8000 to the left-hand side, the result is equal to $(x + 20)^3$, making it easy to find x. Dardi's equation arose from a problem involving loans and interest which later appeared in the *Trattato d'abaco* (Treatise on the abacus) of Piero della Francesca (1420–1492), so we can see how the abacist tradition of commercial arithmetic and the tradition of solving algebraic equations were linked. In fact the first printed Renaissance algebra, the influential *Summa de arithmetica, geometrica, proportioni et proportionalita* (1494) by Luca Pacioli (1445–1514), was essentially a summary of the work of earlier abacists, and included not only arithmetic and the solving of equations but also elementary geometry and double-entry bookkeeping. Interestingly, Pacioli said—incorrectly, as it turned out—that the general cubic equation could not be algebraically solved.

The Italian tradition stimulated interest in algebra in many countries. In France Nicolas Chuquet wrote his *Triparty en la science des nombres* (The science of numbers, in three parts, 1484), which introduced a notation for exponents and gave the rules for multiplying powers by adding their exponents, even allowing the exponents to be zero or negative. In Portugal, Pedro Nunes (1502–1578) wrote a *Libro de algebra* (written 1532; published 1567), which, instead of being oriented toward applications, emphasized solving quadratic equations and the properties of square roots. The *Coss* (1525; the title is a German rendering of the Italian *cosa* for "unknown") of Christoph Rudolff (c. 1500–c. 1545) was the first large-scale German algebra. Also in Germany the *Arithmetica integra* (1544) of Michael Stifel (1487–1567), included negative coefficients in equations, thereby reducing all cases of quadratic equations to a single form and enabling Stifel to express the general solution verbally. In England, the royal physician Robert Recorde (1510–1558), drawing on German sources, published the first English-language algebra, *The Whetstone of Witte* (1557), which, incidentally, introduced the equal sign.

Solving the General Cubic.

In Italy in the sixteenth century, mathematicians often engaged in problem-solving competitions, with victory resulting in prestige, university positions, and monetary rewards. In the 1530s one such competition produced the solution of the general cubic equation. Special cases had been treated earlier, but cubics of the forms $x^3 + px = q$ and $x^3 + rx^2 = q$ had not yet been solved.

The solution to the cubic of the first form seems to have been discovered by Scipione del Ferro (1465–1526), professor of mathematics at Bologna, who told his student Antonio Maria Fior how to solve it. Niccolò Tartaglia (1499 or 1500–1557) claimed he could solve cubics of the second form. In 1535 Fior challenged Tartaglia to a public mathematical contest. Tartaglia worked out the solution to cubics of the first type and won the competition. News of this reached Girolamo Cardano (1501–1576), known as an astrologer (he had cast a horoscope of Christ), a physician, and a gambler who wrote the first treatise on applying mathematics to games of chance, the *Liber de ludo aleae* (Book on games of chance; c. 1526); Cardano was then lecturing on mathematics in Milan. By swearing himself to secrecy, Cardano wormed out of Tartaglia the method of solving the cubic.

In 1545 Cardano published the solution of the general cubic in the most famous of Renaissance algebras, *Ars magna* (Great art). Although he cited Tartaglia as being one of the discoverers, Tartaglia was outraged and retaliated by publishing the text of the oath Cardano had violated. This episode illustrates how the social circumstances of Renaissance mathematicians often caused them, unlike mathematicians today, to suppress new results just to win contests. Ironically, the method is today known as

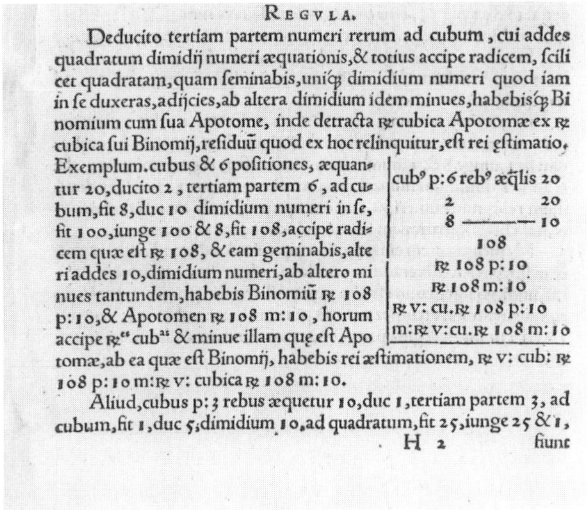

REGVLA.

Deducito tertiam partem numeri rerum ad cubum, cui addes quadratum dimidij numeri æquationis, & totius accipe radicem, scilicet quadratam, quam seminabis, unicq dimidium numeri quod iam in se duxeras, adijcies, ab altera dimidium idem minues, habebisq Binomium cum sua Apotome, inde detracta ℞ cubica Apotomæ ex ℞ cubica sui Binomij, residuü quod ex hoc relinquitur, est rei æstimatio, Exemplum, cubus & 6 positiones, æquantur 20, ducito 2, tertiam partem 6, ad cubum, fit 8, duc 10 dimidium numeri in se, fit 100, iunge 100 & 8, fit 108, accipe radicem quæ est ℞ 108, & eam geminabis, alteri addes 10, dimidium numeri, ab altero minues tantundem, habebis Binomiü ℞ 108 p:10, & Apotomen ℞ 108 m:10, horum accipe ℞cu cub & minue illam quæ est Apotomæ, ab ea quæ est Binomij, habebis rei æstimationem, ℞ v: cub: ℞ 108 p:10 m:v: cubica ℞ 108 m:10.

Aliud, cubus p:3 rebus æquetur 10, duc 1, tertiam partem 3, ad cubum, fit 1, duc 5, dimidium 10, ad quadratum, fit 25, iunge 25 &1,

H 2   fiunt

cub⁹ p:6 reb⁹ æqlis 20
2   20
8 ———— 10
108
℞ 108 p:10
℞ 108 m:10
℞v: cu.℞ 108 p:10
m:℞ v:cu.℞ 108 m:10

Figure 1. Cardano's Solution. The solution to the cubic equation from Girolamo Cardano's *Ars Magna* (Nürnberg, 1545). BY PERMISSION OF THE HOUGHTON LIBRARY, HARVARD UNIVERSITY

"Cardano's solution" (figure 1). Using analogous techniques, Cardano's student Lodovico Ferrari (1522–1566) solved the general fourth-degree equation by reducing it to the solution of a cubic. Ferrari's method was also published in *Ars magna*.

Cardano's book marked the first substantive advance beyond the algebra of the Islamic world. Even so, the importance of giving exact solutions of cubic and fourth-degree equations lies less in the solutions themselves than in the wealth of new problems and topics they inspired. For instance, Cardano's formula produces square roots of negative numbers when solving a cubic equation known to have only real roots. Addressing this problem in his *Algebra* (1572), Rafael Bombelli (1526–1572) introduced the laws of the arithmetic of complex numbers. Also, mathematicians began to raise general questions about equations of all degrees. They investigated whether arbitrary equations of a degree higher than four could be solved with the same techniques as those of the *Ars magna* (in the early nineteenth century it was proved that this could not be done). They asked how many roots an equation of a given degree could have and what the general relationships between the roots and coefficients of such an equation were.

General Notation and Concepts in Algebra.

Equations like $3x^2 + 2x = 5$ and $3x^2 = 2x + 5$ had once been considered as distinct types, but by the Renaissance they were recognized as different cases of the general quadratic. Today we express this generality by saying that every quadratic equation has the form $ax^2 + bx + c = 0$. It may be surprising to learn that such notation was invented only at the end of the sixteenth century. Earlier, although mathematicians had occasionally used symbols or abbreviations to represent an individual quantity, even the solution to the general cubic was presented verbally, with an individual numerical example treated as a model. In 1591, however, François Viète (Franciscus Vieta; 1540–1603) devised a way of writing an entire class of equations at once. Instead of using individual numbers, Viète used letters to refer to the entire "species" of numbers. (Viète used the capitalized vowels A and E for his unknowns where we use René Descartes's x and y, but such differences are unimportant.) The power of Viète's innovation is enormous. Saying that the solutions to the quadratic $x^2 - 5x + 6 = 0$ are 2 and 3 gives little help in solving some other equation, since we cannot be sure how the 2 and 3 were produced from the equation. But solving $ax^2 + bx + c = 0$ gives us

$$x = \frac{-b + \sqrt{b^2 - 4ac}}{2a}$$

and

$$x = \frac{-b - \sqrt{b^2 - 4ac}}{2a}$$

Since we can see exactly how these two expressions were produced from the original equation, they solve *every* quadratic equation. As Viète put it, the separate operations leave their footsteps behind. Viète's work changed the goal of algebra from searching for individual solutions to studying general processes and the structure of algebraic objects. Algebra became at once more abstract, more general, and more powerful.

Viète's immediate successors Thomas Harriot (1560–1621) and Albert Girard (1595–1632) extended these notational innovations to the theory of equations of any degree. For instance, consider the quadratic case. Let $(x - a)(x - b) = 0$ be the quadratic equation with the roots a and b. Multiplying its two factors yields $x^2 - (a + b)x + ab = 0$. The notation itself lets us discover that, in any quadratic equation beginning with x^2, the constant term is the product of the roots, and the negative of the coefficient of x is the sum of the roots. Similar considerations show, as Girard stated in his *Invention nouvelle en l'algèbre* (1629), that an equation of degree n has n roots, a result now known as the fundamental theorem of algebra.

Viète also established the now familiar "let $x =$ the unknown" approach to solving word problems. Pappus of Alexandria (fourth century A.D.) had discussed a Greek method for solving geometrical construction problems called "solution backward" or "analysis." Assume that the problem has already been solved, so that the desired line has already been constructed, and then work backward from that assumed construction until reaching something whose construction is already known. As Viète recognized, the "let x equal the unknown" way of solving word problems is indeed "solution backward"— analysis—because, when we give an unknown quantity a name like x, we can treat it as if it were known: double it, add 7 to it, take its square root, as we translate the conditions of the word problem into the language of algebraic equations. The equations we write can then be solved. Viète called algebra "the analytic art," which, he wrote, "claims for itself the greatest problem of all, which is *To solve every problem*" (*Analytic Art*, p. 32).

Other, humbler notational innovations of the Renaissance include the now familiar symbols $+$, $-$, $=$, $\div$, $>$, $<$, and $\sqrt{}$. The widespread use of rapid decimal calculations in commerce and banking strongly encouraged the invention of such succinct symbols. Their use in arithmetic, together with Viète's symbolic algebra, reinforced the abstract thinking about operations and operators essential for the later mathematics of Descartes (1596–1650), Gottfried Wilhelm Leibniz (1646–1716), and their successors.

Trigonometry, Geometry, and Navigational Maps. The new age of exploration required more accurate maps. At the start of the sixteenth century, although land maps were based on some form of projection, "plane charts," in which the distances between meridians of longitude were the same at all latitudes, were still generally used at sea. In seeking possible improvements, Pedro Nunes discovered in 1537 that on a sphere a constant compass course—a course that makes the same angle with every meridian of longitude—is (unless the angle is 0 or 90 degrees) a spiral that eventually ends at a pole. He then tried to find a projection that would represent constant compass courses as straight lines on a flat map. But it was Gerard Mercator (1512–1594), a mathematical instrument maker of Louvain, who, elaborating on earlier work by Erhard Etzlaub, successfully developed such a projection and applied it to navigation.

Mercator's is a variation on a simple cylindrical projection. First, imagine the sphere of the earth inscribed inside a cylinder that is tangent to the earth at the equator. To plot the point on the cylindrical map corresponding to a point on the earth's surface, draw a straight line beginning at the center of the earth that passes through the point on the earth's surface and ends where it hits the cylinder. Unroll the cylinder into a rectangular map. Second, adjust the spacing of the parallels of latitude so that, at any given point on the map, a degree of latitude and a degree of longitude are measured by the same distance. This projection succeeded in representing constant compass courses as straight lines. Unfortunately, there was a practical problem in using Mercator charts to plot courses, since the "scale of miles" varies with latitude, and Mercator's solution to this was empirical and not general. However, in 1599 Edward Wright (1558–1615), both a mathematician and an experienced seaman, solved the problem by working out the trigonometric theory underlying the Mercator projection. In modern terminology, Wright found the distances at any latitude by numerically integrating the secant function over intervals of one minute. He now could calculate distances on the earth from a Mercator map as accurately as desired. Although the Mercator map distorts shapes and sizes and therefore is misleading as a geopolitical picture of the world, it is still the projection used in most deep-sea navigation today.

Trigonometry, Astronomy, and Angle Division.

Johann Müller of Königsberg (1436–1476), better known as Regiomontanus, conceived a grand plan to translate and print Greek scientific work. Though he died before carrying out the project, he did complete a Latin version of Ptolemy's *Almagest*. Regiomontanus also wrote *De triangulis omnimodis* (On triangles of all kinds; 1464), which drew both on the work of Ptolemy and on Islamic plane and spherical trigonometry. Regiomontanus's was the first systematic European trigonometric work. When Nicolaus Copernicus (1473–1543) proposed the idea that the earth revolved around the sun, he needed a great deal of trigonometry to work out the mathematical details of his theory. Copernicus relied not only on his Islamic predecessors but on his student Georg Joachim Rheticus (1514–1576), a German familiar with Regiomontanus's work. Rheticus also published an even more extensive treatise on trigonometry, with elaborate tables of all six trigonometric functions.

Meanwhile Viète, working both from his knowledge of Islamic and Greek mathematics and from the work of Regiomontanus and Rheticus, developed multiple-angle formulas for the trigonometric functions and used them to solve algebraic equations, including the cubic that arises in trisecting an angle. In response to a challenge from the Dutch mathematician Adrien van Roomen, Viète solved a forty-fifth-degree equation by trigonometric substitution. Viète's work helped broaden the scope of algebra and trigonometry, bringing together these previously disparate branches of mathematics.

Geometry and Art.

Many Renaissance artists used geometry to give the viewer the visual sense of three dimensions. To be sure, a convincing painting does not require complete mastery of the geometry of perspective. Still, stimulated by the rediscovery of Euclid's geometrical work on optics, several Renaissance artists did original work in geometry. Most notable were Piero della Francesca (c. 1412–1492) and Albrecht Dürer (1471–1528).

Piero's *Trattato d'abaco* included original work on polyhedra, and he was one of the artists, along with Dürer, Daniele Barbaro, and Leonardo da Vinci, who helped rediscover the beautiful objects that are now called the Archimedean solids (polyhedra whose faces, though regular polygons, are not all the same regular polygon; an example, made up of twenty hexagons and twelve pentagons, may be seen on a modern soccer ball). In his *De prospectiva pingendi* (On perspective in painting), the first mathematical treatise on perspective for painting, Piero showed, constructing one point at a time, how to depict objects in three dimensions, viewed from an arbitrary standpoint, on the picture plane. Since he did not relate every step in his constructions to a general theory of perspective, the work is largely a contribution to the practical tradition. Nonetheless, it contains both some original theorems and some abstract geometrical proofs. Even though Piero's treatise was not printed, it influenced later writers on the geometry of perspective (figure 2).

Dürer's *Underweysung der Messung* (Treatise on measurement; 1525) was the first geometric text written in German and it included applications of geometry to constructing regular polygons and polyhedra, to architecture, and to typography. Dürer is sometimes considered the inventor of descriptive geometry because he showed, constructing one point at a time, how to project three-dimensional curves onto two perpendicular planes, including studying spirals as projections of helical space curves (figure

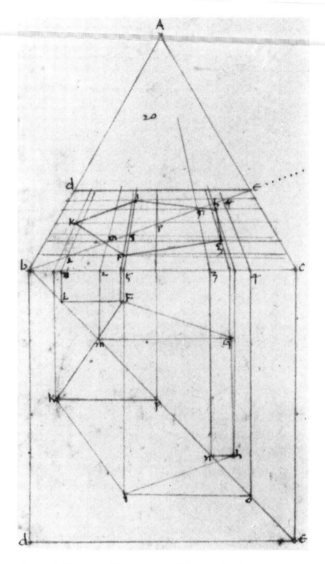

Figure 2. Piero and Perspective. Piero della Francesca's perspective construction of a regular pentagon. Piero worked out the perspective in his *De prospectiva pingendi* in the 1480s. BY PERMISSION OF THE HOUGHTON LIBRARY, HARVARD UNIVERSITY

3). The methods of perspective developed in the Renaissance helped direct attention to many of the key ideas of projective geometry, a subject initiated in the seventeenth century by Girard Desargues and Blaise Pascal.

Logarithms and Rapid Calculation. As astronomy and navigation became more mathematically sophisticated, the computations required became harder. Trigonometric functions often needed to be multiplied together, and it is much harder to multiply multidigit numbers than it is to add them.

In treating some problems, Renaissance mathematicians could use identities like

$$2 \sin \frac{x + y}{2} \cos \frac{x - y}{2} = \sin x + \sin y$$

which made it easier to find products like the one on the left because they could be calculated from sums like the one on the right. Inspired by this idea, and also by the technique Chuquet, Rudolff, and Stifel had used to multiply numbers raised to powers by adding the powers, John Napier (1550–1617) of Scotland devised a system of numbers he called "logarithms" whose sums would enable him to calculate any possible product.

Napier explained his system by means of points moving on two number lines, on one according to an increasing *arithmetic* progression, on the other according to a corresponding decreasing *geometric* progression. He used this idea to calculate a table of logarithms numerically and published it in his *Mirifici logarithmorum canonis descriptio* (Description of the marvelous canon of logarithms; 1614), translated into English in 1616 by the navigator Edward Wright. Logarithms soon became widely used, especially in the simplified base-10 form devised by Henry Briggs (1561–1630), and vastly increased the power of trigonometric calculation. Furthermore, the slide rule, essentially a simple analog computer that multiplies numbers by adding their logarithms, put fast calculation within the reach of every navigator and tax collector.

Another influential writer on calculation was Simon Stevin of Bruges (1548–1620), an engineer, mathematician, and physicist. Stevin wrote *De thiende* (On the tenth, 1585) on decimal fractions, which, though they had been developed earlier in the Islamic world, became commonly used in Europe only after his work. If one uses decimals, said Stevin, arithmetic can be performed with fractions just the way it is with whole numbers. Indeed, he was willing to raise numbers to fractional powers, and to accept irrational numbers far beyond those which had been allowed by Euclid (300 B.C.E.). Stevin's work thus extended the very idea of number.

Mathematics and the European Future.
Already in the Middle Ages, mathematicians had approached problems whose answers were not finite. As the seventeenth century began, Galileo Galilei speculated about the mathematical properties of infinite sets. His pupil Bonaventura Cavalieri (1598–1647) suggested thinking about areas as made up of infinitely many indivisible lines in the same way in-

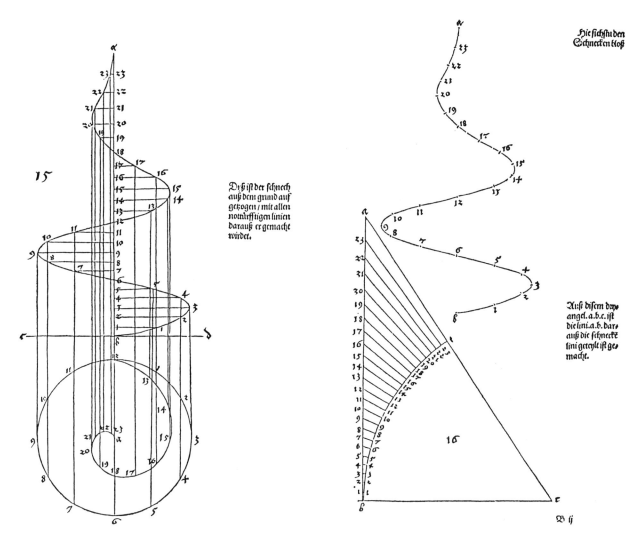

Figure 3. Two Diagrams by Albrecht Dürer. Helical space curve (one turn around a cylinder, numbers 1–12, then one turn around a cone, numbers 12–23), projected onto two perpendicular planes. Note that 12–23 on what we would call the *x*–*y* plane is a spiral, while 1–12 on what we would call the *y*–*z* plane is in fact a sine curve. From Albrecht Dürer's *Unterweisung der Messung* (1525), diagrams 15 and 16.

divisible atoms make up physical matter, and he was able to determine areas and volumes by means of this idea. Johannes Kepler (1571–1630), curious about the approximations wine merchants used to find the volumes of barrels and drawing on the work of Archimedes as published by Federico Commandino (1509–1575), invented methods using infinitesimals to find exact volumes for solids of revolution.

The new generalized algebra, and Greek and Renaissance work on geometric constructions, were synthesized in the analytic geometry of Pierre de Fermat (1601–1665) and Descartes. The broadened idea of number, and new mathematical objects like logarithms and infinitesimals, ultimately produced the

calculus. And the ever increasing applications of mathematics to the world led, through the work of Copernicus, Kepler, and Galileo, to the Newtonian revolution. What, finally, was the broader cultural meaning of Renaissance mathematics? It taught European thinkers the ideas of efficient calculation and symbolic reasoning; it emphasized abstraction and general structures; and it made clear that many aspects of the world could be treated mathematically. Above all, the mathematics of the Renaissance exemplified a general sense of intellectual power and progress.

See also **Space and Perspective**; *and biographies of figures mentioned in this entry.*

BIBLIOGRAPHY

Primary Works

Cardano, Girolamo. *The Great Art; or, the Rules of Algebra.* Translated by T. Richard Witmer. Cambridge, Mass., 1968. Translation of *Ars magna* (1545).

Dürer, Albrecht. *Unterweisung der Messung mit dem Zirkel und Richtscheit.* Zürich, 1966. Facsimile reprint *Unterweysung der messung* (1525).

Struik, Dirk J., ed. *A Source Book in Mathematics, 1200–1800.* Cambridge, Mass., 1967. The best mathematics source book. Contains well-annotated selections from figures discussed in the present entry, including Regiomontanus, Recorde, Stevin, Napier, Chuquet, Cardan, Ferrari, Viète, Kepler, Cavalieri, Girard, Desargues, and Descartes.

Swetz, Frank. *Capitalism and Arithmetic: The New Math of the Fifteenth Century.* Translated by David Eugene Smith. La Salle, Ill., 1987. Includes full text of the first mathematical work printed in Europe, the abacist-inspired Treviso *Arithmetic* of 1478, and a discussion of the work and its social context.

Viète, François. *The Analytic Art.* Translated by T. Richard Witmer. Kent, Ohio, 1983. Translation of *In artem analyticem isagoge* (1591).

Secondary Works

Bagrow, Leo. *History of Cartography.* Revised by R. A. Skelton. 2d ed. Chicago, 1985.

Boyer, Carl B., and Uta C. Merzbach. *A History of Mathematics.* 2d ed. New York, 1989. Comprehensive revision, with an updated bibliography, of a seminal work originally published in 1967. Chapters 15 and 16 cover the Renaissance.

Brown, Lloyd A. *The Story of Maps.* 1949. Reprint, New York, 1979.

Cajori, Florian. *History of Mathematical Notations.* 2 vols. Chicago, 1928.

Coolidge, Julian Lowell. *The Mathematics of Great Amateurs.* 2d ed. Oxford, 1990. Chapters on mathematical ideas of Piero della Francesca, Leonardo da Vinci, Albrecht Dürer, and John Napier.

Cromwell, Peter R. *Polyhedra.* Cambridge, U.K., 1997. Much information on the mathematical importance of polyhedra and, though not a historically sophisticated work, includes many wonderful illustrations from the Renaissance.

Field, J. V. *The Invention of Infinity: Mathematics and Art in the Renaissance.* Oxford, 1997. Excellent study, especially the chapters on Piero della Francesca, on Masaccio, and on the birth of projective geometry.

Gillispie, Charles Coulston, ed. *Dictionary of Scientific Biography.* 18 vols. New York, 1970–. The major biographical dictionary for all deceased scientific figures.

Grabiner, Judith V. "The Centrality of Mathematics in the History of Western Thought." *Mathematics Magazine* 61 (1988): 220–230.

Hay, Cynthia, ed. *Mathematics from Manuscript to Print, 1300–1600,* Oxford, 1988. A collection of articles on many aspects of Renaissance mathematics.

Katz, Victor J. *A History of Mathematics: An Introduction.* 2d ed. Reading, Mass., 1998. The best one-volume history of mathematics. Chapters 9 and 10 cover the Renaissance; Chapter 7 covers mathematics in the Islamic world.

Ore, Oystein. *Cardano: The Gambling Scholar.* Princeton, N.J., 1953. Readable biography.

Rose, Paul Lawrence. *The Italian Renaissance of Mathematics: Studies on Humanists and Mathematicians from Petrarch to Galileo.* Geneva, 1975.

Shirley, John W., ed. *Thomas Harriot: Renaissance Scientist.* Oxford, 1974.

Struik, Dirk J. *The Land of Stevin and Huygens: A Sketch of Science and Technology in the Dutch Republic During the Golden Century.* Dordrecht, Netherlands, and Boston, 1981.

Van der Waerden, B. L. *A History of Algebra: From al-Khwarizmi to Emmy Noether.* Berlin, 1985.

JUDITH V. GRABINER

MATTER, STRUCTURE OF. Renaissance teachings on corpuscles or atoms as constituents of natural bodies originated in Greek philosophy and were developed during the Renaissance along three different lines. The first was associated with the classical Greek concept of *atomos,* or atom, favored by many humanists; the second, with the Aristotelian concept of natural minima, fostered by Aristotelians; and the third, with a problem posed in the pseudo-Aristotelian *Mechanics* and known as the "wheel of Aristotle," advanced by Galileo (1564–1642). Each of these is here considered in turn.

Greek Atomism Revisited. In Greek the term "atom" means indivisible. It was used to designate invisible, unchangeable components of bodies, separated from each other by voids, or empty spaces, whose movements and arrangements account for the changing appearances of reality. Originally proposed by Leucippus (fl. 450 B.C.) and his student Democritus (c. 460–c. 370 B.C.), the doctrine was developed by Epicurus (341–270 B.C.) and received its fullest formulation by the Roman poet Lucretius (c. 95–c. 55 B.C.). As a philosophy it was closely associated with atheism and materialism in antiquity, and works expounding it rarely survived the Middle Ages.

Atomism entered the Renaissance when a manuscript of Lucretius's poem *De rerum natura* (On the nature of things) was discovered at Constance by Poggio Bracciolini (1380–1459) sometime in 1417. Lucretius's teachings were taken up by Giordano Bruno (1548–1600), whose writings in turn exerted an influence on Thomas Harriot (1560–1621) and Francis Bacon (1561–1626). A subsidiary source for atomist teachings was Hero of Alexandria (fl. A.D. 62), whose *Pneumatica* (Pneumatics) was published in Latin translation in 1575 by Federico Commandino (1509–1575). This work emphasized the importance of the size and shape of the empty space between the particles of bodies.

Bruno's atomism is best explained in his *De triplici minimo et mensura* (On the threefold minimum and measure; 1591). The minimum he treats there, which he also calls the monad, is of three kinds—metaphysical, geometrical, and physical—and is the source of all measurement. The work itself is chaotic and pantheistic, imitating the style of Lucretius, but its philosophical message is twofold. It is directed against Aristotle's teaching that the continuum is infinitely divisible, and it makes the minimum the key to all physics and mathematics. It explains variability in nature by the motion and arrangement of atoms, which themselves do not change. Atomic movement persists under the action of the World-Spirit, which is everywhere. Nothing is at rest; nothing is full, except atoms; and nothing is void, except the spaces between them.

Unlike Bruno, for whom "science" was purely speculative, Harriot made important contributions to physics, astronomy, and mathematics. The sources of his atomism are obscure, but he seems to have known the works of Bruno, Hero, and Lucretius, and indirectly, Democritus and Epicurus. As a mathematician he held that infinites are generated from finite divisibles or mathematical atoms; these he seems to have transposed to nature, seeing it as constructed of eternal and indestructible atoms. For Harriot, physical qualities arise from the motion of atoms, as do chemical changes and even optical phenomena. Though trained in scholasticism, he abandoned its explanations and used matter and motion as his basic principles.

Bacon is sometimes cited as an atomist, but the grounds here are less secure. In works written up to 1612 he favored a theory of matter resembling that of Democritus and Epicurus. But by the publication of his *Novum Organum* (New organon) in 1620 he had discarded that theory as a mere *a priori* construction, probably because of the new method he was then advancing for science.

The Concept of Natural Minimum.

Related to atomist explanations is Aristotle's idea of a smallest quantity without which a particular nature such as flesh cannot exist, advanced by him in the *Physics* against a teaching of Anaxagoras. Simplicius, Aristotle's early sixth-century commentator, extended the application to include inorganic natures, referring to them as "smallests" (Gr. *elachistai*). In the Middle Ages these became *minima naturalia,* or natural minims, which Albert the Great (c. 1200–1280) likened to the atoms of Democritus. For Albert's student, Thomas Aquinas (1225–1274), the mathematical continuum is infinitely divisible but the physical continuum is not, since natures or natural forms require minimum quantities below which they cannot exist.

In the Renaissance this teaching was further developed, mainly by Agostino Nifo (c. 1473–c. 1538), Julius Caesar Scaliger (1484–1558), and Daniel Sennert (1572–1637). The result was an extension of the concept in which minims were conceived as parts of substance with a more independent existence than previously thought, and were used to explain various physical and chemical processes.

Nifo, under Averroist influences, applied the idea of minimum to qualities as well as to substances, seeing qualitative changes as taking place discontinuously. Moving beyond the *Physics,* he employed the concept in his exposition of Aristotle's *De generatione et corruptione* (On generation and corruption; 1526), holding that when elements react upon each other they are divided into minima.

Scaliger further employed the concept of natural minima to explain how a stone is gradually excavated by drops of water. He also saw minima as not only limits of division, but as the first components of which substances are composed. He related the density of a substance to the size of its minima and the degree of separation between them. And he altered Aristotle's definition of chemical composition from "the union of the reagents" to "the motion of the minima towards mutual contact so that union is effected." (Melsen, *From Atomos to Atom,* p. 76)

The fullest development of minima theory in the Renaissance was effected by Sennert, who used it to reconcile the teachings of Democritus (c. 460–c. 370 B.C.), Galen (c. 129–c. 199), and Paracelsus (1493–1541) with those of the Paduan Aristotelians. Like Albert the Great, Sennert saw minima as Democritean atoms, which he thought fitted Scaliger's definition of chemical composition. He held that atoms are not all of one kind, that there are several kinds in accord with the diversity of natural bodies, and that atoms of simple bodies or elements are different from those of composed bodies. When elements combine, moreover, a new unity arises from the plurality of components, which are united through the higher form of the compound.

The Wheel of Aristotle (*Rota Aristotelis*).

A different line of thought was used by Galileo Galilei (1564–1642) in his *Due nuove scienze* (Two new sciences) of 1638 to justify his belief in the atomic structure of matter. In writings before 1638 Galileo had expressed an interest in atomism, but there are few keys to suggest what form he then had in mind. By 1638 it had become clear that his was a

Figure 1. The Wheel of Aristotle.

mathematical atomism somewhat like Harriot's, despite his speaking of "minims" in the Aristotelian sense.

Galileo took his inspiration from the wheel problem posed in the pseudo-Aristotelian *Mechanica* (Mechanics or Mechanical problems), which may be understood with the aid of figure 1. The two concentric circles on the left represent Aristotle's wheels, the larger with radius AB and the smaller with radius AC. The two wheels are tied together, and as the circles move to the right the center traces out path AD, while the larger wheel rolls along line AB and the smaller along line AC. By the end of one full rotation, point B on the larger circle reaches point F; at the same time, point C on the smaller circle reaches point E. But how can the smaller wheel, with its smaller circumference, traverse the same distance as the larger wheel, when both make only one revolution? That is the puzzle presented by the *rota Aristotelis*.

Galileo's solution to the puzzle is shown in figure 2. Trained in the use of Archimedean approximations and limit concepts, Galileo replaces Aristotle's wheels or circles with regular polygons, in this case two hexagons, or six-sided figures. When the larger hexagon "rolls" or clumps to the right, its sides touch all the parts of figure 1's line BF. But with the same motion, the sides of the smaller hexagon do not touch all the parts of figure 1's line CE. Rather, as shown in figure 2, segments IO, PY, and so on, are skipped over as the center G of the hexagons jumps to C and R, and so on, during the motion. (The dashed arcs in figure 2 show the jumps.) Now, proposes Galileo, let the number of sides of both hex-

agons increase to infinity, so that they approach circles as their limit. Then, in the limit, the parts HI, OP, become quantified minims or atoms, whereas the skipped-over parts become nonquantified minims or vacuums. Thus, for Galileo a finite length is composed of an infinite number of smallest particles and an infinite number of vacuums.

The point of Galileo's argument was to use the axiom "Nature abhors a vacuum" to explain the tensile strength of columns and why pumps cannot lift water over thirty feet. Its defects with regard to the wheel of Aristotle were first pointed out by Giovanni di Guevara (1561–1641), a bishop and friend of Galileo. With regard to indivisibles and pumps, its shortcomings were remedied by two of Galileo's disciples, Bonaventura Cavalieri (1598–1647), in his *Geometria indivisibilibus* (Geometry of indivisibles; 1635), and Evangelista Torricelli (1608–1647), in experiments with a barometer performed around 1644.

See also **Natural Philosophy**; **Science**; *and biographies of scientists mentioned in this entry.*

BIBLIOGRAPHY

Atanasijevic, Knesija. *The Metaphysical and Geometrical Doctrine of Bruno, As Given in His Work* Detriplici minimo. Translated by George Vid Tomashevich. St. Louis, Mo., 1972.

Furley, David J. "Lucretius." In *Dictionary of Scientific Biography*. Edited by Charles Coulton Gillispie. Vol. 8. New York, 1973. Pages 536–539.

Kargon, Robert H. *Atomism in England from Hariot to Newton*. Oxford, U.K., 1966.

Le Grand, H. E. "Galileo's Matter Theory." In *New Perspectives on Galileo*. Edited by Robert E. Butts and Joseph C. Pitt. Dordrecht, Netherlands, 1978. Pages 197–208.

Melsen, Andrew G. van *From Atomos to Atom: The History of the Concept Atom*. New York, 1960.

Shea, William R. "Descartes As Critic of Galileo." In *New Perspectives on Galileo*. Edited by Robert E. Butts and Joseph C. Pitt. Dordrecht, Netherlands, 1978. Pages 139–159.

Wallace, William A. "The Problem of Apodictic Proof in Early Seventeenth-Century Mechanics: Galileo, Guevara, and the Jesuits." *Science in Context* 3, no. 1 (1989): 67–87.

WILLIAM A. WALLACE

MATTHIAS CORVINUS. *See* **Corvinus, Matthias.**

MAURICE OF NASSAU (1567–1625), count of Nassau, stadtholder of United Provinces of the Netherlands (from 1585), and prince of Orange (from 1618). Maurice was the second son of William the Silent. He was born at Dillenburg in the German region of Nassau at a time when his father had been banished from the Dutch provinces and was leading the struggle for Dutch independence from Spanish

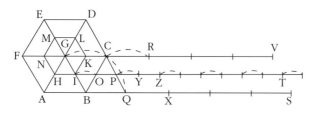

Figure 2. Galileo's Reconstruction.

Maurice of Nassau. Portrait by Michiel Jansz van Miereveld (1567–1641). Oil on wood; 221.5 × 146 cm (87 × 57 in.). RIJKSMUSEUM, AMSTERDAM

rule; and his older half-brother, Philip William (1554–1618), was being held hostage by Philip II of Spain. Maurice was raised in Cologne until his mother was detained for adultery in 1572. Thereafter he was educated by his uncle, John of Nassau, at Dillenburg. He never married, though he had many illegitimate children.

In 1584, when William the Silent was assassinated, Philip William was still a hostage in Spain. Thus was Maurice appointed to his father's responsibilities: in 1584, president of the Council of State; in 1585, statdholder (chief executive) of Holland and Zeeland; in 1589, of Overijssel; 1590, of Utrecht; 1591, of Gelderland; and 1620, of Groningen; and from 1590 he was commander-in-chief and admiral of the Union.

Maurice's greatest legacy was his ability to reorganize the military of a republic that was struggling for its very existence. In pursuing this achievement Maurice was able to rely on the knowledge of his cousin, William Louis of Nassau (1560–1620), of ancient military history; on the advice and observations of a noted mathematician, Simon Steven (1548–1620); and French and English military assistance arranged by Johan van Oldenbarnevelt (1547–1619), *landsadvocaat* (pensionary) of Holland. Between 1590 and 1597 Maurice quickly liberated all the provinces north of the great Rhine and the Maas Rivers. Regions to the south, however, were less tractable. His famous victory near Nieuwpoort in 1600 was short-lived and marked the end of his unchecked military successes. From 1600 onward his great adversary, Ambroglio Spinoza, the Italian general of the Spanish army in the Netherlands, successfully defended Spanish territories, and even regained some.

Despite his slowed military progress, Maurice opposed any agreement with Spain, in part because he owed his position to the war. Against Maurice's will, Oldenbarnevelt engineered a truce with Spain in 1609. The truce did not, however, end the religious disputes between the rigid Contra-Remonstrants—Maurice among them—who demanded the submission of the state to the Calvinists and the more tolerant Remonstrants—including Oldenbarnevelt—who sought to have the church submit to civic authorities. Fearing a civil war, between 1617 and 1618 Maurice initiated an internal purging of Oldenbarnevelt's supporters and the arrest, in 1619, of Oldenbarnevelt himself on the grounds of treason, for which he was beheaded. Maurice publicly ended the truce with Spain in 1621 and the war continued well beyond his own lifetime.

Although his great military successes expanded the borders of the United Provinces, Maurice's political actions intensified internal divisions. When he died his older half-brother, no longer a hostage, was loyal to Spain. Thus in the Union, Maurice was succeeded as stadtholder and prince of Orange by his younger half-brother, Frederick Henry (1584–1647).

BIBLIOGRAPHY

De Schepper, Hugo, and M. Vrolijk. "Vrede en Orde door Gratie in Holland en Zeeland onder de Habsburgers en de Republick 1500–1650." In *Mensen van de Nieuwe Tijd. Een liber amicorum voor A. Th. van Duersen.* Edited by M. Bruggeman et al. Amsterdam, 1996. Pages 98–117.

Van Deursen, A. Th. "Maurits." In *Nassan en Oranje in de Nederlandse geschiedenis.* Edited by C. A. Tamse. Alphen aan den Rijn, Netherlands, 1979. Pages 83–110.

HUGO DE SCHEPPER

MAXIMILIAN I (1459–1519), Holy Roman Emperor (ruled 1493–1519), the eldest surviving son and heir of Holy Roman Emperor Frederick III (ruled 1452–1493) and Eleonora (1457–1467), daughter of King Edward of Portugal (ruled 1433–1438).

Early Life and Marriage.
Maximilian grew up at Wiener Neustadt, one of the most cultivated courts of Europe. There he learned seven languages, as he boasted, and developed his love of learning and appreciation of history, astrology, philosophy, and the arts. He also loved the physical challenge of fencing, jousting, archery, and hunting. As a child Maximilian was robust and healthy. As a man he was lithe and athletic with a tall, robust frame, reddish gold hair, large nose, and prominent Habsburg jaw. The portraits by Hans Holbein and Albrecht Dürer reveal Maximilian's commanding presence, powerful personality, and sense of self-confidence.

In 1477 he wed Mary of Burgundy, heiress of Charles the Bold, duke of Burgundy, and one of the wealthiest women in Europe. Maximilian, however, immediately found himself defending his wife's patrimony from Louis XI of France who, after the death of Mary's father, hoped to seize Burgundy, Flanders, Artois, Luxembourg, the Franche-Comté, Hainaut, Brabant, Holland, Limburg, and Guelderland. The battle of Guinegate (1479) proved Maximilian's prowess on the battlefield and his mastery of tactics. Relying not on heavy cavalry but on artillery and infantry, he defeated the French. The untimely death of Mary in 1482 proved a personal and political tragedy. Mary, who deeply loved her husband and shared his mania for hunting, was thrown from her horse and died shortly thereafter of internal injuries. Two children survived to adulthood: Philip the Fair and Margaret. The French forced Maximilian to assent to the Treaty of Arras (1482), which provided that Margaret would marry the dauphin and that her dowry would include Artois and the Franche-Comté. Despite this settlement, an unpopular war with France broke out and the city of Bruges temporarily detained Maximilian. In 1489 he concluded another peace with France and several of the Netherland estates recognized him as their ruler and guardian of his son, Philip. Maximilian's subsequent attempt to wed yet another wealthy heiress, Anne of Brittany, failed when French troops captured Rennes. The French king, Charles VIII, had Maximilian's marriage by proxy annulled and in 1491 wed Anne himself, sending Margaret, Maximilian's daughter, home.

King of the Romans.
Maximilian, chosen king of the Romans in 1486, persuaded his relative Sigismund in 1490 to abdicate and turn over the Tyrol, with its strategic access to the Brenner Pass and

Emperor Maximilian I. Portrait by Albrecht Dürer. Oil on limewood; 1519; 74 × 61.5 cm (29 × 24 in.). Kunsthistorisches Museum, Gemäldegalerie, Vienna/Erich Lessing/ Art Resource

its lucrative silver and copper mines. These helped to finance Maximilian's wars. Innsbruck always remained Maximilian's favorite residence but after his death the city never again served as the imperial capital.

At this time Maximilian faced enemies in both the east and the west. After the death of Hungarian king Matthias Corvinus in 1490, Maximilian unsuccessfully sought the throne of Hungary but did succeed in driving the Hungarians out of Vienna, Styria, Carinthia, and Carniola. In the ensuing Treaty of Pressburg (1491), he regained lands that his father had lost. The treaty also provided that should Ladislaw Jagiello, king of Bohemia, recently elected king of Hungary, have no legitimate male heirs, the Habsburgs would inherit. Maximilian went on to defeat the Turks at Villach (1492) and then turned his attention to the west and signed the Treaty of Senlis (1493) with France, in which he regained Artois and the Franche-Comté.

Holy Roman Emperor.
On the death of his father in 1493, Maximilian became head of the house

of Habsburg and Holy Roman Emperor. Chronically short of money, Maximilian in 1494 married another wealthy heiress, Bianca Maria Sforza, daughter of the deceased duke of Milan, Galeazzo Sforza (ruled 1466–1476). The marriage was not a success. Bianca Maria remained childless but extravagant and spent most of her time either overeating or alone in Innsbruck. In that year too a revolt in the Netherlands occupied Maximilian. In 1495 he became embroiled in the Italian wars, joining the Holy League with Spain, the pope, Milan, and Venice to force the French out of Italy. To mobilize support he convened an imperial diet at Worms. From 1494 to 1516 Maximilian was involved in wars in Italy, invasions of France, and a war against the Swiss, who had refused to pay imperial taxes or contribute to the war effort. Quixotically, when Pope Julius II became ill, Maximilian also contemplated running as a candidate for the papal throne. His attempts to force the French to give up Milan, an imperial fief, failed, as did his efforts to force the Venetians to cede imperial territory, in large part because the estates of the Holy Roman Empire refused to give him financial support. Maximilian's relations with the German estates were often difficult. He did, however, issue a proclamation of eternal peace, ban private warfare, and establish a supreme court, a Reichskammergericht, financed in part by a poll tax, a "common penney." Many of the princes refused to collect it because part of this tax was to be used to provision an army. Maximilian's attempts to centralize power in the Holy Roman Empire encountered stiff resistance, especially from powerful electors such as the archbishop of Mainz. Maximilian's intervention in the Bavarian Succession War added a significant amount of territory to the Habsburg patrimony in 1505.

Maximilian proved most adept at brokering successful marriage alliances for his offspring, prompting Matthias Corvinus to remark allegedly that "where others wage war, you lucky Austria marry." He married his granddaughter Mary to Louis, the son of Ladislaw Jagiello, king of Bohemia and Hungary, and his grandson Ferdinand to Ladislaw's daughter Anna. Even though both of Ladislaw's thrones were elective, these alliances along with the Treaty of Pressburg paved the way for the eventual succession of Ferdinand. In 1496 Maximilian married his son Philip to the Spanish infanta, Joanna the Mad, and in 1497 his daughter Margaret to the Spanish infante, Don Juan. These settlements not only put Castile and Aragon in the anti-French camp but also ultimately ensured that Maximilian's grandson, Charles, would inherit both Castile and Aragon.

Although Maximilian had little money, he reorganized the University of Vienna and brought the renowned Conrad Celtis there. Although he was an important patron of both church and court music, Maximilian's most prominent cultural achievement lay in the numerous beautifully illustrated works he commissioned to glorify not only his achievements but also those of his house. He also wrote prolifically on various subjects such as hunting and composed extensive sections of his three-part autobiography. In Innsbruck his greatest architectural achievements can be seen; he remodeled the imperial palace and built a new palace and an arsenal. He also commissioned an elaborate sarcophagus not completed until after his death.

Because of his numerous military commitments, Maximilian borrowed from bankers such as the Fuggers. Given his limited resources and his many enemies, Maximilian accomplished a great deal. He reconquered the hereditary countries and added land to the Habsburg patrimony not only militarily but also diplomatically through his astute marriage policies. Admittedly, some of his military adventures against Venice were just that. But it would have been impossible for Maximilian to avoid war with France over the Burgundian inheritance or over the seizure of Milan, which provided strategic access to the hereditary countries.

In his extensive correspondence Maximilian emerges as engaging, committed, caring, articulate, and humorous. The death of his son Philip in 1506 darkened his later years, as did his failure to see his grandson Charles crowned king of the Romans. His last weeks were spent with his dogs and his caged birds who accompanied him everywhere. Before expiring, he requested that he be buried not in the tomb prepared at Innsbruck but under the altar steps at Wiener Neustadt, and that his heart be carried to Bruges and buried with his first wife.

See also **Habsburg Dynasty**; **Holy Roman Empire**; *and biography of Charles V.*

BIBLIOGRAPHY

Benecke, Gerhard. *Maximilian I (1459–1519): An Analytical Biography.* London and Boston, 1982. Excellent coverage in English. Integrates biography with social analysis.

Scholz-Williams, Gerhild. *The Literary World of Maximilian I: An Annotated Bibliography.* St. Louis, 1982. A valuable source.

Wiesflecker, Hermann. *Kaiser Maximilian I: Das Reich, Österreich, und Europa an der Wende zur Neuzeit.* 5 vols. Munich and Vienna, 1971–1986. The definitive biography.

LINDA FREY and MARSHA FREY

MAXIMILIAN II (1527–1576), Holy Roman Emperor (1564–1576), king of Bohemia (1549/1562–1576), king of the Romans (1562–1576), king of Hungary (1563–1576). Maximilian was a member of the Habsburg family and was born in Vienna, the son of the future emperor Ferdinand I and the Bohemian princess Anna, daughter of Vladislav II. He spent his early years in Innsbruck in the Tyrol, where one of his tutors was Wolfgang Schiefer from Alsace, who supposedly introduced Maximilian to Protestant ideas.

The Way to the Throne. From 1544, Maximilian was at the court of his uncle Charles V. In September 1548 he married, by arrangement, the emperor's daughter Maria in Valladolid in Castile. They had sixteen children, among whom were the future emperors Rudolf II and Matthias. In 1549 the Bohemian estates accepted him as king. For a time, Maximilian's succession as Holy Roman Emperor was insecure not only because his Spanish relatives attempted to present Philip II as the future emperor but also because it was opposed by the popes Paul IV and Pius IV, who feared that Maximilian would convert the empire into a Protestant state. In 1560, at the critical point of the discussions about his denomination, his declarations presaged his future program in religious matters—that he wanted to be neither Catholic nor Protestant but simply Christian. Finally, in September 1562, he was crowned king of Bohemia in Prague, in November 1562 king of the Romans in Frankfurt, and in September 1563 king of Hungary in Pozsony (Bratislava). He became Holy Roman Emperor after the death of his father on 25 July 1564. The Austrian hereditary lands were divided among Maximilian and his brothers: Maximilian governed lower and upper Austria; Charles, inner Austria; Ferdinand, the Tyrol and the further Austrian territories in Swabia and Alsace.

The Reign of Maximilian. As emperor Maximilian was not a very successful statesman. He did, however, have many excellent ministers and advisers. The most important members of his secret council were the nobles Hans Trautson, Vratislav z Pernštejna, and Leonhard von Harrach; and the doctors of law Georg Sigmund Seld, Johann Ulrich Zasius, and Johann Baptist Weber. Others played important roles in his political decisions: Ogier Ghislain de Busbecq, a famous collector of ancient and Greek inscriptions and manuscripts; the soldier and diplomat Lazarus von Schwendi; and Maximilian's ambassadors, such as Adam von Dietrichstein and Hans Khevenhüller in Spain and Prospero d'Arco in Rome,

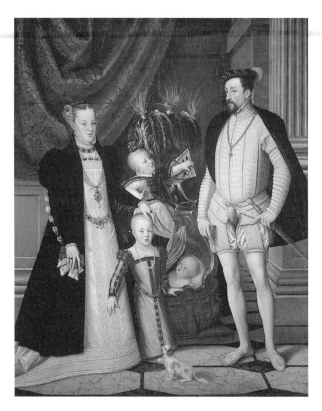

Emperor Maximilian II and His Family. Portrait of the emperor, his wife, Maria of Spain, and his children, Anna, Rudolf, and Ernst, by Giuseppe Arcimboldo (c. 1527–1593). Oil on canvas; 1553; 240 × 188 cm (94.5 × 74 in.). PORTRAITGALERIE, SCHLOSS AMBRAS, INNSBRUCK, AUSTRIA/ERICH LESSING/ART RESOURCE

as well as Francesco della Torre and Vito di Dornberg in Venice.

Maximilian tried to negotiate between the Catholic and Protestant confessions but did not succeed in restoring religious unity. From 1566 on, his religious policy was defensive, trying to secure the Peace of Augsburg of 1555, which protected the Protestant and Catholic confessions within the empire. In lower Austria and Bohemia Maximilian allowed freedom of religion to the Protestant nobles and their subjects. His religious tolerance provoked conflicts with Philip II, especially because of the emperor's attempts to negotiate a peace with the Dutch provinces that had started to revolt against the Spaniards in the 1560s. He was more successful in imperial Italy, where he stopped both Spanish and papal attempts to destroy the imperial system of feudalism that protected the smaller territories in northern Italy from their powerful neighbors.

The war against the Ottoman Empire in 1566–1567 did not significantly change the Hungarian-

Ottoman border, but this frontier became more or less quiet with the Peace of Adrianople (1568) between the Habsburgs and the sultan. Trying not to endanger the situation in Hungary, Maximilian refused to join the Holy League between Venice, the pope, and Spain (1571). When he presented himself as candidate for the Polish throne during the interregnum of 1574–1575, he was only elected by a minority of the Polish *szlachta* (gentry). Only Maximilian's untimely death at Regensburg on 12 October 1576 prevented war from breaking out between the Habsburgs and Poland.

Maximilian was not a very successful statesman. Unwilling to participate in the process of confessionalization, the consolidation of the Catholic, Lutheran, and Calvinist churches took place. Maximilian was destined to have difficulties. Maximilian's chronic lack of money hampered many of his political aims.

The Renaissance Culture at the Court.

His flaws as a statesman notwithstanding, Maximilian was a very popular emperor. He spoke German, Spanish, Czech, Italian, French, and Latin. He was open-minded and was always well received by people who met him. He was an important catalyst of Renaissance culture in central Europe. At his multinational court in Vienna he founded a "court academy" whose members included many famous scientists and scholars: the physicians Pietro Andrea Mattioli, Rembert Dodoens, and Johann Crato von Crafftheim; the botanist Charles de l'Écluse; the mathematician Paulus Fabricius, who was one of the experts working with Pope Gregory XIII on the reform of the calendar; the librarian Hugo Blotius; and the historiographers Wolfgang Lazius and Johannes Sambucus. The Renaissance palace (Schloss Neugebäude) that Maximilian built southeast of Vienna held an important collection of rare and non-European plants and animals, which influenced natural science in central Europe.

Maximilian was also the patron of many artists: the sculptors and painters Giulio Licinio, Giuseppe Arcimboldo, and Antonio Abondio; the architects Hermes Schallautzer and Pietro Ferrabosco; and the antiquarian Jacopo Strada. Maximilian had a famous collection of paintings with works such as those of the Spanish painter Alonso Sánchez Coello, which are still in the Viennese collections. The emperor was also a music lover. The Venetian ambassador Giovanni Michele characterized the musical activities at the court as exceptional. The court music was headed by Filippo di Monte, a leading master of the Italian madrigal with an international reputation. Af-

ter a visit to Vienna, Orlando di Lasso described the chamber music there as being so wonderful that neither tongue could describe it nor ears ever take enough of it.

See also **Habsburg Dynasty**; **Holy Roman Empire**.

BIBLIOGRAPHY

Primary Works

Bibl, Viktor, ed. *Die Korrespondenz Maximilians II.* 2 vols. Vienna, 1916–1921. Maximilian's correspondence with the members of the Habsburg family, 1564–1567.

Edelmayer, Friedrich, Leopold Kammerhofer, and others, eds. *Die Krönungen Maximilians II zum König von Böhmen, Römischen König und König von Ungarn (1562–1563) nach der Beschreibung des Hans Habersack, ediert nach CVP 7890.* Vienna, 1990. Description of the coronations in Prague, Frankfurt, and Pozsony.

Edelmayer, Friedrich, ed. *Die Korrespondenz der Kaiser mit ihren Gesandten in Spanien.* Vienna and Munich, 1997. Maximilian's correspondence with Adam von Dietrichstein, his ambassador in Spain, 1563–1565.

Lanzinner, Maximilian, ed. *Der Reichstag zu Speyer 1570.* Göttingen, Germany, 1988. Edition of the documents of the Imperial Diet, 1570.

Secondary Works

Bibl, Viktor. *Maximilian II. Der rätselhafte Kaiser. Ein Zeitbild.* Hellerau bei Dresden, Germany, 1929. Biography of Maximilian II.

Edelmayer, Friedrich. *Maximilian II, Philipp II. und Reichsitalien: die Auseinandersetzungen um das Reichslehen Finale in Ligurien.* Stuttgart, Germany, 1988. Spanish-imperial relations in northern Italy.

Edelmayer, Friedrich, and Alfred Kohler, eds. *Kaiser Maximilian II. Kultur und Politik im 16. Jahrhundert.* Vienna and Munich, 1992. Collection of articles about all aspects of culture and politics at the court of Maximilian II. The articles about Busbecq (by Zweder von Martels), Strada (by Dirk Jacob Jansen), and music (by Robert Lindell) are written in English.

Evans, R. J. W. *The Making of the Habsburg Monarchy, 1550–1700: An Interpretation.* Reprint, Oxford and New York, 1985.

Kaufmann, Thomas DaCosta. *Variations on the Imperial Theme in the Age of Maximilian II and Rudolf II.* New York, 1978.

Lanzinner, Maximilian. *Friedenssicherung und politische Einheit des Reiches unter Kaiser Maximilian II. (1564–1576).* Göttingen, Germany, 1993. Imperial policy in the age of Maximilian II.

Louthan, Howard. *The Quest for Compromise: Peace-makers in Counter-Reformation Vienna.* Cambridge, U.K., 1997.

FRIEDRICH EDELMAYER

MAZZONI, JACOPO (1548–1598), Italian philosopher, literary theorist. Born in Cesena, Jacopo Mazzoni studied at the University of Padua between 1563 and 1566 or 1567, worked on the Gregorian calendar in Rome from 1578 to 1581, then became a university professor. He taught Aristotelian and Platonic philosophy at the University of Pisa from 1588 to 1597, and he was appointed to the University of Rome just before his death. In the late 1580s Mazzoni became a member of the Accademia Fiorentina and of the Accademia della Crusca.

In his *Della difesa della Comedia di Dante* (A defense of Dante's *Comedy;* part 1, 1587, part 2, 1688), Mazzoni drew on Plato for a theory of literary aesthetics. According to Mazzoni, a poet creates images for their own sake, in such a way as to make them credible. Thus he delights his audience and achieves his aim. Further, a poet's ability to describe real detail, in the light of his own artistic sensibility, is a measure of his skill. This notion is the basis on which Mazzoni developed his theory of imitation.

In *De comparatione Platonis et Aristotelis* (Comparison of Plato and Aristotle; 1597), Mazzoni updated Marsilio Ficino's interpretation of Platonism by emphasizing the importance of skepticism and mathematics. In Mazzoni's view, skepticism allowed individuals to free themselves of dogmatic belief in accepted philosophical systems, in order to select in each those theoric elements useful for the progress of knowledge. Mazzoni then developed a theory of matter as made up of imperceptible geometrical corpuscles. This metaphysical foundation justified the use of mathematical demonstration in natural investigation. So, against the attacks of Aristotelian philosophers, he defended the truth of Archimedes's principles and propositions used by Renaissance mathematicians in the study of the motion of bodies. Mazzoni was one of the most interesting exponents of late-Renaissance Platonism, a major literary theorist, and a significant figure in the changing scientific world in the years of Galileo's intellectual development.

BIBLIOGRAPHY

De Pace, Anna. "Archimede nella discussione su aristotelismo e platonismo di Jacopo Mazzoni." In *Archimede: Mito, tradizione, scienza.* Edited by Corrado Dollo. Florence, 1992. Pp. 165–197.

De Pace, Anna. *Le matematiche et il mondo: Ricerche su un dibattito in Italia nella seconda metà del Cinquecento.* Milan, 1993. See pages 261–336.

Purnell, Frederick. "Jacopo Mazzoni and Galileo." *Physis* 14 (1972): 273–294.

Purnell, Frederick. "Jacopo Mazzoni as a Student of Philosophy at Padua." *Quaderni per la storia dell'Università di Padova* 7 (1974): 17–25.

ANNA DE PACE

Translated from Italian by Paul F. Grendler

MEASURES.   *See* **Weights and Measures.**

MECHANICS.   Mechanics in its early form was a science dealing with weights and the movement of heavy bodies. This science developed during the Renaissance and prepared for the emergence in the seventeenth century of classical mechanics, with its threefold division into statics, kinematics, and dynamics. The main sources of Renaissance mechanics were the works of Greek mathematicians such as Archimedes (c. 287–212 B.C.), Hero (first century A.D.), and Pappus (c. 300 A.D.), newly available in the Renaissance through the efforts of Federico Commandino (1509–1575) and others; printed editions of treatises relating to the medieval science of weights; commentaries on portions of Aristotle's *Physics* dealing with quantitative aspects of motion; and the Pseudo-Aristotle's *Mechanics* or *Mechanical Problems,* unknown in the Latin West until 1497. The first two prepared for the branch of mechanics known as statics, the last two, for kinematics and dynamics. Allied to the development of these sciences were various mechanical arts dealing with the construction and use of machines by artist-engineers.

The Early Phase: Statics.   Statics is concerned with the study of forces exerted by bodies at rest, that is, by their weight alone and without motion. The basic principle that underlies this discipline is the law of the balance, which tells how weights or forces applied at varying distances from a fulcrum will be in equilibrium, bringing them to rest. Two proofs of this law were known to the Greeks: one static, by Archimedes, which employed mathematical ratios between the forces and the linear distances involved; the other dynamic, by the Pseudo-Aristotle in the *Mechanics,* which employed the concept of "virtual" motion in a circle around the fulcrum to achieve the same result. The second method of proof was known to Jordanus de Nemore (first half of the thirteenth century), who used it to investigate the balancing of weights on inclined planes. The arrival of the *Mechanics* in the Renaissance revived interest in mechanics as a science and in both methods of proof.

Two humanist philosophers, Niccolò Leonico Tomeo (1456–1531) and Alessandro Piccolomini (1508–1578), were the first to promote the *Mechanics.* Both were Aristotelians and both were professors at Padua; Piccolomini also taught at Siena and was later an archbishop there. Their commentaries on the work served to identify mechanics as a speculative science that is concerned with causes and principles, is partly natural and partly mathematical but more the latter, and is thus similar to the sciences

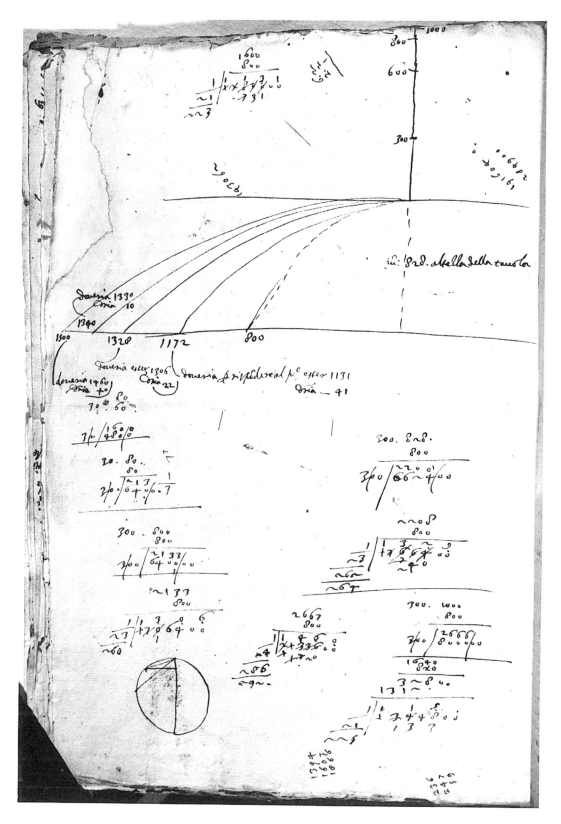

Galileo's Experiment in Mechanics. A "tabletop" experiment recorded by Galileo around 1608–1609. Balls were dropped from various vertical heights above a table and deflected horizontally from the table's edge to describe a series of semiparabolic curves in their descent to the floor. Measurements of the corresponding horizontal projections from the foot of the table, checked against calculations, yielded the modern laws of falling bodies. BIBLIOTECA NAZIONALE CENTRALE, FLORENCE, MSS. GALILEIANA, VOL. 72, FOL. 116v

of optics and astronomy. Neither Tomeo nor Picco-lomini was expert in mathematics, however, and neither was acquainted with ancient or medieval works on mechanics.

The situation was different with regard to the next mathematicians to embrace the *Mechanics,* Niccolò Tartaglia (1449/50–1557) and Francesco Maurolico (1494–1575), both having worked on earlier treatises on mechanics. Maurolico, the more proficient in mathematics, preferred the static type of proof over the dynamic and so tended to slight the physical aspects of the science. Tartaglia, on the other hand, favored the dynamic approach. He made available Latin translations of both Archimedes and Jordanus, translated Euclid and Archimedes into Italian, and, in his *Nova scientia* (New science) of 1537 and *Questi et inventioni diverse* (Various queries and inventions) of 1546, advanced the science considerably. Throughout his writings he stressed, as had Jordanus, the need for suppositions (*suppositiones*) when applying mathematics to natural motions. In proving the law of the balance, for example, he would "suppose" that all natural movements of heavy bodies are parallel to each other, even though the lines of fall can never be exactly parallel, since they must converge at the center of the earth.

Unfortunately, mathematicians who continued work on the *Mechanics,* such as Guidobaldo del Monte (1545–1607), decided against Tartaglia and followed Maurolico, rejecting this type of supposition. Guidobaldo's *Liber mechanicorum* (Book of mechanics) of 1577 became the most influential in the field. It built on the works of Archimedes, Hero, and Pappus to offer a completely static approach to mechanics, leaving little room for the dynamic alternative.

The Later Phase: Kinematics and Dynamics. The next two branches of mechanics are concerned with bodies in motion rather than at rest: kinematics with spatiotemporal aspects of the motion, dynamics with the forces that produce it. An approximation to this distinction was made at Oxford University by fourteenth-century natural philosophers, who analyzed velocities of motion with respect to their causes (the forces that produce them), and with respect to their effects (the distances and times of their travels). Two advances there are noteworthy: one in dynamics, by Thomas Bradwardine (c. 1209–1349), who developed laws more sophisticated than Aristotle's for analyzing the forces that move bodies (see below), the other in kinematics, by William Heytesbury (c. 1313–1372), who provided rules for calculating the distances bodies travel in various times. Influenced by nominalism, however, their calculations were made in an imaginary way and without explicit reference to motions in the real world.

The thought of these "Calculators," as such scholars were called, passed quickly to Paris, where basic applications were made in physics and astronomy. Brought to Padua by Paul of Venice (c. 1369–1429), their techniques were further developed by Paul's disciple Gaetano da Thiene (1387–1465), who prepared editions of the Oxford treatises along with commentaries on Heytesbury, illustrated with numerous physical examples. These prompted considerable interest in the early sixteenth century, first at Paris with John Major (1469–1550) and then by his disciples, many of whom were from Spanish universities. The major contribution in kinematics came from Domingo de Soto (1495–1560), who had studied at Paris and later taught at Salamanca. There he proposed, in 1551, that the motion of falling bodies is *uniformiter difformis* (uniformly varying) with respect to time, equivalent to saying that such motion is uniformly accelerated. Soto also did work in dynamics, adopting Bradwardine's "laws" of motion in his commentary on Aristotle's *Physics* and attempting to reconcile them with Aristotle's, but with limited success.

The final chapter in Renaissance mechanics was effectively written by Galileo Galilei (1564–1642). At Pisa he was taught at the university by Francesco Buonamici (1533–1603) and Girolamo Borro (1512–1592), with whom he probably engaged in disputations, and tutored privately by Ostilio Ricci (1540–1603), reputedly a student of Tartaglia. He began teaching there in 1589 and a year later had composed his "older treatise on motion" (*De motu antiquiora*), in which he attacked Aristotle's dynamic law, namely, that the speed of fall of a body in a medium is directly proportional to its weight and inversely proportional to the resistance the body encounters. The "true cause" (*vera causa*) of the motion, Galileo argued, was not the absolute weight of the body but rather its weight less the weight of a volume of the medium equal to its own volume. With this cause, already advanced in 1585 by Giovanni Battista Benedetti (1530–1590), bodies of the same material but of unequal size fall at the same speed in the same medium, contrary to Aristotle. Galileo was particularly ingenious in his use of suppositions, holding, for example, that if all impediments are removed, a body on a plane parallel to the horizon will be moved by a minimal force, that is, a force less than any given force. He further investigated the decrease in weight that results from a body's position on an inclined plane, slowing down its motion, and began performing experiments to confirm his results.

At Padua, Galileo's course in mechanics, dating from 1593–1594, was based directly on the Pseudo-Aristotle's *Mechanics,* as was his more complete course in Italian, the *Le meccaniche* of 1602, modeled on the works of Tartaglia and Commandino. Fundamental to his analysis was the principle of the balance, which he used to calculate the mechanical advantage of simple machines, namely, the steelyard (or balance), the lever, the windlass, and the screw. He also calculated correctly the force required to move an object up an inclined plane, a problem Pappus had been unable to solve.

Between 1602 and 1609 Galileo experimented more intensively with pendulums and inclined planes. By 1609 he had determined the basic principle of his "new science," namely, that the speed of a falling body varies directly as its time of fall, not with its distance of fall, as he had thought up to 1604. In a series of clever "tabletop" experiments, whose existence was discovered only in the 1970s, he finally succeeded in demonstrating, with the aid of suppositions, that falling motion is uniformly accelerated, that is, *uniformiter difformis* with respect to time. (Whether Soto influenced his result is questionable, but the possibility cannot be ruled out.) With this finding in hand, he was able to demonstrate that distances of fall are proportional to the squares of the times of fall, that the path of a body projected horizontally is a semiparabola, and other properties of falling motion.

Immediately after these demonstrations, Galileo perfected the telescope and made the discoveries recorded in his *Sidereal Messenger* of 1610. These sidetracked him on a fateful twenty-three-year detour to dissuade the church from condemning Copernicanism. Only after the trial of 1633 and the solitude of his "house arrest" at Arcetri did he put together his *Two New Sciences* in 1638, which is fundamental for the modern science of mechanics. He never did solve the problem of what force moves the falling object. This had to await the *Principia* (1687) of Sir Isaac Newton (1642–1727).

See also **Physics**; **Scientific Instruments**; **Technology**; *and biographies of figures mentioned in this entry.*

BIBLIOGRAPHY

Drake, Stillman, and I. E. Drabkin, eds. *Mechanics in Sixteenth-Century Italy.* Madison, Wis., and London, 1969. Selections from Tartaglia, Benedetti, Guido Ubaldo, and Galileo, translated and annotated by the editors.

Gabbey, Alan. "Between *Ars* and *Philosophia Naturalis:* Reflections on the Historiography of Early Modern Mechanics." In *Renaissance and Revolution: Humanists, Scholars, Craftsmen, and Natural Philosophers in Early Modern Europe.* Edited by J. V. Field and Frank A. J. L. James. Cambridge, U.K., 1993. Pages 133–145.

Laird, W. Roy. "The Scope of Renaissance Mechanics." *Osiris,* 2d series, 2 (1986): 43–68.

Rose, Paul Lawrence, and Stillman Drake. "The Pseudo-Aristotelian *Questions of Mechanics* in Renaissance Culture." *Studies in the Renaissance* 18 (1971): 65–104.

Wallace, William A. *Galileo and His Sources: The Heritage of the Collegio Romano in Galileo's Science.* Princeton, N.J., 1984.

Wallace, William A. *Galileo's Logic of Discovery and Proof: The Background, Content, and Use of His Appropriated Treatises on Aristotle's* Posterior Analytics. Boston Studies in the Philosophy of Science. Vol. 137. Dordrecht, Netherlands; Boston; and London, 1992. Chapter 6.

Wallace, William A. *Prelude to Galileo: Essays on Medieval and Sixteenth-Century Sources of Galileo's Thought.* Boston Studies in the Philosophy of Science. Vol. 62. Dordrecht, Netherlands, and Boston, 1981.

WILLIAM A. WALLACE

MEDALS. *See* **Coins, Medals, and Plaquettes.**

MEDICI. [The following four entries deal with the Medici family, which dominated Florence from the fourteenth to the eighteenth century, and three of its most famous members. The first, Medici, House of, provides an overview of the family's history. The following three entries, in chronological order, are biographies of Cosimo de' Medici (1389–1464), his son Lorenzo the Magnificent (1449–1492; this entry includes two subentries), and Cosimo I (1519–1574), the first grand duke of Tuscany. Two Medici who became popes (Leo X and Clement VII) and two Medici who became queens of France (Catherine de Médicis and Marie de Médicis) are covered in separate entries at the appropriate places in alphabetical sequence of the Encyclopedia.]

MEDICI, HOUSE OF. The Medici were the most important family of Renaissance Florence, heading Europe's largest bank and steering the city's politics from behind the curtain of Florence's republican constitution during much of the fifteenth century. Tax records show them to have become Florence's richest family by mid-century. In the sixteenth century the Medici set themselves above other Florentine families by managing to have three of their sons elected to the papacy, marrying into Europe's Catholic royal houses, and obtaining hereditary rule over Tuscany.

The Medici and Florence. Although a sixteenth-century court historian drew up a fanciful ge-

House of Medici

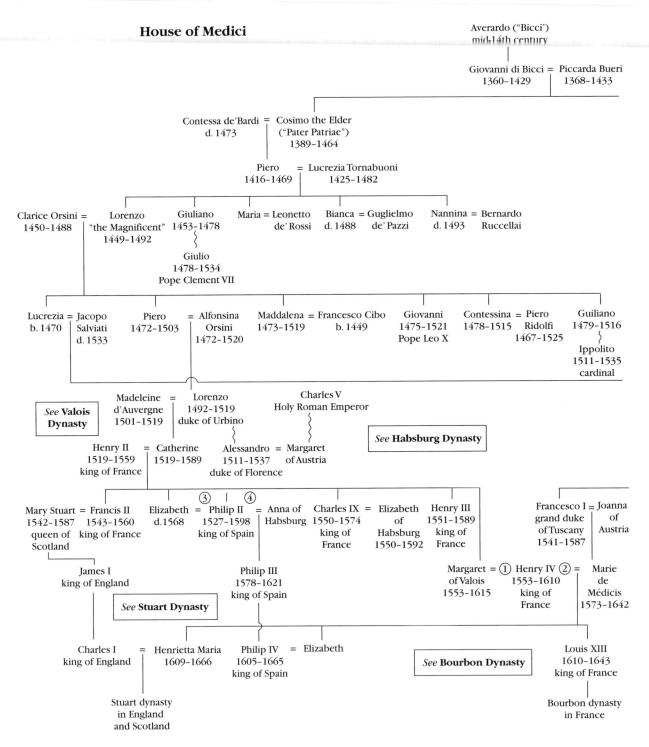

nealogy tracing the Medici to the armies of Charlemagne, the house's origins can be dated with certainty only to 1201, when Chiarissimo di Giambuono de' Medici served in the Florentine *signoria* (city council). His progeny sired the two most important lines: the Cafaggiolo, named after a village in the Mugello region and descended from his great-

grandson, Averardo; and the Lippo (or Popolani), descended from his great-grandson of that name. The Medici crest featured a set of *palle* (balls), and their adherents came to be called Palleschi.

The family's role in Florence's history remained secondary until Salvestro de' Medici, a successful merchant of the Lippo branch, was exiled for having

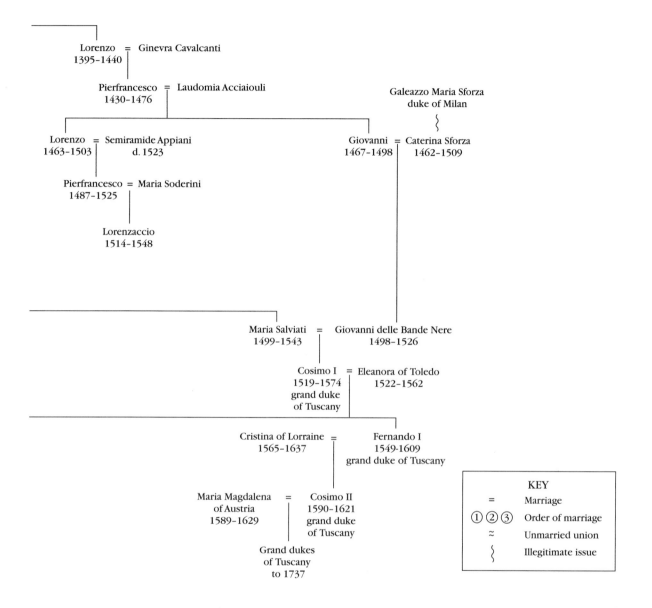

Lorenzo = Ginevra Cavalcanti
1395-1440

Pierfrancesco = Laudomia Acciaiouli
1430-1476

Galeazzo Maria Sforza
duke of Milan

Lorenzo = Semiramide Appiani
1463-1503   d. 1523

Giovanni = Caterina Sforza
1467-1498   1462-1509

Pierfrancesco = Maria Soderini
1487-1525

Lorenzaccio
1514-1548

Maria Salviati = Giovanni delle Bande Nere
1499-1543   1498-1526

Cosimo I = Eleanora of Toledo
1519-1574   1522-1562
grand duke
of Tuscany

Cristina of Lorraine = Fernando I
1565-1637   1549-1609
                       grand duke of Tuscany

Maria Magdalena = Cosimo II
of Austria   1590-1621
1589-1629   grand duke
                   of Tuscany

Grand dukes
of Tuscany
to 1737

KEY

=	Marriage
① ② ③	Order of marriage
≈	Unmarried union
∫	Illegitimate issue

supported the 1378 revolt of the *ciompi* (unguilded cloth workers). The exile notwithstanding, Francesco de' Medici served as a prior in 1397. By the 1420s two factions emerged in Florence: one headed by Cosimo de' Medici (1389–1464), known as the Elder, and the other by the Albizzi, a rival banking family. City elections in September 1433 led to the

dominance of the Albizzi and the exile of the Medici. The following year, however, the elections reversed the Medici's fortunes, and Cosimo returned to Florence to oversee the banishment of his enemies.

Outwardly an ordinary citizen who rarely held significant political office, Cosimo became the power behind the scenes. While preserving Florence's republican constitution, the Medici placed power in the hands of *balìe* (extraordinary councils) packed with their supporters. They also replaced the old communal assemblies with smaller legislative bodies like the Council of One Hundred in 1458. Above all, for the Medici wealth furthered political power and vice versa. Cosimo, for instance, paid some of Florence's military expenses from his own pocket, thus tying some of the city's *condottieri* (mercenary captains) to him personally and adding to his influence in foreign policy. He developed close relationships with the Sforza dukes of Milan and the kings of Naples. He manipulated Florence's electoral system, which called for frequent rotation of offices (most terms were two to four months). The Medici built up a core of adherents by the astute use of wealth, patronage, and marriage alliances. They also spent large sums on charity and public works. Balancing the family's books in 1469, Lorenzo the Magnificent (1449–1492) declared the hundreds of thousands of florins devoted to such expenditures honorable and wise investments.

The brief period of dominance of Cosimo's son Piero *il Gottoso* (1416–1469), or the Gouty (a reference to the disease that afflicted the family), was highlighted by his survival of an attempted coup by Medici opponents, including Diotisalvi Neroni, Luca Pitti, Niccolò Soderini, and Angelo Acciaiuoli. A second plot by a coalition of exiles failed in 1467–1468. As a result, the Medici's position was strengthened as they won increased powers for the *balìe;* Lorenzo himself was named to the *balìa* even though he was technically too young.

Lorenzo succeeded Piero as head of the family and as virtual ruler of Florence in 1469. The perception that the Medici were in fact, if not in law, lords of Florence was one cause of a conspiracy, allegedly approved in advance by Pope Sixtus IV, headed by members of the Pazzi and Salviati families. During mass in the Florentine cathedral in April 1478, assassins stabbed Lorenzo's younger brother, Giuliano (1453–1478), to death; Lorenzo, though wounded, escaped. The Medici and their supporters hunted down dozens suspected of involvement with a vengeance that the patrician and historian Francesco Guicciardini later called uncivilized. The deaths of the principal conspirators were depicted in paintings commissioned of Sandro Botticelli. The aftermath, however, led to a war in which the papacy and Naples united against Florence. A personal embassy by Lorenzo to King Ferdinand I of Naples (known as Ferrante), brought the war to an end.

The Medici quickly pushed through constitutional changes, including the creation of the Council of Seventy with its two standing committees, the twelve Procuratori and the Otto di Pratica, which gained extensive control over appointments to office, foreign affairs, and finance. Extensive fiscal and tax reforms were undertaken by the newly established Seventeen Reformers, Lorenzo among them. The Medici and their friends lent money to the state, paying themselves high rates of interest—as much as 16 percent during the mid-1480s—while securing the loans against tax revenues or the funded public debt (*monte comune*). The directors of the *monte* were, between 1482 and 1494, chosen from only twenty-six families, most of them Palleschi; Lorenzo himself sat for a two-year term beginning in 1488. These reforms gave a small Medicean oligarchy close control over, as well as the ability to exploit, the state's financial resources.

With Lorenzo's untimely death in 1492, leadership of Florence fell to his eldest son, Piero (1471–1503), who was soon faced with the invasion of Italy in 1494 by King Charles VIII of France. When Piero quickly acceded to Charles's demands, Florentine republicans in league with followers of the influential Dominican Girolamo Savonarola revolted. Piero and his brothers, Giuliano (1479–1516) and Giovanni (1475–1521), were declared rebels, exiled, and deprived of their property. Some of their distant cousins, however, remained quietly in Florence, among them Lorenzo di Pierfrancesco (1463–1503), who spoke in the *pratiche* (advisory sessions) and sat on the board of Florence's charitable pawnshop, the Monte di Pietà. In 1502 the Soderini emerged as the principal obstacle to the return of the Medici with the election of Piero Soderini as *gonfaliere* (standard-bearer) for life.

With Piero's death in 1503, leadership of the house of Medici, its prominent members still in exile, passed to his brother Cardinal Giovanni. With allies in the form of the pope and Spain, Giovanni reinstalled his family in Florence in a bloodless coup of 1512. Niccolò Machiavelli reported that cries of "Palle, palle!"—a reference to the Medici coat of arms—led the Florentine city council to call a *parlamento* (people's assembly), which demanded the restoration of the Medici. The Florentine patriciate, disillusioned with broad-based government, acquiesced reluctantly in Medici domination. Under Lorenzo (1492–1519), duke of Urbino, and Giuliano, duke of Nemours, the family proceeded to solidify its position in Florence. Machiavelli himself, implicated unjustly in an abortive anti-Medici plot, was arrested, tortured, and sent into exile, where he wrote *Il principe* (*The Prince*), dedicated to Lorenzo in the vain hope that it might win him a government position.

The Sack of Rome in 1527, during the pontificate of the Medici pope Clement VII (reigned 1523–1534), gave impetus to a rebellion against the Medici in Florence. On 17 May 1527 the family was exiled once again. But Clement made his peace with the emperor, who acquiesced in the installation of Alessandro de' Medici (1510–1537), illegitimate son of Duke Lorenzo of Urbino, as head of Florence in 1531 after a ten-month siege that ended in 1530. In 1532, Alessandro received the hereditary title of duke. The Florentine patriciate, weary of decades of civil strife, coups, and exile, accepted Medici lordship in return for stability. Moreover, men like Guicciardini now looked back on the era of Lorenzo the Magnificent as a golden age and identified the exile of the Medici in 1494 as the beginning of Florence's misfortune. Such men, who called themselves Ottimati (the best men), hoped to constrain the Medici; after all, though Medici ruled as pope and as duke, the family bank and wealth were long gone.

The new regime quickly abolished the Great Council, established a Senate of Forty-Eight, revived the practice of ruling Florence through small councils, and dismissed most city officials, replacing them with Medici friends and allies. Following Alessandro's assassination on 6 January 1537 by a disgruntled kinsman, Lorenzaccio (or Lorenzino) di Pierfrancesco de' Medici (1514–1548), the Ottimati faced the problem of succession. They needed an adult male Medici of legitimate birth, but Alessandro had left two illegitimate infants; the only legitimate survivor in the line of Cosimo the Elder was Catherine, the future queen of France. Looking to the progeny of Cosimo the Elder's brother, they discovered another Cosimo (1519–1574), the son of Giovanni delle Bande Nere (1498–1526), or John of the Black Bands (a reference to the military troops he led), and of Maria Salviati, a granddaughter of Lorenzo the Magnificent.

The eighteen-year-old Cosimo had few connections in Florentine politics and lacked an independent territorial or financial base. He appeared, therefore, to be the perfect candidate, one subject to direction by the Ottimati. That he proved one of the strongest and most independent rulers in Florentine history came as a surprise to everyone. By the mid-1540s he had freed himself from domination by both the Florentine patriciate—Guicciardini, among others, was driven into retirement—and his Spanish al-

lies. Making astute use of republican institutions like the Monte di Pietà, which he used as a source of cheap loans and of patronage, Cosimo proved a tireless ruler who sought as much control as possible. In 1555 he expanded his possessions to include Siena, which he held from the emperor as a fief, and in 1569 won from the pope the coveted hereditary title grand duke of Tuscany. His reign elevated the House of Medici to parity with the great Roman Catholic houses of Europe. In 1564 Cosimo handed over everyday governance to his son Francesco (1541–1587) in what may have been the smoothest transfer of power in the history of Florence.

The Medici Bank. The Medici's fortunes rose with the phenomenal success of their bank. The original institution was founded in Rome by Vieri di Cambio de' Medici, from the line of Lippo. In 1397 Giovanni di Bicci de' Medici (1360–1429) of the Cafaggiolo line transferred some operations to Florence and set the stage for the bank's growth to Europe-wide prominence under his son Cosimo, its director from 1429 until his death. Offices existed in Lyon, Bruges, London, Milan, Geneva, Venice, Pisa, and elsewhere; a mobile branch followed the papacy. Among the partners and managers were men from families allied to the Medici: Tornabuoni, Martelli, Bardi, Portinari, and others. The bank's papal business yielded not only wealth but immense powers of patronage, for the Medici were sometimes able to win ecclesiastical appointments for favored clients. Like its modern counterparts, the Medici bank diversified, investing in enterprises like alum production and silk and wool manufacturing.

The establishment declined under Cosimo's son Piero and Piero's son Lorenzo. Following the Pazzi Conspiracy of 1478, the bank's decline became precipitous. Its very size contributed to its downfall, as branch managers spread throughout Europe could not act in coordination. Moreover, neither Piero nor Lorenzo continued Cosimo's close, astute control over its activities, and they sometimes forced the bank to serve their political interests at the expense of its own. The bank collapsed with the exile of the Medici in 1494.

The Medici and the Church. Guicciardini wrote that to dominate Florence the Medici "need popes." They obtained what they needed; three of their line attained the papacy. Lorenzo the Magnificent's son Giovanni reigned as Pope Leo X from 1513 to 1521. After the brief rule of Adrian VI in 1522–1523, Giovanni's cousin Giulio (1478–1534), the illegitimate son of Lorenzo's brother, Giuliano, fol-

Giuliano de' Medici. Portrait by Sandro Botticelli, 1478. ACADEMIA CARRARA, BERGAMO, ITALY/ET ARCHIVE/SUPER-STOCK

lowed as Clement VII (reigned 1523–1534). A distant Medici relative also became pontiff: Leo XI (1535–1605; reigned April 1605), who came from a collateral branch of the Florentine Medici. Virtually every generation of the Medici from the late fifteenth century on produced at least one cardinal.

Winning high ecclesiastical office did not happen by chance. Lorenzo maneuvered for years before obtaining in 1489 what he called the greatest achievement of the house of Medici: an appointment as cardinal for Giovanni, then aged thirteen. In the next century the Florentine architect, art historian, and court painter Giorgio Vasari would paint a fresco showing Giovanni acknowledging his father's role by presenting him his cardinal's hat. After Giovanni's departure for Rome, Lorenzo sent him a letter urging him to piety but adding that, in serving the church, Giovanni would surely find occasion to serve the house of Medici as well. With this advice Lorenzo implied that the state's interests had become identical with the Medici's interests. Contemporaries al-

leged a change in Medici behavior with Giovanni's election. According to Bernardo Segni's *Istorie fiorentine* (Florentine history; completed in 1555), the Medici, having returned from exile in 1512, lived in the city like other inhabitants; once Giovanni became Pope Leo X, however, they ignored the republican constitution and went about with armed retainers—in short, they behaved like lords, not citizens.

Leo X and Clement VII strove for one paramount goal: the establishment of the Medici as rulers of Florence. Leo X attained the papacy in 1513, only a year after he, then an influential cardinal, had helped engineer the Medici's return from exile. At his death eight years later, the family's position in Florence was far more secure because of his efforts. Similarly, Clement reigned during the terrible sack of Rome in 1527 and the Medici's consequent expulsion from Florence. Three years later he brought about the Medici's return and the creation of the Medici dynasty. These popes' pursuit of policies that advanced Medici interests, however, diverted their energies from vital matters like the challenge from Martin Luther and the Protestant Reformation.

Medici Property and Marriages. The Medici dominated the area around the church of San Tommaso, near Florence's Old Market, but made the ancient basilica of San Lorenzo virtually their family church. Redesigned between 1420 and 1442 by Filippo Brunelleschi, San Lorenzo housed works commissioned of the great masters of the period, including Andrea del Verrocchio, Donatello, and Michelangelo. The nearby family palace, which later became the headquarters of the prefecture, was designed by the architect Michelozzo for Cosimo the Elder. During the duchy the Medici lived first in the Palazzo Vecchio and then, as of 1549, in the Palazzo Pitti. The family also owned substantial property outside Florence, including villas at Careggi and Poggio a Caiano.

For most of the fifteenth century the Medici followed a pattern common among their peers: making *parentadi* (marriage alliances) for political and economic reasons with other Florentine patrician families. Cosimo the Elder married Contessina de' Bardi, while his son Piero married Lucrezia Tornabuoni. Both women came from wealthy merchant families with connections to the Medici bank. Lucrezia, whose brother Giovanni began work in the Rome branch as a fifteen-year-old in the same year that she married Piero, shared in her family's business acumen, making successful investments in mineral springs.

The Medici proved astute at using *parentadi* to reconcile to themselves past or potential opponents. That the Pazzi had headed an assassination attempt against him did not stop Lorenzo from approving a marriage between his sister Bianca and a member of the Pazzi clan in 1488. Another sister married into the Rucellai; a cousin, Pierfrancesco (1487–1525), married a Soderini; Lorenzo's granddaughter Clarice and a cousin, Laudomia, married into the Strozzi. All these families had been Medici rivals.

Lorenzo the Magnificent broke a pattern, for he turned not to the Florentine patriciate but to the Roman aristocracy, wedding Clarice Orsini. With this arrangement, brokered in part by his Tornabuoni in-laws, Lorenzo signaled an expansion of the family's ambitions and horizons, for the Orsini were powerful magnates with influence on the papacy. From this time on the Medici sought enhanced status, not only in Florence but throughout Europe, through their marriages. Lorenzo arranged *parentadi* for two offspring with the Orsini and the house of Savoy. In 1536 Alessandro wed Margaret of Austria, a daughter (albeit illegitimate) of the Holy Roman Emperor Charles V and later the duchess of Parma and regent of the Netherlands. Cosimo I's marriage in 1539 to Eleonora of Toledo, the daughter of the viceroy of Naples, brought both wealth and a Spanish connection. His accomplishments are reflected in the marriages of some of his fourteen children, who married into the Albizzi family, the Orsini, the house of Toledo, the house of Este, the house of Habsburg (this time to a legitimate daughter of the emperor), and the house of Lorraine. Catherine (1519–1589), a great-granddaughter of Lorenzo the Magnificent, married Henry II Valois, the king of France, in 1533 and ruled as queen mother for years from behind the scenes; it was she who was blamed for masterminding the St. Bartholomew's Day Massacre of 1572. Maria (1573–1642), the daughter of Francesco I, took as her husband Henry IV Bourbon, the king of France, in 1600. Cosimo III married Marguerite-Louise, the daughter of Gaston, duke of Orléans, and a granddaughter of Henry IV, an alliance that poised the house of Lorraine to take the Tuscan throne when the Medici line ended in 1737.

The Medici and Renaissance Culture.
The Medici were important patrons of intellectuals and artists. Cosimo the Elder, anxious that some of his riches might have come from usury, rebuilt the monastery of San Marco and the church of San Lorenzo in atonement. He arranged for the classical Greek manuscripts—some of which were pur-

chased through his own generosity—in the estate of the humanist Niccolò de' Niccoli to be deposited in the library of San Marco, which he had Michelozzo build. This collection became the core of the best Greek library in Florence and was later integrated into the Laurentian Library, whose building was designed by Michelangelo. Cosimo and his successors were patrons of the Neoplatonist Marsilio Ficino, and they encouraged the discussion of Platonic philosophy among humanist circles. Lorenzo the Magnificent studied Greek and Latin under some of the foremost humanists, including Cristoforo Landino and Marsilio Ficino. This training, along with sheer economic interest, may have influenced Lorenzo's toleration for the Jews of Florence. Both he and his mother, Lucrezia, were poets. Giovanni, the future Leo X, received an outstanding humanist education from tutors like Poliziano (Angelo Ambrogini).

Among the painters, goldsmiths, sculptors, and architects who worked for the Medici were Brunelleschi, Filippo Lippi, Domenico Ghirlandaio, the Della Robbias, Verrocchio, Michelangelo, and Benvenuto Cellini. Some of Botticelli's most important paintings, notably *Primavera* and *The Birth of Venus,* were done for Lorenzo di Pierfrancesco. Leo X and Clement VII continued the tradition of Medici patronage: during their pontificates Rome became the center of the Renaissance, luring or retaining the services of artists like Michelangelo, Cellini, and Raphael, until the sack in 1527. Catherine de Médicis brought Italian manners and style to France and built the Tuileries gardens, a new wing of the Louvre, and the castle of Monceau. She also collected a great classical library.

Cosimo I Medici did much to restore Florence's position as a center of art and culture. He established the Accademia Fiorentina (Florentine Academy) and promoted the University of Pisa. Exiled intellectuals like the Medici opponent Benedetto Varchi were encouraged to return to Florence. Cosimo's treasury subsidized printers, including Lorenzo Torrentino, or Laurens Laenaerts, whom Cosimo had lured from Brabant. Cosimo commissioned works or gave positions to such artists as Vasari, Bartolommeo Ammannati, Baccio Bandinelli, Jacopo da Pontormo, Bernardo Buontalenti, Francesco da Sangallo, Agnolo di Cosimo (Il Bronzino), and Cellini. Cosimo's wife, Eleonora, purchased the Palazzo Pitti and redid it and its gardens. Grand dukes Francesco, Ferdinando (1549–1609), and Cosimo II (1590–1621) showed particular interest in literature, science, and mathematics. Francesco founded the Accademia della Crusca to purify and promote the Tuscan language. The young Galileo Galilei studied with Francesco's court mathematician, Ostilio Ricci, and later was appointed chief mathematician and philosopher by Cosimo II. His passionate treatise arguing that scripture was the infallible record of God's revelation but not a guide to the natural world was addressed to Ferdinand's wife, Christina of Lorraine.

See also **Clement VII; Florence; Leo X; Medici, Cosimo de'; Medici, Cosimo I; Medici, Lorenzo de'.**

BIBLIOGRAPHY

Primary Works

Ficino, Marsilio. *The Letters of Marsilio Ficino.* 5 vols. Translated by the School of Economic Science, London. London, 1975–1994. Includes numerous letters between this important fifteenth-century humanist and his Medici patrons.

Guicciardini, Francesco. *The History of Italy.* Translated by Sidney Alexander. New York, 1969. An account covering 1490 through 1532 by an important contemporary Florentine historian, political figure, and patrician.

Machiavelli, Niccolò. *History of Florence and of the Affairs of Italy.* Introduction by Felix Gilbert. New York, 1960. Another history by an eyewitness of the Medici during the turbulent late fifteenth and early sixteenth centuries.

Medici, Cosimo I de'. *Lettere.* Edited by Giorgio Spini. Florence, 1940. A selection of the letters, in Italian, of this Medici duke.

Medici, Lorenzo de'. *Lettere.* Edited by Nicolai Rubinstein et al. 6 vols. Florence, 1977–. The edited letters, in Italian, of Lorenzo the Magnificent.

Ross, Janet. *Lives of the Early Medici as Told in Their Correspondence.* London, 1910. Contains facsimiles of early Medici letters.

Secondary Works

Acton, Harold. *The Last Medici.* New York, 1980. Rev. ed., with illustrations. A lively classic, first published in 1932; still the standard account of the Medici from Cosimo III to the succession of Lorenzo.

Ady, Cecilia M. *Lorenzo dei Medici and Renaissance Italy.* New York, 1955. Dated, but still the best biography of Lorenzo the Magnificent as the central figure of his time.

Brown, Alison. *The Medici in Florence: The Exercise and Language of Power.* Florence, 1992. A collection of scholarly essays by one of the foremost historians of fifteenth-century Florentine politics.

Clarke, Paula C. *The Soderini and the Medici: Power and Patronage in Fifteenth-Century Florence.* Oxford, 1991. Shows that individuals within these two families could sometimes cooperate, sometimes behave as bitter rivals, as politics and family needs dictated.

DeRoover, Raymond. *The Rise and Decline of the Medici Bank, 1397–1494.* Cambridge, Mass., 1963. Reprint, New York, 1966. A readable yet scholarly account, based on archival research, of the bank's history.

Goldthwaite, Richard. "The Medici Bank and the World of Florentine Capitalism." *Past and Present* 114 (February 1987): 3–31. Argues that the Medici's use of their bank in the service of politics helped bring about the bank's decline.

Hale, John. *Florence and the Medici: The Pattern of Control.* London, 1977. well-written history that emphasizes the continuity in Medici domination of Florence.

Kent, Dale. *The Rise of the Medici: Faction in Florence, 1426–1434.* Oxford, 1978. A scholarly account of how the Medici survived exile and obtained power.

Marks, L. F. "The Financial Oligarchy in Florence under Lorenzo." In *Italian Renaissance Studies.* Edited by E. F. Jacob. London, 1960. Pages 123–147. A technical discussion of fiscal and political reform under Lorenzo the Magnificent.

Rubinstein, Nicolai. *The Government of Florence under the Medici (1434–1494).* 2d ed. Oxford, 1997. Newly revised version of the 1966 classic account of how the Medici came to, and preserved, power in the fifteenth century.

CAROL BRESNAHAN MENNING

MEDICI, COSIMO DE' (1389–1464), leading citizen, statesman, banker, and patron of the arts in Renaissance Florence.

Patrimony: The Bank. The Medici were part of the Florentine ruling class from at least 1291, when the first member of the family took office as a prior, one of the group of nine that made up the city's governing magistracy, known as the Signoria. In the course of the fourteenth century they acquired extensive landholdings in the Mugello, the mountainous district just north of Florence; this territorial base guaranteed Cosimo a country retreat and a reliable supply of faithful retainers in times of civic unrest. The family also acquired a reputation for populism that may have provided a foundation for Cosimo's reputed popularity with the city's lower classes; in 1378 Salvestro de' Medici was one of the patrician leaders of a revolt of woolworkers, the Ciompi.

By 1393 Cosimo's father, Giovanni di Bicci, had founded the bank that became the basis of the revived fortunes of his branch of the family, building on his association with the earlier-established business of his distant cousin Vieri di Cambio de' Medici, and cooperating with the bank of his nephew, Averardo di Francesco de' Medici, in Rome. By 1421, thanks to Pope John XXIII's earlier appointment of Giovanni di Bicci's general manager as depositary general of the Apostolic Chamber, the Medici bank handled a large part of the lucrative business of the papal court. Giovanni's tax report of 1429, filed shortly before his death, revealed him to be the richest citizen of Florence. He had retired from the actual direction of the bank as early as 1420, in favor of his sons Cosimo and Lorenzo. Their business continued to expand steadily and to benefit from papal favor, except for a short period in the 1440s when Cosimo fell out with Pope Eugenius IV. Cosimo demonstrated great natural aptitude for the banking profession in which he was trained, and under his direction the Medici bank reached its zenith, expanding and diversifying until the mid-1450s, when it had branches or affiliates throughout western Europe.

Politician and Patron. As the elder son, Cosimo inherited his father's considerable prestige as a statesman and diplomat. By the late 1420s he was a frequent contributor to the councils advising the Signoria, and was often a leading figure in diplomatic missions to other states involved in the wars in which the Florentine republic was almost constantly engaged. In his extensive correspondence, both personal and official, Cosimo showed himself an aficionado of military strategy and an admirer of the most talented mercenary captains hired by the Florentine state. These interests are apparent in three huge panels, *The Battle of San Romano* (against Lucca in 1432), painted by Paolo Uccello, which dominated the Medici living space. Cosimo also owned a substantial quantity of armor, both ceremonial and functional.

Like most Florentine patricians the Medici, a large family of twenty-seven households in 1427, cultivated personal ties for mutual advancement and protection with kinsmen, neighbors, and associates in business and other activities. Due to his family's great wealth and increasing reputation, in the late 1420s and early 1430s Cosimo became the most powerful personal patron in the city. His private correspondence shows that the Medici exploited loopholes in the city's complex electoral system to promote their friends to public office, and encouraged them, once elected, to exercise their power in the interests of the group, a practice strictly forbidden by law although indulged in by most prominent citizens. By 1433 the Mediceans, under the leadership of Cosimo and his cousin Averardo, had become the predominant political party or faction in Florence. At this point their chief opponents in the governing regime, among them the Albizzi, Peruzzi, and Gianfigliazzi families, fearing the erosion of their own influence, attempted to preempt this by exiling Cosimo and the other leaders of the Medici clan.

However, Cosimo's absence from Florence served chiefly to demonstrate that his wealth and his talents as a statesman had made him indispensable to his city. The commune relied heavily on Cosimo and his wealthier friends to finance and advise on the conduct of its wars, and the international operations of the Medici bank and its association with the papacy

Cosimo de' Medici. Painting by Jacopo Pontormo (1494–1557). GALLERIA DEGLI UFFIZI, FLORENCE/ALINARI/ART RESOURCE, NY

greatly enhanced Cosimo's personal influence with leaders of states throughout Italy and beyond it, including the kings of France and England and the Holy Roman Emperor. In September 1434, precisely a year after he was exiled, an almost entirely pro-Medicean Signoria was drawn from the electoral purses. An attempt on the part of the anti-Mediceans to defy the Signoria and the constitution it represented was deflected by Pope Eugenius IV, then staying in Florence. Cosimo was recalled and openly acknowledged as Florence's leading citizen. His enemies were exiled in their turn, and their lingering attempts at rebellion, with Milanese support, were finally defeated by the communal forces led by Cosimo's cousin, Bernardetto de' Medici, and his close friend Neri Capponi, at the Battle of Anghiari in 1440.

Patronage of Art. Like other prominent citizens of this period, in which the visual arts were inspired by the recovery of classical forms, the Medici commissioned works of art honoring their family, their city, and God. As prominent members of the Bankers' Guild, Giovanni di Bicci and Cosimo played a major role in financing and commissioning from Lorenzo Ghiberti in 1419 a bronze statue of the guild's patron, St. Matthew, for the facade of the oratory of Orsanmichele. A few years later, as executors of Pope John XXIII's estate, father and son oversaw the making of his magnificent tomb in the Baptistery by the renowned sculptors Donatello and Michelozzo Michelozzi. Cosimo's first major independent commission, begun in the mid-1430s, was the rebuilding of the Dominican convent of San Marco, just north of the Medici houses on Via Larga. To paint the austerely moving frescoes for the cells and communal rooms Cosimo chose Fra Angelico, both a member of the monastic community and an artist admired for his religious works.

In 1419 Giovanni di Bicci commissioned Filippo Brunelleschi, the architect of the cathedral's famous dome, to build a sacristy for the Medici parish church of San Lorenzo, to serve as his burial chapel. Cosimo and his brother Lorenzo oversaw its completion and its decoration by Donatello. After Lorenzo's death in 1440, Cosimo assumed sole responsibility for the neighborhood project to rebuild the entire Church of San Lorenzo, dedicated to his brother's patron saint, in the Renaissance style. The church was the devotional center of the district from which came the core of Medici partisans; Medici friends and neighbors furnished its chapels, and under Medici leadership the rebuilding of San Lorenzo became a metaphor for the consolidation of the family's ascendancy over their party.

In the mid-1450s, in accordance with his interest in the monastic life, Cosimo rebuilt the convent of the Badia at Fiesole, just outside Florence. As at San Marco he reserved a cell there for his own use. The late 1450s saw the completion of a magnificent new residence for Cosimo and his sons, the Palazzo Medici, begun in 1445. It was the first monumental palace of the mid-fifteenth century building boom, blending classical elements with traditional Florentine features. Within, it was opulently decorated; as the architect Filarete observed, "[Cosimo] has neglected nothing which would add to the comfort of his accommodations." It was filled with objects of beauty and distinction, including Donatello's classicizing bronze statue *David,* a symbol for Florentines of civic morality and freedom. The centerpiece of the palace was a chapel, one of the few built in private houses in the fifteenth century. It was brilliantly decorated by Benozzo Gozzoli with frescoes depicting a popular devotional subject, *Journey of the Magi*

(1459), of which Cosimo and his friends commissioned many other representations.

Literary Patronage. Cosimo acquired an informal literary education by frequenting the discussions of humanists like Roberto de' Rossi and Ambrogio Traversari, who promoted the revival of classical studies, particularly Roman literature and history, and the early Christian writers. From his youth the scholars Niccolò Niccoli and Poggio Bracciolini were Cosimo's close friends, and he subsidized their search for classical manuscripts. With their aid he assembled a large library of his own, which by 1418 amounted to more than seventy volumes. He donated many books to the library he had built at the convent of San Marco to house Niccoli's collection of manuscripts after his death, and to the Badia. Many were provided by the bookseller Vespasiano da Bisticci (1421–1498), who came to know Cosimo well and was his only contemporary biographer. A variety of works were dedicated and presented to Cosimo, from Panormita's *Hermaphrodite* to Leonardo Bruni's Latin translation of the *Economics* then attributed to Aristotle. In the mid-1450s translations of Aristotelian works were made for Cosimo by John Argyropoulos (1415–1487), who came to Florence after the fall of Constantinople in 1453. Cosimo's lively interest in Platonic ideas, which became increasingly popular in Florence around mid-century, is expressed in his patronage of Marsilio Ficino (1433–1499), son of the former Medici family physician. He gave Ficino the use of a house on the Medici estates near their villa at Careggi, and Ficino presented him with translations of a number of Plato's works.

Image and Legacy. Both patrician and popular writers criticized the "great authority" contemporaries attributed to Cosimo, seen by some as a serious threat to traditional republicanism. However, he was also much admired. His extensive patronage of churches, and his membership in and promotion of religious confraternities earned him praise as the "preserver of churches and holy places." The general populace appreciated his skill as a diplomat and statesman who defended Florentine independence and liberty in time of war, and eventually negotiated the Peace of Lodi in 1454, which put an end to half a century of warfare, with its attendant expense for the Florentine taxpayers. Ironically, the resolution of foreign conflicts opened the way in the mid-1450s for the strongest challenge in Cosimo's lifetime to Medici influence over internal affairs, not only from his opponents but even from his own supporters.

Although other challenges to Medici authority were to arise after Cosimo's death, his problems were largely resolved in 1458 by the revival of the *catasto,* a more equitable form of taxation, and the consolidation of the regime in a new Council of Seventy.

All the men of Cosimo's line suffered from chronic gout. His younger son, Giovanni, predeceased him in 1463; Cosimo's last years were overshadowed by this loss and his own advancing illness. Nevertheless, although he officially ceded the direction of the bank to his sons Piero and Giovanni in 1453, he never entirely relinquished the reins of business and politics, both areas in which he was conspicuously more gifted than they. Always strongly interested in devotional and philosophical literature, he was increasingly preoccupied with the good death that was the goal of every devout man of his age. Cosimo arranged for his burial in a tomb beneath a marker in the pavement of San Lorenzo immediately in front of the high altar, and commissioned from Donatello, the artist he had favored most throughout his life, an adjacent pair of pulpits depicting the central redemptive events of the Christian revelation, the Crucifixion and the Resurrection. He ordered that his funeral be simple, and attended mainly by the members of the extensive Medici households, in town and at the country villas of Careggi and Cafaggiolo, and by clergy from the foundations he had patronized—San Marco, San Lorenzo, and the Badia. Less than a year after his death in August 1464, the commune issued a decree conferring upon him the title *Pater patriae* (father of his country) with which Cosimo's favorite classical writer, Cicero, had been honored, and which Cosimo had incorporated in the inscription on the tomb he commissioned for his father.

Regarded from the perspective of his grandson Lorenzo the Magnificent's (1449–1492) increasingly authoritarian government of Florence, and the installation of his descendants, some sixty years after Cosimo's death, as dukes of Florence by the authority of the emperor, Cosimo is often described as effectively the "prince" of Florence. In fact, despite his modifications of the constitution to ensure the predominance of his partisans in the leading offices, Florence remained a republic in which many families of its enduring and resilient ruling class participated, until the city was conquered by imperial troops in 1530. The testimony of Cosimo's own words and actions suggests that he may best be described as a man absolutely convinced of his own superior qualifications to serve his *patria* as its leading citizen, promoter, and protector.

See also Faction; Florence, *subentries on* Florence in the Renaissance *and* Art in the Fifteenth Century; Medici, House of; *and biographies of figures mentioned in this entry.*

BIBLIOGRAPHY

Primary Work

Vespasiano da Bisticci. *Vite de uomini illustri del secolo XV.* Edited by Aulo Greco. 3 vols. Florence, 1970–1976.

Secondary Works

Ames-Lewis, Francis, ed. *Cosimo "il Vecchio" de' Medici, 1389–1464.* Oxford, 1992. Includes articles offering various perspectives on Cosimo.

Brown, Alison M. "The Humanist Portrait of Cosimo de' Medici, *Pater Patriae.*" *Journal of the Warburg and Courtauld Institutes* 24 (1961): 188–214.

Brucker, Gene A. "The Medici in the Fourteenth Century." *Speculum* 32 (January 1957): 1–26. Reprinted in Gene A. Brucker, *Renaissance Florence: Society, Culture, and Religion.* Goldbach, Germany, 1994.

Cherubini, Giovanni, and Giovanni Fanelli, eds. *Il Palazzo Medici Riccardi di Firenze.* Florence, 1990. Contains essays on the origins of the Medici family and their patronage, and various aspects of the palace.

De Roover, Raymond. *The Rise and Decline of the Medici Bank, 1397–1494.* Cambridge, Mass., 1963.

Gutkind, Curt S. *Cosimo de' Medici,* Pater Patriae, *1389–1464.* Oxford, 1938. Still the standard biography.

Kent, Dale. *Cosimo de' Medici and the Florentine Renaissance.* New Haven, Conn., 2000. A comprehensive study of Cosimo's artistic commissions.

Kent, Dale. *The Rise of the Medici: Faction in Florence 1426–1434.* Oxford, 1978.

Rubinstein, Nicolai. *The Government of Florence under the Medici (1434 to 1494).* Oxford, 1966.

DALE KENT

MEDICI, LORENZO DE' (1449–1492), Florentine statesman and ruler, called Il Magnifico. [This entry includes two subentries, the first on Lorenzo's role as ruler of Florence and patron of the arts, the second on his literary works.]

Political Leader and Patron of the Arts

Lorenzo the Magnificent managed the domestic and foreign affairs of the Florentine Republic from 1469 to 1492, while substantially strengthening the position of his immediate family through the exercise of what has been termed a "veiled lordship."

Early Years. As the eldest son of Piero di Cosimo de' Medici and Lucrezia Tornabuoni, born 1 January 1449, Lorenzo inherited both the political following and the considerable wealth and business interests of his Medici forebears. Grooming for his future role began at an early age. His mother (a distinguished poet), and a humanist tutor, Gentile Becchi (for whom he later secured the bishopric of Arezzo), trained him in letters, and he participated as a young man in the discussions of the circle of the Platonic philosopher Marsilio Ficino. In 1459, at the age of ten, he "organized" a show of arms for the arrival in Florence of fifteen-year-old Galeazzo Maria Sforza. Six years later he traveled to Venice and Milan for the wedding of Ippolita Sforza and Alfonso of Aragon. In 1466 he went to Rome to meet Pope Paul II and, foreshadowing a future political triumph, he secured the support of Ferrante of Aragon for the Medici at Florence. His marriage, arranged by his father, to Clarice Orsini took place on 4 June 1469. The next months, when he became godfather to Gian Galeazzo Sforza, he was treated as a prince. In these early years he traveled about Tuscany, and from 1465 the subject communities of the dominion began to look to him in their dealings with Florence.

Political Control.   Two days after the death of his father (2 December 1469), the leaders of the Medici party visited Lorenzo to invite him to assume the care of the city and the state. He accepted their offer, as he wrote in his *Ricordi,* "for the conservation of our friends and wealth, since in Florence you live badly if you are rich but do not control the state." Lorenzo did not serve on the Florentine Signoria, but during his lifetime he sat on numerous important governing bodies and executive committees, sometimes during crucial moments for the regime. His officeholding included terms in the Council of One Hundred, the Eight of Security (1478; he resigned after only eighteen days), the Ten of War (1478–1479), the Monte (1487–1490), and the Seventeen Reformers (1481–1482, 1490–1491). True to the established Medici pattern, it was especially through the control of electoral commissions and the awarding of offices to others, rather than through his official positions, that Lorenzo kept control of the city.

More than his forebears, however, Lorenzo displayed a willingness to intervene personally in public events. This was especially clear in his policy toward subject areas of Tuscany, where his accession to power was marked by a dramatic increase in the level of his involvement. Matters came to a head at Volterra, in southern Tuscany, in 1471–1472, in a conflict over the concession of mining rights at a newly discovered alum deposit at Sasso, in Volterran territory. Lorenzo was himself an investor in a Florentine, Sienese, and Volterran company that secured the mining rights, but when a faction in Volterra that was opposed to the Medici (and to the lead Volterran investor) came to power, the formerly independent

Lorenzo the Magnificent. Terra-cotta bust by Andrea del Verrocchio (c. 1435–1488). NATIONAL GALLERY OF ART, WASHINGTON D.C., SAMUEL H. KRESS COLLECTION, 1939

commune (which still enjoyed great autonomy) itself took control of the mine in June 1471, excluding the original investors. The situation deteriorated in the months that followed, resulting first in the siege, then the sack (18 June 1472) of Volterra—contrary to the negotiated terms of the city's surrender. The tragic event became one of the chief counts in the charges of "tyranny" leveled against Lorenzo by his detractors.

An increasing personal role for Lorenzo diminished the power of other leaders in the coalition of families that had long constituted the Medici party. Some formerly loyal Miceans distanced themselves from the regime, while others engaged in conspiratorial opposition. The Pazzi conspiracy had its origins in a conflict involving the papacy. When, in 1473, Sixtus IV purchased Imola for his nephew, Girolamo Riario, Lorenzo tried to block the sale. The Pazzi family of Florence, who were longtime Medici supporters, had loaned the pope the money for the purchase, and, as a reward for this service, Sixtus made the Pazzi bank the new papal depository instead of the Medici bank. Hostility between the papacy and Lorenzo grew in 1474, when Sixtus named Francesco Salviati archbishop of Pisa and Lorenzo refused to allow him to take up his office.

A conspiracy against Lorenzo was formed, and on 26 April 1478, in the Florentine cathedral, his brother Giuliano was killed; Lorenzo managed to escape with light wounds. The conspirators, including the leaders of the Pazzi family, were hanged or were torn to pieces by the crowd. Sixtus then tried to arouse opposition to Lorenzo by excommunicating him and by placing Florence under interdict, but the city responded by creating an armed guard for Lorenzo. An invasion from the south by troops of the pope's ally, Ferrante of Naples, was initially successful, and the Val d'Elsa and part of the Val di Chiana were occupied and pillaged. His personal control and Florentine independence both threatened, Lorenzo turned for help to the French, whose overtures to Ferrante of Naples paved the way for Lorenzo's dramatic voyage (6 December 1479) to Naples. He returned to Florence with a preliminary peace accord on 15 March 1480, and Sixtus—after receiving a Florentine embassy requesting pardon—extended his renewed blessing.

The Pazzi conspiracy and subsequent war with the papacy represented a watershed for the Laurentian regime. The crisis surmounted, Lorenzo faced only negligible opposition at home, and his now relatively secure relationships with the major Italian powers permitted him to take on the role that the historian Francesco Guicciardini would later describe as that of "the needle between the scales" (*l'ago del bilancio*) of Italian diplomacy. Security was reinforced by a network of client states and friendly neighbors. In addition, in the 1480s and early 1490s Lorenzo attempted to ring the Florentine state with a series of imposing fortresses. Territorial expansion took on renewed vigor, with the acquisition of Pietrasanta (1484), Sarzana (1487), and Piancaldoli (1488).

In the political arena Lorenzo would appear to have done everything possible to secure the future of his family line. His eldest son and heir, Piero, was trained by his father as political arbiter and patron, and in 1487 he was married to Alfonsina Orsini, an alliance that renewed the important tie with the Neapolitan clan of Lorenzo's wife, Clarice. Most important to his plans was a friendly relationship with Pope Innocent VIII. After negotiating a peace (11 August 1486) in the Barons' War between the papacy and Ferrante of Naples, Lorenzo obtained the mar-

riage of his daughter Maddalena to the pope's nephew, Franceschetto Cibò, in 1487/88 followed by the naming of his son Giovanni (the future Pope Leo X) to the cardinalate (9 March 1489) as cardinal deacon of the Roman church of Santa Maria in Domnica, at the unheard-of age of thirteen. Only in the management of the Medici bank, which suffered large losses in the 1480s and early 1490s, can Lorenzo be said to have been remiss in pursuing his interests and those of his heirs.

Artistic Patronage. In addition to his special role in the history of Italian humanism and literature, Lorenzo was an important patron of the plastic arts and of music. His most important architectural commission was at Poggio a Caiano, on the road to Pistoia, where from 1480 Giuliano da Sangallo designed a villa on antique principles. Lorenzo commissioned murals by Sandro Botticelli, Perugino, Filippino Lippi, and Domenico Ghirlandaio for a villa (now destroyed) at Lo Spedaletto, in the vicinity of Volterra. And he commissioned two bronze statues from Andrea del Verrocchio for his villa at Careggi, probably *Boy with a Fish* (now in the Palazzo Vecchio) and *David* (in the Museo Nazionale del Bargello). He gave a strong impetus to gem carving and to the manufacture of smaller bronzes of the kind produced by Bertoldo di Giovanni, who resided in the Medici Palace.

If Lorenzo, in his personal patronage, focused on his villas and the "minor" arts, he nonetheless provided stimulus or support for a number of public and ecclesiastical projects, including a plan for neighborhood renewal in the quarter of San Giovanni, Verrocchio's work on the tombs of Piero and Giovanni de' Medici in San Lorenzo, a monastery for the Augustinian Observants at San Gallo (now destroyed), the sacristy of Santo Spirito, and a competition to design the cathedral facade (for which he submitted a plan). Lorenzo was especially significant in encouraging the spread abroad of Florentine style. Artists he recommended for projects outside of Florence included Verrocchio (as architect and sculptor for the funeral monument to Cardinal Niccolò Forteguerri at Pistoia), Giuliano da Sangallo (as architect of the church of Santa Maria delle Carceri at Prato), Filippino Lippi (to Cardinal Oliviero Carafa in Rome), and Giuliano da Maiano (to the duke of Calabria). Important works of art were sent as gifts to the kings of Naples and Hungary.

In music Lorenzo was influenced from an early age by Antonio Squarcialupi, who asked Guillaume Dufay to set one of Lorenzo's verses to music. Lorenzo also brought the Flemish composer Heinrich Isaac to Florence, where he became musical tutor to the Medici children.

Lorenzo died in his villa at Careggi on 8 April 1492, almost certainly of gout. Girolamo Savonarola heard his last confession and gave absolution. Lorenzo's doctor, Piero Leoni, accused of negligence, was thrown in a well. A death mask survives. Isaac composed the haunting music for a funeral lament by Angelo Poliziano. An inventory of Lorenzo's palace and country estates is preserved in a copy from 1512.

See also **Florence**; **Medici, House of**; *and biographies of figures mentioned in this entry.*

BIBLIOGRAPHY

Primary Works

Del Piazzo, Marcello, ed. *Protocolli del carteggio di Lorenzo il Magnifico per gli anni 1473–74, 1477–92* (Protocols of the correspondence of Lorenzo the Magnificent for the years 1473–74, 1477–92). Florence, 1956.

Medici, Lorenzo de'. *Lettere*. Vols. 1–2 edited by Riccardo Fubini, 3–4 edited by Nicolai Rubinstein, 5–7 edited by Michael Mallett. Florence, 1977–1998.

Poliziano, Angelo. "The Pazzi Conspiracy." Translated by Elizabeth B. Welles. In Benjamin G. Kohl and Ronald G. Witt, eds., *The Earthly Republic: Italian Humanists on Government and Society*. Philadelphia, 1978. Pages 293–322. Translation of *Coniurationis pactianae commentarium* (1478).

Spallanzani, Marco, and Giovanni Gaeta Bertelà, eds. *Libro d'inventario dei beni di Lorenzo il Magnifico* (Book of the inventory of the goods of Lorenzo the Magnificent). Florence, 1992.

Valori, Niccolò. *Magnanimi Laurentii Medices viri illustris vita* (The life of the magnanimous Lorenzo de' Medici, an illustrious man). Edited by Enrico Niccolini. Vicenza, 1991.

Secondary Works

Ames-Lewis, Francis, ed. *The Early Medici and Their Artists*. London, 1995.

Brown, Alison. *The Medici in Florence: The Exercise and Language of Power*. Florence, 1992.

De Roover, Raymond. *The Rise and Decline of the Medici Bank, 1397–1494*. Cambridge, Mass., 1963.

Fubini, Riccardo. *Italia quattrocentesca: Politica e diplomazia nell'età di Lorenzo il Magnifico*. Milan, 1994.

Garfagnini, Gian Carlo, ed. *Lorenzo il Magnifico e il suo mondo*. Florence, 1994.

Gombrich, E. H. "The Early Medici as Patrons of Art." In his *Norm and Form: Studies in the Art of the Renaissance*. London, 1966. Pages 35–57.

Morelli Timpanaro, Augusta, Rosalia Manno Tolu, and Paolo Viti, eds. *Consorterie politiche e mutamenti istituzionali in età laurenziana*. Florence, 1992.

Rochon, André. *La jeunesse de Laurent de Médicis (1449–1478)*. Paris, 1963.

Rubinstein, Nicolai. *The Government of Florence under the Medici (1434 to 1494)*. 2d ed. Oxford, 1997.

WILLIAM J. CONNELL

The Literary Figure

The literary production of Lorenzo de' Medici, substantial and ranging across a variety of genres, attests to his active participation in the cultural life of Renaissance Florence and to his considerable literary ambition. His humanistic studies were supervised by some of the most noted scholars of the age, including Cristoforo Landino and Marsilio Ficino, but his early work is best represented by poems such as "Uccellagione" (The partridge hunt) and "Nencia da Barberino," suggestive of the rustic amusements of the young Lorenzo and his friends in the Medici villas outside the city; the latter is a particularly fine example of his close observation of country life. Humor, satire, and a bawdy realism mark much of his youthful writing; the "Canzone di Bacco" (Triumph of Bacchus and Ariadne), one of his exuberant songs written for the pageantry of the Florentine Carnival, ends with the famous dictum "Let him who chooses to, be merry: Of tomorrow nothing's sure."

In a period of linguistic flux in Italy, Lorenzo's choice of the Tuscan idiom for his own poetry was a political as well as a literary strategy. His preference is defended in the prefatory letter, possibly drafted by the humanist-poet Angelo Poliziano, that accompanied the selection of poems known as the *Raccolta Aragonese* (1476?), the earliest known anthology of poems in Italian, that he addressed to Frederick of Aragon, son of the King of Naples. The major literary currents of the late fifteenth century are reflected in his later writing, notably in his combination, following the example of Dante's *Vita Nuova* (New life), of forty-one of his many love-sonnets into a prose frame known as *Commento ad alcubi dei suoi sonetti* (Commentary on some of my sonnets). The work's prologue is in fact a treatise in favor of the vernacular as a language of poetry, and the *Commento* itself reveals the influence not only of Petrarch and his followers but of Ficino's recasting of Platonic doctrine.

Lorenzo's appreciation of humanist letters continued into his later years. His contact with Poliziano, who served as tutor to his children, and with the philosopher Giovanni Pico della Mirandola led to preparations for the major library that would later bear his name as the Laurenziana. It resulted also in the composition of ambitious mythological poems, among them "Corinto" and "Ambra." The latter exemplifies Lorenzo's fusion of conventional literary themes and a more personal perspective revealing his attachment to his native Tuscany: it follows Ovid's story of Arethusa, but the name of its protagonist Ambra, a wood-nymph saved by metamorphosis from a pursuing river god, is also that of Lorenzo's villa at Poggio a Caiano.

A different blend of conventional and private elements is found in the debate on the relative merits of city and country life in "Altercazione" (The supreme good), whose Neoplatonic explanation of the nature of true happiness is dominated by the expression of a personal longing for tranquility. In his single dramatic work, a religious play or *sacra rappresentazione* on the martyred saints John and Paul that was performed in Florence in the year preceding his death, Lorenzo's own preoccupations again come to the fore: its real protagonists are not the two saints but two emperors, who debate the possession and proper use of power.

BIBLIOGRAPHY

Primary Work

Medici, Lorenzo de'. *Lorenzo de' Medici: Selected Poems and Prose*. Edited by Jon Thiem. Translated by Jon Thiem et al. University Park, Pa., 1991.

Secondary Work

Sturm, Sara. *Lorenzo de' Medici*. New York, 1974.

SARA STURM-MADDOX

Cosimo I de' Medici. Portrait by Agnolo Bronzino (1503–1572). GALLERIA DEGLI UFFIZI, FLORENCE/ALINARI/ART RESOURCE, NY

MEDICI, COSIMO I (1519–1574), duke of Florence (1537–1574), duke of Siena (1555–1569), grand duke of Tuscany (1569–1574). Born in Florence on 12 June 1519, Cosimo was the only child of Maria Salviati, the granddaughter of Lorenzo "the Magnificent" de' Medici, and of Giovanni delle Bande Nere (of the Black Bands) de' Medici. Cosimo thus claimed descent from both main branches of the house of Medici.

Maria's decision to send her young son abroad after Giovanni's death in 1526 proved prudent, for 1527 saw the exile of the Medici from Florence. Not until 1530 did they return, with Alessandro de' Medici receiving the title of head (*capo*) and, soon, duke. With Alessandro's assassination in 1537, a cadre of Florentine patricians chose Cosimo as head of the city. They saw nominal rule by a Medici—particularly a teenager believed to be agreeably pliable—as preferable to the detested popular government of the last republic. Cosimo, however, quickly asserted his independence. He defeated a rebellion led by the powerful patrician Filippo Strozzi at Montemurlo on 31 July 1537, and forced others, including

the historian Francesco Guicciardini, to withdraw from politics.

Cosimo next turned to foreign affairs. Through a combination of payments, favors, political maneuvering, and astute marriage alliances, he made himself both independent from and an ally of the emperor. He won the title of duke, and completed construction of the Florentine fortress, the Fortezza da Basso. In 1555 he conquered Siena, holding it in fief from the emperor; in 1569 Pope Pius V bestowed on him the title of grand duke of Tuscany.

In 1539 Cosimo wed Eleonora of Toledo (d. 1562) daughter of the viceroy of Naples. Their union produced eleven children, including his eventual successor, Francesco (1541–1587), and Ferdinando (1551–1609), who resigned his cardinalate to succeed his older brother. Cosimo's offspring helped raise the prestige of the house of Medici through marriage alliances with important families, including the house of Habsburg and the house of Lorraine. Cosimo also fathered three illegitimate children, and in 1570 married Camilla Martelli, the mother of the third.

A discerning patron, Cosimo employed such artists as Bartolommeo Ammannati, Agnolo Bronzino, Giorgio Vasari, Benvenuto Cellini, Baccio Bandinelli, Jacopo Pontormo, and Francesco da Sangallo. Vasari, ducal superintendent of buildings, redesigned the Palazzo Vecchio (old palace), the traditional seat of government, where the duke lived during the early part of his reign. Vasari also built the Uffizi, the government office building that now houses the great art museum, along with the quarter-mile corridor connecting it to the Pitti Palace, purchased in 1550 by Eleonora as the ducal residence and renovated by Ammannati. Cosimo employed engineers to restructure the banks and bed of the Arno River, patronized education in Tuscany, appointed the poet Benedetto Varchi to a position at the Florentine Academy, and subsidized Laurents Lenaerts (or Torrentino), whose press became one of the most important in Italy.

Though textbooks often dismiss Italy as in decline by the late fifteenth century, Tuscany under Cosimo was a tightly run, expanding territorial state. His reign was characterized by remarkable personal control over even day-to-day governance. His interests can be seen in his comments in the voluminous documentation in the Florentine state archives. Small but powerful advisory councils like the Pratica Segreta and Magistrato Supremo made decisions that were carefully scrutinized by the duke. All public servants who handled money were made accountable to a central auditing office during their tenure. The duke made astute use of existing Florentine institutions like the *monte di pietà* (charitable pawnshop), authorizing large loans at low interest for himself, his friends, and clients while encouraging its development as a bank. He organized a network of health boards in Tuscany, its main aim the prevention of plague. He oversaw the reorganization and codification of laws in the subject towns and called for the reform of hospitals and charities. In 1561 he founded the knightly Order of Santo Stefano (St. Stephen); admission was open only to "gentlemen" and subject to Cosimo's scrutiny. He established a navy and supplied twelve galleys to fight against the Turks in 1572.

Although Cosimo surely wanted absolute power, late twentieth-century scholarship emphasized the obstacles—ranging from occasional shortages of cash to official corruption to the sheer size of his state—that he faced in his search for order. His style made him enemies, who spread the false rumor that he had murdered one of his own sons in 1562. In 1564 the ailing duke stepped aside, allowing Francesco to carry out the quotidian tasks of governance. Cosimo died on 21 April 1574 in the Pitti Palace, and was buried in the basilica of San Lorenzo in Florence.

BIBLIOGRAPHY

Fasano Guarini, Elena. *Lo stato mediceo di Cosimo I.* Florence, 1973. Discusses the organization of Cosiminian Tuscany and the constraints, including physical ones, on Cosimo's power.

Hale, John R. *Florence and the Medici: The Pattern of Control.* London, 1977. A well-written book for the general reader, with excellent chapters on the Medici dukes.

Menning, Carol Bresnahan. *Charity and State in Late Renaissance Italy: The Monte di Pietà of Florence.* Ithaca, N.Y., 1993. Examines Cosimo's use of the Florentine state pawnshop in personal and state finance and in patronage.

Richelson, Paul W. *Studies in the Personal Imagery of Cosimo I de' Medici, Duke of Florence.* New York, 1978. Discusses the ideas and perceptions of duke and duchy that Cosimo wished art to convey.

CAROL BRESNAHAN MENNING

MEDICINE. Medical skills were spread throughout society in Renaissance Europe. They were available for money from university-educated physicians, apprentice-trained surgeons, and the apothecaries who made up medicines, as well as from the usually cheaper empirics, quacks, and mountebanks who traveled from place to place advertising and selling their nostrums, panaceas, or cure-alls. At the cheaper end of the commercial medical marketplace were also uroscopists (who diagnosed illness from the urine), medical astrologers, and specialists like toothdrawers, oculists, and lithotomists (operators on bladder stones). Midwives were in charge of births, with surgeons only being called on the rare, disastrous occasion to extract a dead fetus from the womb. Wisewomen or white witches provided a mix of magical and naturalistic services, such as detecting and countering witchcraft that had caused illness or other misfortune and also selling herbal remedies.

Laypeople also possessed medical skills. Patients often treated themselves or were treated by their families. Unlike modern Western society, Renaissance women not only cared for their families but also tried to cure them, even if they were suffering from the most serious of illnesses, such as smallpox, plague, or consumption (usually forms of tuberculosis). They often produced drugs in the home from herbs and chemicals, and sometimes distilled remedies. This work was part of the general household self-sufficiency that existed before the widespread commercialization in the eighteenth century of consumer items such as bread, beer, and clothes. Mothers handed down their medical knowledge to their daughters, and successive generations would often

Der schad ist der massen gestalt/
Das ym werd angelegt ein gwalt/
Mit eim Cauterio/behendt
Gold/feür/vnd eisen das vollendt.

Cauterization. Cauterizing a thigh wound. Woodcut from Hans von Gersdorff, *Feldtbuch der Wundartzney* (Strasbourg, 1540). PHILADELPHIA MUSEUM OF ART, SMITHKLINE, BEECHAM CORPORATION FUND FOR THE ARS MEDICA COLLECTION

note the ingredients of favorite medicines in a manuscript book of family remedies, together with recipes for food and cosmetics. In the countryside well-off women provided charitable medical services to the sick poor, while clergymen also acted as charitable practitioners.

The discussion of Renaissance medicine that follows will concentrate largely on the medicine of the physicians, surgeons, and apothecaries, who considered themselves at the top of the medical ladder, but they practiced within the larger context of a widespread medical marketplace, whether based on money, familial obligation, or charity. They did not have a monopoly of medical practice, and although the regulation of medicine differed across the countries of Europe, it was nowhere effective enough to exclude empirics, wisewomen, and laypeople. The

formally constituted medical occupations faced competition, and their authority could be challenged at the bedside by lay onlookers who could substitute their own treatment or call in another type of practitioner. However, the physicians, especially, made vociferous claims that their medicine was the best.

The Demographic Facts of Life and Death. Death was an ever-present threat to all age groups. Infant mortality was very high compared to present-day figures for the developed world. Depending on location and class, around a quarter of live births would have died by the age of one (250 per 1,000 live births compared with under 10 per 1,000 live births in Western countries today). By the age of fifteen, 500 out of 1,000 live births might have died. Life expectancy was greater in the countryside and worse in the overcrowded poor areas of towns and cities and in unhealthy parts of the countryside such as in malarial low-lying ground. The killers of the young were infectious diseases such as smallpox, diphtheria, measles, influenza, and a variety of gastrointestinal infections. Once past this danger period, a further twenty to thirty years of life expectancy was usual. Epidemics of plague, however, which occurred every twenty to thirty years, could reduce a population by a third. Illnesses were often acute and short-term and always had the potential to be mortal, but conditions like paralysis, some types of cancers, gout, and tuberculosis could be chronic. Renaissance medicine made little impact upon disease, for it was not until the 1850s, with better diet, sanitation, and living conditions, that the demographic regime of Western countries began to change. The only exception is plague, for which the preventive measures instituted in the Middle Ages and Renaissance were probably responsible for its disappearance from Europe in the eighteenth century.

Hospitals and Town Physicians. Some of the sick poor were looked after in hospitals. In Catholic countries church-run hospitals continued to provide a variety of charitable care for the poor, including medical treatment, as they had done from the Middle Ages. In Italy the hospital of Santa Maria Nuova in Florence, founded in the 1280s, and with over three thousand male patients by 1500 (the number of women patients is unknown), was famous throughout Europe for its organization and standards of care, so much so that Henry VII of England drew upon its statutes when planning his new hospital in London, the Savoy. However, this high standard was exceptional. Many hospitals were overcrowded and dirty, and their inmates experienced poor care, nutrition, and treatment.

The first thirty years of the sixteenth century saw the poor experiencing a much more repressive attitude from city and state authorities. Both Catholics and Protestants revised their attitude to the poor, whom they no longer viewed as placed on earth by God but as dangerous potential criminals and carriers of infection. The sick poor were often put in institutions which also confined the disorderly. In France, the medieval *hôtels-dieu* located in many cities and towns provided a mix of poor relief and therapeutic care. In the mid-seventeenth century the Catholic Company of the Holy Sacrament built *hôpitaux-généraux* which housed both the "disreputable" poor, who were provided with a harsh regime, and the "shamefaced," reputable poor, who, if they were sick, were given medical care. In England, the Reformation meant that most church-owned hospitals were closed, though some, such as St. Bartholomew's in London, survived. The care of the sick poor was largely undertaken by the parishes, funded from 1601 by a compulsory poor rate and by donations.

Across Europe hospitals served a limited clientele, the poor, and they still had a variety of nonmedical functions, such as general charitable poor relief and the incarceration of those who were perceived as disorderly. Among the particular social group they took in, Renaissance hospitals often excluded incurable and infectious cases (plague victims were often housed in separate lazarettos, or isolation hospitals). Most people were ill at home.

Civic doctors (*medici condotti*), paid by the town authorities as well as by the fees of well-off citizens, were widespread throughout Italy by 1500, especially in the smaller towns, which had difficulties in retaining a doctor. In the rest of Europe, cities like Basel, Zurich, Berlin, Amsterdam, and Delft also employed town physicians. They gave advice to the magistrates on hygiene, and during times of epidemics they helped in the regulation of medicine, provided free medical care to the poor, and were available for consultation by the well-to-do. Although outside Italy there were not many town physicians, their appointment indicates a concern by some civic authorities to bring medicine within the scope of government.

It was only in relation to plague that governments were heavily involved in implementing health measures. The most sophisticated systems of quarantine were set up by Italian states like Venice, Florence, and Milan following the Black Death of 1348–1352.

By the sixteenth century the Italian magistracies of health had developed compulsory notification systems, isolation facilities, travel passes, inspection of goods, and efficient means of communicating news to each other of plague outbreaks. The rest of Europe followed the Italian example in the sixteenth century, with some variations such as England's "shutting up" policy, whereby all the members of a house, the well together with the sick, were locked up whenever one of their members became infected.

The Physicians and Humanistic Medicine. The love of all things Greek and Roman which characterized much of Renaissance culture also profoundly affected medicine. By re-creating the *prisca medicina* (pure ancient medicine), medical writers wanted to effect a reformation of medical knowledge, which would improve medical practice. The Middle Ages, despite having experienced an intense study of Greek medicine, was seen as having defiled the medicine of the ancients with incorrect and barbarously inelegant translations. Greek texts, especially, were seen as possessing the purest wisdom.

The translation and editing of classical texts was centered in Italy at the beginning of the sixteenth century, with Niccolò Leoniceno (1428–1524) at the forefront, and from the 1530s onward Paris led the way. Humanists focused especially on the two principal sources of classical medical knowledge: the Hippocratic works (composed by a variety of writers mainly between 420 and 350 B.C.) and those of Galen (129–c. 216), who had created a coherent and encyclopedic medical system that brought together different strands of ancient medicine and philosophy as well as his own researches. In 1525 the Venetian Aldine Press published the complete works of Galen in Greek; in the same year the Hippocratic corpus was first published in Latin and the next year in Greek. Between 1500 and 1600 some 590 separate editions of Galen were published. The result of this activity was to clear up ambiguities in medical terminology, such as the precise meaning of "cinnamon," and to substitute classical terms for Arabic. In anatomy and physiology, Galen's *On the Natural Faculties* was newly translated by Thomas Linacre (c. 1460–1524) in 1523, and in 1531 the previously lost *On Anatomical Procedures* was translated, though incomplete, by Johann Guinther von Andernach (1505–1574), one of the teachers of Andreas Vesalius (1514–1564).

In the practice of medicine, the new translation of Galen's *Method of Healing* by Linacre in 1519 exerted an enormous influence on Giambatista da

Interior of a Hospital. Woodcut from an edition of Paracelsus's *Opus chirurgicum* (1565). NATIONAL LIBRARY OF MEDICINE, BETHESDA, MD.

Monte (1498–1551), a professor of the practice of medicine in Padua, the dominant European university in the sixteenth century. Da Monte, who introduced bedside teaching at a Padua hospital for his students, tried through his lectures (published posthumously by his students as *Opuscula varia* [Various little works; 1558] and *Medicina universa* [Universal medicine; 1587]) to recreate a Galenic practice of medicine. This meant replacing the medieval compendia on practice, the *practica,* which only related treatment to the causes of disease, with a medical practice that also took the constitution, lifestyle, and environment of the patient into account. Although few medical writers after da Monte followed in his footsteps because it was too time consuming, the need to tailor therapy to the individual patient was used as ideological rhetoric by the learned physicians, educated in the universities in Galenic medicine, to separate themselves from their competitors.

Just as in religion, the reformation of medicine meant going back to the original sources and rejecting later additions. Progress was linked to scholar-

ship because the highest form of knowledge was believed to have been created in the past. However, in anatomy, especially, the re-creation of classical knowledge was the step that helped to overthrow it.

Medical Theories and Practices. The humoral theory of health and illness which is found in different versions in the Hippocratic treatises was given its final form by Galen, and it was this theory that the learned Galenic physicians of the Renaissance followed. Four humors (blood, phlegm, yellow bile, and black bile or melancholy) made up the body, and just like the Aristotelian four elements (air, water, fire, and earth), out of which was composed the sublunary world, they were the product of the four qualities of hot, cold, dry, and wet that Aristotle (384–322 B.C.) had stated were the primary constituents of the world. The figure below indicates how the microcosm or little world of the body was linked to the macrocosm, or the world at large, and also to the seasons, so that, for instance, blood was in greatest quantity in spring, when a routine annual bleeding would then be carried out. The four ages of man also corresponded to the four humors, so that in old age phlegm was preponderant. Each person had a temperament or constitutional mix of humors in which one humor held sway and shaped their physical and psychological predispositions: phlegmatic, melancholic, sanguine, or choleric.

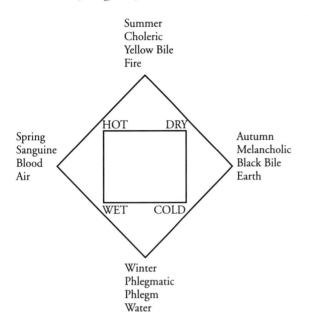

Summer
Choleric
Yellow Bile
Fire

Spring
Sanguine
Blood
Air

HOT   DRY

WET   COLD

Autumn
Melancholic
Black Bile
Earth

Winter
Phlegmatic
Phlegm
Water

The temperament of the individual was supposed to be taken into account when devising regimens or rules of living healthily. Phlegmatic patients, for example, should avoid watery foods and eat dry and hot ingredients. Illnesses were also categorized in humoral and qualitative terms. Treatment was based on the principle that opposites cure opposites (allopathic), so that a cold illness was cured by a hot remedy. The assessment of the degree of hot, cold, wet, and dry in a patient was usually subjective, though Santorio Santorio (1561–1636), professor of the theory of medicine at Padua and an acquaintance of Galileo, invented at the beginning of the seventeenth century a thermometer and a hydrometer so that the four qualities could be measured objectively.

The body was viewed as porous and interconnected by means of arteries, veins, and nerves. Humors could clog up the body and cause disease. Putrefying material was an especially potent source of disease, whether located in the intestines, stomach, lungs, brain, or blood vessels. Plague and syphilis were often seen as being caused by a contagious putrid poison. Disease could also travel from one part of the body to another, so headache was viewed sometimes as originating in smoky vapors in the stomach which traveled to the brain. Bleeding, purging, sweating, cupping, vomiting, and blistering were procedures that expelled noxious humors from the body. Bleeding and purging were also often carried out prophylactically and were frequently automatic responses in any illness.

This pathological view of the body was common to both physicians and surgeons. The latter, in addition to operating on broken limbs and wounds caused by falls from horses, accidents at home and at work, and by warfare, also treated cancers and skin conditions, including syphilis. They saw the day-to-day progress of their patients in the same humoral framework as physicians and applied the same procedures. This was especially the case with those surgeons who were learned in the medical and surgical texts of the Greeks. A number of surgical treatises were translated into the vernacular: for instance, Jacques Daléchamps (1513–1588) brought together ancient surgical learning in his *Chirurgie françoise* (French surgery; 1569). Ambroise Paré (1510–1590), the most distinguished surgeon of the sixteenth century, who wrote in French, gained status through royal patronage, surgical innovation (using salves rather than boiling oil on gunshot wounds), and an immense knowledge of classical medicine and its framework of thought.

The learned physicians also gave advice on aspects of lifestyle as a means of both preventing illness and treating it. This advice was usually structured around the Galenic "six nonnaturals" (food and drink; air; sleep and waking; evacuation and repletion; motion and rest; and the passions of the soul or the emotions). Because the advice was meant to be tailored to the individual, in the eyes of the physicians it helped distinguish their medicine from that of the empirics. A number of popular works, such as the *Regimen sanitatis Salernitanum* (Guide to health; in manuscript from the thirteenth century and then widely printed) and Sir Thomas Elyot's *Castel of Helth* (c. 1536 and often reprinted), brought health advice to a lay readership, while Luigi Cornaro (1500–1558) combined the inherent moralizing aspect of regimen with a strictly regulated diet in his *Trattato de la vita sobria* (Treatise on the temperate life; 1558), which proved popular throughout Europe. However, in therapeutics it was medicines, usually made from plants, which transcended all procedures and advice and were common to all types of medical practitioner.

Pharmacy and Botany. Plants (their leaves, stalks, flowers, roots, and seeds), animals, and minerals had been used since classical times to cure disease. Simples consisted of remedies of one ingredient, while compounds could involve a large number. *On Materia Medica* by Dioscorides (c. 40–c. 90), together with the botanical works of Theophrastus (c. 372–288 B.C.) and the pharmacological works of Galen, gave classical authority for the use of simples and compounds, and the often quoted passage from Ecclesiasticus 38:4, "The Lord hath created medicines out of the earth," provided religious sanction. In the Renaissance medical students began to be taught how to recognize plants and their virtues. Towns and universities built botanical gardens (Pisa and Padua in 1544/45; Bologna, 1567; Leipzig, 1580; Leiden, 1587; Basel, 1588; Montpellier, 1593), and the holders of the newly created chairs of medical botany (first in Padua, 1533) took their medical students on field trips into the countryside. Herbalists produced large realistically illustrated works which newly described northern European and western Mediterranean plants as well as those of the classical writers, which grew in the eastern Mediterranean and in Asia Minor. A search for the lost drugs of antiquity, such as the true rhubarb, also developed. Among these drugs was theriac, a panacea and antidote for poisons made from at least eighty-one ingredients, many of which in the 1540s could not be found, though by the end of the century physicians and pharmacists were confident that they had been recovered. Pier Andrea Mattioli (1500–1577) acted as the center for information on the lost drugs. In the successive editions of his *Di pedacio Dioscoride* (Commentaries on Dioscorides; first published 1554) he publicized the researches of herbalists and travelers in Greece, the Mediterranean islands, and Asia Minor, who rediscovered balsam, myrrh, petroselinum, and other drugs known to the ancients.

The European vision of the world greatly expanded in the Renaissance, looking not only backward into the past but also outward to new lands. The Portuguese voyages in the fourteenth and fifteenth centuries brought Africa, India, the East Indies, and even Japan and China into direct trade with Europe, bypassing Arabic and Indian intermediaries. The legendary Spice Islands, the Moluccas, had been discovered in the Pacific in 1512–1513 by the Portuguese. The spices and remedies of the East flowed more freely into Europe, and new medicines also traveled west. In 1563 the Portuguese physician and trader Garcia de Orta (1501/02–1568) publicized some of India's medicines in his *Coloquios dos simples, e drogas he cousas mediçinais da India* (Dialogues about simples and drugs and medical matters from India).

The totally new land of America also provided new medicines, which the Spanish physician Nicolás Monardes popularized in his *Dos libros. El uno que trata de todas las cosas que traen de nuestras Indias Occidentales* (Two books. One which deals with all the things that are brought from our Western Indies; in three parts, 1565, 1571, and 1574). Tobacco, sarsaparilla, sassafras, and especially guaiac wood (*Guaiacum officinale*) were welcomed by European physicians and patients, ever eager for exotic remedies from faraway countries, whose powers were magnified by distance. But the exotic was also domesticated; Monardes and other physicians had no difficulty in placing the new drugs into the humoral system.

New and Old Diseases. In the disease exchange between Europe and America, the American Indians suffered immeasurably the worse. They had not been exposed to the Old World mix of diseases and consequently had no immunity to them. In the century following Columbus's landing in the New World in 1492, "virgin soil" epidemics of tuberculosis, measles, mumps, influenza, scarlet fever, and other infectious diseases helped to devastate the indigenous populations of America. Europe only received syphilis from America, and whether this was really the case is still disputed. It was the subject of a poem by Girolamo Fracastoro (c. 1478–1553), *Syphilis sive morbus gallicus* (Syphilis, or the French disease; 1530), in which he argued that syphilis and other diseases were spread by "seeds of disease" which, when in a receptive body, produced putrefaction. Fracastoro's was but one variant of the dominant putrefactive theory of syphilis. The initial treatment for syphilis was with mercury, whose side effects of a sea of sweat, saliva, and rotting bones were graphically described by Ulrich von Hutten (1488–1523) in *De guaiaci medicina et morbo gallico* (On the guaiac remedy and the French disease; 1519). Hutten advertised the virtues of guaiac instead of mercury. The Spanish had seen the American Indians using decoctions of the wood to treat syphilis or perhaps yaws, and on the principle that God provides local remedies for local diseases, they had imported it into Europe with huge profits.

The initial acute form of syphilis changed to a less virulent type, and by the end of the sixteenth century Europeans were asserting that syphilis had burned itself out. By this time mercury was back in vogue, guaiac having proved ineffective. Syphilis linked sexual intercourse, disease, and morality together for the first time. Surgeons like William Clowes (1544–1604), the English writer on syphilis, were especially concerned with the treatment of syphilis as it showed itself as a skin disorder, and they did not hesitate to condemn prostitutes, the poor, and the sexually promiscuous, while making it clear that the well-to-do respectable classes could acquire it by nonvenereal means, such as by sitting on contaminated toilets.

New diseases like syphilis and the "English sweat" of the sixteenth century (perhaps influenza) were viewed as part of God's continuing punishment for the Fall of Adam and Eve, when death and illness first came into the world. Original sin and further sins since the Fall were believed to merit punishment with new and old diseases.

Paracelsianism and Radical Change.

Paracelsus (1493–1541) and his followers fundamentally criticized Galenic medicine. For them the world and human beings were made of chemical principles (the *Tria Prima:* salt, sulphur, and mercury), with physiological processes within the body being equated with chemical processes, and chemical remedies being used in therapeutics. Disease was seen in specific terms, as having an essential nature—the "ontological" view of disease—rather than being a disorder of the humoral balance of the body. However, although Paracelsian medicine looks in some respects like modern medicine, it was highly mystical. The microcosm and macrocosm were seen as connected by a series of correspondences, and astral influences could send disease to individuals. Treatment was based on the homeopathic principle that like cures like, and the doctrine of signatures justified the use of remedies for particular parts of the body (the walnut for the brain and the root of the orchid for the testicles, as they look like the brain and testicles, respectively). Above all, Paracelsian medicine was initially antiacademic. For Paracelsus the physician's ability was God-given and not taught. Learning from nature rather than from books also underlay Paracelsus's philosophy.

The ideas of Paracelsus slowly spread after his death, first to the courts of the German princes and then to France, especially in Montpellier and in the royal court, dominated by Montpellier physicians. In the courts the politically radical message of Paracelsus was toned down (he had been a supporter of the German peasants in their wars against their rulers) and the mystical, chemical side of his writings emphasized. In England during the Civil War (1642–1649), reformers of medicine were attracted by Paracelsus's religious, social, and medical radicalism and hoped to create a new medicine based on charitable Christian principles and Paracelsian theory. However, the influence of Paracelsian medicine showed itself most in the wider dissemination of chemical remedies often bereft of Paracelsian theory. Indeed, some writers, like Guinther von Andernach (in *De medicina veteri et nova* [On the old and the new medicine; 1571]), claimed that Paracelsian and Galenic medicine could be reconciled.

By the 1660s, with the advent of the new mechanical and corpuscular philosophies of René Descartes (1596–1650), Robert Boyle (1627–1691), and others, chemistry was increasingly accepted within natural philosophy and medicine, but no longer in the guise of the vitalistic, magical, and mystical medical chemistry of Paracelsus. Also by this time Galenic medicine was in decline, yet much of therapeutics and regimen remained the same into the eighteenth century, despite the replacement of Aristotelian philosophy, one of the foundations of Galenic medicine, with the mechanical philosophy and its new vision of the body as a machine.

See also **Anatomy; Botany; Demography; Galen; Hospitals and Asylums; Plague; Poverty and Charity;** *and biographies of Fracastoro, Linacre, Paracelsus, and Vesalius.*

BIBLIOGRAPHY

Arizabalaga, Jon, John Henderson, and Roger French. *The Great Pox: The French Disease in Renaissance Europe.* New Haven, Conn., 1997.

Beier, Lucinda McCray. *Sufferers and Healers: The Experience of Illness in Seventeenth-Century England.* London, 1987.

Brockliss, Laurence, and Colin Jones. *The Medical World of Early Modern France.* Oxford, 1997.

Cipolla, Carlo. *Public Health and the Medical Profession in the Renaissance.* Cambridge, U.K., 1976.

Conrad, Lawrence I. et al., eds. *The Western Medical Tradition.* Cambridge, U.K., 1995. See the chapter on "Medicine in Early Modern Europe, 1500–1700," pp. 215–361.

Debus, Allen G. *The French Paracelsians.* Cambridge, U.K., 1991.

Flinn, Michael. *The European Demographic System, 1500–1800.* Brighton, U.K., 1981.

Gélis, Jacques. *History of Childbirth.* Translated by Rosemary Morris. Cambridge, U.K., 1991.

Grell, Ole, and Andrew Cunningham, eds. *Medicine and the Reformation.* London, 1993.

Livi Bacci, Massimo. *Population and Nutrition: An Essay on European Demographic History.* Cambridge, U.K., 1991.

Numbers, Ronald L., ed. *Medicine in the New World.* Knoxville, Tenn., 1987.

Pagel, Walter. *Paracelsus.* New York, 1958. Classic study of Paracelsian ideas.

Park, Katharine. *Doctors and Medicine in Early Renaissance Florence.* Princeton, N.J., 1985.

Reeds, Karen. *Botany in Medieval and Renaissance Universities.* New York, 1991.

Siraisi, Nancy G. *Medieval and Early Renaissance Medicine.* Chicago, 1990. Excellent introduction to the subject.

Slack, Paul. *The Impact of Plague in Tudor and Stuart England.* London, 1985.

Wear, A., R. K. French, and I. M. Lonie, eds. *The Medical Renaissance of the Sixteenth Century.* Cambridge, U.K., 1985.

ANDREW WEAR

MEDITERRANEAN SEA. From ancient times the Mediterranean Sea was a great highway that connected all the lands around its shores. It was at the heart of the Roman Empire, geographically, culturally, and economically. As the Roman Empire collapsed in the West, and as Islam created a new world along its southern shores, Western Europeans for a time played a minor part on the Middle Sea. As the western economy revived, Italy's central geographic position again proved advantageous. From the time of the First Crusade, the Italian maritime cities had treated the Mediterranean as their own, to use and to fight over. The years around the start of the fifteenth century marked the beginning of yet another turn of fortune's wheel.

Politics, War, and the Conflict of Empires.

The region that surrounded the Mediterranean Sea was not tranquil in the centuries before the Renaissance. Only a few years before, in 1400, Venice and Genoa had ended the fourth of their major wars. Aragon had become a power in the western Mediterranean. For more than a century the kings of Aragon had been heavily contesting the Angevins for control of Sicily and southern Italy. France used the chaotic politics of Genoa and Milan as a means of entering northern Italy. In 1401, the marshal of France, Jean le Maingre, marshal Boucicaut, took control of Genoa, hoping to use it as a base for a new crusade. Venice, nearly vanquished by Genoa in the War of Chioggia (1378–1381), began to recover and to gain control over the lower Po valley. The Byzantine Empire, under Turkish assault, sought aid from western Europe. During the fourteenth century the Ottoman Turks had gained control of Anatolia and consolidated their control in the Balkans. Tamerlane (1336–1405) seized Syria from the Mamluke sultans of Egypt by 1401. The French and Genoese tried and failed to take Mahdia in 1390, and a relative peace then prevailed across the Mahgreb.

From this turbulent and unsettled beginning, the region's political and military developments of the next two hundred years show surprising coherence. These were, in a sense, the Ottoman centuries in which the Turks quickly regained momentum and began a steady expansion after the disintegration of Tamerlane's empire. They conquered not because they were invincible, but because they exerted steady and relentless pressure. Sultan Murad II failed to take Constantinople in 1422 and was twice defeated by John Hunyadi in the 1440s. Nonetheless, in that same period he extended his control beyond the territory held by the Ottomans at the beginning of the century. In 1453 Mehmed II took Constantinople. The final remnants of the Byzantine Empire were eliminated by the end of that decade. Constantinople remained unrivaled in strategic position; using its harbor and naval resources, the Ottomans were able to become a major naval power.

The Turks had a naval presence in the eastern Mediterranean since the fourteenth century, but the naval superiority of Venice had restricted their activity to piracy and the occasional raid from the Turkish bases along the Anatolian coasts. With the newly acquired resources of Constantinople, they were poised to do much more. Venice had established a chain of strategic strong points along the eastern coast of the Adriatic Sea and across the Aegean. They relied on galleys, which had very large crews and small capacity to carry food and water, so that fleets could not operate very far from the logistical support of strong bases. The Venetians, with the support of the Knights Hospitalers (a military order originally constituted to aid pilgrams) based at Rhodes, effectively hemmed in the Turks. The Ottomans could break out only by laboriously capturing the Venetian bases one by one. The Venetians also had centuries of experience in naval warfare that gave them a superiority in ships and crews that made the Turkish task even more difficult. The Turks, however, had much greater reserves of manpower, as well as tremendous determination. The amphibious nature of galley warfare made siege operations on land, at which the Turks were very skilled—and for which they could marshal large armies—as important as fleet operations. In the first Turkish-Venetian War (1463–1479) the Turks won no great naval victories, but captured the key Venetian base at Negroponte (1470), as well as others. The strategic significance of this became clear in 1480 when Sultan Mehmed attacked the Hospitaler base at Rhodes and landed an army at Otranto with the aim of conquering Italy. Although they failed at Rhodes and abandoned the Italian expedition when Mehmed died in 1481, the Ottomans nevertheless had broken through the Venetian chain.

The Ottomans kept up their pressure on the Venetian bases in the eastern Mediterranean. They won

A Mediterranean Empire. Map of the Roman Empire from Abraham Ortelius, *Theatrum orbis terrarum* (1595). THE GRANGER COLLECTION, NEW YORK

naval victories at Zonchio in 1499 and 1500 and at Prevesa in 1538 in support of land attacks on Venetian bases in Greece and Dalmatia. By this time the Turks had established overwhelming numerical superiority over the fleets of Venice and its allies, but knew that the real key to maritime domination was the possession of strategically located bases. The capture of Egypt by Selim the Grim in 1517 brought the entire eastern Mediterranean coast under Ottoman control. The capture of Rhodes in 1522 further enhanced the Turkish naval position in the eastern Mediterranean. They then recaptured Tripoli from the Spanish in 1551, and Ottoman control extended across North Africa. Thus, by the mid-sixteenth century the Ottoman sultanate controlled the mainland shores of the Mediterranean from Dalmatia to Morocco and many of the most strategic island bases. In 1570 the Ottoman assault on Venetian-held Cyprus created a naval alliance of Spain, the papacy, Genoa, and Venice. The ensuing Battle of Lepanto (7 October 1571) was a resounding Christian victory, but was not followed up, and the Turks quickly built a new fleet. Their occupation of Cyprus was of far more strategic consequence than their defeat at Lepanto. Though Lepanto was not, in itself, a turning point, it—along with the failure of the Turkish siege of Malta in 1568—marked a kind of

high-water mark of the Ottoman Empire. By the end of the century Turkish armies were no longer a match for Europeans in the Balkans. They had also reached the end of their logistical tether at the frontier of Austria. Still, it was not for another hundred years that the tide of conflict reversed, and the War of the Holy League (1684–1697) forced the Ottomans to yield Transylvania, Hungary, and other territories to European powers.

A state of almost continual piratical warfare, commerce raiding, and small actions—the *guerre de course*—obtained throughout the Mediterranean from the middle of the fifteenth century through the sixteenth. As they lost bases in the eastern basins of the Mediterranean, western raiders had a progressively harder time projecting their power into that area. At the same time, Ottoman raiders based in the Balkans and along the coast of the Mahgreb were well-placed to raid western Mediterranean commerce. The age of the Barbary pirates had begun.

The Mediterranean Economy. In the late Middle Ages Italian merchants effectively controlled the commerce of the Mediterranean. Northern Italian cities were prosperous because of commerce between the Mediterranean and northern Europe.

Manufacturing and banking were of secondary importance. Of the great commercial cities, Venice and Genoa were the largest and wealthiest. With their superficial similarities and conflicts, their economies and spheres of influence overlapped rather than coincided. Through the fifteenth century Venice was the hub of European commerce. For the Venetians the most profitable—if not the largest—part of their trade was in spices, especially of the very valuable pepper, which came to the Mediterranean through Alexandria and the ports along the eastern shores of the sea. Well-manned galleys transported and protected these small but immensely valuable cargos. Greek malmsey wine, North African and Apulian grain, cheese, salt, Egyptian cotton, hides, and timber were imported in round ships that held more cargo. These goods were paid for in cash or by a transit trade in cloth, mostly from Germany. Venetian commercial interests led to ambiguous relations with the Ottoman Turks and a reluctance to engage in or support military actions against them except under extreme provocation. At the end of the fifteenth century the Portuguese attempted to divert the spice trade from the Mediterranean to their route around Africa. They succeeded only briefly, and the attempt quickly proved more expensive than the Venetians' dealing with the Turks. The Mediterranean spice trade survived well into the next century. In the long run, that the Serenissima's merchants were gradually squeezed out of the Aegean was more important than the spice trade. Eventually, the growing Venetian state on the Italian mainland proved a more dependable source of profit for the republic's elites than the steadily diminishing overseas trade.

What the spices of Alexandria were to the Venetians, silks, and to a lesser extent spices, were to Genoa, coming through the Black Sea ports of Caffa, Tana, and Trebizond. Since they gained control of Constantinople's suburb of Pera in 1261, the Genoese had a virtual monopoly on trade from the Black Sea. In contrast to the many possessions of Venice in the Aegean, Genoa possessed only Chios. But that island gave them control of the alum of Focea, a raw material necessary in the manufacture of cloth. Alum was exported to England and Flanders in "great galleys" through the Straits of Gibraltar. These ships returned laden with wool. With so few ports and such concentrated commerce in the East, Genoa's trade with that area was extremely vulnerable. The Ottoman capture of Constantinople did not immediately end Genoese trade with the Black Sea, but it did put it in jeopardy. The Turks seized the alum mines of Focea by 1455; by 1475 they had taken Caffa. The

Genoese held on to Chios until 1566, but without access to the alum of Focea its economic importance was vastly lessened. Increasingly, most of Genoa's trade was shifted to the western Mediterranean, carrying bulk goods between the ports of France, Spain, and the Mahgreb. Its economy in decline in the late fifteenth century, Genoa would stage a remarkable recovery in the next century.

As the Italians were squeezed out of the eastern Mediterranean, subjects of the polyglot Ottoman Empire were beginning to take over trade there. The addition of Egypt to the empire at the beginning of the sixteenth century revived the old trade from north to south—from the Black Sea to Egypt. Not long after, merchants from the Turkish Balkans traded across the Adriatic. With the peace that came after the Battle of Lepanto, a *Fondaco dei Turchi* was set up: a warehouse and residence for Turkish merchants like that for the long-established Germans.

The collapse of the Medici bank in 1494 visibly ended Florentine domination of European banking, and financial leadership shifted to Antwerp and Augsburg. Genoa's involvement in Spain and Portugal had been increasing steadily since the fourteenth century; indeed the most famous navigator of the fifteenth century, Christopher Columbus, was a Genoese sailing for the crown of Castile. Thus, Genoese bankers were well placed to step in when the Spanish bankruptcy of 1557 ruined the bankers of Augsburg. Genoese financiers dominated the European scene into the seventeenth century with a complicated web of loans to the Spanish crown, investment in precious metals, and management of exchange instruments. Although Genoa maintained this dominant position in the European economy for a long lifetime, and a large presence in Spain for much longer, the center of Europe's economy had shifted away from the Mediterranean. Nevertheless, for the two centuries of the Renaissance, the Mediterranean Sea was the major route between East and West, the place where Christian and Muslim met for trade, in peace and in conflict.

See also **Lepanto, Battle of; Naval Warfare; Ottoman Empire.**

BIBLIOGRAPHY

Braudel, Fernand. *The Mediterranean and the Mediterranean World in the Age of Philip II.* 2d ed. Translated by Sian Reynolds. New York, 1973.

Epstein, Steven A. *Genoa and the Genoese, 958–1528.* Chapel Hill, N.C., 1996.

Guilmartin, John F. *Gunpowder and Galleys: Changing Technology and Mediterranean Warfare at Sea in the Sixteenth Century.* Cambridge, U.K., 1975.

Inalcik, Halil. *The Ottoman Empire: The Classical Age, 1300–1600*. Translated by Norman Itzkowitz and Colin Imber. New York, 1973.

Lane, Frederic C. *Venice: A Maritime Republic*. Baltimore, 1973.

Lock, Peter. *The Franks in the Aegean, 1204–1500*. London, 1995.

Pryor, John H. *Geography, Technology, and War: Studies in the Maritime History of the Mediterranean 649–1571*. Cambridge, U.K., and New York 1988.

JOHN E. DOTSON

MEHMED II (the Conqueror; 1432–1481), Ottoman sultan (1444–1446, 1451–1481). The third son of Murād II, Mehmed succeeded his father to power at the age of nineteen. Known in history as "the Conqueror" because he engineered the military action that ended in the conquest of the capital of the Byzantine Empire in 1453, his military achievements following the fall of Constantinople were perhaps of greater significance than delivering the fatal blow to the dying empire.

Committed to the expansion and consolidation of what was to become the great Ottoman Empire of the "golden age," from 1453 through the reign (1520–1566) of Süleyman I the Magnificent, he subjugated the southern Slavs by incorporating Serbia, Bosnia, and Herzegovina into the Ottoman Empire, conquered Greece, and took several Venetian possessions in the Aegean islands. However, his armies were unable to annex Albania and Montenegro or to conquer Belgrade. The Romanian provinces of Wallachia and Moldavia retained their own rulers but accepted de facto vassalage after years of protracted military confrontations with the Turks. Similarly, the Ottoman fleet was unable to subdue Crete, Cyprus, or Rhodes, and the landing in Italy, at Otranto in 1480, which alarmed western Christendom more than any other Turkish military action, was inconsequential. The annexation of Azov, Crimea, Trebizond, and Karamania complemented the process of aggrandizement and consolidation of the empire during Mehmed's reign.

The military successes of the Ottoman armies were recorded primarily against weak enemies, and the Turks were held in check, or even defeated, by János Hunyadi, the prince of Transylvania, Stephen the Great of Moldavia, and for a time even Vlad Ţepeş of Walachia and George Castrioti Scanderbeg of Albania. It is also noteworthy that efforts to rouse Christendom against the "Infidel," most notably those of Pope Calixtus III and humanists sympathetic to that cause, fell largely on deaf ears. The preoccupations and concerns of Renaissance Europe were other than restoring the Byzantine Empire or liberating the Balkans from Ottoman domination.

Mehmed II. Portrait by an anonymous Turkish artist, fifteenth century. TOPKAPI MUSEUM, ISTANBUL

The historic significance of Mehmed II, however, is as much based on his internal actions and policies as on his military achievements. The fall of Constantinople did not entail the uprooting of eastern Christendom. In fact, Christians were still allowed to practice their faith and enjoy a significant degree of self-governance under the authority of the Ottoman patriarch. Although not directly influenced by the western Renaissance, Mehmed II was a patron of the arts and an emulator of Byzantine imperial traditions. Finally, he laid the foundations for giving the Ottoman Empire a coherent structure by codification of existing laws into three codes (*Kanoun Namé*) dealing with the structure of the state, the welfare and duties of its subjects, and land ownership and taxes.

BIBLIOGRAPHY

Babinger, Franz. *Mehmed the Conqueror and His Time*. Edited by William C. Hickman. Translated by Ralph Manheim. Princeton, N.J., 1978.

Inalcik, Halil. *The Ottoman Empire: The Classical Age, 1300–1600.* New York, 1973.

Schwoebel, Robert. *The Shadow of the Crescent: The Renaissance Image of the Turks, 1453–1517.* New York, 1967.

STEPHEN FISCHER-GALATI

MELANCHTHON, PHILIPP (Philipp Schwartzerdt; 1497–1560), German humanist, teacher, and Lutheran Reformer. Melanchthon was born in Bretten, an important trading center in the Rhenish Palatinate. His father, Georg (d. 1508), was armorer at the Heidelberg court of the Palatine elector Philipp the Upright, after whom the child was named. His mother, Barbara Reuter (d. 1529), was the daughter of an important merchant in Bretten. In 1509 Philipp and his brother Georg were sent to the Latin school in Pforzheim and lived with a relative by marriage, Elizabeth Reuchlin, whose brother was the famous humanist Johann Reuchlin (1455–1522). It was he who, in rewarding Philipp at the Pforzheim school for his astounding mastery of the Greek and Latin languages, gave him a Greek grammar inscribed with the Greek form of the boy's name, Melan (*schwartz,* black) chthon (*Erdt,* earth).

In 1511, at the age of only fourteen, Philipp received his bachelor of arts at the University of Heidelberg. He earned his master of arts at the University of Tübingen (1514), where he worked with John Oecolampadius, the later Reformer of Basel, at the printing office of Thomas Anshelm. In 1518, at the recommendation of Johann Reuchlin, he became the first professor of Greek at the relatively new (founded 1502) University of Wittenberg, where he taught and lived for the rest of his life.

University Professor. Once in Wittenberg, Melanchthon received the first theological degree, the *baccalaureus biblicus* (bachelor of the Bible), at a disputation chaired by Martin Luther in September 1519. By this time he was an avid supporter of Luther, having helped him during the Leipzig debates with John Eck. From 1523 to 1524 he was rector of the university, and in 1527 the university's patron, Elector John of Saxony, gave to him and Luther extraordinary positions, allowing them to lecture on any subject. As a result, Melanchthon, although never receiving a doctorate of theology, taught in both the arts and theology faculties throughout his career. After the defeat of Elector John Frederick of Saxony in the Schmalkald War of 1547, the city and university fell into the hands of Maurice of Saxony, to whom Emperor Charles V awarded the electorship. After the war Melanchthon returned to Wittenberg, where he rewrote the university's plan of stud-

ies. His most well-known students included Joachim Camerarius (1500–1574), teacher in Nürnberg, Tübingen, and Leipzig; Kaspar Peucer (1525–1602), Melanchthon's son-in-law and professor in Wittenberg; Johann Stigel (1515–1562), the Neo-Latin poet; and theologians such as Martin Chemnitz (1522–1586) and David Chytraeus (1530–1600), signers of the Lutheran Formula of Concord (1577); Tilemann Heshusius (1527–1588), Paul Eber (1511–1569, pastor in Wittenberg), and George Major (1502–1574), all Lutheran university professors; and Zacharias Ursinus (1534–1583), a Reformed teacher and coauthor of the *Der Heidelberger Katechismus* (Heidelberg catechism).

Educator. Melanchthon, himself molded by the advances in learning fostered by the Renaissance, shaped the pedagogy of Germany, earning thereby the nickname *Praeceptor Germaniae* (preceptor of Germany). In August 1518 Melanchthon delivered his inaugural address at the University of Wittenberg, "*De corrigendis adolescentiae studiis*" (Concerning the correction in the studies of the young). There he set out proposals for a reform of university curriculum along humanist lines and emphasized the three classical languages (Latin, Greek, and Hebrew) and such disciplines as rhetoric, dialectics, and history. During his rectorate he realized these reforms by revising the curriculum for the arts faculty. Among his innovations was the replacement of some required disputations with declamations, polished Latin speeches often written by Melanchthon. In the 1530s and again at the time the University of Wittenberg was reconstituted in 1548, Melanchthon also provided new statutes for the theology faculty.

When the poet and later teacher in Nürnberg, Helius Eobanus Hessus (1488–1540), worried that evangelical theology might destroy the new interest in the humanities, Melanchthon composed a detailed response, the so-called *Encomium eloquentiae* (Praise of eloquence). There he distinguished the gospel's righteousness of faith from human righteousness (both gifts of God) and insisted that students in all subjects, including theology, needed proper training in languages and classical literature. Thus, when in 1527 the elector of Saxony organized a visitation of the churches in his territories, Melanchthon collaborated with Luther in the writing of *Unterricht der Visitatoren an die Pfarrherrn im Kurfürstentum Sachsen* (Instruction by the visitors for the parish pastors of Saxony), published in 1528. In it Melanchthon included a lengthy description of the

Philipp Melanchthon. Portrait by Albrecht Dürer. Engraving; 1526. FOTO MARBURG/ART RESOURCE, NY

curriculum for local schools. He also was deeply involved in the founding of a new Latin school in Nürnberg in 1525, drawing up the school's plan of studies, encouraging the hiring of several professors, including his close friend Camerarius, and delivering an oration at the school's opening in 1526, "*In laudem novae scholae*" (In praise of a new school). He also maintained close contacts with other Latin schools, especially in Magdeburg and Eisleben.

Humanist. Already at a very early age, Melanchthon demonstrated an enormous capacity to absorb the most recent studies in the classical languages and literature of Greece and Rome. His very first works were an edition of Terence's plays with his own extended introduction and an oration on the importance of the liberal arts. Published while still in Tübingen, where he also worked on the defense of Reuchlin, these compositions brought him to the attention of no less a scholar than Erasmus of Rotterdam. Once in Wittenberg, Melanchthon produced two works on rhetoric (in 1519 and 1521) and another on dialectics (in 1520). He also wrote a very popular Greek grammar, first published in 1518, and an even more widely used Latin grammar, which first appeared in 1526.

Throughout his career, he saw to the publication of a variety of texts by Greek and Latin authors for his own students. Often these texts included intro-

ductions and brief annotations; they show Melanchthon's broad interests in poets such as as Homer, Euripides, and Virgil, orators such as Demosthenes and Cicero, and the philosopher Aristotle. Despite an initial criticism of Aristotle, he later produced commentaries on several of his works, including *De anima* (*On the Soul*).

Melanchthon wrote in an unadorned Latin style, particularly appreciated by students for its simplicity and clarity. This style served him well in his many important theological works, especially the Augsburg Confession of 1530 and its Apology of 1531. Besides numerous orations, he wrote many poems and influenced an entire generation of Neo-Latin poets, including Johann Stigel. His letters, one of the first of which Erasmus published in 1519, were preserved, copied, and printed widely throughout the sixteenth century.

Already as a worker in Anshelm's print shop, Melanchthon took an interest in historical works and assisted in the publication of Francis Irenicus's *Exegesis Germaniae* (1518). He lectured on both Herodotus and Thucydides and, starting in the 1530s, began to lecture on and completely rework the chronicle on world history of Johann Carion (1499–1537/38). At the time of his death Melanchthon had reached the period of Charlemagne. Kaspar Peucer completed the work after his death.

One of his most important contributions to the humanities came in his second work on rhetoric, the *Institutiones rhetoricae* (Principles of rhetoric). There he created, next to the three classical genres of speech (the demonstrative, the deliberative, and the judicial), a fourth kind: the didactic. Intended for use in the classroom and in commentary, this genre used as its rules of invention not rhetorical categories but dialectical ones. Thus, after the manner of Aristotle's logic, it asked whether a thing exists, what it is, what are its parts, genus, species, causes, effects, and the like. Here the speaker's goal was no longer governed by the probabilities of oratory but by the certainties of syllogism. In this blending of dialectics into rhetoric, Melanchthon owed a debt to Rudolf Agricola (1443/44–1485), the south German humanist whose book on dialectic Melanchthon first read in Tübingen.

Already in the book on rhetoric from 1519 and in every handbook on dialectics and rhetoric he produced thereafter, Melanchthon emphasized the importance of *loci communes* (commonplaces). Whereas Erasmus in *De copia* and in his introductions to the Greek New Testament had defined them in rhetorical terms as headings under which to arrange an author's statements, Melanchthon, again following Rudolf Agricola, used them as the basic topics and structure inherent in an author's work.

Theologian. Older scholarship often pitted Melanchthon's humanist training and interests against his encounter with Luther and his supposed transformation into a Reformer under Luther's influence. Most now accept the view that Melanchthon's humanism coexisted with Luther's evangelical theology. In fact, Melanchthon's contributions to Reformation theology were manifold and demonstrate at every turn his debt both to Luther and to methods learned from such humanists as Rudolf Agricola and Erasmus. Melanchthon encouraged study of the humanities and their preservation as a propaedeutic for theology.

In commentaries on the Pauline epistles, Melanchthon rigorously applied the rules of rhetoric and dialectic to analyze the content and style of Paul's letters. In place of the standard topics provided by the medieval theological textbook of Peter Lombard, Melanchthon used the basic topics (*loci communes*) of Romans to provide the scope of early lectures on theology. Reworked for publication, the *Loci communes rerum theologicarum* (1521) became the first theological textbook of the Protestant Reformation. It influenced generations of Protestants, including such disparate figures as Martin Chemnitz, who lectured on the 1543 edition of the work at the University of Wittenberg in 1554, and John Calvin, whose second edition of the *Christianiae religionis institutio* (1539; trans. *Institutes of the Christian Religion*) bore the marks of Melanchthon's topical arrangement of theology.

See also Humanism, *subentry on* Germany and the Low Countries; Protestant Reformation.

BIBLIOGRAPHY

Primary Works

Melanchthon, Philipp. *Loci communes 1543* (Commonplaces). Translated by J. A. O. Preus. St. Louis, Mo., 1992. Translation of the final Latin edition of the premier summary of Protestant theology, first published in 1543.

Melanchthon, Philipp. *Loci communes theologici* (Theological commonplaces). Translated by Lowell J. Satre. In *Melanchthon and Bucer*. Edited by Wilhelm Pauck. Philadelphia, 1969. The first Protestant textbook of theology, published in 1521.

Melanchthon, Philipp. *A Melanchthon Reader*. Translated by Ralph Keen. New York, 1988.

Secondary Works

Manschreck, Clyde. *Melanchthon: The Quiet Reformer*. Nashville, Tenn., 1958. The standard, though somewhat outdated, biography of Melanchthon in English.

Scheible, Heinz. *Melanchthon: Eine Biographie*. Munich, 1997. The most up-to-date German biography of Melanchthon, written by the editor of Melanchthon's correspondence.

Schneider, John. *Philip Melanchthon's Rhetorical Construal of Biblical Authority: Oratio sacra*. Lewiston, N.Y., 1990. A detailed analysis of Melanchthon's earliest writings and career, showing the ways he combined Renaissance rhetoric and Protestant theological categories.

Wengert, Timothy J. *Human Freedom, Christian Righteousness: Philip Melanchthon's Exegetical Dispute with Erasmus of Rotterdam*. New York, 1998. A comparison of Melanchthon's and Erasmus's methods of biblical interpretation, centered on Paul's letter to the Colossians and the dispute over the freedom of the will.

TIMOTHY J. WENGERT

MEMLING, HANS (c. 1430/1440–1494), Flemish painter of German origin. Memling was born in Seligenstadt near Frankfurt. He probably began training in the Rhineland (possibly at Cologne), traveled to Flanders to further his education, and presumably completed his instruction in the workshop of Rogier van der Weyden in Brussels. These hypotheses arise from the study of Memling's style, sources, and technique. On 30 January 1465, Memling became a citizen of Bruges, where he remained for the rest of his life. Because he failed to register in the Bruges painters' guild and held no public office, he probably enjoyed special privilege, although there is no evidence that he held a position at court. Instead, he worked mainly for the wealthy merchant class, resident foreign communities, and the local clergy of Bruges.

The writers Giorgio Vasari, in 1550, and Lodovico Guicciardini, in 1567, called Memling a disciple of van der Weyden, and a triptych belonging to Margaret of Austria is described in an inventory of 1516 as having a central panel by Rogier and side panels by Master Hans. This could be proof of collaboration between the two artists. Although some scholars recognize Memling's hand in several pictures attributed to Rogier, unanimous consent is lacking. Several paintings attributed to Memling follow Rogierian prototypes; however, this is hardly extraordinary, as van der Weyden was so influential.

The St. John Altarpiece (Bruges, Memlingmuseum), signed and dated 1479, was ordered for the new high altar of the chapel of St. John's Hospital in Bruges. This monumental triptych shows the Virgin enthroned as queen of heaven, crowned by two angels, with two angels kneeling by her side. The Christ child seated on Mary's lap proffers a ring to St. Catherine, thereby binding her in mystic wedlock. Catherine is balanced on the right by St. Barbara, likewise sitting in the foreground, while John the Baptist and

Hans Memling. *Mystical Marriage of St. Catherine of Alexandria.* Central panel from the *Altarpiece of St. John,* Hôpital Saint-Jean, Bruges, Belgium. HÔPITAL SAINT-JEAN, BRUGES/GIRAUDON/ART RESOURCE

John the Evangelist—the patron saints of the hospital—stand in the middle ground before a colonnade through which a landscape and city view can be seen. The left wing shows the beheading of John the Baptist, and the right wing shows the visions of John the Evangelist on Patmos. On the exterior of each wing, two donors kneel—with their patron saints standing behind them—inside a niche.

The St. John Altarpiece—a symmetrical *sacra conversazione* (a gathering of saints around the virgin) depicting Mary seated before a rich brocade and underneath a baldachin, with a superb oriental carpet extending toward the bottom of the composition—is indebted to Jan van Eyck, who was active in Bruges and whose warm palette inspired Memling. Memling's attenuated figure types are, on the other hand, derived from van der Weyden. The serene beauty of this altarpiece seems at odds with the dramas recorded on the side panels.

Also in 1479 Memling signed and dated the small triptych *Adoration of the Magi* (Bruges, Memlingmuseum) for the friar Jan Floreins.

The approximately ninety paintings attributed to Memling indicate that his style remained remarkably consistent, thereby complicating the chronology of roughly seventy pictures that are not or cannot be exactly dated.

The subject depicted in *Virgin and Child with Angels* (Vienna, Kunsthistorisches Museum; Florence, Uffizi) was one Memling repeatedly returned to, occasionally adding a great classicizing arch filling the entire height of the composition and Italian motifs— unknown until then in Flemish painting—such as putti and festoons of fruits and leaves.

Memling's skill in perfecting the appearance of things made him a much-sought-after portrait painter. In the diptych *Virgin and Child* and *Maarten van Nieuwenhove* (1487; Bruges, Memlingmuseum), the bust-length Virgin, shown frontally and in close-up on the left wing, holds the naked Christ child with one hand while with the other she offers Jesus the apple that identifies him as the new Adam who will redeem humankind. Mary is depicted in a bourgeois interior, with a view of a landscape out a window. The young, bust-length Maarten, seemingly sharing the same space on the right wing, is turned in three-quarter profile toward the left as he worships the Virgin and child. The combination of a Virgin and child with a donor's portrait in a diptych harks back to van der Weyden. Memling also painted single bust-length portraits against blank grounds or interior backgrounds with views of the outdoors and was apparently the first Flemish painter to set single bust-length portraits against landscape backgrounds. However, for all their technical accomplishment, Memling's pictures differ from van der Weyden's in their remarkable lack of expressiveness and psychological insight.

Memling's paintings were admired in Italy and Spain. In Bruges his works influenced Michel Sittow as well as a series of anonymous minor artists, among them the Master of the Legend of St. Ursula and the Master of the Legend of St. Lucy.

BIBLIOGRAPHY

Verougstraete-Marcq, Helene, et al., eds. *Memling Studies: Proceedings of the International Colloquium, Bruges, 10–12 November 1994.* Louvain, Belgium, 1997.

Vos, Dirk de. *Hans Memling: The Complete Works.* Ghent, Belgium, 1994.

Vos, Dirk de. "Memling, Hans." In *The Dictionary of Art.* Edited by Jane Turner. Vol. 21. New York, 1996. Pages 100–106.

MICHAËL J. AMY

MENASSEH BEN ISRAEL (1604–1657), rabbi and preacher in the Portuguese Jewish community of Amsterdam. Menasseh was born as Manuel Dias Soeiro in Lisbon or La Rochelle to a family of conversos (converted Jews). His father was condemned by the Portuguese Inquisition for Judaizing, and the family emigrated to Amsterdam around 1613. There they returned openly to the Jewish faith. In 1626 Menasseh established the first Hebrew printing house in Amsterdam, which published nearly two hundred Hebrew books in less than thirty years. He served as preacher and later as the third rabbi of the rabbinical college of the community. Although he never stood out as an authority in rabbinical law, his broad theological education, his mastery of several languages, and his determined effort to arouse sympathy for Judaism made him the most famous rabbinical figure among Christian scholars in western Europe. He claimed to have written more than three hundred epistles to Christian correspondents, including Hugo Grotius, Caspar Barlaeus, Christian Ravius, and Gerardus Vossius. He supplied Hebrew books to Queen Christina of Sweden, whom he met in Antwerp in 1654. Among his acquaintances was the painter Rembrandt van Rijn, who produced four engravings for his book *Piedra gloriosa* (Glorious stone; 1655) which presents Jewish messianism in terms of universal spiritual values.

Menasseh combated heterodox tendencies within his community, mostly composed of former conversos, some of whom denied divine revelation and providence and the immortality of the soul. His *De resurrectione mortuorum* (On the resurrection of the dead; 1636) was mainly an attack against the views of Uriel da Costa, who rejected Pharisaic Judaism and had been excommunicated in Hamburg and Amsterdam. In his four-volume work in Spanish, *El conciliador* (The conciliator; 1632–1651), Menasseh attempted to resolve apparent contradictions within the Old Testament. Following Jewish thinkers of the Renaissance, he sought to reduce all theological traditions to a single one, presenting the Hebrew prophets and sages as the source of pagan philosophy. In his *Nishmat hayyim* (Book of the living soul), an eclectic Hebrew tractate on the immortality of the soul, he mingled kabbalistic and philosophical concepts with popular beliefs, placing strong emphasis on the affinities between Kabbalah and Neoplatonism. Almost all his works are based on a belief in *prisca theologia* (ancient theology) that contains the shared truth of all the ancient religions and cultures, pagan as well as monotheistic, but like other Renaissance Jewish thinkers, he argued that the highest truth is found in the ancient Jewish sources.

In Menasseh's latter years he formed close connections with Christian millenarians, who found support in him for their hopes for imminent redemption. Though he realized that their sympathy for the Jews was motivated by faith in their future conversion, he made use of his connections with the English millenarians John Dury and Henry Jessey to obtain a proclamation regarding the return of the Jews to England. In 1650, in hopes of gaining approval for this project, he dedicated the English edition of his *Miqweh Israel* (The hope of Israel), which included a report of the discovery of some of the Lost Tribes of Israel in South America, to the English Parliament. To that end he also traveled to England in 1655 and presented *The Humble Addresses,* an apologetic treatise describing the usefulness and loyalty of the Jews, to Cromwell. His effort did not obtain the hoped-for results, though Jews in London were allowed to pray privately and received a burial plot. Shortly afterward Menasseh died in Middelburg.

BIBLIOGRAPHY

Primary Works

Menasseh ben Israel. *The Conciliator of R. Menasseh ben Israel: A Reconcilement of the Apparent Contradictions in Holy Scripture.* Translated by E. H. Lindo. 2 vols. London, 1842. Translation of *El conciliador* (1632–1651).

Menasseh ben Israel. *The Hope of Israel.* Translated by Moses Wall. London, 1652. Reprint, with introduction and notes by Henry Méchoulan and Gérard Nahon. Oxford and New York, 1987. Translation of *Miqweb Israel* (1650). This book was published simultaneously in Latin and Spanish and also translated into Dutch, Hebrew, French, and other languages.

Secondary Works

Coppenhagen, J. H. *Menasseh ben Israel: Manuel Dias Soeiro, 1605–1657: A Bibliography.* Jerusalem, 1990. A comprehensive bibliography of his life and work.

Kaplan, Yosef, Henry Mechoulan, and Richard H. Popkin, eds. *Menasseh ben Israel and his World.* Leiden, Netherlands, and New York, 1989. A collection of articles about his cultural and religious ambience and his intellectual connections.

Katz, David S. *Philo-Semitism and the Readmission of the Jews to England, 1603–1655.* Oxford, 1982. The most up-to-date study of the return of the Jews to England and the activities of Menasseh ben Israel in that matter.

YOSEF KAPLAN

MENDOZA, PEDRO GONZÁLEZ DE. *See* González de Mendoza, Pedro.

MERCANTILISM.

Government intervention in economic life for fiscal, political, social, and other reasons has recurred throughout history. Following Adam Smith, who in *The Wealth of Nations* (1776) described—and denounced—what he called "the mercantile system," many scholars hold that state efforts in Europe between the fifteenth and eighteenth centuries became more determined and comprehensive. To foster both economic development and national power and plenty, officials, businessmen, and publicists proposed measures with several related objectives: expanding domestic industry, capturing larger shares of foreign trade, augmenting bullion stocks, and assuring favorable commercial balances. Spurred by economic crisis, sharp competition in international and colonial trade, and military ambitions in Europe, and sustained by elaborated theoretical underpinnings and strategically placed ministers, mercantilism (a term introduced by German economic historians about 1860) was at its height in western Europe during the seventeenth century. Although increasingly criticized in their original heart-

land, mercantilist tenets and practices were thereafter adopted by so called enlightened absolutists in central and eastern Europe.

Early Steps. The Renaissance period constituted the first stage in the gradual and unsystematic implementation of mercantilist political economy. As in the Middle Ages, guilds and municipalities were intimately concerned with economic affairs. Corporate bodies enforced local production monopolies by dictating labor supply and training, output maxima, and quality standards. Civic administrators directed their attention toward benefiting their producers and consumers at the expense of the surrounding countryside and other towns. Thus, they enacted provisioning policies to secure adequate, cheap supplies of foodstuffs and raw materials for urban needs and struggled to impose regional market monopolies for their artisans and merchants.

While acknowledging these efforts as crucial forerunners, interpretations of mercantilism concentrate on central governments' policies and projects. Italian city-states took important early steps. Venice operated the Arsenal, long the largest work site in Europe, to build and outfit the galley fleet that was so vital to the city's domination of eastern Mediterranean trade and finance. In Lombardy, novel crops like rice and mulberries were planted, and substantial irrigation works built, with the backing of the Visconti and Sforza dukes. Like the Bentivoglio at Bologna, the Medici in Florence, and other princes, the rulers of Milan assisted with privileges (and, at times, funds) and the establishment of new crafts, most notably in metal and weapons trades, though including textiles, glassmaking, and luxury goods as well.

Measures to quicken the economy and strengthen the state likewise accompanied the rise of monarchies in western Europe. From an early date England sought to protect woolens, its chief industry. It temporarily banned raw wool exports in 1258, subsequently taxed wool sent abroad, and, in the mid-fifteenth century, forbade entry to foreign woolens and silks. Other enactments attempted to prevent the outflow of precious metals and restrict foreign merchants to the benefit of natives. In France the crown's financial needs at the close of the Hundred Years' War (1337–1453) and its goal of rebuilding state and economy led Louis XI (ruled 1461–1483) to assist mining ventures and cheap woolens manufactures for export, to try to hinder bullion transfers abroad, and, by fostering silkmaking, to curb luxury imports and thereby contribute to a positive balance of payments. These two countries also pioneered monopoly trading companies such as the English Merchants of the Staple and Merchant Adventurers, and several associations authorized by the French crown to manage international commerce and develop maritime shipping in the Mediterranean.

The Sixteenth Century. In response to several forces during the sixteenth century, mercantilist schemes of some kind were adopted by most major states and many of those of the second rank. These forces included the costs of centralized state-building, the growth of Europe's first New World colonial empires, and the accelerating export of gold and silver necessitated in particular by rising trade with Asia. In this period, too, tracts began explicitly to back interventionist approaches. Some called for protecting existing industry and developing new ones whose products could supplant imports. Others focused on retaining or, if possible, augmenting bullion supplies, a demand that reinforced the preoccupations of political leaders who believed that the size of monetary reserves determined the extent of state power.

Individual polities pursued strategies that varied according to the specific combinations of opportunities and threats they faced, although all relied on some mix of privileges and exclusions. In Elizabeth I's reign (1558–1603), England sought with cash subventions and temporary monopolies to attract foreign artisans who would start manufactures hitherto unknown there. Charles V (ruled 1516–1556) hoped to aid Spanish industry by forbidding raw materials exports. The Medici dukes, in contrast, relied on interdictions of competing imports to assist Tuscan textile crafts. Monetary awards, exclusive rights, high tariff barriers, and even—under Francis I (ruled 1515–1547)—the founding of a tapestry workshop near the royal palace in Fontainebleau were ventured in France. At the end of the period there began to appear the direct predecessors of the great chartered companies that, building on earlier staple organizations, were to loom so large in seventeenth-century overseas trade. Regulations designed to enhance monetary stocks became yet more numerous, diverse, and extreme; they ranged from placing all exchange transactions under the control of government officials to prohibiting outright all bullion exports.

An Assessment. Renaissance mercantilism was less ambitious than its successors, and it enjoyed weaker conceptual and ministerial support. Few of the projects so hopefully initiated were destined to flourish; indeed, most successful economic innovations owed very little to state assistance. To be sure, ducal edicts helped agricultural projects around Milan to overcome landlord and peasant recalcitrance. Again, England progressively restricted wool exports; limited the activities of foreign merchants; and protected paper, glass, sugar refining, and other nascent manufactures. But no government had sufficient revenues to fund new industries adequately, so nearly all of those dependent on state largesse soon foundered. Nor did states dispose of the bureaucratic resources needed to enforce restrictions on bullion flows or other financial dealings. Despite efforts to reduce tolls, moreover, internal barriers continued to hobble market operations. Finally, fiscal needs typically prevailed over protectionist goals, so that, for instance, tariffs on exported manufactures were often higher than levies on imported raw materials.

The balance sheet of Renaissance mercantilism is therefore largely negative. Nevertheless, nonmarket policies of this period prefigured many of those later undertaken by governments seeking to foster national wealth and power through industrial development, commercial expansion, favorable trade balances, and precious metals stockpiling.

See also **Renaissance, Interpretations of the,** *subentry on* **Economic Interpretations.**

BIBLIOGRAPHY

Cole, Charles W. *French Mercantilist Doctrines before Colbert.* New York, 1931. A solid study, now in need of replacement, that discusses some medieval and Renaissance texts along with seventeenth-century classics.

Ekelund, Robert B., and Robert D. Tollison. *Mercantilism as a Rent-Seeking Society: Economic Regulation in Historical Perspective.* College Station, Tex., 1981. An up-to-date treatment informed by modern economic theory.

Heckscher, Eli. *Mercantilism.* Edited by E. F. Soderlund. Translated by Mendel Shapiro. Rev. ed. 2 vols. New York, 1955. Much criticized for exaggerating the uniformity and systematic nature of the phenomenon it analyzes, but a comprehensive work that remains fundamental.

ROBERT S. DUPLESSIS

MERCENARIES. Mercenaries are usually defined as soldiers fighting for wages for a country to which normally they do not belong. They have no particular stake in the society they are recruited by—no property to defend, no family to protect against the enemy. Their loyalty is directed to the person who pays their wages. When payment is withheld or late, or if their contract is ended or thought to have been broken by the employer, mercenaries may feel entitled to switch their service to anyone else, even to the enemy they were fighting the previous day.

States may employ mercenaries for a variety of reasons—they possess a necessary skill; they are willing to engage in violent activities shied from by the state's citizens; or they may be used in addition to or in place of citizen soldiers.

Renaissance Mercenaries. Although most aspects of the above definition should be acceptable to early-modern historians, the most important characterics of Renaissance mercenaries were the rather large size of their units (600 to 4,000) and the way they received their pay. The state that hired them paid their wages to the captain of the mercenary unit, who in turn distributed them to the men under his command. Unlike their predecessors, Renaissance mercenaries sometimes came from within the borders of the state for which they eventually fought—a situation that suggests either the social alienation of the soldier or the powerlessness of central governments to enforce the law within all the territories theoretically under their sovereignty.

The use of mercenaries was a long-standing practice in the history of warfare. They were part of armies beginning in the ancient Near East, continuing in the Hellenistic period, and in the early Middle Ages. They became increasingly common during the later-Middle Ages, and by the time of the Renaissance they had become the basis of most armies, especially in Italy. The number of mercenaries in Europe in the sixteenth and seventeenth centuries has been estimated at between 100,000 and one million. In spite of Niccolò Machiavelli's (1469–1527) vitriolic portrait of mercenaries, the profession of war was considered a highly honorable occupation during the Renaissance. It lost its luster only during the eighteenth century.

Unlike medieval companies, which were comprised of individuals from many different parts of Europe, most Renaissance mercenaries were recruited in blocks from certain regions—Switzerland, Germany, and Italy, for instance. The most popular medieval mercenary was initially the crossbowman, who was superseded in the fifteenth century by the longbowman in northern Europe. For the most part Renaissance armies required pikemen, arquebusiers (gunmen), and artillerymen. In the Italian states the core of Renaissance armies were squadrons of heavy cavalrymen, joined in the late-fourteenth century by companies of arquebusiers. Knights for instance were the core of the army of the Italian Holy League, which battled the French at the battle of Fornovo in northern Italy in 1495.

The increase in the tempo of warfare and the geographical expansion of Renaissance conflicts also meant a large growth in the number of soldiers in general and of mercenaries in particular. This process had already begun on a large scale in the fifteenth century. The city of Metz for instance hired French, Italians, Burgundians, Spaniards, Germans, and Albanians in 1490 while engaged against the duke René of Lorraine. The process accelerated in the sixteenth century, when international armies fought the so-called national wars of France against the empire. Armies were a "Noah's Ark" in the words of the Venetian Marino Sanudo writing in about 1500. This process became a normal practice in the sixteenth century in France, which had already engaged Swiss mercenaries in long-term contracts during the fifteenth century.

The Mercenary Life. The attractions of mercenary service were varied, but did not necessarily include good pay. Although normally higher than the pay of native troops, mercenary pay was based on subsistence. Actual pay was only one of the perks of mercenary life. First of all, even subsistence alone must have been attractive to many in a period of chronic un- and underemployment. Moreover, there were other financial attractions for the soldier, like the lure of ransacking the effects of the enemy army, which could happen even if they lost the battle—this happened at Fornovo in 1495 with the Holy League's stradiots, that is, light cavalrymen often recruited from the Dalmation coast. Derelict in their duties of attacking the enemy soldiers, the stradiots looted the French baggage train. Taking prisoners was another lucrative enterprise, since some could be ransomed for a price. Even at Fornovo, where the commander in chief of the Holy League Army, Gianfrancesco Gonzaga, ordered his men-at-arms to take no prisoners, the order was ignored because the lure of gain was stronger than the general's wishes. The greatest temptation was to sack the enemy city. The winners of a battle frequently enjoyed complete control over the liberty, property, and life of the city dwellers. As at Rome in 1527 and Antwerp in 1576, the rewards could be very high. At Rome the treasures of the city churches fell into the hands of the sackers; it is said that the sack of Antwerp resulted in a loot of over twenty million ducats. In addition to financial gain, mercenary service offered a sense of freedom from the constraints of everyday life; the attraction of adventure; the possibility of escaping prison or the drudgery of family existence at home; or, in the case of the sociopath, the acceptance of sexual license and excesses, which in civilian life would end with the perpetrators on the gallows.

Many times people of the same background fought on opposite sides. This was true not only of Italians, who had done so for centuries, but of other people like the Swiss, who had a much closer ethnic identity. In such cases the loyalty of the troops, especially after a defeat, was questioned. The mercenaries, it was said, engaged in mock fights, happy only to collect their pay, not to defeat their comrades on the other side. Accusations of this kind were common throughout Europe, although Machiavelli's condemnations have left the greatest mark on the awareness of successive generations. In reality most mercenaries were reliable as long as they received their pay on time. But frequently the pay was late or did not come at all; then their behavior defied prediction. The beast of disorder could be unleashed, as in the case of the Sack of Rome of 1527; mercenaries could force their commanders to attack when they did not want to, like the landsknechts (German pikemen) at Pavia in 1525 (with a happy result for the Spanish forces), or the Swiss at the order of the French at Bicocca in 1522 (with unhappy results); they could proceed with great ferocity in taking revenge against the civilian population in spite of their leader's prohibition, as the Swiss did at Pontremoli, in the mountains between Florence and Genoa, during Charles VIII's dangerous trek back to France in 1495. Situations like these fueled the contemporaries' suspicions that mercenaries, once unleashed, were lawless and unpredictable. Still, in spite of all these fears the trend in the sixteenth century was not a decrease in the use of mercenaries, but a steady increase. The commanders' most common complaint was that there were not enough of them.

Condottieri. The most famous of all Renaissance mercenaries were the Italian condottieri, a name derived from the word *condotta,* which referred to a contract that guaranteed the employment of a specified number of soldiers for a certain period of time under the leadership of a captain, the condottiere. Later, the term *condotta* came to refer also to the company of soldiers itself. Organized companies of professional soldiers, ready to be hired or to engage in warfare for their own interest, had appeared in Italy in the Middle Ages under the leadership of foreigners. By the fifteenth century, however, most of the condottieri were Italian. Their companies were the best of the kind in terms of the sophistication of their organization and efficiency on the battlefield.

The emergence of these companies of professional fighters was on one hand a symptom of the commercial success of the Italian civilian population, able to pay strangers for the dangerous business of arms, and on the other of the alienation of the majority of the population from the states they were born in. The prosperity of the Italian economy and the continuing tension between enemy groups within the city-states often led to an aversion on the part of the ruling classes to personally mixing business with war. Yet, they grew increasingly reluctant to rely on the rest of their own populations in warfare for many reasons—lack of trust, desire to keep commoners out of a profession considered dangerous to the security of the state, and in the long run inefficiency on the battlefield.

Most of the condottieri and their soldiers came from outside the borders of the state that hired them, although it was not uncommon, especially in the lands of the pope, that theoretically they were subjects of their employer. An inordinate number of mercenaries originated from the Papal States—the Marche, Romagna, and Umbria regions—yet there was practically no Italian area that was unrepresented. Although a few, such as Erasmo da Narni, called il Gattamelata (1370–1443), a baker's son, and Niccolo Piccinino (1386–1444), whose father was a butcher, came from humble backgrounds, the majority were from the ranks of nobility, some claiming ancient origins like the Roman noble families of the Colonna and Orsini. In many cases they were the *signori* (lords) of a particular state, like the Montefeltro of Urbino, the Este of Ferrara, or the Gonzaga of Mantua, people often shoring up the revenues of relatively economically disadvantaged principalities with the profits of war.

The condottieri companies, or *condotta,* could be composed of both cavalry and infantry, and sometimes even artillery, but the dominant soldier was the heavy cavalryman. Usually a *condotta* was defined by how many "lances" it comprised. In general each "lance" included two cavalrymen and at least one infantryman, often a page or squire, who would help his master on the battlefield by rescuing him if wounded, keeping control of prisoners taken by the lord, looking after his warhorse, replacing the warhorse if the animal was killed, or providing the lord with a new lance after the first charge. In general, Italian "lances" were much smaller than the "lances" from across the Alps. They included two to three soldiers, while the French "lances" had about four men and the forces of the duke of Burgundy even more.

The size of the companies varied. Early in the fifteenth century it was not unusual to find companies of as few as ten "lances"; later in the fifteenth century, they became increasingly larger, sometimes numbering in the hundreds. The tendency, however, as the century progressed, was for a captain of renown to gather around him not only his own condotta but the companies of other minor condottieri as well. Although initially the state signed contracts with each individual condottiere, this changed as the century moved on. Gianfrancesco Gonzaga, the leader of the Holy League at Fornovo in 1495, personally led a condotta that included the forces of many other condottieri, such as his uncle Rodolfo, who had fought also for the duke of Burgundy.

Contracts, Loyalty, and Efficacy. In the fifteenth century there was also a change in the length and the type of the contract. Initially contracts were divided into a period of *ferma,* that is a term of firm employment, and a period *di rispetto,* that is a term during which the employer had the option of signing the condottiere to another contract. In Venice, the normal length of the *ferma* was three months. This was a system that suited the employer: soldiers were available when required (most frequently during the spring, summer, or fall), and dispensable when war was unlikely (during the winter). The second half of the fifteenth century witnessed a crucial change in the practice of war, as the emergence of permanent armies led to a continuous need for soldiers. The process began in France and spread to Italy, especially in the northern states of the Duchy of Milan and the Republic of Venice, but also in the southern Kingdom of Naples. The purpose of standing armies was to prepare for war during peacetime. This translated into much longer terms of service for the condottieri, and in most cases practically permanent service. For instance, the condottiere Guido Rangoni in 1441 was required to maintain a *condotta* of seven hundred cavalrymen in war and five hundred in peacetime. In the Venetian territories, the implementation of a standing army led to important changes in the Republic's relationship to its condottieri. Various methods were used to assure their loyalty to Venice: very long terms of contract; territorial rewards, like a fief or a house in Venice; inclusion within the ranks of the Great Council, that is, the nobility eligible for public office (a very unusual concession to foreigners); annual pensions (often extended to wives and families of condottieri); gracious care of people maimed on the battlefield; state funerals; and in some cases permission to erect posthumous monuments to their fame, like Gattamelata's 1453 equestrian statue by Donatello standing in front of St. Anthony's Church in Padua.

Although the loyalty of the condottieri employed by Venice was well known during the period, condottieri were more likely to be criticized for their cunning and duplicitous ways (see Machiavelli's works for instance); but criticism of the condottieri was one of the mandatory commonplaces of the literature of the fifteenth and sixteenth centuries, similar to the often venomous indictment of courts and courtiers. Numerous ills were attributed to mercenaries: they lacked loyalty, were treacherous, changed sides at will, refused to wage real battles preferring skirmishes to pitched encounters, and encouraged the citizens of the state to avoid a career of arms, thus making the state militarily weak. J. R. Hale and Michael Mallett have worked to dispel this picture of the Italian condottieri and to portray the condottieri instead as resourceful, clever, and loyal. Insisting on the inefficacy of condottiere warfare is generally inaccurate. They were professional soldiers, paid wages for a certain time. It was normal and certainly not treacherous if at the end of the contract they decided to offer their services elsewhere. Moreover, the presence of treacherous individuals was also always balanced by men whose loyalty was unquestioned, like Sir John Hawkwood (c. 1320–1394) or Gattamelata, people who were not in the minority, as often claimed. Furthermore, their skill in warfare has been underestimated. The beginning of the Renaissance saw the confluence of two schools of military art—the shock impact of French armies, and the skillful maneuvers of the Italian condottieri. It is no surprise that the eventual winner of continental hegemony in the sixteenth century was Spain, which blended both traditions.

It is also inaccurate to claim, on the basis of Machiavelli's words, that condottieri battles ended with one or two casualties or none at all. The battle of Anghiari of 1440, where, according to Machiavelli, only one man was killed because he was trampled to death by the horses when he fell to the ground, actually ended with three hundred casualties. It is true that the condottieri preferred maneuvers to confrontations, but often this was a requirement dictated by the type of armies they led (small in comparison to the French armies) and by the reluctance of their employers to commit all their soldiers in a crucial encounter. One defeat could have meant complete disaster for the state. Venice, for instance, gave specific orders not to endanger the integrity of all her forces at Fornovo. Decades earlier Venice had kept its condottiere Gattamelata in great esteem in spite of a number of defeats not only because Gattamelata was a soldier worthy of such esteem but because his defeats did not end in the total destruction of the republic's armies.

See also **Gattamelata, Erasmo da Narni, il; Pavia, Battle of; Warfare; Wars of Italy.**

BIBLIOGRAPHY

General Works

Contamine, Philippe. *War in the Middle Ages.* Translated by Michael Jones. New York, 1984.

Corvisier, Andre. *Armies and Societies in Europe, 1494–1789.* Translated by A. T. Siddall. Bloomington, Ind., 1979.

Hale, J. R. *War and Society in Renaissance Europe 1450–1620.* London, 1985. Rev. ed., 1998.

Hall, Bert S. *Weapons and Warfare in Renaissance Europe.* Baltimore, 1997.

Pieri, Piero. *Il Rinascimento e la crisi militare italiana.* 2d ed. Turin, Italy, 1982.

On Mercenaries

Ancona, Clemente. "Milizie e condottieri." In *Storia d'Italia.* Vol. 5. Turin, Italy, 1973. Pages 646–665.

Mallett, Michael. *Mercenaries and Their Masters. Warfare in Renaissance Italy.* Totowa, N.J., 1974.

Mallett, Michael. "The Condottiere." In *Renaissance Characters.* Edited by Eugenio Garin and translated by Lydica C. Cochrane. Chicago, 1988. Pages 22–45.

"Preparations for War in Florence and Venice in the Second Half of the Fifteenth Century." In *Florence and Venice: Comparisons and Relations: Acts of Two Conferences at Villa I Tatti in 1976–1977.* Vol. 1, *Quattrocento.* Florence, 1979. Pages 149–164.

Ricotti, Ercole. *La storia delle compagnie di ventura in Italia.* 2 vols. 2d ed. Turin, Italy, 1884.

"Venice and Its Condottieri, 1404–1454." In *Renaissance Venice.* Edited by J. R. Hale. Totowa, N. J., 1973. Pages 121–145.

Antonio Santosuosso

MERICI, ANGELA (1474?–1540), saint, founder of the Company of St. Ursula, the original model for several communities and congregations bearing the name "Ursuline," notably the Order of St. Ursula, the oldest and most influential Roman Catholic women's teaching order.

Born to peasant parents in Desenzano, on Lake Garda in northern Italy, Angela Merici was orphaned in early childhood and later became a Franciscan tertiary (a member of the third, or lay, order of St. Francis), teaching poor girls the essentials of Catholic faith and caring for sick women in her native town. In 1516 she was invited to undertake similar tasks in Brescia, to which she returned after making pilgrimages to the Holy Land and Rome in 1524–1525.

Dedicated to her educational and caritative activities, she gradually organized, and in 1535 established more formally, a group of young women, then numbering twenty-eight, called the Company of St. Ursula. As a society of virgins dedicated to the teaching of girls, Angela and her companions bound themselves to devote their lives to the service of their patron, St. Ursula. Taking no vows and wearing simple clothing rather than religious habits, these women lived not as an organized community, but rather in their own homes or in suitable private households, as a kind of sisterhood, each serving an apostolate among her family, friends, and neighbors.

In the beginning, their company reflected not only the tertiary influence, but in its twofold structure the patronage system of contemporary urban confraternities. Its full-fledged members were the young virgins, twelve or older, originally girls of lower social status. Affiliated with them as patrons or "governesses" were the upper-class women who supported them and who supplied the four "colonels" chosen to guide the young members.

Recognizing the pressures and opportunities of change, in her *Regola* (composed 1535–1540) Angela Merici advised her first followers that "if according to times and needs you should be obliged to make fresh rules and change certain things, do it with prudence and good advice." Without binding her "company" by rigid rules to any single mode of life, she combined models from the distant past, the "house virgins" of the early church and the patronage of St. Ursula, with features of the tertiaries, *pinzochere* (pious laywomen), and confraternities of her own time and place. In this way she constructed a "new company" capable of assuming different forms, including communities of sisters taking simple vows and a cloistered order of teachers, the Ursulines of France, founded in the early seventeenth century and later established in Canada, where it became the first female missionary order.

Although Angela Merici lived to direct her company for only a few years, she had already joined the "living saints" of her time and immediately after her death a campaign for her beatification began. Disclaiming the charismatic gifts to which other "holy women" aspired, Angela Merici holds a special place among the extraordinary number of women striving for, but rarely achieving, sainthood in sixteenth-century Italy. Her great achievement was the creation of an active and flexible model of women's religious life, adaptable not only to her own limited environment, but to the diverse needs of women in changing circumstances and societies. Angela Merici was beatified in 1768 and canonized in 1807; her feast day is 1 June.

BIBLIOGRAPHY

Primary Works

Ledóchowska, Teresa. *Angela Merici and the Company of St. Ursula According to the Historical Documents.* Rev. ed., 2 vols. Translated by Mary Teresa Neylin. Rome, 1969.

Mariani, Luciana, Elisa Tarolli, and Marie Seynaeve. *Angela Merici: Contributo per una biografia.* Milan, 1986.

Merici, Angela. *Regola, ricordi, legati: Testo antico e testo moderno.* Edited by Luciana Mariani e Elisa Taroli. Brescia, Italy, 1976. English trans. in Ledóchowska (1969), vol. 1, pp. 272 ff.

Secondary Works

Blaisdell, Charmarie J. "Angela Merici and the Ursulines." In *Religious Orders of the Catholic Reformation: Essays in Honor of John C. Olin on His Seventy-fifth Birthday.* Edited by Richard L. De Molen. New York, 1994. Pages 99–136.

Zarri, Gabriella. "Ursula and Catherine: The Marriage of Virgins in the Sixteenth Century." In *Creative Women in Medieval and Early Modern Italy: A Religious and Artistic Renaissance.* Edited by E. Ann Matter and John Coakley. Philadelphia, 1994. Pages 237–278.

MARY MARTIN MCLAUGHLIN

METAPHYSICAL POETRY. *See* **Poetry,** *subentry on* **Early Stuart and Metaphysical Poetry.**

METAPHYSICS. Aristotle describes metaphysics in three ways: as a "divine science" that studies immaterial reality not subject to change, a science that studies being as being, as well as a science that grounds the principles of the special sciences. The encounter in the Renaissance between Aristotle's idea of God as first substance and the Christian notion of a God active as triune creator opened the way from the ancient dialectical constructions to the dynamic metaphysical systems of modern times.

Lullian Metaphysics. The static Aristotelianism established in the medieval schools by Thomas Aquinas was challenged as early as the fourteenth century by a conception of knowledge and reality which belonged to the Renaissance. This new conception first appeared in the territories bordering on Islam. The Majorcan Ramon Lull (1232–1316)—wanting to make the Christian Trinity and Incarnation intelligible to Moslems and Jews—spoke of the dynamism of the divine names common to all religions. Because activity presupposes a principle, that which is produced, and a bond between them, he defined these "correlatives" as the intrinsic principles of activity which are valid for all reality. He conceived his "Art" as a means of ascent which proceeds by transcending first sense knowledge and then rational knowledge to discover at a higher level the supreme being.

By the early fifteenth century Lull's dynamic understanding of reality as tending to the infinite began to attract followers. Ramon Sibiuda (d. 1436) of Toulouse associated Lull's doctrine with that of Anselm of Canterbury, holding Anselm's definition of God as "that greater than which cannot be thought" to be the basis for a new metaphysics. The first signs of a permanent Lullism appear in Italy. While studying at Padua, the young Nicholas of Cusa (1401–1464) became acquainted with Lull's ideas. In his *De docta ignorantia* (On learned ignorance), Nicholas proposed a vision of all reality. Making use of Anselm's maximum, and relating Lull's correlatives to the triad associated with the school of Chartres, *unitas, aequalitas, connexio,* Nicholas treats God in book 1 as the absolutely infinite unity which produces all things. Book 2 sees the second moment of the triad in the production of the universe. The created universe is the "contracted" equal of the primal unity—as the limit of its striving for perfection. Book 3 presents Christ as the perfect man, connecting the two infinities.

A new period in the history of Renaissance metaphysics began with the Council of Ferrara-Florence. The Greek philosopher George Gemistus Pletho (c. 1360–1452) maintained that the Latin theologians at the council had been misled by Averroes (Ibn Rushd), the twelfth-century Islamic philosopher, to believe that Aristotle's works contained the sum total of human wisdom. He found the source of the Latin errors concerning the creation of the world and God's providence over it in their ignorance of Platonic philosophy. In the context of the ensuing controversy concerning the relative superiority of Plato and Aristotle, Nicholas made a profound contribution to the theory of knowledge. In his *De non aliud* (Concerning the not-other), he looked for the roots of Aristotle's errors, arguing that Aristotle failed in metaphysics because he never ascended beyond sense and rational knowledge to the certitude of intellectual vision.

Platonic Metaphysics. Marsilio Ficino (1433–1499) sought an alternative to Latin Aristotelianism in Platonic metaphysics. He gave his Neoplatonic vision a dynamic turn by breaking with the Plotinian idea which made Mind subordinate to the One and Soul to Mind. He assigned some of Mind's attributes to God, others to the angels. The status of Mind as supreme thinker and supreme thought belongs to the One. In his doctrine of Soul, the humanistic character of Ficino's approach appears. Man is the bond of all things, who can ascend in thought from the senses to Soul, thence to Mind and to the One itself. But his constant struggle to transcend himself projects him into the future. He is destined for the infinite and can find fulfillment only in immortality.

Taking his departure from Ficino's Christian Platonism, Giovanni Pico della Mirandola (1463–1494) sought in his early works to establish the concord between the wisdom of the ancients—Proclus, the *prisci theologi* (ancient theologians), and Jewish Kabbalah—and Christian wisdom. But with the condemnation of several of his theses by Pope Innocent VIII in 1487 on the ground that they led to the reappearance of pagan ideas and in effect reduced faith to rational knowledge, Pico came to abandon his undertaking. The abandonment of the idea of a degree of knowledge higher than rational knowledge marked a turning point in the history of metaphysics as the science of divine things and coincided with the establishment of Thomism as the dominant theological school in the West. The earlier tradition of a dynamic understanding of reality became associated with Renaissance magic and occultism in the new philosophies of nature sketched by authors like Giordano Bruno (1548–1600), Francesco Patrizi (1529–1597), and Tommaso Campanella (1568–1639).

Catholic Aristotelian Metaphysics. The victory of the papacy over conciliarism (the theory of the supremacy of a general council in the government of the church) at the Council of Basel (1431–1449) was accompanied by the appearance of the notion of a Christian Aristotelianism meant to underline the necessity of revelation. At Paris the secular master Johannes Versor (d. c. 1485) commented on Aristotle's *Metaphysics* on the basis of Aquinas's doctrine. God is treated in metaphysics only as the cause of being. Versor preserved the Aristotelian idea of physics as dealing with *corpus mobile* (physical bodies as changeable), but he introduced the doctrine of creation into Aristotle's science by holding that corporeal reality is also treated in metaphysics *sub ratione entis creati* (as created being).

This understanding of Aristotle's philosophy was challenged by Pietro Pomponazzi (1462–1525). In his *De immortalitate animae* (On the immortality of the soul; 1516), Pomponazzi maintained that according to Aristotle—who knew nothing of creation—the doctrine of the soul belongs as *corpus animatum* (physical bodies as animate) to physics and that it is consequently impossible to prove its immortal-

ity. To meet this challenge, the proponents of a Christian Aristotelianism sought metaphysical rather than physical proofs for the soul's immortality. Dominicans like Thomas de Vio (Cajetan; 1468–1534) and Crisostomo Javelli (1470/72–c. 1538) and Jesuits like Benito Perera (c. 1535–1610) and Francisco Suárez (1548–1617) constructed a science of metaphysics based on the idea of creation, transforming Aristotle's natural philosophy into metaphysics.

Because metaphysics can treat incorporeal reality only as cause, Perera proposed a division of traditional metaphysics into two distinct sciences: "first philosophy," treating being as being, and "divine science," dealing with God, the intelligences, and the soul. In his *Disputationes metaphysicae* (Metaphysical disputations; 1597), Suárez made the principle of noncontradiction the foundation of his Christian reinterpretation of Aristotle's philosophy. Finite being is that which can be constituted in actual existence by God's absolute power because its essence contains no contradictory notes. Suárez's division of reality into infinite being, created immaterial being, and created material being provided a basis for the scholastic apologetics and rendered the growing crisis of the Aristotelian physics as the science of *corpus mobile* irrelevant to Scholastics.

Lutheran Metaphysics. Despite Martin Luther's rejection of Aristotle, the Aristotelian conception of science gained, within a century of the Reformer's disputation *Contra scholasticam theologiam* (Against scholastic theology) of 1517, a central place in Protestant universities. Lutheran Orthodoxy regarded metaphysics as the condition for the presentation of revealed theology. The textbooks on metaphysics which appeared in German universities in the 1590s looked to Aristotle for the terminology needed in controversy with Calvinists and agnostic Socinians (adherents of a movement that denied the Christian doctrine of the Trinity of Persons in the Godhead). They looked to Aristotle's theory of truth to defend the harmony between reason and revelation against Lutheran extremists who saw the doctrines of faith as contrary to reason. German metaphysical works, like the *Exercitationes metaphysicae* (Metaphysical exercises; 1603–1604) of Jacob Martini (1570–1649) and the *Metaphysica commentatio* (A metaphysical commentary; 1605) of Cornelius Martini (1568–1621), turned to Suárez's notion of a confessionally neutral, possible world which all those who admitted the idea of creation could accept. But Lutheran writers also came, in the early seventeenth century, reluctantly to admit the necessity of an independent natural theology. Following Perera, Christoph Scheibler (1589–1653) published the first separate treatise on *Theologia naturalis* in 1621.

Calvinist Metaphysics. Reformed theologians of the early seventeenth century followed the synthetic order in the presentation of doctrine but also adopted the Lullian notion of an art. Bartholomaeus Keckermann (1571/73–1609) considered the philosophical disciplines not as Aristotelian sciences but as productive "arts." Ordered compilations of doctrine were described as "systems" and each of the systems of the arts brought together in a new encyclopedia in the works of Keckermann, Clemens Timpler (1567–1624), and Johann Heinrich Alsted (1588–1638). The new conception of scientific knowledge affected the traditional role of metaphysics. For the Marburg professor Rudolph Goclenius (1547–1628), who used the word for the first time in his *Lexicon philosophicum* (A philosophical lexicon; 1613), "ontology" had the function of assigning each of the disciplines its proper place in a new encyclopedia of knowledge. Alsted enlarged and transformed the encyclopedia of the disciplines into a system of systems, governed by a theory of the arts, entitled "technologia." Timpler drew the consequences for metaphysics of this theory of the arts. The discipline which coordinates the arts must itself be less a theory of being than a theory of knowledge. For Timpler the subject matter of metaphysics is not being, but rather the intelligible, *pan noēton.*

See also biographies of figures mentioned in this entry.

BIBLIOGRAPHY

Lohr, Charles H. *Latin Aristotle Commentaries.* Vol. 2, *Renaissance Authors.* Florence, 1988.

Lohr, Charles H. "Medieval Latin Aristotle Commentaries." *Traditio* 23–30 (1967–1974).

Lohr, Charles H. "Metaphysics." In *The Cambridge History of Renaissance Philosophy.* Edited by Charles B. Schmitt et al. Cambridge, U.K., 1988. Pages 537–638.

CHARLES H. LOHR

MEXICO, CONQUEST OF. *See* **Americas; Cortés, Hernán.**

MICHELANGELO BUONARROTI (Michelangelo di Lodovico Buonarroti Simoni; 1475–1564), Italian sculptor, painter, architect, and poet. [This entry includes two subentries: Michelangelo the Artist and Michelangelo the Poet.]

Michelangelo the Artist

Michelangelo is universally recognized to be among the greatest artists of all time. His career spanned from the final years of Lorenzo de' Medici's Florence to the first stirrings of the Counter-Reformation. He lived through the pontificates of thirteen popes and worked for nine of them. Although his art occasionally has been criticized (he was accused of impropriety in the *Last Judgment*), Michelangelo's influence and reputation have always been acknowledged. Many of his works—including the *Pietà, David, Moses,* and the Sistine Chapel ceiling—are ubiquitous cultural icons. Despite the familiarity of Michelangelo's art and the large quantity of primary documentation (more than any previous artist), many aspects of Michelangelo's art and life remain open to interpretation. Only Shakespeare and Beethoven have inspired a comparable scholarly and popular literature, which may be expected given that each is the exemplary genius of his respective field of endeavor.

Early Life and Works. Michelangelo was born in the small town of Caprese in rural Tuscany. His father, Lodovico Buonarroti, was the local governor (*podestà*) who, after his six-month term of office, moved his family back to Florence. Michelangelo grew up in the small town of Settignano on the outskirts of Florence, and here he received his first lessons in stone and marble carving.

Much of Michelangelo's life is colored by myth, especially the undocumented early years. The contemporary biographies written by Giorgio Vasari (1550) and his pupil and assistant Ascanio Condivi (1553) are fictionalized accounts tinged by the self-fashioning recollection of an artist more than seventy years old and at the height of his international fame. Employing literary topoi, rhetorical description, and anecdote, the biographies were written primarily to praise Michelangelo's genius and unprecedented achievements (Vasari) and to tell the artist's own story (Condivi). Their evidential value as primary documents, therefore, should be qualified by recognition of their status as works of literature. Nonetheless, it is notable that within his lifetime Michelangelo inspired a considerable body of writing.

Despite petty concerns and frequent bickering, Michelangelo was very attached to his father and three younger brothers (his mother died when he was just six years old and his eldest brother became a Dominican friar). Michelangelo ardently believed that his family was descended from the medieval counts of Canossa, as is emphatically stated in the opening lines of Condivi's life of the artist. This belief in the antiquity and noble origins of his family fueled Michelangelo's lifelong ambition to improve their social and financial situation. Michelangelo's pride of ancestry is evident in his dress and comportment, as well as in his frequent admonitions to his brothers and nephew to behave in a manner befitting their elevated social station.

Florence. Appropriately for a son whose family had noble pretensions, Michelangelo attended Latin school until the age of thirteen. It is uncertain when he first aspired to be an artist, but it is understandable that his father opposed such a predilection since painting and sculpture were considered manual crafts and lowly occupations. In 1488 Michelangelo was apprenticed to Domenico Ghirlandaio, then the most fashionable painter in Florence. From Ghirlandaio, Michelangelo learned fresco painting; perhaps more important, Ghirlandaio practiced the arts of drawing and design (*disegno*) that Michelangelo made foundational principles of his art.

Michelangelo never completed his apprenticeship nor did he ever own or operate a conventional artist's workshop (*bottega*). Rather, he obtained a place in the large entourage of Lorenzo de' Medici, probably thanks to the intervention of his father, who could claim a distant relationship to the Medici family. Here he was introduced to some of the finest works of ancient and modern art and some of the most important literary and intellectual figures of the day, including Marsilio Ficino, Angelo Poliziano, Cristoforo Landino, and Giovanni Pico della Mirandola. Michelangelo spent nearly two years in the Medici household (c. 1490–1492). He received the beginnings of a humanist education, which was unique for an artist, alongside two of his future patrons, Giovanni de' Medici (Pope Leo X) and Giulio de' Medici (Pope Clement VII). He never mastered Latin, but he was exposed to a world of books, learning, and refined culture.

Among Michelangelo's surviving early works are exercises in low relief (*Madonna of the Stairs,* Casa Buonarroti) and higher relief (*Battle of the Centaurs,* Casa Buonarroti), respectively revealing the artist's emulation of Donatello and classical antiquity. After the death of Lorenzo de' Medici in 1492, Michelangelo actively sought patronage among the Strozzi and probably carved for them a lifesize marble *Hercules* (lost). Without a regular artistic practice or steady patronage, however, Michelangelo's future and economic security remained tenuous. When the Medici were expelled from Florence in 1494, Mi-

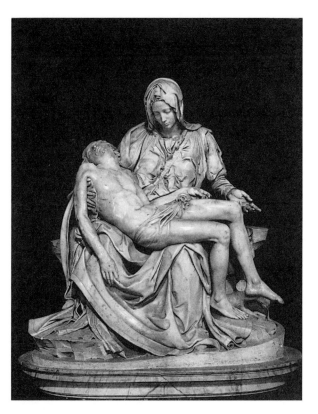

Michelangelo. *Pietà.* St. Peter's Basilica, Vatican City. 1497–1500. ALINARI/ART RESOURCE

chelangelo elected to follow the family to Bologna, where he lived for nearly a year in the house of the Bolognese patrician Giovanni Francesco Aldovrandi (Aldrovandi). Aldrovandi encouraged Michelangelo's interest in vernacular literature, especially Dante and Petrarch, and arranged for the twenty-year-old artist to carve several small statuettes for the still incomplete tomb of St. Dominic (*S. Petronius, S. Proclus,* and an angel candelabrum in San Domenico, Bologna).

Late in 1495 Michelangelo returned to Florence, then under the sway of the fiery Dominican preacher Girolamo Savonarola. In need of a patron, Michelangelo curried favor with Lorenzo di Pierfrancesco de' Medici, a member of the younger branch of the Medici family. For Lorenzo, Michelangelo carved a marble *St. John the Baptist* and a *Sleeping Cupid* (both lost). Lorenzo recommended Michelangelo to Cardinal Raffaele Riario, nephew of Pope Sixtus IV and one of the richest and most powerful men in the Roman Curia. Thus, armed with letters of introduction, Michelangelo arrived in Rome for the first time, in the summer of 1496.

Rome. The ancient monuments of Rome must have been a revelation, inspiration, and challenge to

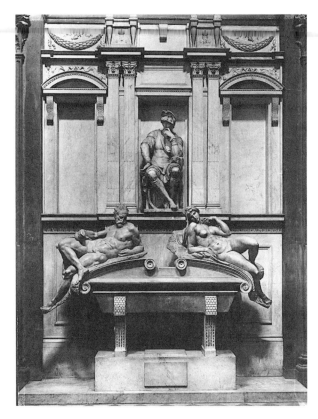

Michelangelo. Tomb of Lorenzo de' Medici. Lorenzo (1492–1519), grandson of Lorenzo the Magnificent, was duke of Urbino; he sits in meditation above. On his sarcophagus are Dawn and Dusk. The tomb is in the Sagrestia Nuova (New Sacristy) of the church of San Lorenzo, Florence. SAN LORENZO, FLORENCE/ALINARI/ART RESOURCE

Michelangelo for he immediately attempted some extremely audacious works, beginning with the *Bacchus* (Bargello, Florence). He carved this *all'antica* (in imitation of the antique) figure at the behest of Cardinal Riario, but it ended up in the collection of the Roman banker Jacopo Galli, who encouraged and supported the artist. Galli commissioned a *Cupid* and a *St. John* (both variously but dubiously identified with surviving sculptures), and he guaranteed the contract for Michelangelo's commission to carve the *Pietà* for the French cardinal Jean Villiers de La Grolais (1497–1499, Saint Peter's, Rome). A tour-de-force of aesthetic design and technical realization, the two-figure composition was created from a single, large block of Carrara marble. It is the only work Michelangelo ever signed and is one of the best-loved religious images of all time.

Altogether, the first few years of Michelangelo's artistic career were highly unconventional, but they provided an important foundation for the singular artist he became. Despite the success of the *Pietà* and evidence for an aborted painting commission for the church of Sant'Agostino, however, Michelangelo had few opportunities in Rome.

David *and other sculpture.* Michelangelo readily accepted a commission in 1501 from Cardinal Francesco Piccolomini to carve some marble statuettes needed for the Piccolomini Altar in Siena. He completed small figures of Saints Peter and Paul, but his interest in the commission waned that same year when he was offered a large and partly worked marble that had lain abandoned in the cathedral workshop for some forty years. From the narrow block he carved the *David* (Accademia, Florence). In this figure Michelangelo successfully combined classical and Christian traditions, conceiving the youthful biblical hero on the scale of an ancient nude colossus and endowing him with immanent physical movement and intense mental alertness. With the twin successes of the *Pietà* in Rome and the *David* in Florence, Michelangelo firmly established his public reputation, and he would never again lack for commissions.

Between 1501 and 1508 Michelangelo sustained an astonishing level of productivity, which included the *David,* the Bruges *Madonna* (Notre-Dame, Bruges), the *St. Matthew* (Accademia, Florence), marble tondi (sculptured medallions) for the Taddei and Pitti families (Royal Academy, London; Bargello, Florence), a painted tondo for Angelo Doni (Uffizi, Florence), a bronze *David* sent to France (lost), a monumental bronze statue of Pope Julius II for Bologna (destroyed), and a commission for a giant fresco, *Battle of Cascina* (never completed). The number, stature, and international character of Michelangelo's patrons during these years are equally impressive. They included a cardinal and a pope; Piero Soderini, the head of the Florentine government; four prominent Florentine families; the Florentine Cathedral Board of Works (*Opera del Duomo*); a company of rich Flemish merchants; and the French minister of finance. The first years of the sixteenth century—a period sometimes called the High Renaissance—were characterized by prodigious production for an extremely diverse, international clientele. Yet Michelangelo's simultaneous commitment to an impossible number of commissions inevitably meant that many were destined to remain incomplete. Nonetheless, Michelangelo's activities during the years prior to the commission for the Sistine Chapel ceiling placed Michelangelo firmly on a world stage.

Julius II. In 1505, at the recommendation of his friend and colleague, Giuliano da Sangallo, Michelangelo was called to Rome to work for Pope Julius II. Together, the ambitious pope and equally ambitious artist conceived a giant tomb that would rival those of the Roman emperors. And so began the long, convoluted history of a project that Condivi aptly called "the tragedy of the tomb." At least six designs, four contracts, and some forty years later, a much reduced but still grand monument was installed in San Pietro in Vincoli, the titular church of Pope Julius.

In characteristic fashion, Michelangelo began the tomb project in the marble quarries, supervising the selection and quarrying of the large quantity of material needed to construct the giant mausoleum. Returning to Rome eight months later, Michelangelo discovered that the pope's attention had turned elsewhere, mainly to war and the rebuilding of the venerated basilica of Saint Peter, then more than a thousand years old. Incensed that papal attention and resources had been deflected from the tomb project, Michelangelo left Rome for Florence despite the pope's intense displeasure and repeated efforts to lure him back. Not until Julius was on campaign in nearby Bologna was Michelangelo persuaded to appear before the pope and ask for forgiveness. Michelangelo then spent a taxing year in Bologna (1507–1508) casting a monumental seated bronze of Pope Julius, which, just three years later, was destroyed by an angry mob. Thus was erased a chapter in Michelangelo's career and his greatest achievement in the demanding medium of bronze.

Almost immediately after completing the statue in Bologna, Michelangelo was once again in Rome, and once again given a task ill-suited to a marble sculptor: the painting of the ceiling of the Sistine Chapel (1508–1512). As with many commissions that Michelangelo initially resisted, once he reconciled himself to the task, he devoted immense energy and creative powers to carrying it out in spectacular fashion. The ceiling—replete with narrative scenes from the book of Genesis, alternating male Prophets of the Bible and female Sibyls of classical antiquity, a series of nude youths (*ignudi*), lunettes with representations of the ancestors of Christ, and a host of secondary figures and decoration—is a transcendent work that never fails to instill wonder. In the words of Johann Wolfgang von Goethe, "Until you have seen the Sistine Chapel, you can have no adequate conception of what man is capable of accomplishing."

The ceiling was officially unveiled on 31 October 1512, shortly before the death of Pope Julius in February 1513. For a brief period Michelangelo turned once again to the pope's tomb (1513–1516). During these years he carved the *Moses* as well as the so-called *Rebellious Slave* and *Dying Slave* (Musée du Louvre, Paris).

Medici Patronage, 1516–1534. The newly elected pontiff, Giovanni de' Medici (Pope Leo X, 1513–1521), was Michelangelo's boyhood acquaintance from the Medici palace and the first Florentine ever elected pope. Although Leo's tastes ran to painting and precious objects, he commissioned Michelangelo to design a facade for the Medici church of San Lorenzo in Florence. With little previous training in architecture, Michelangelo set out to create a magnificent all-marble facade that he promised would be "the mirror of architecture and sculpture of all Italy." A large wooden model was constructed (Casa Buonarroti, Florence), and tons of marble were quarried and shipped to Florence. It was an ambitious undertaking that, although never realized, prepared the way for Michelangelo's subsequent architectural projects.

The exceptional cost of the facade may have contributed to its suspension in March 1520, but equally important was the pope's urgent desire to turn Michelangelo's attention to the construction and adornment of a Medici mausoleum at San Lorenzo. The untimely deaths of the two young scions of the family, Giuliano (1516) and Lorenzo (1519), served as the immediate impetus to build the Medici Chapel (1519–1534). Statues of Giuliano and Lorenzo now grace the chapel's interior along with the *Medici Madonna* and the famous allegories of *Night, Day, Dawn,* and *Dusk.*

In the midst of this project Giulio de' Medici was elected Pope Clement VII (1523–1534). Clement was another boyhood acquaintance of the artist and a highly astute patron. In addition to the chapel, Clement commissioned Michelangelo to build the Laurentian Library, a reliquary tribune balcony on the inside facade of San Lorenzo, and a number of other minor projects. From 1516 to 1534 Michelangelo devoted himself to the Medici commissions at San Lorenzo. In hiring and supervising the work of more than three hundred individuals, Michelangelo demonstrated that he could be an effective business manager as well as a versatile and immensely inventive artist. During these same years he carved the *Risen Christ* (Santa Maria sopra Minerva, Rome) and the highly enigmatic *Victory* (Palazzo della Signoria, Florence).

Michelangelo. *Crucifixion of St. Peter.* Pauline Chapel, Vatican. 1542–1549. ALINARI/ART RESOURCE

The Sack of Rome in May 1527 and the subsequent expulsion of the Medici from Florence resulted in a curtailment of work at San Lorenzo. Michelangelo, a lifelong republican but also a Medici client, found himself in an extremely awkward situation. Despite Pope Clement's efforts to dissuade him, Michelangelo elected to side with his native city against the combined forces of the pope and the Holy Roman Emperor, Charles V. During the next three years Michelangelo devoted himself to the design and construction of temporary fortifications for Florence, a painting of *Leda* for Duke Alfonso I d'Este of Ferrara (lost), and a never realized statue of *Hercules and Cacus* that was intended as a pendant to his *David*.

In 1530 the Medici were restored to power in Florence and Clement magnanimously forgave Michelangelo his defection. The artist turned once again to his Medici projects, albeit somewhat less enthusias-

tically. More work was relegated to assistants and the artist spent more and more time in Rome. Between 1530 and his definitive move to Rome, Michelangelo carved the smallish figure of *David/Apollo* for Baccio Valori (Bargello, Florence), and he made a number of highly finished presentation drawings for his new friend, Tommaso de' Cavalieri. Increasingly disaffected with Florence, where the last vestige of liberty was erased when Alessandro de' Medici abolished the republican constitution in 1532, Michelangelo finally settled in Rome in 1534, where he spent the remaining thirty years of his life. In 1534 the energetic and reform-minded Alessandro Farnese was elected Pope Paul III (1534–1549).

Painting and Architecture in Rome.
Probably the greatest and most discerning of Michelangelo's many patrons, Paul lost no time in employing the artist's talents, first in the painting of the

Last Judgment (1534–1541) in the Sistine Chapel. Thus, some twenty-five years after completing the ceiling decoration, Michelangelo painted an eschatological vision of the Second Coming for the altar wall of the same chapel.

Shortly after completing the *Last Judgment,* Michelangelo painted two large frescoes, the *Conversion of Saul* and the *Crucifixion of Peter,* for the Pauline Chapel (1542–1550). Far less accessible and familiar than the frescoes of the Sistine Chapel, those in the nearby Pauline Chapel are sometimes considered exemplars of the artist's old age or "mannerist" style. They are, in any case, profound meditations on matters of faith by the aged and deeply religious artist, painted for an equally sensitive patron.

Paul III also patronized Michelangelo as an architect, appointing him in 1546 to direct the construction of Saint Peter's and the Farnese Palace. Saint Peter's was Michelangelo's torment and final triumph: it is the largest church in Christendom, an imposing manifestation of papal authority, and a crowning achievement of Renaissance architecture. Despite numerous changes inflicted on the building during its approximately 150-year construction history, we properly think of the church as largely Michelangelo's creation. In less than twenty years he corrected what had gone before and largely shaped what came afterward. Michelangelo devoted his final years to the project, despite intrigue, construction debacles, and the repeated efforts of Duke Cosimo I de' Medici to persuade him to return to his native Florence.

Also during the pontificate of Paul III, Michelangelo undertook in 1538 to redesign and refurbish Rome's Capitoline Hill (Campidoglio), the geographical and ceremonial center of ancient Rome. As with many of Michelangelo's architectural commissions, most of the Capitoline project was realized after the artist's death, but the force and clarity of his design ensured that the final result largely reflected his intentions.

With each successive pope Michelangelo was confirmed in his position as supreme architect of Saint Peter's, all the while taking on additional responsibilities from the popes and select patrons. During the reign of Pius IV (1559–1565), Michelangelo designed the Porta Pia, transformed the Baths of Diocletian into the Christian church of Santa Maria degli Angeli, and designed the Sforza Chapel in Santa Maria Maggiore. Thus did Michelangelo become an urban planner as well as an architect, helping to transform the face of Rome in ways that may be labeled proto-baroque.

Personal sphere. While working as an architect in the public sphere, Michelangelo also plumbed the depths of his personal faith in poetry, drawings, and a few sculptures. For an artist who early in his career proudly signed himself "Michelangelo scultore," in the last thirty years of his life he completed just three sculptures: the *Rachel* and *Leah* for the tomb of Julius II, and the *Bust of Brutus* carved for Cardinal Nicolò Ridolfi (Bargello, Florence). The *Florentine Pietà* (Museo dell'Opera del Duomo, Florence) was destined for the artist's own grave but was given away broken and unfinished, and the *Rondanini Pietà* (Castello Sforzesco, Milan) was worked so obsessively that it probably never could be brought to satisfactory completion. As the artist grew older, drawing and poetry became increasingly important vehicles of creative expression. His late religious drawings, especially the series of haunting and intensely worked Crucifixion sheets, are the visual equivalent to his deeply felt penitential poetry.

During his lifetime Michelangelo had a large circle of friends and acquaintances. Indeed Michelangelo's extensive correspondence (nearly 1,400 letters to and from the artist) offers a cross section of Renaissance society in the first half of the sixteenth century. Acutely conscious of his claim to nobility, the artist was particularly attracted to persons of high social station as well as to persons of intellect and fine sensibility. His friendship with the young Roman nobleman Tommaso de' Cavalieri inspired an outpouring of intense love poetry and some of the most remarkable drawings of all time. These highly finished presentation drawings, most notably *Ganymede, Tityus,* and *Fall of Phaeton,* attained instant fame thanks to their circulation among appreciative cognoscenti and their frequent reproduction in a variety of media. Michelangelo's friendship with Cavalieri continued to the artist's death, even if somewhat diminished from its initial passionate intensity. Two other friends, Donato Giannotti and Luigi del Riccio, encouraged Michelangelo to publish his poetry, a project that was suspended with del Riccio's untimely death in 1546.

Michelangelo found sustained spiritual nourishment from a long friendship with Vittoria Colonna, the scion of an old Roman family and an accomplished poetess whom he met while he was painting the *Last Judgment.* Vittoria Colonna served as something of a spiritual guide and refuge during the tumultuous early years of the Counter-Reformation. Through Colonna, Michelangelo was exposed to the leading reform thinkers of his day, including Juan

Michelangelo. *Creation of Adam.* Central panel of the Sistine Chapel ceiling before the restoration of 1982–1985. [For the complete ceiling, see the color plates in this volume.] SISTINE CHAPEL, VATICAN PALACE/ALINARI/ART RESOURCE

Valdés, Bernardino Ochino, and Cardinal Reginald Pole.

Living nearly twice the average Renaissance life span, Michelangelo outlived his entire family and many of his friends. He died just two weeks shy of his eighty-ninth birthday. He was given a magnificent funeral and was buried in Santa Croce, Florence. That same year Galileo and William Shakespeare were born.

Character and Reputation.   Although it is a cherished myth, Michelangelo hardly ever lived or worked alone. For most of his long life he resided with one or more male assistants, a male servant, and one or more female housekeepers. He never married, but this was not uncommon among Renaissance artists. Instead he formed lasting attachments with a few friends and was loyally committed to his immediate and extended family. He was pleased when his favorite brother Buonarroto married the sister of the famous writer Giovanni della Casa. In addition, his nephew and niece also wedded Florentine aristocracy by marrying into the Ridolfi and Guicciardini families, respectively. Thus was fulfilled Michelangelo's ardent wish to perpetuate the Buonarroti line, which survived to the mid-nineteenth century. Acutely conscious of his family's social station, he was ashamed that he had a brother "who trudges after oxen." He was particularly sensitive about being treated like an artisan, insisting "I was

never a painter or sculptor like those who run workshops." He began insisting in his later years on using his family surname.

In his old age Michelangelo suffered from excruciatingly painful kidney stones, and he worried incessantly about his nephew's marriage, property investments, and general comportment. He was suspicious, kept his money hidden in socks, and died a wealthy man, though he scarcely lived like one. At the same time he was eminently human, capable of extreme grief at his servant's death, and generous in providing financial security for the widow and her children. He took pleasure in the occasional company and conversation of friends, and he had an acerbic wit.

Michelangelo's legacy is more than the sum of his many works. From a highly successful marble sculptor, Michelangelo became an artistic impresario, transforming himself into an aristocrat of art whose humble origins as a stone-carver are obscured by myth and his greatest accomplishments. Throughout his career Michelangelo was remarkably adept in maintaining the life of a sort of artist-courtier, in which mutually beneficial and reciprocal relations blurred the distinction between patronage and friendship, between professional and personal ties. More than any of his contemporaries, he contributed to the elevation of the artist, from craftsman to genius, from artisan to gentleman. Fully conscious of his hero's place in history, Giorgio Vasari wrote to Duke Cosimo in 1560: "the ancients are surpassed by the beauty and grace of what his divine genius has been able to achieve." In the Renaissance there could be no higher praise than to have surpassed antiquity.

Few artists have achieved as much in such diverse fields of endeavor; few so completely embody the notion of artistic creativity. Although the term is currently unfashionable, Michelangelo exemplifies genius. The life of such an individual is prey to the embellishments of myth, as was particularly the case in the nineteenth and early twentieth centuries. Romantic interpretations of his art and life abound, and he continues to be a figure of mythic proportions in our time. Both fact and fiction about Michelangelo are fascinating; often the truth is every bit as astonishing and illuminating as the embellishments of the romantic novelist.

[Michelangelo's *Last Judgment* is the frontispiece to this volume; his Sistine Chapel Ceiling and *Holy Family* (Doni Tondo) appear in the color plates in this volume. His *David* and the reading room of the Laurentian Library in Florence, which he designed, appear in the color plates in volume 3.]

BIBLIOGRAPHY

Primary Works

Buonarroti, Michelangelo. *Il Carteggio di Michelangelo.* Edited by Giovanni Poggi, Paola Barocchi, and Renzo Ristori. 5 vols. Florence, 1965–1983. Critical edition of all letters to and from Michelangelo. Michelangelo's letters have been translated in *Letters of Michelangelo.* Edited by E. H. Ramsden. 2 vols. London, 1963.

Buonarroti, Michelangelo. *Corpus dei disegni di Michelangelo.* Edited by Charles de Tolnay. 4 vols. Novara, Italy, 1975–1980. A complete catalog of the artist's drawings, reproduced in color and full size, both recto and verso.

Secondary Works

Ackerman, James S. *The Architecture of Michelangelo.* 2 vols. London, 1961. Classic overview and catalog of Michelangelo's architecture.

Argan, Giulio Carlo, and Bruno Contardi. *Michelangelo Architect* Translated by Marion L. Grayson. New York, 1993. Lavish monograph on the artist's architecture.

Barolsky, Paul. *Michelangelo's Nose: A Myth and Its Maker.* University Park, Pa., and London, 1990. Innovative examination of myth and artistic identity.

Condivi, Ascanio. *The Life of Michelangelo.* Translated by Alice S. Wohl, edited by Hellmut Wohl. Baton Rouge, La., 1976. An important contemporary biography of Michelangelo.

Einem, Herbert von. *Michelangelo.* Translated by Ronald Taylor. Rev. ed. London, 1973. Excellent general study.

Hibbard, Howard. *Michelangelo.* New York and London, 1974. An accessible and readable one-volume introduction to the artist.

Hirst, Michael. *Michelangelo and His Drawings.* New Haven, Conn., and London, 1988. A handy introduction to the artist's drawings.

Liebert, Robert S. *Michelangelo: A Psychoanalytic Study of His Life and Images.* New Haven, Conn., and London, 1983. The artist and his creations from a psychoanalytic perspective.

Pope-Hennessy, John. *Italian High Renaissance and Baroque Sculpture.* London, 1963. Best introduction in English to the sculpture of Michelangelo and his contemporaries.

The Sistine Chapel: Michelangelo Rediscovered. Edited by André Chastel. London, 1986. The first of many books published in conjunction with the restoration of the Sistine Chapel, including *The Sistine Chapel: A Glorious Restoration.* Edited by Pierluigi de Vecchi. New York, 1994; and *Michelangelo, the Last Judgment: A Glorious Restoration.* Translated by Lawrence Jenkins. New York, 1997.

Summers, David. *Michelangelo and the Language of Art.* Princeton, N.J., 1981. Renaissance artistic theory as revealed in the language used by Michelangelo and his contemporaries.

Symonds, John Addington. *The Life of Michelangelo Buonarroti.* 2 vols. London, 1893. The classic biography.

Tolnay, Charles de. *Michelangelo.* 5 vols. Princeton, N.J., 1969–1971. A comprehensive examination of the artist and his work.

Vasari, Giorgio. *Lives of the Artists.* Translated by George Bull. Harmondsworth, U.K., and Baltimore, 1965. An important contemporary biography.

Wallace, William E. *Michelangelo at San Lorenzo: The Genius as Entrepreneur.* Cambridge, U.K., and New York, 1994. A documentary study of Michelangelo's Medici commissions at San Lorenzo.

Wallace, William E., ed. *Michelangelo: Selected Scholarship in English.* 5 vols. New York, 1995. A collection of more than one hundred articles in English on all aspects of Michelangelo's art and life.

WILLIAM E. WALLACE

Michelangelo the Poet

Although better known as a visual artist, Michelangelo composed more than three hundred sonnets, madrigals, and other poetic verses. Despite his self-deprecating humor, Michelangelo took this avocation seriously, consulting literary advisers and revising extensively. A project to publish a third of his output was canceled by his editor's death, but the verses circulated privately and were highly regarded. Prominent composers set a few to music, and the Florentine humanist Benedetto Varchi delivered two lectures in 1547 quoting several poems as praiseworthy examples of Varchi's theories. As part of the earliest extended corpus of autobiographical writings by an artist, Michelangelo's verse commentary on personal and aesthetic matters has long provided a fruitful mine for students of art history and theory, history and philosophy, and psychology and gender.

Themes and Content. The poems are inspired by his own experience, sometimes work and politics but most often love, the animating force of

Michelangelo's life and art. He seldom strayed far from his central concern, the conflict of desire and spirit—the poignant tension between ephemeral earthly beauty and the passing time that brings death and judgment. Both a passionate pagan and a passionate Christian, he found temporary release from this dilemma in the Neoplatonic philosophy current in the Florence of his apprenticeship, where he enjoyed the support of the city's first citizen and accomplished poet, Lorenzo de' Medici, patron of the philosopher Marsilio Ficino and the poet Angelo Poliziano, who trained the young prodigy in classical mythology.

Many early poems are student exercises in courtly love, addressed to probably imaginary women with formulaic ardor or, occasionally, whimsical humor ("You have a face sweeter than boiled grape juice," no. 20). His humor turned darker when treating the tribulations of real life: wry complaints at the discomfort of painting the Sistine Chapel ceiling (no. 5), satirical invectives against clerical abuses in Rome (no. 10), and macabre details about the infirmities of age (no. 267). A cluster of poems discuss art theory in Neoplatonic terms, exalting the ideal *concetto,* or mental image, that preexists its less perfect physical realization (no. 151). He viewed poetry and visual art, both products of the creative intellect, as interchangeable: fifty epitaphs for the nephew of his editor Luigi del Riccio substituted for a tomb portrait that the overworked artist delegated to an assistant.

The bulk of his mature work is love poetry inspired by his two most profound personal relationships, with Vittoria Colonna and Tommaso de' Cavalieri. The pious noblewoman Colonna, who published religious verse, served as friend, muse, and colleague; Michelangelo celebrates her inspirational yet distant beauty in terms familiar from Dante's Beatrice or Petrarch's Laura. His enraptured evocations of the beloved's uplifting effect on him invoke the ideal of anagogy, in which "a pure desire / for something beautiful / can bear us from earth to God" (no. 117). Some fifty poems to Cavalieri, a handsome young aristocrat, constitute the first large body of homoerotic poetry in a modern Western language, its mood swinging from ecstatic delight to frustrated rejection to guilt. In old age, he turned to contemplating ebbing desire and looming eternity; though he sometimes railed against the inevitable ("Bring back to me the time," no. 272), he increasingly welcomed with relief the freedom to prepare for Christian salvation. In no. 285, written when he was nearing eighty, he vowed to abandon all earthly distractions, including art itself: "Neither painting nor sculpture will be able any longer / to calm my soul, now turned toward that divine love / that opened his arms on the cross to take us in."

Style and Form. Michelangelo's literary talent was genuine but modest. He worked hard to develop it, both because poetry afforded him an essential outlet for his often tortured emotional life and because artists were expected to prove their eligibility for the liberal arts by their ability to express themselves in writing. Although he based his poetry on the established lyric tradition of Dante and Petrarch, large sections of which he knew by heart, his results were uneven. At their best, his verses display the virtues of their author, a moving combination of blunt artisan and heartfelt intellect; but they often overreach into obscurity or give up in incompletion. His interest was above all in self-expression, and contemporaries like fellow poet Francesco Berni admired him for ideas rather than elegance.

His plainspoken vocabulary and wrenching confessionalism, deviations from prevailing standards of decorum, are decried by some critics but acclaimed by the twentieth-century poet Eugenio Montale among others as a deliberately "rocky" escape from the stylistic straitjacket of polished but impersonal classicism exemplified by the Venetian author Pietro Bembo. His unresolved poems are like the sculptures he abandoned still unfinished, one of many striking parallels between Michelangelo's literary and visual forms: in both media, he pioneered the shift from Apollonian high Renaissance canons toward a more dynamic and open-ended mannerist aesthetic, perhaps even paving the way for the Dionysian theatricality of the baroque.

One significant innovation, mirroring his unorthodox subject matter, was a deliberate fluidity of gender. Seeking suitable language for his novel desires, friendships, and self-image, he sometimes addresses the same verse simultaneously to a woman and a man; calls Colonna "a man within a woman"; imagines his own creative androgyny in such feminine terms as a bride; and turns Petrarch's courtly love for a woman, ever unconsummated, into an acceptable trope for chaste homosexual yearning. This novelty was long obscured by Michelangelo's grandnephew, who printed a bowdlerized first edition of the poems in 1623. Publication of the autographs in the 1860s stimulated critics to a broader view: Walter Pater, in his essay on Michelangelo's poetry (1871), dramatized the artist's fateful choice between "two great traditional types" of culture and deemed him "the disciple not so much of Dante as of the Platonists."

In fact Michelangelo followed both, but it was his pursuit of platonic love that led to his latter-day canonization as the patron saint of homosexual self-expression.

See also Italian Literature and Language; Plato, Platonism, and Neoplatonism.

BIBLIOGRAPHY

Primary Works

Alexander, Sidney. *The Complete Poetry of Michelangelo.* Athens, Ohio, 1991. English translation with brief notes and commentary.

Saslow, James M. *The Poetry of Michelangelo: An Annotated Translation.* New Haven, Conn., and London, 1991. Bilingual edition with extensive commentary. The Italian is based on the standard edition by Enzo Noè Girardi, *Michelangelo Buonarroti: Rime.* Bari, Italy, 1960.

Secondary Works

Cambon, Glauco. *Michelangelo's Poetry: Fury of Form.* Princeton, N.J., 1985. Examines literary style and the sophisticated effort of composition.

Clements, Robert. *The Poetry of Michelangelo.* New York, 1965. Still the comprehensive critical study of themes, language, and biographical relevance.

Ryan, Christopher. *The Poetry of Michelangelo: An Introduction.* Madison, N.J., 1998. A more concise and chronological treatment of themes and imagery than Clements.

Saslow, James M. "Michelangelo: Sculpture, Sex, and Gender." In *Looking at Italian Renaissance Sculpture.* Edited by Sarah Blake McHam. Cambridge, U.K., and New York, 1998. Pages 223–245.

JAMES M. SASLOW

MICHELET, JULES. *See* **Renaissance, Interpretations of the,** *subentry on* **Jules Michelet.**

MIDDLE AGES. Like the names of all historical periods, the idea of a distinct or "middle" epoch between antiquity and modernity has assumed a false reality. Georg Horn first applied the Latin term *medium aevum* (middle age—in the singular) in 1666 to the history of the church. In 1688 Christoph Cellarius extended the idea to secular history. Yet whatever convenience a name for the millennium between 410 and 1453 may provide, two major faults result: (1) it exaggerates contrasts between the Middle Ages and the surrounding eras, and (2) it conceals important distinctions within the period itself. A partial solution divides the period into "early" (c. 400–c. 950), "central" or "high" (c. 950–c. 1300), and "late" (c. 1300–c. 1500) phases. Nonetheless, the idea of an unambiguous "Middle Age" distorts more truth than it conveys.

Antiquity versus the Middle Ages. Contrasts between classical antiquity and the subsequent age began very early. Tertullian (d. c. 225) pejoratively used the term *romanitas* (Romanness) to distinguish Roman ways from Christian. Once the emperor Constantine the Great began to favor Christianity after 312, and Theodosius I prohibited all worship but Christian in 392, Roman order (or the idea of it) and a professed Christianity combined partially and confusedly for centuries. St. Jerome (c. 347–419/420) provides one example of this difficulty. Although his translations from Hebrew and Greek became the Vulgate Bible, he dreaded being accused of preferring Cicero's Latin to scripture. Yet even before Alaric's Visigoths sacked Rome in 410, Jerome looked to the Roman Empire for defense against "ferocious" tribes. For Jerome, Roman order was a fading ideal but an ideal nonetheless.

The Renaissance versus the Middle Ages. The Renaissance thirst for the Roman ideal was less ambivalent than Jerome's, but its institutional base was more securely Christian. In one of the first signs of Renaissance self-portrayal, Petrarch (1304–1374) imagined himself looking back across barren centuries to a distant and superior antiquity. He confided in a "letter" to the first-century Roman historian Livy how he cultivated classical studies to escape from the "present evils" and "thievish company" of his own day. He yearned to mix with ancient greats such as Regulus, Brutus, Scipio, Cato (and Nero!). He confided his *Book of Secrets* to St. Augustine (354–430). Giovanni Boccaccio (1313–1375), in his *Life of Dante,* credited the poet (1265–1321) with enticing the muses back to Italy. Boccaccio also hailed the painter Giotto (1267/1277–1337) for recovering the visual arts from centuries of error. Petrarch's call to Cicero's ideal of "a more polished humanity" drove a cohort of humanists around 1400 to emulate ancient literary and artistic models.

Giorgio Vasari incorporated this view of the Middle Ages in his *Lives of the Artists* (1550, revised 1568), where he perceives three stages in the history of art: perfection (in antiquity), decadance (after Constantine), and restoration (after Giotto). Beyond the physical ruin occasioned by the "Goths and other barbarous and foreign peoples," and the consequent scattering of craftsmen, Christian opposition to pagan gods devalued the art that celebrated them, leaving it "rude," "vile," even "monstrous." Then, in Florence, a new light appeared, in the person of Giotto, who began the return to ancient skills. Gradually, as they had in antiquity, the arts, like living beings, revived to progress through childhood, youthful, and mature phases. Michelangelo (1475–1564) consummated this development, surpassing not only his own generation and nature, but also the artists of antiquity.

The standards of ancient Rome also inspired the philosophes of Enlightenment Europe, whose disparagement of religion entailed scorn for the Middle Ages. In his *Decline and Fall of the Roman Empire* (1776–1788), Edward Gibbon declared the period from the reign of the emperor Nerva to that of Marcus Aurelius (96–180) the happiest of history. For him Christianity brought only a decline into ignorance, superstition, and a princely-clerical alliance that joined military might to spiritual terrors. Gibbon annihilated the Middle Ages by having antiquity agonize until 1453, when the Ottoman Turks conquered Constantinople. In 1860 Jakob Burckhardt sharply separated the Renaissance from the Middle Ages. For Burckhardt, the achievements of Renaissance Italy rent a veil of faith and illusion.

Scholarship since Burckhardt has rejected the idea of a homogeneous medieval period or "Dark Age," but polemicists still use "medieval" to evoke cruelty and credulity. This denigration stems largely from attacks on Catholicism and the regret some feel not so much for its prominence in the Middle Ages as for its tenacity. Conversely, however, some supporters of Catholicism, or of Christianity in general, have exaggerated the uniformity and extent of these beliefs. This trend has produced the cliché of an Age of Faith or the Greatest of Centuries. Modern scholars distinguish varieties of religious expression and behavior among different medieval populations.

Medieval Self-Awareness. The self-congratulatory comparisons fostered by Petrarch and his followers presuppose a uniform and bleak Middle Ages. But medieval leaders had themselves identified distinct stages in their own history. The idea of reconnecting with Roman greatness was common. Byzantine emperors from the fourth century declared themselves rulers of a "Second Rome." Mid-eighth-century clerics around the pope appropriated Roman authority when they forged a "Donation of Constantine," ostensibly bestowing the Roman Empire's western half on the pope and his successors. In 800 Pope Leo III (and possibly Charlemagne's advisers) orchestrated a coronation ceremony that acclaimed the Frankish conqueror as "Augustus" and "emperor." This "New Constantine" proclaimed a "restoration of the Roman Empire." After Byzantine church leaders accepted rapproche-

ment with the Roman church in 1439, at the Council of Ferrara-Florence, Tsar Basil II declared Moscow the "Third Rome."

Revivals occurred in religion, too. Clergymen, especially members of religious orders such as the Premonstratensians and canons regular in the twelfth century and the Dominicans and Augustinian Hermits in the thirteenth, each adopted a monastic rule attributed to Augustine of Hippo, thus building a fresh start on ancient origins. Other reforms sought a return to the primitive church or apostolic life, while yet others looked ahead to a purging, apocalyptic cataclysm, or, like Joachim of Fiore (c. 1135–1202), to a dawning Age of the Spirit. Some twelfth-century scholars claimed that they, as Christians, could see farther than the ancients—but, they modestly added, only in the manner of dwarfs standing on the shoulders of giants.

Renaissance Appreciation of the Middle Ages. Despite the scorn proclaimed by many from Petrarch on, the Middle Ages offered much of interest to Renaissance thinkers. In his *History of Florence,* Leonardo Bruni (1370–1444) treated impartially the interval from Rome to his own day. Flavio Biondo (1392–1463) matched a history of Rome's "triumph" with another (1438–1453) on its decline, devoted to the intervening millennium. Niccolò Machiavelli's *History of Florence* (1525) analyzed thirteenth-century politics dispassionately; he blamed the city's expulsion of the nobility for much of the republic's subsequent weakness. In sixteenth-century France the jurist Jacques Cujas commented on the *Libri feudorum,* a twelfth-century compilation of legal texts. This interest in things medieval, treated with the new critical perspective of the Renaissance, often had political overtones. Lorenzo Valla's unmasking of Constantine's "Donation" is a prime example. In his *Francogallia* (1573), which reviewed early medieval custom, François Hotman argued that the assembly of the nation had limited French kings from the very beginning.

In the realm of epic poetry, Matteo Boiardo (*Orlando innamorato,* 1487) and Ludovico Ariosto (*Orlando furioso,* 1516, 1521, and 1532) developed the Old French *Song of Roland,* turning Charlemagne and the peers of France into Renaissance literary figures. Developing a plot line from the late twelfth-century Saxo Grammaticus, Shakespeare updated *Hamlet.* Catholic religious studying the history of their faith saw no need to break with the Middle Ages—except to apply Renaissance scholarly techniques of critical analysis. The Jesuits Heribert Rosweyde (d. 1629) and Jean de Bolland (d. 1665) began the systematic and critical analysis of saints' lives in what was to become the *Acta sanctorum,* an enterprise continuing to this day.

Unlike the negative view of medieval law, which began to give ground in the sixteenth century, Vasari's model for the visual arts endured until the eighteenth century. In the influential essay "Of German Architecture" (1772), Goethe likened the formal articulation of the cathedral of Strasbourg to a tree, an affinity he regarded as particularly German. He contrasted this natural impulse to the frivolity of the French, who at the Church of the Madeleine in Paris were still imitating Greek columns! Romanticism and nationalism, therefore, joined to encourage a reevaluation of each European country's medieval past. The French architect Eugène-Emmanuel Viollet-Le-Duc (1814–1879) supervised the restoration of medieval French monuments as the English artist William Morris (1834–1896) unfavorably compared English industrial production to medieval craftsmanship. In music and literature, Richard Wagner, Victor Hugo, and Sir Walter Scott represent parallel inspirations. In scholarship, too, the states of Europe set up institutions to publish medieval records via the Rolls Series in England, Germany's Monumenta Germaniae Historica, and others. Late Roman (as distinct from classical art) and Romanesque art came into their own much later, after Alois Riegl (1901) and Henri Focillon (1934, 1938) devised methods for giving each age its due. Iconographers such as Anna Jameson (1794–1860) and Émile Mâle helped overcome one obstacle to appreciating medieval art by explaining narrative cycles and complex series of symbols.

"The Revolt of the Medievalists." Disparagement of the medieval period led some modern scholars to question its homogeneity and to characterize its high points as "renaissances" in their own right. In 1839, only six years after Jules Michelet first called the French fifteenth and sixteenth centuries a renaissance (in *Histoire de la France,* 1833–1867), Jean-Jacques Ampère applied the term "renaissance" to Charlemagne's reforms improving grammatical texts, liturgical books, clerical discipline, and the mechanisms of his government (*Histoire littéraire de la France avant le douzième siècle*). Ampère also awarded a renaissance to the Ottonians, who ruled Germany from 962 to 1002. Charles Homer Haskins termed "revivals" the efforts of medieval scholars in Latin classics, jurisprudence, science, and philosophy, and, following a suggestion of Dana C. Munro

(1906), called them *The Renaissance of the Twelfth Century* (1927). A 1984 publication edited by Warren Treadgold collected articles on six "renaissances," from the fourth to the fifteenth century, excluding the one to which this Encyclopedia is devoted. Giles Constable has uncovered a reformation in the twelfth century. The Middle Ages, then, was replete with reforms, renewals, and renaissances.

Not only did the "middle" centuries reach outstanding peaks of creativity, some of their ideas and institutions led directly into aspects of life later considered essential to the Renaissance. Paul Oskar Kristeller traced the origins of Italian humanism back into medieval rhetoric. For Walter Ullmann, the medieval revival of Roman law secularized society and produced Renaissance humanism. Lynn Thorndike connected medieval experimentation with magic to Renaissance science. Thomas Tentler linked the casuistry of sixteenth-century Europe to the penitential literature consequent upon the Fourth Lateran Council (1215).

Gradually, therefore, the Middle Ages have come to appear longer, especially outside of Italy. Examining art and religious symbolism, Johan Huizinga showed continuity with medieval forms of courtliness and artistic expression in fifteenth-century Netherlands. Focusing more on theology, Heiko Oberman blended late medieval Catholic with early Protestant questioning. Eamon Duffy traced into sixteenth-century England many of those characteristics of medieval religion that first attracted scorn. He argues, however, that they were not supplanted by reason, but forcibly uprooted through political pressure.

Other scholars have gone farther. Joseph Strayer, R. I. Moore, Colin Morris, and Marcia Colish have claimed for the Middle Ages the "foundations" of modern institutions and mental outlooks as diverse as the state (from feudalism), dissent (from popular heresy, especially Catharism), individualism (from aspects of religion and "courtly love"), and the "Western intellectual tradition." These views posit a medieval origin for these phenomena and a modified but unbroken development into the present.

Working on the earlier boundary, other historians have extended antiquity and postponed (but not, like Gibbon, obliterated) the Middle Ages. Henri Pirenne charted the ancient Mediterranean economy until the Muslim conquests of the seventh century. Peter Brown called "late antiquity" the blend of ancient institutions and sensibilities variously discernible in the European West, North Africa, Byzantium, and early Muslim culture. What these works show is how much depends on the centuries, regions, and cultural phenomena one chooses to emphasize. As the focus shifts, so does certitude about historical periodization.

Modern Definitions. After World War II, and particularly after 1968, investigators broadened the range of historical inquiry. Inspired by the French journal *Annales,* and by the methods of anthropology, they sought the underlying durable or structural elements in society, which change very slowly. They also examined a different, marginalized population: women, ethnic minorities, religious and sexual nonconformists, people regarded in their own day as deviant. These scholars believe that this marginalization marks the past and affects the present. Thus researchers in women's and social history like Suzanne Wemple and JoAnne McNamara identified a break in the history of kinship before which women benefited more under the extended family than later, after primogeniture increasingly dominated.

The efforts of Georges Duby, Thomas Head, Richard Landes, and others to see the connection of politics and religion at the affective and behavioral levels, as opposed to the doctrinal and ideological levels, uncovered a new synthesis that blends the Peace of God movement of the late tenth century with the establishment of monarchies and regional dynasties. These political powers were far better able than local lords to oppress "deviants" and "others" such as women, heretics, Jews, and homosexuals, as John Boswell and R. I. Moore have shown. Scholars such as Caroline Bynum learned how to elicit testimony from, and assess the social agency of, such marginalized figures. Via the history of "mentalities," Jacques Le Goff and Aron Gurevich have integrated some of the ideas scorned by Renaissance critics into a more complex fabric, suggesting new relationships between societies and the ideas they profess.

Further breaking down the supposed uniformity of the Middle Ages, many local histories find great regional variations in practices like land tenure, inheritance, and military service. Pointing to these variations, Elizabeth A. R. Brown and Susan Reynolds rejected the term "feudalism" to describe all rural society or all government (whether at the local or the monarchical level) in the Middle Ages. They attributed the exaggeration of "feudalism" to those sixteenth-century lawyers, cited above, whose interest in the Middle Ages undercut Renaissance scorn for the earlier period. These analytical techniques produced a new, more nuanced understanding of the centuries between Jerome and Petrarch, a far more heterogeneous middle age than those who coined the phrase ever imagined.

See also **Renaissance**, *subentry on* **The Renaissance in Historical Thought**.

BIBLIOGRAPHY

Barraclough, Geoffrey G. "Medium Aevum: Some Reflections on Medieval History and on the Term 'the Middle Ages.' " In his *History in a Changing World.* Oxford, 1956. Pages 54–63.

Benson, Robert L., and Giles Constable, eds. *Renaissance and Renewal in the Twelfth Century.* Cambridge, Mass., 1982.

Boswell, John. *Christianity, Social Tolerance, and Homosexuality: Gay People in Western Europe from the Beginning of the Christian Era to the Fourteenth Century.* Chicago, 1980.

Brown, Elizabeth A. R. *Politics and Institutions in Capetian France.* Aldershot, U.K., and Brookfield, Vt., 1991.

Brown, Peter R. L. *The World of Late Antiquity.* New York, 1971.

Burckhardt, Jakob. *The Civilization of the Renaissance in Italy.* Edited by S. G. C. Middlemore. New York, 1929. First published as *Die Kultur der Renaissance in Italien,* 1860.

Bynum, Caroline Walker. *Holy Feast and Holy Fast: The Religious Significance of Food to Medieval Women.* Berkeley, Calif., 1987.

Colish, Marcia. *Medieval Foundations of the Western Intellectual Tradition, 400–1400.* New Haven, Conn., 1997.

Constable, Giles. *The Reformation of the Twelfth Century.* Cambridge, U.K., 1996.

Duffy, Eamon. *The Stripping of the Altars: Traditional Religion in England, c. 1400–c. 1580.* New Haven, Conn., 1992.

Ferguson, Wallace K. *The Renaissance in Historical Thought.* Boston, 1948.

Haskins, Charles Homer. *The Renaissance of the Twelfth Century.* Cambridge, Mass., 1927.

Huizinga, Johan. *The Autumn of the Middle Ages.* Translated by Rodney J. Payton and Ulrich Mammitzsch. Chicago, 1996. First published as *Herfsttij der Middeleeuwen,* 1919.

McNamara, JoAnn, and Suzanne Wemple. "Sanctity and Power: The Dual Pursuit of Medieval Women." In *Becoming Visible: Women in European History.* Edited by Renate Bridenthal and Claudia Koonz. Boston, 1977. Pages 90–118.

Moore, R. I. *The Formation of a Persecuting Society: Power and Deviance in Western Europe, 950–1250.* Oxford, 1990. First published in 1987.

Oberman, Heiko A. *The Harvest of Medieval Theology: Gabriel Biel and Late Medieval Nominalism.* Cambridge, Mass., 1962.

Pirenne, Henri. *Mohammed and Charlemagne.* Translated by Bernard Miall. London, 1939. First published, in French, in 1937.

Reynolds, Susan. *Fiefs and Vassals: The Medieval Evidence Reinterpreted.* Oxford and New York, 1994.

Treadgold, Warren, ed. *Renaissances before the Renaissance: Cultural Revivals of Late Antiquity and the Middle Ages.* Stanford, Calif., 1984.

Ullmann, Walter. *Medieval Foundations of Renaissance Humanism.* Ithaca, N.Y., 1977.

Van Engen, John. "The Christian Middle Ages as an Historiographical Problem." *American Historical Review* 91 (1986): 519–552.

ALAN E. BERNSTEIN

MIDDLETON, THOMAS. *See* **Drama, English,** *subentry on* **Jacobean Drama.**

MIDWIVES AND HEALERS. Throughout the Renaissance a wide variety of options were available to those in need of medical attention. In addition to the "learned medicine" of university-trained practitioners and the services of other licensed medical personnel were the ministrations of renegade physicians (for example, followers of Paracelsus), clergy, magicians and alchemists, religious healers, family members, and various types of "empirics": for example, local "wise women" or "cunning men," itinerant healers, and specialists in particular disorders or body parts. A further distinction can be made between those who casually dabbled in medical pursuits and individuals identified both by themselves and their communities as healers. Itinerant healers or "charlatans" performed "miraculous" cures in public squares and used showmanship to sell patent medicines. Specialists such as oculists, bonesetters, dentists, and midwives might draw clients through a reputation for success. Most villages had a "wise" man or woman believed to have a talent for magic or a divine gift for healing. However, healing could occur on a more occasional basis: local women (in particular, noblewomen or the wives of medical men), priests, students, and apothecaries were also frequently consulted for medical advice, which was often dispensed at no charge.

Transmission of Knowledge.

The secrets—whether patent medicines or special techniques—that were the stock in trade of itinerant healers and specialists were often closely guarded and transmitted orally or via some form of apprenticeship, in many cases passed down through families for generations. Informal or "folk" medical knowledge, both herbal and magical, also circulated in this manner. However, such knowledge also appears in written sources. There was often no clear demarcation between popular and learned medicine in matters of therapy—folk remedies and classical pharmacy were intermingled in learned medical texts. Furthermore, because folk wisdom was valorized by Paracelsists and by the authors of various "books of secrets," which proliferated in the sixteenth century, many traditional remedies made their way into print. With the appearance of vernacular medical treatises (such as midwifery texts directed at both lay readers and midwives), a substantial amount of medical information, both learned and popular, was available to anyone who could read.

Yet those who practiced medicine outside the sanction of the universities and the guilds were increasingly characterized as dangerous imposters and ignorant frauds throughout this period. Religious

Midwives Attend a Birth. Woodcut by Jost Amman, c. 1580. PHILADELPHIA MUSEUM OF ART, SMITHKLINE, BEECHAM CORPORATION FUND FOR THE ARS MEDICA COLLECTION

and secular authorities, in addition to the university-trained practitioners keen to eliminate their competitors in the medical marketplace, became ever more concerned with restricting the practice of nonaccredited or unlicensed practitioners. Despite these efforts, traditional healers remained the practitioner of choice for much of the population, many of whom would not be able to afford the services of a learned physician.

Women who engaged in medical activities were among the first to be singled out as "illegitimate" practitioners. Although midwives represent only one variety of female practitioner, their changing fortunes throughout the Renaissance provides a unique illustration of the complex negotiations between "official" and "unofficial" medicine in this era.

Midwives. Throughout the Renaissance midwifery was more often practiced as a skill than as a trade or profession. Although by the late Middle Ages women for whom midwifery constituted a social or occupational identity can be found in urban centers, midwifery was also practiced as a form of casual community service, particularly in more rural areas. The primary attendant at a birth might be an experienced and skilled midwife who had served an apprenticeship under a senior midwife; but she could also be a friend, neighbor, or family member with some experience in these matters. Given this diversity of practitioners, it is difficult to assess the methods and competence of Renaissance midwives. In addition, there is little textual evidence outside the predictably biased accounts of hostile physicians until midwives begin to publish their own works in the seventeenth and eighteenth centuries.

Licensing and regulation. National, regional, and local differences also make it difficult to describe a "typical" midwife, although certain common trends can be identified. Records indicate that on the Continent from the fourteenth century onward midwives were employed by some municipalities to ensure care for their female residents. Even in the absence of such official status, midwives often testified as expert witnesses in matters of rape, abortion, infanticide, and illegitimacy, and assessed the pregnancy claims of female prisoners standing trial.

The practice of licensing and regulating midwives first arose in the towns of southern Germany during the fifteenth century. Examinations were administered by a committee of physicians or women of high social standing as part of the licensing process. The growing web of regulations that circumscribed the activities of midwives in this period reflects a greater concern with the moral, rather than technical, qualifications of the midwife; these regulations often included directives intended to define the midwife's place in the medical hierarchy (for example, those banning midwives from prescribing drugs or performing surgery or requiring them to call for a learned physician in difficult cases). Interestingly, in England, where physicians became organized as a professional body much later, the licensing of midwives was left entirely to the bishops and appears cursory by comparison to the increasingly demanding requirements to which urban midwives on the Continent were subject.

Witchcraft. The onset of this regulatory movement at approximately the same time that prosecutions for witchcraft became more frequent has led a number of scholars to theorize a connection between the two phenomena. John Riddle has suggested that midwives came under suspicion because they possessed a dangerous knowledge associated with witches, specifically of herbal remedies that inhibited conception and induced abortion. The explicit condemnation of midwives in Renaissance treatises on witchcraft, such as the *Malleus maleficarum* (The hammer of witches; 1487), would appear to support such a thesis, but examinations of trial records have consistently shown that midwives appeared more often as expert witnesses than victims in witchcraft trials, and that "wise women" were more likely to be targeted for prosecution.

Thus it appears that although midwives were not widely prosecuted by witchcraft tribunals they did come under greater scrutiny by both religious and secular authorities during this period, with increasing restrictions placed on their activities. It is interesting to note that midwives were often vilified as agents of ignorance and superstition not only in the growing obstetrical literature of this period, but also in books debunking "popular errors" (indeed, Scipione Mercurio [1550–1595?] was the author of one of the most specific and detailed obstetric texts of the period as well as a work on "popular errors"). The gradual erosion of the midwives' authority and the growing involvement of male surgeons in obstetrics from the late sixteenth century onward set the stage for the eventual dominance of this field by male practitioners in the modern period.

See also **Birth and Infancy; Motherhood; Obstetrics and Gynecology; Pregnancy.**

BIBLIOGRAPHY

Green, Monica. "Women's Medical Practice and Health Care in Medieval Europe." *Signs: Journal of Women in Culture and Society* 14, no. 2 (1989): 434–473. Brilliant rebuttal of several longstanding assumptions about female practitioners, through the fifteenth century.

Lingo, Alison Klairmont. "Empirics and Charlatans in Early Modern France: The Genesis of the Classification of the 'Other' in Medical Practice." *Journal of Social History* 19 (1986): 583–603. Oft-cited, classic article.

Marland, Hilary, ed. *The Art of Midwifery: Early Modern Midwives in Europe.* London and New York, 1993. Collection of essays that examines midwifery practice in England, Germany, Holland, France, Italy, and Spain.

Perkins, Wendy. *Midwifery and Medicine in Early Modern France: Louise Bourgeois.* Exeter, U.K., 1996.

Riddle, John M. *Eve's Herbs: A History of Contraception and Abortion in the West.* Cambridge, Mass., and London, 1997. Intriguing, if ultimately unconvincing, thesis.

JEANETTE HERRLE-FANNING

MILAN. [This entry includes two subentries, one on the history of the city and territory of Milan in the Renaissance and the other on artists active in Milan and Lombardy.]

Milan in the Renaissance

Since the late Roman Empire, Milan has been one of Italy's largest and wealthiest cities. During the early

Renaissance the Milanese city-state became one of the five dominant powers in Italy, with an influential political, cultural, and economic presence throughout Europe. In the sixteenth century, however, Milan lost its political autonomy and influence, becoming just another element in the Habsburgs' global empire.

During the Middle Ages and early Renaissance, Milan was often at the leading edge of developments, first as a free commune resisting the power of its imperial overlord and later as a splendid princely state with a sophisticated administration. Renaissance Milan was a great commercial and industrial center and a pioneer in the development of both civil and military administrations. Culturally, Renaissance Milan boasted northern Italy's dominant princely court, blending Italian neoclassicism with the Gothic magnificence of late medieval northern Europe.

Society and Economy. Renaissance Milan and its dominion occupied a strategic position at the crossroads of major routes between the Italian peninsula and northern Europe. The dominion extended from what is now Italian Switzerland to the Apennine Mountains. The fertile Po Valley provided a stable and prosperous agricultural base, but it was the commercial activity of Milan and other cities that furnished the dominion with its greatest economic strength. Those cities were major centers of commercial activity. Milan itself was renowned particularly for luxury goods, especially cloths and clothing (silks, satins, velvets), as well as arms and armor. The other cities of the dominion, including Pavia, Milan's traditional rival, also had their specialties. However, none had the size or commercial scale of the capital, except perhaps Genoa, Italy's second largest port, which was ruled by Milan in the later fifteenth century. Merchants of the dominion had active and sophisticated trading relationships with most of the Western world and the eastern Mediterranean.

Every town and region within the Milanese state had a strong sense of local patriotism. In rural areas traditional feudal relationships dominated throughout the Renaissance. Great noble families, such as the Pallavicini, Rossi, and Malaspina, held sway over both the agricultural plains and the rugged mountain districts. In the urban areas medieval traditions of communal republicanism continued long after Milan became a princely state. One of the primary political concerns of the dominion's rulers was to overcome the divisive effects of local factional disputes and feuds.

In the dominion's cities the leaders of urban political factions were often the same nobles who dominated the surrounding countryside. In fifteenth-century Parma, for instance, the four factions were identified with the families of Pallavicini, Rossi, Sanvitale, and Da Correggio. Lombardy and adjacent regions never expelled their noble families from cities and replaced them with mercantile aristocracies. Nevertheless, Milanese rulers needed to deal with continuing tensions between the different elements of society, including influential professional groups such as lawyers and physicians. During the Renaissance those tensions rarely erupted into open conflict except during periods of contested princely succession. Milan's rulers valued and enforced order and security.

The Milanese dominion was relatively diverse and tolerant of foreigners. Traditional prerogatives and privileges were still under local control but were ultimately subject to princely approval. Those on whom the princes and their advisers relied were able to find places in Milanese society, but only the most favored recipients of princely support could take places of influence.

Women had little opportunity for full participation in Milanese public and commercial life. Traditional medieval limitations on women's roles in society were exacerbated in areas subject to Lombard law, which severely restricted women's ability to take most types of legal action in their own name. These limitations did not stop some women from managing family properties and businesses with great skill and effectiveness, but they did make it necessary to enlist at least nominal assistance from cooperative men.

Political Developments. The political aspirations of Renaissance Milan were rooted in the late Roman Empire, when the city was briefly the capital of the Western Empire (395–402). Later it was the capital of the Lombards' kingdom and of the Carolingian kingdom of Italy. When northern Italian cities challenged the Holy Roman Emperor's authority in the twelfth century, Milan led the way.

In the fourteenth century Milan came to be dominated by a single noble family, the Visconti. During much of the century, two or three of the Visconti shared the dominion at any given time as co-lords. They made that dominion a major force on the Italian and European stages, strengthening the civil and military establishments and marrying their many

Rulers of Milan: Visconti and Sforza

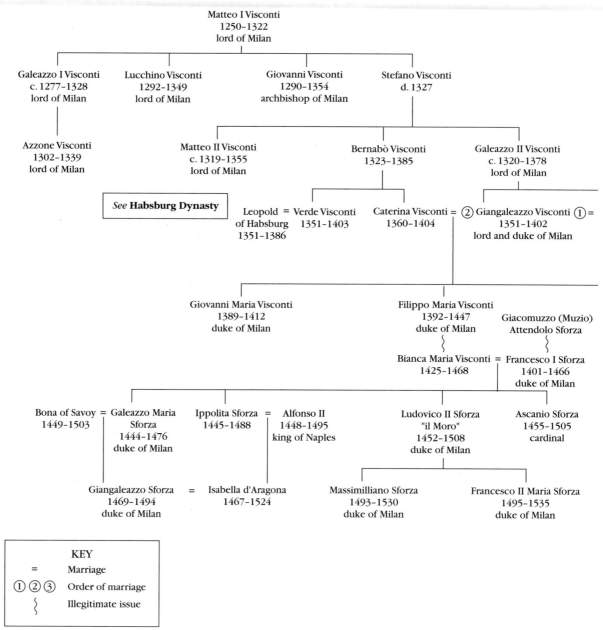

children to ruling families throughout Europe. Giangaleazzo Visconti (lord, 1378–1395; duke, 1395–1402), the son of co-lord Galeazzo II Visconti (lord, 1354–1378), was married to Isabelle, daughter of King John of France. By 1385 the ambitious Giangaleazzo had succeeded his father and imprisoned and surreptitiously disposed of his co-ruler and uncle, Bernabò, paving the way for establishment of a true princely state. In 1395 Giangaleazzo bought from his imperial overlord the title of duke of Milan,

providing this wealthy dominion with a formal dignity exceeded in Italy only by the papacy and the kingdom of Naples.

Giangaleazzo expanded and stabilized the Milanese political administration and enlarged the Milanese state considerably. Had he not died of the plague in 1402, he might have conquered Florence and brought all of Tuscany under his rule. As it was, the duchy shrank after his death while his young sons and ambitious nobles vied for political control.

environment, and he spent many years as a virtual recluse in Milan's fortresslike castle, scheming and plotting to rebuild Milan's fortunes.

Filippo Maria had no sons to inherit the ducal office. His only acknowledged child, Bianca Maria (1425–1468), was born to his mistress, a Milanese noblewoman. Bianca Maria was reared in the Visconti court; because she was seen as his presumptive heiress, Filippo Maria tried to use her as a political bargaining chip. He was ultimately constrained to marry her to the commander of his armies, Francesco Sforza (1401–1466; duke, 1450–1466), a mercenary general who was probably the greatest military leader of his age.

When Filippo Maria died in 1447, the elements of Milanese society that had felt ill treated and marginalized under him sacked the castle where he had lurked. They proceeded to establish the Ambrosian Republic, an attempt to return to the communal governments of the medieval past. This experiment in republicanism failed to hold the allegiance of Milan's subject territories or maintain the economic well-being of the capital itself. Within three years Francesco Sforza had brought his powerful army and his wife's legacy into the city of Milan, where most of the populace welcomed him.

Francesco Sforza restored much of the well-being and greatness of the Milanese dominion. He rebuilt, and added to, both the physical and administrative structures of the duchy. In doing so, he relied heavily on the help of "new men" from outside the duchy who came into power with him. The most influential of these newcomers in the ducal administration were the Simonetta family from Calabria, especially Francesco (Cicco), the indispensable secretary-chancellor to the first two Sforza dukes.

Francesco was as skilled in diplomacy as in warfare. He valued stability and entered into alliances that endured throughout his reign, particularly with the Medici of Florence, the kings of Naples, and the kings of France. The alliance with Florence brought Francesco the funding needed for his expensive civil and military administrations, and the other alliances brought prestigious marriage connections and related political advantages. Francesco secured a feudal grant from Louis XI of France of the lordship of Genoa, Italy's second largest port and an outlet for Milanese commerce. He also made a marriage alliance, matching his eldest son, Galeazzo Maria (duke, 1466–1476), with the king's sister-in-law, Bona of Savoy (1449–1503).

Francesco's greatest diplomatic achievement, for which Cosimo de' Medici shared responsibility, was

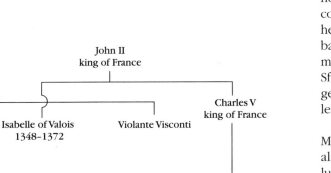

John II
king of France

Isabelle of Valois
1348-1372

Violante Visconti

Charles V
king of France

Valentina Visconti
1370-1408
=
Louis of Valois
1372-1407
duke of Orleans

See **Valois Dynasty**

For ten years his son Giovanni Maria (duke, 1402–1412) reigned without effectively ruling. After Giovanni Maria's death Giangaleazzo's younger son, Filippo Maria (duke, 1412–1447) succeeded. Filippo Maria ruled for thirty-five years in a period of constant diplomatic intrigue; the many states of Italy formed and broke alliances with alarming regularity and warfare was conducted mainly by mercenary generals with little sense of loyalty. Filippo Maria's almost paranoid personality was well suited to this

the Peace of Lodi, a multilateral peace treaty agreed in 1454 between all the major (and most minor) states of Italy. The Peace of Lodi ended a century of constant intrigue and warfare between those states, creating a dynamic balance of power that proved to be a precursor of modern international relations. That balance of power lasted until the French invasions of Italy in the 1490s.

Under Francesco and his successors Milan developed one of Europe's most effective bureaucracies, an early network of resident ambassadors (both within and outside Italy), and one of Europe's first professional standing armies. Unfortunately, Francesco's great military and political abilities were not inherited fully by his children or grandchildren. His immediate successor, Galeazzo Maria, was assassinated after ten years of mixing princely magnificence and effective governance with spectacular and corrosive personal excesses. Galeazzo Maria's young son and heir, Giangaleazzo (duke, 1476–1494), never had the opportunity to rule; his ducal reign was dominated by his mother, Bona, and then his uncle, Ludovico "il Moro" Sforza (duke, 1494–1500). Ludovico succeeded Giangaleazzo Maria after the latter's death in 1494.

Although this era is considered Milan's golden age, it also marked the end of Milan's political autonomy. In 1494 Charles VIII of France invaded Italy, in part at Ludovico's prompting. Charles tried to assert a claim to the royal throne of Naples, but he did not have adequate support. He left the peninsula after fighting a major battle in Milanese territory at Fornovo in 1495. In 1499, however, Charles's successor, Louis XII, returned to Italy with an army led by a Milanese nobleman and asserted a claim to the ducal throne. That claim was based on the fourteenth-century marriage of Giangaleazzo Visconti's daughter Valentina into the French royal family. Louis conquered Milan easily and captured Ludovico, who died as a French captive in 1508.

From 1494 to 1559, during the Italian Wars, Milan became a prize to be fought and bargained over by the kings of France, the Holy Roman emperors, the kings of Spain, and even the Swiss Confederation. During this period the last Sforza dukes reigned in the shadow of those powers. In 1525 one of the century's most notable battles was fought at Pavia, where King Francis I of France was captured by the Habsburg army. The French tried once more to invade and conquer Milan, but Francesco II Sforza (duke, 1521–1525, 1529–1535) remained on the throne with Habsburg support until he died in 1535 and the emperor Charles V claimed the duchy. Milan

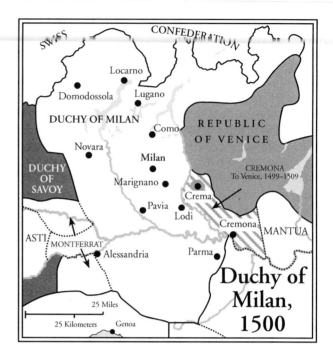

became part of the Habsburg Empire, held by the Spanish crown until 1706.

Culture, Arts, and Religion. Although Milan has never enjoyed the same reputation as Florence, Rome, or Venice, it was the site of some of the most crucial and influential cultural, artistic, and religious manifestations of the Renaissance.

For much of the fourteenth and fifteenth centuries, Milan was a center of princely culture in northern Italy, benefiting from its close contacts with France and other parts of northern Europe. During this period some of the greatest minds of the Renaissance lived and worked in Milan. Indeed, Petrarch (Francesco Petrarca; 1304–1374) lived at the court of Milan for several years in the 1350s and 1360s. By that time the Visconti lords had already begun collecting books, creating a large library at Pavia Castle that the Sforza dukes later expanded. In the fifteenth century the crown jewel of the library was Petrarch's copy of Virgil's *Aeneid,* with his marginal annotations.

Understanding the importance of learning and education to the prestige of his dominion, Galeazzo II Visconti founded the University of Pavia (1361). His son Giangaleazzo supported and expanded the university further, even commanding that no Milanese subject attend universities outside the dominion. Throughout the fifteenth century Milan continued to be a home for humanist writers and thinkers, chief among them Francesco Filelfo (1398–1481). He spent over thirty years in the mid-fifteenth century serving the dukes and providing a focus for humanism in Lombardy. Although Filelfo's works are not widely read today, his unpublished Sforziad remains an important landmark in historiography, an early full-scale attempt to cast the life and work of a Renaissance prince (Francesco Sforza) as a classical epic.

Filelfo's main rival among Milanese humanists and historians was Pier Candido Decembrio (1392–1477), who wrote a biography of the last Visconti duke, Filippo Maria. Decembrio served in the ducal administration, as did many of Milan's and Lombardy's leading intellectuals. Another influential Renaissance figure in the service of Francesco Sforza was Filarete (Antonio di Pietro Averlino, c. 1400–1469), who wrote a systematic and imaginative neoclassical *Treatise on Architecture,* featuring a utopian city called Sforzinda.

Milan's culture of secular literature was aided by the relatively early start of the printing industry there in 1469. By the early sixteenth century, as Milan's political autonomy was fading, a new literary art form featuring poems in local dialect arose. Other writers in that era reflected the neoclassical conventions of the time, and Milan produced some early historians of note, particularly Bernardino Corio (1459–1519).

In the later fifteenth century Milan became one of the first centers of Renaissance court culture. Galeazzo Maria Sforza spent lavishly to establish a systematic foundation for the court and to embellish it. His brother Ludovico, both as regent and later as duke in his own right, invested further in court splendor, creating the golden age of Milan. The magnificence and sophistication of the Milanese court in that era were recalled by one of its alumni, Baldassare Castiglione (1478–1529), in *The Book of the Courtier.* Castiglione, who was born into a distinguished Lombard family, received much of his training in courtiership during several years at the court of Milan. By the time he published his masterpiece, though, Milan had been conquered by Spain, and the culture of the Milanese court followed that of the Spanish kings.

Milan also played an influential role in Renaissance music, an important component of daily and ceremonial life at every princely court. Galeazzo Maria Sforza recruited a ducal choir that may have been the largest princely choir of the time, and it was full of exceptional singers and composers. His choir was also a center of musical innovation, developing the peculiar form of mixed sacred and secular music known as *motetti missales* (motets written to take the place of the usual sung parts of the medieval mass). Some of the singers responsible for these unusual works became recognized later as some of the greatest composers of the Renaissance, particularly the brilliant Josquin des Prez (c. 1450–1521), Gaspar van Weerbecke (c. 1445–1514), Alexander Agricola (1446–1506), and Loyset Compère (d. 1518).

Milan also held a prominent place in the visual arts and architecture during the Renaissance. In the fourteenth and fifteenth centuries the rulers and nobles of the dominion embarked on ambitious programs of building castles, palaces, and churches. The fruits of those programs included the grand ducal castles at Milan, Pavia, and Vigevano; the magnificent Duomo of Milan and Certosa (Charterhouse) of Pavia; and urban noble palaces such as the Palazzo Borromeo and Casa Marliani. In the 1450s and 1460s, the humanist architect Filarete put some of his theoretical concepts into concrete form for the design of the poorhouse Ospedale Maggiore (Great Hospital), one of northern Italy's great public buildings of the period. Later in the century the first architect of the high Renaissance, Donato Bramante (1444–1514), began his illustrious career in the duchy of Milan. His early major projects included the cathedral in Pavia and the monumental churches of Sant' Ambrogio and Santa Maria delle Grazie in Milan.

Santa Maria delle Grazie is also the site of *The Last Supper,* by Leonardo da Vinci (1452–1519), one of the world's most famous frescoes. Leonardo spent much of the 1480s and 1490s in Milan, originally as a military engineer and architect. He returned for several years during the early sixteenth century. Other prominent painters active in Renaissance Milan included Vincenzo Foppa (c. 1430–c. 1515) and Bernardino Luini (d. 1532), most of whose surviving works are religious. Among the extant secular works of visual art is the Visconti-Sforza tarot deck, painted around 1450, one of the earliest decks of cards that still survives.

During the fourteenth and fifteenth centuries, when Milanese power was at its height, the role of the church tended to be overshadowed by the secular authority. The cities of Lombardy had long had substantial local control over their religious establishments, and the Visconti-Sforza dukes enjoyed even broader powers over church offices and revenues. The dukes assumed even greater authority over religious matters if order and security were implicated. Galeazzo Maria Sforza prohibited the Franciscans and Dominicans from debating the doctrine of the Immaculate Conception, because the debates were causing ordinary subjects to question authority.

On another occasion the same duke commanded that no baptisms be performed for infants in Milan whose births had not yet been recorded with the his office of public health, a remarkable requirement for the fifteenth century.

By the later sixteenth century the Catholic Church played a more dominant role in Milanese life. Worried about northwestern Italy's heretical traditions and proximity to Protestant Switzerland, the Spanish made the city a bastion of the Catholic Reformation. In this period Milan's dominant figure was its archbishop, Saint Charles Borromeo (1538–1584), the greatest religious reformer in sixteenth-century Italy. Saint Charles's triumphant leadership exemplifies the ways in which Milan had changed in the sixteenth century from a medieval city ruled by its nobles and a Renaissance city led by secular princes to a Counter-Reformation city dominated by Spain and the church.

See also **Visconti, Giangaleazzo**; **Wars of Italy**; *and biographies of figures mentioned in this entry.*

BIBLIOGRAPHY

Bueno de Mesquita, Daniel. *Giangaleazzo Visconti, Duke of Milan (1351–1402): A Study in the Political Career of an Italian Despot.* Cambridge, U.K., 1941. The only scholarly book-length treatment in English on the first Milanese duke.

Caroselli, Susan. *The Casa Marliani and Palace Building in Late Quattrocento Lombardy.* New York, 1985. A study that presents the perspective of Lombardy's native elites.

Cognasso, Francesco. *I Visconti.* Milan, 1987. A useful Italian-language overview of the Visconti dynasty. (1st ed. 1966).

Fondazione Treccani degli Alfieri per la Storia di Milano. *Storia di Milano.* 16 vols. Milan, 1953–1962. See especially volumes 6–9 for the Renaissance period, covering political, social, and cultural history in essays by leading Italian scholars, with illustrations.

Ianziti, Gary. *Humanistic Historiography under the Sforzas: Politics and Propaganda in Fifteenth-Century Milan.* Oxford, 1988. An interesting study on the roles of Milan's leading humanists.

Ilardi, Vincent. *Studies in Italian Renaissance Diplomatic History.* London, 1986. Essays, mostly on Milan, by the dean of American historians of Milan.

Lubkin, Gregory. *A Renaissance Court: Milan under Galeazzo Maria Sforza.* Berkeley and Los Angeles, 1994. A wealth of interesting information about the Sforza court and other aspects of Renaissance Milan.

Noblitt, Thomas. "The Ambrosian Motetti Missales Repertoire." *Musica Disciplina* 22 (1968): 77–104. Seminal paper on the most innovative aspect of musical activity in Renaissance Milan.

Robin, Diana. *Filelfo in Milan.* Princeton, N.J., 1991. The best source in English on Milan's greatest humanist.

Santoro, Caterina. *Gli Sforza,* Milan, 1968. A good Italian-language introduction to the Sforza dukes and their family.

Smyth, Craig, and Gian Carlo Garfagnini, eds. *Florence and Milan: Comparisons and Relations.* 2 vols. Florence, 1989. A wide-ranging collection of papers by leading scholars in various disciplines.

Ward, Lynn Halpern. "The Motetti Missales Repertoire Reconsidered." *Journal of the American Musicological Society* (fall 1986): 491–524. Valuable reconsideration of Renaissance Milan's most innovative musical activity.

GREGORY P. LUBKIN

Art in Milan and Lombardy

In the fifteenth century Milan was the largest and wealthiest city in Italy, and it dominated the artistic production of most of the Lombard region. Although the "Renaissance" of classical style in the arts did not begin to flourish in Milan until the 1460s, we shall define the Renaissance in Lombardy as the time from the reign of Giangaleazzo Visconti in the late fourteenth century, through the period of Sforza rule, down to 1522, when the forces of Charles V, the Holy Roman Emperor, entered Milan. The two greatest Lombard centers of artistic production, the Cathedral of Milan and the Certosa di Pavia, were founded, respectively, in 1386 and 1396, and work on them continued steadily until about 1525, when it was interrupted by warfare and plague.

Lombard Renaissance art has not been sufficiently studied and appreciated. Scholarship on it lags generations behind that on Florentine art. Scholars of Milanese art are still working as if in the age of Berenson, sorting out identities of artists, establishing chronologies, and collecting documents. Milanese art has suffered from several erroneous biases or oversimplifications: that it is the art of a despotism; that it resulted mostly from ducal patronage; that its progress was due to Florentine influence; that it was debased by a love of mere surface decoration; and that its working methods were so collaborative that it is fruitless to try to identify hands of execution. Most of the attention that has been focused on Lombard Renaissance art has been paid to the great foreigners who worked there, especially Donato Bramante of Urbino and the Tuscans Masolino, Filarete (Antonio Averlino), and Leonardo da Vinci. However, native Lombard Renaissance art was far richer than has been realized, and it is surprisingly well documented.

To outline this material, we shall give monumental projects higher priority than individual artists. The alternative, to give priority to artists and their works, would be to adopt a Vasarian emphasis on the individual. This Florentine mannerist concept is ill suited to Lombard Renaissance patterns of patronage and working methods. Lombard artistic projects were often grandiose, even when the patron was not the duke, so that many artists had to work together

Art in Milan. *Madonna of the Book* by Vincenzo Foppa (c. 1427–1515) in the Sforza Castle, Milan. ALINARI/ART RESOURCE

to complete the projects within a reasonable time. The Florentine paradigm of the individual artist making his own masterpiece should be replaced, for Milan, by a more collaborative model in which many artists formed ad hoc consortia to execute projects. It was typical for many architects to consult about the design of a building, and sculptors often worked after designs made by painters. This is not to say that we cannot know a great deal about many individual Lombard artists and that we cannot sort out hands of execution. The richness of Milanese archives makes it possible to document the lives of Milanese artists in great detail, and careful analysis of their works reveals a distinct character which enables us to attribute works to individual hands, even when they took part in large collaborative projects.

The Cathedral of Milan. The cathedral, begun in 1386 and constructed intensively throughout the period in question, was Milan's largest and most important center of artistic activity. Prior to the construction of Saint Peter's in Rome, the Fabbrica del Duomo was the largest cathedral building project in Europe. The Fabbrica was a secular, public corporation, dominated by neither the duke nor the archbishop. Although the duke made significant contributions of privileges and money, and although the Fabbrica had to maintain cooperative relations with the duke and the archbishop, the work on the cathedral should not be classified as resulting from either ducal or ecclesiastical patronage. Nor was its patronage civic, in the sense that the Milanese Commune supported it. It was civil, in the sense that it was supported by practically everyone in Milan. The Fabbrica reported to a large board of citizens elected by the various neighborhoods of Milan, hiring a large professional staff of managers, notaries, and bookkeepers, and employing an enormous salaried staff of artisans.

Designed from the beginning to be covered with marble, statues, and reliefs and to sport a vast array of stained-glass windows, the cathedral was intended to be Europe's richest, and it employed impressive numbers of stonecutters and many fine sculptors and painters. In the earliest years, many distinguished architects from Germany, France, and other Italian cities were hired, and many sculptors and stonecutters were imported from Germany and Burgundy, but by the early fifteenth century these were replaced by native Lombards as Milan developed its own school of resident artisans capable of executing all aspects of the cathedral. The Lombard architects of the cathedral (or engineers, as they were called) included Marco da Campione, Simone da Orsenigo, Giacomo da Campione, Giovannino de' Grassi (painter), Marco da Carona, Lorenzo degli Spazii, Antonio da Paderno, Filippino da Modena, Franceschino da Canobio, Giovanni Solari, Guiniforte Solari, Giovanni Antonio Amadeo, Giovanni Giacomo Dolcebuono, Cristoforo Solari, Bernardo Zenale (painter), and Cristoforo Lombardo. Given that Marco da Carona was the father of Giovanni Solari, that Amadeo was a son-in-law of Guiniforte Solari, and that a niece of Giovanni Solari married a grandson of Simone da Orsenigo, it is clear how important the Solari family was to church building in Milan. Northern architects who worked for the Fabbrica in its early years included Nicolas de Bonaventura, Hans von Freiburg, Heinrich von Gmünd, and Jean Mignot. The Fabbrica also employed Italian architects from outside of Lombardy, including Bernardo da Venezia, Filarete, Francesco di Giorgio, Leonardo, and Bramante, usually to make and critique architectural models, but the ideas of the Lombard architects largely prevailed in the construction of the cathedral. Although the Duomo is usually considered one of the last great Gothic cathedrals, and although its plan and elevation were carried out according to the designs of the International Gothic period, the cathedral is not a good example of truly Gothic style. Rather, it is a distinctly Lombard interpretation of the Gothic, being broader and more horizontal than northern Gothic churches, lacking an enlarged clerestory, and having no functional need for flying buttresses since the thrust of the vaults is supported by iron tie-rods. The early sculpture is in the International Gothic style, but the styles of all the subsequent periods are apparent in the ornamentation, including the Renaissance, mannerist, baroque, rococo and neoclassical styles.

A list of some of the most important sculptors who worked for the cathedral provides an inventory of the whole Lombard school of sculpture. They included Giacomo da Campione, Paolino da Montorfano, Giorgio Solari, Matteo Raverti, Jacopino da Tradate, Francesco Solari, Cristoforo Mantegazza, Martino Benzoni, Luchino Cernuschi, Giovanni Antonio Piatti, Giovanni Antonio Amadeo, Lazzaro Palazzi, Gabriele da Rho, Francesco Cazzaniga, Benedetto Briosco, Tommaso Cazzaniga, Biagio Vairone, Giovanni Battista da Sesto, Giovanni Stefano da Sesto, Cristoforo Solari, Agostino Busti (called Bambaia), and Cristoforo Lombardo. A similarly important list of painters and stained-glass makers worked for the cathedral, including Giovannino de' Grassi, Paolino da Montorfano, Michelino da Besozzo, Stefano da Pandino, Niccolò da Varallo, Franceschino Zavattari, Ambrogio Zavattari, Vincenzo Foppa, Constantino da Vaprio, Gottardo Scotti, Cristoforo de Mottis, Pietro da Velate, Ambrogio da Fossano (called Bergognone), Antonio da Pandino, and Cesare Cesariano.

The Certosa di Pavia. The Certosa, the most elaborately decorated of all Renaissance monasteries, was founded by Giangaleazzo Visconti as his dynastic mausoleum, and he endowed it with the income from rich surrounding agricultural territories. The subsequent Visconti and Sforza dukes renewed the privileges of the Certosa, thereby identifying themselves with Giangaleazzo's pious and politically astute donation. However, like the cathedral, the Certosa is not a simple case of ducal patronage, for the Carthusian order owned the property that Giangaleazzo had given, and the Carthusians played an important role in supervising the work. The Certosa must be understood as a satellite of the cathedral, in that the two monuments had, to a surprising extent, the same architects, the same sculptors and stonecutters, the same stone dealers, and even the same stained-glass-window makers. They were not ducal artists but private, bourgeois entrepreneurs, mostly Milanese citizens, who worked for the Fabbrica, the Certosa, the duke, or any other employer they could find.

The Certosa is an assemblage of the finest work by the best Lombard Renaissance artists. The style of the church ranges from a Lombard variant of the International Gothic in its earliest parts, in the sacristies and the choir, through the early Renaissance in the transept and the nave, to the high Renaissance on the facade. Similarly, the sculptural details show the same range of period styles, while the most important painting is from the Renaissance and high Renaissance styles. The structure of the church was largely built by Giovanni and Guiniforte Solari, who also built the small and large cloisters. The stone and terra-cotta sculpture decorating the two cloisters was largely made in the 1460s and early 1470s by Francesco Solari, Cristoforo Mantegazza, Amadeo, and others. The terra-cotta sculpture of the cloisters was made about the same time by Rinaldo de Stauris, Francesco Solari, Amadeo, and others, and it is here that the classical influences of the Renaissance first appear at the Certosa. The sculptured keystones in the church were made in the late 1460s and early 1470s by Cristoforo Mantegazza, Amadeo, and others. There were paintings by Vincenzo Foppa in the cloisters, but these have perished. The colossal roundels of the *Four Fathers of the Church* were made shortly before 1478, two by Cristoforo and Antonio Mantegazza and two by Amadeo. Stained-glass windows were made, about the late 1470s, by Niccolò da Varallo, Antonio da Pandino, Jacopino de Motti, Pietro da Velate, and Cristoforo de Motti. The facade of the church, designed by Amadeo, Dolcebuono, and Bergognone in the 1490s, and later finished according to designs by Cristoforo Lombardo, is the most richly decorated church facade in Europe, with reliefs and statues by Cristoforo and Antonio Mantegazza, Amadeo, Antonio della Porta, Benedetto Briosco, Cristoforo Solari, Giovanni Pietro and Gabriele da Rho, Tommaso Cazzaniga, Biagio Vairone, Pasio Gaggini, Giovanni Battista da Sesto, and Stefano da Sesto, and others, probably including the young Bambaia. The portal of the facade, made between the late 1490s and about 1510, is decorated with relief sculpture by Amadeo, Benedetto Briosco, Biagio Vairone, Giovanni Battista da Sesto and Stefano da Sesto. The tomb of Giangaleazzo Visconti, made largely in the 1490s, contains sculpture by Gian Cristoforo Romano, Benedetto Briosco, and others. The church contains marble altarpieces, in-

Milan Cathedral. Begun 1386. ALINARI/ART RESOURCE

cluding that of the Capitolo dei Padri, largely by Cristoforo Mantegazza, and that of the Capitolo dei Fratelli, by Antonio Mantegazza and assistants. There is a large marble lavabo in the right-hand sacristy made by Alberto Maffioli da Carrara, Antonio della Porta, and others, in the early 1490s. The marble frontal of the main altar was probably made by Biagio Vairone, about 1497. The marble portal of the Sacrestia Vecchia was made in the mid-1490s by Cristoforo Solari and Benedetto Briosco. The marble portal of the Sacristy of the Lavabo was made about the same time by Tommaso Cazzaniga, Benedetto Briosco, and Gian Cristoforo Romano. Many fine altarpieces were painted in the 1490s, including several by Bergognone and others by Pietro Perugino, Macrino d'Alba, and Bartolomeo Montagna. There are frescoes by Bergognone, Bernardino de Rossi, and Bernardino Luini, mostly painted in the 1490s. The inlaid choir stalls by Bartolomeo Polli and others were made in the late 1480s and early 1490s, with the images of

saints on the backs of the seats probably designed by Bergognone. The marble Sacrario to the left of the main altar was made about 1513 by Biagio Vairone, Stefano da Sesto, and Giovanni Battista da Sesto, while the marble lavabo to the right of the altar was made by Antonio della Porta and Pasio Gaggini about the same time. The central panel of the altarpiece of the Sacrestia Nuova was painted by Andrea Solari about 1524. Many of the projects in the church were collaborative.

The Castles of Pavia, Milan, and Vigevano. The Visconti and Sforza dukes had castles in Pavia (constructed largely in the late fourteenth century), Milan (constructed in the late fourteenth and early fifteenth centuries, demolished during the Ambrosian Republic, 1447–1450, and rebuilt under the Sforza), Vigevano (constructed between the 1470s and 1490s), and in many other locations throughout Lombardy. The campaigns to build, rebuild and decorate these castles were the only examples of exclusively ducal patronage of all the projects discussed in this article. These castles were built by teams of engineers and contained rooms frescoed by teams of painters. The castles of Milan and Vigevano both involved the services of Bartholomeo Gadio, Ambrogio Ferrari, Benedetto Ferrini, Mafeo da Como, Bramante, and Leonardo. An altarpiece for the chapel in the Castello Sforzesco of Milan was designed by Benedetto Ferrini and painted by an ad hoc team of Vincenzo Foppa, Bonifacio Bembo, and Zanetto Bugatto. Often one team of painters would bid against another team to see who would be willing to do a project for the lowest price. These were not simply court artists. Most of them worked also for other patrons. The duke would avail himself of whatever artistic services he needed, without necessarily having a permanent relationship with the artists. For example, Francesco Solari, as a private entrepreneur, supplied stone elements of the Castello Sforzesco in the 1460s, and Guiniforte Solari was called to consult about structural problems at the castle.

Other Church-Building Projects. Many other churches were built in Lombardy in the fifteenth century, and many of them involved artists named above. The following churches were built with the participation of members of the Solari family, if Amadeo is considered a Solari by marriage, and none of them is an example of purely ducal patronage. They all involve Florentine influence, but they remain distinctively Lombard buildings. The Collegiate Church in Castiglione Olona was built in the late 1420s and 1430s, under the patronage of Cardinal Branda Castiglione, by Giovanni Solari and his brothers. The presence of frescoes by Masolino shows that the Solari were aware of Tuscan advances in pictorial naturalism. The Solari were probably also involved in the construction of the Chiesa di Villa in Castiglione Olona and thereby exposed to the domed construction developed by Filippo Brunelleschi. The Portinari Chapel, annexed to the church of San Eustorgio in the 1460s under the patronage of the Florentine banker Pigello Portinari, and the Colleoni Chapel in Bergamo, built under the patronage of Bartolomeo Colleoni in the 1460s and 1470s, are both similarly Brunelleschian structures, consisting of a dome on a cube. We do not know who was the architect of the Portinari Chapel, but circumstantial evidence suggests that the Solari built it. The chapel features pilasters by the young Amadeo, terra-cotta dancing angels by Francesco Solari and other artists

who worked in the Certosa cloisters, and a very progressive cycle of frescoes by Vincenzo Foppa, who also worked at the Certosa under the direction of Guiniforte Solari. The Colleoni Chapel, one of the most impetuously classicizing of all Renaissance buildings, was built with Amadeo as its architect, and it contains the tomb of Bartolomeo Colleoni and that of his daughter Medea, both by Amadeo and assistants. The facade of the Colleoni Chapel is covered with sculpture by Amadeo and collaborators.

Santa Maria presso San Satiro in Milan, built in the 1480s, is usually attributed to Bramante, but he was a painter-architect, not a builder, and we know that Amadeo had some responsibility for the facade. The facade was decorated with reliefs made about 1486 by Antonio Mantegazza. Santa Maria delle Grazie is usually considered to have been built under ducal patronage, but this is an oversimplification. The Dominican order was also a patron, as were hundreds of citizens who made donations to the monastery. The nave of the church seems to have been built by the Solari about the 1460s, and the chancel, designed by Bramante, was built in the 1490s with the participation of Amadeo and Dolcebuono. At the same time as Leonardo was painting his *Last Supper* in the refectory, Cristoforo Solari was making for the church the tomb of Ludovico il Moro and Beatrice d'Este, a project that was never finished, the gisants (recumbent effigies) of which have been in the Certosa di Pavia since the sixteenth century. The Cathedral of Pavia was another project in which both Amadeo and Bramante participated in the 1490s.

Other Secular Buildings. The Ospedale Maggiore in Milan is generally thought to have been designed by Filarete and built under ducal patronage. However, many documents indicate that Guiniforte and Francesco Solari were heavily involved in the construction, starting about 1456, and many charitable organizations helped to support it. The Medici Bank was built under the patronage of Pigello Portinari in the 1460s. We do not know who designed it. The drawing of it in Filarete's *Treatise on Architecture* probably does not indicate that he was the architect; if he were, he would have claimed credit for it. The facade was decorated by large terracotta medallions, attributable to Francesco Solari, and Vincenzo Foppa painted frescoes in the court. This combination and date suggest that the Solari were occupied in its construction. Its imposing marble portal is now in the Castello Sforzesco.

See also biographies of Bramante, Filarete, and Giangaleazzo Visconti.

BIBLIOGRAPHY

Albertini Ottolenghi, Maria Grazia, Rossana Bossaglia, and Franco R. Pesenti. *La Certosa di Pavia.* Milan, 1968.

Brown, David Alan. *Andrea Solario.* Milan, 1987.

Hartt, Frederick. *History of Italian Renaissance Art: Painting, Sculpture, Architecture.* New York, 1987.

Morscheck, Charles R. *Relief Sculpture for the Facade of the Certosa di Pavia, 1473–1499.* New York, 1978.

Natale, Mauro, ed. *Scultura lombarda del Rinascimento: I monumenti Borromeo.* Turin, Italy, 1997.

Paoletti, John T., and Gary M. Radke. *Art in Renaissance Italy.* Upper Saddle River, N.J., 1997.

Pope-Hennessy, John. *Italian Renaissance Sculpture.* 3 vols. London, 1996.

Rossi, Marco. *Giovannino de Grassi: La corte e la cattedrale.* Milan, 1995.

Schofield, Richard V., Janice Shell, and Grazioso Sironi, eds. *Giovanni Antonio Amadeo: Documents/I documenti.* Como, Italy, 1989.

Shell, Janice. *Pittori in Bottega: Milano nel Rinascimento.* Turin, Italy, 1995.

Welch, Evelyn S. *Art and Authority in Renaissance Milan.* New Haven, Conn., and London, 1995.

CHARLES R. MORSCHECK JR.

MILTON, JOHN (1608–1674), English poet and prose controversialist. Milton was born 9 December 1608 in Bread Street, London, the eldest child of John and Sarah Milton. His father, who had converted to Protestantism at the cost of his inheritance, prospered in legal and financial affairs as a member of the Company of Scriveners and was a notable composer of music. His mother was, according to Milton's nephew and pupil Edward Phillips, "of the family of the Castons," of Welsh descent, and "a woman of incomparable virtue and goodness" (Hughes, p. 1026). An assiduous scholar from childhood, Milton was tutored at home by the Scottish Presbyterian Thomas Young and in 1620 entered St. Paul's School, where he formed a close friendship with Charles Diodati and doubtless heard sermons by John Donne. He entered the reformist Christ's College, Cambridge, in 1625, the year of the accession of Charles I, and proceeded to the M.A. in 1632, the year of his first published poem, "On Shakespeare," printed in the Second Folio of Shakespeare's *Works.* He spent the next five years in study at family residences in the Hammersmith district of London and rural Horton, Buckinghamshire. Although he had expected to enter the clergy, he would not conform to the church of Archbishop William Laud and felt himself "Church-outed by the Prelates" (*Complete Prose,* vol. 1, p. 823).

In 1638–1639, already an accomplished poet in English, Latin, and Italian, Milton traveled in Europe, met Hugo Grotius in Paris, and in Italy visited the Svogliati, Apatisti, Della Crusca, and Florentine academies, meeting, among others, Jacopo Gaddi, Carlo Dati, Pietro Frescobaldi, Benedetto Buonmattei, and Torquato Tasso's friend and patron Giovanni Battista Manso, for whom he wrote a Latin poem, "Mansus." He also visited Galileo Galilei, "a pris[o]ner to the Inquisition, for thinking in Astronomy otherwise then [*sic*] the Franciscan and Dominican licencers thought" (*Complete Prose,* vol. 2, p. 538). In Rome, where he defended his religion when he heard it attacked, Milton saw the Vatican Library at the invitation of its librarian, Lucas Holstien, and probably the Barberini Palace. From Venice he shipped home books including music by Luca Marenzio, Claudio Monteverdi, Orazio Vecchi, Antonio Cifra, and Carlo Gesualdo. He returned to London in 1639, partly because of "the sad tidings of civil war," thinking it base to travel abroad "while my fellow-citizens at home were fighting for liberty" (*Complete Prose,* vol. 4, pt. 1, p. 619). There he taught privately, his nephews being his first pupils, and wrote on behalf of the religious and political reformation of England.

Career and Relation to Contemporaries. Milton sensed his poetic calling early and considered it his primary vocation "to fix all the industry and art I could unite to the adorning of my native tongue" in order "to be an interpreter & relater of the best and sagest things among mine own Citizens throughout this Iland in the mother dialect." He believed poetic talent to be "the inspired gift of God . . . of power beside the office of the pulpit, to imbreed and cherish in a great people the seeds of vertu, and publick civility, to allay the perturbations of the mind, and set the affections in right tune" (*Complete Prose,* vol. 1, pp. 816–817). But finding that he could not fulfill this calling, nor his country her reformation, in a repressive political and religious order (marked by the refusal of Charles I to call Parliament for eleven years and by the Laudian church's persecution of dissident preachers), Milton felt obliged to invest his talent and privileged education in advancing the liberty without which he thought full humanity unattainable.

In 1649, after the Royalists' defeat by the Parliamentarians, Milton published *The Tenure of Kings and Magistrates,* upon which the Council of State appointed him secretary of foreign tongues, responsible for foreign correspondence and other commissions. Among the first was a commission to write an answer to *Eikon Basilike,* purportedly written by Charles I and casting him as a martyr; Milton produced *Eikonoklastes,* declaring that the king is not above the rule of law and accusing him of murder and treason. He became totally blind in 1652, his eyes "over ply'd / In Liberties Defence" ("To Mr. Cyriack Skinner upon His Blindness") and expressed the frustration and rededication of his ability to serve in "When I Consider How My Light Is Spent." He continued his work with the help of an amanuensis and the learned assistance of Andrew Marvell, who also helped secure his release from imprisonment after the Restoration and who wrote a prefatory poem for *Paradise Lost.*

The epic was published in ten books in 1667 (reissued in 1668 with prefatory "arguments") and in twelve books in 1674. (The cottage in Chalfont St. Giles where he probably worked on it in 1665–1666 is the only one of his residences still standing, and receives visitors.) *Paradise Regained* and *Samson Agonistes* appeared together in 1671, and an augmented collection of his earlier poems in 1673, a year before his death.

Poetic Vocation.

For Milton his religious, poetic, and political callings were inseparable. Both his upbringing and "every instinct and presage of nature" led to a poetic vocation enabled by a life of the highest integrity, for "I was confirm'd in this opinion, that he who would not be frustrate of his hope to write well hereafter in laudable things, ought him selfe to be a true poem; that is, a composition and patterne of the best and honourablest things; not presuming to sing high praises of heroick men, or famous Cities, unless he have in himselfe the experience and the practice of all that which is praiseworthy" (*Complete Prose,* vol. 1, p. 890). This dedication did not prevent him from being a devoted friend, a genial companion, a musician, and a lover of plays, country walks, and temperate feasts, as *L'Allegro* and *Il Penseroso* and his elegies and sonnets show. Something of his character may be seen in the invocation to Book 3 of *Paradise Lost,* concerning the deprivations of blindness:

> Seasons return, but not to me returns
> Day, or the sweet approach of Ev'n or Morn
> Or sight of vernal bloom, or Summer's Rose,
> Or flocks, or heards, or human face divine;
> But cloud in stead, and ever-during dark
> Surrounds me, from the chearful wayes of men
> Cut off, and for the Book of Knowledge fair
> Presented with Universal blanc
> Of Nature's works to me expung'd and raz'd,
> And wisdom at one entrance quite shut out.
> So much the rather thou Celestial light,
> Shine inward, and the mind through all her powers
> Irradiate, there plant eyes.

Milton's fortitude exemplifies the heroic patience that the chorus of *Samson Agonistes* recommends to their blinded leader, who nevertheless, stirred inwardly by "rouzing motions," acts. Blind Samson breaks the Temple of the idol Dagon, and blind Milton breaks the idols of the mind by renewing the powers of the imagination and their receptivity to light.

Relation to the Renaissance.

Milton chose, transformed, and naturalized Renaissance poetic genres, and classical and neoclassical poets and commentaries figured largely in his decorum, his moral penetration, and his allusive inclusion of the haunting suggestiveness of myth into his lyrics and, subordinately but enrichingly, into his biblical poetry.

Shakespeare and Milton share highest honors among English poets for Aristotle's highest genres: Shakespeare for drama and Milton for epic and (along with other seventeenth-century poets) for hymn and encomium. Shakespeare was concerned primarily with the human; Milton, with the integration of "divine and humane things" (*Complete Prose,* vol. 2, p. 406). Milton makes evident his admiration for both Shakespeare and Spenser in early poems, especially *A Mask* (*Comus*), and praises Shakespeare in his memorial poem and "our sage and serious Spen[s]er" in *Areopagitica* (*Complete Prose,* vol. 2, p. 516). Both poets contributed abundantly to the enrichment of the English language and to the modern conception of the self: Shakespeare, through representation of developed and dynamic subjectivity; Milton, of free and active consciousness having the responsibility of moral choice among the complexities and perplexities of a living cosmos full of contending claims. Both probed the social and political order and broke the hold of categorical thinking.

Early Poems.

In 1645 Milton published his collected English, Italian, and Latin poetry, largely poems of praise: odes, hymns, epigrams, elegies, epitaphs, sonnets in English and Italian, masques, and metrical translations from the Hebrew (done at age fifteen) of Psalms 114 and 136, both songs of liberation. The *Poems* include a prophetic ode, "On the Morning of Christ's Nativity" (1629), in form appropriate to angelic and cosmic music able to "hold all Heav'n and Earth in happier union"; companion poems on the active and the contemplative life, "L'Allegro" and "Il Penseroso" (both 1631); and "At a Solemn Musick" (1633), in praise of the power of words and music to raise imaginations to the ever-

and do not comprise a typical sequence. Many of them praise particular men and women.

Milton's two entertainments, *Arcades* and *A Mask Presented at Ludlow Castle* (subsequently also called *Comus*), were written for members of the aristocratic Egerton family: the dowager countess of Derby, patron of Spenser and other poets, and the earl of Bridgewater, with members of the family as participants. Among the actors in *A Mask,* performed at Michaelmas to celebrate the earl's inauguration as lord president of Wales, were three Egerton children and the composer of its music, Henry Lawes, who oversaw the publication of an expanded version in 1637. *A Mask* is remarkable for the beauty of its poetry, its integration of locality and occasion with entwined themes of justice and personal integrity, and the seriousness of its treatment of the embattled Lady, played by fifteen-year-old Alice Egerton, in her defense of chastity, her eloquent rebuttal of Comus's lures to a wastefully lavish life (perhaps a parody of the Caroline court), and her argument for just and temperate use of Nature's gifts.

The Latin *Poemata,* Stella Revard argues, should be read as companions to the English *Poems:* "Lycidas" with "Epitaphium Damonis," for example. They are divided into two books, prefaced by commendatory poems from Mansus, Giovanni Salzilli, Selvaggi, and Antonio Francini, some of whom praise the author as the English Homer, Virgil, and Tasso. *Elegiarum liber primus* includes early elegies on the coming of spring and on young love in the spirit of an innocent Ovid; to Charles Diodati and Thomas Young; and on the deaths of Lancelot Andrewes, bishop of Winchester, and the Cambridge University beadle; and epigrams on the Gunpowder Plot, the inventor of gunpowder, and the accomplished singer Leonora Baroni. The *Sylvarum liber* consists of poems in various meters, including a longer poem on the Gunpowder Plot, "In quintum novembris" (1626), two funereal poems and two academic ones, replies to the tributes of Mansus and Salzilli, a Greek translation of Psalm 114, a Greek epigram, a serious, revealing verse letter to his father, and his poignant elegy for Charles Diodati. "Ad patrem" thanks his father for long supporting his studies, but resists apparent urgings to undertake business or the law and reaffirms his vocation: poetry manifests the divine origins of the mind, and as poet and musician—the elder Milton composed primarily vocal music—they share between them the gifts of Apollo; music is barren without the human voice.

John Milton. Portrait by William Faithorne. Engraving; 1670. THE GRANGER COLLECTION, NEW YORK

lasting "Song of pure concent" that "we on Earth . . . May rightly answer," as we did before sin "Broke the fair music that all creatures made"—a prelude to *Paradise Lost.* "Lycidas" (previously printed in *Justa Edouardo King,* 1638) is a pastoral elegy lamenting a drowned Christ's College classmate, rooted in classical and neoclassical tradition applied to the current state of poetry and the church. The poem is pastoral in two senses: it casts Edward King both as a shepherd-poet and as a promising pastor of the church at a time when England sorely needs both. "Lycidas" asks hard questions about God's ways: "What boots it" to sacrifice pleasure by preparing for these high callings if such a life can be cut off so inexplicably? Among the procession of mourners is St. Peter, through whom the poem, Milton says in a headnote, "foretels the ruine of our corrupted Clergy then in their height."

The 1645 volume contains five sonnets and a canzone in Italian praising, especially for her speech and singing, a dark beauty named Emilia for her native region. Its five English sonnets, and those written later, are Italian in form but non-Petrarchan in tenor,

Milton's *Poems, &c. upon Several Occasions*, published with *Of Education* in 1673, includes the 1645 poems and adds others. "On the Death of a Fair Infant" (1628), the earliest English poem in his printed collections, was written to console his sister, Anne Phillips. Some sonnets denounce detractors of his divorce tracts and "the New Forcers of Conscience under the Long Parliament," and others respond to deeply felt personal experiences of friendship, blindness, and bereavement. "On the Late Massacre in Piedmont" (1655) is a cry of outrage against violent persecution of the Protestant Waldensians. Other new inclusions are verse translations of Psalms 1–8 and 80–88 and a Latin ode to John Rous, librarian of Oxford University, who had requested for the Bodleian Library copies of Milton's early pamphlets and the 1645 poems shortly after their publication. Sonnets found only in the Trinity Manuscript praise and advise the revolutionary leaders Thomas Fairfax, Oliver Cromwell, and Henry Vane.

Major Prose. Milton's prose works concern primarily religious, political, and domestic liberty. They are collected and annotated in Wolfe's edition. While practicing close and learned reasoning, Milton was not averse to "vehement Expressions" (*Complete Prose*, vol. 1, p. 535), and engaged in rallies of vituperation. He was most notorious for *Eikonoklastes,* which earned him revilement as a regicide, though he did not participate in the decision to execute the king, and *The Doctrine and Discipline of Divorce; Restored to the Good of Both Sexes* (1643), which earned him the name of divorcer, though his emphasis is on the right to end a yoking that does not fulfill the true purposes of marriage, and to remarry.

Five tracts promoting religious reformation appeared in 1641–1642: *Of Reformation Touching Church-Discipline in England; Of Prelatical Episcopacy; The Reason of Church-Government Urg'd Against Prelaty,* which contains an account of Milton's poetic calling and principles; *Animadversions upon the Remonstrant's Defence, Against SMECTYMNUUS* (the acronym deriving from the initials of five antiprelatical clergymen, including Thomas Young); and (by short title) *An Apology for SMECTYMNUUS,* with a further passage on Milton's moral and poetic practices and his admiration for Plato, Xenophon, Dante, and Petrarch (*Complete Prose,* vol. 1, pp. 889–893).

Of Education (1644) proposes to Samuel Hartlib a plan for replacing "the Scholastick grossness of barbarous ages" (*Complete Prose*, vol. 2, p. 374), which required composition and logical dispute from empty heads, and equipping future statesmen and members of the professions with means to wise and humane leadership. Its curriculum is humanistic; its purposes, religious, ethical, and practical: "The end then of learning is to repair the ruins of our first parents by regaining to know God aright" and "possessing our souls of true vertue . . . by orderly conning over the visible and inferior creature." Pupils would begin by learning the rudiments, quickly followed by praxis, of the languages "of those people who have at any time been most industrious after wisdom" (*Complete Prose,* vol. 2, pp. 366–369). He advises reading to pupils such "easie and delightful" books (he mentions Cebes, Plutarch, Socratic discourses, and Quintilian) as will enflame them with love of learning, and proceeding with a comprehensive program of Latin, Greek, Hebrew, and modern languages and literature, mathematics, science, law, economics, theology, music, military exercises, and the observation of building, fortification, navigation, and other arts. The literary curriculum begins with agricultural authors and culminates in rhetoric and poetry. For poetics he recommends Aristotle, Horace, Ludovico Castelvetro, Tasso, and Jacopo Mazzoni.

Probably Milton's best-known argument for liberty, sometimes credited with a part in the founding principles of the American republic, is *Areopagitica* (1644), named for the Areopagus, or Hill of Ares, seat of the judicial court in Athens and addressed to Parliament in opposition to an act requiring prepublication licensing of books. Milton argues not for absolute freedom from government control, but that "a good Booke is the pretious life-blood of a master spirit, imbalm'd and treasured up on purpose to a life beyond life" (*Complete Prose,* vol. 2, p. 493); to suppress a book before it is printed is a kind of murder. He points out to the reformed Parliament that their only predecessors in this form of oppression were their chief enemies the inquisitors, and that "God uses not to captivat [a man] under a perpetuall childhood of prescription, but trusts him with the gift of reason to be his own chooser"; the "doom *Adam* fell into" may be "knowing good by evil" (*Complete Prose,* vol. 2, pp. 513–514). Sin cannot be removed by law, and if it could, "how much we thus expell of sin, so much we expell of virtue: for the matter of them both is the same"; that is, sin and virtue are different uses of the same things: "Wherefore did [God] creat passions within us, pleasures round about us, but that these rightly temper'd are the very ingredients of virtu?" (*Complete Prose,* vol. 2, p. 527).

"Truth is compar'd in Scripture to a streaming fountain; if her waters flow not in a perpetuall progression, they sick'n into a muddy pool of conformity and tradition," and to believe anything without exercising reason and choice, even if it is true, makes one "a heretick in the truth; . . . the very truth he holds, becomes his heresie" (*Complete Prose,* vol. 2, p. 543).

Four "divorce tracts" were published in 1643–1645: *The Doctrine and Discipline of Divorce* (in two editions), *The Judgement of Martin Bucer, Tetrachordon,* and *Colasterion.* These may be seen as a logical extension of Milton's ideas of individual liberty, based on the argument that the laws of God were meant for human happiness and should be interpreted by the rule of charity. Among the remarkable features of Milton's tracts is the elevation of companionship and spiritual compatibility above procreation and the benefices of bed and board as the chief purposes of marriage. Whether the first of these may have been motivated in part by the return to her parents of his young wife, Mary Powell, soon after their marriage in 1642, is disputed; whether for personal reasons or because the Powells were Royalists in a Royalist stronghold, she did not return for three years. The reconciliation seems to have been complete. Mary asked forgiveness; the Powell family, in financial difficulties, soon joined the Milton household; and Mary gave birth to four children: three daughters, the eldest apparently disabled, and a son who died, a year old, shortly after his mother's death following childbirth in 1652.

Tracts against absolute monarchy (and eventually any) include *The Tenure of Kings and Magistrates* and *Eikonoklastes,* both published in 1649. *Pro populo anglicano defensio contra . . . Salmasii* (*A Defense of the People of England* against Claude de Saumise's defense of Charles I, 1651), commissioned like *Eikonoklastes* by the Council of State, was condemned in France and Germany and ordered burned by Charles II in 1661. The *Defensio secunda* (*A Second Defense of the English People,* 1654) contains much biographical information. *Pro se defensio* (*A Defense of Himself* against Alexander More) followed in 1655.

On the eve of the Restoration, in 1659 and 1660, duty again called Milton to the exercise of his "left hand" (*Complete Prose,* vol. 1, p. 808) in matters announced by their titles: *A Treatise of Civil Power in Ecclesiastical Causes Showing That It Is Not Lawful for Any Power on Earth to Compel in Matters of Religion; Considerations Touching the Likeliest Means to Remove Hirelings out of the Church;* and The

Ready and Easy Way to Establish a Free Commonwealth, and the Excellency Thereof Compared with the Inconveniences and Dangers of Readmitting Kingship in This Nation. In 1673 he published *Of True Religion, Heresy, Schism, Toleration; and What Best Means May Be Used Against the Growth of Popery.* Other printed works include his academic prolusions, his commonplace book, numerous letters and state papers, the textbook *Accidence Commenc't Grammar* (1669), *The History of Britain* (1670), and an *Art of Logic* following the approach of the sixteenth-century French logician Petrus Ramus (1672).

The reputation of *Paradise Lost* as the sublime expression of Christian orthodoxy was shaken by the publication in 1825 of the newly discovered *De doctrina christiana,* which gave explicit expression to literal—hence heterodox—readings of the Bible. The treatise denies the coessentiality of the persons of the Trinity, propounds the creation of matter *de Deo* rather than ex nihilo, opposes Calvinist predestinarianism, and defends the polygamy of the biblical patriarchs. Milton's authorship has been both disputed and defended.

Later Poems. Milton's three major poems, in three major genres, are founded on typologically related biblical texts, Adam and Samson being forerunners whose imperfect virtues Christ perfects. Trial is thematic in all three. To what extent the characters and outcomes are heroic is a matter of dispute. Milton, opposed to heroisms of force and acquisition and in favor of meritocracy, proposes to "rise above the Aonian mount" and redefines heroism and merit. Rather than a national epic, he wrote an epic of humanity as found in Genesis and the rest of the Hebrew and Greek (Christian) testaments, and also generously allusive to classical predecessors. These poems have been associated with aspects of biblical tradition that postcolonial, gender-conscious, multicultural readers reject. It is important to distinguish Milton's work from the tradition of interpretation; he knew it well and used it when he chose, but avoided customary thinking, raised hard questions, and provoked complex responses. He would not lead his readers to be idolators even "in the truth."

Paradise Lost. Milton wrote *Paradise Lost* in unrhymed pentameter, defending that practice in a preface (1668) as "an example set, the first in *English,* of ancient liberty recover'd to Heroic Poem from the troublesome and modern bondage of Rimeing." He structured it first in ten books, divisible into the five acts of tragedy, then revised it into the

Virgilian twelve-book form. The invocation asks the aid of the Celestial Muse and the "Spirit, that dost prefer / Before all Temples th' upright heart and pure," who "from the first / Wast present," that the poet "may assert Eternal Providence, / And justifie"—show to be just—"the wayes of God to men" (Book I, ll. 17–18, 19–20, 25–26).

Much debate has arisen as to whether and how Milton succeeded, or whether he intended to succeed, in that aim. What he produced is an epic so rich in diverse perspectives that the epic question, "what cause / Mov'd our Grand Parents in that happy State . . . to fall off / From their Creator?" and the epic answer, "Th' infernal Serpent," raise myriad more (Book I, ll. 28–29, 30–31, 34). According to their preconceptions, credos, politics, and cosmologies, readers have seen Milton as orthodox Christian or heretic, Satan as hero or destroyer, God as repressive monarch or beneficent creator, Eve as weaker vessel or talented and responsible partner, the Fall as fortunate or tragic, the authorial voice as univocal or contradictory. Few current scholars would agree with the polarizations that such clusters of assumptions produce, but much useful discussion has emerged from them.

Readers are attracted to Satan because he exhibits both sublime energy and human traits: not only pride and ambition but also courage, charismatic leadership, suffering, frustration, confusion, crises of conscience (evil, like goodness, has to be chosen), and even tears. He is not the clawed and tailed demon of the Middle Ages, but a Renaissance overreacher who does huge damage and suffers cosmic defeat. Romantic poets, responding to historic revolutions, found him heroic; but his energy and indignation are not motivated by a desire to replace an oppressive system with freer and more just conditions, but by envy, vengefulness, and a plot to destroy the new creation or institute a repressive system of his own. Nevertheless, in his original magnificence, crowd-swaying oratory, and processive deterioration he challenges all the repressive systems and exertions of unjust power that he alleges of the monarchy of heaven, and his rebel government shows what damage self-serving earthly monarchies, parliaments, and colonial enterprises can inflict.

Some feminists and new historicists blame monotheism for the repressions of monarchy, patriarchy, and technocratic capitalism: the God of Judaism, Christianity, and Islam exercises autocratic rule, transcends nature and gives human beings disastrous control of it, and is grammatically male gendered.

Milton's theodicy anticipates and provokes these responses and addresses them by reading Scripture in ways deemed heretical. Confutations of received opinion in *Paradise Lost* include God's exemplary subordination of his own sovereign volition to the Law of Nature, which decrees the freedom of rational beings, in order to preserve angelic and human choice, and the rational intelligibility of his actions toward rational beings; the separate begetting and subordination of the Son, who in the Articles of Religion is "of one substance, power, and eternity" with the Father; and the creation of all things not out of nothing but out of God's own substance. Consequent from these are monism and mortalism: all forms of life are "one first matter" (Book V, l. 472), not separate body and soul, and proceed from God, who even after the Fall fills "Land, Sea, and Aire, and every kinde that lives" (Book XI, l. 337), and to whom all things will return when God is All in All: body and soul, being one substance, are not separated at death, and will be resurrected together. This monist materialist theology allows Milton's "integration of the natural and the spiritual" that Arthur Barker identifies as a major Miltonic principle. This integration affirms both "humanism" in its broadest sense and liberationist individualism; all created beings are kindred, and the divine image in human ones, though tragically obscured by the Fall, is more fully reparable on Earth in those who choose than predestinarian and dualistic believers could imagine. Milton's heresies, by drawing the human and the divine closer together without violating the Father's transcendence, contribute to his theodicy.

The agent of this creation and integration is the Son, the conduit of divinity to angels and the inhabitants of the universe. The first two chronological, not textual, occurrences in the epic are the proclamation of the new creation (reported in Book II, ll. 345–353 and Book X, ll. 480–482) and the Almighty's appointment of the Son as vicegerent to the angels (Book V, ll. 600–615), who had been created through his agency (Book V, ll. 835–837); this announcement admits no debate and precipitates the epic action. Later, as the Father's "Omnific Word" (7.217), the Son effects the new creation and a new race of free beings to whom he becomes mediator and, after the Fall, redeemer.

Milton strongly adhered to the Renaissance precept of the original dignity of man—and woman—and incorporates it into an innovatively extended dramatization of prelapsarian life. To sustain the theodicy, he needed to find ways for the Fall to result not from weakness, predestination, or necessity, but

"**Of mans first disobedience.**" First page of Milton's *Paradise Lost*. Manuscript; c. 1665.
THE PIERPONT MORGAN LIBRARY/ART RESOURCE, NY

from Satan's perversions of human virtues, including virtues that could be exercised only through the general decree of freedom that gives Satan, too, his liberty. He does not present a *felix culpa* implying that God needed human sin in order to produce grace; grace is perpetual, and the Fall resists it, wounds the Earth, and admits death, violence, and misery. Rather, Milton portrays a human pair who are sufficient but freely developing, confronted with basic human perplexities about love, work, temptation, and the founding of a community that can preserve freedom in the presence of evil. Unlike other rep-

resentations, Milton's provides both Adam and Eve a full education, through the archangel Raphael, in the history and enmity of Satan as well as the creation of the world and its diverse inhabitants, and depicts an extended, unfallen life of joyful labor, sexual bliss, informative temptations, and an egalitarian, improvised liturgy invoking all of nature to join in.

It is possible to find traces in *Paradise Lost* of the patristic teaching that Eve fell because of pride and vanity, but Milton makes that view difficult to defend. In his theodicy God makes nothing intrinsically vain—certainly not the woman he gave as Adam's meet help, whom Milton gives talents, responsibilities, and volition of her own. Eve looks into a watery mirror, like Narcissus, but is persuaded to abandon her reflection in favor of a living Adam. Satan pours an evil dream into her sleeping ear, but she rejects it. She parts from Adam for a morning not, as other Eves do, because she is attracted to what is forbidden, but to devote herself creatively to the primary human vocation: taking care of a responsive natural world. Most important, in the separation debate with Adam, who rightly points out the danger, she raises crucial issues of government, among them the question whether they are going to let the presence of evil hamper their liberty, and therefore their virtue. Unfortunately she neglects to reopen this conversation with Adam when confronted with the Serpent.

Critics have read these ameliorations as disruptions of hierarchy, but for Milton hierarchies are flexible and negotiable, whether in the angelic orders, the human family or nation, the scale of nature, or even the Godhead: the Son will be exalted through his humility and receive his scepter by merit. For feminist and Foucauldian critics ameliorations are not enough, but women in the eighteenth century found his portrait of the first woman liberating. Like *Areopagitica,* Milton's treatment of Eve propels a trajectory toward more liberal views than he inherited.

Adam engages in a debate with his Creator when, after he has named the mated animals with intuitive knowledge and found no mate among them, he insists on a companion "fit to participate / All rational delight" (Book VIII, ll. 390–391). He asks Raphael about angelic digestion, learning that angels really eat, not seemingly, and about astronomy, receiving an answer that does not assert, but suggests, a Copernican cosmology; politically corrects a gendered stereotype of Earth and sun—"great / Or Bright inferrs not Excellence" (Book VIII, ll. 90–91)—and counsels temperance in speculative science. Adam tells Raphael of his passion and admiration for Eve, is rebuked, replies that their delights "subject not" (Book VIII, l. 607), and asks how angels love, receiving an ardent though nonsexual reply: "Total they mix" (Book VIII, l. 627). He advises Eve wisely after her dream and during the separation debate, without hampering her freedom.

At the Fall, both are fully responsible because fully warned, and Milton has set himself the demanding task of showing how such beings could fail; yet each reader can share their experience. Their fall is the more tragic because of their potentialities for active and interesting kinds of goodness, but their renovation is the more promising also. Stanley Fish has argued that *Paradise Lost* sets traps for readers, so that by falling into sinful responses they recognize their own depravity. However, it also sets opportunities to recognize their own and others' capacity for regeneration, defined in *Christian Doctrine* as the renewal of God's image in the intellect and the will: "But what can this renovation of the will mean except the restoration of the will to its former liberty?" (*Complete Prose;* 6:462).

Paradise Regained.   Milton's other major poems, licensed in 1670, came forth in 1671 as *Paradise Regain'd. A Poem. In IV Books. To Which Is Added Samson Agonistes.* Whether they should be read as companion poems in spite of their different genres is unclear. If read as thematically paired, does the type compare or contrast with the antitype?

Paradise Regained is modeled in part on the "brief epic" exemplified by the book of Job and in part on the mode and structure of Virgil's *Georgics,* and dramatizes with elaborations the temptation of Christ as ordered in the Gospel of Luke with features from Matthew 4 and Mark 1. After the fullness of *Paradise Lost, Paradise Regained* may seem relatively plain; the words of Jesus are simple and to the point. This simplicity is both appropriate to the character and, like the sayings of the biblical Jesus, unfathomably deep, with spacious invitations to meditation. Though the agent of creation, mediator, judge, and ultimate king in *Paradise Lost,* the Son incarnate is fully human, but neither powerful nor ambitious, and has to discover his divine origins and his mission on the basis of Scripture, his mother's witness, God's voice at his baptism, and his debate with Satan. Finding out who he is, is also Satan's motive.

Satan tries to draw his rival into admirable but corruptible ambitions: to turn stones to bread, not just to feed himself after his forty-day fast but to feed the wretched; and to bow down to Satan in return for the kingdoms of the world, not only for his own glory but to defeat the oppressors of his people. These plausible enticements inject suspense into scenes whose outcomes cease to be forgone conclusions and test the young savior with the ethical reader's most perplexing problems. Milton also transforms the third test, when, having found Jesus invincible to temptations of "Honours, Riches, Kingdoms, Glory" (Book IV, l. 536), Satan catches him up and transports him to the Temple pinnacle. The Gospel writers do not fully resolve this challenge; Jesus' reply, "It is said, Thou shalt not tempt the Lord thy God" (Luke 4:12), ends the temptation. In *Par-*

adise Regained, Jesus must either stand, cast himself off so as to test God by requiring a miracle, or die. His answer demonstrates his identity: " 'Tempt not the Lord thy God,' he said, and stood" (Book IV, l. 561). The tensions and balances of the whole work are caught up in the word "stood," the reversal of the Fall. He stands, apparently not by fiat but by the temperance he has achieved through these initiatory trials. It is Satan, who had flown there "without wing / Of *Hippogrif*" (4.542), who is cast from the pinnacle by this reply.

Milton not only expands the biblical three temptations through his four books; he also interpolates linking episodes. The first is reminiscent of *A Mask,* a temptation to luxury and riches begun with the question "Hast thou not right to all Created things?" (Book II, l. 324) and confronting the hungry savior with a banquet, attended by nymphs and fair stripling youths, of "beasts of chase, or Fowl of game, / In pastry built, or from the spit, or boyl'd, / Grisamber-steam'd" (Book II, ll. 342–344) and other "pompous Delicacies" easily contemned (Book II, l. 390). A more perplexing interpolation ensues in book 4, the offer of mastery of the poetry, art, and philosophy of Greece and Rome, the learning appropriate to a philosopher-king. "Light from above," Jesus replies, and Hebrew "Law and Story strew'd / With Hymns" (Book IV, ll. 289, 334–335), have all the wisdom and art one needs. Are we to take this renunciation as Milton's own? By putting first the Kingdom of God, the young Messiah has all else added unto him—including a better banquet and a new anthem delivered by the angels, who do indeed lift him from the pinnacle on which he has shown who he is, and who now tell him his unremembered history: the "Thief of Paradise . . . of old / Thou didst debel, and down from Heav'n cast / With all his Army, now thou has aveng'd / Supplanted *Adam,* and by vanquishing / Temptation, hast regain'd lost Paradise, / And frustrated the conquest fraudulent" (Book IV, ll. 604–609).

Samson Agonistes.

Samson Agonistes, though not intended for the stage, is structured as a Greek tragedy, evoking a homeopathic catharsis through a series of encounters that stimulate Samson's recovery from the disordered affections that his interlocutors display, with a chorus of Danites who comment, not always percipiently, on the action. Some readers see in Samson, whose story is told in the Book of Judges, correspondences with Milton's own situation: blind and exiled in an alien land—though his own—the people he tried to save from oppression having preferred monarchy to strenuous freedom. Controversy has arisen over the problems of Samson's repudiation of Dalila and his use of violence. Is Dalila a meretricious opportunist, a heroine whose claims combat national and religious bias, the instrument of a totalitarian state, or all of these? Does Samson's inward struggle with shame and despair issue in a revived relation to a universal God and an icon-breaking attempt at liberating his own people, and by extension all people, from political and religious slavery? How does his use of violence compare to Jesus' refusal of warfare and conquest as means to oppose oppression? Milton's three major poems do not offer easy answers, but exercise readers' capacities for complex moral reasoning, debate, and action.

Language and Voicing. Some critics, from Samuel Johnson and John Keats to F. R. Leavis and T. S. Eliot, have censured Milton's language as un-English. However, Milton purposefully employs the etymological, syntactic, and mensural resources of the languages he knew, especially Latin, for the "adorning of [his] native tongue." Writing at a time of linguistic exuberance and change, he often uses words of polysemous implication that invite the reader to decide whether the more etymological or the more modern definition predominates. His syntax surprises, suggests alternatives, and teaches the reader to hold complex relations in mind—as one must in order to be politically responsible. His prosody aurally and his syntax kinetically mime the image or action in progress. It is remarkable that a poet of cosmos-making-and-shaking sublimity should see God in the details, and present them—dictating, blind—in language of which every syllable counts, every line is full of linguistic and prosodic interest, every moment is filamented to every other.

Is Milton's bard a controlling voice or the orchestrator of a dialogic republic of voices? Milton's dramatic characters present a range of autonymous views; yet behind these diverse voices one may sense a master spirit for whom "reason is but choosing" and who frees readers from bondage to unscrutinized assumptions by exercising them in interpretive choice. A reading community debating these choices will become more able to perceive complexity and less apt to mistake propaganda for wisdom.

Literary Reputation and Influence. Although in his lifetime Milton's poetry was only moderately well known, and his hope of helping to establish an English republic was disappointed, the audience for his poetry and his powerful arguments for liberty and individual conscience has steadily enlarged. In America his volumes accompanied colonists and pioneers, and their contents entered the thought of, for example, Thomas Jefferson, William Ellery Channing, Margaret Fuller, Ralph Waldo Emerson, Henry David Thoreau, and John Muir. His work became well known in continental Europe, gained circles of admirers in India and Japan, and was read in the Soviet Union and the People's Republic of China.

Milton's influence has so pervaded subsequent English literature that for many he was the poet one had to rebel against to carve a poetic identity. Each age finds a matrix of meaning intensely relevant to its own concerns within his poetic texts' multilayered integrity: the eighteenth century, visionary sublimity and universality; the Romantic period, revolutionary zeal; the nineteenth century, aesthetic excellence; the twentieth century, Puritanism, Christian humanism, orthodox, heretical, and politically untenable theology, indeterminacy, and anticipations of quantum mechanics, chaos theory, and ecology. Late twentieth-century scholars have historicized Milton's politics and subjected his texts to the hermeneutics of suspicion. These continuing debates, when the participants are attentive to his close weaving of divinity, humanity, and art, would not displease the writer, who believed that "Where there is much desire to learn, there of necessity will be much arguing, much writing, many opinions" (*Complete Prose,* vol. II, p. 554). By provoking controversy in language that never shuns difficulty or lacks radiance, Milton engages responsive readers in the exercise of disciplined liberty.

BIBLIOGRAPHY

Primary Works
All quotations from Milton's works are from these "complete" collections.
John Milton's Complete Poetical Works: A Critical Text Edition. Edited by Harris Francis Fletcher. 4 vols. Urbana, Ill., 1943–1948. Reproduced in photographic facsimile.
Complete Prose Works of John Milton. General editor Don M. Wolfe. 8 vols. New Haven, Conn., 1953–1983.

Selected Editions
Carey, John, and Alastair Fowler, eds. *Poems of John Milton.* London, 1968; revised ed., 1980.
Flannagan, Roy, ed. *The Riverside Milton.* Boston, 1998.
Hale, John K., ed. and trans. *John Milton: Latin Writings. A Selection.* Assen, Netherlands, and Tempe, Ariz., 1998.
Hughes, Merritt Y., ed. *John Milton: Complete Poems and Major Prose.* Indianapolis, Ind., 1957.
Leonard, John, ed. *Milton: The Complete Poems.* London, 1998.
Patterson, Frank Allen, gen. ed. *The Works of John Milton.* 18 vols. New York, 1931–1938.

Secondary Works

Biography
Brown, Cedric C. *John Milton: A Literary Life.* New York, 1995.
Campbell, Gordon. *A Milton Chronology.* New York, 1997.
Masson, David. *The Life of John Milton: Narrated in Connexion with the Political, Ecclesiastical, and Literary History of His Time.* 7 vols. Edinburgh, 1881–1894; rprt., New York, 1946.
Parker, William Riley. *Milton: A Biography.* 2 vols. Oxford, 1968.
Phillips, Edward. "The Life of Mr. John Milton." Prefaced to *Letters of State. Written by Mr. John Milton.* Edited by Phillips. London, 1694. Rpt. in Hughes, *Complete Poems and Major Prose.*

Reception and Influence
Rudrum, Alan, ed. *Milton: Modern Judgments.* London, 1968; Nashville, Tenn., 1970.
Sensabaugh, George F. *Milton in Early America.* Princeton, N.J., 1964.
Shawcross, John T., ed. *Milton: The Critical Heritage.* London, 1970.
Thorpe, James Ernest, ed. *Milton Criticism: Selections from Four Centuries.* New York, 1966.
Van Anglen, Kevin P. *The New England Milton: Literary Reception and Cultural Authority in the Early Republic.* University Park, Pa., 1993.
Variorum Commentary on the Poems of John Milton. New York, 1970–.

Serial Publications
Milton Quarterly. Edited by Roy C. Flannagan. Baltimore.
Milton Studies. Edited by James D. Simmonds (1967–1991) and Albert C. Labriola (1992–). Pittsburgh.

Scholarship and Criticism
Barker, Arthur E. *Milton and the Puritan Dilemma, 1641–1660.* Toronto, 1942.
Bennett, Joan S. *Reviving Liberty: Radical Christian Humanism in Milton's Great Poems.* Cambridge, Mass., 1989.
Brown, Cedric C. *John Milton's Aristocratic Entertainments.* Cambridge, U.K., 1985.
Corns, Thomas N. *Milton's Language.* Oxford, 1990.
Danielson, Dennis. *Milton's Good God.* Cambridge, U.K., 1982.
Danielson, Dennis, ed. *Cambridge Companion to Milton.* Second edition. Cambridge, U.K., 1999.
DuRocher, Richard. *Milton and Ovid.* Ithaca, N.Y., 1985.
Empson, William. *Milton's God.* London, 1961; revised, 1965.
Evans, J. Martin. Paradise Lost *and the Genesis Tradition.* Oxford, 1968.
Fallon, Robert Thomas. *Milton in Government.* University Park, Pa., 1993.
Fallon, Stephen M. *Milton Among the Philosophers: Poetry and Materialism in Seventeenth-Century England.* Ithaca, N.Y., 1991.
Fish, Stanley Eugene. *Surprised by Sin: The Reader in* Paradise Lost. 2nd edition. Cambridge, Mass., 1998.
Frye, Roland Mushat. *Milton's Imagery and the Visual Arts: Iconographic Tradition in the Epic Poems.* Princeton, N.J., 1978.
Hill, Christopher. *Milton and the English Revolution.* New York, 1977.
Honigmann, E. A. J. *Milton's Sonnets.* London and New York, 1966.
Leonard, John. *Naming in Paradise: Milton and the Language of Adam and Eve.* Oxford, 1990.

Lewalski, Barbara Kiefer. *Milton's Brief Epic: The Genre, Meaning, and Art of* Paradise Regained. Providence, R. I., 1966.

Lewalski, Barbara Kiefer. Paradise Lost *and the Rhetoric of Literary Forms*. Princeton, N.J., 1985.

Lieb, Michael, and John T. Shawcross, eds. *Achievements of the Left Hand: Essays on the Prose of John Milton*. Amherst, Mass., 1974.

Low, Anthony. *The Georgic Revolution*. Princeton, N.J., 1985.

McColley, Diane Kelsey. *Milton's Eve*. Urbana, Ill., 1983.

Norbrook, David. *Writing the English Republic: Poetry, Rhetoric and Politics, 1627–1660*. Cambridge, U.K., 1998.

Nyquist, Mary, and Margaret W. Ferguson, eds. *Re-membering Milton: Essays on the Texts and Traditions*. New York, 1987.

Radzinowicz, Mary Ann Nevins. *Milton's Epics and the Book of Psalms*. Princeton, N.J., 1989.

Rajan, Balachandra, and Elizabeth Sauer, eds. *Milton and the Imperial Vision*. Pittsburgh, Pa., 1999

Revard, Stella Purce. *Milton and the Tangles of Neaera's Hair: The Making of the 1645* Poems. Columbia, Mo., 1997.

Ricks, Christopher. *Milton's Grand Style*. Oxford, 1968.

Samuel, Irene. *Dante and Milton: The* Commedia *and* Paradise Lost. Ithaca, N.Y., 1966.

Sims, James H., and Leland Ryken, eds. *Milton and Scriptural Tradition: The Bible into Poetry*. Columbia, Mo., 1984.

Steadman, John M. *Milton and the Renaissance Hero*. Oxford, 1967.

Stein, Arnold. *Heroic Knowledge: An Interpretation of* Paradise Regained *and* Samson Agonistes. Hamden, Conn., 1965.

Stevens, Paul. *Imagination and the Presence of Shakespeare in* Paradise Lost. Madison, Wis., 1985.

Summers, Joseph H. *The Muse's Method: An Introduction to* Paradise Lost. London, 1962.

Turner, James Grantham. *One Flesh: Paradisal Marriage and Sexual Relations in the Age of Milton*. Oxford, 1987.

Werman, Golda. *Milton and Midrash*. Washington, D.C., 1995.

Wittreich, Joseph. *Feminist Milton*. Ithaca, N.Y., 1987.

DIANE KELSEY MCCOLLEY

MINERALOGY. *See* **Geology; Mining and Metallurgy.**

MINING AND METALLURGY. The extraction of metals and the exploitation of mines have been practiced by most civilizations since antiquity. Detailed reports of the extension and technological advancement of mining procedures can be found in Pliny the Elder's *Natural History* and Strabo's *Geographical Sketches*. During the fifteenth and sixteenth centuries, however, several developments changed the traditional form of these activities. First, the number and size of mining districts rapidly increased throughout Europe. Second, the availability of large amounts of capital encouraged investment in the mechanization of mining. Finally, as a consequence of mechanization, an elaborate division of labor regulated the administration and the organization of mining.

Economic Growth. The rapid changes in mining were due mainly to economic conditions.

Mining. Mining scene in Hungary from Georgius Agricola's *De re metallica* (1556).

During the Middle Ages prices of iron and other metals remained fairly stable. From the second half of the fifteenth century the frequency of wars and the mechanization of European armies and warfare radically increased the consumption of iron, resulting in a steady increase in prices. The need for and consumption of metals for military purposes during the Renaissance was enormous. The average daily consumption of cannonballs during a siege at the beginning of the seventeenth century was about thirteen thousand. Warfare was not the only activity that stimulated the mining industry during the Renaissance. The development of housing, architecture, arts, and crafts stimulated the trade and consumption of metals and alloys such as lead, brass, copper, and tin.

As a consequence of the widespread need for metals and alloys, the search for alternative fuels increased rapidly. Until the first half of the fifteenth century wood had been the most common fuel used in metalworking and mining. With the expansion of mining, concerns arose about deforestation and the shortage of wood. In response to this acute problem coal reserves in the Low Countries began to be exploited. The rapid growth of coal mining, unknown to the ancients, was remarkable. During the first half of the sixteenth century the production of coal from the Liège district nearly quadrupled. The effects of coal use was evident in John Evelyn's *Fumifugium: or the Inconvenience of the Aer and Smoak of London Dissipated* (1661), in which he proposed some measures to fight increased air pollution due in part to coal consumption.

The strategic importance of coal along with other economic activities stimulated the creation of new means of transportation and new infrastructures to ease trade and circulation. In many respects the Renaissance mining industry represented the most developed and sophisticated form of economic production at the time. The organization of labor was by far the most complex, and the extensive use of mechanical devices in production constituted the first example of the industrialization of a strategic sector in the sixteenth-century economy.

Division of Labor. The highly developed division of labor in Renaissance mines and the rich system of laws regulating their organization made metallurgy a body of knowledge shared by and essential to the prosperity of entire communities. It is certainly not by chance that while finishing *De re metallica* (On metals; 1556), Georgius Agricola announced the publication of a legislative treatise entitled *De jure et legibus metallicis* (which he was not able to complete), and that the final part of the fourth book of *De re metallica* provided a detailed description of the division of labor in mining and of its economic organization. Agricola introduced names for at least twenty-five different duties, including *praefectus metallorum* (mining prefect), *magister metallorum* (mine director), *decumanus* (tithe gatherer), *praefectus fodinae* (manager of the mine), *fossores* (diggers), and *excotores* (smelters or metallurgists). During the sixteenth and seventeenth centuries extremely complex and articulated bodies of laws regulating the activities of the main European mining districts were published. From the perspective of a community in which the economy was based on the exploitation of mines, the clarity of mineralogical, technological, and legislative notions was necessary for its economic development.

Technical Improvements. The need for large quantities of metals and alloys required changes in the technical means by which mines were exploited. The most apparent change was the mechanization of metallurgical and mining processes. The systematic introduction of hydraulic pumps, mechanical devices for ventilating the shafts, water-powered sieving and roasting devices, large laboratories, and progress in the use and construction of blast furnaces brought mining to a level of productivity and complexity that had not been conceivable prior to 1450. Although the machines and tools used by Renaissance miners were often similar to those devised during the Middle Ages, the elevation of machines to the center of the productive process was a new feature of sixteenth-century mineralogists. The mechanization of labor was an effect of the increasing demand for metals and the need to reduce the costs of production; but it also showed miners the opportunities and the possibilities of a more systematic improvement of mechanical and technical devices. Among the numerous treatises on machines published during the sixteenth century, those dealing with metallurgy and mining contributed toward a general reevaluation of the economic and scientific role of machines in the exploitation of natural resources. In this respect, Agricola's *De re metallica* represented, for more than two centuries, the model for constructing, using, and improving mechanical devices. The importance of machines in mining and metallurgy and the notable progress achieved in understanding metals and metalworking posed the problem of how to organize and to make accessible the acquired knowledge. Since mining was primarily a public activity, largely dependent on economic factors, the solution of this problem was of crucial importance.

Scientific Treatises. Mining and metallurgy fully exploited the opportunities provided by the invention of printing, which allowed the collection and dissemination of metallurgical knowledge from different mining districts. Among several specialized treatises that were published during the sixteenth century on mining and metallurgy, two deserve special mention. In 1540 the Sienese engineer Vannoccio Biringuccio published in Venice *De la pirotechnia* (On pyrotechnics), a systematic treatise in Italian on mining and metallurgy. Biringuccio's work provided detailed description of metalworking, the principal techniques and equipment, the process for making glass, the purification of saltpeter, and the preparation of gunpowder. *De la pirotechnia* included eighty-three woodcuts illustrating in detail the instruments, furnaces, and machines used during metallurgical operations. The initial success of Biringuccio's treatise was soon overshadowed by Georgius Agricola's *De re metallica,* a monumental work in folio divided into twelve books and adorned with 292 woodcuts. *De re metallica* was the most comprehensive treatise on metallurgy ever to be published. Operations, machines, laboratories, mining sites, and surveying were described in minute detail. Furthermore, Agricola's humanistic background allowed him to reform the technical nomenclature by introducing a standardized language to describe mining.

This clarity of terminology played a decisive role in demarcating the limits of scientific investigation and experimentation. For, if an experimental procedure could not be described in a plain prose, or if a substance or compound could not be named in a way everybody could recognize, then such a work was useless. Agricola's emphasis on the openness and descriptiveness of technical language was a necessary condition for the accessibility of metallurgical knowledge.

Following the success of Agricola's work other sixteenth-century authors began to write treatises and books on mining and metallurgy, thus elevating this practical activity to a scientific discipline. Of great importance for the later development of analytic chemistry was Lazarus Ercker's *Beschreibung allerfürnemnisten mineralischen Ertzt und Berckwercksarten* (Description of mining and processing lead ore; Prague, 1574), which accurately described techniques and instruments for testing ores and minerals. During the seventeenth century metallurgical literature became a specialized genre, so much so that in 1631 the first mining school, Bergskollgium, was founded in Stockholm.

See also **Agricola, Georgius.**

BIBLIOGRAPHY

Long, Pamela. "The Openness of Knowledge: An Ideal and Its Context in 16th-Century Writings on Mining and Metallurgy." *Technology and Culture* 32 (1991): 318–355.

Nef, John U. "Industrial Europe at the Time of the Reformation (ca. 1515–ca. 1540)." *Journal of Political Economy* 49 (1941): 1–40.

Tylecote, R. F. *A History of Metallurgy.* London, 1992.

MARCO BERETTA

MIRANDOLA, PICO DELLA. *See* **Pico della Mirandola, Giovanni.**

MISSIONS, CHRISTIAN. Among the principal motives of European explorers of the Renaissance period was the conversion of native populations to Christianity. Because these men came from Catholic countries, they brought this religion to the lands they discovered: the Portuguese to Africa, Asia, and Brazil; the Spanish to the Americas and the Philippines; and the French to Canada.

Africa. The second stage of the mission in Africa (after the ancient mission in North Africa) began with the exploration of the western coast by the great naval power Portugal. Pope Nicholas V recognized the discoveries of Portugal. With the bull "Romanus Pontifex" (1454), he confirmed the right of the Portuguese to the peaceful occupation of the lands of the non-Christians on the west coast of Africa. Pope Calixtus III gave to the great prior of the Order of Christ spiritual supervision of all the overseas dominions of Portugal: Senegal (1444), Ghana (1482), Benin (Nigeria, 1514–1538), and Angola (1520). The missionaries were well received in the kingdom of Congo. Numerous inhabitants were converted to Christianity, the most famous being Nzinga Nkuwu, or John, the king of Congo (1491). He was followed by Alphonso I (1506–1543), who cultivated good relations with Portugal. One of his sons, Dom Henrique (c. 1495–c. 1531), was ordained a priest and appointed bishop in 1518. Some of the Africans who studied in Portugal became priests. However, the mission did not have lasting results and by the midsixteenth century had died out. The reasons for this involve the slave-trade and Portuguese interference in African politics.

Along the eastern coast of Africa Portuguese navigators founded trading centers in Mozambique and Mombasa. The Jesuit Gonçalvo da Salveira began the missionary activity in Mozambique with two other Jesuits. The king of Monomotapa was baptized in 1561. However, in the same year Muslim Arabs at court convinced the king to apostatize and execute Salveira as an enchanter and spy. There was no follow-up.

The Portuguese also labored to bring the ancient Ethiopian church into union with Rome. Appreciative of Portuguese military assistance in their struggles with aggressive Muslim neighbors and impressed by the learning and discipline of the Jesuit missionaries, some Ethiopian leaders, notably the negus Susenyos (1607–1632), converted to Catholicism. The imprudent attempts (1622–1632) of the Latin patriarch Alfonso Mendes, S. J. (d. 1659) to impose a Latin form of Christianity on the Ethiopian church led to civil war and the destruction of the mission.

The Americas. Catholic missionary activity in the New World was carried out by the kings of Spain and Portugal under the *patronato* (Spain) and *padroado* (Portugal), and by religious orders. Papal documents granted privileges to the Spanish and Portuguese kings that corresponded to the duty of encouraging the spread of the faith. The kings paid for the traveling expenses of the missionaries, the building of churches and monasteries, and also for the living expenses of the clergy. The kings collected tithes to pay these costs.

The missionary expansion began from Hispaniola, Puerto Rico, and Cuba. It continued in Mexico (New Spain) and Peru, which became important centers of missionary activity. In 1510 the first Dominicans arrived in Haiti and Cuba. They saw from the very beginning the shortcomings of the *encomienda* system, which consisted of the distribution of land and peoples to Spanish administrators to work the land in return for instruction in the faith and further merits. The laws of Burgos (1512) mitigated some abuses of the native peoples. It was especially Bartolomé de Las Casas (c. 1474–1566) who defended the human rights of the Indians. He made a substantial contribution to the new laws (1544) that replaced the *encomienda* with *repartimiento,* which required short periods of forced labor at token wages.

After the fall of the Aztec Empire (1519), the viceroyalty of New Spain was established (1535). The missionary expansion started with the arrival of the first twelve Franciscans (1524), called the "Twelve Apostles of Mexico." They had great success and baptized large crowds of Indians. The result was often a superficial Christianity. A Franciscan, Juan de Zumárraga (c. 1468–1548), was appointed the first bishop of Mexico (1527), and in 1546 he was named archbishop of the new church province of Mexico. Like the great humanists, he highly appreciated the printed word, and he brought the first printing press to Mexico. The Franciscans were followed by the Dominicans, the Augustinians, and later by the Jesuits. Three provincial councils (1555, 1565, 1585) dealt with pastoral questions especially with regard to social justice toward the Indians.

Franciscans and Dominicans founded the church in Colombia and Ecuador (New Granada). After the fall of the Inca empire the viceroyalty of Peru was established (1542–1543). Lima became a center of missionary expansion; from 1541 it was a diocese, and in 1543 it became an archdiocese. Franciscans were also the first missionaries in Argentina and Paraguay.

The evangelization of the Philippines began in earnest in 1565 under the leadership of Augustinian friars coming from Mexico. Various island territories were assigned to them and to the Franciscans, Dominicans, Jesuits, and Recollects to Christianize. The see of Manila was established in 1579 and raised to an archbishopric with three suffragans in 1595. The native populations readily converted from nature worship to Christianity.

In French Canada missionary activity among the native populations began in the early seventeenth century and was the work initially of the Recollects, and later (1632) of the Jesuits, whose heroic exploits and martyrdoms were recorded in the famous *Jesuit Relations.*

According to the Treaty of Tordesillas (1494) Brazil belonged to Portugal; therefore the region was under the *padroado,* or patronage of the king of Portugal. The first Franciscans were followed by the Jesuits. The Jesuit José de Anchieta (1534–1597) is commonly considered the "Apostle of Brazil." He became proficient in Tupi, and wrote the first Tupi dictionary and grammar. He opened a college in Piritinanga (São Paulo). In his missionary apostolate he made use of chants and drama.

Erasmus (c. 1466–1536), an influential scholar called the "prince of the humanists," argued for new missionary methods. In his treatise *Ecclesiastes sive concionator evangelicus* (Ecclesiastes, or the evangelical preacher; 1535), he laid out strong missionary motives, which were meant to inspire the missionaries to work for the expansion of the kingdom of Christ. For Erasmus Europe was only a small part of the world. He called attention to non-Christian countries, especially in Africa and Asia, that should be converted by preaching the Gospel. He also considered preaching to Jews and Muslims. Erasmus appealed to the clergy, especially to the Franciscans and Dominicans. He drew up a catalog of missionary virtues and claimed that missionaries cannot convert non-Christians if they do not offer themselves totally to God. He also shunned avarice: "It is better to give than to rob." He demanded missionary zeal without material recompense, and with unshakable patience, freedom from arrogance, friendly modesty, and continence. According to him Christianization is incompatible with any form of colonization, or with slavery

Christian Missionaries in Japan. At top, priest and altar boy worship at an altar. *Southern Barbarians Screen* (detail); early seventeenth century. SUNTORY GALLERY, TOKYO/LAURIE PLATT WHITNEY

and exploitation. The noble office of preacher aims at winning souls, not for oneself, but for Christ.

The scholar Joaquín García Icazbalceta discovered the origin of one of the catechisms of Zumárraga. The first part was taken from the writings of Constantino Ponce de la Fuente (c. 1502–c. 1559); the second was taken from the works of Erasmus. The reasons Zumárraga did not mention Ponce probably included his inability to contact him. Moreover, in Spain Ponce's works were put on the 1559 Index and Ponce died in prison during the Inquisition, charged with Lutheranism. The catechism, however, circulated in Mexico and is in its substance Catholic.

Missionary Methods in the Americas.
The first missionaries initially built convents and churches, and soon added schools and hospitals. They were eager to learn the many different languages. In this regard native children helped them. In the beginning the missionaries also made use of

pictures, music, and choral chant. Peter of Ghent, O.F.M. (1486–1572) wrote in 1528 a famous pictographic catechism, making use of Aztec pictography by adding new Christian pictures. He also created numerous catechetical centers and taught practical arts and crafts. Bernardino de Sahagún (1499–1590) is considered the greatest ethnologist of the sixteenth century. With the help of students he was able to master the Nahuatl language. His most famous work is *Historia general de las cosas de Nueva Espagna* (1558–1569; originally written in Nahuatl and translated into Spanish in 1577), an encyclopedia in twelve volumes, in which he described the religion, culture, and history of the Aztecs.

The humanist and protector of the Indians, Vasco de Quiroga (c. 1477/79–1565), became well known for his pueblo-hospital of Santa Fe, near Mexico City. The missionaries also had a share in founding "reductions" (from the Latin word "*reducere*"), where they gathered the Indians in stable settlements that facilitated their evangelization. The settlements were based on the European agricultural model, with animals brought from Spain and new agricultural methods.

From the beginning missionaries opened schools and colleges for the education of the youth. Six universities were founded in the sixteenth century: Santo Domingo, Mexico, Lima, Santiago de la Paz, Bogotá, and Quito. Chairs of linguistics served for the study of local languages. Professors of linguistics guided the translation of the many catechisms, the most famous of which was the catechism of Lima (1584), which gives an insight into the transmission of faith; the Aymara and Quechua texts together with the Spanish is a unique historical and linguistic document. It was the first book printed in the southern hemisphere.

Grave obstacles to conversion were the *encomienda* and *repartimiento* systems. Erasmus was right in explaining the incompatibility of evangelization with any form of colonization. The documents of the third Mexican provincial council (1585) are an excellent illustration in this regard. Different reductions tried new approaches, including separating the colonial administration from the native population. The best known examples of the seventeenth century are the Jesuit reductions in Paraguay. The missionaries considered idolatry a great obstacle to Christianization. They destroyed pagan temples and pictures, repressing the public cult. In spite of the prohibitions for new Christians, idolatry continued, especially in the more remote places.

Asia. Six years after the discovery of America, the Portuguese Vasco da Gama (c. 1469–1524) arrived in India (1498) and two years later Pedro Álvares Cabral (c. 1467–1520) landed at the small port of Cannanore with more missionaries. There they encountered the community of Thomas Christians, which numbered 100,000 and claimed the apostle Thomas as its founder. They used the Syriac language in their liturgy. The Thomas Christians welcomed the Portuguese as allies against Muslim aggression. Only later did difficulties appear. The Portuguese who represented the pope were interested in having the control of the Nestorian patriarch of Seleucia-Ctesiphon in Mesopotamia over the Thomas Christians eliminated. The center of Portuguese dominion was Goa, where a bishopric dependent on the archbishop of Funchal in Madeira was established in 1533. In 1557 Goa became an archbishopric, with suffragan sees of Malacca and Cochin, to which were later added Macao in China (1576), Funai in Japan (1588), Cannanore (1600),

and Mylapore (1606). The archbishop of Goa was thus the chief representative of the Western Church throughout the whole of East Asia.

The Portuguese brought Dominicans, Franciscans, Augustinians, and some secular clergy to look after their pastoral needs, but these made hardly any attempt to do missionary work. For such an activity they would have to learn the local language. Also the moral behavior of many Portuguese did not help to propagate the faith, but rather was an obstacle. The newly founded Jesuit order (1534) later became the leading force of the missions in India and Asia. The most famous Catholic missionary was the Basque Jesuit Francis Xavier (1506–1552), a companion of Ignatius Loyola. "To a passionate but disciplined nature, profound devotion, and an eager longing for the salvation of souls, Xavier added the wide outlook of the statesman and the capacity of the strategist for organization on a large scale" (Neill, *Christian Missions*, p. 148). He reveals his boundless love for mankind in his letters to his colleagues. In 1542, Xavier landed in Goa as the representative of John III of Portugal. For some months he worked among the licentious colonists and the superficially converted Christians. Then he spent three years among the Paravas, the pearl divers and fishermen of the Coromandel coast. He himself baptized entire villages in Travancore. In 1545, Xavier traveled via Madras and Malacca to the Moluccas. There on Ambon he comforted the Christians, and on Ternate he tried to establish a mission center. In Japan (1549), he changed his method, working with the feudal lords and adopting local customs. Returning to Goa in 1551 as provincial of the Society of Jesus, he sailed in 1552 to China, where he died worn out by his labors on the island of Shangchuan (St. John Island).

Xavier's Method and Influence. In southern India Xavier acquired a rudimentary knowledge of Tamil. Local people procured him a rough translation of the Lord's Prayer, the Creed, and the Ten Commandments. In the villages Xavier gathered boys who were willing to help him in teaching the essentials of faith and in learning them by heart. They also attracted other youths. At Sunday services all the members repeated the prayers and the articles of faith in their own language.

In Japan Xavier adopted a policy of cultural adaptation that was later put into practice by Matteo Ricci (1552–1610) in China, Roberto de Nobili in India (1577–1656), and many Jesuits. Ricci obtained imperial permission to preach Christianity. A good number of Chinese, among them members of noble families and distinguished scholars, converted to Christianity. Ricci considered the honors that scholars were required to offer to Confucius "to be academic rather than religious acts and that the ancestor veneration was perhaps not superstitious" (Witek, "Ricci, Matteo," in *BDCM*, p. 566).

Nobili adopted the lifestyle of an Indian brahmin, dressing and living like a *sanyasi* (holy man). He mastered the pure, or "court," Tamil and Sanskrit and studied the Hindu Vedas thoroughly. He permitted converts to Christianity to keep their local customs, which he judged to be a cultural expression rather than of religious significance. Thus he also accepted the social discrimination of the caste system. Nobili succeeded in obtaining converts among the Hindus from high and low castes. He insisted on the idea of the dignity of the human person. The mystery of the incarnation was not a limitation, but led to the revelation of the three divine persons.

Alessandro Valignano (1539–1606) practiced the same positive approach to native culture in Japan. There he took into consideration Buddhism and Shintoism. He began the dialogue with a consideration of the light of reason, which enables us to judge "in the splendor of the true Light" what is true and false, what is good and bad. He presented Christ as the teacher of all nations and as the giver of the law, who perfects the commandments with the spirit of love.

In Japan Xavier encountered a civilization different from the fishermen of India. He realized that the gospel must transform it and need not reject it. This positive approach is reflected in the catechisms of Ricci, Nobili, Valignano, and Alexandre de Rhodes (1591–1660) who worked in Vietnam. These take into consideration the different religious contexts of Confucianism, Taoism, Buddhism, Hinduism, and Shintoism. Ricci related the Christian message to the true significance of the Lord of Heaven (T'ien Chu). Nobili referred to the person of God as well as to the person of Jesus Christ. Valignano presented God as the Creator, Rhodes as the "noble Lord of Heaven." Such a dialogue produced fruitful results. Unfortunately, later controversies interrupted the missionary activity, and misunderstandings led to persecutions.

Protestants. Martin Luther (1483–1546) judged paganism and its religious and ethical manifestations in the light of the central principle of his theology, which is justification by faith alone (*sola fides, sola gratia, solus Christus*). This constitutes the christological difference from all the other religions. In Jesus Christ, God has revealed the one saving truth to humankind. Any other claim of religious truth is excluded as well as any tolerance of relativism. Christian faith is for Luther the unique "religio vera." There exists an irreconcilable opposition between true and false religion. Luther did not judge non-Christian religions as would a phenomenologist or a humanist, but as a theologian, who is bound to the Bible. By this he differed from the optimistic view of humanists, who saw elements in pagan religions that were compatible with Christianity and could be used as a basis for evangelization. The European lands which followed his teachings (for example, Sweden, Denmark, and Germany) did not enter the quest for colonies until after the period under discussion here.

John Calvin (1509–1564) followed in principle Luther's line of thought. However, he equated the *regnum Christi* with the obligation to proselytize. He collaborated with the first Protestant mission enterprise in Brazil, where he sent some members of the Calvinist church (1557). This undertaking failed.

Art. The Renaissance popes welcomed experiments in art. They favored humanist scholars who recovered ancient ways of thinking. Some scholars apply the term "baroque" to the late Renaissance to characterize the influence of the Jesuits. The interior of the principle Jesuit church in Rome, the Gesù, is almost a confirmation of Renaissance style. Sant' Ignazio, also in Rome, is primarily baroque in all its dimensions. There the Jesuit lay brother Andrea dal Pozzo (1642–1709) painted the frescoes on the ceilings of the central nave, which present the glorification of St. Ignatius and the worldwide expansion of his spiritual sons in the Jesuit order.

Spaniards and Portuguese imported the arts into the New World. Artisans accompanied the colonists in the Philippines and in Asian centers. In the new environments of Latin America, European art was influenced by the artistic traditions and skills of the Indians. Franciscans, Augustinians, and Dominicans built churches in this style. "The cathedrals combined the architectural tendencies of New Spain. They show medieval elements but also elements of the classical Renaissance order, as in the cathedrals of Mexico City and Puebla, culminating in the baroque of the cathedral of Zacatecas" (Obregón, p. 420). Many parish churches and chapels show the splendor of the baroque. Palaces with patios and galleries were built in baroque style. The Spanish masters, especially the friars, found in the Indians excellent students of sculpture and painting. Sometimes this art is a mixture of pre-Columbian elements and Renaissance details.

The oldest painting of Francis Xavier is preserved in the chapel of Sant' Ignazio near the Gesù in Rome. The iconography is based on a painting that today is preserved in the Vatican picture gallery. It was replaced by another painting of great artistic value, which is also in the Vatican picture gallery. This was painted in 1622 or 1623 by Anthony van Dyck (1599–1641), and shows Xavier walking and a village in the background. The saint looks to heaven in ecstasy while opening his tunic seeking relief from the ardor that inflames his heart. A group of angels coming from heaven puts a crown of roses on his head. In the background one sees a dream he had: he was carrying an old Indian on his shoulders—indicating the mission for which he offered his life.

But this painting was removed from the Gesù when in 1674–1678 Pozzo and Carlo Maratta (1625–1713) painted the death of Xavier. Peter Paul Rubens (1577–1640) painted Xavier preaching; others painted the pilgrim Xavier with a stick and Xavier teaching the Indians.

From the beginning of their mission (1580) to the Mogul court of Akbar (ruled 1556–1605) and his son Jahāngir (ruled 1605–1627) in northern India the Jesuits used European pictures as aids to evangelization and as objects of veneration. Indian painters copied these paintings in miniatures, wall paintings, and portraits. Some attempts at a Christian Chinese art were made, also under the influence of the Jesuits. The Jesuit painter Giuseppe Castiglione (1688–1766) transformed the Western European style into Chinese expressions. Some more attempts at an adaptation to the local style were made; however, these remained exceptions. The churches of the important missionary centers followed European models. Generally speaking local art was considered pagan in opposition to Christian art.

See also **Americas**; **Francis Xavier**; **Ricci, Matteo**.

BIBLIOGRAPHY

Primary Works

Ricci, Matteo. *The True Meaning of the Lord of Heaven* (T'ien-chu shih-i). Edited by Edward Malatesta. St. Louis, Mo., 1985.

Sahagún, Bernardino de. *Florentine Codex: General History of New Spain*. Translated from Aztec into English by Arthur J. O. Anderson and Charles E. Dibble. Salt Lake City, Utah, 1950–1974.

Xavier, Francis. *The Letters and Instructions of Francis Xavier*. Translated with an introduction by M. Joseph Costelloe. St. Louis, Mo., 1992.

Bibliographies

Rommerskirchen, Giovanni, and Willi Henkel. *Bibliografia Missionaria*. 61 vols. (yearly). Rome, 1935–1998. See Dindinger, Johannes, and G. Rommerskirchen, "Bibliografia dell'arte indigena agli usi liturgici," vol. 7 (1940), pp. 85–133.

Streit, Robert, and Johannes Dindinger. *Bibliotheca Missionum*. 30 vols. Rome and Freiburg, Germany, 1916–1974.

Dictionaries

Anderson, Gerald H., ed. *Biographical Dictionary of Christian Missions (BDCM)*. New York, 1998. See the following articles including essential bibliography: A. Camps, "Peter of Ghent," p. 528; J. Klaiber, "Quiroga, Vasco de," pp. 551–552; J. W. Witek, "Ricci, Matteo, S. J." pp. 566–567; A. Camps, "Sahagún, Bernardin," p. 586; López-Gay, "Xavier, Francis," p. 751.

Neill, Stephen, Gerald H. Anderson, and John Goodwin. *Concise Dictionary of the Christian World Mission*. London, 1970.

History of Missions in General

Latourette, Kenneth Scott. *History of the Expansion of Christianity*. 7 vols. New York, 1937–1945.

Neill, Stephen. *Christian Missions*. London, 1965.

Schmidlin, Joseph, and Mattias Braun. *Catholic Mission History*. Techny, Ill., 1933.

Other Works

Arokiasamy, Soosai. *Dharma, Hindu and Christian according to Roberto de Nobili*. Rome, 1986.

Blöchle, Herbert. *Luthers Stellung zum Heidentum in Spannungsfeld von Tradition, Humanismus, und Reformation*. Frankfurt am Main, Germany, 1995. Pp. 252ff.

Costantini, Celso. *L'arte cristiana nelle missioni*. Vatican City, Italy, 1940.

Hanke, Lewis. *The Spanish Struggle for Justice in the Conquest of America*. Philadelphia, 1949.

Jones, William B. "Evangelical Catholicism in Early Colonial Mexico." *The Americas* (1966–1967): 423.

Lavagnino, Emilio. "Francesco Saverio, Iconografia." In *Enciclopedia Cattolica*. 12 vols. Vatican City, 1954. Vol. 5, pp. 1619–1620.

Lokuang, Stanislaus, ed. *International Symposium on Chinese-western Cultural Interchange in Commemoration of the 400th Anniversary of the Arrival of Matteo Ricci, S. J. in China*. Taipei, 1983.

Obregón, Gonzalo Pérez-Siliceo. "Latin America, Art and Architecture." *New Catholic Encyclopedia*, vol. 8, pp. 418–440.

Schurhammer, Georg. *Francis Xavier: His Life, His Times*. Translated from the German by M. Joseph Costelloe. 4 vols. Rome, 1973, 1982.

WILLI HENKEL, O.M.I.

MODENA. The city of Modena is located in the province of Emilia-Romagna, in northern Italy. Modena came under the control of the Este family in 1289 and was made a duchy in 1452. Through the fourteenth and fifteenth centuries, the ascent of the feudal families in the territory (the Rangoni, Contrari, Calcagnini, and Cesi) posed an obstacle to the d'Este. These families sometimes headed the urban factions and thus were useful to the city's autonomy, in a difficult dialectic between municipal freedom and growing privileges of the nobility.

The wars within Italy initiated a period of anarchy, during which the Rangoni handed over the city to Pope Julius II (1514). Nevertheless, Modena continued to consider itself the "Republic of Modena," with an assertion of identity. A strong civic spirit survived, even when Alfonso I d'Este reestablished his rule over the city in 1527.

A strong integration between municipal guilds and institutions characterized Modena during the Renaissance, while elsewhere the guilds were losing political power. The ruling Council of Conservators, from which feudal nobles were excluded, was dominated by families of guildsmen and merchants; members were chosen from a broad slate of candidates that included commoners. On numerous occasions the Este attempted in vain to change the mechanisms of municipal elections. During the second half of the sixteenth century, out of a population of approximately 20,000 over the age of two, 5,500 persons were enrolled in guilds. The city's great economic vitality was illustrated by the fact that in 1577 more than three hundred textile looms were operating and four hundred families were employed in the wool-making trade.

The strongly bourgeois character of the city favored independence from the court and control over religious and cultural institutions. In 1539–1542 the Council of Conservators set in motion one of the most advanced attempts in Italy to reform the system of assistance, concentrating the assets of charitable institutions into a "Holy Union," responsible to the city rather than to the bishop. The city maintained the studium, founded in the twelfth century but reduced to three lectureships (humanities, law, and medicine) in the sixteenth century. The lecturers included Lodovico Castelvetro (c. 1505–1571), a prominent literary critic, and Filippo Valentini, an influential member of the patrician class. They promoted Giovanni Grillenzoni's informal "Academy," where a large group of lay persons gathered to discuss literature (or humane letters) and Holy Scripture in Italian. This was the beginning of a Protestant movement, one of the largest in Italy, made up of patricians, artisans, and merchants. Castelvetro and Valentini were accused of heresy, and although defended by the Council, they were forced to flee. The offensive of the Roman Inquisition routed the "community of brothers," as the reformers called themselves, and its members were faced with condemnation or flight. Even the bishop of Modena, Giovanni Morone (1509–1580), though ultimately

released, was arrested and tried by the Inquisition. In 1598 Ferrara came under papal rule, and the Este moved their capital to Modena.

See also **Este, House of.**

BIBLIOGRAPHY

Berselli, Aldo, ed. *Storia dell'Emilia Romagna.* 3 vols. Bologna, Italy, 1976–1980.

Chittolini, Giorgio. "Il particolarismo signorile e feudale in Emilia fra Quattro e Cinquecento." In his *La formazione dello stato regionale e le istituzioni del contado. Secoli XIV e XV.* Turin, Italy, 1979. Pages 254–291.

Marini, Lino. *Lo stato estense.* Turin, Italy, 1987.

Peyronel Rambaldi, Susanna. *Speranze e crisi nel Cinquecento modenese: tensioni religiose e vita cittadina ai tempi di Giovanni Morone.* Milan, 1979.

Susanna Peyronel Rambaldi

Translated from Italian by Marguerite Shore

MODENA, LEON (1571–1648), Venetian rabbi, polemicist, and author. Born in Venice, Modena was raised in northern Italy where he studied rabbinic subjects and poetry, letter writing, voice, music, dancing, Italian, and Latin. At the age of thirteen, he wrote a macaronic poem, sounding and meaning the same in Hebrew and Italian, and translated sections of Ludovico Ariosto's *Orlando furioso*. He later wrote a pastoral dialogue on gambling, many sermons, and his own epitaph and many others for the tombstones of the Venetian cemetery.

In 1592 Modena returned to Venice ready for a rabbinic career, but the Jewish lay leaders, challenging the authority of the rabbis, raised the age of ordination to forty. Instead, he taught, preached, served as a clerk for the rabbinate, worked for Hebrew publishers, and composed letters and occasional poems, including a poem for the future Louis XIII and one for *Arca Noë* (Noah's ark) by the Christian Hebraist Marco Marini. He also turned to gambling.

In addition to teaching, serving as a rabbi, and pioneering in synagogue music in Ferrara (1604–1607) and Florence (1609–1610), Modena made a successful presentation concerning Jewish moneylending before the papal legate, Cardinal Orzario di Giovani Spinola (d. 1616). He met with and taught English Christians, including Henry Wotton (1568–1639), the English ambassador to Venice; William Bedell (1571–1641), Wotton's chaplain, who would later become a Protestant bishop in Ireland and translator of the Bible into Gaelic; Samuel Slade (1568–1612), a vicar; and perhaps Thomas Coryat (1577–1617), author of a travelogue. Modena corresponded with David Farar of Amsterdam regarding his disputations with Hugh Broughton (1549–1612), an English Hebraist and dissenter, and had relations with the French Catholic Jean Plantavit de la Pause (1576–1651) and perhaps Paolo Sarpi (1552–1623), a Venetian government adviser, philosopher, and political writer. Modena was offered a chair in oriental languages in Paris and was commissioned by an English lord to write a description of Judaism for James I, the *Riti hebraici,* the first vernacular description of Judaism, which provided Christians with information about Judaism for many generations.

Modena's services were sought by many synagogues, schools, confraternities, and the government. His advice on Jewish controversies, in particular those involving Iberian converts to Catholicism who reverted to Judaism and challenged rabbinic tradition and authority, was requested by other Italian Jewish communities as well as those in Hamburg and Amsterdam. He continued to receive distinguished visitors, among them Gaston, duc d'Orleans (1608–1660), Henri, duc de Rohan (1579–1638), once leader of the French Huguenots and commander of the Venetian military; Henri, duc de Candale, a French ambassador; Claude Mallier, M. De Houssay, another French ambassador; and the scholars Jacques Gaffarel, Louis Iselin, Gabriel Naudé, Andreas Colvius, Giovanni Vislingio, and Vicenzo Noghera.

Modena's family life was not without difficulty. His oldest son died attempting alchemy with a priest, in the house the son shared with the priest—testimony to harmonious relations between Jews and Christians. His youngest son was murdered by a Jewish gang in the ghetto—testimony to violent relations in the Jewish community. Modena banished his middle son at the age of twelve to the Greek islands for many years because he felt he could no longer control the boy's behavior, and he was estranged from one son-in-law. In his autobiography Modena also ridiculed his wife incessantly.

Modena's important writings remained unpublished during his lifetime. These manuscripts include his autobiography, *Hayyei Yehudah;* a text challenging the authenticity of Kabbalah, *Ari Nohem;* a tract against reincarnation, *Ben David;* defenses of rabbinic Judaism, *Sha'agat Aryeh* and *Magen Ve-Zinnah;* a defense of the Talmud, *Diffensa;* replies to queries on points of Jewish law, known formally as responsa, *Ziknei Yehudah;* poetry, *Shirei Yehudah;* an attack on Christian Kabbalah, *Magen va-Herev;* and many sermons, letters, and Bible commentaries.

During the nineteenth century Modena's loyalty to traditional Judaism was questioned and he was identified as a secret heretic determined to undermine traditional Judaism. This view of Modena became accepted in modern Jewish history.

Leon Modena's life, however, is not only an important example of the struggles of early modern rabbinic authority but also of social history. His letters, autobiography, three testaments, and an inventory of his possessions provide details about the social and economic conditions of the family and of women, and about daily life, community, and religion, including the occult, magic, amulets, and, especially, Jewish-Christian relations.

BIBLIOGRAPHY

Primary Works

Cohen, Mark, ed. and trans. *The Autobiography of a Seventeenth-Century Venetian Rabbi: Leon Modena's Life of Judah.* Princeton, N.J., 1988.

Fishman, Talya. *Shaking the Pillars of Exile: "Voice of a Fool," an Early Modern Jewish Critique of Rabbinic Culture.* Stanford, Calif., 1997.

Secondary Work

Davis, Robert C., and Benjamin Ravid, eds. *The Jews of Venice: A Unique Renaissance Community.* Baltimore, forthcoming.

HOWARD TZVI ADELMAN

MOLINA, TIRSO DE (Fray Gabriel Téllez; 1579–1648), Spanish playwright, short-story writer, and chronicler of the Mercedarian order. Once thought to be the illegitimate son of the second duke of Osuna, the future dramatist was actually born poor, the son of Andrés López and Juana Téllez, and baptized in the Madrid parish of San Sebastián. Virtually nothing is known of Téllez's youth. At some point he acquired fluent Portuguese and Gallego, as shown by the beautiful Portuguese verse passages in plays such as *El amor médico* (Love the physician; 1635). He became a novice in the Order of Mercy in 1600, was ordained in 1601, and studied theology with the Mercedarians in Alcalá de Henares until about 1609. How he gained his knowledge of love, passion, and the peculiarities of the human psyche is unknown.

Between 1605 and 1610 Téllez launched his vocation as dramatist alongside an ecclesiastical career, taking Lope de Vega as his model. In a prose and drama miscellany called *Los cigarrales de Toledo* (The country houses of Toledo; 1621), he stoutly defended Lope's anticlassical, three-act, polymetric structure for popular tragicomedy. An early masterpiece, *Don Gil de las calzas verdes* (Don Gil of the green breeches; 1615), is a hilarious and brilliantly complicated comedy featuring his favorite figure: the heroine, disguised as a man, in pursuit of her unfaithful lover. On 10 April 1616, Fray Gabriel embarked for Santo Domingo to catechize the local Indians and spread the doctrine of the Immaculate Conception. Returning to Madrid in 1618, he mixed with aristocrats, poets, and dramatists at academic soirees. *Los cigarrales de Toledo,* his first book, came out under the pseudonym Tirso, the phallic wand (*thyrsus*) of the Greek Dionysiac orgies.

In the early 1620s, Tirso wrote the work that immortalized him, *El burlador de Sevilla* (The seducer of Seville). It gave the world the figure of the original Don Juan Tenorio (Don Giovanni). Unsurpassed by later imitations, Tirso's Don Juan play portrays a rake who defies society at large, but God explicitly. Don Juan's poetic damnation to hellfire upbraided complacent attitudes toward salvation and human freedom promoted by some laxist Jesuits. A related masterpiece, *El condenado por desconfiado* (Damned for despair; 1635), paradoxically showed a criminal saved and a religious damned in order to prove that no one in this life has certainty about the fate of their soul.

After the accession of Philip IV in 1621, Tirso increasingly attacked the king's favorite, the count-duke of Olivares. Consequently, the count-duke's Committee of Reform banned him (6 March 1625), because he "composed profane plays [full of] evil incentives and examples." Tirso continued to produce, however, bringing out a second prose and drama miscellany, *Deleitar aprovechando* (To delight and profit) in 1635 and, as official chronicler, composing his *Historia general de la orden de la Merced* (History of the Mercedarian Order; 1632–1639). Francisco Lucas de Avila, his nephew, also edited four volumes of Tirso's dramas during the 1630s. Then, in 1640, the year of the Catalan Revolt, Fray Marcos Salmerón condemned Tirso on trumped-up political charges and in 1642, as general of the order, rejected his great *History.* Tirso died in obscurity as prior of the Mercedarian monastery at Almazán (Soria).

Tirso is ranked with Lope de Vega and Calderón de la Barca as the three greatest playwrights of the epoch. Tirso's work forms the technical and experimental bridge between the other two. He left behind about eighty dramas (he may have written many more): transvestite comedies, tragedies, hagiographical plays, plays from Spanish history, the Spanish New World, the Old Testament, Greek mythology, and Byzantine antiquity, as well as five one-act allegories for the Feast of Corpus Christi. Firm dates of composition cannot be assigned to the bulk of his dramatic production, and the authorship of several key works has been questioned.

Tirso was the funniest, most lubricious, and most outrageous of the great Spanish dramatists. He exploited cross-dressing to probe the question of sexual identity and created a ludic, topsy-turvy world. He attacked money's ability to corrupt the new Madrid, and mocked Neoplatonic love's fatuities. His poetry has the uncanny rhyming ease of Molière's; his satiric wit and erudition make him comparable to Ben Jonson. He is undoubtedly one of the great dramatists of the Western world.

BIBLIOGRAPHY

Primary Works

Molina, Tirso de. *Los cigarrales de Toledo* (The country houses of Toledo). Edited by Victor Saíd Armesto. Madrid, 1913.

Molina, Tirso de. *Damned for Despair.* Adapted and translated by Laurence Boswell with Jonathan Thacker. In *Two Plays.* Bath, U.K., 1992. Translation of *El condenado por desconfiado.*

Molina, Tirso de. *Deleitar aprovechando* (To delight and profit). Madrid, 1635. There is no modern edition of this work. Two of its stories have been published separately: *El bandolero* (The bandit). Edited by André Nougué. Madrid, 1979; and *La patrona de las musas* (The patroness of the muses). Edited by Rinaldo Froldi. Milan, 1959.

Molina, Tirso de. *Don Gil of the Green Breeches.* Adapted and translated by Laurence Boswell with Deirdre McKenna. In *Two Plays.* Bath, U.K., 1992. Translation of *Don Gil de las calzas verdes.*

Molina, Tirso de. *Historia general de la Orden de Nuestra Señora de las Mercedes* (A general history of the Order of Our Lady of Mercy). Edited by Manuel Penedo Rey. 2 vols. Madrid, 1973–1974.

Molina, Tirso de. *Obras dramáticas completas* (The complete dramatic works). Edited by Blanca de los Ríos. 3 vols. Madrid, 1946–1958.

Molina, Tirso de. *Obras de Tirso de Molina* (The works of Tirso de Molina). Edited by María del Pilar Palomo. 6 vols. Madrid, 1970–1971.

Molina, Tirso de. *The Trickster of Seville and the Stone Guest.* Translated by Gwynne Edwards. Warminster, U. K., 1986. Translation of *El burlador de Sevilla y el convidado de piedra.*

Secondary Works

Albrecht, Jane. *Irony and Theatricality in Tirso de Molina.* Ottawa, Ont., Canada, 1994.

Bushee, Alice H. *Three Centuries of Tirso de Molina.* Philadelphia, 1939.

Sullivan, Henry W. *Tirso de Molina and the Drama of the Counter Reformation.* Amsterdam, 1976.

Sullivan, Henry W., and Raúl A. Galoppe, eds. *Tirso de Molina: His Originality Then and Now.* Ottawa, Ont., Canada, 1996.

Williamson, Vern G., and Walter Poesse, eds. *An Annotated, Analytical Bibliography of Tirso de Molina Studies, 1627–1977.* Columbia, Mo., and London, 1979.

Wilson, Margaret. *Tirso de Molina.* Boston, 1977.

HENRY W. SULLIVAN

MONARCHOMACHS. *See* **Monarchy; Resistance, Theory of.**

MONARCHY.

The most common form of government in Europe during the Renaissance was monarchy. But not all monarchies were created equal: they varied greatly in size and type. Some, such as Scotland under the Stuarts, England under the Tudors, and France under the Valois, were ruled by hereditary dynasties. Some, such as Poland, Hungary, Bohemia, and the Holy Roman Empire, were elective. Some were relatively uniform in language or ethnic membership, but most kingdoms contained disparate tongues and regions that had come together under different circumstances over long periods of time. The English king, for example, was also lord of Ireland and ruler of the Welsh; the union of the various Spanish kingdoms occurred only in the sixteenth century. Dialects of the same language could be almost incomprehensible in other parts of the realm: the *langue d'oil* of northern France and the *langue d'oc* of the south divided Frenchmen as surely as Castilian and Catalan divided Spaniards. Some lands were united with others under the rule of a joint king: Poles and Lithuanians as well as Danes, Swedes, and Norwegians lived under a union of crowns. The notion of a "nation-state" was an aspiration of some intellectuals but was a long way from reality.

Claims of Monarchy.

Many of the monarchies made high-flown claims to power and independence. The administrators who served Charles Habsburg and who had overseen his elevation to the rule of Spain and the Holy Roman Empire, the largest empire in history to that time, assured him: "God has set you on the path to universal monarchy." As the emperor Charles V (1519–1556), he would see himself occupying his thrones for the purpose of leading Christendom against the enemies of God: Islam, the Lutherans, and other heretics. Henry VIII of England proclaimed in the 1533 preamble to one of the acts that would bend the English church to his will:

Where by divers sundry old authentic histories and chronicles it is manifestly declared that this realm of England is an empire, and so hath been accepted in the world, governed by one supreme head and king having the dignity and royal estate of the imperial crown of the same, unto whom a body politic, compact of all sorts and degrees of people divided in terms and by names of spiritualty and temporalty, be bounden and owe next to God a natural and humble obedience; [the king] being also institute and furnished by the goodness and sufferance of Almighty God with plenary, whole and entire power, preeminence, authority, prerogative and jurisdiction. . . .

There was always an abundance of councilors and intellectuals at European courts who were willing to advance the imperial and theocratic pretensions of their masters with proof-texts from Roman law and antiquity. They might quote the third-century jurist Ulpian: "Quod principi placuit legis habet vigorem"—What pleases the prince has the force of law—or they might remind him of the maxim "Rex in regno suo est imperator"—A king is an emperor in his own realm. French Renaissance monarchs had humanist admirers who came close to deifying their rulers, calling the king a "vicar of Christ in his kingdom" or a "second sun on Earth" and even likening him to a "corporeal god." (British humanists seem to have been more cautious in their appraisals of monarchy. In Scotland, John Mair and George Buchanan argued for the right to depose evil kings; in England, Thomas More and Richard Starkey proposed limitations on royal power.)

Images of Monarchy.

Renaissance kings spent vast sums on upholding the highest image of the monarchy. They commissioned painters, sculptors, and engravers; patronized poets and playwrights, and mandated architects, heralds, and iconographers to inflate the reputation of the monarch and his dynasty. Kings displayed themselves in the most magnificent of finery wherever subjects needed to be reminded of their ruler's authority and majesty. In 1535, Francis I showed himself to the people of Paris, bareheaded and clad in black, marching behind the Host and the Crown of Thorns in a procession to demonstrate the strength of the crown's devotion to the Catholic Eucharist, which had been defamed by Protestants. There were numerous pageants of entry on monarchs' accession to the throne as well as coronation and wedding processions. Royal portraits in painting, statuary, or on coins and medallions served the same purpose when the king's physical body was absent. The preening and display of majesty reached its peak in 1520 when Francis I and Henry VIII met at the aptly-named Field of Cloth of Gold, where the splendor of the French king's tent was said to outdo the Egyptian pyramids and the Roman amphitheaters, and the dress of the participants was so costly that it was said they "carried their mills, forests, and meadows on their backs." The only exception to the notion that monarchy rested at least in part on conspicuous magnificence seems to have been in Scandinavia, where kings adopted a policy of plainness of dress and decorum.

Powers of Monarchy. Some have taken such claims of royal authority at face value and detected in Renaissance monarchy a new kind of state, distinct from the older, medieval model—a state marked by its centralizing tendencies, crushing feudal and local privileges, and arrogation of power to the hands of a bureaucracy staffed by "new men" drawn from the ranks of the educated middle class. Representative institutions such as the Spanish Cortes, the French Estates General, or the English Parliament were seen to be either ignored or overawed by the king. National legislation and new legal codes triumphed over a tangled myriad of customs and provincial franchises and liberties.

Almost certainly many monarchs had dreams of this sort and longed for a day when the nobles, towns, and churches would be subordinated to the royal throne, when assemblies would no longer block their drives for enhanced and secure revenues, and when the king's writ would run supreme in a realm free of local exemptions and privileges. However, no European monarchy of the time ever achieved absolute rule and all had to deal day to day with the complex and confusing machinery of government and political obligation that the Middle Ages had bequeathed them. There seems to have been no master plan on the part of Renaissance monarchs to solve these challenges and their responses were essentially pragmatic.

Monarchy and church. If kings were ever to be free of outside interference they had first to come to grips with their relationship with the church and particularly the papacy. In order to achieve dynastic security, Henry VIII felt it necessary to wrench the Church of England entirely out of the jurisdiction of the pope and make himself supreme head. The Spanish monarchs Ferdinand and Isabella won the right to name ecclesiastical officeholders and, in the Spanish Inquisition, had control of the highest church court in the realm, virtually independent of Rome. In his Italian dominions Ferdinand asserted the right to prevent the publication of any papal bull and threatened to withdraw from obedience to the papacy when Pope Julius II challenged him on this. The French monarchy negotiated a concordat in 1516 with Pope Leo X by which it could control the choicest church offices in the realm, and it long exercised a censorship on papal bulls. Thus the leading Western European monarchies had won significant victories over the church before the Reformation: freedom from meddling by Rome and the power that came with oversight of the national churches. Patronage of the church guaranteed monarchs not only certain economic benefits but also the influential loyalty of the clergy and of the nobility who would look to the crown as the source of ecclesiastical careers for their family and clients.

Financing monarchy. An unceasing problem for Renaissance monarchs was finding enough money to support their administrative responsibilities and ambitions. The medieval notion that a king could "live of his own," depending only on crown lands to finance the operations of government, had long since become impracticable, even before the price revolution of the sixteenth century. The cost of warfare had escalated: mercenary infantry such as the vaunted Swiss pikemen did not come cheaply, nor did warships, artillery trains, musketeers, or fortresses. An agenda of calculated magnificence, such as the building programs of Henry VIII and Francis I, were also drains on royal treasuries. Kings met this challenge in a number of ways: crown land (or church lands in England and Protestant countries) could be sold off; in Spain the three great orders of chivalry could be tapped; and long-forgotten feudal dues could be revived. Offices of state could also be sold, from the lowest collectorship of customs to seats on the sovereign courts; in fact many kings invented new offices strictly for the purpose of sale. These sales opened careers for the middle class and reinforced the view of royalty as the fount of authority. Loans could be raised from the Western European banking houses or extorted from prosperous subjects; annuities could be sold, guaranteed by future revenue. In the end, however, monarchs had to consider raising taxes.

Monarchical Government. In most countries it was recognized that a king seeking new taxation required the consent of his subjects, expressed through the approval of a representative institution. These assemblies were seldom eager to see taxes raised but neither were they anxious to thwart what they saw as the legitimate demands of government. Even kings who claimed a "plenary, whole and entire power" bargained with their parliaments and found ways to use them to the royal advantage. Many kings looked to the French monarchy with envy. It was able to levy certain taxes without the need of consulting the Estates General: the *taille* was a direct personal and property tax (from which the aristocracy, clergy, and certain territories were exempt) and the gabelle taxed the consumption of salt. But even in France the crown had to dicker with local estates, assemblies of the clergy, and parlements. Throughout the sixteenth century the need for these institutions continued; in some counties they thrived, in all they survived, and the idea that increasingly "absolute" kings were able to do without them cannot now be supported.

As kings developed a growing administrative framework for enforcing their wills, they also increasingly had to contend with the opinions of their subjects. Royal vassals had always claimed the right to give counsel to their monarch and be considered part of the rule of the kingdom; even in the sixteenth century, when most kings had won the right to staff their councils as they saw fit, they still had to accommodate the magnates. Kings had to acknowledge the powerful loyalties that old noble families could generate in their traditional territories. Increasingly, however, monarchs looked outside the great families for their professional administrators and came to favor the sons of the lesser nobility and the prosperous middle class. There often was tension between the older nobility and the bureaucrats, but historians have come to recognize that both were needed in the context of Renaissance government—none but the noble, for example, could govern a province or command a fleet, army, or fortress. Indeed we can see that the nobility prospered from royal service and filled most of the offices in church and state during this period.

Rather than witnessing a triumph of a new breed of centralizing national monarch, the Renaissance saw the growth of government itself, with kings, royal councils, sovereign courts, some parliaments, and regional assemblies all gaining power. No realm could function without cooperation between these various organs of the body politic. Nobles continued to predominate in the military and politics, middle-class professionals contributed their legal and administrative expertise, and the king served as patron, conciliator, and motive force of the growing state. Such developments marked a departure from the semiautonomous feudal relations of the Middle Ages, but a truly absolute monarchy, free of all limitations save those owed to God, was still a thing of the future.

Theory of Monarchy. Contemporaries were aware that changes were occurring in Renaissance monarchy, and many political writers commented astutely on the nature of kingship. Niccolò Machiavelli's *The Prince* (1513) and Erasmus's *Education of a Christian Prince* (1516) take two remarkably different approaches to the formation of a king. The Swiss humanist Claude de Seyssell's *La monarchie de France* (1515), written for the young Francis I, argued for a monarchy limited by fundamental laws, justice, and respect for the privileges of other state institutions. François Hotman's *Francogallia* (1572) lead the way later in the century for a wave of Protestant and Catholic League advocates of resistance to kings when they crossed the line into tyranny, the most important of which might be *Vindiciae contra tyrannos* (A defense of liberty; 1579) of Philippe Duplessis Mornay and *De justa reipublicae Christianae in reges impios et haereticos authoritate* (The just authority of a Christian commonwealth over impious and heretical kings; 1590) of "Gulielmus Rossaeus" (William Reynolds). Jean Bodin's treatment of the question of sovereignty in his *Six Books of the Commonwealth* (1576) has been called "a major event in the development of European political thought . . . [which] helped turn public law into a scientific discipline." Thomas More's *Utopia* (1516), Bishop Stephen Gardiner's *De vera obedentia* (On true obedience; 1553), and Bishop John Ponet's *Shorte Treatise of Politicke Power* (1556) offered differing views of English monarchy, ranging from humanist satire pleading for a just Christian commonwealth, to theocratic pretensions, to talk of the need for tyrannicide. In 1579 the Scottish humanist George Buchanan produced the best analysis of his country's monarchy in *De juri regno apud Scotos* (The powers of the crown in Scotland), where he too argues for a monarchy tempered by traditional restraints and the ultimate sanction of assassination. By the late sixteenth century advocates of an absolute monarchy were beginning to appear more frequently in print, such as Adam Blackwood of Scotland, Charles Merbury of England, and the man who would be ruler of both nations, James VI and I, in his 1595 *Trew Law of Free Monarchies,* where he claimed that he and his fellow kings exercised "a manner or resemblance of divine power upon earth."

See also **Field of Cloth of Gold; Finance and Taxation; Nation-State; Prince; Resistance, Theory of; Royal Iconography, English;** *and biographies of figures mentioned in this entry.*

BIBLIOGRAPHY

Primary Works

Bodin, Jean. *The Six Books of a Commonweale.* Translated by Richard Knolles. Edited by Kenneth Douglas McRae. Cambridge, Mass., 1962. Translation of *Six livres de la république* (1576).

Buchanan, George. *The Powers of the Crown in Scotland.* Translated by C. F. Arrowood. Austin, Tex., 1949. Translation of *De juri regno apud Scotos* (1579).

Hotman, François. *Francogallia.* Translated by J. H. M. Salmon. Edited by Ralph E. Giesey. Cambridge, U.K., 1972.

Seyssel, Claude de. *The Monarchy of France.* Translated by J. H. Hexter. Edited by Donald R. Kelley. New Haven, Conn., 1981. Translation of *Le monarchie de France* (1515).

Secondary Works

Burke, Peter. "State-Making, King-Making, and Image Making from Renaissance to Baroque: Scandinavia in a European Context." *Scandinavian Journal of History* 22, no. 1 (1997): 1–8. Argues that Nordic kings used a plain style of dress and speech and a less formal court manner to relate to subjects.

Burns, J. H., ed. *The Cambridge History of Political Thought 1450–1700.* Cambridge, U.K., 1991. Comprehensive and authoritative.

Guy, John, ed. *The Tudor Monarchy.* New York, 1997; London, 1998. The Tudors as Renaissance monarchs.

Knecht, R. J. *French Renaissance Monarchy: Francis I and Henry II.* 2d ed. London and New York, 1996. Original edition, London and New York, 1984. Fundamental documents and analysis.

Knecht, R. J. *Renaissance Warrior and Patron: The Reign of Francis I.* Cambridge, U.K., and New York, 1996. An important revision of an earlier biography.

Koenigsberger, H. G., George L. Mosse, and G. Q. Bowler. *Europe in the Sixteenth Century.* 2d ed. London and New York, 1989. Two pertinent chapters on "Empires" and "Monarchies."

Major, J. Russell. *From Renaissance Monarchy to Absolute Monarchy: French Kings, Nobles, and Estates.* Baltimore and London, 1994. The leading advocate of a constitutional trend in Renaissance monarchy.

GERRY BOWLER

MONEY. *See* Banking and Money.

MONTAIGNE, MICHEL DE

(1533–1592), French thinker and essayist. Michel de Montaigne was born on the family property, the Château de Montaigne near Bordeaux. His father, Pierre Eyquem, was a soldier and lawyer whose family came from a line of French merchants; his mother, Antoinette de Louppes, was a Catholic of Spanish-Jewish origin. Until the age of six, Montaigne spoke only Latin, his German private tutor having no knowledge of French. He then attended the College of Guyenne in Bordeaux, eventually went on to study law (probably at the great law center at Toulouse), and began a legal career at age twenty-one. While a magistrate at the Bordeaux Court of Justice, Montaigne met Étienne de La Boétie, who died prematurely in 1563 and who had a profound, lasting influence on him. (Montaigne composed the essay "Of Friendship" in memory of La Boétie and the brief but "perfect friend-

ship" they enjoyed.) In 1565 Montaigne married Françoise de la Chassaigne, the daughter of another magistrate of the court. They had six children together, with only a daughter surviving infancy and early childhood. Often bored and growing increasingly skeptical about his legal career, Montaigne resigned his duties at the Court of Justice in 1570 and retired from active life. In 1571 he took up residence at the Château de Montaigne, in his "tower," where he could devote himself for the remainder of his life to reading, meditating, and writing. This contemplative life was interrupted only by a fifteen-month travel tour in 1580–1581 of Germany, Switzerland, and especially Italy, which he minutely documents in his *Travel Journal,* and two-year terms as mayor of Bordeaux from 1581 to 1585.

Montaigne's *Essays*. The first edition of Montaigne's *Essais* (trans. *Essays*), containing the first two "books" or volumes, was published in 1580. A new edition containing all three volumes of the *Essays* appeared in 1588. A much enlarged edition, containing Montaigne's many textual alterations and additions, was subsequently edited by Marie de Gournay, whom Montaigne considered his "adopted daughter." This annotated edition was published posthumously in 1595. Within the text of many editions of the *Essays* the letters *A, B,* and *C* refer to the printings of 1580, 1588, and 1595, respectively.

Montaigne is of singular importance for understanding the Renaissance. He was largely responsible for creating and perfecting the literary (as opposed to the formal philosophical) genre of the essay in the Renaissance. (In 1597, Francis Bacon, the first great English essayist, would borrow from Montaigne not just the style of essay writing but the very title for his own *Essays.*) Coming from the French *essai,* meaning a "trial" or an "attempt" (or more literally, a "testing"), the word "essay" was first used by Montaigne for short prose discussions. The informal essay as Montaigne understood it and developed it is the instrument for formulating and testing the author's judgment and views on life and on himself. Although the traditional approach to reading Montaigne is to recognize three stages in his ideological evolution (the Stoic, the skeptic, and the Epicurean, with these thought patterns corresponding to three specific groups of essays), this approach does present a critical problem since Montaigne's thought can seldom be fully accounted for and partitioned into neat and closed categories. Montaigne was truly an eclectic, with ideas from one field of thought often being syncretically interwoven in the exposition of

Michel de Montaigne.

another. To appreciate Montaigne's eclectic mind, the reader has only to consider, among many essays that could be cited, "Of Experience," the last he wrote, which is composed of elements drawn from various sources, Stoic as well as Epicurean. Montaigne's correspondence with Justus Lipsius is further testimony to his syncretic thinking. Like Lipsius, Montaigne is often an exponent of a Christianized Stoicism.

In his *Essays,* Montaigne is above all trying to relate the "*essais* [experiences] of [his] life." To accomplish this end, he combines the personal or autobiographical element of his essays (which includes self-revelation, particular tastes and experiences, and an intimate and confidential manner) with humor, a sane and graceful style, rambling structure, unconventional themes, freedom from stiffness and affectation, and a typically incomplete or tentative treatment of topic. His essays are also full of pithy sayings—maxims, aphorisms, adages, apothegms, proverbs—as well as of anecdotes, sententiae, and exempla taken from his readings in the classics such as, among others, works by Cicero, Seneca, Tacitus, and Plutarch. Ingeniously blending personal concerns and perspectives with the wisdom literature of the Greeks and Romans, Montaigne's essays cover a wide range of topics: "Of Idleness," "Of Liars," "Of the Power of the Imagination," "Of the Education of Children," "That It Is Folly to Measure Truth and Error by Our Own Capacity," "Of Cannibals," "Of Pre-

sumption," "Of the Art of Conversation," "Of Experience, and so on. Though Montaigne's essay writing began as a commentary on his readings, interspersed with anecdotal material, it quickly evolved into the use of anecdotes and quotations to illustrate and justify Montaigne's own ideas, especially his interest in introspection and his concern with self-portraiture that developed around 1578.

Skepticism and Beyond. For Montaigne, the new essay art form was essential for coming to terms with the central epistemological question that haunted him: "What do I know?" Answering this question was ultimately responsible for propelling him in the direction of self-study and self-portraiture. The Pyrrhonian perspective of "What do I know?" appears in the famous essay "The Apology for Raymond Sebond" (begun 1575), at the skeptical low point in Montaigne's thinking and writing on human epistemological powers and on human reason as a means of acquiring any certain knowledge. (Montaigne translated this work for his father. It was, paradoxically, a fifteenth-century claim for the sufficiency of human reason.) Montaigne is really attacking human presumption here when he compares man's reason to a weak and wavering reed. Such doubt about the human mind and its ability to know anything with certainty had so overcome Montaigne that "What do I know?" ("Que sais-je?") became his personal motto. He even had a medallion struck containing these words.

Montaigne does not, however, let himself remain in such a state of skeptical impasse. With the negatives dispatched, he proceeds to the things he is capable of affirming. In a truly reconstructive sense, the essays that follow the "Apology" were written to demonstrate precisely what the "I: Michel de Montaigne, essayer" *does* know. In his "attempts" at answering this uncertain question and thus possibly reversing a pervasive sense of skepticism, Montaigne takes the reader on a journey that culminates in a singular and powerful self-portrait of the essayist himself. Since, as we see in Montaigne's critique of reason, it is impossible for anyone to really "know" anything about a world in flux and full of contradiction, Montaigne soon discovered that the only subject he might truly acquire some knowledge of was himself. (In spite of focusing on his inner self, Montaigne did not hesitate, when circumstances required it, to confront the real world. This can be seen especially in the conciliatory role he played as an intermediary between Guise and Henry of Navarre during the religious wars.) Personal experience and the private method of self-evaluation and self-knowledge provided by the informal essay and its discursive and revelatory style became Montaigne's true obsession. "Thus, reader," he tells us and shows us time and again in these "essays" of his self and his life, "I am myself the subject matter of my book." Or elsewhere in his *Essays,* as he restates this all-important concept, "I offered myself to myself for argument and subject"; "Everyone recognizes me in my book, and my book in me."

Montaigne's Individualism and Influence. In this very personal literary way, Montaigne incarnates perfectly the intense individualism of the Renaissance—that is, the best qualities of the art of living well. Montaigne's ultimate faith in the human condition, despite its limitations, is characteristic of the Renaissance. This art or modus vivendi requires the knowledge and enjoyment of oneself, the realization that fulfillment and happiness are to be found not outwardly but inwardly in one's self, even in one's everyday life, one's experience. Knowledge grounded in self, experience, and everyday life became Montaigne's goal. He was constantly evolving from a normative to an existential perspective in his unique exploration of the self. "When I dance, I dance; and when I sleep, I sleep" is how Montaigne describes, simply yet profoundly, this art of living, which was for him so intense an enjoyment of life here and now.

This art, so much a part of Montaigne's being, is the art of combining awareness with action, knowledge with living, to achieve a proper relation between self and event, desire and reality. Montaigne's last essay in book 3, entitled "Of Experience," contains his best statements about the principle of self-revelation and on the human value of knowledge through personal experience. On the last page of this final essay, he writes: "The man who knows how to enjoy his existence as he ought has attained to an absolute perfection, like that of the gods. We seek other conditions because we do not understand the proper use of our own, and go out of ourselves because we do not know what is within us." The writing of essays becomes, for Montaigne, the writing of his life's experiences: "All this medley that I am scribbling here is but a record of my life's experiences [*essais* is the word used in French]." Writing and living were truly synonymous for Montaigne.

Montaigne's individualism or self-concern is not selfish but has universal appeal and readerly application. He became convinced and fascinated by the idea that he was representative of mankind in general: "Every man contains within himself the form of the human condition." His unique undertaking as a writer of essays was, ironically, to show the universality of individualism, the "universal being" of his individual self: "Authors communicate themselves to people by some special and peculiar mark; I, the first of any, by my universal being, as Michel de Montaigne." In the self, one can find all that is necessary to human knowledge: "I study myself more than any other subject. That is my metaphysics, that is my physics." And Montaigne's self-portraiture provides a method for others to learn how to look at and appraise themselves and work out their own art of living.

Montaigne had a tremendous influence on later thinkers and writers like René Descartes, Blaise Pascal, Montesquieu, Jean-Jacques Rousseau, Gustave Flaubert, and André Gide, to name just a few. The success of the editions of the *Essays* in the Renaissance and afterward, with more than a hundred having been published, testifies to the value of Montaigne's self-study and self-portraiture for his readers. Montaigne's belief in universality and his desire to discover and portray in himself that which is common to all individuals greatly shaped classicism and influenced the French and English writers in the next century, including Shakespeare, who quotes directly from the *Essays* in *The Tempest.* Montaigne was also the forerunner of the great French *moralistes* from the seventeenth through the twentieth century, thinkers and writers who also employed the seductive, enlightening resources of literature to study human conduct and the human condition.

BIBLIOGRAPHY

Primary Work
Montaigne, Michel de. *The Complete Works of Montaigne: Essays, Travel Journal, Letters.* Translated by Donald M. Frame. Stanford, Calif., 1980.

Secondary Works
Brush, Craig B. *From the Perspective of the Self: Montaigne's Self-Portrait.* New York, 1994.
Cottrell, Robert D. *Sexuality/Textuality: A Study of the Fabric of Montaigne's Essais.* Columbus, Ohio, 1981.
Frame, Donald M. *Montaigne: A Biography.* New York, 1965.
Henry, Patrick, ed. *Approaches to Teaching Montaigne's Essays.* New York, 1993.
La Charité, Raymond C. *The Concept of Judgment in Montaigne.* The Hague, Netherlands, 1968.
McGowan, Margaret M. *Montaigne's Deceits: The Art of Persuasion in the Essais.* Philadelphia, 1974.
McKinley, Mary B. *Words in a Corner: Studies in Montaigne's Latin Quotations.* Lexington, Ky., 1981.
Regosin, Richard L. *The Matter of My Book: Montaigne's Essais as the Book of the Self.* Berkeley, Calif., 1977.

Regosin, Richard L. *Montaigne's Unruly Brood: Textual Engendering and the Challenge to Paternal Authority.* Berkeley, Calif., 1996.

Sayce, R. A. *The Essays of Montaigne: A Critical Exploration.* Evanston, Ill., 1972.

Screech, M. A. *Montaigne and Melancholy: The Wisdom of the Essays.* London, 1991.

JERRY C. NASH

MONTE, GUIDOBALDO, MARCHESE DAL

(1545–1607), Italian mathematician. Guidobaldo was a leading figure in the mathematical disciplines during the sixteenth century and an influential patron and correspondent of Galileo Galilei (1564–1642). Guidobaldo was born into a noble family at Pesaro in the duchy of Urbino, in central Italy, on 11 January 1545. His father Raniero, knowledgeable in architecture and astrology, was rewarded for military services by the duke of Urbino with the fief of Montebaroccio, near Pesaro, which was inherited by Guidobaldo.

In 1564 Guidobaldo studied philosophy at Padua without taking a degree. On his return to the duchy of Urbino he was instructed in mathematics by Federico Commandino (1509–1575), one of the leading mathematicians of his age.

After having fought in Hungary against the Turks, dal Monte in 1571 accompanied his duke to the Battle of Lepanto, but fell ill and had to remain at Messina in Sicily. There he may have met Francesco Maurolico (1494–1575), another important mathematician.

In 1577 dal Monte published at Pesaro his masterpiece, *Liber mechanicorum* (Mechanics), in which he brought together the science of machines and Archimedean statics. He greatly admired Greek mathematics for its rigorously deductive formulations and despised the medieval tradition of Jordanus de Nemore (fl. thirteenth century) and the practical mathematics of Niccolò Tartaglia (1500–1557). He often tried to display the consequences of his theoretical views by means of instruments built to the purpose by the Urbino instrument maker Simone Barocci (d. 1608). His collaboration with Barocci involved many instruments, including a compass that he improved over earlier designs.

At Pesaro in 1588 dal Monte published an edition and translation of Archimedes, *In duos aequiponderantium libros paraphrasis* (Paraphrase of the two books on the equilibrium of planes). That year dal Monte supervised the publication of Commandino's edition of *Mathematicae collectiones* (Mathematical collections) by the Greek mathematician Pappus of Alexandria (fl. fourth century C.E.). In the same year he was appointed visitor general to the fortresses

and cities by the grand duke of Tuscany. Thanks to Guidobaldo and his brother, the cardinal Francesco Maria, Galileo obtained the chairs of mathematics at Pisa in 1589 and Padua in 1592. In his correspondence with Guidobaldo, Galileo announced his discovery of the isochronism of pendular oscillations, a claim received with scepticism by Guidobaldo, who believed that motion did not belong to the realm of the mathematical disciplines. Galileo's *Discorsi e dimonstrazioni matematiche intorno a due nuove scienze* (Dialogue concerning two new sciences; Leiden, 1638) contains statements that can also be found in dal Monte's manuscripts, notably the claim that an inked ball rolled on an inclined plane describes a parabola, although it is not clear whether this idea originated with dal Monte or Galileo.

After having published *Planisphaeriorum universalium theorical* (Theory of the universal planispheres; 1579), dal Monte produced *Perspectiva libri sex* (Six books on perspective; 1600). It expanded on previous treatises on the same subject and included a general theory of vanishing points.

Unlike other sixteenth-century mathematicians, dal Monte did not see the emergence of the mathematical disciplines as a challenge to philosophy. He refused to accept with Christopher Clavius (1538–1612) and Galileo that the 1604 nova was in heaven, for example, on the grounds that the heavens were incorruptible.

Guidobaldo died in January 1607 at Montebaroccio. His *Problemata astronomica* (Problems in astronomy; 1609) and *De cochlea* (The cochlea; 1615) were published posthumously by his son Orazio.

See also **Mathematics** *and biography of Galileo Galilei.*

BIBLIOGRAPHY

Bertoloni Meli, Domenico. "Guidobaldo dal Monte and the Archimedean Revival," *Nuncius* 7 (1992): 3–34.

Drake, Stillman, and I. E. Drabkin. *Mechanics in Sixteenth-Century Italy.* Madison, Wis., 1969.

Rose, Paul Lawrence. *The Italian Renaissance of Mathematics.* Geneva, 1975.

DOMENICO BERTOLONI MELI

MONTEFELTRO FAMILY.

Of five fifteenth-century Montefeltro rulers, one was guilty of those violent crimes and depraved excesses so vividly portrayed by Jakob Burckhardt in his *Civilization of the Renaissance in Italy,* as characteristic of Italian Renaissance princes. The other four were exemplary Christian princes.

According to tradition the family's name (sometimes contracted to Feltro) originated in the locality

Montefeltro Family

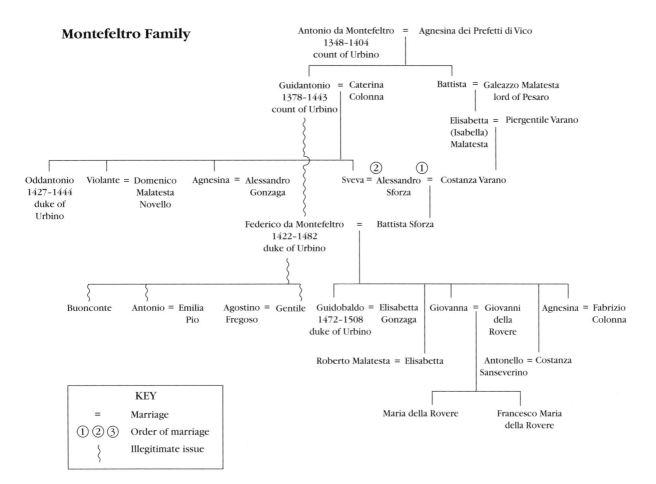

KEY

=   Marriage

① ② ③   Order of marriage

⟨   Illegitimate issue

of Montefeltro (now called San Leo) in the Marches (a region of central Italy bordering the Adriatic Sea), which the family received from the emperor in 1155, the males then being ascribed to the imperial nobility as counts. Some two centuries later, when the Marches were under papal authority, the family was granted as vicariates territory recently acquired by the emperor, together with Urbino. In 1369, however, the papal legate dispossessed the family and sent it into exile.

Ecclesiastical misgovernment of the territory followed, with the result that in 1375 Urbino's citizens requested Count Antonio (1348–1404), living in Florence, to return as their signore (lord), an offer he accepted. Within a decade a compromise with the church was reached whereby the count ruled again as papal vicar, thus legalizing his authority. He was able to thwart expansion by the Malatesta family, his neighbors to the north and east, in part by marrying into that family both of his children, Guidantonio and Battista. His vicariates were further secured by the incorporation of the towns of Cagli, Gubbio, and Cantiano, which controlled passes in the mountains.

Urbino was the center of his state. From his residence there he maintained contact with Florentine humanists, formed the nucleus of a library, and ensured that both his children should acquire courtly accomplishments and Latin humanities. Of his original family palace, which has since been rebuilt, there remains the main portal, also his arms carved in stone, and likewise those of his wife, Agnesina dei Prefetti di Vico, of the ruling family of Viterbo. He died on 29 April 1404 and was buried in the Church of San Francesco in Urbino, where the tomb, commissioned by his son, can still be seen, decorated with chivalric emblems.

The son, Guidantonio (1378–1443), inherited a well-governed state. As an esteemed mercenary general, he enhanced its prosperity and his own reputation on the Italian peninsula. His service to Pope Martin V was rewarded on 7 January 1419 by the duchy of Spoleto for life, and the associated title of duke. Links with Rome were strengthened by his second marriage in 1424, to the pope's niece Caterina Colonna. Already by about 1420 Buonacorso da Montemagno, dedicating his "De nobilitate" (Concerning nobility) to Guidantonio, declared him "the light of our age," so comparable with the epithet "the light of Italy" accorded by Baldassare Castiglione in *Il cortegiano* (*The Book of the Courtier*) to Guidantonio's illegitimate son, Federico. The similarity between father and son goes further. The first wife of each proved sterile, and each sought the continuance of the dynasty by means of a papal bull legitimizing a bastard son (Federico was so legitimized); late in life each was able to remarry and each engendered a legitimate heir, who had precedence over the legitimized son. Guidantonio died on 21 February 1443. Robed in Franciscan habit he was buried in the cemetery of the Franciscan Church of San Donato, a mile outside Urbino's wall.

Oddantonio (1427–1444), Guidantonio's legitimate son, was an aberrant Montefeltro ruler. He succeeded at the age of sixteen, hence without restraint of a regency, to be flattered by Pope Eugenius IV, who created him the first duke of Urbino, and also by Sigismondo Pandolfo Malatesta, a few years his senior. Malatesta held the neighboring vicariates of Rimini and Fano, and sought Oddantonio's debauchery in order to precipitate a revolt, when Malatesta might be able to acquire territory. Oddantonio, with cruelty reminiscent of a Nero, had a page decked out as a candle and burned alive. With two cronies, he gang-raped some wives and some daughters of Urbino's citizens. His profligacy also emptied the treasury, and necessitated high taxation. After just over a year in authority Oddantonio and his two associates were murdered on 23 July 1444 by disaffected citizens.

Federico was summoned to replace his half-brother as signore. The new signore consistently modeled his rule on his father's, and like his father, he acquired wealth and reputation as an outstanding condottiere. In 1474 he was created duke of Urbino by the pope in recognition of his military service. When Federico died, his heir, Guidobaldo (1472–1508), was ten, too young to receive profitable military contracts. Furthermore he inherited a severe form of congenital dropsy, which increasingly incapacitated him, thus explaining his absence from the court activities described in Castiglione's *The Courtier* (the fictitious dialogue of which is set at the court of Urbino in the year before Guidobaldo's death). Moreover, Guidobaldo was impotent, so that his marriage in 1488 to Elisabetta Gonzaga of Mantua was childless. The Montefeltro line ended with his death on 12 April 1508. Four years previously Pope Julius II had prevailed on him to adopt their common nephew, Francesco Maria I della Rovere, who succeeded as duke of Urbino.

See also **Castiglione, Baldassare; Urbino.**

BIBLIOGRAPHY

Primary Works

Castiglione, Baldassare. *The Book of the Courtier.* Translated by Charles S. Singleton. Garden City, N.Y., 1959. Translation of *Il cortegiano* (1528).

Michelini Tocci, Luigi. "I due manoscritti urbinati dei privilegi dei Montefeltro." In *La bibliofilia* 60 (1958): 206–257.

Secondary Works

Clough, Cecil H. "Montefeltro." In *Die grossen Familien Italiens.* Edited by Volker Reinhardt. Stuttgart, Germany, 1992. Pages 360–371.

Dennistoun, James. *Memoirs of the Dukes of Urbino.* 3 vols. London, 1851. Revised and edited by Edward Hutton. 3 vols. London, 1909.

Franceschini, Gino. *I Montefeltro.* Milan, 1970.

CECIL H. CLOUGH

MONTEMAYOR, JORGE DE

MONTEMAYOR, JORGE DE (c. 1520–1561), Iberian poet and prose author. Little is known about the life of Jorge de Montemayor, whose name presumably refers to the small Portuguese town where he was born, Montemor-o-Velho. The dearth of biographical information about the author has led many to conclude that he was either illegitimate or from a Jewish family that had converted to Catholicism. All evidence suggests that Montemayor enjoyed little formal education and spent most of his short life in the service of Spanish nobility and royalty as a musician, soldier, and courtier, enjoying access to aristocratic literary production and patronage.

Montemayor was a singer in the imperial chapel in Madrid from 1548 to 1552, then served as chamberlain for Princess Joan of Castille during her marriage to John IV of Portugal from 1552 to 1554. The untimely death of the prince led to Joan's return to Spain, after which Montemayor disappeared from official records. Fanciful rumors about his death in a love duel in Piedmont, Italy, although unsubstantiated, captured popular fancy and reflect the association between Montemayor and exaggerated love that still dominates interpretation of his works.

Montemayor's religious writings, his most numerous works, earn him a primary place in the history of European devotional literature. From 1545 to 1554 he wrote poems as well as a prose dialogue dated 1548, the "Diálogo spiritual" (Spiritual dialogue), in which a courtier converses with a courtier-turned-hermit about fundamental questions of Catholic doctrine and delicate matters of faith. In 1554, a two-part volume of his religious and secular verse, the *Obras*

(Works), was published in Antwerp. Twin volumes followed in 1558, the *Segundo cancionero* (Second songbook) and *Segundo cancionero spiritual* (Second spiritual songbook; Antwerp), including new contemplative poetry in the religious verse and pastoral works in the secular volume. The "Diálogo spiritual" and Montemayor's religious poetry reflect the relatively open spiritual and political environment of early-sixteenth-century Iberia, and promote major reformist themes of the day: unmediated access to God; individual, affective interpretation of the scriptures; and the exaltation of infused wisdom. Unique to Montemayor, and characteristic of his works in general, is a pronounced melancholy and profound sense of loss rendered by the recollection of an idealized past in light of a disillusioning present.

An unlettered courtier's emotional writings about God and Catholicism were unacceptable to the Counter-Reformation Catholic Church, and all of Montemayor's religious writings were prohibited by the 1559 Spanish inquisitorial Index. By that date, he had the famous *Los siete libros de la Diana* (The seven books of Diana) ready for press. Not surprisingly, that work displays many of the author's religious themes projected onto a secular canvas: human love doctrine replaces Catholic theology; and personal lament and recollection of individual experience, contrasted with idealized expectations, constitute the primary narrative blocks.

Diana (1559?), the prototype of Spain's many pastoral narrations, was an immediate international success, inaugurating a vogue of pastoral culture that was still sweeping through Europe at the beginning of the seventeenth century. A seven-part collection of love stories told by their protagonists, the book is loosely held together by the shepherd Sireno's frustrated affection for the married shepherdess Diana, but it includes chivalric and fantasy interludes, all united by the protagonists' common quest for mutual love. The *Diana* marks an important step in prose fiction from the plot-dominated romances then popular to more novelistic, psychologically profound works, which developed fully in Cervantes's *Don Quixote* (1605).

BIBLIOGRAPHY

Primary Work

Montemayor, Jorge de. *La Diana*. Edited by Juan Montero. Barcelona, Spain, 1996. Thorough, scholarly edition of text including an insightful introduction.

Secondary Works

López Estrada, Francisco. *Los libros de pastores en la literatura española*. Madrid, 1974. Comprehensive study of the socio-cultural factors that influenced the genre of pastoral fiction in Renaissance Spain.

Rhodes, Elizabeth. *The Unrecognized Precursors of Montemayor's* Diana. Columbia, Mo., and London, 1992. Analysis of *Diana* in light of Montemayor's religious works.

ELIZABETH RHODES

MONTEVERDI, CLAUDIO (1567–1643), Italian composer. Monteverdi studied composition with Marc'Antonio Ingegneri in his native Cremona. He was active in the court of Mantua from c. 1590 to 1612, first as member of the instrumental ensemble and later as *maestro di cappella* (chorus master), and in Venice from 1613 until the end of his life as *maestro di cappella* at St. Mark's basilica.

Monteverdi's long career—sixty-one years separate his earliest published musical work, the *Sacrae cantiunculae* (1582), from his last work, *L'incoronazione di Poppea* (The coronation of Poppea; 1642)—spans a period of profound change in the aesthetics of musical composition that led to the establishment of a new style as well as to the creation of new genres. The end of the sixteenth century and the beginning of the seventeenth saw the replacement of the equal-voiced, predominantly linear, polyphony of the Renaissance, with its strict adherence to the rules of counterpoint, by the new textures of Baroque music. The new style relied on an instrumental basso continuo to support a predominantly soloistic texture of one or more parts, and frequently set aside contrapuntal propriety, particularly regarding the treatment of dissonance, in the interest of affective expression.

Monteverdi's output exemplifies this change: until 1605, his musical compositions consisted primarily of a cappella madrigals for five voices; after the turn of the century, in both sacred and secular music, he experimented with new combinations of voices and instruments, as well as with such emergent genres as monody and opera. To the latter he contributed the earliest works still in the active repertory: *Orfeo* (1607), *Il ritorno di Ulisse in patria* (The return of Ulysses to his native country; 1640), and *L'incoronazione di Poppea*. Indeed, Monteverdi's reputation as the towering figure of his generation is due to a great extent to his remarkable flexibility, which to the very end of his career allowed him to adapt successfully to the rapidly changing aesthetic climate of his time.

Monteverdi's historical position as the creator of modern music who marks the end of the Renaissance was fixed by the public dispute with the Bolognese theorist Giovanni Maria Artusi, who, in two

Claudio Monteverdi. Portrait by Bernardo Berozzi (1561–
1644). TIROLER LANDESMUSEUM FERDINANDEUM, INNSBRUCK/
ERICH LESSING/ART RESOURCE

homage to the conservative tradition of the contrapuntal *missa ad imitationem.* As maestro at St.
Mark's, he composed, in addition to more modern
motets for voices and instruments, a cappella Masses
for Christmas and possibly other feasts; two survive
in the late collections *Selva morale e spirituale*
(Moral masses; 1641) and *Messa et salmi* (Mass and
psalm; 1650). Finally, evidence of his finely crafted
contrapuntal technique and nuanced text-setting in
the best sixteenth-century tradition can be found
even in such modern works as the *Madrigali guer-
rieri et amorosi* (Madrigals of war and love; 1638)
and the late operas.

BIBLIOGRAPHY

Primary Works

Artusi, Giovanni Maria. *L'Artusi, overo Delle imperfettioni della
    moderna musica* (L'Artusi, or, On the imperfections of mod-
    ern music). 2 vols. Venice, 1600, 1603. Facsimile ed. Bolo-
    gna, 1968.
Monteverdi, Claudio. *L'incoronazione di Poppea.* Edited by Alan
    Curtis. London, 1989.
Monteverdi, Claudio. *The Letters of Claudio Monteverdi.* Trans-
    lated and edited by Denis Stevens. Oxford, 1995. A revised
    edition of the original volume published in Cambridge, 1980.
Monteverdi, Claudio. *Lettere.* Edited by Éva Lax. Florence, 1994.
Monteverdi, Claudio. *Tutte le opere.* Edited by Gian Francesco
    Malipiero. 2d ed. Vienna, 1954–1968.
Treitler, Leo, ed. *Source Readings in Music History.* New York,
    1998. A revised edition of the original volume edited and
    translated by Oliver Strunk, New York, 1950. Contains trans-
    lations of passages from *L'Artusi,* as well as of Monteverdi's
    reply in the preface to the fifth book of madrigals (1605),
    and of his brother Giulio Cesare's gloss on the preface, the
    "Dichiarazione," in the *Scherzi musicali* (1607).
Zarlino, Gioseffo. *Le Istituitoni harmoniche* (The principles of
    harmony). Venice, 1558. Facsimile ed. New York, 1965. Par-
    tial translation in *The Art of Counterpoint: Part Three of "Le
    istitutioni harmoniche," 1558.* Translated by Guy A. Marco
    and Claude V. Palisca. New Haven, Conn., and London, 1968.

Secondary Works

Arnold, Denis, and Nigel Fortune, eds. *The New Monteverdi
    Companion.* London, 1985.
Chafe, Eric. *Monteverdi's Tonal Language.* New York, 1992.
Fabbri, Paolo. *Monteverdi.* Translated by Tim Carter. Cambridge,
    U.K., 1994. Translation of *Monteverdi.* Turin, Italy, 1985.
Leopold, Silke. *Monteverdi: Music in Transition.* Translated by
    Anne Smith. Oxford, 1991. Translation of *Claudio Monte-
    verdi und seine Zeit.* Laaber, Germany, 1982.
Schrade, Leo. *Monteverdi: Creator of Modern Music.* New York,
    1950.
Tomlinson, Gary. *Monteverdi and the End of the Renaissance.*
    Berkeley, Calif., 1987.

MASSIMO OSSI

treatises criticizing the excesses of modern music
(1600 and 1603), singled him out as representative
of the new generation's disregard for counterpoint
as taught by such masters as the theorist Gioseffo
Zarlino, whose treatises codified the rules of counterpoint. Artusi's attack on Monteverdi's *seconda
prattica* (new style) helped to establish the term as
a manifesto for composers writing in the Baroque
style; Monteverdi himself later claimed credit for the
term (although it is likely to have been in common
use before Artusi invoked it as an aesthetic label) and
planned to use it as the title of a never-realized treatise explaining the principles of the new style.

In fact, Monteverdi was a reluctant, if unrepen-
tant, "rebel" who, in spite of pursuing new genres
and developing new techniques to suit them, never
abandoned the Renaissance foundations of his training. His madrigals include some of the finest examples of the genre as practiced by such masters as
Cipriano da Rore, Luca Marenzio, and Giaches de
Wert, and after Artusi's criticisms he seemed to go
out of his way to emphasize his roots. His Marian
Vespers (1610) opens with the "Missa in illo tem-
pore" based on a motet by Nicolas Gombert, an

**MONTLUC, BLAISE DE LASSERAN-MASSEN-
CÔME, SEIGNEUR DE** (c. 1501–1577), French
soldier, memoirist, commentator on the art of war in

the sixteenth century. Born in Armagnac, Montluc (or Monluc) came from an impoverished branch of the house of Montesquiou. His military career began in 1521 in Italy, where he was an archer in the armies of Francis I. Thereafter, he served in most of that monarch's campaigns, including Pavia (1525), Marseilles (1536), Ceresole (1544), and Siena (1554–1555). In reward for his skill and bravery, Montluc rose rapidly to become interim colonel general of the French infantry in 1558.

With the outbreak of the French Wars of Religion in 1562, Montluc commanded the royal forces in the southwest against the Huguenots. Promoted to lieutenant general and admiral of Guyenne in 1565, he became noted for the rigor of his repression of the Calvinists, which even contemporaries found excessive. Forced to retire briefly from battle (1570–1572) by a wound to the face, Montluc wrote his famous *Commentaries* (first published in 1592) during his convalescence. Part autobiography and part reflection on the art of war, his purpose—besides self-aggrandizement—was to formulate useful lessons drawn from personal experience for the instruction of future commanders. Called "the bible of soldiers" by Henry IV, Montluc's military axioms also influenced Napoleon. Shortly after returning to action in 1573, Montluc was created marshal of France (1574). He died at Condom three years later, on 26 August 1577.

BIBLIOGRAPHY

Primary Works

A modern edition of Montluc's *Commentaries* and letters was published by Alphonse de Ruble for the Société de l'histoire de France in 1864–1872, followed by a second version in 1911–1925 by Paul Courteault. An English edition by Charles Cotton was published in 1674, while selections, translated by A. W. Evans, appeared as *Blaise de Monluc* in 1913.

Secondary Works

Courteault, Paul. *Blaise de Montluc historien*. Paris, 1908.
Fonclare, Elie de. *Le maréchal de Monluc, sa vie, son temps*. Paris, 1949.
Le Gras, Joseph. *Blaise de Monluc, héros malchanceux et grand écrivain*. Paris, 1926.

RONALD S. LOVE

MONTMORENCY FAMILY. The French family of Montmorency led one of the three extensive clienteles that fought for control of the crown on the eve of and during the Wars of Religion (1562–1598). Familial ties and religious positions ultimately allied the Montmorency with the second family, the Bourbon, against the Guise, the third of the competing clans.

Leaders of the Montmorency Family. Drawing of the leaders of the family during the Wars of Religion, the brothers Cardinal Odet de Coligny, Admiral Gaspard de Coligny, and François d'Anelot de Coligny. Drawing; 1580. MUSÉE CONDÉ, CHANTILLY, FRANCE/GIRAUDON/ART RESOURCE

From Barony to Dukedom. The Montmorency underwent a renaissance in the sixteenth century. The family had a brilliant medieval past in the service of the French king, holding high offices and winning such major battles as Bouvines (1214). With fifteenth-century civil wars and Anglo-French conflict, the family's fortune declined as its members joined various parties, compromising the integrity of the baronial holding. Guillaume (d. 1531), who had remained loyal to the French king Louis XI (1423–1483) during the War of the Public Weal (1464–1465), was able to reunify and expand the patrimony in Île-de-France comprising the lordships of Ecouen, Montmorency, and Chantilly, which formed the territorial basis of the peer-duchy constituted in 1551 by King Henry II (1519–1559) in favor of Guillaume's son, Anne (1493–1567), the constable of France. The duchy of Montmorency passed on to Anne's own sons, first to the eldest, François (1530–1579), and then to Henri de Montmorency-Damville (1534–1614), whose namesake son's decapitation

Montmorency Family

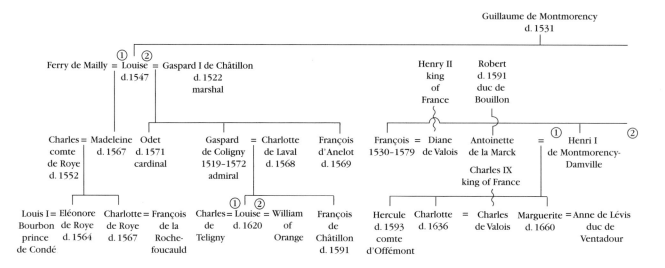

(in 1632, at Richelieu's behest) brought the first ducal line of Montmorency to a brutal end.

When Anne was made first duke of Montmorency, he considerably expanded the landed assets of the family through heritages, donations, acquisitions, and confiscations. As a result the Montmorency, already solidly ensconced in Paris, Île-de-France, and Picardy, also became firmly established in the center of France (Auvergne, Champagne, Berry, and Bourgogne), and in its western provinces, where their possessions spanned Normandy, Brittany, and Anjou. To the considerable revenues derived from these estates were added the lucrative offices and benefices held by various members of the family who were marshals (Anne, François, and Henri), constables (Anne and Henri), governors (of Paris: La Rochepot [d. 1551], Anne's younger brother, and François; of Languedoc: Anne and Henri), lieutenant governor (of Picardy: La Rochepot), admiral (Henri; Gaspard de Coligny [1519–1572], Anne's nephew; and Charles de Méru, Anne's third son), and cardinal (Odet de Coligny, Gaspard's brother).

Family Structure and Clientele Network.
Control of land, government office, and military command furthered Montmorency influence at court and abroad, and strengthened the family's inner coherence and political effectiveness. The constable-duke Anne, architect of a vast clientage, favored kin over patronage and vassalic relations, carefully building upon blood relationships and marriage. Through his sister Louise, Anne was the uncle of the

Châtillon brothers—Cardinal Odet, Admiral Gaspard de Coligny, and François d'Andelot—and the granduncle of Louis de Bourbon, prince de Condé (1530–1569), who had married Louise's granddaughter Eléonore de Roye. From his own marriage to Madeleine de Savoie, a niece of the mother of King Francis I (1494–1547), Anne sired five sons and seven daughters. Four of these daughters married: François de Turenne, Louis de La Trémoille (vicomte de Thouars and prince de Tarente), Gilbert de Lévis (duc de Ventadour), and Henri de Foix (comte d'Estarac), bringing the four most prominent families in Aquitaine within the Montmorency orbit. Anne's five sons all embraced military and governmental careers, with the eldest, François, making a profitable marriage with the natural daughter of King Henry II.

Family Dynamics, Religious Divisions, and State Politics.
Conspicuous in their ambition, the Montmorency were at times manipulated by the monarchy, which sought to balance them against the Bourbon and Guise, especially during the royal minorities following Henry II's death. This latter event at first signaled the dramatic ascendancy of the Guise, uncles to the now reigning king, Francis II (1544–1560). When her second son ascended the throne in 1560 as Charles IX, Catherine de Médicis turned to the Bourbon and Montmorency families to promote religious toleration, thereby checking the Guise, who championed an aggressively anti-Protestant policy. This experiment at tolerance failed, opening a thirty-six-year period of civil war during

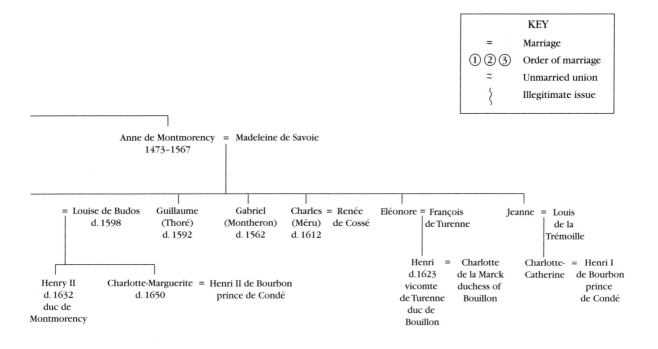

which religious passions and factional struggles among the nobility greatly weakened the monarchy.

Although religious affiliation complicated the loyalty of the Montmorency, they ultimately rallied across confessional lines to oppose the Guise. Anne's nephews, the Châtillon and Louis de Bourbon, prince de Condé, were Protestants. Condé was the leading Huguenot general, succeeded thereafter by Gaspard de Coligny. Anne remained a staunch Catholic. His sons François and Henri stayed on the Catholic side but advocated Politique policies of toleration, supporting Coligny's program for a patriotic war against Spain, alliance with England, and marriage of the king's sister, Margaret of Valois, with the then Calvinist Bourbon Henry of Navarre (the future Henry IV). The reaction of the Guise, ousted from court by Coligny, and of the ultra-Catholics, brought about the Saint Bartholomew's Day massacre (23–24 August 1572), of which Coligny was the chief victim.

While the Guise formed the Catholic League in 1576, placing it on a military footing to destroy heresy in France and later making an alliance with Spain to oppose Henry of Navarre's inheritance of the French throne, Henri de Montmorency-Damville permitted the Huguenots in his government of Languedoc to form their own armies, law courts, and fiscal system, even encouraging opponents of the Guise across denominational lines to join forces with this Protestant contingent. In the joint assembly of the Politiques, Catholic Malcontents, and Huguenots held at Nîmes in Languedoc in 1574, Montmorency-Damville appeared to be "uncrowned king" of the south, having carved for himself a virtually independent state. His younger brothers—Charles, seigneur de Méru (d. 1612), and Guillaume, seigneur de Thoré (d. 1592)—actively supported the Huguenot cause at this time. Unable to maintain a posture of indifference to King Henry III's distrust or to the attacks of the league, Montmorency-Damville made an alliance with Henry of Navarre in 1585.

As the most important Catholic nobleman to join the royal cause after Navarre's succession to the throne in 1589 as Henry IV, Montmorency-Damville was promised the office of constable (which he received in 1593) and helped Navarre to stabilize his crown, to end the religious wars (by the Edict of Nantes issued in 1598), and to revive the power of the monarchy, including, ironically, its centralization over the semi-independent French south. Montmorency-Damville died in 1614. Whether he had joined forces with the Huguenot party as head of the Catholic Malcontents or as leader of the Politique party is a point still debatable to those historians who doubt the existence of a specific Politique party. However, the Politique program, which favored political unity under the crown at the expense of uniformity of worship, was one that the Montmorency espoused as individuals and furthered as heads of a large clientele.

See also **France,** *subentry on* **Kingdom of France; Wars of Religion.**

BIBLIOGRAPHY

Bedos, Brigitte. *La châtellenie de Montmorency des origines à 1368. Aspects féodaux, sociaux et économiques.* Pontoise, France, 1980. A social history of the Montmorency and their lordship between the early eleventh and the mid-fourteenth centuries.

Davies, J. M. *Languedoc and Its Governors: Henry de Montmorency-Daimville, 1563–1589.* London, 1974.

Desormeaux, Joseph-Louis. *Histoire de la maison de Montmorency.* 5 vols. Paris, 1764.

Palm, Franklin Charles. *Politics and Religion in Sixteenth-Century France: A Study of the Career of Henry of Montmorency-Damville, Uncrowned King of the South.* Boston, 1927. A detailed chronicle with a slightly apologetic tone.

Shimizu, J. *Conflict of Loyalties: Politics and Religion in the Career of Gaspard of Coligny, Admiral of France.* Geneva, 1970.

BRIGITTE M. BEDOS-REZAK

MONTMORENCY, ANNE DE

MONTMORENCY, ANNE DE (1493–1567), leading French statesman and patron of the arts. Anne, who died duc de Montmorency and a peer of France, was born to a baronial lineage of ancient and distinguished, if impoverished, antiquity, the second son of Guillaume de Montmorency and Anne Pot. In reviving the family's grandeur and wealth, elevating both to unprecedented heights, Anne acquired assets and developed a network central to his strategy of self- and state-promotion. To a man upholding traditional values and governed by a firm set of loyalties to both kin and king, the dynamic of the time brought conflict, failure, and opportunity. Through his capacity for work, his courage on the battlefield, and his taste for the arts, Anne became an architect of the French Renaissance.

His godmother, Queen Anne of Brittany, bequeathed him his unusual name. His intimacy with French royalty was intensified by an education at court, a boyhood friendship with the future King Francis I (1494–1547), a marriage with Madeleine of Savoy (niece of Francis's mother, Louise of Savoy) in 1527, and an affectionate relationship with King Henry II (1519–1559) and the two central female figures of Henry's entourage, Queen Catherine de Médicis and Diane de Poitiers, the king's mistress. On the basis of such intimacy, Anne early launched a career at court, proving his utility by a distinguished record in the Valois wars against the Habsburgs and by astute diplomacy capable of minimizing his king's military disasters.

Rewarded with the offices of marshal (1522–1526), grand master (1526–1538), governor of Languedoc (1526–1563), and constable of France (1538–1567), and made duke and peer in 1551, Anne was granted official leadership in every aspect

Anne de Montmorency. Portrait by Léonard Limousin. Enamel on leather; 1556; 72 × 56 cm (28 × 22 in.). MUSÉE DU LOUVRE, PARIS/GIRAUDON

of state governance. His policies fostered centralized absolutism, favored peace, achieved unification and expansion of the national territory (but not the Valois dream of French sovereignty over Italy), respected imperial and papal supremacy (though not to the detriment of French majesty), and, after a short-lived attempt at religious tolerance, promoted action against Protestantism.

Emulating the Valois politics of art, Anne engaged in a vast program of artistic patronage that reinforced his social and official status. Elegant Montmorency emblems still identify his architectural creations (Ecouen, Chantilly, Parisian mansions), the book bindings enshrining the translations he commissioned of favorite authors (Thucydides, Cicero, Livy, Sallust), and the ceramics, tapestries, and other luxurious objects he either gathered or commissioned. In the course of surrounding himself with fame and the art that trumpeted it, Anne gave impetus to several careers and furthered major aesthetic trends. He discovered and promoted the architect Jean Bullant (c. 1520–1578) and the sculptor Jean Goujon (d. c. 1564/68), while supporting the ceramicists Bernard Palissy and Masséot Abaquesne and the painter Niccolò dell'Abbate (1512–1571).

Anne's policies as chief minister provoked factional opposition and brought him into disgrace (from 1541 to 1547 and 1559 to 1560). Although none exceeded the Guise family in its rivalry with Anne and his clan for supreme influence at court, the two antagonists joined to form the extreme Catholic party (the Triumvirate, 1561) against Protestantism. This coalition sparked the Wars of Religion upon whose battlefields Anne found his death, fighting for the trinitarian order of God, faith, and king.

BIBLIOGRAPHY

Bedos-Rezak, Brigitte. *Anne de Montmorency: Seigneur de la Renaissance*. Paris, 1990. A comprehensive biography with a new focus on Anne's artistic patronage.

De Crue de Stoutz, Francis. *Anne de Montmorency, grand maître et connétable de France: A la cour, aux armées et au conseil du roi François Ier*. Paris, 1885. Reprint, Geneva, 1978.

De Crue de Stoutz, Francis. *Anne, duc de Montmorency, connétable et pair de France sous les rois Henri II, François II, et Charles IX*. 2 vols. Paris, 1889. Detailed chronological studies of Anne's career, emphasizing its political significance.

BRIGITTE M. BEDOS-REZAK

MORAL PHILOSOPHY. During the Renaissance, moral philosophy was largely based on the thought of classical antiquity. Most thinkers elaborated on ancient systems of philosophy, adapting them to the needs of their own Christian society. Even Niccolò Machiavelli's undermining of traditional morality, by placing the claims of political expediency above those of private virtue, derived as much from his analysis of Roman history as from his observation of contemporary political behavior.

Renaissance practical philosophy was divided into three disciplines: ethics, politics, and economics, or household management. This division, traceable to Aristotle and his Greek commentators, was adopted by scholastic philosophers of the thirteenth century and institutionalized in the curriculum of medieval and Renaissance universities. Following a scheme elaborated by Thomas Aquinas, Renaissance philosophers regarded ethics as concerned with the individual, economics with the family, and politics with the state: ethics trained the good man, economics the good head of household, and politics the good citizen. Some held that politics was superior to economics and ethics because the good of the state was more important than that of the family or the individual. Others, however, argued that ethics was the most fundamental and comprehensive of the three disciplines.

Human Dignity. The dignity of human beings was a popular theme during the Renaissance; the arguments on which it was based, however, were not new but derived mainly from classical, biblical, patristic, and medieval sources. Drawing on Cicero and Lactantius, for instance, fifteenth- and sixteenth-century authors listed the bodily attributes, from head to toe, that made the human body more beautiful than any other created being. These authors admitted that human beings lacked certain physical gifts possessed by animals, but their mental powers could more than compensate for their bodily weakness.

The most powerful argument for human dignity, however, came from the Bible, where God said: "Let us make man in our image, after our likeness" (Gen. 1:26). The divine status of human beings was further underlined by Christ's becoming incarnate as man. Such views were reinforced by the belief, popularized by Renaissance Platonists, that human beings provide the vital cosmic link connecting the immaterial realm of God and angels to the material world perceived by the senses. For the princely philosopher Giovanni Pico della Mirandola (1463–1494) it was freedom that gave human beings their unique position in the universe. We alone among all creation, Pico maintained, have within ourselves the seeds to grow into whatever type of being we choose: we can vegetate like a plant, wallow in the brutish existence of an animal, live the rational life of a human, or rise to the celestial level of an angel.

Aristotelian Ethics. Aristotle's *Nicomachean Ethics* was the main university textbook on ethics throughout the Renaissance, as it had been since the thirteenth century. Professors of moral philosophy, whether scholastic or humanist, Italian or English, Catholic or Protestant, all looked to Aristotle as their authority. This was partly due to the clarity of his definitions and the organization of his treatise, making it very suitable for pedagogic purposes. A vast number of commentaries, most growing out of classroom lectures, were written on the *Ethics*. It was also summarized, paraphrased, translated into vernacular languages as well as Latin, turned into dialogues, and even put in the form of an epic poem. In 1566 the Swiss scholar Theodor Zwinger produced an elaborate series of diagrams, providing detailed outlines of the ten books of the *Ethics*.

A most influential teaching was Aristotle's definition of moral virtue as a mean between two extremes. For him, each virtue occupies a middle position between two vices, one characterized by excess, the other by deficiency. Thus, courage is the mean between rashness and cowardice, generosity, between profligacy and miserliness. Only the most committed of anti-Aristotelians, such as the Italian humanist Lorenzo Valla (1407–1457), objected, arguing that the middle course was not always the best and the extremes were sometimes preferable. Was it not better to be exceedingly wise than only moderately so?

Aristotle's treatments of virtue were generally thought to be in line with Christian teaching. Indeed, according to the Scottish scholastic John Major (1469–1550), Aristotle's divinely inspired account of the moral virtues diverged in no way from Christian orthodoxy. Nevertheless, Aristotle's pagan conviction that our highest good, which for him could be achieved in the present life through contemplation, needed to be adapted to the otherworldly perspective of Christianity. This had been largely achieved in the late Middle Ages, when scholastic philosophers described the Aristotelian supreme good as a staging post on the way to man's ultimate goal: union with God in the next life.

Most Renaissance Aristotelians accepted this outlook. Some, like the sixteenth-century Oxford philosopher John Case (c. 1540–1600), went even further, asserting that Aristotle had believed that the soul was immortal and would receive rewards and punishments after death. The Italian Dominican Crisostomo Javelli (1470–1538) took a more cautious approach, and pointed out that Aristotle had neither affirmed nor denied the possibility of attaining the supreme good in the future life. His countryman Agostino Nifo (1469/70–1538) agreed, but argued that Aristotle had nevertheless hinted at a belief in happiness after death. The Lutheran theologian Philipp Melanchthon, by contrast, distinguished between the pagan ethics of Aristotle and the Christian teachings of the Gospels. Although both were necessary, they served very different ends: the former protected civil society from the evil effects of original sin, the latter brought unearned salvation to fallen humanity.

Platonic Ethics. Renaissance Platonists regarded the supreme good as achieving contemplative knowledge of God, which could only be perfectly attained in the next life. The Spaniard Sebastian Fox-Morcillo (1526/28–1560) claimed that Platonic moral philosophy, far more than Aristotelian, was unambiguously in accord with Christianity. This agreement was of crucial importance to the Florentine Marsilio Ficino (1433–1499), a priest as well as a philosopher, who played the key role in the fifteenth-century revival of Platonism in the West. One of his followers, Francesco de' Vieri (1524–1591), carried on Ficino's program by producing a *Compendio* (1577) of all Platonic doctrines that conformed with Christianity.

Although Platonic ethics never made serious inroads into university teaching, some of its doctrines infiltrated the vernacular literary culture of the Renaissance. Chief among these was the theory of Platonic love. In his commentary on the *Symposium* (1469), Ficino had turned Plato's intellectual ascent from physical beauty to the realm of Ideas into a spiritual journey whose final destination was God. His younger contemporary Giovanni Pico della Mirandola adopted this religious interpretation of Platonic love, that he, like Ficino, saw as a profound and nonsexual relationship between two men. By 1505, however, the humanist and future cardinal Pietro Bembo (1470–1547), in *Gli Asolani* (The lovers of Asolo), took up the theme and Platonic love, while remaining deeply religious and nonsexual, came to be applied to relations between men and women. This ensured the doctrine a wide diffusion in popular works on love. In Baldassare Castiglione's dialogue *Il cortegiano* (1528; trans. *The Book of the Courtier*), a character named Bembo presents an idealized vision of Platonic love. Transcending more hackneyed treatments of the theme, Castiglione has the other speakers challenge Bembo. His philosophical musings on beauty and love are thus confronted by a more down-to-earth and psychologically realistic view of physical attraction between the sexes.

Stoic and Epicurean Ethics. In addition to the classical philosophies of Plato and Aristotle, Renaissance ethical thought was influenced by two other ancient groups, the Stoics and the Epicureans. Stoicism attracted many Italian humanists, among them Niccolò Niccoli (1364–1437), who admired its association with the stern morality of the Roman Republic and its high-minded belief that virtue alone was sufficient for the good life. Others, however, felt that Stoicism's moral demands, which included a complete extinction of the emotions, were inhuman and even unchristian: Christ, after all, had revealed his humanity through his expression of anger and sorrow. This ambivalent attitude continued until the late sixteenth century, when the Flemish humanist Justus Lipsius (1547–1606) promoted a new brand of Stoicism, more accommodated to the Christian religion, as a remedy for the turmoil caused by the wars of religion. This neo-Stoicism found a wide audience throughout Europe. In Spain, for example, Francisco Sanches (1550/51–1623) translated the *Enchiridion* (Manual) of the Greek Stoic Epictetus into Spanish, emphasizing the work's near complete conformity with the Bible. This theme was developed by his countryman Francisco de Quevedo (1580–1645), who maintained that Epictetus's philosophy of patient resignation derived ultimately from Job.

Epicurean ethics had far less impact on Renaissance thinkers. The doctrine that pleasure was the supreme good had long been misinterpreted as an endorsement of sensual indulgence, while Epicurus's rejection of divine providence and immortality were clearly unacceptable to Christians. When the epic poem *De rerum natura* (On the nature of the universe), by Lucretius, a Roman follower of Epicurus, was rediscovered in 1417, humanists admired its consummate artistry but carefully distanced themselves from its impious philosophical teachings. A few attempts were nonetheless made to adapt Epicureanism to Christianity. In the fifteenth century, Lorenzo Valla transferred the earthly pleasures of Epicurus to the heavenly ones enjoyed by the virtuous in the next life. Inspired by Valla, Erasmus maintained that Christ was the true Epicurean, since his disciples led the most pleasurable life.

BIBLIOGRAPHY

Primary Works

Castiglione, Baldassare. *The Book of the Courtier.* Translated by George Bull. Harmondsworth, U.K., 1976. Translation of *Il cortegiano* (1528). Book 4 contains one of the most popular Renaissance expositions on Platonic love.

Kraye, Jill, ed. *Cambridge Translations of Renaissance Philosophical Texts.* 2 vols. Cambridge, U.K., 1997. Vol. 1: *Moral Philosophy.* Contains selected texts covering Aristotelian, Platonic, Stoic, and Epicurean ethics, as well as concepts of man.

Secondary Works

Copenhaver, Brian P., and Charles B. Schmitt. *Renaissance Philosophy.* Oxford, 1992.

Kraye, Jill. "Moral Philosophy." In *The Cambridge History of Renaissance Philosophy.* Edited by Charles B. Schmitt, Quentin Skinner, Eckhard Kessler, and Jill Kraye. Cambridge, U. K., 1988. Pages 303–386.

Lines, David. "The Importance of Being Good: Moral Philosophy in the Italian Universities, 1300–1600." *Rinascimento* 36 (1996): 139–188.

JILL KRAYE

MORATA, OLYMPIA (1526–1555), humanist writer. Olympia Morata learned Greek and Latin from her father, Fulvio, court tutor in Ferrara. Her early writings include declamations and poems on classical subjects. She lived at court (1540–1546) as companion to Anne, daughter of Ercole II d'Este (1534–1559) and Renée of France, a sympathizer of religious reform. Olympia became ill (1546–1548), her father died (1548), and Catholic orthodoxy was reasserted at court (1548–1550). She turned to religion, writing *Lavinia Ruverensis Ursina et Olympia colloquuntur* (Dialogue between Lavinia della Rovere and Olympia; 1550), which resolved a conflict related to study by a decision to focus on religion. In 1550 Olympia married Andrew Grunthler, a doctor and a Protestant. While he was in Germany seeking a position, she wrote *Theophila et Philotima colloquuntur* (Dialogue of Theophila and Philotima; 1551), her most significant work. Philotima, annoyed by her husband's absence, is admonished by Theophila to study the Bible and lives of the saints to understand life's trials. Both express a resolution to turn to religious studies. In 1551 Olympia and Grunthler left for his native city of Schweinfurt, but in April 1553 the city came under siege. After leaving for Heidelberg in 1554 Olympia described the siege, which had broken their health and led to their deaths in 1555. In her last year she interpreted her religious faith in terms of suffering.

BIBLIOGRAPHY

Primary Works

Morata, Olympia. *Olympia Morata Opere.* Edited by Lanfranco Caretti. In *Deputazione Provinciale Ferrarese di storia patria, atti e memorie,* n.s. 11 (1954). Part 1 (*Epistolae* and *Orationes, dialogi et carmina*). Contains a critical biography and a bibliography.

Parker, Holt N., trans. "Latin and Greek Poetry by Five Renaissance Italian Women Humanists." In *Sex and Gender in Medieval and Renaissance Texts: The Latin Tradition.* Edited by Paul A. Miller, Barbara K. Gold, and Charles Platter. Albany, N.Y., 1997. Pages 247–285.

Secondary Works

Bainton, Roland H. *Women of the Reformation in Germany and Italy.* Minneapolis, Minn., 1971. Pages 253–268.

Rabil, Albert, Jr. "Olympia Morata (1526–1555)." In *Italian Women Writers: A Bio-Bibliographical Sourcebook.* Edited by Rinaldina Russell. Westport, Conn. Pages 269–278.

ALBERT RABIL

MORE, THOMAS (c. 1478–1535), English humanist, statesman.

Early Life. Like many other prominent Renaissance figures, Thomas More was a product of the well-to-do middle class. His father, John More, was an important London lawyer who was eventually raised to the King's Bench. John More could give his son the best possible education the times allowed, and he knew important men. Young Thomas went to grammar school early and, when he was about twelve, went to live in the household of Cardinal John Morton, not only a prince of the church but also lord chancellor of England under Henry VII.

From Cardinal Morton's house, More went to Oxford. There he seems to have been tempted to become a priest or a monk (depending on which early biographer one believes), but following his father's lead More entered the Inns of Court in London and emerged a barrister. Even while he studied law, he came under the influence of John Colet, an influential scholar and preacher who had been to Italy and, although unlearned in Greek, brought back to England the new Italian method of reading ancient texts in their historical contexts. Colet caused a sensation by lecturing on Paul's Epistle to the Romans, and about 1498 More drew attention by lecturing on Augustine's *City of God*.

In 1499 Erasmus went to England for the first time, met More, and was impressed by More's powerful friends (including the boy who would become Henry VIII) and by his wit and learning. More studied Greek, and the two collaborated in translating short works of Lucian of Samosata (c. 120–c. 190). Lucian wittily mocked pagan superstitions, and he was widely regarded as an atheist. More and Erasmus learned from him the art of humorous ridicule for a serious purpose, aiming to criticize superstitious and immoral practices among Christians without questioning the fundamentals of Christian doctrine.

More translated Greek epigrams in later years and wrote poems and epigrams of his own, using ironic wit to teach the virtuous and sensible life. He mocked the follies of physicians and their bogus remedies, of women questing for artificial beauty, and of astrologers. Often he commented on the shortness and uncertainty of life.

In the meantime he advanced in his career and into family responsibilities. He married Jane Colt, a young woman from the country, in 1504 or 1505. After bearing four children she died in 1511. Within a month More was married again to a widow named Alice Middleton, whom one of his biographers, Nicholas Harpsfield, called "aged, blunt, and rude." More believed in education as a road to virtue. He took great care for the education of his children and the wards assigned to him, and contemporaries reported his determined efforts to educate both his wives.

When Henry VII died in 1509, More greeted his death with exuberant poems dedicated to young Henry VIII. He was sharply critical of the old king, making Henry VII seem tyrannical and vindictive. When these poems were finally published in a collection of 1518, More included one expressing his preference for a republic over a monarchy. Senators, he said, are chosen by reasoned argument, monarchs by "blind chance." But he recognized that people seldom had any choice in the government that ruled them. Twelve of More's poems condemned tyranny. Perhaps these strong feelings were inculcated in a London accustomed to the judicious republican forms of the city's government.

Among More's poems published in 1518 were several mocking a French writer, Germanus Brixius, who enthusiastically had written epic verses praising a French naval captain, Hervé de Porzmoguer. Hervé had gone down with his ship during a naval battle with an English vessel that had also been sunk in the engagement. Brixius responded with *Antimorus,* a blistering attack that included a scathing critique of More's Latin diction. More fired back, and this petty squabble raged until Erasmus managed to cool tempers on both sides.

History of Richard III.   Sometime during these years More undertook a history of King Richard III, writing one version in English and a shorter one in Latin. Richard S. Sylvester, the modern editor of this work, demonstrated the influence of the Roman historian Tacitus on More's conception. In More's *History,* Richard III played the villainous role of Tiberius, as Tacitus described it, following the peaceful reign of Augustus.

Most of the events in More's account occurred during his childhood. Among his most likely sources were his father and Cardinal Morton. Doubtless some of the scenes, including conversations, have an element of fiction in them, More putting in direct discourse speeches passed down to him at second- or thirdhand. Doubtless, too, he followed the lead of many classical historians, including Thucydides and Plutarch, who gave characters the words they ought to have spoken. More leaves out some things—including Richard's hugely ceremonial coronation and its indication of large popular support. Some of his details, such as his claim that Richard was a hunchback, are vigorously but inconclusively debated by modern scholars. Especially effective in blackening Richard's reputation was More's detailed

Sir Thomas More and His Descendants. Painting by R. Lockey, 1593. NATIONAL PORTRAIT GALLERY, LONDON

account of how he engineered the murder of the two young sons of Edward IV.

Whatever More's rhetorical devices, the substance of the story seems accurate. Modern historians have little good to say about Richard III, and few doubt that he had the little princes killed. For him it was kill or be killed, and he was as ruthless as the times required. There is every reason to believe that More tried to tell the truth. But he was also teaching a lesson, that a tyrant will subvert all law to ensure his own authority and that under tyranny neither people nor property is safe.

The ruthless dissimulation of More's Richard III has affinities with Machiavelli's ideal prince, who chose to be feared rather than loved and who kept his word only when to do so furthered his interests. But More wanted to believe that the evil prince was doomed to failure while Machiavelli supposed that men were so selfish and corrupt that only a ruthless prince devoted to a theatrical display of power could hope to survive in an evil world. And could More have had faith that tyrants must fall, given that Richard III was succeeded by Henry VII, whom More clearly regarded as a tyrant and who died in bed?

Utopia. More may have given up writing about Richard III to undertake his *Utopia,* published late in 1516 after he returned from a diplomatic mission to Burgundy in 1515. *Utopia* is a fiction inspired by the discovery of the Americas. In the first part of the little book, More recounts a meeting in Antwerp between himself and a sunburned Portuguese mariner named Raphael Hythloday, who has been with Amerigo Vespucci to the New World.

Hythloday is a philosophical traveler, opinionated and virtuous, and as he, More, and More's friend Peter Giles converse, he makes a scouring critique of the ills of Europe. Every place he has seen in his voyages seems superior in both wisdom and practice. With burning eloquence, he castigates the injustice of an economic system that allows a few to amass great wealth while multitudes endure such poverty that they must beg or steal to survive.

Included in Hythloday's diatribe is a denunciation of the European practice of punishing thieves with death: "I think it altogether unjust that a man should suffer the loss of his life for the loss of someone's money. In my opinion, not all the goods that fortune can bestow on us can be set in the scale against a man's life."

In creating Hythloday, More extended cause and effect beyond human will and fortune—Machiavelli's categories—to embrace an economic theory with profound and enduring moral implications. Necessity could overcome virtue at any level of society but especially among the poor. A man faced with no prospect of gainful employment would not shrink from theft and robbery if these were his only chances to live. The commonwealth must bear some responsibility for creating circumstances that compel vice; the relentless pursuit of wealth by the few left the many in distress—to the danger of all.

At the end of the first part of *Utopia,* More urges Hythloday to enter the council of some prince—a decision More himself may have been pondering as he wrote—because a man of such wisdom ought to give advice for the good of the commonwealth. Hythloday responds with an acerbity that may reflect More's own doubts at the time: for a philosopher to advise kings is a waste of time because kings refuse all good counsel.

More replies that Hythloday should not seek perfection. All things, More says, cannot be good unless all people are good, and such a condition is not to be. Therefore, the duty of the councillor is not to suggest radical change that no prince will accept but to do what he can, as tactfully as possible, to make things better rather than worse.

Hythloday is unconvinced. The root of society's ills, he says, is private property, and he denounces the pursuit of wealth as a result of *superbia,* the pride that, he says, following Augustine, is the mother of all sins, making individuals live unto themselves without regard to the good of the whole or to the moral order of the universe. He will describe for More and Giles the Utopian commonwealth to show what good may come when private property is abolished and all laws and customs are built on a virtuous communist economy.

This description of Utopia is the subject of the second part of the book. Hythloday speaks enthusiastically of a republic on an island off the coast of Brazil where, 1,760 years before, a benign conqueror named Utopus established a constitution based on a communist system intended to make its citizens virtuous and its society secure. Not only does Utopia not have a king; it lacks even a ceremonial head of state. Every city has a mayor elected by a republican assembly. The mayor, very much like the doge of Venice, has ceremonial functions but little real power. Authority resides in two elected councils, a smaller one to deal with day-to-day government and a larger one to handle important matters of policy. Political decisions are made deliberately; there is no place in Utopia for the rhetorician who dazzles with eloquence. Reasonableness is everything.

Each Utopian city is divided into eating units of about thirty households each. A household is a clan presided over by the oldest father unless he is senile, in which case the next oldest father rules. Every Utopian male works six hours a day at a craft, and everyone does a two-year term as a farm laborer. All Utopians dress alike except the priests of a tolerant Utopian religion that embodies Christian virtues although without a knowledge of Christ. (When they learn of Christ from Hythloday, Utopians begin to convert.) Since all property is held in common and no money exchange exists, people are able to satisfy their simple needs for food, clothing, and such by applying to a common supply through their representative in the large council.

Yet More fudges the issue a bit by giving them a huge trading surplus with surrounding nations and makes the Utopians precursors of the mercantilism developed later in the century. The surplus provides them with enormous stocks of gold and silver, but since they denigrate precious metals, they use these metals for chamber pots, prisoners' chains, and other base purposes. When they are threatened from abroad, the Utopians can melt these objects down and pay savage mercenaries to do their fighting for them.

Mention of prisoners' chains indicates disquieting features of Utopia. Utopian society is filled with laws that effectively abolish private life and individuality, and those who break these laws are punished by enslavement or death. Husbands and wives are alone, it seems, only in their beds; Utopians eat, work, travel, and spend their leisure in groups. In Utopia, Hythloday boasts, there is no hiding place: all are observed by all. Private political discussion and two convictions for adultery are punished by death. Slaves who revolt are slaughtered like mad dogs. The Utopians also put to death any extradited foreigner who has injured a Utopian traveling in his territory.

Punishment is essential to their religion, for all Utopians are required to believe that God exists and that in a future life he will reward good and punish evil deeds done in this one. Without such belief, Hythloday says, no one can be a good citizen. The punishments of human law must be backed up by the threat of divine vengeance. It is altogether a bleak estimate of the human condition, far removed from that of the Neoplatonists of the Italian Renaissance or even of an Aristotelian philosopher such as Pietro Pomponazzi (1462–1525), who taught that virtue and vice were reward and punishment in themselves.

Politics, Religion, and Death. More rose steadily in his career, first as undersheriff of London,

Thomas More. Portrait by Hans Holbein the Younger (1497–1543). Oil on panel; 1527. THE FRICK COLLECTION/ THE GRANGER COLLECTION, NEW YORK

then as, in succession, member of the Royal Council, speaker of Parliament, chancellor of the duchy of Lancaster, and, finally, in 1529, lord chancellor of the realm after the fall of Thomas Cardinal Wolsey. His eminent status made him at first a powerful figure in defense of the new learning. He intervened to defend Greek studies against conservatives at Oxford University who opposed them. When a continental theologian named Martin Dorp attacked Erasmus's *Praise of Folly,* More wrote Dorp a vigorous defense of the work. When a monk attacked Erasmus's edition of the Greek New Testament, More wrote him a stinging letter of rebuke.

But his ascetic tendencies remained close to the surface of his life. According to his son-in-law William Roper, More wore a hair shirt next to his skin to mortify his flesh, and he beat himself with whips as a religious exercise. Sometime before 1520 he translated into English a brief biography of the Italian humanist Giovanni Pico della Mirandola that had been written by Pico's nephew. This little work made much of Pico's ascetic practices and little of his Neoplatonic philosophy. About 1524 More wrote a somber meditation called *The Four Last Things.* These

were supposed to be death, judgment, heaven, and hell, but he wrote only of death and dying to remind his readers and perhaps himself not to take too much pleasure in this life. The treatise, unpublished while More lived, has affinities with the stark iconography of death and corruption common in the Renaissance.

With the advent of Luther, More was drawn into defending the Catholic Church against the Protestants. In 1521 he was one of those who helped Henry VIII compose *Assertio septem sacramentorum* (Assertion of the seven sacraments) against Luther's radical revision of sacramental theology. After Luther replied to this treatise with a savage book against Henry VIII, More responded (using a pseudonym) with an equally savage, but much longer, assault on Luther and his doctrines.

But Luther had English disciples, most notably William Tyndale, who translated first the New Testament and then much of the rest of the Bible into English. Tyndale also translated Luther and wrote sharp theological treatises promoting the radical teaching of Huldrych Zwingli on the Eucharist. In 1528 Cuthbert Tunstall, the bishop of London, authorized More to write in English against heresies. More then published harsh polemical works one after another almost until his arrest.

More steadfastly held that heretics should be burned alive for their blasphemy against God's true church, for the safety of souls they might lead astray, and for the peace of the realm. In his view Jesus had founded the Catholic Church and promised to be with it to the end of the world, leading it by the Holy Spirit into all truth. If the Catholic Church had gone astray, as the Protestants claimed, God had broken his promise and nothing was certain. The church could not err in its understanding of scripture, but if everyone interpreted scripture for himself, Christianity would be subject to infinite fragmentation. Moreover, the church was the custodian of an oral tradition, handed on by Jesus to his disciples but not immediately written down, and this tradition was a guide to interpreting scripture. True doctrine was the consensus of the faithful, what the vast majority of Christians would affirm if they were all gathered in one place. But More made little of papal authority and in both published works and private letters made it clear that he thought the general council was superior to the pope.

More had little influence as lord chancellor because he did not support Henry's method of pursuing his divorce from Catherine of Aragon. Yet Henry kept him in office, allowing him to resign only after Parliament passed the Act of Supremacy on 15 May

1532, making the king supreme head of the church in England. More retired to more polemical writing against the Protestants now being courted by Henry VIII. Late in 1533 the Royal Council ordered him to stop publishing.

He was arrested in April 1534 for his refusal to sign the oath attached to the Act of Succession, an oath that confirmed all Henry's moves against the Catholic Church. Imprisoned in the Tower for more than a year, More doggedly refused the oath, and on 1 July 1535 he was tried and convicted of "misprision of treason." He was beheaded on Tower Hill on the morning of 6 July 1535. In 1935 he was canonized a saint of the Catholic Church.

See also **Humanism,** *subentry on* **The British Isles;** **Utopias.**

BIBLIOGRAPHY

Primary Works

More, Thomas. *The Complete Works of St. Thomas More.* New Haven, Conn., 1963–.

More, Thomas. *Selected Letters.* Edited by Elizabeth Frances Rogers. New Haven, Conn., 1961.

Stapleton, Thomas. *The Life and Illustrious Martyrdom of Sir Thomas More.* Translation of *Vita Thomae Mori* by Philip E. Hallett. Edited and annotated by E. E. Reynolds. New York, 1967.

Secondary Works

Ackroyd, Peter. *The Life of Thomas More.* New York and London, 1998.

Adams, Robert P. *The Better Part of Valor: More, Erasmus, Colet, and Vives on Humanism, War, and Peace, 1496–1535.* Seattle, 1962.

Gogan, Brian. *The Common Corps of Christendom: Ecclesiological Themes in the Writings of Sir Thomas More.* Leiden, Netherlands, 1982.

Kenney, Anthony. *Thomas More.* Oxford and New York, 1983.

Marc'hadour, Germain. *The Bible in the Works of Thomas More.* 5 vols. Nieuwkoop, Netherlands, 1969–1972.

Marius, Richard. *Thomas More: A Biography.* New York, 1984.

Pineas, Rainer. *Thomas More and Tudor Polemics.* Bloomington, Ind., 1968.

Sylvester, R. S., and G. P. Marc'hadour, eds. *Essential Articles for the Study of Thomas More.* Hamden, Conn., 1977.

Trapp, J. B. *Erasmus, Colet and More: The Early Tudor Humanists and Their Books.* London, 1991.

RICHARD MARIUS

MORISCOS. On 12 February 1502, the sovereigns Isabel of Castile and Ferdinand of Aragon issued an edict forcing Muslims, or *mudejars,* within the dominion of Castile to choose between exile and conversion to Christianity. Charles V made a similar pronouncement on 9 December 1525 regarding the *mudejars* of Aragon. With these proclamations, the age-old policy of recognizing minority religious communities in all their rights, beginning with that of freedom of religion, came to an end. The changes were all the more significant because of the many thousands of people they affected. Faced with a cruel dilemma—homeland or faith—the majority of the people preferred to remain and receive baptism.

The Moriscos in Spanish Society. Documents from the period call these subjects of the kings of Spain *cristianos nuevos de moros* in order to distinguish them from the *cristianos nuevos de judíos,* but they soon became known by the pejorative term *moriscos,* which unambiguously evoked their Muslim origin. In the mid-sixteenth century the Moriscos numbered between 350,000 and 400,000. While they were less numerous and very dispersed in Catalonia, Castile, Estremadura, and Andalusia, they constituted a significant portion of the population of Aragon (50,000 inhabitants, about 20 percent) and of Valencia (100,000 inhabitants, about one-third of that population). The majority of the Moriscos were peasants who were valued either as experts in the techniques of irrigation (in the Alpujarras of the Kingdom of Granada, and the Duchy of Gandía to the south of Valencia, for example) or as cultivators of the arid lands (*cultivo de secano*). Their activity was chiefly divided between the cultivation of cereals and arboriculture (everything from oranges to olives, including mulberries, which were one of their principal sources of wealth). In Ávila, Segovia, and Valladolid, however, groups of Moriscos actively participated in local craftwork. These groups occupied a unique situation in Granada where the Moriscos, numbering about 25,000, were very present in the textile (silk), construction, and leather industries. In addition, the Moriscos readily embraced small business activities, so much so that the character of the *arriero* (mule driver) or the *buhonero* (peddler) had great success in the literature of the period.

From an economic perspective, the positions of the Moriscos were all the more varied since many of those living in the kingdoms of Aragon and Valencia were under the control of lords. Similarly, there were important cultural differences between Moriscos from Castile or Catalonia whose ancestors had long lived among Christians, and those from Granada who had been more recently brought under the protection of the Catholic kings. The divergence with regard to language, for example, is clear. While the Aragonese and Castilian Moriscos were completely ignorant of Arabic, the Moriscos of Valencia and Granada knew nothing else. Of course, all the intermediary levels of diglossia and of bilingualism could

Baptism of Moriscos. Relief by Felix Bigarny, c. 1522. CAPILLA REAL, GRANADA/
ORONOZ

also be found. Finally, the differences within a single regional group were, at times, more than simply nuanced: day workers in the area of Almería had little in common with people of standing in Granada. Such notables were sometimes of princely lineage and had been baptized before the surrender of their city in 1492.

Measures against the Moriscos. Throughout the sixteenth century, Moriscos were subject to the difficulties occurring in the relations between the Spanish monarchy, the Muslims of the Mediterranean basin (Ottoman Empire and Berbers of North Africa), and the Moriscos themselves. Four periods can be distinguished during this time. From 1502 to 1526 the authorities took the Moriscan problem in hand and increased the measures intended to reduce their cultural particularities. These measures redefined the word "morisco," changing the sense of the word from strictly religious to cultural. They specifically prohibited the ritual slaughter of cattle and the wearing of traditional dress, and they oversaw the frequenting of baths and the observance of customs pertaining to birth, marriage, and burial. This period ended with the enforced conversion or expulsion of Muslim subjects of the Crown of Aragon; with the assembly of the Royal Chapel of Granada (1526),

presided over by Charles V where the list of prohibitions imposed upon the Moriscos of the Crown of Castile was drafted; and with the establishment of an inquisitorial tribunal in Granada.

Meanwhile, the Moriscos did receive a respite. The measures designed to promote assimilation fell dormant after the payment of considerable sums of money by the communities of Granada and Valencia. The resulting modus vivendi was characterized by an increase in ecclesiastical presence and by evangelical campaigns led first by the Franciscans and then by the Jesuits. The Moriscos attempted to live their Muslim faith by adopting the *taqiyya,* or dissimulation—a practice available to Muslims placed under the yoke of adversity. This second period lasted until around the mid 1550s. The growing impatience of Christians faced with the meager results of catechizing, increasingly fierce repression on the part of the inquisitorial tribunals, more frequent recourse to active forms of opposition on the part of the Moriscans (destruction of businesses, emigration to North Africa, incidents in numerous villages), and the rising tensions between the Spanish and the Ottoman Empires in the Mediterranean were all factors anticipating future widespread conflict. Madrid's decision in 1566 to enforce the prohibitions that had been enumerated in 1526 provoked a retaliation on the part of the Granada Moriscos, whose rebellion on 24 December 1568 kept the loyal armies at bay for two years. The combat was merciless. In 1569 Philip II ordered that all Moriscos be dispersed in Castile, Estremadura, and western Andalusia, including those who took no active part in the conflict. In all, more than eighty thousand people were deported.

Expulsion. The last run of events occurred during the period from 1571 to 1609. Debate concerning possible solutions to the Moriscos question set this period apart. The partisans of a better catechization, a more authentic conversion, never relented in their efforts, but had to face increasing numbers of opponents. Among these latter, some went so far as to entertain the idea of genocide, while others recommended the deportation of all Moriscos to the New World, and still others proposed castration. Some simply preferred definitive expulsion from Spanish territory, but the clergy, who had little desire to see those in question flee to the lands of Islam, received this option with reluctance, and the titular nobility of the señorios (landed gentry) were no less alarmed by the prospect of losing the Moriscan labor that had become indispensable to them. The expulsion of Valencian Moriscos was proposed in 1582 but was not acted upon at the time.

Despite these events, the myth of a Moriscan threat and of their purported complicity with both Muslim and Protestant enemies had taken root in Spanish society. On 9 April 1609, Philip III, following the counsel of his favorite, the duke of Lerma, signed a decree of expulsion. During the years spanning 1609 and 1614, between 300,000 to 350,000 people were forced to leave their homelands, resettling for the most part in North Africa. Some more modest contingents went to Turkey, France, and Italy. Children, slaves, and "good Christians" numbering in the tens of thousands received authorization to remain behind. The regions with the highest density of Moriscos (Valencia, Aragon, eastern Andalusia) had great difficulty surmounting the consequences of this expulsion.

See also Islam; Philip III.

BIBLIOGRAPHY

Chejne, Anwar G. *Islam and the West: The Moriscos, a Cultural and Social History.* Albany, N.Y., 1983.

Epalza, Michel de. *Los moriscos antes y después de la expulsión.* Madrid, 1992.

Hess, Andrew. *The Forgotten Frontier.* Chicago, 1978.

Lea, Henry Charles. *The Moriscos of Spain: Their Conversion and Expulsion.* Philadelphia, 1901.

Ortiz, Antonio Domínguez, and Bernard Vincent. *Historia de los moriscos. Vida y tragedia de una minoría.* Madrid, 1978.

Villanueva, Francisco Márquez. *El problema morisco (desde otras laderas).* Madrid, 1991.

BERNARD VINCENT

MORISON, RICHARD (c. 1510–1556), English humanist, politician, reformer. Morison came of humble stock in Hertfordshire and made his career on the strength of his academic accomplishments and thrusting personality. He was educated at Eton and Cardinal Wolsey's new college at Oxford (B.A. 1528) and perhaps also in Paris. He certainly studied in Padua, where he read law and languages and hung on the fringes of Reginald Pole's household before successfully ingratiating himself with Henry VIII's chief minister, Thomas Cromwell, in 1535.

Almost immediately after his return to England the next year, Morison served as secretary to the committee that read Pole's *Pro ecclesiasticae unitatis defensione* (Defense of the unity of the church). He managed to summarize its arguments while largely masking the vehemence of Pole's language. At very nearly the same time, at Cromwell's request, Morison wrote *Apomaxis calumniarum* (meaning uncertain: *apomaxis* is a neologism, and the sense appears to be something like "Grand refutation of slanders"; London, 1538). The text was aimed at Johann Cochlaeus's attacks on Henry's religious policy and amounted to an official review of events over the last seven or eight years. Although finished in mid-1536, the work was not printed until 1538, overtaken by the Pilgrimage of Grace, the rebellion that broke out in October 1536. Cromwell redirected Morison's efforts, and Morison rapidly produced *A Lamentation in Which Is Showed What Ruin and Destruction Cometh of Seditious Rebellion* (London, 1536) and *A Remedy for Sedition* (London, 1536). *A Remedy* is by far the more important of the two tracts. In it Morison argued a strictly hierarchical view of the English commonwealth. In a draft plan for the reform of the common law, Morison also suggested positive propaganda in the form of plays against papal supremacy. It may be significant that Morison had by then read Machiavelli's *Istorie florentine* (Florentine histories), which he praised in his own work. Machiavelli's ideas may also have lain behind the distinctly Italianate view of the English polity put forward in *A Lamentation* and *A Remedy*.

In early 1539 Morison wrote *An Invective against the Great and Detestable Vice of Treason* (London, 1539) and *An Exhortation to Stir All Englishmen to the Defence of Their Country* (London, 1539). Both were intended to counter the threat posed by Cardinal Pole in particular and a wider web of English traitors in general, known as the Exeter conspiracy. *An Invective* impressively attacked Pole before turning to Morison's explanation of why England had little to fear: Henry's conversion to true religion. *An Exhortation* built on that foundation and underlined the weakness of the pope and his minions by contrast with the military strength of England. By now a stout Protestant, Morison continued in Cromwell's favor, but Henry did not like him, and when Cromwell proposed him in 1539 as a member of the king's privy chamber, Henry refused the appointment. After Cromwell's fall in 1540, Morison got only one more diplomatic assignment during Henry's reign. After Edward's accession in 1547, Morison was knighted in 1550 and made ambassador to the emperor, where he remained until recalled when Mary became queen in 1553. He thereupon went into exile in Strasbourg, where he corresponded with John Calvin and Heinrich Bullinger and died in 1556.

See also biography of Reginald Pole.

BIBLIOGRAPHY

Berkowitz, D. S., ed. *Humanist Scholarship and Public Order: Two Tracts against the Pilgrimage of Grace by Sir Richard Morison.* Washington, D.C., 1984.

Elton, G. R. *Reform and Renewal: Thomas Cromwell and the Common Weal.* Cambridge, U.K., 1973.

Zeeveld, W. Gordon. *Foundations of Tudor Policy.* Cambridge, Mass., 1948.

THOMAS F. MAYER

MORRA, ISABELLA DI (c. 1520–1545), Italian poet. The opus and tragically short life of Isabella di Morra, daughter of Giovan Michele di Morra, baron of Favale, in southern Italy, are inextricably bound. Subjected to virtual imprisonment by her three brothers in the wake of her father's exile, she wrote poetry that speaks to the pain of isolation and the vain hope that her condition would improve with his return. This hope was brutally dashed when she was finally murdered by her brothers.

Isabella's opus of ten sonnets and three *canzoni* reflects these circumstances by a profound longing for companionship and literary recognition as well as a mournful lament over her forced isolation and loneliness. No other poet prior to Isabella di Morra infused such personal depth into poetry, bringing new drama to the lyric precisely because it so closely addresses the tragic circumstances of her life.

Autobiographical as her work is, however, it is her skillful adaptation of the traditional Petrarchan rhetoric to a broader set of overtly subjective concerns that defines her contribution to a revitalized lyric. An impressive prefiguration of romanticism, her poetry is also eerily echoed by Torquato Tasso in his "Canzone al Metauro" where he expresses his own personal vendetta with Fortune for having similarly ruined both his political and familial life. Isabella di Morra's work thus contributed to the development of a new sensibility in poetic language, one grounded in a kind of life writing that raises the biographical, the political, the familial, and the personal to a genuinely lyric stature.

BIBLIOGRAPHY

Primary Work

Morra, Isabella di. *Canzoniere: A Bilingual Edition.* Edited and translated by Irene Musillo Mitchell. West Lafayette, Ind., 1998. In English and Italian.

Secondary Work

Caserta, Giovanni. *Isabella Morra e la società meridionale del cinquecento.* Matera, Italy, 1976.

JULIANA SCHIESARI

MOSTAERT, JAN (c. 1475–1555/56), North Netherlandish painter. Mostaert was born to a noble Haarlem family and was trained by Jacob van Haarlem, a painter about whom little is known. From 1500 onward, Mostaert is frequently mentioned in the records of the Haarlem painters' guild, of which he became dean in 1507 and again in 1543 and 1544. He is documented at the court of Margaret of Austria, regent of the Netherlands, in 1519 and 1521 but presumably spent more time in Malines, for there is no evidence that he was in Haarlem between 1516 and 1526. As a court artist, Mostaert was primarily engaged in painting copies after original court portraits.

The Dutch painter and writer Karel van Mander described a *West Indies Landscape* by Mostaert—"in which are many naked people, a protruding cliff, and strangely constructed houses and huts"—which matches an extraordinary picture in the Frans Hals-museum at Haarlem. The painting shows a procession of nude armed men, marching down paths to confront armored troops that have been brought to a standstill by a small group of stone-throwing nude men on a cliff. Some huts are half buried under the hills of the rolling landscape, while others are erected against the sides of the fantastic rock formation in the middle ground. Scholars consider this picture an imaginative re-creation of a recent historical event. The landing of Columbus on the island of Goanin (1493), the conquests of Cortés in central Mexico (1519), and the expedition of Coronado in search of the Seven Cities of Cibola in modern-day New Mexico and surrounding regions (1540–1542)

Jan Mostaert. ***Zuni Indians Resisting Coronado's Troops.*** Painting, c. 1545. FRANS HALS MUSEUM, HAARLEM, THE NETHERLANDS/FOTO MARBURG/ART RESOURCE

have all been proposed—the last identification being the most compelling. The Renaissance discovery of unknown lands, peoples, and societies in America inspired Mostaert to explore the new subject of the invasion of a culture, untouched by Western civilization, by a domineering and technologically advanced one.

Mostaert was fond of imaginary, atmospheric landscapes punctuated with small, agitated figures (see, for example, his *Landscape with St. Christopher,* Antwerp, Mayer van den Bergh Museum), in the line of the Flemish painter Joachim Patinir. Mostaert also produced more traditional devotional paintings, such as the crowded *Adoration of the Magi* (Amsterdam, Rijksmuseum) and the triptych of the *Last Judgment* (Bonn, Rheinisches Landesmuseum), in which his debt to the figure types of the Haarlem painter Geertgen tot Sint Jans is apparent.

Mostaert's fame as a court artist led to commissions for portraits of lesser members of the aristocracy. In the elegant, Geertgenesque, though expressionless *Portrait of Abel van de Coulster* (Brussels, Musées Royaux des Beaux-Arts), the nobleman—identified by his coat of arms and initials—is shown behind a parapet, in half length and in three-quarter profile toward the left, with both hands raised on a pillow as he counts his rosary beads. The vision of

the Virgin and child appearing to Augustus and the Tiburtine Sibyl is depicted in the middle ground before a mountainous landscape set off by a palace on the right. This sitter's pose and dress reappear in the delicate *Portrait of a Young Man* (Liverpool, Walker Art Gallery), before a landscape with hunters that seems influenced by German or even north Italian painting.

BIBLIOGRAPHY

Snyder, James. "The Early Haarlem School of Painting, III: The Problem of Geertgen tot Sint Jans and Jan Mostaert." *Art Bulletin* 53 (1971): 445–458.

Snyder, James. "Jan (Jansz.) Mostaert." In *The Dictionary of Art.* Edited by Jane Turner. Vol. 22. New York, 1996. Pages 199–201.

van Mander, Karel. *The Lives of the Illustrious Netherlandish and German Painters.* Doornspijk, Netherlands, 1994. See vol. 1, pages 174–177, and vol. 3, pages 190–204.

MICHAËL J. AMY

MOTHERHOOD. The modern idealization of motherhood dates from no earlier than the eighteenth century. Before that time the maternal role was not usually singled out for praise.

The Ideal of Motherhood. The one exception to the absence of an early idealization of motherhood was the veneration of the Virgin Mary, whose maternal qualities received almost as much attention as the divinity of her son. Implicit in those qualities is an idea of perfect motherhood. Depictions in Renaissance art show her not only nursing a more and more natural-looking baby but also caring for him on the flight to Egypt and later grieving at his death. Men imagined her caring for them. She was thought of as kind and forgiving, a rescuer and intercessor, and was frequently shown standing by the side of Christ at the Last Judgment. Women allowed themselves to identify with her. In the ongoing Renaissance debate on the worth of women it was always argued in women's favor that God chose to have his son born of a woman. Women asked for her help in their maternal role and visited shrines of the Virgin when they had trouble becoming pregnant or were worried about sick children.

Ideas about mothers were influenced by ideas about fathers, who represented familial authority. Fathers were supposed to supervise their children's upbringing and make decisions about their futures. In the final analysis the mother also had to obey the father. It was taken for granted that if a choice had to be made, children should be with their fathers. Bearing children belonged among the many duties a wife owed to her husband and his family. If married women were rarely praised for being able to offer the Virgin's kind of maternal love, they were frequently praised for unswerving fidelity to their husbands.

Mothers in Renaissance Society. It is difficult to know whether people in all walks of life shared the ideas just described. Children in poor households had closer physical contact with their mothers than children in wealthier families, who spent their earliest years with wet nurses. Little information is available concerning the formative years of children in the Renaissance.

Mothers provided their children with links to kinship groups. Names from the mother's family were often given to some of her children, to honor her father or to appropriate the glory associated with distinguished ancestors. Children were beneficiaries of the wealth and prestige of their mothers' families, whether they lived in the village society of peasants or the great world of the nobility. Although a wife was supposed to become absorbed in her husband's lineage, she and her children remained a concern of her father and brothers. Maternal grandparents, aunts, uncles, and cousins have always loomed large in the emotional life of Western culture. The cardinals of the Roman church, and the popes themselves, were proverbially generous uncles to their sisters' children.

Mothers also played a role in inheritance. Although they did not usually transmit real property themselves they were important instruments in the transmission from fathers. A common procedure was for the children to inherit everything, while the widowed mother received a certain proportion set aside for her use until she died. Not only was the proportion quite large if the father's will or the marriage contract so provided, but some men also simply made their wives outright heirs if the children were still young. Mothers were assumed to be temporary holders of property. They were not owners so much as stewards, guarding it for others. The poor widow who had a hard time supporting her children was a common figure who was regarded with respect and pity, whereas a poor widow who lived alone was likely to be an object of fear and suspicion. Motherhood made a difference here.

Maternal obligations were put to the test if a woman remarried, especially if she had children by her second husband. Conflicts between the children of the "first bed" and those of the "second bed" were frequently fought out in law courts (as well as in the world of imagination that demonized the stepmother). The threat to the first bed was that her loyalty and obedience to her second husband would take precedence over everything else. A French royal edict of 1560 came down on the side of "motherhood," guaranteeing the property rights of children by limiting what a widowed mother could carry into a new marriage. Such a law actually protected the rights of children as members of their father's lineage.

See also **Birth and Infancy**; **Pregnancy**; **Women**, *subentry on* **Women in the Renaissance**.

BIBLIOGRAPHY

Primary Work

Selected Letters of Alessandra Strozzi. Translated by Heather Gregory. Berkeley, Calif., and London, 1997. The complete Italian edition is *Lettere di una gentildonna fiorentina del secolo XV ai figliuoli esuli* (Florence, 1877). Shows an upper-class widow's concern for the "honor and profit" of her family, especially through arranging good marriages for her children.

Secondary Works

Hanawalt, Barbara A. *The Ties That Bound: Peasant Families in Medieval England.* New York and Oxford, 1986.
Klapisch-Zuber, Christiane. *Women, Family, and Ritual in Renaissance Italy.* Translated by Lydia Cochrane. Chicago, 1985.

BEATRICE GOTTLIEB

MÜNTZER, THOMAS (c. 1489–1525), German radical Protestant reformer, leader in the Peasants' War. Müntzer was among the first and most astute critics of Martin Luther (1483–1546) to emerge within the ranks of the Protestant reformers. He was a founder of the distinctive Radical Reformation within the Protestant movement and he was one of the most influential leaders of the German Peasants' War (1525).

Thomas Müntzer was born at Stolberg in the Harz mountains of Germany. Little is known about his family background. He studied at the universities of Leipzig (1506) and Frankfort on the Oder (1512). Between 1517 and 1519 he was at Wittenberg, where he came into contact with Luther. Renaissance humanism and medieval mysticism were among the cultural currents that influenced Müntzer's thinking. In 1520–1521 he preached at Zwickau. Later in 1521 he traveled to Bohemia; he preached at Prague and in November wrote his *Prager Manifest* (Prague protest), the first of his surviving tracts.

At Easter 1523 Müntzer became pastor of the church of Saint John in the small market town of Allstedt in electoral Saxony. At Allstedt, Müntzer married the former nun Ottilie von Gersen. Here he also introduced the first vernacular liturgy of the German Reformation. His Allstedt reform program was successful, and he soon enjoyed a wide following in the town and surrounding countryside, which led to conflict with local Catholic lords, especially Count Ernst of Mansfeld. By the end of 1523, following a Wittenberg-inspired investigation into his reforms, Müntzer definitively broke with Luther. In March 1524 a group of Müntzer's followers burned the small pilgrimage chapel at nearby Mallerbach. Müntzer defended the deed and hindered its prosecution by electoral officials. On 13 July 1524 he preached his famous *Fürstenpredigt* (Sermon to the princes; or, An exposition of the second chapter of Daniel) at the Allstedt castle before Saxon rulers and officials. These authorities called Müntzer and members of the Allstedt council to Weimar for a hearing and afterward ordered him to end his agitation.

Müntzer fled Allstedt for Mühlhausen, a free imperial city in Thuringia, where he joined another radical reformer, Heinrich Pfeiffer. In late September 1524, city authorities expelled both reformers following their involvement in a rebellion. Later that fall, both of Müntzer's final polemical treatises against Luther, *Ausgedrückte Entblössung des falschen Glaubens* (A special exposure of false faith) and *Hochverursachte Schutzrede* (A highly provoked defense), were secretly printed at Nürnberg.

Thomas Müntzer Preaching.

Müntzer traveled to southwestern Germany at this time, where he made contact with fellow radicals and preached to peasants who had risen in rebellion in the Klettgau and Hegau regions.

In early 1525 Müntzer returned to Mühlhausen. In March a revolution in the city led to the formation of a new government. When the Peasants' War swept Saxony and Thuringia in April, Mühlhausen became an important urban center supporting the insurrection. Müntzer and Pfeiffer campaigned with rebel military bands and worked assiduously to promote the cause of the commoners. Following the defeat of the peasants at the battle of Frankenhausen, Müntzer was captured. After interrogation and torture, he was beheaded outside the walls of Mühlhausen on 27 May 1525.

BIBLIOGRAPHY

Primary Works

The Collected Works of Thomas Müntzer. Translated and edited by Peter Matheson. Edinburgh, 1988.

Revelation and Revolution: Basic Writings of Thomas Müntzer. Translated and edited by Michael G. Baylor. Bethlehem, Pa., 1993.

Secondary Works

Goertz, Hans-Jürgen. *Thomas Müntzer: Apocalyptic, Mystic, and Revolutionary.* Translated by Jocelyn Jaquiery; edited by Peter Matheson. Edinburgh, 1993. A translation of the most influential German interpretation of Müntzer's thought.

Scott, Tom. *Thomas Müntzer: Theology and Revolution in the German Reformation.* New York, 1989. The best short biography; strong on Müntzer's political career.

MICHAEL G. BAYLOR

MURET, MARC-ANTOINE (1526–1585), French humanist, poet. Marc-Antoine Muret was born close to Limoges in the town of Muret (hence the frequent version of his name "de Muret"), the son of a jurisconsult. After irregular studies in the provinces, he began his teaching career at the Collège de Guyenne in Bordeaux, where Michel de Montaigne was among his pupils. He moved to the Collège de Boncourt in Paris, where he taught Latin from 1551 to 1553 and developed friendships with the humanist Jean Dorat and the group of young poets later called the Pléiade. Accused of heresy and sodomy at the end of 1553, he left Paris for Toulouse, where similar troubles forced him to travel to Italy in 1554, teaching first in Venice, then in Padua. In 1559 he left for Ferrara and became secretary to the cardinal Ippolito d'Este. From 1563 until his retirement in 1584, Muret taught moral philosophy, jurisprudence, and rhetoric at the University of Rome. Muret's work includes commentaries on Aristotle's *Nicomachean Ethics* and *Rhetoric,* Cicero's *Tusculanae disputationes* (*Tusculan Disputations*), *De finibus* (Of ends), and *De officiis* (Of duties), works of Horace, Plato, Tacitus, and Seneca, as well as the *Corpus iuris civilis* (The body of Roman law). But Muret also composed French and Latin verses himself (such as his *Juvenilia* of 1553) and provided a commentary for Pierre de Ronsard's 1553 *Les amours*. He was known for his orations in the service of the papacy and the French monarchy, including a speech defending the Saint Bartholomew's Day massacre, and for his opening lectures at the university.

BIBLIOGRAPHY

Primary Works

Muret, Marc-Antoine. *Commentaires au premier livre des* Amours *de Ronsard.* Edited by Jacques Chomarat, Marie-Madeleine Fragonard, and Gisèle Mathieu-Castellani. 2 vols. Geneva, 1985–1986.

Muret, Marc-Antoine. *Opera omnia.* Edited by Carl-Heinrich Frotscher. 3 vols. Leipzig, Germany, 1834–1841. Reprint, Geneva, 1971.

Secondary Works

Céard, Jean. "Muret, commentateur des *Amours* de Ronsard." In *Sur des vers de Ronsard (1585–1985).* Edited by Marcel Tetel. Paris, 1990. Pages 37–50.

MacPhail, Eric. *The Voyage to Rome in French Renaissance Literature.* Saratoga, Calif., 1990.

ULLRICH LANGER

MURNER, THOMAS (1475–1537), German Franciscan preacher and satirist, foremost opponent of Luther during the early phase of the Reformation. As a theologian, poet, jurist, satirist, preacher, and translator, Murner was a man of astonishing versatility and broad intellectual interests. Fluent in both Latin and German, he authored numerous Latin texts and some of the best satires in the vernacular.

Born in Obernai, Alsace, Murner was educated in Strasbourg at the cloister school of the Franciscans, whose order he entered in 1490. Four years later he was ordained a priest. Between 1494 and 1501 he traveled widely throughout Europe and studied at seven universities (Freiburg, Cologne, Paris, Rostock, Cracow, Prague, and Vienna). He received his bachelor of arts degree from the University of Paris (1498), his master of arts degree from the University of Freiburg (1499), and his bachelor of theology degree from the University of Cracow (1500). Later he was promoted to doctor of theology (Freiburg, 1506), and doctor of law (Basel, 1519). In 1501, after his return to Strasbourg, Murner became embroiled with the Alsatian humanist Jakob Wimpheling in a controversy that foreshadowed the numerous disputes he participated in throughout his restless life. While Wimpheling argued that Alsace had always been part of Germany, Murner took the opposite stand, claiming that the region had once belonged to France. Although this attack on Wimpheling resulted in Murner's virtual banishment from the circle of humanists in Strasbourg, it did not harm his career in the Franciscan order, in which he served as preacher, guardian, and reading master in Strasbourg, Speyer, Frankfurt, and Freiburg.

Between 1510 and 1521 Murner wrote a number of satires, which secured him a firm place in German literary history. In *Doctor Murners Narrenbschwerung* (The exorcism of fools; 1512) Murner tries to exorcise all the fools Sebastian Brant had drawn to Germany in his *Narrenschiff* (Ship of fools; 1494). Like Brant before him, he denounces the follies of all social groups, including the clergy and nobility. In contrast to the *Narrenbschwerung,* which, at least in its conception and the accompanying woodcuts, is dependent on Brant, Murner found his own satirical voice in *Der Schelmen Zunfft* (The fools' guild; 1512). In colorful, realistic, and folksy language, Murner pillories human weaknesses, follies, and vices. In *Die Mülle von Schwyndelszheym* (The mill of Swindleton; 1515) Murner appears in the guise of a miller who assembles an astonishing company of lechers, drunks, and fools on the anniversary of his wife's death. While these works present a broad spectrum of human society, *Die Geuchmat* (The lovers' meadow; 1519) focuses on the follies of love-stricken men, and abounds with examples from the Bible and ancient and medieval literature. A stay in the baths might have inspired Murner to write *Ein andechtig geistliche Badenfart* (A devout and spiritual journey to the baths; 1514), an allegorical poem in which the various procedures of taking the baths are equated with taking a spiritual journey or obtaining a cure that results in the physical and spiritual rejuvenation of the participant.

In addition to these German satires, Murner translated a number of important Latin works into German. He was the first to translate Virgil's *Aeneid* into German (1515), and he rendered Justinian's *Institutiones* (Institutes) into the vernacular in 1519. His translation of Marcus Antonius Sabellicus's (1436–1506) *Enneades* as *Hystory von anbeschaffener Welt* (History of the world order) with 344 excellent ink drawings, probably from Murner's own hand, exists only as an autograph (facsimile published in 1987).

Although Murner was one of the loudest critics of clerical abuses before the Reformation, he turned against Luther once he saw the unity of the church threatened. Initially moderate in tone, his numerous anti-Reformation treatises, sermons, and satires became increasingly strident. His most ambitious and witty indictment of the Reformation is the satire *Vom dem grossen Lutherischen Narren* (The great Lutheran fool; 1522), in which the "Lutheran Fool" is not Luther but the embodiment of all the destructive elements unleashed by the reformer. In 1524 Murner left Strasbourg after a mob had raided his cell and destroyed his printing equipment. He spent the years 1525–1529 in Lucerne, Switzerland, which had remained Catholic, but again his outspokenness led to his forced departure. After a stay at court in Heidelberg, he returned in 1530 to Obernai, where he spent his last years.

Reviled by Protestants because of his vehement attacks on Luther, and not wholly embraced by Catholics who were embarrassed by his verbal violence, Murner is one of the most controversial figures of the Reformation period. Only in the late twentieth century did a more balanced assessment of him emerge.

See also **German Literature and Language**; **Protestant Reformation**; **Satire**, *subentry on* **Satire in Germany**.

BIBLIOGRAPHY

Primary Works

Murner, Thomas. *Scheming Papists and Lutheran Fools: Five Reformation Satires*. Selected and translated by Erika Rummel. New York, 1993. Contains portions of Murner's *Great Lutheran Fool*.

Murner, Thomas. *Thomas Murners Deutsche Schriften mit den Holzschnitten der Erstdrucke*. 9 vols. Edited by Franz Schultz. Berlin and Leipzig, Germany, 1918–1931.

Secondary Works

Gaus, Linda L. "Thomas Murner." In *Dictionary of Literary Biography,* vol. 179. *German Writers of the Renaissance and Reformation 1280–1580*. Detroit, Mich.; Washington, D.C.; and London; 1997. Pages 184–197. Concise article with a bibliography of the most important works of primary and secondary literature.

Heger, Hedwig. "Thomas Murner." In *Deutsche Dichter der frühen Neuzeit (1450–1600)*. Edited by Stephan Füssel. Berlin, 1993. Pages 296–310. Balanced account of Murner's life and work.

ECKHARD BERNSTEIN

MUSEUMS. While collecting artifacts predates the Renaissance, no preceding era made the collection and display of things so important to its definition of culture. In the Middle Ages princely treasuries and churches displayed gems, gilded and bejeweled swords and drinking cups, ostrich eggs, saintly relics, and a variety of other precious objects that signified power and authority. But medieval patrons and collectors did not yet see culture as a systematically collectible entity. This idea, on which the development of the museum as an institution to house culture and knowledge is based, emerged in the course of the fifteenth and sixteenth centuries. Its appearance was a direct result of attitudes and values associated with Renaissance humanism.

Collections of Antiquities and Novelties.

The humanist sense of the past encouraged scholars to accumulate tangible remnants of the Greco-Roman past. By the late fifteenth century a nascent market for antiquities had arisen. Collectors avidly sought the best examples of Roman coins, statues, and manuscripts; in some instances, they traveled to the Greek islands, and later to Egypt, in search of new archaeological treasure troves. The broad-based interest in antiquity meant that early collections—such as the princely ones of Cosimo de' Medici in Florence, Federico da Montefeltro in Urbino, and Isabella d'Este in Mantua, and the private ones of humanists such as Poggio Bracciolini and Pomponio Leto in Rome—did not distinguish the museum from the library. As the Vatican Library developed after the initial bequests made by Nicholas V and Sixtus IV between the 1454 and 1475, it seemed natural to place other kinds of papal collections adjacent to its rooms. By the mid-sixteenth century visitors could also enjoy the statuary in the Belvedere courtyard and tour the papal physician Michele Mercati's mineralogical collection. Preserving culture and pursuing knowledge had not only become complementary activities but also tangible signs of the emergence of a strong Renaissance state.

The largely antiquarian emphasis of fifteenth-century collecting, dominated by a handful of princely collectors and prominent humanists, gave way in the sixteenth century to a more encyclopedic image of the museum as a temple of all the arts and sciences. They increasingly used the word "museum" to define their collections. Inspired by the image of the museum of ancient Alexandria, which had purportedly contained all knowledge of the ancient world, and by the image of the nine Muses as guardians of the arts and sciences, late Renaissance collectors expanded the scope of their collecting activities to include natural curiosities and technological marvels. Well-known collectors such as the naturalist Ulisse Aldrovandi (1522–1605) in Bologna prided themselves on collecting the ingredients to write the new encyclopedia of knowledge, challenging Aristotle's and Pliny's stature as the ancient encyclopedists. They saw collecting as a means of reflecting the changes in knowledge that had occurred since antiquity and of displaying a fuller and more accurate view of antiquity than earlier humanists such as Petrarch had had.

European travel to and conquest of the Americas also challenged the geographic parameters of the known world. Interest in the Americas contributed to the greater fascination with natural and ethnographic objects, since they were the most tangible signs of America's difference from Europe. Renaissance museums responded to this new idea of knowledge by becoming repositories of both Old World and New World artifacts in order to fulfill their claims of complete mastery of nature and knowledge. Armadillos and porcupines confronted Nile crocodiles; Tupinamba capes from Brazil competed for shelf space with fragmentary Venuses from Latium. The museum became a place in which the contest of culture was played out through the display and interpretation of objects.

Private and Public Collections. By the seventeenth century such collections were routinely called "cabinets of curiosity." They had become an important part of the cultural itinerary of educated travelers. Men and occasionally women saw the world by touring the cabinets of Europe, punctuating their stops in each city with visits to the most noteworthy museums. Published travel accounts and museum catalogs guided them along the way, telling them where to go and what to see. While museums continued to fulfill a scholarly function, as a meeting place for academies and a repository of the materials of scholarship, they increasingly served a more public and social function. Cultural tourism, the origins of the famous "grand tour," began in the Renaissance museum. Generations of educated elite came to see possessing a private collection and visiting other collections as a crucial part of their identity.

Despite the growing popularity of museums by the late sixteenth century, they enjoyed a fairly ephemeral existence. In this preinstitutional phase of the history of museums, most collections did not survive the death of their creator. Accumulating objects took at least a lifetime but dissipating them seemed to take only a matter of a few years, especially as the market for collectibles expanded and professionalized. Quite often heirs did not see a collection as a public treasure but instead regarded it as a patrimony to transform into more tangible forms of wealth that might easily divide among themselves. Collectors responded by finding ways to leave their cultural legacy to their city. For instance, in 1523 Cardinal Domenico Grimani gave his ancient statuary collection to Venice in order that it be preserved and publicly displayed; eighty years later, Ulisse Aldrovandi signed an agreement with the Senate of Bologna transforming his collection into a civic museum. In both instances, their collections survived for at least another hundred years intact.

Such agreements on the part of private collectors reflected a growing understanding of the museum as a public institution, a form of cultural patrimony best managed and maintained by a state. And yet the Renaissance state's concept of culture was itself fairly privatized. Rulers such as Isabella d'Este (1474–1539) showed their collections only to fellow courtiers. Initially the Uffizi galleries in Florence were simply a set of converted offices in one of the city government buildings, appropriated by the grand duke Francesco I in 1584 so that he could have a more suitable space in which to contemplate his favorite collectibles. Few visitors entered the Uffizi in those early years, and the majority of those who did were either family members or diplomats. Gradually the grand dukes came to see their galleries as a public treasure open to visitors. Yet not until the eighteenth century did they separate the scientific and artistic parts of the collection. In this respect, they upheld the encyclopedic ideal of the museum.

The Italian model of the courtly museum, embodied by Isabella d'Este's *grotta* and *studiolo* and by the Medici's Uffizi galleries, was imitated and refined in northern Europe. By the early seventeenth century no respectable monarch could be without some sort of collection to display to visitors. As the wealth and power of the Italian rulers declined, the princely cabinets of English, French, and central European monarchs grew in splendor and magnificence. The collection of Holy Roman Emperor Rudolf II (1552–1612) and the wonders of Fontainebleau amazed even Italian visitors, while astute observers of the Stuart collection would have recognized many paintings from the court of Mantua in this English gallery. By the seventeenth century the museum was on its way to becoming an enduring cultural institution—enough so that royalty preyed upon the carcasses of their weaker brethren in order to enhance their own magnificence through objects.

BIBLIOGRAPHY

Bredekamp, Horst. *The Lure of Antiquity and the Cult of the Machine.* Translated by Allison Brown. Princeton, N.J., 1995.

Findlen, Paula. *A Fragmentary Past: Museums and the Renaissance.* Stanford, Calif. 2000.

Findlen, Paula. *Possessing Nature: Museums, Collecting, and Scientific Culture in Early Modern Italy.* Berkeley, Calif., 1994.

Grafton, Anthony, ed. *Rome Reborn: The Vatican Library and Renaissance Culture.* Washington, D. C., 1993.

Impey, Oliver, and Arthur MacGregor, eds. *The Origins of Museums: The Cabinet of Curiosities in Sixteenth- and Seventeenth-Century Europe.* Oxford, 1985.

Jardine, Lisa. *Worldly Goods: A New History of the Renaissance.* London, 1996.

Olmi, Giuseppe. *L'inventario del mondo: catalogazione della natura e luoghi del sapere nella prima età moderna.* Bologna, Italy, 1992.

Thornton, Dora. *The Scholar in His Study: Ownership and Experience in Renaissance Italy.* New Haven, Conn., 1997.

PAULA FINDLEN

MUSIC. [Discussion of music is divided into two types of entries, a general survey of music and six entries on music in various countries. Following an introductory subentry entitled Renaissance Music, this general survey entry is divided into eleven other subentries:

Music in Renaissance Culture
Music in Renaissance Society
Music Treatises
Transmission of Music
Performance Practice
Musical Instruments
Instrumental Music
Sacred Vocal Music
Secular Vocal Music
Intermedi
Opera

The six entries on music in various countries are:

Music in England
Music in France
Music in Italy
Music in Spain and Portugal
Music in the Holy Roman Empire
Music in the Low Countries

For discussion of texts set to music, see Poetry and Music.]

Renaissance Music

The concept of "Renaissance music" has come under pressure at both chronological ends, as on one hand, medieval structures and procedures have been perceived as lasting well into the sixteenth century, and, on the other, studies taking their cue from history have emphasized the "early modern" aspects of the context and content of music. Traditionally, and following Jakob Burckhardt's definitions of the essentially Renaissance features of the period, European music between 1400 and 1600 has been seen to reflect the principal characteristics of the cultural life of the era.

The classic accounts of the period drew an implicit parallel between the first major stylistic shift—the newly consonant (to later ears) style of Guillaume Dufay (c. 1400–1474) and Gilles Binchois (c. 1400–1460) (the *countenance angloise,* learned from English music around 1400, evident most clearly in Dufay's chansons and motets composed during his Italian sojourns of the 1420s)—and the rediscovery of ancient culture and the diffusion of perspective painting. Central to the evolutionary perspective of this view was the development of imitative polyphony, a musical style in which the parts or lines (vocal or instrumental) were equal and linear, employed a succession of identical (or similar) melodic motifs, and relied on consonant musical intervals in regular succession. This view, first stated explicitly by August Wilhelm Ambros in his *Geschichte der Musik* (1862–1878), considered the Renaissance's first musical peak to have been expressed in the works of Josquin des Prez ([c. 1440–1521] seen, in his individuality and compositional genius, as a parallel to Beethoven as a central figure in modern European music). It was evident, even in Ambros's day, that many composers of the fifteenth and early sixteenth centuries had been trained in the Low Countries and then fanned out to work all over Europe.

In the late sixteenth century music was considered to have reached another high point in the works of Giovanni Pierluigi da Palestrina (c. 1525–1594) before giving way to the baroque era with the appearance of Florentine court opera and the basso continuo (generative instrumental chordal bass line), both appearing in printed editions of 1600. Because of an emphasis on individuals, much of this development was cast in contrasting composer pairs; in chronological order they are: Dufay and Binchois; Jacob Obrecht (c. 1450–1505) and Johannes Ockeghem (c. 1410–1495); des Prez and Heinrich Isaac (c. 1450–1517); Adriaan Willaert (c. 1490–1562) and Cipriano de Rore (1516–1565); Palestrina and Orlando di Lasso (Orlandus Lassus; 1532–1594); William Byrd (1543–1623) and Tomás Luis de Victoria (c. 1548–1611). Borrowing a term from art history, the post–Palestrina generation in Italy (notably the madrigalists Giaches de Wert [1535–1596], Luca Marenzio [1553/54–1599], and Carlo Gesualdo [1560–1613]) was perceived by twentieth-century scholars to have manifested musical traits of Mannerism in its use of extreme contrast, hyperextended gesture, and chromatic inflection. Although the "end" of the Renaissance was normally situated in the works of Claudio Monteverdi (1567–1643), in the periphery (England, Iberia, Poland) it was seen as lasting well into the seventeenth century.

The two perspectives to have transcended the simple dichotomy of this view or its negation are relatively recent. For Reinhard Strohm (1993) the fifteenth century represented a slow, halting, but eventually triumphant consolidation of a pan–European musical language, while J. A. Owens (1990) cautioned against the uncritical importation of Burckhardtian terms and called for a historicist critique of some of the "foundation myths" associated with the central figures of the traditional view.

Musical Philosophy, Procedures, and Genres.

The medieval divisions between musical philosophizing (*musica speculativa*) and the theory of music composition and performance (*musica practica*) retained their validity for most of the Renaissance. Although Augustine and Boethius continued to be cited by most writers, the influence of Plato's comments on music (especially in *Timaeus*) remained important. More recondite speculation on music's role in inducing poetic furor was to be found in some of the writings of Marsilio Ficino (1433–1499) while neo-Pythagorian theory, emphasizing the *symphonia* of the cosmos (the "music of the spheres"), led a more marginal life. Toward the end of the sixteenth century, an Aristotelian view of music's utility and the possibilities of mixed styles became more prevalent in Italy.

The rediscovery of actual Greek writings on music occurred in the sixteenth century, sparking polemics on the power and musical (scalar) structures of ancient music such as that which broke out in the 1550s between Nicola Vicentino (1511–1576?) and Vicente Lusitano. In the 1580s, a group of Florentine academicians (organized in various groups called *camerate*), under the leadership of Girolamo Mei (1519–1594), began to engage better textual recensions of Greek treatises, leading to speculations about the simplicity and audible textual projection of Greek music that would be realized in solo song of the end of the century.

The actual setting of Greek and Roman texts to music was relatively rare; refined settings in the spirit of the contemporary madrigal are found in the works of Rore and Lassus. A more scholastic approach, with meters geared to those of classical literature, is evident in the German scholastic settings of Horace by Petrus Tritonius (1507) and the choruses from the Italian translation of *Oedipus Tyrannus* composed by Andrea Gabrieli (Vicenza, 1585).

More important were the various national schools of contemporary literary theory. The modified classicism of Pietro Bembo, which established both a literary language and a stylistic taxonomy, has been seen as having direct results in the madrigals (and, one might add, the motets) of Willaert and Rore, composed in the decades after the publication of Bembo's treatises. Similarly, the experiments of the French literary academies around 1570 resulted in the highly text-bound *chansons* of Claude Le Jeune (c. 1530–1600) published in the last decades of the century. At the very end of the period, rhetorical terms and structures were applied to musical pieces (for example in Johannes Burmeister's analysis of a motet by Lasso in his *Musical Poetics* of 1606).

The relationship between word and text was central in the categorization of musical style. Thus, in the 1607 preface to his brother Claudio's *Scerzi musicali*, Giulio Cesare Monteverdi made the retrospective, polemical, and historiographically famous distinction between two approaches to composition: a *prima prattica*, in which the beauty of contrapuntal line and the priority of number were privileged over close textual reading (typical, in this view, for composers from Ockeghem, through Josquin and Gombert, up to Willaert), and a *seconda prattica*, whose representatives from Rore onward (Marenzio, Wert, and Claudio Monteverdi himself) took licence with, and introduced changes in, previous compositional practice so as to provide greater fidelity to the affect and literary structures of the texts set to music.

The period also witnessed the production of treatises that attempted to systematize rules for music composition. The works of Johannes Tinctoris (c. 1474–1511?) and Franchinus Gafurius (1451–1522) provided a synthesis of fifteenth-century practice. The sixteenth century witnessed the more systematic essays of Pietro Aron, Francesco Rossetti, and especially *Dode cachordon* (written 1539; published 1547) of Heinrich Glareanus (1488–1563) and *Le istitutioni harmoniche* (1558; rev. 1573) of Gioseffo Zarlino (1517–1590). These works provided clear rules of counterpoint, expanded the medieval system of church modes (octave species) from eight to twelve, and linked such modes to various affects of text. Their innovations met with controversy; some later Italian theorists (Pietro Ponzio) retained the system of eight modes, while English music as theorized by such figures as the madrigal and church composer Thomas Morley (c. 1577–1602) displayed a typically insular idiosyncratic system of modal organization. Rhythm and meter from the beginning of the period were governed by a proportional method, the mensuration system, in which units of duration were subdivisible into two or three, and different rhythmic levels could be combined in the same piece, a procedure especially helpful in multivoice (polyphonic) works based on a pre-existant melody, sacred or secular (a cantus firmus).

The essential compositional technique was that of counterpoint, the combining of independent melodic lines in a harmonic and consonant manner. For most Renaissance music, the third lowest part in a four-voice texture, the tenor (often but not necessarily sung by an tenor voice) was the structural voice, often forming with the top line ("cantus" or "superius") a duet that projected the mode. The two other voices in the texture ("altus" and "bassus") provided other counterpoint. Indeed, in the sixteenth century, the duet (or *bicinium*) became a favorite means of pedagogy and amateur music-making. The imitation of the counterpoint was crystallized in a series of melodic ideas or motives, the points of imitation, stated successively by the various lines of a composition.

The priority of vocal music, and the formative experience of chant, continued throughout the period. Many genres of sacred music in the fifteenth century employed a cantus firmus. Dufay seems to have championed one of the major forms, the polyphonic setting of the Ordinary of the Mass (the Kyrie, Gloria, Credo, Sanctus-Benedictus, and Agnus Dei) in works from the 1420s. Contrapuntal ingenuity characterized the masses of Ockeghem, Obrecht, Josquin, and Isaac. In the fifteenth century, the use of *imitatio* (less happily titled "parody") of a pre-existant polyphonic (that is, not simply single-line melody) piece became increasingly important for the composition of masses and the Magnificat. For this service, both the canticle and the appropriate psalms were sung, first in chant or in *alternatim* practice (in which vocal polyphony or organ versets alternated with chant), then increasingly in the sixteenth century in recitation formulas (*falsobordone*, four-part harmonization) or full imitative polyphony.

The other major genre of sacred music was the motet, the setting of a Latin text. The texts for these pieces ranged from the familiar Marian antiphons (such as *Salve Regina*) to humanistically crafted texts commemorating a political occasion or a patron (such as Isaac's *Virgo prudentissima*). Many of these pieces were to be sung in votive services of various kinds, ranging from memorial masses for a deceased patron (or composer, in Dufay's own case) to the remarkable amount of pre-Reformation English polyphony for Marian services. Although some motets quote or paraphrase chant, most are independent, free compositions. Most composers of the period, even those working in Lutheran Germany, wrote motets; in the second half of the sixteenth century, the works of Willaert and especially Lasso, marked a new sensitivity to the rhetorical structures and affects of such texts. A number of settings, by Lassus and others, of secular Latin motets survive.

Settings of vernacular texts began with the priority of the French *formes fixes* of the fourteenth century: rondeau and ballade, even for composers working in Italy. Binchois in particular cultivated the chanson at the court of Burgundy. In the 1520s Claudin de Sermisy (c. 1490–1562) perfected a newly simplified, often quasi-chordal ("homophonic") approach to the form, setting classicizing or popular texts by Clément Marot and others (the "Parisian chanson"); his work was carried forward in the following generations (Thomas Crecquillon [d. c. 1557], Lasso, and the composers of the generation of the Pléiade and metrically-governed verse settings, *musique mesurée*). The chanson also inspired a purely instrumental form of the late sixteenth century in Italy, the *canzona francese* (best-known in the works of Giovanni Gabrieli, active in Venice in the last decades of the century).

Vernacular settings in Italy were well-known in the fifteenth century; the most famous (and best-paid) performers at the courts were poet-improvisers (such as the famous Serafino d'Aquila [1466–1500]), whose works were largely not recorded. The transmission of such music thus begins with the major vernacular genres of the courts around 1500, the various poetic types (*barzeletta, strambotto*) that comprised the *frottola* and the sacred *lauda,* both cultivated in Mantua and Ferrara by Marchetto Cara (d. c. 1525) and Bartolomeo Tromboncino (c. 1470–c. 1535). The first example of the various non-strophic poetic forms set to was music, the madrigal, was owed to two northerners working Italy around 1530, Jacques Arcadelt (c. 1505–1568) and Philippe Verdelot (c. 1470 or 1480–c. 1552).

Yet under the influence of mid-century literary theory, and due to the contrapuntal style of Willaert and Rore, the madrigal acquired greater generic weight, becoming the most preferred and prestigious genre of European secular vocal music. At the hands of the post-Rore generation (Wert, Luca Marenzio [c. 1553–1599], and Monteverdi), the form used directly representational gestures (musical "madrigalisms," for example, ascending scales to represent the idea of rising to the heavens), contrasted imitative with chordal sections, and normally employed at least some rhetorical features (the exordium) of an oration or sermon. In the later 1500s, lighter (often strophic) forms such as the villanella, *napolitana,* and *canzonetta* came north from Naples, achieving pan-European circulation in the works of Orazio Vecchi (1550–1605) and Giovanni Giacomo Gastoldi (c. 1550s–c. 1622).

These forms also achieved a late popularity after their importation to England by Nicolas Yonge (d. 1619; *Musica transalpina,* 1588). Madrigals were composed by Byrd, Morley, Thomas Weelkes (1576–1623), and John Dowland (1563–1626) well into the seventeenth century. Germany and the Low Countries also felt the influence of the madrigal, due to the numerous printed editions of the genre emanating from the printing presses of Nürnberg and Antwerp, imitated by local composers. German song of the early sixteenth century features a pre-existant tune in the tenor part (the *Tenorlied*), while Dutch devotional songs for domestic use in both Catholic and Reformed households (the *souterliedekens*) were evidently popular. The outline of Spanish song is not as clear; several important manuscripts were prepared for court use, featuring the poetic-musical forms of *villancicos* and romances.

The sixteenth century also witnessed the standardization of different-sized families of instruments while retaining the distinction between loud (shawms, cornetts, and trombones) and soft (viols and recorders) ensembles. An independent keyboard repertory developed both in Italy and Ger-

many. But the single most widely-used instrument of the century (whose function was equivalent to that of the piano in the nineteenth century) was the lute, played by the most celebrated virtuosos of the time (like the Italian Francesco Canova da Milano [1497–1543]) and amateurs alike. Whether as a solo instrument playing both single lines and chords, as an accompaniment to solo or ensemble singing, or as an aid in pedagogy and composition, the lute was the premier instrument from Italy to the English lutenist-songwriters (Dowland) into the early seventeenth century.

BIBLIOGRAPHY

General surveys include the classic accounts: Gustave Reese, *Music in the Renaissance,* 2d ed. (New York, 1959), a monumental but dated work; and Howard M. Brown, *Music in the Renaissance,* 2d ed., rev. by L. Stein (New York, 1999), concentrating largely on individuals. A more culturally organized textbook is Allan W. Atlas, *Renaissance Music: Music in Western Europe, 1400–1600* (New York, 1998). For an ambitious synthesis of fifteenth-century music, Reinhard Strohm, *The Rise of European Music, 1380–1500* (Cambridge, 1993); for the best overview of historiography, J. A. Owens, "Music Historiography and the Definition of 'Renaissance,'" *Notes* 47 (1990): 305–330. Two other reference books are likely to become standard: J. Haar, ed., *New Oxford History of Music,* 2d ed., vol. 4, and Stanley Sadie, ed., *The New Grove Dictionary of Music and Musicians,* rev. ed. (London, 1999). For helpful brief articles and a glossary of musical terms, David Fallows and Tess Knighton, eds., *Comparison to Medieval and Renaissance Music* (New York, 1992). Musical sources are catalogued in the series Repertoire International des Sources Musicales (Kassel, 1971–), which has separate volumes for musical anthologies, theory, and manuscripts; for manuscripts a better guide is *Census-Catalogue of Manuscript Sources of Polyphonic Music, 1400–1550,* 4 vols. (Neuhausen-Stuttgart, 1979–1987), compiled by the Musicological Archives for Renaissance Manuscript Studies at the University of Illinois.

There is no single overview in English of Renaissance musical theory; another work in progress, *The Cambridge History of Music Theory,* edited by T. Christensen, will fill this gap. For translations of some of the key musical theorists, see J. Tinctoris, *The Art of Counterpoint,* edited by Albert Seay (n.p., 1961); Franchino Gaffurius, *The Theory of Music,* edited by Claude V. Palisca and translated by Walter Kurt Kreytzig (New Haven, Conn., 1993); and Gioseffo Zarlino, *The Art of Counterpoint,* edited and translated by Claude V. Palisca (New York, 1976). For compositional methods, J. A. Owens, *Composers at Work: The Craft of Musical Composition, 1450–1600* (New York, 1997). For humanism and music, the collected essays of Nino Pirrotta, *Music and Culture in Italy from the Middle Ages to the Baroque: A Collection of Essays* (Cambridge, Mass., 1984), and those of Claude V. Palisca, *Humanism in Italian Renaissance Musical Thought* (New Haven, Conn., 1985) and *Studies in the History of Italian Music and Music Theory* (Oxford, 1994); for scholarship, Ann E. Moyer, *Musica scientia: Musical Scholarship in the Italian Renaissance* (Ithaca, N.Y., 1992). The basic article on *imitatio* remains H. M. Brown, "Emulation, Competition, and Homage: Imitation and Theories of Imitation in the Renaissance," *Journal of the American Musicological Society* 35 (1982):

1–48. For the tracing of Neoplatonic threads through Ficino and Italian philosophy, Gary Tomlinson, *Music in Renaissance Magic: Toward a Historiography of Others* (Chicago, 1993). And for the influence of Bemboist literary theory and the relations between literary academies and one genre, Martha Feldman, *City Culture and the Madrigal at Venice* (Berkeley, Cal., 1995).

ROBERT L. KENDRICK

Music in Renaissance Culture

The concept of a renaissance in the music of the period 1350–1600 is problematic. Some musicologists deny that a rebirth was possible, since no ancient music could serve as a model for imitation, for the few late Greek odes that survived were neither deciphered nor performed. Besides, it is said, the music of the period was dominated by composers from northern Europe, while the Renaissance movement began in Italy.

These views overlook the slow penetration of humanist ideas in Italy and their spread to the north, eventually transforming the musical culture of the continent and England. The movement affected musical practice only slightly until the sixteenth century. But inspired by ancient Greek and Roman ideals, the urge toward text-expression evident in the Italian madrigal of the 1530s oriented music in a direction that it maintained for the next two centuries and shifted musical leadership, held by France and the Netherlands in the fifteenth century, to Italy.

Italy. During the fifteenth and early sixteenth centuries music in Italy spoke a different language from that of the other arts. The painters, sculptors, architects, poets, and other writers were indigenous Italians. But in the ducal and papal chapels professional choirs made up almost wholly of singers trained in places like Cambrai, Bruges, or Antwerp sang music by Guillaume Dufay, Antoine Busnois, Jacob Obrecht, Johannes Ghiselin, Johannes Ockeghem, and Jean Mouton, all of whom made short visits to Italy but whose principal employment lay across the Alps. Others, like Josquin des Prez in Milan and Rome, Heinrich Isaac in Florence, Philippe Verdelot and Jacques Arcadelt in Florence, Adrian Willaert in Ferrara and Venice, and Jacquet (Colebault) of Mantua in Ferrara pursued the major part of their careers in Italian cities. In Venice, Willaert through his teaching spawned a veritable school of composers, which included Andrea Gabrieli, Gioseffo Zarlino, and Nicola Vicentino.

The patronage of the Italian courts made the Italian cities, bustling with civic, economic, educational, artistic, and literary activity, caldrons of fermenting new ideas and influences. They imported transalpine singers, instrumentalists, music, and instruments. The Venice printing press of Ottaviano Petrucci supplied both foreign and domestic music to these centers, while Greek scholars brought their manuscripts, language, and learning, and edited and translated major works of ancient philosophy, history, and literature.

Secular Music. The secular music of the Italian courts consisted largely of polyphonic chansons in French and unwritten lyric, epic, and narrative songs recited on standard tunes by Italian singers and poet-composers. Contrasted with the artful music enjoyed by aristocratic circles, the people sang dance and carnival songs, religious songs called *laude,* and popular songs often accompanied by stringed instruments or by improvised choral harmony. Toward the end of the century several native composers of a semipopular genre, the frottola (a largely homophonic part-song), emerged in the northern courts, among them Bartolomeo Tromboncino and Marchetto Cara in Mantua and Michele Pesenti in Verona. Although written for three or four voices, frottole were usually performed by a soloist singing the uppermost part, the other parts being played on one or more instruments.

Church Music. Highly trained musicians and composers dominated church music throughout Europe. Plainchant continued to be the mainstay of Catholic services, but on solemn occasions polyphonic Masses and motets took its place. In the fifteenth century the medieval custom of basing these on plainchant cantus firmi continued, but popular songs, of which *L'homme armé* is the most famous, increasingly replaced plainchant in Masses as the tenor's melody around which other parts wove imitating or paraphrasing counterpoints. When in the sixteenth century a succession of fugues (called points of imitation) on different or related subjects became the preferred means of constructing polyphonic music, composers adopted the custom of borrowing wholesale entire points of imitation from a motet, madrigal, or chanson to begin phrase-sections of a mass.

Humanism. Through the translations and commentaries of Marsilio Ficino (1433–1499), Plato's *Timaeus, Republic,* and *Laws* nourished a Neoplatonic intellectual strain that emphasized cosmic harmony and its relation to human sensibilities and the divine origin of artistic creativity. Boethius (480–524), whose treatises on music and arithmetic dominated mathematical and musical instruction in the early Renaissance, divided music into *mundana, humana,* and *instrumentalis,* that is, the unheard harmony of the cosmos and of the human soul, the harmony that united it with the body, and, lastly, the music made audible by voices and instruments. The latter could be experienced through the ear and its cause understood as rapid motion of the air. But the other two kinds acted silently and blindly in the heavens, on earth, and in space, and their nature was occult and magical. Plato in his *Timaeus* described a world-soul composed of disparate, opposite, and discordant elements held together through simple number ratios. He thought of the human soul as an analogous harmony, and the body's parts and its relation to the soul as also ideally a harmony, but one that could fall into dissonance.

Marsilio Ficino developed these ideas particularly in *De vita libri tres* (Three books on life; 1489). He claimed that sounding music could magically resolve the discordances of the human soul and could even affect the planets and stars if the appropriate combination of pitches (such as modes) were sent up in song. Franchino Gaffurio, in *Musica theorica* (Music theory; 1492) and *De harmonia* (On harmony; 1518)—influenced by Ficino but also directly by Plato, Aristides Quintilianus, and Ptolemy, whose musical works he read in translation—considered the part-music composed in his time an imitation of the cosmic harmony revealed to the artist through divine suffusion. Music could thus lead a soul to retrace the path back to harmony's divine origin. Numerous philosophers elaborated the magical and astrological aspects of music, particularly in the early years of the sixteenth century—notably Henry Cornelius Agrippa and Pietro Pomponazzi—but also later in the century, including such writers as Tommaso Campanella, Pontus de Tyard, and Francesco Patrizi.

The most frequently cited passage from the *Republic* (3.399–400) defines music as made up of words, rhythm, and melody, with the words "by far the most important of the three, being the very basis and foundation of the rest." Invoked by Jacopo Sadoleto in *De liberis recte instituendis* (On the proper education of children; Venice, 1533), where he complained that he could not understand the text in the current church music, the dictum was later quoted also by, among others, Giovanni Bardi, Giulio Caccini, and Claudio Monteverdi to support word-centered new styles.

Although the logical works of Aristotle were well known and studied in the universities and elsewhere, the writings most important to music—*Politics, Poetics,* and the *Problems*—only now received renewed attention through Latin translations and commentaries. Aristotle's view that all arts are based on imitation, that the tragedy and music could purge people of certain undesirable emotions, and that music may "imitate" and stir a wide variety of passions won many adherents in the sixteenth century.

The Greek musical treatises of pseudo-Euclid, Cleonides, Ptolemy, Aristides Quintilianus, Bacchius Senior, and pseudo-Plutarch were translated into Latin in the 1490s, and Aristoxenus finally in 1562. They helped correct misreadings of the *De institutione musica* (trans. *Fundamentals of Music*) of Boethius as well as his Pythagorean biases, and his music treatise was now reread as a document about Greek music rather than as a foundation of western music theory. Johannes Gallicus (Legrense), Franchino Gaffurio, Lodovico Fogliano, Gioseffo Zarlino, Girolamo Mei, Francisco de Salinas, and Vincenzo Galilei interpreted and spread this ancient musical thought and laid new foundations for music theory.

Aspiring to the Power of Ancient Music. Humanists who read the ancient literature about music, especially that of Plato, Aristotle, and pseudo-Plutarch, could not understand why the music of the ancients had such power over moral character and emotions, while the art music of their own time, though pleasurable, was ineffective. Among those who took up this question were Carlo Valgulio (*Prooemium in musicam Plutarchi;* Introduction to the music treatise of Plutarch; Brescia, 1507), Jacopo Sadoleto, Bernardino Cirillo (Letter to Ugolino Gualteruzzi; 1549), Heinrich Glarean (*Dodecachordon;* The twelve modes; Basel, 1547), Nicola Vicentino (*L'Antica musica ridotta alla moderna prattica;* Ancient music adapted to modern practice; Rome, 1555), Girolamo Mei (letters to Galilei and Giovanni Bardi; 1572–1581), Bardi ("Discorso . . . sopra la musica antica"; Discourse on ancient music; c. 1578), and Galilei (*Dialogo della musica antica et della moderna;* Dialogue on ancient and modern music; Florence, 1581).

Glarean expanded the system of modes from eight to twelve, believing (mistakenly) that he had restored those of Aristoxenus. Vicentino advocated resurrecting the ancient chromatic and enharmonic scales and implementing whatever melodic and harmonic means were effective in moving the affections even if conventionally prohibited. Mei urged a return to monody, because his research showed that the ancient Greeks always, even in a chorus, sang only a single line and never accompanied this with consonances. Bardi and Galilei, deploring the complexities of counterpoint and excessive embellishment, urged simplicity of melody and harmony, greater attention to the meaning of a text and not just word painting, and a return to the Greek tonal and modal systems. Galilei also promoted freer use of dissonance (*Discorso intorno all'uso delle dissonanze;* Discourse on the use of dissonance; 1589–1591). In France a group around the poet Jean-Antoine de Baïf founded in 1570 the Academie de poésie et de musique (Academy of poetry and music) to experiment with a classically inspired quantitative poetry, *vers mesurés à l'antique.* Because French pronunciation observed accent rather than quantity, the group devised rules for determining the quantity of vowels and vowel-consonant combinations. Claude Le Jeune observed the short and long quantities in setting this poetry as well as the psalms in a tuneful homophonic style.

Mei's revelation that ancient tragedies and comedies were performed musically inspired a group of Florentine intellectuals and musicians who met under Bardi's leadership in an informal academy later known as the camerata to stage pastoral plays as sung dramas modeled on the ancient. Ottavio Rinuccini's *Euridice,* with music by Jacopo Peri, performed at the Henry IV–Maria de' Medici wedding in Florence in 1600, was the first drama sung throughout that survives complete, and marked the beginning of opera.

Poetics. Meanwhile poetic theory turned from the Neoplatonic belief in the divine origin of creativity—the *furor poeticus*—to the Aristotelian principle of imitation as the impulse for artistic expression. A composer should "imitate" the text, that is, express its literal and emotional message through musical means. The adoption of this goal led to a breakdown of the homogeneous fugal texture of the 1520s in favor of a variety of textures and devices that made the words come to life and move listeners. Every line and sometimes every hemistich (half a line) of a poem now received a different treatment in terms of rhythmic movement, proportion of consonance and dissonance, relationship between the voices, degree of floridity, diatonicism or chromaticism, and purity or adulteration of mode by accidentals. A composition became a heterogeneous collection of manners instead of manifesting a uniform style, eliciting from modern critics the term "mannerism." This tendency is already evident in some Italian madrigals by Arcadelt and Willaert of the 1530s and 1540s and became pronounced in the madrigals and motets of

Rore, Orlando di Lasso, Luca Marenzio, Giaches de Wert, Luzzasco Luzzaschi, Carlo Gesualdo, Claudio Monteverdi, and certain of their contemporaries. The English madrigals of Thomas Morley, Thomas Weelkes, John Wilbye, and Orlando Gibbons reflect this movement somewhat later.

Rhetoric. Although several Italian writers had compared music to oratory in its power to move the emotions, it was only at the end of the sixteenth century that Joachim Burmeister, a Lutheran church musician and preceptor of Latin at the Rostock town school, systematically applied rhetorical principles to the teaching of musical composition. He claimed that a good composition, like an oration, should not only be correct and fluent but also should forcefully move listeners to the affections represented in its text. He described more than twenty devices composers used to convey the text's sense and sentiments, making his pupils aware of the variety of figures available to them. He gave most of the figures names borrowed from Latin rhetoric. Burmeister's aim was to hold up models of expressive writing, many of them drawn from the motets of Lasso, to beginners in composition. But he also emphasized the need to organize a piece as one would an oration, with an enticing exordium, a persuasive middle, and a fitting conclusion.

See also **Music,** *subentry on* **Music Treatises***; biographies of figures mentioned in this entry.*

BIBLIOGRAPHY

Primary Works

Atlas, Allan W. *Anthology of Renaissance Music.* New York, 1998.

Burmeister, Joachim. *Musical Poetics.* Translated by Benito Rivera. New Haven, Conn., and London, 1993.

Palisca, Claude V., ed. *Girolamo Mei (1519–1594): Letters on Ancient and Modern Music to Vincenzo Galilei and Giovanni Bardi.* 2d ed. Stuttgart, Germany, 1977.

Palisca, Claude V. *The Florentine Camerata: Documentary Studies and Translations.* New Haven, Conn., and London, 1989.

Tomlinson, Gary, ed. *The Renaissance.* Vol. 3: *Source Readings in Music History.* Edited by Oliver Strunk. Rev. ed. Edited by Leo Treitler. New York, 1998.

Secondary Works

Blume, Friedrich. *Renaissance and Baroque Music.* New York, 1967.

Lowinsky, Edward E. "Music in the Culture of the Renaissance." *Journal of the History of Ideas* 15 (1954): 509–553.

Maniates, M. Rika. *Mannerism in Italian Music and Culture.* Durham, N.C., 1979.

Palisca, Claude V. *Humanism in Italian Renaissance Musical Thought.* New Haven, Conn., and London, 1985.

Palisca, Claude V. *Studies in the History of Italian Music and Music Theory.* Oxford, 1994.

Rempp, Frieder. *Die Kontrapunkttraktate Vincenzo Galileis.* Cologne, Germany, 1980.

Schrade, Leo. "Renaissance: the Historical Conception of an Epoch." In *Congress Report, International Musicological Society, Utrecht 1952.* Amsterdam, 1953. Pages 19–32.

Tomlinson, Gary. *Music in Renaissance Magic.* Chicago and London, 1993.

Walker, D. P. *Spiritual and Demonic Magic from Ficino to Campanella.* 2d ed. Notre Dame, Ind., 1975.

CLAUDE V. PALISCA

Music in Renaissance Society

From the works that Guillaume Dufay (c. 1400–1474) composed for the Malatesta at Rimini, to the madrigals and motets written by Giaches de Wert (1535–1596) and Claudio Monteverdi (1567–1643) for the Mantuan Gonzaga, Renaissance music has been viewed as a court product. Major Italian centers included Aragonese Naples; the papal court with its prestigious ensemble; the Medici establishments of Florence; and the musical chapels of the dynastic rulers of Ferrara, Mantua, and Milan. North of the Alps, the emperor Maximilian I expanded the traditions of Burgundian court music, recruiting Heinrich Isaac (c. 1450–1517) for his imperial chapel, and Charles V's chapel continued the tradition with its employment of the other major contemporaries of Adriaan Willaert (c. 1490–1562), the Netherlanders Nicolas Gombert (c. 1490–c. 1556) and Thomas Crecquillon (c. 1480/1500–1557). Later the Wittelsbach rulers of Bavaria hired and supported Orlando di Lasso (Orlandus Lassus) for nearly forty years. The French court maintained important singers and composers, starting with Johannes Ockeghem (c. 1410–1495), and Netherlanders were recruited for the Castilian court for over a century. Most known English composers served at some time in the Chapel Royal.

The musical patronage of popes and dukes was important but different in some ways from that of the visual arts. The ducal centers of the fifteenth century (for instance, the Este of Ferrara) were often in fierce competition for Netherlandish singers and chapel masters, and the two papal chapels (the Sistine Chapel and the Julian Chapel, founded by Sixtus IV and Julius II, respectively) in particular hosted the best musicians of Europe. Still, one must be careful to avoid an anachronistic view of musicians as artistic free agents who translated patrons' specific wishes into musical terms. The traditions of these courts continued; the revised biography of Josquin des Prez (c. 1440–1521) now places his first important position at the papal chapel in the late 1480s, and the court at Ferrara engendered some of Wert's most daring madrigal experiments, composed for the

most famous ensemble of late sixteenth-century Italy, the spectacular women singers who made up part of the semiprivate ducal *concerto delle donne.*

The choir schools of the cathedrals of the Low Countries produced singers who worked in all of Europe, and such centers as Ghent and Bruges maintained permanent instrumental ensembles. Religious houses and confraternities also supported polyphony, as Reinhard Strohm has documented for Bruges in its heyday and Blake Wilson for fifteenth-century Florence. By the early sixteenth century Venice and Antwerp, with their basilica or cathedral ensembles, production of musical instruments and printed editions, and merchant confraternities sponsoring polyphony, became continental musical centers. Later in the century, on a smaller scale, Nürnberg (with its tradition of urban artisan-musicians, the Meistersinger, such as Hans Sachs) filled an analogous role for Protestant Germany.

The Printing of Music. Urban culture as well as the technological innovations of music printing contributed to a marked spread of musical literacy in the course of the sixteenth century. The first (multiple-impression) method for printing music was developed by Ottaviano dei Petrucci in Venice; his first edition, the *Harmonice musices Odhecaton A* (1501), consisted of motets and chansons by the leading composers of the day. Petrucci's prints featured the music of Josquin, Isaac, Pierre de La Rue, and Loyset Compère. Around 1520, the Parisian printer Pierre Attaignant employed a single-impression method for musical editions, drastically cutting production times and costs; Attaignant's prints disseminated both the new Parisian chanson and the sacred works of the generation after Josquin.

Music printing spread quickly through Italy and central Europe, with major centers in Venice (the competing firms of the Gardano and Scotto families), Rome, Nürnberg, Antwerp (the presses of Tylman Susato and of the partnership of Hubert Waelrant and Jan Laet, succeeded by the famous Phalèse dynasty), and Paris. Lesser centers important for the transalpine trade were Lyon and Milan. Most music, except for special sacred repertories, was printed in sets of part books, each of which contained only the music for a single line of each polyphonic piece in the book. The speed with which the most recent music could travel through Europe was remarkable; by the 1590s merchants in Gdansk had a standing order with the Venetian presses that brought the works of Luca Marenzio and Giovanni da Palestrina to Poland within months, and the inventories of the Portuguese court in Lisbon contained imported recent Italian music.

Although printing was vital in the propagation of music (it was essential in the pan–European reputation of Lasso, the single most widely performed composer of the second half of the sixteenth century; his music was sung by such diverse groups as Milanese nuns and Nürnberg burghers), the production of manuscripts for institutions and individuals remained important (some of Lasso's most valued music for the Bavarian court, his settings of the penitential psalms, circulated only in manuscript until after the death of his patron, Duke Albert V). Continuing an earlier tradition, many ecclesiastical codices (e.g., those of the Sistine Chapel) were written in choir-book format, in which all the voices of a piece were fit onto a single opening, so that ensembles could perform (or memorize) directly from the book. Insofar as such choir books transmitted local composers, devotional music, or liturgy, they became musical monuments to an institution's or a city's traditions.

Music and Christianity. Music's relationship to the changes in devotion and structure of Christianity has been viewed largely through a northern European prism, in which its role in magisterial Protestant traditions has been emphasized and its parallel "decadence" in Catholicism has been seen as being "reformed" by omnipotent Tridentine strictures (epitomized by the famous, and apocryphal, story in which the Council of Trent intended to ban polyphony until dissuaded by the clarity and intelligibility of Palestrina's mass settings, such as the *Missa Papae Marcelli*). As we obtain a more nuanced view of both religious life and musical practice, greater continuity across both temporal and confessional divisions is evident.

Martin Luther's admiration for music is well known, and the establishment of a set of vernacular hymns plus melodies, the basic German chorale repertory, was central not only to musical life but also to the self-understanding of Reformed communities. In similar if less formal ways, imprisoned Anabaptists in the Netherlands used hymns and sacred songs to console each other and reaffirm their faith. Anglican music under Henry VIII first showed continuity with pre-Reformation style; then, under Thomas Cranmer's radical reforms, John Marbeck compiled a vernacular psalter and hymns. This was more similar to the Calvinist repertory of metrical psalms printed in Geneva than to the Lutheran chorale repertory. After the brief (but musically fruitful) Catholic interlude of Mary, Elizabeth's Chapel Royal cultivated the particularly English form of the verse anthem as well as vernacular services, examples of both being written by composers such as Thomas Tallis and William Byrd (both Catholics whose personal faith evidently did not obstruct their service to the queen).

Similarly, as the various waves of Catholic reform in the sixteenth century become apparent, the continuity of the underlying sentiments that gave rise to musical expression become evident. Much music around 1500 had been generated by the spectacular Marian devotion across Europe. The motets of Willaert's *Musica nova* (1559) display a clear, balanced structure geared toward projecting a sacred text to audiences. Far from an aural world of unintelligible contrapuntal artifice, midcentury sacred music in Catholic Europe strove for clarity. The Tridentine guidelines were vague in their recommendations for the clear declamation of liturgical Latin texts; they were hurriedly passed, and left most actual decisions to the discretion of the local bishop. The simplification of style evident in the masses that Vincenzo Ruffo wrote for the Milan cathedral in the first years of Archbishop Charles Borromeo's tenure was relatively short-lived, and Ruffo's experiments should be considered in the broader context of midcentury neoclassicism.

More significant in the postconciliar years was the musical expression of the devotional waves that spread throughout Catholic Europe, and its linkage to the post-Bemboist changes in sacred rhetoric inaugurated by Gabriele Fiamma and Angelo Grillo, which were contemporary with new standards for sacred oratory. Polyphony was practiced by religious houses and sponsored by the numerous urban confraternities of Palermo, Rome, Bologna, and Venice. The most striking example was in Rome, where these bodies sponsored annual cycles of music outside the framework of the papal chapel or the basilicas. North of the Alps, sacred music continued to be important at the imperial court of Vienna (with the last of the Netherlanders, Philippe de Monte), at the French court, and, especially as a mark of Catholic identity, at the war-torn Brussels court in the Spanish Netherlands, this last employing English Catholic exiles (Peter Phillips and John Bull). Some of the most heartfelt settings of Latin texts were due to Byrd, an English recusant writing his masses and motets for noble Catholic households; several of the latter seem to refer indirectly to the English Catholic martyrs of the 1580s.

The major political events of the time also called forth music. The entries of the Burgundian dukes or emperors into the cities of the Low Countries were normally marked not only by the civic trumpeters but also by the composition of sacred music (e.g., the entrance of the future Charles V into Antwerp in 1515). Some of the most elaborate pieces were composed for dynastic occasions: the meeting of the Spanish and English court chapels in London at the betrothal of Philip II and Mary Tudor, or the series of increasingly elaborate, "multimedia" Medici wedding festivities in Florence that began with the madrigals of the 1539 events, continued through the spectacular theatrical *intermedi,* songs, and instrumental pieces of 1589, and spawned a newly comprehensive kind of theatrical music, the *opera in musica,* created for those of 1600.

The Musician's World. Little is still known about Renaissance music education. Some institutional instruction occurred in the cathedral choir schools of France and Flanders, and similar training was part of the choirboys' training at the major Italian cathedrals. But much learning was essentially due to individual instruction and domestic practice (the latter especially for girls). In the later sixteenth century musical primers began to be printed, but the essential relationship was that of a master passing down the art to a student. In both sacred and secular repertories improvisation of entire pieces (e.g., the stock harmonic formulas used to recite stanzas of ottava rima by Ludovico Ariosto) and the melodic ornamentation of lines in an existing piece played a central role. Noteworthy is the dissociation of musical from general literacy; in postconciliar Italy confraternities used *laude* (hymns of praise) as a means of imparting Catholic doctrine because they could not rely on their public to be able to read.

Many singers and composers were clerics (especially in Catholic Europe), and thus qualified for (often absentee) benefices (notably in the somewhat looser pre-Tridentine atmosphere). A few, like Dufay, had pan-European careers or held honored places at the imperial court, like Isaac. But the situation for most was quite precarious; they were subject to firing after the accession of a new duke at court or in the wake of financial cutbacks at a major church. To publish music, normally one had to find a patron who would subsidize (prepay) the printing costs, and most Renaissance musical editions are dedicated to such a figure. Although some musicians (Palestrina, who had had decades of service at the major Roman basilicas and then in the Julian Chapel) achieved relative wealth, many were dependent on their jobs as chapel masters or directors of music in institutions for their income.

Until recently it appeared that the relative freedom of women in late medieval Europe had become restricted in terms of musical activity in the course of the Renaissance. However, the actual situation was much more nuanced, with important if somewhat hidden counterexamples. These included the patronage of French, Flemish, and Savoyard noblewomen to which many of the manuscripts containing the early chanson repertory is owed; the catalyzing effect of Isabella d'Este in the development of frottole (strophic vernacular songs in a variety of poetic forms, often but not necessarily on amatory or light-hearted topics, normally set for four voices but often arranged in practice for voice and lute) and instrumental music in early-sixteenth-century Mantua; and the famous performers like Laura Pevernara from Ferrara's *concerto delle donne.* Outside the court this was evident in female printers like Catherina Gerlach in Nürnberg; the participation of women and girls in the domestic musicmaking targeted by the Antwerp presses; the burgeoning musical life of Italian nuns in late-sixteenth-century Bologna, Milan, and Verona. One association between music and gender was the classification of musical activities into more narrowly defined male and female spheres. In addition, a part of the classical revival, taking its cue from aspects of Platonic thought, disdained music as an "effeminate" activity.

The gender segregation formed part of a more general view of the musical accomplishments "appropriate" to the courtier and the general role of amateurs. Although it considered music part of noble education for both genders, Baldassare Castiglione's *Book of the Courtier* praised the art as appropriate to women because of its sweetness, although his idea of courtly *sprezzatura* (elegance, poise, nonchalance) was picked up by Florentine singer-composers like Giulio Caccini (1545–1618) later in the century. The growth of amateur music making among both patricians and the middle class was one of the most striking features of the sixteenth century. The best-known English Renaissance guidebook to reading music, singing, and even simple composition, Thomas Morley's *A Plaine and Easie Introduction to Practicall Musicke* (1597), takes such music lovers as its intended audience.

BIBLIOGRAPHY

The best introductory volume accessible to nonspecialists is Iain Fenlon, ed., *The Renaissance from the 1470s to the End of the 16th Century* (Englewood Cliffs, N.J., 1989), organized around places (courts and cities). Monographs on court music include Iain Fenlon, *Music and Patronage in Sixteenth-Century Mantua,* 2 vols. (Cambridge, U.K., 1980–1982); Lewis Lockwood, *Music in Renaissance Ferrara, 1400–1505* (Cambridge, Mass., 1984), and Allan W. Atlas, *Music at the Aragonese Court of Naples* (Cambridge, U.K., 1985). Studies of music in cities include Reinhold Strohm's remarkable *Music in Late Medieval Bruges* (Oxford, 1985); other centers are covered in Fenlon's *The Renaissance* and in such monographs as Frank Dobbins, *Music in Renaissance Lyons* (Oxford, 1992) and the later sections of Frank A. d'Accone, *The Civic Muse: Music and Musicians in Siena during the Middle Ages and Renaissance* (Chicago, 1997). National surveys include Tim Carter, *Music in Late Renaissance and Early Baroque Italy* (Portland, Oreg., 1992); and the still-valuable if dated works of Robert Murrell Stevenson, *Spanish Music in the Age of Columbus* (The Hague, 1960; repr. Westport, Conn., 1979) and *Spanish Cathedral Music in the Golden Age* (Berkeley, Calif., 1961). John Caldwell, ed., *The Oxford History of English Music,* vol. 1 (Oxford, 1991), provides a good overview of insular developments; a still-useful book is Walter L. Woodfill, *Musicians in English Society* (Princeton, N.J., 1953; repr. New York, 1969). Some of the essays in John Kmetz, ed., *Music in the German Renaissance: Sources, Styles, and Contexts* (Cambridge, U.K., 1994) cover an area without a large English-language bibliography.

A standard work on genres is Alfred Einstein, *The Italian Madrigal,* trans. Alexander H. Krappe, Roger H. Sessions, and Oliver Strunk, 3 vols. (Princeton, N.J., 1949; repr. 1971); instrumental music is cataloged in Howard M. Brown, *Instrumental Music Printed before 1600: A Bibliography* (Cambridge, Mass., 1965). On sacred music, Howard M. Brown, "The Mirror of Man's Salvation: Music in Devotional Life About 1500," *Renaissance Quarterly* 43 (1990): 747–773; and M. J. Bloxam, "Obrecht as Exegete: Reading *Factor orbis* as a Christmas Sermon," in D. Pesce, ed., *Hearing the Motet: Essays on the Motet of the Middle Ages and Renaissance* (New York, 1997), 169–192, provide stimulating points on music and religious life. The first chapter of Robin A. Leaver, *"Goostly Psalmes and Spirituall Songes": English and Dutch Metrical Psalms from Coverdale to Utenhove, 1535–1566* (Oxford, 1991), gives a basic introduction to Reformation attitudes toward music. On England see Peter Le Huray, *Music and the Reformation in England, 1549–1660* (New York, 1967; repr. Cambridge, U.K., 1978). For the place of *laude* in Florentine life, see Blake McDowell Wilson, *Music and Merchants: The Laudesi Companies of Republican Florence* (Oxford, 1992). Noel O'Regan, *Institutional Patronage in Post-Tridentine Rome* (London, 1995), provides a detailed and balanced study of confraternity music in the time of Palestrina.

For women musicians see A. Newcomb, "Courtesans, Muses, or Musicians? Professional Women Musicians in Sixteenth-Century Italy," and J. Bowers, "The Emergence of Women Composers in Italy, 1566–1700," in Jane Bowers and Judith Tick, *Women Making Music: The Western Art Tradition, 1150–1950* (Urbana, Ill., 1986), 90–115 and 116–167, respectively; for representative works the selection of compositions in Martha Furman Schleifer and Sylvia Glickman, eds., *Women Composers: Music through the Ages,* vol. 1 (New York, 1996); and for a microhistorical account of music's role in one female foundation, Craig A. Monson, *Disembodied Voices: Music and Culture in an Early Modern Italian Convent* (Berkeley, Calif., 1995).

ROBERT L. KENDRICK

Music Treatises

Music treatises in the period 1425 to 1550 tended to be either theoretical, following the precedent set by Boethius in *De institutione musica* (Fundamentals of music; c. A.D. 500), which examined music as a branch of mathematics within the quadrivium, or practical, dealing with musical composition, improvisation, and performance. After 1550 the distinction blurred, as authors strove for greater integration of musical knowledge.

Music Theory. Theorizing about music split into two categories: *musica theorica,* which dealt with the foundations of music, such as the nature of sound, intervals, consonance and dissonance, scales, modes, tunings, durations, and other matters defining the medium of musical sound; and *musica practica,* comprising instruction in singing, playing instruments, and composition of melody, rhythm, and counterpoint.

The most comprehensive treatise of the late Middle Ages, the *Speculum musicae* (Mirror of music; c. 1330) of Jacques de Liège (c. 1260–c. 1330), divides music into *theorica* and *practica*. Marchetto da Padova (fl. 1305–1326) mixes the two in his *Lucidarium* (c. 1318) and *Pomerium* (c. 1326), but Prosdocimo de' Beldomandi (c. 1380–1428), who taught mathematics, astronomy, and music at the University of Padua, wrote separate treatises on practical and theoretical matters—*Contrapunctus* (Counterpoint; 1412) and *Tractatus musicae speculativae* (Treatise on theoretical music; 1425), the former addressed to musicians, the latter to theorists and university students. Treatises after Prosdocimo until the mid-sixteenth century reflect this division of subject matter, often specifying one or the other in their titles.

Ugolino of Orvieto (c. 1380–1457) in his *Declaratio musicae disciplinae* (Exposition of the musical discipline; c. 1430) follows this pattern. He dedicated the first three books to *musica practica*—the subjects of the choir school, including the basic scale, the church modes, the rules of discant and counterpoint, and the system of time durations. Books 4 and 5, mostly based on Boethius but drawing some insights from Aristotle, explained the arithmetical ratios of musical intervals.

Although Boethius was cited frequently throughout the Middle Ages and early fifteenth century, important chapters of his *De institutione musica,* particularly those in book 4 dealing with the modes, were poorly understood. Johannes Gallicus (c. 1415–1473), who studied the text with the humanist Vittorino da Feltre in Mantua, appears to have been the first to realize that the modes described by Boethius were a Greek system altogether different from the modern modes of plainchant and that the Boethian treatise was a compilation of translations from the Greek. But neither he nor Franchino Gaffurio (1451–1522), who took up the matter of the modes, was able to explain the difference between the tonal systems adequately or to identify Boethius's sources.

Nicola Burzio of Parma (c. 1445–1518), another pupil of Gallicus, remained faithful in his *Musices opusculum* (A little work on music; Bologna, 1487) to the Pythagorean definition of consonance at a time when this was challenged by practitioners. Boethius had defined consonance in terms of ratios of string lengths according to the Pythagorean tradition: the terms of the ratios of a consonance must be drawn from the first four numbers and must be of the multiple (mn/n) or superparticular ($n+1/n$) classes. The only ratios and intervals that qualify are: 2:1, octave; 3:2, fifth; 4:3, fourth; 3:1, octave plus fifth; and 4:1, double octave. This excludes the major and minor thirds and major and minor sixths, intervals that practitioners treated as consonances already in the thirteenth and fourteenth centuries. The tuning of the scale resulting from the Pythagorean ratios provides fourths and fifths in their most harmonious sounding forms, but the major thirds and minor sixths are too large and the minor thirds and major sixths too small to blend well in the simultaneous chords essential to polyphony. Nevertheless Gaffurio defended this tuning in his *Theorica musice* (Milan, 1492), although in his *Practica musice* (Milan, 1496) he admitted that keyboard players tuned their instruments otherwise to produce more agreeably sounding chords.

Bartolomé Ramos de Pareja (c. 1440–1491), a Spanish mathematician who settled and lectured in Bologna around 1470, aimed in his *Musica practica* (Bologna, 1482) to bring theory more in line with practice. He proposed a new way of dividing the single string of the monochord—an instrument used since antiquity for tuning the musical intervals by measuring string lengths. He derived not only the "perfect consonances," the octave, fifth, and fourth, in their true ratios but also the "imperfect" consonances: the major third, 5:4; minor third, 6:5; major sixth, 5:3; and minor sixth, 8:5. However, Ramos admitted that a few consonant combinations within his scale were not in their just tuning.

Ramos's pupil Giovanni Spataro (1448?–1541), a Bolognese composer and choirmaster, defended his teacher's solution against Gaffurio and Burzio in *Honesta defensio* (Honest defense; Bologna, 1491). The differences between Ramos, Spataro, Burzio, and Gaffurio were truly theoretical in that practitioners—composers and musicians—paid little attention to

ratios when they composed, performed, or tuned their instruments, and the debate subsided.

The theoretical side of the question was not resolved until Lodovico Fogliano of Modena—at one time a singer and composer but also a master of Greek and Latin—in his *Musica theorica* (Venice, 1529) applied logical and natural principles from Aristotle's *Posterior Analytics, De anima,* and *Physics.* He rejected number as the sole criterion for consonance, pointing out that according to Aristotle sound was a natural, not mathematical, phenomenon, placing harmonics or the theory of pitch relations in an intermediate position between the mathematical and the natural. Consequently the judgment of the ear was as much to be trusted as mathematics, and sense experience taught that thirds and sixths were as acceptable consonances as the fourths and fifths, if not more so. Without citing either Ramos or Ptolemy, Fogliano proposed a tuning similar to theirs as ideal for polyphonic music.

Meanwhile the attention of literate musicians turned to defining the standards for musical composition. The fifteenth century was a time of transition from treble-dominated vocal music on both secular and sacred texts to music for several equally active vocal parts. A few simple rules, mostly about the succession of consonances, guided the writing of part-music, leaving composers to follow personal taste in the use of dissonances.

Dissatisfied with the haphazard way dissonances were introduced by his predecessors, Johannes Tinctoris (c. 1435–1511) subjected them to careful control in his *Liber de arte contrapuncti* (Book on the art of counterpoint; 1477). Tinctoris was born in the province of Brabant and trained partly under Guillaume Dufay in Cambrai. After a period of service as a singer and choir director in Orléans and Chartres, Tinctoris settled around 1472 in Naples in the service of King Ferdinand I. In his instructions on counterpoint Tinctoris limited dissonances to short notes of local motion and to syncopated cadence formulas. He distinguished *res facta,* written composition in which his rules were to be strictly followed, from *supra librium cantare,* the freer improvised counterpoint in which singers made up parts impromptu around a melody read from a plainchant choirbook. Among his twelve treatises, he also addressed mensural proportions, the modes (based largely on Marchetto da Padua), and the emotional effects of music, and he wrote a dictionary of musical terms, *Terminorum musicae diffinitorium,* the first such dictionary printed (Treviso, Italy, 1495). In these works Tinctoris revealed not only a mastery of practical theory but also a broad acquaintance with classical literature.

If Tinctoris reflected the humanist propensity for treatise writing and classical allusions, Franchino Gaffurio was a true humanist searching in Greek theoretical and philosophical writings for answers to musical questions. He tried in his *Theoricum opus musice discipline* (A theoretical work on the discipline of music; Naples, 1480) to corroborate or complement with more ancient and modern sources the doctrine transmitted by Boethius, not letting his inability to read Greek stand in the way. Gaffurio probably finished this work in Naples between 1478 and 1480. Although he based this treatise mostly on Boethius, he utilized, for example, Pietro d'Abano's commentary on the *Problems* of Aristotle. (*Expositio problematum Aristotelis;* 1475). For his revision and expansion, the aforementioned *Theorica musice,* Gaffurio relied heavily on the *Paraphrases* of Themistius, the *De anima* of Aristotle in the translation by Ermolao Barbaro (Treviso, 1481), the *De musica* attributed to Plutarch in the translation of Carlo Valgulio published later (Brescia, 1507), and a translation of the *Introduction to the Art of Music* by Bacchius Senior (3rd–4th century A.D.).

In 1484 Gaffurio was named choirmaster of the Cathedral of Milan and from 1492 he lectured on music in the gymnasium created by Duke Lodovico Sforza. At about this time he commissioned Giovanni Francesco Burana, who may have already translated the Bacchius, to translate into Latin the music treatises of the ancients Aristides Quintilianus and Manuel Bryennius, and a compilation known as Bellermann's Anonymous. These were completed by 1494, but Niccolò Leoniceno's translation of Ptolemy's *Harmonica* (trans. *Harmonics*), also intended for Gaffurio's use, was not ready until March 1499, by which time Gaffurio had almost finished his last theoretical work, *De harmonia musicorum instrumentorum opus* (A work on the harmony of musical instruments; Milan, 1518). Because of the changing political situation in Milan, alternating between local and French rule, Gaffurio found a sponsor only after presenting illuminated manuscript copies of the book to several prospects on both the Sforza and French sides. Ultimately the famous book collector Jean Grolier, the French king's treasurer in Milan and later the treasurer of France, helped to get this richly illustrated and complex book into print eighteen years after it was finished. In the meantime Gaffurio used some material from the translations in his *Practica musicae* (Milan, 1496), most significantly a

table of Greek temporal signs from Bellermann's Anonymous.

De harmonia expands the field of music theory beyond the Boethian curriculum to many topics, including modern practice, cosmic harmony, the elements, the muses, and the harmony of the human soul. Gaffurio also delves much more deeply into some of the traditional areas, such as the various tunings proposed by Greek authors for the three genres of melody: diatonic—made up of tones and semitones, that is, whole steps and half steps; chromatic—made up of a minor third and two half-steps; and enharmonic—made up of a major third and two minute intervals approximately a quarter tone each. He also treats the division of an interval such as the octave into three means. Where two notes of an interval are represented by their relative string lengths, a and b, and where $a > b$, the arithmetic means equals $a - \frac{1}{2}(a - b)$; the geometric mean equals the square root of ab; and the harmonic mean equals ($2ab / a + b$). For example, in an octave C–c whose ratio is 12:6, the arithmetic mean is F (9), the harmonic mean is G (8), and the geometric mean is F♯ (approximately 8.5). He also now admits that it is possible to divide a string to produce the thirds and sixths in simple ratios, but he rejects them as consonant intervals because, though consonant to the sense of hearing, they do not fit Aristides's definition of "rational."

Gaffurio reveals for the first time in *De harmonia* Ptolemy's own solution for diatonic tuning: his syntonic, or tense, diatonic, whose tetrachord, or four-note module, has the descending order of ratios 10:9 (smaller tone), 9:8 (larger tone), and 16:15 (semitone). It was new to nonreaders of Greek because Boethius suspended translation of Ptolemy's book 1 just before he reached this tuning.

A method to adapt the plainchant modes to polyphony came under increasing investigation in the sixteenth century. Pietro Aron in his *Trattato della natura et cognitione di tutti gli tuoni di canto figurato* (Treatise on the nature and identification of all the modes of measured song; Venice, 1525) analyzed a large number of published polyphonic secular and sacred compositions to determine what characteristics could be assigned to the eight church modes. His main criteria were the final note and the characteristic species of fourth and fifth—that is, the arrangement of tones and semitones within these intervals as observed particularly in the tenor part. He found that analyzing compositions in this way usually yielded a positive determination of mode, but

Music Theorist. Francesco Gafori (Gaffurio; 1451–1522) lecturing on music, from the title page of a collection of his three musical treatises, *Theorica musicae, Practica musicae,* and *De harmonia.*

results were sometimes ambiguous, particularly when a composition did not end on one of the recognized finals—D, E, F, or G—but rather on A or C.

Heinrich Glarean in his *Dodekachordon* (Basel, 1547) solved this problem by adding four new modes with A and C as legitimate finals. Two were authentic and two were plagal or collateral modes, which shared a final with the authentic but were a fourth lower in range. In an elaborate rationalization for the new modes, he called on the authority of Aristoxenus and other Greek writers. To the names Dorian, Phrygian, Lydian, Mixolydian and their plagal or hypo forms (for example, Hypodorian), which had been applied to the eight plainchant modes, he added the names "Aeolian" for the final on A and "Ionian" for the final on C. The names were borrowed from Aristoxenus, but Glarean did not realize that the Greeks had assigned these names not to modes but to tonoi—which are more akin to our keys—and to the octave species that resulted from them, none of which agreed with those synonymously named by Glarean. Nevertheless, his twelve-mode system was adopted by some composers and

theorists, including Zarlino, because it made the determination of mode more consistent both for the analyst and composer.

The long-abandoned Greek chromatic and enharmonic genres of melody also beckoned to be revived. In a music treatise then attributed to Plutarch, the enharmonic was extolled as the noblest and most beautiful of the genres but, the Greek author lamented, it was disdained by the musicians of his time (1st century A.D.). Nicola Vicentino dedicated most of his treatise *L'antica musica ridotta alla moderna prattica* (Ancient music adapted to modern practice; Rome, 1555) to a practical method of adapting the chromatic and enharmonic genres to modern composition, showing how the octave could be divided into semitones throughout for the chromatic and into quarter-tones for the enharmonic. He devoted much of his career to composing in this idiom and training singers to perform it. Although many derided Vicentino's campaign, it inspired a few composers to experiment with chromatic music, notably Orlando di Lasso, Cipriano de Rore, Luca Marenzio, Luzzasco Luzzaschi, and Carlo Gesualdo.

213

Vicentino at the same time brought the rules of counterpoint up to date with the current practice. Gaffurio in his *Practica* and Aron in his *Thoscanello de la musica* (Venice, 1523) had already liberalized and expanded the rules of Tinctoris. Aron showed with his tables of consonant combinations how to achieve full harmony in a four-part texture, and toward that end encouraged composing all the parts at once rather than one voice at a time. The goal now was always to accompany the lowest voice with a third and fifth or a third and sixth. Vicentino freed the composer even more from the older strictures, insisting that the verbal text and the function of a piece should determine how strictly a composer should observe melodic and harmonic conventions.

Nostalgic like Vicentino for ancient practices, Pontus de Tyard published his dialogue on music, *Solitaire second,* the same year (Lyons, 1555). Unlike Vicentino, who found Boethius largely irrelevant, Pontus reviews the Boethian theory didactically, mostly through Gaffurio's *Theorica* and *De harmonia*. Tyard prefers monody to polyphony and longs for the union of music and poetry that reigned in ancient Greece. Otherwise, his reliance on Gaffurio, on Plato's *Timaeus,* and on Marsilio Ficino's commentaries allies him with the Neoplatonic movement current in Italy at the end of the fifteenth century.

Musical Treatises after 1550. *Musica theorica* and *musica practica* received a new integration and synthesis in the monumental *Le istitutioni harmoniche* of Gioseffo Zarlino (Venice, 1558). In this book Zarlino dedicated parts 1 and 2 to theory and parts 3 and 4 to practice. He provided the theoretical first half as a foundation for the practical second half, for he considered theory and practice inseparable. Like modern architects and painters, musicians should know the reasons for what they do, based on the nature of sounds and tones and on the numerical ratios of the consonances.

Followers of Boethius and the Pythagoreans, like Gaffurio, were content to limit the ratios of consonances to the first four numbers, which admitted only the perfect consonances. Zarlino raised the bar to the number six—the senary number, or *numero senario*—because, if theory was to serve as a basis for practice, the major third (5:4), minor third (6:5), and major sixth (5:3) had to be included. Zarlino also tentatively rationalized the admission of the minor sixth (8:5), as a composite of the fourth and the minor third.

The tuning that best yielded the imperfect consonances in these ratios was the syntonic diatonic of the Greek astronomer and mathematician Claudius Ptolemy, who in his *Harmonics* (2nd century A.D.) had preferred it for its arithmetical simplicity and because all the primary interval ratios were superparticular. Spataro had identified this tuning with Ptolemy, thanks to Gaffurio's exposition of it in *De harmonia,* and Lodovico Fogliano had adopted it without crediting it to anyone. Zarlino, acknowledging Ptolemy but not Spataro or Fogliano, pointed to the additional property that only the first six numbers were needed for the ratios of the consonances. Moreover, six was a "perfect" number, because 1 + 2 + 3 equals 6, and 1 × 2 × 3 also equals 6. The number six became the cornerstone of Zarlino's harmonic edifice, marking the boundary that made the special rules for the employment of dissonances in composition necessary and rational.

Counterpoint. In the third part of the *Istitutioni* (trans. *The Art of Counterpoint*) Zarlino laid down in great detail precepts of counterpoint based on a practice that had reached a pinnacle of refinement in the music of his teacher Adrian Willaert (c. 1490–1562), one of his predecessors as choirmaster of St. Mark's in Venice. Willaert's close attention to the proper accentuation of Latin and Italian and to the spirit of the texts also served Zarlino as a model. In the fourth part, Zarlino reviewed the best information then available about the ancient tonal system and the practice of the twelve modern modes. In the dialogue *Dimostrationi harmoniche* (Demonstrations in harmonics; Venice, 1571), in which Willaert is an interlocutor, Zarlino renumbered the modes, so that modes 1 and 2 were now the Ionian and Hypoionian with their final on C rather than the Dorian and Hypodorian on D. He adopted this system also for the second edition of *Istitutioni* (Venice, 1573), but few subsequent authors went along with the change.

Although Zarlino's rules for the composition of part-music remained the standard for at least a century, his theoretical underpinnings were soon challenged. If singers in their effort to hold to the natural tuning of consonances sang two different sizes of tones (and semitones) of the syntonic diatonic, they would ascend or descend a greater or lesser interval to reach a particular pitch at one time than at another, leading to a fluctuation in the pitch level of the performance.

This was demonstrated by the physicist Giovanni Battista Benedetti (1530–1590) with an ingenious set of musical examples, accompanied by an analysis of the relevant ratios, in a letter to the composer Cipriano de Rore (1515?–1565), then choirmaster of St. Mark's in Venice. Benedetti later published the letter in his *Diversarum speculationum mathematicarum et physicarum liber* (A book of diverse mathematical and physical theories; Turin, 1585).

Another serious fault of the syntonic also involved the size of the tones and semitones. Not all the consonances usable within the diatonic scale could be defined by the ratios of the *senario* because when two different sizes of whole tones—9:8 and 10:9—were combined in consonances, some turned out too large or too small.

When Vincenzo Galilei pointed out this and similar discrepancies in his *Dialogo della musica antica, et della moderna* (Dialogue on ancient and modern music; Florence, 1581), Zarlino minimized the differences, reluctant to renounce the wondrous power of number. Attracted to Plato's and Ficino's ideals of universal harmony, he clung to the idea that proportion lay behind the beauty and power of music. Zarlino admitted that builders and tuners of "artificial" instruments "tempered" or altered the pure tuning of consonances in order to spread the errors inherent in the tonal system among all the usable intervals, but he insisted that voices, which were God-given and natural, sang only the true and natural consonances.

The Zarlino-Galilei Debate.
Thus ensued the most important musical controversy of the sixteenth century, between Zarlino and his defenders and Galilei and his circle. The debate was fueled by discoveries about ancient Greek music made by Girolamo Mei, a Florentine classicist working in Rome. Mei read in Greek all the sources that Gaffurio knew in translation and many more, including all the Greek music treatises that have survived. In a series of letters to Galilei, Mei undermined Galilei's faith in Zarlino, with whom Galilei had studied in the mid-1560s. A number of the letters were discussed in Florence in the informal academy, later known as the "camerata," hosted by Galilei's patron Giovanni Bardi, count of Vernio. The subject matter went beyond the area of tuning to such matters as the relation of science to art, the absence of polyphony among the Greeks, the reason the Greeks did not recognize the imperfect consonances, the emotional power of music that Greek writers boasted about, the nature of the Greek modes, the instruments with which they accompanied vocal music and how, the music of the tragedies, and many other questions

that had a bearing on the aesthetics, uses, and reception of modern music. Mei was a disciple of the Aristotelian philosopher and humanist Piero Vettori. In the Zarlino-Galilei debate Neoplatonic metaphysics clashed head-on with Aristotelian natural science and poetics.

A single theme holds the diverse contents of Galilei's *Dialogo* together: the degree of applicability of the theory and practice of ancient Greek music to the musical practice of Galilei's time. In the first third of the book Galilei refutes Zarlino's claim that Ptolemy's syntonic diatonic tuning was or should be the basis of modern vocal intonation. In the next thirty pages the interlocutors, Giovanni Bardi and an aristocratic musical amateur, Piero Strozzi, consider the differences between the ancient and modern tonal and modal systems with the aim of showing the superiority of the ancient. The brief section that follows—often cited in modern anthologies—is a critique of polyphony, particularly as practiced by the madrigal composers, and a plea for more effective means of moving the affections through monody. The last third of the dialogue concerns ancient and modern instrumental music and the notation of both vocal and instrumental music, including the presentation of four Greek hymns now attributed to Mesomedes (early second century A.D.) in their original notation, as well as the Alypius tables that permitted their transcription. Mei had sent him both the hymns and the notation tables, and Galilei had access also to Mei's treatise in four books, *De modis musicis* (On the musical modes; 1567–1573). Although the *Dialogo* owed much to Mei and probably to Bardi, it was a daring and original work in its conception, argumentation, and execution.

Zarlino's expansive retort in *Sopplimenti musicali* (Musical supplements; Venice, 1588) shows that Galilei stimulated him to read or reread the Greek theoretical literature by then available in translation, especially Antonio Gogava's *Aristoxeni . . . Harmonicorum elementorum libri iii . . . Ptolemaei Harmonicorum . . . libri iii. Aristoteli de objecto auditus* (Aristoxenus's three books of harmonic elements . . . Ptolemy's three books on harmonics . . . Aristotle's three books concerning the object of hearing; Venice, 1562). Zarlino dipped liberally into the ancient sources to bolster his positions in the *Istitutioni* and *Dimostrationi*. Although he seemed now to embrace some of his disciple's ideas, Zarlino did not abandon any of his basic principles and biases.

Galilei answered with his *Discorso intorno all'opere di Gioseffo Zarlino da Chioggia* (A discourse concerning the works of Gioseffo Zarlino of Chioggia; Florence, 1589). Already in the *Dialogo* Galilei had asserted that the path to truth was not in appeals to authority but in sense experience and experiment. Galilei now reveals the most devastating evidence that he discovered through experiment and that undermined Zarlino's reliance on number. The ratios of the consonances were not necessarily those traditionally associated with them. The statement made in many older sources that weights attached to a string in the ratio of 2 to 1 produced an octave was incorrect; the weights had to be in the ratio of 4 to 1. There was no reason to accept 2:1 as the ratio of the octave, when it could be 4:1 in tension, or 3:2 for the fifth, rather than 9:4. Galilei's son, Galileo, later made this same argument in his *Discorsi* (1638; trans. *Dialogues Concerning Two New Sciences*) but ended up defending the traditional ratios by attributing them to frequency of vibration rather than to the dimensions of sounding bodies. Vincenzo further asserted that the ratio of cubic volumes in pipes that sounded an octave was 8:1, which was corroborated by Marin Mersenne in *Traité de l'harmonie universelle* (Treatise on universal harmony; Paris, 1627).

Meanwhile Francisco de Salinas, a nearly blind organist educated at the University of Salamanca, spent twenty years in Naples and Rome between 1538 and 1558 studying the ancient writings on music, helped undoubtedly by a fluent reader of Greek and Latin. Back in Spain, where he taught at Salamanca, he published his *De musica libri septem* (Seven books on music; Salamanca, 1577), a comprehensive volume on music theory. It was unique in its extended chapters on the neglected subject of rhythm based on classical metrics and rhythmics. He also investigated the Greek tonal system and was the first in a published book to distinguish clearly between the tonoi and octave species and between these and the plainchant modes. He also identified Nicomachus and Ptolemy as the main sources that Boethius had translated from the Greek. Salinas borrowed much from Fogliano, Zarlino, and Vicentino, though he also dedicated some chapters to what he considered their errors. Perhaps more than any other music treatise, Salinas's work shows the achievement of the Renaissance in the best light.

The music treatises of the Renaissance reflect both the changing aesthetic philosophies and epistemologies of the period and the shifts in musical taste and style. While Gaffurio, Tyard, and Zarlino responded to the Platonic thought in the first half of the sixteenth century, Fogliano, Mei, Benedetti, and Galilei manifest the revival—with needed correction—

of Aristotelian poetic and scientific thought in the second half. Vicentino, Zarlino, Mei, and Galilei all embraced in varying degrees the goal of moving the affections, which permeated all the arts in that period.

See also **Acoustics**; *biographies of figures mentioned in this entry.*

BIBLIOGRAPHY

Primary Works

Aron, Pietro. *Toscanello in music.* Translated by Peter Bergquist. Colorado Springs, Colo., 1970.

Barker, Andrew. *Greek Musical Writings.* 2 vols. Cambridge, U.K., 1984–1989. Includes translations of Aristoxenus, Plutarch, and Ptolemy.

Beldomandi, Prosdocimo de'. *Contrapunctus.* Edited and translated by Jan Herlinger. Lincoln, Nebr., and London, 1984.

Beldomandi, Prosdocimo de'. *Tractatus musice speculative.* In D. Raffaello Baralli and Luigi Torri, "Il *Trattato* di Prosdocimo de' Beldomandi contro il *Lucidario* di Marchetto da Padova." *Rivista musicale italiana* 20 (1913): 707–762.

Blackburn, Bonnie J., Edward E. Lowinsky, and Clement A. Miller. *A Correspondence of Renaissance Musicians.* Oxford, 1991.

Boethius, Anicius Manlius Severinus. *Fundamentals of Music* (*De institutione musica*). Translated by Calvin M. Bower. New Haven, Conn., and London, 1989.

Gaffurio, Franchino. *De harmonia musicorum instrumentorum opus.* Translated by Clement A. Miller. Stuttgart, Germany, 1977.

Gaffurio, Franchino. *The Theory of Music.* Translated by Walter K. Kreyszig. New Haven, Conn., and London, 1993. Translation of *Theorica musicae* (1492).

Galilei, Vincenzo. *Dialogue on Ancient and Modern Music.* Translated by Claude V. Palisca. New Haven, Conn., and London, forthcoming.

Glarean, Heinrich. *Dodecachordon.* Translated and edited by Clement A. Miller. 2 vols. Rome, 1965.

Jacques de Liège. *Speculum musicae.* Edited by Roger Bragard. Rome, 1955.

Mei, Girolamo. *De modis.* Edited by Tsugami Eisuke. Tokyo, 1991.

Mei, Girolamo. "Letters." In Claude V. Palisca, *Letters on Ancient and Modern Music to Vincenzo Galilei and Giovanni Bardi.* Rome, 1960; 2d. ed., Neuhausen and Stuttgart, Germany, 1977.

Pontus de Tyard. *Solitaire second.* Edited by Cathy M. Yandell. Geneva, 1980.

Ramos de Pareja, Bartolomeo. *Musica practica.* Translated by Clement Miller. Neuhausen and Stuttgart, Germany, 1993.

Tinctoris, Johannes. *Opera theoretica.* Edited by Albert Seay. Rome, 1975.

Ugolino of Orvieto. *Declaratio musicae disciplinae.* Edited by Albert Seay. Rome, 1959.

Vicentino, Nicola. *Ancient Music Adapted to Modern Practice.* Translated by Maria Rika Maniates. New Haven, Conn., and London, 1996.

Zarlino, Gioseffo. *The Art of Counterpoint* (*Le Istitutioni harmoniche*, part 3). Translated by Guy A. Marco and Claude V. Palisca. New Haven, Conn., and London, 1968.

Zarlino, Gioseffo. *On the Modes* (*Le Istitutioni harmoniche,* part 4). Translated by Vered Cohen. New Haven, Conn., and London, 1983.

Secondary Works

Damschroder, David, and David Russell Williams. *Music Theory from Zarlino to Schenker.* Stuyvesant, N.Y., 1990.

Gallo, F. Alberto. "La trattatistica musicale." *Storia della cultura veneta dal primo Quattrocento al concilio di Trento.* iii/3 (Venice, 1981): 297–314.

Lowinsky, Edward E. *Music in the Culture of the Renaissance and Other Essays.* Edited by Bonnie J. Blackburn. 2 vols. Chicago, 1989.

Moyer, Ann. E. *Musica Scientia: Musical Scholarship in the Italian Renaissance.* Ithaca, N.Y., and London, 1992.

Palisca, Claude V. *The Florentine Camerata: Documentary Studies and Translations.* New Haven, Conn., and London, 1989.

Palisca, Claude V. *Humanism in Italian Renaissance Musical Thought.* New Haven, Conn., and London, 1985.

Palisca, Claude V. *Studies in the History of Italian Music and Music Theory.* Oxford, 1994.

Vendrix, Philippe. *La musique à la Renaissance.* Paris, 1999.

CLAUDE V. PALISCA

Transmission of Music

Like spoken language, music is an acoustical phenomenon that exists in real time; its moment-to-moment substance changes as the work of music unfolds in performance. That characteristic makes it unlike others of the arts that are distinguished by their more-or-less static materiality: painting, sculpture, architecture. However, music, like spoken language, can be approximated or represented in static, material form, as a series of written signs, or musical notation. Like spoken language, whose principal constituent elements are words and sentences, among others, music consists of discrete syntactic elements that are arranged linearly: notes and phrases.

During the Renaissance music was transmitted either orally, by means of live performance, or in written form as a series of signs. The history of the transmission of music becomes more interesting—and more complicated—during the Renaissance because of the invention of the printing press. This technology was developed as an alternate means of recording musical notation and gradually replaced manual copying as the preferred method of rendering music in written form.

Oral Transmission. Entire musical traditions and compositional genres must have been transmitted exclusively by oral means during the Renaissance, particularly those traditions and genres where improvisation figured prominently. For example, the *bassedance* (in Italian, *bassadanza*) was a slow, stately dance-type of the fifteenth and sixteenth centuries. There were standard melodies or tunes asso-

ciated with the *bassedance* that served as its musical accompaniment. Several of these tunes are preserved, and the theory is that each note of the melody corresponded to one step in the choreography. However, the extant melodies are single melodic lines or tunes, which in performance were almost surely elaborated upon and enriched with supplemental countermelodies, the accompaniment of percussion instruments, and so on.

Indeed, the extant musical sources occasionally preserve pieces that look like the written record of an improvisation upon a *bassedance* tune; the lower voice of a two-voice piece contains the familiar *bassedance* tune, while the upper voice has all the characteristics of an improvised countermelody, frozen in written form as if by happenstance. Although standard *bassedance* tunes are preserved in musical notation, in their time they must have been transmitted orally, as part of a repertory of stock materials that a practicing musician would have known; their melodic "logic" is simple and compelling enough that they could easily have been transmitted by oral means. Similarly, there are occasional written records of other types of stock, formulaic materials that typically must have been transmitted orally. Among them are the famous tunes known as the *folia,* the *passamezzo,* the *romanesca,* and so on, which served as the basis for musical elaboration. Printed musical sources from the early sixteenth century preserve a series of stock melodic formulas used to set poetry in particular verse types. Some of these formulas are known as *aëre da cantar* or *modo de cantar sonetti* (air for singing, or manner of singing sonnets) or *modus dicendi capitula* (manner of singing *capitoli*). Such formulas, in Nino Pirrotta's words, were "intended to be used with any text of a given metrical structure." Here, too, although the formulas are preserved in written form, they might well have been transmitted orally at one stage in their evolution, given their relative simplicity and melodic cogency.

One may conjecture that much of the musical culture of Renaissance Europe was an oral culture, that whole traditions existed almost entirely in an oral state and that the extant written reflections of these oral practices imperfectly document only a tiny part of the oral musical traditions of the time. Fanfares, the music of the heralds of the Florentine signoria used in announcing newsworthy developments, processional music for triumphal state entries, music for dancing, instrumental music performed at banquets, music for sacred and secular theatrical productions: all such musical traditions presumably employed stock materials transmitted orally from teacher to pupil, from one musician in one town to another musician in another, who had occasion to hear a piece he liked and asked to be taught it, and by other unknown means and processes.

Written Transmission. With the written traditions of music, one can speculate with somewhat more confidence about the dynamics of the process of transmission, precisely because written documents provide evidence about that process.

Although works in the oral tradition occasionally found their way into the written record, the practice of preserving works in written form tended to be reserved for compositional genres and musical traditions that required it. Works transmitted orally were not ordinarily committed to notation precisely because there was no need to do so. Their characteristics were such that they could be readily transmitted by oral means, and indeed the process of notating them may have even destroyed some essential characteristic. Conversely, works transmitted in written form could hardly have been transmitted by any other means; their essential characteristics were such that notation was indispensable to the process of transmission. It is sometimes assumed that the improvisatory practices of the oral tradition produced works that were in some sense "freer," but in the written tradition the results are more varied precisely because the composer had the luxury of time denied the improvisor.

Manuscripts. Before the development of music printing, the written transmission of music entailed transporting manually copied documents—manuscripts—from one location to another. A large number of extant letters document the process. Musical manuscripts traveled in diplomatic pouches, with the belongings of family members traveling from one residence to another, and by other such means. Documentary evidence helps explain why the same musical work may be contained in manuscript sources copied in different centers of patronage. In one case an exchange of letters between two members of the Medici family includes a musical setting of the text of the Roman Catholic Mass. A mass by the Medici employee Heinrich Isaac is copied into both a Florentine manuscript and a papal manuscript that are roughly contemporary and contain strikingly similar versions of the work, similar enough that the editor of the Isaac masses suggested that the two manuscripts must surely have been copied from the same parent source. The mass might well have been one of those transmitted from Florence to Rome in 1513

by the mother of Lorenzo di Piero di Lorenzo de' Medici.

In some cases, a particular musical composition from the Renaissance is transmitted in as many as thirty-five different manuscript and printed sources (Josquin des Prez's motet *Stabat Mater dolorosa,* for example), resulting in hundreds of variants for the work. Stemmatic evidence—the ways in which similarities among variants suggest groupings of sources—is often substantiated by historical evidence: sources that can be shown with reasonable certainty to have been copied or printed at a particular center of patronage at a particular time preserve versions of the same work that are similar or virtually identical. Such a congruence of stemmatic and historical evidence suggests that there may have been regional scribal practices—conventions about how to handle certain kinds of notational challenges, or how to render certain elements of the musical syntax—as well as a single version of the musical work in question that was in circulation in that region.

Printed music. With the invention of music printing in the late fifteenth century, the dynamics of the process of transmission became more complicated. We have become accustomed to appreciating the advantages of printing over manual copying, but the invention of printing in the mid-fifteenth century occasioned debate. The fifteenth-century Florentine humanist Angelo Poliziano assessed the virtues of printing as follows: "The most stupid ideas can now in a moment be transferred into a thousand volumes and spread abroad." Although music printing made musical works much more readily available, and served—indeed, helped to create—a new market for them, until editing procedures were refined it also greatly increased the potential for greater numbers of erroneous and corrupt versions of musical works to circulate. Historians of music printing have demonstrated the existence of corrected copies of printed music books.

The printing of musical notation began in a limited way in the late fifteenth century in music theory works and in earnest in 1501 with the publication in Venice of the first "practical" work, Ottaviano dei Petrucci's *Odhecaton.* Initially, musical works were printed using the less efficient "multiple impression" method, where each sheet was passed through the printing press several times, first in order to print the five-line musical staves, then the actual musical notation, and so on. Eventually printers developed the more efficient "single impression" method, where all notational elements were printed on the sheet during a single pass through the printing press. After an initial period of monopoly by Italian printers—Petrucci in Venice and other locations, Andrea Antico in Rome and other locations (first music publication in 1510: *Canzoni nove con alcune scelte de varij libri de canto;* New songs with some selected from various [existing] songbooks)—northern European printers succeeded in challenging the Italian monopoly, notably the Frenchmen Pierre Attaingnant in Paris (first music publication in 1528: *Chansons nouvelles en musique à quatre parties;* New songs with music in four parts) and Jacques Moderne in Lyon (first music publication in 1532: *Liber decem missarum a praeclaris musicis contextus*). There were also a number of renowned German printers.

As suggested, printing made the process of transmission of music considerably more complex. Textual traditions were no longer exclusively manuscript traditions; on the contrary, printers could gain access to works in manuscript and subsequently publish them, and, conversely, scribes could assemble manuscripts from printed sources, leading to a confrontation and interaction of manuscript and print "cultures."

The invention of music printing had another profound consequence. Traditionally, repertories of art music had been the more or less private preserve of those in a position to employ scribes or enlist their services: wealthy individual patrons and institutions of patronage like the church. Music printing made it possible for prospective consumers who would not otherwise have had access to such repertories to enjoy such access, and such a notable figure as Ferdinando Columbus, the natural son of the explorer and a prolific book collector, accumulated a vast collection of printed music. Because printing served new markets, it in turn led to the emergence of new compositional genres and musical traditions that catered to the tastes of those new markets. The great secular genres of the sixteenth century—the French chanson and the Italian madrigal—to some extent emerged and developed as they did precisely because of the market created and served by music printing. The revolutionary effects of the new technology can scarcely be overestimated.

See also **Dance.**

BIBLIOGRAPHY

Cummings, Anthony M. "Medici Musical Patronage in the Early Sixteenth Century: New Perspectives." *Studi musicali* 10 (1981): 197–216.

Cummings, Anthony M. "The Transmission of Some Josquin Motets." *Journal of the Royal Musical Association* 115 (1990): 1–32.

Heartz, Daniel. *Pierre Attaingnant, Royal Printer of Music: A Historical Study and Bibliographical Catalogue.* Berkeley and Los Angeles, 1969.

Maas, Paul. *Textual Criticism.* Oxford, 1958.

Palisca, Claude V. *Baroque Music.* Reprint, Englewood Cliffs, N.J., 1991.

Pirrotta, Nino, and Elena Povoledo. *Music and Theatre from Poliziano to Monteverdi.* Translated by Karen Eales. Cambridge, U.K., 1982. Translation of *Li due Orfei* (1969).

Pogue, Samuel. *Jacques Moderne: Lyons Music Printer of the Sixteenth Century.* Geneva, 1969.

ANTHONY M. CUMMINGS

Performance Practice

The performance of music in various regions of Europe during the Renaissance included traditional practices inherited from the Middle Ages as well as new practices that developed in conjunction with new repertories, new styles, and new instruments. Each area continued to perform its own regional music in the traditional manner, while adopting the new practices that went along with the international Franco-Flemish style. Although initially the two types of music—local and international—were performed quite differently, inevitably the two practices influenced one another, thus compromising the regional styles and localizing the international. In general, both performance practices can be described in the same terms as the music itself: local practices are relatively simple or straightforward in presentation and involve contrasting sounds. International practices are characterized by complexity of presentation and a blend of sound.

The local practices grew from each region's unwritten tradition of monophonic song, hymns, and dance. The texts and melodies were passed on by rote from generation to generation, and the accompaniment was improvised. When we see written polyphonic examples of this repertory from the late fourteenth and early fifteenth centuries they maintain the essential ingredients of their past: the melodies are dominant and relatively simple, and the accompaniment is subservient to the melody.

The international style of composition developed in the North—Paris, Burgundy, and the Netherlands—during the late fourteenth century and then moved to the other areas of Europe. The style is quite complex, having a texture that is melodically, harmonically, and rhythmically intricate in all parts. As the fifteenth century progressed the individual parts in these compositions became increasingly integrated, until by 1480 the most striking characteristic of this repertory is that all parts shared the same melodic and rhythmic material.

Voices. The usual practice during most of the period was performance by one singer to a part for all of the secular music and much of the sacred repertory. Performance by chorus, that is, several singers to a part, usually was reserved for unison singing, both for refrains in songs or for monophonic chant. In a few large cathedrals polyphony was sung with several voices on a part, but for most of the period it was performed by soloists. The use of larger vocal ensembles for polyphonic performance developed in the latter half of the sixteenth century, notably the British Chapel Royal with over thirty voices, and in conjunction with the large ceremonial motets in Venice.

Both males and females participated in amateur performances of the repertory; musical training was considered to be an important part of the education of highborn children, and domestic performance by members of the family was a part of the daily routine in an aristocratic household. Most professional musicians, however, were male, and the ensembles that performed sacred polyphony usually employed male falsettists, castrati, or boys on the highest part. There were exceptions: a female is recorded as a member of the papal chapel choir during the mid-sixteenth century, and of course all singing in convents, monophonic and polyphonic, would have been exclusively by females.

In the performance of a polyphonic vocal composition, the text was not necessarily sung by all of the performers. In both the sacred and the secular repertory, one or several of the voices might vocalize without words. As late as 1597 the English theorist Thomas Morley noted that motets were sometimes sung completely without their texts, although he did not approve of the practice.

Instruments. Until the late fifteenth or early sixteenth century, very little music was written expressly for instruments, with the exception of that written for keyboard. The instrumentalist's repertory consisted mostly of music improvised or learned by rote memorization, although those who could read music also performed the vocal repertory. There were three more-or-less standard instrumental ensembles during the period: trumpets, "loud bands," and "soft ensembles."

Groups of large trumpets (from two to over a hundred, depending on the occasion), often performing with drums and cymbals, were present in every town and court and represented the majesty and authority of the government and the elevated status of noblemen. Because the trumpets could play only the notes of the overtone system, their repertory was limited to fanfare-like sounds. They often accompanied the military in the field and heralded the presence of government officers or the nobility as they processed through the streets. Throughout the period these instruments maintained their traditional symbolic role, and remained separate from the other musical groups.

The "loud band" is first noted in the court records of Philip the Bold of Burgundy in the late fourteenth century, and by the mid-fifteenth century most European centers and courts included such an ensemble. Originally it consisted of various combinations of reed and brass instruments, but eventually stabilized as three shawms (members of the oboe family) and a sackbut (trombone). This combination of instruments was capable of performing all of the repertory, and their volume made them ideal for large outside gatherings, including dances. In the Netherlands, Germany, and England the ensemble originally served as watchmen, but their function gradually evolved to one that was mostly musical. The members of this group (usually called "pipers") were often quite versatile, playing bowed and plucked strings in addition to their usual instruments, and often singing. Beginning in the last decades of the fifteenth century they were required to read music, and in many communities they entertained the citizens during the summer months by performing composed polyphony in the village square.

The "soft ensembles" were not fixed ensembles but could consist of any combination of soft woodwinds and strings, and eventually included voice. The combinations of soft instruments changed along with the repertory; early in the fifteenth century they were made up of contrasting sounds (for example, fiddle, lute, and recorder), but as the period progressed this changed to a preference for ensembles of like sounds (for example, four viols, or four lutes), mirroring the influence of the Franco-Netherlandish blended compositions.

The increasing popularity of polyphonic music had a profound effect on instruments. Some that had been prominent in all social circles during the Middle Ages were relegated to the lower classes; these were mostly the instruments that were best suited to perform monophonic music, such as the vielle (fiddle), hurdy-gurdy, and bagpipe. Others, such as the lute, were modified in order to accommodate the several simultaneous lines of the new polyphonic music. "Families" of smaller and larger sizes were developed for traditional instruments such as recorder and shawm, in order to encompass the extended ranges

Musicians Playing. Four musicians performing in a meadow. Anonymous Italian painting, 16th century. MUSÉE DE L'HÔTEL LALLEMANT, BOURGES, FRANCE/LAUROS-GIRAUDON

of polyphonic music; and new instruments were invented: the most important of this group in terms of later developments was the violin family that is first seen at the end of the fifteenth century. The loud and soft ensembles, similar to voices, usually performed one to a part; two or more players on a part occurred only on very special occasions such as massive theatrical interludes known as intermedi, or other lavish entertainments intended for large audiences.

Voices and Instruments. Similar to the medieval practices, performance of secular monophonic music during the Renaissance often involved an instrument, frequently played by the singer. The instruments most often chosen for this were those that could play chords and which allowed the performer to sing: lute, harp, keyboard, and the bowed strings—vielle, rebec, and lyra da braccia. This practice remained throughout the period, although it was relegated to the less prestigious local repertory.

The performance of polyphonic music changed during the course of the Renaissance. Until the early decades of the sixteenth century the usual custom was that instruments and voices performed separately, but shortly after 1500, probably influenced by the local monophonic practices, instruments and voices were combined, although usually retaining only one to a part. When joining with voices only the "soft" instruments were used: plucked strings (lute, harp, guitar), bowed strings (viol, violin), soft woodwinds (recorder, cornetto), and the strung keyboards (harpsichord, clavichord) or a small portative organ. The large church organ usually performed alone, often alternating verses with singers or setting the pitch for choral performance. Not until the very end of the period did large organs play with voices and other instruments, and then only on special occasions when there was a large number of voices or other instruments or both. In the second half of the sixteenth century the trombone sometimes was employed to play along with large choruses. Throughout the period trumpets were never combined with voices or with any instruments other than drums and cymbals and occasionally trombones.

In the sixteenth century, performance practices moved in the direction of an integration of voices and instruments, including the substitution of instruments on one or more of the lines in a vocal performance. From the beginning of the period there had been a tradition of transcribing vocal music for a single continuo instrument—lute or keyboard—and that practice was expanded to include a solo voice on one line (usually, but not exclusively, the top part) with continuo performance of all other parts. By the end of the period this practice evolved into a new composed repertory of music called monody, written expressly for performance by solo voice and continuo. Another repertory that developed in the middle of the sixteenth century was one written expressly for performance by a set of instruments with vocal solo. A good example of this genre is the English consort song, intended for solo voice with three or four viols. By the end of the sixteenth century a very large part of both the sacred and secular repertories consisted of music for one or more solo voices with instrumental accompaniment.

Improvisation. Improvisation was an important part of both vocal and instrumental performance. Improvised instrumental accompaniment of monophonic vocal music has been mentioned above as a tradition inherited from the Middle Ages—this format often included improvised melody as well. The practice involved the use of set formulas that were developed to fit the meter and rhyme scheme of the different poetic types. This tradition continued through the Renaissance and was especially revered in Italy, where the printer Ottavio Petrucci published some of the patterns at the end of the fifteenth century. As late as 1623, Francesca Caccini is recorded as a participant in a "contest" in Rome that required her to improvise a melody for a poem she had not previously seen, and to accompany herself while singing.

Instrumentalists routinely improvised music for dancing. When they were accompanying "generic" dances—those that were made up of a repetition of a single step pattern—all that was necessary was to know the rhythms and phrase lengths of the dance. When accompanying a choreographed dance such as a *basse danse,* however, the musicians followed a sustained-note "tenor" that was constructed to reflect the phrase patterns of the choreography. Typi-

cally, when improvising to a tenor, the ensemble (usually a "loud band") would assign one instrumentalist to the tenor while another improvised harmonies to the tenor and a third musician would improvise a rapid soprano melodic line to fit the other two parts.

Vocal improvisation of polyphonic music was also practiced throughout the period. Theoretical treatises as late as the sixteenth century provide instructions for improvisation in the imitative style, and narrative accounts describe that it was often practiced both in secular and sacred performance.

Ornamentation. All performances, both vocal and instrumental, involved spontaneous ornamentation: the addition of melodic gestures that served to personalize a composition. The first practical manual of instructions on how to ornament was published in Italy in 1535 by Sylvestro di Ganassi, but information on the subject is included in theoretical treatises from the Middle Ages. Variants found in different copies of the same compositions from as early as the ninth century through to the end of the Renaissance give ample evidence that the practice of ornamentation was widespread. It is from these variants, together with instrumental intabulations of vocal music and the instruction manuals, that we can form an impression of the ornamentation practices and how they changed over the centuries.

An ornament could consist of as little as a single note to fill in a melodic pattern, a quick gesture of two or three notes, or long, elaborate runs of scales that continued on for several bars. The type, quantity, and placement of the ornaments depended on the style of the composition and were related to the amount of melodic activity in the individual parts. In those pieces that were mostly a single prominent melody with accompaniment (usually the regional styles), ornaments were applied principally to the melodic part. In those compositions where the other parts were more melodically equal and active, ornaments were also applied to those lines. Pieces with repetitions—verse songs, dance tunes—were ornamented more elaborately with each repeat, in the fashion of "theme and variations."

BIBLIOGRAPHY

Brown, Howard M. *Embellishing Sixteenth-Century Music.* Oxford, 1976.

Brown, Howard M., and Stanley Sadie. *Performance Practice: Music Before 1600.* New York, 1989.

Jackson, Roland. *Performance Practice, Medieval to Contemporary: A Bibliographic Guide.* New York, 1988.

Kite-Powell, Jeffrey, ed. *A Performer's Guide to Renaissance Music.* New York, 1994.

McGee, Timothy J. *Medieval and Renaissance Music: A Performers' Guide.* Toronto, 1985.

Montagu, Jeremy. *The World of Medieval and Renaissance Musical Instruments.* London, 1976.

TIMOTHY J. MCGEE

Musical Instruments

Many of the instruments of the Middle Ages continued to be played during the fifteenth and sixteenth centuries, although some were adjusted in shape and size to meet new needs and tastes. Contributing to these changes were the rise of amateur interest in instrumental performance; a growth in the number and size of theatrical presentations; and the increasing integration of instruments in vocal performance. The growing popularity of polyphonic music (music in many parts) also profoundly influenced instruments and their use. It changed the social status of some; caused alterations in the construction and playing technique of others; and inspired the creation of new instruments and the expansion of those already in use. Those instruments that had drones, such as hurdy-gurdy and bagpipe, were relegated to folk or peasant music, in which a drone enhanced the single line of music. Some instruments were altered so that they no longer played drones, and many traditional instruments were constructed in new larger and smaller sizes.

Beginning in the 1480s composers began to integrate the lines of their compositions, emphasizing equality and similarity among the parts. To represent the blend, instrumentalists performed the repertory on the newly developed families of instruments—soprano, alto, tenor, and bass instruments of the same type—that reflected the homogeneity of the music. Those instruments that were capable of playing chords and several lines at a time, such as lute and the keyboards, were in increasing demand for solo performance, accompaniment of solo lines, to consolidate the harmonies in larger ensembles, and for domestic music-making by amateurs.

The growth of theatrical productions and spectacles during the sixteenth century encouraged the composition of music for ever-larger ensembles that would be able to fill the spacious halls with sound. These events involved large groups of instruments of all types, often in combination with singers, and new instruments were invented to meet the demands of the theater.

Bowed Strings. The medieval bowed instruments still played during the early Renaissance period were the viol (tenor range, six-string instrument, curved bridge, held by the legs), viola da braccio (alto

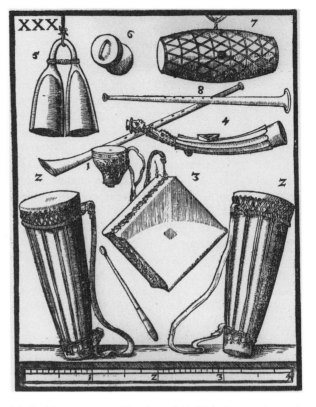

Musical Instruments. Woodcut of Turkish, Muscovite, and Indian instruments by Michael Praetorius, 1620.

range, seven strings including drones, held on the shoulder), vielle (alto range, four strings with a flat bridge), and rebec (soprano range, three strings, flat bridge). Of these, only the viol was adjusted to meet the new demands; its size was increased, making it capable of the bass range, and also decreased, in the form of a small, treble size. The other instruments gradually faded from use. By the end of the sixteenth century the family of viols (also called viola da gamba, or viol held by the leg) had become one of the most popular instrumental ensembles for amateur performance, a popularity that lasted until after the time of Johann Sebastian Bach (1685–1750).

Shortly before 1500 the violin was developed, in a form that combined the shoulder position of the viola da braccio, the small number of strings of the medieval rebec and vielle, and the curved bridge of the earlier viol. Originally the violin was used only to perform dance music, but professional musicians recognized its adaptability to the needs of the newest music and it became the instrument of choice for a wide variety of repertory and occasions. It expanded quickly to a family of matched instruments in the tenor and bass ranges (viola and cello). Since then neither the popularity nor the basic shape of the violin family has changed.

Plucked Strings. Of the several plucked strings popular during the Middle Ages, those instruments that were left with closely spaced strings that produced drones (cittern, citole, mandora) were relegated to folk music. Only the lute and harp were physically adjusted to meet the needs of the new repertory.

The Renaissance harp added bass and treble strings to expand the range from the medieval norm of twenty-four to twenty-six notes to more than twice that number. By the end of the sixteenth century double and triple harps had been developed with as many as ninety-four strings in two and three rows. This allowed the performer access to a full range of chromatic notes and so accommodated the requirements of new compositions in large theatrical works.

By the middle of the fifteenth century the lute was adjusted by widening the space between the strings and changing its tuning. Both changes eliminated the constant presence of drone and allowed for the performance of multiple melodic lines. In the sixteenth century the lute expanded from five to seven courses of strings (a "course" refers to double-stringing; a seven-course lute would have thirteen strings, all but the highest string doubled). By the end of the century, in answer to a need for large-scale chordal and contrapuntal accompaniment, a family of archlutes was developed. New instruments were called theorbo or chitarrone, depending on their stringing (gut = theorbo, metal = chitarrone), with a second, longer neck attached next to the traditional lute neck, on which additional strings were added to the bass range. The new instruments could be as long as six feet with up to eight additional bass strings, thus adding an extensive low range to enhance the chordal support of the traditional lute for accompaniment. Because of their versatility and portability, archlutes remained in constant demand as accompaniment instruments for solo and ensemble performance throughout the seventeenth century.

The four-string (or four-course) guitar developed from the variety of plucked instruments that survived from the Middle Ages. The instrument served in France and England both for solo and accompaniment, and in Spain a six-course version, known as the *vihuela de mano,* was extremely popular during the sixteenth century.

Woodwinds. The number and sizes of woodwinds expanded greatly during the Renaissance. Whereas previously most woodwind instruments had played in the alto range, new sizes, both larger and smaller, were developed. The double-reed instrument known as the shawm, frequently found in the late Middle Ages with the bagpipe as a dance instrument duo, was paired with a new tenor range size (known as "bombard" because of its resemblance to a small cannon). During the fifteenth century an ensemble of two or three shawms, often including a trombone, became the favorite instrumental music group employed by civic governments and courts. This ensemble was quite flexible in terms of its repertory and is frequently depicted playing for outdoor dances and entertainments. Such ensembles were known variously as the town pipers (England), *pifferi* (Italy), *pyperen* (The Netherlands), and *Pfeifer* (Germany). In the sixteenth century the shawm family was expanded to include a soprano (schalmey) and bass.

Both flute and recorder were developed in small and large sizes during the Renaissance period. The recorder traditionally had been popular throughout Europe for domestic music-making, whereas the flute was usually associated with the military until the fifteenth century. From the late fifteenth century both instruments were played in discreet consorts (that is, groups of the same instruments) or mixed with other "soft" instruments (plucked or bowed strings, keyboard, voices).

By the end of the fifteenth century the crumhorn, a double-reed instrument in a bent shape, was popular in Germany. By mid-sixteenth century its popularity had spread to England, where it too could be found in both large and small sizes. Other, less popular woodwind instruments invented during the period include rackett, kortholt, and rauschpfeife, all of which had short lifespans, and the curtal, which in the seventeenth century developed into the bassoon.

"Brass." The term "brass" for instruments of the Middle Ages and Renaissance is a misnomer. They should be more correctly referred to as "cup-mouthpiece" instruments since that is their one common characteristic. The materials they were made of included silver and wood, as well as brass.

Trumpets, in both straight and folded shape, continued to be used as signal instruments and for heraldic purposes. They were used singly (ship signalmen), in pairs (noblemen's heralds), or in large numbers along with drums to represent a government on ceremonial occasions or with the military in the field. When used to perform heraldic functions, the instruments were usually made of silver and were adorned with pennants that were emblazoned

Musical Instruments. Detail from *Hearing,* from the series *The Five Senses* by Jan Brueghel the Elder (1568–1625). PRADO, MADRID/SCALA/ART RESOURCE.

with the symbol of the nobleman or government they represented. Lacking either a slide or valves, the trumpet range was limited to the overtone system, and its repertory consisted of fanfare-type sounds.

Because of its ability to play the entire chromatic scale, the trombone (French *saicqueboute,* English sackbut), from its origin in the late fifteenth, had a more versatile function than the trumpet. It was preceded in the early decades of the century by a slide trumpet—a trumpet with a single movable slide extending from the mouthpiece. The single-slide mechanism gave the trumpet access to the entire scale, and the instrument was used to perform polyphonically with the early shawm bands from about 1430. By the end of the century, however, the slide trumpet had been replaced by the more efficient double-slide mechanism of the trombone. The date of the invention of the double-slide is not known, but the earliest secure image of a trombone is in a Roman fresco painted by Filippino Lippi (1457–1504) in 1490. During the sixteenth century the trombone was employed various ways: with trumpets on ceremonial occasions; to perform dance music and a variety of polyphonic chamber music with ensembles of shawms; to support the lower voices in church choirs; and to play with orchestras of strings and woodwinds in theater productions.

The cornet (German *Zink*), which became one of the favorite virtuoso instruments of the Renaissance, evolved from a medieval folk instrument. It was made of wood bound with leather, had a cup mouthpiece, and was fingered like a flute. Cornets were popular in both the soprano and alto sizes. They performed with a wide variety of chamber and theater ensembles and supported the high voices in church choirs.

Keyboards. The small portative organ, held on the lap or placed on a table, continued to be popular for domestic music-making during the period and remained more or less in its medieval form and size. The positive (that is, large, stationary) organ, however, underwent an enormous expansion and development during the fifteenth and sixteenth centuries. The instruments were installed in all cathedrals and major churches throughout Europe. All were built with many ranks of pipes; some were provided with additional keyboards and foot pedals, all of which added range, volume, and a variety of sounds.

Harpsichords (having plucked strings) and clavichords (having hammered strings) are first noted in the late fourteenth century and became increasingly popular over the next several centuries. The clavichord, because of its extremely soft volume, remained a domestic instrument throughout its history. The harpsichord, however, was far more versatile and by the mid-sixteenth century it served as the most popular instrument for large and small ensembles, solo performance, and accompaniment. Harpsichords were constructed in large and small sizes, some with two and three strings per note, and some with an additional keyboard, allowing a variety of sound color and intensity.

BIBLIOGRAPHY

Brown, Howard Mayer, and Stanley Sadie, eds. *Performance Practice: Music before 1600*. New York and London, 1989. See chapter 9.

Marcuse, Sibyl. *A Survey of Musical Instruments*. London, 1975.

Montagu, Jeremy. *The World of Medieval and Renaissance Musical Instruments*. London, 1976.

Munrow, David. *Instruments of the Middle Ages and Renaissance*. London, 1976. Part 2.

Remnant, Mary. *Musical Instruments of the West*. New York, 1978.

TIMOTHY J. MCGEE

Instrumental Music

Because the earliest notated music is accompanied by text, historians of instrumental music have often put their focus on two main areas: the role of the improvising minstrel and the participation of instruments in vocal polyphony. Both are extremely uncertain subjects that can be treated only after a survey of the musical sources that seem to be intended for instruments. Throughout the Renaissance there is ample evidence of highly skilled instrumental performance on a wide variety of instruments; but until the sixteenth century there is a distressing shortage of written music, and even after 1500 the surviving music needs to be treated with care.

Keyboard Tablature. The earliest known manuscripts that are definitely for instruments are all in what is normally called keyboard tablature, that is, with the music in score and textless, often with some component in letter notation. The only surviving document before the fifteenth century is the "Robertsbridge fragment," two leaves copied in about 1350 and added at the end of a book from Robertsbridge Abbey in England. Like the fifteenth-century keyboard tablatures from Germany, it has the upper line in staff notation and most of the rest written in letters to represent the note names. Even though no comparable source survives, the notation is consistent enough to suggest that the Robertsbridge fragment was by no means unique and that there was a substantial tradition of this kind of music played on instruments. It contains three pieces that

appear to be dances and three that are embellished intabulations of vocal polyphony (one of them based on Philippe de Vitry's motet *Tribum quem non abhorruit*).

That repertory seems characteristic, for there is a comparable repertory in the first substantial manuscript in keyboard tablature, the Faenza Codex, copied in northern Italy in the first quarter of the fifteenth century: it contains nearly fifty pieces, mostly embellished versions of French and Italian songs but including some apparent dances and liturgical pieces—works in which the lower voice carries a plainchant and the upper voice weaves a florid fantasy. A similar repertory again appears in the next large source, the Buxheim Organbook, copied in southern Germany around 1460 and containing over 250 pieces: here the main extra component is in the *Fundamenta*, long series of freely composed examples of embellishment over particular tenor patterns. There are perhaps twenty further fragmentary sources of keyboard tablature from the fifteenth century, and between them they show the same repertorial pattern.

On the face of it, these documents would all seem to be intended for performance on the organ, but other possibilities must be accepted. Given the high proportion of dances and secular songs that they contain, they were evidently not exclusively for church use. The notation of the Robertsbridge fragment would be perfectly usable for any instrument capable of playing simple polyphony, such as a lute or a harp. The Faenza Codex has both lines written in staff notation and contains several passages of overlapping voices that would be almost impossible on a single keyboard instrument; it has been suggested that many of its pieces may be designed for two melody instruments. Moreover, the only specific information about instruments in any of these sources is the statement above one of the Buxheim pieces, "in cytaris vel etiam organis" (for stringed instruments or also for organ)—a statement that can be taken to suggest, among other things, that the piece could be performed by two lutes. Given that the style of the piece is indistinguishable from the remaining music in that collection, it seems likely that the "keyboard" sources could have been used for a variety of purposes. Certainly the more specific printed sources of the early sixteenth century show very little stylistic difference between lute and keyboard music, sometimes presenting identical music in both forms.

Surprisingly, the sixteenth-century keyboard sources present very little advance on the kinds of music found earlier, though the styles of course evolve; the only fully new genres are the variation set and the imitative polyphonic fantasia (both of which appear first in the lute sources). Moreover, the quantity of keyboard music remains far less than the quantity of lute music, and there is relatively little that is of much technical difficulty. Only with the rise of the English virginalists do we begin to find a musically ambitious and technically demanding keyboard repertory that seems to reflect a style that is truly idiomatic for the keyboard. Of those composers, William Byrd (1543–1623) was the supreme genius and generally counts as the first great composer of keyboard music, paving the way for the brilliance of Jan Pieterszoon Sweelinck (1562–1621) and Girolamo Frescobaldi (1583–1643).

Lute Tablature. There can be no serious questioning of the purpose of lute tablature, since this is a notation that instructs the player where to stop the strings and is thus irrevocably tied to the technique and tuning of the lute (or similarly constructed instruments such as the flat-backed vihuela). But although there is clear evidence of the lute's existence in western Europe from at least the thirteenth century, there is no trace of lute tablature before the late fifteenth century: Conrad Paumann (1410–1473) is credited with having invented German lute tablature, a system that gives a different letter or symbol for each intersection of string and fret on the instrument, and an Arab musician around 1470 was claimed to have introduced an adaptation of the much earlier Arabic system.

The known repertory of European lute tablature effectively begins with the series of lutebooks printed by Ottaviano Petrucci at Venice, starting in 1507, while a few manuscript sources may be slightly earlier. What is important, though, is that in the course of the sixteenth century over two hundred lutebooks were published: this is enormously more than any other form of instrumental music, and the books contain an increasing amount of highly idiomatic music that is extremely hard to play. It can be argued that keyboard players had no need of an elaborate tablature and could therefore play from other kinds of sources; but to judge from the surviving sources of instrumental music, the sixteenth century is emphatically the age of the lute.

Petrucci printed six large lutebooks, including a fair amount of music that requires considerable virtuosity (particularly in the two books by Francesco Spinacino, both published in 1507), but perhaps the most astonishing early collection is the beautifully painted manuscript of Vincenzo Capirola (c. 1517), which demands quite exceptional skill from the player and includes devices that are only possible on the lute.

By the 1530s, the lute was firmly established as the leading virtuoso instrument. Players like Francesco Canova da Milano (1497–1543), called "Il Divino," and Alberto da Ripa (c. 1480–1551) were praised in ecstatic terms and have left substantial repertories of their music, mostly printed. Both had a substantial impact on their many followers in Italy and France, respectively. In Spain Luis de Milán (c. 1500–c. 1565) published a collection of the most astonishing stylistic and formal originality in *El maestro* (1536). If the handful of later Spanish publications have slightly less originality of style, they all show a strong awareness of music in France and Italy back to the very beginning of the sixteenth century, and Alonso Mudarra's *Tres libros de musica* (Three books of music; 1546) contains some of the loveliest music of the entire century. In Germany the printed lutebooks of Hans Judenkünig (1523), Hans Gerle (1532 onward), and Hans Newsidler (1536 onward) started a flourishing tradition of music that was mostly much easier to play but evidently found a large audience. On the other hand, England saw very few lute publications in the sixteenth century: the solo music of John Dowland (1562–1626) survives almost exclusively in manuscripts, though the large tradition of printed songbooks with often quite complex accompaniments in lute tablature—starting with Dowland's *First Book of Songs* of 1597—is clear evidence that tablature was perfectly possible for the printers and attracted a reasonable market.

In all these collections, the repertory is based on the same few genres: abstract imitative fantasias; simple preludes (initially called "ricercar," "tastar de corde," or something of the kind); intabulations of polyphonic songs or motets, ranging from the most literal to embellished versions that leave the original almost unrecognizable; simple dance music, sometimes decorated; and relatively restrained accompaniments to solo songs. Variation sets are much rarer here than in the keyboard repertory.

Ensemble Sources. It is extremely hard to be confident about which collections in ordinary staff notation were intended for instruments. There is plenty of evidence quite early in the fifteenth century of instrumental ensembles playing composed polyphonic music, and they could obviously have read it from manuscripts with text. But from around 1480 there is a substantial increase in apparent song-

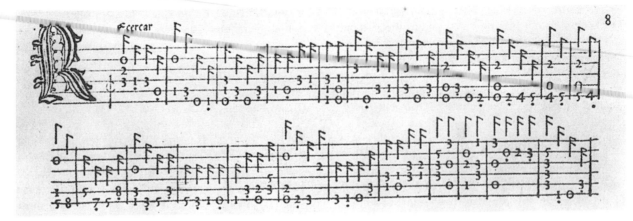

A Musical Score. Lute music printed from movable type by Ottaviano Petrucci (Venice, 1508).

books that have little or no text added to the music. One of the clearest such cases is the manuscript from the Ferrara court now in the Biblioteca Casanatense (Rome): this beautifully copied and evidently complete manuscript has no text beyond the names or text openings of the pieces, and evidence indicates that it represents the repertory of the court instrumental ensemble, not least in adjustments made to certain pieces as though to keep them within the range of particular instruments. While much of the music in the Casanatense manuscript is from the polyphonic song repertory and survives with full texts elsewhere, other pieces seem from their style and design as though they were composed specifically for an instrumental ensemble. The same is the case in the Glogauer Liederbuch, copied in eastern Germany at around the same time, and in several other manuscripts over the next twenty years, many of them Italian.

On the other hand, a surprisingly large group of earlier manuscripts seem to be songbooks but have either virtually no text or such garbled and incomplete text as to be virtually useless for vocal performance. While it is easy enough to point out that the best performances would have been done from memory and that the texts could easily be taken from elsewhere, it is notable that most of these manuscripts are from areas where the language of the texts was unfamiliar. Thus a songbook from the Rhineland and now in Prague, copied in about 1400, has only the opening words for its music, and much of its music originally had French texts. The St. Emmeram Choirbook (early 1440s), mostly copied in Vienna but now in Munich, contains a large number of French songs with either no text at all or a poorly fitting substituted text in liturgical Latin. The same is

true of many other fifteenth-century manuscripts copied in the German-language area where French was very little known. It is hard to resist the conclusion that these were mostly used by instrumental groups. The research of Keith Polk has shown with startling clarity not only how many highly skilled professional instrumentalists were active in fifteenth-century Germany but how these musicians became leading figures in the instrumental ensembles of courts all over Europe.

This evidence indicates that a small number of pieces in these manuscripts seem from both stylistic and formal viewpoints to have been composed specifically for an instrumental ensemble. Among the earliest of these are a setting of the apparently monophonic Dutch tune "T'Andernaken" (At Andernach) by a certain Tyling, an arrangement of the English polyphonic song "Love woll I withoute eny variaunce," and a setting of a *basse danse* (the principal court dance of the time): all were written down in the 1440s; all have their top line in a very free improvisatory style, not unlike that of the keyboard tablatures; all have often messy counterpoint; and all are three-voice works built around a cantus firmus tenor in relatively even note values, perhaps for dancing. Too few of these pieces survive to allow confident reconstruction of the genre and its history, but they do seem to stand as evidence that the common *alta cappella* (loud ensemble) of a sackbut and two shawms probably had a substantial and viable repertory of written polyphony from quite early in the fifteenth century.

Moving closer to solid ground, however, the group of late fifteenth-century songbooks without text culminated in the three grand publications of Ottaviano Petrucci: *Harmonice musices odhecaton*

A (A hundred polyphonic pieces, volume A; 1501; the first ever book of printed polyphonic music), *Canti B numero cinquanta* (Songs, fifty in number, volume B; 1502), and *Canti C numero cento cinquanta* (Songs, one hundred, fifty in number, volume C; 1504). Between them they contain almost three hundred pieces, almost all of them without text beyond the opening words (the exceptions have sacred Latin texts). As with the Casanatense manuscript, a large proportion of these pieces either survive with text elsewhere or leave every impression of having been conceived as songs, but there are many others that seem designed specifically for an instrumental ensemble (particularly in *Canti C*). Most of these are based on a borrowed tenor line—most often the tenor of a known polyphonic song, but sometimes apparently of monophonic songs (settings of "T'Andernaken" again) and occasionally of known dance tones (such as "La Spagna"). But the most important difference between these and the few examples of apparent instrumental ensemble music from a century earlier is that their counterpoint is immaculate and none of them contains any hint of improvisatory style. It is as though the somewhat rough-and-ready music of the minstrels had become civilized.

Oddly, though, this tradition seems to have died out fairly soon. Certainly these and related pieces continue to appear in manuscripts down to the middle of the century, but there is no evidence of any fresh compositions in that style after about 1510, and the main body of this kind of repertory seems to have been composed in the years 1480–1500. The next publications of instrumental polyphony are either very simple and homophonic dance music (the editions of Pierre Attaingnant and Tielman Susato, for example) or sternly imitative fantasias, such as those of Adrian Willaert (1551) and Julio Segni da Modena (1540). Beyond these, there continues to be a rich harvest of manuscript partbooks (sets of books, each containing the individual line for a single performer) in which polyphonic songs and madrigals are copied without any text added; they would seem to be evidence that instrumental ensembles habitually played vocal polyphony. Perhaps the most striking such partbooks are two manuscript sets in the Copenhagen Royal Library, copied in the 1550s and 1560s, evidently for the wind band at the royal court. Between them they contain over three hundred pieces, all with only their text openings. Their repertory includes mass movements, motets, chansons, German lieder, Italian madrigals, and works that were apparently designed for instruments from

the outset. Just occasionally a specific instrument is named by a part—an exceptional novelty that is not found in printed music until Giovanni Gabrieli's *Sacrae symphoniae* (Venice, 1597), and even there only sporadically.

Repertory. Those three categories of music books for instrumentalists contain a surprisingly consistent range of styles over the 250 years surveyed here.

Dance music appears in the earliest sources in the form of *estampies*, music composed in sections of irregular length, each repeated. In the fifteenth century the dances are mostly based on cantus firmus tenors of the *basse danse* or *bassadanza* variety. All these genres of dance are graceful and irregular; one must presume that if sharply periodic dance music (marked by simple, regular, parallel phrases) was used, nobody needed to write it down. Such music appears for the first time in the printed lutebook of Joan Ambrosio Dalza (Venice, 1508), which includes a series of elaborately composed dances in groups of three, called *pavana, saltarello,* and *piva;* later in the same collection there are similarly periodic dances called *calata*. Similar groups of dances appear in Hans Judenkünig's lutebook (Vienna, 1523), entitled *Hoff dantz* and *Nachdantz,* as well as in Pierre Attaingnant's *Dixhuit basses danses* (Paris, 1530), where the groups are called *Basse danse, Recoupe,* and *Tourdion*. These and related traditions continue throughout the sixteenth century, culminating in William Byrd's magnificent series of pavan-galliard pairs for keyboard; but these last, and many others, can hardly have been music for dancing so much as free instrumental pieces based on the form and style characteristics of those dances.

Intabulations—the presentation of vocal polyphony in a manner suitable for instruments, usually slightly adapted—are perhaps the largest genre of written instrumental music during these centuries. Sometimes the lower voices are simplified, and very often the top voice is embellished: that was a scheme common enough from the Robertsbridge fragment through to the end of the sixteenth century, with the different kinds of embellishment suggesting a fascinating picture of the changing musical preferences over the years. On the other hand, there is also a surprisingly large repertory of entirely unchanged intabulations, starting with several pieces in the Buxheim Organbook and becoming extremely common in ensemble books throughout the sixteenth century. The more advanced musicians, if they used these books at all, would surely have embellished them heavily. But there are also many straight intabulations of highly complex polyphony in six voices, for example in the Spanish vihuela publications. that of Diego Pisador (1552) even includes eight entire masses by Josquin des Prez.

Fantasias—abstract imitative instrumental pieces—become common from around 1530 and are often hard to distinguish from intabulations, since they are cast in an imitative form very much like the motets of the time. But as the century progresses they become more idiomatic and distinctive, whether for lute, for keyboard, or for an ensemble of melody instruments. Like the other genres, these come under various different names: "canzona," often intended to suggest an origin in the French chanson style; "ricercar," often meaning that it was more methodical (but the term is also used for preludes, as discussed below); "toccata," meaning strictly just something touched, and thus played on a keyboard instrument; and "tiento," meaning a piece usually more relaxed in design than the formal fantasia.

Chant settings are also very common throughout these years, normally carrying the chant in relatively long notes in the lower voice, with the upper voice adding an often surprisingly irrational florid descant above the chant. This kind of playing was evidently the main function of the organ in the churches of the Renaissance (there is very little direct evidence of exactly what they did before the seventeenth century), and the sixteenth-century sources contain many examples of *alternatim* organ music—settings of short sections of the chant so that the choir could sing the remainder of the chant between those sections.

Fundamenta are related to these chant settings. The term is taken from the earliest such documents, from the mid-fifteenth century, such as the *Fundamentum organisandi* (Fundamentals of polyphonic playing) by Conrad Paumann. These are effectively instruction manuals, examples of how a descant could be played over a variety of lower-voice patterns. Although the earliest of these are apparently for organ, there are several printed books from the late sixteenth century that show how a solo wind or string player could improvise on an existing line.

Sets of variations (sequences of embellished or otherwise changed variants of a known tune or chord sequence stated at the outset) almost inevitably arose from these. First found in the Spanish vihuela publications, they remained relatively rare (perhaps again they were often improvised) until they were avidly cultivated by the Elizabethan virginal composers in England.

"Preludes" is perhaps the best general term for another variety of instrumental music that takes visible root only in the early sixteenth century, in the keyboard and lute books. They are mostly very short, often intended merely to set the tonality before the intabulation that was to follow: in the Capirola Lutebook, for example, most of them are specifically designated for particular pieces that will follow.

Improvisation and Embellishment. The kinds of musical sources and repertory described in this entry make it inevitable that a large part of the instrumentalist's art was in improvisation and embellishment. Instrumental ensembles in the courts of the fifteenth century were paid quite as much as the leading singers, but we have only indirect traces of their music. Pietrobono de' Burzellis (c. 1417–1497) was widely described as one of the greatest musicians of his century, but not a note of his music survives. Certainly there are hints from descriptions of Pietrobono's lute playing that he took the top line of existing polyphony and decorated it, perhaps in the manner of the Buxheim Organbook; and in later years he seems normally to have worked with a *tenorista,* who presumably played the lower voices (again as in Buxheim). In principle, none of this is particularly difficult, and twentieth-century jazz demonstrates that an ensemble can play sophisticated polyphonic music without anything being written down. But the available evidence indicates that the concept of known and established chord progressions evolved only in the mid-sixteenth century, when patterns such as the *passamezzo moderno, Ruggiero,* and *romanesca* abound, particularly in the Italian lutebooks.

In the fifteenth century, the main information about instrumental ensemble performance indicates that it was based around the long-note tenors of the French *basse danse* and the Italian *bassadanza.* Any three-voice counterpoint would need to have evolved from extensive experience and rehearsal, but in an age when memory was far more central than it is today, this too would be far easier than it may seem at first glance. The very sparsity of the written record, however, does mean that any modern attempt to reconstruct the work of those ensembles is fraught with difficulty: on the one hand, it must treat the available evidence with scrupulous delicacy; on the other, it must recognize that excellence presumably existed, as it does today, only in an atmosphere of fertile imagination.

What we do have, particularly from the later sixteenth century, are manuals explaining how melodic lines could be decorated. Beyond that, the lute and keyboard sources contain a large number of indications for ornamentation, particularly in manuscripts of the late sixteenth century.

But there is also evidence that composers were ambivalent about ornamentation. A story survives about Josquin des Prez (around 1500) exploding at a singer who added ornamentation with the words: "You idiot: Why do you add embellishment? If I had wanted it I would have put it in myself." And in 1586 Francisco Guerrero specified in his ordinances for the players in Seville Cathedral that only one of the players on the top line could gloss the music, but if the top line was resting, then the player on the next line down could "add all the glosses that he desires and knows so well how to execute on his instrument."

Participation of Instruments in Vocal Polyphony. This topic has come in for renewed examination and controversy particularly in the 1980s and merits a brief summary, partly because its outlines point to a more fundamental question. Most polyphonic songbooks of the fourteenth and fifteenth centuries have text supplied only to the highest voice; and, while no polyphonic source before the sixteenth century specifies any instrument, it has seemed likely that the untexted lines would normally be played on instruments. But three main considerations cast doubt on that apparently obvious conclusion. First, a remark in the poetry treatise of Eustache Deschamps (1392) can be taken to state that the three-voice songs of Guillaume de Machaut are best heard performed by three singers, and that is supported by a certain number of fifteenth-century descriptions that quite unambiguously state that all lines were taken by singers. Second, no such description before about 1475 has yet been found that describes voices and instruments working together in what was definitely composed polyphony. Third, the history of instruments begins to suggest that very few of the many available instruments were at all suited to taking part in composed polyphony during these years. For example, the available pictorial evidence of bowed string instruments shows that they seem generally to have had flat bridges that would be suitable for playing against a drone but not for a single polyphonic line, and that the few that definitely had curved bridges are so small they could not reasonably have played the lower polyphonic lines for which instruments seem so necessary.

For a short time in the early 1980s some scholars thus concluded that instruments had no role in these polyphonic songs, which were conceived for voices alone: that is, that the music recovered from the surviving manuscripts has nothing to do with what was played on the instruments reconstructed on the basis of pictures. But that was an extreme position, for several reasons. First, there are many other instruments perfectly capable of playing those lines, among them the harp, the lute, and the *douçaine* (a woodwind). Second, in much of this song repertory the texted line is patently articulated in a way that matches the lines and structure of the poem, whereas the lower voices are often quite differently structured. (Singers can of course simply vocalize those lines, but that is by no means the only possible solution.) Third, the direct information about small performing ensembles in the early Renaissance is so sparse and scattered that it can hardly serve as a basis for general historical conclusions. While it is hard to resist the evidence that this music was sometimes performed by voices alone, it is almost certainly wrong to conclude that instruments never took part.

But the story can stand as a paradigm for our understanding of early instrumental music in general. Much of the available evidence can be interpreted in many different and even contradictory ways. The history of sacred vocal music is far easier to trace because there are so many more manuscripts and the musicians were associated with churches that were run by highly literate administrators. The history of instrumental music before 1500 must be pieced together very cautiously from a scattering of miscellaneous information, though the trail becomes much firmer in the sixteenth century.

See also **Music,** *subentries on* **Performance Practice** *and* **Musical Instruments.**

BIBLIOGRAPHY

Apel, Willi. *Keyboard Music of the Fourteenth and Fifteenth Centuries.* American Institute of Musicology, 1963.

Brown, Howard Mayer. *Embellishing Sixteenth-Century Music.* London, 1976.

Brown, Howard Mayer. *Instrumental Music Printed before 1600: A Bibliography.* 2d printing. Cambridge Mass., 1967.

Brown, Howard Mayer, and Stanley Sadie, eds. *Performance Practice.* Vol. 1. Basingstoke, U.K., 1989.

Boetticher, Wolfgang. *Handschriftlich überlieferte Laute- und Gitarrentabulaturen des 15. bis 18. Jahrhunderts.* Munich, 1978.

Fallows, David. *Songs and Musicians in the Fifteenth Century.* Aldershot, U.K., 1996.

Ferand, Ernst T. *Die Improvisation in der Musik.* Zurich, Switzerland, 1938.

Gombosi, Otto J., ed. *Compositione di meser Vincenzo Capirola: Lute-Book (circa 1517).* Neuilly-sur-Seine, France, 1955.

Holman, Peter. *Four and Twenty Fiddlers: The Violin at the English Court, 1540–1690.* Oxford, 1993.

Neighbour, Oliver. *The Consort and Keyboard Music of William Byrd.* Berkeley, Calif., 1978.

Page, Christopher. *Music and Instruments of the Middle Ages: Studies on Texts and Performance.* Aldershot, U.K., 1997.

Polk, Keith. *German Instrumental Music of the Late Middle Ages: Players, Patrons, and Performance Practice.* Cambridge, U.K., 1992.

Schrade, Leo. *Die handschriftliche Überlieferung der ältesten Instrumentalmusik.* 2d ed. Tutzing, Germany, 1968.

Vaccaro, Jean-Michel. *La musique de luth en France au seizième siècle.* Paris, 1981.

DAVID FALLOWS

Sacred Vocal Music

Sacred vocal music in the Renaissance, as in the late Middle Ages, consisted of monophonic and polyphonic settings of religious or liturgical texts augmenting the ever-present Gregorian chant. However, Renaissance polyphony employed a musical style with a radically new conception of meter and counterpoint (this was true of sacred and secular music) and sounded very different from music of the earlier period (musicologists generally date this change to c. 1420). Polyphony in the liturgy also became more common, and in the late fifteenth century, polyphonic choirs were founded and strengthened in cathedrals, churches, and secular courts throughout Europe.

The major polyphonic genres of the late Middle Ages, motet and Mass, were basically redefined in the Renaissance, as the motet became unambiguously sacred and the Ordinary of the Mass was treated for the first time as a musical unity. Further, more of the liturgy became available in polyphony, as hymns, magnificats, lamentations, psalms, and complete items from the Proper of the Mass were set in increasing numbers. On a structural level, compositions based on a few pitches drawn from preexistent monophonic melodies (almost always chant) were gradually replaced by compositions based on complete melodies (which could be chant, a popular melody, or a voice drawn from a secular polyphonic work). Sometimes, these borrowed melodies were made clearly audible, and, eventually, sacred and secular polyphonic works themselves became the bases of new compositions. Further, as the sixteenth century progressed, ever more attention was given to clarifying the musical settings of phrases and individual words of texts. The relation of any of this to the general idea of the "Renaissance" as expressed in art and literature continues to be debated.

The Motet. In the fourteenth century, the motet—derived from the French *mot,* or "word," a polyphonic work in which one or more of the voices sing specific text or texts—consisted usually of two rapidly moving voices (often with different texts in Latin or French) over a slow-moving tenor that comprised a cantus firmus (a preexistent melody, usually a snippet of chant) organized in repeated rhythmic patterns (the compositional technique known as isorhythm). The extent to which these pieces can be classified as "sacred music" is unclear as the texts were often not religious. Fifteenth-century composers continued the isorhythmic idea for a while (the last isorhythmic motets were composed in the 1440s), but the technique was reserved for motets celebrating very special state or religious occasions as in Guillaume Dufay's *Nuper rosarum flores,* an isorhythmic motet written for the consecration of the cathedral of Florence in 1436.

But a new type of motet, with a single Latin religious text set in four voices moving at the same speed, was introduced and soon predominated. A chant cantus firmus is sometimes present in these motets, but it is not isolated from the other voices through long note values and rhythmic patterns as in the isorhythmic motet. Often, however, there is no cantus firmus and the entire motet is newly composed. At the end of the fifteenth century a structural principle related to the syntax of the text being set emerged. Each line or phrase of the text is set off by a "point of imitation"—a short motive that is sung by each of the voices of the motet in sequence at the beginning of the line or phrase (whether this has any relationship to humanistic concerns about texts is a matter of debate). This procedure, called syntactic imitation, appeared first in the four-voice motets of Josquin des Prez (c. 1450–1521) and his contemporaries (the rare five- and more-voice motets that were composed in the late fifteenth century expanded the four-voice texture through use of the old cantus firmus long-note procedure or canonic imitation). Eventually, syntactic imitation became the main method of setting motet texts in any number of voices.

By the middle of the sixteenth century, the motet had become the most popular of the sacred music genres throughout Europe. It was not unusual for composers to produce two hundred or more motets, and music publishers printed many motet volumes. The texts of these motets are of many types, sometimes drawn from the liturgy, sometimes newly created, and the function of the works seems to have been as "filler," used to take up time during liturgical actions (in the papal chapel, the motet was generally sung after the Offertory), although they sometimes were performed in nonliturgical situations. Some-

Sacred Music. *Scola cantorum* (choir) singing from an oversized music book, portrayed in the initial K of the *Kyrie eleison*. From a prayerbook made for the bishop of Lodi in Lombardy in the third quarter of the fifteenth century. PIERPONT MORGAN LIBRARY, NEW YORK/ART RESOURCE, NY

times composers tried to express not merely the syntax, but also the meaning of the words they were setting, but the motet never took this idea to the extreme that secular music did.

The Mass. The fifteenth century saw the rise of a new type of polyphonic Mass composition. While settings of the five elements of the Ordinary of the Mass (texts that did not change from day to day: the Kyrie, Gloria, Credo, Sanctus, Agnus Dei) had existed since the fourteenth century, these were usually composed as isolated pieces.

Initially composers of the early fifteenth century continued this tradition of individual settings, but eventually turned almost exclusively to a different conception in which the five elements of the Ordinary (which, with the exception of the Kyrie and Gloria, do not follow one another directly in the Mass liturgy) are related by musical means, in a sense becoming movements in a five-movement work. Such Masses are known as cyclic Masses. The reasons composers hit upon this idea are obscure, since there is no liturgical impetus for uniting the elements of the Ordinary, and, indeed, the five-movement Mass could never be heard as such during the liturgy (its only performance venue). The innovation appears to have been the product of English composers, and was taken up, as were other elements of English style, by continental composers.

In the fifteenth century, there were two basic musical means of achieving musical relationships among the settings of the five Ordinary texts. The first and easiest to hear is the technique of beginning every movement with the same music, or music that was extremely similar, sometimes called a "head motive" or "motto beginning." The second and more important means was unification at the structural level that came about when every movement was based on the same borrowed melody or cantus firmus, placed in the tenor voice (the lowest voice of a three-voice piece, the third voice in a four-voice piece); Masses were named after the borrowed melody. The melody was usually made distinct from the other voices by being presented in long-note values (an idea possibly borrowed from the isorhythmic motet), although this was not always the case. In the early English examples of the genre, composed in the first decades of the fifteenth century, the borrowed melody was drawn from chant, but Guillaume Dufay introduced a major innovation when he based what is possibly his first cyclic Mass, the *Missa "Se la face ay pale"* (If [my] face is pale; c. 1450), not on chant but on the tenor line of one of his own polyphonic chansons.

After Dufay's innovation, secular music was just as likely as sacred music to provide the basis of the cyclic Mass. A favorite cantus firmus was a tune called "L'homme armé" (The armed man), which formed the basis for over thirty Masses written by composers all over Europe in the space of about eighty years. This mixture of sacred and secular elements in the sung liturgy bothered some people a good deal and still occasionally perplexes modern listeners. At the same time, completely original Masses (called *sine nomine*) were also composed. In central Europe, the area of the Holy Roman Empire, composers also set many of the texts of the Proper of the Mass (texts that changed from day to day) often as strict chant-based compositions.

Composers of the late fifteenth and sixteenth centuries expanded on the original concept of the cyclic

Mass. The cantus firmus was treated in a wide variety of ways; eventually it left the tenor voice and migrated to all the voices of the composition. Josquin des Prez seems to have used a different method of cantus firmus treatment in every one of his twenty-odd Masses, even inventing some new ones (for example, the use of a cantus firmus made up of solmization syllables denoting the tones of a musical scale).

Although the cantus firmus idea was never completely abandoned, around 1500 composers begin to base their Masses not on single-line melodies but on polyphonic borrowings, in particular the points of imitation that had become the major constructive principle of the motet; that is, polyphonic motives from a model arranged in a variety of ways now formed the basis of the structural unity of the Mass as opposed to a single melody repeated in every movement. Such Masses were said to be "in imitation" of a polyphonic model, usually a motet, sometimes a secular work (*ad imitationem moduli*). The modern term for this procedure is "parody Mass," a designation that has no historical justification but still has not dropped out of currency. This was a favorite method of Mass construction of late-sixteenth-century composers such as Giovanni Pierluigi da Palestrina (c. 1525–1594) and Orlando di Lasso (c. 1532–1594), and was even used by Claudio Monteverdi (1567–1643) when in 1610 he presented a Mass based on a motet to the pope in order to demonstrate that he, a major destroyer of the style of Renaissance polyphony, actually did know "how to compose."

The decisions of the Council of Trent that ecclesiastical music should be composed so that the "words be clearly understood by all," a reflection of ongoing concerns about the effect of the imitative style on the presentation of text (imitation forces different voices to sing different words at the same time), finds its expression in Masses where the imitative principle is abandoned and homophonic writing is applied to the long texts of the Gloria and Credo. The most famous of these Masses is Palestrina's *Missa Papae Marcelli* (Pope Marcellus Mass, whose date of composition is unknown, although scholars favor c. 1562), but there were others as well (some commissioned by reform-minded prelates). The council also decreed that music in the liturgy should contain no references to things secular (a response to the many Masses based on chansons and madrigals). Nonetheless, Masses employing all the old techniques were written well into the seventeenth century; Giacomo Carissimi (1605–1674) composed a Mass based on the "L'homme armé" tune as late as the 1630s.

Liturgical Genres. Some polyphonic settings of liturgical texts are to be distinguished from Masses and motets. Hymns, sung mainly at the office of vespers throughout the year, consisted of many verses sung to the same chant melody. The response of composers setting hymns in polyphony was to provide music for only half of the verses, so that in performance the singing alternated between chant and polyphony (*alternatim* practice). The first flurry of such hymn composition occurred in the beginning of the fifteenth century; this seems to have provided enough repertory to satisfy demand for about one hundred years. In the cycle of hymns for the church year that Dufay composed sometime in the 1430s, the hymn verses are presented as simple three-voice pieces with a rhythmicized and slightly altered hymn melody clearly audible in the top voice.

When composers of the sixteenth century turned their attention to hymns (beginning c.1530), they also provided *alternatim* cycles, but the musical means employed in the polyphonic verses are much more varied, although the hymn melody is always present. The Magnificat, the canticle of the Virgin, sung at the end of vespers, also inspired many polyphonic settings. In most of these, the *alternatim* procedure was also employed (there are some exceptions). In setting Magnificats, however, composers were not dealing with a melody but with recitation tones (basically chant formulas for reciting text on one pitch), which are the usually audible basis of the polyphonic verses. The Lamentations of Jeremiah, a major component of Holy Week services, which inspired numerous polyphonic settings in the sixteenth century, also incorporated recitation tones in polyphonic settings similar to Magnificats. Psalms were sometimes also treated in this way with settings based on the psalm tone (although psalm texts could also be set as freely composed motets). In the middle to late sixteenth century, composers also published collections of settings of the Proper of the Mass, particularly Introits, based on chant and intended for *alternatim* performance.

Polychoral Music. Polyphonic music for two alternating (antiphonal) four-voice choirs (*cori spezzati*, literally, broken choirs) seems to have originated in the Veneto and in Venice in the early to middle sixteenth century. Although the different choirs were occasionally separated physically, polychorality did not require this and did not, as is sometimes supposed, originate because of the existence of two facing organ lofts in the basilica of San Marco in Venice. The technique was first applied to psalm texts, with examples of *salmi spezzati* (literally, broken psalms) published in 1550 by the influential composers Adrian Willaert (c. 1490–1562) and Jacquet of Mantua (c. 1483–1559).

Yet the idea of dividing large vocal forces into antiphonal groups was also present in works for more than five voices produced by northern composers even before this date; all that was needed was to designate the groups as separate choruses and true polychoral music would result. By 1600, polychorality had spread throughout Italy and Europe and was employed in setting all types of religious and liturgical texts in a way that both emphasized the separateness of the performing forces (which could consist of as many as four choirs of voices and instruments) and the monumental aural effect that ensued when they all sang at the same time.

Monophonic Music: Gregorian Chant.
Although the Renaissance is a great age of polyphony, it must not be forgotten that Gregorian chant continued to supply the majority of the music that was sung during the Catholic rite. This enormous monophonic repertory was the first thing that choirboys learned, and the members of church and cathedral choirs often had to memorize all of the chants that were to be sung during the year. Since most Renaissance composers actually made their adult living as singers in ecclesiastical establishments, they, too, spent a good deal of their time performing chant, so it is not surprising that chant is to be found in myriad subtle and not so subtle ways in the polyphony that these composers produced.

But there were problems with chant that increasingly bothered the reform-minded clerics of the sixteenth century with their great concern for the integrity of liturgical texts. The old chant melodies were increasingly viewed as "incorrect" because they put melismas (many pitches sung over a single syllable) on "short" syllables, and did not observe the modal system as the sixteenth century construed it. These practices were described as corruptions that had entered into the repertory as a result of its many centuries of oral and written transmission. In the late sixteenth century a concerted effort in Rome to reform Gregorian chant led to a commission by Pope Gregory XIII (reigned 1572–1585) to Palestrina and Annibale Zoilo (c. 1537–1592) to produce an authoritative edition of chant that would purge it of its "barbarisms." The final result of the commission, the *Editio Medicea* of 1613 (not edited by Palestrina) was

a drastic revision of the entire chant repertory. Melismas were shortened or cut entirely, beginnings of chants were altered to correctly indicate the mode, text placement was changed to conform to correct metrical readings; not a single chant melody remained untouched. Yet this edition was not in fact imposed on the church as a whole, and was not even always used in Rome itself. It was not until the late nineteenth century that successful efforts were made to standardize chant in all Catholic churches, the final result being a total repudiation of the edited melodies of the *Editio Medicea*.

Gregorian chant also provided the basis for what we know to have been a common practice during the entire period: the improvisation of polyphony directly upon the chant. The ability to add music "at sight," often called *discant, contrapunctus,* or *cantare supra librum,* was required of all professional singers (it was specifically part of the audition process of the papal chapel, for instance). Since this music by definition was not written down, we have no direct record of it, but it is possible that some examples of "contrapunctus" built over chant that Johannes Tinctoris (c. 1435–1511) provided in his *Liber de arte contrapuncti* (usually taken to be a manual for composers) actually reflect the unwritten tradition. This type of music may actually have been more prevalent during the liturgy than composed (written down) polyphony, and indeed, when performed by skilled singers, may not have sounded much different.

Sacred Music in the Vernacular: The *Lauda.*
Sacred songs in the vernacular existed in many countries (the carol in England, the *noël* in France), but the Italian *lauda* (song of praise) was perhaps most closely connected with sacred ritual. In thirteenth-century Italy, the performance of *laude* was cultivated in the services held by confraternities (religious lay corporations) that were established in major cities, in particular Florence, Venice, and Rome. The poems were sung to specially composed monophonic melodies or as contrafacta (works created when previously written music is provided with new text) of polyphonic settings of secular texts. In the fifteenth and sixteenth centuries, polyphonic *laude* in two or more voices, usually in a simple chordal homophonic style, were composed (the contrafactum tradition also continued). It has been suggested that the simple choral style of the *lauda* had an effect on some of the sacred music composed by northern musicians who worked in Italy; a similar style can be observed in some of the motets of Jos-

quin des Prez and his contemporaries, for instance. Girolamo Savonarola (1452–1498), who was opposed to sacred polyphony, nevertheless encouraged the singing of *laude,* and he and his followers provided many new texts. In the period of the Counter-Reformation the publication of polyphonic *laude* increased, particularly in Rome where *lauda* singing was connected particularly to Filippo Neri's Congregation of the Oratory, and dominated the music of their meetings until supplanted by the Oratorio.

Music in Reformation Churches. The three major Reformers had different ideas about the use of music in the service. Luther did not object to the elaborate polyphony of the Catholic rite; indeed many of the sources of the music of Josquin des Prez and his contemporaries were produced in Lutheran areas in the sixteenth century. But Luther also created a new class of sacred vocal work, the chorale, to be sung in his new vernacular liturgy. Chorales were originally monophonic melodies, often contrafacta created by putting German words to Gregorian chant, but also often newly composed. Luther himself wrote a number of chorales ("Ein' feste Burg ist unser Gott" [A mighty fortress is our God] is one of the most famous) and also encouraged composers to set the melodies in polyphonic contexts. Eventually, the chorale became the basis of almost all the music of the Lutheran liturgy. Calvin and Zwingli, on the other hand, were hostile to the use of music in church. Calvin restricted it to simple monophonic settings of the psalms, and Zwingli banned it entirely. The Anglican rite employed monophonic melodies, but also allowed more complicated polyphonic settings of English liturgical texts.

See also **Liturgy**.

BIBLIOGRAPHY

Atlas, Allan W. *Renaissance Music.* New York, 1998.

Carver, Anthony F. *The Development of Sacred Polychoral Music to the Time of Schütz.* Cambridge, U.K., 1988.

Garside, Charles, Jr. "Some Attitudes of the Major Reformers toward the Role of Music in the Liturgy." *McCormick Quarterly* 21 (1967): 151–168.

Kelly, Thomas Forrest, ed. *Plainsong in the Age of Polyphony.* Cambridge, U.K., 1992. Eight essays on the relationships between chant and polyphony, three dealing with music of the fifteenth and sixteenth centuries.

Lockwood, Lewis. *The Counter-Reformation and the Masses of Vincenzo Ruffo.* Venice, 1970.

Lowinsky, Edward E. "Humanism in the Music of the Renaissance." In *Medieval and Renaissance Studies: Proceedings of the Southeastern Institute of Medieval and Renaissance Studies, Summer 1978.* Edited by Frank Tirro. Durham, N.C., 1982. Pages 87–220.

Macey, Patrick Paul. *Bonfire Songs: Savonarola's Musical Legacy.* New York and Oxford, 1998.

Owens, Jessie Ann. "Music Historiography and the Definition of 'Renaissance.'" *Notes* 47 (1990): 305–330.

Pesce, Dolores, ed. *Hearing the Motet: Essays on the Motet of the Middle Ages and Renaissance.* New York, 1977. Of the sixteen essays in the volume, twelve concern the motet in the fifteenth and sixteenth centuries.

Sparks, Edgar H. *Cantus Firmus in Mass and Motet, 1420–1520.* Berkeley, Calif., 1963.

Strohm, Reinhard. *The Rise of European Music, 1380–1500.* Cambridge, U.K., 1993.

Wegman, Rob C. "From Maker to Composer: Improvisation and Musical Authorship in the Low Countries, 1450–1500." *Journal of the American Musicological Society* 49 (1996): 409–479.

Wilson, Blake. *Music and Merchants: The Laudesi Companies of Republican Florence.* Oxford, 1992.

RICHARD SHERR

Secular Vocal Music

Lyric poetry set for voices was a principal kind of music written in the fifteenth and sixteenth centuries and rivaled sacred music (Masses and motets) in importance. Over the course of this two-century span, genres and styles with predetermined structures inherited from medieval musicians gradually metamorphosed into the free, more expressive and personal art that characterizes the sixteenth century. As a concomitant of this change, the prevalent style of early Renaissance music fragmented to create, during the sixteenth century, a complex of stylistic dialects that set poetry in many languages—Italian, Spanish, Dutch, German, and English—in addition to French, which dominated the secular vocal music of the fifteenth century as it had that of the Middle Ages. Two kinds of secular vocal music, the French chanson and the Italian madrigal, are central in the Renaissance. Each of these, in addition, threw off satellite subgenres; all of them taken together constitute the most popular and often the most innovative music of the period.

The Chanson. Defined simply as a song with French words, the chanson was the most prominent secular music of the fifteenth century, written by composers throughout Europe. The musical form of chansons, especially in the first half of the century, was determined by the fixed patterns of the poetry being set. These *formes fixes,* as they are collectively termed, which may be recognized historically as a final flowering of medieval chanson practice, are the rondeau, the ballade, and the virelai. (The closely related Italian ballata and the Spanish villancico are formal variants of the virelai.) Usually using poems of several stanzas, chansons were typically written for three solo voices, one to a part, in a treble-dominated texture that placed the chief melody in the uppermost voice (the cantus or superius) with simpler melodic lines in the supportive tenor and the contratenor, a voice that filled in gaps in the musical space. Although chansons were suited to purely vocal performance, iconographic and other evidence indicate that instruments sometimes doubled (that is, played along with) the voices or even replaced them.

All the finest composers of the fifteenth and early sixteenth centuries were born and trained in the region near Flanders, most especially, during the early 1400s, in the Duchy of Burgandy. Some of these musicians stayed in the north, but many of them took up positions in the elegant Italian courts and in the papal chapel, creating a brilliant musical culture in Italy that for much of the Renaissance eclipsed those of Spain, France, England, and Germany. Only in the later sixteenth century did native Italian musicians gain prominent positions and status in Italy, finally overturning the musical hegemony of the foreigners in their homeland and themselves becoming the most significant group of composers for the next hundred years.

The greatest of the Burgundian musicians, and the best chanson composers before the mid-fifteenth century, were Guillaume Dufay (c. 1400–1474) and Gilles Binchois (c. 1400–1460). Dufay, the more versatile and influential, wrote more then seventy chansons, most of them settings of love poems in the courtly-love tradition and most in the *formes fixes,* especially rondeaux, which he preferred. Dufay and Binchois were followed most notably by the innovative composers Johannes Ockeghem (c. 1410–1497), who served the royal court of France for more than forty years, and Antoine Busnois (c. 1430–1492) who was chiefly active at the Burgundian court. Ockeghem brought to full realization the melodic and polyphonic tendencies of the Dufay chanson, with the result that the treble-dominated style nearly vanished in an interweaving of more homogeneous melodic lines. Busnois, meanwhile, anticipated the future by writing about a third of his chansons with four lines rather than three, a grouping that would become the norm by the turn of the century.

In the last years of the fifteenth century a radical change in musical style occurred with the generation of Franco-Netherlandish composers that included Josquin des Prez (c. 1440–1521), Jacob Obrecht (c. 1450–1505), Heinrich Isaac (c. 1450–1517), Alexander Agricola (c. 1446–1506) and Loyset Compère (c. 1445–1518). The tradition of a hierarchical texture in which each voice had a special function was now replaced by a new one in which each voice, while independent, was similar in melodic style and nearly equal in importance. The balance among voice parts was further enhanced by the sharing of thematic matter in a procedure that typically resulted in sections whose melodic lines presented the same textual-musical matter through *imitatio,* that is, overlapping imitation. These sections, called points of imitation by modern scholars, were so linked as to produce a seamless continuity in the musical flow. This significant advance in design, which may be recognized as reflecting the same ideals of moderation and balance that characterize the visual arts of the period, brought about the abandonment at last of the old *formes fixes.* Now music was shaped not by standardized poetic forms but by impulses that sought to project the meanings and even the emotions of the words being set. Emphasis was also placed on a clear declamation that respected the natural rhythms of the words being sung.

From about 1520 a new French style, distinct from the dense polyphony of the all-pervasive Franco-Flemish or Netherlands style, began to appear in publications brought out in Paris. (The printing of secular music dates from the *Odhecaton* published in Venice in 1501.) The new Parisian chanson was simple, light, and elegant. Characteristically, an easy and graceful melody was harmonized with simple chords in the three lower voices, which also followed the rhythms of the words being set. Thus, text was generally set syllabically (a single note for each syllable) and varied only toward the ends of phrases by short melismas (passages in which a succession of notes sets a syllable), with the melismas employed not for expressive reasons but as decoration. The leading masters of the Parisian chanson were Clément Janequin (c. 1485–1558), Claudin de Sermisy (c. 1490–1562) and somewhat later, Pierre Certon (d. 1572). Among the sorts of chansons written by these men, and by other composers of the Paris school, were descriptive chansons, some of the best of which are Janequin's *La guerre* and *Le chant des oiseaux. La guerre,* probably written in commemoration of Francis I's victory in 1515 at the Battle of Marignano, with its stylizations of trumpet fanfares, battle cries, cannon fire, and rallying calls to arms, became one of the most popular pieces of the century, much copied and arranged by subsequent composers for various solo instruments and instrumental ensembles.

During the second half of the sixteenth century both the polyphonic chanson of the Netherlands and the generally chordal Parisian chanson continued to evolve. In the latter case, the most significant of the composers who came to the fore in the 1550s and 1560s were Jacques Arcadelt (c. 1505–1568), Claude Goudimel (c. 1514–1572), and Orlando di Lasso (1532–1594), although the latter was resident in Munich where he held the important position of choirmaster to the dukes of Bavaria. The greatest of all the native French composers in the second half of the sixteenth century was Claude Le Jeune (c. 1528–1600). Some of his chansons, which he began to publish in the 1570s, can be linked to the Pléiade, the group of poets led by Pierre de Ronsard that sought to imitate classical meters and forms in poetry and that called for a new musical style appropriate to them. One of the Pléiade, Jean-Antoine de Baïf, established a means to these ends in his "Vers et musique mesurés à l'antique" (Verse and music according to the ancient model). Here, French verse shaped by the metrical patterns of classical poetry was to be sung in a kind of chordal chanson that used long notes for long syllables of text and short notes for short syllables (resulting in an irregular musical meter). The Académie de Poesie et Musique that Baïf founded in 1570 with the support of Charles IX lasted only a few years, but the music it fostered—by Le Jeune and others—influenced French composers for the rest of the century. Notable in this regard is the *air de cour* (sometimes termed a vaudeville), which came to prominence at this time. These very simple and usually chordal airs set strophic court poetry for four or five unaccompanied voices or for solo voice with lute accompaniment. Their characteristic irregular meter shows the direct effect of the "musique mesurée" of Baïf and his company. The popularity of the airs with the French court carried them well into the first half of the seventeenth century, during which period they were the most important secular vocal music in France.

The Frottola and the Madrigal.

The Italian madrigal of the Renaissance emerged in the sixteenth century (it has no connection to the fourteenth-century madrigal), and by about 1550 it came to equal or surpass the French chanson in importance. The madrigal was preceded by, and to some extent grew from, the frottola, an indigenous, short-lived genre that was cultivated at several courts in northern Italy, including those at Ferrara and Mantua. It flourished from about 1480 to 1520 and had among its chief composers Marchetto Cara (c. 1470–c. 1525) and Bartolomeo Trombocino (c. 1470–c. 1535), both professional musicians at the court of the Gonzaga in Mantua. The frottola was a short song for four

parts with a characteristic melody of narrow range and many repeated notes. Like the Parisian chanson, its lines usually moved together in chords, with a syllabic setting of text and with musical phrases whose distinct articulation produced a structure of very clear-cut design. The highest and lowest voices in the frottola had the more important roles with the two middle voices filling out the harmony. Most often only the top part was sung, with the lower three "voices" presumably performed by accompanying instruments, as is indicated by the fact that the uppermost voice had the full text while only textual incipits appeared for the lower parts. The tone of the frottola mirrored that of its words, light, frivolous poetry written specifically for the composer.

The Madrigal.

It was a change in poetic taste within Italian courts that began the dissolution of the frottola. During the first two decades of the sixteenth century, poetry of a more serious and "literary" quality began to gain favor, and the frottola, unable to cope with the new, increasingly impassioned texts, was replaced by the madrigal. The most important stylistic alteration that defined the madrigal was the changed conception in the part-writing. The two middle voices were now accorded the same status as the two outer voices, so that melodic lines of equal importance were created. The four voices now came together, often in a polyphonic ensemble, with each part having the entire text. Other new features included a more flexible rhythmic and metric organization that allowed the composer to comply more closely with the changing moods and meanings of the text. Along with this, the sectional form of the frottola gave way to the through-composed (continuous and nonrepetitive) structure of the madrigal. The musical form responded more to the unfolding content of the poem than to the poem's shape. Of significance, too, was the replacement of the harmonic simplicity that had belonged to the frottola by a freer harmonic flow that also had its raison d'être in a desire to express the poetic idea.

All of this taken together made the madrigal resemble the Renaissance motet—a motet with a secular text as it were. The motetlike structure came about not through an adaptation of the contemporary motet, however, but through an infusion into the frottola of elements from the Franco-Netherlandish style. It was the combining of the two styles that produced the madrigal and gave the genre its vigor. Traces of the old frottola style remained with the Italian madrigal throughout its life and prevented it from

Plate 1. Andrea Mantegna. *The Gonzaga Family and Court.* Mantegna portrays Ludovico Gonzaga, marquis of Mantua (reigned 1444–1478), and his wife, Barbara of Hohenzollern, and their daughters. Mural (1465–1474) in the Camera degli Sposi of the Ducal Palace in Mantua. [See the entries on Mantegna and Mantua in this volume.] PALAZZO DUCALE, MANTUA, ITALY/SUPERSTOCK

Plate 2. Masaccio. *The Tribute Money.* Mural in the Brancacci Chapel of the church of Santa Maria del Carmine, Florence. The painting illustrates a passage in the Gospel of Matthew (17:24–27). At the right, a tax collector asks Peter for the tribute money; in the center Jesus tells Peter that he will find the coin to pay tribute in the mouth of a fish; at the left, Peter finds the coin. Fresco; 1425–1428. [See the entry on Masaccio in this volume; for another treatment of this subject, see Perugino's *Christ Giving the Keys to Peter* in the color plates in volume 5.] SANTA MARIA DEL CARMINE, FLORENCE, BRANCACCI CHAPEL/SUPERSTOCK

Plate 3. Masaccio. *The Holy Trinity.* Mural in the church of Santa Maria Novella, Florence. Fresco; 1428. [See the entry on Masaccio in this volume.] SANTA MARIA NOVELLA, FLORENCE/CANALI PHOTOBANK, MILAN/SUPERSTOCK

Plate 4. Michelangelo. Sistine Chapel Ceiling. Michelangelo painted the ceiling of the Sistine Chapel between 1508 and 1512. [See the entry on Michelangelo in this volume.] VATICAN MUSEUMS AND GALLERIES, VATICAN CITY/THE BRIDGEMAN ART LIBRARY

Plate 5. Michelangelo. *Doni Tondo*. *Holy Family* (called the *Doni Tondo;* a tondo is a circular painting). 1503; 1.2 m (47 in.) diameter. [See the entry on Michelangelo in this volume.] GALLERIA DEGLI UFFIZI, FLORENCE/SCALA/ART RESOURCE

Plate 6. Myth. *The Birth of Venus,* early 1480s, by Sandro Botticelli (1445–1510). [See the entry on Myth in this volume and the entry on Botticelli in volume 1.] GALLERIA DEGLI UFFIZI, FLORENCE/SUPERSTOCK

Plate 7. Art in the Netherlands. Hugo van der Goes. *Adoration of the Shepherds.* From the Portinari Altarpiece. [See the entry on Art in the Netherlands in this volume.] GALLERIA DEGLI UFFIZI, FLORENCE/SUPERSTOCK

Plate 8. Art in the Netherlands. *The Mérode Altarpiece* by Robert Campin (c. 1378–1444). In the left panel, the donors—possibly Ingelbrecht of Mechelen and his wife—kneel in veneration. In the center panel is the Annunciation. In the right panel, St. Joseph makes a mousetrap, a means to catch the Devil. Oil on wood; side panels 64.5 x 27.3 cm (25.4 x 10.75 in.); center panel 64.1 x 63.2 cm (25.25 x 25 in.). [See the entry on Art in the Netherlands in this volume.] METROPOLITAN MUSEUM OF ART, THE CLOISTERS COLLECTION, 1956, 56.70

Plate 9. Palladian Architecture. La Rotunda, villa near Vicenza, Italy. Built 1567–1591. [See the entry on Palladio in this volume.] ERICH LESSING/ART RESOURCE

Plate 10. Procession in Piazza di San Marco, Venice. *Procession of the Reliquary of the True Cross*, 1496, by Gentile Bellini (c. 1429–1507). [See the entry on Parades, Processions, and Pageants in this volume. For a depiction of the rescue of the relic, see the painting by Gentile Bellini illustrating the entry on Art in Venice in volume 6; for another depiction of the reliquary, see the painting of the Vendramin family by Titian in the color plates in volume 6.] ACCADEMIA, VENICE/SCALA/ART RESOURCE, NY

TEMPLA·DOMVM·EXPOSITIS·VICOS·FORA·MOENIA·PONTES·
VIRGINEAM·TRIVII·QVOD·REPARARIS·AQVAM·
PRISCA·LICET·NAVTIS·STATVAS·DARE·COMMODA·PORTVS·
ET·VATICANVM·CINGERE·SIXTE·IVGVM·
PLVS·TAMEN·VRBS·DEBET·NAM·QVAE·SQVALORE·LATEBAT·
CERNITVR·IN·CELEBRI·BIBLIOTHECA·LOCO·

Plate 11. The Papacy as Patron of Learning. *Sixtus IV Names Platina as Prefect of the Vatican Library,*
1477, by Melozzo da Forlì (1438–1494). Bartolomeo Sacchi, called il Platina, kneels before the pope; the
prelate standing between Platina and the pope is the pope's nephew Giuliano della Rovere, who became
Pope Julius II in 1503. [See the entry on the Papacy in this volume.] PINACOTECA, VATICAN MUSEUMS AND
GALLERIES, VATICAN CITY/SCALA/ART RESOURCE

Plate 12. Parmigianino. *Madonna dal collo lungo* (Madonna of the Long Neck). Painted 1534–1540.
[See the entry on Parmigianino in this volume.] GALLERIA DEGLI UFFIZI, FLORENCE/SCALA/ART RESOURCE

ever reaching the academicism that occasionally marks the sixteenth-century motet.

In light of this it is not surprising that the first great masters of the madrigal were the three northerners Jacob Arcadelt, Philippe Verdelot (c. 1470–c. 1552), and Adriaan Willaert (c. 1490–1562). Within the careers of these composers and their contemporaries the transition was completed from the early madrigal, with its generally simple style, to the middle-period madrigal, which emphasized more learned, northern techniques. Willaert's early madrigals, for example, composed in the third decade of the century, display a predominance of chordal writing (like that of the frottola and the Parisian chanson) with imitative passages used infrequently; phrases still plainly marked off by the tendency of all the voices to close together; and, even though the voices are relatively independent, the upper part retaining the most important role. By contrast, in Willaert's late madrigals phrases are often not so well defined; imitation and other contrapuntal techniques are more in evidence, with chordal passages used mostly for expressive purposes; and the upper voice is no longer so prominent.

The madrigal: middle period. Five voices became the norm for the madrigal in its middle period, and decisive changes took place as well in its expressive character, changes that were due to the composers' desire to translate into musical terms the full meaning of the text. This applied not only to the explicit statements of the text but to its imagery and mood. Thus, on the one hand, a more dramatic and more emotional style sometimes attempts to catch the general spirit of the text, while on the other, new interest is shown in "painting" or illustrating specific words or phrases. In their zeal to translate the full content of the poetry into musical language, many madrigalists now devoted particular attention to portraying physical or natural phenomena in musical terms. For instance, such concepts as "highness" or "lowness" may be represented by high or low musical pitch; speed (slow or fast) and its change are frequently matched by analogous tempo and rhythms; and such actions as falling, rising, climbing, and jumping may be illustrated by appropriate melodic movements.

In addition to these audible devices of word-painting, the musical notation itself was enlisted to provide visual equivalents for matters mentioned in the madrigal text. Thus, black notes might be used to set such words as night, darkness, death, black; open note-heads might depict eyes, the moon, pearls; or material objects such as chains or ropes might be indicated by melodic lines that offer a pictorial image of the object. These visual metaphors, collectively referred to by modern students of the madrigal as "eye-music," are generally viewed by them with varying degrees of disapproval. For the madrigal performer of the time, however—and madrigals were primarily addressed to the performer—the extramusical devices must have offered an intellectual fillip to heighten the enjoyment of madrigal singing.

The middle-period madrigal also has more contrast in textures and sonorities. These traits, which arose from the ever-increasing desire for faithful rendering of the words, became especially pronounced as more poetry having a dramatic cast was set to music. Such texts—for instance, many among the monologues and dialogues frequently excerpted from Torquato Tasso's *Gerusalemme liberata* (1581) and Giambattista Guarini's *Il pastor fido* (1590)—were favored by madrigalists from the 1580s on. As an additional tool for expressing passion or melancholy (feelings that were coming to dominate the poetry of the time), chromaticism, with its enrichment of both melody and harmony, was often relied upon. The leading composers of the middle-period madrigals include Cipriano de Rore (c. 1515–1565), Andrea Gabrieli (c. 1510–1586), and their younger contemporary Giaches de Wert (1535–1596).

The madrigal: late period. In the next generation a host of excellent composers were drawn to what was by this time the most advanced and important of all the musical genres. In the late madrigal the stylistic traits that had previously evolved were carried still further, but now these conflicted with the very spirit of the form, that is, a vocal art in which every line shares equally in the upbuilding of the whole and each singer is entitled to the full expression of the text. This spirit, however, was no longer compatible with the new aesthetic demands for dramatic and subjective utterance. In this sense what brought the madrigal to its breaking point was the same force that had driven it throughout its history: the search for ever more expressive means with which to translate the meaning and mood of words into musical language. Indeed, this ideal, coupled with the growing refinement of literacy taste during the sixteenth century, is chiefly accountable for the entire development of the madrigal as a textual-musical genre.

Three great masters served the Italian madrigal in its last period: Luca Marenzio (c. 1553–1599) who, while remaining within traditional aesthetic confines, brought the genre to its ultimate perfection; Carlo Gesualdo (c. 1561–1613), whose daring experiments with chromaticism produced a melodic and harmonic language of such richness and diversity as occasionally to approach the bizarre; and Claudio Monteverdi (1567–1643), whose realization of the madrigal's implicit tendencies led ultimately to the establishment of the new stylistic conventions of the seventeenth century. Among the most telling of his advances was the arrival in his later madrigals at a style and texture that resulted from his giving a soloistic presentation to highly personal and intimate texts. Coupled with this was his explicit demand for instrumental components in the madrigal, and the two together destroyed the genre's basic premise as a homogeneous and balanced a cappella art drawing together four or five voices of equal status.

In addition, an external factor helped to bring about the decline of the madrigal: the new taste within Italian courts (especially those at Ferrara, Mantua, and Florence) for virtuoso voices. This trend motivated a recasting of the genre as a composition meant for an attendant audience, and so the intimate, social basis of the madrigal as music for the personal enjoyment of its performers was lost. It was in part out of these changes in style and technique that seventeenth-century monody and opera were born, and the madrigal in Italy became passé.

England, Spain, and Germany. Beyond Italy, the madrigal had a vigorous production by Italian as well as by native-born composers. This was true in German-speaking lands; in Poland, Denmark, and the Netherlands; and especially in England. As the madrigal began its decline in Italy it had a new lease on life in the England of Elizabeth I and James I. Italian madrigals were popular with the English from early in the genre's history, but following publication of *Musica transalpina,* an anthology of Italian madrigals with their texts translated into English that appeared in London in 1588, an English school began to flourish, with its composers writing distinctive madrigals to original English poetry. Perhaps the most notable of these composers were Thomas Morley (c. 1557–1602), Thomas Weelkes (1576–1623), and John Wilbye (1574–1638). The English madrigal more often than not was modeled on the lighter Italian madrigal or in some cases on the Italian canzonetta, a simpler satellite genre (along with the villanella) of the madrigal in Italy. Beginning in the last years of the sixteenth century, the English produced another kind of music, the lute song or ayre, which was much composed from the late 1590s into the third decade of the next century. Madrigalists such as Morley composed ayres, but preeminent was John Dowland (1563–1626), a virtuoso lutenist whose compositions for solo voice and lute (as well as his instrumental music for lute alone) stand among the finest musical works of the age.

An important song literature existed as well in Spain in the late sixteenth century with the villancico and the romance. The villancico had emerged earlier, during the reign of Ferdinand II and Isabella I, when a true Spanish style in music was created. It was at that point a genre much like the Italian frottola, with a principal melody in the top voice and (usually) three lower parts, all moving in a clearly directed chordal harmony. The more expressive range of the villancico, however, carried it beyond the light tone of the frottola into more serious and lyrical moods. The best of the villancico composers in the late fifteenth and early sixteenth centuries were Juan Vasquez (c. 1510–c. 1560) and Joan Brudieu (c. 1520–1591), who composed madrigals as well to both Italian and Catalan poetry.

In Germany, as in Italy and Spain, secular vocal music developed only in the late fifteenth and early sixteenth centuries. The dominant genre there was the lied (or tenorlied), with its placement of the chief melody in the tenor voice and the accompaniment of three others, two higher voices somewhat faster-moving above and a supportive bass below. Among the earliest composers who, while borrowing from the Franco-Flemish style, still created a distinctly German music, were Heinrich Isaac, Henrich Finck (c. 1444–1527), and Paul Hofhaimer (1459–1537). In the lied's next period, the most notable of the composers was Ludwig Senfl (c. 1486–c. 1543), in whose secular music the German style reached its high point and began its decline. From about 1565 to the end of the century, the finest composers were the Munich-based Orlando di Lasso and Hans Leo Hassler (1562–1612). In their works the influence of foreign music, especially the Italian madrigal and the villanella, began to push aside distinctive German elements to produce a new, synthetic style. Thus did German music, like that of England and Spain, find itself at the end of the Renaissance engulfed by a powerful wave of Italian musical art, an art that would be dominant throughout Europe for the next century and beyond.

See also biographies of figures mentioned in this entry.

BIBLIOGRAPHY

Atlas, Allan W. *Renaissance Music: Music in Western Europe, 1400–1600.* New York, 1998.

Brown, Howard Mayer, and Louise K. Stein. *Music in the Renaissance.* 2d ed. Upper Saddle River, N.J., 1998.

Einstein, Alfred. *The Italian Madrigal.* Translated by Alexander H. Krappe, Roger H. Sessions, and Oliver Strunk. Reprint, 3 vols. Princeton, N.J., 1971.

Kerman, Joseph. *The Elizabethan Madrigal.* New York, 1962.

Reese, Gustave. *Music in the Renaissance.* Rev. ed. New York, 1959.

EDMOND STRAINCHAMPS

Intermedi

Intermedi (singular, intermedio) were musical interludes performed between the acts of plays during the Renaissance, with or without staging. The practice of inserting intermedi apparently began in connection with revivals of plays by Terence and Plautus at Ferrara in 1486 and quickly spread from there to every major Italian cultural center.

The Earliest Intermedi.

The earliest known description of intermedi tells us that instruments were played between the acts of Niccolò da Correggio's *Fabula di Caephalo* (The tale of Cephalus) at Ferrara in 1487. Instruments also provided the intermedi for Baldassare Taccone's *Danae* at Milan in 1496 and for Ludovico Ariosto's *I suppositi* (The substitutes) at Rome in 1519. Generally the instruments were played behind the scenes, and the minor tradition of unseen intermedi continued in Italy for most of the sixteenth century.

Staged intermedi were used in the production of three plays at the ducal court of Ferrara in 1499: *Eunuco* (The eunuch) by Terence and *Trinummo* and *Penulo* by Plautus, all three in Italian translations. The sixteen intermedi used in these productions required 144 performers costumed as peasants, pages, nymphs, fools, and parasites. Their themes included pastoral scenes, the hunt, mythology, and comedy. Each intermedio included a mimed dance occasionally interrupted by poetic recitation or singing. Some of the vocal music was performed by costumed singers who acted. Likewise at Ferrara in 1502 four plays by Plautus were staged with intermedi including music by court composer Bartolomeo Tromboncino.

Diaries record intermedi performed with plays produced at private homes in Venice during the early sixteenth century. At a performance of *Miles gloriosus* (The boastful soldier) at Ca' Pesaro in 1515 one intermedio ended with singing nymphs riding a parade cart and another portraying the judgment of Paris. Baldassare Castiglione described four intermedi performed at Urbino in 1513 with connected themes: the search for the golden fleece, Venus in a cart pulled by two doves, Neptune on a cart pulled by seahorses, and Juno on a cloud-shaped cart drawn by two peacocks. At the end, Cupid explained that the intermedi were intended to portray the victory of love over discord and war. Similar themes from ancient mythology became ever more important in intermedi of the sixteenth century, particularly in Florence.

Florentine Court Intermedi.

Niccolò Machiavelli's comedies *Clizia* and *La mandragola* (The mandrake) were performed in Florence at least in 1525, perhaps as early as 1518, with madrigals by Philippe Verdelot sung as intermedi between the acts. But it is the series of court intermedi celebrating Medici-family dynastic events that brought fame to Florentine musical spectacle in the sixteenth century. These began with the six intermedi for Antonio Landi's *Il commodo* (The convenience) produced to celebrate the marriage of Duke Cosimo I de' Medici and Eleonora of Toledo in 1539. An elaborate description was published, as would become the general practice with this series; exceptionally, so was the music by Francesco Corteccia. The scenes of these six intermedi are set at specific times of day—dawn, early morning, mid-morning, midday, evening, and night—a progression symbolized by magnified lantern light that represented a sun that changed position in the sky for each intermedio. Each of the intermedi incorporated seemingly magical transformations of personages and objects, and the music included accompanied solo singing.

Likewise, the five madrigals by Corteccia performed as intermedi for Francesco d'Ambra's *Il furto* (The theft) in 1544 were published as a group. For the 1565 wedding of Francesco de' Medici and Joanna of Austria, sister of the emperor, Ambra's *La cofanaria* (Cabinetry) was performed with intermedi designed by Giorgio Vasari and Bernardo Buontalenti in which a plot is carried out from one intermedio to the next and that relates to the plot of the play: in effect the story is told on two levels, alternating between the divine and the human spheres. Of the music by Alessandro Striggio and Francesco Corteccia, only Corteccia's moving lament sung by Psyche remains.

The four intermedi performed with *Il granchio* (The crab) by Leonardo Salviati in 1566 represented the four ages of human life—childhood, youth, virility, and senility—which were intended to refer to the four parts of the twenty-four-hour day—morning, noon, evening, and night—in which the action of the comedy unfolds. To celebrate the baptism of Francesco de' Medici and Joanna of Austria's first-born in 1568, *I Fabii* (The Fabii) by Lotto del Mazza was staged with six intermedi, music by court music director Striggio, set by Baldassare Lanci, and costumes by Buontalenti. From these intermedi survives a ten-voice madrigal that was sung by the monsters conquered by Hercules.

The 1569 state visit by Joanna's brother, Archduke Charles, was celebrated with a production of *La vedova* (The widow) by Giovanni Battista Cini staged in the Salone dei Cinquecento of the Palazzo Vecchio with six intermedi representing episodes from Aristophanes, Ovid, and Dante. The music was again by Striggio. And the staging, which depicted the facade of the very palace in which the performance took place, included magical transformations: peasants turned into frogs; ghosts of poets, painters, sculptors, musicians, and alchemists appeared, sang, then disappeared. The performance of *L'amico fido* (The faithful friend) by Giovanni de' Bardi for the 1586 wedding of Cesare d'Este and Virginia de' Medici was staged in a new theater specially constructed in the Uffizi. The intermedi, planned by Bardi himself, were the first (in Florence) to evoke the myth of the Golden Age as an allegory for the glory, hopes, and accomplishments of the Medici dynasty. In each intermedio, one of the principal gods of mythology brings a tribute to the wedding couple: Jove sends the Virutes, Hell swallows the Evils, Zephyrus and Flora proclaim eternal spring, Neptune calms the ocean, and Juno contains the elements.

The series of Florentine courtly intermedi climaxed in 1589 with the series performed with Girolamo Bargali's comedy *La pellegrina* (The pilgrim lady) to celebrate the marriage between Grand Duke Ferdinand de' Medici and Christine of Lorraine. The themes of its six intermedi, planned by Giovanni de' Bardi, summarize the aspirations of Bardi's Camerata, an informal academy that had been investigating the nature of ancient Greek music since the early 1570s. The first five intermedi portray, one by one, several of the celebrated myths of music's miraculous powers during the original Golden Age of the gods: the harmony of the spheres, the singing contest between the Pierides and the Muses, Apollo's slaying of the Python, the conquest of the inferno, and Arion's rescue by dolphins. The finale of the sixth intermedio took place in the present time. In answer to Ferdinando's entreaties, the gods return to earth with the gift of (ancient-style) music and dance as a token of the new Golden Ages that is seen to commence with the reign of Ferdinand and Christine. Notable in the music (almost all of which was printed afterward) are solo songs by Giulio Caccini,

Jacopo Peri, and Emilio de' Cavalieri, who a decade later would vie for recognition as inventor of opera.

Other Intermedi. A series of ten intermedi for religious plays (*commedie sacre*) performed in the oratories of Florentine lay confraternities run parallel to the much more famous court intermedi of the sixteenth century. Nearly all of them now known were authored by Giovanni Maria Cecchi between 1549 and 1587. Whereas Florentine court intermedi often feature virtuosic solo singing and accompaniment by instruments, the religious intermedi employ a cappella madrigals almost exclusively. And whereas the themes of the court intermedi were nearly always drawn from ancient mythology, those of the religious intermedi tend to be taken from the Old Testament. In fact, they tend to reflect careful study of the original Hebrew texts as much as the humanistically inspired court intermedi are founded upon classical philology. And whereas the Florentine court intermedi often foster the political myth of the Medici family's ancient right to rule and the advent of a new Golden Age symbolized by a rebirth of ancient learning and arts in Florence, the religious intermedi refer to such civic virtues as modesty and piety.

Musical intermedi did not disappear with the emergence of opera (in 1598). In 1608, for example, the Florentine wedding between Cosimo II de' Medici and Maria Maddalena of Austria was celebrated by *Il giudizio di Paride* (The judgment of Paris) by Michelangelo Buonarroti *il giovane* (the younger; 1568–1646) with intermedi by the same author, which included the new style of recitative singing that had been recently introduced in the earliest operas. The early operas themselves often incorporated intermedi into the conclusions of their acts, as a static series of dances and choruses. The last vestiges of intermedi can be found in the French *comédie-ballet* at the court of Louis XIV and the dramatic operas of Restoration England.

See also **Drama**, *subentry on* **Religious Drama**; **Music**, *subentry on* **Opera**; **Parades, Processions, and Pageants**.

BIBLIOGRAPHY

Brown, Howard Mayer. *Sixteenth-Century Instrumentation: The Music of the Florentine Intermedi*. Rome, 1973. A survey of the Florentine intermedi of broader scope than the title implies. Concerns the relations between musical style and dramatic purpose.

Carter, Tim. "A Florentine Wedding of 1608." *Acta Musicologica* 55 (1983): 89–107. Focuses on the preparations for and creation of the last major Florentine wedding intermedi.

Hill, John Walter. "Florentine *Intermedi Sacri e Morali*, 1549–1622." *Actes du XIIIe congrès de la société internationale de musicologie: La musique et le rite sacré et profane.* Vol. 2, *Communications libres.* Edited by Marc Honegger and Paul Prévost. Strasbourg, France, 1986. Pages 265–301. Uncovers a series of religious intermedi running parallel to the courtly intermedi of Florence during the sixteenth century.

Nagler, Alois Maria. *Theatre Festivals of the Medici, 1539–1637.* New Haven, Conn., 1964. A basic descriptive account of the Florentine court intermedi of the Renaissance, with references to other, related pageants and spectacles.

Pirrotta, Nino, and Elena Povoledo. *Music and Theatre from Poliziano to Monteverdi.* Translated by Karen Eales. Cambridge, U.K., 1982. Translation of *Li due Orfei: Da Poliziano a Monteverdi* (1969). A masterful survey and interpretation of the entire history of the Renaissance intermedi.

JOHN WALTER HILL

Opera

The term "opera," a modern convenience, refers to full-length musical drama with costumes and staging, sung entirely throughout. Its origins can be traced to the 1590s, and its emergence is often considered to be the event that signals the end of the Renaissance and beginning of the baroque era of music history in Italy. This entry, in keeping with the scope of this encyclopedia, will emphasize the roots of opera in late-Renaissance Italian music, literature, theater, and Humanist thought.

The First Operas. The earliest known opera is generally regarded to have been *La Dafne,* first performed in Florence during Carnival of 1598 with music by Jacopo Peri (1561–1633) on a text by Ottavio Rinuccini (1562–1621). It was originally planned and sponsored by the Florentine silk merchant Jacopo Corsi (1561–1602), who also composed some music for it before Peri joined the endeavor. Only six short fragments of music are preserved from this work.

A complete, printed musical score survives from Peri and Rinuccini's second operatic collaboration, *L'Euridice,* first performed in Florence in October 1600, as part of the celebration of the politically important marriage of Maria de' Medici to King Henry IV of France. This is usually thought to be the first surviving opera, although the *Rappresentatione di anima e di corpo* (Pageant of soul and body) was performed in Rome during Carnival of 1600 with music by Emilio de' Cavalieri (c. 1550–1602). The latter work is sometimes discounted because it is squarely within the tradition of the *sacre rappresentazioni* (religious pageants) and because it does not really have a plot in the usual sense. However, in the preface to the printed score of the *Rappresentatione,* Cavalieri's spokesman, Alessandro Guidotti, mentions three earlier, short, entirely sung pastorals by Cavalieri—*Il satiro* (The satyr) and *La disperazione di Fileno* (Fileno's desperation) of 1590 and *Il giuoco della cieca* (Blind man's bluff; 1595), based on an episode from Giovanni Battista Guarini's *Pastor fido* (The faithful shepherd; 1590)—which were performed in Florence, where Cavalieri served the grand ducal court as superintendent of the arts. Of these three pastorals there is no trace of either text or music. However, in a letter of 1616, the Florentine composer Giulio Caccini (c. 1551–1618) asserts that the three works did not incorporate what came to be known as recitative style, which Caccini, in the preface to the printed score of his own setting of *L'Euridice* (1600) and elsewhere, claims to have invented as early as 1585.

The Camerata. Caccini's claim to have invented recitative style includes a striking reference to a camerata, or informal academy, devoted to discussions of ancient Greek music, organized and hosted by the Florentine courtier and amateur composer Giovanni de' Bardi, count of Vernio (1534–1612), in which were gathered "not only many of the nobility but also the foremost musicians, intellectuals, poets, and philosophers of the city." The names of two further members of the camerata figure in the *Dialogo della musica antica et della moderna* (Dialogue on ancient and modern music; 1581) by the Florentine nobleman, lutenist, and composer Vincenzo Galilei (c. 1520–1591), which takes the form of a dialogue between Bardi and Piero Strozzi. In his other writings, Galilei refers to Florentine humanist Girolamo Mei (1519–1594), whose letters from Rome to Galilei in Florence, written between 1572 and 1581, provided the camerata with most of its information about ancient Greek music, many of its ideas for the reform of modern music, and many specific thoughts and expressions that are repeated or paraphrased in Galilei's *Dialogo* and in a *Discorso mandato a Giulio Caccini* (Discourse addressed to Giulio Caccini) written by Bardi about 1580.

The ideas that Bardi and Galilei derived from Mei, which we take to be the main conclusions of the Florentine camerata, are these. The music of the ancient Greeks derived its legendary power to move listeners—a power thought to be lacking in modern music—from the fact that it was vocal, that it adhered closely to the text, especially as regards rhythm and inflection, and that it consisted of only one melody (unaccompanied according to Mei, accompanied by simple harmony according to Galilei). All three agreed that modern polyphonic madrigals failed to move because the melodic inflections in one voice were canceled by opposite motion in another voice. From his study of the ancient modes and genres, Mei concluded that Greek melodies encompassed a narrow range of pitches and often focused upon a single note. Although Peri was only twenty years old when the camerata concluded its meetings, his preface to the score of *L'Euridice* repeats Mei's opinion that the ancient Greeks sang their tragedies throughout in a style midway between speech and song, a characterization echoed in the writings of both Cavalieri and Caccini.

It appears that Caccini, Strozzi, and perhaps others of Bardi's camerata transferred their meetings to the house of Jacopo Corsi, at least by the time Bardi moved to Rome, in 1592. Peri and Rinuccini were part of this later group, which, as has been said, produced the first operas. On the occasion of the wedding performance of 1600, the duke of Mantua came to Florence with his musicians, chief among whom was Claudio Monteverdi (1567–1643), whose first opera, *L'Orfeo* (1607), was closely modeled—as regards both music and text—on *L'Euridice* by Peri.

All the individuals named so far, with the exception of Cavalieri, were also members of the Florentine lay confraternity called the Compagnia dell'Arcangelo Raffaello detta della Scala. Following on earlier traditions of performing *sacre rappresentazioni* and *commedie sacre* (religious plays), the members of this confraternity performed or produced, beginning in 1582, a series of brief dramatic musical skits, illustrating the themes of such important religious holidays as All Saints' Day, Christmas, and Easter. Caccini and Peri are frequently named as composers and performers in these, along with other early singers and composers of operas. In time, longer and more dramatic musical vignettes were performed in the oratory of this organization, and their outlines resemble works known in Rome as sacred dialogues in the 1610s. By the 1630s, the Compagnia dell'Arcangelo Raffaello did away with stage sets and costumes for their festival performances, and the works they presented from that point onward can be regarded as early oratorios.

The Development of Recitative.

The innovative musical style crucial to the emergence of opera and oratorio became known as recitative early in the seventeenth century. Today it is widely recognized that neither Peri nor Caccini really invented it, nor did they hit upon it in an attempt to copy ancient Greek singing, of which they knew no examples. Rather it was a baroque modification of a Renaissance type of recitational singing using stock formulas, called *arie* (airs), that can be traced back to the fifteenth century. Galilei advised using these *arie* as models for serious solo vocal compositions in a recitational style. Caccini devised a method of capturing in musical notation the nuances of rhythm and embellishment of *aria* singing, which were formerly preserved only by oral tradition. And Peri can be credited with molding this style into something a good deal more expressive. The general characteristics of early recitative style are syllabic text setting (one note per syllable of text), a narrow range of pitches, frequent use of repeated pitches (monotone recitation), avoidance of rhythmic and melodic patterning, rhythmically free performance that obscures the beat and meter, and accompaniment by simple chords played on a harpsichord, lute-family instrument, organ, or some combination of these.

Those portions of early opera libretti set in recitative style were written in *versi sciolti*, that is, lines of seven and eleven syllables without discernible rhyme scheme. Other parts of the texts, called *luoghi oziosi* (idle scenes) by Mei and others, employed the classical forms of ottava rima (eight-line stanzas), terza rima (three-line stanzas), quarta rima (four-line stanzas), and so on, or were strophic *canzonette* (songs). These were composed either in the dance-like style of earlier *canzonette* for three voices, or they employed the strophic variation procedures derived from the nonrecitational manner of singing based on formulaic *arie*.

Opera as a Musical Genre.

Opera was not an entirely new dramatic genre. In its general outlines, it can be considered a form of pastoral tragicomedy in the tradition of Guarini's *Pastor fido*. The first opera, *La Dafne*, begins exactly like one of the *intermedi* performed between the acts of the play *La pellegrina* (The pilgrim lady) in Florence for the wedding of Grand Duke Ferdinand I de' Medici in 1589. This set of intermedi was based on the invention of Giovanni de' Bardi, with music by Cavalieri, Caccini, and Peri, among others, celebrating ancient myths of the miraculous powers of music. Many of the earliest operas in Florence, Mantua, and Rome incorporate intermedi into the conclusion of their acts.

The earliest operas were sung throughout, like most intermedi, but they had plots (unlike intermedi) resembling pastorals, which, however, mixed singing with spoken dialogue. *L'Euridice* was proclaimed a tragedy on the title page of its libretto, whereas Caccini's *Il rapimento di Cefalo* (1600) was advertised as a comedy. Traces of the *mascherata* (masquerade) and *bariera* (joust) can also be found in early operas. Early Roman operas, beginning in the 1630s, included comic scenes derived from the scenarios of commedia dell'arte. Madrigal comedies, which can be found as early as but no earlier than the first operas, set dialogue to music sung by ensembles rather than soloists representing individual interlocutors. They never use recitative style. For these reasons, they bear no relation to early operas.

It is generally agreed that all forms of pageantry, including musical spectacle, at Renaissance courts had a hortatory function. The pageantry surrounding the Medici weddings during the sixteenth and early seventeenth centuries tended to project what has been called a prevailing "political mythology," the major tenets of which were that the Medici family had a long-established right to rule, that their patronage of the arts was a sign that Florence was the new Athens, and that their role in reviving the arts and learning of antiquity signaled the return of the golden age. These themes run throughout the Florentine intermedi of the sixteenth century and are carried over into the earliest operas. This mythology helps to explain why Bardi, the members of his camerata, and their successors in Corsi's household sought a musical style and a dramatic form that paralleled or emulated those of antiquity. For the same reason, the plots and characters of *La Dafne, L'Euridice,* and several other of the earliest operas revolve around heroes of ancient mythology who find their salvation through prowess in or support of the arts.

See also **Commedia dell'Arte**; **Drama**, *subentry on* **Religious Drama**; **Music**, *subentry on* **Intermedi**; **Parades, Processions, and Pageants**.

BIBLIOGRAPHY

Primary Work

Palisca, Claude V. *The Florentine Camerata: Documentary Studies and Translations.* New Haven, Conn., 1989. Translations of the original documents surrounding the creation of opera.

Secondary Works

Brown, Howard Mayer. "How Opera Began: An Introduction to Jacopo Peri's *Euridice* (1600)." In *The Late Italian Renaissance.* Edited by Eric Cochrane. New York, 1970. Pages 401–444. Reprinted in *The Garland Library of the History of Western Music.* Edited by Ellen Rosand. Vol. 11, *Opera, I: Up to Mozart.* New York, 1985. Pages 1–44. A very reliable overview that avoids controversy and focuses on the essential innovations that define the musical styles of the earliest operas.

Hanning, Barbara Russano. *Of Music's Power: Humanism and the Creation of Opera.* Ann Arbor, Mich., 1980. The best overview of the musical, literary, and aesthetic theories that surrounded the creation of the first operas.

Hill, John Walter. "Oratory Music in Florence, I: *Recitar Cantando,* 1583–1655." *Acta musicologica* 51 (1979): 108–136. Reprinted in *The Garland Library of the History of Western Music.* Edited by Ellen Rosand. Vol. 5, *Baroque Music, I: Seventeenth Century.* New York, 1985. Pages 86–115. Concerns the Compagnia dell'Arcangelo Raffaello detta della Scala, in which the poets and musicians who wrote the first operas transferred the same creative processes to the sphere of religious music drama.

Palisca, Claude V. "The 'Camerata Fiorentina': A Reappraisal." *Studi musicali* 1 (1972): 203–236. Reprinted in *The Garland Library of the History of Western Music.* Edited by Ellen Rosand. Vol. 11, *Opera, I: Up to Mozart.* New York, 1985. Pages 45–79. A masterful summary of the writings of Mei, Galilei, and Bardi brought to bear on early recitative style.

Pirrotta, Nino, and Elena Povoledo. *Music and Theatre from Poliziano to Monteverdi.* Translated by Karen Eales. Cambridge, U.K., 1982. A translation of *Li due Orfei: Da Poliziano a Monteverdi.* Turin, Italy, 1969. A major challenge to the notion that recitative style and the genre of opera were exclusively the products of late-Florentine humanism. Documents earlier manifestations of recitational style and musical drama in various other parts of Europe.

Smither, Howard E. *A History of the Oratorio, I: The Oratorio in the Baroque Era: Italy, Vienna, Paris.* Chapel Hill, N.C., 1977. The early chapters fill in the background to Cavalieri's *Rappresentatione di anima e di corpo* (1600) and the early Roman sacred dialogues and oratorios.

JOHN WALTER HILL

MUSIC IN ENGLAND. As early as 1516, Thomas More's *Utopia* articulated the humanistic ideal that music should express textual meaning and work upon hearers' minds, but Renaissance musical aesthetics were generally taken up considerably later and less wholeheartedly in England than on the Continent. John Dunstaple (c. 1390–1453) and other English composers of the early fifteenth century such as Leonel Power (c. 1370/1385–1445) have been credited since their own time with influencing the beginnings of Renaissance musical style in continental music, particularly with regard to the use of "sweet" harmonies, rich in thirds and sixths. They had also provided influential models for paraphrasing a preexistent cantus firmus melody and for settings of the "cyclic" Mass Ordinary based on a borrowed cantus firmus returning in each movement. (The Catholic Mass is divided into the Ordinary, which is the unchanging liturgical texts of the mass, and the Proper, which consists of prayers and the readings from the Old and New Testaments, which change daily in order to emphasize different events and themes in the life of Christ.) But after the mid-fifteenth century English music betrays little influence of the musical Renaissance it had helped to provoke across the Channel. The theorist and composer Johannes Tinctoris's oft-quoted remark in his treatise

Proportionale musices (1473–1474) that the English "are still using one and the same manner of composition (which is the mark of lamentably deficient invention)" might have been echoed by other continentals until well into the sixteenth century. Indeed, Frank Ll. Harrison's *Music in Medieval Britain* suggests that an essentially medieval attitude toward music continued in England until as late as the 1550s.

Sacred Music. A "medieval" outlook was most apparent in English sacred music, which was particularly slow to reflect the humanistic attitudes toward music developing on the continent. Until the English reformation, Latin church music, cultivated in the Chapel Royal, cathedrals, and various collegiate chapels, remained intimately linked to the liturgy. Because early-sixteenth-century English sacred music was still conceived to adorn specific rites of the Mass and office, there was no equivalent to the freer Latin "motet" widely cultivated across the Channel. Although lengthy festal Masses, based on a cantus firmus borrowed from plainchants of the Sarum rite (the version of the Roman Liturgy peculiar to Britain), and usually lacking a polyphonic Kyrie (the first prayer of the Ordinary of the Mass) became less common after the early decades of the sixteenth century, large-scale votive antiphons (songs praising Mary, independent of any psalm) and Magnificat settings (the Magnificat is Mary's canticle, sung at Vespers; the text is Luke 1:46–55) were composed until the eve of the English Reformation. Verbal texts could be all but lost in the expansive, overlapping, lavishly ornate, highly melismatic, and largely non-imitative contrapuntal lines of this style.

Around the 1520s John Taverner and his contemporaries introduced Renaissance musical elements such as sequence (melodic figure repeated on successive scale steps), various sorts of imitation, ostinato (a repeated melodic figure), and antiphonal textures, chiefly in smaller forms; this provided a greater sense of order and clarity in the texture, which, however, retained its distinctively florid, decorative character until the Reformation. This complex, exuberant style also enjoyed an intense but brief final flowering, particularly in the responds of Thomas Tallis and John Shepherd (Sheppard), during the Catholic restoration of Mary Tudor's reign (1553–1558).

Throughout Henry VIII's reign (1509–1547), Latin daily services had remained the rule in English churches, with increasing emphasis on intelligibility and some use of English, most notably in the English litany (a set of petitions by the priest, briefly answered by the congregation), published in 1544, for use in times of special need. The Chantries Acts of 1545 and 1547 had disbanded many significant choral institutions, and church organs and Latin service books were common objects of iconoclasm during Edward VI's reign (1547–1553). The First Act of Uniformity of January 1549, requiring the replacement of Latin service books with the new Book of Common Prayer in English for uniform use throughout the realm, was supplanted in 1552 by the more severe Second Prayer Book, which drastically trimmed many perceived remnants of the Roman rite that had survived the previous act. Music had a place in the new English rite, even if it was not particularly encouraged during Edward's reign.

If Edward VI had reigned longer there might never have been the "golden age of English church music" of the later sixteenth century. After the temporary restoration of Catholicism during Mary Tudor's reign, Elizabeth I followed more liberal policies regarding church music than her younger brother had. The Elizabethan Act of Uniformity of 1559 re-established the prayer book of 1552, while allowing for less austere artistic adornments of the liturgy than the reforms of 1552 had originally intended. Nevertheless, the use of music was extensively cut back, compared to pre-Reformation times. Despite vehement opposition from Protestant reformers, Elizabeth permitted the use of elaborate anthems and services, provided that musical complications did not obscure the text.

It was only during the reign of Elizabeth I (1558–1603), who did not wholly forbid the use of Latin in Anglican services, that English Latin sacred music began more closely to resemble its continental equivalent. William Byrd (1540–1623) proved most adept at imitating stylistic features of the continental Renaissance motet, such as systematic imitation, clear, flexible declamation of the text, and expressive musical rhetoric to convey textual meaning. It was in fact in his Latin sacred music, rather than his secular music, that Byrd most enthusiastically espoused late Renaissance ideals of textual expressivity.

The intended use of Byrd's Latin *Cantiones sacrae* (Sacred songs), published in 1589 and 1591, remains somewhat ambiguous. But many of their texts speak to the plight of England's Catholic recusants. Byrd's last Latin collections, settings of the Mass Ordinary in three, four, and five voices (1592–1595), and *Gradualia* (1605 and 1607) were clearly intended for use in Catholic services, quite systematically providing music for Propers of the Catholic church year, as well as for the standard Ordinary texts.

Music in England. A page with the opening of "O Mistress Mine" from the Fitzwilliam Virginal Book, a collection of keyboard works copied in the early seventeenth century. FITZWILLIAM MUSEUM, UNIVERSITY OF CAMBRIDGE, CAMBRIDGE, ENGLAND

Compared to the soaring brilliance of pre-Reformation Latin polyphony and the flexible, highly expressive style of Byrd's Elizabethan Latin motets, much sacred music in English, for the new Anglican rite, seems rather straightforward. The Renaissance ideal of textual comprehensibility in church music, articulated in the 1540s by Archbishop Thomas Cranmer's dictum, "for every syllable one note," was espoused emphatically during Edward VI's reign in the determinedly simple, syllabic, largely chordal style of many anthems, much service music, and metrical psalms set to music. The Elizabethan Anglican repertory, which underwent a marked expansion during the early years of Elizabeth's reign, is characterized by syllabic text setting, relieved by occasional, modest melismas (several notes on one syllable), some text repetition, the free mixture of imitation and chordal textures, and a generally reserved attitude toward wordpainting, that is, making the music literally express the words. A substantial body of more demonstrative, expressive settings of English sacred texts, which usually survive only in sources of secular origin, was intended for domestic performance as a kind of "grave chamber music," not for use in church, though many of these "anthems" are commonly heard in churches today.

While "full" anthems for the choir are roughly comparable in musical style to continental motets, there was no equivalent across the Channel to the English verse anthem. The verse anthem was first extensively cultivated during Elizabeth's reign, most notably by Byrd. This new idiom, in which one or more vocal soloists and instrumental accompaniment alternate with sections for chorus, offered a notable means of meeting ideals of textual intelligibility, since the vocal soloists could present their words comparatively unobscured.

The impressive corpus of Elizabethan church music must have been chiefly a product of Elizabeth's own Chapel Royal and other churches within the courtly sphere: Westminster Abbey, St. Paul's Cathedral, and St. George's Chapel, Windsor. The Chapel Royal, a uniquely national institution, drawing upon the best men's and boys' voices of the realm, but no foreigners, remained surprisingly stable in its membership, despite the quick succession of doctrinal and liturgical changes between 1547 and 1558. In Elizabeth's time its membership included thirty-two gentlemen of the chapel and twelve boys, though only half the men were required to attend the less important services. The queen's chapel was almost certainly the only choir capable of performing elaborate Elizabethan services such as Byrd's great service in ten vocal parts or William Mundy's first service "in medio chori" in as many as nine parts. Many anthems, such as Byrd's "O Lord Make Thy Servant Elizabeth our Queen," "Behold O God the Sad and Heavy Case," and "Thou God That Guid'st," all incorporating petitions for Elizabeth, must have resulted directly from the needs of the Chapel Royal.

Outside the sphere of the court, church music appears to have been rather drab, and performance standards lax. Provincial bishops were allowed to reform and simplify the music and ritual of their cathedrals and dioceses, and the same was true of London parish churches, where organs were often allowed to fall into disrepair and funds originally intended for music were diverted to other uses. In these churches elaborate music was eclipsed by the congregational singing of metrical psalms, which achieved great popularity in the second half of the sixteenth century. Thomas Sternhold and John Hopkins's metrical translations of the psalms, first published with music in Geneva in 1556 and in London in 1562, were reprinted literally hundreds of times and constituted the only successful music publishing in England before the late 1580s.

Secular Vocal Music. Secular vocal music in England began to betray some evidence of Renaissance aesthetic ideals in the early sixteenth century, in the carols and part-songs for courtly and domestic entertainments, including numerous examples by Henry VIII in "Henry VIII's Songbook." Some pieces reflect the imitative textures of early-sixteenth-century French chansons, which occasionally appear beside them in the sources or provide models for English reworkings of French originals. Others employ a simpler, more chordal style, projecting the texture comparatively clearly. But many features, forms, and styles that appeared in continental secular music of the early 1500s only found their way across the Channel around mid-century or later.

Some of the best composers, such as Byrd and Orlando Gibbons (1583–1625), cultivated a contrapuntal style of vocal part-song or songs for solo voice accompanied by a consort of viols. Both consort song and part-song shared a preference for non-Italianate, sober, frequently sentennous texts. Their rather undemonstrative, polyphonically complex musical settings tend to reflect textual shape, declamation, and general mood, rather than the more diverse textures and literal-minded textual depiction of the Italian madrigal. Two songs by Byrd ("Constant Penelope" and "Come to Me, Grief, Forever") notably reflect humanistic concerns in their experimentation with quantitative meters on classical models, after the manner of Jean de Baïf's humanistic *musique mesurée*. Several surviving consort songs are associated with spoken drama, particularly choirboy plays, in which the boy actors lament impending death or that of a beloved—hence, the name "death songs." The genre also remained a favorite for elegies, most notably Byrd's lament on the death of Thomas Tallis (c. 1505–1585), "Ye Sacred Muses" (1585).

When Byrd published his songs in 1588 and 1589, their identity as accompanied solo songs was disguised by the addition of words to the original accompanying instrumental parts, thereby enhancing their resemblance to the madrigal, then coming into fashion in England. Several of Gibbons's songs were treated similarly in his *First Set of Madrigals and Motets* of 1612. "Madrigal" publications of lesser composers such as Richard Alison (fl. 1592–1606), Richard Carlton (c. 1558–1638?), and John Mundy (c. 1555–1630) likewise betray the continued influence of the more restrained, polyphonic song tradition rather than the madrigal.

The Italian madrigal vogue only caught on in England in the 1570s and 1580s, marked most notably by the publication of Nicholas Yonge's *Musica Transalpina* (1588) and Thomas Watson's *Italian Madrigals Englished* (1590), offering selections of Italian madrigals in translation, either relatively literal or freely rewritten. Both collections prominently feature the works of the Italian composer Luca Marenzio (c. 1553–1599), and tend toward serious rather than light styles, also abjuring the bolder and more dramatic Italian experiments in text setting. Such reticence proved characteristic of English composers' own madrigals in the spate of publications over the next two decades.

Thomas Morley (c. 1557–1602), whose work as a madrigalist dominates the early 1590s, is credited with adopting and adapting the Italian madrigal style to English taste. Morley's five published collections favored the canzonet (a lighter, less overtly expressive song) and ballet, with frivolous texts whose attractiveness derives largely from their musical setting. For Morley the working out and elaboration of the music, particularly in the expanded sections to the words "fa-la-la," clearly eclipses the text. It is the music that matters, and Morley is loath to disrupt its unfolding in order to reflect moment-to-moment changes in the words. Morley's generally light naturalization of the Italian model, stressing musical over textual values, became the model for most subsequent English madrigalists.

Of the Englishmen who most aspired toward the Italian model in their choice of serious texts, more elevated musical style, and greater use of five- and six-part textures—John Wilbye, Thomas Weelkes, George Kirbye, and John Ward—Wilbye and Weelkes were, by common consent, the most accomplished. Wilbye, whose two madrigal collections appeared in 1598 and 1609, is the more elegant, restrained, and refined composer of the two, leaving bolder, more dramatic or disruptive gestures to Weelkes, who published madrigals and ballets in 1597, 1598, 1600, and 1608. Of all the English madrigalists, Weelkes most readily resorts to arresting, boldly chromatic harmony, much more familiar in the Italian models of Carlo Gesualdo (c. 1516–1613) and Claudio Monteverdi (1567–1643).

The air (or ayre), for solo voice accompanied generally by the lute, began to appear in print in 1597 with John Dowland's unusually popular *First Booke of Songes or Ayres*. Some two dozen collections of airs were published over the next twenty-five years. They incorporate a significant body of lyric verse, of comparatively greater literary interest than that of the English madrigal, and including texts by some of the better poets of the age, such as John Donne, Philip Sidney, and Ben Jonson. The air's most obvious antecedents were the consort song, whose expansiveness and contrapuntal complexity are reflected especially in Dowland's airs, and the native part-song, most akin to the simpler textures of the accompanied tunes in the frequently strophic, light airs of Thomas Campion (1567–1620). It is in the air repertory that late-Renaissance Italian humanistic experiments with monody came to be reflected in England after the turn of the century, most notably in Dowland's expansive, declamatory songs such as "Sorrow Stay" and "In Darkness Let Me Dwell."

Ensemble Music. The development of an idiomatic instrumental repertory represented another significant aspect of Renaissance music in England. The English monarchs' secular corps of musicians underwent a notable expansion during the sixteenth century, from about twenty instrumentalists at the end of Henry VII's reign to almost sixty during Henry VIII's. The Queen's Music under Elizabeth I settled at about thirty members. By contrast with the Chapel Royal, the equivalent secular body was decidedly international in character, heavily recruited from abroad and including a notable number of Jewish musical families, such as the Bassano, Lupo, and Galliardello, who escaped more intense persecution across the Channel.

City "waits," notably the company of London Waits, who served both as public watchmen and as public musicians, were the other permanent secular musical institutions of the sixteenth century. The musical responsibilities of the London Waits, the diversity of their ensemble, and the complexity of their music greatly expanded during this period, as is evident from Morley's *First Book of Consort Lessons* (1599), dedicated to the London Waits. Beginning in 1571 the London Waits inaugurated the first regular public concerts in England, performed every Sunday atop the Royal Exchange.

Until near the end of the sixteenth century these musical companies must have been the primary performers of the rapidly expanding Elizabethan repertory for instrumental ensemble. A sizable body of consort music had developed by the early years of Elizabeth's reign, in the form of dance music, contrapuntal fantasias (free works, in no fixed form), and the many polyphonic elaborations on the cantus firmus *In Nomine,* whose original impetus had been Taverner's polyphonic setting of the words "*in nomine Domini*" from the "Benedictus" of his *Missa Gloria Tibi Trinitas*. Around mid-century much of this music may actually have been sung to solmization syllables ("ut-re-mi-fa," etc.) rather than played, though in later decades the growing repertory became the province of the consort of viols or the distinctive, characteristically English mixed consort, admired and emulated on the Continent, consisting of lute, the plucked, wire-strung pandora and cittern, bass viol, treble viol (or violin), and flute (or recorder). Morley's highly successful *First Book of Consort Lessons* was intended for this type of ensemble.

Lute and Keyboard Music. More distinctive styles of lute and keyboard music also developed in England during the sixteenth century. A highly idiomatic style based on the intense working out of patterned figuration was already apparent in the keyboard works of John Redford (d. 1547), John Blitheman (c. 1525–1591), and Tallis, all still largely linked to the organ and liturgical repertory. During Elizabeth's reign and its immediate aftermath, keyboard music enjoyed a remarkable expansion at the hands of Byrd, John Bull, Gibbons, and a number of lesser figures, cultivating a wide variety of genres, ranging from highly contrapuntal fantasias and cantus firmus settings, to stylized dance movements, most commonly pavane-galliard pairs (joining a solemn, slow dance with a lively, quick one), and sets of variations on popular tunes or set bass or harmonic patterns. Hundreds of such works survive in manuscripts such as the Fitzwilliam Virginal Book and My Lady Nevell's Book, and in the small, published collection, *Parthenia* (1612). The idiomatic, highly varied figurations systematically worked out in these works provided an important model for continental keyboard composers such as Jan Sweelinck (1562–1621).

Music Printing. Music printing caught on very slowly in England, and as an industry pales by comparison with continental equivalents. Apart from published settings of metrical psalms, less than a half dozen musical publications appeared before Tallis and Byrd's *Cantiones sacrae* (1575), which heralded Elizabeth I's awarding them a monopoly on the printing of music and music paper. The monopoly proved financially unsuccessful because of lack of interest on the part of the public and their printer, the Huguenot émigré Thomas Vautrollier. A steady stream of music publications only began to appear in 1588, after Vautrollier's death, and maintained some impetus through the first decade of the seventeenth century, when it went into decline. The total output of English musical presses remained very small by comparison with continental music printing.

See also biographies of figures mentioned in this entry.

BIBLIOGRAPHY

Primary Works

Brett, Philip, ed. *The Byrd Edition.* 17 vols. London, 1976–. Replaces *The Collected Vocal Works of William Byrd.* Edited by Edmund H. Fellowes. London, 1937–.

Buck, Percy, Alexander Ramsbotham et al., eds. *Tudor Church Music.* 10 vols. Oxford, 1922–1929. Includes English and Latin sacred music of Byrd, Gibbons, Tallis, Taverner, Tomkins, White, et al.

Early English Church Music. London, 1963–. The ongoing series includes English and Latin sacred music of the most significant sixteenth-century English composers besides William Byrd.

Fellowes, Edmund H., ed. *The English Lute-Songs,* 1st ser. (17 vols.) and 2d ser. (21 vols.). Revised by Thurston Dart et al. London, 1959–. A revision and expansion of Fellowes's earlier *The English School of Lutenist Songwriters.*

Fellowes, Edmund H., ed. *The English Madrigalists.* Revised by Thurston Dart et al. 37 vols. London, 1956–. A revision and expansion of the earlier *The English Madrigal School,* including virtually the entire repertory.

Musica Britannica. London, 1951–. The ongoing national series incorporates much English Renaissance music, particularly for instrumental ensemble and solo keyboard.

Secondary Works

Doughtie, Edward. *English Renaissance Song.* Boston, 1986.

Harrison, Frank L1. *Music in Medieval Britain.* London, 1958.

Kerman, Joseph. *The Elizabethan Madrigal.* New York, 1962.

Krummel, Donald. *English Music Printing, 1553–1700*. London, 1975.

Le Huray, Peter. *Music and the Reformation in England*. London, 1967.

Monson, Craig. "Elizabethan London." In *The Renaissance*. Edited by Iain Fenlon. London, 1989. Pages 304–340.

Stevens, John. *Music and Poetry in the Early Tudor Court*. London, 1961.

Turbet, Richard. *Tudor Music: A Research and Information Guide*. New York, 1994.

CRAIG A. MONSON

MUSIC IN FRANCE. At the beginning of the fifteenth century, the kingdom of France and its dependencies were embroiled in the Hundred Years' War with England, and in an escalating civil war with the duchy of Burgundy. At the same time, the century-long reign of French popes at Avignon was coming to an end. Each of these political entities maintained an active musical life at their courts and chapels, bringing to a brilliant close the late Gothic "international" style descended from the *ars nova* of the early fourteenth century.

The Fifteenth Century (c. 1425–1515).

In the 1420s and 1430s a new musical style emerged, particularly in Burgundy, which had absorbed the Low Countries, including Flanders, Hainaut, and Brabant, into its domain and was allied militarily with England. Under dukes Philip the Good and Charles the Bold, cousins and nominal vassals of the French king, Burgundy assimilated English and Flemish musical practices into its predominantly French musical culture, resulting in a new "international" style that ultimately spread to every corner of Europe. After the death of Charles the Bold and reabsorption of Burgundy by the victorious French state in 1477, the politically orphaned Low Countries continued to maintain their Burgundian traditions and Franco-Flemish musical culture into the next century as part of the vast Habsburg empire of Maximilian I, Charles V, and Philip II.

Features of the new style included harmonically organized polyphony based on triadic consonance varied by controlled dissonance, and motivic interplay and imitation, combined with projection of the text in vocal music. The first important masters of this style were Guillaume Dufay (c. 1400–1474) and Gilles Binchois (c. 1400–1460), both born in the border area between France and Flanders and therefore generally identified as "Franco-Flemish." By the beginning of the sixteenth century this style had evolved into one that modern scholarship identifies with the Renaissance. The pitch range of polyphonic music had expanded from two and a half to four octaves, harmony had become governed by the bass, and rhythms and melodic shapes began to reflect the requirements of humanistic rhetorical expression.

The new style did not appear suddenly. Emerging from the layered polyphony, complex rhythms, and pointed dissonance favored both in Paris and at the papal court at Avignon at the turn of the fifteenth century, it absorbed the consonant harmonies brought to France by the English invaders and the flowing vocal idiom of fourteenth-century Italian music. Later in the century the Flemish theorist Johannes Tinctoris (c. 1436–1511) recognized the novelty and importance of the new style, stating that "a new art . . . whose fount and origin is held to be among the English" had come into being about forty years before his time (*Proportionale musices;* c. 1473–1474). Naming as its most prominent practitioners Dufay and Binchois, Tinctoris went on to cite more nearly contemporary representatives, such as Johannes Ockeghem (c. 1410–1497), Antoine Busnois (c. 1430–1492), and Johannes Regis (c. 1430–c. 1485). The style matured in the generation after Tinctoris, in the work of such composers as Josquin des Prez (c. 1450–1521), Loyset Compère (c. 1445–1518), Jean Mouton (c. 1459–1522), Antoine Brumel (c. 1460–c. 1520), and Antoine de Févin (c. 1470–c. 1512), most of whom can be characterized as Franco-Flemish and all of whom spent a significant part of their careers in France.

The musical forms favored by the generations of Dufay and Ockeghem included medieval survivals such as the *formes fixes* of courtly French lyric poetry (*rondeau, ballade, virelai*) and the Latin "isorhythmic" motet based on a rigorously repeated rhythmic pattern and associated with ecclesiastical and civic ceremony. At the same time, these medieval forms underwent fundamental transformation or gave way to new ones—strophic and freely composed chansons and motets, and the cyclic Mass. In addition, four rather than three polyphonic voices became the norm in sacred music around 1450, and in secular music around 1490. The cyclic Mass, made up of the five movements constituting the Ordinary (Kyrie, Gloria, Credo, Sanctus, Agnus), was based on English models dating from around 1430 and became the most important large musical form of the Renaissance after 1450. This cycle is unified by having all movements incorporate a single borrowed or original melody, sacred or secular, and common structural devices. The largest family of such Masses is that based on the battle song "L'homme armé" (The armed man), to which over thirty composers from Dufay, Busnois, and Ockeghem to Morales and

Palestrina contributed. The tradition of these Masses may have originated in the ceremonies of the chivalric Order of the Golden Fleece founded by Philip the Good in 1429 to promote a crusade against the Turks. Failing in that mission, the order nevertheless succeeded in stimulating artistic and musical, not to mention gastronomic, display at the Burgundian Court. Typical of court festivities was the Feast of the Oath of the Pheasant, which was held at Lille in 1454 for the order, combining a banquet with *tableaux vivants* and music by Philip's court composer Binchois.

Composers of the Josquin generation made extensive use of thematic imitation, which quickly became pervasive in all forms of music. These new musical forms and techniques, introduced by Franco-Netherlanders in France, the Low Countries, and at Italian courts, remained the dominant features of music in France and throughout Europe in the sixteenth century.

Institutions that supported music in the fifteenth and sixteenth centuries included not only the French royal court but other noble courts, some of which, notably those of Burgundy, Anjou, and Savoy, rivaled the royal court in musical activity and artistic splendor, employing skilled chapel singers and chamber musicians. Additionally, many ecclesiastical centers had professional choirs and choir schools. These included such cathedrals as Paris, Cambrai, Chartres, Bourges, and Amiens, and also collegiate churches and abbeys, the most important of which was the royal abbey of Saint Martin at Tours, where Ockeghem held the post of treasurer. Ockeghem may have been a teacher at Tours of Antoine Busnois (c. 1430–1492), who honored Ockeham in his motet "In hydraulis" and served in the Burgundian chapel of Charles the Bold.

At a lower level, town musicians and itinerant players (*menestriers*) were available for civic ceremonies, dances, and other festivities. These instrumentalists had been organized in guilds or confraternities under royal charter since the fourteenth century. The chapel singers and cathedral choirs were usually made up of clerics who, in addition to receiving salaries, held lucrative benefices, such as canonries, at the pleasure of the local bishop or prince, approved by the pope. In the fifteenth century musicians received remuneration as clerics, administrators, scribes, singers, organists, and players of instruments, but at the beginning of the sixteenth century their employers began to recognize the profession of the composer, and some musicians were rewarded for performing that function.

After the collapse of the Burgundian state, the French royal court at Paris became the unrivalled center of French culture. Under Charles VIII, Louis XII, and Francis I, the most important French and Franco-Flemish musicians, among them Ockeghem, Josquin, Compère, Févin, and Mouton, served at court and at the Sainte-Chapelle, which took pride of place as the chief royal musical institution.

The Sixteenth Century (c. 1515–c. 1615). A distinctively French style, differing from the international Franco-Flemish style that had dominated the fifteenth century, emerged in the early sixteenth century, especially in the field of secular music. Its use was centered at the court of Francis I in Paris, and it reflected the extrovert character of the monarch and the culture that he encouraged, strongly influenced by the Italian Renaissance. The dissemination of this style was facilitated by the rapid development of music printing, notably in the editions of the Parisian publisher Pierre Attaingnant (c. 1494–1552). Active as early as 1514, Attaingnant began his independent publishing career in 1528 with a volume entitled *Chansons nouvelles* (New songs), featuring music by Claudin de Sermisy (c. 1490–1562). Attaingnant's process involved single-impression printing from movable type, a much cheaper method than those employed in Italian music printing at the time. Attaingnant's method came to dominate music printing for the rest of the sixteenth century. Attaingnant obtained the title "imprimeur et libraire du Roy" (printer and bookseller of the king) in 1537, and continued to publish sacred music and music for lute, keyboard, and instrumental ensemble, as well as secular chansons, until his death. His widow continued these publications until 1557, by which time his successors Nicolas Du Cheminy (c. 1515–1576) and the firm of Adrian Le Roy (c. 1520–1598) and Robert Ballard (c. 1525–1588) had entered the field.

Claudin de Sermisy was the archrepresentative of the style of the so-called Parisian chanson: light in spirit, simple in form and character, elegantly blending courtly and popular elements in a strongly harmonic idiom. Sermisy served at the courts of Louis XII, Francis I, and Henry II in their private chapels and at the Sainte-Chapelle from 1508 until his death in 1562. In addition to chansons, he composed traditional masses and motets. Another chanson composer favored by Attaingnant was Clément Janequin (c. 1485–1558), active at Bordeaux and Angers but who did not settle in Paris until 1549, entering the chapel of Henry II after 1550. Although he composed mainly light chansons similar to Claudin's, he is identified more with large-scale programmatic chansons characterized by imitations of natural and environmental sounds such as birdsongs and battle (*La bataille,* celebrating the French victory at Marignano in 1515). Extending the stylistic range of the chanson around mid-century and reflecting the influence of the Italian madrigal was Pierre Certon (c. 1510–1572), choirmaster at the Sainte-Chapelle and *compositeur* (composer) in the royal chapel of Charles IX.

Paris was not the only musical center, however. Many cities, courts, and ecclesiastical institutions continued to support music and musical publication. In 1528 in Lyon, Estienne Gueynard (d. 1529) published a book containing Mass Propers and motets by a transplanted Florentine, Francesco de Layolle (1492–c. 1540), and at Avignon in 1532–1533 Jean de Channey (c. 1480–c. 1540) published three volumes of music by Elzéar Genet of Carpentras (c. 1470–1548). It was also in Lyon that Attaingnant's principal rival, Jacques Moderne (c. 1495–c. 1561), a printer of Slovenian origin who settled in Lyon in 1523, began to produce music books starting in 1532. Moderne hired Layolle as an editor and followed Gueynard's publications with his own volumes of Layolle's masses and motets. In 1538 Moderne initiated a series of eleven volumes entitled *Le parangon des chansons* (The paragon of chansons) containing a broad representation of Franco-Flemish and French chansons, while continuing his publication of sacred music, instrumental works, and treatises, as well as secular songs, until 1560. In many ways his output was similar to that of Attaingnant, but it was broader in its representation of non-Parisian music, including Italian madrigals.

After the middle of the century new ideas entered the mainstream of French music. One of these was *vers mesurés à l'antique* (measured verse in the ancient manner) based on the quantitative meters of classical poetry, a product of the Académie de poésie et de musique (Academy of poetry and music) founded in 1571 by the humanist poet Jean-Antoine de Baïf (1532–1589) and the musician Joachim Thibault de Courville (c. 1530–1581). Courville and after him Claude Le Jeune (c. 1530–1600) and Jacques Mauduit (1557–1627) set Baïf's poetry to music utilizing two durations, one twice the length of the other. Despite the rigidity of this system, composers of the Académie successfully adopted it for both lyric poetry and psalm translations, and it had a lasting effect on the rhythms of the *airs de cour* in the late-

sixteenth century and the monodic *récits* of the seventeenth.

A second influence was that of the Italian madrigal, which introduced richer textures, chromaticism, and a deeper expressiveness into the idiom of the chanson. The most influential practitioner of this new style of chanson was the Franco-Flemish composer Orlando di Lasso (Roland de Lassus; 1532–1594), who lived in Italy for much of his early life and spent his later career in Germany. Although he was only tangentially associated with France, his chansons were well known to French musicians and profoundly influenced them. Among the French composers who followed a path similar to Lassus's was Guillaume Costeley (c. 1531–1606), a member of Baïf's Académie and composer to Charles IX. He is credited with being the first composer of *airs* (he called them *chansons en façon d'airs*).

The Reformation had a profound influence in France, as in other countries of northern and central Europe. Its French standard-bearer was John Calvin (1509–1564), whose radical rejection of the doctrines of the Roman church led to his exile in Basel, where he introduced the idea that polyphony, instruments, and formal choral music should be banished from worship, and that only unison congregational singing in the vernacular should be permitted. In 1539 he published a songbook with verse translations of psalms and other texts by Clément Marot (c. 1496–1544) and himself, which he set to hymn tunes used in the Reformed liturgy of Strasbourg. In 1542 he carried this idea further in a new psalm collection published in Geneva, which was now the center of his church. This became the basis of the Huguenot (as his followers in France were called) psalter, which ultimately contained all 150 psalms in translations by Marot and Theodore de Bèze (1519–1605), with melodies composed or arranged by Louis Bourgeois (c. 1510–c. 1561), published in 1562 in Geneva, Paris, Lyon, and elsewhere. Few musical publications of any period had as wide an impact. The Huguenot psalter was adopted, wholly or in part, in Reformed churches in Germany, Holland, England, Scotland, and America over the next century, and remains in wide use today.

Polyphonic settings of the psalm tunes composed by Bourgeois and by such composers as Certon, Le Jeune, and Claude Goudimel (c. 1515–1572) were originally intended to replace popular chansons for domestic and social use. Some of these psalm settings were elaborate and motet-like, but most were in simple, four-part harmony with the psalm tunes unadorned in the middle or top voice. As the century progressed Calvin's stern commands were moderated by some of his followers, and Protestant churches began to replace unison singing with the kind of simple polyphony originally designed for domestic use, a practice that continues to this day.

Fierce attempts to suppress the Huguenots culminated in the St. Bartholomew's Day Massacre (1572) in which thousands of Protestants throughout France, among them the composer Goudimel, were killed by soldiers and the mob. French Protestantism survived, mainly in the southern provinces, although its long-term musical influence was stronger in other countries.

Many threads of French Renaissance culture were brought together in court entertainments, especially the *Balet comique de la Royne,* an elaborate theatrical portrayal of the triumph of reason over magic, presented at the court of Henry III in 1581. Created by the émigré Italian dancing master Balthasar de Beaujoyeulx (Baldassare de Belgioioso; c. 1535–c. 1587) with music by Lambert de Beaulieu and Jacques Salmon and a text by La Chesnaye, the *Balet comique* combined dance, drama, and song around a unified plot, foreshadowing the *ballet de cour* (court ballet) and operatic *tragédie lyrique* (lyric tragedy) of the following century. Its songs with their metrical patterns translated into pointedly irregular musical rhythms reveal the influence of *vers mesurés,* even while anticipating the character of the French baroque *récit.* The *Balet* was the most ambitious theatrical/musical conception of its time, and it brought music in Renaissance France to an appropriate climax.

See also **Dance**; **Music**, *subentries on* **Sacred Vocal Music** *and* **Secular Vocal Music**; **Wars of Religion**; *and biographies of Guillaume Dufay, Josquin des Prez, and Johannes Ockeghem.*

BIBLIOGRAPHY

Primary Works

Arbeau, Thoinot (pseud. for Jean Tabourot). *Orchesography.* Translated by Mary S. Evans, with a new introduction by Julia Sutton. New York, 1967. The most important French dance treatise of the sixteenth century, originally published in 1588, with descriptions and illustrations of the dances, and extensive examples of the music.

"Le Balet Comique" by Balthazar de Beaujoyeulx, 1581. A facsimile edition with an introduction by Margaret M. McGowan. Binghamton, N.Y., 1982. Originally entitled *Balet Comique de la Royne* and published in Paris, this facsimile includes the full text, with the music of many songs and dances, and copious illustrations.

Mersenne, Marin. *The Books on Instruments.* Translated by R. E. Chapman. The Hague, Netherlands, 1957. An English translation of a portion of Mersenne's *Harmonie universelle* (Universal harmony; Paris, 1636), an encyclopedic survey of late-sixteenth- and early-seventeenth-century music.

Secondary Works

Cazeaux, Isabelle. *French Music in the Fifteenth and Sixteenth Centuries.* New York, 1975.

Dobbins, Frank. *Music in Renaissance Lyons.* Oxford, 1992.

Lesure, François. *Musicians and Poets of the French Renaissance.* Translated by Elio Gianturco and Hans Rosenwald. New York, 1955.

Marix, Jeanne. *Histoire de la musique et les musiciens de la cour de Bourgogne sous le règne de Philippe le Bon (1420–1467).* Strasbourg, 1939. Reprint, Geneva, 1972, and Baden-Baden, Germany, 1974. A documentary study.

Wright, Craig. *Music and Ceremony at Notre Dame of Paris, 500–1550.* Cambridge, U.K., 1989. A documentary study.

Yates, Frances A. *The French Academies of the Sixteenth Century.* London, 1947. Reprint, Nendeln, Liechtenstein, 1973; London, 1988. Study of humanist academies and their influence on literature and music.

Note: A comprehensive bibliography can be found in *The New Grove Dictionary of Music and Musicians.* Edited by Stanley Sadie. London, 1980. See S. Boorman and F. Dobbins, "France: Bibliography of Music to 1600, B: 1450–1600," vol. 6, pp. 766–780.

MARTIN PICKER

MUSIC IN ITALY. From the early fifteenth century to the mid-sixteenth, virtually every important composer of religious (liturgical and nonliturgical) and secular vocal "art music" in Italy came from the north (Burgundy, Netherlands, Flanders, and France) or west (Spain) at the behest of the courts and chapels of Italian rulers and the pope in Rome. They brought with them the so-called international style, a hybrid of the late medieval continental Gothic style with a new sense of triadic consonance and control of dissonance between parts. As the Renaissance continued, the number of voice parts increased to five; the individual parts, initially rather angular and independent of one another, became less frenetic and more similar between parts; and imitation between parts became a stylistic constant, often in contrast with a chordal (homorhythmic) texture in which texts were easier to hear. By the end of the sixteenth century, this balance between linear and vertical elements had produced melodic, harmonic, contrapuntal, and cadential patterns that anticipated tonal practices of the next three centuries.

Although the music of Italian fourteenth-century composers (especially Francesco Landini, c. 1325–1397) was comparable in quality to the French *ars nova,* surviving Italian music manuscripts of fifteenth and sixteenth centuries and publications of the sixteenth century demonstrate the monopoly held by non-Italian musicians in Italy, including Guillaume Dufay (c. 1397–1474), Jacob Obrecht

(1450 or 1451–1505), Alexander Agricola (c. 1446–1506), Heinrich Isaac (c. 1450–1517), Gaspar van Weerbeke (c. 1445–after 1517), Pierre de La Rue (c. 1460–1518), Antoine Brumel (1460–after 1520), Josquin des Prez (c. 1440–1521), Philippe Verdelot (c. 1470/80–before 1552), Cristóbal de Morales (c. 1500–1553), Jachet di Mantua (1483–1559), Adrian Willaert (c. 1490–1562), Cipriano de Rore (1515 or 1516–1565), Jacques Arcadelt (c. 1505–1568), Orlando di Lasso (1532–1594), Giaches de Wert (1535–1596), and Tomás Luis de Victoria (c. 1549–1611).

Native musicians began writing music of comparable quality, however, in the sixteenth century. In secular music, vocal and instrumental genres were dominated by Italian composers by mid-century; by 1600 they had invented a monodic style that would in effect define baroque music. In religious music, Italy provided the backdrop for a battle of musical ideologies between stylistic proscriptions of the Counter-Reformation (represented by Rome) and evolutionary tendencies (represented by Venice) in the years leading up to the seventeenth century. The distribution of music benefited incalculably from the invention of music printing, replacing the laborious task of copying music by hand, beginning in the first decade of the sixteenth century—and nowhere more so than in Italy, where music printing began.

The Fifteenth Century.

The lack of manuscript evidence for music by Italian composers during the fifteenth century is often cited as proof of a dearth of native skill and talent. But other evidence suggests that fifteenth-century Italian musicians performed much northern repertoire in Italy, learned by ear or from the numerous manuscripts of western European polyphony found in Italy. This points to a continuing practice of performing solo song with improvised accompaniment (usually on the lute) ranging from occasional strummed chords to extemporized parts of equal interest to the melody. There is also iconographic and written evidence for Neapolitan villanellas (rustic partsongs) being heard as part of the commedia dell'arte.

The early fifteenth century saw a reaction to Petrarchan and other poetic vernacular models of the previous century, inspiring a return to stylized Latinate forms. But this trend was later reversed, notably through the cultural politics of Lorenzo de' Medici (the Magnificent, 1449–1492), the ruler of Florence. He favored vernacular poetry and wrote in the Tuscan dialect, using the *ballata* (a poem in several verses, each followed by a refrain) and other Petrarchan forms. He also transformed his city's pre-Lenten celebrations from a processional into a more theatrical presentation and encouraged the inclusion of *canti carnascialeschi* (carnival songs) with ribald texts. Three-part writing gave way to four-part; chordal textures were prevalent; the music was performed outdoors with instruments doubling vocal parts. While many of these pieces were destroyed when the Dominican reformer Girolamo Savonarola dominated Florence from 1494 to 1498, some were preserved with new sacred texts as *laudi spirituali* (spiritual praise songs). But the carnival song's point was made: the influence of Italian urban or rural popular music on composed genres.

Secular Vocal Music.

Italian composers continued writing in the lighter manner of the Florentine carnival songs. From the 1470s, these pieces were classed under the general category of *frottola,* a polyphonic song with origins in the practice of reciting poetry to musical accompaniment. The genre encompassed pieces based on fixed poetic forms—including poems by Petrarch (then undergoing a revival)—and the refrain-based villanella and *canzonetta* (canzonet, a genre that survived the Renaissance). In the sixteenth century, the *frottola* inspired the development of other forms, especially strophic dialect songs.

Following Lorenzo de' Medici's example, Isabella d'Este of Mantua (1474–1539) made her court into a salon for native Italian culture. She encouraged poets (notably Pietro Bembo, 1470–1547) and composers to challenge the hegemony of the French chanson. She took the unusual step of employing two Italians as court composers: the lutenist Marchetto Cara (c. 1470–c. 1525) and Bartolomeo Tromboncino (c. 1470–c. 1535), remembered primarily for their *frottole*. Ottaviano dei Petrucci (1466–1539), the first to print music (in Venice in 1501), published eleven books of frottolas (1504–1514) for a new audience of noble dilettantes who performed social music for their own pleasure and to prove their education and courtliness (as described by Baldassare Castiglione in *The Courtier,* 1528).

As in the fifteenth century, sixteenth-century *frottole* had unsentimental strophic texts full of mock-suffering and mock-rapture; the composer's goal was to provide a neutral, even absurd platform, with little or no aural depiction of the emotional, visual, or metaphorical. But four-part pieces become the norm; triads are almost constantly used, and harmonic progressions resemble major and minor tonality (not yet a compositional principle); a reduction of frivolous ornamentation provides a sense of sobriety. Rhythms remain simple, with strong emphasis on primary beats; there is little syncopation and no frenetic subdividing of beats as had prevailed in the fifteenth-century international style.

The *frottola* is often considered to have been a lesser genre, its composers less able than their northern contemporaries. But Florentine and Mantuan patronage of vernacular-based composition symbolized a trend toward an Italian response to the Franco-Flemish chanson, in place by the 1520s: the five-part madrigal, with comparatively short texts, unrestricted choice of poetic scheme—the fourteenth-century madrigal used a specific fixed form—and a through-composed musical design, in which each stanza of a piece could be set to different music. The neo-Petrarchan fixed forms of Bembo were replaced by freer linguistic schemes. Text setting became paramount, as appropriate expression of mood (including shifts) or pictorialism (word-painting), where minute musical gestures (or, somewhat pejoratively, "madrigalisms") represented the physical or metaphorical. The madrigal retained elements of the later frottola: the dominance of the upper voice (the basis of alternative performances for solo voice and accompaniment); direct contrast between chordal and contrapuntal passages; faster tempos; and expressive exploitation of dissonance and chromaticism.

With the exception of Costanza Festa (c. 1480–1545), the first madrigalists, Verdelot and Arcadelt among them, were of northern origin. Attracted to the later *frottola* and its untapped possibilities, these "internationalist" composers applied their technical skill to the new genre's expressivity and created works of greater weight than the *frottola*. Rore was the last important northern madrigalist working in Italy; the native composers Luca Marenzio (1553 or 1554–1599), Carlo Gesualdo (c. 1560–1613), and Claudio Monteverdi (1567–1643) produced the most distinctive late-Renaissance madrigals. Marenzio was the consummate composer of the "sublime" literary madrigal. Gesualdo, who worked outside the mainstream, took Rore's chromatic melodic motion and harmony to hyperexpressive lengths, the musical equivalent of mannerism in painting. Monteverdi redefined the madrigal; his fifth collection (1605) called for *basso continuo,* a form of accompaniment in which harmony was improvised according to a bass line (and other *obbligato* or required parts). He later composed "madrigals" for solo voices, antiphonal choirs, solo instruments, and basso continuo, with homophonic refrains, passages for instruments alone, and ostinato (repeating) bass lines—all part of the new "concerted" baroque style, worlds away

from the sixteenth-century five-part madrigal. The earlier dispute between proponents of the Roman and Venetian religious styles anticipated controversies around 1600 in which the "old style" or "first practice" was defended by Giovanni Maria Artusi (c. 1540–1613) against the harmonic, text-setting, and structural liberties of Monteverdi's "modern style" or "second practice."

Even as the Renaissance madrigal was running its course on the Continent, however, the Italian madrigal was being brought north by composers and publishers; one example was a collection of madrigals in English translation, *Musica transalpina* (1588). In *A Plaine and Easie Introduction to Practicall Musicke* (1597), Thomas Morley (1557 or 1558–1602) recommended the madrigals of Marenzio and others; he also applauded Marenzio's lighter canzonets and the even lighter *balletti,* or "fa la's," of Giovanni Giacomo Gastoldi (active from 1572–c. 1622). England's madrigal school, much like its Renaissance as a whole, outlived Italy's by a half-century or more.

The commedia dell'arte and pastorale (a rustic play with shepherds and other archetypes) also influenced madrigal composition. Orazio Vecchi (c. 1550–c. 1604), Alessandro Striggio the Elder (c. 1540–1592), and Adriano Banchieri (1568–1634) wrote madrigal narratives or descriptive songs. Vecchi, Banchieri, and others wrote narrative sets of madrigals misleadingly designated "madrigal operas" by historians (they were not staged). Vecchi's *L'Amfiparnasso* (1594) is the genre's masterpiece.

Sacred Vocal Music. The Mass Ordinary cycle, liturgical hymns, and the nonliturgical sacred motet were the most respected Renaissance genres. Composers working with similar texts—in the case of the Mass Ordinary, the same text—could take a more generalized approach in terms of expressing its meaning appropriately than with the madrigal. Masses were based on preexisting melodies from Gregorian chant or elsewhere, even entire sections from earlier works; hymns and motets were usually freely composed.

Religious music remained under the sway of Rome, with the papal chapel the exemplar. The international style that had solidified during Dufay's lifetime flourished throughout Italy; des Prez refined the imitative procedures used, and was considered the greatest composer of the time by his contemporaries. Of the Italians who extended this style, Giovanni Pierluigi da Palestrina (1525 or 1526–1594) was the most successful.

But theological politics intruded with the Council of Trent. In its discussions of music (1562–1563), many prelates argued for a return to Gregorian chant or for strictly chordal settings. The more musical constituency crafted an official statement favoring textual clarity (with a consequent reduction in contrapuntal complexity) and the use of only sacred melodies or pieces as models. Palestrina and others who had written madrigals and secularly based religious works strove to redeem themselves by composing spiritual madrigals, settings of religious texts in madrigal style. In order to abide by the council's will, composers designated as "sine nomine" any new masses based on secular music. During the Counter-Reformation, more court chapels were established and castratos were admitted into the papal choir (1562), joining the boy sopranos added earlier in the century.

While religious Rome struggled with the impact of the council, Venice's St. Mark's Basilica, already the center of Venetian worship and pageantry, became the center for new Italian religious music. Its choirmaster, Adrian Willaert, more Italian than the Italians, taught excellent pupils such as Rore (who succeeded Willaert briefly), Costanzo Porta (1528 or 1529–1601), Gioseffo Zarlino (1517–1590; who succeeded Rore), Nicola Vicentino (1511–1572), and Andrea Gabrieli (c. 1510–1586); significantly, all but Rore were Italians. St. Mark's rich acoustics and divided balcony provided a perfect setting for music: the organ playing of virtuosos (Gabrieli and Claudio Merulo, 1533–1604); the introduction of an instrumental ensemble (1568); and the *cori spezzati* (broken choirs), the practice of separating choruses and ensembles to achieve powerful antiphonal textures. This new "concerted style" reached its first fruition in the Venetian sonatas and canzonas of Andrea Gabrieli's nephew Giovanni (between 1554 and 1557–1612). Even as Palestrina's style was being codified as the model for future contrapuntalists, the new style was sweeping the religious a cappella style into obscurity.

Instrumental Music. While keyboard music had appeared in late medieval manuscripts, instrumental idioms had their first flowering in the sixteenth century. The lute—a European outgrowth of the Arab oud—was the primary beneficiary of the Italian instrumental music publishing boom. A lack of surviving fifteenth-century music for lute suggests that performers extemporized on vocal music; but in the following century, works by virtuoso lutenist-composers in tablature form (showing how to play a note, not what note to play) proliferated, beginning with Petrucci's first book of lute music (1507). The three main genres were intabulations (arrangements) of mostly secular vocal pieces, from bare-bones presentations to difficult written-down improvisations; fantasias and ricercars, freely structured pieces, sometimes functioning as toccatas (touch pieces) for warming up; and dance music suites. Lute duets, accompanied songs, and ostinato-based courtly *bassadanzas* were also published. Important Italian lute composers included Francesco Spinacino (fl. 1507), Joan Ambrosio Dalza (fl. 1508), Franciscus Bossinensis (fl. 1509–1511), Francesco Canova da Milano (1497–1543), Vicenzo Capirola (1474–after 1548), Pietro Paolo Borrono (fl. 1531–1549), and Alberto da Ripa (c. 1480–1551).

The printer Andrea Antico (c. 1480–after 1539) first published keyboard intabulations in 1518; the Venetian printer Antonio Gardano (Gardane; c. 1500–1569) followed with several collections. Composers also wrote canzonas, toccatas, and versets. Keyboard ricercars, originally modeled after the motet, paralleled the lute ricercar in their prelude-like mixture of imitation, chordal writing, and toccata-like passages. But the short motives, ornamentation, and syncopation led to the baroque ricercar, predecessor of the fugue. Both St. Mark's and Naples were centers for late-sixteenth-century keyboard music.

Attention to performance practice manifested itself in prefaces to music collections and diminution (ornamentation) manuals. From 1535 on, Italian methods were published for recorder, viol, cornetto, voice, and keyboard. There were also discussions of the composition of free-ranging "viola bastarda" parts, instrumentation, and basso continuo.

Monody and Recitative. In Florence, the lutenist-composer Vincenzo Galilei (c. 1520–1591) began to attack the international style, criticizing its contrapuntal complexity as detrimental to understanding the text and expressing feeling. Like other Renaissance aestheticians (notably Vicentino), he cited Plato's argument that "the *harmonia* and the rhythm must follow the sense of the words" (*Republic* 3). In the Florentine Camerata gatherings presided over by Giovanni de' Bardi (1534–1612) in the 1570s and early 1580s, Galilei and others developed the monodic style: solo voice with basso continuo accompaniment. The melodic qualities of the *frottola* and madrigal were replaced by the equivalent of the pathos and intensity of reciting actors. While solo song had never disappeared during the sixteenth century, the setting of dramatic poetry to music of even greater dramatic intensity was new.

The theatrical implications of the new "representing" (later "reciting") style were tentatively realized in the great 1589 Florentine wedding intermedi, overseen by Bardi. But the history of opera begins with the first examples of *dramma per musica* (that is, opera) by the Camerata veterans Jacopo Peri (1561–1633), Giulio Caccini (c. 1550–1618), and Jacopo Corsi (1560–1604). Without the Mantuan operas of Monteverdi (*Orfeo,* 1607; *Arianna,* 1608, of which one famous lament survives), however, the new genre might not have lasted. The impetus for opera, after shifting from Florence to Mantua, moved on to Rome, then Venice (where the first public opera house opened in 1637) and other cities. As an alternative during Lent, the oratorio emerged as religious music theater minus the staging that would have been unacceptable during that solemn period.

Monody also found outlets in domestic genres, especially at the salons. Another inspiration was the skills of particular singers, notably the "three singing ladies" of Ferrara for whom composers wrote solos, duets, and trios with accompaniment. Caccini published two books of monody (1602, 1614), more songlike than early recitative. Other important monodists were Peri, Luzzasco Luzzaschi (c. 1545–1607), Sigismondo d'India (c. 1580–c. 1629), Steffano Landi (1586 or 1587–1639), and Marco da Gagliano (1582–1643). Composers fully exploited the expressive contrast between tonal simplicity and highly charged chromaticism. Other monodic genres included the strophic aria, sometimes with introductory recitative; solo and duet cantata, alternating recitative-like passages with strophic sections; and the old canzonetta.

Conclusion. It is worth recalling the two great musicians who framed the Renaissance. Dufay and Monteverdi were successful and highly respected in their lifetimes: they composed in every important genre of their day and contributed significantly to stylistic development—Dufay especially in religious music, Monteverdi in the madrigal and opera. But Dufay was a foreigner who brought into fifteenth-century Italy a northern international style, while Monteverdi was a native who laid the foundation for a post-sixteenth-century Italian international style. The music of Renaissance Italians had evolved from a popular culture criticized for limited learned musicianship into a cultivated avant-garde culture that remained in touch with its native *sprezzatura.*

BIBLIOGRAPHY

Primary Works

Strunk, Oliver, ed. *Source Readings in Music History.* Edited by Leo Treitler. Rev. ed. New York, 1998. Translations of selections from writings by Artusi, Pietro Bardi (on his father's Camerata), Castiglione, Galilei, Monte verdi, Palestrina, Zarlino, and other important figures.

Vicentino, Nicola. *Ancient Music Adapted to Modern Practice* (1555). Edited by Claude V. Palisca. Translated by Maria Rika Maniates. New Haven, Conn., 1996.

Zarlino, Gioseffo. *On the Modes: Part Four of* Le istitutioni harmoniche. Edited by Claude V. Palisca. Translated by Vered Cohen. New Haven, Conn., 1983.

Zarlino, Gioseffo. *The Rules of Harmony* (1558, 1573). Part 3: "The Art of Counterpoint." Translated by Guy A. Marco and Claude V. Palisca. New Haven, Conn., 1968.

Secondary Works

Brown, Howard Mayer. *Embellishing Sixteenth-Century Music.* London, 1976. A study of diminution manuals and other sources for instrumental and vocal ornamentation.

Brown, Howard Mayer, ed. *A Florentine Chansonnier from the Time of Lorenzo the Magnificent.* Monuments of Renaissance Music, vol. 7. Chicago, 1983. An introduction to fifteenth-century international secular style in Italy.

Brown, Howard Mayer, and Louise K. Stein. *Music in the Renaissance.* 2d ed. Upper Saddle River, N.J., 1999. A succinct survey of the period by one of its best scholars. Posthumous rev. ed. of 1976 by Brown.

Einstein, Alfred. *The Italian Madrigal.* 3 vols. Princeton, N.J., 1949. An as yet unsurpassed source study and style analysis of the cinquecento genre in the tradition of central European musicology.

Fenlon, Iain, and James Haar. *The Italian Madrigal in the Early Sixteenth Century.* Cambridge, U.K., and New York, 1988. Supplements Einstein on the birth of the genre.

Lockwood, Lewis. *Music in Renaissance Ferrara, 1400–1505: The Creation of a Musical Center in the Fifteenth Century.* Cambridge, Mass., 1984. A model study on northern musicians in Italy.

Lockwood, Lewis. "Renaissance." In *The New Grove Dictionary of Music and Musicians.* Edited by Stanley Sadie. London, 1980. Vol. 15, pages 736–741.

Pirrotta, Nino. "Italy, I." In *The New Grove Dictionary of Music and Musicians.* Edited by Stanley Sadie. London, 1980. Vol. 9, pages 365–368. Followed by an extensive entry by several authors, "Italy: Bibliography of Music to 1600," pages 392–401.

Reese, Gustave. *Music in the Renaissance.* Rev. ed. New York, 1959. The classic musicological study of the period, still unmatched in its breadth.

Strohm, Reinhard. *The Rise of European Music, 1380–1500.* Cambridge, U.K., 1993. A more technical survey of the fifteenth century incorporating the copious amounts of research since Reese's survey.

RICHARD KASSEL

MUSIC IN SPAIN AND PORTUGAL. Music in Spain during the Renaissance can be understood by dividing the period into three segments: the late medieval/transitional period, roughly 1400 to 1469, from which very little music survives; 1469 to about 1530, in which a uniquely Spanish school of composition emerged; and 1530 until around 1620, a period when Spanish and Portuguese composers garnered unprecedented international acclaim. Although this scheme is based primarily on sacred, Latin-texted polyphony or "part" music, vernacular vocal repertories as well as instrumental genres followed a similar course of development. Very little Renaissance music composed prior to 1500 survives in Portugal; therefore, later traditions there will be discussed separately.

Spain, circa 1400–1469. There is little evidence, at least in terms of surviving music, for Renaissance music in Spain before the marriage of Ferdinand and Isabella and the unification of Aragon and Castile in 1469; there is, however, archival evidence about musical life. One witness to this musical culture is Fernand Estevan (fl. 1410), whose treatise *Reglas de canto plano è de contrapunto, è de canto de organo* covers only the rules of chant despite the broader subject matter, including polyphony, indicated in the title. Ecclesiastical documents such as the records or *actas* of cathedrals in various regions of Spain give some information about music. Through such records, it is known that polyphonic music had been written in Toledo—where dozens of polyphonic music manuscripts survive from the mid-sixteenth century—by 1418. Before 1450 several instrumentalists/composers gained some international recognition through periods of employment in Spanish Naples or short trips with patrons to other countries. Juan Cornago, employed in Naples at mid-century, was the only internationally prominent Spanish composer of vocal music during this period.

The New Spanish Nation, 1469–1530. This "middle" period in Spain witnessed the development of a school of composers centered in the courts of Ferdinand and Isabella; the most important composers of sacred music were Francisco de Peñalosa, Juan de Anchieta, and the Portuguese native Pedro de Escobar, each of whom produced masses; motets, which are freely composed devotional works; and settings of liturgical items with a required function in the various daily Divine Office services. Works in honor of Mary and those for Holy Week figure very prominently among the oeuvre of most composers active during this time. Peñalosa is the most important both because of the quality of his extant works and because of his influence on other

Spanish composers; he used musical style and techniques developed by the Franco-Flemish composers, still at this time the leaders in creating Renaissance-style music. When Charles I (later Emperor Charles V) took control of the crown of Spain in 1516, Spanish music began to have a much lower profile at court. Between 1510 and 1530 many regional centers of musical composition began to develop; these included the Cathedral of Seville, home to several internationally recognized composers in the mid- and later sixteenth century.

Although the emergence of sacred Latin music is crucial for the history of music in Spain, the appearance of genres with "Spanish" texts, followed by their rapid growth in popularity, is another fundamental element of musical life during this time. The primary poetic form used in these songs was the *villancico,* which has an opening refrain repeated at the end of each stanza, making it very similar to the French *virelai;* this would become the standard poetico-song form for Spanish composers until the eighteenth century. The most important early composer was Juan del Encina (1468–1529/1530), whose songs feature quick changes of mood and subtle rhythmic effects.

During this time the *vihuela*—a relative of the guitar and one of the most popular instruments in sixteenth-century Spain—is first documented. Although there was a bowed version of the instrument, it is the plucked *vihuela, vihuela de mano,* that was played throughout Spain. Little music specifically for *vihuela* survives from before 1530, but there are references to players at the courts of Ferdinand and Isabella as well as several documents that link the instrument to Moorish culture. Likewise, almost no music survives from this time for the organ and other keyboard instruments, though scholars have found numerous references to performances in religious institutions and noble houses.

Spain's International Renaissance, 1530–1620. Although Peñalosa and several other composers from Spain had served the papal choir in Rome, it was Cristóbal de Morales (ca. 1500–1553), with his ten years of work there (1535–1545) and his internationally acclaimed publications, who firmly established Spanish music on a par with that of other nations. Morales, a Sevillian, worked in Ávila and Plasencia before going to Rome, and after his return, in several Spanish cities, including Toledo. His music displays consummate technique, incorporating devices of counterpoint and skill developed by the international schools while expressing the meaning of text. He displays his awareness of Spanish traditions with such works as his Requiems and Office for the Dead, settings that follow a uniquely Spanish approach. Morales's masses, twenty-two in all, Magnificats, Lamentations of Jeremiah, and more than eighty motets include some of the most widely disseminated works created in Spain during the Renaissance.

Francisco Guerrero (1528–1599), Morales's student for a brief time, continued this high level of achievement. In addition to his sacred Latin works, Guerrero wrote Spanish-texted *villancicos* and several lighter genres. His Latin works display the consummate technique found in those of Morales but also a use of harmonic expressive devices that foreshadow techniques of baroque music after 1600. Guerrero composed more than 150 motets, texts that could be used in a number of different contexts—added to a mass, devotional service, funeral, and so on. His approach in these works displays a heightened awareness of the texts with contrasts of harmony, texture, voicing, and melodic contour that emphasize each new phrase of text. Works by Morales and Guerrero were performed throughout Spanish America as well as in Spain.

The third in this triumvirate of great Spanish Renaissance composers is Tomás Luis de Victoria (c. 1548–1611), a native of Ávila who worked at several religious institutions in Rome from 1565; in 1587 he returned to Spain to serve the dowager Empress Maria, who then lived in retirement in a convent in Madrid. Victoria seems to have composed only works with Latin texts; he also created fewer pieces than did the two earlier Spanish composers, and only a fraction of those composed by Giovanni da Palestrina, the leading Roman composer, to whose works Victoria's music is often compared. In addition to masses, Victoria composed motets, Magnificats, hymns, music for Holy Week, and Marian items—principally the Salve Regina, for which he wrote four settings. Victoria created some of the most emotionally intense works of the late Renaissance, a fact obvious from his requiems and items for the Office for the Dead, his most popular works today.

A number of composers, including Juan Vásquez, Juan Navarro, Rodrigo de Ceballos, Alonso Lobo, Sebastián de Vivanco, and Juan Esquivel Barahona—all of whom were active in the mid- and later sixteenth century, and such later composers as Pedro Ruimonte—wrote works with many of the same techniques and similar expressive language as the three great composers. Perhaps no other country

during this time had so many truly fine composers of sacred music than did Spain.

Instrumental music. The *vihuela,* as mentioned above, emerged as the principal lute-family instrument in late-fifteenth-century Spain. The traditions and compositional practices associated with the *vihuela* are much better known between 1536 and 1576, during which period composer/arrangers Luis Milán, Luis de Narváez, Enríque de Valderrábano, Diego Pisador, Miguel de Fuenllana, and Esteban Daza issued books for it. Much of the surviving music was indeed "arranged," being adapted from vocal pieces. Although some composers during this time developed *fantasías* that were more idiomatic and less vocally conceived, the basis for the repertoire continued to be adapting vocal works to the *vihuela.* It seems that improvisation, demonstrating the good taste of the gentleman player, was a required aspect of *vihuela* playing. Not long after 1576 the *vihuela* began to be displaced in popularity by the guitar, a situation lamented by writers who thought the guitar a poor substitute lacking the refinement of the *vihuela.*

Keyboard music is also much better understood in the mid- and later sixteenth century. This is true in terms of both writings on how to play keyboard instruments and the number of composers who emerged. Two theorists active around 1550 wrote treatises with guidelines for playing keyboard instruments and making settings of chant melodies at the keyboard. Both Juan Bermudo and Tomás de Santa María included examples explaining techniques, such as imitation, that could be incorporated in creating music for the keyboard. The most important composer was Antonio de Cabezón. He cultivated as his principal form the *tiento,* a freely composed piece similar to the *fantasía* then developing in *vihuela* repertory. Cabezón's *tientos* vary from shorter, contemplative works to longer ones with contrasts of texture and melodic material. His *diferencias* (variations) are interesting for the various ways that the composer works the melody into the texture, each time in a different "voice" or register. In addition to these more idiomatic keyboard works, Cabezón wrote a number of liturgical pieces that incorporate chant melodies intended for services.

Wind and string ensemble music has received growing attention in recent years. It is known through archival records that numerous minstrels were hired on special occasions and often performed with the singers in cathedrals. Barcelona, and probably other cities, hired trumpeters for specific occasions, which followed the medieval practices of using brass instruments as signs of royal entries and for military pomp. In the church, it seems that minstrels performed only occasionally in the late fifteenth century, but by the mid-sixteenth century were contracted to play on numerous important days. Manuscripts from the later sixteenth century demonstrate that groups of minstrels had a mixed repertory from Spanish and foreign composers that included international "greatest hits" for instrumental groups. These imported works were probably not sung by choirs but remained a specialized repertory for the instrumental ensembles.

Portugal in the Sixteenth Century. The history of Renaissance music in Portugal before 1500 is based largely on interpretations of references to music, not actual musical manuscripts. Recent research has shown that many works composed in Ferdinand and Isabella's courts were disseminated in Portugal and that a repertoire by Portuguese composers grew around it, but little can be established about composers who added to this body of music. The dissemination of Spanish music in Portugal is not surprising since Pedro de Escobar, one of the three most important composers in Spain around 1500, was from Portugal. A number of sixteenth-century composers in Portugal wrote sacred Latin works: Fernão Gomes Correia, Vasco Pires, Heliodoro de Paiva, Pedro da Gamboa, and António Carreira. Each of these men composed competent polyphonic music but did not create a style that incorporated distinct Portuguese elements. The great names of Portuguese Renaissance composers begin with Duarte Lobo, who published his own works in Antwerp beginning in 1605; Lobo's music shows much of the same intensity of expressive power that Francisco Guerrero's had. Other outstanding later composers were Manuel Cardoso and Filipe de Magalhães. Instrumental music in Portugal was noted by Spanish visitors as being even more magnificent than that in Spain, but research has not demonstrated how such repertoires may have differed.

BIBLIOGRAPHY

Primary Works

Anglés, Higinio, ed. *Cristóbal de Morales: opera omnia.* Vols. 11, 13, 15, 17, 20–21, 24, 34, *Monumentos de la Música Española.* Madrid, 1952–. See editions of numerous other composers' works in this series.

Snow, Robert J. *Obras completas de Rodrigo de Ceballos.* In four volumes. Granada, Spain, 1995–.

Secondary Works

Griffin, John. "The Vihuela: Performance Practice, Style, and Context." In *Performance on Lute, Guitar, and Vihuela: His-*torical Practice and Modern Interpretation.* Edited by Victor Anand Coelho. Cambridge, U.K., and New York, 1997.

Kreitner, Kenneth. "Minstrels in Spanish Churches, 1400–1600." *Early Music.* 20/4 (1992): 532–548.

Nery, Rui Viera. "Aontónio Carreira, o Velho, Fr. António Carreira e António Carreira, o Moço: Balanço de um enigma pro resolver." In *Livro de Homenagem a Macario Santiago Kastner.* Edited by Maria Fernandez Cidrais Rodrigues. Lisbon, 1992. Several other essays in this volume contain important information on music in Portugal.

Parkins, Robert. "Spain and Portugal." In *Keyboard Music before 1700.* Edited by Alexander Silbiger. New York, 1995.

Rees, Owen. *Polyphony in Portugal, c. 1530–c. 1620: Sources from the Monastery of Santa Cruz, Coimbra.* New York, 1995.

Ros-Fábregas, Emilio. "Historiografía de la música en las catedrales españolas: nacionalismo y positivismo en la investigación musicológica." *Codexxi: Revista de la Communicación Musical.* 1 (1998): 68–135.

Rubio, Samuel. *Desde el "ars nova" hasta 1600.* Vol. 2: *Historia de la música española.* Edited by Pablo Lopez de Osaba. Madrid, 1983–.

Stevenson, Robert Murrell. *Spanish Cathedral Music in the Golden Age.* Berkeley, Calif., 1961.

Stevenson, Robert Murrell. *Spanish Music in the Age of Columbus.* The Hague, Netherlands, 1960.

Ward, John Milton. "The Vihuela de mano and Its Music (1536–1576)." Ph.D. diss., New York University, 1953.

G. GRAYSON WAGSTAFF

MUSIC IN THE HOLY ROMAN EMPIRE. Almost at the same time as in Italy (which has traditionally been taken as the most advanced country in musical development in the Renaissance), the latest musical style of the Franco-Flemish school became known in Prague and Vienna. Composers such as Johannes Brassart and Johannes de Sarto, both from Liège, represented the high quality of court music under Albert II (ruled 1438–1439) and his successor, Frederick IV (ruled 1440–1493), who resided mainly in Graz and Wiener Neustadt. Many distinguished musicians came to Frederick's court, among them Johann Hinderbach, who supposedly commissioned the series of musical manuscripts known as the Trent Codices. This collection bears testimony to the acquaintance at the imperial court with the best music of the day and is an invaluable source of fifteenth-century Franco-Flemish music. Works by leading composers such as Gilles Binchois, Brassart, Guillaume Dufay, and John Dunstaple are included, as well as those of a later generation, among them Loyset Compère, Heinrich Isaac, and Johannes Ockeghem.

Music as Imperial Representation. Music played an important role in Habsburg imperial representation (festivities such as weddings, coronations, entries at imperial and local diets), but this did

Music in the Holy Roman Empire. The emperor Maximilan I with his musicians. Illustration from *Weisskunig* by Hans Burgkmair the Elder. Woodcut. FOTO MARBURG/ART RESOURCE, NY

not necessarily mean that individual emperors were not also genuine music lovers. Frederick IV played the lute and actively sought to attract English musicians to his court. The emperor Maximilian I (ruled 1493–1519) claimed he wanted to write his own *Musica-Puech* (compositions), and Maximilian II (ruled 1564–1576) gathered some of the best musicians in Europe at his court for his chamber music. Part of this musical representation has survived because the music was preserved in luxurious, elegantly illuminated manuscripts that found their way into the imperial treasuries.

One of the most important developments for the arts in general and music in particular was the connection to Burgundy through the marriage of Maximilian I and Mary of Burgundy in 1477. This wedding had particular impact on musical life because it co-incided with the demand throughout Europe for musicians and composers from the Low Countries (mostly the northern part of the duchy of Burgundy). This gave Maximilian and his descendants a particular advantage in choosing the best musicians for their court chapels. Many of the precious musical manuscripts that Maximilian and his daughter Margaret of Austria commissioned as presents and for other purposes were produced here, especially those by the scribe Pierre Alamire. This period dominated by Franco-Flemish musicians came to a close at the imperial court in 1619, when Ferdinand II became emperor and Italians took over the most important positions at court.

Imperial representation was also expressed in the size of the music chapel and particularly in the number of trumpets that announced the emperor's arrival at public occasions. Here the impressiveness of the forces was important, and the musical qualities of the ubiquitous Te Deum were secondary. On the most important occasions polychoral works were common, especially after the middle of the sixteenth century. This called for an impressive demonstration of the abilities of a choirmaster to conduct from two to six choirs singing works in homophonic style that emphasized the clarity of the texts. Such special occasions also called for the *Staatsmotette,* a musical setting for a Latin poem in praise of the ruler (or other dignitaries); it differs from the motet used in church services only in that the text records a specific, usually secular, occasion.

Maximilian I.   Maximilian I continued the Burgundian traditions of festivals on a specific theme and generous musical patronage. As the sovereign of Burgundy's Order of the Golden Fleece, he welcomed much of the founding mythology and a musical program for its meeting on the day of its patron saint (St. Andrew) that influenced many composers in the sixteenth century. Both Maximilian and his successor, Charles V, were "traveling" sovereigns, in that they never chose a particular city as their permanent residence. This usually meant much fluctuation in the number of singers in their court chapels and the composers they commissioned. The major composers Heinrich Isaac, Jacob Obrecht, and Pierre de La Rue were associated with Maximilian I's court. Isaac's lied "Innsbruck ich muss dich lassen" has survived as a folk song, expressing sadness at leaving a much-loved place. His compositions in his posthumously published *Choralis Constantinus* (a large collection of mass propers composed in 1507) reflect the need for reform in the Catholic Church. Although the title stems from the Council of Constance (1414–1418), many of the masses included were written for use in the imperial chapel. An important part of Maximilian's legacy is the publications that record his festivals and his life in general; they include many engravings showing the importance of musicians in all his activities. A very famous engraving shows the court musicians on a float as a part of an idealized festival parade, and another depicts his favorite organist, the famous Paul von Hofhaimer.

Although Maximilian favored Innsbruck on the whole, he chose Vienna as the place to found a permanent musical institution. On 20 July 1498 he wrote the order that boy singers should be trained as a part of the court chapel, at the time under the direction of Georg Slatkonia (later bishop of Vienna). This arrangement was necessary because women were not allowed to sing the upper voices in chapel. The institution of the boys' choir also served the practical purpose of training future composers.

In 1515 the double wedding that crowned Maximilian's marriage policies took place in Vienna. His grandson Ferdinand married Anne, heiress of Bohemia and Hungary, and his granddaughter Mary married Louis of Hungary. The festivities included a play in Latin (*Voluptatis cum virtute disceptio*) dedicated to the future Charles V, who was present, and *Humanistenoden* (Humanist odes), New Latin poems set to music in a purely homophonic style. Humanist poets were organized in Vienna in the Sodalitas Danubianae, a kind of "academy" like that popular in Italy.

In 1524 the young king Louis Jagellon was killed in battle against the Turks at Mohács, and Ferdinand of Habsburg became king of Hungary and Bohemia. This meant that the chapel in Vienna did not again become "imperial" until Ferdinand became emperor at the abdication of his older brother, Charles V.

Charles V, Ferdinand I, and Maximilian II.   Charles V's long reign (1519–1556) saw the beginnings of the Protestant Reformation and the Catholic reaction: the Council of Trent (1545–1547, 1551–1552, and 1562–1563). The musical implications of Protestantism can be seen in the greater participation of the faithful in church services, particularly by singing simple songs in the vernacular. The contrast to the complicated polyphonic works (masses and motets in Latin; chansons in French) composed by Charles's court composers Nicolas Gombert, Thomas Crequillon, and Jacob Clemens non Papa could hardly be greater. Although Charles had a natural inclination to the musicians from the Low Countries, where he was born, he also began to employ musicians from Spain. This resulted in a division into a *capilla flamenca* (Spanish term for continuation of the Burgundian chapel choir) and a choir of Spaniards, a system that his son Philip II continued. The influence of Spanish keyboard players can be seen in the choice of organists for the chapel, such as Antonio Cabezón. Gombert accompanied the emperor on trips throughout Europe, including the capitals of his most important lands: Vienna and Madrid. At the end of Charles's reign, his son Philip II married Mary Tudor. In 1555 Philip's chapel choir accompanied him to England. A Fleming, Philippe de Monte, was hired as a singer but abandoned the position shortly thereafter, justifying his actions by claiming that, as the only non-Spaniard among Philip's musicians, he was not treated well by the Spanish musicians. Monte was recommended to the position of chapel master at the court of Albert of Bavaria at Munich in 1556, and his singing talent and knowledge of the latest style were mentioned in his favor. Monte became the chapel master of Maximilian II in 1568.

Ferdinand I (ruled 1558–1564) maintained what was to become the imperial music chapel in Vienna. Flemish musicians, such as the chapel master, Arnold de Brouck (from Bruges), were preferred. Vienna had a promising start in the new business of publishing music. Movable type for music was perfected in Venice around 1500, and although many imperial composers published their works in Venice, Antwerp and Nürnberg were the major music-printing centers in the empire itself. Hans Judenkünig's *Ain schone kunstliche underweisung zu lernen auff der Lautten und Geygen,* the first printed lute book, was published at Vienna in 1523 by Johann Singreiner. Since the lute was the most popular instrument among dilettantes as well as many professional musicians, the importance of this book's publication is obvious. Throughout the rest of the sixteenth century and well into the seventeenth, music publishing remained sporadic in most of Middle Europe. After the abdication of Charles V (1558), the imperial residence became Vienna.

Maximilian II (ruled 1564–1576) was married to Mary, the daughter of Charles V, and spent several years as his father-in-law's representative in Spain. His strong Protestant sympathies caused something of a crisis by 1560. His chapel master, Jacobus Vaet, composed a conciliatory text about the different paths to truth taken by Peter and Paul, and published this *Staatsmotette* on parchment in that year. The Council of Trent was meeting again (from 1562 to 1563), and Ferdinand I was under great pressure to confirm his son Maximilian's Catholic beliefs. The Council of Trent reconfirmed a special privilege of the emperor to reserve ecclesiastical benefices known as the *precum primaria.* Probably the most important benefice awarded to an imperial musician was that of treasurer of the Cathedral of Cambrai, which Maximilian II gave to Philippe de Monte in 1572.

The *Thesauri musici atque catholici . . . ,* in five volumes, can be considered another form of imperial representation. It is a compendium uniting compositions by most of the leading court musicians serving Ferdinand I and Maximilian II. The fifth volume contains mostly *Staatsmotetten* written for the house of Habsburg. Maximilian II was a genuine music lover who enlarged the court chapel and established a group of virtuoso musicians to perform his chamber music. These musicians and the music they performed were Italian. Virtually no north European music seems to have been included, although the Flemish composer Jacob Regnart later became identified mainly with his German *napolitane* in the Italian style. Maximilian II also continued the festival traditions of his namesake, as best seen in the festivities for his brother's wedding in 1571. Archduke Charles married Mary of Bavaria in Vienna, and a weeklong festival celebrated the event. Some of the jousts and costumed parades were organized by another brother, Archduke Ferdinand of the Tyrol, but the main event was a *tournois à thème,* based on the number four, conceived by the eclectic painter Giuseppe Arcimboldo. This festival was also recorded with a printed description, much as the first Maximilian would have done.

Rudolf II and Matthias. Rudolf II, only twenty-four when he became emperor (ruled 1576–1612), was considered to be very conservative because of his education at the court of Philip II in Spain. He seems to have appreciated music mainly as a form of imperial representation. He kept the music chapel almost exactly as it had been under Maximilian II, and only slowly began to hire new musicians. A case in point is the imperial chapel master, Philippe de Monte, who wanted to retire in 1578 and live in Cambrai, where he had important benefices. Rudolf did not permit this, and the composer died at Prague in 1603, still officially in imperial service. Around 1580, Rudolf moved his residence to Prague. The Italian musician Camillo Zanotti seems to have gained Rudolf's respect, for he was the only composer allowed to reproduce the imperial crown on the frontispiece of a printed work, a collection of Italian madrigals dedicated to the emperor. He was assistant chapel master (under Monte) until his death in 1591. Zanotti's successor as assistant chapel master, the trumpeter and composer Alessandro Orologio, was never appointed to the higher rank, which was left vacant. After Rudolf II renewed the wars against the Turks in 1594, his cousin Francesco Gonzaga traveled to Vienna and Prague; in his entourage were several musicians, including the young Claudio Monteverdi. Although the imperial court was a stronghold of the music of the Counter-Reformation, the most common type of mass composition was the so-called parody mass, which had been prohibited by the Council of Trent. (The parody mass basically is a composition that reworks the musical material of the model [e.g., madrigal, chanson, or even motet] to create a new composition.) It was this secular aspect that the church condemned. Monte composed *madrigali spirituali* (spiritual madrigals), a form of private devotional music in Italian that was strongly influenced by the Jesuits.

In 1585 Rudolf, his brother Ernst, and their uncle Archduke Charles were accepted into the Order of the Golden Fleece, which was headed by Philip II. On this occasion Monte wrote a work for three choirs that was sung in St. Vitus's Cathedral in Prague; trumpets also played fanfares as a part of the celebrations. The customary *Tafelmusik* (table music) was played at the banquet that followed the ceremony, and a luxurious manuscript roll, in addition to an illustrated printed description, was created to commemorate the event.

One form of composition that was particularly prevalent around 1600 was the *battaglia,* a description of a battle by musical means (trumpet fanfares, swords and spears swinging). Apparently inspired by the wars against the Turks, Christoph Demantius wrote his *Tympanum militare . . .* (1600), which included obligatory praise of the great military conqueror Rudolf II. However, Rudolf lost control over his lands in the succeeding years. The person who virtually dethroned him was his brother Matthias.

Matthias's short reign (1612–1619) was the culmination of his growing activities as a younger brother of the ruler over the preceding twenty years. As soon as he became emperor, his chapel master, Lambert de Sayve (from Liège), published the monumental work *Sacrae symphoniae . . . ,* which collects compositions from the early 1590s to 1612. The title indicates a connection to the polychoral compositions of Andrea Gabrieli, and many of the works in this collection are set for several choirs requiring up to sixteen parts (probably some of them instruments). This kind of composition was one of the current possible forms that might be called modern, but about the same time the rise of monody (and eventually opera) in Italy pointed to what the future would bring. On a state visit to Dresden in 1617, Matthias heard music written by Heinrich Schütz that has not survived. He also began the italianization of the court musicians by employing the lutenist Pietro Paolo Melli and Angela Stampa, the first female musician to be named as receiving payments directly. One of Matthias's musicians expressed the decisive event that ended the Renaissance at the imperial court: the battle of the White Mountain (1620). Jan Sixt z Lerchenfelsu composed a *battaglia* celebrating the victory of the Catholic (imperial) forces that marked the beginning of the Thirty Years' War.

See also biographies of figures mentioned in this entry.

BIBLIOGRAPHY

Anglés, Higenio. *La musica en la corte de Carlos V.* Barcelona, 1944.

Blume, Friedrich. *Renaissance and Baroque Music.* Translated by M. D. Herter Nelson. New York, 1967.

Bossuyt, Ignace. *Flemish Polyphony.* Louvain, Belgium, 1996.

Cuyler, Louise. *The Emperor Maximilian I and Music.* London, 1973.

Dunning, Albert. *Die Staatsmotette 1480–1555.* Utrecht, 1970.

Haggh, Barbara. "The Archives of the Order of the Golden Fleece and Music." *Journal of the Royal Music Association* 120, no. 1 (1995): 1–43.

Kmetz, John, ed. *Music in the German Renaissance: Sources, Styles, and Contexts.* Cambridge, U.K., 1994.

Lindell, Robert. "Music at the Imperial Court after Charles V." In *Le concert des voix et des instrument à la Renaissance.* Edited by J.-M. Vaccaro. Paris, 1995. Pages 273–285.

Lindell, Robert. "The Wedding of Archduke Charles and Maria of Bavaria in 1571." *Early Music* 18, no. 2 (May 1990): 253–269.

Palisca, Claude V. *Humanism in Italian Renaissance Musical Thought.* New Haven, Conn., 1985.

Pass, Walter. *Musik und Musiker am Hof Maximilians II.* Tutzing, 1980.

Reese, Gustave. *Music in the Renaissance.* 2d ed. New York, 1959.

Salmen, Walter. *Musikleben im 16. Jahrhundert.* Leipzig, 1976.

Stevenson, Robert. *Spanish Cathedral Music in the Golden Age.* Berkeley, Calif., 1958.

Wessely, Othmar. "Arnold von Bruck: Leben und Umwelt. Mit Beiträgen zur Musikgeschichte des Hofes Ferdinands I. von 1527 bis 1545." Habilitationsschrift. University of Vienna, 1959.

ROBERT LINDELL

MUSIC IN THE LOW COUNTRIES. The area commonly referred to as the "Low Countries"—including present-day Belgium, the Netherlands, and Luxembourg, as well as parts of northern France—began to develop its own political and cultural distinctiveness when Duke Philip the Bold of Burgundy (1342–1404) inherited the counties of Flanders and Artois in 1384; his successors added much of the rest of this region to their domain. After the death of Charles the Bold in 1477, rule of the Low Countries devolved to the Habsburgs when Charles's only child, Mary, married Maximilian I of Austria (1459–1519). Subsequent Habsburg rulers added the remaining portions of the Low Countries to their dominion.

Throughout the Renaissance, the Low Countries were the birthplace of not only a disproportionately large number of the major composers but also of a vast number of lesser-known musicians who filled the courtly and ecclesiastical chapels of Europe, particularly France and Italy. No single reason can fully explain this phenomenon, but several factors not found together elsewhere fostered the development of so many musicians. First, the Low Countries (along with northern France) had choir schools associated with their cathedrals and large churches, such as those at Cambrai and Antwerp; comparable institutions were not nearly as prevalent elsewhere in Europe. In the *maîtrises,* choirboys learned the art of singing, and the more talented ones received their first lessons in composition. The curriculum, held over from the late Middle Ages and noted for its rigor, included theoretical as well as practical studies. Second, the Burgundian dukes and later the Habsburg emperors were important patrons of music who spent large sums of money on singers, composers, instrumentalists, and books of music. Some of the composers associated with the Burgundian court include Baude Cordier, Gilles Binchois, Antoine Busnoys, Hayne van Ghizeghem, and Robert Morton. Finally, the dukes, emperors, and cathedrals were not the only patrons, and as the Low Countries grew in prosperity, smaller churches were able to support modest chapels; towns were able to support trumpeters and wind bands; and the increasingly large middle class was able to support music through its guilds and confraternities.

Institutions. The chivalric Order of the Golden Fleece, established by Philip the Good of Burgundy in 1430, met for the last time in 1559. The order usually consisted of thirty-one knights who met on an irregular basis in different towns belonging to the sovereign, usually one in the Low Countries. Music—both monophonic and polyphonic—played an important role at these meetings; it is likely that the order commissioned works specifically for their meetings, including motets by Agricola and La Rue, as well as some of the Masses based on "L'homme armé."

Confraternities and guilds, as well as wealthy individuals and families, were also important patrons of music. Confraternities—groups of devout men and women dedicated to the veneration of a saint or mystery—associated themselves with a church or convent, and individual churches could have several confraternities attached to them (St. Gudule in Brussels had four associated with it during the fifteenth century, dedicated to Mary, and SS. Anne, Barbara, and Mary Magdelen). Confraternities were especially popular during the fourteenth and fifteenth centuries: most towns had several and the larger towns had many (more than fifteen were active in Brussels during the Renaissance). Confraternities dedicated to Mary were the most common (four were dedicated to Mary in Brussels), and the Marian confraternities in Antwerp, Bergen op Zoom, and 's-Hertogenbosch were important musical establishments in their own right. The wealthier guilds and confraternities engaged some of the most important composers of their time, including Johannes Ghiselin (fl. c. 1492–1507), La Rue, Obrecht, and Matthaeus Pipelare (c. 1450–1515). The earliest polyphony sung in a church not associated with a religious order in the Low Countries was introduced by the Marian Confraternity in Brussels in 1362. Confraternities regularly endowed special services such as weekly Lady Masses, anniversaries of patron saints, and commemorative services in honor of deceased members. These endowed services frequently specified the use of polyphony, and the clergy who sang this music often had to learn the necessary skills not for the sake of performing the official liturgy but in order to fulfill the wishes of confraternities and benefactors who endowed the music; when their skills were inadequate or their number insufficient, the confraternities occasionally hired other musicians to perform the music. Confraternities occasionally commissioned their own manuscripts for use in their services; six manuscripts for the Marian Confraternity in 's-Hertogenbosch contain principally Masses, motets, Magnificats, and hymns. Three of these manuscripts were copied in 's-Hertogenbosch during the 1540s, and the others were copied by the Netherlandish court scribe Pierre Alamire in Brussels and Mechlin in 1530–1531.

Many of the large cities of the Low Countries had a scriptorium where manuscripts were produced; the most important of these was the Netherlandish court of Margaret of Austria and Charles V in Brussels and Mechlin. Pierre Alamire was a principal scribe there from 1495–1534, and the main copyist of at least fifty-one manuscripts on commissions from private individuals such as Pompejus Occo of Amsterdam to important rulers such as Frederick the Wise of Saxony. Alamire also worked as a spy for Henry VIII of England, keeping an eye on the pretender Richard de la Pole, as a counterspy for de la Pole, and as a courtier for Charles V.

Tylman Susato (c. 1500–1564) established the first important music press in the Low Countries in Antwerp. After two failed partnerships with other printers, he received his own privilege in 1543, and for the next eighteen years published at least fifty-seven books of music, including chansons, motets, Masses, and *Musyck boexken* (music books, which included dances, Flemish songs, and *Souterliedekens*). Susato's rival in Antwerp was the firm of Jean de Laet and Hubert Waelrant, who published only sixteen books of music, although Laet on his own also printed a few other music books, including a volume of Lasso's motets in 1556, as well as many other books (Bibles, histories, classical texts, Spanish books, and so forth). Pierre Phalèse (c. 1510–c. 1576) was an important music printer in Louvain who began publishing in 1545, and for a while specialized in instrumental music; his first books of vocal music did not appear until 1552. Phalèse's son took over the firm after his father's death and moved to Antwerp in 1581.

During the Reformation, singing the psalms in the vernacular became very important in all Protestant countries. The first Dutch metrical Psalter was published in 1540 by Symon Cock in Antwerp. Known as *Souterliedekens,* these psalms were set to preexisting popular tunes (mostly Dutch folk songs but also some French and German folk songs as well) and were meant for use at home. Several composers made polyphonic settings of all the *Souterliedekens,* including Jacob Clemens (1556–1557), Gherardus Mes (1561), and Cornelis Buscop (1568).

Composers. One of the first major composers to emerge from this milieu was Johannes Ciconia. Probably born in the 1370s, he was a choirboy in Liège, but spent much of his adult career in northern Italy, thus setting a precedent followed by many of his compatriots throughout the Renaissance. He combined elements of the *ars subtilior* (the rhythmically and notationally complex style of fourteenth-century France) with those of Italian fourteenth-century music. The principal genres of this time were motets (loosely defined as any setting of a Latin text except the Ordinary of the Mass), independent Mass movements, and chansons in the three *formes fixes* (ballade, rondeau, and virelai). Guillaume Dufay (1397–1474), a choirboy at Cambrai from 1409 until at least 1414, spent much of his early career in Italy, including the papal chapel, and at the court of Savoy; he returned to Cambrai in 1439 and spent much of his remaining career there. His music, a synthesis of Ciconia and the triadic and very consonant music of the English composers Leonel Power and John Dunstaple, became the standard for the rest of the century, the starting point from which other composers transformed the style to suit their own purposes. Dufay's contemporaries include Binchois, Hugo and Arnold de Lantins, Johannes de Lymburgia, and Johannes Brassart, all of whom were born and worked in the Low Countries.

The next generation of composers included Johannes Ockeghem (c. 1410–1497), who was born in the Low Countries and spent part of his career in

Music in the Low Countries. Guillaume Dufay (left, with portable organ) and Gilles Binchois (with harp). Illumination from *Champion des dames* by Martin Lefranc, fifteenth century. THE GRANGER COLLECTION

Antwerp and Moulins before joining the French royal court. His music is denser and less often relieved by changes of texture or full cadences than that of his predecessors. He expanded the range of musical space and gave each voice approximately equal prominence. Some of his important contemporaries from the Low Countries include Johannes Regis, Hayne van Ghizeghem, Gilles Joye, and Jacques Barbireau; Busnoys, who was born in France, was one of the most important composers at the Burgundian court during the 1460s and 1470s. By the middle of the century, the principal genres were the same but independent Mass movements gave way to settings of the complete Mass Ordinary, and composers showed a decided preference for the rondeau over the ballade and virelai.

Josquin des Prez (c. 1450–1521), one of the most important musical figures of the Renaissance, may have been born in Condé-sur-l'Escaut in Hainault, and after a career that took him to France and Italy, he retired there in 1504. Although there are still some major gaps in his biography, we do know that he worked for René of Anjou (1477–1478), king of Sicily, the papal choir (1489–1495), and the duke of

Ferrara (1503–1504); however, recently discovered documents indicate that he was not associated with Milan from 1459 to the early 1470s as had been supposed. Some of his technical innovations include a closer relationship between text and music and the use of imitation. He and his contemporaries from the Low Countries—Jacob Obrecht (1457/8–1505), Heinrich Isaac (c. 1450–1517), Pierre de la Rue (c. 1460–1518), Alexander Agricola (c. 1446–1506), and Gaspar van Weerbeke (c. 1445–after 1517), to name but a few—were sought after in courts and churches throughout Europe. During this generation, the chansons ceased to be confined to the *formes fixes* and were now frequently either through-composed (that is, with no internal repetitions) or based on popular monophonic tunes. The Mass and especially the motet were of much greater interest to composers; for example, Ockeghem composed 14 Masses and 4 motets whereas Isaac wrote more than 40 Masses and over 350 motets.

The so-called post-Josquin generation also was dominated by composers from the Low Countries. Adrian Willaert (c. 1490–1562), born in Bruges or Roulaers, spent most of his career in Italy, working in Ferrara and then as *maestro di cappella* at St. Mark's in Venice from 1527–1562; Nicolas Gombert (c. 1495–1560), born in Flanders, worked at the imperial chapel of Charles V; Thomas Crecquillon (c. 1480/1500–1557) worked for Emperor Charles V as well as in Béthune and Louvain; and Jakob Clemens (c. 1510/1515–c. 1555) stayed in the Low Countries all of his life, working in Bruges, 's-Hertogenbosch, and Ypres. This generation continued the innovations of Josquin, particularly his use of imitation and his attention to the text-music relationship. Their music, usually built around points of imitation, privileges seamless counterpoint uninterrupted by changes of texture or full cadences over structural clarity; in this respect it is a synthesis of Ockeghem and Josquin. The madrigal, an Italian form that first appeared during the 1520s, was dominated for some time by composers from the Low Countries working in Italy, including Willaert and Cipriano de Rore (c. 1515–1565).

Although there were several important composers from the Low Countries during the late Renaissance, the hegemony they once held was over. Orlando di Lasso (1532–1594), born in Mons, spent most of his career in Italy and at the imperial chapel. A far more dramatic composer than his Italian contemporary Palestrina, Lasso wrote in every genre and in a wide variety of styles, and was passionately committed to the idea that music should heighten and even embody the meaning of the texts he set. Giaches de Wert (1535–1596) and Philip de Monte (1521–1603) excelled in madrigal composition.

See also biographies of figures mentioned in this entry.

BIBLIOGRAPHY

Forney, Kristine K. "Music, Ritual, and Patronage at the Church of Our Lady, Antwerp." *Early Music History* 7 (1987): 1–58.

Forney, Kristine K. "The Role of Secular Guilds in the Musical Life of Renaissance Antwerp." In *Musicology and Archival Research.* Edited by Barbara Haggh, Frank Daelemans, and André Vanrie. Brussels, 1994. Pages 441–461.

Haggh, Barbara. "The Archives of the Order of the Golden Fleece and Music." *Journal of the Royal Music Association* 120 (1995): 1–43.

Haggh, Barbara. "Music, Liturgy, and Ceremony in Brussels, 1350–1500." Ph.D. diss., University of Illinois at Urbana-Champaign, 1988.

Prizer, William F. "Music and Ceremonial in the Low Countries: Philip the Fair and the Order of the Golden Fleece." *Early Music History* 5 (1985): 113–154.

Strohm, Reinhard. *Music in Late Medieval Bruges.* Rev. Ed. Oxford and New York, 1990.

Weaver, Robert Lee. *Waelrant and Laet: Music Publishers in Antwerp's Golden Age.* Warren, Mich., 1995.

Wegman, Rob C. *Born for the Muses: The Life and Masses of Jacob Obrecht.* Oxford, 1994.

Wegman, Rob C. "From Maker to Composer: Improvisation and Musical Authorship in the Low Countries, 1450–1500." *Journal of the American Musicological Society* 49 (1996): 409–479.

Wegman, Rob C. "Music and Musicians at the Guild of Our Lady in Bergen op Zoom, c. 1470–1510." *Early Music History* 9 (1989): 175–250.

Wright, Craig. "Musiciens à la cathédrale de Cambrai 1475–1550." *Revue de musicologie* 62 (1976): 204–228.

Wright, Craig. *Music at the Court of Burgundy, 1364–1419: A Documentary History.* Henryville, Pa., 1979.

MURRAY STEIB

MUSLIMS. *See* **Islam.**

MYSTERY PLAYS. *See* **Drama,** *subentry on* **Religious Drama.**

MYTH. The humanist revival of classical antiquity caused myth to resonate powerfully in Renaissance consciousness. Various strands of mythology were important. Chivalric romance remained vital; ancient history was a popular form of myth; the matter of Troy projected the imperial aspirations of Habsburgs and Tudors; and the mythology in Plato was virtually a new discovery. This necessarily selective account will concentrate on the pagan gods as they were transmitted by Homer, Virgil, and Ovid, and for which Ovid's *Metamorphoses* was the central text. From the later fifteenth century, pagan myth began to challenge the dominance of religious subjects in both literature and visual arts. Although traditions of allegorical commentary continued strongly through the sixteenth century, in practice artists and writers tended to shift from allegory to symbolism, creating local types of myths or freely adapting established meanings to reflect the particularity and complexity of the human condition.

Texts, Translations, Commentaries. Recovery requires the availability of texts. Throughout the Middle Ages, Homer's epics were unknown firsthand, except for scattered quotations. Petrarch (1304–1374) recorded both his search for a manuscript of Homer and, when he obtained one, his frustration at his inability to read Greek. Given the predominant latinity of the humanist movement, translation assumed signal importance. Although Giovanni Boccaccio (1313–1375) had commissioned a Latin prose Homer, a complete verse translation was not available until the sixteenth century. As with Homer, direct knowledge of Plato had been limited and fragmentary; in the fifteenth century, humanists mastered enough Greek to begin putting the dialogues into Latin, culminating with the complete translation (1484) by Marsilio Ficino (1433–1499). If for Latin authors language was not an obstacle, editorial issues of authenticity and canon still could be vexing. Virgil was believed to have written the *Priapea,* which poems frequently were included in his works; and, from 1471, the "Thirteenth Book" of the *Aeneid* by Maffeo Vegio regularly was attached to editions.

Allegorical commentary on Homer started early with the pre-Socratics; for Virgil it began in the fourth century A.D. The Renaissance saw no reason to break with these traditions. In Ficino's Neoplatonic circle alone, Angelo Poliziano (1454–1494) undertook a Latin *Illiad,* completing five books; Cristoforo Landino (1424–c. 1492) both edited Virgil (1487) and wrote a remarkable allegorization of the *Aeneid;* and Giovanni Pico della Mirandola (1463–1494) promised, but did not deliver, a "Poetic Theology" revealing the magical doctrines hidden in Homer. If the urgent project of the fifteenth century was providing Latin editions of essential works, in the sixteenth century it shifted to vernacular translation. This did not mean, however, that translators put aside the vision of the commentators. Lodovico Dolce (1508–1568) prefaces each section of his verse translation of the *Odyssey, L'Ulisse* (1573), with a statement of the allegory; and George Chapman (1559?–1634), who translated all of Homer into English, boasted that the reader "shall easily see I understand the understandings of all other interpreters and commenters."

Since texts were not lacking, far more than with Homer and Virgil the allegorization of Ovid was a medieval industry, exemplified by the twelfth-century *Ovide moralisé,* which turns the *Metamorphoses* into French verse and supplies a Christian allegory. A fourteenth-century competitor, Pierre Bersuire's *Metamorphosis Ovidiana moraliter,* enjoyed an extended popularity from its fable-by-fable, positive and negative allegories. In 1493 Rafaello Regio, professor of rhetoric at Padua, published his commentary, incorporating summaries by Lactantius Placidus; after a dozen reprints, the commentary of Petrus Lavinius was added in 1510. This edition sold fifty thousand copies in Regio's lifetime. Venetian printers found Ovid to be a particularly marketable classic and responded with numerous editions. The first Italian translation, *Ovidio Methamorphoseos vulgare* (1497), a prose redaction written by Giovanni Bonsignori in the fourteenth century, was printed there. Bonsignori's allegories resurfaced in *De Ovidio le Metamorphosi* (1533) with a verse translation by Nicolò degli Agostini. This, in turn, was followed by *Le trasformationi* (1553) of the diligent Lodovico Dolce.

The impetus to vernacular translation coexisted peacefully with a steady demand for Latin editions with commentaries, often intended as school texts; indeed, the vision of the commentaries bridged classical and modern languages. In France, from the advent of printing in 1487 to 1600, 266 Latin editions of Ovid have been recorded, nearly half with commentaries; and in 1614 Nicolas Renouard issued the *Metamorphoses* in French prose, with discourses on "l'explication moralé" of the fables, an edition that was reprinted thirteen times. In England the plodding, moralistic translation of Arthur Golding (1567) was succeeded by George Sandys's *Ovid's Metamorphosis Englished* (1626, 1632), in which the commentaries are an epitome of the entire tradition.

Mythographers and Meanings. The systematic study of classical mythology was largely a creation of the Renaissance. First came Boccaccio, whose *De genealogia deorum* (Genealogy of the gods) occupied the last twenty-five years of his life. His encyclopedic study does, indeed, offer genealogies and explains that myths have multiple senses: beyond the historical sense as real events, they can be understood morally, allegorically, and analogically. Boccaccio is traditional in revealing the Christian truths underlying fables but modern in the flex-

Picturing the Gods. *Danaë* by Titian. The story of Danaë, who was visited by Jupiter in the form a shower of gold, is told in the *Biblioteca* (Library) of Pseudo-Apollodorus of Athens (second or first century B.C.). It is referred to in Ovid's *Metamorphoses* 4.611 and 6.113. Painted 1545. CAPODIMONTE GALLERY, NAPLES/SUPERSTOCK

ibility of his readings, and the *Genealogy* was widely influential.

This flexibility becomes supreme in Ficino's extensive commentaries on Plato (1496), which in many respects constitute a discursive mythography. All of the traditional allegorical senses can be detected intermittently; however, in Ficino's subtle and complex system, individual fables do not have fixed values, but are changeable vocabulary in a mythic syntax, parts of a poetic theology. His commentary on the *Symposium* (1484) in particular had an extraordinary literary impact. Lilio Gregorio Giraldi (1479–1552) produced the most scholarly history of the gods (1548). Its popularity, however, was limited by his etymological method, leaving the field to be swept by the *Mythologies* (1551?) of Natale Conti (Natalis Comes; 1520–1582), which ran to at least thirty reprints and editions, including a French translation. Learned, but more accessible than Giraldi, Conti firmly returns the science to familiar allegorical territory with historical, natural, and moral interpretations.

Although cosmology and astrology are significant elements, the cardinal principle of all Renaissance mythographers is the assumption that classical mythology is consonant with Christian morality and doctrine; hidden beneath the often trivial and absurd surfaces, Christian archetypes may be discerned. Such assumptions were reinforced by the belief in an "ancient theology," a secret tradition of wisdom stretching from Zoroaster to Moses to Plato, and by the *Hieroglyphics* of Horapollo (printed 1505), a pictorial dictionary of symbols seeming to project the same consonance. The most succinct expression of the syncretic principle may be Desiderius Erasmus's invocation, "Saint Socrates, pray for us."

Picturing the Gods. Bersuire devoted part of his treatise to explaining how the ancients depicted the gods. Among the mythographers, the German Georg Pictor emphasized physical descriptions in his *Mythological Theology* (1532). The preface to Vicenzo Cartari's *Imagini delli dei de gl'antichi* (Images of the gods; 1556) claims that no one before Cartari has described their statues, thereby making the book very useful to artists and poets, a feature greatly enhanced by the eighty-five engravings added to the 1571 edition. A similar concern can be observed with Cesare Ripa's *Iconologia* (1593; illustrated 1603), a handbook explaining how to personify various concepts, such as truth, envy, and magnanimity.

From Bersuire to Ripa there is a concentration on iconography—representation by conventional symbols and attributes—that coalesces with several other elements: heraldry, hieroglyphics, the Neoplatonic cult of esoteric symbolism, the vogue for personal devices on medals and hat badges, and the popularity of emblem books initiated by Andrea Alciato (1492–1550), whose *Emblemata* (1531) went through 175 editions. Gabriele Simeoni even managed to convert the *Metamorphoses* into an emblem book (1559). The same tendency also manifested itself in programs of mythological decoration. In one family, Isabella d' Este (1474–1539) commissioned moral allegories figured in myth; her brother Alfonso (1476–1534) wanted bacchic revelries; and her son Federigo II Gonzaga (1500–1540) had a taste for erotic mythology. Learned and popular traditions of illustration intermingled in the sixteenth century. The woodcut illustrations to the vernacular Ovids influenced compositions of such major artists as Giovanni Bellini (c. 1430–1516) and Titian (c. 1488–1576).

Visual Arts. Leon Battista Alberti (1404–1472) advised painters to read poets to find such subjects as the *Calumny* of the fourth-century B.C. Greek painter Appelles and the Three Graces. His *On Painting* (1435) assumes two crucial concepts: as poetry and painting are "sister arts," so a painting is like a silent poem; and modern should emulate ancient. His advice was taken by Sandro Botticelli (1445–1510), who placed the Three Graces prominently in his *Primavera* (c. 1477; see the color plates in volume 1) and whose *Calumny* (c. 1495) rivals that of Apelles. Botticelli's *Primavera* and *Birth of Venus* (c. 1480–1485; for the *Birth of Venus,* see the color plates in this volume) were the first large-scale paintings of pagan gods since antiquity; and the former audaciously represents a metamorphosis in progress. Botticelli's links with Florentine Neoplatonism have caused these paintings, along with his

Mars and Venus, to be read as complex allegories. Other critics see only the illustration of such texts as Ovid's *Fasti* and Poliziano's "Stanze per la qiostra" (Stanzas for the joust; 1475–1478); all, however, acknowledge their humor, sensuality, and haunting loveliness.

A monograph could trace the metamorphoses of a particular myth—say, Leda and the Swan in paintings by Leonardo da Vinci, Michelangelo, Correggio, and Tintoretto, as well as in woodcuts, engravings, bronze, and marble—but here summary is necessary. If the medieval sense of self looked inward, the Renaissance paused long over its outward manifestations, preoccupied with accurate human anatomy, the sexuality of Christ, and the varieties of human sexuality. For the last, whether imaged through Leda, Hercules, Io, or Europa, the *Metamorphoses* became the artists' bible. With new reproductive technology, those Ovidian images could be widely copied and disseminated; Giovanni Jacopo Caraglio depicted *The Loves of the Gods* (1527) in twenty engravings.

The career of Titian, the greatest mythological painter of the age, can represent sixteenth-century developments. Artistic continuities are shown by posthumous collaborations in which Titian completed Giorgione's *Sleeping Venus* (c. 1510) and touched up Bellini's *Feast of the Gods* (c. 1514), a representation of the Olympians in the throes of very human sensuality. His own *Sacred and Profane Love* (1514) has been read as Neoplatonic allegory, but seems to have been a portrait of Niccolò Aurelio's bride. From 1518 to 1523 Titian produced three large paintings in a mythological program for Alfonso d' Este; the most remarkable, *Bacchus and Ariadne,* dramatizes precisely gestures from Ovid. Of his numerous Venus paintings, the most significant is the *Venus of Urbino* (1538), which shocked Mark Twain with its frank eroticism. [For Titian's *Sacred and Profane Love, Bacchus and Ariadne,* and *Venus of Urbino,* see the color plates in volume 6.]

Many of the earlier mythological paintings are recreations of classical works described by Philostratus or Pliny. In the 1550s Titian created for Philip II of Spain a series of *poesie*— *Venus and Adonis, Danaë, Perseus and Andromeda, Diana and Actaeon, Diana and Callisto, The Death of Actaeon,* and *The Rape of Europa*—that take the genre to another dimension. As the term *poesie* suggests, these are the pictorial equivalent of narrative poetry; here Titian's competition is with Ovid himself. In contrast to Botticelli's Florentine emphasis on concept and design, which results in a frescolike surface, Titian's Venetian devotion to execution, color, and process responds more immediately to Ovid's projections of psychological change. Again, the debate as to whether the *poesie* are Neoplatonic mysteries or sophisticated pornography has been waged. The question does not arise with Titian's *Flaying of Marsyas* (c. 1571–1576), which certainly is not erotic, but profoundly mysterious.

Literature. Here the story begins with Petrarch, whose *Canzoniere* radically exploits the myth of Apollo and Daphne. Like Apollo, Petrarch is both poet and lover, whereas, with the endless plays on her name, Laura metamorphoses into the laurel that crowns poetic achievement. Petrarch instituted an international vogue for sonnet sequences and made mythic structure a requisite feature of them. In other genres, Poliziano's "Stanze" celebrate the powers of Venus and Cupid, and his *Favola di Orfeo* (Fable of Orpheus; 1480) is the first pastoral drama written in Italian. Among the carnival songs of Lorenzo de' Medici (1449–1492), his "Canzona di Bacco" (Song of Bacchus) gives us a poetic precursor to Titian's Bacchanals. In Ovidian fashion, Lorenzo's *Ambra* recounts the river god Ombrone's pursuit of the eponymous nymph, who escapes when Diana turns her to stone. Both artist and poet, Michelangelo Buonarroti (1475–1564) expressed his conflicting, erotic feelings through Ovidian myths— Ganymede, Tityus, and Phaethon—in both drawings and sonnets. To Pico della Mirandola metamorphosis symbolized the self-transformational power of humans with free will; and in this spirit Ludovico Ariosto (1474–1533) understands the myths that he reweaves into the narrative of the century's most famous poem, *Orlando furioso* (1532), whether it is Angelica chained to a rock like Andromeda to be rescued by Perseus-Ruggiero, Ariadne-like Olimpia abandoned by Theseus-Bireno, or a Circean Alcina who turns Astolfo into a tree.

As Italian art had penetrated France with the decorative program at Fontainebleau, so the Italian enthusiasm for myth captivated French writers. The Prologue to the *Gargantua* (1534) of François Rabelais (1494–1553) adapts the Silenus metaphor for Socrates, revived by Ficino and Pico, to describe the seriousness beneath the play of his own book. The ascendance at court of Diane de Poitiers, mistress of Henri II (ruled 1547–1559), generated a cult of Diana, expressed in both art and poetry. Virtually all the poets associated with the Pléiade drew upon classical myth, but none more extensively and brilliantly than Pierre de Ronsard (1524–1585). Ronsard's ekphrastic poems—for example, "La defloration de Lede" (Rape of Leda), which describes mythological scenes on her basket—have affinities with the decorative style of Fontainebleau. In his later hymns, Apollo and Bacchus symbolize the transcendent experience of poetic inspiration.

After several false starts, the Renaissance arrived in England with full force during the reign of Elizabeth (ruled 1558–1603). The *Faerie Queene* by Edmund Spenser (1552–1599) is an amalgam of medieval chivalry, Virgil, Chaucer, and Ariosto, but it is also distinctly Ovidian. In Book 3, the Garden of Adonis presents a generative myth informed by Ficino's concept of love as first mover, while Venus, Adonis, and Diana recurrently figure the activities of fictive characters, who often see their situations mirrored in Ovidian tapestries. The 1590 edition ends by evoking the image of Hermaphroditus; in 1596 the climax is a vision of the Three Graces. Christopher Marlowe (1564–1593) translated Ovid's *Amores* and left unfinished *Hero and Leander,* which launched a fashion for mythological narratives. Marlowe's poem was completed (1598) by Chapman, whose *Shadow of Night* (1594) imitates Orphic hymns and whose *Andromeda liberata* (1614) partially versifies Ficino.

Venus and Adonis (1593), Shakespeare's notable contribution to mythological narrative, captures both the humor and the tragic tonality of Ovid's own verse. The familiar claim that Ovid was Shakespeare's favorite poet is one admission of the extent to which he ransacked the *Metamorphoses* for material, from Philomela for *Titus Andronicus* (1593) to Actaeon for *The Merry Wives of Windsor* (1597). No more shining example is needed than the climax of *The Winter's Tale* (1610–1611), in which the statue of Hermione, executed by "that rare Italian master" Giulio Romano, is restored to life, an event modeled on Pygmalion but extending the competition between the sister arts to that of art with nature herself. Metamorphosis, for Shakespeare as for his predecessors, became an essential metaphor for artistic creation.

See also **Classical Antiquity, Ovid**; **Paganism**; *and biographies of figures mentioned in this entry.*

BIBLIOGRAPHY

Primary Works

Alberti, Leon Battista. *On Painting*. Translated by Cecil Grayson. London, 1991. Translation of *De pictura* (1435).

Alciato, Andrea. *Emblemata: Lyons, 1550.* Translated by Betty I. Knott. Aldershot, U.K., 1996. Facsimile, with facing-page translation and notes, of the first complete edition.

Cartari, Vicenzo. *Imagini delli dei de gl' antichi.* Introduction by Stephen Orgel. New York, 1976. Facsimile of the Venice 1571 edition (the first illustrated).

Conti, Natale. *Natale Conti's Mythologies: A Select Translation.* Translation by Anthony DiMatteo. New York, 1994. Based on the Venice 1567 and Padua 1616 editions.

Ficino, Marsilio. *Commentary on Plato's Symposium on Love.* Translated by Sears Jayne. Dallas, Tex., 1985. Translation of the Latin *De amore* (written 1469, printed 1484).

Ripa, Cesare. *Baroque and Rococo Pictorial Imagery.* Edited and translated by Edward A. Maser. New York, 1971. Translation of the German and Latin edition of *Iconologia* by Johann Georg Hertel (1758–1760?) with the eighteenth-century illustrations.

Sandys, George. *Ovid's Metamorphosis Englished, Mythologized, and Represented in Figures.* Edited by Karl K. Hulley and Stanley T. Vandersall. Lincoln, Neb., 1970.

Secondary Works

Allen, Don Cameron. *Mysteriously Meant: The Rediscovery of Pagan Symbolism and Allegorical Interpretation in the Renaissance.* Baltimore, 1970. Essential study.

Allen, Michael J. B. *The Platonism of Marsilio Ficino: A Study of His Phaedrus Commentary, Its Sources and Genesis.* Berkeley, Calif., 1984. Valuable on mythology.

Barkan, Leonard. *The Gods Made Flesh: Metamorphosis and the Pursuit of Paganism.* New Haven, Conn., 1986. Primarily on literature, with some attention to painting.

Bush, Douglas. *Mythology and the Renaissance Tradition in English Poetry.* New York, 1963. Foundational 1932 study.

Cave, Terence. "Ronsard's Mythological Universe." In *Ronsard the Poet.* Edited by Terence Cave. London, 1973. Pages 159–208.

Fehl, Philipp P. *Decorum and Wit: The Poetry of Venetian Painting.* Vienna, 1992. Several important studies of mythological painting.

Gombrich, E. H. *Symbolic Images: Studies in the Art of the Renaissance.* Oxford, 1978.

Hulse, Clark. *Metamorphic Verse: The Elizabethan Minor Epic.* Princeton, N.J., 1981.

Panofsky, Erwin. *Studies in Iconology: Humanistic Themes in the Art of the Renaissance.* New York, 1962. Classic 1939 study.

Reid, Jane Davidson. *The Oxford Guide to Classical Mythology in the Arts, 1300–1990s.* New York, 1993. Useful reference book.

Saslow, James M. *Ganymede in the Renaissance: Homosexuality in Art and Society.* New Haven, Conn., 1986. A significant break with the intellectual-history approach.

Seznec, Jean. *The Survival of the Pagan Gods: The Mythological Tradition and Its Place in Renaissance Humanism and Art.* Translated by Barbara F. Sessions. Princeton, N.J., 1972. Translation of *Le Survivance des dieux antiques* (1940).

Waddington, Raymond B. *The Mind's Empire: Myth and Form in George Chapman's Narrative Poems.* Baltimore, 1974.

Wind, Edgar. *Pagan Mysteries in the Renaissance.* New York, 1968. Revised edition of a stimulating and influential 1958 study.

RAYMOND B. WADDINGTON

NAOGEORGUS, THOMAS (Thomas Kirchmeyer, Kirchmair, Kirchmaier, also Neubauer; 1508–1563), German Protestant theologian, humanist poet, dramatist. Born in Straubing, Bavaria, Naogeorgus entered the monastery of the Dominicans in Regensburg at an early age. However, he left it in 1526 to study at various German universities. During this time he converted to Lutheranism. Recommended by Philipp Melanchthon, he became a Protestant minister in the Saxon towns of Mühltroff (1535), Sulza (1536), and Kahla (1542). Personal and theological conflicts led to his having short stints as minister in six more towns before he died in 1563 during a plague epidemic.

A nonconformist, Naogeorgus got into conflict not only with the papacy but also with the orthodox Lutherans. Wittenberg theologians and the Kahla city council forced him to flee to Augsburg. Following short stints as minister in the south German towns of Kaufbeuren (1546) and then Kempten (1548), which he had to leave because it had adopted the Interim (Charles V's mandate demanding a complete return to the medieval church), he began to study law at the University of Basel (March–October 1551). In the same year Duke Christoph of Württemberg called him to Stuttgart, where he stayed until 1560, when conflicts with his superiors resulted in his transfer to Backnang (1560) and then Esslingen (May 1560–January 1563). Because of his Calvinist leanings and his involvement in a witch trial he was dismissed from that post. The Calvinist elector Frederick III of the Palatinate appointed him minister in Wiesloch, near Heidelberg.

Naogeorgus's literary significance is based on his six dramas. The *Tragoedia nova pammachius* (The new tragedy Pammachius; 1538) is a grandiose blend of salvation history, world history, and topical anti-papal polemics. Its function was to show that the rule of the papacy is the work of Satan. The play ended with an unprecedented theatrical trick. A speaker announced that the expected fifth act would be written by Christ himself on the day of the Last Judgment. The play *Mercator seu Judicium* (The merchant; 1540) uses the basic structure of the morality play to present Luther's doctrine of justification by grace alone; Naogeorgus used a chorus to sum up his theological message. His third play, *Incendia seu Pyrgopolinices* (Arson, or Pyrgopolinices; 1541) seeks to demonstrate in coded form the alleged criminal acts of the "papists." In the three dramas *Hamanus* (1543), *Hieremias* (1551), and *Judas* (1552), biblical themes serve as a foil for the criticism of contemporary issues and persons.

Reviving the Roman tradition of verse-satire in Germany, Naogeorgus wrote *Satyrarum libri quinque* (Five books of satires; 1555). In all of his works, Naogeorgus articulated an Erasmian optimism, expressing the belief that human beings could be improved by education. In his satires Naogeorgus does not spare the Lutherans, whom he accuses of establishing a new papacy in Wittenberg, or those Protestant princes who expropriated church property for their own personal gain. In his *Agriculturae sacrae libri quinque* (Five books of the sacred agriculture; 1550), Naogeorgus develops his ideas about the qualifications and functions of a good (Protestant) pastor.

Unlike many Reformation writers who wrote in the vernacular to reach a broad audience, Naogeorgus addressed himself to the educated humanist elite by writing exclusively in Latin. Naogeorgus's plays, especially *Pammachius,* had a great impact in Europe and were staged until the seventeenth century.

BIBLIOGRAPHY

Primary Work

Naogeorg, Thomas [Thomas Naogeorgus]. *Sämtliche Werke.* Edited by Hans-Gert Roloff. 6 vols. Berlin and New York, 1975–1987. Contains all of the plays, in Latin and in German translations.

Secondary Works

Fauth, Dieter. "Kirchmeyer, Thomas." In *The Oxford Encyclopedia of the Reformation.* Edited by Hans J. Hillerbrand. New York and Oxford, 1996. Vol. 2, p. 378.

Roloff, Hans-Gert. "Naogeorg, Thomas." In *Autorenlexikon: Autoren und Werke deutscher Sprache.* Edited by Walther Killy. Gütersloh and Munich, Germany, 1990. Vol. 8, pp. 330–332. Concise article by Germany's foremost Naogeorgus scholar.

Roloff, Hans-Gert. "Thomas Naogeorg und das Problem von Humanismus und Reformation." In *L'humanisme allemand (1480–1540).* Paris and Munich, 1979. Pages 455–475. Argues convincingly that Naogeorgus represents a successful synthesis of humanism and Reformation.

ECKHARD BERNSTEIN

NAPLES. [This entry includes two subentries, one on the history of the city and kingdom of Naples in the Renaissance and the other on artists active in Neapolitan territory.]

Naples in the Renaissance

When Petrarch went to be examined by King Robert the Wise of Naples before his coronation as poet laureate in 1341, he was acknowledging Robert's moral and intellectual leadership in Italy. Robert's Angevin court had likewise enthralled the young Giovanni Boccaccio, who spent thirteen formative years, 1327–1341, in Naples. Angevin Naples before the plague of 1348, like fifteenth-century Aragonese Naples and late sixteenth-century Spanish Naples, was a political and cultural capital. It played a large role in Italian and European affairs and was one of Italy's great powers at the center of Renaissance crises and debates.

The Kingdom of Sicily, forged by the eleventh- and twelfth-century Norman conquest of Byzantine, Lombard, and Muslim lands in southern Italy and Sicily (Sicily on either side of the straits), passed to the Holy Roman Empire through marriage and inheritance by the end of the twelfth century. The Angevin-papal alliance of the thirteenth century against Frederick II (ruled 1198–1250) and his heirs wrested Naples and Sicily from the empire in the battles of Benevento (1266) and Tagliacozzo (1268) and established Charles of Anjou (ruled 1266–1285) at the head of a new Angevin dynasty ambitious to replace the Byzantine with a Mediterranean empire under French leadership. After the revolt of Sicily known as the Sicilian Vespers (1282) placed the island kingdom under Peter III of Aragon (the husband of the Hohenstaufen heiress Constance), the Kingdom of Naples, which was the lower third of the Italian peninsula, remained in Angevin hands. Angevin-Aragonese rivalry for kingship in Naples and Sicily continued the medieval conflict between papal and imperial factions through the fourteenth and fifteenth centuries, with the 1442 conquest of Alfonso V of Aragon temporarily reunifying the kingdom. After Alfonso's death in 1458, Sicily reverted to the king of Aragon and Naples passed to his illegitimate son, King Ferdinand I, called Ferrante. With the French invasions of Italy in 1494 and the Habsburg-Valois wars of the sixteenth century, the unified Spanish monarchy conquered Naples in 1503 and held it under a viceroy as a cornerstone of Spain's Italian policy until it passed to the Austrian Habsburgs in 1713 at the end of the War of the Spanish Succession.

Angevin Naples (1268–1442) flourished under Robert the Wise (ruled 1309–1343), who assumed the role of leader of the Italian Guelfs and nourished hopes that he would unite and liberate Italy. The problematic rule of his childless granddaughter, Joanna I (ruled 1343–1382)—her alleged complicity in the murder of her husband, Prince Andrew of Hungary (1345), the resultant invasion by his brother King Louis I of Hungary, alliance with the Avignon papacy, and naming of a French prince as her heir—precipitated a divisive dynastic struggle within the house of Anjou. The line of Durazzo, descended from Robert's younger brother, allied itself with the Roman popes, Florence, and the city of Naples to crown Charles III (ruled 1381–1386), one of Robert's grandnephews, king. His son Ladislas (ruled 1386–1414), despite being a minor at his coronation, repelled the rival claims of Louis II of Anjou and grew to become a military conqueror who not only restored the Neapolitan kingdom but also expanded into central Italy, taking Rome, Latium, and Umbria by exploiting the uncertainties around the Great Schism. As Ladislas moved into Tuscany, Florence and Siena joined his Angevin rivals to thwart his advance. His sister Joanna II (ruled 1414–1435), even more notorious in her amours than Joanna I, ruled an ever-dissolving kingdom as the last of the Nea-

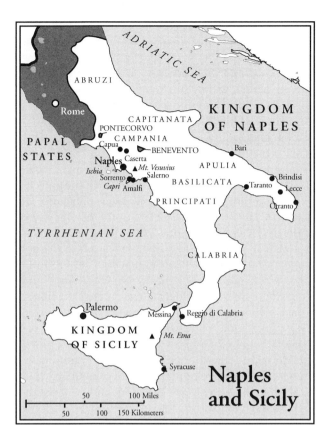

ABRUZI

Rome

CAPITANATA

PONTECORVO

CAMPANIA

Capua

Caserta

BENEVENTO

KINGDOM
OF NAPLES

Bari

PAPAL
STATES

Naples

Ischia

Sorrento

Capri Amalfi

▲ Mt. Vesuvius

Salerno

APULIA

BASILICATA

PRINCIPATI

Taranto

Brindisi

Lecce

Otranto

TYRRHENIAN SEA

CALABRIA

Palermo

Messina

Reggio di Calabria

KINGDOM
OF SICILY

▲ Mt. Etna

Syracuse

50   100 Miles

50   100   150 Kilometers

ADRIATIC SEA

**Naples
and Sicily**

politan Angevins. Upon her death the contested succession between her disputed heirs, René of Anjou (supported by the pope) and Alfonso V of Aragon (supported by the Visconti in Milan), brought war for almost a decade.

Aragonese Naples (1442–1503), after the 1442 conquest by Alfonso V (King Alfonso I of Naples, ruled 1442–1458), became the cornerstone of a Mediterranean empire bound by Aragon, Sardinia, Sicily, and Naples that was fueled by Catalan merchants and trade. Once his court was established at Naples, Alfonso intervened in the Milanese war of succession, drove the Genoese into French hands, signed the Peace of Lodi in 1454, and promoted his Catalan servant and ecclesiastic Alfonso de Borgia, Pope Calixtus III (reigned 1455–1458), with whom he later quarreled. Alfonso's illegitimate son, Ferrante (1458–1494), succeeded him in Naples, while his brother, John II (ruled 1458–1479), took over the Aragonese possessions. Ferrante's reputation as a subtle yet duplicitous and cruel diplomat, forged by the propaganda victory of his enemies after the demise of the Aragonese dynasty, arose from the ruthless internal wars against his succession that joined two baronial revolts (1458–1465 and 1485–1486) with continued

Angevin claims to the kingdom. Ferrante was, in fact, little different from his contemporaries and a critical force in maintaining the precarious peace in Italy during the late fifteenth century. In the high-stakes game of Renaissance diplomacy, he was a wily player who recognized the wisdom of supporting Lorenzo de' Medici in Florence, reestablished ties with the Sforza in Milan through marriage alliances, and married his daughter Beatrice to Matthias Corvinus, the king of Hungary, to bolster defense against the Turks, who had seized the Apulian town of Otranto in 1480–1481.

In 1494 Ferrante's unpopular son Alfonso II (ruled 1494–1495), who was adept in military affairs, mistakenly sent an army to northern Italy under his son Ferdinand II, called Ferrandino (ruled 1495–1496), to head off the French invasionary forces of Charles VIII (ruled 1483–1498). Evading the Neapolitan army, Charles VIII continued his uncontested march to Naples, where Alfonso II abdicated in January 1495. Ferrandino failed to rally Neapolitan resistance and fled Naples in February when Charles triumphantly entered the city. Only three months later, in May 1495, Charles left Naples, never to return. The remaining French troops were defeated in June a year later, but Ferrandino died in October 1496 and was succeeded by his uncle Frederick (ruled 1496–1501), the second son of Ferrante I. Despite Frederick's abilities, he found himself expendable as Naples had now proven a vulnerable prize coveted anew by King Louis XII of France (ruled 1498–1515), whose army invaded Italy in 1499, and Frederick's Aragonese cousin, Ferdinand II, called the Catholic, of Spain (ruled Naples as Ferdinand III 1504–1516), who had aided Ferrandino's restoration. France and Spain partitioned the kingdom by the treaty of Granada (1500), but in 1502 Gonzalo Fernández de Córdoba, the Great Captain, led his Spanish *tercios* (troops trained to repel cavalry using pikes and firearms in tight square formations) from Calabria and Apulia to expel the French and conquer the whole kingdom by the end of 1503.

Spanish Naples (1504–1713), from Gonzalo Fernández de Córdoba's entrance into the capital in January 1504 and appointment as first Spanish viceroy until the dissolution of the last invading French army in southern Italy in 1528, acted as the military staging ground for Spanish policy in Italy. Under the Holy Roman emperor Charles V (ruled 1519–1556; ruled Spain as Charles I, 1516–1556), the Francophile nobility was eradicated and replaced with loyalist vassals, such as the Genoese Andrea Doria, who was made one of the kingdom's most powerful feudal lords as prince of Melfi. The viceroy Pedro de Toledo's long tenure (1532–1553) oversaw the stabilization of Spanish rule in Naples as well as the Spanish pacification of Italy with the annexation of Milan and the marriage of Eleonora of Toledo (the viceroy's daughter) to Cosimo I Medici (ruled 1537–1574) of Florence. Famine and food-provisioning needs precipitated short-lived revolts in the fast-growing capital in 1508, 1533, and 1585, but only two cases are recorded when nobles and *popolo* sided together against the Spanish monarchy—the two failed attempts to introduce the Spanish Inquisition (1510 and 1547). Under Philip II (ruled 1556–1598), Neapolitan (along with Sicilian and Milanese) affairs were overseen by the Council of Italy after 1558. The viceroyalty fostered the development of a new class of nobles of the robe (*togati*), whose legal and administrative expertise furthered the bureaucratization of the kingdom and acted as a wedge against baronial authority. Genoese merchants entered Neapolitan trade and finance with greater frequency to tie it ever tighter to Philip's imperial structure. Although an absentee monarch meant the loss of Neapolitan political independence, Spanish rule provided for political stabilization through protection against foreign invasion from France or the Ottoman Turks, subordination of the unruly nobility, and establishment of long-lasting bureaucratic and legal traditions.

Economic, Social, and Cultural Life.

The 79,477 square kilometers of the mid-sixteenth-century kingdom had a population density of about thirty-five people per square kilometer but with wide regional variation among the twelve provinces and extreme differences between the capital and provincial towns. Dense population in the city of Naples, which, with 250,000 inhabitants in 1600, rivaled Paris as western Europe's largest city, spilled over along the Bay of Naples into Principato Citra and could also be found in the Adriatic provinces of Terra di Bari and Terra d'Otranto as well as around certain cities in Calabria, whereas the interior provinces of Basilicata, Molise, Capitanata, and the Abruzzi had a sparse population. The fourteenth-century socioeconomic crisis had especially depopulated the provincial interior as the number of rural communes declined by 40 percent from 2,356 in 1268 to 1,462 in 1505. The pre-plague population of about 2.5 million fell to about 1.5 million in the fifteenth century before redistributing itself and recovering to 2.5 to 3 million by 1600. The capital had surpassed its medieval, pre-plague peak of 100,000 (from a loss of as many as two-thirds of its inhabitants) by 1500, but no other town in the kingdom numbered more than 20,000. The gulf between center and periphery was enormous, and the concentration of population in unarticulated, widely separated coastal enclaves impeded the kingdom's economic development.

Localized markets in Bari, Taranto, Reggio di Calabria, and Salerno served as export outlets to Tuscan, Venetian, Catalan, and Genoese merchants shipping raw agricultural products—wheat, silk, wool, and olive oil—to their respective industrial cities, which enjoyed a ten-to-one trade imbalance in favor of exports in about 1580, at the height of the brief and illusory prosperity of the Indian summer of the Italian economy. Two economies, silk and wool textiles from the capital and agricultural exports from the provincial centers, and two societies, large and small agricultural producers, exacerbated the differences between city and countryside, rich and poor. The agricultural interests of the feudal nobility sustained them in their regional power bases and allied them with foreign merchants against communal towns and the development of native commerce and industry. Such regional isolation and association with foreign industrial centers increased factiousness among the feudal nobility and made the kingdom easy prey for foreign intervention and conquest. The capital and its court remained a world apart—home to conspicuous consumption and display of a dominant aristocracy, arena for an ambitious professional class of lawyers and bureaucrats, marketplace for an artisanal workforce servicing demand, and refuge to an ever-growing teeming mass that was escaping provincial taxation and feudal jurisdiction.

The disproportionate wealth of the city and its myriad noble courts fostered a vibrant cultural life. Angevin Naples commissioned works by Tuscan artists such as Giotto di Bondone, Donatello, and Michelozzo di Bartolommeo and was influenced by the French Gothic in its art and architecture, literature and learning. Church architecture from the beginning of Angevin rule—San Lorenzo Maggiore, San Domenico Maggiore, Santa Chiara, San Eligio, Santa Maria Donna Regina, and the Duomo—attests to a late medieval confluence of piety and aesthetics. Aragonese patronage attracted the well-known humanists Antonio Beccadelli (Panormita), Bartolomeo Facio, Lorenzo Valla, Giannozzo Manetti, and Giovanni Pontano; sustained the native humanists Giovanni Brancati, Giovanni Albino, Giuniano Maio, Gabriele Altilio, and Elisio Calenzio; and nourished a local variant of "feudal" humanism, inspired by the exigencies of the French invasions and Italian wars, in Pietro Jacopo De Jennaro, Andrea Matteo Acquaviva, Belisario Acquaviva, Antonio de Ferrari (Galateo), and Tristano Caracciolo. The poet Jacopo Sannazaro may be the most exemplary of the political and cultural players spawned in the late-fifteenth-century Italian Wars. Spanish Naples witnessed the establishment of a reformist circle around Juan de Valdés and the religious fervor of Gian Pietro Carafa (Paul IV, reigned 1555–1559), the rebuilding of the city under Pedro de Toledo, and the formation of numerous secret and learned academies. In the second half of the sixteenth century the philosophical ideas of Bernardino Telesio, Giordano Bruno, and Tommaso Campanella, the scientific inquiries of Giambattista Della Porta and his naturalist circle, and the literary stimulus from the Sorrento-born exile Torquato Tasso all played important roles in Neapolitan cultural life. Neither a minor participant in nor a cultural backwater during the Renaissance, Naples was later marginalized by its decline and the anti-Spanish propaganda of eighteenth- and nineteenth-century nationalist historiography.

See also **Sicily.**

BIBLIOGRAPHY

Primary Work

Bacco, Enrico. *Naples: An Early Guide.* Edited and translated by Eileen Gardiner. New York, 1991.

Secondary Works

Abulafia, David, ed. *The French Descent into Renaissance Italy, 1494–95: Antecedents and Effects.* Aldershot, Hampshire, U.K., 1995.

Bentley, Jerry H. *Politics and Culture in Renaissance Naples.* Princeton, N.J., 1987.

Calabria, Antonio, and John A. Marino, eds. and trans. *Good Government in Spanish Naples.* New York, 1990.

Croce, Benedetto. *History of the Kingdom of Naples.* Edited by H. Stuart Hughes. Translated by Frances Frenaye. Chicago, 1970.

Galasso, Giuseppe. *Il regno di Napoli: Il mezzogiorno angioino e aragonese (1266–1494).* Turin, Italy, 1992.

Ryder, Alan. *Alfonso the Magnanimous: King of Aragon, Naples, and Sicily, 1396–1458.* Oxford, 1990.

Ryder, Alan. *The Kingdom of Naples under Alfonso the Magnanimous: The Making of a Modern State.* Oxford, 1976.

JOHN A. MARINO

Art in Naples

Naples, one of Europe's largest and most prosperous cities, was subjected to government by three separate foreign powers between the years 1400 and 1600: the Provençal house of Anjou, the Aragonese dynasty established by Alfonso I "the Magnanimous" in 1442, and finally, from 1504 onward, a viceroy delegated by Spain. Each government favored its own artistic style, but in Naples, a city whose own history reached back over two thousand years of cosmopolitan exchanges among vastly differing cultures, these external traditions developed a strong local flavor.

Founded by Greeks, surrounded by Italic nations like the Latins, Etruscans, Samnites, and Oscans, connected by trade with the seafarers of Phoenicia and Egypt, ancient Neapolis, the "new city," was eventually absorbed into the Roman Empire. Its physical layout still preserves the old Greek street grid (with Roman modifications) and its rich repertory of standing ruins ensured that Renaissance Naples, like Rome itself, always expressed a particularly deep and immediate engagement with the Greco-Roman past.

Angevin Period, to 1442. The rise of merchant capitalism in the Middle Ages brought this important Italian emporium into close contact with Arab traders and trading cities, with noticeable effect on local tastes in architecture and design (the ornamental brick and tile of the Cathedral of San Matteo at Salerno, the arabesques in the Cloister of Paradise in the cathedral at Amalfi). To this rich mix, the Provençal lords of Anjou added during the fourteenth and early fifteenth centuries a French Gothic aesthetic, further refining the early Renaissance flavor of the Naples in which Giotto painted for the Angevin king, Petrarch evoked the memory of Virgil, Boccaccio met his Fiammetta, and chivalry mixed with the ancient classics to shape the tastes of the city's aristocrats.

The legacy of Angevin Naples included a pronounced taste for Gothic arches and soaring architecture, gracefully stylized sculpture, and the precise oil paintings perfected by Burgundian artists in the fourteenth and fifteenth centuries; Naples indeed became a particularly important market for Burgundian oils and manuscript illuminations. One of the very first examples of recognizably Renaissance art in Naples (if we exclude Giotto's works, mostly destroyed) is the tomb (1428) of the Angevin king Ladislas of Durazzo (ruled 1386–1414) in the Augustinian church of San Giovanni a Carbonara, an imposing succession of marble arches topped by an equestrian statue of Ladislas himself. Commissioned by his sister and successor, Queen Giovanna II (ruled 1414–1435), and executed by a team of Florentine sculptors that included Andrea and Marco di Nofri da Firenze, the monument combines Gothic spires and classical pilasters in an elegant, if idiosyncratic, expression of the Angevins' dynastic hopes.

Art in Naples. *Virgin of the Annunciation* by Antonello da Messina (c. 1430–1479). GALLERIA NAZIONALE, PALERMO/ ANDERSON/ALINARI/ ART RESOURCE

The Aragon Period, 1442–1504. In 1442, René of Anjou was defeated in battle by the Aragonese monarch Alfonso the Magnanimous (1396–1458), who transferred his court to Naples and spent the next sixteen years transforming its kingdom into an evocation of both its classical past and its Spanish present. Alfonso restored narrowed Neapolitan streets to their old Roman breadth, added spacious new piazzas, and girdled the city with the latest in fortifications. Spurred by his Florentine bankers, he imported Florentine architects and sculptors to embellish the city according to the aesthetic principles of humanists like Leone Battista Alberti and Alfonso's own advisers, prominent among whom were the inveterate enemies Lorenzo Valla (Alfonso's secretary) and Antonio Beccadelli "Il Panormita." Alfonso's son Ferrante (ruled 1458–1494) shared and continued many of his father's aesthetic preferences.

Perhaps the most definite statement of Aragonese ambitions, and the most succinct synopsis of the Aragonese contribution to art in Naples, is the lofty marble triumphal arch (begun 1443) inserted between two fat towers of the Castel Nuovo. With architecture based on Roman triumphal arches and sculpture that draws its inspiration from Roman historical reliefs, Roman coins, and Roman portraiture, Alfonso's commemorative monument places him firmly in the tradition of ancient Imperial rule. Design and execution of the arch fell to an impressively international group of artists, led by the Dalmatian architect Onofrio di Giordano: Pietro di Milano, an Italian who had been working in Dalmatia; the Dalmatian Francesco Laurana; the Italians Paolo Romano, Isaia da Pisa, Andrea dell' Aquila, and Domenico Gagini; and the Catalan Pere Joan. Alfonso's legitimized son and successor Ferrante added an inner arch in 1465 (by Andrea dell' Aquila and Antonio Chellini, both pupils of Donatello) and a set of bronze doors by the Italian metallurgist Guglielmo Lo Monaco in the 1470s. All told, castle and arch were meant to convey an image of consolidated power that Alfonso and his successors were hard pressed to maintain in reality.

Patronage of Neapolitan Nobility. Naples did not belong entirely to its foreign monarchs, whether they were French or Spanish. Local baronial families like the Carafa and Sanseverino dominated city politics, setting their mark on the cityscape by erecting imposing palazzi, endowing churches, commissioning works of art, and conspiring with the deposed Angevins against the Aragonese dynasts; in 1485 the rebellion known as the "Barons' Conspiracy" temporarily drove Ferrante, Alfonso's son, into exile. Florentine style—inspired by the Palazzo Rucellai of Alberti, Palazzo Strozzi, and Palazzo Medici—governs the appearance of rusticated, blocklike baronial residences like the Palazzo Como (intermittent work 1464–1490) and the Palazzo of Diomede Carafa (1466; now Palazzo Carafa Santangelo), testimony to the close ties Naples maintained with Florentine financiers as well as the Tuscan city's concerted efforts to become Italy's cultural center. The Palazzo of the Orsini of Gravina (1513–1549), by contrast, evokes the style of papal Rome, where the Orsini were as important as they were in Naples. The Sanseverino family, perhaps the most powerful of all the Neapolitan baronial clans with extensive feudal holdings in Southern Italy, adopted a Spanish and Sicilian tradition by using diamond-point masonry for the forbidding palazzo (1470) that was transformed in the later sixteenth century into the Jesuit church of the Gesù Nuovo (1584–1601).

Baronial families also dominated artistic patronage in Neapolitan churches alongside the monarchy. The Caracciolo family maintained its profile through elaborate chapels in the Augustinian church of San

Giovanni a Carbonara. The most notable of these, the rotunda of the Caracciolo di Vico, was completed in 1516 by a group of artists that included the Spanish sculptors Bartolomé Ordoñez and Diego Siloe, who brought their Italian experience back to their homeland with significant effects on the subsequent development of Spanish art.

The Dominican mother house at San Domenico Maggiore, endowed by the Angevins in 1283, received close attention from the Orsini family, who boasted its famous resident Thomas Aquinas as one of their relatives, and from the Carafa, whose wooden creche scene by Pietro Belverte (1507–1511) still survives. The Aragonese also contributed when they chose the sacristy of the church as their mausoleum and erected the monumental staircase that dominates the piazza beneath the apse of the church.

The church of Monteoliveto, founded by the Angevins in 1411 and extensively elaborated thereafter, also represents a combination of Aragonese patronage, especially by Alfonso, and the sponsorship of nominally private citizens, although the Florentine banking family of the Strozzi and the Ferrarese ruling family of the Este were in fact tied to the Aragonese monarchy by intricate financial and political bonds. The important foreign presence in this thoroughly Renaissance church is augmented by the presence of foreign artists, including marble reliefs by the Tuscan sculptor Benedetto da Maiano (tomb of Maria d' Aragona, 1479; *Annunciation,* 1489), intarsiated choir stalls (c. 1510) by Fra' Giovanni da Verona, and a life-size terra-cotta statue group portraying the Aragonese monarchs in *Lamentation over the dead Christ* (1492) by Guido Mazzoni of Modena.

The Angevin-founded Duomo, or Cathedral of Naples, particularly reflects the Roman-inspired patronage of Cardinal Oliviero Carafa, who in the first years of the sixteenth century commissioned a large *Assumption of the Virgin* by the Umbrian painter Pietro Perugino. Carafa also commissioned the Soccorpo, an extraordinary chapel reputedly designed by Bramante and executed by the local architects Tommaso and Giovan Tommaso Malvito to house the relics of the patron saint of Naples, St. Januarius (San Gennaro), translated to the Cathedral in 1497.

Perhaps the most distinctively Neapolitan of all Renaissance buildings in Naples is the mausoleum or chapel (1490–1492; architect disputed) of the city's foremost humanist: the writer and diplomat Giovanni Gioviano Pontano (1422–1503). Modeled on ancient Roman tombs, studded with learned inscriptions, Pontano's stately, severely classical chapel,

with its pilasters in the local gray stone known as piperno, also served before and after his death as the meeting place for his Academy. This learned gathering of like-minded men felt that their efforts to revive the literary culture of ancient Rome in a new Christian spirit had transformed Naples into a new Arcadia, to borrow an image from Pontano's good friend and fellow Neapolitan humanist, Jacopo Sannazaro.

Like Pontano, Sannazaro (1457–1530) adapted classical literary forms to Christian purpose, but he also endowed a church to the Virgin Mary, Santa Maria del Parto (completed 1525), in conjunction with the writing of his Christian epic, *De partu Virginis* (On the Virgin's giving birth). A second church, dedicated to his name saints, James and Nazarius, was never completed. Sannazaro's white marble funeral monument, by Giovanni Angelo Montorsoli and Bartolommeo Ammannati (1536), reflects the influence of Michelangelo. Had the Aragonese-founded villa of Poggioreale survived into the present century, we might have a still more vivid picture of the Arcadian life in Renaissance Naples, for records suggest that its gardens and sumptuous architecture made it a worthy successor to the Arabic tradition of the "paradise," the enclosed garden of which the Paradise Cloister at Amalfi is a rare remnant.

Naples under Spanish Rule. In 1504, Naples and its kingdom were subjected to a Spanish viceroy. Now Iberian influences that had long been implicit in the art and urban planning of Aragonese Naples became much more explicit expressions of political domination, a dependency brought into still clearer focus with the accession of the brilliant Habsburg power-broker Charles V to the Spanish throne in 1516. The viceregal government of Don Pedro de Toledo (1532–1553) made late Renaissance Naples a model of city planning; the broad straight thoroughfare of the Via Toledo, laid out in 1536, developed whole new areas of the city, protecting them by a greatly expanded tract of fortification walls. The tiny city blocks of the Spanish Quarter still preserve Don Pedro's urban design.

From the time that Giotto made his visit in the fourteenth century, painting in Naples remained under heavy foreign influence, from the French painters favored by the Angevins to the Flemings preferred by the Aragonese to the Tuscan and Roman styles of the sixteenth century. Native Neapolitans had little chance to develop their own distinctive style. But the arrival in 1606 of one particular foreigner to Naples, the Lombard expatriate Michelangelo Merisi da Caravaggio (1573–1616), had a different effect. Caravaggio's style, nurtured in Lombardy and ripened in Rome, featured dramatic effects of dark and light and a clarity of presentation that looked especially refreshing when contrasted with the elaborately stylized gestures of much contemporary religious and mythological painting.

But Naples added something more. Caravaggio arrived as a fugitive from Rome, where he stood charged with murder; his work under this duress shows a new concentration and a still greater compositional and expressive power. His sensitivity to the burgeoning vitality of Neapolitan life showed forth in paintings like his *Seven Works of Mercy,* executed shortly after his arrival (1606) for the young nobles of a Neapolitan confraternity founded in 1601, the Pio Monte della Misericoria. According to contemporary reports, perhaps the best painting of his entire career was the *Resurrection of Christ* he painted for his "native" church of Sant' Anna dei Lombardi; tragically, it was destroyed in an earthquake in 1798. Caravaggio's presence in Naples, however brief (it was intermittent between 1606 and 1610), was enough to galvanize a local painterly tradition, exemplified by followers like Battistello Caracciolo and Artemisia Gentileschi, who would shortly help to transform Naples into one of the international centers for Baroque art.

See also **Caravaggio, Michelangelo Merisi da**; **Pontano, Giovanni**; **Sannazaro, Jacopo**.

BIBLIOGRAPHY

Abbate, Francesco. *Storia dell' Arte nell' Italia Meridionale.* Vols. 2, *Il Sud angiono e aragonese,* and 3, *Dal Viceregno spagnolo al Regno borbonico.* Rome, 1998.

Cole, Alison. *Art of the Italian Renaissance Courts: Virtue and Magnificence.* London, 1995. See especially chapter 2.

Langdon, Helen. *Caravaggio: A Life.* New York, 1998.

Pane, Roberto. *Il Rinascimento nell' Italia meridionale.* Milan, 1977–1979.

INGRID D. ROWLAND

NASHE, THOMAS. *See* **Fiction,** *subentry on* **Elizabethan Fiction.**

NATION-STATE. "Nation-state" is a modern term designating a political entity in which, ideally, all the people of a nationality live, where political authority resides in members of that nationality, with the state's policies reflecting the general will of those people.

Most of the available evidence can be marshaled against the existence of nation-states in the Renaissance. Religion created more unity or disunity in a state than nationality did, and the dynastic ambitions of rulers were the major motivation for war. The existence of numerous joint monarchies—Poland and Lithuania, the Scandinavian Union of Kalmar (from which Sweden seceded in 1523), Ferdinand and Isabella's Spain—in which rulers from one ethnic background were accepted peaceably as monarchs in another realm, and elective monarchies—Bohemia, Poland, Hungary—in which foreign princes were often chosen as monarchs, reveal that there was little sense that a ruler had to come from the native ethnic group. The widespread use of mercenaries indicates the same about fighting men. Citizenship, if that word can be used for the Renaissance, often resided in a fragment of the larger geographical unit, as was true of Germany and Italy, or in an empire made up of numerous ethnic groups, such as the Ottoman Empire. When political entities in Italy and Germany, such as Venice, Florence, or Brandenburg, began to create larger territorial units, that enlargement was intended to increase the power of those states, not to create a unified nation-state.

Several states, however, coincided entirely or closely with modern nation-states. For them the evidence of true nation-statehood is mixed. The Swiss Confederation, for example, was a nation without a state. France's major military episodes in the Renaissance, the invasions of Italy and the Valois-Habsburg wars, were products of dynastic claims, although there were discussions of what constituted the natural boundaries of France. The several revolts in the old kingdom of Aragon after 1516 suggest that the Aragonese did not regard themselves as Spaniards. England, Sweden, and Portugal came closest to being true nation-states. While Henry VIII involved England in several wars on the Continent largely in pursuit of the old dynastic claim to the French throne, the Spanish Armada episode in Elizabeth's reign tapped a powerful patriotism among the English, well displayed in Shakespeare's historical plays, with their paeans for "this realm, this England." The Swedish revolt of 1523 against the Danish monarchy, establishing the native Vasa dynasty, closely prefigures the modern creation of nation-states, but religious concerns and the desire to become Holy Roman Emperor were major motives for the Swedish king Gustavus Adolphus's involvement in the Thirty Years' War. Portugal, with its homogeneous population and its nationalistic epic *Os Lusíadas,* by Luíz Vas de Camões, can be described as a nation-state, yet King Sebastian met his death on a crusade against the Muslims in Morocco in 1578, leading to the Spanish monarchy's rule over Portugal for the next sixty years.

While the evidence for the existence of nation-states in the Renaissance era is limited, the period is full of nationalistic sentiment, even in those countries clearly not yet nation-states. Some of the best examples come from the works of Machiavelli, Ulrich von Hutten, and Joachim Du Bellay. This sense that a person belonged to a distinct ethnic group different from its neighbors, which sixteenth-century religious divisions enhanced, was fundamental to the later creation of the nation-state.

See also **Political Thought.**

BIBLIOGRAPHY

Bean, Richard. "War and the Birth of the Nation-State." *Journal of Economic History* 33 (1973): 203–221.
Marcu, Eva Dorothea. *Sixteenth-Century Nationalism.* New York, 1976.
Tivey, Leonard, ed. *The Nation-State: The Formation of Modern Politics.* Oxford, 1981.

FREDERIC J. BAUMGARTNER

NATURAL HISTORY. *See* **Botany; Geology; Zoology.**

NATURAL PHILOSOPHY. A branch of philosophy concerned with the study of sensible or corporeal being, natural philosophy is mainly Aristotelian but includes a considerable accretion of Neoplatonic elements, plus distinctive interpretations of Christian and Islamic commentators. This study, hallowed by tradition in the Latin West from the twelfth century onwards, formed a major part of university studies in the Renaissance. Novel views of nature also appeared at that time, but these are treated elsewhere. Traditional philosophy of nature was complex and its written expression prolix, yet it provided the seedbed from which disciplines now respected as parts of "modern science" emerged.

A General Science of Nature. The two expressions, natural science (Latin *scientia naturalis*) and natural philosophy (Latin *philosophia naturalis*), were used interchangeably throughout the Renaissance. The overall subject of consideration was material being as it appears to the senses; thus, it was differentiated from mathematics, which considered quantitative being, and metaphysics, which considered being in general. Aristotle's *Physics* and *De anima* (On the soul) supplied its general principles and the rest of his *libri naturales* (natural treatises) instantiated these principles with studies of the heavens, elements and compounds, the atmosphere, and

various types of living organisms. As the centuries progressed, study of the *Physics* became natural philosophy and study of *De anima,* psychology, whereas the special disciplines took on new identities as sciences in the modern sense.

Natural philosophy, in this understanding, studied natural bodies as composed of matter and form; causality and chance; motion and the infinite; time, space, and the void; the continuum; and sequences of movers and moveds, culminating in a First Unmoved Mover. It was part of a systematic worldview expressed in a technical Latin language that reflected the structure of its Greek source. It was further characterized by divisions into schools arising from students of the Greek text versus those of the Latin text, from geographically diverse universities such as those at Paris and Padua, and from religious orders such as the Dominicans and Franciscans. In the context of Thomist, Scotist, and Ockhamist thought—in the traditions, respectively, of medieval commentators Thomas Aquinas, Duns Scotus, and William of Ockham—it was oriented toward metaphysics and theology. On the other hand, in Latin Averroist circles (following Ibn Rushd, or Averroes; 1126–1198), notably at Padua, it was ordered toward medicine. In all cases it was pursued for its instructional value, providing general knowledge of nature that was open to intellectual or practical development. The approach was largely speculative, with little reliance on experimentation and, especially among Averroists, a mistrust of mathematics in unveiling the secrets of nature.

Humanism and the return to sources. Against this background, changing emphases manifested themselves throughout the Renaissance. The major innovation was the humanist return to classical sources and the increased knowledge it provided of the Greek text of Aristotle and Greek commentaries on his works. The medieval development showed little critical awareness and was based on Greek-Latin translations of varying, often inferior, quality. This, plus the pervasive desire for systematization, led to interpretations favorable to a particular system that could seriously depart from Aristotle's thought. Fifteenth- and sixteenth-century commentaries were more faithful to the text and more intent on discerning its original meaning. Yet the resulting emphasis on language and philology encouraged an inherent conservatism among Renaissance natural philosophers, for the study of texts closed the eyes of many to the world of nature surrounding them.

Associated with this study was increased knowledge of alternative approaches to nature. The complete works of Plato (428–348 B.C.) became available and, along with this, Neoplatonic interpretations of Aristotle that conciliated him with his teacher. A fuller knowledge of Neopythagorean doctrines also resulted, as did that deriving from the tradition of the mythical Hermes Trismegistus. Stoic and Epicurean texts also became available, offering new insights into problems relating to atoms and the void. In this atmosphere Lorenzo Valla (1407–1457), combining what has been called a "simple empiricism and biblical literalism" (Trinkaus, "Lorenzo Valla's Anti-Aristotelian Natural Philosophy," p. 285), launched a wholesale attack on the corrupt Latinity and abstract terminology of the Aristotelians and looked instead to Scripture and personal experience for his understanding of nature. Within Aristotelianism, a more tolerant attitude toward opposing schools became evident. Nominalist positions insinuated themselves within both Thomist and Scotist traditions, and when the Jesuits attained prominence a studied eclecticism characterized their works. To a remarkable degree the physical works of Aristotle supplied common ground on which followers of the Greek commentators Alexander of Aphrodisias (fl. second–third centuries C.E.) and Simplicus (fl. c. 530), as well as the medieval Averroes, along with Scholastics and Neoplatonists, could argue out their differences.

Technology and medicine. Another development was the emergence, especially in sixteenth-century Italy, of strong technological and artisan traditions. Work in architecture and military engineering fostered interest in the mechanics of Archimedes (c. 287–212 B.C.), and the recovery of the *Mechanica* (Mechanics), attributed to Aristotle, induced natural philosophers to be more sympathetic to that discipline. Similar developments in painting and the fine arts led to renewed interest in optics, and the proposal by Nicolaus Copernicus (1473–1543) of a Pythagorean, as opposed to a Ptolemaic, universe gave new life to astronomy. In the Middle Ages these "mixed sciences" pertained to preparatory studies, the *quadrivium,* but in the Renaissance they entered into the university curriculum. The fact that disciplinary fields were jealously guarded did not prevent some crossing over between the physical and the mathematical domains. It was in these areas that experimentation began to appear in its modern dress. Court patronage subsidized studies in this field for their practical value, further promoting their development.

A related infusion into natural philosophy came from the close alliance of the practice of medicine with its speculative underpinnings in the study of nature. Physicians in the Renaissance saw themselves as both *philosophi* and *medici,* with their university degrees qualifying them in this way. This led to refined observation in analyzing symptoms, to contrasting methods used by Aristotle and Galen (129–c. 199 C.E.), and to the study of the organs of the human body through the practice of surgery and accurate pictorial representation.

Along with these developments came a shift of interest within logic as an academic discipline. The late Middle Ages saw an extensive development of the *summulae* (little summaries) tradition and a nominalist concern with formal logic and *sophismata* (sophisms), both of which served mainly the instructional needs of the young. The Renaissance reacted against the hairsplitting such teaching involved and directed attention instead to Aristotle's *Analytica Posteriora* (Posterior analytics) and *Topica* (Topics), along with related treatises such as his *Rhetorica* (Rhetoric) and *Poetica* (Poetics). Significant advances were made in the logic of discovery associated with the demonstrative *regressus* and related methods of resolution and composition.

Commentaries and Treatises. The major vehicle for communicating all of this knowledge was commentaries on the text of Aristotle, supplemented by collections of special questions, called "questionaries," then by compendia useful for teaching, and finally by treatises on individual topics such as motion and the infinite. Among the Italian commentators, all of whom were influenced by Averroes, the more notable were Pietro Pomponazzi (1462–1525), Alessandro Achillini (1463–1512), Agostino Nifo (c. 1473–c. 1538), Jacopo Zabarella (1533–1589), and Cesare Cremonini (1550–1631). Their works are characterized by careful exposition of the text and much disputation over details of interpretation. At Paris, substantial textbooks appeared in the first two decades of the sixteenth century under the influence of John Major (1469–1550), who wrote an important treatise on the infinite. These works, by Major, John Dullaert of Ghent (c. 1470–1513), Peter Crockaert (c. 1470–1514), and Juan de Celaya (c. 1490–1558), among others, combined commentaries with questionaries and featured extensive studies of motion employing calculatory techniques. They had an important influence in Spain on the questionaries of Diego Diest (fl. 1511), Diego de Astudillo (c. 1480–1535), and Domingo de Soto (1495–1560).

Among compendia the more notable were those produced in Italy by Crisostomo Javelli (1470–1538), in the Netherlands by Frans Titelmans (1502–1537), in Germany by Philipp Melanchthon (1497–1560) and Jakob Schegk (1511–1587), and in Spain by Pedro Margallo (fl. 1520) and Alonso Gutierrez a Vera Cruce (1504/7–1584). These were composed in various intellectual traditions: Javelli's in the Dominican or Thomist; Titelmans's in the Franciscan; Vera Cruce's in the Augustinian; Melanchthon's and Schegk's in the Lutheran; and Margallo's in the nominalist. The treatments were perforce speculative and systematic, ordered toward incorporation into larger philosophical syntheses.

Calculatory treatises took up problems that could be formulated as "thought experiments," mainly relating to motion and the void, but it is difficult to ascertain when these were put to actual test. The main advance came in the study of local motion, and particularly in contesting the Aristotelian doctrine that the speed of fall of a body varies directly with the weight of the body and inversely with the resistance the body encounters. As early as 1544 tests were reported showing that this relationship could not be true, and in 1554 Giovanni Battista Benedetti (1530–1590) offered its rational disproof. Experimental disproofs were offered in 1575 by Galileo's teacher at Pisa, Girolamo Borro (1512–1592), in 1576 by Giuseppe Moleti (1531–1588) at Padua, and finally by Galileo Galilei (1564–1642), initially on the basis of tests made from the Leaning Tower of Pisa around 1590, more fully by experiments with inclined planes at Padua about 1609. With Galileo's discoveries, the "new science" of nature had begun.

See also **Anatomy**; **Astronomy**; **Chemistry**; **Logic**; **Matter, Structure of**; **Mechanics**; **Medicine**; **Optics**; **Physics**; **Psychology**; **Science**; **Science, Epistemology**; **Scientific Method**; *and biographies of Galileo Galilei, Lorenzo Valla, and other figures mentioned in this entry.*

BIBLIOGRAPHY

Primary Works

Aristotle. *Physics.* Translated by Hippocrates G. Apostle. Bloomington, Ind., and London, 1969.

Galilei, Galileo. *On Motion and On Mechanics.* Edited and translated by I. E. Drabkin and Stillman Drake. Madison, Wis., 1960.

Galilei, Galileo. *Galileo's Early Notebooks: The Physical Questions.* Translated by William A. Wallace. Notre Dame, Ind., 1977.

Secondary Works

Schmitt, Charles B. *Studies in Renaissance Philosophy and Science.* London, 1981.

Trinkaus, Charles. "Lorenzo Valla's Anti-Aristotelian Natural Philosophy." *I Tatti Studies: Essays in the Renaissance* 5 (1993): 279–325.

Wallace, William A. *Prelude to Galileo: Essays on Medieval and Sixteenth-Century Sources of Galileo's Thought.* Dordrecht, Netherlands, and Boston, 1981.

Wallace, William A. "Traditional Natural Philosophy." In *The Cambridge History of Renaissance Philosophy.* Edited by Charles B. Schmitt. Cambridge, U.K., and New York, 1988. Pages 201–235.

WILLIAM A. WALLACE

NAVAL WARFARE. The Renaissance was an era of accelerated warfare at sea by western European states, the Byzantine Empire until 1453 when it was defeated by the Ottoman Turks, and maritime powers including Venice, Genoa, and the states of North Africa. Naval warfare changed due to advances in ship construction and technological innovations that produced the full-rigged ship capable of carrying hundreds of men with their equipment and armed with cannon that could be fired from ships designed and built to accommodate these new weapons.

The age of exploration and the ability of Europeans to impose their control on people as distant as America and Asia were made possible by the creation of large multimasted sailing ships that incorporated both lateen and square sails within a hull layered by several decks. The ship could accommodate the improved cannon of the fifteenth and sixteenth centuries, principally by the addition of a gun deck. Gun ports pierced the hulls of ships beginning in the early sixteenth century, and the lids of the gun ports were raised to allow the carriage-mounted cannon to be positioned for firing. The men worked behind the thick planking of the hull. Placement of the cannon lower in the ship, rather than on the main deck, allowed more cannon to be carried because this lowered the center of gravity of the ship and provided greater stability.

The principal warship for most of this era was the galley, an oared vessel with a ram that had been in use since the time of the ancient Greeks. Galleys remained valuable warships because they did not depend on wind for movement and could attack, position, or retreat in most weather conditions. In contrast, sailing ships could sail against the wind only by tacking, that is, by going back and forth at an angle to the wind. Galleys could carry only limited amounts of cargo, weapons, supplies, or men because the vessels had long and narrow hulls, needed oarsmen to man them, and carried huge amounts of water for the crew. A large number of cannon could not be mounted aboard a galley. Heavy cannon had to be mounted along the centerline of the ship in the stem or stern. Galleys fought in most major naval engagements in the Mediterranean and often in the northern seas.

The medieval cog, a high-sided cargo vessel with a single mast, square sail, and sternpost rudder, was superseded in the early fifteenth century by the carrack. The carrack was a more versatile sailer with a new sail plan that included a square sail on a fore and main mast and a lateen sail on a mizzenmast. It also had a large forecastle and aftercastle that served as fighting platforms. This new design blended northern (clinker-built with overlapping hull planking and square sails) and Mediterranean (carvel-built, with hull planks placed edge to edge to form a smooth hull and lateen rigging) shipbuilding traditions. The introduction of the northern cog into the Mediterranean was noted by the Florentine chronicler Giovanni Villani in 1304. The cog influenced the construction of *coche,* Mediterranean carracks, especially in Genoa and Venice.

Caravels became widespread in the fifteenth century and were made famous by early Spanish and Portuguese explorers. In the sixteenth century they were used increasingly as fighting ships after modifications that produced the *caravela de armada* of over one hundred tons. Unlike the caravel, with its two or more masts and lateen sails, this vessel carried square rig on the main and fore masts and a lateen sail on the mizzen. Christopher Columbus rerigged the caravel *Niña* in this fashion on his first voyage. The *caravela de armada* was more suited for fighting than were earlier, smaller caravels. From North Africa to Brazil, and by the 1530s, India, the caravel was involved in naval engagements as well as military transport duties.

The galleon emerged in the sixteenth century as a fine-lined full-rigged ship with a high length-to-breadth ratio. Crescent shaped with a higher stern than forecastle, the galleon was a faster and better sailer than the carrack. The Spanish Armada of 1588 included twenty galleons, and not one was lost in the fight with the English or during the journey home. The only galleon preserved today is the 800-ton *Vasa* built by Dutch shipwrights for the king of Sweden, which sank in Stockholm harbor in 1628 and was raised and conserved for public display in the 1960s. The instability of the *Vasa* and Henry VIII's *Mary Rose* indicated the challenge of placing heavier guns on ships by incorporating gun decks low to the waterline. The 600-ton carrack *Mary Rose* sank while heavily loaded with sailors and marines in 1545 off Portsmouth while engaging the French. The cause was the design of her gun decks, which placed the gun ports close to the waterline.

Cannon appeared aboard ships in the fourteenth century. Their effect was unremarkable until developments in cannon founding and gunpowder produced weapons that changed naval warfare. Cannon on land were used from the 1420s to blast through castle walls. At sea, special mounts and carriages were necessary to use cannon effectively on the main deck of a sailing ship; a gun deck and gun ports were added after 1500. By mid-century the four-wheeled truck carriage for cannon was in use. At the Battle of Zonchio in 1499 the Turks used heavy ordnance against the Venetians. Early cannon fired balls of stone or iron and also small pieces of shot. Bronze guns were lighter but several times more expensive than iron. Weight of shot fired increased when gun decks became standard on large sailing ships. Spanish galleys used bow guns that fired twenty-four- to fifty-pounders by the 1540s. Sailing vessels used large cannon and many more of them. Ships could be destroyed or disabled through shots that damaged the masts and rigging or rudder. Stone or iron balls could pierce the planking of ships, thus sending splinters flying at those on board.

Naval battles proved pivotal in determining the outcome of major conflicts. The English defeated the French and their allies at the Battle of Sluys in 1340, early in the Hundred Years' War (1337–1453). They won again in 1350 at Les Espagnols sur Mer off Winchelsea against large Spanish vessels, but lost at La Rochelle in 1372. Several English expeditions successfully navigated the English Channel to France, carrying thousands of men, horses, and matériel. Stones and heavy objects were fired from various devices, but battles were usually decided by grappling and boarding.

Naval warfare also figured in trade and shipping. A confederation of trading towns on the Baltic and North seas was formed in the twelfth century, the German Hanse or Hanseatic League. The league was composed of nearly two hundred towns, centered on Lübeck, and dominated Baltic commercial shipping and finance. Hanse fleets fought to control markets and shipping routes. Danish rulers waged war against the Hanse from the mid-fourteenth century until the sixteenth century, and a Swedish fleet defeated the Hanse forces in 1565–1566.

The Venetians dominated trade to Constantinople and the east, though challenged by Genoa. This rivalry erupted in four separate wars and ended with a Venetian victory in 1380. The powerful Ottoman Turks overran Constantinople in 1453, bringing an end to the Byzantine Empire and tempering further Italian conflicts. The Turks continued to challenge at

Naval Warfare. *The Christian Fleets before Messina* by Giorgio Vasari, commissioned by Pope Gregory XIII to celebrate the Christian victory at Lepanto. Allegorical figures of the Christian allies, Spain, the papacy, and Venice, are at the lower left; Death harvests the defeated Turks at the lower right. [For another depiction of the three victors, El Greco's *Adoration of the Name of Jesus,* see the color plates in volume 5.] THE GRANGER COLLECTION

sea, building large fleets of war galleys armed with cannon. This culminated with their conquest of Cyprus in 1570–1571, although they failed to take Malta in 1565. The Western states, including Venice and Spain, briefly united in the Holy League. Ultimately two fleets met in 1571 at the Gulf of Patras on the western coast of Greece near the town of Lepanto in the last great battle of oared fighting ships. The Battle of Lepanto (7 October 1571) was a ferocious naval battle involving more than five hundred ships. Firing at point-blank range, the Christian side destroyed or captured about two hundred Turkish ships, killing or injuring perhaps twenty thousand men. Cannon were a primary factor in the fight. But further Christian assaults did not follow the victory; the Turks retained control of the eastern Mediterranean.

The commercial conflict between England and Spain in the New World and Europe was compounded by England's acceptance of Protestantism. The Spanish Armada of 130 ships departed from Lisbon in summer 1588 to unite with the army of the duke of Parma in Flanders and invade England. The English "Sea Dogs," including Sir Francis Drake and John Hawkins, attacked the Armada with faster vessels and long-range cannon. The Armada could not reach Parma's army. The battle was fought over two weeks ending when violent storms scattered the Spanish fleet which sailed north around Scotland and Ireland. About thirty-five ships were lost in the conflict, most due to the severe weather.

See also Lepanto, Battle of; Mediterranean Sea; Ships and Shipbuilding.

NAVAL WARFARE

BIBLIOGRAPHY

Guilmartin, John F., Jr. *Gunpowder and Galleys: Changing Technology and Mediterranean Warfare at Sea in the Sixteenth Century.* Cambridge, U.K., 1995.

Padfield, Peter. *Tide of Empires: Decisive Naval Campaigns and the Rise of the West.* Vol. 1, *1481–1654.* London, 1979.

Unger, Richard W., ed. *Cogs, Caravels, and Galleons: The Sailing Ship, 1000–1630.* London, 1994.

TIMOTHY J. RUNYAN

NEBRIJA, ANTONIO DE (1441–1522), Spanish humanist. Born to an hidalgo family at Lebrija, near Seville, Nebrija got his primary education at Lebrija, then went to the University of Salamanca in 1455. Five years later he obtained a position at the Spanish College at the University of Bologna, where he spent ten years studying theology and familiarizing himself with Italian humanist scholarship. He returned to Spain in 1470 and took a position with his powerful patron, Alonso de Fonseca, archbishop of Seville, and later with Fonseca's successor, Don Juan de Zuñiga. By the early sixteenth century Nebrija was teaching grammar at the University of Salamanca. In 1513 he went to the newly founded University of Alcalá to participate in the editing of the Complutensian Polyglot Bible at the invitation of Cardinal Francisco Jiménez de Cisneros, the archbishop of Toledo and primate of Spain. In 1514 or early 1515 Nebrija, a notoriously prickly character, had a falling out with the other editors and left the Complutensian project. He remained at Alcalá, however, where he held the chair of rhetoric until his death in 1522.

Like many other humanists, Nebrija wrote poetry, commented on classical literary works, and promoted the study of classical languages and literature. He was more notable, however, for seeking to introduce the critical philological scholarship of Italian humanism into Renaissance Spain. His most important efforts were connected with linguistic analysis and biblical scholarship.

While studying in Bologna, Nebrija became acquainted with the works of Lorenzo Valla and other Italian humanist scholars. In 1481 he published *Introductiones latinae* (Introduction to Latin), a textbook on Latin grammar and literature that promoted the observance of classical literary standards; it appeared in fifty editions during the author's lifetime. In spite of his classical interests, Nebrija's most famous literary scholarship focused on Castilian rather than Latin language. In 1492 he published his *Gramática de la lengua castellana* (Grammar of the Castilian language), which he dedicated to Queen Isabella of Castile. This work represented one of the earliest efforts to codify a European vernacular language, and it had considerable political as well as scholarly influence. Like Lorenzo Valla, Nebrija recognized that language played a crucial role in the maintenance of state power. In offering the work to Queen Isabella, he characterized language as "the companion of empire," indeed as "the perfect instrument of empire," suggesting that his grammar would prove politically useful as the Catholic kings extended their rule to peoples who spoke languages other than Castilian.

About 1495 Nebrija decided to give up secular studies and turn his attention to biblical scholarship. He sought to improve the text and interpretation of the Bible by subjecting it to the same kind of critical philological scholarship that Italian humanists had applied to classical literature. He soon produced a set of critical notes on the text and translation of the Bible, but about 1504 he fell under the suspicion of Diego de Deza, the conservative inquisitor general of Spain, who confiscated and destroyed his work. In 1507 Deza died, and Cardinal Jiménez succeeded him as inquisitor general. Under the protection of Jiménez, Nebrija resumed his studies and eventually published a series of works that defended humanist scholarship and employed philological tools to solve problems of biblical translation and interpretation. For a short time Nebrija was a star member of the editorial team assembled by Jiménez to prepare the Complutensian Polyglot Bible, but he clashed with his more conservative co-editors, who resisted his efforts to employ critical philological criteria in the editing of scriptural texts. Jiménez respected Nebrija but sided with the other editors, who established a very conservative text for the Complutensian Bible.

In seeking to place biblical scholarship on a solid philological foundation, Nebrija stood alongside Lorenzo Valla (1407–1457) and Erasmus of Rotterdam (1466?–1536). Yet his efforts had little lasting influence in Spain, where church leaders clamped down on humanist biblical scholarship after the outbreak of the Protestant Reformation. His linguistic scholarship, however, had great influence throughout the sixteenth and seventeenth centuries, both in Spain and in the expanding Spanish Empire. His attention to the Castilian language influenced Juan de Valdés (1490?–1541) and Luis de León (1527–1591), who promoted vernacular religious publications in Spain. It also served the interests of missionaries who followed conquering Spanish forces into Andalusia, the Caribbean, Mexico, Peru, and the Philippine Islands. Just as Nebrija had suggested to Queen Isabella in 1492, the Castilian tongue—together with Roman

Catholic Christianity—was indeed the companion of the Spanish Empire.

See also **Alcalá de Henares, University of; Complutensian Polyglot Bible; Humanism;** *and biographies of Francisco Jiménez de Cisneros and Lorenzo Valla.*

BIBLIOGRAPHY

Primary Work

Nebrija, Elio Antonio de. *Gramática castellana.* 2 vols. Edited by Pasqual Galindo Romeo and Luis Ortiz Muñoz. Madrid, Spain, 1946. Modern edition of Nebrija's Castilian grammar with a facsimile of the original.

Secondary Works

Bataillon, Marcel. *Erasmo y España.* Translated by A. Alatorre. 2d ed. Mexico City, 1966. Places Nebrija in context of the Spanish Renaissance.

Bentley, Jerry H. *Humanists and Holy Writ: New Testament Scholarship in the Renaissance.* Princeton, N.J., 1983. Deals with Nebrija's biblical scholarship.

Mignolo, Walter D. *The Darker Side of the Renaissance: Literacy, Territoriality, and Colonization.* Ann Arbor, Mich., 1995. Assesses the influence of Nebrija's Castilian grammar.

Olmedo, Felix G. *Nebrija (1441–1522): Debelador de la barbarie, comentador eclesiastico, pedagogo-poeta.* Madrid, Spain, 1942. The most complete biography, which emphasizes Nebrija's literary and scholarly pursuits.

JERRY H. BENTLEY

NEO-LATIN LITERATURE AND LANGUAGE.

The word "Neo-Latin" is frequently used to denote the classicizing tendency that is the hallmark of the prose and poetry of the humanists. Some scholars would contend that Neo-Latin begins with the classicizing verse of the Paduan pre-humanists of the late thirteenth and early fourteenth centuries, the most important of whom was probably Lovato dei Lovati (c. 1240–1309), while others consider the pre-humanists to be essentially medieval and would place the origins of Neo-Latin in the rise of full-fledged Italian humanism in the fourteenth and fifteenth centuries. The term Neo-Latin is also applied to modern Latin in general up to the most recent times. It may be argued, however, that the Renaissance is not only the period of the greatest Neo-Latin authors but also that of the greatest prestige and influence of Neo-Latin as an instrument of communication.

Stylistic Developments and Preferences.

Many factors could be enumerated that led the humanists to stress the importance of classical Roman authors as models for their own Latin writings, perhaps not least of which was the general enthusiasm for classical arts and institutions that prevailed in the Renaissance. But it is worth noting that a return to the standards of classical Latin offered some special advantages in the late Middle Ages, a time when increasing specialization in the academic disciplines led to the development of highly technical subspecies of Latin adapted to particular disciplines, such as canon law, theology, or speculative grammar, and when the language of local documents often came to be so infiltrated with regional terminology as to be hardly recognizable as Latin. Humanist Latin provided a universally recognizable norm and a chance to regularize the language of learning according to universally acceptable standards. Far from turning the living tradition of medieval Latin into a "dead" language, the humanist revolution ensured that the lingua franca of learned Europe would have several more centuries of vigorous life.

But the establishment of ancient Latin as the hallmark for modern Latin was not without complications. For one thing, classical Latin, if understood to include the "golden" and "silver" ages of pagan Latin literature from the first century B.C. to the second century A.D., is far from a monolithic and uniform entity and embraces a vast variety of usage. If we add the corpus of Christian Latin of later antiquity to the supply of available models, we find that most of the idiosyncracies commonly held to be typical of literary medieval Latin syntax and usage—such as declarative *quod* or *quia*-clauses instead of the accusative and infinitive, the ablative of the gerund as a present participle, erratic tense sequence and use of mood, erosion of distinctions in use of pronouns, new use of cases and prepositions, increased use of auxiliary verbs, and many other features—are all amply attested in Latin literature written before the end of the Roman Empire in the West.

In view of such considerations, it is hardly surprising that controversies arose among the humanists concerning which ancient authors should be imitated and how far such imitation should be taken. Some of the most influential humanistic Latin writers, such as Lorenzo Valla (1407–1457), author of one of the most widely circulated humanistic works on Latin usage, *Elegantiarum linguae latinae libri sex* (Six books of the elegances of the Latin language; 1471), and Desiderius Erasmus (c. 1466–1536), advocated a more or less eclectic approach to imitating ancient Latin writers. Others, especially in Italy during the late fifteenth and sixteenth centuries, were proponents of Ciceronianism, the view that Cicero should be the model for contemporary prose. Ciceronianism probably received considerable impetus from the works of the Roman authors themselves, in which the treatment of Cicero as the supreme example of Roman eloquence and his period as the age of the best Latin oratory was already a commonplace. However, the Renaissance Ciceronians may perhaps be divided into extremists and moderates: the latter contended that Cicero should be the primary model but acknowledged that usages might also be borrowed from other classical authors too. Imitation (and creative adaptation) was carried in a different direction by the so-called Apuleians, who zealously quarried rare expressions from early Latin authors and the archaizing or antiquarian writers of the second century A.D., such as Aulus Gellius and Apuleius. This "archaizing" movement seems to have had considerable influence on the idiosyncratic Latin prose style developed by the Flemish scholar and moral philosopher Justus Lipsius (1547–1606), a style that also owed much to the usage of Seneca and Tacitus.

Lipsius had not a few admirers and even some imitators, but by the turn of the sixteenth and seventeenth centuries a reaction against the various forms of extremism seems to have set in. A style such as the one developed by Lipsius is not easy to read and would have been quite difficult to learn. A moderate Ciceronianism (a position, in fact, not very far from the electicism of Erasmus) such as that advocated by the German educational theorists Philipp Melanchthon (1497–1560) and Johannes Sturm (1507–1589) or the influential French orator Marc-Antoine Muret (1526–1585), undoubtedly represented a more viable model for an international learned language, since it combined the stability and clarity of classical syntax with a ready acceptance of late or entirely new words where necessary. The use of new words to describe new things is nearly universal in Neo-Latin: only a very few of the most extreme Ciceronians argued that the vocabulary of Neo-Latin should be restricted to that of classical Latin. A moderate Ciceronianism, which allowed a considerable element of eclecticism, was not only championed by some of the leading pedagogues in the Protestant countries, it was also adopted as the main stylistic doctrine in the colleges of the Jesuit order, a factor that undoubtedly helped to secure its supremacy in Catholic Europe too. We should keep in mind that these remarks on stylistic evolution are based on the precepts and theories of humanist teachers and modern studies based on them. Much more can be learned from the style, syntax, and vocabulary of Neo-Latin texts themselves.

Survival and Influence of Medieval Latin.

Despite the classicizing precepts of humanistic teachers and the virulent polemics of certain humanists of the fifteenth and early sixteenth centuries directed against "barbarous" medieval Latin, a considerable medieval element remains in Neo-Latin. This element is most obvious in vocabulary, since many of the Latin words for political, ecclesiastical, and especially academic institutions had developed entirely in the Middle Ages, and of necessity Neo-Latin writers continued to use the same terminology. Sometimes ancient Latin words are employed with meanings that were added only in the Middle Ages.

Elements of medieval syntax can also sometimes be detected in the works of Neo-Latin writers, though this is more frequent in the earlier than the later periods of humanism. The "classicization" of Latin was a protracted development that moved more slowly in some places than in others. Not a few medieval grammars, such as the *Doctrinale* of Alexander de Villa Dei, and medieval lexica, such as the *Catholicon* (c. 1286) of Giovanni Balbi, remained in use for much of the Renaissance.

Similarly, the establishment of a classicized spelling of Latin was a gradual process, and in many manuscripts and printed books of the fifteenth and early sixteenth centuries medieval orthography remains, especially in the treatment of diphthongs. For example, the letter *e* or *ę* with a cedilla is employed where classical Latinists would expect *ae* or *oe*. Sometimes the diphthong *ae* appears where we might expect a long vowel *e*. Other variants of this type persist well into the sixteenth century and sometimes beyond.

Finally, we should note that some Renaissance Latin works produced in the context of academic disciplines that had been thriving long before the advent of humanism, especially law and theology, retain a strongly medieval and scholastic flavor in both syntax and vocabulary. This is scarcely surprising if we recall that scholastic theology was still flourishing at institutions like the University of Paris at the end of the fifteenth and the beginning of the sixteenth centuries.

Influence of the Vernacular Languages and Regional Features.

We might expect that there would be points of contact between Latin and the many vernacular tongues all over Europe, some of which were developing considerable literary traditions and were even coming to rival Latin in certain areas of discourse where the learned language had formerly been supreme. Such contacts are perhaps most obvious in vocabulary, since some of the neologisms (especially those used to describe local and popular institutions) employed by Neo-Latin writers are derived from one or another vernacular tongue. However, the proportion of neologisms derived from the vernaculars seems to have remained relatively small, and the great majority of new words were built on Latin or Greek roots.

Neo-Latin works occasionally contain vernacular proverbs translated into Latin, but the translations normally do little violence to the properties of Latin syntax and semantics. Indeed, as far as the actual syntax and usage of literary Neo-Latin is concerned, the influence of the vernacular languages is very rare and very difficult to prove. One of the primary objects of humanist pedagogy was to eradicate the tendency of little children to transliterate the phrases of their native tongue into their second language. This effort (bolstered by the emphasis, ubiquitous in humanist pedagogy, on memorizing vast numbers of whole Latin phrases pertaining to various spheres of life) seems to have been usually quite successful, if we may judge by the typical products of adult writers. In general, modern scholars have been rather too ready to attribute apparent oddities that are occasionally found in Neo-Latin to the influence of the author's native language. More often than not, such peculiarities result from usages found in ancient Latin works well studied by humanists but no longer widely read in modern classical curricula, or from variants excised from more recent critical editions of classical texts, or from usages that have origins in late and medieval Latin. Moreover, some parallels between the vernaculars and Neo-Latin usage result from the fact that learned Latin has influenced vernacular usage, rather than the other way around.

However, importation of vernacular elements into less formal works is more frequent. School commentaries, for example, sometimes contain vernacular words and phrases. We occasionally find texts that are deliberately macaronic, and in a few works, such as the anonymous *Epistolae obscurorum virorum* (Letters of obscure men; 1515), vernacular phrasing is obviously imitated on purpose for the sake of parody.

Geographical Distribution. The spread of Neo-Latin more or less followed the spread of humanism. Neo-Latin literature was already flourishing in Italy thoughout the fifteenth century, a time when most Latin authors in northern Europe wrote in styles that can be only described as medieval. However, toward the end of the fifteenth century the humanist approach to Latin began to spread to northern Europe, eastern Europe, and Britain. This transforma-

tion was effected partly through the agency of Italians who traveled and sought employment or patronage in other parts of Europe and partly by non-Italians who traveled to Italy to study with humanist teachers. By the mid-sixteenth century Neo-Latin was becoming the prevailing style in Scandinavia too, and the seventeenth and early eighteenth centuries saw a "golden age" of Latin writing in the Nordic countries, especially in Sweden and Denmark. Neo-Latin traveled with Europeans to the Americas, and the corpus of Neo-Latin produced before 1740 in both Spanish America and the regions of the New World colonized by other Europeans is considerable, though so far little studied by modern scholars.

Extent and Spheres of Usage. Latin was the typical language for diplomatic correspondence for most of the period under consideration here, although by the second half of the seventeenth century French became the primary language of diplomacy. Latin had also been the language of civil administration and public documents in many areas of Europe during the Middle Ages, but during the Renaissance local vernaculars tended to be used more and more for this function. This evolution happened at different times in different places. French became the official language of public documents in the kingdom of France from the reign of Francis I (1515–1547). In Hungary, by contrast, Latin remained the language of public administration until well into the nineteenth century.

Latin, being the official language of the Catholic Christendom, was regularly used in the correspondence of church officials, church councils, and seminaries until well into the twentieth century. Latin also remained the primary language of learning and science throughout the Renaissance, as it had been in the Middle Ages. In the later Renaissance, especially in regions where the vernacular was relatively highly developed, such as Italy, France, and England, the number of philosophical and academic works written in the national languages began to increase rapidly. But a strong tradition of scientific and learned Latin persisted in many areas, especially in the Low Countries, Germany, Scandinavia, and eastern Europe, into the eighteenth century and in some cases even later.

The choice of Latin offered a writer several advantages. First and foremost, a work in Latin was at once accessible to an international audience in a way that a text written in a vernacular language could never be. But even if reaching an international audienoe was not the primary goal, Latin, which had a continuous tradition as the intellectual language of European Christendom since the late Roman empire, was endowed with a prestige and authority that could be rivaled by few, if any, vernacular languages during the Renaissance period. The mere fact of writing in Latin would impose upon the author forms and techniques peculiar to this tradition and put the work in the context of the Latin heritage. Moreover, vernacular languages were in a state of flux and changed rapidly, a fact pointed out by many humanists, while Latin offered a stable, well-defined medium, which undoubtedly seemed to many people of the Renaissance to provide a much more secure way to preserve material for posterity than one's native language.

The replacing of Latin in its traditional areas of discourse was a gradual process that was the result of a complex variety of factors. To a person of our own age, when language and culture are so often considered an inseparable aspect of nationhood, the result of this evolution may perhaps seem inevitable, but to many thinkers of the Renaissance this would not have been apparent at all. Even at the end of the sixteenth century the number of Latin works being printed in Germany was still larger than the number of vernacular books that issued from presses in the same area.

Genres. Philosophical, theological, and other learned works produced in the context of the various academic disciplines make up a substantial portion of the Neo-Latin texts written in this period, but Renaissance Neo-Latin was not limited to these areas of discourse. Neo-Latin poetry flourished throughout the Renaissance and early modern periods, and verses by Baptista Mantuanus, Girolamo Fracastoro, Jacopo Sannazaro, and Angelo Poliziano were widely read all over Europe. Neo-Latin poetry, epistolary prose, and dialogues were often studied in schools along with the Latin authors of ancient Rome. Important Neo-Latin genres also include epistolography, historiography, travel accounts, drama (both comedy and tragedy), oratory, and satire. It is perhaps not sufficiently appreciated that a tradition of prose fiction in Latin existed during the Renaissance. Quite a few of these works may be classified as "utopias," of which perhaps the earliest and most important is the well-known *Utopia* by Thomas More. Not a few Latin novels, such as *Argenis* by the Scottish humanist John Barclay, an international best-seller first printed in the early seventeenth cen-

tury, were actually written in the "Menippean" style, a mixture of prose narrative with verse interludes.

Spoken Usage. Neo-Latin is primarily a literary language, the norms of which are defined by a body of texts, not the usage of people in the streets. Nevertheless, Latin was also a spoken language in certain circles during the Renaissance, and a spoken usage persisted as long as there was an active tradition of writing in Latin. In many regions of northern Europe—for example, in Germany, Scandinavia, the Low Countries, and France—students in Latin schools (often after the second year) were required to speak only Latin in school, and similarly in the schools and academies of the Jesuit order the spoken use of Latin was required. The authors of textbooks used for conversational Latin, which are usually described by the generic term "colloquia," included some famous humanists, such as Juan Luis Vives and Erasmus.

The ability to follow a discourse in Latin and some ability at spoken expression in the language would have been necessary for those who entered universities, since Latin was the primary teaching language at most universities in the period. Spoken usage was maintained for some diplomatic communication and gatherings within the hierarchy of the Roman church, although the testimony of Erasmus indicates that if participants at such meetings knew the same vernacular language, Latin might be quickly reduced to ceremonies. Nevertheless, there is substantial evidence that Latin could enable learned people from different linguistic backgrounds to communicate without an interpreter and that the spoken or conversational usage of Latin was not restricted to academic circles or the functioning of the Catholic hierarchy, but included a considerable variety of international communication.

Pronunciation. During the Renaissance and early modern periods there were probably almost as many pronunciations of Latin as there were vernacular languages and dialects, for we know that Latin during the Renaissance, as in the Middle Ages, tended to be pronounced according to the norms of the local vernacular language. In one respect, this was not much different from the period of the Roman Empire, in which there was certainly a considerable variety of regional pronunciation, although the ancient world possessed a cadre of native, or at least Roman, speakers of the language, who perhaps set some sort of standard.

Divergent pronunciations undoubtedly constituted impediments to intelligibility from time to time at most periods in the history of Latin as a widely diffused language, and this was certainly the case in the Renaissance. We learn a great deal about regional pronunciations in the early sixteenth century from Erasmus's *De recta Latini Graecique sermonis pronuntiatione* (On the correct pronunciation of the Latin and Greek languages; 1528). From this work and other sources it is clear that some regional variants of Latin pronunciation could be so diverse that someone from another region who heard such a variant for the first time might be unsure whether the speaker was actually using Latin.

Two factors probably reduced the obstacles to understanding that might arise from divergent pronunciations. First, we know from a number of sources, including Erasmus and, at a later period, John Milton, that the Italian pronunciation enjoyed the highest prestige. Many humanists who studied in Italy would have acquired this pronunciation, and an Englishman in the seventeenth century, for example, who wanted to use Latin in different regions of continental Europe might be advised to adopt the Italian pronunciation because it was widely accepted. Second, although some varieties of Latin pronunciation might be so large as to render comprehension difficult for someone unused to them, many regional variants were smaller, and Latin speakers who fell within such vernacular language groups would not have needed the same period of adjustment in order to understand each other. Perhaps we can gain the best idea about regional varients in Latin pronunciation from the evidence collected by music scholars. The material presented by Harold Copeman in *Singing in Latin,* for example, gives us a good indication of the similarities and differences between various Latin pronunciations.

See also **Cicero** *and biographies of figures mentioned in this entry.*

BIBLIOGRAPHY

Primary Works

Erasmus, Desiderius. *The Ciceronian: A Dialogue on the Ideal Latin Style.* Vol. 28 of *Collected Works of Erasmus.* Translated by Betty I. Knott. Toronto; Buffalo, N.Y.; and London, 1986. A fundamental work on the stylistic controversies of the sixteenth century.

Erasmus, Desiderius. *Copia: Foundations of the Abundant Style.* Vol. 24 of *Collected Works of Erasmus.* Translated by Betty I. Knott. Toronto; Buffalo, N.Y.; and London, 1978. Pages 279–659.

Erasmus, Desiderius. *De copia verborum ac rerum* (On abundance of words and things). In *Opera omnia Desiderii Erasmi Roterodami, ordinis primi tomus sextus.* Edited by Betty I. Knott. Amsterdam, 1988. An important text illustrating the humanistic approach to acquiring Latin fluency.

Erasmus, Desiderius. *De recta Latini Graecique sermonis pronuntiatione* (On the correct pronunciation of the Latin and Greek languages). In *Opera omnia Desiderii Erasmi Roterodami, ordinis primi tomus quartus.* Edited by M. Cytowska. Amsterdam, 1973. Pages 1–103.

Erasmus, Desiderius. *The Right Way of Speaking Latin and Greek: A Dialogue.* Vol. 26 of *Collected Works of Erasmus.* Edited by Maurice Pope. Toronto; Buffalo, N.Y.; and London, 1985. Pages 348–475, 580–625.

Valla, Lorenzo, *Elegantiarum linguae latinae libri sex* [Six books of the elegances of the Latin language]. Vol. 1 of *opera omnia.* Edited by Eugenio Garin. Torino, Italy, 1962.

Secondary Works

Benner, Margareta, and Emin Tengström. *On the Interpretation of Learned Neo-Latin.* Göteborg, Sweden, 1977. One of the few studies that gives us some notion of the latinity of authors who used learned or scientific Latin in the seventeenth century.

Binns, J. W. *Intellectual Culture in Elizabethan and Jacobean England: The Latin Writings of the Age.* Leeds, U.K., 1990. A fundamental source on Latin writing in England in the sixteenth and seventeenth centuries.

Bömer, Alois. *Die lateinischen Schülergespräche der Humanisten.* Berlin, 1897–1899. The basic source on "colloquia," or school dialogues used for teaching conversational Latin.

Copeman, Harold. *Singing in Latin.* Oxford, 1992.

Hoven, René. *Lexique de la prose latine de la Renaissance.* Leiden, Netherlands, 1994. The first modern lexicon of Neo-Latin prose. Based only on a selection of authors and texts, but nevertheless an essential resource.

IJsewijn, Jozeph. *Companion to Neo-Latin Studies: Part I, History and Diffusion of Neo-Latin Literature.* 2d ed. Louvain, Belgium, 1990. This work, together with volume 2, listed below, constitutes a starting point for virtually any inquiry into Neo-Latin language or literature.

IJsewijn, Jozeph, with D. Sacré. *Companion to Neo-Latin Studies: Part II, Literary, Linguistic, Philological and Editorial Questions.* 2d ed. Louvain, Belgium, 1997.

Jensen, Minna Skafte, ed. *A History of Nordic Neo-Latin Literature.* Odense, Denmark, 1995.

Mantello, F. A. C., and A. G. Rigg, eds. *Medieval Latin: An Introduction and Bibliographical Guide.* Washington, D.C., 1996. Articles by many contributors. A starting point for almost any question about the medieval background to Neo-Latin.

Mazzocco, Angelo. *Linguistic Theories in Dante and the Humanists: Studies of Language and Intellectual History in Late Medieval and Early Renaissance Italy.* Leiden, Netherlands, 1993.

Tavoni, Mirko. *Latino, grammatica, volgare: Storia di una questione umanistica.* Padova, Italy, 1984. Another contribution on the question of humanistic attitudes to the vernacular languages, their origin, and development. To be read with Mazzocco, listed above.

Tournoy, Gilbert, and Terence O. Tunberg. "On the Margins of Latinity? Neo-Latin and the Vernacular Languages." *Humanistica Lovaniensia* 45 (1996): 134–175. A detailed examination of several instances in which usages in Neo-Latin have been said to be influenced by the vernacular languages.

Tunberg, Terence O. "Ciceronian Latin: Longolius and Others." *Humanistica Lovaniensia* 46 (1997): 13–61. An examination of the actual language of a Ciceronian author. Main emphasis on Christophe de Longueil (1488–1522), but with references to other Ciceronians also. Part II concerns the effects of Ciceronianism on the Latin of the later Renaissance.

Tuynman, P., G. C. Kuiper, and E. Kessler, eds. *Acta conventus neo-latini Amstelodamensis: Proceedings of the Second International Congress of Neo-Latin Studies, Amsterdam 19–24 August 1973.* Munich, 1979. Many useful articles on various aspects of Neo-Latin.

TERENCE TUNBERG

NEOPLATONISM. *See* Plato, Platonism, and Neoplatonism.

NEO-STOICISM.

"Neo-Stoicism" is a term historians often use to refer to the revival of interest, during the Renaissance, in a group of ancient philosophers, notably Epictetus, Plutarch, Marcus Aurelius, and, above all, Seneca. The key idea of these philosophers was that of "constancy" (*constantia* in Seneca's Latin) or tranquillity of mind: the capacity to withstand what Hamlet called "the slings and arrows of outrageous fortune." Linked ideas included self-discipline; detachment from worldly things—or traveling light through life, as Seneca described it; and being able to distinguish between a few important matters and all the rest (*adiaphora,* or "indifferent things").

Early History. Some fathers of the church, notably Jerome, were sympathetic to Stoicism, regarding this pagan philosophy as compatible with Christianity, although the Stoic defense of suicide was difficult for them to accept. Some of the works of Seneca were known in the Middle Ages, notably his *Epistulae morales* (Letters to Lucilius; c. A.D. 50), and an apocryphal story of his correspondence with St. Paul was in circulation.

What was new in the Renaissance was the enthusiasm for Stoicism shown by Petrarch (who addressed a letter to Seneca in 1350) and his follower Coluccio Salutati. In fifteenth-century Italy, Gasparino da Barzizza wrote a commentary on Seneca's letters; Leon Battista Alberti wrote a treatise, *De tranquillitate animi* (On tranquillity of mind); and Niccolò Perotti translated Epictetus into Latin. In France, Jean de Montreuil studied Seneca's letters, while in Spain interest in Seneca on the part of the marqués of Santillana and others was encouraged by the fact that the philosopher had been born on the peninsula. In the early sixteenth century, Pietro Pomponazzi, Guillaume Budé, Niccolò Machiavelli, and Francesco Guicciardini were all in their different ways interested in Stoic ideas. Erasmus edited the works of Seneca in 1515 and again in 1529. Antonio de Guevara, whose *Reloj de príncipes o libro aureo del emperador Marco Aurelio* (Dial of princes; 1529) was a European best-seller, was steeped in Seneca. An early work by John Calvin, published in 1532, took the form of a commentary on Seneca's treatise on clemency. The poet Thomas Wyatt translated Plutarch and told his son, "I would Seneca was your study and Epictetus."

The Fashion for Stoicism. It was in the later sixteenth and early seventeenth centuries that an interest in Stoicism became a fashion in the sense that it spread beyond a circle of intellectuals and colored, if it did not penetrate, the everyday life of some European elites. Central to the process of the reception of Stoicism was the scholar Justus Lipsius, who taught at the universities of Leiden and Leuven (Louvain), in the northern and southern Netherlands respectively, during the religious wars. Lipsius made his reputation with his Latin dialogue *De constantia* (On constancy; 1584), which presented the Stoic philosophy as a remedy for the troubles of the time. By the early seventeenth century the dialogue had been translated into Dutch, French, English, German, Spanish, Italian, and Polish. Lipsius went on to produce an introduction to Stoicism (*Manuductio ad stoicam philosophiam,* 1604) and a scholarly edition of Seneca's works (1605) that bore a dedication to Pope Paul V suggesting that the philosopher was "virtually a Christian."

The example of Lipsius was followed by the French magistrate Guillaume Du Vair, who translated Epictetus into French and published his own dialogue *De la constance et consolation ès calamitez publiques* (On constancy; 1595), once again presenting it as a remedy for "public calamities." Michel de Montaigne abandoned his early enthusiasm for Stoic ideas, but his follower Pierre Charron remained close to Stoicism in his book *De la sagesse* (On wisdom; 1601). In Spain, the writer Francisco de Quevedo produced a translation of Epictetus into Spanish verse and an introduction to Stoic philosophy (1635). In Italy, Cardinal Carlo Borromeo, archbishop of Milan and one of the leaders of the Catholic Reformation, sang the praises of Epictetus. In Germany, the poet Martin Opitz wrote on tranquillity of mind. In England, Stoicism was popularized by Joseph Hall, bishop and satirist, and Thomas James, the translator of Du Vair, who claimed that "no kind of philosophy is more profitable and nearer approaching unto Christianity . . . than the philosophy of the Stoics." Its appeal should also be viewed as a reaction to civil war and to the rise of absolute monarchies in which (as in Rome in the age of Seneca and

Nero) the individual was at the mercy of the government.

Stoicism affected late Renaissance culture in a number of ways. DuVair's claim that weeping was "contrary to virility" would be taken seriously, at least in northern Europe, for centuries. The reform of military discipline by Maurice of Nassau (a former pupil of Lipsius) was influenced by Stoic ideals and in turn influenced the practice of other European armies. Emblems, medals, and paintings offered vivid images of Stoic doctrines, notably the image of the hero resisting the onslaughts of fortune like a tree buffeted by the winds or a rock struck by the waves. Literature, from Montaigne's *Essais* (1580–1588) to Philip Sidney's *Arcadia* (completed in 1580 and revised in 1593), was colored by Stoic ideas and by the Stoic love of aphorisms. Sidney's Pamela, for example, is presented as a Stoic heroine. Of all the art forms, the one most affected by Stoicism was drama, a genre that had been practiced by Seneca himself. In Robert Garnier's *Porcie* (1568), for instance, Portia, daughter of the Stoic hero Cato, kills herself after affirming her constancy. Shakespeare's Brutus and his Cleopatra also demonstrate constancy through suicide. In a Latin play about St. John the Baptist by the Scottish humanist George Buchanan, the fearless hero is compared to a rock among the waves.

See also biographies of Pierre Charron, Guillaume Du Vair, Justus Lipsius, and Michel de Montaigne.

BIBLIOGRAPHY

Morford, Mark. *Stoics and Neostoics: Rubens and the Circle of Lipsius.* Princeton, N.J., 1991.
Oestreich, Gerhard. *Neostoicism and the Early Modern State.* Cambridge, U.K., and New York, 1982.

PETER BURKE

NEPOTISM. The word "nepotismo" (Italian for "nepotism," the word is derived from *nepote,* the Italian word for nephew.), charged with negative connotations, emerged in Italy at the beginning of the seventeenth century. The phenomenon itself, however—the preferential treatment of relatives and friends by secular and religious leaders when bestowing offices, titles, and material benefits—goes back to the ancient world.

In the ancient world, especially in Rome, favoring relatives was an act of *pietas.* Mediterranean societies believed that the individual could only be guarded against a hostile environment by kin or by patronage. *Pietas* was understood as dutiful behavior, of human beings showing respect and deference toward their gods, and between parents and children, including all living relatives and commemorated ancestors (*di parentes*). Romans felt bound to observe *pietas* toward the state (*patria*) as well. The ancient notion of *pietas* survived in the language of Roman law, remaining in use in the Middle Ages and the Renaissance without being reduced to its religious meaning (piety toward God, charity).

Nepotism was widespread and normal practice in Renaissance society. Rulers favored relatives with offices and riches because they felt that the recipient, in turn, would support the ruler. Moreover, the money stayed within the family. Similarly, civic officials favored relatives by appointing them to offices, while businessmen preferred to hire relatives. Indeed, society—and especially the person's relatives—criticized the ruler, civil official, or merchant if he did not favor his own flesh and blood. But customary secular practice had complicated results and sometimes received sharp criticism when high church officials, and especially popes, the spiritual leaders of Catholic Christendom, practiced nepotism.

Power and Support. Papal nepotism initially was also an act of *pietas.* The pope favored his relatives because the accepted values and norms allowed, or even required, him to do so. He acted accordingly in order to safeguard his reign and to provide for his family and their social advancement. Nepotism thus had a double function for the papacy: it secured power and provided support. In specific historical contexts either function could be manifest or latent.

During the crisis of the Great Schism (1378–1415) and the reconquest of the Papal States, nepotism regained much of its former function to secure power. The Roman popes Innocent VII (1404–1406) and Gregory XII (1406–1415) in their severe afflictions relied heavily on their relatives. Martin V (1417–1431) was also able to lean on his mighty family when confronted with the Papal States's disastrous condition. He provided his relatives with fiefs in the Kingdom of Naples and with possessions in the Papal States, culminating in the establishing of a *fideicommissum* (a gift of property with the provision that the recipient transfer it to another specified individual, as a way of evading inheritance laws). This became standard nepotistic procedure during the next centuries.

The popes' nepotism during the Renaissance is particularly known for Alexander VI's excesses. In contrast, Nicholas V (1447–1455) proved to be moderate, making his half brother Filippo Calandrini cardinal and transferring to him the diocese of Bologna.

Papal Nepotism. *Pope Paul III with His Grandsons* by Titian. Cardinal Alessandro Farnese *(left)* was appointed by his grandfather to be vice chancellor of the Roman church; he was noted as a patron of the arts. Ottavio Farnese *(right)* succeeded his father, Pierluigi, as duke of Parma and Piacenza in 1547. Paul III alienated the territories from the Papal States in 1545 to provide a duchy for his family. Painted 1545– 1546. GALLERIA NAZIONALE DE CAPODIMONTE, NAPLES/ALINARI/ART RESOURCE

Calixtus III (1455–1458) favored numerous relatives and compatriots, among them the twenty-four-year-old cardinal Rodrigo Borgia, subsequently Pope Alexander VI. Pius II (1458–1464) professed the ideal of *pietas* through the selection of his pontifical name. He appointed his nephew Francesco bishop of Siena and cardinal; the latter's brother Antonio became castellan of the Castel Sant' Angelo in Rome, commander in chief of the papal forces in Italy, grand justiciary of the Kingdom of Naples, duke of Amalfi, and son-in-law of King Ferrante of Naples. Many

relatives and compatriots also received positions in the Papal States.

Although deploring and attempting to diminish nepotism's abuses, the councils that initiated the reform movement during the late Middle Ages (Pisa, Constance, Basel) did not abolish nepotism entirely. On the contrary, the quarrel between the papacy and the sacred college openly demonstrated nepotism's function of power maintenance. Sixtus IV (1471–1484) was able to decide the conflict in his favor: he changed the structure of the college completely by appointing thirty-four new cardinals, among them six relatives. These new cardinals, often lacking a religious orientation, contributed significantly to the peculiar character of the expanding Renaissance papacy. The enormous extension of the system, the notorious amoralism of various favorites, and the re-establishment of the principality of Imola in the territory of the Papal States set new standards for nepotism under Sixtus IV. With Alexander VI (1492–1503), the pope's favors for his numerous children culminated the power maintenance and support functions of papal nepotism. The brutal destruction of the small princedoms in the Romagna by the pope's son Cesare Borgia and the elimination of the Roman barons in the capital's environs freed the papacy once and for all from the dangers of dependency on Roman noble factions and from the feudal disintegration of the Papal States.

Obviously, however, there remained the danger of the total alienation (by inheritance) of the church's secular property, which was owned almost exclusively by the house of Borgia. The situation changed when Pope Julius II (1503–1513) subjected much of the church territory to the central authority of Rome without the help of his kinsmen. His nepotism was meant exclusively for the support of his family: Galeotto della Rovere received the lucrative post of vice-chancellor, and the secular favorite Francesco Maria della Rovere, who was made heir to Urbino as the adopted son of a Montefeltro even before the election of his uncle to the pontificate, received Pesaro as fief.

Nepotism as Support. The transition from Alexander VI to Julius II marks a decisive shift in the history of nepotism because it lost its traditional power maintenance function; once again the support element came to the fore. Now the popes' nephews threatened to separate new feudal principalities out of the Papal States' territory, as they did when Pope Paul III (1534–1549) erected Farnese rule in Parma-Piacenza in 1545. The inclination of favorites to found their own principalities did not end even after Pius IV (1559–1565) sentenced the nephews of Paul IV (1555–1559) to death. Even the ban on new feudalities that Pius V (1566–1572) decreed in his bull *Admonet nos* on 29 March 1567 did not prevent the Barberini from pursuing such plans in the middle of the seventeenth century—with disastrous consequences.

Nepotism's support function also was subject to change from the middle of the sixteenth century: social change from the fourteenth to the seventeenth centuries led to the rise of the new bourgeois plutocracy that largely replaced the nobility. The papacy became a channel of social mobility, with Rome attracting patricians from northern and central Italy in particular. Having an uncle in the pontificate was an important event for a family's social status. The house of Farnese obtained a dukeship under Paul III, and the family of Julius III (1550–1555) was elevated from small-town patricians to barons. Most families of succeeding popes in the sixteenth and seventeenth centuries reached the same social status. The stages of such upward social mobility were largely similar. Direct or indirect financial allocations—gifts, benefices, or privileges—given by the papal uncle were decisive for the enrichment of the families, who were thus enabled to acquire real estate in the Papal States and in Naples, which was the basis of their baronage.

Cardinal-Nephews. In 1538 Pope Paul III put the young cardinal Alessandro Farnese in charge of the diplomatic correspondence, thereby creating the new office of *cardinal-nepote* (cardinal-nephew). Thus a pope's nephew with ecclesiastical status became cardinal, was entrusted with far-reaching, bureaucratic powers defined by briefs (papal instructions), and acted as the pope's deputy for secular affairs. He became head of foreign policy and held the position of *sopraintendente dello stato ecclesiastico,* that is, head of the most important administrative congregations as well as being the corresponding partner of the legates in the provinces of the Papal States. The new office must be seen in the context of the position of "superintendent" that appeared in Europe in the sixteenth and seventeenth centuries. A parallel can also be drawn to the position of prime minister as held by Cardinal Richelieu in France under Louis XIII or the count-duke of Olivares in Spain under Philip IV. Like these favorites of the kings, the *cardinal-nepote* was superseded by an "expert minister," the secretary of state, toward the end of the seventeenth century.

Judged by formal criteria, it was only then that nepotism reached its manifest function to maintain power, since the office became fully institutionalized. Legal provisions and assertions, however, hide political and social realities. The new office allowed the pope to maintain the illusion of a ruling favorite, while he himself actually determined the Vatican's policy with the help of his secretary of state. Papal nepotism around 1600 was primarily a systematic arrangement to siphon off church proceeds for the pope's family, thus raising sufficient means for the dynasty's usual social advancement and for securing the newly acquired status even after the end of the present pontificate. This Roman system was based on the papal finances and on the benefice system of the church as a whole. The bulk of the revenues stemmed from the Papal States and Spanish southern Italy.

The office of *cardinal-nepote* relieved the pope of social pressure and allowed him formally to distance himself from routine affairs. As *padre comune* he was above factious disputes over both international policy and internal matters. The *cardinal-nepote* replaced the pope as patron of the pope's clientele and head of the family. Yet there were also politically more active cardinal favorites, like Paolo Emilio Sfondrato, Pietro Aldobrandini, and Ludovico Ludovisi.

Reform and Abolition. The reform bull proclaimed during the Fifth Lateran Council in 1514 explicitly approved limited nepotism as *iustum et laudabile* (right and praiseworthy) on the basis of *pietas*. The Council of Trent strictly prohibited the bishops' and cardinals' nepotism (session 25, decree on reform 1) without, however, disassociating itself completely from the command of *pietas*. Like other poor, relatives in need were to receive alms. At Trent, Gabriele Paleotti had moderated as far as possible the rigorous reform measures drawn up by the Portuguese prelate Barthomoaeus a Martyribus. But the popes rejected even the revised decree.

It was the crisis of the papal finances caused by the general economic depression in Europe in 1621 that jeopardized nepotism. During this time Kaspar Schoppe (1576–1649) in *Funiculus triplex* (The threefold gage; 1622) made concrete reform proposals: all cardinals, including the nephews, were to receive a regular annual income of twelve thousand scudi; their number was to be reduced to thirty-three; and the pope himself was to dispose of only a small sum of money, being accountable for the remainder to the College of Cardinals. Further criticism and more difficulties with papal finances eventually brought the official papal nepotism of the Renaissance to an end in the late seventeenth century.

See also **Papacy.**

BIBLIOGRAPHY

Felix, Gilbert. *The Pope, His Banker, and Venice.* Cambridge, Mass., 1980.

Jaitner, Klaus. *Die Hauptinstruktionen Clemens' VIII für die Nuntien und Legaten an den europäischen Fürstenhöfen, 1592–1605.* 2 Vols. Tübingen, Germany, 1984.

McClung Hallman, Barbara. *Italian Cardinals, Reform, and the Church as Property.* Berkeley and Los Angeles, 1985.

Partner, Peter. "Papal Financial Policy in the Renaissance and Counter-Reformation." *Past and Present* 88 (1980): 17–62.

Partner, Peter. *The Pope's Men: The Papal Civil Service in the Renaissance.* Oxford, 1990.

Pastor, Ludwig von. *History of the Popes from the Close of the Middle Ages.* 39 vols. Translated and edited by Frederick Ignatius Antiobus et al. St. Louis, Mo., 1891–1938.

Reinhard, Wolfgang. *Papstfinanz und Nepotismus unter Paul V (1605–1621).* 2 vols. Stuttgart, Germany, 1974.

Reinhard, Wolfgang. "Nepotismus. Der Funktionswandel einer papstgeschichtlichen Konstanten." *Zeitschrift für Kirchengeschichte* 86 (1975): 145–185.

KLAUS JAITNER

NETHERLANDISH LITERATURE AND LANGUAGE.

The development of Dutch Renaissance language and literature should be considered against the background of rebellion and uprising against the sovereign, Philip II of Spain, and the struggle for independence that followed, the Eighty Years' War, which lasted from 1568 to 1648. The Dutch Republic broke away from the Habsburg (Spanish) Netherlands, whose territory was roughly the size and location of what is today the Benelux countries (Belgium, The Netherlands, and Luxembourg). The division of the northern and southern Netherlands was finalized in the 1580s, with the recapture of Antwerp by the Spanish in 1585 as the turning point. Consequently, a stream of merchants, intellectuals, artists, and craftsmen left the South to settle in the northern Netherlands, where they contributed to the boom in the economy as well as the arts and sciences, known as the Dutch golden age. In 1579 the northern provinces had formed a defensive alliance, the Union of Utrecht. By 1588 this had grown into a confederation of seven provinces, the Dutch Republic, waging the war of independence against Spain. The Twelve Years' Truce (1609) meant a de facto acknowledgment by the Spanish king of the Netherlands' independence, which was finally pledged in the Peace of Münster (Peace of Westphalia; 1648). The South was to remain under Habsburg rule for nearly another century and a half. These political events strongly influenced the development of language and literature: various sixteenth-century developments that had begun in the South now continued in the North, and came to fruition there during the first half of the seventeenth century.

Development of the Dutch Language. In the Habsburg Netherlands of the sixteenth century there was no uniformity of language. Rather, several related dialects were spoken, known collectively as "Diets."

Appreciation of the vernacular. It was not until the second half of the sixteenth century that—following France and Italy—interest in the vernacular language began to grow. The native tongue was now exalted in many ways. In the North as well as in the South attempts were made to structure, purify, and cultivate the written language so as to allow its use at different levels but especially in the production of a vernacular literature equal in stature to the classics.

Standardization. Some essential requirements for the creation of a standard language are that it should obey rules of grammar and spelling; it should be untainted by foreign (notably French) elements; and its vocabulary should be enlarged with new terminology for contemporary concepts in the fields of economy, culture, and science. This process was headed by the Amsterdam *rederijkerskame* (chamber of rhetoric), De Egelantier (the wild brier), whose leader was the merchant and poet Hendrick Laurensz Spiegel (1549–1612). He is the author of *Twe-spraack vande Nederduitsche letterkunst* (Dialogue on Dutch language), the first Latin-based Dutch grammar, published by De Egelantier in 1584. The booklet contained a preface by Spiegel's friend, the writer Dirck Volckertsz Coornhert (1522–1590), emphasizing the social relevance of the work. In the following years De Egelantier continued the educational program with the publication of small rhetorical and dialectical guidebooks in the vernacular. In that same period Simon Stevin (1548–1620), a mathematician from the university town of Leiden, was writing his Dutch-language scientific works on arithmetic, mathematics, and fortification; he invented a large number of new scientific terms, demonstrating that his native tongue was suitable as a language of science.

Lexicography. In the field of lexicography, the main events took place in the South. The prominent Antwerp printer and publisher Christophe Plantin (c. 1520–1589) produced the first glossaries and dictionaries, for example, the *Thesaurus theutonicae linguae* (1573). In 1574 Plantin's editor, Cornelis Kiliaen (c. 1530–1607), published the first scholarly description of Dutch vocabulary, known since its third impression in 1599 as *Etymologicum teutonicae linguae*. Kiliaen here distinguishes between native and nonnative words; his work constitutes a milestone in sixteenth-century Dutch lexicography.

Further evolution. The seventeenth century witnessed the evolution of a standard language that was derived mainly from the dialect of the province

Netherlandish Poet. Joost van den Vondel (1587–1679).

of Holland—the political, economic, and cultural heart of the Republic—but that also contained southern elements due to the influx of immigrants. For the learned, however, the process was too slow; the new norms, they felt, were as yet too noncommittal and arbitrary. That is why, in the winter of 1622–1623, a group of prominent poets, Pieter Cornelisz Hooft (1581–1647) and Joost van den Vondel (1587–1679) among them, held regular sessions on language and literature. Their aim was to find agreement in such matters as word order, collocations, cases, and spelling; they also advocated various changes in poetic technique. The new rules were first implemented in 1625 with Vondel's translation of Seneca's tragedy *Troades*. In retrospect, the choices made by these leading poets greatly affected further seventeenth-century literary developments.

Statenbijbel. Far more important for the development of the Dutch language, however, was the publication of the Statenbijbel in 1637. This Calvinist translation of the Bible from its source languages, financed by the States General, soon became the bible of the Protestant population. For more than three centuries the Statenbijbel has profoundly influenced the Dutch language, enriching it with a wealth of words and phrases. The Statenbijbel has remained the most authoritative version of the Bible to many Dutch Protestants to this day. The learned translators purposely worked at the creation of a uniform language that would transcend the limitations of any specific dialect area. That is why the language of the Statenbijbel shows influences from the south and east of the Netherlands as well as from Holland. The Statenbijbel may be regarded as the greatest monument of the seventeenth-century Dutch language.

Development of Dutch Renaissance Literature.

Surveying the area of Renaissance literature, we find that five authors were trend-setting: the poet, dramatist, and historian Pieter Cornelisz Hooft; the poet and dramatist Gerbrandt Adriaensz Bredero (1585–1618); the poet, satirist, and dramatist Joost van den Vondel; the poet Constantijn Huygens (1596–1687); and the poet and emblematist Jacob Cats (1577–1660). Bredero, Hooft, and Vondel lived in Amsterdam; Cats in Zeeland and later in The Hague (due to his political career); and Huygens in The Hague. The most versatile of them was Vondel, who practiced just about every literary genre. Cats was the most didactic and moralistic; his highly popular emblem books and didactic works, *Houwelyck* (Marriage; 1625) and *Trou-ringh* (Wedding ring; 1637), for instance, were printed in vast quantities. Cats and Huygens were the personifications of stylistic ideals: Cats stood for perspicuity and a simple style, Huygens for obscurity and complexity. Cats, the educator of the people, wrote for the broad masses of the literate, whereas Huygens's work was intended for the happy few of the literati. Both these poets were proficient in English, an unusual achievement in their day; Huygens even translated a number of John Donne's poems into Dutch. But Vondel was the poet whose style was to become the ideal example for generations of poets to come. Even during his lifetime, Vondel was a classic like Hooft before him.

Chambers of rhetoric.

Throughout the sixteenth century, the literary life of Dutch and Flemish towns took place mainly in the chambers of rhetoric, where poets, artists, and intellectuals together practiced the arts in the vernacular, where literary works were passed around in manuscript and plays were staged. The chambers had a major function in public cultural life and were involved in the organization of all kinds of municipal manifestations.

After 1585 Amsterdam became the main literary center. Apart from De Egelantier, Amsterdam, like other towns in Holland, had another chamber especially for immigrants from the South: the Brabant chamber, Het Wit Lavendel (The white lavender). One of its members was the young Vondel, who made his debut here with his play *Het Pascha* (The Passover; 1612), treating the deliverance of the Israelites from slavery in Egypt. Although there were contacts between poets of the two chambers, innovations took place chiefly within the circle of De Egelantier, the breeding ground of talents like Hooft, Bredero, and Samuel Coster (1579–1665). These poets were modern, humanistically oriented idealists whose intention was to develop a national type of Renaissance drama.

Jan van der Noot.

The earliest real evidence of literary innovation is found in the work of an individualist who published outside the chambers: the Antwerp patrician Jan van der Noot (c. 1535–1595), whose lengthy stay in France had acquainted him with Ronsard and other Pléiade poets. His volume *Het bosken* (The copse), published in London circa 1570, in exile, is the first collection of Dutch poetry to carry the new Renaissance lyric to full fruition. Platonic notions like love leading to virtue, insights into a higher reality through poetic vision, and the poet as bestower of immortality are presented in genres new to Dutch literature, such as the sonnet, the epithalamium, and the ode, as well as in new verse forms. Probably due to political developments, Van der Noot remained a fairly isolated phenomenon; his work did not have any noticeable impact.

Nederduytsche Academie.

In 1617, a conflict—presumably about literary beliefs—arose in De Egelantier, which resulted in Coster, Hooft, and Bredero leaving the chamber. Coster then founded the Nederduytsche Academie, an educational project, offering scientific education as well as the modern Renaissance drama in Dutch. Coster's project met with great opposition and was therefore short-lived; he had to close down in 1622. Still, the Academie has earned a specific place in literary history as the oldest Dutch theater. Some classic Dutch comedies had their premieres here: Bredero's *Het Moortje* (The Moorish woman; 1615), an adaptation of Terence's *Eunuchus;* Bredero's *Spaanschen Brabander* (The Spanish Brabanter; 1617), an adaptation of the Spanish picaresque novel *Lazarillo de Tormes;* and Hooft's *Warenar* (1617), an imitation of Plautus's *Aulularia.*

Joost van den Vondel.

After the closing of Coster's Academie, the authorities of Amsterdam forced the two chambers of rhetoric to cooperate. This was followed, in 1637, by the foundation of the Schouwburg, Amsterdam's first permanent theater, whose inauguration took place in January 1638 with the presentation of the "Amsterdam tragedy" *Gysbreght*

Netherlandish Historian and Poet. Pieter Cornelisz Hooft (1581–1647). NEW YORK PUBLIC LIBRARY, ASTOR, LENOX, AND TILDEN FOUNDATIONS

van Aemstel, a glorification of the city's history. During the first decades of its existence, the theater occupied a prominent position in Amsterdam's literary life, mainly because Vondel's plays were performed there.

Vondel as a playwright had initially followed the more Senecan tradition of Hooft, but he increasingly concentrated on Aristotle and Greek drama, and began writing tragedies on the classical model. His tragedy *Jeptha* (1659)—a Christian imitation of Euripides's *Iphigenia*—was presented as model drama in the Aristotelian sense. Vondel is exceptional in that he took the material for most of his thirty-two plays from the Scriptures, which makes him the most important seventeenth-century author of biblical drama in Europe. Works like *Joseph in Dothan* (1640), *Salomon* (1648), *Lucifer* (1654), *Adam in Ballingschap* (Adam in exile; 1664), and *Noah* (1667) are proof of his mastery of stagecraft. Vondel's best-known play is *Gysbreght van Aemstel.* It was performed in Amsterdam every New Year, a tradition that continued until 1967. Vondel was also skillful in other genres, as seen in his pastoral play *Leeuwendalers* (1647), written in 1648 when the Peace of Münster was signed.

Individualization. In the second decade of the seventeenth century, a process of individualization set in. Poets began to publish under their own names; as a consequence the influence of individual poets increased to the detriment of the chambers of rhetoric. One of those who acquired great authority was Daniel Heinsius (1580–1655), a classical scholar and neo-Latin poet from the University of Leiden. In 1616 a friend published his vernacular poems titled *Nederduytsche poemata.* The fact that Heinsius prefered his mother tongue over classical Latin was a matter of the greatest consequence, since it showed that the Dutch language was fit for the production of high quality literature. This volume, which became exemplary, may therefore be regarded as the final breakthrough of Renaissance literature in the northern Netherlands. For Heinsius, classical literature was the absolute norm, and creative imitation of the classics was a leading principle. Writers such as Carel van Mander (1548–1606), Hooft, Vondel, and others also took this idealistic line, using much mythological ornament in their style. A far more realistic course was taken by Coornhert, Spiegel, Bredero, Dirk Rafaelsz Camphuysen (1586–1627), and others.

Women. Women writers were active in the republic, but their role in literary circles was very minor, even though they often received glowing praise from their contemporaries. The two daughters of the poet Roemer Visscher, Anna (1583–1651) and Maria Tesselschade (1594–1649), for example, both enjoyed much appreciation in their circle but never published collections of their own work. Indeed, it was not until the nineteenth century that their poetry became available. Women writers on the whole did not begin to publish until 1650.

Literary networks. Communication among poets took place in various ways: through visits, letters, or the mutual exchange of poems. In the early seventeenth century, the home of Roemer Visscher (1547–1620) and his gifted daughters became a meeting place for artists and poets. The so-called Muiderkring has also attained some fame: after his second marriage, in 1627, Hooft and his wife would entertain their learned and literary friends at Muiden Castle, Hooft's summer residence not far from Amsterdam. Huygens, Maria Tesselschade Visscher, Vondel, and Vos were among Hooft's visitors. Jacob Steendam (1616–1673) emerged from the literary circle surrounding the minor Amsterdam poet Jan Zoet; Steendam settled as a colonist in New Netherland and wrote about the Dutch colony in North America:

Klacht van Nieuw Amsterdam (Complaint of New Amsterdam; 1659) and *'t Lof van Nieuw Nederland* (Homage to New Netherland; 1661), the latter earning him the honorary title of earliest poet of New Amsterdam.

Other Dutch cities had varying degrees of literary life: Leiden, Dordrecht, and Rotterdam are some examples. In Zeeland, Cats became the center of a kind of circle of poets in the town of Middelburg, which in 1622 produced a collection ironically titled *De Zeeuwsche nachtegael* (The Zeeland nightingale, i.e., the frog).

Popular Genres and Nonfiction Prose.

Songbooks. In the early seventeenth century, songbooks became popular. These were anthologies of songs and poetry intended to be performed by the young sons and daughters of the wealthy social elite. The booklets were often expensively made and contained a miscellany of Petrarchan texts from both well-known and lesser-known poets. Many of Hooft's and Bredero's songs were first printed in songbooks such as *Den bloemhof van de Nederlantsche Jeught* (The flower garden of Dutch youth; 1602), *Apollo oft ghesangh der Musen* (Apollo or the singing of the Muses; 1615), and *Thronus Cupidinis* (1618). Bredero was highly popular; his poetry was assembled and published posthumously, in 1622, in a sumptuous volume titled *Boertigh amoureus en aendachtigh groot lied-boeck* (Comical, amorous, and devotional great songbook). Not surprisingly, after the outbreak of the rebellion, politics and religion were major themes besides love. The many editions of the *Geuzenliedboek* (Beggar's War songbook), with new songs added each time, are proof of the widespread popularity of these songs. The oldest existing copy (c. 1577–1578) already contains the "Wilhelmus," now the Netherlands' national anthem.

Emblem books. There was also a large production of emblem books. Three types of emblem flourished in the Netherlands: first, the love emblem with a strong Petrarchan bias. Introduced by Heinsius and also practiced by, for example, Hooft (*Emblemata amatoria;* 1611), this category began its existence fairly lightheartedly. Its character changed with Cats's *Sinne- en minnebeelden* (Meaningful pictures and pictures on love; 1618), since Cats was first and foremost a moralist. He gave each picture a threefold interpretation: an amorous one for the young, a social one for the grown-ups, and a religious one for the elderly. The second category, the religious love emblem, emanated from the love emblem and

caught on chiefly among the Jesuits in the South as an aid to education and propaganda. Finally, the realistic emblem, which took its subject matter from everyday life, was introduced in 1614 by Roemer Visscher with *Sinnepoppen* (Meaningful figures). Here, too, Cats became the undisputed master for his contemporaries. His *Spiegel van den ouden ende nieuwen Tijdt* (Mirror of the old and new times; 1632) offers advice on all aspects of human existence from infancy to old age. The pictures for most of these emblem books were made by important artists, which contributed greatly to their appeal.

Poetry. The country house poem was another very popular genre. Inspired by the Horatian *beatus ille* theme, poets sang the praises of country life and the estates of the well-to-do, eulogizing not only their houses and gardens but their libraries as well. Cats's *Hofgedachten op Zorghvliet* (Garden thoughts at Zorghvliet; 1655) and Huygens's *Hofwijck* (1657) are country house poems in praise of their own estates.

Practically every poet wrote religious poetry or translated Psalms. Many members of the clergy published volumes of songs for the edification of their parishioners. Among the best are Huygens's *Heilighe dagen* (Holy days; 1645) and the "metaphysical" poetry by the Deventer clergyman Jacobus Revius (1586–1658). *Stichtelyke rymen* (Edifying rhymes; 1644), an anthology published by the Arminian minister Dirk Rafaels Camphuysen (1586–1627) was a best-seller. By 1700 it had been reprinted more than thirty times.

Major public and social events were likewise celebrated in verse. One example is Vondel's *Inwydinghe van 't stadthuis* (Inauguration of the town-hall; 1655), a long poem extolling Amsterdam and its regents. In effect, Vondel became the official city poet of Amsterdam.

Of course poets also expressed their anxieties about Dutch society. In his *Costelick mal* (Costly folly; 1622) Huygens ridiculed fashion quirks, while the poet Willem Godschalck van Focquenbroch (1640–1670) composed a razor-sharp comment on the greed and spiritual poverty of the city of Amsterdam, aptly called *Op Amsterdam*.

Prose. In comparison with drama and poetry, the number of significant prose writings remained limited. In 1569 Marnix van St. Aldegonde (1538–1598), a fervent Calvinist, published *Biencorf der H. Roomscher Kercke* (Beehive of the holy Roman church), an unprecedentedly trenchant attack on the Roman Catholic Church. Entirely different in nature is *Zedekunst, dat is wellevenskunste* (Ethics, that is, the art of living well; 1586) by Coornhert; it is the first ethics text in vernacular prose, and in it Coornhert proves himself an original, independent thinker with a profound understanding of human behavior. A book that has preserved its significance is Carel van Mander's *Het Schilder-boeck* (Book of painters; 1604); a series of lively biographies of Dutch, Flemish, German, and Italian painters in the manner of Giorgio Vasari, it is still a major source of information about early Flemish and Dutch painting. The most impressive example of Renaissance prose is offered by Hooft's *Nederlandsche historien* (Dutch history), a monumental history of the Dutch revolt against Philip II, written in the high style. The first part came out in 1642, but Hooft's work remained unfinished. *Nederlandsche historien* is the epic of William the Silent, leader of the rebellion and the uncontested protagonist of the history. He is brought to life as a wise, tolerant, and resolute leader, who willingly subordinates his own interests to the common good. As regards both content and style, Hooft has followed his ideal, the Roman historian Tacitus.

Travel Stories. A different, and immensely popular, type of nonfiction prose was the travel story. Descriptions of remote lands (America, Indonesia, China) appealed greatly to the imagination, and numerous translations provided for an international reading public. The most famous example is *Journaal van Bontekoe* (1646), the stirring account of a voyage to the Dutch East Indies that leads the skipper, Bontekoe, into all kinds of adventures (including shipwreck) and ends happily with his safe arrival. Translations, adaptations, and reprints of this book have continued to the present.

The deaths of the two literary giants—Vondel in 1679 and Huygens in 1687—ended the prime years of Dutch Renaissance literature. The next few generations of poets lacked literary genius and remained under the shadows of their great predecessors.

BIBLIOGRAPHY

Primary Works

Barnouw, Adriaan J. *Coming After: An Anthology of Poetry from the Low Countries.* New Brunswick, N.J., 1948.

Levenson, Christopher, trans. *Light of the World: An Anthology of Seventeenth-Century Dutch Religious and Occasional Poetry.* Windsor, Ont., 1982.

Levenson, Christopher, trans. *Searching Heart's Solace: An Anthology of Sixteenth- and Seventeenth-Century Dutch Love Poetry.* Toronto, 1982.

Secondary Works

Augustinus, Dierick P. "European Baroque and Dutch Seventeenth-Century Lyric Poetry." *Canadian Journal of Netherlandic Studies* 2 (1980–1981): 1–32.

Boheemen, Christine van. "Dutch-American Poets of the Seventeenth Century." In *The Dutch in North-America: Their Immigration and Cultural Continuity.* Edited by Rob Kroes and Henk-Otto Neuschäfer. Amsterdam, 1991. Pages 114–130.

Harmsel, Henrietta ten. "The Metaphysical Poets of Holland's Golden Age." *Revue of National Literatures* 8 (1977): 70–96.

Parente, James A. *Religious Drama and the Humanist Tradition: Christian Theater in Germany and in the Netherlands.* Leiden and New York, 1987.

Schama, Simon. *The Embarrassment of Riches: An Interpretation of Dutch Culture in the Golden Age.* New York, 1987.

Schenkeveld, Maria A. *Dutch Literature in the Age of Rembrandt: Themes and Ideas.* Amsterdam and Philadelphia, 1991.

Spies, M. "The Amsterdam Chamber De Egelentier and the Ideals of Erasmian Humanism." In *From Revolt to Riches: Culture and History of the Low Countries 1500–1700: International and Interdisciplinary Perspectives.* Edited by Theo Hermans and Reiner Salverda. London, 1993. Pages 109–118.

Spies, M. "Woman and Seventeenth-century Dutch Literature." *Dutch Crossing* 19 (1995): 3–23.

Weevers, Theodore. *Poetry of the Netherlands in Its European Context 1170–1930.* London, 1960.

HENK DUITS

NETHERLANDS. [This entry includes two subentries, one on the history of the Netherlands in the Renaissance and the other on artists active in the Netherlands.]

The Netherlands in the Renaissance

The Burgundian Netherlands. The geographic, economic, social, and political entity known variously as the Netherlands, the Low Countries, the Seventeen Provinces of Charles V, and in more recent times as the Benelux Countries (Belgium, Netherlands, and Luxemburg) had its medieval origins in and around the provinces of Flanders and Brabant in the south, and Holland and Zeeland in the north.

The complexity of the region during Burgundian (1384–1477) and Habsburg (1477–1795 in the south, 1477–1579 in the north) rule is illustrated by the bewildering number of lands that passed into (and sometimes out of) their effective authority, among which were the parts or the whole of Luxembourg; Limburg; Namur; Hainaut; the castellanies of Lille, Douai, and Orchies; Cambrai; Tournai and Artois in the south; and Gelderland, Utrecht, Overijssel, Lingen, Drenthe, Friesland, and Groningen in the north.

Separated by the westward course of the two great rivers (the Waal, principal branch of the Rhine, and the Meuse or Maas), north and south developed within different economic and political orbits. The area south of the rivers was oriented toward France and Burgundy and its economic development revolved around high-value manufactured goods (such as textiles) for export. The area north of the rivers was largely oriented toward northern Germany and the Baltic, and its trade in bulk goods brought it into conflict with the cities of the Hanseatic League. While Flanders and Brabant had the greatest concentrations of population and wealth (and the concomitant industry and commerce), Holland became predominant in the north as earthwork, flood control, and reclamation projects began to yield systematic and effective benefits from the early thirteenth century onward.

Both north and south were brought together under the rule of the Burgundian dukes. Flanders in 1384 passed to Duke Philip the Bold (1342–1404) via his wife, Margaret, the daughter of the deceased Louis de Mâle, count of Flanders. By 1428 the dukes of Burgundy had extended their territory to Holland and Zeeland (under Philip the Good, ruled 1419–1467). With the goal of assimilating and unifying his territories, Philip created a number of common institutions, among which were the Order of the Golden Fleece, the States General, and a central Chamber of Accounts. Yet these institutions did not entirely resolve the historic divisions among hitherto separate provinces. The center of courtly and political activity remained in the south, anchored to the duke's residence in Brussels, and officeholders and members of the new institutions were drawn largely (in some cases almost exclusively) from the south.

Hence ducal appointees—like the French-speaking southern nobles who succeeded one another as provincial governors, or stadtholders, of Holland—were seen as alien within their respective jurisdictions. Towns and provinces north and south remained stubbornly attached to traditional privileges and loath to sacrifice their own interests to the alleged common interest of the larger Burgundian patrimony. For example, during Holland's wars with the Hanseatic League from 1438 to 1441, Bruges in Flanders had to be constrained by ducal authority to break off commercial relations with its Hanseatic trading partners.

The last Burgundian duke, Charles the Bold (ruled 1467–1477), significantly advanced his father Philip's program of centralization; taxes were now voted not by the provincial states or parliaments individually, but by their representatives assembled in the States General. But Charles's death brought a reaction in favor of local autonomy as his daughter, Mary (ruled 1477–1482), was forced to concede a set of Great Privileges, first to the States General of the entire Burgundian Netherlands, and then to the states of the separate provinces. The provinces sought greater privileges (such as initiative of assembly, approval of taxation) at the provincial level, not only at the expense of the central government, but also to the exclusion of "foreigners" from the other provinces. The privilege granted to Holland and Zeeland, for example, excluded outsiders from governmental positions and provided for the use of Dutch as the official language of government, as opposed to the French of the southern provinces (and the court language of most of the high nobility).

Under the Habsburgs. During the confusion following Charles the Bold's death, France reclaimed the duchy of Burgundy and built a clientele in Flanders, historically a fief of the French crown. Mary's marriage in 1477 to Maximilian of Habsburg (from 1493, the emperor Maximilian I) provided protection against France, but it also tied the Low Countries to events in the Holy Roman Empire.

Like the Burgundians, Habsburg rulers found a formidable array of privileged towns standing in the way of any plan for centralization. This was due in part to the high level of urbanization in the Netherlands. From 1300 on Flanders and Brabant had several cities with populations of 10,000 or more, including Ghent, Bruges, and Antwerp. Even more urbanized was Holland, which by the mid-sixteenth century had a ratio of town and city (populations of 5,000 or more) inhabitants to rural (country and village) approaching 50 percent.

Within the towns, civic associations were concerned with their own "privileges," which were usually codified and endorsed by the city government. Guilds, especially strong in Flanders and Brabant, served a number of functions, from quality control and consumer protection to monopolistic control of trade. Guilds also assumed a social role for their members that included poor and sick relief and ceremonial and religious observance. In some cities, individual quarters also were represented by similar associations. Of specific consequence to the Reformation in the Netherlands were the "shooting guilds," or militias, of individual towns. These were often the deciding factor in determining a town's allegiance, either for or against the States or the emperor, the old church or the new, since town councils—regardless of their own sympathies—could not enforce regulations upon an unwilling populace without the militias. Chambers of rhetoric (civic theatrical and literary organizations) also played a role in spreading the ideas of humanism and the Protes-

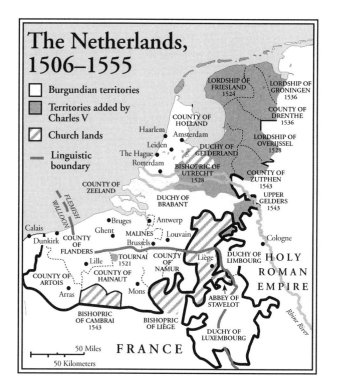

The Netherlands, 1506–1555

- ☐ Burgundian territories
- ▨ Territories added by Charles V
- ▥ Church lands
- — Linguistic boundary

tant Reformation, though often in a covert and ironic way, owing to efforts of the emperor Charles V (ruled 1519–1556) and King Philip II of Spain (ruled 1556–1598) to suppress heresy.

Guilds and related associations could exert real political pressure on town councils. But those holding civic offices, often referred to collectively as the regents, mainly represented the great merchant and patrician families, and were tied in many ways to the interests of the Habsburg and Burgundian dynasties. "Democratic" elements in the town governments—especially the guilds, in Flanders and Brabant—were less reliable politically. Habsburg rulers sometimes took advantage of civic unrest to strip the guilds of their political role, as Charles V did at Ghent in 1540. As important as the towns were in this highly urban society, they were not unchallenged. Great nobles, often members of the Order of the Golden Fleece, usually spoke for the government in its dealings with the towns, conscious that their own authority and that of the prince were mutually dependent.

When Maximilian I became Holy Roman Emperor in 1493 his son, Archduke Philip the Handsome (d. 1506), was already recognized as "natural prince" in each of the separate Low Countries provinces. The resistance to control by a foreigner that had marred Maximilian's reign did not continue under Philip; for example, Philip was able to reestablish the High

Court or Grand Council of Mechelen (attempted under Charles the Bold), which over time became an important instrument of centralization. Philip was succeeded in the Low Countries by his young son Charles, for whom the boy's aunt, Margaret of Austria, served as regent until 1515, and again from 1517 to 1530, while Charles (elected Holy Roman Emperor as Charles V in 1519) became acclimated to the Spanish realms of his maternal grandparents, Ferdinand of Aragon and Isabella of Castile. Charles would return in 1531, long enough to effect some further administrative reforms and name a new regent, his sister, Mary of Hungary, who would serve in that capacity until 1555. By 1538 the perennial factionalism of the guild town of Ghent, aggravated by a dispute with the regent over raising funds for the military defense of the southern provinces in the wars with France (1521–1529, 1536, 1542–1544, and 1551–1559), had deteriorated into sporadic mob violence and civil strife, which was spreading through the most contentious of the fractious towns in Flanders and Brabant. Mary had appealed to Charles for help, and this, combined with an invitation from the king of France, convinced Charles to leave Spain and travel through France on his way to Flanders, finally returning to the place of his birth, the Prisenhof in Ghent, in 1540.

By the time of Charles's abdication in the Netherlands in favor of his son, Philip II, in 1555, a new, university-trained class of civil servants had moved increasingly into positions of authority, thereby reducing somewhat the dynasty's historic dependence on the great nobility. The Council of State (responsible for foreign affairs) remained dominated by the great nobles, but the Privy Council (which addressed internal affairs and some judicial appeals) and the Council of Finance were dominated by university-trained commoners.

Philip II was in the Low Countries from 1555 until 1559, returning to Spain after he had concluded the last of the Habsburg-Valois wars (1551–1559) of this period. Philip's plan for taxation to support the war, whereby revenues were controlled by the States General, proved unsatisfactory, and he directed the new regent (his half sister and Charles's illegitimate daughter, Margaret of Parma) to deal separately with the provincial states and not to convene the States General. Within the Council of State, Margaret faced a growing rivalry between the two great magnates (William of Orange and Lamoraal, count of Egmont) and two of the dynasty's most trusted servants, Antoine Perrenot, lord of Granvelle in Franche-Comté, and the jurist Vigilius van Aytta. Complicating this increasingly volatile situation was Philip's plan (approved by the pope) to create new bishoprics in the Netherlands. The new bishoprics were formed by dividing the existing sees (Thérouanne, Arras, Tournai, Cambrai, and Liège in the south, and Utrecht in the north) into a total of nineteen, eight of which were in the north. The endowments for these new bishoprics were to come not from the government, but rather from monastic lands and revenues. This generated much resistance from members of the clerical elites and from their brothers and cousins among the nobility. In the towns, Philip's plan brought the realization that each new bishopric would have its own inquisitorial tribunal, stoking a growing opposition to the enforcement of Habsburg anti-heresy laws.

Religious and Cultural Life. The Netherlands was a culturally diverse region in which a number of languages were used: French and Dutch dialects, and Low German in the border areas. Latin, however, was the language of the scholars, diplomats, and the church. The first university in the region opened in Louvain in 1426. In the sixteenth century, when religious wars separated the northern from the southern region, the University of Douai (1559) became the bulwark of the Catholic party, and the University of Leiden (1575) the center of the reformed party. During the seventeenth century the universities of Groningen (1614) and Amsterdam (1632) came into existence.

Humanism entered the Netherlands at the turn of the sixteenth century as a result of the travel between the Low Countries and Italy. Rudolf Agricola and Jacob Canter were among the first scholars to return from Italy imbued with the new learning. The establishment of the first printing press (1473) is a significant date for the dissemination of humanist culture; the foundation of a trilingual college at Louvain (1517) was another milestone. Desiderius Erasmus, who took a personal interest in the college, was the leading light of northern humanism. His contributions to biblical studies, textual criticism, pedagogy, and political thought were widely recognized and applauded. The religious strife and the censorship connected with it, however, had a dampening effect on scholarship. At the beginning of the seventeenth century the University of Leiden led an intellectual revival. It became a center of classical learning where scholars like Justus Lipsius and Joseph Scaliger set new standards of excellence. Lipsius and Hugo Grotius did the same for political thinking, Vesalius for medicine.

The religious and intellectual foment of the sixteenth century had (to some extent) roots in the fifteenth century. During the fifteenth century the Devotio Moderna (also known as the Brothers and Sisters of the Common Life) spread from its origins in the northern provinces of Overijssel and Groningen into the southern Low Countries and northern Germany. Followers of the Devotio Moderna stressed the interior religious life of the individual, in part through the writings of such authors as Wessel Gansfort (1419–1489) and Thomas à Kempis (1379?–1471), the author of *De imitatione Christi* (The imitation of Christ). Leading humanists of this region, such as Rudolf Agricola (1444–1485) and Desiderius Erasmus (c. 1466–1536) both spent time at schools run by Devotio teachers. Unlike his teachers, Erasmus in particular attacked what he saw as medieval Christendom's excessive dependence on "ceremonies."

His "philosophia Christi" sought in "learned piety" a mean between the extremes of a "paganizing" obsession with classical literature divorced from commitment to Christ and Christian truth and the destruction of true piety by a fearful and anti-intellectual clinging to the externals of ceremony, ritual, and legalism (which Erasmus condemned as "Judaism"). While Erasmus himself was terrified of the schismatic consequences of the Reformation and worked to preserve the unity of the church, his writings provided ammunition for the reformers' criticisms of monasticism, scholasticism, and papal authority.

By the 1530s Anabaptists of various sorts had established themselves in the Netherlands, and their activity ranged from the pacifist (such as the original Melchiorites, and the Davidites, derived from founders Melchior Hofmann and David Joris) to the militant (followers of Jan of Leiden, a Melchiorite who claimed a new divine revelation, and Jan van Batenburg). The volatile eschatological expectations of militant Anabaptists peaked in the "revolutionary kingdom" that they temporarily established just outside the Netherlands in Münster in 1534 and 1535, until its conquest by an alliance of Lutheran and Catholic princes. Of enduring significance for Dutch Anabaptism was the pacifist movement that now coalesced around Dirk Philips and Menno Simons.

While barely detected at the time, tightly organized Calvinist churches, starting from the French-speaking towns in the south in the 1540s, would later prove to be a more serious threat to the authorities. The Netherlands also proved to be a fertile ground for various sorts of Spiritualism. The Familists (or

Family of Love) practiced an outward conformity to the existing church while pursuing an interior process of salvation based on direct communication with God. Perhaps the most notable Spiritualist was Dirk Volkertszoon Coornhert, who rejected the dogmatism of Catholics and Protestants alike, criticized the doctrines of original sin and predestination, and argued for a civil order in which the state had no right to control the religious beliefs of its citizens.

The common environment for religious dissenters of all kinds in the Netherlands was the campaign against heresy begun by Charles and continued by Philip. In 1521 Charles issued the first posted notices of the edicts, or "placards," forbidding the possession of Luther's books under penalty of death. The placards would continue, aided and abetted by the Inquisition promulgated by the crown in the Netherlands, which would execute approximately 1,300 individuals between 1523 and 1566. While town governments and some provincial officials were loath to enforce heresy laws strictly, there were also zealous inquisitors, notably Pieter Titelmans, active in Flanders, who heard an average of 75 to 80 cases a year during his twenty-year tenure.

By 1565 the situation had become so volatile that the Council of State (now without Granvelle, who had been dismissed at the insistence of the magnates) wrote to Philip in Spain petitioning him to suspend harsh measures against heresy. Philip's rejection of this request occasioned widespread protest, organized in November 1565 into a League of Compromise, led by noblemen such as Hendrik van Brederode and Floris of Culemborg. On 5 April 1566 the League—dismissed as "beggars" by one of Margaret's advisers—presented the regent the Petition of Compromise in Brussels, demanding the end of the Inquisition. Fueled by a wave of iconoclastic riots organized by refugees returning from England, the protest turned into a revolt. Outdoor preaching by Calvinists (called hedge-sermons) often attracted thousands of listeners in areas where consistories had not yet been organized. Yet by the time of the arrival of the Spanish army under the duke of Alba in August 1567, the central government in Brussels had already begun to reestablish itself, and a great many nobles and Protestants supporting the revolt had left the country.

The Great Revolt. Alba hastened the flight of the exiles by arresting and subsequently executing Lamoraal, count of Egmont, and Philip de Montmorency, count of Horn, two magnates loyal to the established church, yet whom Alba believed were im-

plicated in the League of Compromise and their Petition of Compromise. Alba's Council of Troubles would eventually investigate and sentence 8,950 individuals for their part in the revolt, of whom more than 1,000 were executed. Prospects for the revolt looked grim at first. Only in 1568, after attempting to play an intermediary role between the crown and the rebels, did William of Orange finally declare himself for the revolt, and this only after his lands had been confiscated and he had been condemned by the Council of Troubles. William's prominence immediately made him the leader of the revolt, but the rebels' initial efforts to seize and hold fortified towns failed. The situation on the ground improved only with the famous seizure, on 1 April 1572, of the port city of Brill in Holland by the Sea Beggars, as the maritime branch of the rebel movement was called.

The seizure of Brill marked a turning point. Town by town, much of Holland and Zeeland fell to the Great Revolt, and the rebels there were able to hold back the Spanish counterinsurgency in the rebellion's first years. Alba's tactics against the rebels included the intentional massacre of entire towns, such as Zutphen and Naarden in 1572.

It was an unplanned atrocity, however, that led to the last major effort to unite north and south in revolt against Spain. In 1576 the Spanish army in the Netherlands mutinied after being unpaid, unfed, and unsupplied owing to Philip's financial difficulties. In November 1576 the mutineers attacked Antwerp. This assault on the greatest commercial and financial center of Europe galvanized southern and northern provinces, which reacted by signing the agreement known as the Pacification of Ghent, which sought to unite the entire Netherlands in an effort to drive out the Spanish mutineers and also in defense of traditional privileges with tacit recognition for the Calvinist regime established by rebel troops in Holland and Zeeland.

This unity was fractured, first by the unwillingness of Calvinist minorities to tolerate Catholics in the major southern cities that they had seized, and then by the tactical successes of the new Spanish commander, Alexander of Parma. Despite William of Orange's proclamation of the Religious Peace, allowing freedom of practice to both Catholics and Protestants in 1578, the unity behind the political goals of the pacification of Ghent became untenable. In 1579 the rebel provinces formed the nucleus of the later republic in the Union of Utrecht, signed by the delegates of Holland, Zeeland, Utrecht, and the Ommelanden of Groningen, and the nobles of the quarters of Arnhem and Zutphen. A rival Union of Arras

(1570), Catholic in religion and loyal to Spain, prefigured the Spanish Netherlands.

Hostilities between the nascent Dutch Republic in the north and the Spanish Netherlands in the south would continue for the next thirty years. A division between the two countries was recognized provisionally in the Twelve Years' Truce (1609–1621), and permanently in the Treaty of Westphalia (1648). The freedom of religion envisioned in the Religious Peace of 1578 was not realized on either side. But Catholics in the north enjoyed more liberties than Protestants in the south, and in the decades following the Synod of Dordrecht (1618–1619), the Dutch Republic tolerated many non-Calvinist communities in practice, if not in law. This was as close as the seventeenth century would come to the ideal of peaceful coexistence for several religious confessions within one civil society, envisioned by figures as different as William of Orange and Dirk Volkerstszoon Coornhert.

See also **Amsterdam**; **Antwerp**; **Devotio Moderna**; *and biographies of Charles V, Margaret of Parma, Philip II, and William the Silent.*

BIBLIOGRAPHY

Brandi, Karl. *The Emperor Charles V: The Growth and Destiny of a Man and of a World-Empire.* Translated by C. V. Wedgwood. 1939. London, 1980.

DuPlessis, Robert S. *Lille and the Dutch Revolt: Urban Stability in an Era of Revolution, 1500–1582.* Cambridge, U.K., 1991.

Fernández Alvarez, Manuel. *Charles V: Elected Emperor and Hereditary Ruler.* London, 1975.

Hibben, C. C. *Gouda in Revolt: Particularism and Pacifism in the Revolt of the Netherlands, 1572–1588.* Utrecht, the Netherlands, 1983.

IJsewijn, Jozef. "Humanism in the Low Countries." In *Renaissance Humanism: Foundations, Forms, and Legacy.* Edited by Albert Rabil, Jr. Vol. 2. Philadelphia, 1988. Pages 156–215.

Israel, Jonathan. *The Dutch Republic: Its Rise, Greatness, and Fall, 1477–1806.* Oxford, 1995.

Krahn, Cornelius. *Dutch Anabaptism: Origin, Spread, Life, and Thought (1450–1600).* The Hague, the Netherlands, 1986.

Marnef, Guido. *Antwerp in the Age of Reformation: Underground Protestantism in a Commercial Metropolis, 1550–1577.* Translated by J. C. Grayson. Baltimore, 1996.

Parker, Geoffrey. *The Dutch Revolt.* 1977. Rev. ed. London, 1988.

Tracy, James D. *Holland under Habsburg Rule, 1506–1566: The Formation of a Body Politic.* Berkeley, Calif., 1990.

GORDON WILLIAM BYNUM

Art in the Netherlands

The Burgundian Netherlands, so called after the Burgundian dukes who ruled or had in their sphere of influence much of present-day Belgium, Holland, and Luxembourg, witnessed a great flowering of arts in the fifteenth and early sixteenth centuries. The dukes, paragons of princely magnificence who shaped taste and demand for Burgundian arts across Europe, stimulated artistic production through extensive patronage; ducal courtiers, functionaries, and foreign visitors also actively patronized these arts. In the first half of the sixteenth century, Margaret of Austria, daughter of Maximilian I and regent of the Netherlands for her nephew, Charles V, established a small but impressive court at Mechelen. Her collection of artifacts elicited the admiration of its beholders, including Albrecht Dürer, who sojourned in the Netherlands in 1520 and 1521.

The central position of the Burgundian Netherlands at the crossroads of international commerce and the extensive economic relations of the region with the rest of Europe contributed to the production of arts for cosmopolitan clientele and facilitated the wide dissemination of Netherlandish artifacts. Bruges and Antwerp constituted major business and art emporiums: Bruges as a world market and center of international banking, Antwerp as the site of great fairs. The luxury goods produced in the Burgundian Netherlands—gold and silver work, tapestries, embroideries, illuminated manuscripts, sculpted altarpieces, and paintings—thus enjoyed broad domestic and international consumption.

Gold Work. Works of Renaissance goldsmiths are today largely viewed as decorative arts. Yet contemporary written sources and depictions demonstrate the preeminence of gem-embellished gold work as a tangible symbol of power and status. The inventories and accounts of the Burgundian dukes burst and shimmer with vast quantities of such precious metalwork. Brussels and Bruges, which hosted the Burgundian court and vibrant merchant communities, served as centers of the goldsmith's craft in the fifteenth century; Antwerp became the main center of jewelry production in the southern Netherlands in the sixteenth century, retaining its reputation for gem cutting to this day. Some names and works of Netherlandish masters survive: Jan de Leeuw, the dean of the goldsmiths guild at Bruges in 1441, was immortalized by Jan van Eyck in a portrait (1436; Vienna, Kunsthistorisches Museum) in which he appears in a fur-trimmed dress holding a gold ring. Gérard Loyet produced an exquisite gold reliquary representing the kneeling duke of Burgundy, Charles the Bold, accompanied by his patron saint, George (1466–1467), presented by the duke to Saint Lambert's Cathedral of Liège in 1471 (in situ). The goldsmith also made life-size statues and portrait

Art in the Netherlands. Beaker known as " The Monkey Cup." Silver, gilt, enamel; c. 1460; 20 cm (8 in.) high. THE METROPOLITAN MUSEUM OF ART, THE CLOISTERS COLLECTION, PURCHASE, 1952

busts of the duke in silver with gold detailing (lost) and embellished his clothes and hats with jewels. Other goldsmiths are known only from documents: Lodewijk van Berchem worked for Charles the Bold in Bruges, devising a new technique for splitting, faceting, and polishing precious stones. Jean Peutin of Bruges supplied Philip the Good with countless gold work and decorated numerous garments and pieces of armor with gold and silver heraldic devices and figures in relief.

Surviving Burgundian gold work by unknown artists includes a betrothal pendant containing a young couple rendered in enameled gold and embellished with diamonds and garnets (Boston, Museum of Fine Arts) and a brooch with a similar couple (Vienna, Schatzkammer). Princely inventories list numerous such adornments, presented and worn not only as jewels but also as badges of membership in knightly orders, of loyalty to a ruler, and of diplomatic friend-

ship. Also linked to the Burgundian court on the basis of style and provenance are several enamel vessels and spoons decorated with fine and lively drawings in opaque white enamel applied to a dark metal background (c. 1425–1475): the *Monkey Cup* (New York, Metropolitan Museum of Art) depicts a group of apes robbing a sleeping peddler while other monkeys climb around the foliage; a spoon (London, Victoria and Albert Museum) shows a monkey riding through a forest on a deer; another spoon (Boston, Museum of Fine Arts) presents a fox in ecclesiastical garb preaching to a congregation of geese while its companion steals one of the flock. Such objects appear in the inventories of the late fifteenth-century rulers Charles the Bold and Piero de' Medici. Lorenzo the Magnificent de' Medici, moreover, owned a Burgundian-made reliquary shaped like a crystal goblet resting on a foot guarded by wild men rendered in gold and enamel; its gold lid is decorated with gems and pearls (Florence, San Lorenzo). The splendid half-meter-tall *Cup of Saint-Michael* (c. 1530–1540; Vienna, Kunsthistorisches Museum), rendered in gold, enamel, diamonds, emerals, rubies, and pearls, was acquired by King Francis I of France from the Antwerp merchant Josse Vezler; it was subsequently presented by King Charles IX to Archduke Ferdinand II in 1570.

Petrus Christus's painting of St. Eligius (New York, Metropolitan Museum of Art) portrays the patron of goldsmiths as a master in his shop visited by a fashionably and richly dressed couple. To such prosperous city clientele he offers a range of products: rings with stones, brooches, a belt buckle, a crystal container, pewter pitchers with gold bases and lids, and raw precious materials.

Other Metalwork. Several splendid princely tombs reveal Netherlandish metalworking expertise. Ten bronze statuettes attributed to the Brussels founder Jacques de Gérines (1476; Amsterdam, National Museum) derive from the tomb of Isabella of Bourbon, the second wife of Charles the Bold. The tomb, situated in Saint Michael's Abbey in Antwerp (destroyed), originally included twenty-four figures of the relatives of the deceased on the sides of the stone sarcophagus. The late fifteenth-century tomb of Mary of Burgundy (Isabella's daughter) in the Church of Nôtre-Dame in Bruges engaged the talents of several artists: the sculptor Jan Borman probably provided a wooden model; the founder Renier van Thienen cast the bronze effigy; the goldsmith Pieter de Backere gilded it; Hubert Nonnon carved the marble sarcophagus on which the court painter

Jacques van Lathem composed the family tree bearing coats of arms and figures. The painter Jan de Hervy of Bruges appears to have designed and overseen the project.

The southern Netherlands also enjoyed a continuous tradition of brass founding and extensively exported funerary monuments, baptismal fonts, chandeliers, and lecterns, the latter exemplified by the eagle lectern from the Collegiate Church of Saint Peter at Louvain (New York, Metropolitan Museum of Art). Domestic brass ware, ubiquitous in contemporary paintings, was also mass-produced and exported.

Tapestry and Embroidery. Tapestries, particularly those incorporating silk, silver, and gold, were among the most precious and prestigious art forms in the Renaissance. Arras, Tournai, and Brussels were the greatest Renaissance tapestry centers not only in the Burgundian Netherlands but in the whole of Europe; by the mid-sixteenth century, Antwerp had become the main center of the international tapestry trade. This industry was sponsored and promoted by the Burgundian court and by the continuous demand from worthies abroad. Philip the Good (ruled 1419–1467) owned ninety to one hundred tapestry cycles, ranging from single pieces to sets of up to ten weavings, which he stored in a specially designed fireproof vaulted hall at Arras, staffed with guards, servants, and menders.

The manufacture and sale of tapestries were managed by merchants who put up the capital, kept stocks of cartoons, and employed weavers, often dividing large orders among weavers in different cities. Pasquier Grenier of Tournai supplied rulers throughout Europe. Philip the Good purchased from him at least eight tapestry sets between 1455 and 1467, including armorial weavings, *Passion of Christ, History of Alexander, History of Esther, History of the Swan Knight, Woodcutters and Peasants at Work,* and *Orange Pickers.* The range of subjects exemplifies the variety of themes desired and enjoyed by rulers. Some of these ensembles were used by the duke, others were presented as gifts to relatives and peers. Philip the Good's most splendid tapestry ensemble, *History of Gideon,* commissioned in 1449 from Robert Dary and Jehan de Lortye, included not only great quantities of precious metals but also gems.

The prestige of tapestries derived from their costly imported materials—gold, silver, silk, wool, and dyestuffs—and from the fact that they were extremely labor-intensive. Tapestries, like gold work, ranged widely in quality and price and could be purchased, secondhand, ready-made, or custom-ordered. They served numerous purposes: they decorated residences, created programmatic settings for special events through their carefully chosen subject matter, distinguished the person of the ruler by lining his war tents or barges, and produced magnificent backgrounds for great processions and entries. Philip the Good dazzled the citizens of Paris and upstaged Louis XI, whose return from exile and coronation as France's new king he attended in 1461, by hanging at his Hôtel d'Artois a great number of tapestries; *History of Alexander,* the paragon of a great ruler, was prominently displayed on the facade.

The worthies of England, Hungary, Italy, Spain, and other European kingdoms avidly accumulated Netherlandish tapestries and recruited their weavers. Shortly after his military triumph in Morocco (1471), King Afonso V of Portugal (ruled 1438–1481) ordered from Flanders, possibly from the Grenier workshop, four tapestries depicting and celebrating the victory (Pastrana, Museo Parroquial). The Medici of Florence not only collected Netherlandish tapestries but also engaged in lucrative sales of this prestigious merchandise to such customers as the dukes of Savoy, the popes, the Sforza of Milan, and the Este of Ferrara. One of the most popular tapestry sets of the late fifteenth century, the Trojan War ensemble, was originally presented to Charles the Bold (1472), and replicas were produced for Henry VII of England, Charles VIII of France, Ferdinand I of Naples, and Matthias Corvinus of Hungary. The quality and renown of Flemish weavings was such that Pope Leo X, having commissioned Raphael to design tapestries for the Sistine Chapel (1515–1516; Rome, Vatican), dispatched the cartoons to be turned into weavings in Brussels, in the workshop of Pieter van Aelst. The completed tapestries cost 15,000 ducats, compared to the 1,000 ducats Raphael received for their designs.

Embroidery was another specialty of the Netherlands. The vestments and altar hangings of the Burgundian Order of the Golden Fleece (Vienna, Kunsthistorisches Museum) exemplify this sumptuous art form. The pieces are embroidered in the *or nué* technique, in which parallel gold threads are laid on the surface of the cloth and couched with colored silk stitches; shading and areas of color are achieved by the density of such stitches. A distinct needle-painting technique served to depict skin and hair; it imitates brush strokes by using tiny stitches in extremely subtle color ranges of silk to modulate the hues and produce minute gradations of tone. Embroideries were further embellished by seed pearls

Netherlandish Tapestry. *The Boar and Bear Hunt* from the Devonshire Hunting Tapestries. Tapestry; c. 1435–1445; 4 × 10.2 m (13.25 × 33.5 ft.). VICTORIA & ALBERT MUSEUM, LONDON/ART RESOURCE

outlining figures and objects. While the artist of this ensemble is unknown, Philip the Good frequently commissioned similar objects from his court embroiderer and valet de chambre Thierry du Chastel. Numerous Netherlandish embroiderers also resided in Florence: Coppino di Giovanni of Mechelen probably supervised the production of the lavish ceremonial vestments depicting the life of St. John, commissioned for the Baptistery of Florence and designed by Antonio Pollaiuolo (Florence, Museo dell' Opera del Duomo).

Illuminated Manuscripts. Manuscript illumination was already flourishing in the Netherlands in the fourteenth century, when French kings employed Netherlandish miniaturists. In the fifteenth century the Burgundian dukes and their entourages nourished this art through their patronage, as did the kings and prosperous men of the northern Netherlands, Germany, Bohemia, England, France, Italy, Spain, and Portugal. Philip the Good assembled the largest library in northern Europe: he had approximately one thousand volumes at the time of his death, about half of them illustrated by artists, including Dreux Jean, Simon Marmion, Jean Le Tavernier, Willem Vrelant, Lievin van Lathem, and Loyset Liédet. A famous miniature from *Chroniques de Hainaut* shows the duke receiving the manuscript from its author, Jean Wauquelin (1446; Brussels, Bibliothèque Royale). Charles the Bold commissioned fewer manuscripts, but their quality was very high. He continued to employ some of the illuminators who had served his father, as well as Philippe de Mazerolles.

The so-called Ghent-Bruges school of manuscript illumination, an umbrella term for book illustrations in the southern Netherlands in the last quarter of the fifteenth and the first half of the sixteenth century, replaced the courtly, somewhat mannered style of decoration found in the books of Philip the Good and Charles the Bold (c. 1440–1475). The new style was characterized by more realistic figures, spacious interior and exterior settings, and increasing use of pastel shades in place of formerly favored primary colors. Marginal decorations—previously vegetal motifs and occasional narrative scenes painted on undyed parchment page—now exhibited volumetric, trompe l'oeil flowers and objects, often casting shadows on the page tinted with golden yellow or other colors. The Grimani Breviary (c. 1510; Venice, Biblioteca Marciana), produced for an Italian patron, exemplifies the finest achievement of such leading miniaturists of the Ghent-Bruges school as Simon Bening and Gerard Horenbout (who subsequently emigrated to England to work for the Tudor court).

Manuscript manufacture was a highly organized industry in which the ateliers divided work between specialists in miniatures, borders, and scripts; popular texts, decorated with standardized pictorial cycles, could be customized by an addition of separate gatherings of pages containing local calendars or special suffrages (short prayers), and were mass-produced and marketed.

Sculpture. Wooden altarpieces carved in Antwerp, Brussels, and Mechelen in the fifteenth and sixteenth centuries enjoyed great demand both domestically and in Scandinavia, Poland, Germany,

311

France, Portugal, and Spain. These artifacts were cheap compared with gold work, textiles, and illuminated manuscripts and catered to middle-class ecclesiastic and lay clientele. The commercial success of these altarpieces was intertwined with the international trade taking place at the fairs and ports of the Burgundian Netherlands, particularly Antwerp. The altarpiece *Infancy of Christ* (c. 1500; Clerey, France), carved in Mechelen, bears a mark of Antwerp, which guaranteed its quality and approval for sale in that city. Foreign merchants trading in the Burgundian Netherlands took carved altarpieces, among other products, as return cargo for resale in their native lands.

In response to their popularity, the production of carved altarpieces developed into an industry. Workshops were run by master craftsmen, who took orders, invested in raw materials, distributed tasks, marketed the finished products, and delivered the commissioned altarpieces to their intended locations. The majority of retables were produced not to commission but for the open market, their mass manufacture facilitated by standardization of subjects and sizes and inclusion of reused or prefabricated parts. The altarpieces most often consisted of a rectangular elevated center panel and flanking sections. While their interiors bore carved narratives, their outer wings were often painted, necessitating a collaboration between sculptors and painters.

One of the most talented carvers was Jan Borman II (fl. c. 1479–1520), who settled in Brussels but produced sculptures for a wide area, including Antwerp, Bruges, Diest, and Louvain. He is credited with a wooden model for the tomb of Mary of Burgundy, cast in bronze by Renier van Thienen, and is the author of the altarpiece (originally polychromed) narrating the life of St. George (1493; Brussels, Musées Royaux d'Art et d'Histoire), commissioned by the Guild of Crossbowmen for their chapel in Louvain. Borman's figures are better proportioned, their faces more individualized, their clothing and hair finely detailed, and their spatial arrangement more coherent than those of other contemporary altarpiece makers. Borman's skill earned him a commission (1511) for wooden models of the dukes and duchesses of Brabant, designed by Jan van Roome, to be cast by Renier van Thienen and placed on the grand esplanade of the Palais Royale in Brussels (destroyed), as well as for a carved stone lion for the facade of the palace (destroyed).

In addition to carved altarpieces, freestanding sculptures in wood, stone, alabaster, or plaster of paris were also produced in the Burgundian Neth-

erlands for local and foreign clientele. These typically represented Christ, the Virgin Mary, and crucifixes. An Antwerp-made wooden statue of the Virgin Mary, *Granada Madonna,* is said to have been carried into battle against the Moors by Ferdinand and Isabella of Spain and subsequently presented by them to the Granada Cathedral. Rosaries of various sizes and materials—glass, bone, wood, agate, amber, coral, silver, and gold—were another common artifact, with Bruges particularly engaged in their manufacture. Costly rosaries, items of luxury and prestige, were frequently passed on to heirs.

Painting. Painting is the best-studied Netherlandish art form. Paintings were most commonly commissioned for religious institutions by church authorities and individual clerics, confraternities, and pious laymen—patrons similar to those purchasing carved altarpieces. Civic authorities ordered religious pictures, scenes of justice, and portraits of rulers. Paintings produced in the Burgundian Netherlands were admired across Europe. Rogier van der Weyden's *Columba Altarpiece* was in Cologne by c. 1450 (Munich, Alte Pinakothek). The polyptych *Virgin and Child with Saints,* attributed to the Master of the Legend of St. Lucy, was commissioned in Bruges in 1481 by the Blackheads Fraternity of Tallinn and installed in 1495 in the Dominican Church of Saint Catherine (Tallinn, Art Museum). Numerous altarpieces by Gerard David were exported to Genoa in the late fifteenth and early sixteenth centuries. There is ample documentation for the acquisition of Flemish altarpieces and portraits by the English, Italians, and Spaniards.

Netherlandish painters were consummate masters of oil painting. Although this technique had been employed since the Middle Ages, fifteenth-century masters took it to new levels of proficiency and refinement. By systematically layering multiple coats of tinted oil glazes, they created enamel-like surfaces that possessed both depth and translucency. The use of fine glazes also enabled them to blend brush strokes to the point of imperceptibility and to build up painted images gradually and in minute detail. Netherlandish painting is distinguished by meticulous depictions of the physical world: textures of textiles and metals, reflections in objects and glimmer of jewels, particularities of distant cityscapes, and elaborately rendered landscapes. Netherlandish masters were also admired by contemporaries for conveying deep emotions in religious narratives. In addition to oil painting, Netherlanders also used tempera and watercolors.

Petrus Christus. *St. Eligius.* Eligius is patron saint of goldsmiths. Oil on wood; mid-fifteenth century; 99 × 85 cm (39 × 33.5 in.). The Metropolitan Museum of Art, Robert Lehman Collection, 1975

Jan van Eyck (before 1395–1441) was and remains the most famous Netherlandish painter. He served as a court painter and valet de chambre to Philip the Good, for whom he executed a variety of projects, including the decoration of residences, designed lavish festivities, and undertook diplomatic assignments. Jan also painted six statues and tabernacles for the facade of the town hall of Bruges and portraits and altarpieces for prominent officials in ducal circles, such as the *Ghent Altarpiece* (1432; Ghent, Saint Bavo Cathedral), the *Virgin and Child with Chancellor Rolin* or *Rolin Madonna* (c. 1435; Paris, Louvre), and the *Arnolfini Betrothal* (1434; London, National Gallery). [For the *Ghent Altarpiece* and *Rolin Madonna,* see the biography of Eyck in volume 2; for the *Arnolfini Betrothal,* see the color

plates in volume 2.] Jan's fame resounded well outside Burgundian territories: he was eulogized by Italian humanists, and his works were sought by King Alfonso the Magnanimous of Naples, the Medici of Florence, the Este of Ferrara, and others.

Rogier van der Weyden (1399?–1464), born in Tournai, was likewise much admired in his day both in the Netherlands and abroad. He worked for the Burgundian court, painting portraits and coloring two funerary monuments for Philip the Good. From about 1436 on he was the city painter of Brussels, where he decorated the wall of a courtroom of the town hall with scenes on the theme of justice (c. 1439–1450; destroyed). His works were eagerly acquired by Italians, Germans, and Spaniards. Rogier's authenticated works include *Descent from the Cross* (before 1443; Madrid, Prado; see the illustration in the biography of Weyden), *Miraflores Triptych* (before 1445; Berlin, Gemäldegalerie), and *Crucifixion* (before 1455; Madrid, Escorial). Among the more tenable attributions are *St. Luke Painting the Virgin* (c. 1435; Boston, Museum of Fine Arts), *Last Judgment Altarpiece* (c. 1443–1451; Beaune, Musée Hôtel-Dieu) commissioned by the chancellor of Burgundy Nicholas Rolin, and several portraits, including those of Philip the Good and members of his court. Rogier ran a busy workshop, and his compositions and style were widely imitated.

Dirck Bouts (c. 1400–1475), who was born in Haarlem, spent most of his working life in Louvain. The commissions of his *Holy Sacrament Altarpiece* (1464–1468; Louvain, Saint Peter's; see the illustration in the biography of Bouts) and *Justice of Emperor Otto III* (1470–1482; Brussels, Musées Royaux des Beaux-Arts) are recorded in surviving documents: the former by members of the Confraternity of the Holy Sacrament for their chapel in Saint Peter's; the latter by the local government for the council room of the newly erected town hall of Louvain, for which he also painted the triptych *Last Judgment* (1468–1470). Paintings associated with Bouts or his workshop were exported to Spain and Italy and emulated at home and abroad.

Hugo van der Goes (c. 1440–1482) of Ghent worked for private, civic, and foreign clientele and participated in the embellishment of the marriage festivities of Charles the Bold and Margaret of York in Bruges in 1468. His great *Nativity Altarpiece* (c. 1473–c. 1477; Florence, Uffizi; see the color plates in this volume) painted for Tommaso Portinari, an agent of the Medici Bank in Bruges, was greatly admired and emulated in Florence, where it was shipped by its owner in 1483. In the same years Hugo produced another large altarpiece, commissioned by Edward Bonkil, the provost of the Collegiate Church of the Holy Trinity in Edinburgh for his church; the wings depict the donor and the royal patrons of the church, James III of Scotland and his queen, Margaret of Denmark (1473–1478; British Royal Collection, on loan to Edinburgh, National Gallery). Other paintings attributed to Hugo include a diptych of *Fall of Man* and *Lamentation* (c. 1468–1470; Vienna, Kunsthistorisches Museum), *Nativity* (c. 1472–1475; Berlin, Gemäldegalerie), and *Death of the Virgin* (c. 1480; Bruges, Groeningemuseum).

Hans Memling (c. 1430 or 1435–1494), a German-born painter, emigrated to Bruges and established a thriving practice patronized by rich burghers and churchmen as well as foreigners doing business in the city. He was a superb portraitist, capturing the likeness of his sitters with remarkable tangibility. Memling produced several works for the Hospital of St. John in Bruges, including the triptych *St. John the Baptist and St. John the Evangelist* (1474–1479) and *St. Ursula Shrine* (1489; both Bruges, Memlingmuseum). For Angelo Tani, an agent of the Medici bank in Bruges, Memling painted a large triptych, *Last Judgment* (1467–1471; Gdańsk, Muzeum Narodowe), which was captured by Hanseatic pirates as it was being shipped to Florence in 1473 and taken by them to the Church of Saint Mary in Gdańsk. For Tommaso Portinari and his wife Memling produced *Panorama with Scenes from the Passion* (c. 1470; Turin, Galleria Sabauda), as well as their half-length likenesses rendered with striking veracity (c. 1470; New York, Metropolitan Museum of Art). Sir John Donne of Kidwelly, serving Richard, the duke of York, commissioned a triptych (1479–1480; London, National Gallery) depicting himself and his wife in prayer before the enthroned Virgin and Child flanked by saints, a composition typical of Memling's output.

Hieronymus Bosch (Jeroen van Aken, 1450–1516) was admired for his fantastic tableaux that drew on moralizing literature, proverbs, and biblical parables. His Haywain tryptych (c. 1500–1505; El Escorial, Monasterio de San Lorenzo) depicts a pilgrim passing through the evil world on the outer shutters, and the Haywain of sins in the center, which elaborates on the proverb "All the world is a haystack and each man can pluck from it what he can." On the inner left wing, Heaven already witnesses the fall from grace; the right wing, toward which the Haywain proceeds, contains the image of Hell populated by hybrid beasts torturing sinners in innumerable ways. Bosch's paintings were in demand throughout Europe: Philip II of Spain collected his works along with those of Titian; Duke Ernst of Austria, King Francis I of France, and the Venetian Cardinal Grimani also sought his creations that were, moreover, copied in tapestries.

Joachim Patinir (fl. 1515–d. c. 1524) specialized in landscape painting and was very successful in his day, as the vast output of his studio attests. His landscapes and those inspired by him were widely exported and collected. While all his works contain identifiable and usually religious themes, such as *St. Jerome in a Rocky Landscape* (London, National Gallery), the subject is dwarfed by a panoramic vista with crisply described fantastic rock formations. Patinir collaborated with colleagues specializing in figure paintings, such as Quentin Massys and Joos van Cleve.

Several sixteenth-century Netherlandish painters journeyed to Italy and incorporated classicizing imagery and subject matter into their works upon their return. Jan Gossaert (Jan Mabuse; c. 1478–1532) went to Rome in 1508 in the suite of Philip of Burgundy, who was traveling on a diplomatic mission to the Vatican. Philip was keenly interested in architecture and antiquities, and Gossaert made sketches of the sites they encountered. In the aftermath of the Roman trip, Gossaert included numerous Italian compositional and thematic elements into his pictures, but he also looked to fifteenth-century Flemish painting for both technique and style. His *Neptune and Amphitrite* (1516; Berlin, Staatliche Museen) recalls Dürer's *Adam and Eve* engraving (1504), itself based on Apollo Belvedere and the Medici Venus the German artists saw in Italy; but while Gossaert's figures resemble statues placed in a classical portico, they are Flemish in attention to detail and facial type. Maerten van Heemskerck (1498–1574) also visited Rome, sketched antique ruins and statues, and was impressed by Raphael, Michelangelo, and Salviati (he also likely stopped in Mantua in late 1536 or early 1537 to view the work of Giulio Romano). Heemskerck's *Self-portrait with the Colosseum* (1553; Cambridge, Fitzwilliam Museum) recalls his formative Italian journey. Heemskerck brought to the north a classical subject matter and conception of the human body inspired by Italian high Renaissance and mannerist art. His style of "Romanism" was widely disseminated through prints. Italian influence, which became pronounced in the Netherlands around 1540, is evident in the works of Cornelis Floris, Pieter Coecke van Aelst, and Hans Vredeman de Vries.

At the same time, Pieter Brueghel the Elder (c. 1525/30–1569) continued the moralizing, proverbial, and rustic themes in his richly populated paintings, such as *Harvesters* (1565; New York, Metropolitan Museum of Art; see the color plates in this volume) and *Hunters in the Snow* (1565; Vienna, Kunsthistorisches Museum), created for an Antwerp financier, Niclaes Jongelink. Brueghel's *Wedding Feast* (c. 1565; Vienna, Kunsthistorisches Museum; see the illustration in the biography of Brueghel) exemplifies his ability to communicate an impression of veracity through strongly characterized faces and gestures, as well as a seemingly casual composition cut off abruptly at the sides and suggestive of an instantaneous record. Even in paintings concerned with classical mythology, such as *Fall of Icarus* (c. 1555–1556; Brussels, Musées Royaux des Beaux-Arts), a peasant tilling the land dominates the scene.

Lucas van Leyden (c. 1494–1533), trained in painting and engraving, is the most celebrated Netherlandish printmaker. His prints possess remarkable softness of forms and tonalities achieved through a fine shading that creates a painterly rather than a linear quality; he is able to convey atmospheric perspective and soft chiaroscuro effect in the printed medium. *David Playing the Harp before Saul* (c. 1508) exhibits not only Lucas's mastery of the printing medium, but also the psychological complexity of narrative, capturing the moment at which David soothes the melancholy of the mad king.

See also **Burgundy; Decorative Arts.**

BIBLIOGRAPHY

Cavallo, Adolfo. *Medieval Tapestries in the Metropolitan Museum of Art.* New York, 1993.

Flanders in the Fifteenth Century: Art and Civilization. Detroit, Mich., 1960. Exhibition catalog.

Flemish Illuminated Manuscripts, 1475–1550. Edited by Maurits Smeyers and Jan van der Stock. Ghent, Belgium, 1996.

Friedländer, Max J. *Early Netherlandish Painting.* 14 vols. New York, 1967–1976.

Jacobs, Lynn F. *Early Netherlandish Carved Altarpieces, 1380–1550: Medieval Tastes and Mass Marketing.* Cambridge, U.K., 1998.

La miniature flamande: Le mecenat de Philippe le Bon. Brussels, Belgium, 1959.

Nieuwdorp, Hans, ed. *Antwerp Altarpieces, 15th–16th Centuries.* Antwerp, Belgium, 1993. Exhibition catalog.

Paravicini, Werner. "The Court of the Dukes of Burgundy: A Model for Europe?" In *Princes, Patronage, and the Nobility: The Court at the Beginning of the Modern Age, c. 1450–1650.* Edited by Ronald G. Asch and Adolf M. Birke. Oxford, 1991. Pages 69–102.

Prevenier, Walter, and Willem Pieter Blockmans. *The Burgundian Netherlands.* Cambridge, U.K., 1986.

Smith, Jeffrey Chipps. "The Artistic Patronage of Philip the Good, Duke of Burgundy (1419–1467)." Ph.D. diss., Columbia University, 1979.

Smith, Jeffrey Chipps. "Portable Propaganda: Tapestries as Princely Metaphors at the Courts of Philip the Good and Charles the Bold." *Art Journal* 48, no. 2 (1989): 123–129.

Snyder, James. *Northern Renaissance Art: Painting, Sculpture, the Graphic Arts from 1350 to 1575.* New York, 1985.

Souchal, Genevieve. *Masterpieces of Tapestry from the Fourteenth to the Sixteenth Century.* New York, 1974. Exhibition catalog.

Stechow, Wolfgang. *Northern Renaissance Art, 1400–1600: Sources and Documents.* Englewood Cliffs, N.J., 1966.

Wilson, Jean C. *Painting in Bruges at the Close of the Middle Ages.* University Park, Pa., 1998.

MARINA BELOZERSKAYA

NEW WORLD.   *See* **Americas.**

NICHOLAS V (Tommaso Parentucelli de Sarzana; 1397–1455), pope (1447–1455). Born at Sarzana near La Spezia, Parentucelli's father was a physician of modest means who died when his son was seven. Tonsured at the age of ten, Parentucelli studied the arts at the University of Bologna (c. 1413–1416), excelling in scholastic disputations and in the study of Aristotle's *Physics*. When his family could not support him, Parentucelli interrupted his studies to become a tutor in the households of Rinaldo Albizzi and Palla Strozzi in Florence (c. 1417–1420), where he came into contact with the new humanist learning, including the study of Greek. Returning to Bologna (c. 1420), Parentucelli became a master of arts (c. 1420/21) and found a patron in Niccolò Albergati, the bishop of Bologna (1417–1443), whom he served as a chaplain and then as secretary and governor of the household for more than twenty years. Albergati was named a cardinal in 1426 and sent by Pope Martin V (1417–1431) and Pope Eugenius IV (1431–1447) on numerous peace-making missions, regularly accompanied by Parentucelli.

Parentucelli's entry into the household of Albergati coincided with a shift in his studies to theology, followed by ordination as a priest (c. 1422) and the award of minor benefices in Bologna. By 1437 Parentucelli had become a canon and chamberlain of the cathedral chapter at Bologna. In 1444 Eugenius IV appointed Parentucelli bishop of Bologna. In 1446 the pope sent him, together with Juan de Carvajal, an auditor of the Roman Rota, and Nicholas of Cusa, on an embassy to the Empire (the Germanies) to secure the support of King Frederick III against the Council of Basel. The pope's envoys succeeded in their mission by making substantial concessions in matters of benefices and were thus able to undermine the Empire's policy of neutrality in the church conflict. A grateful Eugenius IV rewarded Carvajal and Parentucelli by raising them to the cardinalate on 16 December 1446. A little more than two months later Eugenius IV died and Parentucelli unexpectedly was elected pope, taking the name Nicholas V, in honor of his former patron Niccolò Albergati.

The first priority of Nicholas V as pope was to secure the return of the Empire (the Germanies) to the "obedience" of the Roman pope. To accomplish this, Nicholas V sent his former colleague Cardinal Carvajal to Frederick III in order to negotiate a concordat for the Empire. Usually called the Concordat of Vienna (February 1448), this settlement was accepted only reluctantly by the other German princes and bishops since it abrogated the reform decrees of the Council of Basel that had insured local control of benefices and abolished taxes exacted by the Roman Curia. Published as a papal privilege, the Concordat of Vienna recognized absolute papal control over benefices in theory but limited it in practice. In France, where the reform decrees of the Council of Basel concerning church benefices were enforced in French royal courts since 1438 through the Pragmatic Sanction of Bourges, Nicholas V did not have the same success in setting aside the conciliar decrees through a concordat.

When Nicholas V was elected pope, a remnant of the Council of Basel was still in session and its antipope Felix V continued to have a limited following. Nicholas V ended the schism with a conciliatory settlement: in return for recognizing him as pope, many of the dissident conciliarists were allowed to keep their benefices, the antipope Felix V being "recognized" as a cardinal-bishop, while the judicial actions of the Council of Basel were allowed to stand. By June 1449 Nicholas V was acknowledged as the undisputed pope throughout the Latin church. This heightened the mood of celebration in the jubilee year 1450, when thousands of pilgrims visited the holy sites of Rome, implicitly paying tribute to its bishop as successor of St. Peter.

As ruler of the Papal States, Nicholas V pursued a policy of conciliation. In the politics of the Italian peninsula, he acknowledged existing power relationships. In carrying out his policies, Nicholas V was aided by the fact that, unlike other popes of his time, he did not use his office to secure principalities for his next of kin. On 19 March 1452 Nicholas V crowned his political ally Frederick III as Holy Roman Emperor in Rome in a ceremony that underlined the pope's symbolic authority but which was otherwise of little political significance. In his relation with Jewish communities, Nicholas V reiterated prohibitions against attempts to baptize Jewish children without their parents' consent and supported an extension of the rights of Jews in the duchy of Ferrara in the Papal States. In Castile, he intervened to safeguard the rights of Jewish converts (conversos) to Christianity. The last two years of the pontificate were overshadowed by the fall of Constantinople to the Ottoman Turks (29 May 1453), which led to calls for a crusade against the Turks.

The most distinctive features of the pontificate were the new direction Nicholas V gave to the urban development of Rome and his support of humanist and scholastic learning. He envisaged making St. Peter's basilica and the adjacent Vatican Palace (outside the "city") the principal church and residence of the pope. Only a fragment of these plans, the massive

Tower of Nicholas V, was actually built, since most resources were needed to repair the city's walls and restore older churches. The most celebrated aspect of the pontificate was the role of Nicholas V in making the papal court a center of literary patronage, where the copying of Latin manuscripts and the translation of Greek texts into Latin found liberal support. A collector of manuscripts even before he became pope, Nicholas V sought to establish a papal library at the Vatican "for the common convenience of men of learning." By the time of his death, the pope had assembled over 800 Latin and 353 Greek manuscripts.

By comparison with the libraries of popes in the preceding centuries, the new Vatican Library contained proportionately fewer works on canon or civil law, and it differed from the libraries of contemporary princes by its emphasis on Greek and Latin works of a theological nature and by its relatively smaller holdings of works in vernacular languages. While it was left to Pope Sixtus IV (1471–1484) to complete the institutional framework for the Apostolic Library in the Vatican Palace, it was Nicholas V's personal interests as a theologian and his commitment to scholastic and humanist learning that defined its collection of Latin and Greek texts. It was also his liberality that first envisaged making these texts available to other scholars. In keeping with the intellectual formation of Nicholas V, his library included not only the Latin and Greek classics of pagan and early Christian antiquity but also medieval authors from St. Augustine through Thomas Aquinas and John Duns Scotus. The first pope with an appreciation of the new humanist learning, Nicholas V was also the first to place the Feast of St. Thomas Aquinas on the liturgical calendar of the papal court, celebrating in person a mass on the saint's feast day. Centering the residence of the pope at the Vatican, promoting the rebuilding of Rome with a conscious reference back to ancient architecture, and founding the Vatican Library were the major contributions of Nicholas V to a program of celebrating the papacy's victory over the conciliar movement and, in the process, establishing Rome as a center of Renaissance culture.

See also **Basel, Council of; Papacy; Vatican Library.**

BIBLIOGRAPHY

Primary Works

Manetti, Giannozzo. "Vita Nicolai V, Summi Pontificis." In *Rerum Italicarum Scriptores.* Edited by Ludovico Muratori. Volume 3, Part 2. Milan, 1734. Columns 905–960.

Vespasiano da Bisticci. *The Vespasiano Memoirs: Lives of Illustrious Men of the Fifteenth Century.* Translated by William George and Emily Waters. 1963. Reprint, Toronto, 1997.

Secondary Works

Caravale, Mario, and Alberto Caracciolo. *Lo stato pontificio da Martino V a Pio IX.* Turin, Italy, 1978. See pages 65–76.

Esposito, Anna. "Nicolas V." In *Dictionnaire historique de la papauté.* Edited by Philippe Levillain. Paris, 1994. Pages 1168–1170.

Manfredi, Antonio. *I Codici latini di Niccolò V.* Vatican City, Italy, 1994. With a preface by Leonard E. Boyle on the founding of the Vatican Library by Nicholas V, not by Sixtus IV.

Meyer, Andreas. "Das Wiener Konkordat von 1448: Eine erfolgreiche Reform des Spätmittelalters." *Quellen und Forschungen aus italienischen Archiven und Bibliotheken* 66 (1986): 108–152.

Mollat, Guillaume. "Nicolas V." In *Dictionnaire de Théologie Catholique.* Vol. 11. Paris, 1931. Columns 541–548.

Stieber, Joachim W. *Pope Eugenius IV, the Council of Basel, and the Secular and Ecclesiastical Authorities in the Empire: The Conflict over Supreme Authority and Power in the Church.* Leiden, Netherlands, 1978. See pages 302–330, on the settlement of the conflict with the Council of Basel and the German Concordat of 1448.

Toews, John B. "Formative Forces in the Pontificate of Nicholas V, 1447–1455." *The Catholic Historical Review* 54 (1968): 261–284.

Joachim W. Stieber

NICHOLAS OF CUSA (1401–1464), philosopher, theologian, cardinal, reformer, mathematician. Nicholas of Cusa (Nicolaus Cusanus) rose from his origins in a small town to the pinnacles of power, but his experience of power often was bitter. He espoused the cause of reform but many times he faced entrenched opposition, much of it aroused by his intransigence. Nevertheless, Cusanus excelled as a writer, leaving behind a body of treatises, dialogues, and sermons that remain the object of study. They include works of political theory, proposals for reform, and speculative works couched in a frequently difficult style.

Origins and Early Career. Born at Kues in the Moselle Valley, the son of a boat owner and merchant, Niclas Krebs was educated at the universities of Heidelberg, Padua, and Cologne. Although his degrees were in canon law, he also studied theology and became acquainted with the new learning of the Renaissance. His discovery of twelve previously unknown works of Plautus made him famous even before he began his ascent to high office. By 1432 Nicholas was a cleric and successful lawyer, and he had begun accumulating benefices. In that year he joined the Council of Basel in order to present the case for one of the claimants to the archdiocese of Trier. Al-

Nicholas of Cusa. Nicholas venerates St. Peter, who is being released from his chains by the angel at right. Funeral monument by Andrea Bregno (1418–1503) in the church of San Pietro in Vincoli, Rome, 1500. ALINARI/ART RESOURCE, NY

though he lost the case, Cusanus wrote the most famous treatise on questions of institutional structure and reform, *De concordantia catholica* (On Catholic concordance; 1433). This work, dedicated to Cardinal Giuliano Cesarini and the emperor Sigismund, balanced hierarchy and consent while advocating reform of church and empire. Cusanus became affiliated with Cesarini in his efforts to direct the council. He supported the cardinal in disputes over the presidency of the council (1434) and over the site of a council of union with the Greeks (1436–1437). By 1437 Nicholas, representing the minority faction at Basel, was working with Pope Eugenius IV to bring the Greeks to Italy. He visited Constantinople to advance this cause. Later Nicholas reported having had a shipboard experience that altered his perception of the universe and set him to work attempting to explain how one might attain a truer knowledge of God.

Legate and Cardinal. During the period of the Council of Florence (1438–1445), Cusanus was often in Germany, working to win the allegiance of the princes for the pope, whom the Council of Basel declared deposed in 1439. These labors won Nicholas of Cusa recognition as "the Hercules of the Eugenians." In this same period, he wrote his first significant speculative works. *De docta ignorantia* (On

learned ignorance; 1440) explored the limits of human abilities in the quest to know God. Its fundamental doctrines were "learned ignorance," which involved going beyond human abilities in order to grasp the divine, and "coincidence of opposites," seeing all things from the perspective of infinity in order to grasp how they meet in God. God was the absolute Maximum, whereas the universe was the contracted Maximum. The incarnate Word, absolute and contracted Maximum, was the point at which, in this doctrine, the infinite God and the universe coincide. Faith in the Word was the way to truth. *De coniecturis* (On conjectures; c. 1443) outlined the effort to rise from the sensory realm by way of reason to intellect, which strains—with divine aid—to grasp God in image and metaphor. The art of conjecture, which used icons and metaphors, left maximum room for human creativity. Nicholas also composed brief tracts exploring further the implications of his idea of learned ignorance. Among these were *De deo abscondito* (On the hidden God; 1442) and *De quaerendo deum* (On seeking God; 1445), which spoke of the need to go into the darkness beyond unaided human faculties in the quest for God. Cusanus addressed the ecclesiastical issues of the day in his own idiom, outlining in his letter to Rodrigo Sánchez de Arévalo (1442) an ecclesiology founded on the hypostatic union and on the unfolding of the church from the apostle Peter.

After the accession of Nicholas V in 1447, the Basel schism came to an end. Although the Council of Basel dissolved itself and its pope, Felix V, resigned, bitter feelings over its failure to reform the curia remained. Cusanus had to write an apologetic work, *Apologia doctae ignorantiae* (Apology of learned ignorance; 1449), answering Johann Wenck's accusation of heresy, which was inspired in part by these resentments. In 1450 Cusanus received publicly the cardinal's hat that Eugenius IV had awarded him in secret. He also composed the *Idiota* (Layman) dialogues, which made an uninstructed layman the spokesman for learned ignorance. Late that year Nicholas was sent to the Holy Roman Empire as papal legate, both to proclaim the indulgences of the Jubilee year and to attempt reform of ecclesiastical institutions. Despite distant travels and hard work, the cardinal found his reforming efforts thwarted at every turn, except where local reformers were able to make use of his support. Moreover, as happened when he tried to act against excessive veneration of a bleeding-host relic, the legate found his efforts undercut by a timid pope.

Nicholas repaired at last (1452) to the see of Brixen, given to him by the pope in 1450. There he found life even less pleasant. His own failings, including inflexibility and lack of tact, together with resentment of an outsider bishop of low birth and resistance to stringent reforms he tried to impose on the wealthy convent of Sonnenberg, put him at odds with many, most notably with Sigismund, count of Tyrol. Cusanus carried on the struggle until 1457, when he found himself a refugee at the castle of Andraz. He would remain there until Pope Pius II called him to Rome in 1458.

Despite these adversities, Cusanus's first residence at Brixen was not a barren period in his literary life. Word of the fall of Constantinople (1453) inspired him to write *De pace fidei* (On the peace of faith), a visionary account of religious accord achieved by seventeen representatives of various nations and religions at a heavenly colloquy presided over by Christ, the divine Word. An inquiry from the monks at Tegernsee about his doctrines inspired him to write his most accessible speculative work, *De visione dei* (On the vision of God; 1453), which used an icon of Christ, with its all-seeing gaze, to teach the way in which we see and are seen by God. Once more it is the Word that is crucial, enabling us to get a glimpse beyond "the wall of paradise."

Cusanus's return to Rome involved him in Pius II's efforts to organize a crusade against the Turks. When the pope went to Mantua to meet with representatives of the princes, Cusanus was left behind as his vicar. This led to an effort to reform the diocese of Rome. After Pius returned, the cardinal composed his *Reformatio generalis* (General reform; 1459), a plan for the reform of church and curia. This program included correction of the pope himself in order to set an example for others. Pius included passages from the work in a draft of a reform bull, but the project died there.

Against the pope's advice, Cusanus decided to return to Brixen (1460). Count Sigismund soon drove him back to his refuge at Andraz. Soon thereafter Nicholas fled back to Italy. The only bright spot of this second residence in the diocese of Brixen was the treatise *De possest* (On "possest"; 1460), a speculative work based upon a neologism he coined that described God as beyond the coincidence of absolute possibility and actuality.

Late Career. Cusanus returned to Rome. There he was involved yet again in efforts to promote reform. Frustration with curial indifference and the pope's political preoccupations led him to cry out during a consistory that he was mocked for even mentioning reform. The cardinal continued to write on the quest for God, producing *De non aliud* (On the not-other; 1462), which stressed the complete otherness of God in relationship to the limited human effort to understand. *De venatione sapientiae* (The hunt of wisdom; 1462 or 1463) spoke of Cusanus's hunt for wisdom, and *De ludo globi* (On the game of spheres; 1463) used a game of spheres to explore the soul's relationship with God. *Compendium* (c. 1463) offered a summary of its author's epistemological and semiotic theories, while *De apice theoriae* (On the summit of contemplation; 1464) spoke of God as "possibility itself," Cusanus's last neologism for divinity. In these late works, the self-diffusive yet ineffable Word remained the touchstone of all truth. Pope Pius II had Nicholas intervene in a debate between the friars over whether all the blood shed on Calvary had gone up into heaven with Jesus.

This Roman residence saw Nicholas of Cusa's health begin to fail; but he remained active, attempting reform of Orvieto. The Brixen controversy died down with a draft agreement that Cusanus would remain an absentee bishop. Cusanus supported the crusade by writing a more typically medieval work on interreligious relations, *Cribratio alkorani* (A scrutiny of the Koran; 1461), a critique of Islam as it was understood in the West. Pope Pius left Rome in the summer of 1464 in the hope of leading a crusade against the Turks. Cusanus was left behind to resolve some unfinished diplomatic business involving Bohemia. Once it was concluded he was to follow the ailing pope with any laggard crusaders. Instead, when he reached Todi, Cusanus fell mortally ill. He made his will and expired in that city on 11 August 1464. His body was buried in Rome at San Pietro in Vincoli, but his heart was returned for burial in Kues. It was interred in the chapel of the hospice that he had founded there, which still exists. The hospice possesses his scientific instruments and many of his books, some of them annotated by the cardinal himself.

BIBLIOGRAPHY

Primary Works

Nicholas of Cusa. *The Catholic Concordance*. Edited and translated by Paul Sigmund. New York, 1991.

Nicholas of Cusa. *Selected Spiritual Writings*. Translated by H. Lawrence Bond. New York, 1997.

Secondary Works

Bond, H. Lawrence. "Nicholas of Cusa and the Reconstruction of Theology: The Centrality of Christology in the Coincidence of Opposites." In *Contemporary Reflections on the Medieval Christian Tradition*. Edited by George H. Shriver. Durham, N.C., 1974. Pages 81–94.

Izbicki, Thomas M. "The Church in the Light of Learned Ignorance." *Medieval Philosophy and Theology* 3 (1993): 186–214.

THOMAS M. IZBICKI

NIFO, AGOSTINO (c. 1470–1538), Italian Aristotelian philosopher. Nifo was born in Sessa Aurunca and received a basic arts education in Naples before moving to Padua, where one of his teachers was Nicoletta Vernia. He was awarded a degree around 1490 and taught at Padua from 1492 to around 1499. He returned to his hometown and began an association with a circle of humanists led by Giovanni Pontano that resulted in a lifelong interest in humanist themes. He learned ancient Greek and apparently taught philosophy at both Naples and Salerno in the early sixteenth century. Pope Leo X appointed him ordinary professor of philosophy at the University of Rome in 1514, and he later taught at Pisa and returned to Naples and Salerno. In the last few years of his life he was elected mayor of Sessa Aurunca.

Nifo's writings cover a wide spectrum. He wrote commentaries on Aristotle and Ibn Rushd (Averroes), wrote systematic treatises and several works dealing with humanist themes, including one on beauty and love in which he developed an Aristotelian counterpart to the well-known Platonic view on these topics. In addition, his work *De regnandi peritia* (On the practical knowledge of ruling; 1522) is a restatement of some of the central issues of Machiavelli's *Il principe* (*The Prince;* 1513). Nifo was unafraid of controversy and in his years at Padua attacked in writing the views of his teacher, Nicoletto Vernia, as well as those of Pietro Pomponazzi and other faculty members.

In his commentary on Aristotle's Physics, published in 1508, Nifo considered the notion of demonstrative knowledge. He argued that scientific knowledge of the reason or cause for some effect is possible. From the observation of some effect, the mind is able to reason to the proximate cause of the effect. However, since scientific knowledge properly proceeds from causes to effects, something is necessary so that the cause first reasoned to becomes capable of providing the basis for a proper demonstration. Nifo posited a sort of mental "consideration" (*negotiato*) whereby the mind transforms the knowledge of the cause derived from observation of the effect in such a way as to make that cause the basis of a demonstration of the reason for the effect. Nifo came to have doubts about this account of scientific procedure. He rejected the theory of a special process of consideration on the basis of the authority of the ancient Greek commentators Alexander of Aphrodisias, Philoponus, and Simplicius of Cilicia. In place of this consideration, Nifo suggested that the knowledge of the cause that makes proper demonstration possible is based on a "conjectural" syllogism because the knowledge of the cause can never be as certain as the effect since the latter is arrived at through sensory experience.

In his thought concerning the human soul and intellect, he began as a strong advocate of Averroes (Ibn Rushd), whom he called "Aristotle transposed," but in *De intellectu* (On the intellect; 1503) he rejected Ibn Rushd's account of the unity of the human intellect. The dramatic shift in opinion, Nifo claimed, was brought about by his newfound command of the Greek language. Ibn Rushd's lack of Greek had caused him to misread Aristotle. Drawing on a wide range of sources, including the views of Plato as propounded by Marsilio Ficino, the Greek commentators Simplicius of Cilicia, Themistius, and Alexander of Aphrodisias, as well as the Latin tradition of Thomas Aquinas and Albertus Magnus, Nifo held that the immortality of the human soul is demonstrable. He placed great weight on arguments based on moral considerations and human happiness derived from Ficino, and in stating his own position relied on several suggestions of Albertus Magnus. In his later work, *De immortalitate animae libellum* (Small book on the immortality of the human soul; 1518), Nifo reaffirmed his commitment to the demonstrability of personal immortality in response to Pomponazzi's attacks on the notion, and he placed special emphasis on the ability of humans to choose freely as an indication of immortality.

Nifo's basic metaphysical outlook showed a marked affinity for a cluster of views derived from the Neoplatonic tradition as mediated by Thomas Aquinas and Albertus Magnus. In several early works, especially his commentary on Ibn Rushd's *Destructio destructium* (Incoherence of the incoherence; 1497), Nifo developed a metaphysical picture in which all creatures other than God exist insofar as they participate in God's existence. Since all things other than God exist by virtue of God's existence, Nifo argued that creatures differ inasmuch as they participate more or less fully in God's existence. Consequently, he viewed the world of creatures as hierarchical, with those creatures highest on the "chain of being" who more closely approach God and those creatures lowest on the chain who are more distant from God. God, thus, acts as the measure of all things.

BIBLIOGRAPHY

Ashworth, E. J. "Agostino Nifo's Reinterpretation of Medieval Logic." *Rivista critica di storia della filosofia* 31 (1976): 354–374.

Mahoney, Edward P. "Philosophy and Science in Nicoletto Vernia and Agostino Nifo." In *Scienza e filosofia all'Università di Padova nel Quattrocento.* Edited by A. Poppi. Padua, Italy, 1983. Pages 135–202.

Mahoney, Edward P. "Plato and Aristotle in the Thought of Agostino Nifo (ca. 1470–1538)." In *Platonismo e aristotelismo nel Mezzogiorno d'Italia (secc. XIV–XVI).* Edited by Giuseppe Roccaro. Palermo, Italy, 1989. Pages 81–102.

JAMES B. SOUTH

NOBILITY. *See* **Aristocracy.**

NOGAROLA, ISOTTA (1418–1466), Italian humanist. The first major female humanist, Isotta Nogarola produced a large body of works that were recognized in their day and remain important for the learning they display and the themes they address. Born to an old Veronese noble family with a considerable literary tradition, Isotta Nogarola, along with her older sister Ginevra, received a serious humanist education at the direction of her widowed mother. During their adolescence, both sisters won the attention of northern Italian humanists and courtiers, mostly of the circle of the educator Guarino da Verona. With these learned men, they exchanged books and letters that were testimonies to their classical training and lively intelligence. In 1438, Ginevra married and ceased to participate in humanist discourse. Isotta continued to do so until 1441. Then, discouraged by scurrilous attacks on her character (evidently due to hostility to learning in women) and Guarino's indifference at a crucial moment, she withdrew from humanist circles and retired to join her mother in her brother's house and live, as she put it, in a "book-lined cell." There, on the model of the holy women of the medieval tradition, she continued her studies in solitude.

Nogarola's works fall into two groups, before and after the great divide of her retirement. In the earlier period (from about 1434 to 1441), she composed an extensive letterbook consisting of her own letters to humanist friends and relatives and some of their responses. These letters demonstrate her knowledge of patristic and classical authors such as Lucius Lactantius, John Chrysostom, and Livy, show her engaged in discussion of current political events and the historical tradition of heroic women, and attest to her relationships with the intellectual and political figures of her northern Italian milieu. Letters from admirers, though hyperbolic, suggest that Nogarola's exceptional achievements were widely known.

The chorus of praise from learned correspondents continued in the second, longer period of Nogarola's life from 1441 to 1466. She received tributes from such eminent figures as Ermolao Barbaro the Elder, bishop of Verona, and the Greek expatriate Cardinal Bessarion, as well as from various humanists. Of special interest are letters from the Venetian humanists Lauro Quirini and Ludovico Foscarini, the latter also an eminent Venetian statesman and governor of Verona. Quirini's letter outlined a program of study that urged her to reach beyond the Latin literary tradition to read philosophical works in the original Greek. In this, Quirini both argued (as was not unusual among Venetian humanists) for the supremacy of philosophy over rhetoric, and, implicitly, for the capacity of a learned woman to master its difficulties. Foscarini's acquaintance with Nogarola is witnessed in several laudatory letters, and the peak moment of their relationship is marked by the composition, in 1451, of her dialogue "On the Equal or Unequal Sin of Eve and Adam." Here Nogarola counters Foscarini's powerful restatement of the traditional view of Eve's primary guilt for original sin with arguments based, ironically, on Eve's moral incapacity. Her work marks a first contribution in a subsequent feminist rethinking of the Adam and Eve narrative.

Also in this second period, Nogarola wrote a small study of Saint Jerome (1453), a letter to Pope Pius II (1459) urging a crusade, and a letter of consolation (1461) to the Venetian nobleman Jacopo Antonio Marcello on the death of his son Valerio. Her last five years were marked by illness. In 1468, two years after Nogarola's death, the humanist Giovanni Mario Filelfo (son of the more famous Francesco) dedicated a lengthy poem to her brother, celebrating her achievement as a holy woman but omitting any mention of her intellectual work.

BIBLIOGRAPHY

Primary Works

Nogarola, Isotta. "On the Equal or Unequal Sin of Eve and Adam." In *Her Immaculate Hand: Selected Works by and about the Women Humanists of Quattrocento Italy*. Edited and translated by Margaret L. King and Albert Rabil, Jr. 2d ed. Binghamton, N.Y., 1992. Pages 57–68.

Nogarola, Isotta. *Opera quae supersunt omnia; accedunt Angelae et Zeneverae Nogarolae epistolae et carmina*. Edited by Eugenius Abel. 2 vols. Vienna, 1886.

Secondary Works

King, Margaret L. "Isotta Nogarola." In *Italian Women Writers: A Bio-Bibliographical Sourcebook*. Edited by Rinaldina Russell. Westport, Conn., 1994. Pages 313–323.

King, Margaret L. "The Religious Retreat of Isotta Nogarola." *Signs* 3 (1978): 807–822.

MARGARET L. KING

NONFICTION PROSE. *See* **Prose, Elizabethan.**

NORWAY. *See* **Scandinavian Kingdoms.**

NOSTRADAMUS (Michel de Nostredame; 1503–1566), French physician and astrologer. Born in Saint-Rémy, Provence, Nostradamus studied arts at Avignon and medicine at Montpellier (1529), where he also taught briefly. Years of travel and treating plague victims solidified his medical reputation, although plague claimed his first wife and children at Agen, where he had settled at the invitation of Julius Caesar Scaliger. After moving to Salon and remarrying, he turned his attention increasingly to prognostication, and began by producing the first of his annual almanacs in 1550. His famous *Prophecies* or *Centuries* began to appear in 1555. The latter name is derived from their form; Nostradamus planned (and mostly completed) a series of verses organized into ten "centuries" of one hundred quatrains.

Written in an obscure style modeled upon ancient oracles and sibyls, the *Prophecies* earned Nostradamus strong supporters and equally strong detractors. Among the former were Catherine de Médicis, who requested that he prepare horoscopes for her royal children; King Charles IX, who named him physician in ordinary; and the poet Pierre de Ronsard. Attackers included especially supporters of Calvinism, for whom Nostradamus seemed to predict a harsh future.

Nostradamus asserted that his prophecies arose from divine inspiration that he received while contemplating the heavens, combined with predictive astrology and strengthened by comparison with similar past events. The works' lasting fame as well as their notoriety both come from the difficulty of either corroborating or disproving such evidence and sources, the veiled language of the verses, and his claim that the prophecies extended to the year 3797. They have enjoyed constant reprintings and translations, often with colorful interpretive commentary, since their first publication. Nostradamus's other writings included a French version of Galen's exhortation to Menodotus, a loose verse translation of the *Hieroglyphics* of Horapollon, and recipes for cures and cosmetics.

BIBLIOGRAPHY

Primary Works

Nostradamus, Michael. *The Elixirs of Nostradamus: Nostradamus' Original Recipes for Elixirs, Scented Water, Beauty Potions, and Sweetmeats*. Edited by Knut Boeser. Transcribed by Carola Friedrichs-Friedlander. Translated by Guy Slatter. London, 1996.

Nostradamus, Michael. *Interprétation des hiéroglyphes de Horapollo*. Edited by Pierre Rollet. Aix-en-Provence, France, 1968.

Nostradamus, Michael. *Lettres inédites*. Edited by Jean Dupèbe. Geneva, 1983.

Nostradamus, Michael. *Nostradamus au XVIe siècle: 10 fac-similés*. Verna, France, 1995.

Nostradamus, Michael. *Les premières centuries, ou, Propheties*. Édition Macé Bonhomme de 1555. Edited by Pierre Brind'Amour. Geneva, 1996.

Nostradamus, Michael. *La seconde partie contenant la façon et manière de faire toutes confitures liquides, tant en sucre, miel, qu'en vin cuit. . . .* Montreal, 1982.

Nostradamus, Michael. *Le vray et parfaict embellissement de la face . . . ; & La facon et maniere de faire toutes confitures liquides . . .* Reprint, Paris, 1979.

Secondary Works

Brind'Amour, Pierre. *Nostradamus astrophile: Les astres et l'astrologie dans la vie et l'oeuvre de Nostradamus*. Ottawa, Canada, 1993.

Leoni, Edgar. *Nostradamus: Life and Literature*. New York, 1961.

ANN E. MOYER

NOTARIES. A notary (*notarius* or *tabellio*) is a scribe who attests or certifies private human affairs, recording them in a public form and giving them public validity. He sometimes held no office, so was a private person, but his writings carried public validity, so he was also a public person. The kinds of documents notaries redacted, as stated by the anonymous *Formularium tabellionum* (c. 1205; once attributed to Irnerius), included legal instruments, emphitities, wills, donations, adoptions, emancipations, manumissions, conversions, transactions, covenants, guarantees, and contracts. To draw up a public instrument, the notary asked the customer the nature of his business and determined the kind of instrument he needed. Then the notary asked the customer all the questions necessary to handle the legal technicalities, make the required statements in the instrument, and set out the case, taking notes. He drew up a summary, which he then read back to the customer (the *recitatio*), making all necessary corrections with witnesses present. The corrected summary, called the *abbreviatura,* or protocol, was registered in the register of protocols. Both the transaction and its publication were necessary steps. The instrument became a public instrument because it was registered by a notary. However, notaries could be of different kinds and social classes, and have different functions and training.

Notaries were established in classical Roman law, the *Code* and *Digest* containing the basic ideas of an authentic instrument and a public person. Notarial practice survived throughout the Middle Ages in places where debased Roman law was used, taking on much greater importance in Italy with the revival of Roman law and foundation of the communes in the twelfth century, while not spreading north until the thirteenth century. The first mention of a notarial faculty at Bologna is from approximately 1250. From that time on the notarial art in Italy became more closely affiliated with the law as the range of legal documents became greater and also became more technical and more based in the Roman law.

In Italy, notaries and lawyers were organized into the same guilds. The lawyers were a small portion of a guild; in fifteenth- and early sixteenth-century Florence, for instance, there were usually twenty-five lawyers to four hundred notaries. But the lawyers were of a higher social class and were more politically important and conservative than the notaries, and so the governing bodies of the guilds were disproportionately loaded with lawyers. To matriculate in the guild notaries took an examination that consisted of three parts: Latin grammar, handwriting and composition, and forms of contracts and public instruments. Preparation for the examination could be done through apprenticing or attending classes for two years. The notarial arts were sometimes taught by teachers hired by the commune and sometimes taught within a university.

The notaries who became most important in France were those who headed the royal chanceries and departments of the bureaucracy. They developed into a corps of powerful and wealthy men whose position rivaled the hereditary nobility, especially under Francis I (ruled 1515–1547), when they numbered some 125. They were especially useful because they could wield a great deal of independent power without incurring the jealousy of the royal family. By the fifteenth century, the secretaries and notaries were given hereditary noble status for their offices. They were able to rise into the nobility because of demographic changes caused by the Hundred Years War (1338–1453). They became dynasties held together by professional and familial ties, and also were cultural leaders.

Notaries in England played a limited but essential role. They had almost no role in the common law courts, where oral evidence was preferred to written documents because of the jury system, and where private documents were authenticated by seals and the signatures of the parties before witnesses. Private documents could also be made into deeds that would be recorded by the court. Notaries were employed by merchants and by the courts of the church and Admiralty. A Scriveners Company guild was first mentioned in 1357 in London. The notaries of the church courts were appointed by the papacy before the Reformation and by the archbishop of Canterbury after. The *Summa* by Giovanni of Bologna was compiled for use by the English bishops and archbishops and reflected the unique practices in England.

Notaries were important in the papal curia. For both high and low posts in the papal chancery, a notarial degree was required. There were six main classes of notaries: *notarii cardinalium* (notaries of the cardinals), *notarii sacri platii* (notaries of the sacred palace), *notarii camere* (notaries of the treasury), *notarii audientiae contradictarum* (notaries of the audience of protestations, a public audience in which letters posing an objection to a motion or judgment were heard), *notarii curie marescalli* (notaries of the court of the marshal, the guard of the conclave), and *notarii commissariorum* or *notarii quorumcunque aliorum in Romana curia causas auctoritate apostolica audientium* (notaries of the commissaries or the notaries of whatever other cases come to the Roman court by apostolic authority). Besides these mainly legal notaries, there were administrative notaries as well. As the older offices of the curia degenerated into sinecures, the notarial offices became the backbone of the curia by the late Middle Ages. These notaries evolved their own formularies, starting with Thomas of Capua's formulary under Innocent III (reigned 1198–1216), which eventually contained the formulas for all papal documents, and contained the most important parts of Rolandino Passageri's and Rainerius of Perugia's work. In 1483 Sixtus IV temporarily established, and in 1507 Julius II permanently established, a college of seventy-two notaries with exclusive rights to work in the curia. There were also a great number of notaries who surrounded the papal court and represented private and corporate interests there.

BIBLIOGRAPHY

Banker, James R. "The Ars Dictaminis and Rhetorical Textbooks at the Bolognese University in the Fourteenth Century." *Medievalia et Humanistica,* n.s., 5 (1974): 153–168.

Barraclough, Geoffrey. *Papal Notaries and the Papal Curia: A Calendar and a Study of a "Formularium Notariorum Curie" from the Early Years of the Fourteenth Century.* London, 1934.

Brooks, C. W., R. H. Helmholz, and P. G. Stein. *Notaries Public in England since the Reformation.* Norwich, U.K., 1991.

Grendler, Paul F. *Schooling in Renaissance Italy: Literacy and Learning, 1300–1600.* Baltimore, 1989.

Martines, Lauro. *Lawyers and Statecraft in Renaissance Florence.* Princeton, N.J., 1968.

LAURA IKINS STERN

NOVELLA. The novella is a short narrative tale, especially popular in Italian and German literature, that often has an unexpected or comic ending. In antiquity as well as in modern times, the novella has rarely been considered among other literary genres. It was ignored not only by Aristotle and Horace, but also by the Aristotelian critics of the sixteenth century, even by Nicolas Boileau (1636–1711). There were few exceptions, such as the *Lezione sopra il comporre delle novelle* (*Lesson upon composing novella*) by F. Bonciani (1574).

Not until the 1960s did critical discussions about the novella in the medieval and Renaissance periods become more frequent. The emphasis on the novella, at least at the level of literary history, may be due in part to an urge to counter the indifference with which for years literary critics dealt with the so-called minor literary genres, the novella included. This interest may also be seen as the result of the lively critical attention focused on the various types of *narratio brevis,* or brief narrative, initiated at the beginning of the twentieth century by the Russian Formalists, and particularly by the studies on Pushkin by Boris Tomashevsky (1916) and on Dostoyevsky by A. Cejtlin (1926), until it found its definitive formulation in the more complete theoretical studies by Victor Shklovsky (*The Theory of Prose,* 1925) and by Boris Eichenbaum ("Theory of the Formal Method," 1927). Later, the French theorists interested in the *analyse du recit,* or analysing narrative, drew inspiration from the critics of the Prague-school and from Vladimir Propp's studies on the fable. The French *recit* critics officially drew critical attention to the *narratio brevis,* thereby creating interest for the novella in Italian literature.

Origins and Influences. Important contemporary critical studies dealing with the medieval novella and with Boccaccio's *Decameron* (1349–1351) provide significant data concerning the influence of the rules of classical rhetorics on the compositional form of the novella and elucidate the close connection between the narrative form of the novella and such classical or medieval narrative forms as the cursus, the controversia, the exemplum, the legend, the parable, the fabliau, the lai, the provencal nova. According to Letterio di Francia, a prominent historian of the novella, the novella is the only literary genre that is of Oriental, not classical, origin. Several translations of important Oriental works appear to predate the Italian novella. The first of these was *Barlaam and Josaphat* (translated into Latin in the tenth century), which transformed the great master of Buddhism into a Catholic saint, St. Josaphat, whose cult was observed for centuries before the mistaken identity was recognized and corrected. Two other important works of Oriental origin were the *Book of Calila and Dimna* (or *Panchatantra,* translated into Greek in the early eleventh century) and the *Book of the Seven Sages* (or *Sindibad;* translated into Greek at the end of the eleventh century). The diffusion of these works was greatly facilitated by the frequent commercial exchanges that were taking place by the twelfth century between important Italian cities— such as Venice, Genoa, or Pisa—and the Orient. The Crusades also brought more traffic between Europe and the Arab world.

These three Oriental works were the source of a collection of stories in Latin that became very popular in medieval Italy, the *Disciplina clericalis,* a moral treatise aimed at preparing a young man for life through examples drawn from lively, pleasant Oriental stories and written by the Spaniard Petrus

Alfonso (1062–1106). Several other collections of exempla used as sermons were equally popular at about the same time, such as the *Sermones vulgares* by Jacques de Vitry (one of the best known preachers of medieval times; 1180–1240) or the *Alphabetum narrationum* (an anonymous work of the thirteenth century) or the *Legenda aurea* by Jacobus de Voragine (c. 1228 or 1230–1298). These collections used brief narratives with popular tone and themes in order to reach an audience of men and women belonging to the middle and low social classes and teach them moral behavior presented in accessible language and style.

Early *Novelle*. The first works to use the *narratio brevis* in the Italian vernacular while employing some of the narrative material found in the above-mentioned collections appeared in Italy by the thirteenth century. The most remarkable of them were: (1) the *Fiori dei filosofi e di molti savi* (Flowers of philosophers and of many sages), (2) *Fiori di virtù* (Flowers of Virtue) and (3) The *Novellino* or *Cento novelle* (the One hundred novelle). The *Fiori dei filosofi e di molti savi* was a collection of brief narratives (probably composed between 1260 and 1280) derived almost exclusively from Vincent de Beauvais's *Speculum historiale*. The *Fiori di virtù*, probably written between 1280 and 1300 by a Benedictine monk from Bologna, was very popular, especially in the fourteenth century, when it was translated into such languages as Armenian, Arabic, Greek, German, French, Spanish, and even Romanian. Its popularity might have been in part due to its topic—the definition of virtue and of vice—and in part to its narrative organization. In the forty-two chapters of the book each virtue and its opposite vice are presented with several exempla taken from pleasant narrations sometimes animated also by animal fables.

The *Novellino* was the most important and extremely popular collection of the time, as its several manuscripts confirm. It shows the first use of the term "novella" as representative par excellence of the medieval narratio brevis. The term can be found in the prologue of the work, which is also called *Libro di novelle e di bel parlare gentile* (Book of novella and of beautiful and gentle conversing), where for the first time a connection is made between *novelle* as *ars narrandi,* the art of narrating, and *bel parlare* or *ars loquendi,* the "art of speaking"—that is, rhetoric. The *Novellino* as a book confirms the presence of an author who intends to establish a clear connection with a narrative oral tradition that

he reproposes in good written style, through which he gives religious and historical sources a new rhetorical formulation suitable to his readers' interests and contemporary issues (Picone, p. 129, 133).

The term "novella" probably came from the French word *nouvelle,* which means new information, or from the diminutive Latin form *novella* (from *novus*), meaning new things. It has been argued that the *Novellino,* rather than the *Decameron,* should be considered the beginning of the novella genre, although the latter remains the work that brought the genre into literary prominence. One basic definition of novella characterizes it as a brief narrative in prose (in contradistinction to the fabliau or the lai, which are in verse) that deals with human characters (not with animals, as the fable usually does) and represents events that are likely true, even if not historical, events (as one finds in the anecdote) without moralistic intentions or moralizing conclusions (as with the exemplum). The author of this type of narration will then make certain choices between (1) oral narration versus written narration and (2) insertion within a frame versus autonomy.

Boccaccio. Boccaccio faced some of these choices in his *Decameron,* which became the official model of prose writing for at least three centuries in Europe. He chose a written narration and added a new dimension to the literary physiognomy of the genre by avoiding any didascalic or moralistic finality, while conferring linguistic distinction to everyday discourse. Thus on the formal level he broke with the courtly tradition, paying attention to a new social group of readers, the bourgeois, merchant class who recognized themselves in his fictional characters. Boccaccio shows terminological uncertainty in the preface of his *Decameron:* "I intend to relate one hundred novellas or fables or parables or stories—whichever you choose to call them" (*Decameron*).

He seems still to vacillate between the new term "novella" and the other terms ("fable," "parable," "story") belonging to an old and well-known narrative tradition. Yet this uncertainty was soon overcome in the course of the *Decameron* with the definitive choice of the term "novella" used anytime he intended to define the type of narrations contained in the book. In this passage of the preface, he clearly makes additional choices in favor of a framework for his novella; in this case, he utilizes a narrative occasion in which a group of ten young people escape the Black Death of 1348 by moving away from the city of Florence in order to find relief in the Tuscan countryside and find distraction from the plague by telling and listening to novelle, singing songs, and dancing.

The presence of death, as suggested by the mention of the plague and the contrast that it creates with the serene atmosphere of the country setting, alludes to the real sense of the precariousness of life, of the risks that human beings constantly face in their everyday confrontation with chance and fortune. These are themes that recur frequently in the novelle of the *Decameron,* as well; while the ten young people of the frame seem determined and able to overcome the dangers of the plague and show an unshakeable faith in their own ability to stand up to death and misfortune, they convey a positive message for mankind, just as the novellas do in their celebration of life, joy, and natural love. As the mirror of a society that sees itself correctly represented in it, the *Decameron,* through the powerful positive message conveyed by both its frame and novellas, signals its novelty within the narrative tradition to which it belongs as it clearly addresses the earthly, bourgeois world as it is, rather than proposing an afterlife world as it should be, as Dante's *Divine Comedy* had done half a century earlier. The *Decameron* as the "merchants' epic" reached an enormous popularity especially within the bourgeois, mercantile society that Boccaccio had intended to address, and this popularity continued for the next three centuries even at the upper echelon of literary circles, especially after being endorsed by Pietro Bembo (1470–1547), the most authoritative voice on the sixteenth-century literary scene.

After Boccaccio. Naturally such a prestigious model offered the opportunity to be followed in different ways, both at the microlevel of the novella and at the macrolevel of the organization of the work. At the microlevel, some authors opted for limiting the choice of narrations to one single type, such as the *motto* or witticism, as is the case of Franco Sacchetti's (c. 1330–c. 1400) *Trecentonovelle* (Three hundred novelle) or the several collections of *Motti* or *Witticisms* typical of the fifteenth and sixteenth centuries. Others chose to work mostly with fables, like Gianfrancesco F. Straparola (1480–1557?) in his *Piacevoli notti* (Pleasant nights), imitated from the *Fabulae* in Latin by Girolamo Morlini. At the macrolevel of the work itself, some dropped the frame device, as did Sacchetti in his *Trecentonovelle* in the fourteenth century, Masuccio Salernitano in his *Novellino* in the fifteenth century, or Matteo Bandello in his *Novelle* in the sixteenth century, while some, especially in

the fourteenth century, preferred to try their hand at the so-called *novella spicciolata* or "loose novella," which is not included in a group or in a collection, such as the famous *Novella del grasso Legnaiolo* attributed to Filippo Brunelleschi (1377–1446) or *La tragica Storia di due amanti,* that is, the novella of Romeo and Juliet, written by Luigi Da Porto (1485–1529).

Throughout the sixteenth century and part of the seventeenth century, the novella was the most popular narrative genre in Italy, even if some areas of the country were more productive than others. Tuscany was indeed one of the strongest centers of novella production; Agnolo Firenzuola (1493–1543), Anton Francesco Doni (1513–1574), Anton Francesco Grazzini (1503–1584), Pietro Fortini (d. 1562), the Bargagli brothers, Girolamo (1537–1586) and Scipione (d. 1612), are some of the Tuscan novella writers who were very successful in those centuries. Another very successful group of novella writers came from the Veneto region and included well-known letterati like Straparola, Sebastiani Erizzo (1525–1585), Giambattista Giraldi (Cinzio, 1504–1573), Francesco Pons, Girolamo Brusoni (b. 1614), and Giovanni Sagredo (1617–1682). With such writers, the novella continued gaining literary prestige, and it could be said that in Italy, between the sixteenth and seventeenth centuries, the novella occupied a more important narrative space than that of the *romanzo* or novel, which did not develop in Italy until the nineteenth century.

See also biographies of figures mentioned in this entry.

BIBLIOGRAPHY

Cherchi, P. "From *Controversia* to *Novella.*" In *La nouvelle.* Actes du Colloque Internationale de Montréal. Montréal, 1983. Pages 89–99.

Cottino-Jones, Marga. "Narrative Structures and Interrelations, and Narrative Techniques." In *Order from Chaos: Social and Aesthetic Harmonies in Boccaccio's* Decameron. Washington, D.C., 1982. Pages 4–32.

Di Francia, Letterio. *Novellistica.* 2 vols. Milan, 1924–1925.

Gillespie, Gerald. "Novella, Nouvelle, Novella, Short Novel? A Review of Terms." *Neophilologus* 51 (1967): 117–127, 225–230.

Lewalski, B. Kiefer. *Renaissance Genres: Essays on Theory, History, and Interpretation.* Cambridge, Mass., and London, 1986.

Picone, M. "L'invenzione della novella italiana." In *La novella italiana.* Edited by E. Malato. Rome, 1992. Pages 119–154.

Segre, C. "La novella e i generi letterari." In *La novella italiana.* Edited by E. Malato. Rome, 1992. Pages 47–57.

MARGA COTTINO-JONES

NUDE IN RENAISSANCE ART. *See* **Human Body in Renaissance Art.**

NUMEROLOGY. Renaissance numerology is concerned with the symbolic import of the numbers often used to structure a text, for example into books and chapters, or lines, stanzas, and cantos. Such preplanned designs were seen as signs in their own right, often pointing beyond themselves to a higher reality than that of mere sense perception. Symmetrical and graded arrangements are a related phenomenon created by the repetition of the same or similar words, phrases, and topoi (commonplaces, or concepts). In such structures number symbolism is not necessarily present beyond the fact of the ratio. Whereas verbal texturing reveals conscious intent, purely numerical patterns are a matter of decorum only (that is, agreement between form and content). When verbal and numerical patterns combine, the verbal texture lends strong support to the numerical design. This fusion is typical of Renaissance epics like Torquato Tasso's *Gerusalemme liberata* (1581; translated as *Jerusalem Delivered* by Edward Fairfax, 1600), Edmund Spenser's *The Faerie Queene* (1590–1595) and John Milton's *Paradise Lost* (1667).

Sources. The science of numbers dates back to antiquity, when philosophers like Plato and Pythagoras used numbers, which they thought of geometrically, as concepts defining various aspects of creation. The tradition of philosophizing by means of numbers persisted through the Middle Ages and the Renaissance so that it was possible for Sir Thomas Browne (1605–1682) to refer to "arithmetical theology." Pythagoras referred everything back to the first four numbers (the *tetractys*) and their sum, 10, whereas Plato in the *Timaeus* played with seven numbers: 1 (that is, Unity), which engenders 2 and 3, each subsequently squared to form a planar world, and then each cubed to form a three-dimensional world. These numbers express the harmony of the world because they define the ratios that create the perfect consonances, chief of which is the diapason (1:2 or 2:1). Hence the distances between the planets could be construed musically as ratios, and the same principle was applied to the "distances" established by textual divisions. Because cosmic and textual space were conceived analogically, it was possible for Augustine, the greatest of the church fathers, to refer to the universe as God's *carmen* (song or poem).

The tradition of thinking by way of numbers and ratios was Christianized on the basis of the assumption that the classical philosophers were "ancient theologians" indebted for their insights either to Moses and the Hebrew prophets or to such Gentile prophets as Hermes Trismegistus and Zoroaster. Thus Plato's seven numbers were linked to the Mosaic week of creation, the "week" being a metaphor for God's orderly way of proceeding as he created everything "in number, weight, and measure" (Wisdom 11:20). This view was elaborated by Renaissance philosophers like Marsilio Ficino and Giovanni Pico della Mirandola, and the subject of number symbolism featured prominently in medieval and Renaissance encyclopedic treatises.

Exegetes, too, paid careful attention to the textual structures in the Bible and to the numbers featured in the text (for example, the 40 years in the desert and the 40 days Christ remained in the wilderness; the number served to define the meaning of these events). Balanced patterns were traced everywhere. Among the important biblical numbers are 15 (for ascent, as in the fifteen Psalms of Ascent), 33 (Christ's age at death), and 42 (the 3×14 generations from Abraham to Jesus listed in Matthew 1). These numbers were often used to structure prose treatises and poems. Augustine explicitly advised all artists to imitate God's "eternal art" in their own works so as to reflect the beauty of his harmonious order.

Principles and Examples. Decorum is the basic principle. If a text contains concepts that invite numerical expression, appropriate numbers may be found to condition the form. Milton's "At a solemn Musick" (*Poems,* 1645) illustrates the point. Its 28 lines are divided in the sequence 16–8–4 lines as indicated by the syntax and the rhyme scheme, thus forming a double diapason in honor of the divinely ordained diapason celebrated in the contents. The poem moves rhythmically "in tune with Heaven" in "perfect diapason." In his treatise *On the Trinity* (book 4), Augustine traces this rhythm throughout God's works of creation and redemption. Another example is Edmund Spenser's *Epithalamion* (1595) whose 24 stanzas take us through the 24-hour cycle. Such is the textual precision that night falls after 16 stanzas and a quarter, exactly when it would occur on the date celebrated in the poem.

The description of an estate could be made to praise the owner by reflecting the structures attributed to God's works of creation and redemption. Andrew Marvell's "Upon Appleton House" is a good example. This estate poem is dedicated to Thomas, Lord Fairfax, one of Cromwell's leading generals. The 97 stanzas form a sequence of 10—25—50—12 stanzas. The family history is narrated in the group of twenty-five stanzas, while the description of the estate in the group of fifty stanzas contains witty allusions to major events in redemption history (Noah and the Ark, Moses). The 1:2 ratio between these groups proclaims the harmony between the family history and God's plan of redemption. By virtue of this harmony, Lord Fairfax is made to seem like a new Noah and a new Moses, in short a new national redeemer. The ten introductory stanzas on Lord Fairfax stress the idea of Justice (connected with the Ten Commandments of the Law), while the twelve last stanzas on his daughter Maria present her as being perfectly in command of all languages—a proposition that associates her with the Holy Spirit bestowed on the Twelve Apostles. Father and daughter, therefore, represent the justice of the Old Testament and the grace of the New.

The numerical structuring of salvation history is found also in Spenser's *The Faerie Queene*, book 2, canto 10, where stanzas are aligned with generations, the basic numbers being 33 and 42, each subdivided in the ratio 2:1.

Verbal Texturing. Symbolic numbers are often coordinated with, and subordinated to, symmetrical and graded structures created by the location of topoi within the body, or *morphé*, of the text. Such "topomorphs" have their origin in such rhetorical schemes as *epanados* (linking the beginning and the middle, or the middle and the end), *epanalepsis* (linking the beginning and the end), and *chiasmus* (linking through repetition in inverse order).

Diagram 1 shows that such linkages are created by means of repetition within a sentence or a single stanza, but the scope may be extended to a nine-stanza segment (diagram 2) or to a canto as a whole (diagram 3). Segments, cantos, and verse paragraphs may have numerically significant unit totals (diagram 3). The presence of these patterns shows that readers and writers alike had a spatial approach to the text so that special attention was paid to beginnings, middles, and ends and to points equidistant from the center. The basis of this structural tradition is in classical rhetoric. The schemes appropriate for a sentence were applied to a composition as a whole. In an epic (diagram 4), topomorphs serve to unify and

DIAGRAM 1. Linkage through verbal repetition (Spenser, *The Faerie Queene*, book 1, canto 4, stanza 8)

High above all a cloth of State was spred,
       A   B   C
And a rich throne, as bright as sunny day,   A B C

On which there sate most brave embellishéd

With royall robes and gorgeous array,
              D   C
A mayden Queene, that shone as Titans ray,   D C

In glistring gold, and peerelesse pretious stone,
  B
Yet her bright blazing beautie did assay
  B
To dim the brightnesse of her glorious throne, B A
                        D
As envying her selfe, that too exceeding shone. D

These rhetorical schemes highlight the line at the center.

DIAGRAM 2. Linkage through repetition of identical rhyme words in a 9-stanza segment (Spenser, *The Faerie Queene*, book 1, canto 5, stanzas 45–53)

Stanza		
45	Pride / spide / lay	A B C
48	Pride	A
49	stall / fall	D E
53	lay / spide / Pride / stall / fall	C B A D E

In this narrative segment (on Redcrosse's escape from the House of Pride), repeated words are key concepts emphasized by being placed in rhyme position. Repetitions within the lines support this pattern.

DIAGRAM 3. Balanced canto structure in Spenser's *The Faerie Queene* (book 1, canto 3)

Stanza	Stanza totals		Events
1–2		2	*Lament* for Una
3–9		7	The *power* of Una *unveiled*
	19		
10–21		12	Una in the *false* house of holiness
22–23		2	Una *cursed* by Corceca and Abessa
24–32		9	Una and the *false* Redcrosse knight
	19		
33–42		10	Archimago's *weakness* when *unveiled*
43–44		2	*Lament* for Una

The topos of lament links the beginning, middle, and end, and other topoi link the segments in between. The structure highlights the antithesis between truth and falsehood, strength and weakness. The number 19 signifies addiction to sin and punishment for it.

DIAGRAM 4. Examples of topomorphs that unify Tasso's *Jerusalem Delivered* (translated by Fairfax, 1600)

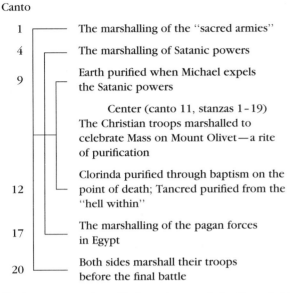

Canto

1 — The marshalling of the "sacred armies"

4 — The marshalling of Satanic powers

9 — Earth purified when Michael expels the Satanic powers

Center (canto 11, stanzas 1–19)
The Christian troops marshalled to celebrate Mass on Mount Olivet—a rite of purification

12 — Clorinda purified through baptism on the point of death; Tancred purified from the "hell within"

17 — The marshalling of the pagan forces in Egypt

20 — Both sides marshall their troops before the final battle

Further topomorphs unify the epic as a whole. Stanza totals often have a symbolic import as in the 144 stanzas of the last canto, where 144 represents the dimensions of the heavenly Jerusalem (that is, 12 × 12), thus aligning the earthly and the heavenly.

to assist interpretation by foregrounding basic concepts. The center around which an epic pivots is often a self-contained episode possessed of its own textual structure. In *Gerusalemme liberata,* Tasso placed the center so exactly that it is preceded and followed by the same number of stanzas (949). Spenser emulated this practice in book 1 of *The Faerie Queene.* To avoid structural monotony and to permit an important reversal (*peripeteia*) to be located two thirds of the way through a text, a division in the ratio 2:1 is usually imposed upon the centering pattern.

The numerical and verbal patterns sketched here should be seen as part of the preoccupation with expressive form typical of Renaissance art, and especially, perhaps, architecture and music.

Methodical Problems. Textual units must be clearly defined and preferably indicated by verbal schemes or topomorphs as shown in the diagrams. The principle of numerical decorum should be invoked only when the text speaks plainly about its own form in so-called self-referring passages. Analysis of verbal texture must be given priority; such analysis will reveal the writer's plan or "fore-conceit" (Sir Philip Sidney's crucial term). Examples of preplanned

structures may be found also in prose texts, one example being Sir Thomas Browne's *Religio Medici* (1642). To recognize self-referring passages, familiarity with Renaissance rhetoric and number symbolism is called for. *Unity* and *multiplicity,* for example, are key concepts discussed at length in Renaissance treatises concerned with number symbolism.

It must also be stressed that the same number may have a wealth of possible meanings—for example the number 7—so that the contents must decide which meaning is relevant. Moreover, the same number (or sign) may be interpreted *in bono* or *in malo* (in a good or a bad sense) according to a basic exegetical principle explained by Augustine in his treatise *De doctrina christiana* (*On Christian Doctrine*). Further complexities are created by the simultaneous use of symmetrical and grade arrangements in the ratio 1:2 or 2:1. This flexibility helps to explain the popularity, during the Renaissance, of preplanned textual structures. Structures, too, may be *witty* in the Renaissance sense of this word.

See also Bible, *subentry on* Christian Interpretation of the Bible.

BIBLIOGRAPHY

Allen, Michael J. B. *Nuptial Arithmetic: Marsilio Ficino's Commentary on the Fatal Number in Book VIII of Plato's Republic.* Los Angeles, 1994. Contains an introduction to ancient and Renaissance numerology and number-ratio theory.

Butler, Christopher. *Number Symbolism.* London, 1970.

Fowler, Alastair. *Spenser and the Numbers of Time.* London and New York, 1964.

Fowler, Alastair. *Triumphal Forms: Structural Patterns in Elizabethan Poetry.* London, 1970.

Heninger, S. K., Jr. *Touches of Sweet Harmony: Pythagorean Cosmology and Renaissance Poetics.* San Marino, Calif., 1974.

Røstvig, Maren-Sofie. " 'Arithmetical Divinitie' and the Unity of Sir Thomas Browne's *Religio Medici.*" In *Contexts of Baroque,* edited by Roy T. Eriksen. Oslo, 1997. Pages 119–146. Shows the presence of symmetrical and graded arrangements in the ratio 2:1 and their unifying effect.

Røstvig, Maren-Sofie. *Configurations: A Topomorphical Approach to Renaissance Poetry.* Oslo, Norway, and Oxford, 1994. Pages 1–112. This large-scale study places the Renaissance use of preplanned textual structures in a historical context extending from late antiquity to the early eighteenth century.

Røstvig, Maren-Sofie. "The Hidden Sense: Milton and the Neoplatonic Method of Numerical Composition." In *The Hidden Sense and Other Essays.* Edited by M.-S. Røstvig. Oslo, Norway, 1963.

MAREN-SOFIE RØSTVIG

NÜRNBERG. Nürnberg was one of the largest and most important cities in the Holy Roman Empire during the Renaissance. As Niccolò Machiavelli com-

Nürnberg. View of the city by Hans Wurm. GERMANISCHES NATIONALMUSEUM, NÜRNBERG

mented in his *Report on the Affairs of Germany,* "the power of Germany certainly resides more in her cities than in her princes." He also argued that the cities "are the real nerves of the Empire" because they have "plenty of money, stable governments, and are free to act" (quoted in Strauss, p. 4). Despite the fact that German imperial towns held only about 1 percent of the empire's land and about 3.5 percent of its population according to an early eighteenth-century report made in Vienna, the economic and cultural significance of towns like Nürnberg was indisputable during the Renaissance.

The "Dutch Venice."

By the sixteenth century, Nürnberg was second only to Cologne among German towns. More than forty thousand people lived within its walls, with a similar number dwelling in the immediate vicinity. Although the Pegnitz River, which ran through the heart of the city, was not navigable, twelve trade routes converged in its territory. Through those trade routes Nürnberg was connected to the water traffic along the Main River via Bamberg, thirty miles to the northwest, which linked the town to the commerce of the Rhineland and beyond. In the southeast via nearby Regensburg, Nürnberg was joined to the trade with the Danubian territories. Indeed, Nürnberg's location in the heart of Europe placed it in an enviable economic situation by the start of the Renaissance.

Furthermore, Nürnberg's social and business elite wisely took the economic and political steps necessary to exert control over the trade traffic and to add its own products to the channels of commerce that moved within and around it. The city won trading concessions (including toll-free zones) throughout the fourteenth and fifteenth centuries. Nürnberg's craftspersons became world famous for the high quality of their goods, especially metal goods such as cannons, clocks, and armor.

Political Life. Nürnberg's political life had always been closely tied to that of the Holy Roman Empire. In 1219 the emperor Frederick II granted the town its Great Charter, which made it free from all authority except that of the emperor and his representative, the burgrave, and confirmed its market privileges. The emperor Charles IV proclaimed the famous Golden Bull of the Empire at an Imperial Diet in the city. One of the provisions of the Golden Bull granted Nürnberg the honor of holding the first diet for each newly elected emperor. In 1424 the emperor Sigismund transferred the imperial regalia (*Reichskleinodien*) from Prague to Nürnberg, where they remained for the next three hundred years. Ten years later, Sigismund turned over the imperial castle in the heart of the city to the authority of the ruling, merchant-dominated town council. The burgrave Frederick VI of nearby Brandenburg-Ansbach sold the remainder of his rights over the city in 1427, although the town and the margraves remained in frequent conflict until the late 1520s.

Holy Roman emperors continued to visit the city on a regular basis throughout the Renaissance. The emperor Maximilian I was a frequent visitor and resided in Nürnberg for six months in 1491. His grandson, Charles V, made Nürnberg the seat of the Imperial Council of Regency and the Imperial Chamber of Justice (*Reichskammergericht*) in 1521. Given Charles's investment in the city, Nürnberg's support of Lutheranism in the early 1520s put the convinced Catholic emperor in an awkward position. Nürnberg could not be allowed to continue as the ceremonial capital of the Holy Roman Empire; therefore, Charles V moved the Imperial Council and the Chamber Court to Esslingen in 1524. In March 1525 after a public religious debate, Nürnberg officially adopted Lutheranism. Its diplomats continued to assure the emperor and his regent, Ferdinand, of the city's loyalty, and Nürnberg refused to join the Protestant Schmalkaldic League. Nürnberg also continued to send generous subsidies and even troops for the Habsburg wars with the Ottomans.

Intellectual Life. Not only was Nürnberg a major economic and political center, but it was also an important focal point for Renaissance art and thought. Throughout the fifteenth and early-sixteenth centuries, as the city grew in wealth and population, new buildings and the expansion of older ones gave employment to architects and artists. The town's parish churches and monastic houses also provided abundant patronage. While Nürnberg's claim to being a "German Athens or Florence," was greatly exaggerated, the city could count a number of major Renaissance artists among its citizenry. The great Albrecht Dürer (1471–1528) was foremost among them. The son of a Nürnberg goldsmith, Dürer spent much of his career in his native city and owned a pleasant home in the shadow of the city's imperial castle.

While no other Nürnberg artist achieved the international reputation of Dürer, sculptors such as Adam Krafft (d. 1507), Veit Stoss (c. 1447–1553), and Peter Vischer (1460–1529) earned important local and imperial commissions. Both Stoss and Vischer, for example, were invited to contribute to the great tomb of Maximilian I in Innsbruck. The painter and engraver Michael Wolgemut (1434–1519) operated an extremely busy studio after his arrival in Nürnberg in the 1480s and became one of Dürer's teachers.

Although Nürnberg was not a university town during the Renaissance, it was a thriving intellectual center. A city doctor and humanist, Hartmann Schedel (1440–1514) achieved great recognition for his popular *Liber chronicarum* (World chronicle) and his widely used *Book of Songs*. Other major Nürnberg humanists included Willibald (1470–1530) and Caritas Pirckheimer (1467–1532), the lawyer Christoph Scheurl (1481–1542), and the city secretary Lazarus Spengler (1479–1534). During the great crisis of the Reformation, Abbess Caritas Pirckheimer led a spirited defense of her Poor Clare convent that remained Catholic until 1590. The celebrated astronomer Regiomontanus (1436–1476) settled in Nürnberg in 1471, while the cosomographer Martin Behaim (1459–1507) was a native Nürnberger. The cobbler-poet Hans Sachs (1494–1576) was Nürnberg's most prolific Renaissance author, with more than four thousand *Meisterlieder* (master songs), seventeen hundred verse tales and fables, and two hundred dramas to his credit. Like Dürer, Sachs was an important early supporter of the Reformation and hailed Martin Luther as "The Wittenberg Nightingale." The glories of Renaissance Nürnberg can be seen not only in the surviving art and writings of these individuals, but also in a host of Renaissance buildings in the center of the city, reconstructed following the massive destruction of World War II.

See also **Nürnberg Chronicle.**

BIBLIOGRAPHY

Primary Work
Pfeiffer, Gerhard, ed. *Quellen zur nürnberger Reformationsgeschichte.* Nürnberg, Germany, 1968. Excellent collection of official documents transcribed from the city's archives.

Secondary Works
Grimm, Harold. *Lazarus Spengler: A Lay Leader of the Reformation.* Columbus, Ohio, 1978. Meticulous study of the humanist city secretary.
Smith, Jeffrey Chipps, ed. *Nuremberg, A Renaissance City.* Austin, Tex., 1983. Essays about Dürer, his art, and his world.
Strauss, Gerald. *Nuremberg in the Sixteenth Century.* 1966. Reprint, Bloomington, Ind., 1976. Outstanding survey.
Zophy, Jonathan. *Patriarchal Politics and Christoph Kress (1484–1535) of Nuremberg.* Lewiston, N.Y., 1992. Looks at a leading urban politician.

JONATHAN W. ZOPHY

NÜRNBERG CHRONICLE. The history of the world commonly known as the *Nürnberg Chronicle* is one of the greatest examples of book design and production in the history of printing. It was published in Nürnberg in 1493 in a Latin edition (*Liber chronicarum*) and a German translation (*Das Buch der Chroniken und Geschichten*), both illustrated with more woodcuts than had ever before appeared in a printed book. It is remarkable as well for the survival of manuscript "exemplars" or layout books for both editions, and of documents recording the contractual agreements for the *Chronicle*'s illustration and printing.

The work was compiled by Hartmann Schedel, a physician and bibliophile who was part of the humanist circle in Nürnberg. His library of some 370 manuscripts and 600 printed books survives in the Bavarian State Library in Munich. Schedel recorded the history of the world from the Creation to his own day and, leaving six blank pages for the purchaser to fill in, concluded with an account of the Apocalypse and Day of Judgment. Although he did rely on humanist sources, Schedel's text is essentially of the medieval Scholastic tradition. As history it soon was surpassed by others, but the work remains significant for its illustrations and its graphic design.

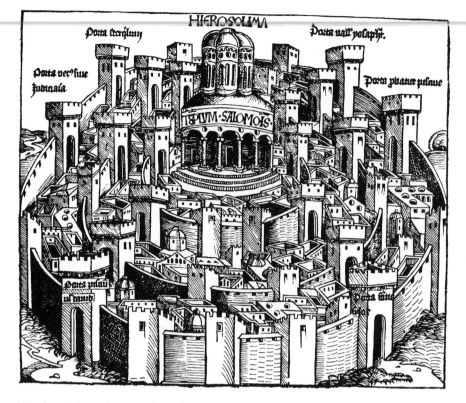

Nürnberg Chronicle. Woodcut of Jerusalem. While the woodcuts of most European cities in the Chronicle are reasonably accurate, the view of Jerusalem is imaginary.

The *Nürnberg Chronicle* contains over 1,800 illustrations printed from 645 woodcuts. The total number of repeated cuts is 1,164. They depict major events from the Old and New Testaments; episodes in the lives of the saints; portraits of prophets, kings, popes, and other important figures; images of monsters and curiosities; and maps and panoramic views of the cities described. The woodcuts were produced in the workshop of artists Michael Wolgemut (1434–1519) and Wilhelm Pleydenwurff, whose apprentices included the young Albrecht Dürer (1471–1528). The workshop was known for fine altarpieces, sculptures, paintings, and playing cards, as well as woodcuts. According to the contractual agreement for the *Chronicle,* dated 29 December 1491, the artists were responsible for the production of all the woodcuts and the preparation of the exemplars, which served as the printer's copy. The artists also were required to be on hand while the printing was carried out to insure that there were no defects in the blocks.

The printer was Anton Koberger, one of the great scholar-printers of the fifteenth century, whose activities encompassed all aspects of book production and distribution. His shop housed twenty-four presses, and the quality of its products is evident in the *Chronicle*. Koberger also had an extensive network for distribution with agents in Budapest, Cologne, Frankfurt, Lyon, Paris, Vienna, and Warsaw. He took on the work of printing the *Chronicle* as a commission, as documented in a contract of 16 March 1492. Although the size of the pressrun is not recorded, it is estimated that the Latin edition was produced in fifteen hundred copies, while the German was done in one thousand copies.

The production of this lavishly illustrated history was financed by Sebald Schreyer and his brother-in-law, Sebastian Kammermaister. Schreyer was a wealthy merchant of the city who sponsored a number of artistic, religious, and civic projects and numbered among his honorary offices that of churchwarden of the cathedral of Saint Sebald. Upon the completion of the printing, he had the exemplar sheets for each edition bound. The volumes survive in the Nürnberg City Library.

See also **Graphic Arts**; **Printing and Publishing**.

BIBLIOGRAPHY

Cockerell, Sydney C. *Some German Woodcuts of the Fifteenth Century*. Hammersmith, U.K., 1897.

Duniway, David Cushing. "A Study of the Nuremberg Chronicle." *The Papers of the Bibliographical Society of America* 35 (1941): 17–34.

Wilson, Adrian. *The Making of the Nuremberg Chronicle*. Amsterdam, 1976.

MARIE ELENA KOREY

OBSTETRICS AND GYNECOLOGY. A variety of writings on obstetric and gynecological topics was in circulation during the Renaissance, including a number of ancient and medieval works devoted entirely to this field: several versions and adaptations of Soranus's first century A.D. *Gynecology,* pseudonymous treatises attributed variously to Priscianus and Cleopatra, and the twelfth-century Salernitan texts attributed to Trotula, including one that may actually have been written by a female practitioner of that name. There was also a significant amount of scholastic commentary touching on these subjects, which were discussed in many of the ancient and Arab works that formed the basis of late medieval academic medicine and natural philosophy.

Although topics of a more purely philosophical import—theories of generation, female physiology, and sexual difference—drew by far the greatest amount of learned attention, fifteenth-century Italian physicians such as Antonius Guainerius and Giovanni Michele Savonarola included lengthy discussions of gynecological disorders and obstetric complications in their larger Latin publications. In addition, a growing body of anatomical works by university medical professors described the structures of the reproductive tract, occasionally challenging traditional concepts such as the notion of a seven-cell uterus, falsely attributed to Galen.

The relationship between this Latin medical literature and actual practice is not readily apparent, particularly given the significant role of nonacademic practitioners (midwives) in this area of medicine. There is evidence that male physicians did in fact treat gynecological disorders in the course of their practice—for example, both Guainerius and Savonarola incorporated case histories alongside their references to the standard authorities. However, it appears that in such cases physical examinations leading to diagnosis were performed by midwives rather than the practitioners themselves and that most births were managed by women, except perhaps among the highest classes (for example, royalty) and in cases that required surgical intervention.

A further complication is presented by the proliferation of vernacular texts on these topics in the fifteenth and sixteenth centuries. Original works appeared alongside translations or recapitulations of traditional sources, such as the extremely popular work by the Frankfurt city physician Eucharius Rösslin, *Der swangern Frawen und hebammen Rosegarten* (1513), translated into English in 1540 as *The Byrth of Mankynde.* Savonarola treated gynecological matters not only in his Latin commentaries on Avicenna's *Canon,* but also in *Il trattato ginecologico-pediatrico* (1460), written in Ferrarese dialect and dedicated to the women of Ferrara. In fact, much of the vernacular literature explicitly invokes female readers, or declares its intent to assist in the reform of midwifery (as did a small number of the earlier Latin texts). It is unclear whether these appeals reflect real expectations of a female readership or function merely as a rhetorical device. It does seem that literacy may have been commonplace among urban midwives, who were increasingly subject to prescriptive regulation and licensing procedures by ecclesiastical and municipal authorities. Perhaps the most significant development occurred at the end of the sixteenth century, with the appearance of (mostly French) obstetrical literature written by and for male surgeons—for example, Ambroise Paré's *De la génération de l'homme* (On the generation of man; 1573) or François Rousset's *Traitté nouveau de l'hystérotomotokie; ou, Enfantement caesarien* (New treatise on uterine surgery; or caesarian childbirth; 1581)—foreshadowing the eventual absorption of obstetrics into male medical practice.

See also **Midwives and Healers**; **Motherhood**; **Pregnancy**.

BIBLIOGRAPHY

Primary Works

Rösslin, Eucharius. *When Midwifery Became the Male Physician's Province: The Sixteenth-Century Handbook* The Rose Garden for Pregnant Women and Midwives. Edited and translated by Wendy Arons. Jefferson, N. C., 1994. Translation of *Der swangern Frawen und hebammen Rosegarten.*

Soranus of Ephesus. *Soranus' Gynecology.* Translated by Owsei Temkin. Baltimore, 1956.

Trotula of Salerno (attrib.). *The Diseases of Women.* Translated by Elizabeth Mason-Hohl. Los Angeles, 1940. Translation of pseudo-Trotula texts.

Secondary Works

Benton, John F. "Trotula, Women's Problems, and the Professionalization of Medicine in the Middle Ages." *Bulletin of the History of Medicine* 59, no. 1 (1985): 30–53. Important article, which resolves the longstanding debate over the identity and works of Trotula by identifying a previously unknown, genuine work of that author.

O'Neill, Ynez Viole. "Giovanni Michele Savonarola: An Atypical Renaissance Practitioner." *Clio Medica* 10, no. 2 (1975): 777–793.

Siraisi, Nancy. *Medieval and Early Renaissance Medicine: An Introduction to Knowledge and Practice.* Chicago, 1990.

JEANETTE HERRLE-FANNING

OCKEGHEM, JOHANNES (c. 1410–1497), Franco-Flemish composer. Ockeghem was born in St.-Ghislain, in the Belgian province of Hainaut. Nothing is known of his education, but he may have been a student of the composer Gilles Binchois (c. 1400–1460) and thus would have had an early connection to the Burgundian court of Philip the Good.

Ockeghem was a singer at the church of Our Lady in Antwerp in 1443–1444, and then in the chapel of Charles I, duke of Bourbon, at Moulins in 1446–1448. A few years later he joined the French royal chapel, in which he served until his death. In 1459 Charles VII, hereditary abbot of the large and wealthy abbey of St.-Martin at Tours, appointed Ockeghem to the important post of treasurer of St.-Martin's. He became master of the chapel in 1464.

Some time before 1472, possibly in 1464, Ockeghem was ordained a priest at Cambrai, where he met Guillaume Dufay (c. 1400–1474), whose work had a major influence on him.

Ockeghem composed in various sacred and secular genres, but his most important works are his fourteen Masses, each consisting of a cycle of movements unified by a common melody, motive, or technical procedure, following examples set by English composers such as John Dunstaple (c. 1390–1453) and his older Franco-Flemish contemporary Dufay. His Requiem Mass, which may have been written on the death of Charles VII in 1461, is the earliest polyphonic example of such a work that survives. He also wrote an isolated Credo, five motets, twenty-five French chansons, and an arrangement of a Spanish *canción*. A handful of doubtful works are also attributed to him.

Ockeghem was renowned for his contrapuntal skill, especially in canonic writing. His masterpiece in that technique is his *Missa Prolationum*, consisting almost entirely of double canons at all intervals within the octave, each voice being in a different "prolation" (meter). Distinctive features of his music include intricate contrapuntal textures, complex and often unpredictable rhythms, and long, overlapping phrases. Conservative in many respects, his style also displays progressive features that became standard in the music of the emerging Renaissance, such as the equal importance of all voices and extension of the bass range.

Ockeghem had an immense impact on later musicians. Antoine Busnois, singer and composer in the chapel of Charles the Bold, duke of Burgundy, honored Ockeghem in his motet "In hydraulis" as "a true image of Orpheus." The Flemish music theorist Johannes Tinctoris dedicated his treatise on the modes (*Liber de natura et proprietate tonorum*, 1476) jointly to Ockeghem and Busnois, and in his treatise on counterpoint (*Liber de arte contrapuncti*, 1477) called Ockeghem first among "the most excellent of all the composers I have ever heard." In his last treatise (*De inventione et usu musicae*, c. 1481), Tinctoris describes Ockeghem as the finest bass singer known to him. The poet Guillaume Cretin mentions a number of his works including an "exquisite and most perfect Requiem Mass," and praises his "subtlety" in composing a thirty-six-voice motet. The poet Jean Molinet (1435–1507) wrote a lament on Ockeghem's death that was set to music by the Franco-Flemish musician Josquin des Prez (c. 1450–1521), the great composer of the next generation. In 1523 the poet Nicole Le Vestu wrote a *chant royal* praising Ockeghem, a manuscript of which contains a miniature painting depicting Ockeghem with singers of the royal chapel.

BIBLIOGRAPHY

Primary Works

Ockeghem, Johannes. *Collected Works*. Edited by Dragan Plamenac and Richard Wexler. 3 vols. New York, 1947.
Ockeghem, Johannes. *Masses and Mass Sections*. Edited by Jaap van Benthem. Utrecht, Netherlands, 1994–.

Secondary Works

Picker, Martin. *Johannes Ockeghem and Jacob Obrecht: A Guide to Research*. New York, 1988.
Vendrix, Philippe, ed. *Johannes Ockeghem: Actes du XLe Colloque international d'études humanistes, Tours, 3–8 février 1997*. Paris, 1998.

MARTIN PICKER

OECOLAMPADIUS (Johannes Huszgen; 1482–1531), German humanist, clergyman, editor and translator of church fathers. The son of a citizen of Weinsberg (Swabia), related on his mother's side to a leading family of Basel, Oecolampadius attended the Latin school in Heilbronn and studied at the University of Heidelberg (1499–1506). Additional studies in Bologna and later in Tübingen and Basel led him into the *via antiqua* (the old way) and humanism; as a young instructor he composed a Greek grammar. Jacob Wimpheling influenced his early development; other humanists, including Wolfgang Capito, Conrad Peutinger, Willibald Pirckheimer, and Johann Reuchlin were among his earliest teachers and associates. After serving as a tutor for the sons of Elector Philip of the Palatinate, he assumed a position as preacher in Weinsberg in 1510, apparently following ordination. Moving to Basel in 1515, he assisted Erasmus with the editing of Jerome and of the Greek New Testament, offering particularly his expertise in the Hebrew language. The two broke over Oecolampadius's rejection of Erasmus's assertion of the freedom of the will against Luther.

Oecolampadius received a doctorate in theology from the University of Basel in 1518 and served as the cathedral preacher at Augsburg (1518–1520), where he continued his Hebrew studies and translation of patristic texts into German and Latin. These scholarly activities continued during his short stay in the Brigittine monastery in Altomünster (1521–1522). After brief service as chaplain for Franz von Sickingen, the military leader of the imperial knights, he returned to Basel in 1523. As a professor in the Bible, alongside Conrad Pellikan, Oecolompadius lectured on Isaiah, Jeremiah and Lamentations, Eze-

kiel, Daniel, most of the minor prophets, Job, and Genesis, the gospels of Matthew and John, and the epistles to the Romans and Hebrews. The Wittenberg faculty regarded his commentary on 1 John as part of its "commentary series" (1524). In 1523 he also assumed pastoral duties at the Church of St. Martin and worked on behalf of ecclesiastical reform in the city, which ended when he became pastor of the Münster in 1529. In 1528 he married Wibrandis Rosenblatt, the widow of his fellow Basel Reformer Ludwig Keller; they had three children, one of whom survived childhood. His widow married Wolfgang Capito and, after Capito's death, Martin Bucer.

In 1520 Oecolampadius had begun corresponding with Martin Luther and writing tracts that promoted the Wittenberg Reformer's understanding of the justification of the sinner by grace through faith in Christ. Oecolampadius wrote a number of significant presentations of Reformation doctrine. Reactions to certain elements of medieval dogma and practice differed, however, among the Reformers, and Oecolampadius did not share Luther's understanding of the sacraments. In the controversy between Huldrych Zwingli in Zurich and Luther regarding the real presence of Christ's body and blood in the Lord's Supper, Oecolampadius based his support of Zwingli on a citation from Tertullian, which defined Christ's reference to his body in the Lord's Supper as a *"figura corporis"* (representation of the body). He again defended Zwingli at the Colloquy of Marburg in 1529, where his partner in the negotiations was Luther himself.

Oecolampadius represented a reforming point of view in a public disputation with Roman Catholic representatives in Swiss Baden in 1526, where the judgment of local authorities went against him. In a similar disputation at Bern in 1528 the Reform party under the leadership of Oecolampadius, Zwingli, Capito, and Bucer won the argument. Local Anabaptists were exiled at his direction. His most important contribution to ecclesiastical practice came in his formulation of the Protestant view of church discipline (as a means of restoring sinners to salvation rather than as punishment). He proposed that the church handle discipline through a commission of four members each from the ministry, city council, and congregation. The Basel city council rejected this plan because it gave the church more independence than the council was willing to grant.

Oecolampadius's greatest scholarly contributions were in editing and translating ancient texts. His work on the New Testament was criticized, but Erasmus defended him by pointing out that he had worked in haste. He rendered a number of church fathers into Latin, including John Chrysostom, Cyril of Alexandria, Gregory of Nyssa, Basil the Great, John of Damascus, Theophylactus of Ochrida, and Gregory of Nazianzus. Oecolampadius left a legacy of church reform in Basel, significant theological treatises, and scholarly contributions to patristic studies that aided the study of the church fathers for generations.

BIBLIOGRAPHY

Rupp, Ernest Gordon. *Patterns of Reformation*. Philadelphia, 1989.

Staehelin, Ernst. *Briefe und Akten zum Leben Oekolampads*. 2 vols. Leipzig, Germany, 1927–1934.

Staehelin, Ernst. *Oekolampad-Bibliographie*. 2d ed. Nieuwkoop, Netherlands, 1963.

Staehelin, Ernst. *Das theologische Lebenswerk Johannes Oeko-lampads*. Leipzig, Germany, 1939.

ROBERT KOLB

OLIGARCHIES. Rule by oligarchy, government by a small number of wealthy men, was a common form of urban government. This model had three variants during the Renaissance period. In early Renaissance republican city-states, the Italian communes had been succeeded by new forms of government in which small numbers of men occupied key offices and moved easily between them while others were excluded. In Italy, Venice retained this model throughout the period, and Siena, Florence, Lucca, and Genoa retained a strong republican tradition until the late fifteenth and sixteenth centuries. In Germany, the oligarchical constitutions of cities such as Lübeck, Hamburg, and Frankfurt lasted from the late Middle Ages until Napoleon's arrival in 1806.

The second type of oligarchy was to be found in those city-states, mostly in Italy, where the ruling group had lost power to signorial rule. It suited the new rulers of Florence, Milan, Ferrara, and Mantua to continue working with at least those members of the formerly republican oligarchy who had offered them political support. These became the new princely ruling class, closely identified with the new regime because most of their powers were dependent on its patronage. The same applied to city-states that were absorbed by larger territorial units both inside and outside Italy. Brescia, Verona, and Padua all fell to Venice during the fifteenth century, but the Venetians carefully retained existing organs of government and encouraged the cooperation of the old ruling class. Milan, on the other hand, became part of the Spanish Empire, whose rulers enhanced the privileges of members of the oligarchy by assuring them of noble status.

The final form of urban oligarchy was the most widespread and enduring of all. These were the men who ruled over urban centers within the emerging territorial states in western Europe. Here, conditions varied from one region to another, but with the exception of capital cities and viceregal centers in the Spanish Empire, urban government remained in the hands of a restricted circle of men.

From the fifteenth century the trend toward oligarchical government was intensified, both in the surviving city-states and in the towns within the territorial states. Although the range of responsibilities undertaken by urban governments grew at this time, fewer men exercised real power. Survivals of older constitutional forms that required large assemblies of privileged men, such as the Great Councils in Venice and Nice, were supplanted by smaller groups, often numbering no more than twenty or thirty, in whose hands lay major decisions and policy-making. In Venice this group was made up primarily of members of the Senate and the Council of Ten. In some cities membership in this inner group was for life. In others membership rotated among a small number of families, giving a semblance of constitutional flexibility that masked a considerable degree of continuity. Everywhere members of the oligarchy exercised a strong influence on the selection of their successors. Few members of larger governmental bodies or other outsiders could aspire to membership in these restricted groups unless they had access to considerable wealth and influential political and familial connections.

That is not to say that such oligarchies were impermeable. A distinction needs to be made between the heavily aristocratic oligarchies of Spain, Italy, and some south German cities like Nürnberg, and the more open oligarchies of northern Europe, where, as long as a town's economy remained buoyant, there were opportunities for outsiders to acquire the necessary wealth and connections to take their place. The commercial expansion of Amsterdam in the early seventeenth century enabled many new men to prosper and join the ranks of the city's regents. However, at times of commercial and industrial stagnation, especially from the early seventeenth century, largely landowning and rentier elites closed their ranks everywhere. Even English towns, whose openness has often been contrasted with the oligarchic nature of government in continental western Europe, displayed a major degree of continuity in government. Members of the Twenty-Four in Exeter, for example, were typical in the way in which their political power was based on overlapping networks of family links, trading partnerships, and the exercise of other important offices.

The response of urban oligarchies to threats to their unity, especially during the religious and political changes of the sixteenth century, varied. One thing remained constant, however; no matter how strong the religious or political pressures that threatened to end the political power of an oligarchy through internal dissension, the end result was invariably a partial change in the composition of the oligarchy rather than any kind of radical revolution from below. In some towns, such as Münster, strong attempts were made to reduce the impact of religious diversity on the unity of the oligarchy. Faced by an external political threat from the prince-bishops of Münster, the Catholic majority on the council joined forces with Lutheran councillors to assert the city's independence. Even in cities like Lübeck, where victory for Lutheran councillors was followed by an exodus from the city of papal supporters, and a temporarily radical shift in policy, the continuity in council membership before and after the crisis was striking.

The growth in centralized power in the territorial states was matched by a corresponding decline in urban autonomy. The persistence of oligarchic government in the face of this overall loss of political power owed much to the capacity of territorial rulers to incorporate members of urban oligarchies into broader systems of high status. The close association between leading urban families and the landed nobility was one that had characterized urban elites in southern Europe since the Middle Ages. It was only from the later sixteenth century, though, that their northern counterparts began to follow suit, combining land acquisition with the accumulation of feudal rights and titles intended to raise their social profile. Opportunities to mix with members of rural elites at the university, at princely courts, and in state office did much to encourage a partial fusion of the two, although many of the former retained close links with their towns of birth.

See also articles on individual cities and city-states mentioned in this entry.

BIBLIOGRAPHY

Amelang, James. *Honored Citizens of Barcelona: Patrician Culture and Class Relations, 1490–1714.* Princeton, N.J., 1987.
Burke, Peter. *Venice and Amsterdam: A Study of Seventeenth-Century Elites.* London, 1974.
Cowan, Alexander. *Urban Europe, 1500–1700.* New York, 1998.
Cowan, Alexander. *The Urban Patriciate: Lübeck and Venice, 1580–1700.* Cologne, 1986.
Diefendorf, Barbara. *Paris City Councillors in the Sixteenth Century.* Princeton, N.J., 1983.
Ferraro, Joanne. *Family and Public Life in Brescia, 1580–1650.* Cambridge, U.K., 1993.
Friedrichs, Christopher R. *The Early Modern City, 1450–1750.* New York, 1995.
Hsia, R. Po-chia. *Society and Religion in Münster, 1535–1618.* New Haven, Conn., 1984.
Reinhard, Wolfgang. *Power Elites and State Building.* Oxford, 1996.

ALEXANDER COWAN

OPERA. *See* **Music,** *subentry on* **Opera.**

OPTICS. The science of optics is concerned with the geometrical study of light in reflection and refraction; it also deals with the nature of light and theories of human vision. Originating in antiquity with Euclid, it developed through the Middle Ages and began to assume its modern form by the end of the Renaissance.

Early Treatises. The most influential medieval writer on optics was the tenth-century Arab thinker Abu Ali al-Hasan ibn al-Haytham, known in the Latin West as Alhazen (965–1039). He integrated the anatomical, physical, and mathematical approaches from the ancient Greeks and developed a theory of vision in which he suggested that each point or area on the surface of a body radiates in all directions and light enters the eye through refraction. His major work was translated into Latin as *De aspectibus* during the twelfth century and disseminated in the Latin West during the thirteenth by the English Franciscan Roger Bacon. Around 1270 Bacon's follower Witelo wrote *Perspectiva*, primarily a reworking of Ibn al-Haytham's *De aspectibus*. It also used Ptolemy's *Optics* and the works of other Arab writers and twelfth- and thirteenth-century Latin authors.

Early Renaissance optics neglected these developments in medieval optics and returned instead to the writings of ancient authors. For example, the Carthusian monk Gregorius Reisch (c. 1467–1525) produced an encyclopedic work, *Margarita philosophica* (Philosophical pearl) that went through at least fourteen editions in the hundred years after its appearance in 1486. Reisch followed the optical tradition of the ancient Stoics that considered vision as a product of a series of images that moves from the visible object to the eye of the viewer.

A notable work from the mid-sixteenth century was *Photismi de lumine et umbra* (Illuminations concerning light and shadow, 1575) by Francesco

Maurolico (1494–1575), a Benedictine monk and mathematician at Messina. *Photismi* was primarily a review of the science of optics in his time. Maurolico discussed the extent of illumination obtained with rays of different inclination, shadows, the passage of light through a hole, and mirrors of all kinds—plane and spherical, concave and convex, cylindrical and pyramidal. He proposed a geometrical theory of the camera obscura and discussed the refracting properties of the crystalline humor, though he erred in seeing it as the source of vision. He further described the causes of myopia and hypermetropia. Not published until 1611, Maurolico's *Photismi* consequently had little effect on the groundbreaking developments of the first decade of the seventeenth century.

Optics and Renaissance Art. The relationship between vision and the plastic arts gave artists a reason to inquire into optics. Piero della Francesca (c. 1416–1492) based *De prospectiva pingendi* (On the perspective of painting, c. 1472), on Leon Battista Alberti's *De pictura* (On painting, 1435; an Italian translation, *Della pittura,* appeared in 1436), a codification of the geometry of linear perspective. However, Piero went further to explore the optics of perspective. He used Euclid's *Optics* to provide a geometrical foundation, but concentrating on the intersection of the visual pyramid relative to the size of the object. He attempted to establish geometrical laws showing how the apparent size of an object corresponds to its distances from the human eye and the pyramid intersection.

The notebooks of Leonardo da Vinci (1452–1519) contain his musings on vision and the eye. Leonardo believed that light radiated from the object viewed in all directions and spread like the waves caused by dropping a stone into a pond. The rays move in straight lines and form pyramids through which it enters the pupil of the eye and then forms another pyramid that is directed through the lens and to the optic nerve. Leonardo also studied the varying diameter of the pupil and related the variation to the intensity of light. He compared the eye to a camera obscura both in his notebooks and in a treatise on the eye. Leonardo's work, though suggesting important advances in optics, was never published and not studied until the end of the eighteenth century.

Major Advances. The impetus to major advances in optics during the Renaissance came from the collaboration between Petrus Ramus (1515–1572) and Friedrich Risner (d. 1580). The result was Risner's publication of *Opticae thesaurus* (Thesaurus of optics, 1572), a single-volume edition of both Ibn al-Haytham's *De aspectibus* and Witelo's *Perspectiva.* This was the first printed edition of *De aspectibus* and was produced from two manuscripts that Ramus had discovered. Risner added citations and subdivided the book into propositions. Although *Perspectiva* had already been printed twice before, Risner's edition was a substantial improvement because he prepared it by comparing the texts of several manuscripts. He also redrafted the figures and added citations to corresponding propositions from Ibn al-Haytham's work. Thus, two important works on optics became available and changed the direction future discussion would take.

Another influential work was *Magia naturalis* (Natural magic), a collection of secrets of nature in the tradition of Renaissance Neoplatonism by the humanist scholar Giambattista della Porta (c. 1535–1615). The second edition, published in 1589, included a section on refraction. This was expanded in *De refractione* (On refraction, 1593). In these works he described experiments in which he juxtaposed concave and convex lenses, which proved important in the development of the telescope. Della Porta was also the first to report about the addition of a concave lens to the aperture in the camera obscura. He provided a geometrical explanation of the refracting properties of the lenses. Moreover, by comparing the camera obscura to the pupil in the eye, he provided an easily understood proof that the source of visual images was outside the eye.

The optical studies of the astronomer Johannes Kepler (1571–1630) laid the foundation of modern geometrical optics. His *Ad Vitellionem paralipomena, quibus astronomiae pars optica traditur* (Supplement to Witelo, in which the optical part of astronomy is handed down) was published in 1604. As the title suggests, Kepler's starting point was the optics of Ibn al-Haytham and Witelo. He also followed Della Porta in understanding the relationship of vision to the camera obscura. But Kepler went much further than his predecessors. In the first part of his work Kepler wrote about the nature of light and its relationship to color, reflection and mirrors, and refraction. He described a process of vision whereby light rays from the visible object enter the eye and how an inverted image is imprinted on the retina. Kepler thus established the geometrical mechanism of vision, was the first to understand the function of the retina, and came close to formulating a law of refraction. His chapters on astronomy dealt with the measurement of light intensity, parallax, and refraction.

Optical Devices. Roger Bacon in *Opus maius* (Major work, 1267) suggested that magnifying lenses could be used to correct the presbyopia that comes with the aging process. The Dominican Alessandro della Spina (d. 1313) is reported in a contemporary chronical as the first to make eyeglasses. In the middle of the fifteenth century concave lenses were commonly used to correct for myopia. By 1500 the use of lenses to improve vision was widespread through Europe, but they were the work of craftspeople and unrelated to writings on optics.

Spyglasses made from a combination of two lenses as suggested by Della Porta were first reported in the Netherlands in 1608, but they were of limited value because they could only magnify threefold. The next year Galileo Galilei started experimenting with his own version and succeeded in constructing an instrument that could magnify thirty times. In 1610 he published *Sidereus nuncius* (The sidereal message or messenger) describing what he saw when he viewed the sky through his telescope: mountains and valleys of the moon, four satellites around Jupiter, a Milky Way composed of individual stars, and new fixed stars.

Reactions to Galileo's discoveries were mixed. Francesco Sizi, a Florentine knight, wrote *Dianoia astronomica, optica, fisica* (Astronomical, optical, and physical thought, 1611), which attempted to combat the implications of Galileo's report by denying the reality of anything seen through a telescope. On the other hand, Kepler responded with *Dissertatio cum nuncio sidereo* (Conversation with the sidereal messenger, 1610), a strong endorsement of the capabilities of the telescope and the reality of Galileo's observations. Shortly thereafter Kepler published *Dioptrice* (1611), the first application of the science of optics to lenses.

The Emerging Science. The Jesuit scholar François d'Aguilon (1546–1617) organized the teaching of the exact sciences in Belgium, leading to his composition of a textbook on optics that synthesized the work of Euclid, Ibn al-Haytham, Witelo, and Kepler. It was intended to have three parts, but only the first, on the way the eye perceives objects, was completed. The book, *Opticorum libri sex* (Six books of optics), was published in 1613 with six frontispieces drawn by Peter Paul Rubens. One of the drawings was of an experimental apparatus that Aguilon proposed for studying variations in intensity of the light according to variations in distance and comparing lights of different intensities, a precursor to the photometer.

The law of refraction of light rays was then formulated by the Dutch mathematician Willebrord Snel (1580–1626) around 1621. His work was contained in a manuscript that was never published and that subsequently disappeared, but its existence was confirmed by the Dutch physicist Christian Huygens and others. The law was first published by René Descartes in his *Dioptrique* (1637), but it is possible that Descartes got the law from Snel because in *Dioptrique* the law is stated without experimental proof and Descartes visited Leiden both while Snel was living there and after Snel died.

See also **Scientific Instruments; Space and Perspective.**

BIBLIOGRAPHY

Primary Works

Della Porta, Giambattista. *Natural Magick.* London, 1658. Reprint edited by Derek J. Price. New York, 1957. Translation of *Magiae naturalis* (1589).

Galilei, Galileo. *Sidereus Nuncius, or, The Sidereal Messenger.* Translated and annotated by Albert Van Helden. Chicago and London, 1989. Translation of *Sidereus nuncius* (1610).

Kepler, Johannes. *Optics.* Translated by William H. Donahue. Sante Fe, N.Mex., forthcoming. Translation of *Ad Vitellionem paralipomena, quibus astronomiae pars optica traditur* (1604).

Kepler, Johannes. *Dioptrice.* In *Gesammelte Werke*, vol. 4. Edited by Max Caspar and Franz Hammer. Munich, 1941. Modern critical edition of *Dioptrice* (1610).

Kepler, Johannes. *Kepler's Conversation with Galileo's Sidereal Messenger.* Translated and annotated by Edward Rosen. New York and London, 1965. Translation of *Dissertatio cum nuncio sidereo* (1610).

Leonardo da Vinci. *The Notebooks of Leonardo da Vinci.* Translated by Edward MacCurdy. 2 vols. New York, 1939. Reprint New York, 1958.

Secondary Works

Kemp, Martin. *The Science of Art: Optical Themes in Western Art from Brunelleschi to Seurat.* New Haven and London, 1990.

Lindberg, David C. *Theories of Vision from Al-Kindi to Kepler.* Chicago and London, 1976.

Ronchi, Vasco. *The Nature of Light: An Historical Survey.* Translated by V. Barocas. Cambridge, Mass., 1970. Translation of *Storia della luce* (1939).

SHEILA J. RABIN

ORATORY. *See* **Rhetoric; Preaching.**

ORCAGNA, ANDREA (Andrea di Cione; 1315/20–1368?), Florentine painter, sculptor, architect. Orcagna's brothers Nardo and Jacopo were also painters, and Matteo, a third brother, was a sculptor.

Early Activity (1343–1348). Orcagna (a nickname derived from *arcagnuolo*, archangel) is first mentioned in 1343, the year in which he was involved in a commission for Santa Maria Novella.

Andrea Orcagna. *Christ, Virgin, and Saints.* Altarpiece in the Strozzi Chapel in the Church of Santa Maria Novella, Florence. The saints are (to the left of Christ) Michael, Catherine, the Virgin Mary, Thomas Aquinas (kneeling and receiving the book of wisdom), (to the right of Christ) Peter (kneeling and receiving the keys), John the Baptist, Lawrence, and Paul. Painted 1357. ALINARI/ART RESOURCE, NY

At this time, or slightly later, he enrolled in the Arte dei Medici e Speziali, the guild of doctors and apothecaries in which painters also matriculated. Among his earliest surviving works are thought to be a fresco of the *Expulsion of the Duke of Athens* (1340s; Florence, Palazzo Vecchio), fragments of a fresco cycle on the *Triumph of Death* and *Hell* (1344–1345; Florence, Santa Croce), and a panel depicting the *Annunciation* (1346; private collection). In this early phase Orcagna, indebted to the art of Taddeo Gaddi and Maso di Banco, displays an interest in spatial organization, an awareness of the delicate effects of light, and a preference for figures designed with volumetric forms.

Maturity: Painting (1348–1359). From 1348 to 1352 Orcagna frescoed the choir chapel of Santa Maria Novella, Florence. Almost everything

was destroyed; decorations in the vault, the sole surviving fragments, depict busts of vigorously characterized, solid figures from the Old Testament. Although not all of the prophets were painted by Orcagna himself, at least two were executed in a style that resembles his autograph work. Shortly after the plague of 1348 his name was included in a list of Tuscany's nine best painters; the *operai* (members of the board of works) of a church in Pistoia required this information so that they could appoint a suitable painter to work on a polyptych.

Around 1350 Orcagna worked in the Baronci chapel in Santa Maria Maggiore, Florence, executing frescoes on the *Life of the Apostle Saint Thomas* (hidden behind an altar) and a triptych of the *Virgin and Child with Saints* (Amsterdam, Rijksmuseum). The stocky forms of the attendant saints from the triptych contrast with the lighter appearance of the floating

Virgin at the center of the same picture. The style of another of his works, a pentaptych (c. 1353; Florence, Accademia), comes close to the manner of the Baronci triptych. Both paintings, in fact, display a similar approach to modeling and contain frontal figures whose forms are defined by sharp outlines that clearly stand out from the gold background.

Some of the above-mentioned qualities of the Baronci and Accademia altarpieces reappear in Orcagna's most famous painting, the Strozzi altarpiece (signed 1357; Florence, Santa Maria Novella). However, the overall style of this work, commissioned by Tommaso di Rossello Strozzi in 1354, reflects the changes that took place in Orcagna's art while he designed and executed the Orsanmichele tabernacle. The Strozzi altarpiece, once criticized for the apparent flatness of its composition, is now considered to be innovative in design. Of particular importance are its frame (it helps to articulate the carefully planned pictorial space) and unified picture plane (the work has not been subdivided into compartments with saints standing in flanking panels, as in standard polyptychs). The staring Christ, in full frontal pose, is suspended in air, and the visionary quality of the scene is enhanced by the lack of space around him. The iconographic program has been carefully devised, and it focuses on the message that the church is the source of divine intercession.

Sculpture and Architecture.

In 1352 Orcagna joined the Arte dei Maestri di Pietre e Legnami (guild of stonemasons and carpenters) so that he could embark on the prestigious commission of the Orsanmichele tabernacle. This work, finished by Orcagna and collaborators in 1360, is an independent domed structure that contains a painting of the Virgin. Over a hundred reliefs and statues decorate its surfaces, and the Marian cycle culminates in the east wall with a double relief of the *Death and Assumption of the Virgin*. This section contains a lavish display of polychromatic marble and glass inlays, and the style of the carvings closely resembles the painter's contemporary work on the Strozzi altarpiece, exhibiting similarities in the volumetric figures, the well-defined contours, and the plasticity of the drapery forms.

Orcagna was involved in the building plans for Florence Cathedral, especially the area of the chancel, from 1357 into the 1360s. Furthermore, he is thought to be responsible for the idea of including the drum beneath the dome because a drum supports the dome of the Orsanmichele tabernacle. These important experiences in Florence almost cer-

tainly explain why, on 14 June 1358, he was invited to take on the role of *capomaestro* (chief master) of the masons' workshop in Orvieto Cathedral from 1359. He worked in Orvieto over a period of nine months, in which time he completed a mosaic of the *Baptism of Christ* for the cathedral facade.

Late Activity (1360s) and Reputation.

In the 1360s Orcagna is thought to have executed the fresco of the *Crucifixion* in the convent of Santa Marta outside Florence; stylistically close to this is the triptych with the *Pentecost* (Florence, Accademia). One of the painter's last known commissions dates to 15 September 1367, when the Arte del Cambio (moneychangers' guild) invited him to paint an altarpiece dedicated to Saint Matthew for Orsanmichele; on 25 August 1368 the painter became too ill to paint, and this commission was given to his brother Jacopo.

Orcagna's influence on mid-fourteenth-century Tuscan painting was considerable. The calm monumentality and solidly constructed figures of the Strozzi altarpiece affected the style of his brothers and, among others, Giovanni del Biondo and Niccolò Gerini. The term "Orcagnesque" describes, rather loosely, the oeuvre of a number of painters; their designs display the vigorous forms of frontal figures who, with intent gazes, seem to float on vertically hanging, richly patterned floor coverings.

BIBLIOGRAPHY

Boskovits, Miklòs. "Orcagna in 1357—and in Other Times." *Burlington Magazine* 113 (1971): 239–251.
Kreytenberg, Gert. *Orcagna's Tabernacle in Orsanmichele, Florence.* New York, 1994.
Offner, Richard. *A Critical and Historical Corpus of Florentine Painting.* Sect. 4, vol. 1. New York, 1962.
Padoa Rizzo, Anna. "Per Andrea Orcagna pittore." *Annali della Scuola Normale Superiore di Pisa: Classe di Lettere e Filosofia* 11, no. 3 (1981): 835–893.

FLAVIO BOGGI

ORPHANS AND FOUNDLINGS. Orphans, along with widows, were prominent among the vulnerable and helpless people who normally became the special concern of princes, governments, and the church, receiving their protection. Orphans were perceived as young people who had been born in wedlock and separated from their parents by death; the stricter charities would insist on seeing evidence to that effect before agreeing to take care of them.

Orphans commanded more respect than did foundlings or abandoned children who had been disavowed by living parents. Contemptuous names current in Renaissance Italy, such as *proietti* or *get-*

Orphans and Foundlings. Detail of a fifteenth-century fresco by Domenico de Barrolo in the foundling hospital of Santa Maria della Scala, Siena, depicts the care of foundlings, including wet-nursing, education, and marriage. ALINARI/ART RESOURCE

tatelli, meaning "castoffs" or "throwaways," signified their rejection by their embarrassed parents, their lack of family, and their consequent loss of social identity. Florence's principal foundling hospital, however, was dedicated to the Innocents, and the word stressed the difference between the sinful parents and the children who, as victims of their shameful acts, deserved public pity. But in the words of a sister in the nursing order founded by St. Vincent de Paul, speaking in Paris in 1643, "As their little bodies are doubly conceived in sin, there is reason to think that the Devil may have more power to lead them into sin and that he will do his best to send most of them to hell" (Leonard, trans., *The Conferences of St. Vincent de Paul to the Sisters of Charity,* vol. 1, p. 117).

Not all foundlings were born out of wedlock, but their origins were uncertain, and the stigma of being associated with bastards and bad parents inevitably clung to them; the foundling hospital of Santi Pro-

colo e Pietro in Bologna was unfairly known as the Bastardini. Abandonment by poor families unable or unwilling to keep all their children became increasingly common. As the English priest Gregory Martin wrote of the so-called Exposed Infants of the hospital of Santo Spirito in Rome about 1580, "these are such as the parents are either ashamed of as begotten in fornication, or not able to keepe them, and therefore but for this provision they should perish."

In principle, orphans and foundlings represented different categories of poor children, but in practice they were often admitted by the same large institutions. The Hospital of the Pietà in Venice, originally designed by Fra Pietro of Assisi to take in abandoned children, accepted a number of orphans after plague outbreaks in the 1350s and 1440s. For the Venetian Senate in 1488 it was "the refuge of many, indeed numberless, orphans and other children of destitute persons who have no means to feed them" (Grandi, in Grieco and Sandri, eds., *Ospedali e città,* p. 98). During the sixteenth century more care was taken to distinguish orphans from foundlings by setting up separate establishments for their upbringing. These so-called conservatories were sometimes attached to general hospitals and sometimes intended to stand on their own as relatively small and select institutions. To some extent attention shifted from rescuing infants to educating, or at least training, young children of impressionable ages (between three and ten in Florence during the 1540s).

Many children and adolescents who were not exactly orphans or foundlings were also in obvious need of care and protection. Parents left alone by the death of a wife or a husband's desertion would sometimes be allowed, by special arrangement, to hand over a young child to a hospital's care. From the sixteenth century there was a growing anxiety to protect the honor of the attractive daughters of irresponsible parents (called "girls in danger"), of mothers who were not abandoning so much as exploiting their children. One of Matteo Bandello's stories introduces a Greek woman of Venice who, "being anxious to escape privation, began to instruct [her daughter Cassandra] and hire her out to the person who would give her most money" (*Tutte le opere di Matteo Bandello,* vol. 1, p. 691). Rome, the model for the Catholic world, which sought to practice every conceivable form of charity, recognized the problem of *fanciulli spersi,* meaning waifs and strays, children who seemed to belong to nobody and ran wild in the streets. Some were assembled by a groom known ironically as Il Letterato (for he could not read) and organized into scraping a living as street sweepers. Certain children, too, were reclaimed by their parents from hospitals after the crisis that led to their abandonment had passed: the status of "abandoned child" was not necessarily permanent or irrevocable.

Foundlings.   Special concern for foundlings sprang from the fear that mothers of base-born children, terrified of social condemnation, might not only kill their children but also deprive them of baptism—thus taking away two lives, both temporal and eternal, when they had given only one. To provide facilities for abandoning children might seem a highly questionable policy. If parents and their agents, such as midwives, were allowed to abandon their children anonymously and were even encouraged to do so by the provision of shelves or rotating wheels at hospitals on which children could be safely deposited, there was a danger of condoning

immorality. But the practice could be defended as a necessary concession to the sinful nature of human beings, a pragmatic decision to choose a lesser evil for the sake of avoiding one infinitely greater. Unfortunately, when hospitals became overwhelmed with children abandoned on account of poverty, the death rate threatened to rise to such levels that abandonment seemed to have become a legalized form of infanticide.

Provisions for foundlings differed from country to country. In some parts of France, lords with rights of justice were entitled to inherit the goods of bastards who were born and died within their jurisdictions. This right created a reciprocal obligation to maintain them, a duty that the lord would sometimes discharge by paying a local hospital to look after them on his behalf. Such arrangements fostered the belief that foundlings, insofar as they were presumed to be illegitimate children, were not proper subjects for private charity, which ought rather to concentrate on orphans. By the early seventeenth century, two different approaches to the problem had arisen.

In England, and perhaps in most parts of Protestant Europe, there was greater reluctance to make overt provision for child abandonment, though exceptions to the rule can always be found. General hospitals or orphanages would discreetly accept foundlings but not advertise the fact or make them their speciality. With other paupers, they had a claim on parish relief. Where poor relief was financed by parish rates, there was great hostility to bastard-bearers. In England and parts of France, other measures were taken to guard against infanticide and to track down the fathers of illegitimate children, by closely watching unmarried pregnant girls and endeavoring to extract the father's name from them.

But elsewhere in Europe metropolitan hospitals received abandoned children and some orphans, not only from their own cities but from a large surrounding area, small country hospitals accepting them and passing them on to the great institution that dominated the region. The farther infants had to travel, the greater the risk of mortality. Preventive measures designed to encourage the poor to keep their children were tried in Milan, where subsidies were granted to the parents of twins and to others in extreme poverty.

Nursing and Adoption.   Institutions that cared for large numbers of infants, whether orphans or foundlings, faced the problem of finding and paying wet nurses to suckle them. Hospitals that had maternity wards would enlist the services of expectant mothers; after giving birth, they would be paid for nourishing other people's children as well as their own. It was common practice to keep abandoned children in the hospital for a couple of weeks after reception but then to send them to foster parents, often in the surrounding countryside. Complaints that nurses were poorly paid and badly supervised were legion.

Surviving children—a small proportion of the whole—were generally returned to the hospital between the ages of four and seven. Those admitted as infants, and those taken in at a more advanced age, were subsequently prepared either for absorption into society as laborers, craftsmen, domestic servants, textile workers, or housewives, or else for enlistment in the service of the hospital, perhaps for life. Apprenticeships to craftsmen, assignments to farming families, and attachments to households often led to adoption under the hospital's surveillance. Alternatively, an adoptive parent might arrange an apprenticeship with somebody else, as Antonio di Leonardo Capello dal Banco of Venice did, taking a child of the Pietà as his adopted son in 1526 and placing him with a Rialto goldsmith to be taught the trade.

Children without family were the creatures most subject to social engineering, to attempts to mold them into useful subjects complying with the demands of the society in which they lived. Educating them to a modest station in life was more common than any attempt to promote social mobility. Charities generally sought to preserve social order, striving at most to turn potential beggars into industrious artisans, potential whores into good wives (if dowries could be found to enable them to marry steady husbands). Exceptionally good prospects seemed to lie ahead of Matteo Dicomano, the Florentine child from the Innocenti whose adoptive father (c. 1450) promised to make him a gentleman, a theologian, or at the very least a merchant.

See also Childhood; Education; Hospitals and Asylums.

BIBLIOGRAPHY

Boswell, John. *The Kindness of Strangers: The Abandonment of Children in Western Europe from Late Antiquity to the Renaissance.* New York and London, 1988.

Charpentier, Jehanne. *Le droit de l'enfance abandonnée, son évolution sous l'influence de la psychologie (1552–1791).* Paris, 1967.

Gavitt, Philip. *Charity and Children in Renaissance Florence: The Ospedale degli Innocenti, 1410–1536.* Ann Arbor, Mich., 1990.

Grieco, Allen J., and Lucia Sandri, eds., *Ospedali e città: L'Italia del centro–nord, XIII–XVI secolo.* Florence, 1997. Includes essays about orphans and foundlings.

Hunecke, Volker. *I trovatelli di Milano: Bambini esposti e famiglie espositrici dal XVII al XIX secolo.* Bologna, Italy, 1989. Despite its title, contains interesting material from the fifteenth and sixteenth centuries.

Pullan, Brian. *Orphans and Foundlings in Early Modern Europe.* Reading, U.K., 1988. Reprinted in *Poverty and Charity: Europe, Italy, Venice, 1400–1700.* Aldershot, U.K., 1994.

BRIAN PULLAN

ORZECHOWSKI, STANISŁAS (Stanislaus Orichovius; 1513–1566), Polish writer, polemicist, orator. Born to a noble family, Stanisłas Orzechowski was the son of an educated land official. Orzechowski went to the cathedral school in Przemyśl and then studied at the University of Cracow from 1526 to 1528. He continued his education abroad, in Vienna, Wittenberg, and Leipzig (1528–1531) as well as in Padua (1531/32–1537). After a short stay in Przemyśl in 1538, he came back to Italy, visiting Bologna and Venice, where he studied history under the supervision of Giambattista Egnazio. He also spent about a year in Rome. Studying abroad enabled Orzechowski to become familiar with the ideas of the Reformation in Germany (the circle of Martin Luther and Philipp Melanchthon) and with Italian humanism.

These experiences had such a powerful influence on him that Orzechowski took holy orders after his return to Poland sometime before 1543. He worked as a parish priest in Żurawica. At the same time, however, he publicly stood up against the celibacy of clergymen. In his work *De lege coelibatus . . . oratio* (Oration on the law of celibacy; 1547), he participated in the debate over *Baptismus Ruthenorum* (The baptism of the Ruthenians; 1544) as an advocate of the rights of the Greek Orthodox Church and the use of native languages in the liturgy. His marriage to Magdalena Chełmska in 1551, as well as his earlier support for the marriage of another Catholic priest, led Orzechowski to open conflict with the church. He was removed from his parish and temporarily deprived of his income.

By that time Orzechowski was known as a splendid orator and political writer. Already in his Latin treatise *Fidelis subditus sive de institutione regia ad Sigismundum Augustum* (The loyal subject; or, on the education of kings, to Sigismund II Augustus; 1543), he presented himself as an advocate of democracy among the nobility and also spoke against the intended marriage between the king and a Lithuanian aristocrat, Barbara Radziwiłł. His oratorical talents were also appreciated at the funeral celebrations of Sigismund I, at which Orzechowski made a speech, *Funebris oratio habita . . . ad equites Po-*

lonos in funere Sigismundi Jagiellonis (Funeral oration addressed . . . to the Polish knights at the funeral of the Jagiellon King Sigismund; 1548). His speeches concerning war against the Turks—*De bello adversus Turcas suscipiendo . . . ad equites Polonos oratio* (On undertaking war against the Turks: . . . A speech addressed to the Polish knights; 1543) and *Ad Sigismundum Poloniae regem Turcica secunda* (Second speech concerning the Turks, to King Sigismund of Poland; 1544)—made him known throughout Europe. His Latin works were also printed abroad and translated into Polish and German.

Orzechowski's radical views advocating both Catholic learning (doctrine) and political reforms to strengthen the political influence of the nobility are presented in his popular works, such as *Rozmowy albo dialog około egzekucyjnej Polskiej Korony* (Talks or dialogue about the execution of laws in Polish crown lands; 1563), *Quincunx to jest wzór Korony Polskiej* (Quincunx is the model of the Polish crown; 1564), and *Policja Królestwa Polskiego* (The policy of the kingdom of Poland; 1565). Orzechowski also wrote valuable historiographical works: *Annales Polonici ab excessu divi Sigismundi primi* (Polish annals, from the death of Sigismund I; published 1611) and *Żywot i śmierć Jana Tarnowskiego* (Life and death of Jan Tarnowski; published 1773). Both the Polish and Latin prose of Orzechowski exemplify the work of a well-educated representative of the flourishing literary culture of the Polish Renaissance.

BIBLIOGRAPHY

Barycz, Henryk. "Studia włoskie Stanisława Orzechowskiego." In *Studia z dziejów kultury polskiej.* Edited by Ksiazka Zbiorowa. Warsaw, 1949. Pages 209–231.

Starnawski, Jerzy, ed. Introduction to *Wybór pism,* by Stanisław Orzechowski. Wrocław, Poland, 1972.

Stolfi, Lanfranco. *Il rinascimento in Polonia.* Bologna, Italy, 1979. See chapter 19, pp. 273–284.

ANDRZEJ BOROWSKI

OTTOMAN EMPIRE. The Ottoman Empire, which was founded in the late thirteenth century in Anatolia by Osman I and ruled by his descendants until its dissolution at the end of World War I, evolved from a minor emirate into the vast, multicontinental empire ruled at its height in the sixteenth century by Süleyman I the Magnificent (c. 1495–1566). That evolution encompassed gradual expansion westward at the expense of the ever-diminishing Byzantine Empire. This expansion eventually resulted in the Fall of Constantinople in 1453 and the ensuing aggrandizement—through successful military actions at the expense of weak rulers of Balkan and southeast European political formations—of the kingdom of Hungary, of territories coveted by the rising Holy Roman Empire of the Habsburgs, of territorial acquisitions in the Mediterranean area, and, through consolidation and additions, of Ottoman holdings in the non-European world.

Historical Overview. Ottoman expansion into modern Iraq, Yemen, and the East African coast during the "golden age," from the Fall of Constantinople (1453) to the death of Süleyman the Magnificent (1566), was significant for the history of the Islamic world. But the importance of these developments was overshadowed by the impact of the Ottoman expansion into Europe.

The conquest of the Balkan Peninsula was virtually completed with the incorporation of Serbia (1459), Bosnia (1463), and Herzegovina (1482). Only Montenegro and Albania remained de facto independent. Morea was annexed to the Ottoman Empire in 1459, and Venice was forced to surrender Lemnos, Euboea, and Scutari in 1479. Süleyman the Magnificent pursued more ambitious goals. Belgrade fell to the Turks in 1521. The expanding Holy Roman Empire ruled by Charles V (ruled 1519–1556) and the empire of the Ottoman Turks confronted each other first in Hungary, following the destruction of the armies of King Louis II of Hungary (ruled 1516–1526) at the Battle of Mohács in 1526, then in the celebrated Ottoman siege of Vienna in 1529, which resulted in Habsburg recognition of the incorporation of most of Hungary proper, as the pashalik of Buda, into the Ottoman Empire, and of Turkish suzerainty over Transylvania by 1547. The earlier acceptance of Turkish suzerainty by rulers of the Romanian provinces of Moldavia and Wallachia, together with the consolidation of Ottoman control over the Black Sea through the conquest of Azov and the Crimea in 1475, marked the greatest territorial expansion of the empire in Europe. The Habsburg-Ottoman conflict also extended to the Mediterranean, where, as allies of France, the Turks engaged in protracted confrontations with Spanish and Venetian naval forces. Ultimately, these confrontations ended in the destruction of the Turkish fleet at the Battle of Lepanto (1571). That battle has traditionally been regarded as the beginning of the decline of the Ottoman Empire.

Ottoman Social and State Structure. Evidence of the existence and beneficial character of the *Pax Ottomanica* may be seen in the efficiency of the governmental order and the toleration of re-

Ottoman Ruler. Procession of Süleyman the Magnificent (ruled 1520–1566) through the Atmeidan (Hippodrome) in Constantinople. Woodcut after Pieter Coecke van Aelst from *Ces moeurs et fachons de faire de Turez,* 1553. THE METROPOLITAN MUSEUM OF ART, HARRIS BRISBANE DICK FUND, 1928

ligious diversity through the *millet* system. However, this contrasts with the inherently despotic nature of the political system, which may be seen as tyrannical. In reality, one may hardly speak of a governmental structure comparable to any of those of the Christian Europe of the fifteenth and sixteenth centuries, but rather of one rooted in the Muslim world with elements derived from Byzantine imperial traditions.

The Ottoman state. The central institution of the Ottoman Empire was the sultanate, in which the monarch acted as leader in battle, lawgiver, and ecclesiastical official. As supreme military commander, the sultan led his armies in the jihad (holy war) against unbelievers. As lawgiver, the sultan—in close association with the *ulema,* the theologians and jurists expert in the interpretation of the *Sharī'a* (the sacred law of Islam) and the principal representatives of Sunnite orthodoxy—became de facto the head of a legal and theological hierarchy that wielded immense power over every field of human conduct. Thus, in 1538 Süleyman the Magnificent assumed the role of caliph (successor to the Prophet).

The extraordinary powers of the sultan in this theocracy were exercised through a system of governance whose architect was Mehmed II the Conqueror (ruled 1451–1481). The fundamental law of the empire, the so-called *Kanoun Namé,* defined the peculiarities of the Ottoman social order and state structure. The sultan's power was absolute and the throne hereditary in the Ottoman ruling house. The *Kanoun Namé,* in accordance with the injunction of

the Koran, also provided for the establishment of a central council. The principal members of the imperial council—the *Divan-i-Hümanyun*—were the grand vizier, the judge advocate, the minister of finance, and the secretary of state. The grand vizier was the equivalent of a European chancellor and was expected to lead armies in the field. All these officials were personally appointed by the sultan, and they served only at his pleasure.

In provincial government no distinction was drawn between military and civilian authority. The administration of large cities or great provinces was entrusted to high-ranking officials (*pashas*), who in the European parts of the empire were granted fiefs, the so-called *çiftliks*. The *çiftliks* gradually became the dominant form of nonhereditary landholding, replacing the *timars* that were granted, also on a nonhereditary basis, to the military followers of the sultans, the so-called *sipahis* of the land.

Ottoman social structure. The institutions that most clearly distinguished the Ottoman Empire from the European political and social orders of the fifteenth and sixteenth centuries were those related to slavery and to the dual division of society. The first division distinguished Muslims from non-Muslims (*zimmi*); the second distinguished those who were connected with the state and its institutions, the so-called professional Ottomans, from the rest of the population, well over 90 percent, the so-called *reaya* (members of the flock), who could be either Muslim or *zimmi*.

One feature of the Ottoman governmental system was the sultan's exercise of absolute powers through "slaves of the Porte." The majority of the "professional Ottomans" were secured through the *devşirme*, whereby male children (ages eight to twenty) of Christian peasants were converted to Islam, enslaved, and initially used in the celebrated Janissary (infantry) corps, later for palace duties, and finally in government. In fact, aside from the *devşirme*, slavery was practiced in the Ottoman Empire through the slave trade, raids, and other means that were looked upon as reprehensible in the age of the Renaissance and Reformation. However, these slaves were not maltreated, and whereas most of them were servants or bodyguards of households, some served in the harems of sultans and lesser dignitaries, and several attained important governmental positions at both the central and regional levels.

Another distinct aspect of Ottoman rule was the tolerance of religious diversity, most clearly expressed in the *millet* system. This system of social organization according to religion was practiced before the establishment of the Ottoman Empire in Europe, and it was formalized under Mehmed II by legislation creating two formal *millets*, the Orthodox and the Armenian, in addition to the unofficially recognized Jewish *millet*. The largest was the Orthodox, which like the others was headed by the leader of the religious community. The patriarch of Constantinople had full ecclesiastical powers and jurisdiction over his flock. He was also responsible for the collection of taxes and was entrusted with a great number of administrative and legal functions in addition to his ecclesiastical one. In this he was assisted by a smaller bureaucracy. The Jewish *millet*, headed by the chief rabbi of Istanbul, and the Armenian *millet*, headed by the Gregorian patriarch of Istanbul, enjoyed rights and privileges similar to those of their Orthodox counterpart.

Military character of the state. Whereas the *millet* system was entirely compatible with Islamic religious precepts, it was also established for pragmatic political purposes related to the securing of the allegiance of the *zimmis*, and to the corollary interests of the Ottoman state. For, in the last analysis, this fundamental aspect of the *Pax Ottomanica* was closely related to the ultimately military character of that state. An overwhelmingly Christian agricultural society was subject to a political and economic order far more tolerant than that prevalent before the Turkish conquest and even, in many ways, than that in parts of eastern Europe not Ottoman-dominated. As for the Jews, the Ottoman Empire welcomed persecuted Iberian Jews for their commercial and diplomatic expertise and for their contacts with the outside world.

Nonetheless, the positive elements of Ottoman governance were invariably and fundamentally connected with the military objectives legitimized by the jihad and with the powers and interests of conservative Sunnite Islamic ideology. Thus, the theocratic Ottoman political and social orders ultimately depended on military successes that allowed the reconciliation of potentially conflicting interests of its inhabitants. In the fifteenth and sixteenth centuries, changes in the European political, military, and economic system exposed and exploited the inherent weaknesses of the Ottoman political, military, and economic system. The *Pax Ottomanica* disintegrated and the decline of the empire became apparent.

The Ottoman Impact on European History and Civilization. It has been suggested that the age of geographic exploration with the corollary shifting of the European trade routes from East to West was precipitated, if not caused, by the Ottoman conquest of Constantinople and control of the eastern Mediterranean and the Near East. There is little basis for taking that presumption at face value, although it is evident that the predominant role played by Venice and Genoa in eastern Mediterranean trade was undermined by the Turks' presence in Constantinople, control of the Straits, and expansion of maritime power in the Mediterranean.

The Turkish landing at Otranto in 1480 was less ominous than originally perceived, but it increased western apprehensions over the intentions and capabilities of "the Infidel." The Turkish conquest of most of the Balkan Peninsula and the establishment of Turkish suzerainty over the Romanian provinces elicited no response from Catholic Europe. However, the Ottoman campaigns against Hungary, Styria, and Carniola led to centuries-long military confrontations between the Habsburgs and the Ottomans.

This conflict led to the Ottoman-French alliance of the 1530s, and the "Turkish menace" assumed a European significance far beyond the hypothetical threat of an expansion of the holy war beyond the borders of the medieval Hungarian kingdom. But those fears were more imaginary than real and, in fact, were promoted to serve the Habsburgs' more ambitious imperial goals, which were merely delayed by the Turkish presence in Hungary and Transylvania.

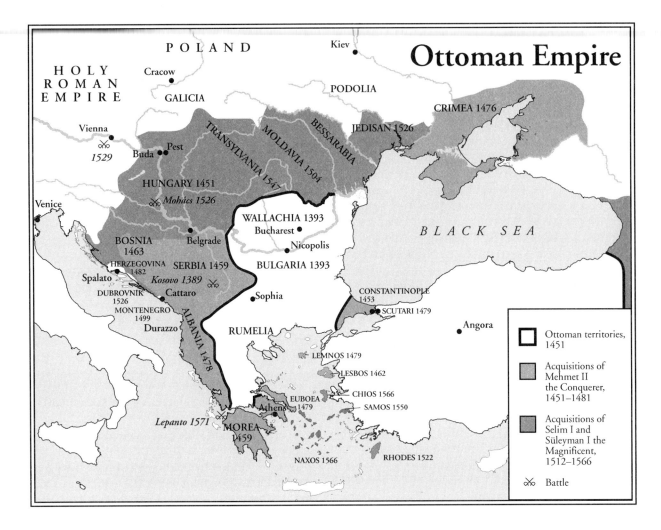

The confrontation between Ottoman and Habsburg imperialism may have contributed to the legal recognition of Protestantism in 1555, as the Habsburgs' need for Protestant support was a major factor in avoiding military conflict with Martin Luther's followers. Furthermore, Ottoman tolerance of religious diversity may have contributed to the evolution of Lutheranism, Calvinism, and Unitarianism in Transylvania. Beyond this, the Ottoman relationship with the Renaissance in Europe was of minor significance.

To the Islamic Ottoman rulers, the Shi'a-Sunni controversy was infinitely more significant than European ideological and religious conflicts in the fifteenth and sixteenth centuries. As the sultans aligned themselves with the cause of Sunnite orthodoxy, they rejected those elements in the intellectual heritage of Islam that might have enabled them to understand or adapt to the cultural and economic changes taking place in Europe. Thus, all ideological controversy, all innovative ideas or departure from

the past in all aspects of political, social, and economic life were suppressed.

European writers generally condemned the Ottoman conquest as brutal and depicted the invaders as barbaric, although some, like Luther and Erasmus, saw them as the "scourge of God" and called for repentance and reformation rather than military action. The advanced administrative-governmental structures in the Ottoman Empire, its tolerance of religious and ethnic diversity, and its cultural and scientific achievements went largely unappreciated. More often than not, the Turk was depicted as the ultimate threat to Christianity and to civilization as such. Thus, Cardinal Bessarion (1403–1472) viewed the conquest of Constantinople as the work of "the fiercest of wild beasts" and as a prelude to similar actions against Italy, while an endless number of inflammatory pamphlets by various authors stressed the Turkish threat and the need for war against "the Infidel." However, many humanists admired the efficiency of the Turkish government, against which they contrasted the disorder of the European west. Even Luther agreed with this view, but he also viewed the Turk, just as he did the pope, as anti-Christ.

The Turkish threat was exploited for political purposes and was not persuasive in rallying crusades or another anti-Turkish actions on the part of western Christendom. Realistic observers of the workings of the Ottoman Empire—such as the Venetian ambassadors to Constantinople, the Flemish diplomat Ogier de Busbecq (1522–1592), Charles V's special ambassador to Istanbul, the Italian humanist Paolo Giovio (1483–1552), and the French political philosopher Jean Bodin (1530–1596) in his celebrated *Six livres de la république* (Six books of the commonwealth; 1576)—minimized the presumed threat by providing accurate descriptions of the Ottoman order.

Eventually, as the Renaissance bypassed the Ottoman Empire, the Turk and his "threat" became increasingly remote and of little concern to Renaissance and Reformation Europe as the sixteenth century neared its end.

See also **Austria; Crusade; Europe, Idea of; Habsburg Dynasty; Hungary; Islam; Mediterranean Sea; Venice.**

BIBLIOGRAPHY

Ascher, Abraham, Tibor Halasi-Kun, and Béla K. Király, eds. *The Mutual Effects of the Islamic and Judeo-Christian Worlds: The East European Pattern.* New York, 1979.

Braude, Benjamin. *Christians and Jews in the Ottoman Empire.* New York, 1982.

Coles, Paul H. *The Ottoman Impact on Europe.* London, 1968.

Finkel, Caroline. *The Administration of Warfare: The Ottoman Military Campaigns in Hungary, 1593–1606.* Vienna, 1988.

Fischer-Galati, Stephen A. *Ottoman Imperialism and German Protestantism, 1521–1555.* Cambridge, Mass., 1959.

Fleischer, Cornell H. *Bureaucrat and Intellectual in the Ottoman Empire: The Historian Mustafa Âli (1541–1600).* Princeton, N.J., 1986.

Gibb, Hamilton A. R., and Harold Bowen. *Islamic Society and the West.* London, 1957.

Inalcik, Halil. *The Ottoman Empire: The Classical Age, 1300–1600.* New York, 1973.

Schwoebel, Robert. *The Shadow of the Crescent: The Renaissance Image of the Turk, 1453–1517.* New York, 1967.

Shaw, Stanford J., and Ezel Kural Shaw. *History of the Ottoman Empire and Modern Turkey.* New York, 1976.

Sugar, Peter F. *Southeastern Europe under Ottoman Rule, 1354–1804.* Seattle, Wash., 1977.

STEPHEN FISCHER-GALATI

OVID (Publius Ovidius Naso; 43 B.C.–A.D. 17), Roman poet. The descendant of an old family of knights, Ovid held minor judicial posts, but abandoned public life for poetry. He offended the emperor Augustus (the exact nature of his indiscretion is not known) and was exiled to Tomis on the Black Sea coast in A.D. 8. He is the author of *Metamorphoses,* a collection of mythological stories in hexameters; amatory elegies (the semiautobiographical *Amores* and *Heroides,* laments of mythical heroines, cast in letter form); *Ars amatoria* (The art of love), facetious advice on seduction, *Remedia amoris* (Remedies for love), a mock recantation; and the poetical calendar *Fasti* (incomplete). In exile he wrote *Tristia* (Sorrows), *Ibis* (a curse against an unnamed enemy), and *Epistulae ex Ponto* (Letters from the Black Sea).

Ovid's fame in the twelfth and thirteenth centuries (the *aetas Ovidiana*) rested on his love poetry and *Metamorphoses*. Petrarch had his own text but condemned Ovid as wanton and thought his *Ars* rightly caused his exile. Giovanni Boccaccio, who used Ovid's love stories for the *Decameron,* praised them in the *Filocolo* as a "holy book that showed how to kindle the sacred fires of Venus in cold hearts." Chaucer too saw him as a love poet, "Venus' clerk Ovide," drawing on *Heroides* for the *Legend of Good Women* and on *Metamorphoses* for the *House of Fame,* the tale of Ceyx and Alcyone in the *Book of the Duchess,* and the crow's narrative in the "Manciple's Tale."

In France *Remedia* had long been a schoolbook, and *Metamorphoses* was popular in the moralized paraphrase and commentary *Ovidius Moralizatus* of Pierre Bersuire (d. 1362), who offered, for example, four allegorizations of Daedalus and Icarus: historical, moral (Daedalus was the sinner imprisoned by the devil Minos), domestic (boys should obey their fathers), and religious (Daedalus was God the architect and Icarus the Christian at risk of falling).

But readers were more sophisticated in the late fifteenth and sixteenth centuries. In Italy Lorenzo Valla, Marsilio Ficino, and Giovanni Pico della Mirandola adopted Daedalus's escape by flight in *Metamorphoses* as a symbol of human freedom, and humanist philology made advances in refining the text of the love poetry, as Angelo Poliziano worked correcting his manuscript from a superior text. Renaissance authors still turned to Ovid as an encyclopedic source of mythology, but he became predominantly a model of brevity, elegance, and wit, whose elegiac poetry set the style and vocabulary for neo-Latin poets. While allusions and adaptations of tales from *Metamorphoses* are found in every genre, *Heroides* (especially the Letter of Sappho) greatly influenced women authors such as Louise Labé. Conceits and precepts from the didactic love poetry appear repeatedly in Spenser, Elizabethan lyrics, and the metaphysical poets.

The editio princeps (first printed edition) appeared at Bologna in 1471. Raphaele Regio's learned commentary to his text of *Metamorphoses* (Venice, 1493; Paris, 1496; remodeled by Josse Badius in 1501, reprinted 1504, 1506, etc.) treated Ovid as an encyclopedia of mythology and history, and the "tropological" commentary to *Metamorphoses* 1.1–451 added to the edition of 1510 by the Dominican Petrus Lavinius constructed a careful parallel between Genesis and Ovid's creation myth up to the flood. All Ovid's works, even the spurious *Nux*, had been separately printed in France by 1500, and the Aldine press text of *Omnia opera* of 1502 was quickly pirated at Lyon (1503 and 1506).

But while Erasmus's friend Gilles van Delf was still moralizing his commentary on *Remedia* in 1493 (reprinted seven times before 1506), Bersuire was becoming discredited: attacked by *Epistolae obscurorum virorum* (Letters of obscure men) in 1516, mocked by Erasmus's *Praise of Folly* and by Rabelais, he would be condemned by the Council of Trent in 1559. Ovid himself became suspect in the shadow of reform. Another contemporary of Erasmus, Noel Beda, actually banned the teaching of *Heroides* at the College of Montaigu in Paris. However, Erasmus himself shows detailed knowledge of *Metamorphoses* in the early *Antibarbarus* (Antibarbarians) and cites Ovid as a source of good style in *De ratione studii* (On the method of study), just as he recommends Ovid's descriptions of places and personifications in *Metamorphoses* as a source of abundance in *De conscribendis epistolis* (On the writing of letters). In old age he wrote a commentary on *Nux* for young students.

The sixteenth century saw wide diffusion of Ovid's work in translation: French versions of *Heroides* in 1500, *Remedia* in 1509, and the first two books of *Metamorphoses* in 1532; in England Arthur Golding's influential *Metamorphoses,* the version Shakespeare knew (1565–1567). Edmund Spenser and lyric poets like George Chapman and Michael Drayton knew Ovid as a source of myth and model of technique, and John Dryden both criticized and praised him, publishing witty, elegant versions of the tale of Ceyx and Alcyone from *Metamorphoses* 11 and all of *Metamorphoses* 12. The fundamental text of all Ovid's works was established by Nicholas Heinsius's collation of some thirty-four manuscripts for his 1661 edition (Amsterdam).

Ovid also greatly influenced the visual arts: painters like Pieter Brueghel the Elder (*The Fall of Icarus*), Titian (*Rape of Europa, Bacchus and Ariadne,* the *Flaying of Marsyas*), and Peter Paul Rubens; sculptors (Giovanni Bernini's *Apollo and Daphne*); and tapestry makers.

See also **Neo-Latin Literature and Language; Poetry,** *subentry on* **Classical Poetry.**

BIBLIOGRAPHY

Anderson, William S., ed. *Ovid: The Classical Heritage.* New York, 1995.

Martindale, Charles, ed. *Ovid Renewed.* Cambridge, U.K., 1988.

Moss, Ann. *Ovid in Renaissance France.* London, 1982.

Reynolds, L. D., ed. *Texts and Transmission: A Survey of the Latin Classics.* Oxford, 1983.

Reynolds, L. D., and N. G. Wilson. *Scribes and Scholars.* 3d ed. Oxford, 1991.

Sandys, John Edwin. *A History of Classical Scholarship.* Vol. 2. Hafner, N.Y., 1958.

Stroh, Wilfred. *Ovid im Urteil der Nachwelt.* Darmstadt, Germany, 1969.

ELAINE FANTHAM

OXFORD, UNIVERSITY OF. The university at Oxford came into being in the course of the twelfth century, with the first evidence of its importance as a center of learning dating from the reign of Henry I (d. 1135). The evolution of a corporate body or *universitas* out of an inchoate community of masters was a gradual development affected by the interests of the Plantagenet dynasty. In the later years of the century the office of Master of the Schools at Oxford was established by the bishop of Lincoln, and it is almost certain that the masters had formed a corporate body by 1215. Yet well before that date, in the 1190s, Alexander Neckam, who had studied in Paris and was later to write *De natura rerum* and *Speculum speculatiorum,* was lecturing to an appreciative audience on a work of Aristotelian science still very new in the west, *De anima* (On the soul) of Avicenna, and there is other evidence of such vitality by 1200. By the latter half of the thirteenth century, with the arrival of the religious orders, the university was well established as a thriving institution. The learning of its masters carried its reputation abroad, and in the first half of the fourteenth century the schools of Oxford attained an unparalleled reputation throughout the academic world. By 1310 there were perhaps more than two thousand scholars, and although evidence suggests a later decline in numbers, the medieval university is unlikely to have fallen below fifteen hundred, the majority of whom were in the Faculty of Arts.

Government. The medieval government of the university was a broad democracy of the regent (teaching) masters, whose parliament was congregation, presided over by the chancellor. By the mid-thirteenth century the masters had won the right to elect their own chancellor. A larger body, convocation, consisting of both regents and more senior non-regents, had sole authority to promulgate statutes, but the ongoing business was done in congregation, presided over usually by the chancellor's deputy, or commissary. The university enjoyed wide immunities from secular jurisdiction along with extensive powers to regulate various trades in Oxford, all authorized by a series of royal charters. During the long reign of Henry VI (1422–1461 and 1470–1471), the university began to select nonresident chancellors from powerful lords spiritual and temporal in order to advance its interests in a political world of warring factions.

This habit led Oxford to the fateful step of courting the favor of Thomas Wolsey, cardinal archbishop of York and papal legate, by far the most powerful ecclesiastical and political figure in the realm. In 1506 the university had elected the archbishop of Canterbury, William Warham, to the chancellorship, a post he held until his death in 1532. He was an able, practical man who was prompt to give the university advice and assistance, but he was overshadowed by Wolsey. In 1514 Cambridge offered Wolsey the chancellorship, which he declined, and Oxford was quick to follow with blandishments of its own. Although Wolsey never became chancellor, he became Oxford's political mainstay, to the neglect and even humiliation of Warham.

The transformation of Oxford's government was a by-product of the organization of the Tudor regime under Thomas Cromwell, aided and abetted by the university's resistance to the Reformation. Wolsey's fall from power in 1529 deprived the university of his patronage and the kind of clear political direction it needed almost immediately with respect to the royal divorce question. Both universities were asked in February 1530 to give opinions about the validity of Henry VIII's marriage to Catherine of Aragon. At Cambridge the chancellor persuaded the senior members to refer the matter to a committee of theologians, and convocation by 9 March produced a decision in the king's favor. At Oxford a similar suggestion backed by Warham was resisted by the powerful arts faculty, and the university continued in deadlock until angry intervention by the king's agents produced the desired decision on 8 April.

The episode foreshadowed Oxford's fate under the Tudors, when its dominance of the medieval English church was surrendered to Cambridge. Oxford was also rightly suspected of being, by and large, less enthusiastic about the new religion than was its sister university. Like Cambridge, but with even more dramatic consequences, Oxford was subjected to a succession of royal visitations to enforce the religious policies of successive regimes. The result was the subversion of the ancient democracy and self-government of congregation and convocation under the reiterated batterings of the Tudor new monarchy.

A royal visitation in 1535 aimed to enforce subscription to the royal supremacy over the English church, supplant scholasticism, and establish public lectures introducing new disciplines (see below). Under Henry's successor, Edward VI, there was another visitation (1549) intended to give formal recognition to Protestantism while purging Catholic influences and to forward the renewal of the curriculum. Under Edward's successor, Mary, the Catholic cause was pressed in a counterattack of 1559 designed chiefly to undo the previous changes, and under her successor, Elizabeth I, yet another royal visitation (1559) reversed the Marian reversal. The university polity was given final form for the Tudor age by Elizabeth's appointed chancellor, Robert Dudley, earl of Leicester. Measures were introduced to ensure conformity to the Elizabethan settlement, and changes in government were designed to the same end: to ensure that, henceforth, Oxford would be Protestant and orderly. In 1570 Dudley made it clear that in the future he would effectively appoint the commissary, now called the vice chancellor, a change in title appropriate for the new and subordinate relationship of the university to the state. As chancellor, Dudley was active in regulating the ordinary business of the university, even in matters of detail. A steering committee was established to regulate the business of convocation and extinguish what Leicester called its "immoderate liberty." That committee was typically formed of a small oligarchy of heads of colleges, themselves no longer elected by the fellows but appointed by the government.

This reshaping of the ancient polity was enshrined in a comprehensive set of university statutes in 1634, formally establishing oligarchic control. They gave statutory form to the changes of Leicester's rule and further reduced the powers of congregation and convocation. A weekly meeting of the vice chancellor with the heads of colleges and halls henceforth enforced and coordinated official policy as well within collegiate walls as without. This state of affairs prevailed still in November 1640, when the meeting of the Long Parliament introduced an era of political change in which, as in 1530, Oxford associated its interests with the losing cause, and the issues of both its government and its studies were suspended for three decades.

Renaissance Influences. The advent of Italian humanism at Oxford may be identified with the gift of books to the university by Humphrey, duke of Gloucester from 1435 to 1444. He was the fourth son in the literate family of Henry IV and one of the noble patrons to whom the university had appealed for support. The gift came into a receptive environment. The fifteenth-century university was the scene of an eclectic intellectual culture, some of whose characteristics—such as a marked interest in biblical theology, patristics, and sermonizing and pastoral care—also typified much of the humanist agenda.

Duke Humphrey's benefaction was followed by those of other nobles who had studied at Oxford, such as John Tiptoft, earl of Worcester, and the powerful Henry Beaufort, bishop of Winchester. Tiptoft endowed both Oxford and Cambridge from his extensive library, gathered in Italy, to improve the quality of Latin scholarship (humanistic script enters the records at Oxford after 1450). William Grey and Richard Bole, English pupils of Guarino da Verona, left books to Balliol College, and Robert Flemming left his collection, especially important for its Greek manuscripts, to Lincoln College. These men were the predecessors of such as the better-known Thomas Linacre and William Grocyn, who returned from Italy with good Greek. Grocyn was seemingly the first to lecture on the subject, although Greek had been available at least in theory since the 1460s, when Emmanuel of Constantinople arrived to work as a scribe for the chancellor and evidently taught in the university as well. Emmanuel of Constantinople, whose origins are obscure, had been brought to Oxford by George Neville, the powerful archbishop of York and chancellor of the university.

A parallel development, the most important single instrument of curricular change, was the provision of endowed lectureships to replace the teaching of the regent masters recruited from recent graduates. This was associated with the growing importance of undergraduate colleges and appeared first at Magdalen College, founded in the last decades of the fifteenth century, where extramural lectures were provided to the university at large in moral and natural philosophy and in theology. This was followed closely by the endowment of readerships in theology at Oxford and Cambridge in 1497 by Lady Margaret Beaufort, the widowed mother of Henry VII. Such efforts were favored as instruments of policy by the governments of Henry VIII and Edward VI, the greatest emphasis being on the establishment of public lectures in colleges. Two new Oxford colleges were of paramount importance: Corpus Christi (1517), the foundation of Richard Foxe, bishop of Winchester, and Wolsey's Cardinal College (1527). At the former there was provision for public lectures in humanity (classical humanistic Latin), Greek, and theology, taught not from the *Sentences* of Peter Lombard (written 1148–1151) in the traditional fashion but from scripture.

Cardinal College as a foundation supplanted the public lectures in humanity and theology of Wolsey's earlier provision and envisaged six professorships in canon law, philosophy, theology, civil law, medicine, and humanity. Wolsey's fall prevented the realization of his scheme, but after many vicissitudes his college was reborn under royal patronage as Christ Church, where his initiatives bore fruit in the regius professorships (that is, of royal foundation) in theology, Greek, Hebrew, civil law, and medicine. Holders of these chairs were usually Oxford men, some of whom had also studied abroad, but foreigners such as Juan Luis Vives, Alberico Gentili, Peter Martyr Vermigli, and Juan de Villa Garcia were included.

Such initiatives occurred in other colleges, including the two newly founded under Queen Mary: St. John's and Trinity. The early seventeenth century saw a fresh wave of enthusiasm for new professorships. In 1619 Sir Henry Savile established chairs in geometry and astronomy; in 1621 Sir William Sedley established a chair in natural philosophy. Also in 1621 Thomas White founded one in moral philosophy, and the university was endowed with the earliest botanical garden in England. The Camden chair in (ancient) history was established in 1622. A chair in anatomy was founded by Richard Tomlins in 1624. Public lectures in Arabic began in 1625, foreshadowing the foundation of a chair by Archbishop William Laud in 1636.

Social Change. No alteration was more representative of the Renaissance than the laicization of the university and the influx of laymen to take advantage of the new studies. The first, imperfect census of the university in 1552 gives just over one thousand masters and scholars in residence, reflecting the political and religious uncertainties of the reign of Edward VI. By the early seventeenth century the same positions had risen to between two and three thousand people. With this development came stratification and distinctions of social rank—from servants and scholars to gentlemen commoners and nobles—all enshrined as much in voluminous regulations as in architectural arrangements. Accompanying this was the entirely new emphasis on strict discipline. In collegiate building, as in the statutory curriculum, outward traditionalism concealed interior change: there were now garrets for the influx of commoners, separate lodgings for heads of house now allowed to marry, common rooms for fellows, and libraries altered to replace lecterns with book presses.

The mechanics of change can convey but the meanest impression of what was involved. From Tudor Oxford came Sir Philip Sidney (killed in battle, 1586), John Donne (d. 1631), and Robert Burton (d. 1640), among writers and poets; John Jewel (d. 1571), Edmund Campion (executed, 1581), Richard Hooker (d. 1600), and William Laud (executed, 1645), among churchmen; Sir Walter Ralegh (executed, 1618), Sir Henry Savile (d. 1622), and William Camden (d. 1623), among savants and statesmen; Richard Hakluyt (d. 1616), Thomas Harriot (d. 1621), and Nathaniel Torporley (d. 1632), among scientists and mathematicians; and, in Sir Thomas Bodley (d. 1613), the creator of the greatest Renaissance library in England. In the following century the names of John Pym (d. 1643), Thomas Hobbes (d. 1679), Elias Ashmole (d. 1692), and John Locke (d. 1704) convey their own story, and that of Sir Christopher Wren (d. 1723) provides an epitome of the age. Wren's first commission, the theater completed in 1669 for Gil-bert Sheldon, was meant to remove university ceremonies from the university church. His bell stage that caps Wolsey's great Gothic tower at Christ Church forms a signature on the Renaissance in Oxford.

See also **Cambridge, University of; Universities**.

BIBLIOGRAPHY

Primary Work

Statua antiqua universitatis oxoniensis (Ancient statutes of the University of Oxford). Edited by Strickland Gibson. Oxford, 1931. The statutes promulgated by the University of Oxford prior to 1634.

Secondary Works

T. H. Ashton, ed., *The History of the University of Oxford,* vols. 2 (*Late Medieval Oxford,* edited by J. I. Catto and Ralph Evans, Oxford, 1992) and 3 (*The Collegiate University,* edited by James McConica, Oxford, 1986), contains much of relevance. In vol. 2, see especially J. I. Catto, "Theology after Wycliffism," an important account of the religious culture of the late medieval university; J. M. Fletcher, "Developments in the Faculty of Arts, 1370–1520"; M. B. Parkes, "The Provision of Books," a comprehensive account of the nature and contents of the medieval libraries in the university, including the humanist benefactions of Duke Humphrey and others; and J. I. Catto, "Conclusion: Scholars and Studies in Renaissance Oxford," a summary of the advent of humanism and the medieval university. In vol. 3, see James McConica, "The Rise of the Undergraduate College," on the evolution of college teaching and the response to new intellectual currents; Claire Cross, "Oxford and the Tudor State from the Accession of Henry VIII to the Death of Mary"; G. D. Duncan, "Public Lectures and Professional Chairs," which is more far-ranging than its title suggests and is particularly important for understanding the nature and extent of royal initiative in reforming the university's teaching; Penry Williams, "Elizabethan Oxford: State, Church, and University"; and James McConica, "Elizabethan Oxford: The Collegiate Society," which enlarges on the social dimension of the Elizabethan university. See also Roberto Weiss, *Humanism in England during the Fifteenth Century* (3d edition; Oxford, 1967) first published in 1941 and still the standard account.

James McConica

PACIOLI, LUCA (c. 1445–1517), Italian teacher and writer on mathematics. Born in Borgo San Sepolcro, Tuscany, Pacioli began his career as tutor to the sons of a rich Venetian merchant, Antonio Rompiasi, and while in Venice attended classes of mathematician Domenico Bragadino. In 1470 he spent some months in Rome, a guest of Leon Battista Alberti, and in 1475 was teaching mathematics at the University in Perugia. Around this time he was ordained as a Franciscan friar. Over the next forty years he taught mathematics throughout Italy, in the major universities and at the courts of noble patrons, particularly those of Federico da Montefeltro in Urbino and the Sforza family in Milan. One of his colleagues in Urbino was the artist and mathematician Piero della Francesca, who included Pacioli in the detail of his Montefeltro Altarpiece. A better-known painting, by Jacopo de' Barbari, shows Pacioli demonstrating a point of geometry to a young man. In Milan (1496–1499) Pacioli became a close friend of Leonardo da Vinci, advising him on mathematics and collaborating with him on a work on geometry, *De divina proportione* (On divine proportion), for which Leonardo drew the perspective illustrations.

Almost all Pacioli's published works were printed in Venice: *Summa de arithmetica, geometria, proportione et proportionalità* (1494; second edition Tuscolano, 1523), dedicated to Guidobaldo da Montefeltro, Federico's son; a Latin edition of Euclid's *Elements* (among the first printed editions; 1509); and an expanded version of *De divina proportione* (1509). Two other unpublished manuscripts exist: a book on arithmetic and algebra (1478) written for his

pupils in Perugia, from which he drew for his *Summa,* and "De viribus quantitatis," a collection of recreational problems in arithmetic and geometry. Elsewhere, Pacioli mentions a book on arithmetic and algebra dedicated to the Rompiasi brothers, an Italian translation of Euclid, and "La schifanoia," a work on games, including chess, but these have not survived.

The *Summa,* the most influential of Pacioli's books, contains over six hundred pages of closely printed Gothic type, full of common abbreviations for the time, and contains accounts of theoretical and practical arithmetic; the first printed account of algebra; a catalog of moneys, weights, and measures in many European states and cities; the first printed account of double-entry bookkeeping; and a summary of Euclid's *Elements,* followed by a variety of practical geometrical problems, many solved using algebra. The practical aspects of the *Summa* belong to the "abacus" tradition of Italian teachers of commercial arithmetic and algebra, who preserved and developed the mathematics of Leonardo Fibonacci of Pisa, whose *Liber abaci* (1202) introduced the Hindu-Arabic numerals and their operation, together with the algebra of al-Khwarizmi (c. 780–c. 850). Most wrote informal vernacular treatises on practical mathematics, and many of the same commercial and recreational problems appear in them with only minor variations; the originality is in the solutions rather than the problems themselves.

The *Summa* marks a turning point in mathematical texts, being the first such work to combine the practical tradition with the scholarly theoretical tra-

Luca Pacioli. Portrait of Pacioli teaching by Jacopo de' Barbari (c. 1440–c. 1516). GALLERIA NAZIONALI DI CAPODIMONTE, NAPLES/ALINARI/ART RESOURCE

dition of ratios, geometry, and Boethian number theory. Its aim was to make all aspects of mathematics available to everyone. Thus it represents the state of mathematics at a point just before the discovery of a general solution to the cubic equation inspired the strides that were made in algebra in the following century. Italian algebraists such as Gerolamo Cardano, Niccolò Tartaglia, and Rafael Bombelli acknowledge their debt to the *Summa,* and many sixteenth-century mathematical treatises are modeled on it.

In the *Summa,* Pacioli demonstrated a discerning understanding of algebra, selecting the most effective techniques of his predecessors, such as the use of two unknowns in an equation, and abandoning others, such as the practice of supplying a large number of solutions to special case equations, preferring instead to look at the structure behind them. He competently manipulated equations of high degree and was among the first to accept a negative solution to an equation. He showed occasional originality. For example, he is the first known to have added a constant to each side of an equation in order to factorize, a technique that Cardano used advantageously, and he was the first to give a general formula for the solution of a compound interest problem. Many problems from earlier abacus treatises are found in the *Summa,* typically with a different solution, either a correction or with an algebraic method instead of an arithmetic one.

Always an enthusiastic teacher, Pacioli made his contribution to mathematics by combining its different traditions and presenting them together in a form that enabled the subject to be absorbed and further developed by his sixteenth-century successors.

BIBLIOGRAPHY

Brown, R. Gene, and Kenneth S. Johnston. *Pacioli on Accounting.* New York, 1963. For Pacioli's place in accounting.

Franci, Raffaello, and Laura Toti Rigatelli. "Towards a History of Algebra from Leonardo of Pisa to Luca Pacioli." *Janus* 72 (1985): 17–82. Useful survey article.

Jayawardene, S. A. "Luca Pacioli." In *Dictionary of Scientific Biography.* Edited by Charles Coulston Gillispie. Vol. 10. New York, 1974. Pages 269–272.

Rankin, F. K. C. "The Arithmetic and Algebra of Luca Pacioli (c. 1445–1517)." Ph.D. diss., University of London, 1992.

Taylor, R. Emmet. *No Royal Road: Luca Pacioli and His Times.* Chapel Hill, N.C., 1942. A lively but unreliable narrative.

FENELLA K. C. SMITH

PADUA, UNIVERSITY OF. The university of Padua was the most famous university of the Renaissance. A good university during the Middle Ages,

Padua reached its zenith during the fifteenth and sixteenth centuries, when its scholarly innovations and professors made it the European leader in research and teaching. Many well-known Italian and non-Italian figures studied at Padua. In the century and a quarter between Pietro Pomponazzi's appointment in 1488 and Galileo Galilei's departure in 1610, the University of Padua had one of the most glorious periods of any university at any time in history.

Origins to 1509. The University of Padua began with a migration of teachers and students from Bologna in 1222. In 1262 the government of the free commune of Padua guaranteed the privileges of students and professors and agreed to pay the salaries of professors of canon and civil law. Pope Urban IV granted papal recognition in 1264 by affirming that the doctors of the schools might examine students for degrees and that the bishop would confer degrees on successful candidates. In effect, the pope chartered the University of Padua. The communal government of Padua, later the Carrara family, which ruled Padua from 1318 to 1405, supported and guided the university. By the late fourteenth century, the University of Padua boasted some well-known scholars and students.

In 1405 the Republic of Venice conquered Padua. It incorporated the city into the Venetian state and took control of the university. This change in political leadership ushered in the greatest era of the university. From the beginning the Venetian overlords made it clear that they would strongly support the university. The Venetian government decreed that Padua would be the only university in the state. It ordered all the Republic's subjects desiring university degrees to study at Padua under pain of a fine of five hundred ducats, although the law was not rigorously enforced. Most important, the Venetian government appointed very able scholars to the faculty.

In the course of the fifteenth century the Venetian government developed a system of financial support for the university. Like other Italian governments, Venice believed that the town hosting a university should bear the costs. Most of the expenses of the university were met by two taxes levied on the people of the town and territory of Padua: a tax to be paid by the owners of vehicles and a head tax. The government also diverted some tax revenues from other towns in the Venetian state to the expenses of the university.

The first surviving roll, that of 1422–1423, showed that Padua had sixteen professors for arts and medicine, eleven for law, and two teaching students. This made it fourth in faculty size, behind Bologna, Pavia, and Perugia, among Italian universities at the time. The faculty grew to at least forty professors in the 1430s.

Foundations of Greatness. The university experienced an enrollment crisis shortly after the middle of the fifteenth century, as the number of students dropped from the normal eight hundred to only three hundred. The Venetian government responded with a series of measures to strengthen the university. It added professorships, often providing three concurrent professors (professors lecturing on the same text at the same hour), which offered more instruction and stimulated competition. It exempted all the professors except the holders of the most junior professorships from the traditional student vote of approval. And if the students voted against someone the government preferred, it overruled the students.

The government severely restricted localism in university appointments by forbidding Venetian nobles and original citizens (a legal caste just below the nobility conferring certain privileges) from holding professorships at Padua. It also restricted the number of Paduans who might hold university professorships; in any group of three concurrent professors, only one might be a Paduan. The Venetian legislation was a remarkable departure from the usual Renaissance practice of staffing the faculty with local men, often at the expense of quality. By contrast, the Venetian government habitually appointed distinguished scholars from beyond its borders to its major professorships. Most important, the Venetian government raised the salaries of many of its professors and recruited good scholars from other universities.

The measures of the last forty years of the fifteenth century laid the foundations for the brilliance of the next century. The University of Padua filled the key positions in canon law, civil law, medical theory, and natural philosophy with distinguished scholars drawn from the entire peninsula of Italy and beyond. It also kept them filled, thus avoiding the extended vacancies that drove away students.

Padua had sixty professors in 1500–1501: fourteen professors of canon law, seventeen for civil law, twelve for medicine (six for medical theory, four for medical practice, and two for surgery), four professors of natural philosophy, two moral philosophers, four logicians, two humanists, two theologians, two metaphysicians, and a professor for mathematics, astronomy, and astrology. Many of these were major scholars such as the natural philosopher Pietro Pomponazzi (1462–1525), who obtained a doctorate in arts at Padua in 1487, then taught at Padua from 1488 to 1509, with the exception of three years of private study from 1496 to 1499.

Until the end of the fifteenth century, professors rented lecture rooms in various parts of the city, with some financial help from the government. In 1493 the Venetian government acquired a large building called *Hospitium bovis* (Hotel of the ox) in the center of the city to be used for law lectures. The Venetian government made extensive renovations, which continued through the following century and beyond, in order to make the building more suitable for teaching. In 1530 arts and medicine professors also began to teach there. A permanent anatomical theater was added in 1594. Now called the Palazzo del Bò, the building still houses the offices of the rector and the central administration of the university, and it hosts doctoral examinations.

Closure from 1509 to 1517.

When the Venetian army suffered a crushing defeat at the Battle of Agnadello (14 May 1509) at the hands of a coalition of enemies, the leading citizens of Padua threw off Venetian rule and welcomed imperial forces into the city. Professors and students fled, and the university closed down. Paduan independence lasted only until Venetian troops recaptured the city in mid-July 1509. The Venetians hanged a professor of canon law, a native Paduan, as a traitor because he held high civic office during the imperial occupation, and they meted out lesser penalties to two other professors. But the university remained closed, except for a handful of lectures and a few degrees conferred.

The Venetians finished reconquering their mainland state in early 1517, then formally reopened the university in November 1517. It began with a skeleton faculty of nineteen professors, mostly second-rank figures. The university rebuilt its faculty over the next few years until it reached the former figure of about sixty, divided between twenty-six legists and thirty-four professors of arts, medicine, and theology.

As it rebuilt the university faculty, the Venetian Senate increasingly relied on three of its members for advice. Senate documents began to refer to the trio as "Reformers of the University" (*Riformatori dello Studio di Padova*). In the following decades the trio became an elected commission of senior Venetian nobles who oversaw all aspects of the university, including appointments, salaries, and curriculum.

Medical Studies.

Padua was the leading university of Europe from about 1525 to about 1610. Indeed, few universities at any time in history have contributed as much to learning as did Padua in those years.

The University of Padua probably had its greatest impact on the research and teaching in medicine. Padua was the locale for what is sometimes called "the medical Renaissance of the sixteenth century." In December 1537 the Venetian Senate appointed Andreas Vesalius of Brussels (1514–1564) professor of surgery and required him to teach anatomy "with the obligation to dissect human bodies." Between 1537 and 1543, when he left to become one of the physicians at the court of Emperor Charles V, Vesalius revolutionized the understanding of the human body. He made the study of anatomy a far more important part of medical education than it had ever been before. Other professors of anatomy at Padua and other Italian universities followed Vesalius's lead and made numerous anatomical discoveries. Some of them gave their names to parts of the human body that their research highlighted. For example, "fallopian tubes" are named for Gabriele Fallopio (1523–1562), one of Vesalius's successors as professor of surgery and anatomy at Padua.

The University of Padua established the first continuing professorship of simples in 1532. The term "simple" came from the classical Latin adjective *simplex, simplicis,* meaning undivided, then acquired the meaning of medicinal plant in the Middle Ages. The professorship was for the study of the medicinal properties of plants, what might be called medical botany or pharmacology. Earlier medical professors had included limited discussion of simples as part of medical theory; the subject now had an independent existence in the curriculum. Most other Italian universities quickly followed Padua's lead.

In June 1545 the Venetian Senate authorized construction of a botanical garden, which was in operation by the summer of 1546. Padua and the University of Pisa almost simultaneously established the first university botanical gardens in Europe. The curator of the Paduan botanical garden was expected to display the plants and explain their properties to all who came. In other words, the physical examination of plants became an essential part of instruction in medical botany. This led to the modern study of botany and zoology.

Padua began the practice of clinical medicine in the 1540s. Although professors of medicine had occasionally taken students to the bedsides of patients in order to discuss diseases, Giovanni Battista Da

University of Padua. A sixteenth-century view of the building in which classes of the University of Padua met. The building, called the Palazzo del Bo (because the original edifice seems to have been a "Hotel of the Ox" [Bovis]), was acquired in 1493 by the Venetian government, the ruler of Padua and the ultimate authority over the university; over the door is a bas-relief of the Lion of St. Mark, the symbol of Venice. Today it houses the senior administration of the university and oral examinations for the doctorate are held in some of the historic rooms; if the candidate is successful, the square in front of the building becomes the site of celebration. CLICHÉ BIBLIOTHÈQUE NATIONALE DE FRANCE, PARIS. VB 24 FOL

Monte (1489–1551), professor of medical theory at Padua, made this a regular part of his instruction. In 1543 he led his students from the Palazzo del Bò to a hospital next door. Da Monte lectured on the symptoms, diagnosis, pathology, and cure of diseases, using patients to illustrate his points. Clinical discussions in the presence of ill patients became a regular part of medical training, supplementing classroom lectures.

Other Studies. Padua also had leading scholars in other fields, notably natural philosophy (which included elements of physical science and human psychology) and mathematics. A series of distinguished professors of mathematics culminated with Galileo Galilei, who taught at Padua from 1592 to 1610.

Padua made changes in the teaching of law in the 1540s by placing greater emphasis on specialized practical law and by reducing the number of professorships in canon law. Padua created a professorship of criminal law in 1540, plus another professorship

to focus on practical legal applications. In 1578 Padua added a professorship of humanistic jurisprudence, the second Italian university to do so.

Students. Padua attracted numerous students from all over Italy and Europe in the sixteenth century. Annual enrollment probably rose from eleven hundred students in the 1530s to a peak of sixteen hundred in the 1560s, then declined slightly later in the century. Only Bologna had more students. Probably slightly more than half were law students; the rest studied arts and medicine. Padua also had a few theology students.

Many famous Renaissance figures studied at Padua between 1405 and 1600. Among Italians, they included the historians and political philosophers Donato Giannotti, Paolo Giovio, Francesco Guicciardini, and Paolo Paruta. Humanists who studied at Padua included Giovanni Pico della Mirandola, Giovanni Pontano, and Pier Paolo Vergerio the Elder. Well-known Italian scholars in other fields who studied at Padua included Ulisse Aldrovandi, Girolamo Cardano, Francesco Patrizi da Cherso, and Bernardino Telesio. The poet Torquato Tasso studied at Padua in 1561–1562 and 1564–1565. Popes Eugenius IV and Sixtus IV studied at Padua, as did Saints Gaetano Thiene and Antonio Maria Zaccaria. Elena Lucrezia Cornaro Piscopia, a Venetian noblewoman, was the first woman to receive a university degree. She obtained a doctorate of philosophy at Padua on 25 June 1678 through examination, as she did not attend university lectures.

The largest group of non-Italians was the Germans. A total of 10,536 Germans studied at Padua from 1546 through 1630, an average of 124 per year. (Students normally attended lectures for five or more years before obtaining doctorates.) Two hundred German law students, plus an unknown number of German arts students, were in attendance in August 1564, possibly the high point of German enrollment. Many Germans obtained law degrees at Padua, then returned to prominent civil and ecclesiastical positions in their homelands. The Germans included Nicholas of Cusa (doctorate in canon law in 1423), plus the future humanists and scholars Joachim Camerarius, Conrad Peutinger, and Willibald Pirckheimer.

As many as a thousand Hungarian students came to Padua between 1526 and 1660, including the humanists Janus Pannonius and Andre Dudith de Sbardellat. The English students included John Colet, William Harvey (medical doctorate in 1603), William Latimer, Thomas Linacre, Richard Pace, the Jesuit Robert Parsons, and Cardinal Reginald Pole. Michael Servetus, the Spanish physician and anti-Trinitarian, studied at Padua, as did the French jurist Michel de l'Hôpital. From Greece came John Argyropoulos, who took his degree in 1444. Padua even had an American student in the seventeenth century. Edmund Davie (died before 1688), the son of an Englishman who emigrated to Boston, obtained a bachelor's degree at Harvard in 1674 and a medical doctorate at Padua in 1681. Davie was the first English-speaking North American known to have attended an Italian university.

The size of the teaching faculty diminished slightly in the last forty years of the sixteenth century, dropping to between forty-five and fifty professors. By the early seventeenth century, signs of decline were evident. Fewer students came, they often avoided the university lectures in favor of private instruction, and the faculty was less distinguished. Nevertheless, Padua established the first known university library in 1631. Students earlier had to rely on their own resources or the willingness of owners of private libraries to open their collections to them.

See also **Medicine** *and biographies of figures mentioned in this entry.*

BIBLIOGRAPHY

Acta graduum academicorum Gymnasii Patavini. Padua, Italy, 1969–1992. Ten volumes published to date covering 1406–1470, 1501–1550, and 1601–1605. Gives brief documentary summaries of doctoral degrees awarded.

Belloni, Annalisa. *Professori giuristi a Padova nel secolo XV. Profili bio-bibliografici e cattedre.* Frankfurt am Main, Germany, 1986. Biographical and bibliographical information on all the law professors of the fifteenth century. Introduction explains the organization of law instruction.

Brugi, Biagio. *Gli scolari dello Studio di Padova nel cinquecento.* 2d ed., revised. Padua, Italy, and Verona, Italy, 1905. Contains a count of German students at Padua.

Bylebyl, Jerome J. "The School of Padua: Humanistic Medicine in the Sixteenth Century." In *Health, Medicine, and Mortality in the Sixteenth Century.* Edited by Charles Webster. Cambridge, U.K., 1979. Pages 335–370. Good summary of innovations in medical research and teaching at Padua.

Dupuigrenet Desroussilles, François. "L'Università di Padova dal 1405 al Concilio di Trento." In *Storia della cultura veneta.* Vol. 3, pt. 2: *Dal primo quattrocento al Concilio di Trento.* Edited by Girolamo Arnaldi and Manlio Pastore Stocchi, Vicenza, Italy, 1980. Pages 607–647. Excellent survey covering 1405 to 1563; particularly good on relations between university and government.

Grendler, Paul F. "The University of Padua 1405–1600: A Success Story." *History of Higher Education Annual* 10 (1990): 7–17. Shows that the enlightened direction of the Venetian government was the foundation of the university's success.

Iorio, Dominick A. *The Aristotelians of Renaissance Italy: A Philosophical Exposition.* Lewiston, N.Y., 1991. Good survey of Aristotelian philosophical thought with particular reference to Paduan professors.

Pesenti, Tiziana. *Professor e promotori di medicina nello Studio di Padova dal 1405 al 1509. Repertorio bio-bibliografico.* Padua and Trieste, Italy, 1984. Biographical and bibliographical information for all the professors of medicine from 1405 to 1509.

Quaderni per la storia dell'Università di Padova. 1968–. Annual volume dedicated to history of the University of Padua in all periods. Includes annual surveys of research on the university.

Rossetti, Lucia. *L'Università di Padova: Profilo storico.* Milan, 1972. Also available in English and French translations. Brief (forty-seven-page) survey.

PAUL F. GRENDLER

PAGANISM. The Renaissance was a Christian culture that devoted considerable effort to the study of ancient pre-Christian art and learning. Inevitably the intensity of study of Greek and Latin literature, art, and philosophy led to suspicions or judgments that concentrating on the works of people whose religious beliefs and practices were not Christian could either undermine Christian faith or lead to contamination of Christian thinking by these ancient religious beliefs. These beliefs were known as "pagan" or "gentile," two words of classical origin meaning an outlook or set of beliefs derived from rural or country people, or popular or native religious beliefs and practices not part of organized religions such as Christianity, Judaism, or Islam.

Accusations of "Paganism."   The charge that scholars during the Renaissance, in their enthusiasm for things ancient, were contaminating their Christian beliefs with "paganism" was made by one of the most prominent scholars of the Renaissance, Erasmus of Rotterdam, in his dialogue concerning contemporary Italian scholars and poets called *Ciceronianus* (The Ciceronian; 1528). One such example was Jacopo Sannazaro's *De partu virginis* (On the Virgin Birth; 1526), a highly classicized poem on the nativity of Christ.

Modern historians have also made this charge. Jakob Burckhardt in his *Civilization of the Renaissance in Italy* speaks of the same poem and of other writings: "Nor could they treat of Christianity without paganizing it." The English Victorian historian John Addington Symonds speaks even more emphatically of the Italian humanists: men "who lived within their own conceits outside of custom and opinion. . . . Far more important, however, than these circumstances was their passion for a Pagan Ideal" (*Revival of Learning*).

Later scholarship would no longer entertain such judgments. First of all, Renaissance knowledge of popular Greek and Roman religious and ritual practices was very limited. In the late nineteenth and early twentieth centuries important studies, influenced by the new discipline of anthropology, established a more authentic and informed understanding of the subject. In the context of the Renaissance, the interest in and concept of "paganism" was more literary, philosophical, and theological. The pagan gods throughout the Middle Ages and the Renaissance were well known in a number of contexts, as Jean Seznec has shown, not as true deities but as minions of Satan, as evil spirits and demons. They were thought of as powerful historical men and women who because of their fame had become deified or demonized. Classical gods and mythical personalities also gave their names to the planets and constellations, and powers were attributed to them in the contexts of astrological beliefs. The pagan gods were also given roles as moral qualities; love and lust, for example, might be attributed to Venus or called venereal. They were well known and written about and carefully distinguished from the true deity during the Renaissance by such humanists as Petrarch, Boccaccio, Coluccio Salutati, Giovanni Caldiera, and Cristoforo Landino who showed how they could be used to represent various qualities in poetry and literature without confusing them with true deities, although popular confusion and superstitions obviously could occur. The classical gods played a well-known role in the poetry and artistic works of the Renaissance, even in churches and religious contexts, without any genuine contamination of Christian beliefs.

Neoplatonism.   There was one area of Renaissance philosophy where an element of paganism truly seems to have intruded, and that was the revival of knowledge and interest in Plato and Neoplatonism. George Gemistus Pletho (c. 1355–1452 or 1454) was a Greek Orthodox layman. He attended the Council of Florence in 1438 as a personal adviser to Emperor John VIII Palaeologus. There he promoted the revival of Plato as a theological influence, and at some point after his return to Greece proclaimed himself a reviver of ancient paganism under Zeus and other Hellenic gods. The question for a supposed Renaissance paganism is whether he, a subject of heated controversy in Italy, had a deeper influence than the revival of the philosophical study of Platonism to which he very likely did contribute.

Marsilio Ficino (1433–1499), the protegé of Cosimo de' Medici and the translator of Plato, reports that Pletho inspired Cosimo to procure the necessary manuscripts of Plato and set Ficino the task of translating Plato. Ficino, himself, after translating the works of Plato, wrote *Theologia Platonica* (1482), a major Christian theological work, and developed a conception of *prisca theologia* (ancient theology), which held that a number of ancient non-Judaic and pre-Christian religious figures anticipated Christianity in their theological notions. Among these were, supposedly, Zoroaster, held by Ficino to be author of the *Chaldaic Oracles;* Orpheus, who possibly inspired the *Orphic Hymns;* and Hermes Trismegistus, mythical author of *Asclepius* and some other works translated in part by Ficino. Also Plato was included among these ancient theologians. Ficino believed that such Christian-era Neoplatonic philosophers as Plotinus (whom Ficino translated and commented on), Porphyry, Iamblichus, and Proclus (whom he partially translated) had been inspired by Pseudo-Dionysius the Areopagite, whom he believed had been converted to Christianity by Saint Paul. Ficino did not regard these figures as "pagan" in their influence on his own thinking and writing of such works as his *Theologia Platonica, De amore* (On love), and *De vita* (On life). At least he would have considered himself able to weed out any pagan elements.

Giovanni Pico della Mirandola (1463–1494) has also occasionally been regarded by a later commentator as opening the door to paganism in his *De hominis dignitate oratio* (Oration on the dignity of man; 1486) and *Conclusiones sive theses DCCCC* (Nine hundred conclusions; 1486). This suspicion would be based on the presence of non-Christian sources included in each work. What is certainly indisputable is that he was influenced by Arabic philosophers such as Ibn Rushd (Averroes), Ibn Sīnā (Avicenna), and others, and even more by medieval and contemporary Jewish thought in which the Kabbalah played a major role. There is no doubt that his piety became more intense after certain of his *Conclusiones* were condemned by Pope Innocent VIII, and this deeper piety was manifested in his disputations against astrology and in his closeness until his death to Savonarola.

It would be the judgment of contemporary scholarship that "paganism" is too diffuse and vague a conception to have much meaning when applied to the Renaissance, an intensely religious, but also conspicuously worldly, period of history.

See also **Classical Antiquity, Discovery of; Leto, Pomponio; Plato and Platonism; Renaissance, Interpretations of the,** *subentries on* **Jakob Burckhardt** *and* **John Addington Symonds;** *and biographies of figures mentioned in this entry.*

BIBLIOGRAPHY

Primary Works

Boccaccio, Giovanni. *Boccaccio on Poetry, Being the Preface and the Fourteenth and Fifteenth Books of Boccaccio's Genealogia deorum gentilium.* Translated by Charles G. Osgood. Indianapolis, Ind., 1956.

Erasmus, Desiderius. *Collected Works of Erasmus.* Vol. 28, *Ciceronianus.* Translated by Betty I. Knott. Toronto, 1986.

Secondary Works

Burckhardt, Jakob. *The Civilization of the Renaissance in Italy.* Translated by S. G. C. Middlemore. New York, 1958. Translation of *Die Kultur der Renaissance in Italien* (1860).

Seznec, Jean. *The Survival of the Pagan Gods: The Mythological Tradition and Its Place in Renaissance Humanism and Art.* Translated by Barbara F. Sessions. New York, 1953.

Symonds, John Addington. *Renaissance in Italy: The Revival of Learning.* New York, 1904.

Trinkaus, Charles. *In Our Image and Likeness: Humanity and Divinity in Italian Humanist Thought.* Notre Dame, Ind., 1995.

Walker, D. P. *The Ancient Theology: Studies in Christian Platonism from the Fifteenth to the Eighteenth Century.* London, 1972.

Wind, Edgar. *Pagan Mysteries in the Renaissance.* New York, 1958.

Woodhouse, C. M. *George Gemistos Plethon: The Last of the Hellenes.* Oxford, 1986.

CHARLES TRINKAUS

PAGEANTRY. *See* **Parades, Processions, and Pageants.**

PAINTING. Paintings in the Renaissance were either on the wall, on wood panels or canvas supports, or exceptionally on metal or stone. Outside of manuscript illumination, paper and parchment rarely were used.

Preparatory Design. In Italy underdrawing was usually done with a brush and dilute ocher, often red sinoper, which gave its name, sinopia, to the kind of underdrawing frequently found before the mid-fifteenth century. When paper became more readily available, cartoons (preparatory drawings) came into use. In a technique called pouncing, the outlines were pricked, and the paper was held against the prepared surface; then a bag of black chalk was flung against it, transferring black dots onto the surface to be painted. In fresco the drawing could also be incised directly onto the damp plaster by tracing the cartoon with a blunt instrument. The earliest full-scale cartoon to have survived is Raphael's *School of Athens* (Milan, Ambrosian Library). Auxiliary cartoons must have been used for transferring the design, permitting the cartoon's preservation. Underdrawings done with black chalk have been detected with infrared radiation in many paintings from northern Europe, and presumably other materials more difficult to detect also were used.

Materials. A panel and its frame were crafted by a carpenter, then delivered to the painter's workshop. The surface was prepared with multiple layers of gesso, which was smoothed and polished. Beneath areas to be gilded a red clay, called bole, was applied because it imparted a warm tone and was slightly elastic, allowing it to receive the tooling without breaking the delicate sheets of gold. Special punches for tooling were part of each workshop's equipment. After the mid-fifteenth century gold leaf was usually replaced with a painted simulation of gold because it demonstrated the painter's skill and allowed him to control the effect of light.

Pigments were prepared in the workshop, each according to the secret techniques of the master, to obtain maximum brilliance. Some needed to be ground fine, some coarse. Precious ultramarine, obtained from the semiprecious stone lapis lazuli imported from Afghanistan, was washed to separate the deep blue crystals from the impurities, then ground. The palette contained only about eighteen pigments in common use, and although some were more successfully worked in oil and others in an egg binder, they remained largely constant throughout the period of the Renaissance, both in Italy and the north. Many of the pigments used in panel painting are incompatible with fresco, so the palette for a fresco was limited chiefly to the earth pigments. Blue was a problem because azurite turned green in water, and ultramarine was too expensive to use on a large scale. Smalt, known but rare before the sixteenth century, gradually came into use, especially for skies and wherever a pale blue was needed. When a deep blue was required in fresco, azurite would be applied *a secco* (on dry plaster) as in Giotto's vault and skies in the Arena Chapel. An exception is Michelangelo's *Last Judgment* (Sistine Chapel), where the pope paid for the ultramarine used in the pigment in the background.

Fresco. Fresco is a technique for painting a mural on lime plaster while it is still damp using pigments dissolved in water. The calcium hydroxide in the plaster combines with carbon dioxide in the air to form calcium carbonate. The pigment particles become cemented to the surface lime, making the painting very durable. Particularly popular in central Italy where the climate is dry, it was less successful in Venice, where all the walls are footed in water, and was not used in northern Europe. First the wall was prepared with layers of plaster, moving from rough to smooth. The next to last layer, called *arriccio,* would receive the sinopia. The painter then applied the final layer (*intonaco*) as a patch of plaster corresponding to the amount of painting expected to be completed that day (*giornata*). When finished, the edges had to be prepared for a smooth seam with the next patch. The *intonaco* could be worked upon for only a few hours. For changes after that the artist had either to chisel out the plaster or paint over on dry plaster with pigment in a binder (*secco*). *Secco* is much less durable and will eventually flake off. Because it was virtually impossible to match the color on adjacent patches, the frescoist normally tried to complete a color field in a day; thus the *giornate* follow contours.

With brilliant colors like ultramarine excluded, Renaissance fresco typically was of a more muted tonality and paler than panel painting. Leonardo da Vinci, seeking deeper tones and a less rigorous

working method, attempted unsuccessful alternative techniques in his *Last Supper* (Milan, Santa Maria della Grazie) and *Battle of Anghiari* (Florence, Palazzo Vecchio, never completed). When the taste for dramatic chiaroscuro took hold in Rome (c. 1515), experiments with oil mural were undertaken (Raphael, Sala di Costantino). Sebastiano del Piombo was successful in inventing such a technique, which allowed him to create dark backgrounds and deep shadows (Borgherini Chapel, San Pietro in Montorio, Rome, c. 1519–1524).

Facades had been painted in the Middle Ages, but in the early sixteenth century it became the fashion to fresco palace facades. In Rome, Polidoro da Caravaggio frescoed as many as forty facades in the 1520s before the Sack of Rome (1527) forced him to flee. The preferred subjects were ancient Roman history or mythology. The facade would be divided into bands in which simulated niches and statues or bands of relief were painted in grisaille (using tones of a single color), giving the look of carved stone. In Venice colors and illusionistic spatial effects were introduced by Pordenone (Giovanni Antonio de Sacchis). In Florence grotesques were frequently used. The sgraffito (Italian: "scratched") technique, described by Giorgio Vasari in the technical introduction to the second edition of the *Vite dé più eccellenti architetti, pittori ed scultori italiani* (*Lives of the Most Eminent Italian Architects, Painters, and Sculptors;* 1568), spread from Italy into northern and central Europe in the sixteenth century. A coat of pigmented plaster was covered with another layer in a different color, and while this top layer was still damp the design was incised through to the undercoat. In sixteenth-century Rome Polidoro's facades were as much copied by visiting artists as the works of Michelangelo and Raphael and the great statues of antiquity.

Egg Tempera. Because of its viscosity, egg required the use of a small brush and short strokes, but its quick-drying character permitted the painter to build up colors without blending them. The technique for painting in egg and in fresco was described by Cennino Cennini in his fourteenth-century howto book for artists, *Il libro dell'arte* (*The Craftsman's Handbook;* 1437). He declared that he was describing the techniques of Giotto as they were handed down through several generations of his workshop in the fourteenth century. The aesthetic of the Cennini technique valued pure, brilliant color. The palette was centered on the primary triad of ultramarine, vermilion, and gold. Modeling was accomplished by adding increments of white to the pure color. A modeling sequence moved from the pure color for the darks, to paler tints for the mid-tones and lights. For variety a hue shift might be employed, in which another pigment was introduced for the mid-tone, and perhaps even a third for the lights. This technique, called *cangiantismo,* fell out of favor, as did the whole Cennini system, in the second quarter of the fifteenth century, when its artificiality conflicted with the naturalism made possible by the invention of linear perspective, but was given new life by Michelangelo on the Sistine vault (1508–1512) and became very popular in frescoes in its wake. A modeling system to replace Cennini's was described by Leon Battista Alberti in his treatise *Della pittura* (*On Painting;* 1435/36) in which black was added to tone down the shadows, pure color represented the mid-tone, and white was added for the lights. This system was widely adopted in panel painting, but only briefly and experimentally in fresco (by, for example, Andrea del Castagno), where the Cennini system continued to prevail.

Oil. Oil was used as a binder in the Middle Ages, but a technique for painting in oil was perfected in Flanders early in the fifteenth century and then transferred to Italy. The means and date of transmission are still uncertain, but the earliest documented use of oil in Italy seems to be 1466, when Piero della Francesca was commissioned to paint a banner in oil. He and others must have been experimenting with the medium, possibly already in the 1440s. Jan van Eyck's technique was to apply multiple thin layers, building up the color thickly for the darks and allowing the white ground to shine through for the lights. A minimum of white or black was added, but a range of tints and shades could also be obtained by using coarser or finer grinds. Antonello da Messina appears to have learned this technique, probably from a follower of van Eyck, and introduced it in Venice when he arrived there in 1475. Giovanni Bellini and perhaps others in Venice were already using oil as a binder, but not with the effects of translucency the Eyckian technique achieved. By the 1490s oil was the medium of choice all over Italy, but egg tempera continued to be used for certain purposes and effects; for underpainting, for example, because it was quick drying.

With the introduction of oil, mixtures, often by superimposition of layers (as in early Netherlandish paintings), became the preferred system in Italy. A layer containing azurite and some lead white might be glazed with red lake to produce a mauve tone.

Leonardo in his *Adoration of the Magi* (1481–1482; Florence, Uffizi) introduced a dark underpainting to provide the modeling, which was intended to show through the thin layers of color bound in oil painted on top. Although he left it incomplete, it was studied and used as a model by the Florentine painters. We have unfinished paintings with such undermodeling, though never so dark, by Fra Bartolommeo, Raphael, Andrea del Sarto, Correggio, and later painters, indicating that it became a widespread technique in central Italy in the sixteenth century.

Sixteenth-Century Developments. Sixteenth-century Venetian painters exploited the texture of canvas and perfected the system of using multiple thin layers to simulate the effects of reflections and atmosphere. Titian developed a spontaneous approach to coloring, avoiding the drawn cartoons that were common in central Italy. Cross sections reveal that he sometimes masked what he had painted with a thick layer of opaque lead white, or he would paint an entire background, then place figures on top (rather than reserving the figures in the way that central Italians, working from cartoons, would do). In the 1540s he introduced a new technique, called open brushwork, putting the aesthetic of pure and brilliant color (*bellezza di colore*) behind him. Rather than the traditional smooth and uniform surface, he used impasto (thickly applied pigment) and left his brushstrokes unblended, sometimes even dipping his brush in another color without cleaning it so that the stroke itself contained multiple colors. When read at a distance the eye blends the colors, as the Impressionists would rediscover. This technique would be enormously influential in later centuries. Tintoretto introduced a dark underpainting in which dramatic effects and spontaneity were achieved with the quick and thin application of paint, sometimes letting the ground serve as the darks and applying only minimal colors for the mid-tones and white for the lights. Caravaggio also used a dark ground (usually reddish-brown or black) and the Caravaggisti, northern and Italian, imitated this technique.

In northern Europe beginning around the second decade of the sixteenth century, there was a general tendency to employ simpler layer structures and thinner paint, resulting in speedier production, partly because it could be executed by the workshop.

In Italy paintings and murals became larger and larger as the century progressed, making workshop execution a necessity. The master increasingly became only the inventor and designer, and less and less the executor. When the iconographical hand-books became available around mid-century, a man of letters would write a program and turn it over to the painter to translate into visual terms. This he might do only in compositional sketches that the workshop transformed into figure studies and eventually into cartoons. Painters and brilliant draftsmen like Giulio Romano, Giorgio Vasari, Francesco Salviati, and Taddeo Zuccaro might only oversee this process but contribute very little with their own hands.

See also biographies of artists mentioned in this entry.

BIBLIOGRAPHY

Borsook, Eve. "Technical Innovation and the Development of Raphael's Style in Rome." *Canadian Art Review* 12 (1985): 127–136.

Borsook, Eve, and Fiorella Superbi Gioffredi, eds. *Tecnica e stile: esempi di pittura murale del rinascimento italiano.* Milan, 1986.

Cennini, Cennino. *The Craftsman's Handbook.* Translated by Daniel V. Thompson Jr. New Haven, Conn., 1933.

The Great Fresco Cycles of the Renaissance. New York, 1994–. A series on individual fresco cycles, some recently restored, such as the Brancacci Chapel and Fra Angelico's frescoes at the convent in San Marco. Each volume explains and discusses the fresco technique used.

Hall, Marcia B. *Color and Meaning: Practice and Theory in Renaissance Painting.* New York, 1991.

Lazzarini, Lorenzo. "The Use of Color by Venetian Painters, 1480–1580: Materials and Technique." In *Color and Technique in Renaissance Painting.* Edited by Marcia B. Hall. Locust Valley, N.Y., 1987. Pages 115–136.

"Methods and Materials of Northern European Painting in the National Gallery, 1400–1500." *National Gallery Technical Bulletin* 18 (1997): 6–55.

Mora, Paolo, Laura Mora, and Paul Philippot. *The Conservation of Wall Paintings.* London, 1984.

Shearman, John, and Marcia B. Hall, eds. *Science in the Service of Art History: The Princeton Raphael Symposium.* Princeton, N.J., 1990.

MARCIA B. HALL

PALACES AND TOWNHOUSES. Private residential architecture achieved a new monumentality in the fifteenth and sixteenth centuries as a result of the Renaissance values of secularism and individualism, and the corollary ascendance of princely rather than church patronage. A fifteenth-century Florentine building boom, fueled by the desire of a rising merchant class to make their mark on the city, coincided with a renewed appreciation for classical antiquity to produce the Renaissance palazzo. While the appellation "palace" was technically reserved for the urban residence of a prince, the Renaissance townhouses of the great Florentine mercantile and banking families were referred to as palaces because of their remarkable scale and grandeur. The innovations in Florence influenced townhouse architecture throughout the Italian peninsula and beyond, interacting with traditional building practices to determine regional Renaissance typologies.

Florence. In medieval Florence powerful families lived in urban compounds: clusters of buildings, very often built of wood, marked by defensive towers, external loggias for social interaction, and the incorporation of shops. In the mid-fifteenth century the medieval compound was replaced by a single tall stone building composed of four wings surrounding a central arcaded court. The facade, usually of three equal stories, was distinguished by the use of heavily rusticated masonry and antique architectural elements such as stringcourses and cornices. While the political security of fifteenth-century Florence obviated the need for defensive towers, the facade rustication of Renaissance palaces recalled the fortified character of the medieval compound and served to set the building apart from the surrounding urban fabric. The Palazzo Medici (now Riccardi), begun in 1444 by the architect Michelozzo di Bartolomeo (1396–1472) for the most powerful Florentine banking family, became the prototype of the Tuscan Renaissance palazzo.

The Florentine merchant class expressed their dramatic political, economic, and social ascendance by building and sumptuously furnishing palaces that both embellished their city and celebrated their families. These patrons believed that they were fulfilling the humanist ideal of the magnificence of a residence corresponding to the status of its owner. But because these families chose to invest a large percentage of their wealth, up to one third of their capital, in building palaces, their residences also functioned as evidence of conspicuous consumption. The monumental palace, with its great height, regularized facade organization, and rusticated blocks, was an urban symbol of the power and wealth of its patron. To ensure the identification of the palace with its builder, facades were ornamented with the family arms and the personal devices of the patron, such as the sails of the Rucellai family and the moons of the Strozzi.

The Renaissance palace was more private in nature than its medieval predecessor. The loggias now faced the central court rather than the street, and the court, often the site of ceremonies, banquets, and theatrical performances, was enclosed within the mass of the building. The nucleus of the family residence was the *camera* (bedchamber) of the patron, located on the *piano nobile* (second floor) and buffered from the more public areas of the palace by the *sala* (main hall). As the century progressed, new room types were added to provide more comfort, privacy, and security: antechambers, closets, studies, and chapels. But the Florentine Renaissance palace was a place of business as well as a private residence, and while shops were rarely found in Florentine palaces, storerooms and other spaces identified with the mercantile activities of the family were located on the ground floor.

In his design for the Palazzo Rucellai (1450s), the humanist, theorist, and architect Leon Battista Alberti (1404–1472) introduced a new element into the palace facade: the antique orders. The mildly rusticated facade is regulated by pilasters stacked in the manner of the Roman Colosseum, a self-conscious reference to antiquity. This combination of rustication and pilasters provided an alternative facade prototype that was influential primarily outside Florence.

The Palazzo Strozzi (built by Giuliano da Sangallo, 1489–1490), the largest palace in Florence at the time of its construction, follows the model set by the Palazzo Medici but introduces a rigorous symmetry typical of the late fifteenth century. The Renaissance values of privacy and individuality are emphasized by the isolation of this almost freestanding palace. The overall symmetry, regular facade fenestration, ornamental use of rustication, and antique-style cornice indicate an increasing classicism in the Florentine palace. The interior organization displays the Renaissance admiration for the centralized plan, with a nearly symmetrical ground plan organized around the central court. Furthermore, Sangallo created a neat correspondence between the regular window spacing on the exterior of the palace and the distribution of interior rooms that Michelozzo was not able to achieve in the Palazzo Medici.

Rome. Whereas Florentine palaces were built by merchant princes, Roman palaces were marked by the patronage of "princes of the church": popes, cardinals, and prelates of the Curia. The Roman Renaissance palace type evolved from the feudal castle of the nobility rather than the merchant compound antecedent of the Florentine palace. The fifteenth-century Roman palace, typified by the Palazzo Venezia (built between 1455 and 1471), was both bulkier and more severe than its Florentine counterpart, its wall mass interrupted by few openings. The fortified character was emphasized by the persistence of medieval towers and decorative elements such as battlements with machicolations intended to denote strength. The second floor, the level of the palace with the elaborate ceremonial rooms so important to the clerical patrons, was given prominence on the facade by the presence of cross-mullioned windows with classical-style moldings, a window type reserved exclusively for this location.

The layout of the Roman palace was less uniform than the foursquare Florentine type, consisting of two or more wings around a semienclosed courtyard. Roman palaces often incorporated extensive gardens, lending a suburban air; loggias at the rear of the palace offered views of these gardens. The interior of the Palazzo Venezia marked an important step forward in the creation of the rationally organized and comfortable Renaissance palace interior. It contained the first true apartment suite, in which the rooms of the residence were organized in a linear fashion and progressed sequentially from public to private. The fully developed apartment suite, which served to control access and to channel visitors through the palace, consisted of *sala* (main hall), *saletta* (dining parlor), *anticamera* (antechamber), *camera* (bedchamber), *studio* (closet), and back stairs. This organization provided a framework for the highly ritualized social life of the popes and cardinals.

The Cancelleria, built for Cardinal Raffaello Riario in 1486–1496, inaugurated a new Roman palace style, a transition to the more classical sixteenth century. Based on the Florentine palace type, the Cancelleria is marked by classical symmetry and regularity. The facade is clad with flat rustication and organized by pilasters, as at the Palazzo Rucellai in Florence; other classical elements include a frieze inscription and windows modeled on antique types. This classical style was also evident at the Palazzo Caprini (also known as Raphael's House; 1501–c. 1512) designed by Bramante. The rusticated ground floor was conceived as a plinth visually supporting the orders, paired Doric half-columns, on the *piano nobile*. The entire facade is articulated by classical elements used in a way that expresses the structural logic of the building.

The masterpiece of the sixteenth-century Roman palace was the Palazzo Farnese (begun 1517, redesigned 1534, completed in 1548), a residence on an enormous scale designed by Antonio da Sangallo the Younger for Cardinal Alessandro Farnese and enlarged when Farnese became Pope Paul III (1534–1549). The flat three-story facade of the freestanding palace, composed of a record thirteen bays, is punctuated only by window surrounds, cornices, and quoins; aedicules with alternating triangular and arched pediments distinguish the *piano nobile*. The horizontality and austerity of this papal palace, which are emphasized by the enormous overhanging cornice designed by Michelangelo in 1546, place it firmly within the Roman palace tradition while its classical order and simplicity embody the artistic values of the high Renaissance.

Venice. Venice had a developed palace architecture tradition prior to the Renaissance. The grand Gothic palaces lining the canals were characterized by wall surfaces with multiple arcade openings, placed asymmetrically, and by a lavish polychrome ornamentation influenced by Byzantium. When the Renaissance arrived in Venice at the end of the fifteenth century, this Gothic palace tradition was merged with classical elements to create the Venetian Renaissance palazzo.

The Venetian Republic, fueled by the belief that it was the true successor to ancient Rome, encouraged the adoption of a Roman style, especially after the sack of Rome in 1527. In addition, aristocratic Venetian families with close ties to Rome, such as the Corner and Grimani, self-consciously promoted the new "Roman" Renaissance style by commissioning palaces from Roman architects with a firsthand knowledge of ancient buildings.

In the early Renaissance Palazzo Dario (1487) asymmetry and polychromy are still the defining features of the facade, although round arches have replaced Gothic arcades. At the Palazzo Corner (1545) Jacopo Sansovino adapted Bramante's Roman palace type to the Venetian tradition and introduced strict symmetry to the Venetian palace facade. Above the rusticated lower level the two upper stories are pierced by seven bays of tall, round-arched windows divided by a double order of columns. The center of the facade, which corresponds to the interior great hall on the *piano nobile,* is emphasized by three wider bays and the corresponding arched entryways on the ground floor. The three-story Palazzo Grimani facade (Michele Sanmicheli, 1539) presents a forceful grid of classical elements: vertical Corinthian columns and horizontal projecting cornices. The three central bays present a triumphal arch motif, a clear reference to the glory of ancient Rome.

France. The French equivalent of the Italian palazzo was the *hôtel particulier,* the townhouse of a noble family. The strict social hierarchy of France dictated a clear distinction between the *hôtels* of the courtly elite and the *maisons* (houses) of the wealthy middle class during the Renaissance; whereas the

Italians built according to their wealth, the French built according to their status.

Francis I's announcement in 1528 that he intended to make Paris the capital of his realm encouraged the building of townhouses. Although the peripatetic court never did settle in Paris, Francis moved from the Loire Valley to the Ile-de-France, thus assuring the importance of the city. The destruction of several royal palaces in Paris and the subsequent subdivision of the land on which they had stood into building lots, undertaken in the 1540s to raise money to wage war, further spurred townhouse construction.

It was the example of Italy that converted the medieval "castle in a city" type of residence, such as the Hôtel de Cluny (1485–1510), into the Renaissance *hôtel* type. Francis I's court was a center for Italian artists who brought the Renaissance to France; among them was the Venetian architect Sebastiano Serlio. In a townhouse he designed at Fontainebleau between 1542 and 1546, known as the Grand Ferrare, Serlio applied the Italian Renaissance principles of symmetry, order, and regularity to the existing French townhouse type. This building became the model for such later townhouses as the Hôtel Carnavalet in Paris (1546–1550).

The Renaissance townhouse type consisted of a main block set between a court and a garden, with side wings flanking the court and ending in pavilions on the street. The court was enclosed by a wall separating the townhouse from the street, thus ensuring privacy for the aristocratic residents. The focus of the street facade was a monumental portal, composed of classical elements such as columns, pierced in the screen wall. The Renaissance townhouse, built of stone, presented court and garden facades of two or three stories capped by tall slate roofs punctuated by dormer windows.

An important characteristic of the Renaissance *hôtel* plan that distinguishes it from late Gothic townhouses is its bilateral symmetry, a feature valued by Italian Renaissance architects and evident in Serlio's Grand Ferrare. The interior of the *hôtel* is organized into apartment suites, as in Rome, but with fewer rooms; the French Renaissance apartment sequence consisted of just three rooms, the *grand salle* (main hall), *chambre* (bedchamber), and *cabinet* (study). The Renaissance townhouse type embodied in the Hôtel Carnavalet, heavily influenced by Italy, determined the course of French townhouse architecture for the next two centuries.

BIBLIOGRAPHY

Babelon, Jean-Pierre. "Du grand Ferrare à Carnavalet: Naissance de l'hôtel classique." *Revue de l'art* 40–41 (1978): 88–108.

Frommel, Christoph Luitpold. "Living all'antica: Palaces and Villas from Brunelleschi to Bramante." In *The Renaissance from Brunelleschi to Michelangelo: The Representation of Architecture*. Edited by Henry A. Millon and Vittorio Magnano Lampugnani. New York, 1994.

Goldthwaite, Richard A. *Banks, Palaces, and Entrepreneurs in Renaissance Florence*. Aldershot, U.K., and Brookfield, Vt., 1995.

Howard, Deborah. *The Architectural History of Venice*. New York, 1981.

Lotz, Wolfgang. *Architecture in Italy, 1400–1600*. Rev. ed. New Haven, Conn., 1995.

Magnuson, Torgil. *Studies in Roman Quattrocento Architecture*. Stockholm, 1958. English trans. by Mary Holtinger. Harmondsworth, U.K., 1974.

Thornton, Peter. *The Italian Renaissance Interior, 1400–1600*. New York, 1991.

NINA LEWALLEN

PALATINATE. Heidelberg, the capital of the Palatinate, a German historical principality, became a center of literary and cultural activity during the Renaissance and Reformation.

History. The historical Palatinate consisted of two territories: the Rhine or Lower Palatinate (Rheinpfalz), often called simply the Palatinate, an area in western Germany along the Rhine and Neckar; and the Upper Palatinate (Oberpfalz), an area north of Bavaria and separated from the Rhine Palatinate by the lands of other rulers. From 1257, the count palatine served as one of the seven electors of the Holy Roman Emperor and as the emperor's representative (*Reichsvikar*) during a vacancy. As with other territories in the German empire, territorial losses and gains frequently changed the borders of the principality. Under Elector Frederick I "the Victorious" (ruled 1449–1476), for instance, the territory greatly expanded, while under his successor and nephew Philip "the Upright" (ruled 1476–1508), the principality suffered the loss of numerous lands as the result of the Bavarian War of Succession in 1504.

In the second half of the sixteenth century, the Palatinate became Protestant, oscillating between Lutheranism and Calvinism. Whereas the Elector Ottheinrich (ruled 1556–1559) placed the Palatinate in the Lutheran camp, his successor, Frederick III (ruled 1559–1576), made it into an intellectual and diplomatic center for European Calvinism, and Ludwig VI (ruled 1576–1583) reestablished Lutheranism. The election in 1619 of Elector Frederick V (ruled 1610–1623), the leader of the Protestant Union, as king of Bohemia represented a provocation to the Catholic Habsburgs and precipitated the first phase of the Thirty Years' War. Frederick's army was defeated, the Palatinate was ravaged by imperial forces, and Frederick was stripped of his electoral dignity, which was transferred to the duke of Bavaria. Only at the Peace of Westphalia (1648) was the electoral vote restored to the counts palatine by the creation of a new, eighth vote, and the territory became known as the *Kurpfalz* (Electoral Palatinate).

Princely Patronage in the Palatinate. Throughout its history, the Palatinate had rulers who actively supported scholarship, literature, and the arts. In 1386 Elector Rupert I, though reportedly barely able to read or write, founded the University of Heidelberg, the third university in the empire after Prague and Vienna. During the second half of the fifteenth century, cultural life flourished at the university and the court under the two electors Frederick I and his nephew Philip, who for fifty years became the main princely patrons in the empire. Frederick invited humanists such as Peter Luder (c. 1415–1472) and the Italian Petrus Antonius Finariensis (c. 1435–1512) to the university.

But it was Philip who in the last two decades of the fifteenth century made Heidelberg the paramount center for humanists, poets, historians, and musicians. The focal point of the Heidelberg circle became Johann von Dalberg. As bishop of Worms, chancellor at the court, and friend of many scholars at the university, Dalberg embodied the close links at Heidelberg between church, court, and university. He invited the famous Frisian humanist Rudolf Agricola (1444–1485), who in turn, during his short stay in the mid-1480s, attracted other humanists, such as Conrad Celtis and Johann Reuchlin, to Heidelberg. Both returned a decade later. Celtis in 1495 founded the Sodalitas litteraria Rhenana (Literary Society of the Rhine), the best documented of the numerous humanist circles that emerged in Germany at that time. With Dalberg presiding, it included Reuchlin, Jacob Wimpheling, Johann Trithemius, and others. For a short time Reuchlin, who had been appointed princely tutor, also made Heidelberg a center for the study of Hebrew and Greek. In addition, Elector Philip actively sponsored literature written in the vernacular and commissioned German translations of Latin and Greek works. The University of Heidelberg continued to play an important role in the sixteenth century, although after 1520 it was eclipsed by Wittenberg as the most important university of Protestant Germany.

The Bibliotheca Palatina. As a preeminent center of scholarly and literary activity, Heidelberg had one of the best libraries in Germany. Founded in 1421 when Elector Louis III (ruled 1410–1436) donated his library to the university, the Bibliotheca Palatina (as it became known in the seventeenth century), grew in the following centuries through donations, purchases, and appropriations. Elector Ottheinrich in particular used every opportunity to acquire manuscripts and books. He appropriated, for instance, the famed library of the Monastery of Lorsch. The Palatina was greatly expanded by the donation of Ulrich Fugger (1526–1584), a member of the Augsburg family of merchants and bankers. A Lutheran from a largely Catholic family, Ulrich had moved to Heidelberg in 1567 and upon his death left his enormous collection (approximately 1,300 manuscripts and 8,200 printed books) to the elector. By the beginning of the seventeenth century, the Heidelberg library was considered the "best treasure of educated Germany" (*optimus literatae Germaniae thesaurus*), as it was often called. It included priceless manuscripts, such as a Virgil manuscript from late antiquity (Vat. Pal. Lat. 1631), the ninth-century gospel book from the monastery of Lorsch (Lorscher Evangeliar, Vat. Pal. lat. 50), the book of falconry of Frederick II (Vat. Pal. Lat. 1071), and the famed *Manessische Liederhandschrift* (Manuscript of songs) of the early fourteenth century, containing 138 illustrations of the minnesinger (Cod. Pal. Germ. 848).

The library's fame, however, proved to be its undoing, at least for Heidelberg. When Protestant Palatinate was defeated in the Thirty Years' War and Heidelberg was occupied in 1622 by Catholic troops under the command of Graf von Tilly, the Catholic duke Maximilian I of Bavaria "donated" the library of his vanquished opponent to Pope Gregory XV, upon whom he was dependent for financial and political support. Under the watchful eye of the papal legate Leone Allaci, a total of 11,000 volumes, among them 3,600 invaluable manuscripts, were transported in fifty wagons across the Alps to Rome. Efforts to regain the library were largely unsuccessful, until 1816 when thirty-six manuscripts that Napoleon had brought to Paris were returned, after his defeat, to Heidelberg. In the same year, the Vatican voluntarily returned 852 manuscripts (mostly German) to Heidelberg, a quarter of the total number.

See also **Holy Roman Empire.**

BIBLIOGRAPHY

Backes, Martina. *Das literarische Leben am kurpfälzischen Hof zu Heidelberg im 15. Jahrhundert: Ein Beitrag zur Gönnerforschung des Spätmittelalters*. Tübingen, Germany, 1992. Informative study of literary life at the courts of the Palatine electors.

Berschin, Walter. *Die Palatina in der Vaticana: Eine deutsche Bibliothek in Rom*. Stuttgart, Germany, and Zürich, Switzerland, 1992. Concise, excellent bibliography and chronology.

Cohn, Henry J. "The Early Renaissance Court in Heidelberg." *European Studies Review* 1 (1971): 295–322.

Cohn, Henry J. *The Government of the Rhine Palatinate in the Fifteenth Century*. Oxford, 1965.

Mittler, Elmar, and Wilfried Werner. *Mit der Zeit: Die Kurfürsten von der Pfalz und die Heidelberger Handschriften der Bibliotheca Palatina*. Wiesbaden, Germany, 1986.

Press, Volker. *Calvinismus und Territorialstaat: Regierung und Zentralbehörden der Kurpfalz, 1559–1619*. Stuttgart, Germany, 1970. Classic study of the Palatinate in the sixteenth century.

Walter, Peter. "Johannes von Dalberg und der Humanismus." *1495: Kaiser, Reich, Reformen. Der Reichstag zu Worms*. Koblenz, Germany, 1995: 139–171.

ECKHARD BERNSTEIN

PALESTRINA, GIOVANNI PIERLUIGI DA

(c. 1525–1594), Italian singer and composer. Palestrina began his career in the 1530s as a choirboy in the basilica of Santa Maria Maggiore in Rome. In 1551 he became the *magister cantorum* (in charge of the choirboys), and later the *magister capellae* of the choir of Saint Peter's (the Cappella Giulia). In January 1555, he was made a member of the papal chapel by direct order of Pope Julius III (formerly bishop of Palestrina, reigned 1550–1555), bypassing the requirement that prospective singers be auditioned and admitted by vote of the other members of the choir. However, in September of the same year, Palestrina (who had married in 1547) and two other married singers were removed from the papal choir by order of Pope Paul IV (elected 23 May). Palestrina remained in Rome as the *maestro di cappella* of major Roman ecclesiastical institutions and refused offers of employment elsewhere. He returned in 1571 to the Cappella Giulia where he spent the rest of his life. Beginning in October 1565, he was given special payments for producing music for the papal chapel and became in effect its official composer. After the death of his wife in 1580, he contemplated entering the priesthood, but instead married a wealthy widow. He died on 2 February 1594 and was buried in Saint Peter's; his funeral was attended by all the musicians of Rome and many other people. He was survived by his son Iginio (1558–1610) who supervised the posthumous publication of a number of his works.

Palestrina was a prolific composer of sacred music for the Catholic rite. His first publication was a book of Masses printed in Rome in 1554 and dedicated to his patron, Pope Julius III; he went on to produce 104 settings of the Mass and about 250 motets, along

Giovanni Pierluigi da Palestrina. Palestrina presents his first book of masses to Pope Julius III in 1554. From the title page of *Missarum liber primus* (1572).

with hymns, lamentations, Magnificats, Offertories, and litanies. These were disseminated in an increasing number of prints and manuscript copies as the sixteenth century progressed. Yet among his most popular works were Italian madrigals. His second publication of 1555 was a book of madrigals that eventually went through as many as eight reprintings before 1600. In later life, Palestrina professed to be embarrassed by his youthful secular works. While Palestrina was well known in his lifetime as a composer and was the preeminent member of the Roman musical community and an influential teacher, he hardly had the mythic status while he lived that he acquired after his death. Some of his posthumous fame is due to a legend begun in the seventeenth century that he had "saved music" from being banned by Pope Marcellus II (reigned April–May 1555) by composing the *Missa Papae Marcelli* (Pope Marcellus Mass), a work in which the prevailing imitative style of the day is abandoned in the Gloria and Credo, allowing the words to be clearly understood (scholars now date this Mass c. 1562, but no one has yet explained the title).

Beginning in the seventeenth century, Palestrina's remarkably consistent contrapuntal style was adopted as the pedagogical model to be followed by those who wished to learn the art of Renaissance counterpoint (the *stile antico*), culminating in the immensely influential treatise *Gradus ad Parnassum* (1725) by the Viennese *Kapellmeister* and composer Johann Joseph Fux. Countless students have struggled since then to produce the kind of music Palestrina wrote as a matter of course. Because of this reputation, Palestrina was the first Renaissance composer to engender any serious scholarly inquiry. In 1828, a two-volume hagiographical biography was written by the papal singer Giuseppe Baini, and a scholarly edition of the composer's entire output was begun in 1862 (completed after thirty-three volumes in 1907). Palestrina as composer, as opposed to pedagogical model, has been the subject of a number of modern studies.

BIBLIOGRAPHY

Primary Works

Bianchi, Lino, Giancarlo Rostirolla, et al. *Iconografia Palestriniana: Giovanni Pierluigi da Palestrina: immagini e documenti del suo tempo.* Lucca, Italy, 1994. Picture book with facsimiles of title pages of prints, documents (some in Palestrina's hand), portraits, maps, and other items relating to Palestrina's career. Organized chronologically. Text in Italian.

Lockwood, Lewis, ed. *Palestrina Pope Marcellus Mass.* New York, 1975. An authoritative score, backgrounds and sources, history and analysis, views and comments of Palestrina's most famous (notorious) work.

Palestrina, Giovanni Pierluigi da. *Opere complete.* Edited by Raffaele Casimiri, et al. 35 vols. Rome, 1939–.

Palestrina, Giovanni Pierluigi da. *Werke.* 32 vols. Edited by F. X. Haberl. 32 vols. Leipzig, Germany, 1862–1907.

Secondary Works

Bianchi, Lino, and Giancarlo Rostirolla, eds. *Atti del II convegno internazionale di studi Palestriniani: Palestrina e la sua presenza nella musica e nella cultura europea dal suo tempo ad oggi.* Palestrina, Italy, 1991. Twenty-eight articles, two in English.

Bianchi, Lino. *Palestrina nella vita, nelle opere, nel suo tempo.* Palestrina, Italy, 1995. In Italian. Most up to date biography, individual discussions of every Mass and motet, general discussion of all other works.

Jeppesen, Knud. *The Style of Palestrina and the Dissonance.* 2d edition. Oxford, 1946. Reprint, New York, 1970. The classic study of Palestrina's contrapuntal style.

Lockwood, Lewis, and Jessie Ann Owens. "Giovanni Pierluigi da Palestrina." In *The New Grove High Renaissance Masters.* New York, 1984. Pages 93–156.

RICHARD SHERR

PALLADIO, ANDREA (Andrea di Pietro della Gondola; 1508–1580), architect active in the Veneto. Andrea Palladio was born in Padua, where at the age of thirteen he became apprenticed to a local stonemason, Bartolomeo Cavazza da Sossano. He did not stay long with Cavazza, and by 1524 he was formally registered in the Vicentine guild of stonemasons. In

Vicenza, Palladio joined the Pedemuro workshop run by Giovanni di Giacomo da Porlezza and Girolamo Pittoni da Lumignano; the former specialized in architecture, and Palladio continued collaborating with him after leaving the workshop. Through Porlezza, the young Palladio probably had the chance to meet the architect and military engineer Michele Sanmicheli (1484–1559).

By 1537 Palladio's presence in the Pedemuro workshop was waning as he entered the circle of Gian Giorgio Trissino (1478–1550). A local aristocrat and humanist who had retired to Vicenza after a diplomatic career, Trissino gathered in his villa in Cricoli an academy of intellectually promising young Vicentines. Trissino's impact on Palladio was great; it was through Trissino that he was first exposed to humanist education, probably learned some Latin, first encountered Vitruvius's treatise on architecture, and made many important acquaintances in the intellectual circles of the Veneto. The name Palladio, which he adopted in about 1545, also came from Trissino's circle. During the 1540s Palladio made a number of trips to Rome (1541, 1545, 1546/1547, 1549), some in the company of Trissino. During the trip in 1546/1547, he met Michelangelo. Preserved drawings show that Palladio spent much of his time in Rome studying and surveying the Roman ruins.

Early Works. Palladio's first independent design was Villa Godi in Lonedo (near Vicenza). Designed in the late 1530s, the villa was inhabited by 1542. Two palazzi in Vicenza; Thiene and Civena, as well as Villa Pisani in Bagnolo, are also from the early 1540s. Palladio's buildings from this period however do not yet show many of the design aspects that later become characteristic of his work. His use of the classical orders was still timid on Palazzo Civena and Villa Godi; his expertise in this field was only to develop following his trips to Rome. Palazzo Thiene shows strong mannerist tendencies, atypical of Palladio's work, and clearly indicates the influence of Giulio Romano. The similarity to Romano's work and the fact that Romano visited Vicenza in 1542 have resulted in doubts about Palladio's authorship of this palazzo ever since the early seventeenth century.

The decisive breakthrough in Palladio's career came toward the end of the 1540s, when the Vicentine city council entrusted him to complete the facade of the city's public palace. The Basilica, as this building is commonly called, is actually a complex of medieval buildings that were reorganized into a single structure and surrounded by Gothic arcades during the fifteenth century. A section of the arcades collapsed soon after their completion in 1496, and for the next half century the city looked for an architect to complete the building in the Renaissance idiom and resolve the numerous structural and compositional problems. The solution Palladio proposed shows the thorough understanding of the classical orders he had gained during his trips to Rome. The composition, especially the extensive use of the *serliana,* indicates the influence of Jacopo Sansovino's project for the Library of St. Mark in Venice; yet the reduced presence of secondary ornamentation shows that Palladio was looking more to Donato Bramante's Roman works than to those of his contemporaries. A reluctance to follow the mannerist tendencies of the time became a major characteristic of Palladio's work during the 1550s.

The Mature Palladio. It took three years (1546–1549) for the Vicentine city council to approve Palladio's plans for the Basilica. The work on such a large building proceeded slowly, and the entire structure was only completed in 1614. However this work provided important contacts for Palladio and brought him considerable reputation. His first major commission after having been entrusted with the work on the Basilica was Palazzo Chiericati, also in Vicenza. Placed in a prominent city square, the palazzo demonstrates confidence in facade design and use of the classical orders. It was also a very complex project because of the narrow site. Another Vicentine palazzo, Porto-Festa, was probably designed about the same time.

During this period Palladio was also developing the villa type that later became identified with his name. Villa Poiana in Poiana Maggiore (near Vicenza), built in the late 1540s, was transitional in this sense, but a series of villas built during the 1550s fully represent the model of a villa that eventually became emblematic of Palladio's work. All these villas have a central monumentally vaulted *sala,* or central hall (which can be square, rectangular, or in the shape of a cross or of the letter T) with a row of rooms on both sides and a facade with a Greco-Roman temple portico. The Villas Chiericati in Vancimuglio di Grumolo (near Vicenza), Badoer in Fratta Polesine (near Rovigo), Emo in Fanzolo (near Treviso), Foscari, also known as Malcontenta, in Gambarare di Mira (near Mestre), Cornaro in Piombino Dese (near Treviso), and Pisani in Montagnana were designed during the 1550s or early 1560s, and all belong to this type. The last two have an upper

story as well, in which the same organization is repeated.

That villas constituted the main part of Palladio's
work between the mid-1550s and the mid-1560s had
to do with changes in the Venetian economy and an
increased orientation toward agriculture, because
villas functioned as agricultural estates. From the
mid-1560s, as Palladio returned to the work on palazzi and civic buildings in Vicenza, his style gradually changed. The most remarkable feature was the
use of the colossal order on the facade. Palazzi Val-
marana (begun 1565) and Porto Breganze (begun in
the early 1570s) both show this new boldness in facade design. Palazzo Barbarano, which was being
built in about 1570, was originally planned with a
colossal order, but this design was subsequently
changed. The colossal order is also found on Loggia
del Capitaniato, the seat of the Venetian governor of
Vicenza, begun in 1571. An unusual villa, on which
the motif of the colossal order is also exploited, is
that of Sarego in Santa Sofia near Verona.

Palladio's most famous edifice, Villa Rotonda,
known also as Villa Capra, was also built in the late
1560s, for the retired papal secretary Paolo Almerico.
[See the color plates in this volume.] The villa, located on a hill very close to Vicenza, has a circular
central hall covered by a dome with four big rooms
in the corners and four smaller ones next to them.
Four identical porticoes open on all four facades,
and a great number of symmetries and complex systems of axial alignments are developed within the
structure. Over the centuries, the Rotonda became
emblematic of Palladio's architecture and has been
copied many times in different parts of the world.

**Humanist Contacts and Collaboration
with Daniele Barbaro.** Palladio's early contacts with Trissino coincided with the period when
the latter was studying philosophy in Padua. It is impossible to trace individual contacts in the lively intellectual life of the University of Padua during those
years, but there is no doubt that the association with
Trissino opened many doors to Palladio. It was during those years that he became acquainted with the
Venetian noble and architect Luigi Alvise Cornaro
(1475–1566). After Trissino's death in 1550 Palladio
paid considerable attention to keeping and building
contacts with humanists. Thus his name appears on
the list of the founders of the Vicentine Accademia
Olimpica in 1556.

Among Palladio's humanist contacts, Daniele Barbaro (1513–1570) was particularly important.
Through Trissino's circle in Padua, Palladio got to

know Barbaro, who assumed the role of intellectual
mentor after Trissino died. Barbaro, who was patri-
arch-elect of Aquileia, belonged to high Venetian nobility and was the author of a number of philosophical books, a commentary on Vitruvius, and a treatise
on perspective. The patron of a number of contemporary artists, such as Paolo Veronese (1528–1588)
and Alessandro Vittoria (1525–1608), he helped Palladio establish his reputation in the Veneto and introduced him to prospective Venetian clients. Palladio collaborated on the preparation of Barbaro's
Italian translation of and commentary on Vitruvius,
which came out in 1556; he also prepared a number
of illustrations for it. He made a trip to Rome with
Barbaro in 1554.

Palladio also designed a villa in Maser for Daniele
Barbaro and his brother Marcantonio. The villa was
habitable by 1560, and by 1562 Veronese had completed his frescoes in it. Although the villa is regarded as a masterpiece, it presents some of the most
complex problems for Palladian scholars. Its planning is in many ways atypical of Palladio, and it is
not always easy to determine how far his design was
influenced by Daniele Barbaro. The situation is further complicated by the discord between Palladio's
architecture and Veronese's paintings as well as the
unclear authorship of sculptures, since Daniele Barbaro's brother Marcantonio seems to have interfered
in Vittoria's work. The thesis of a number of scholars
that Palladio's relationship with Barbaro cooled due
to the architect's dissatisfaction with Veronese's frescoes in the villa was, however, later disproved. Until
his death in 1570 Barbaro seems to have helped Palladio acquire commissions in Venice.

Palladio's Published Works. As early as
the mid-1550s, Palladio was working on a treatise on
architecture. The book, however, did not come out
until 1570, when he completed it in haste and under
pressure, as part of his efforts to succeed Sansovino
as main architectural adviser to the Venetian republic. After *Regola delli cinque ordini d'architettura*
(Canon of the five orders of architecture; 1563) by
Giacomo Barozzi da Vignola (1507–1573), Palladio's
treatise is undoubtedly the most influential Renaissance book on architecture and has had great impact
on generations of architects. Book 1 of the treatise
discusses elements of architecture and the theory of
the classical orders; book 2 presents plans of residential buildings Palladio designed; book 3 describes a number of bridges that Palladio designed
and gives a highly idealized version of the project of
the Vicentine Basilica; and book 4 contains Palladio's

surveys of Roman temples. The treatise has many internal contradictions, obviously due to the long period of preparation and the haste in the formulation of the final version. For instance, illustrations in the account of the classical orders systematically contradict the text; plans of projects that Palladio presents in book 2 often fail to correspond to the way these buildings were actually built, while his surveys in book 4 are reliable to varying degrees. The influence of Vignola is particularly obvious in the illustrations of the system of the orders and in some archaeological surveys in book 4.

In 1554, well before the treatise on architecture, Palladio published two short books: *Descritione de le chiese* (The churches of Rome) and *L'antichità di Roma* (Roman antiquities). A few years after the publication of the treatise, in 1575, he published *I commentari di C. Giulio Cesare,* a version of Caesar's *Gallic War.* The edition contains illustrations by Palladio's sons Leonida and Orazio, both of whom died in 1572. Palladio's contribution here is limited to a discussion of Roman military tactics.

Ecclesiastical Architecture and Late Works.

For the greatest part of his life Palladio was occupied with residential architecture, and churches enter his work relatively late.

His first ecclesiastical building was not in fact a church but the convent of Santa Maria della Carità in Venice, which he started in about 1561. Palladio received a commission for the facade of the San Francesco della Vigna church in 1562, largely through Barbaro's assistance. Combining classical orders with the uneven nave heights of a Christian basilica had been a problem for architects since the early Renaissance. Palladio's solution, which imposed two Greco-Roman temple fronts, was later repeated by many architects. His greatest ecclesiastical building, the Benedictine church of San Giorgio Maggiore, was started in 1566. It was a complex project, developed both to suit the well-established Benedictine monastery and to be used for ceremonial purposes.

The year 1570 brought an important change in Palladio's career. Both Barbaro and Sansovino died that year, and Palladio, already well established in the city of Venice, succeeded the latter as the main architectural adviser of the Venetian republic. The ten years from his appointment to this position to his death in 1580 were marked by one grand project: the votive church of Redentore. In his new position Palladio often acted as consultant; he helped with celebrations related to the visit of King Henry III of

Andrea Palladio. Portrait by Giambattista Maganza. Painted 1576. Centro Internazionale degli Studi di Architettura "Andrea Palladio," Vicenza, Italy

France to Venice in 1574 and prepared proposals for the restoration of the ducal palace after a fire in the same year. In those years he also prepared several proposals for the church of San Petronio in Bologna. Two important buildings from this late period should be mentioned in addition to those discussed earlier: the Teatro Olimpico in Vicenza and a small church in Maser, commissioned by Marcantonio Barbaro.

Influence.

There are good reasons to argue that Palladio was the most influential Renaissance architect. The influence of his *Four Books on Architecture* is second only to that of Vignola's *Regola,* whereas no other Renaissance architect's work has been so widely followed. Not only were Palladio's buildings often copied, but his solutions to the problems of applying classical architecture later became so common that they are hardly perceived as innovations when seen on Palladio's buildings. Palladio's influence on generations of architects in Italy was immense. By the seventeenth century his architectural ideas had, due to the efforts of Inigo Jones, arrived in England, and in later centuries they spread across the Anglo-Saxon world. Interest in Palladio's work did not wane even in the twentieth century, when the domination of modernist views in architectural practice and theory made interest in many other Renaissance architects a purely academic pursuit: the ideology of the modernist movement insisted on seeing itself in relation to the principles of Palladio's architecture. This kind of interest in Palladio escalated after the publication of Rudolf Wittkower's *Architectural Principles in the Age of Humanism* in 1949; it coincided with the belief that it was possible to identify the same underlying principles in modernist and Renaissance architecture. While the modernist approach to Palladio's architecture emphasized his anti-mannerist tendencies and his use of proportions, the professional architectural community's increased interest in the classical tradition beginning in the late 1980s again revived interest in Palladio's use of ornamentation and the classical orders.

See also Architecture, *subentry on* Architectural Treatises.

BIBLIOGRAPHY

Primary Works

Palladio, Andrea. *L'antichità di Roma* (Roman antiquities). Rome, 1554.

Palladio, Andrea. *The Churches of Rome.* Translated by Eunice D. Howe. Binghamton, N.Y., 1991. Translation of *Descritione de le chiese* (1554).

Palladio, Andrea. *I commentari di C. Giulio Cesare* (Caesar's Gallic war). Frankfurt, Germany, 1575.

Palladio, Andrea. *The Four Books on Architecture.* Translated by Robert Tavernor and Richard Schofield. Cambridge, Mass., 1997. Translation of *I quattro libri dell'architettura* (1570).

Secondary Works

Ackerman, James. *Palladio.* 2d ed. Harmondsworth, U.K., 1977.

Boucher, Bruce. *Andrea Palladio: The Architect in His Time.* New York, 1994.

Lewis, Douglas. *The Drawings of Andrea Palladio.* Washington, D.C., 1981.

Puppi, Lionello. *Andrea Palladio.* Translated by Pearl Sanders. London, 1975.

Tavernor, Robert. *Palladio and Palladianism.* London, 1991.

Wittkower, Rudolf. *Architectural Principles in the Age of Humanism.* London, 1949.

BRANKO MITROVIĆ

PALMIERI, MATTEO (1406–1475), Florentine humanist and historian. Born in Florence in 1406, Matteo Palmieri was the son of Marco Palmieri, a Florentine pharmacist, and Tommasa Sassolini, daughter of a silk merchant. The Palmieri and Sassolini were middle-class families with prominent positions in the social and political life of the city.

Matteo Palmieri. Classical Roman-style marble bust by Antonio Rossellino, 1468. MUSEO NAZIONALE DEL BARGELLO, FLORENCE/ALINARI/ART RESOURCE, NY

Matteo Palmieri received the foundations of his humanist education in Florence from such great masters as Ambrogio Traversari and Carlo Marsuppini. Following in his father's footsteps, Palmieri pursued a civil career and became one of Florence's most outstanding public officials. He entered public life at the age of twenty-six and held public office from 1432 to 1475, filling numerous posts of distinction. As representative of the Florentine republic, he was sent on several diplomatic missions, including one to King Alfonso of Naples in 1455, and two to Rome, at the papal court of Paul II in 1466 and Sixtus IV in 1473.

Palmieri's deep involvement in the public affairs of his city did not prevent him from engaging in literary activity. He firmly believed the humanist claim that virtue (*virtù*) is a blending of both learning and political action (*scribendo et agendo*), departing, along with his friend and contemporary Leonardo Bruni, from the "contemplative" tradition of Petrarch and his followers. Palmieri wrote both in Latin and Italian. Among his Latin works are the *Liber de tem-*

poribus (Book of epochs), a Latin chronicle of the history of the world from the time of creation to his own days, the *De captivitate pisarum liber* (The capture of Pisa), an account of the Florentine capture of Pisa in 1406, and a biography of Niccolò Acciaiuoli (1310–1365), translated into Italian by Donato Acciaiuoli.

In Italian, Palmieri wrote a poem entitled *La città di vita* (The city of life), which he completed in 1465. It contains three books divided into one hundred chapters in terza rima (third rhyme). The allegorical poem is a late imitation of the *Commedia* (trans. *Divine Comedy*) by Dante Alighieri (1265–1321). In *La città di vita,* the author describes an imaginary journey to the Elysian fields, under the guidance of the Cumaean Sybil. In the afterworld are found the souls of the angels who were neutral to God and Lucifer. They are gathered there to be reborn as humans and suffer their punishment on earth before making their final choice between good and evil. Although the poem remained unpublished, it was subsequently condemned by the church, for it upheld Origen's heretical doctrine concerning the "pre-existence" of the human soul before creation. It is believed that after his death in 1475, Palmieri's body was removed from the Church of San Pier Maggiore and his image burned.

Palmieri's reputation as a humanist, however, is based on his fundamental treatise *Della vita civile* (On civic life; 1528), which he composed in 1429. The treatise, which first circulated between 1435 and 1440, is a dialogue divided in four books, addressing the qualities of the ideal citizen. The scene of the dialogue is a country house in Mugello, during the plague of 1430, with Agnolo Pandolfini as its main participant. Among important topics discussed are the physical and intellectual development of children into adulthood, the moral life of the citizen, in which Palmieri assumes primarily a civic dimension, and the contrasting interaction between what is "useful" and what is "honest" (the *bonum utile* and the *bonum honestum*), later dramatized by Machiavelli in *Il principe* (trans. *The Prince;* 1513). While *Della vita civile* relies heavily on the authority of ancient writers such as Cicero, Quintilian, and Plutarch, it also draws from the element of personal experience that was the highlight of Palmieri's career. What is mainly advocated in his treatise is the necessary correlation between a good education and its practical application in the life of the city. Whether as head of the family or as responsible citizen, the ideal man must create an environment that is productive and advantageous for all members of his community.

For this reason, education becomes critical at an early stage so as to improve the human capacity to do good.

There is a significant connection in *Della vita civile* between the state of the mind and the physical attributes of the body. Both higher and lower faculties must function harmoniously in order to be effective. In *Della vita civile,* physical education, the management of family affairs, and the active involvement of the individual in the life of the community are closely linked to an aesthetic perspective of a reality that is proportionate and balanced. This theme of the individual and the state as a "work of art" is fully grounded in the neoclassical tradition of the fifteenth century. As one of the strongest advocates of civic humanism, Palmieri's main contribution to the history of Italian literature and culture has been to restore the vernacular, in the tradition of Dante's illustrious language (*volgare illustre*), to the same level as Latin.

See also **Humanism,** *subentry on* **Italy.**

BIBLIOGRAPHY

Primary Works

Palmieri, Matteo. *De captivitate pisarum liber.* Edited by G. Scaramella. Città di Castello, Italy, 1904.

Palmieri, Matteo. *Libro del poema chiamato città di vita.* Edited by Margaret Rooke. Vol. 8, nos. 1–2. Smith College Studies. Northampton, Mass., 1927–1928.

Palmieri, Matteo. *La vita civile di Matteo Palmieri e il de optimo cive di Bartolomeo Sacchi.* Edited by Felice Battaglia. Bologna, Italy, 1944.

Secondary Works

Baron, Hans. *The Crisis of the Early Italian Renaissance: Civic Humanism and Republican Liberty in an Age of Classicism and Tyranny.* 2 vols. Princeton, N.J., 1955. Rev. ed. in 1 vol. Princeton, N.J., 1966.

Holmes, George. *The Florentine Enlightenment, 1400–50.* New York, 1969.

Martines, Lauro. *The Social World of the Florentine Humanists, 1390–1460.* Princeton, N.J., 1963.

Woodward, William H. *Studies in Education during the Age of the Renaissance, 1400–1600.* Cambridge, U.K., 1906. Reprint, New York, 1965.

GIUSEPPE FALVO

PANNONIUS, JANUS (1434–1472), humanist active in Hungary. One of the most important Neo-Latin poets of the Renaissance, Janus was a many-sided person whose life and career epitomized the trend of his time. As a mere child he was sent by his uncle, Johannes Vitéz (1408?–1471), bishop of Várad, later archbishop of Esztergom and primate of Hungary, to study in Ferrara with the famed humanist pedagogue Guarino Guarini (1370/74–1460). The boy from "north of the Alps," a region uncouth in the minds of Italians, soon became the pride of the school and was emulated even by his seniors. Guarino's students came from all over Europe, and the world is informed of his activities primarily from Janus's panegyric to his teacher ("Jani Pannonii Silva Panegyrica ad Guarinum Veronensem praeceptorem suum" (*Poemata*, vol. 1; Utrecht, 1774). Among his fellow students Janus was famous for his biting, often erotic epigrams, written in the style of Martial. This genre remained his favorite, although he also wrote a large number of elegies. Janus was sent to Italy to learn what an educated humanist was expected to know, with plans for him to serve in the royal chancery of Hungary. His literary output was an unexpected bonus.

Moving from Ferrara to Padua, Janus studied law and theology at the university. Having completed his studies, after a trip that took him to Rome in 1458, Janus began his administrative and political career at Matthias Corvinus's Buda court. Soon Janus became a confidant of the young king and was elected bishop to the lucrative see of Pécs. He became increasingly engaged in the business of government, and his poetry underwent a marked change. The joyful epigrams were replaced by somber elegies in which loneliness permeates the lines. In his heart Janus remained a poet, longing for Italy, suffering in a place he regarded a cultural desert. "I sing to myself and the muses," he wrote bitterly (*Epigrammata* 1). Also, Janus's consumption flared up in the harsh climate of Hungary. An ambassadorial trip to Italy in 1465, during which he met Marsilio Ficino and spent time with Vespasiano da Bisticci, briefly revitalized his creative energies.

By 1470, in face of the Ottoman danger, Janus became increasingly disappointed in the policies of Matthias and, together with his uncle, he began organizing a plot to replace the king. The conspirators were discovered, however, and Janus had to flee for his life while Vitéz died under house arrest in his see. On his way to Venice, where he hoped to get support against Matthias, Janus reached Zagreb, but there he succumbed to pneumonia and died in the fortress of his co-conspirator, Oswaldus Thuz, bishop of Zagreb.

Born in Croatia and active in Hungary, Janus wrote in Latin only. He was truly universal, belonging to that international network of humanists whose home was the antique world. His oeuvre bears no national characteristics; it is determined by the Latin universalism of the Renaissance. Yet his fate was typically Hungarian: he and Vitéz represented a new force, that of the lesser nobility, which for the following centuries became the carrier of social and cultural change in Hungary and Croatia.

BIBLIOGRAPHY

Primary Work

Pannonius, Janus. *Epigrammata. The Epigrams.* Edited and translated by Anthony A. Barrett. Budapest, Hungary, 1985. Text in English and Latin.

Secondary Works

Birnbaum, Marianna D. *Janus Pannonius: Poet and Politician.* Zagreb, Croatia, 1981.

Thomson, Ian. *Humanist Pietas. The Panegyric of Janus Pannonius on Guarinus Veronensis.* Bloomington, Ind., 1988.

MARIANNA D. BIRNBAUM

PANOFSKY, ERWIN. *See* **Renaissance, Interpretations of the,** *subentry on* **Erwin Panofsky.**

PAPACY. Pope (from the Greek, Latin, and Italian *papa* = "father") was the title given clergy in the ancient church. Eventually it became in the West the exclusive title of the bishop of Rome, considered the successor of St. Peter, the first among the five major patriarchs. Increasingly the pope was accepted in the West as vicar of Christ and head of the whole church. By gifts, purchases, and conquests, the popes became rulers over one of the oldest continuously functioning states of Europe. The Papal States, a territory that stretched from Rome and its environs northeastward to the Adriatic Sea, was composed of six regions (Rome, the Campagna and Marittima, the Patrimony of St. Peter, Umbria, the Marches, and Romagna), and included its vassal Ferrara in the Po River valley. Its economy was primarily agricultural (grain, olive oil, wine, and livestock), but also included the manufacture of woolen textiles and paper (Fabriano), and the mining of salt (Cervia) and alum (after its discovery at Tolfa in 1461). In the first-ever census of the Papal States taken in 1656 the population was determined to be about 1.7 million. The most populous cities were Rome and Bologna; among those of the middling rank were Orvieto, Spoleto, Perugia, Ancona, and Ravenna. The principal ports were Civitavecchia on the Tyrrhenian Sea and Ancona, Rimini, and Pesaro on the Adriatic coast.

Rome and Avignon: The Great Western Schism. During most of the period 1309–1377, the papacy resided at Avignon, but returned to Rome, partly out of fear of losing control over the Papal States. The death of Gregory XI (1370–1378), after only one year in Rome, was followed by a cha-

TABLE 1. Popes, 1294–1644*

Pope	Name	Birthdate	Pontificate
Boniface VIII	Benedetto Caetani	c. 1235	1294–1303
Benedict IX	Niccolò Boccasino	1240	1303–1304
Clement V	Bertrand de Got	c. 1260	1305–1314
John XXII	Jacques Duèse	c. 1244	1316–1334
Nicholas V (Bavaria)[1]	Pietro Rainalducci	after 1275	1328–1329[2]
Benedict XII	Jacques Fournier	c. 1280–1285	1334–1342
Clement VI	Pierre Roger	1291	1342–1352
Innocent VI	Étienne Aubert	1282	1352–1362
Urban V	Guillaume de Grimoard	1310	1362–1370
Gregory XI	Pierre Roger de Beaufort	1329	1370–1378
Urban VI (Rome)	Bartolomeo Prignano	c. 1318	1378–1389
Clement VII (Avignon)	Robert de Genève	1342	1378–1394
Boniface IX (Rome)	Pietro Tomacelli	c. 1350	1389–1404
Benedict XIII (Avignon)	Pedro de Luna	c. 1328	1394–1423
Innocent VII (Rome)	Cosimo Gentile de' Migliorati	c. 1336	1404–1406
Gregory XII (Rome)	Angelo Correr	c. 1325	1406–1415
Alexander V (Pisa)	Pietro Philarghi	unknown	1409–1410
John XXIII (Pisa)	Baldassarre Cossa	unknown	1410–1415[3]
Martin V	Oddone Colonna	1368	1417–1431
Clement VIII (Avignon)	Gil Sanchez Muñoz	c. 1360	1423–1429
Benedict XIV (Avignon)	Bernard Garnier	unknown	1425[4]
Eugenius IV	Gabriele Condulmer	c. 1383	1431–1447
Felix V (Basel)	Amadeo di Savoia	1383	1440–1449[5]
Nicholas V	Tommaso Parentucelli	1397	1447–1455
Callistus III	Alonso de Borja	1378	1455–1458
Pius II	Enea Silvio Piccolomini	1405	1458–1464
Paul II	Pietro Barbo	1417	1464–1471
Sixtus IV	Francesco della Rovere	1414	1471–1484
Innocent VIII	Giovanni Battista Cibò	1432	1484–1492
Alexander VI	Rodrigro de Borja y Borja	1431	1492–1503
Pius III	Francesco Todeschini-Piccolomini	1439	1503
Julius II	Giuliano della Rovere	1453	1503–1513
Leo X	Giovanni de' Medici	1475	1513–1521
Adrian VI	Adrian Florenszoon Dedal	1459	1521–1523
Clement VII	Giulio de' Medici	1479	1523–1534
Paul III	Alessandro Farnese	1468	1534–1549
Julius III	Giovanni Maria Ciocchi del Monte	1487	1549–1555
Marcellus II	Marcello Cervini	1501	1555
Paul IV	Giovanni Pietro Carafa	1476	1555–1559
Pius IV	Giovanni Angelo Medici	1499	1559–1565
Pius V	Antonio (Michele) Ghislieri	1504	1566–1572
Gregory XIII	Ugo Buoncompagni	1502	1572–1585
Sixtus V	Felice Peretti	1520	1585–1590
Urban VII	Giovanni Battista Castagna	1521	1590
Gregory XIV	Niccolò Sfondrati	1535	1590–1591
Innocent IX	Giovanni Antonio Facchinetti	1519	1591
Clement VIII	Ippolito Aldobrandini	1536	1592–1605
Leo XI	Alessandro Ottaviano de' Medici	1535	1605
Paul V	Camillo Borghese	1552	1605–1621
Gregory XV	Alessandro Ludovisi	1554	1621–1623
Urban VIII	Maffeo Barberini	1568	1623–1644

*This table includes all incumbents of or claimants to the office of pope between 1294 and 1644. Claimants elected or appointed while someone already held the office have been called "antipopes," although no one in Western Christendom could be certain of who was pope during the Western Schism (1378–1417). This table therefore indicates the sponsorship or primary residence of popes: Bavaria for one pope elected at the behest of the emperor Louis IV of Bavaria; Avignon for popes who resided at Avignon during most of the schism; Rome for popes who often resided at Rome during the schism; Pisa for the pope elected by the Council of Pisa, Alexander V, and his successor, John XXIII; and Basel for one pope elected by the Council of Basel. Popes without indication of provenance or sponsorship are Roman.

[1] Nicholas V, elected at the behest of the emperor Louis IV of Bavaria, resided mainly in Rome and Pisa.

[2] Abdicated; died 1333.

[3] Abdicated; died 1419.

[4] Date of death unknown.

[5] Abdicated; died 1451.

TABLE 2. The Western Schism

Date of election	Rome	Avignon	Pisa
1378	Urban VI	Clement VII	
1389	Boniface IX		
1394		Benedict XIII	
1404	Innocent VII		
1406	Gregory XII		
1409			Alexander V
1410			John XXIII
1417	Martin V[1]		
1423		Clement VIII	
1425		Benedict XIV	

[1]The schism ended with the election of Martin V by the Council of Constance; he was recognized by followers of the Roman and the Pisan popes. Benedict XIII refused to abdicate and was deposed by the council, though he continued to maintain a court in Peñiscola in the province of Valencia until his death in 1423.

otic conclave. The cardinals were pressured to elect an Italian, who took the name Urban VI (1378–1389). Five months later the cardinals deposed him and elected Robert of Geneva, who became Clement VII (1378–1394) and ruled from Avignon. The rival popes excommunicated each other and attacked and imprisoned their opponent's supporters. All attempts to resolve this Great Western Schism (1378–1415) failed. Convinced that only a general council had the authority to impose a solution, most of the cardinals deserted their popes and together called the Council of Pisa (1409), which deposed the rival popes and elected Alexander V (1409–1410), who won the allegiance of most of Europe and whose army captured Rome. At the Council of Constance (1414–1418) the Pisan and Avignonese popes were deposed and the Roman one resigned. Finally, Martin V (1417–1431) was elected by a conciliar commission composed of cardinals from all three obediences plus thirty deputies. If the papacy emerged from the council with its institutional unity restored, its authority in the temporal and spiritual realms was still in question.

Papal States. During the schism the pope's control over the Papal States was often tenuous. The concordats negotiated at the Council of Constance in 1418 significantly reduced papal spiritual revenues for the next five years. Martin V (Oddo Colonna) therefore looked to the Papal States to supply the lost revenues and moved quickly to assert his authority once he returned to Rome in 1420. By 1424 he eliminated Andrea Fortebracci, known as "Brac-

cione de Montone" of Perugia, and crushed a revolt by Bologna in 1429. His relatives were rewarded for their help with grants of estates, and revenues from the Papal States increased.

In his determination to break the power of the Colonna family, Martin V's successor Eugenius IV (1431–1447) brought turmoil to the Papal States and lost some of its territories to Florence, Venice, and Naples. Nicholas V (1447–1455) succeeded in getting Francesco Sforza (1401–1466) to abandon his claims to Ancona in return for papal acquiescence in his takeover of Milan. The fall of Constantinople in 1453 to the Turks and the failed papal effort to raise a crusade to retake it led Nicholas to work for peace in Italy. He supported the Peace of Lodi (1454), entered the Italian League (1455), and thus secured the freedom of the Papal States from external attacks for years to come. With the help of Federigo II da Montefeltro (1422–1482), Pius II (1458–1464) reduced the power of Sforza's ally, Sigismondo Malatesta (1417–1468), restricting him to the city of Rimini (1463).

The next major elimination of the power of local lords occurred during the pontificate of Alexander VI (1492–1503) whose son, Cesare Borgia (1475–1507), carved out for himself the duchy of Romagna by removing various local families from power. Julius II (1503–1513), who saw to the downfall of Borgia, brought many of these cities and territories under direct papal rule, allowing some families to return to power. In 1509 he forced Venice to return not only territories it had illegally occupied as Borgia's control weakened, but also Ravenna, which it had ruled since 1441. Julius also succeeded in driving the Bentivoglio family from power in Bologna (1506, 1512) and the Baglioni from Perugia (1506). His successors allowed the Baglioni to return, until Paul III (1534–1549) in 1540 permanently excluded them and imposed direct papal governance.

The elimination of local lordships in the Papal States whether by escheat (failure to produce a surviving legitimate male heir) or by the deposition of rebellious vassals and the conquest of their states did not always result in direct papal rule. Some popes used the opportunity to install their relatives as the new lords, the most famous example being when Alexander VI made his son Cesare Borgia duke of Romagna. Pius V (1566–1572) in 1567 forbade further alienation of lands belonging to the Papal States, prohibiting the reinvestiture of fiefdoms that had reverted to their papal overlord. As a result of this decree, the duchy of Ferrara came under direct papal rule with the death of Alfonso II d'Este in 1597, as did Urbino and Pesaro in 1624 with the renunciation of rule by Francesco Maria II della Rovere and his death in 1631. By the early seventeenth century, the process of centralizing power in the Papal States and ruling the major territories and cities directly through papal governors was almost complete.

Popes and General Councils. The popes also labored to restore their spiritual prestige and authority. They considered conciliarism, encapsuled in the decrees *Haec Sancta* (1415) and *Frequens* (1417) of Constance, the most serious threat to this restoration. The first decree gave the general council authority over the pope and the second required that councils be called regularly. Martin V avoided giving explicit confirmation to *Haec Sancta* and initially obeyed *Frequens,* but prevented the Council of Pavia-Siena (1423–1424) from accomplishing its goals. His successor Eugenius IV proved so obstructionist that the Council of Basel deposed him and elected an antipope, Felix V (1439–1449). The rival papal council, meeting at Ferrara, Florence, and Rome (1438–1445), condemned Basel and declared the pope to be the supreme authority in the church.

When Paul III convoked the Council of Trent (1545–1563), he made sure that his legate presidents controlled its procedures and agenda. While the council made no direct pronouncements on the relationship between a pope and general council, its willingness to allow the pope to resolve difficulties in interpreting its decrees led to the establishment in 1564 of the powerful Congregation of the Council, whose ever-expanding rulings bolstered papal power and eliminated for three centuries the need for another council.

Popes and Cardinals. The Renaissance witnessed remarkable changes in the college of cardinals, the group of prominent clerics who elected the pope and functioned as his official advisers and chief administrators. The concordats negotiated at Constance in 1418 and the decree of Basel in 1436 attempted to limit the number of cardinals to twenty-four with no more than a third coming from any one nation, and required of them the minimum age of thirty and an advanced academic degree in scripture or canon and civil law, unless they were the close relative of a great prince. Popes, however, claimed that for the good of the church they needed to increase the number of cardinals. In part to raise money, Sixtus IV (1471–1484) made a large increase in the numbers, and Leo X (1513–1521) in 1517 promoted thirty-one cardinals at one time following a conspiracy on his life. Instead of using twice the

number of Christ's apostles as the norm, Sixtus V (1585–1590) in 1586 set the limit at seventy, the number of elders assisting Moses. Although Italians constituted over half of the cardinals appointed by each pope from Martin V to Calixtus III (1455–1458), the later popes, with the exception of Alexander VI, so advanced the italianization of the college that only a third of its members were foreigners and they usually did not reside in Rome. While many cardinals were well-educated servants of the papacy, others received the honor due to family or political connections, on the payment of large sums of money, and, in the case of princely pedigree, with little regard to the age requirement.

At the beginning of the Renaissance cardinals functioned as powerful, semiautonomous heads of bureaucracies and as protectors of the interests of various nations, religious orders, and factions, often in conjunction with other cardinals. With the increase in numbers and the use of committees, the power of individual cardinals weakened, and the consistory (the meeting of the college of cardinals to advise the pope on policy and appointments), eventually met but weekly, often to give perfunctory praise to decisions already made. The rise of the office of Secretary of State, usually given to a relative of the pope who became his chief adviser and minister, also diminished the power of the cardinals.

Paul III set the college on a new course by appointing many reform-minded cardinals and instituting special congregations of cardinals to deal with

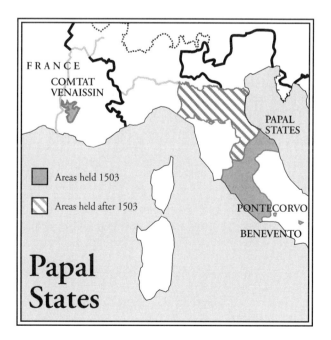

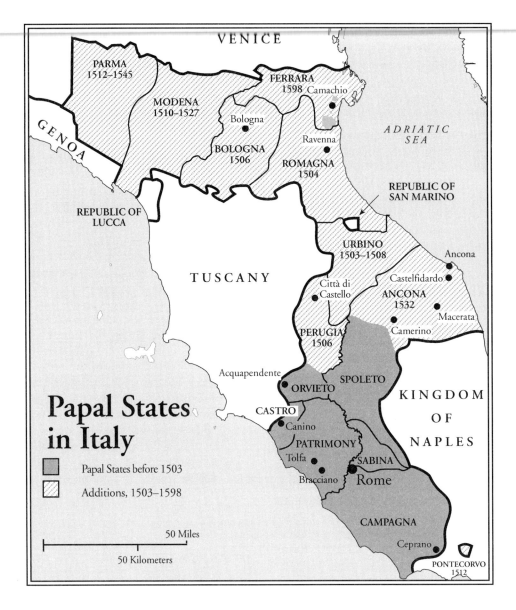

Papal States in Italy

- Papal States before 1503
- Additions, 1503–1598

50 Miles

50 Kilometers

specific issues, for example, Roman Inquisition (1542) and Council of Trent (1545). Pius IV (1559–1565) set up the powerful Congregation of the Council (1564), Pius V that of the Index of Prohibited Books (1571), and Gregory XIII (1572–1585) that for the Affairs of Germany (1572). In 1588 Sixtus V rationalized the whole system by setting up fifteen permanent congregations (six for secular affairs, the others for spiritual), each with its own specific tasks and staffed by three to five cardinals who served fixed terms and were rotated through the various congregations. By such measures, cardinals became docile bureaucrats who fulfilled ceremonial roles at court and in the papal chapel.

If the cardinals lost power during the Renaissance, they managed to maintain their wealth. The reform decrees of the Council of Trent forbade the holding of multiple sees and required residence in the one held. This forced the cardinals to find alternative sources of revenues in commendatory monasteries and pensions drawn on multiple benefices. Cardinals from aristocratic families continued to enjoy private sources of income. All cardinals were entitled to a share in papal revenues. With such wealth, the cardinals resident in Rome maintained lavish palaces with households that averaged about 150 persons. Cardinals so successfully used their wealth and influence to promote their own and their colleagues' family interest by advancing the clerical careers of some relatives and negotiating favorable marriages for others, that by the second-half of the sixteenth century the college had become one big extended family, with three-quarters of the cardinals related to each other by blood or marriage.

Popes and Bishops. Renaissance popes tried to assert their theoretical superiority over bishops while yielding greater influence to secular rulers in their selection. The papacy insisted on its prerogative to confirm the election of a bishop by cathedral chapter or to make the appointment itself, and collected from the new bishop the first year's revenues from his diocese as a fee for this confirmation or direct appointment. Popes frequently allied themselves with increasingly powerful local rulers in order to replace the traditional election of bishops by cathedral canons with the direct appointment by the pope of candidates nominated by the rulers. Such arrangements were incorporated into concordats. Bishops thus appointed tended to be very loyal to the ruler who nominated them and the royal conscience determined in large measure the quality of the episcopate. The Council of Trent raised the educational level of bishops by requiring of them advanced academic degrees in theology or law (1562) and it emphasized their pastoral responsibilities and hence the obligation of residency (1547, 1562). The national colleges, which the popes established in Rome (German, 1552; Greek, 1577; Hungarian [united with the German in 1580], 1578; English, 1579; Polish, 1583, 1600; Maronite and Armenian, 1584; Scots, 1600; and others), produced clergy who went on to become bishops in their native lands. To strengthen the ties between the pope and bishops and to provide closer scrutiny of their ministry, Sixtus V in 1584 required all bishops to visit Rome once every three to ten years, depending on the distances involved, and to submit regularly written reports on their dioceses.

Roman Curia. The central administrative, judicial, favor-granting, and financial offices of the Roman Catholic Church, under the supervision of the pope and college of cardinals, was called the Roman Curia. Its departments were often headed by cardinals and employed hundreds of officials ranging from learned canonists to ignorant sealers of documents, men who composed documents, kept records, and collected fees. In the course of the Renaissance the popes sought to increase their own income by multiplying the number of these offices and selling them for ever higher prices. Those who invested in these lifetime offices were entitled to an annual stipend (valued at 10–12 percent of the cost of office) paid by the Camera Apostolica (the chief financial office of the Papal States), and the third

who actually functioned in their offices were additionally recompensed by their colleges or department for the services rendered. Some officials sought to extract extra revenues from their office by engaging in questionable practices, which earned the Curia much ill-will.

In the fifteenth century numerous reform proposals, and even drafts of bulls, were drawn up, but almost never implemented, primarily for fear of financial losses. In 1466 Paul II abolished the college of abbreviators and reaped thereby the literary wrath of many humanists who had held this post. His successor Sixtus IV restored the college (1479), more than doubled the number of venal offices (up to 625), and created so many other offices to finance his building and military projects that his reign was often cited for introducing abuses into the Curia. His successors created new offices on a lesser scale until Leo X doubled the number of venal offices to over two thousand.

The popes vigorously resisted any attempts by councils to reform the Curia, claiming that they would reform it themselves. To forestall conciliar reform efforts, Julius II on the eve of the Fifth Lateran Council (1512) and Paul III prior to the Council of Trent (1540–1542) issued bulls that regulated fees and removed glaring abuses. Serious reform came gradually and slowly, given the entrenched interests and hostility of cardinals and curialists. Pressure by popes eliminated some of the venal offices, abusive dispensations, and other practices. But under Sixtus V the sale and resale of offices, even of major offices in the Camera (chamberlain, treasurer-general, auditor, and so on) was extensive. The value of the offices at the papal court at the end of his reign is estimated at four million scudi with the obligation of paying out a half-million scudi every year in stipends to office-holders. By the early seventeenth century the Curia, never radically reformed, had been reorganized and regularized with the most glaring abuses abolished.

Papal Finances. Throughout much of the Renaissance, papal finances were difficult to manage. The popes levied no annual income tax on church members, but instead depended on a patchwork of traditional sources of revenues. Fees charged for documents appointing or confirming one in offices—the principal fee was the annate, or first year's revenues from that office—amounted to 13 percent of papal income in 1521. The Roman Curia produced almost half of the pope's income by the fees it charged those using its various services: dispensations from church law, fines for violating it, special favors, reservations and expectatives on benefices, indulgences, costs related to law suits, and so forth. The sale of venal offices produced between 10 and 15 percent of papal revenues. The other major source of revenues was the annual tribute paid by the pope's vassals, vicars, and subject communities in the Papal States, augmented by various taxes, monopolies, and the sale of shares in *monti,* or state bonds. In 1521 the Papal States produced about 37 percent of all of papal revenues. The relative decline in spiritual income over the next eighty-five years can be attributed in part to the loss of revenues from lands that became Protestant and to the elimination of abusive practices in the Curia. The rise in temporal revenues was related to the popes' increasingly direct control over the Papal States with the elimination of many vassals and vicars and more efficient administration. It is estimated that the Papal States accounted for 25 percent of papal fixed income under Gregory XII (1406–1415), and 80 percent under Clement VIII (1592–1605).

Papal expenditures increased throughout the Renaissance. Almost a third of the annual budget went to paying annuities to holders of venal offices. Salaries paid to papal administrators in Rome and the Papal States accounted for another 20 percent. The cost of maintaining an army and building fortifications could consume as much as 60 percent of temporal revenues on occasion. The college of cardinals was entitled to a significant share of papal revenues. Maintaining papal ambassadors in fitting style at the courts of Christendom was expensive. The papal court itself in Rome—with its numerous officials and the meals it provided to them, curialists, and others—was a major annual expense. Popes spent significant sums on their relatives by way of gifts of money and lands, at times for dowries to contract aristocratic marriages. Huge drains on papal revenues were caused by wars and by the subsidies popes paid in support of crusades against the Turks, Hussites, Lutherans, and the Huguenots in France. Also costly were various building projects in Rome, such as the new St. Peter's Basilica; the Vatican, Quirinal, and Lateran palaces; the Roman College with its satellite national residential colleges for students; and various churches around Rome. The Council of Trent required large papal subsidies. Papal funerals, conclaves, and coronation ceremonies were periodic expenses. The popes hoped to build up a reserve fund for such emergencies as famine or warfare. The enormous treasure of 3 million golden scudi and 1.2 million silver scudi that Sixtus V amassed cushioned the papacy for two centuries but had the adverse economic effect of restricting economic growth by removing so much money from circulation.

Papal Claims to Temporal Jurisdiction.

The Renaissance popes tried to maintain the claims of their medieval predecessors to rule not only over the spiritual realm by the Petrine commission (a special office of leadership conferred on Peter by Jesus), but also over the temporal order based both on their interpretation of various scriptural texts and on the supposed *Donatio Constantini* (Donation of Constantine) that recorded the gift to pope Sylvester I (314–335) and his successors of the Western Empire. They claimed the right to approve the election of the emperor and to crown him personally. Leo X failed in his efforts to block the election of Charles V of Habsburg in 1519, and Clement VII crowned Charles in Bologna in 1530. No further emperors were crowned by popes and Paul IV (1555–1559) seriously proposed deposing Charles V because of his formal tolerance of Protestantism. Renaissance popes did excommunicate kings and encouraged neighboring rulers to conquer their territories. Paul III excommunicated Henry VIII of England by a bull dated 1535 that was implemented in 1538, while Pius V excommunicated Henry's daughter, Elizabeth I, in 1570. Sixtus V in 1585 and Gregory XIV (1590–1591) in 1591 both excommunicated the apostate Henry IV Bourbon, lest this Huguenot become king of France.

In the course of the fifteenth century various popes encouraged the rulers of the Iberian peninsula to conquer Muslim territories both there and in Africa and its adjacent islands. The popes acknowledged the Christian kings' sovereignty over these newly won territories and granted to them or to the Portuguese military Order of Christ patronage rights over the churches to be established in these lands. The discovery by Columbus of non-Muslim lands led the pope to invoke his universal temporal sovereignty. By the bull *Inter caetera divinae* of 4 May 1493, Alexander VI granted to the Spanish monarch sovereignty over the islands and mainlands discovered by their agents in the areas one hundred leagues to the west and south of the Azores and Cape Verde islands, provided these lands were not already possessed by another Christian king or prince. The reason given for this grant was to support the monarch's efforts to convert the natives to Christianity.

Popes as Defenders of Orthodoxy.

The Renaissance popes continued to exercise their traditional role, codified in canon law, as the ultimate arbiters of orthodoxy, issuing their rulings on their

Pope and Emperor. *Pope Clement VII and Emperor Charles V* by Giorgio Vasari (1511–1574) in the Sala di Clemente VII of the Palazzo Vecchio, Florence. Clement crowned Charles at Bologna in 1530; Charles was the last Holy Roman Emperor crowned by a pope. SCALA/ART RESOURCE

own authority or with the backing of the council, after an examination by a theological commission. Cases came to the attention of the popes in various ways. Local authorities could send their condemnations of heretics to the popes for confirmation or the party condemned could appeal to the pope to reverse the local decision. Cases on which Renaissance popes ruled included the orthodoxy of the use by Bernardino of Siena (1380–1444) of the symbol "IHS" (letters of the name Jesus; 1426, 1432) and of the liturgical celebration of Mary's Immaculate Conception (1476) and the condemnation of some (seven as heretical and six as suspect; 1487) of the nine hundred theses of Giovanni Pico della Mirandola (1463–1494) and of the feigned prophecies (1498) of Girolamo Savonarola (1452–1498). After careful examination by theological commissions, Leo X issued at the Fifth Lateran Council bulls approving as not usurious the fees charged by public credit organizations (*montes pietatis*) for monetary loans (1515) and condemning the teachings that denied the human soul's multiplicity and immortality, the unicity of truth, and the creation of the world (1513). In 1520 Leo X condemned forty-one propositions extracted from the writings of Martin Luther as heretical, scandalous, and offensive to pious ears

(15 June 1520) and the *Augenspiel* of Johannes Reuchlin (1455–1522) as offensive and scandalous and improperly favorable to Jews (eight days later). The two most famous cases toward the end of the Renaissance involved the condemnation (1599) for his pantheistic and hermetical ideas of Giordano Bruno (1548–1600) and the rejections (1616, 1633) of the Copernican cosmology of Galileo Galilei (1564–1642).

The Renaissance popes established procedures and institutions to deal with heresy. In 1479 Sixtus IV granted to the Spanish monarchs the power to set up inquisitional tribunals in Castile; in 1482 the pope agreed to place the papal inquisition in Aragon under the royally controlled Castilian inquisition. In 1542, inspired by the successes of the Spanish Inquisition, Gian Pietro Carafa (the future Paul IV) urged Paul III to institute the Roman Inquisition to suppress Protestant ideas in Italy and elsewhere. Also known as the Holy Office, it soon became one of the most important papal bureaucracies. Based on earlier papal (1479, 1489, 1559) and conciliar (1515, 1546, 1563) decrees instituting pre-publication censorship of books, Pius IV in 1564 issued the so-called Tridentine Index of Prohibited Books, the first papal index with continuing authority. In 1571 Pius V established the Congregation of the Index composed of six cardinals to oversee the censorship of books. Crucial to the definition of Catholic orthodoxy was the work of the Council of Trent (1545–1563) that met under Paul III, Julius III (1550–1555), and Pius IV. Pius IV also had the Council's central teachings incorporated into the Tridentine Profession of Faith to which he required all bishops, religious superiors, and teachers to subscribe personally with an oath.

Popes and Crusades. The Renaissance papacy often assumed a major role in the defense of Christendom from Islamic threats. Whether because of a default of lay leadership or in order to assert their own claims to universal sovereignty, the Renaissance popes, acting as the common fathers of all Christians, sought to rally Christian princes to help their front-line brethren. The papacy often encouraged these efforts by granting crusade indulgences, special taxes to be levied on the clergy, and patronage rights over the churches to be established in the conquered lands. The popes also provided financial subsidies to support the crusades, and sent their own troops, sailors, and ships to join in the expeditions. In the fifteenth century various popes actively encouraged the efforts of Spanish monarchs to drive the Moors from the Iberian peninsula.

Turkish advances in the Balkans posed a serious threat to the survival of Christendom and also provided a stimulus for greater cooperation among Christians. The Greek Orthodox Byzantine emperors who needed the assistance of their Latin brothers to ward off the Turks suspected that they had to restore church unity before the pope would rally Catholic princes. Once John VIII Palaeologus (1425–1448) and the Greek hierarchy united with the Latin Church at the Council of Florence in 1439, Eugenius IV organized a Western military force composed primarily of the front-line states of Hungary, Poland-Lithuania, and Transylvania. The pope sent eighteen ships to join the combined Venetian, Burgundian, and Ragusan fleet of two dozen ships that guarded the straits to the Black Sea. Nonetheless the Latin army was routed at Varna (1444) by the forces of Murad, which the Venetian contingent of the fleet had allowed to cross the Bosphorus unopposed.

Calixtus III dedicated his papacy to the reconquest of Constantinople, which had fallen to the Turks in 1453, but despite some minor victories aroused animosity among Latin Christians due to his aggressive imposition of crusading taxes. Pius II tried to organize a crusade. When he received only lukewarm support, he tried to lead the crusade person-

The Pope as Crusader. Pius II presides over a assembly in Mantua to plan a crusade. Fresco by Pinturicchio in the Piccolomini Library, Siena Cathedral. ALINARI/ART RESOURCE

ally, but died at Ancona while waiting for the fleet to assemble. The efforts of Leo X to organize a united crusade failed due to the rivalry between the Habsburg and Valois dynasties, which hindered all serious coordinated efforts for the next forty years. Despite French hostility, the Habsburg emperors assumed the leadership of Christian land forces once the disastrous defeat of Hungary in 1526 and seige of Vienna in 1529 made frontline states of their realms. The popes then tried to organize the Mediterranean Catholic naval powers. Adrian VI (1522–1523) and Clement VII protected the Knights of St. John, until Charles V in 1530 granted them the islands of Malta which they herorically defended in 1565. The Holy League (Papacy, Spain, Venice), which Pius V negotiated, scored the temporary naval victory at Lepanto (1571), but Cyprus fell permanently to the Turks in 1571. The death of King Sebastian of Portugal in 1578 while crusading in Morocco brought a symbolic end to the era of crusades against Islam.

Papal Efforts to Restore Church Unity.

The Renaissance popes also promoted crusades against heretics. A series of crusades were unsuccessfully fought against the Hussites in 1420–1431 and again in 1468–1471. A crusade against the Waldensians in the Alpine valleys of the Dauphiné in 1488 resulted in the execution of about 160 heretics, but others escaped. Papal support for military action against Protestants was complicated by fears of Habsburg hegemony and by the frequent reluctance of the Habsburg and Valois rulers to engage in such activities. Paul III sent money and troops to aid Charles V against the Lutherans, while Pius IV and subsequent popes provided financial subsidies to the French kings and the French Catholic League in their armed struggle with the Huguenots.

The popes also tried by means of diplomacy and missionary activities to win back lands that had gone Protestant. Gregory XIII entered into detailed but unsuccessful negotiations to reconcile Sweden. Reversing the policies of his predecessors, Clement VIII accepted the reconversion to Catholicism of Henry IV Bourbon of France and absolved him of ecclesiastical censures (1595). The popes also entertained the hope of reconciliation with the Stuart monarchs of England. To train missionaries to work in German, English, and Scandinavian Protestant lands the popes established seminaries.

The popes also concerned themselves with restoring church unity with Eastern Christians. The reunions negotiated with Greek (1439), Armenian (1439), Coptic (1442), Syrian (1444), and Cypriot Chaldean and Maronite (1445) delegations at the Council of Ferrara-Florence-Rome (1438–1445) did not produce lasting results, but the popes worked through their nuncios and missionaries to restore union. Through the work of the Franciscans, the Maronites of Lebanon made a formal obedience to Leo X at the Fifth Lateran Council (1516); by the efforts of the Dominicans the patriarch of the Assyrian Chaldean Church submitted in person to Julius III in 1553. Clement VIII supported the work of the Jesuits to bring the Syro-Malabar Christians of India into union with Rome, but did not confirm the latinizing decrees of the Synod of Diamper (1599). Eighty years of papal backing for the Jesuit mission to the Orthodox Ethiopian Church culminated in failure in 1632 due to over-latinization. Despite Russian rejection of earlier papal overtures, Gregory XIII warmly received the emissaries sent in 1581 by Ivan IV, tsar and grand prince of all Russia (1533–1584), who asked the pope to mediate a peace with Catholic Poland-Lithuania and suggested his own openness to church union. Once the papal nuncio Antonio Possevino (1533–1611) had negotiated a truce in 1582, he soon discovered that the tsar did not want union with Rome. Fearful of Moscovite domination, the Byzantine-rite bishops of Poland-Lithuania requested union with Rome, which Clement VIII granted on 23 December 1595.

Papal Support for Missionary Activities among Non-Christians.

The Renaissance popes were also concerned with the spread of the Catholic faith into non-Christian lands. Their chief allies in this task were the Iberian rulers whose state-sponsored voyages of exploration opened up new lands for evangelization and the religious orders whose members served as missionaries. By a series of bulls the popes conferred patronage rights and evangelization responsibilities. To aid the friar missionaries in the work of evangelizing America, Adrian VI in 1522 by the bull *Omnimoda* granted them the faculties of a bishop, except for those requiring episcopal orders. Even though a diocesan structure had been established throughout the Spanish lands in America and the Council of Trent had decreed the submission of regular clergy to the local bishop on questions of pastoral care, in 1567, because of the friars' opposition, Philip II was forced to obtain from Pius V a restoration of the friars' privileges. The Third Provincial Council of Mexico in 1585 adopted the decrees of Trent curtailing these privileges, and Sixtus V in 1589 formally confirmed its decrees subjecting members of religious orders to episcopal control in their pastoral work.

The popes intervened on a number of other issues. Paul III by his brief *Pastorale officium* (1537) condemned the enslavement of natives. In his bull *Sublimis Deus* (1537) he taught that the natives are fully human with rights of their own and can become full Christians. His bull *Altitudo divini consilii* (1537) required the traditional rites in administering baptism to converts and assured the converts the right to receive the Eucharist—both implicit criticisms of Franciscan practices. Leo X in his brief *Exponi nobis* (1519) insisted that natives be trained and ordained as clergy. While the Portuguese followed Leo's ruling, the Spanish adopted a contrary policy, which the popes had difficulty modifying.

The foundation of the Congregation for the Propagation of the Faith (1622) indicated greater papal involvement in the missions. Questions of missionary methodology were brought to it for resolution. While the approach of Roberto de' Nobili (1577–1656) in his work among the Hindu Brahmins was approved by Gregory XV (1621–1623) in 1623, Rome eventually rejected some of the cultural adaptations used by the Jesuit missionaries in China. In 1627 Urban VIII (1623–1644) founded the Collegio Urbano in Rome to train missionaries.

The Popes as Patrons of Learning. While most Renaissance popes were trained in canon law or theology and only a few in classical letters (Nicholas V, Pius II, Leo X, Paul IV, and Urban VIII), they were quick to recognize the advantages of employing humanists as their apostolic secretaries and curial officials. Although Petrarch cleverly avoided becoming a papal secretary in Avignon, later humanists were eager to find papal employment. In the early fifteenth century the Roman and Pisan popes hired as their secretaries such noted humanists as Poggio Bracciolini (1380–1459), Leonardo Bruni (c. 1370–1444), Antonio Loschi (1368–1441), and Gasparino Barzizza (1360–1430). The restored papacy continued to hire writers such as Flavio Biondo (1392–1463) and Lorenzo Valla (c. 1407–1457). Leo X had as his secretaries the famous Latinists Jacopo Sadoleto (1477–1547) and Pietro Bembo (1470–1547). Humanists also worked as secretaries for cardinals and other prelates and staffed many posts in the Roman Curia. Their influence is evident in the more Ciceronic prose and humanist script used in the chancery by 1480 and in the classicizing, epideictic style of oratory in the papal chapel. While continuing to support traditional scholastic theology, even encouraging in Rome starting with Nicholas V a revival of Thomism, Renaissance popes also patronized the new humanistic theologies, both poetic/antique theology that borrowed Neoplatonic concepts and tried to syncretize ancient religions with Christianity (Ficino, Bessarion), and rhetorical/philological theology that corrected corrupted scriptural and patristic texts and used Christian antiquity as a model for critiquing the current church (Valla, Erasmus). Popes generally supported the informal academies or literary circles of Rome, unless they proved subversive (for example, Pomponio Leto's academy), and often tolerated the satirical verses emanating from them that were attached to the antique statue dubbed Pasquino.

The popes founded new and supported existing institutions of learning. The Vatican Library founded by Nicholas V "for the convenience of the learned" was reorganized and given enlarged quarters, staff, and endowments by Sixtus IV in 1475. Its present elegant quarters were constructed by Sixtus V in 1585–1590. Of the already existent universities in the Papal States (Rome, Bologna, Perugia, and Ferrara—Macerata was added in 1540–1541), that in Rome (known as the Sapienza since the time of Paul III) received special papal support. Eugenius IV revitalized it with a reorganization and new revenues coming from a tax on imported wine served in Roman taverns; Nicholas V promoted lectureships in classical studies; and Leo X established new professorships, regulations, and a Greek college. While cardinals founded in Rome the Capranica (1475) and Nardini (1484) colleges for the training of priests, Pius IV in 1565 established the Roman Seminary whose students attended lectures at the Collegio Romano, established in 1551 by the Jesuits, for which Gregory XIII provided new quarters and endowments in 1572. With the help of scholars, the popes carried out tasks assigned them by the Council of Trent, revising the Index of Prohibited Books (1564 and 1596), issuing the Roman Catechism (1566), and providing corrected editions of the Breviary (1568), Missal (1570), code of canon law (1582), calendar (1582), Roman Martyrology (1584), and Vulgate (that is, Latin Bible; 1590, 1592). Following the accidental discovery in 1578 of an ancient Roman catacomb, popes encouraged the explorations and scientific studies of Antonio Bosio (c. 1576–1629). Popes also imposed limits on the work of some scholars: they censured the historical writings of Carlo Sigonio (1524–1584) and condemned the philosophical speculations of Giordano Bruno and Tommaso Campanella (1568–1639) and the cosmological theories of Galileo Galilei.

Popes as Patrons of Art. The popes were major patrons of the various arts and Rome was the primary beneficiary of their largesse. As rulers of one of the important Italian states, the popes sought to make their capital city secure and prosperous, but also attractive and a center of culture. One of the first tasks they accomplished was the repair of the city walls. To facilitate the flow of traffic they ordered the removal of refuse from the streets and of porticos and overhanging abutments from bordering buildings. Old streets were regularized and new ones laid out to connect important centers. Sixtus IV ordered the construction of a bridge to link Trastevere with the heart of the city. To encourage the construction of palaces, he changed church law to allow prelates resident in Rome to will to their heirs, instead of having confiscated at death, buildings constructed with money from their benefices. The popes themselves were builders of palaces: the ancient Lateran Palace was found uninhabitable and was almost completely demolished by Sixtus V, who had a new palace built by 1589 according to the design of Domenico Fontana; a new papal summer residence was built on the Quirinale (Montecavallo) for Gregory XIII by the architect Ottaviano Mascarino; and the Vatican Palace, which became the permanent papal residence since the time of Nicholas V, was restored and enlarged by successive popes, Julius II commissioning Donato Bramante to build the long east corridor that connected the palace with the Villa Belvedere of Innocent VIII. The repair of the aqueducts allowed for the construction of fountains and the opening up of new areas for development. The seat of civil government, the Campidoglio, was enriched under Sixtus IV in 1471 by a public collection of ancient statuary and redesigned into a beautiful complex of buildings and paved piazza according to the scheme of Michelangelo commissioned by Paul III. Incorporating the work of his predecessors into a grand master plan, Sixtus V imposed on the city a network of major streets with S. Maria Maggiore as a hub whose radiating streets connected it with other important churches and they with their neighbors.

In their role as head of the Christian Church the Renaissance popes were strong promoters of religious art. They called to Rome some of the most eminent artists and architects of the day to restore old churches and build new ones. For example, Nicholas V hired Leon Battista Alberti to restore the sacred buildings of Rome and Fra Angelico to help decorate the papal chapel (c. 1446–1449); Sixtus IV commissioned Giovanni de' Dolci to build the Sistine Chapel (1473–1484) and artists such as Cosimo Rosselli, Domenico Ghirlandaio, and Sandro Botticelli to fresco its lateral walls with scenes from the lives of Moses and Christ; Julius II commissioned Michelangelo to paint the chapel's ceiling with panels depicting stories from Genesis and Raphael to fresco the walls of the papal apartment with allegorical and historical paintings. The building of a new St. Peter's Basilica, begun under Julius II in 1506, was not finished until 1612 and called upon the talents of Bramante, Antonio da San Gallo the Younger, Michelangelo, Giacomo Barozzi da Vignola, Giacomo della Porta, and Carlo Maderno to bring it to completion. Gian Lorenzo Bernini designed its colonnade.

The Renaissance popes also patronized sacred music, endowing choirs to sing in the Sistine Chapel, St. Peter's Basilica, and S. Maria Maggiore, and commissioning musicians such as Guillaume Dufay, Josquin des Prez, Costanzo Festa, Cristóbal de Morales, and Giovanni Pierluigi da Palestrina to sing and/or compose religious pieces. The popes not only shaped artistic tastes by their commissions but they also regulated its expression in the area of religious art by enforcing the norms laid out at the Council of Trent. Guiding their patronage was a desire to honor God and the saints, promote piety, leave monuments to their own religiosity, make visible to all the majesty and authority of the Apostolic See, and transform Rome into a sacred city, the capital of Christendom and fitting destination of pilgrimage to the shrines of the martyrs and confessors of the faith.

See also **Catholic Reformation and Counter-Reformation; Christianity; Clergy; Conciliarism; Missions, Christian;** *and biographies of figures mentioned in this entry.*

BIBLIOGRAPHY

D'Amico, John F. *Renaissance Humanism in Papal Rome: Humanists and Churchmen on the Eve of the Reformation.* Baltimore, Md., 1983.

Delumeau, Jean. *Vie économique et sociale de Rome dans la seconde moitié du seizième siècle.* 2 vols. Paris, 1957–1959.

Grafton, Anthony, ed. *Rome Reborn: The Vatican Library and Renaissance Culture.* Washington, D.C., 1993. Exhibition catalog.

Hallman, Barbara McClung. *Italian Cardinals, Reform, and the Church as Property, 1492–1563.* Berkeley, Calif., 1985.

Hay, Denys. *The Church in Italy in the Fifteenth Century: The Birbeck Lectures, 1971.* Cambridge, U.K., 1977.

Hofmann, Walther von. *Forschungen zur Geschichte der kurialen Behörden vom Schisma bis zur Reformation.* 2 vols. Rome, 1914.

Jedin, Hubert. *Geschichte des Konzils von Trient.* 4 vols. Freiburg im Breisgau, Germany, 1949–1975. English translation by Ernest Graf of vols. 1–2. London, 1957–1961.

Landi, Aldo. *Concilio e papato nel Rinascimento (1449–1516): Un problema irrisolto.* Turin, Italy, 1997.

Magnuson, Torgil. *Rome in the Age of Bernini.* 2 vols. Translated by Nancy Adler. Stockholm, Sweden, 1982–1986.

McGinness, Frederick J. *Right Thinking and Sacred Oratory in Counter-Reformation Rome.* Princeton, N.J., 1995.

Nussdorfer, Laurie. *Civic Politics in the Rome of Urban VIII.* Princeton, N.J., 1992.

O'Malley, John W. *Praise and Blame in Renaissance Rome: Rhetoric, Doctrine, and Reform in the Sacred Orators of the Papal Court, c. 1450–1521.* Durham, N.C., 1979.

Partner, Peter. *The Lands of St. Peter: The Papal State in the Middle Ages and the Early Renaissance.* Berkeley, Calif., 1972.

Partner, Peter. *The Papal State under Martin V: The Administration and Government of the Temporal Power in the Early Fifteenth Century.* London, 1958.

Partner, Peter. *The Pope's Men: The Papal Civil Service in the Renaissance.* Oxford, 1990.

Partner, Peter. *Renaissance Rome 1500–1559: A Portrait of a Society.* Berkeley, Calif., 1976.

Paschini, Pio. *Roma nel Rinascimento.* Bologna, Italy, 1940.

Pastor, Ludwig von. *The History of the Popes from the Close of the Middle Ages.* Translated and edited by Frederick Ignatius Antrobus et al. St. Louis, Mo., 1891–1938. Vols. 1–39 (1305–1644).

Pecchiai, Pio. *Roma nel Cinquecento.* Bologna, Italy, 1948.

Prodi, Paolo. *The Papal Prince: One Body and Two Souls: The Papal Monarchy in Early Modern Europe.* Translated by Susan Haskins. New York, 1987.

Ramsey, P. A., ed. *Rome in the Renaissance: The City and the Myth: Papers of the Thirteenth Annual Conference of the Center for Medieval and Early Renaissance Studies.* Binghamton, N.Y., 1982.

Reinhard, Wolfgang. "Papal States." In *The Oxford Encyclopedia of the Reformation.* 4 vols. Edited by Hans J. Hillerbrand. New York, 1996. Vol. 3, pp. 208–210.

Stinger, Charles L. *The Renaissance in Rome.* Revised edition Bloomington, Ind., 1998.

Thomson, John A. F. *Popes and Princes, 1417–1517: Politics and Polity in the Late Medieval Church.* London, 1980.

NELSON H. MINNICH

PARACELSUS (Philippus Aureolus Theophrastus Bombastus von Hohenheim; 1493–1541), German-Swiss itinerant physician and reformer, after his death known mainly by the adopted cognomen Paracelsus or as Theophrastus Paracelsus. Paracelsus was born in Einsiedeln, a village in Switzerland where his German father practiced medicine and his mother, of local origin, served at the nearby Benedictine monastery. After his mother's death, Paracelsus and his father moved to Villach, in a mining region of Carinthia. Paracelsus claimed that he was tutored by his father and various clerics, including Abbot Johannes Trithemius, who was well known as an occult philosopher. Paracelsus's written work reveals an unsystematic, but wide-ranging education that reflects not only ecclesiastical and practical medical education, but also an acquaintance with the ideas of late medieval mysticism, Neoplatonism, alchemical theory and techniques, folk healing, popular superstitions, and widespread suppositions about the sources of good and evil in the world. Although he knew some Latin and was conversant with the chief tenets of academic medicine, his bizarre understanding of human anatomy, ideas about human reproduction, and knowledge of the fundamentals of natural philosophy argue against speculations that he attended the University of Vienna, and perhaps also Ferrara, long enough to obtain a degree.

Scholars have focused on Paracelsus as a religious thinker and lay reformer of the sort that wandered central Europe in the early sixteenth century, immersed in the social and intellectual turmoil associated with the Radical Reformation. Certainly this explains Paracelsus's behavior at Salzburg, where he narrowly avoided prosecution for supporting the rebel cause in the violently suppressed Peasants' War of 1525, and also his voluminous theological writings, which are shot through with mystical interpretations of the trinity (and sometimes the four persons of the Godhead, including a female creative principle). His moral and religious beliefs are quite evident in all his writings and undergird his entire worldview. However, this assessment of Paracelsus's essential nature does not explain the tremendous influence of his philosophical and medical ideas on the two generations of natural philosophers, physicians, and even poets that followed him. To those, Paracelsus was remembered primarily as a medical iconoclast, challenging the authority of Aristotle and Galen, whose teachings dominated the university medical curriculum and were staunchly upheld by the elite colleges of physicians. It was not Paracelsus the lay preacher who became an emblem of intellectual reform and revolution, but the Paracelsus who threw Avicenna's *Canon of Medicine,* one of the expensive university medical textbooks, onto a student bonfire at Basel's midsummer celebration (1527). Paracelsus had been hired as municipal physician that year, a post that permitted him to lecture publicly. But his use of that privilege to espouse ideas that were antithetical to traditional medical theory—and practice—aroused the hostility of the local medical establishment, whose authority he sought to undermine.

Paracelsus despised the fundamental Hippocratic and Galenic doctrine of the humors and temperaments and the diagnostic and therapeutic methods that it supported, which he thought were ineffective against the new diseases that raged in Europe. Instead, he advocated the use of powerful, specific drugs, which were in many cases derived by chemical methods from toxic minerals and plants. The art of distillation was developed already in the Middle Ages, but Paracelsus was among the first to utilize for medical purposes improvements in furnace design that enabled the preparation of better solvents and reagents. For this he is regarded today as a pioneer of iatrochemistry. His methods and the theory that accompanied them were viewed as academic heresy, at best fraudulent, and at worst medically dangerous. Not surprisingly, the medical authorities were alarmed and took measures to antagonize the volatile Paracelsus, and thereby bring him into public disfavor. In the course of an ill-conceived lawsuit to recover an exorbitant fee from a leading citizen,

Paracelsus. Portrait attributed to Jan van Scorel (1495–1562). MUSÉE DE LOUVRE, PARIS/LAUROS-GIRAUDON/ART RESOURCE

Paracelsus fled Basel in the night (1528) and resumed his life of wandering.

His unsettled life, reputation for medical and religious heterodoxy, and lack of educational polish militated against his scholarly work; few of his treatises were published in his lifetime, and these are often difficult to understand. Contemporary criticism, even by his supporters, affirms that the opaqueness of Paracelsus's ideas are not merely artifacts of our cultural distance from Renaissance Germany. Were it not for the next generation of medical scholars and publishers, who sought to find meaning in his exciting, sometimes brilliantly insightful utterings, Paracelsus would have had little impact on the scientific and medical world of the seventeenth century.

Gerard Dorn (fl. 1566–1584), like his mentor Adam von Bodenstein (1528–1577), was an eager follower of Paracelsian medicine, locating, editing, and publishing Paracelsus's medical and philosophical manuscripts, sometimes penning works of his own under the master's name. He interpreted Paracelsus's theories in light of Neoplatonic philosophy, which underwent a renaissance in the sixteenth century, and defended Paracelsus against the vigorous attacks of Thomas Erastus (1572–1574), who pointed out that Paracelsus's teachings were anti-

thetical to both orthodox Christian tenets and university-sanctioned medicine. Dorn also compiled a dictionary of the peculiar Paracelsian terminology, which was reprinted and translated into several vernaculars and no doubt helped ease the assessment and assimilation of Paracelsian tracts.

Petrus Severinus (c. 1542–1602), Dorn's younger contemporary, devoted his *Ideal of Philosophical Medicine* (1571) to interpreting Paracelsus in a way that was compatible with certain doctrines of Hippocrates, Galen, and Aristotle, and used them to frame a well-articulated biological theory that explained the physiology and pathology of the organic world in terms of spiritual agencies and divinely ordained patterns of development. Perhaps because of its sophisticated philosophical presentation and manifestly religious (Neoplatonic) vision, Severinus's book proved an influential introduction to Paracelsian ideas, which were taken up by Oswald Croll (c. 1560–1609) and Johann Hartmann (1568–1631), whose work made Paracelsian concepts and drugs the foundation of seventeenth-century chemical medicine.

Johann Hartmann, generally reckoned as the holder of the first university chair in chemistry (Marburg, 1609), adopted Severinus's version of Paracelsian "vital philosophy" and taught medical chemistry as a laboratory subject. Hartmann used and later enlarged Oswald Croll's *Basilica chymica* (1609), which was a popular introduction to chemical methods and recipes for preparing Paracelsian-style medicaments. Croll, who lived and worked as a chemist, physician, and Protestant agent in the imperial capital Prague during the first decade of the century, elaborated Paracelsian chemical philosophy and brought it into accord with Calvinist doctrines and thereby augmented the controversy over Paracelsian ideas, which were often espoused by Rosicrucian sympathizers in the years prior to the outbreak of the Thirty Years' War.

The result of the work of these early Paracelsian scholars and chemists was that chemical drugs, developed by Paracelsian enthusiasts between 1565 and 1615, found acceptance in European pharmacopoeias and were even adopted by orthodox Galenic physicians. Beyond this, however, chemical physicians who were trained in laboratory methods and followed new principles of medical treatment provided a viable alternative to the classical medicine taught in the universities and eventually attained recognition in the medical marketplace. By the end of the seventeenth century, chemical ideas and approaches derived from Paracelsian sources were no longer associated with his name or with religious enthusiasm and were being incorporated into the new philosophical frame of corpuscular medicine. By that time, Paracelsus's once heretical religious teachings were so deeply embedded in pietist and separatist religious thought that if they were remembered at all, they were associated with the names of Valentin Weigel (1533–1588) and Jakob Böhme (1576–1624).

BIBLIOGRAPHY

Debus, Allen. *The Chemical Philosophy: Paracelsian Science and Medicine in the Sixteenth and Seventeenth Centuries.* 2 vols. New York, 1977.

Hannaway, Owen. *The Chemists and the Word: The Didactic Origins of Chemistry.* Baltimore, 1975.

Pagel, Walter. *Paracelsus: An Introduction to Philosophical Medicine in the Era of the Renaissance.* 2d ed. Basel, Switzerland, 1982.

Trevor-Roper, Hugh. "The Paracelsian Movement." In *Renaissance Essays.* London, 1985. Pages 149–199.

Weeks, Andrew. *Paracelsus: Speculative Theory and the Crisis of the Early Reformation.* Albany, N.Y., 1997.

JOLE SHACKELFORD

PARADES, PROCESSIONS, AND PAGEANTS.

The most lavish spectacles of the Renaissance were those taking place in the open air and, of these, particularly the ones that wound through the streets.

Civic Processions.

Much civic pageantry was, of course, inherited from the Middle Ages—not only the pageantry of the Holy Roman Empire and old monarchies like the English and the French, but also that of principalities and republican city-states. Ceremonial costumes and order of precedence, both of intense importance during the Middle Ages, would change little during the Renaissance, but street decorations and chariots were to be transformed by the classical revival.

Triumphal entries into cities. In the early formal entries of the period, decorations consisted mainly of tapestries hung from balconies or windows and arches constructed from branches of greenery, but the greatest occasions entailed dramatic presentations in the street closely related to late medieval theater. Such presentations, more common in the north and termed "pageants" in the English of the time, often involved bands of costumed actors on raised platforms, who portrayed allegories or episodes from mythology, the Bible, and classical history. When the actors were silent and motionless, their poses were called *tableaux vivants* (living paintings). At times, however, as in the London entry of Holy Roman Emperor Charles V in 1522,

actors recited verses, usually vernacular rather than Latin, as the *triumphator* interrupted his or her progress to stop and listen. The tableaux could have poignant contemporary reference, as when those for the 1530 entry of Charles into Munich alluded to religious dissension in Germany. Decorations sometimes also included elaborate "machines" whose main purpose was to amaze. Leonardo da Vinci is thought to have devised an automaton in the form of a lion for the entry of Louis XII to Milan in 1507. To receive Charles V in 1529, Genoa had a globe of the world that opened to release perfumes and a young man costumed as Justice. Florence, receiving Charles VIII of France in 1494, had "giants" that stalked about the Piazza della Signoria.

Tableaux vivants, street pageants, and amazing machines all became less common as planners strove instead to revive the classical Roman triumph. Italy saw several early attempts in this direction during the fourteenth and fifteenth centuries, the best remembered being perhaps the triumphs of Cola di Rienzo in Rome (1347) and Alfonso I in Naples (1443). A series of drawings depicting Roman triumphs done by the artist Andrea Mantegna around 1500 (and now at Hampton Court Palace) became very widely known through engravings, as did soon afterward a triumphal arch and a triumphal procession engraved for the emperor Maximilian. The invasions of the Italian Wars beginning in 1494 had the side effect of acquainting northern nations and the Spanish with the triumphal forms of the peninsula. Fresh documentation was brought in 1571 by the publication of a commentary on triumphs (*De triumpho commentarius*) by the late humanist Onofrio Panvinio that was to have several illustrated editions. By the late sixteenth century, triumphal arches, at least, were expected for entries and grand civic parades all over western Europe. Vienna, for example, well after France and the Low Countries, had its first classical arch for an entry in 1563, of the future emperor Maximilian II. For the coronation parade of Christian IV of Denmark in 1596, Copenhagen built a particularly elaborate three-story arch.

Such arches were a form of "ephemeral architecture," constructed of temporary materials according to the classical orders, and bearing stucco sculpture or chiaroscuro paintings that imitated relief sculpture. Like the permanent stone arches still visible in Rome and elsewhere, they had Latin inscriptions. Most, indeed, had more inscriptions than the permanent structures because of the number of painted or sculpted scenes requiring elucidation. Some planners of entries re-created other ancient architectural

Pageant. Procession of knights pass before King Henry II of France during his ceremonial entry into Rouen, 1 October 1550. BIBLIOTHÈQUE MUNICIPALE, ROUEN/GIRAUDON

forms as well, notably Trajan's Column, as in Mantua in 1530, and the pyramid or obelisk, as at Lucca in 1536 and Paris in 1549.

Not all classical triumphal elements were successfully revived. Unlike the arch (which in ancient times was probably not really built for triumphal marches, time being too short), the authentic chariot for *triumphatores* to ride in did not long find favor, after Louis XII disdained to mount one at the gate of Milan in 1509. There was an occasional classically inspired chariot bearing spoils, as at Messina in 1535, when it was pulled by genuine Moorish prisoners, and there were many allegorical chariots, after the examples of Petrarch's *Trionfi* (The triumphs) and the hermetic *Hypnerotomachia Poliphili* (1499) of Francesco Colonna, but they were seen more often in carnival parades than in entries. Religious processions, of course, often had chariots depicting pious subjects, most notably in Spain but also elsewhere.

Depictions on arches might show contemporary and recent people in majestic attitudes, classical and biblical heroes, purely allegorical personages, or the symbolic animals and plants of emblems. Inscriptions might be verses from Roman poets, especially Virgil, or, more often, paraphrases of such verses. Ancient parallels to contemporary events were eagerly sought. Thus, after Charles V's victories over the Moorish pirate Barbarossa II near Tunis in 1535, humanists in Italy hastened to hail him as a new Africanus for his victories over the "Carthaginians."

With the increased use of Latin inscriptions, less vernacular poetry was written for recital or visual display during entries. This development, which did not always lead to greater expressivity, was more pronounced in Italy than in other countries. Pageants with English verses, for example, remained important in London entries. Even in Italy, moreover, vernacular poetry was still composed for the courtly entertainments that often followed grand entries, as at Florence in 1539.

Flattery of entering personages was the main purpose of decorations and inscriptions, but the effort of a host city to impress an honored guest with its own illustrious history and with the dignity of its local government was nearly as important. Quite down-to-earth messages were also occasionally conveyed through neoclassical conceits. Thus Bruges in 1515, Ferrara in 1598, and Antwerp in 1635 all contrived, through the depictions and inscriptions of street decorations, to complain to new rulers about a decline in commerce. Conscientious *triumphatores* like Charles V and Elizabeth I paused at triumphal arches and other displays to work out the iconography and the underlying messages. Queen Elizabeth is reported to have declared during a progress through London: "I have taken notice of your good meaning toward mee, and will endeavor to Answere your several expectations."

Triumphal progresses. Sovereigns and popes sometimes made whole series of entries during sustained state journeys. Elizabeth I moved periodically around her kingdom, accepting the hospitality of cities or great nobles. Charles V made a point of visiting his dominions in Spain, Italy, Germany, and the Low Countries, entering numerous cities. The most triumphal in spirit of his progresses was across Sicily and up the Italian peninsula in 1535–1536, after the victories over Barbarossa. In 1574, Henry III enjoyed triumphal receptions from Venice to the French border on his roundabout journey home from Poland to take up the French throne. Popes also occasionally made long journeys, as when Clement VIII journeyed grandly across the peninsula and up the Adriatic coast to take possession of Ferrara in 1598. Such journeys inspired many printed entry reports and even comprehensive accounts.

Coronation parades. Actual rituals of coronation, whether imperial, papal, or royal, were medieval in origin and scarcely changed, except for some details in Protestant states. The grand processions that preceded or followed the rites were, however, more subject to fashion. Holy Roman Emperors could, in principle, have two coronations, as king of the Romans at the hand of the electors in Aachen, and as emperor, by the pope, preferably in Rome. There could even be a third, with the Iron Crown of Lombardy in Monza. In practice, only two emperors during the period made the effort to be crowned in Italy. Frederick III received the Lombard and imperial crowns from Pope Nicholas V at Rome in 1452, after a grand entry into the city, and in 1530 Charles V received them from Clement VII at Bologna, which was standing in ceremonially for the Eternal City. Charles's second, imperial coronation was followed by a procession around the city, and the scene of pope and sovereign riding side by side under a single canopy was made known to the rest of Europe in a fine series of engravings by Nicholas Hogenberg. Renaissance popes, after being consecrated in Saint Peter's Basilica, might proceed through decorated streets to take *possesso* of the Roman cathedral of Saint John-in-Lateran. The *possesso* parades of Leo X and Gregory XIV, in 1513 and 1590, were particularly grand. French kings, after consecration in the cathedral of Reims, made *joyeuses entrées* (joyous entries) into the capital, proceeding from a decorated Porte St.-Denis to Notre Dame, and often into certain provincial cities as well. Henry II's entries into Lyon, Paris, and Rouen in 1548–1550 are especially well described and illustrated. New English sovereigns were expected to proceed through the streets of London on the day before their coronations

in Westminster Abbey. The 1559 procession of Elizabeth I was particularly festive and rich in literary manifestations.

Entries of noble consorts. In Italy during the sixteenth century it became customary to stage grand entries, with triumphal arches, for noble brides arriving in their new homes. During the century, more than a dozen noble ladies were thus received into Ferrara, Florence, Mantua, Milan, Pesaro, Turin, and Urbino. Such entries were followed by courtly entertainments, often including the staging of comedies. Elsewhere, France gave entries into Paris or other cities to Mary Tudor, Elizabeth of Austria, Catherine de Médicis, and Marie de Médicis. In England, with a switch of gender, London was required in 1554 to give a formal entry to Philip of Spain, the new husband of Mary I.

Funerals. The grandest funeral procession was staged at Brussels in 1559 in honor of Charles V, who had died in Spain. The centerpiece of the cortege was a moving chariot in the form of a ship that bore allegorical characters and was adorned by painted scenes. Brussels was honoring a sovereign who had died and been buried elsewhere, shortly after having done the same, on a smaller scale, for the English Catholic queen Mary I. In Italy, Florence took a leading role in the staging of proxy funerals, holding ceremonies in the Medici church of San Lorenzo for the emperor Ferdinand I, Charles IX of France, the emperor Maximilian II, Henry III of France, Philip II of Spain, and Henry IV of France. In 1564, it gave an equally magnificent—and more touching—actual funeral in San Lorenzo for its native son, Michelangelo Buonarroti, who had died in Rome. Arrangements were entrusted to the newly formed state academy of design. The architectural catafalque inside the church was as elaborate and dense with symbolic meanings as the great arches erected in streets for triumphal entries.

Religious Processions with Civic Significance. In some cities, annual religious processions acquired civic significance through the habitual participation of civil authorities. Thus the Venetian procession for Palm Sunday as represented in the 1556–1559 engravings of Matteo Pagan, with the doge and other officials at the center, can be seen as a sort of symbolization of the state and its constitution.

***Ommegangen* and the Lord Mayors' Pageants.** Great commercial cities might have annual processions of a civic nature that were animated by

Funeral Procession of Queen Elizabeth. Watercolor by William Camden, 1603. BRITISH LIBRARY, LONDON/THE BRIDGEMAN ART LIBRARY

local guilds. Particularly elaborate were the *omme-gangen* of Antwerp, held on the first Sunday after the Feast of the Assumption (15 August), and the pageants staged in October for the inauguration of new lord mayors of London. The former reached a peak of development in the sixteenth century, while the latter, although important during that period, attained full splendor under King James I. In Antwerp, each guild possessed a chariot, which might be used for a number of years. Most depicted religious subjects, such as Saint John the Baptist in the desert, or the Last Judgment, but there were also secular chariots, such as one showing Mercury, the god of commerce, surrounded by women who personified the trading nations of Europe. The parade was circular, beginning and ending at the cathedral. The new lord mayor of London, always a member of a particular guild, proceeded to Westminster for his oath of office and then back to the Guildhall. The progress to Westminster was sometimes in a decorated boat on the Thames, with the return to the Guildhall via the streets. The mayor's own guild had the principal responsibility for the year's manifestations. It might provide chariots or displays carried on platforms, and there might also be dramatic skits for presentation on fixed or moveable stages along the way. Prominent men of letters came to work on such festivities, as Anthony Munday did on the pageant of 1605, the first for which there was a full printed account. The theme that year, soon after Scotland's union with England under a single ruler, was "The Triumphs of Re-United Britannia." There were various allegorical or mythological characters, and vernacular verses were recited. Elements of the procession included a ship, a chariot, and artificial animals.

The lord mayors' pageants came to rival royal entries and were, of course, much more frequent.

Colonies of foreign merchants, somewhat analogous to the guilds, were expected to make disproportionate contributions to triumphal entries, cutting rich figures in the procession and spending freely for street decorations. At Antwerp in 1549, the Florentine, Genoese, Lucchese, Spanish, German, and English merchants all commissioned arches for the entry of Prince Philip of Spain. In London, the Italian merchants contributed street devices for the 1522 entry of Charles V. Sometimes the Italians were instrumental in introducing the themes of classical revival into the north.

Contributions of Writers, Artists, and Musicians. The collaboration of literati was essential for the planning of pageants, which, with the progress of humanism and classical revival, became a very learned affair. Historical, mythological, or allegorical scenes had to be designed for painting, and classical Latin authors chosen for quotation or paraphrasing. Emblems had to be researched for reproduction or invented for the occasion. Detailed guides had to be drawn up for the artists who were to erect and decorate triumphal arches. Some court humanists, such as Vincenzo Borghini, in the service of the Florentine duke Cosimo I (1537–1574), became expert at such planning, aware of precedents and sensitive to political nuances. A few planners, such as Maurice Scève, in charge of the Lyonese entries of 1548, were poets of the first rank. As for artists, large numbers of them were engaged in advance of entries for very hurried work. Often, as the art historian Giorgio Vasari says in regard to Charles V's Roman entry of 1536, it was necessary to hire "both the good and the bad." Vasari himself became adept at working on decorations and at strawbossing the work of others. Musicians were similarly engaged to play or sing, and special compositions were often commissioned. Most commissions were for courtly entertainments, but in 1539 Francesco Corteccia composed a motet for performance by musicians concealed in a triumphal arch at Florence. Unfortunately, most music written for festivals either is lost or lies unidentified in manuscript.

Festival Books. The triumphal events of the early Renaissance were described, if at all, in manuscript reports for archives, in diaries, or in diplomatic reports (of which those sent to Venice are particularly informative). After the invention of printing, there developed a tradition, or rather two overlapping traditions, of published festival accounts. The simplest took the form of news bulletins, meant to be hawked in the streets, and belong to the infancy of journalism. Most printed reports before 1550 are in that category. As early as 1475, however, for a courtly wedding in Pesaro, there is an isolated example of a more elaborate, more "literary" account. The entry of Prince Charles of Habsburg into Bruges in 1515 inspired another early published description with the text of recited verses, woodcut illustrations, and a good deal of commentary by the author Rémy Du Puys.

Woodcuts were to remain rare, but by 1550 even journalistic authors undertook to include the text of Latin inscriptions from triumphal arches and, often, to hazard some conjecture on their relevance. For the wedding celebrations of Cosimo I de' Medici in 1539, an ambitious description by a learned member of the new Florentine Academy contained Latin inscriptions, much recited poetry, and even the text of a comedy written and performed for the occasion. Moreover, in a far rarer development, the music composed for the wedding was also published. A later Medici wedding, in 1589, generated no fewer than twenty-four publications providing accounts of events, the texts of inscriptions and recited verses, illustrations, and music. Such comprehensiveness remained unusual, but there are perhaps 250 festival books of various kinds for Italy alone between 1475 and 1600. Courts began to compete with each other not just in the splendor of their celebrations but also in the handsomeness of published descriptions. Mas-

Pageantry in the Tuileries Gardens, Paris. Antoine Caron (1521–1599) painted an allegorical scene based on the play *Octavien et les Sybilles* (Augustus and the Tiburtian Sibyl). The painting may depict decor designed by Caron. SCALA/ART RESOURCE, NY

ters of ceremonies and planners of entertainments, like the aforementioned Borghini of Florence, began to collect festival books to consult for precedents and fresh ideas.

See also **Carnival**; **Festivals**; **Ritual, Civic.**

BIBLIOGRAPHY

Anglo, Sydney. *Spectacle, Pageantry, and Early Tudor Policy.* 2d ed. Oxford and New York, 1997. Analyses of progresses and entries through the coronation of Elizabeth in 1559.

Bergeron, David M. *English Civic Pageantry 1558–1642.* Columbia, S.C., 1971. A systematic study, treating lord mayor's shows as well as royal progresses.

Borsook, Eve. "Art and Politics at the Medici Court III: Funeral Decor for Philip II of Spain." *Mitteilungen des Kunsthistorischen Instituts in Florenz* 14 (1969): 91–114. Several studies by the author of other Florentine state funerals also appear in this journal.

Bryant, Lawrence M. *The King and the City in the Parisian Royal Entry Ceremony: Politics, Ritual, and Art in the Renaissance.* Geneva, 1986. Excellent analysis of an evolving tradition, with attention to individual fifteenth- and sixteenth-century entries.

Giesey, Ralph E. *The Royal Funeral Ceremony in Renaissance France.* Geneva, 1960. Reprint, Geneva, 1984. Standard study of the subject.

Jacquot, Jean, ed. *Les fêtes de la Renaissance.* 3 vols. Paris, 1956–1975. The proceedings of three pioneering colloquia on Renaissance festival studies, including focused studies of individual festivals, and valuable syntheses by the editor.

Landwehr, John. *Splendid Ceremonies: State Entries and Royal Funerals in the Low Countries, 1515–1791.* Nieuwkoop, Netherlands, and Leiden, Netherlands, 1971. A descriptive bibliography of festival books.

McGowan, Margaret M., ed. *Renaissance Triumphs and Magnificences.* Binghamton, N.Y., and Tempe, Ariz., 1970–. A series of facsimile editions of Renaissance festival books, with scholarly introductions.

Mitchell, Bonner. *The Majesty of the State: Triumphal Progresses of Foreign Sovereigns in Renaissance Italy (1494–1600).* Florence, 1986. A systematic narrative.

Muir, Edward. *Civic Ritual in Renaissance Venice.* Princeton, N.J., 1981. Excellent study of Venetian processions and other state ceremonies.

Strong, Roy C. *Art and Power: Renaissance Festivals 1450–1650.* Berkeley, Calif., 1984. Although not comprehensive, the best general study, with attention to representative Habsburg, Valois, Medici, and Stuart entries and court festivals.

Wisch, Barbara, and Susan Scott Munshower, eds. *Triumphal Celebrations and the Rituals of Statecraft.* Part 1 of *"All the world's a stage . . .": Art and Pageantry in the Renaissance and Baroque.* Papers in Art History from the Pennsylvania State University, vol. 6. University Park, Pa., 1990. Several focused papers on Renaissance triumphs, and an excellent general bibliography on those of ancient, medieval, and early modern periods.

BONNER MITCHELL

PARAGONE. The word "paragone" (from medieval Greek, "comparison," figuratively, a test for artistic excellence) is used widely today to refer to polemical writings on the comparison of the visual arts regardless of period. The term, however, dates only from 1817, when Guglielmo Manzi published a new edition of *Treatise on Painting* (c. 1570), compiled from the notes of Leonardo da Vinci (1452–1519). Manzi gave this title to the first section of a unique manuscript, which had been recently rediscovered in the Vatican Library, in which Leonardo defended painting against poetry, music, the mechanical arts, and sculpture. His defense is the first major contribution to sixteenth-century literature that documents the social and intellectual struggle of artists to achieve status paralleling that of men of letters. The arguments, which occur in a variety of literary forms, address the nobility, sovereignty, or perfection of individual arts through such ubiquitous comparisons (*paragoni*) as the value of painting versus sculpture relative to seeing a figure from all sides, to performing mental versus physical labor, to the edification and pleasure of the viewer, and to the longevity of the work.

Paragoni are too diverse to be called an independent literary genre, but their varied formal types are interrelated, stemming from common sources in classical and medieval literature reinforced by an oral tradition. Humanist literature leans heavily on late Hellenistic and Roman *ekphraseis* (descriptions of artworks), such as the *Imagines* (Images) and the epigrammatic poetry in the Greek Anthology. Although the debate's ancient origins were known through a variety of classical sources, Leonardo and his successors also acquired particular figures of speech and patterns of justification from medieval poetic contests variously called *certamen, conflictus, altercatio, tenzone,* and *contrasto.* Renaissance culture, particularly the collective pursuits of humanist scholars, aristocrats, and an emerging wealthy bourgeoisie, revived activities associated with the ancient learned gatherings called Musea that offered lectures, discussions, and symposia. At these events learned discourses progressed through the use of comparative analysis following rhetorical models of argumentation, cast as visual discoveries made extemporaneously using actual objects. An oral tradition apparently existed at least since the fourteenth century, with precedents in medieval bucolic verse in which the speakers interpreted paintings, statues, and architecture.

The conception of painting and sculpture as experiment or demonstration piece (the practice of construing painting or sculpture in terms of proofs, trials, or contests) runs throughout Renaissance literature, but rarely names actual productions. Famous ancient demonstrations, like the ones recounted by Pliny the Elder, must have been popular in Renaissance retellings partly because they depict the artist as *aemulus,* competing both with human rivals and with nature. In one famous modern example, Vasari claimed that artists debated the merits of Giorgione's (lost) painting of St. George, where the figure is seen from all sides, in front of an actual sculpture, Verrocchio's equestrian monument of Bartolommeo Colleoni (Vasari, *Vite,* 3:46). A visual tradition can be traced to sculpture simulated in painting and experiments with pictorial effects in relief sculpture beginning in the early fifteenth century with Donatello's reinterpretation of low relief and Lorenzo Ghiberti's bronze panels for the Florentine Baptistery. In 1564, differences of opinion among artists were serious enough to divide the membership of the Accademia del Disegno (the first of its kind, founded under Giorgio Vasari's leadership in Cosimo I de' Medici's Florence). The division occurred over elaborate preparations for Michelangelo's funeral, which included a catafalque with personified allegories of the arts of painting, sculpture, architecture, and poetry, in all of which Michelangelo excelled. The underlying problem can be stated in the following way: how does one select criteria to judge the excellence of artistic productions? According to one argument often credited to Leonardo, sculpture imitated in paint is a more noble invention than actual sculpted relief because it depends on the artist's knowledge of optics, a theoretical science, not simply a manual craft like carving stone or modeling clay.

Literary contributions to the *paragone* were made by central and northern Italians, including Paolo Pino (1548), Anton Francesco Doni (1549), Ludovico Dolce (1557), Raffaelo Borghini (1584), and many others. These writings cannot be called art criticism in the modern interpretive sense. Nevertheless, they introduced substantive concerns with the nature of visual representation. These concerns touched on such matters as the value of pictorial artifice (the equivalent of figurative language). At the same time, the writings provided a context for discussing artistic procedures in theoretical terms. These authors also show direct links via Leonardo with Alberti's *De pictura/della pittura* (composed 1434/35; 1st ed. Basel, 1540), the earliest written account of pictorial perspective and narrative composition, including one of the first comparisons of painting and sculpture; and Baldassare Castiglione's *Il cortegiano* (*The Book of the Courtier;* 1528), a fictional work about ideal courtly conduct that was widely disseminated throughout Europe. A famous document connected with the rivalry of actual painters and sculptors is the questionnaire published in 1550 by Benedetto Varchi to which seven prominent artists and literary figures, including Pontormo, Benvenuto Cellini, and Michelangelo, responded. Vasari also recorded opinions in the preface to his *Lives of Painters, Sculptors, and Architects* (rev. ed. 1568), resolving the rivalry among the three arts in favor of their common foundation in *disegno,* or design.

Vasari's classification of the arts, more than Leonardo's defense of painting as a science of optics, established a theoretical foundation that anticipated the modern system of the fine arts codified in the eighteenth century. Although literary rivalries waned in Italy after the 1560s, similar discussions and a visual tradition developed elsewhere in Europe wherever art academies and humanist culture took root. Comparisons of the arts became a popular topic in eighteenth- and nineteenth-century English, French, and German literature, where they helped define cultural identity in an era of emerging nation-states.

At first these discussions stress criteria for judging different media, whereas later ones emphasize the unity of the arts. It is often assumed that the initiating argument for formalism was expressed in the eighteenth-century philosopher Immanuel Kant's remarks on the beautiful, but the issues have a much deeper history: what began as polemical arguments about the relative merits of painting and sculpture had by the later eighteenth century attained a new level of philosophical credibility. This legacy underlies the first autonomous histories of the "visual arts" (*bildende Kunst*) proposed at the end of the nineteenth century by Heinrich Wölfflin and others, based on the assumption that the work of art, regardless of its cultural and historical origins, was a model of perception—an idea that emerged in turn from the central challenge of the *paragone* that painters and sculptors should outdo each other in surpassing nature.

BIBLIOGRAPHY

Primary Works

Barocchi, P., ed. *Scritti d'arte del cinquecento.* 9 vols. Turin, Italy, 1977. Vol. 3: *Pittura e Scultura.*

Farago, Claire J. *Leonardo da Vinci's "Paragone": A Critical Interpretation with a New Edition of the Text in the Codex Urbinas.* Leiden, Netherlands, and New York, 1992.

Leonardo da Vinci. *Libro di pittura.* Edited by Carlo Pedretti, transcribed by Carlo Vecce. 2 vols. Florence, 1995.

Vasari, Giorgio. *Le vite de' più eccellenti pittori, scultori, ed architettori nelle redazione del 1550 e 1568.* Edited by R. Bettarini and P. Barocchi. 5 vols. Florence, 1966–1987.

Secondary Works

Kristeller, Paul Oskar. "The Modern System of the Arts: A Study in the History of Aesthetics." *Journal of the History of Ideas* 12 (1951): 496–527; 13 (1952): 17–46.

Mendelsohn, Leatrice. *Paragoni: Benedetto Varchi's "Due Lezzioni" and Cinquecento Art Theory.* Ann Arbor, Mich., 1982.

CLAIRE FARAGO

PARÉ, AMBROISE (1510–1590), French surgeon. Ambroise Paré was apprenticed first in the provinces as a barber-surgeon and then in Paris in 1532 or 1533. He was soon afterward appointed resident surgeon at the Hôtel Dieu, the city's main hospital. Much of Paré's career was spent as an army surgeon. In 1536 he was appointed surgeon to the Maréchal René de Montejon on his expedition to Italy. He accompanied the French army in a series of campaigns for the next thirty years. He also gained royal favor. In 1552 Henry II appointed him one of his "surgeons

in ordinary," as did Francis II on Henry's death in 1559; he was made "first surgeon" to Charles IX in 1562 and to Henry III in 1574.

Paré was the most eminent surgeon of the sixteenth century. Despite knowing no Latin and writing in French, he gained the respect of many Latinate "learned" surgeons and physicians, as well as of the apprentice-trained surgeons and barber-surgeons who were taught in French. He introduced a number of surgical innovations based on his war experience, which were quickly taken up. Rather than using boiling oil to cauterize gunshot wounds and to counteract the poisons which were thought to accompany such wounds, Paré used a salve instead, the success of which he noted in his first book, *La méthode de traicter les playes faictes par hacquebutes et aultres bastons à feu* (The method of treating wounds made by harquebuses and other firearms; 1545). Paré also revived the ancient practice of ligaturing the blood vessels in cases of amputations instead of the usual red-hot cautery by iron or oil. He used ligatures first in 1552 at the siege of Danvilliers and publicized the fact in *Dix livres de la chirurgie* (Ten books on surgery; 1564).

What struck contemporaries also was the breadth of Paré's experience and knowledge. He illustrated his points with stories and case histories drawn from campaigns, battles, and his practice in Paris, making him one of the most readable of the Renaissance medical writers. He wrote with authority on surgical and manipulative techniques such as inducing dislocations. He was also famous for his invention of artificial noses, palates, tongues, hands, and, most notably, for iron legs from above the knee for the rich, while he advised the poor to make do with wooden ones. The range of his writings, which covered gynecology, general surgery, therapeutics, anatomy, syphilis, plague, poisons, monsters and prodigies, and the making of forensic reports, gave him the reputation of being an encyclopedic writer. This was especially so after his collected works were first published in 1575 in French (also in 1582 in a poor Latin translation; in Dutch in 1592, German in 1601, and in English in 1634, with many reprints in all five languages). Royal patronage helped to make his a fashionable voice, and it also kept at bay the Paris faculty of medicine, which attacked him in 1575 for writing in the vernacular. Despite such attacks Paré gained the respect of the university-trained physicians. He was steeped in the Galenic humoral tradition and in the intricate knowledge of pharmacy, and he wrote on anatomy, a subject that had once

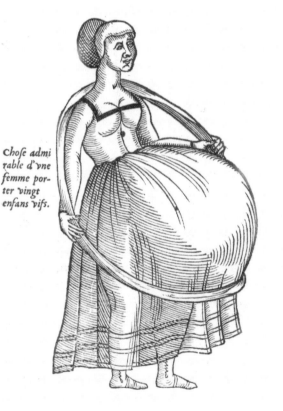

Chose admirable d'vne femme porter vingt enfans vifs.

Ambroise Paré. "An admirable way for a woman to carry twenty live infants." From Paré's *Oeuvres* (1575). NATIONAL LIBRARY OF MEDICINE, BETHESDA, MD.

been solely within surgery but had become intensely interesting to the physicians in the sixteenth century.

Paré exerted most influence on the development of surgery through his writings, in which the subject is presented as capable of rapid, if not revolutionary, development, with ancient and modern knowledge being integrated together. Paré himself provided an example of how a low-status barber-surgeon could achieve high status and learning.

BIBLIOGRAPHY

Primary Works

Paré, Ambroise. *The Apologie and Treatise of Ambroise Paré.* Edited by Geoffrey Keynes. New York, 1968. Contains a good selection of Paré's writings.

Paré, Ambroise. *Oeuvres complètes d'Ambroise Paré.* Edited by J. F. Malgaigne. 3 vols. Paris, 1840.

Secondary Works

Doe, Janet. *A Bibliography, 1545–1940, of the Works of Ambroise Paré, 1510–1590.* Amsterdam, 1976.

Dumaître, Paule. *Ambroise Paré: Chirurgien de Quatre Rois de France.* Paris, 1986.

Packard, Francis R. *The Life and Times of Ambroise Paré.* New York, 1922.

ANDREW WEAR

PARIS.   The largest city in northern Europe through the sixteenth century, Paris was the hub of the French monarchy and a lively intellectual and commercial center. The king and court were still itinerant, moving as dictated by political necessity or personal whim, but after 1528, when King Francis I announced his intention of making Paris his principal place of residence, sixteenth-century kings spent an increasing proportion of their time in or near the city. The financial and judicial organs of state, having long since grown too complex to travel with the court, had already found a home there. The city's role as an administrative capital had a profound impact on its social geography. Service to the king provided a path for upward mobility to prosperous merchants, and the growing ranks of royal officials, along with the frequent presence of the court, stimulated the luxury trades that were the most prestigious sector of Paris's mercantile economy. The city's size and wealth gave it tremendous weight politically, as was demonstrated repeatedly during the Wars of Religion, most dramatically with the revolt of the Holy League in 1588.

Population and Geography.   Scholars estimate that Paris grew from between 150,000 and 200,000 residents in 1500 to a maximum of 250,000 to 300,000 at midcentury. Population declined somewhat in the 1560s on account of the civil wars. It grew again in the 1570s and 1580s, dropped sharply during the crisis of the Holy League, when Paris was besieged by royal armies, and recovered again after the League was vanquished from the city in 1594. Encircled by walls that dated on the left bank of the Seine from the twelfth century and on the right from the fourteenth, the crowded city built upward at its center and sprawled out beyond its gates, despite repeated royal prohibitions against construction in the suburbs. Population was densest in the heart of the medieval city, which had grown out concentrically from the Île de la Cité. The right-bank mercantile quarters opposite the Cité were very tightly packed, as were the areas of the Cité itself not given over to religious or administrative purposes.

When upwardly mobile royal officials began to demonstrate their new status by constructing gracious townhouses, they settled in the more distant, less crowded quarters of the right bank. Here the first signs of Renaissance architecture appeared, though the influences of Italian classicism were generally merged with traditional local styles. An evolving and yet distinctive French Renaissance style emerged from this blending in such projects as the parish church of Saint-Eustache and the new city hall (begun in 1532 and 1533, respectively), the enlargements to the Louvre begun in the reign of Henry II, and the Tuileries Palace constructed by Catherine de Médicis after Henry II's death.

The many colleges that made up the University of Paris clustered on the left bank, along with religious houses founded there for the education of their members. Although the theologians of the University of Paris tended to resist new methods of learning, colleges under the university's mantle provided humanistic studies their first home in Paris. Paris's numerous printing establishments clustered in the vicinity of the university and played an important role in the diffusion of humanistic knowledge. The first books printed in Paris date from 1470. During the remainder of the fifteenth century, religious books outnumbered editions of classical authors and contemporary humanists by two to one. By the middle of the sixteenth century, these proportions had reversed themselves. Philippe Renouard counted 332 editions from Parisian presses in 1549, of which 56 were religious titles and 204 works by Latin, Greek, and humanist authors.

City Government.   A mercantile corporation arose in the Middle Ages to assume responsibility for constructing ports and roads, regulating commerce,

The Louvre in Paris. Procession of Queen Louise de Lorraine (1553–1601), wife of Henry III, leaves the Louvre. Drawing by Nicolas Houel, 1584. CLICHÉ BIBLIOTHÈQUE NATIONALE DE FRANCE, PARIS. PD 30 RES FOL

raising a militia, and collecting the taxes necessary to pay for these services. Despite the many responsibilities assumed by the merchant's corporation, or Bureau de la Ville, authority for governing Paris remained firmly in the hands of the king. He normally delegated these powers but did not hesitate to intervene personally when he believed the occasion warranted it. His authority was exercised through his appointed provost and the provost's subordinate officers, the lieutenants for civil and criminal affairs, but also through his appointed military governor and the officers of the high court of Parlement, as well as through the Bureau de la Ville. Command of the companies of city militias increasingly went to royal magistrates.

Headed by a *prévôt des marchands* (merchant's provost) and four *échevins* (aldermen), and acting through sixteen *quarteniers* (district officers) with the advice of twenty-four (later twenty-six) city councillors, the Bureau de la Ville was in theory elective but in practice operated through a process of co-optation that concentrated most of the highest offices in the hands of an oligarchical civic elite. Families held onto civic office even after they had climbed out of the city's mercantile ranks and into increasingly prestigious positions in the sovereign courts or royal bureaucracy. Only two merchants held office as merchant's provost through the entire sixteenth century, and after about 1570 it was rare

for more than one of the four aldermen to be engaged in commerce. The district officers, by contrast, were usually merchants or tradesmen. Their opportunities to move up into the ranks of the aldermen decreased as the century progressed.

Economic and Social Structures. The rich agricultural belt that surrounded the capital made possible its enormous size. In good years the hinterland did more than feed the city; its surplus grain and other agricultural products were important elements in Paris's export trade. Parisians profited from this commerce as traders and as landowners, for by the middle of the sixteenth century as much as 40 percent of the land in the local countryside belonged to bourgeois city dwellers or officers of the king. Locally produced manufactures and raw materials also played important roles in Parisian commerce, though they were eclipsed in prestige and value by the luxury items for which the city was best known, products of its vast reservoirs of skilled artisans. The presence of the university and the judicial and administrative apparatus of state favored both trade and crafts by providing a ready market for luxury items. The prestige attached to service in the royal bureaucracy nevertheless caused many rich merchants to withdraw from trade to invest instead in royal office, which was for the most part venal, and in land, which was associated with noble status.

The Seine at Paris. The Hôtel de Nevers and the Tour de Nesle, on the Left Bank, are at the left; the Louvre is at the right. Engraving by Jacques Callot (c. 1592–1635). BIBLIOTHÈQUE NATIONALE DE FRANCE, PARIS

Many historians believe that this withdrawal of funds from productive investment in commerce was in the long run harmful to the French economy.

Paris was a guild city. The prestigious Six Corps of wholesale merchants stood at the top of the guild hierarchy. Retail merchants and craftsmen were also organized in closed corporations with their own rules of admission and controls on quality and production. Not all trades were organized into guilds; women's work in particular fell largely outside the guild structures. Where guilds did exist, the opportunity to advance from the rank of journeyman to master tended to narrow as the sixteenth century progressed. Beneath the guilds was a mass of largely unskilled laborers, male and female, who sought work where they could find it, most often on a temporary basis. The precariousness of their situation made itself clear in times of scarcity, when beggars abounded, despite prohibitions against the giving or receiving of alms in city streets. By 1544 old forms of private and ecclesiastical charity no longer sufficed, and a municipally sponsored agency called the Grand bureau des pauvres (greater office for the poor) was created to aid indigent residents deemed worthy of help. Specialized shelters served orphaned children, the congenitally infirm, and the aged. Nonresident indigents and residents deemed unwilling rather than unable to work, by contrast, were summarily expelled from the city. The new poor laws owed much to humanistic theory and rep-

resented a significant departure from medieval notions of Christian charity, which viewed the poor as beloved of God. Whatever the philosophy behind them, the steps taken to deal with the poor failed to keep pace with the growing problem of indigence. All agreed that the problem was worse at the end of the century than when the new poor laws had their start.

Paris as a Political Force. Because of its great population, but also because of the concentration of intellectual and economic resources gathered there, Paris wielded enormous, albeit largely unacknowledged, political power in the realm. Francis I tacitly recognized this when he decided in 1528 to make the city his regular place of residence. Through special tax levies, forced loans, and the sale of annuities guaranteed by the city's good credit, Paris played an important role in funding Francis's wars in Italy, Henry II's wars against the Habsburgs, and the civil wars of the last Valois kings. The city's financial role gave its leaders leverage that could be used to protect local privileges or to moderate, even to protest, royal policies. This leverage was displayed most conspicuously during the Wars of Religion, when the city's fiercely Catholic loyalties more than once prevented the crown from negotiating a compromise settlement with Huguenot leaders.

Reinforced by preaching and religious ritual— most notably, processions that combined Catholic, civic, and monarchical symbols—Paris's Catholic identity resulted in repeated attacks on Protestant (or presumed Protestant) worshipers in the period preceding the outbreak of religious war in 1562. It also hindered the attempts of Catherine de Médicis to negotiate peace in 1563 and to enforce the treaty that concluded the third War of Religion in 1570. Most notoriously, it resulted in the Saint Bartholomew's Day massacre (24 August 1572), when approximately two thousand Protestants were killed in Paris, and in the seizure of city government and expulsion of King Henry III by an ultra-Catholic faction in May 1588. Henry III's hope of negotiating a peaceful settlement with the faction that opposed him abruptly vanished several months later, when he had the ultra-Catholics' leader, Henri, duc de Guise, and his brother Louis, cardinal de Guise, assassinated at Blois.

The radical leaders of the Holy League in Paris, called "les Seize" (the Sixteen), denounced Henry III as a tyrant and led the city into a rebellion characterized by an apocalyptic religiosity and a militant determination to protect the Catholic faith even at the price of its citizens' lives. Many royalists fled Paris; Parlement's magistrates set up courts in exile at Tours and Châlons-sur-Marne. Known royalists who remained in the city were verbally harassed and subjected to punitive taxation. Some endured imprisonment, and a few lost their lives. Forced to ally himself with the Protestant Henry of Navarre in order to try to squelch the League's rebellion, Henry III was preparing to lay siege to his capital when an assassin's knife killed him on 1 August 1589.

Recognized by the dying Henry III as his legitimate heir, Henry of Navarre claimed the throne as King Henry IV and continued Henry III's struggle against the League. The siege he laid to Paris in the spring and summer of 1590 reduced the city to the edge of starvation before the arrival of Spanish reinforcement caused Henry IV to raise the siege. Lessening pressure on the capital while continuing to fight the League elsewhere in the kingdom, Henry IV allowed internal dissensions within the Holy League, particularly between the radical Sixteen and the League's more moderate noble leaders, to undermine its authority in Paris. He also, in July 1593, abjured the Protestant faith so as to be more acceptable to his ultra-Catholic subjects. With the connivance of the merchant's provost, the gates of Paris quietly opened to Henry IV on 22 March 1594. The acclamation that greeted him showed how tired his subjects were of war, though the reduction of the Holy League in the provinces took another four

years. Henry IV's policy of conciliation meant that only the most radical League leaders were punished by exile on their faction's fall. Henry IV did, however, tighten the hold his predecessors had already established on the governing institutions of Paris. He also began an ambitious building program that helped the city's economic recovery and tied it even closer to the crown.

See also **Paris, University of; Wars of Religion.**

BIBLIOGRAPHY

Babelon, Jean-Pierre. *Paris au seizième siècle*. Paris, 1986.

Ballon, Hilary. *The Paris of Henri IV: Architecture and Urbanism*. Cambridge, Mass., 1991.

Descimon, Robert. "Paris on the Eve of Saint Bartholomew: Taxation, Privilege, and Social Geography." In *Cities and Social Change in Early Modern France*. Edited by Philip Benedict. London, 1989. Pages 69–104.

Diefendorf, Barbara B. *Beneath the Cross: Catholics and Huguenots in Sixteenth-Century Paris*. New York and Oxford, 1991.

Diefendorf, Barbara B. *Paris City Councilors in the Sixteenth Century: The Politics of Patrimony*. Princeton, N.J., 1983.

Febvre, Lucien, and Henri-Jean Martin. *The Coming of the Book: The Impact of Printing, 1450–1800*. Edited by Geoffrey Nowell-Smith and David Wootton. Translated by David Gerard. London, 1976.

Roelker, Nancy Lyman. *One King, One Faith: The Parlement of Paris and the Religious Reformations of the Sixteenth Century*. Berkeley and Los Angeles, 1996.

Thomson, David. *Renaissance Paris: Architecture and Growth, 1475–1600*. Berkeley and Los Angeles, 1984.

BARBARA B. DIEFENDORF

PARIS, UNIVERSITY OF. The University of Paris, northern Europe's leading university since its inception around 1200, experienced a decline in revenues, enrollment, and discipline during the last phase of the Hundred Years' War (1415–1453). The violence of the times, Paris's support for the losing Anglo-Burgundian party, and the creation of new universities all played a role. In 1446 the king subjected his "eldest daughter" to the jurisdiction of the Parlement of Paris, weakening the university's traditional autonomy and pontifical status but reinforcing its national character.

New statutes (1452) and reform initiatives by college principals like Jean Raulin (Collège de Navarre) and Jan Standonck (Collège de Montaigu) began the process of recovery. The colleges gradually took over from the "nations" the responsibility for teaching the arts curriculum. In 1470 the first Parisian printing press was installed within the Collège de Sorbonne, and the industry quickly flourished in the Latin Quarter. By 1500 Paris was once again considered to be the leading university in northern Europe.

Faculties and Students. Four faculties (arts, law, medicine, and theology), each led by a dean, made up the university. The arts faculty was composed of four "nations" (France, Normandy, Picardy, and Germany), which elected the rector of the whole university for a term of three months. The M.A. degree was a prerequisite for entry into the three higher faculties. Because the Faculty of Law granted degrees only in canon law, French students wanting civil law went to Orléans, Bourges, or, exceptionally, to Italian universities. The Faculty of Medicine relied on ancient and medieval authorities (Hippocrates, Galen, and Avicenna) and struggled frequently with the surgeons, who received papal permission in 1579 to create a faculty of their own. The doctorate in the Faculty of Theology—the highest academic distinction—required a thirteen- to fifteen-year program consisting of courses on the Bible and the *Sentences* of Peter Lombard and a series of academic disputations assuring the candidate's knowledge, dialectical skills, and orthodoxy. Masters in theology not only taught and wrote but also met regularly on matters of faith and morals submitted to their faculty's judgment.

The student population in the sixteenth century has been estimated between twelve thousand and twenty thousand. Most lived in private rooms or hospices, but many resided in the forty colleges that provided instruction and discipline as well. The largest colleges were Navarre, Montaigu, Sainte-Barbe, Harcourt, Bourgogne, and Cardinal Lemoine. The Sorbonne, a theological college, is often confused with the Faculty of Theology which, after 1554, regularly met there. With the exception of the Faculty of Medicine (and, late in the sixteenth century, the Faculty of Law), teachers had to be celibate. Students, too, were tonsured clerics, although most resumed lay status after leaving the university.

Controlled by secular (diocesan) clerics, the University of Paris lived uneasily with the approximately one thousand Dominicans, Franciscans, Augustinians, and Carmelites who studied theology in Paris—mainly because those orders claimed special pontifical status and exemption from episcopal jurisdiction. For similar reasons, the university refused to accept the Jesuits, who established the Collège de Clermont in Paris in 1550.

The Scholastic Tradition. Although banned between 1474 and 1481, nominalism was the dominant philosophical school in Paris, with Thomas Bricot and then John Major its leading exponents. Together with the leading Scotist, Petrus Tartaretus, all three were lampooned by humanist critics. Before turning his attention to sacred scripture, Jacques Lefèvre d'Étaples provided new translations of Aristotle. From 1503 to 1514 Pieter Crockaert trained a new generation of Thomists at the Dominican *studium,* among them Francisco de Vitoria, whose substitution of Aquinas for Peter Lombard at the University of Salamanca revolutionized the study of Western theology.

Students began grammar studies at about the age of twelve and the five-year arts course at about fifteen. The curriculum stressed logic, natural philosophy, and ethics more than rhetoric. This preference for scholastic learning drew criticism from humanists who wanted to substitute the wisdom and rhetoric of classical authors and to apply philology to theological and scriptural texts. In a watershed event (1514–1517), Paris masters joined those of Cologne and Louvain in opposing Johann Reuchlin's use of Jewish learning to illumine Christian biblical exegesis and commentary. This was followed by a series of skirmishes over new exegetical conclusions of Lefèvre d'Étaples and his disciples.

Humanism. In the late fifteenth century Greek was mostly taught privately and outside the university; but, from 1508, some masters managed to teach it in Paris colleges. In 1547 the humanist Jean Dorat became principal of the Collège de Coqueret, where he taught Pierre de Ronsard, Jean-Antoine de Baïf, and Joachim Du Bellay, the founders of the Pléiade. But in 1533 the Faculty of Arts had warned against the inroads of "grammarians," and most regents maintained the traditional scholastic curriculum. Peter Ramus lost his bid in 1543 to supplant Aristotle with a new logic.

The cause of humanism at the university suffered because its critics believed that, in attacking established traditions, it promoted disorder and even heresy. But it suffered also from lack of patronage during the frequent wars of the time. Only after the Treaty of Cambrai (1529) did Francis I finally accede to the pleas of Guillaume Budé and other humanists to endow lecturers similar to those at the *Collegium trilingue* (Trilingual college) in Louvain. Erasmus, whom they had hoped to attract, chose to avoid Paris, where his works were formally condemned in 1527. In 1530, to the acclaim of humanists, four *lecteurs du roi* (royal lecturers) began to teach Greek and Hebrew. But in 1534, when they announced lectures on the Bible, the Faculty of Theology's syndic, Noël Beda, cited them before the Parlement of Paris—the supreme court in France—for violating the prerogative of doctors of theology in that area. Arts regents objected that same year when a *lecteur royal* in Latin literature was appointed. The royal lecturers did not yet enjoy the independence from the university that they would acquire decades later, when they became known as the Collège Royal and, after the Revolution, as the Collège de France.

Opposition to Heresy. On 15 April 1521 the University of Paris condemned 104 theological propositions of Martin Luther. A year earlier, sensing that the matter was beyond the powers of its dean, the Faculty of Theology had revived the office of syndic and nominated to it Noël Beda, who would marshal the faculty and the whole university against religious and curricular change during the next fifteen years. Another weapon against innovation was the power of censorship granted to the Faculty of Theology in 1521 by the Parlement of Paris. Taking the lead in suppressing heresy, the Parlement regarded the Faculty of Theology as a "permanent council in France" and looked to it for authoritative judgments about a preacher or a book. The kings of France too were accustomed to consult the faculty, which had strong Gallican leanings, about ecclesiastical polity and doctrine.

The university and the Parlement of Paris opposed King Francis I's Concordat of Bologna (1516) with Pope Leo X because it weakened church liberties and strengthened royal control. Although they failed, their efforts cemented an alliance that they later applied effectively against religious change and less effectively against royal absolutism. Until about 1528, the university and the Parlement were usually at odds with Francis I, whose self-image as a tolerant and cultured prince (and encouragement from his sister, Margaret of Navarre), induced him to protect reformist thinkers. During the king's yearlong captivity after the Battle of Pavia (24 February 1525), the jurists and theologians prohibited translations and new versions of the Bible, shut down the evangelical reforms of Bishop Guillaume Briçonnet in the diocese of Meaux, imprisoned several heretics, and even executed some of them. Upon his return the king showed his displeasure with the Parlement in the famous *lit de justice* (1527) and with the Faculty of Theology by censoring Beda's book against Erasmus and Lefèvre d'Étaples. But in May 1528 Francis personally led a procession to atone for the defacement of a statue of the Virgin and Child. And, although he had assured the safety of Louis de Berquin in 1523 and 1527, Francis made no protest when the Parlement executed him in 1529 and appointed Ber-

University of Paris. Meeting of professors. Miniature from *Chants royaux,* early sixteenth century. BIBLIOTHÈQUE NATIONALE DE FRANCE, PARIS. FR 1537 FOL. 27v

quin's worst enemy as its *premier président* later that same year.

In May 1533, however, the king exiled Noël Beda and several other theologians who had attacked the Lenten sermons that Gérard Roussel was preaching under the aegis of Margaret of Navarre. Later, the Faculty of Theology denied censuring her book *Miroir de l'âme pécheresse* (Mirror of a sinful soul). But, in another reverse of policy, Francis reacted strongly against a reformist sermon delivered on 1 November 1533 by the university's rector, Nicolas Cop. And, furious at the circulation of placards (17–18 October 1534) and pamphlets (January 1535) critical of the Catholic Mass, the king led another expiatory procession, watched the execution of several heretics, and then ordered the cessation of all printing in France. He also endorsed the faculty's Articles of Faith (1543), which, even into the seventeenth century, all members of the university and the Parlement swore to uphold. The Parlement enforced the faculty's catalogs of prohibited books from 1544 to 1556, greatly reducing the printing of Protestant books in France and their import from abroad. King Henry II's

Edict of Châteaubriant (1551) solemnized the tripartite repression of heresy by king, Parlement, and university that had already begun under Francis I.

During the Wars of Religion (1562–1598) the university denounced the limited toleration of heretics that the monarchy decreed on different occasions, and in 1568 the institution obtained royal support for exclusion of heretics from the university. This policy hardened into political reaction, supporting the Saint Bartholomew's Day massacre (1572) and the radical Catholic League that welcomed the assassination of King Henry III and preferred a Catholic Spanish king to the Protestant heir Henry of Navarre.

Reform. A royal commission (1595–1600) tightened discipline and assured university loyalty to king and nation. It reduced the time required by the traditional curriculum, thus allowing more scope for new subjects. But Scholasticism remained the dominant methodology at the University of Paris, to be challenged once again in the Age of Enlightenment.

See also **Collège de France**; **Censorship**; **Concordats**; **Gallicanism**; **Humanism**, *subentry on* **France**; **Reuchlin Affair**; **Scholasticism**; **Universities**.

BIBLIOGRAPHY

Primary Works

Du Boulay (Bulaeus), César-Égasse. *Historia universitatis parisiensis.* 6 vols. Paris, 1665–1673. Reprint, Brussels, Belgium, 1966. Volumes 5 and 6 contain numerous original documents from the fifteenth and sixteenth centuries.

Duplessis d'Argentré, Charles, ed. *Collectio judiciorum de novis erroribus qui ab initio duodecimi saeculi post incarnationem verbi, usque ad annum 1735 in ecclesia proscripti sunt et notati. . . .* 3 vols. Paris, 1725–1736. Reprint, Brussels, Belgium, 1963. Largely based on two registers compiled under the aegis of Noël Beda in the 1520s from documents at the University of Paris.

Goulet, Robert. *Compendium on the Magnificence, Dignity, and Excellence of the University of Paris in the Year of Grace 1517.* Translated by Robert Belle Burke. Philadelphia, 1928. Translation of *Compendium recenter editum de multiplici parisiensis universitatis magnificentia, dignitate, et excellentia eius fundatione* (Paris, 1517). An idealistic but contemporary view of the organization and functioning of the University of Paris.

Secondary Works

Crevier, Jean-Baptiste. *Histoire de l'université de Paris, depuis son origine jusqu'en l'année 1600.* 7 vols. Paris, 1761. A thorough analysis in French of Du Boulay's Latin history, but without the documents.

Farge, James K. *Orthodoxy and Reform in Early Reformation France: The Faculty of Theology of the University of Paris, 1500–1543.* Leiden, Netherlands, 1985. An analysis of the university's Faculty of Theology, its relations with church and civil institutions, and its key role in dealing with humanism and religious reform.

Renaudet, Augustin. *Préréforme et humanisme à Paris pendant les premières guerres d'Italie (1494–1517).* Rev. ed. Paris, 1953. Still the best-researched view of the intellectual activity at the university for the period indicated.

Tuilier, André. *Histoire de l'Université de Paris et de la Sorbonne.* 2 vols. Paris, 1994. The first volume is a careful, detailed synthesis of the history of the university from its inception through the reign of Louis XIII.

JAMES K. FARGE

PARKER, MATTHEW (1504–1575), reformer and archbishop of Canterbury (1559–1575). Parker was born in Norwich, the son of William Parker, a prosperous weaver. He received his university education at Corpus Christi College, Cambridge, an institution to which he remained devoted all his life and to which he left much of his extensive manuscript collection. By the end of the 1520s he was influenced by Reformed ideas and began to gain a reputation as a preacher. In 1535 Anne Boleyn appointed him as one of her chaplains and offered him various ecclesiastical promotions. He held the deanery of Stoke-by-Clare in conjunction with Cambridge University offices, becoming master of Corpus Christi in 1544 and twice vice-chancellor of the university. Under Mary I he lost his benefices and other offices but managed to remain in retirement in England.

In 1559 Elizabeth I selected him as her first archbishop of Canterbury, partly because he was not tainted by the radicalism of continental reform movements. Parker accepted with great reluctance and never enjoyed the administrative burdens of his office. But he committed himself energetically to the reconstruction of the Church of England, undertaking regular visitations, seeking to improve the educational standards of the clergy, and ensuring that the Thirty-nine Articles were passed through the convocation of the clergy. From 1566 onward he spent much time defending the uniformity of Elizabeth's religious settlement against the attacks of more zealous Protestants. The queen accepted his ideas of church order but did not offer him the political support necessary to secure conformity. His last years were made bitter by these struggles.

In the last ten years of his life Parker's personal interest was in the scholarly defense of the English church. He was an avid collector of manuscripts, especially those relating to the English church and the Anglo-Saxon past. In the early years of Elizabeth's reign he encouraged John Bale to continue his hunt for treasures from the libraries of the dissolved monasteries, and he collaborated with the historian Matthias Flacius Illyricus in his search for early Christian texts. Parker employed a group of transcribers at Lambeth Palace, and with them edited the earliest printed versions of Asser's *Life of Alfred,* Bishop Aelfric's *Catholic Homilies,* and the chronicles of Matthew Paris and Thomas Walsingham. In 1566 he arranged for the printer John Day to cut a set of Anglo-Saxon characters to facilitate the printing of early texts.

Parker's own major contribution to historical studies was *De antiquitate Britannicae ecclesiae et privilegiis ecclesiae Cantuariensis* (1572), on the rights of the see of Canterbury and on the history of its archbishops. Parker was concerned to demonstrate both the institutional and doctrinal continuity of the English church from the earliest times to his own day. It was also of critical importance to him to show that the scriptures had been available in the vernacular; hence his publication of Aelfric's Gospels "translated . . . into the vulgar tongue of the Saxons" (1571). He did much to stabilize the early Elizabethan church and to save the scattered remains of monastic learning.

BIBLIOGRAPHY

Brook, Victor John Knight. *A Life of Archbishop Parker.* Oxford, 1962. The only full biography, but dated in its interpretation of ecclesiastical politics.

Page, R. I. *Matthew Parker and His Books.* Cambridge, U.K., 1990. Kalamazoo, Mich., 1993.

Wright, C. E. "The Dispersal of the Monastic Libraries and the Beginnings of Anglo-Saxon Studies: Matthew Parker and His Circle: a Preliminary Study." *Transactions of the Cambridge Bibliographical Society* 1, no. 3 (1951): 208–237.

FELICITY HEAL

PARMA. A city of Roman origin in the province of Emilia in northern Italy, Parma was established on the site of earlier settlements. After the end of the Roman Empire in the West in the fifth century, Parma continued its urban existence, coming under the temporal and spiritual rule of its bishops by the early eleventh century. During the high Middle Ages, Parma, like many Italian cities, experienced periods of civic discord and struggles between Guelfs and Ghibellines, between noble families, and between its bishops and the nascent commune. The city came to be governed by a *podestà* (a judicial official), a small council, and a large council. Guilds played an important role in its economic life, as can be seen in statutes and laws of the period. But political independence was rare.

Shifts in Parma's political fortunes in the fourteenth and fifteenth centuries made the city subject to lords like the Correggi, the Scaligeri, and the Visconti and Sforza lords of Milan. During the Italian wars Parma was alternately under French and papal domination before becoming definitively part of the Papal State in 1521. In 1545 Pope Paul III detached the territories of Parma and Piacenza to form a duchy with which he invested his son Pier Luigi Farnese. This controversial action marked the last time a papal family was given a state carved out of the possessions of the church.

The new duchy, with Parma as its capital, was ruled by the Farnese dynasty for 186 years. Upon the death of the last duke in 1731 it passed to the Spanish Bourbons. Under the Farnese dukes Parma's cultural life was focused on the court. Especially significant was patronage of music, much of it performed in the great Teatro Farnese, constructed in 1618–1619. In architecture, Parma had important monuments long before the duchy was formed. Outstanding among them is one of the finest Romanesque complexes of buildings that comprises the cathedral, the bell tower, and the octagonal baptistery with its frescoed cupola. A number of impressive secular buildings and churches dating from the high Middle Ages testify to the wealth of the city, derived from its agricultural hinterland, urban manufacture, and trade. The sixteenth century added splendid new constructions, above all the church of Santa Maria della Steccata, and the huge ducal Palazzo della Pilotta, begun in 1583. A plethora of churches, convents, and monasteries dates from the Farnese period. The most famous Renaissance painters of Parma are Antonio Allegri, known as Correggio, and Francesco Mazzola, called il Parmigianino, both stylistic innovators. Correggio's frescoes in the church of San Giovanni Evangelista, the cathedral, and the Convent of San Paolo are major artistic monuments. Parmigianino, one of the most important and influential mannerist painters, also left many works in Parma.

Although the city had a university already by the early thirteenth century, it was not among the famous Italian institutions of learning and had a discontinuous history. More famous was a college for nobles founded by Duke Ranuccio I in the early seventeenth century in order to educate young aristocrats from Parma and other states in the arts of courtly life. But Parma never reached the educational or artistic status of the major centers of Renaissance culture such as Florence, Venice, or Rome.

BIBLIOGRAPHY

Bernini, Ferdinando. *Storia di Parma.* 3d ed. Parma, Italy, 1979. Short history of Parma from its beginnings to 1914.

Le corti farnesiane di Parma e Piacenza, 1545–1622. 2 vols, vol. 1 edited by M. A. Romani; vol. 2 edited by A. Quondam. Rome, 1978. Scholarly and informative; useful bibliographies.

Marchesi, Gustavo. *Storia di Parma.* Rome, 1994.

ELISABETH G. GLEASON

PARMIGIANINO (Girolamo Francesco Maria Mazzola; 1503–1540), north Italian painter, draftsman, and printmaker. Among the most influential of Italian Renaissance artists, and hailed by sixteenth-century art critics as Raphael reborn, Parmigianino imbued his work with a quality of grace that came to epitomize the highly sophisticated and stylish aesthetic known as mannerism.

Early Life. Born in Parma to the local painter Filippo Mazzola (c. 1460–c. 1505), Parmigianino was raised and first instructed by his uncles, the painters Pier Ilario (c. 1476–after 1544) and Michele (c. 1469–after 1528) Mazzola. The boy demonstrated great precocity in drawing and eventually distinguished himself as one of the most prolific and talented Renaissance draftsmen. At the age of sixteen he painted his first recorded work, a *Baptism of Christ* (Berlin, Bodemuseum). Early pictures such as the *Mystic Marriage of Saint Catherine* (c. 1521; Bardi, Santa Maria) manifest an incipient tendency toward the refined elegance that would later characterize his mature style.

His frescoes in the first two chapels on the left side of San Giovanni Evangelista in Parma (c. 1522) bespeak the influence of the older master Correggio (Antonio Allegri), at the time also working in the church. The attribution to Parmigianino of certain passages in Correggio's cupola decoration in San Giovanni Evangelista invites a renewed consideration of the precise relationship between the two artists. Indeed, Parmigianino's drawings suggest that he had access to and copied Correggio's designs as well as paintings. Parmigianino's frescoes of *Diana and Actaeon* (c. 1523–1524) in the Rocca Sanvitale at Fontanellato, near Parma, similarly reveal his debt to Correggio (c. 1519; Parma, Camera di San Paolo), in terms of subject matter, general organization (trellised bower with putti), and fresco technique. A picture of Count Galeazzo Sanvitale (c. 1524; Naples, Capodimonte) heralds Parmigianino's ability to create original, often hauntingly beautiful portraits.

Rome and Bologna. Accompanied by his uncle Pier Ilario, Parmigianino went to Rome in 1524 in order to study antiquities and the works of Raphael and Michelangelo. Among the presentation pictures he brought to impress the newly elected Pope Clement VII was a virtuoso *Self-Portrait in a Convex Mirror* (Vienna, Kunsthistorisches; see the entry Diaries and Memoirs). The curved panel reproduces effects of mirror distortion to portray the handsome youth offering his hand, a gesture that declares his courtly pretension as much as his creative potential. Such grace in social manners and artistic style soon earned him a reputation as Raphael reborn. Parmigianino began both directly and as a designer to experiment with printmaking techniques such as etching. His Roman paintings, albeit relatively few in number, include a large altarpiece known today as the *Vision of Saint Jerome* (London, National Gallery), commissioned in 1526 by Maria Bufalini as part of the decoration of her husband's chapel in the church of San Salvatore in Lauro. The picture summarizes Parmigianino's Roman experience—the example of Michelangelo (*Bruges Madonna,* c. 1503) and especially Raphael (*Madonna of Foligno,* c. 1510) recast to produce a composition of exceeding elegance and iconographic subtlety. According to Giorgio Vasari, the artist was working on this altarpiece when, during the sack of Rome in 1527, imperial soldiers invaded his studio and captured him. The soldiers protected him from harm, however, and exacted drawings from him as ransom.

The sack of Rome, however traumatic, appears to have had little impact on Parmigianino other than precipitating his departure from the city. His Bolognese works thus refine an already established aesthetic preference for tapering elongated forms and rhythmic, spatially indeterminate compositions, as seen for example in *Saint Roch and a Donor* (1527; Bologna, San Petronio) and the *Madonna with Saint Margaret* (1528–1529; Bologna, Pinacoteca). The latter altarpiece reveals once again his interest in Correggio (*Madonna of Saint Jerome,* c. 1523–1528). Parmigianino continued to paint portraits, including a large allegorical image of the emperor Charles V (whereabouts of original unknown), as well as to draw and make prints. Evidently much celebrated and copied was his *Madonna of the Rose* (c. 1530; Dresden, Gemäldegalerie), so rarefied in sensuality that one eighteenth-century critic would later speculate that the picture originally depicted a Venus and Cupid.

Return to Parma. A commission in 1530 to paint two altarpieces (never executed) for the Parmese church of Santa Maria della Steccata likely prompted the artist's return home. In 1531 the Steccata confraternity enlisted Parmigianino to paint the eastern vault and apse of the church, a project he

Parmigianino. *Madonna and Child with SS. John the Baptist and Jerome.* Oil on poplar wood; 1526–1527; 343 × 149 cm (11.25 × 5 ft.). © NATIONAL GALLERY, LONDON

never brought to term. According to Vasari, a consuming obsession with alchemy led Parmigianino to turn into a bearded savage and neglect altogether his art. The sheer quantity of related preparatory drawings (nearly one hundred of which survive for the Steccata vault alone) suggests, however, that he spent an extraordinary amount of time devising and reworking his ideas, even if he was slow to translate them into paint.

His most famous work, the so-called *Madonna of the Long Neck* (c. 1534–1540; Florence, Uffizi; see the color plates in this volume), made for the chapel of Elena Baiardi and her husband in the Servite church of Parma, involved a similarly protracted graphic search of alternatives for his thematic charge. Although left unfinished at the time of his death, the altarpiece nonetheless offers Parmigianino's most deliberate statement of an exquisitely contrived beauty as sacred content. In this anticipation of the scene of confrontation between Mary and the dead Christ known as the Pietà, a lovely Virgin contemplates her sleeping Infant, as an angel proffers her a vase, itself a formal and iconographic analogy to her elegantly posed body. Such lyrical grace may also be found in the so-called *Wise and Foolish Virgins* that Parmigianino succeeded in painting on the Steccata vault before the confraternity, increasingly frustrated with his slow working pace, had him briefly imprisoned and then debarred from the project in 1539.

The artist fled to nearby Casalmaggiore, outside the jurisdiction of Parma, where he painted a few pictures, notably the *Madonna of Saint Stephen* (Dresden, Gemäldegalerie). Correspondence indicates that he had hoped to return home to resume the Steccata commission, but in 1540, at only thirty-seven years of age, he died and was buried in the Servite church of the Fontana, just outside Casalmaggiore. Parmigianino's refined style was widely imitated across Europe, particularly in court centers (for example, Fontainebleau, Prague), throughout the sixteenth century.

See also **Correggio**; **Mannerism**.

BIBLIOGRAPHY

Freedberg, S. J. *Parmigianino: His Works in Painting.* Cambridge, Mass., 1950. The major English-language monograph on the artist.

Gould, Cecil. *Parmigianino.* New York and London, 1994. A recent English-language monograph on the artist.

Graphische Sammlung Albertina. *Parmigianino und sein Kreis.* Exhibition catalog, Albertina. Introduction by Konrad Oberhuber. Vienna, 1963. Important discussion of Parmigianino's activity as a printmaker.

Popham, A. E. *Catalogue of the Drawings of Parmigianino.* 3 vols. New Haven, Conn., 1971. The most important catalog of Parmigianino's drawings.

MARY VACCARO

PARR, KATHERINE (1512–1548), first Protestant queen of England, sixth wife (and widow) of Henry VIII. Katherine Parr played three important roles in advancing Renaissance humanism and Reformation piety in England: (1) as beloved stepmother in the education and nurture of two eventual monarchs, Edward VI and Elizabeth I, and as guardian of Lady Jane Grey; (2) as patroness of such Reformed humanists as Hugh Latimer, Miles Coverdale, John Cheke, Roger Ascham, Anthony Cooke, Nicholas Udall, and John Parkhurst; (3) as author of two pioneering works in the vernacular, *Prayers or Meditations* and *The Lamentation of a Sinner*.

Katherine received her early education at the family seat of Rye House in Hertfordshire. She was left wealthy, widowed, and childless at thirty-two after marrying twice into great landed families of the north. Returning to court to serve in Princess Mary Tudor's household, Katherine found herself the last nuptial choice of King Henry, whom she married in July 1543. Katherine won Henry's political trust (he formally named her regent of the realm during his military campaign in France in July–October 1544) and his spousal compliance; through her efforts, he reconciled with his daughters, Mary and Elizabeth, and reunited them with the young Edward in the immediate family circle.

Katherine's embrace of Reformed religion proved the crucial development of this same period; apparently she was converted by Thomas Cranmer, with whom as principal councillor she, as regent, consulted daily throughout the summer of 1544. Edward was six, Elizabeth nearly ten, when Katherine became their stepmother. As regent she stepped forward as the guarantor of their education in the "new learning" by securing Cheke's and Ascham's (and subsequently Cooke's) appointment as their tutors.

In 1545–1546 Katherine gained notoriety by reading and discussing scripture in her chambers with a select circle of her ladies. A conservative court faction nearly succeeded in fatally alienating Henry's affections. By a timely act of deference to the king, Katherine was able to save her credit and her life. Now circumspect in continuing her advocacy of a Bible-based Christian humanism, Katherine sponsored an English translation of Erasmus's Latin *Paraphrases upon the New Testament*, published in 1548–1549. The two large volumes would share with the

Katherine Parr. Portrait attributed to William Scrots. NATIONAL PORTRAIT GALLERY, LONDON/SUPERSTOCK

English Bible the privilege of a royal injunction mandating their public access in every parish church of the realm.

In the risky era of Henry's declining years, Katherine dedicated to her irascible spouse her *Prayers or Meditations* in November 1545. This is the earliest printed work by an Englishwoman. Subtly recasting and reordering excerpts from the *Imitation of Christ* (attributed to Thomas à Kempis [1379/80–1471]), in Richard Whytford's translation, Parr makes its Christic affectivity directly accessible to godly laity of both genders. She published her second work in November 1547, after Henry's death. *The Lamentation of a Sinner* proceeds from Lutheran and Pauline self-accounting (including notable declarations on justification by faith and the cross of Christ as the central truth of God's Word) to make a comprehensive survey of the estates of the realm. Katherine exhorts her English readers to a new sense of vocation and zeal for God's kingdom by taking scripture to their hearts as she has done. Her first-person reflections intersect with the social concerns of midcentury Commonwealth men, while her specific pronouncements on wifehood, household duties, and social comportment strikingly anticipate later Puritan treatments of gender roles and marriage.

In or around May 1547, Katherine, now a royal widow, married for the fourth time, but her first time for love—to Thomas Seymour, younger brother of the lord protector, Edward Seymour, duke of Somerset, both uncles of the now boy-king Edward VI. Soon Katherine became a pawn in the struggle between the power-hungry Seymour brothers. The new regime rescinded many of her former prerogatives, including Katherine's intimacy with both Edward and Elizabeth. Her romantic passion for Thomas Seymour resulted in her one and only pregnancy: the daughter born in late August 1548. Katherine died six days later of puerperal fever. The former queen's Protestant funeral, composed of scripture readings, psalm singing, and a sermon by Coverdale, was the first such for royalty in England.

During the half century after her death Parr enjoyed appreciable currency as an author: *Prayers or Meditations* saw twenty-five editions before 1600, *The Lamentation of a Sinner* saw four, including the highly significant presentation of both works in Thomas Bentley's *The Monument of Matrones* (1582), where Katherine's works appear in sequence with devotional compositions by Queen Elizabeth. Thereafter, however, the authorial Parr sank into obscurity, broken only by the publication of *The Lamentation* in *The Harleian Miscellany* (1808). Since the late 1960s there has been renewed interest in her contemporary influence and writings.

BIBLIOGRAPHY

James, Susan E. *Queen's Gambit: The Lives of Kateryn, William, and Anne Parr.* London, 1999.

JANEL MUELLER

PARUTA, PAOLO (1540–1598), Venetian patrician active in politics and literature. Political success came to Paruta in the 1580s and was crowned by his posting to Rome as Venetian ambassador to the court of Pope Clement VIII from October 1592 to October 1595. During his lifetime there was a profound rift within the Venetian patriciate between those who accepted limitations on Venice's autonomy in Habsburg-dominated Italy, favored compromise with the Roman Curia, and were prepared to trade participation in Venetian politics for the power and prestige of an ecclesiastical career; and those who committed themselves to the political struggle in Venice and favored a more independent and assertive role for the republic, especially in defense of Venetian jurisdiction over the church. Paruta has occasionally

been identified with the latter group, but his life also reflects aspects of the former.

Paruta's *Della perfezzione della vita politica* (On the perfection of political life; Venice, 1579) is modeled on the great literary dialogues of the Renaissance. Its participants are Venetian churchmen and statesmen who are represented as meeting in 1563 to debate the classic question of whether humanity's nature is more completely fulfilled in the active life of political engagement (in which the will has a role, and which is enhanced by opulence and distinguished ancestors) or the life of withdrawal into contemplation (where virtue is entirely individual, intellectual, and spiritual). Beneath the veneer of philosophical debate, Paruta portrays the actual rift within the Venetian patriciate and, more broadly, the opposition between Renaissance and Counter-Reformation values.

Paruta's weekly dispatches from Rome are a prime source for European history from 1592 to 1595. His greatest success as an ambassador was to encourage the reluctant pope and Curia to recognize Henry IV as the legitimate Catholic king of France in September 1595, but back in Venice he was accused of not having defended Venetian jurisdiction strongly enough at Rome. In a short *Soliloquio* Paruta expressed a Christian disdain for the active life; while in a *Relazione* delivered to the Venetian government he offered a perceptive political analysis of emerging papal absolutism. In the 1570s Paruta composed *La guerra di Cipro* (The Cyprus war), a vivid account of Venice's role in the recent war (1570–1573) between the Catholic powers and the Turkish empire. He was appointed official historian of Venice in 1580 and composed a history of the years 1513–1552, *Historia vinetiana,* in which he emulated Francesco Guicciardini, the historian of the Italian wars of 1494–1530. *La guerra* and *Historia* were published posthumously in 1605.

Paruta's *Discorsi politici* (Political essays; 1599) responded, half a century later, to the *Discorsi* of Niccolò Machiavelli and to the problems of Italian history raised by Guicciardini. Paruta discusses the relation between the political order of ancient Rome and its success as a conquest state, the validity of the Venetian constitution as an alternative model, and the alliances and the options for war or peace made by the Italian princes during the wars of Italy. Although colored by a partisan defense of the Venetian constitution against the Roman model preferred by Machiavelli, and of the decisions made by Venice during the wars, Paruta's *Discorsi politici* is the work in which he came closest to rivaling his great Renaissance predecessors.

BIBLIOGRAPHY

Primary Works

Paruta, Paolo. *Historia vinetiana* and *La guerra di Cipro*. Vols. 3–4 of *Degli istorici delle cose veneziane*. Venice, 1718–1722.

Paruta, Paolo. *La legazione di Roma di Paolo Paruta*. 3 vols. Venice, 1887. The complete dispatches from Rome.

Paruta, Paolo. *Opere politiche di Paolo Paruta*. 2 vols. Florence, 1852. Includes all of the works discussed except the ambassadorial dispatches and the histories. The most commonly cited edition (except for the *Relazione* on Rome, commonly cited from *Relazioni degli ambasciatori veneti al Senato*. Ser. 2. Vol. 4. Edited by Eugenio Albèri. Florence, 1857).

Secondary Works

Benzoni, G., and T. Zanato, eds. *Storici e politici veneti del Cinquecento e del Seicento*. Milan and Naples, Italy, 1982. The most substantial secondary scholarship on Paruta, plus excerpts from *La guerra di Cipro* and *Della perfezzione*.

WILLIAM MCCUAIG

PASQUIER, ÉTIENNE (1529–1615), French antiquarian scholar and jurist. After graduating from the renowned Collège de Presles in 1546, Étienne Pasquier studied with the greatest legal humanists of his day. From François Hotman (1524–1590), François Baudouin (1520–1573), Jacques Cujas (1522–1590), and Andrea Alciato (1492–1550), he acquired a profound sense of the relativity of laws and institutions, which led him to assert the importance of the French political and cultural inheritance over and against classical Roman and modern Italian models. Upon joining the Paris bar in 1549, he began casting about for a means of expressing this viewpoint and decided in the mid-1550s to concentrate on the study of French antiquities, for which his legal education and profession best suited him. This decision inaugurated his life's work, the monumental *Recherches de la France* (Researches of France), the first book of which appeared in 1560.

Pasquier's public career and private scholarship advanced apace. In 1564 he represented the University of Paris in a famous lawsuit with the Jesuits, whom he portrayed as agents of Romanist tyranny seeking to undermine the liberties of the Gallican church. This Gallican stance left its distinctive mark on *Recherches,* book 2 of which appeared in 1565. In 1585 he became advocate general of the Chambre des comptes in Paris, one of the sovereign courts, and in 1588 he left the city as a deputy to the meeting of the Estates General at Blois. A Politique and staunch opponent of the ultramontane Catholic League that had just seized control of Paris, he did not return to his magistracy until Henry IV officially entered the city in 1594. During this absence from public life, he assembled a new, six-book edition of *Recherches,* which appeared in 1596. After retiring in 1604, he added a seventh book in 1611. Posthumous editions of *Recherches* generally include two additional books culled from work in progress when Pasquier died in 1615.

In form and content, *Recherches* represents a striking departure from traditional French historiography. Pasquier conceived of his project in the unconventional form of a "double research" concerned with "things" and "words," a distinction foreshadowing what in Voltaire's hands would become cultural history. Under the rubric of things, Pasquier included books on the ancient Gauls, French civil institutions, the Gallican church, the kingdom's noteworthy customs and laws, and its neglected historical figures. Under words he included books on French poetry, language, and learning.

The content of *Recherches,* too, breaks new ground. Instead of beginning the history of France with the traditional legend of the first Frenchman, Francus, a fugitive from the destruction of Troy, Pasquier starts with an analysis of the customs, laws, and institutions of the ancient Gauls, an analysis based on a close reading of Julius Caesar's *Gallic War.* This innovative use of a classical text underscores Pasquier's more critical approach to French history, which he reconstructed as much as possible from historical documents, including not only classical texts but also institutional records, like the registers of Parlement. So scrupulous was he in reproducing these documents that humanist historians like Bernard de Girard plagiarized *Recherches* in their own historical accounts of France. At first offended by these scholarly thefts, Pasquier eventually reconciled himself to them, regarding *Recherches* as his "gift" to France.

BIBLIOGRAPHY

Huppert, George. *The Idea of Perfect History: Historical Erudition and Historical Philosophy in Renaissance France.* Urbana, Ill., 1970. See especially chapter 3.

Keating, L. Clark. *Étienne Pasquier.* New York, 1972.

Kelley, Donald R. *Foundations of Modern Historical Scholarship: Language, Law, and History in the French Renaissance.* New York, 1970. See especially chapter 10.

Schiffman, Zachary Sayre. *On the Threshold of Modernity: Relativism in the French Renaissance.* Baltimore, 1991. See chapter 2.

Thickett, D. *Estienne Pasquier (1529–1615): The Versatile Barrister of Sixteenth-Century France.* London, 1979.

ZACHARY S. SCHIFFMAN

PASQUINO. A battered Roman statue of the Greek hero Menelaus standing protectively over the corpse of his comrade Patroclus emerged sometime late in the fifteenth century from the grounds of Palazzo Orsini in Rome. Patroclus had become a limbless trunk. The noseless, helmeted Menelaus had fared little better; his smashed face, upturned at a crazy angle, bore a look of perpetual surprise. No one quite knew what the statues might represent: guesses included Hercules with the slain monster Geryon, or perhaps a pair of gladiators. (An accurate identification was only made possible by the discovery of two more complete versions of the statue group, again in Rome, in 1570.) Quickly, however, the odd looking sculpture acquired the name "Mastro Pasquino," allegedly borrowed from a witty neighbor, reported variously as a tailor, an innkeeper, a barber, or a schoolteacher. By 1501 the cultured Neapolitan cardinal Oliviero Carafa had acquired the statue from his Orsini relatives and installed it on a pedestal in front of his palazzo next to Piazza Navona, where both Michelangelo and Bernini eventually admired its artistry and where it can still be seen today.

In Rome, despite centuries of Christianity, statues of the ancient gods and heroes had never quite lost their power to enchant, and Mastro Pasquino himself partook of that ancient magic. Just as ancient worshipers had decorated their cult statues and affixed prayers to them, so Renaissance Romans continued the practice, and not only with statues of the Madonna, Christ, and the saints. Beginning in the late fifteenth century, Roman students and humanists celebrated 25 April, the feast day of Saint Mark, by dressing Pasquino in the costume of an ancient divinity and festooning him with poems. In 1509 the papal printer Jacopo Mazzocchi first published a pamphlet of the year's "pasquinades": dressed as Janus, the statue had received over three thousand accolades (most of which Mazzocchi regarded as unfit to print). Pasquino's early career also included transformations into Atlas, Mercury, Bacchus, Saturn, Mars, Minerva, Astraea, Venus, Ceres, the Genius of Rome, Apollo, Jupiter, Harpocrates, and Hercules, as well as mourning black for the sudden death of Cardinal Carafa in 1511. Early on, the pasquinades turned toward pointed satires of current events, and eventually they appeared on Mastro Pasquino in every season.

The annual anthology of pasquinades would continue to be published well into the eighteenth century; modern sequels still appear with some regularity in Roman bookshops. In the meantime, Mastro

Pasquino also entered into lively dialogue with other "talking" statues in Rome, especially Marforio, the handsome reclining river god on the Capitoline Hill, and Madama Lucrezia, the colossal bust of a priestess of Isis extracted from the ruins of her temple near Piazza Venezia and installed outside the Palazzo Venezia. Pasquino remains a living Roman tradition; he spent much of the 1980s with a bright red spray-painted feminist graffito—"Pasquina"—and can seldom be seen without a poem or two taped to his pedestal.

See also **Satire**, *subentry on* **Satire in Italy**.

BIBLIOGRAPHY

Bober, Phyllis Pray, and Ruth Rubinstein. *Renaissance Artists and Antique Sculpture. A Handbook of Sources.* London, 1986. Pages 187–188.

Cesareo, Giovanni Alfredo. *Pasquino e pasquinate nella Roma di Leone X.* Rome, 1938.

D'Onofrio, Cesare. *Un popolo di statue racconta: storie, fatti, leggende della città di Roma antica medievale moderna.* Rome, 1990. Pages 27–56.

Giovannini, Cristina. *Pasquino e le statue parlanti.* Rome, 1997.

INGRID D. ROWLAND

PASTORAL. [This entry includes two subentries, one concerning pastoral poetry on the Continent, the other concerning pastoral poetry in Elizabethan England.]

Pastoral on the Continent

Modern sentiment makes it difficult to understand why pastoral was one of the most popular genres of Renaissance Europe. This difficulty has been created in part by the testiness of neoclassicists such as René Rapin and the condemnation of Friedrich Nietzsche, who derided Renaissance pastoral drama as the product of nostalgia and mawkishness. Some pastoral landscape paintings might suggest an essential flatness to the conventions of the genre: shepherds, sheep, a shaded grove, a pipe or lyre. Such judgments, however, reveal a failure to understand what was innovative about a form that engaged the most sophisticated writers, painters, and composers of the Renaissance, among them Jacopo Sannazaro, Torquato Tasso, Miguel de Cervantes Saavedra, William Shakespeare, Peter Paul Rubens, and Claudio Monteverdi.

Origins, Influences, Genres. While it is possible to chart Renaissance pastoral along national lines, it was a phenomenon that transcended such boundaries, albeit one that originated largely in Italy and spread throughout western and eastern Europe.

413

A more useful way to classify Renaissance pastoral is through its relation to the ancient genres of the eclogue, romance, and satyr play. The Latin eclogues of Dante, Giovanni Boccaccio, and Petrarch were the first attempts in the fourteenth century to imitate Virgil's bucolics, even as they largely reduced Virgil's highly innovative poems to allegory; Sannazaro's *Piscatorial Eclogues* and Baptista Mantuanus's eclogues followed in the early sixteenth century. (Although the first seven idylls of Theocritus were translated into Latin in Ferrara in the mid-fifteenth century, their impact on Renaissance pastoral was initially slight—possibly because Theocritus was perceived as far more "rustic," that is, less literary, than Virgil.) With the *Bucoliche elegantissime* (Most elegant bucolics) of 1483, a collection of poems by Florentine and Sienese writers, the Virgilian eclogue was transmitted into the vernacular; and Matteo Maria Boiardo, Garcilaso de la Vega, Pierre de Ronsard, and Edmund Spenser wrote some of the period's most striking pastoral poetry, notable for its tonal and metrical variety as it moves from elegy to debate to epithalamium (a poem in honor of a bride and bridegroom). The pastoral romance of the ancient Greek Longus's *Daphnis and Chloe* had its foremost Renaissance practitioners in Jorge de Montemayor, Sir Philip Sidney, and Honoré d'Urfé; Lucrezia Marinella's *Arcadia felice* (1605) and Lady Mary Wroth's *Urania* (1621) are less-known works in the romance tradition. Finally, pastoral drama, which retrospectively took as its origin the only surviving satyr play, *Cyclops* by Euripides, includes works by Giambattista Cinzio Giraldi, whose *Egle* (1545) conforms more closely to *Cyclops* than any other drama of the period, Tasso Giovanni Battista Guarini, Shakespeare, Ben Jonson, Lope de Vega, and Cervantes.

Nonetheless, approaching pastoral by way of these three genres obscures a great deal. Such attentiveness to pastoral's classical roots ignores its Christian and medieval antecedents. The Nativity scenes of Juan del Encina's *Églogas* and the frequency with which painters such as Titian, Nicolas Poussin, and Rubens set the flight into Egypt in a pastoral setting suggest that pastoral's sources were not limited to classical texts; and the impact of the widespread tradition of the *pastourelle* and the popular forms of the *ballata, frottola,* and *contrasto* on pastoral lyric and drama demonstrates a vital continuity with medieval genres. Focusing only on elements of the three classical genres also fails to take into account the very different settings and audiences for which pastoral was composed. While much pastoral originated in courtly environments—Baldassare Castiglione's *Tirsi* (1506) was composed for the court of Urbino, Ronsard's *Elegies, mascarades, et bergerie* (1565) for Charles IX, and Tasso's *Aminta* (1573) for Alfonso II d'Este—some pastoral plays were performed by commedia dell'arte troupes for crowds in open piazzas and middle-class women read Spanish pastoral novels and the epistolary fiction of d'Urfé.

Finally, Renaissance pastoral itself rarely fit neatly into a single generic category. If anything, the vernacular forms emerged in the mid-fourteenth century to frustrate and mix generic boundaries. Beginning with Boccaccio's *Ameto* (*Comedia delle ninfe fiorentine* [Comedy of the Florentine nymphs]; 1341–1342) and continuing with Sannazaro's wildly popular *Arcadia* (1504), the standard pastoral novel combined narrative and lyric, framing poetic utterance by prose passages that give it a history and an audience. This juxtaposition of genres is particularly apparent in Renaissance epic and eventually the novel, which brought together pastoral and chivalric narratives nowhere more cleverly than in *Don Quixote*. Book 6 of Spenser's *Faerie Queene,* Erminia's stay among the shepherds in Tasso's *Gerusalemme liberata* (Jerusalem delivered; 1581), and the island of the Nereids in Luiz Vaz de Camoës's *Lusiadas* (1572) attest to a conscientious attempt to use pastoral not simply as a foil for heroic endeavor—although it is certainly that—but as a hallmark of a larger tension between an individual's autonomy and his or her incorporation into a larger and sometimes threatening whole. (Such a tension is also evident in classical works that are not often thought of in terms of Renaissance pastoral but clearly influenced it, such as Ovid's *Metamorphosis* and Homer's *Odyssey.*)

Pastoral Space. This tension gives Renaissance pastoral much of its uniqueness. It is certainly an issue in the vigorous theorizing that accompanied the development of pastoral drama, much of it centered on Giovanni Battista Guarini's *Il pastor fido* (The faithful shepherd; 1590). Stung by the Paduan professor Jason Denores's attack on his five-act tragicomic pastoral, Guarini responded in three lengthy treatises to the effect that in the late sixteenth century literature should be emphatically separate from church and state. Although such a view may seem to confirm pastoral's escapist tendencies—one of the criticisms to which it has often been subject— Guarini was asserting art's freedom from censorship and attack in a post-Tridentine era (that is, after the Roman Catholic church council held at Trent from 1545 to 1563) that increasingly scrutinized cultural

Pastoral Setting. *Rest on the Flight into Egypt* by Titian and his workshop. Painted c. 1535. © MUSEO DEL PRADO, MADRID

productions. In so doing, he moved beyond both the traditional association of pastoral with allegory (linked throughout the Renaissance to Virgil) and the claims of Sebastiano Serlio and others that the pastoral setting represented a place of license. Instead Guarini argued that pastoral's distance from the city, and thus from the conventions of civic life, makes it an ideal form for social, political, and even sexual experimentation. While it may not always constitute a "green world"—indeed, it is rarely that—it does emerge as a space for considerable innovation, whether of stylistic, generic, or philosophical, as William Empson argues in *Some Versions of Pastoral*. It is no accident that the great multimedia form of the seventeenth century, opera, developed out of pastoral drama (Monteverdi's *Orfeo,* performed in Mantua in 1609, features a chorus of shepherds and nymphs) nor that some of the most experimental poetry of the period, Luis de Góngora's obscure and unfinished *Soledades* (Solitudes; 1613), is set in a pastoral domain.

Yet although pastoral is often characterized by its separateness from the city, the court, or the constraints of the Counter-Reformation, it is striking how much pastoral portrays the problems of this separation rather than taking it for granted. Theocritus's first idyll serves as a crucial prototype of this. While the main body of the idyll is the goatherd Daphnis's lament as he plunges into a river, the lament takes place within a complex dialogue between an unnamed goatherd and his friend Thyrsis, who per-

forms Daphnis's lament in exchange for a beautifully crafted drinking cup. Thus is Daphnis's solitary song placed within a larger frame that appropriates the lament for its own purposes. Virgil's shepherds also repeat others' songs and put them into a different context, a process that breaks down in the ninth eclogue, where Moeris and Lycidas, distraught by the losses of the civil war, can no longer remember what their teacher once sang. Taking a poem or song from one context and putting it into another setting is at the heart of much Renaissance pastoral, as attested by the interpolation of generally Petrarchan lyrics into prose and drama and the dynamics of many works. The shepherds of Montemayor's *Diana* (1559) are surprised to discover themselves overheard as they sing; the characters in Tasso's *Aminta* are unnervingly placed in the position of voyeurs (as is the courtly audience); Guarini's Corisca in *Il pastor fido* stands offstage to spy on the shepherdess Amarilli and learn of her illicit love for a shepherd; d'Urfé's and Jean Mairet's courtly shepherds are rarely alone even when they imagine themselves to be; Giorgione da Castelfranco's discomfiting paintings feature supposedly disinterested spectators at festivals. A glance at Sidney's revised *Arcadia* or the plates that accompanied the twentieth edition of Guarini's *Pastor fido* (1602) suggests that the Renaissance pastoral space is conceived as densely populated, even crowded.

A Darker Dimension. The critic Paul Alpers has identified what he calls pastoral's responsive-

415

ness: its sympathies and consoling communal practices, which are effective because pastoral uses the lives of shepherds to represent the lives of all men. Yet many pastoral works also have a darker dimension. While Renaissance pastoral offers constant glimpses of an authentic individual, again and again this intimacy is rendered vulnerable as words and at times bodies are revealed to be rarely one's own. Much pastoral thus conveys the risks as well as the pleasures of revealing oneself to others at the same time that it increasingly makes it clear that there is often more than one self and that the process of discovering these selves is more important than the self one discovers. But even in the dizzying games of identity in Giambattista Marino's *Adone* (Adonis; 1623), in d'Urfé's *Astrée* (1607–1627), or on the Fortunate Isles of Tasso's *Gerusalemme liberata,* one encounters a relentless attempt to integrate and interpolate what is initially outside the self. External words, events, or characters are incorporated into a larger whole that may—or may not—affirm and protect individuality.

In its concern with issues of individuality, pastoral raises questions that surpass the strictly literary. Clearly the practice of recalling, interpreting, and interpolating local detail within a larger work was central to a humanism that defined itself vis-à-vis its varied uses of ancient texts. But the historical context—in particular, exploration of the New World—also influenced the subject matter of some pastoral works. That Shakespeare's *Tempest,* Camoës's *Lusíadas,* Lope de Vega's *El nuevo mundo descubierto por Cristobal Colón* (The New World discovered by Christopher Columbus), and many of Ben Jonson's masques for King James I have pointedly pastoral dimensions is hardly accidental.

Finally, much Renaissance pastoral might be construed as a critique of forms of privacy and leisure that were primarily class-based. Hence, in Lope de Vega's *Fuente ovejuna* (1619) the Commendador seizes Laurencia in the countryside, which he erroneously presumes to be a "discreet and silent friend" ("agora no quiere el campo,/ amigo secreto y solo" [Act 1]).

Lope de Vega's play raises the question of pastoral's limits: what does and does not constitute pastoral? A play about peasants who murder their feudal overlord, the Comendador, *Fuente ovejuna* is not pastoral in any strict sense. At the same time, its attack on the Comendador originates in his pastoral idealizations. Indeed, much Renaissance literature may be read as a response to the criticism of pastoral as essentially escapist and connected either to the landed aristocracy and princes, for whom pastorals were often performed, or to an incipient bourgeoisie detached from the real world. The "peasant plays" of Angelo Beolco (more commonly known by his acting name, Ruzzante), the Sienese Congrega dei Rozzi (an academy of artisans dating from the 1530s that played an important part in the history of the Italian comic stage), and Lope de Vega—to name only a few—are grounded in an opposition between shepherds and peasants, between fictionalized characters who see the countryside as an idyllic place and peasants whose difficult lives force them to resort to violence in order to survive.

Even in the early years of theorizing about pastoral, there were strikingly different points of view as to whom the rustic setting should accommodate: the Ferrarese dramaturge Pellegrino Prisciano argued that the satiric stage was ideal for shepherds who sang of love and the pleasures of the countryside, while Sebastiano Serlio suggested that the same setting should feature "rustics" who openly criticize vice and speak without respect for audience or class. The question of the relation of pastoral to local or rustic custom is still open; it is clear that Lope de Vega used chronicles, proverbs, and rustic songs for *Fuente ovejuna* and *Peribañez, y el Comendador de Ocana* (1614) and that Lorenzo de' Medici used popular rhythms and motifs in *Nencia da Barberino* (1468). But when considering the role of the *villano* (boor) in a play by the Congrega dei Rozzi, or that of Sancho Panza in *Don Quixote,* it becomes more difficult to ascertain how and to what extent rural culture affected pastoral. In these works the poets and dramatists refuse to gloss over the realities of shepherds' and peasants' lives, encouraging the reader to reflect on the relation between elite and popular cultures and between written and oral cultures among the rural communities of Europe.

It is difficult to separate most pastoral literature into the works of pure pastoral and those that are reacting to it. European pastoral began to lose its critical edge throughout the seventeenth century. What had been the alluring immediacy of a pastoral moment that was always threatened with dissolution was increasingly lost in dense networks of complicated imagery. Yet, even though the Renaissance pastoral ends with Milton's "Lycidas" (1638), the dynamics of the form did not disappear. The expressions of intimacy that the pastoral stage made possible became part of domestic drama, tragedy, and opera, while the sentimentality and complex plotting of the pastoral romance left a mark on the epistolary novel. Finally, the questions that Renaissance pastoral staged about the relationship of others to the self, and the place of the autonomous song, character, or community in a larger whole, reemerged in a variety of genres.

BIBLIOGRAPHY

Primary Works

Donno, Elizabeth, ed. *Three Renaissance Pastorals: Tasso-Guarini-Daniel.* Binghamton, N.Y., 1993.

Giraldi, Giambattista Cinzio. *Egle: Lettera sovra il comporre le satire atte alla scena favola pastorale.* Edited by Carla Molinari. Bologna, Italy, 1985.

Grant, William Leonard. *Neo-Latin Literature and the Pastoral.* Chapel Hill, N.C., 1965.

Lope de Vega. *Five Plays.* Translated by Jill Booty. New York, 1961.

Marotti, Ferruccio. *Lo spettacolo dall'umanesimo al manierismo.* Milan, 1974. Contains treatises of Serlio and Prisciano.

Paden, William, ed. *The Medieval Pastourelle.* 2 vols. New York, 1987.

Urfé, Honoré d'. *Astrea. Part I.* Translated by Steven Rendall. Binghamton, N.Y., 1995.

General Secondary Works

Alpers, Paul. *What Is Pastoral?* Chicago, 1996.

Empson, William. *Some Versions of Pastoral.* London, 1935.

Ettin, Andrew V. *Literature and the Pastoral.* New Haven, Conn., 1984.

Longeon, Claude, ed. *Le genre pastoral en Europe du XVᵉ au XVIIᵉ siècle.* Saint-Étienne, France, 1980.

Weinberg, Bernard. *A History of Literary Criticism in the Italian Renaissance.* 2 vols. Chicago, 1961.

Pastoral in Specific Regions

Armstrong, Elizabeth. *Ronsard and the Age of Gold.* Cambridge, U.K., 1968.

Clubb, Louise. *Italian Drama in Shakespeare's Time.* New Haven, Conn., 1989.

Dersofi, Nancy. *Arcadia and the Stage.* Madrid, 1978.

Pieri, Marzia. *La scena boschereccia nel rinascimento italiano.* Padua, Italy, 1983.

Rhodes, Elizabeth. "Skirting the Men: Gender Roles in Sixteenth-Century Pastoral Books." *Journal of Hispanic Philology* 11, no. 2 (1987): 131–149.

Salomon, Noël. *Recherches sur le thème paysan dans la "comedia" au temps de Lope de Vega.* Bordeaux, France, 1965.

Rousset, Jean. *La littérature de l'âge baroque en France: Circe et le paon.* Paris, 1963.

JANE TYLUS

Elizabethan Pastoral

Western pastoral began with some twenty poems by Theocritus and Virgil. Writing in Alexandria and conscious of his historical distance from classical Greek culture, Theocritus wrote poems that have an ironized, belated relation to Homeric epic. Although in the same meter as the Homeric poems, they are short, and their central figures are humble people, most frequently herdsmen. These bucolics (now called "idylls") were imitated by Virgil, who was equally conscious of a distant relation to his Greek models. Virgil made Theocritus's herdsmen and their world more homogeneous and thus enhanced the sense in which, as antitheses of the warrior hero, they were seen as representative. He also made his collection of ten bucolics (also called "eclogues," literally, "selections") into a coherent book. Virgil established the fundamental fictions and conventions of pastoral, including the representation of the poet himself as a shepherd.

Sannazaro and Montemayor. Renaissance writers derived several new forms from classical pastorals. The most important are pastoral drama and pastoral romance. Virgil's eclogues are characteristically cast as dialogues or exchanges of song. Hence they could be imitated and performed as court entertainments, from which, in Italy, full-blown pastoral dramas were developed. Pastoral romance also began with an Italian development of Virgilian eclogues. The vernacular *Arcadia* (1504) of Jacopo Sannazaro (1458–1530; he also wrote "piscatory eclogues" in Latin) incorporated Petrarchan love poetry into classical pastoral. Henceforth literary shepherds were viewed, more seriously than their classical predecessors, as representative lovers. Sannazaro also modified the Virgilian eclogue book by connecting the individual poems with short prose passages, which narrate the sojourn of the protagonist, a lover and a figure of the poet, in the pastoral world of Arcadia. Sannazaro's thematic and formal innovations were developed by the Portuguese writer Jorge de Montemayor (c. 1520–1561), who wrote in Spanish. In his *Diana* (1559) the prose narration dominates and the poems (still a mix of eclogues and Petrarchan love complaints) appear embedded in it.

English Versions. A major Elizabethan example exists of each of these pastoral forms. Edmund Spenser's *The Shepheardes Calender* (1579) is an eclogue book, of which the chief innovation is the assignment of each poem to a month of the year. Sir Philip Sidney's *The Countess of Pembroke's Arcadia* is a pastoral romance that exists in two forms. While the so-called *Old Arcadia* (1581) existed only in manuscript, a revision of the first two and a half books, now called the *New Arcadia,* was published in 1590. (A complete version, the revised books completed by the original final books, was published in 1593 and went through several editions.) Shakespeare's interest in pastoral is evident from the beginning of his career; *As You Like It* (1599) is the greatest pastoral drama in English. From the standpoint of continental pastoral, with its roots in classical poetry and its emphasis on Petrarchan and Neoplatonic love, these works brought uniquely English characteristics to pastoral.

Even *The Shepheardes Calender,* which has numerous Virgilian gestures and aims to domesticate privileged forms of European poetry, has less intertextual relation with Virgil than its continental analogues. Its main literary models are two earlier sixteenth-century poets, the Frenchman Clément Marot (c. 1495–1544) and the Italian Battista Spagnuoli (known as Mantuan; 1448–1516), whose moralistic Latin eclogues were a school textbook. In looking to these near-contemporaries, *The Shepheardes Calender* follows the example of the first Elizabethan eclogues, Barnabe Googe's (1563) and George Turberville's translation of Mantuan (1567). Moreover, the *Calender* is markedly ambiguous about the value of love and the authority it gives the poet; hence there has been much critical debate about its central figure, Colin Clout, who is both a figure of the poet and a grief-stricken lover.

Sidney's *Arcadia* is even more critical of love. Its two noble heroes are reduced by love to humbling disguises (as a shepherd and an Amazon), and the plot leads to a rather severe judgment of what love does to men. The most powerful and sympathetic representations of love in *Arcadia* (and in this it perhaps reflects Montemayor's *Diana*) are in three women—the two exiled princesses with whom the heroes are in love and their mother, whose misconceived passion takes on tragic force. Of all the major Elizabethan pastorals, *A Midsummer Night's Dream* (1595–1596) is most willing to imagine that the folly of love is transformative; yet it too expresses ironic reserve, which is even stronger in *As You Like It,* where prose is the dominant medium and the central figure, Rosalind, is both passionate and self-mocking.

Moral, Satirical, Political Pastoral.

The Elizabethan critique of love reflects the moral uses of pastoral. In his humility, the herdsman could be considered representative both of the lover (because a lover is in the power of another person, of a powerful emotion, and, when viewed positively, of the force that runs through the cosmos) and of the poet (humble in his distance from heroic modes and dependent on prior texts). The herdsman could also be a moral representative—sometimes of the clergy (the "shepherd" of his flock, a trope deriving from the biblical parable of the good shepherd, John 10) and sometimes of a wise secular moralist, who knows that to be secure (literally, without care) depends on accepting limitations and on valuing what is simple and essential. Spenser introduced such a pastoral moralist into book 6 of *The Faerie Queene* (1596), where the old shepherd Melibee is paired with Colin Clout, the poet's self-representation, now transported to Mount Acidale, the home of Venus, where he pipes to his beloved and the three Graces.

The satiric use of pastoral is less central than is sometimes thought. But there is no doubt that the moral shepherd can be sharply critical, and that his complaints are sometimes due not simply to ethical security but to the bitterness that comes of painful experience. In the mouth of a herdsman, satire can be directed at abuses in the church or at life at court. But not all herdsmen represented in Elizabethan pastorals are in a position to reject the court. In numerous writings and theatrical pieces (like George Peele's *The Arraignment of Paris,* 1584), literary shepherds, humble and dependent, represent the queen's subjects and her courtly "servants."

Native English Versions. Some versions of Elizabethan pastoral are essentially homegrown products. It is usual to identify native strains, as in the "moral eclogues" of *The Shepheardes Calender,* with archaic diction and conscious rusticity. But English fashions and traditions also produced artful, refined pastorals. These include John Lyly's *Gallathea* (written 1585, published 1592), the finest non-Shakespearean pastoral drama of the Elizabethan period, and Thomas Lodge's *Rosalynde* (1590), a pastoral romance that is the source for *As You Like It.* To this day, perhaps the most familiar Elizabethan pastorals are lyrics with titles like "In the merry month of May," in which poet after poet, "warbling his native woodnotes wild" (Milton on Shakespeare), celebrates springtime, rural festivity, and young love. The most brilliant and famous of these lyrics is Christopher Marlowe's "Come live with me and be my love" (titled "The Passionate Shepherd to His Love," in the pastoral anthology *England's Helicon,* 1600). Marlowe's poem brings together both elements of Elizabethan pastoral—the European and the national—for it reduces the original pastoral invitations of Theocritus and Virgil to a short English lyric, with a characteristic air of innocent sensuousness and refinement.

See also **Virgil** *and biographies of other figures mentioned in this entry.*

BIBLIOGRAPHY

Alpers, Paul. *What Is Pastoral?* Chicago, 1996.
Cody, Richard. *The Landscape of the Mind: Pastoralism and Platonic Theory in Tasso's "Aminta" and Shakespeare's Early Comedies.* Oxford, 1969.

Empson, William. *Some Versions of Pastoral*. London, 1935. Reprint, London, 1995.

Montrose, Louis Adrian. "Of Gentlemen and Shepherds: The Politics of Elizabethan Pastoral Form." *ELH* 50 (1983): 415–459.

Patterson, Annabel. *Pastoral and Ideology: Virgil to Valéry*. Berkeley and Los Angeles, 1987.

PAUL ALPERS

PATER, WALTER. Renaissance, Interpretations of the, *subentry on* Walter Pater.

PATRISTICS. Patristics refers to the writings and doctrines of the church fathers (*patres*), the theologians from the early Christian era. Renaissance humanists, aiming to resuscitate the wisdom of the ancient world, made revival of patristics a counterpart to their cultivation of classical studies.

Discovery of the Fathers. Humanist scholarly efforts did in fact bring to light long-neglected Latin Fathers. These included Lactantius, admired for his Ciceronian elegance, and Tertullian, whose denunciation of philosophy neatly accorded with prevailing humanist attitudes, but whose difficult Latin style and the corrupt state of the extant medieval manuscripts made recovery of his works challenging. The Rhenish humanist Beatus Rhenanus (1485–1547) deployed humanist advances in philology and textual criticism to produce in 1521 the editio princeps (first printed edition) of this second-century African Father.

More consequential was humanist attention to the Greek Fathers. Selected works of the Greek Fathers had been accessible during the Middle Ages in late classical or medieval Latin translations, but humanist expertise in Greek studies made fully available for the first time to the Latin West the theological teachings of all the major Greek Fathers, including John Chrysostom, Basil, Gregory of Nazianzus, and Gregory of Nyssa. The Florentine humanist monk Ambrogio Traversari (1386–1439) was the first major Renaissance scholar of Greek patristics, but he had numerous successors. These included George of Trebizond (1395–1486), who undertook a number of projects for the bibliophile pope, Nicholas V (1447–1455); Pietro Balbi (fl. 1460) and other humanist members of the Greek Cardinal Bessarion's (1403–1472) circle; and humanists associated with the papal court in early sixteenth-century Rome, most notably Raffaele Maffei (1451–1522), who translated Basil and who produced a theological text, *De institutione Christiana* (1518), inspired by a similarly titled work of Lactantius. Italian Benedic-

tine monks in the reformed Benedictine Congregation of Santa Giustina also cultivated Greek patristics as part of their devotional life, and they developed, initially independently of the Reformation controversies, a Christocentric doctrine of grace and salvation based on their understanding of Chrysostom's exegesis of the Pauline Epistles. This linking of patristics to religious reform marked the efforts of northern humanists as well. The humanist circle of Jacques Lefèvre d'Étaples (c. 1455–1536) published numerous Latin translations of the Greek Fathers, for the most part drawing upon earlier versions made by Italian humanists. The foremost Renaissance patristic scholar was Desiderius Erasmus (c. 1466–1536). Between 1516 and his death he produced multivolume complete editions of the major Greek and Latin Fathers, including Jerome, Cyprian, Hilary, Ambrose, Augustine, Chrysostom, Gregory of Nazianzus, Basil, and Origen.

Renewal of Patristic Theology. Renaissance humanists did more than discover, edit, and translate patristic texts. Even for such Latin Fathers as Augustine, Ambrose, and Jerome, whose works had been continually available throughout the medieval centuries, humanist efforts did constitute a renewal of patristic theology. During the later Middle Ages, the Fathers were largely encountered indirectly in compilations like Peter Lombard's *Sentences* (1155–1158), the textbook for scholastic theology. Patristic citations in such texts were organized to facilitate syllogistic analysis, the core curricular methodology for university training of jurists and theologians. The humanists, in contrast to the Scholastics, approached the church fathers less as doctrinal authorities (*auctoritates*) than as sources (*fontes*) of Christian teaching, and for the humanists patristic thought carried special weight because of the Fathers' historical proximity to the ultimate source of Christian revelation, Holy Scripture. Further, humanists valued most those patristic writings, such as letters, poetry, and sermons, that shared the literary elegance or rhetorical characteristics of the classical authors they so admired, and which they strove to emulate in their own works. In turn, the fathers' intellectual formation within the classical rhetorical tradition served as a humanist defense against the charges of religious conservatives, suspicious of their enthusiasm for the pagan classics.

Humanist stress on the literary superiority of the Fathers formed part of their critique of Scholasticism, typically dismissed as barbarous, arid, and full of sophistries. Lorenzo Valla (1407–1457), the Italian humanist whose New Testament studies formed an important precedent for Erasmus's scholarship, found Scholasticism more fundamentally deficient as theology. He regarded the whole scholastic quest for metaphysical knowledge of God, derived as it was from Aristotle's logical categories, as misguided, resulting in the pollution of spiritual truth. Instead, he called for a return to a theology based on the Greek and Latin Fathers as the only authentic way of theologizing, a position Erasmus shared, and he insisted that no adequate theological inquiry could be conducted without Greek, the language of the New Testament.

Moral and Spiritual Guidance. While many humanists expressed an admiration for the learned piety (*docta pietas*) of the Fathers, others saw patristic wisdom as imparting special moral and spiritual guidance, especially for an urban laity confronting the anxieties and vicissitudes of the secular world. This helps explain the humanist attention to Chrysostom, whose homilies on the New Testament tended to develop their ethical implications. Petrarch (1304–1374) went further. In his quest to understand his own psychological afflictions arising from his frustrated ambitions and sense of spiritual malaise, he found a kindred spirit in the Augustine of *Confessions,* a pocket-sized copy of which Petrarch kept as a constant companion, including during his famous ascent of Mt. Ventoux.

Augustine, the most influential theological authority for the Middle Ages, remained a favorite of the humanists, although they tended to see him in a different light. Indeed, Italian humanists, in developing the topos of human dignity as a central theme of their religious thought, took inspiration from how Augustine as well as newly available texts of Lactantius and the Greek Fathers Basil and Gregory of Nyssa placed emphasis upon God's wondrous act of human creation in the divine image and likeness and on the soteriological implications of the Incarnation.

Still, especially indicative of the humanists' patristic proclivities is their celebration of St. Jerome. For Erasmus, whose edition of the works of this Latin Father (1516) was a landmark in humanist philology and historical commentary, Jerome was the greatest Latin Father. In his "Life of Jerome," which prefaced this edition, Erasmus praised the saint's knowledge of languages, erudition in the classics, stylistic elegance, and emphasis on biblical scholarship as comprising the virtues of the ideal Christian scholar, ideals upon which Erasmus modeled his own scholarly work and which he saw as essential to the reform of theology.

See also **Christian Theology; Humanism; Scholasticism;** *and biographies of figures mentioned in this entry.*

BIBLIOGRAPHY

Primary Works

Erasmus, Desiderius. *Patristic Scholarship: The Edition of St. Jerome.* Edited, translated, and annotated by James F. Brady and John C. Olin. Vol. 61 of *Collected Works of Erasmus.* Toronto, 1992. Contains Erasmus's "Life of Jerome."

Lefèvre d'Étaples, Jacques. *The Prefatory Epistles of Jacques Lefèvre d'Étaples and Related Texts.* Edited by Eugene F. Rice Jr. New York, 1972.

Secondary Works

Backus, Irena, ed. *The Reception of the Church Fathers in the West: From the Carolingians to the Maurists.* 2 vols. Leiden, Netherlands, 1997. The most recent scholarship on the subject, with extensive bibliographies.

Camporeale, Salvatore I. "Renaissance Humanism and the Origins of Humanist Theology." In *Humanity and Divinity in Renaissance and Reformation: Essays in Honor of Charles Trinkaus.* Edited by John W. O'Malley, Thomas M. Izbicki, and Gerald Christianson. Leiden, Netherlands, 1993. Pages 101–124. Fundamental treatment of Valla's anti-Scholasticism.

Collett, Barry. *Italian Benedictine Scholars and the Reformation: The Congregation of Santa Giustina of Padua.* Oxford, 1985.

D'Amico, John F. *Renaissance Humanism in Papal Rome: Humanists and Churchmen on the Eve of the Reformation.* Baltimore, 1983. The key source for Raffaele Maffei and his contemporaries.

D'Amico, John F. *Theory and Practice in Renaissance Textual Criticism: Beatus Rhenanus between Conjecture and History.* Berkeley and Los Angeles, 1988.

Rice, Eugene F., Jr. "The Renaissance Idea of Christian Antiquity: Humanist Patristic Scholarship." In *Renaissance Humanism: Foundations, Forms, and Legacy.* Edited by Albert Rabil Jr. Vol. 1. Philadelphia, 1988. Pages 17–28.

Rice, Eugene F., Jr. *Saint Jerome in the Renaissance.* Baltimore, 1985. Includes the representation of Jerome in the visual arts.

Trinkaus, Charles. *In Our Image and Likeness: Humanity and Divinity in Italian Humanist Thought.* 2 vols. Chicago, 1970. Magisterial work on the religious thought of the Italian humanists, including the influence of patristic ideas.

CHARLES L. STINGER

PATRIZI, FRANCESCO (1529–1597), Platonic philosopher and polymath. Born in Cherso (or Cres), a large island in the Adriatic Sea and part of what is now Croatia, Francesco Patrizi (Franjo Petrić in Croatian) was the son of a minor noble. His father gave the boy Francesco into the charge of his uncle, who captained a seagoing galley serving Venice in its battles against pirates. After several years at sea, the thirteen-year-old Patrizi received formal schooling in Venice, Ingolstadt, and Cherso. He began medical studies at the University of Padua in 1547, where he also began to learn Greek on his own. While at Padua, he discovered both Plato and Marsilio Ficino's *Theologica Platonica* (Platonic theology; published 1482), the most important Renaissance Platonic philosophical work. Disillusioned with the Aristotelian philosophy dominating university studies in philosophy and science, Patrizi became an enthusiastic Platonist.

When his father died in 1551, Patrizi sold his medical works and left the university. He pursued various careers in Italy, Cyprus, and Spain over the next twenty-five years. An autodidact and a polymath, Patrizi wrote works on utopianism, historiography, poetics, rhetoric, military affairs, and other subjects, almost all in Italian. In 1571 he published *Discussiones peripateticae* (Peripatetical discussions; expanded edition in 1581), a sustained attack on Aristotle and contemporary Aristotelian philosophy. The University of Ferrara appointed him professor of Platonic philosophy in 1577–1578, the first ordinary professorship of Platonic philosophy in a European university. Before this, a handful of university professors had taught Plato on days on which ordinary lectures did not meet or during holidays. Others inserted limited Platonic material into their lectures. In early 1592 Patrizi moved to the University of Rome, again as ordinary professor of Platonic philosophy. He received a four-year contract at a very high salary.

In 1591 Patrizi published his most important work, *Nova de universis philosophia* (A new philosophy of universes; revised edition 1593). The large, four-part work is a vast encyclopedia of philosophical and scientific material based on Plato and a panoply of ancient Greek sources. Part one deals with the metaphysical and physical properties of light. Part two discusses first principles and hierarchy in a Platonic sense. Part three introduces the Platonic notion of soul (or life principle), including that of the world; Patrizi positioned soul between the spiritual and corporeal world. Part four, the most original section of the work, offers an alternative to Aristotelian physical science. Rejecting Aristotle's four elements of earth, air, fire, and water, Patrizi proposed another four: space, light, heat, and fluid or humidity. These substances combine with each other to form mixed bodies, such as heaven, ether, air, stars, water, and earth. Patrizi gave mathematics a more significant role in science than had Aristotle. And he left room for empirical observation. Part four has many interesting novel views (e.g., that the stars move freely in ether, rather than remain in solid spheres) that would stimulate future scholars.

Patrizi also had a religious agenda. He argued for the compatibility of Platonism and Christian theology on such subjects as the nature of God and the Trinity. He wanted to substitute Plato and a coalition of ancient philosophers and church fathers, notably St. Augustine, for the atheistic Aristotle, who denied divine creation of the world and saw only a First Mover rather than a personal God.

Patrizi's daring philosophical program ran into criticism in Rome. A clerical accuser denounced some of the arguments in *Nova de universis philosophia* as heretical. The Roman Congregation of the Index, charged with assessing the orthodoxy of books, took up the case. For two years Patrizi answered his accusers, arguing that some statements by pre-Christian authors found in his book should not be understood literally. Other statements referred to the physical world, not theological matters. Patrizi continued to affirm that his philosophical synthesis of Plato, a variety of ancient pagan authors and church fathers, was compatible with Catholicism. He also continued to attack Aristotle as anti-Christian. The Congregation of the Index ruled against Patrizi, and the 1596 Index of Prohibited Books prohibited the book unless corrected. But it was never published again. Patrizi died on 7 February 1597. The professorship of Platonic philosophy at the University of Rome ended in 1598, and no other university instituted one.

Patrizi's career and works were the most important attempt to insert Platonic philosophy into the curriculum of Renaissance universities. But church condemnation was not the sole reason for the failure of universities to embrace Platonism. Most scholars saw Platonism as unscientific and disorderly. They preferred to use the well-organized and familiar Aristotle as the philosophical underpinning for both scientific and Christian theological studies. Although few philosophers were Platonists, Renaissance Platonism had a major impact on vernacular literatures, especially love poetry.

BIBLIOGRAPHY

Primary Works

Patrizi da Cherso, Francesco. *Della poetica*. Edited by Danilo Aguzzi Barbagli. 3 vols. Florence, 1969–1971.

Patrizi da Cherso, Francesco. *Lettere ed opuscoli inediti*. Edited by Danilo Aguzzi Barbagli. Florence, 1975. Includes an autobiographical letter and short works.

Secondary Works

Copenhaver, Brian P., and Charles B. Schmitt. *Renaissance Philosophy*. Oxford and New York, 1992. See pp. 187–195.

Kristeller, Paul Oskar. *Eight Philosophers of the Italian Renaissance.* Stanford, Calif., 1964. Chapter 7 deals with Patrizi.

PAUL F. GRENDLER

PATRONAGE. [This entry includes three subentries, the first on patrons and clients in general, the second on patronage of the arts, and the third on literary patronage in England.]

Patrons and Clients in Renaissance Society

Patronage, a term traditionally used to describe the support Renaissance elites gave to artists, writers, and scholars, as well as rights exerted over ecclesiastical property (*ius patronatus*), has been extended by recent historians to embrace certain social and political ties between individuals and groups. Since English, unlike other European languages, does not make the useful distinction between patronage of the arts (*mecenatismo* in Italian), and political and social patronage (Italian *patrocinio* and *clientelismo*), English-speaking historians need to define "patronage" more carefully in any given Renaissance context if the concept is not to become so inclusive as to be almost meaningless.

Renaissance societies were in part animated and sustained by bonds of mutual support between individuals, groups, small communities, and institutions. A minority of historians would argue that in a period of (by modern standards) "small"—not to say weak—central governments, and of considerable social and family dislocation, such ties of patronage and clientage provided individuals and groups with their principal source of protection and even self-identity—certainly more so than did any sense of class solidarity, or even the ubiquitous bonds of kinship and neighborhood (which were, anyway, very often almost indistinguishable from that powerful sense of mutual obligation and affection contemporaries described in Latin and the vernaculars as "friendship"). An English gentleperson's close associates were frequently called "cousins," while in medieval French kinsmen were *amis* (literally, friends) or, more expressly, *amis charnels* (carnal friends); in Italian, variants of the phrase "kinsmen, friends, and neighbors" (*parenti, amici,* and *vicini*) are everywhere to be found. The great patrilineages of Genoa themselves constituted clienteles.

Urban and Postfeudal Patronage. The

workings of the processes of patronage have been most closely studied for well-documented Renaissance republics such as Genoa, Florence, and Ven-

ice, where frequent changes of government and regime may have made more pressing the need to attach oneself to the powerbrokers called *gran maestri* (big shots) in contemporary slang. By the late fifteenth century, a cluster of words associated with Latin *patronus* and *cliens* was self-consciously applied to patronal relationships by a minority of classically trained secretaries. Such considerations have led some scholars to speculate that Renaissance Italian patronage was the direct heir of the urban traditions of classical Rome. However, Renaissance bonds of friendship and dependence, even in Italy, possessed just as clear an affinity with more recent (late- or postfeudal, traditions), and it may be futile to persist in a search for their exclusively classical or feudal, urban or rural, origins.

The respect for *gran maestri,* the processes of informal as well as of seigneurial patronage, can be found in the voluminous records of Italian principalities such as Mantua as well as in those of republics. In Ferrara, the Este lords bound aristocratic followers, their *raccomandati,* to them by a postfeudal contract, the *accomandigia.* Moreover, the "alliances" and "affinities" of late medieval France and England should perhaps be understood as a variety of patronage relationship, as a northern European response to general late medieval conditions which, in the populous southern city-states, created networks of clients. The friends and partisans who crowded into the urban palace of Lodovico Bentivoglio, a magnate to whom Bologna gave a tax concession in order to maintain this clientele, bore more than a passing or coincidental resemblance to the mighty English "affinity" of John of Gaunt (1340–1399), which included a household of 115 men, a retinue of 170, and numerous dependents.

The English quest for "good lordship," and the Italian reverence for *gran maestri,* were two sides of the same coin. If city-state friendships—unlike those of postfeudal Europe—were not sealed by formal contracts, or by oaths of blood brotherhood, they were nurtured by a two-way traffic in favors, maintained by constant visiting and letters expressing fealty and love, and might be solemnized by an exchange of kisses.

Ethos of Friendship. Depending on the par-

ticular context, bonds of friendship and patronage might be a formalization and extension of kinship and neighborhood solidarities, or compensation for the frailty or very absence of such solidarities in an uncertain environment. These bonds could have about them a certain egalitarianism, despite differences of social rank between "friends." Not only rich or politically powerful men and women might be patronage brokers, for a wide acquaintance, access to special information, and personal charm might make a person influential. Renaissance letters, especially private and informal correspondence, are full of references to such fluid relationships—sometimes embracing social equals, sometimes pairing the powerful and not so powerful—in which a person might be a client in one context and the patron in another. Comparatively rare, and almost certainly disingenuous, were claims by individuals such as John Paston (1421–1466) that "I have not usid to meddel wyth lordis materis meche forther than me nedith" (in Walker, *Lancastrian Affinity,* pp. 208–209).

A staple of Renaissance correspondence is the letter of recommendation, by which a patron commended to another his client who, often the bearer of the missive, was to explain his or her business in detail. There was an entire rhetoric of recommendation which, adapted from the medieval *ars dictaminis* (theory and practice of letter writing) and propagated by manuals such as Cristoforo Landino's *Formulario de epistole vulgare* (Handbook of vernacular letters), published in Bologna in 1485, drew its metaphors from the intimacies of family and commercial life and from the familiar vocabulary of Christianity. Patron and client might be "loving brothers," a gentlewoman esteemed "as an elder sister," a powerful patron would have his "creatures" or his "obedient lambs," a client might promise to regard his benefactor as Father, Son, and Holy Ghost should his intervention be successful. It was a common topos of Renaissance letters to insist on an absent friend's duty to maintain his friendships by correspondence, and it needs to be said that, although many letters recommending clients were, inevitably, perfunctory and written for a unique purpose, others clearly reveal that there might be more enduring relationships which crisscrossed many Renaissance societies. There has been interesting speculation that the homoerotic culture of several notable Italian states might have served further to shape their culture of patronage.

Patron-Client Relations and Building States. A bulwark, in part, against social dislocation and unstable regimes, patron-client relations in their various forms might themselves become effective bases for the formation of more or less stable political factions and alliances, and eventually for state-building by ambitious party leaders and princes. The retinues and affinities of northern Europe were neither so destructive of public order, nor inimical to the assertion of central authority, as was once believed; Italian families such as the Bentivoglio of Bologna and the Medici of Florence created one-party regimes composed of their "friends," and did so by making more formal and hierarchical the fluid patronal practices of their ancestors.

From the 1460s onward, the expression *maestro della bottega* (boss of the shop) emerges to describe those Italian leaders, both princes and private citizens, who were masters of the art of political patronage, while around their persons a more courtly and even obsequious language of deference gradually appears in correspondence. This said, the patronal relationship remained a reciprocal one—albeit increasingly unequal—and great lords frequently went out of their way "to serve" even quite humble friends and supplicants, on whose armed support their regimes might depend and on whose devotion their reputations in part rested.

Ethics of Patronage. Some scholars insist upon the ethical dimension of much Renaissance patronage and clientage, though others maintain—in the spirit of Dr. Johnson, who defined a patron as "one who countenances, supports, or protects. Commonly a wretch who supports with insolence, and is paid with flattery" (in Kent and Simons, *Patronage,* p. 11)—that patronal ties constituted Renaissance examples of "I'll scratch your back if you'll scratch mine," of "jobs for the boys," which might even bear comparison with the Mafia. To be sure, patronage was often exerted to obtain office or ecclesiastical benefices for clients and dependents, and was accompanied by much giving and receiving of gifts, but it concerned itself as well with a myriad of contemporary aspirations, touching not only people's purses but also their honor and very existence: the arrangement of marriages, protection against private violence, representation in courts of law, provision of dowries, support of minors, release from prison. A profound belief in the morality of patronal friendship coexisted, somewhat uneasily, with much clerical criticism of its practices, and despite the denunciation of private and special interests by governments committed to equality and justice before the law.

Female Patronage. Women, who were excluded from the political process unless they belonged to dynasties exercising legitimate authority, nevertheless found room to maneuver in the largely informal workings of patronage, especially as brokers and intermediaries—a female role that the shining example of Mary, the mother of Jesus, rendered acceptable to contemporaries. While most women patrons specialized in helping other women and the local poor, real political influence could be exerted by a woman such as Lucrezia Tornabuoni (1427–1482), the Florentine wife and mother of prominent party leaders. Even a marchioness, such as Barbara of Brandenburg (1422–1481) in Mantua, might in part draw her considerable authority from the informal sources provided by patronal networks. The abbesses of Europe's great convents also worked effectively within the prevailing patronal culture of the Renaissance.

Artistic and Literary Patronage. Much literary and artistic patronage took place within this wider patronal context, as its characteristic rhetoric demonstrates; hence the artistic influence, even control, which scholars have observed patrons exerting over creators, a phenomenon which can disconcert the modern observer. It can be difficult to distinguish political from literary patronage, as when the historian Giovanni Simonetta (1410–1480) served the Sforza rulers of Milan both as confidential administrator and gifted apologist, or in the case of the distinguished humanists at the Neapolitan court of the late fifteenth century who were well-rewarded officials and singers of their patrons' praises. Such patrons and creative clients, sharing ideas and enthusiasms in the context of a patronal culture, might influence each other in the very creation of the works of art associated with both of their names. Some of the best known examples are in architecture: the politician Giangiorgio Trissino's fostering of Andrea Palladio's career and Lorenzo de' Medici's close relationship with the up-and-coming Giuliano da San Gallo. Lodovico Gonzaga, marquis of Mantua (1444–1478), liked to joke that he was both the master and the disciple of his architect, Luca Fancelli, a man of humble origin who also enjoyed ringing the changes on their complex social and artistic relationship. The very production of Renaissance art might in another sense express that society's patronal values and practices, as when Michelangelo, working at the church of San Lorenzo in Florence, surrounded himself with a creative retinue of sculptors and artisans drawn from his boyhood friends, kinsmen, and neighbors.

BIBLIOGRAPHY

Bentley, Jerry. *Politics and Culture in Renaissance Naples.* Princeton, N.J., 1987.

Ianziti, Gary. *Humanistic Historiography under the Sforzas.* Oxford, 1988.

Heers, Jacques. *Parties and Political Life in the Medieval West.* Amsterdam, 1977.

Jones, Philip. *The Italian City-State.* Oxford, 1997.

Kent, Dale. *The Rise of the Medici.* Oxford, 1978.

Kent, Francis, and Patricia Simons, eds. *Patronage, Art, and Society in Renaissance Italy.* Oxford, 1987.

Lytle, Guy Fitch, and Stephen Orgel, eds. *Patronage in the Renaissance.* Princeton, N.J., 1981.

Robertson, Ian. *Tyranny under the Mantle of St. Peter: Pope Paul II and Bologna.* Florence, 1999.

Walker, Simon. *The Lancastrian Affinity, 1361–1399.* Oxford, 1990.

Wallace, William. *Michelangelo at San Lorenzo.* New York, 1994.

FRANCIS WILLIAM KENT

Patronage of the Arts

Renaissance patrons commissioned a wide variety of artifacts for diverse purposes. Most works of art conveyed the social, political, religious, or cultural aspirations of their owners; art for art's sake was not the norm. The type of artifact and the intrinsic value of its components usually bespoke the social rank of the patron.

Princely Patronage. Rulers were the most active patrons: they possessed the greatest means and relied on programmatic visual language to convey their authority to subjects and peers. They directed their displays to both domestic and international audiences, for European states were closely linked in a community of shared interests. Rulers employed splendid artifacts crafted from costly materials to demonstrate emphatically their magnificence, an all-important virtue essential for reigning successfully at home and making a strong impression abroad. Architecture (palaces and religious edifices), grand funerary monuments, gem-studded gold work (sculptures, vessels, and items of personal adornment), tapestries (woven with quantities of silk, gold, and silver thread), lavishly embellished armor and arms, embroidered garments (often adorned with gems and pearls), illuminated manuscripts in rich bindings, exotic novelties, and large ensembles of musicians were vital to princely grandeur and thus amassed in quantity. Multimedia displays were staged at tournaments, princely feasts, receptions, and celebrations; their manifold magnificence impressed contemporaries more than any single work of art and served to elevate rulers' standing in pan-European politics. Since religious and secular interests and motivations were closely intertwined in this period, it is less illuminating to divide royal commissions along such lines.

Among the greatest Renaissance princely patrons were the dukes of Burgundy (who ruled the territories of present-day northern France, Belgium, Luxembourg, and the Netherlands), the Habsburg Holy Roman Emperors, Francis I Valois, Henry VIII Tudor, and a series of popes. Other important patrons included the Catholic monarchs of Spain, kings of Naples, dukes of Milan, Medici of Florence, Este of Ferrara, Gonzaga of Mantua, Montefeltro of Urbino, counts and electors of Germany, and other regional potentates.

Philip the Good (ruled 1419–1467) and Charles the Bold (ruled 1467–1477), dukes of Burgundy, were renowned for their splendid court and ceremonials. Little remains of ducal architecture or funerary monuments; the dukes' vast holdings of tapestries and embroideries, gold work and armor, illuminated manuscripts and novelties, and their opulent ephemeral displays are known chiefly through inventories and contemporary descriptions. The dukes assembled an exceptionally fine choir of musicians and were keen patrons of literature, amassing great libraries. A presentation miniature in the *Chroniques de Hainaut* (1446; Brussels, Bibliothèque Royale) depicts the author offering his work to Philip the Good. Jan van Eyck is the best-known Burgundian court artist, but masters of diverse crafts served the dukes. These included the court embroiderer Thierry du Chastel, who both produced and purchased sumptuous garments for Philip the Good; the goldsmith Gérard Loyet, who created gold and silver statuary for Charles the Bold, such as the gold reliquary presented by the duke—portrayed kneeling under the protection of St. George—to Liège Cathedral (1466–1467; in situ); and the armorer Alexandre du Pol of Milan, on whom Charles the Bold bestowed a lofty salary and numerous benefits. The magnitude and brilliance of their commissions made the dukes exemplars of magnificence across Europe and contributed to the international demand for artifacts and artists from their domains.

Through patronage, which emulated Burgundian splendor, Maximilian I Habsburg (ruled 1493–1519) sought to glorify his dynasty. Maximilian summoned humanists to the University of Vienna to advise him on projects and commissioned a vast funerary monument (Innsbruck Hofkirke, begun 1508 under the supervision of Gilg Sesselschreiber but never fully realized) that was to include forty over-life-size bronze statues of his ancestors beginning with Julius Caesar and ending with his children, thirty-four busts of Roman emperors, and one hundred statues of Habsburg family saints. He also ordered a novel piece of visual propaganda—the Triumphal Arch of Maximilian (1515) rendered in 192 woodcuts, assembled into a tableau eleven by ten feet, by Jörg Kölderer, Albrecht Altdorfer, Albrecht Dürer, and Hans Burgkmair. Maximilian wrote autobiographical literature extolling his deeds, which was illustrated by major artists, and commissioned books for his library. His portrait medals were made by the Milanese painter Giovanni Ambrogio de Predis. Maximilian was probably the greatest patron of armorers in his time as well as a keen collector of tapestries and gold work.

Charles V (Charles I of Spain 1516–1556, Holy Roman Emperor 1519–1556), the grandson of Maximilian I, had a strong interest in mathematics, science, and technology and collected splendid globes and maps, scientific instruments, and illustrated books on astronomy and anatomy. His rich collection of tapestries included *Battle of Pavia* (1531; Paris, Louvre) and *Hunts of Maximilian* (1528–1533; Paris, Louvre) designed by Bernard van Orley and *Campaign of Charles V against Tunis* (1546–1554; Madrid, Palacio Real) designed by Jan Cornelisz Vermeyen from firsthand sketches of the action. Charles ordered armor from the great Milanese master Filippo Negroli and collected precious metalwork, jewelry, medals, coins, and feather work from Mexico and Peru. He patronized the Venetian painter Titian, who stayed at the imperial residence in Augsburg in 1547–1548 creating numerous portraits, including the equestrian portrait *Charles V at the Battle of Mühlberg* (1548; Madrid, Prado). Also in these years Charles employed the sculptor and medallist Leone Leoni, who executed for him life-size bronze statues of his kin and one titled *Charles V and Fury Restrained* (1549–1564; Madrid, Prado), representing the emperor nude in a detachable suit of armor.

King Francis I of France (ruled 1515–1547) lavished his greatest attention on his château at Fontainebleau, an old hunting retreat that he refurbished from 1528 onward, turning it into the center of a flourishing court. He charged the Parisian master mason Gilles le Breton (d. 1553) with rebuilding the dilapidated castle. Inside the château, sumptuous tapestries lined the walls, and chambers were embellished with French and Italian paintings, including those by Leonardo da Vinci, Raphael, Andrea del Sarto, Titian, Parmigianino, Giulio Romano, and Bronzino. Leonardo da Vinci spent the last years of his life in Francis's employ, and in the 1530s Francis attracted to his court other Italians—the painters Rosso Fiorentino and Francesco Primaticcio, the goldsmith Benvenuto Cellini, and the architects Giacomo Barozzi da Vignola and Sebastiano Serlio. In addition to executing pictorial commissions, Rosso

Royal Patronage in France. King Francis I invited Rosso Fiorentino (1494–1540) to decorate the Grande Galérie (called the Galérie François Ier) of the Château of Fontainebleau. At the death of Rosso, the king appointed Francesco Primaticcio (1504–1570), who was decorating the Chambre de la Reine, to succeed Rosso as supervisor of buildings, a post he continued to hold under Henry II and Charles IX. Rosso and Primaticcio decorated the Galérie between 1528 and 1537. LAUROS-GIRAUDON/ART RESOURCE

designed costumes for spectacles, tableware, horse trappings, and a tomb. In 1540 Primaticcio went to Rome on an art-collecting spree for the king, procuring casts of *Apollo Belvedere, Cnidian Venus, Hercules Commodus, Laocoön,* Trajan's column reliefs, and Michelangelo's *Pietà.* Francis also devoted great attention to music, literature, and poetry.

The Tudor Kings Henry VII (ruled 1485–1509) and Henry VIII (ruled 1509–1547) of England similarly assembled at their courts artists and artifacts from various countries, a practice followed by all rulers striving to obtain the best assets. The Tudors relied heavily on Burgundian-style visual propaganda to enhance their status in the international arena. Henry VII's Richmond Palace, built of imported Flemish brick, drew on the architectural vocabulary of Burgundian palaces and was embellished by continental arts and artists; the king also imported Bur-

gundian chroniclers and forms of festive displays. Henry VIII, determined to usher in a golden age, lavished great sums on his residences, particularly the Nonsuch and Greenwich Palace. Inventories record that his fifty-five residences were furnished with more than 2,000 pieces of tapestry, 2,028 items of plate, and 1,800 books, as well as quantities of gold artifacts, arms and armor, and richly embellished garments. The king employed native craftsmen to build his palaces, Flemings to make stained glass and create gold work, Italians to fashion sculptural decorations (including Pietro Torrigiano of Florence, who in 1512–1518 produced the gilded-bronze and marble tombs of Henry's parents in Westminster Abbey), and the German Hans Holbein the Younger to execute pictorial projects, including portraits of Henry and his entourage. Passionate about war and tournaments, Henry also imported Milanese, Flemish, and German armorers and armor and established a celebrated armory at Greenwich.

Patronage by Female Rulers. Although female rulers' patronage was often circumscribed by local laws regarding female rights and finances, several nevertheless became renowned patrons. Isabella, the queen of Castile and León (ruled 1474–1504), enjoyed a European reputation for her patronage of scholars and arts. Together with her husband, Ferdinand II, king of Aragon and Sicily, she undertook grand architectural projects. She herself commissioned several religious buildings, notably the Charterhouse of Miraflores near Burgos (1454–1499) to serve as a memorial to her parents, whose splendid alabaster tomb (1489–1493; in situ) was carved by Gil de Siloé, as was the wooden high-altar retable (1496–1499; in situ). Isabella also founded the convent of San Juan de los Reyes in Toledo (1476–1504) to commemorate a key military victory and establish a royal pantheon and the Capilla Real in Granada (1506–1521), the mausoleum of the Spanish royal family. An avid collector of illuminated manuscripts, she assembled her own library, as well as a rich array of tapestries, gold work, painting, and sculpture (predominantly religious) by Spanish, Flemish, and Italian masters. Two Flemish-trained painters, Juan de Flandes and Michel Sittow, served as her court painters.

Margaret of Austria (ruled 1507–1515, 1518–1530), the daughter of Maximilian I and the regent of the Netherlands for her nephew Charles V, established a flourishing court at Mechelen, where she collected tapestries, gold work, manuscripts (she owned the Limburg brothers' *Très riches heures du Duc de Berry* [c. 1411–1416; Chantilly, Musée Condé] and the *Hours of Bona Sforza* [c. 1490; London, British Library]), sculptures, and paintings, including Jan van Eyck's *Arnolfini Portrait* (1434; London, National Gallery) and works by Hieronymus Bosch, Juan de Flandes, and Michel Sittow. Dürer, who admired her treasures during his sojourn in the Netherlands in 1520–1521, was particularly awed by the gold work, arms and armor, and other artifacts imported from Mexico. In 1507 Margaret commissioned funerary monuments for herself and her deceased husband Philibert II, the duke of Savoy, to be erected in the church of St. Nicholas, Brou; she consulted the Italian sculptor Pietro Torrigiano and the Frenchmen Jean Perréal and Michel Colombe but ultimately engaged her master builder Lodewijk van Boghem and the sculptors Jan van Roome and Conrad Meit, who also rendered her portrait bust (1523;

Munich, Bayerische Staatsgemaldesammlungen). She regularly employed the painters Jan Gossaert, Jan Mostaert, Bernard van Orley, Jan Cornelisz Vermeyen, Pieter van Coninxloo, Gerard Horenbout, and Jacopo de' Barbari of Venice.

Isabella d'Este (1474–1539), the marchesa of Mantua, was in her own words "appetitosa," or hungry, for art. Having grown up at the illustrious court of her father, Ercole d'Este, the duke of Ferrara from 1471 to 1505, she was fond of music, played the clavichord, commissioned musical instruments for herself and her musicians, and contributed through her patronage to the development of *frottola*—an Italian genre of songs with instrumental accompaniment. Having a relatively small income, Isabella was unable to underwrite architectural projects, but she had dealers in major Italian cities informing her of prices and sales of antique and contemporary works of art. In her *Grotta* she gathered antique sculpture, gems, cameos, coins, agate, and jasper vases. She ordered floral tapestries with small animals and birds to be woven for her, and in her *studio*, a retreat for study and display of cultured pursuits, she kept paintings by famous contemporary masters, including Leonardo da Vinci, Giovanni Bellini, Andrea Mantegna, and Correggio. She had portraits of herself painted by Leonardo (1499; Paris, Louvre, Cabinet des Dessins), Titian (1534; Vienna, Kunsthistorisches Museum), Lorenzo Costa, and Cosmè Tura and a medal rendered in bronze with enamel and gem embellishment by Giancristoforo Romano (1498; Vienna, Kunsthistorisches Museum), cheaper versions of which she presented to clients and friends. While female patrons traditionally focused on religious foundations and altarpieces, Isabella was keenly interested in antiquities and mythologies, although she also commissioned devotional works.

Papal Patronage. Popes had been important art patrons in the fifteenth century, but they became particularly powerful in the sixteenth century, partly because of the strong personalities and ambitious visions of individual pontiffs. The papal court, accordingly, turned into a preeminent center of culture.

As Pope Julius II (reigned 1503–1513), Giuliano della Rovere sought to convert medieval Rome into a classical city. He rebuilt entire sections of town, laid broad avenues bordered by palaces, and began to replace the dilapidated basilica of St. Peter's with a new structure that would embody the imperial and spiritual splendor of his regime. He employed Donato Bramante to design and construct the new St. Peter's (although the project took twelve architects and twenty-two popes to complete) and to refurbish portions of the Vatican palace. Raphael decorated Julius's private apartments in the Vatican with complex fresco programs: the Stanza della Segnatura (1509–1511), Julius's library, was painted with scenes pertaining to the four branches of humanist learning—theology, philosophy, poetry, and jurisprudence; the Stanza d'Eliodoro (1512–1514), the audience chamber, addressed divine interventions on behalf of the church and alluded to Julius's accomplishments. In 1505 Julius called Michelangelo to Rome to execute a three-story freestanding sepulchral monument combining architecture and more than forty life-size statues. The work on the tomb proceeded sporadically for forty years. It was gradually reduced to a wall monument in the church of San Pietro in Vincoli in Rome. Julius also ordered Michelangelo to fresco the ceiling of the Sistine Chapel (1508–1512). Keen on other princely treasures, Julius was an avid collector of ancient sculpture, and his jewel-studded tiara was valued in 1521 at 62,430 ducats.

As Pope Leo X (reigned 1513–1521), Giovanni de' Medici, the son of Lorenzo the Magnificent, devoted great energy and resources to restoring his family's power through artistic projects. He engaged Michelangelo to build a monumental marble facade for the family church of San Lorenzo in Florence (1516–1520; not completed) and to construct and embellish with a sculptural program the Medici Chapel, where Lorenzo the Magnificent and his brother Giuliano had been buried. The two monumental sepulchres worked on by Michelangelo but not completed (1519–1534) were to be for Lorenzo (1492–1519), duke of Urbino, and Giuliano (1479–1516), duke of Nemours. The Library of San Lorenzo (1524–1559), housing the Medicean book collection, was commissioned by the next Medici pope, Clement VII (reigned 1523–1534). Leo X ordered Raphael to design tapestries for the lower register of the Sistine Chapel walls (1515–1516): the cartoons were dispatched to the tapestry workshop of Pieter van Aelst in Brussels to be rendered in silk, gold, and silver threads. Leo also engaged Raphael to fresco his private dining room in the Vatican, the Stanza dell' Incendio (1514–1517). A lover of music, Leo improved the papal chapel with a superior choral ensemble, building the largest choir in Italy and collecting musical instruments. He was also fond of poetry, lavish multimedia ceremonies and festivities, and theatrical performances. Popes, like secular rulers, commissioned works of art not only for personal use but as diplomatic gifts. In his rapprochement with the French king, Leo X sent a gold cross set with precious stones (valued at 15,000 ducats, the cost of the Sistine Chapel tapestries), a life-size copy of the ancient statue *Laocoön*, and Raphael's paintings *St. Michael* and *Holy Family* (both 1518; Paris, Louvre).

Papal families profited enormously from their mighty relatives; the Medici, Farnese, Barberini, Borghese, Pamphili, Chigi, and others became tremendously wealthy and influential. Papal relatives, frequently appointed cardinals, built lavish palaces and villas, decorating them with tapestry cycles, collections of ancient statuary and coins, metalwork, and paintings. Cardinal Alessandro Farnese erected the largest and most magnificent of such Roman palaces: Palazzo Farnese (1517–1589) occupies the entire side of a vast piazza, with its facade measuring about two hundred by one hundred feet. Antonio da Sangallo the Younger designed the building, and Michelangelo enhanced it in 1546, while Alessandro was Pope Paul III (reigned 1534–1549). Powerful bishops, especially those related to rulers, also commissioned works of art to express and augment their authority. Philip of Burgundy (1466–1524), the illegitimate son of Philip the Good and the bishop of Utrecht from 1517, established his castles of Suyborg and Wijk bij Duurstede as focal points for humanistic scholarship, literature, and art. Philip brought the painter Jan Gossaert to Rome in 1508 to record antiquities, in which he was keenly interested, patronized Hieronymus Bosch and Jacopo de' Barbari, and amassed antiquities, tapestries, and paintings of religious and mythological subjects and a considerable library.

Nobles. The patronage of nobles emulated that of the rulers. They built grand mansions, adorned them with gold work, textiles, woodwork, and paintings, and sported expensive clothes and jewelry.

When Jan van Melle, a patrician of Ghent, was executed during the city's uprising in April 1477, the sale of the contents of his house raised a sum equaling twenty-three years' wages of a skilled worker. Van Melle's possessions consisted of jewelry (30 percent of his wealth), household goods in silver and gold (17 percent), cloth (16 percent), furniture (12 percent), carpets (9 percent), clothing (7 percent), and miscellaneous items. Noblemen also assembled libraries, that of the Bruges patrician Louis Gruuthuse being among the finest. They possessed armor and arms and sponsored religious architectural projects, particularly family chapels, in which they were often buried.

Richard Beauchamp, the earl of Warwick (1382–1439), ordered a costly tomb to be placed in his burial chapel in the church of St. Mary in Warwick (1442–1465). The chapel itself was adorned with stained-glass windows brought from the Continent, paintings, and gilded images of saints. The tomb involved the collaboration of a bronze founder, William Austen; a coppersmith, Thomas Stevyns; a wood carver, John Massingham; and a Netherlandish goldsmith, Bartholomew Lambespring. The monument was likely modeled on the tombs of the Burgundian dukes (Beauchamp had served as a captain of Calais and as lieutenant general of France and Normandy). It comprised a life-size gilded copper effigy of the deceased, in fine Milanese armor, reclining on a marble podium; fourteen gilded copper images of the earl's relatives in niches below; angels with escutcheons alongside these mourners; and a metal canopy over the effigy.

Merchants, Bankers, and Court Functionaries. Merchants, bankers, and court functionaries could rise to remarkable prominence and prosperity in the service of powerful rulers and thus become considerable patrons themselves.

The Sienese banker Agostino Chigi (1466–1520) financed three successive popes—Alexander VI, Julius II, and Leo X—and farmed valuable alum for the Curia. He also had up to one hundred bank offices in Italy and as distant as Cairo and London. Chigi owned a palace in the center of Rome and a suburban residence, Villa Farnesina, designed by Baldassare Peruzzi on the bank of the Tiber (1509–1512). The villa was modeled on those of ancient Rome and embellished with colored marble; it included a garden and dining facilities on the waterfront, where Chigi gave lavish banquets served from precious plate (some designed by Raphael). Peruzzi frescoed a number of rooms with illusionistic perspectival views (1515–1517), while Raphael and his assistants decorated others with mythological and erotic tales (1518–1519). Raphael also worked on the Chigi Chapel in Santa Maria della Pace (c. 1512–1514) and Chigi's exceptionally lavish mausoleum chapel in Santa Maria del Popolo (1507–1520), rendered in polychrome marble, bronze, gold, mosaic, and paint.

Nicolas Rolin rose from modest bourgeois beginnings to enormous power in the service of the dukes of Burgundy, first as the councilor to John the Fearless, then as the chancellor to his son Philip the Good, whose closest adviser he remained for nearly forty years. Rolin's best-known commissions are the Hôtel-Dieu in Beaune, a hospital he founded in 1443, and *Virgin with Chancellor Rolin* painted by Jan van Eyck (c. 1435; Paris, Louvre). The hospital, lavishly decorated with stained-glass windows and statuary, contained twenty-five rooms and a chapel furnished with vestments, chalices, books, and a monumental altarpiece of the Last Judgment painted by Rogier van der Weyden (c. 1445–1448; Beaune, Musée de l'Hôtel-Dieu) and placed over a marble-clad altar on which stood a bejeweled reliquary containing a fragment of the true cross, presented by Rolin's wife, Guigone de Salins. Guigone also gave to the hospital tapestries, six silver cups, wine, and eight hundred gold crowns. The hospital benefited the citizens of Beaune, but it also immortalized its founders.

Wealthy burghers also built imposing town houses. Giovanni Rucellai, a prosperous Florentine merchant, spent the better part of his fortune on his palazzo (designed by Leon Battista Alberti in 1455–1458; later extended by Bernardo Rossellino) and considered it his major achievement. Architecture was seen to elevate a man to a loftier standing and was an arena for keen competition among patrons. The interiors of palazzi were furnished with textiles, carved and painted furniture, and paintings (most often images of the Virgin and child or saints and portraits), as well as ceramics, brasses, and other household wares.

Patrons purchased artifacts for their homes and chapels not only in their own countries but also during diplomatic or mercantile trips abroad. The managers of the Medici bank in Bruges acquired Flemish paintings for themselves and procured tapestries and pictures for their employers. Tommaso Portinari commissioned the *Adoration of the Shepherds* altarpiece (c. 1473–1476; Florence, Uffizi) from Hugo van der Goes and shipped it to Sant'Egidio in Florence. In the opposite direction, a Flemish wool merchant, Alexandre Mouscron, took Michelangelo's marble statue of the Virgin and child, *Bruges Madonna* (1503–1504), to the church of Onze Lieve Vrouwe in Bruges. International activities of patrons thus contributed to the dissemination of artistic products, ideas, and tastes.

Corporate Bodies. Civic authorities, guilds, and religious confraternities also commissioned buildings and artifacts to serve their needs and ambitions. Town magistrates were responsible for constructing communal belfries, town halls, fountains, and fortifications. Town halls were frequently adorned with polychromed sculpture outside (Jan van Eyck painted and gilded statues on the Bruges town hall in 1435) and tapestries and paintings inside. Images of just rule, extolling the government or providing models for lawgivers, frequently adorned these spaces. Rogier van der Weyden executed the narrative panels *Justice of Trajan* for the town hall of Brussels (1439; lost); Dirck Bouts painted *Justice of Otto III* for city magistrates of Louvain (early 1470s; Brussels, Musées Royaux des Beaux-Arts); and Gerard David rendered *Judgment of Cambyses* for the Bruges town hall (1498; Bruges, Groeningemuseum).

City officials also erected defensive walls. Michelangelo was appointed governor and procurator general of Florentine fortifications in 1529. Other artists served in similar capacities: Leonardo da Vinci built fortifications and war engines for Cesare Borgia in 1502–1503 and ranked such service above artistic service in a letter to Ludovico Sforza (ruled 1494–1499), the duke of Milan.

On commission from the board of directors of the Florence Cathedral (Opera del Duomo), Michelangelo carved the colossal statue *David* (1501–1504; Florence, Accademia). His other civic commission was a monumental fresco commemorating Florentine victory at the *Battle of Cascina* (1504–1506), in the Sala del Gran Concilio in the Palazzo della Sig-

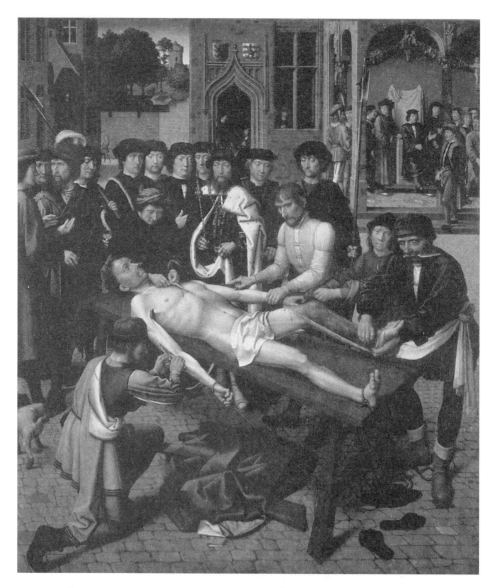

Patronage by Corporate Bodies. Gerard David (c. 1460–1523) painted *The Judgment of Cambyses* (1498) commissioned by the Bruges council for the city hall. Groeningemuseum, Bruges, Belgium/The Bridgeman Art Library

noria; Leonardo da Vinci was to paint *Battle of Anghiari* (1503–1506). Neither fresco was completed, and what they had done was destroyed. City officials also engaged painters to place heraldic devices on banners, flags, arms, and buildings. They ordered gold work and silver work, tapestries, and arms as gifts to rulers and worthies; hired diverse artisans to produce festive displays for state weddings and funerals, visits of dignitaries, and religious celebrations; and engaged musicians to enhance those events.

Guilds and confraternities built meetinghouses; sponsored chapels and furnished them with liturgical implements as well as painted and sculpted images; ordered banners to be borne in public processions; and produced decorations, floats, *tableaux vivants,* and mystery plays for major city celebrations, including triumphal entries of rulers. During Philip the Good's entry into Ghent on 23 April 1458, following his suppression of the rebellious city, guilds and church groups staged plays throughout the city attempting to arouse the duke's clemency.

Leading guilds of Florence financed tabernacles and statues of their patron saints—fashioned by Donatello, Lorenzo Ghiberti, and Nanni di Banco—on the exterior of Or San Michele, the public granary (1411–1429). The wealthier guilds paid for bronze statues, the more modest ones for marble; some of the finely carved niches cost more than the marble figures within. The *scuole,* or religious confraternities, of Venice built meeting halls for which they ordered extensive painted narrative cycles devoted to their patron saints. For the Scuola di Sant'Orsola, Vittore Carpaccio painted nine large canvases (c. 1490–1500; Venice, Accademia), which made his reputation. The *scuole* likewise commissioned banners, vestments, and other portable accoutrements, which confraternity members carried in solemn processions and state ceremonies. Confraternities also furnished chapels: the Brotherhood of the Holy Sacrament in Louvain commissioned Dirck Bouts to paint the *Holy Sacrament* altarpiece for its chapel in the church of St. Peter (1464–1468; in situ).

Church Patronage. The governing bodies of churches undertook the construction, decoration, and maintenance of ecclesiastical buildings. Rich and noble parishioners, guilds, and confraternities frequently endowed chapels and religious services at their altars, which they furnished with liturgical vessels, manuscripts, and vestments and augmented with altarpieces, sculptures, and stained-glass windows or frescoes. Such foundations presented opportunities for prominent families and organizations to demonstrate status and wealth. The burial chapel of Francesco Sassetti (the director of the Medici bank) in Santa Trinità was frescoed by Domenico Ghirlandaio with scenes of the life of St. Francis (1482–1485); Ghirlandaio also painted the chapel's altarpiece, *Adoration of the Magi.* One complete surviving fifteenth-century altar service, commissioned by the Spanish nobleman Don Pedro Fernandez de Velasco and given to the Hospital de la Vera Cruz in Medina da Pomar, near Burgos, in about 1455, consists of chalice and paten, altar crucifix, ciborium, candlesticks, and processional cross, all finely wrought in silver, gold, and enamel inlays. Clerics also embellished churches with private monuments. The French cardinal Jean de Bilhères de Lagraulas commissioned Michelangelo to carve *Pietà* (1498–1500) for the chapel in Old St. Peter's, where he planned to be buried.

Monasteries and their occupants likewise commissioned buildings, liturgical furnishings, and sculptural and painted decorations. Paolo Veronese's *Feast in the House of Levi* (1573; Venice, Accademia) was produced for the convent of San Giovanni e San Paolo. Initially asked to paint the Last Supper, Veronese rendered it in such a grand theatrical manner that he was called before the Venetian Inquisition to account for the inclusion of "buffoons, dwarfs, Germans, and similar vulgarities" in the sacred narrative. Veronese changed nothing of the painting but renamed it *Feast in the House of Levi.*

Middle-Class Patrons. Those with limited means acquired artifacts rendered in cheaper materials—paint and wood, terra-cotta, paper, brass and pewter. Smaller-scale devotional pictures, prayer beads, and modest household implements were aimed at such clientele and produced on speculation rather than commission.

Middle-class women were restricted in their patronage opportunities not only financially but also legally: they were often subject to the authority of their father, husband, or legal guardian, and most governmental, guild, and ecclesiastical patronage was controlled by men. Widows were most at liberty to order works, but even then they often did so for their male relatives—commissioning funerary chapels, altars, or sculpted tombs. Women also had more limited resources and generally undertook more modest projects. *Madonna and Child with Saints* by Carlo Crivelli (1491; London, National Gallery), commissioned by Oradea, the widow of Giovanni Becchetti, for her chapel in the church of San Francesco in Fabriano, is typical of middle-class female patronage: a painted altarpiece bearing a dedication to her family and to the Virgin, it shows Oradea on a diminutive scale, middle-aged, veiled, and dressed in black. Oradea also commissioned a silver-gilded chalice with enameled medallions for the altar of her chapel and obtained indulgences for those who prayed there.

Mechanisms of Patronage. Works of art could be commissioned or bought ready-made. Architecture was always created to order, as were higher-quality tapestries, armor, gold work, manuscripts, paintings, and sculptures. Preserved contracts reveal that patrons were preoccupied with the quality of materials, craftsmanship, and timely delivery. Originality was less important. Indeed, patrons often referred to extant works as examples to be followed, and numerous replicas of successful compositions demonstrate that clients were happy and eager to purchase well-developed schemes. Patrons, moreover, were frequently credited with the authorship of a given project. It is often difficult to ascertain why they chose specific artists: reputation, price, availability, style, and prior relationship may all have decided their selection.

Many artifacts were made on speculation and sold either from the artist's shop or at markets and fairs. A miniature by Jean le Tavernier in David Aubert's *Les chroniques et conquêtes de Charlemagne* (c. 1458–1460; Brussels, Bibliothèque Royale) depicts a small marketplace at the city gates: a jeweler, embroiderer, and potter have set up stalls at this busy and potentially lucrative juncture. Cities could designate special locations—in monastic cloisters or in specially constructed buildings—for the exhibition and sale of artifacts. Fairs served as major commercial outlets for works of art (and other goods): they brought together domestic and foreign artists and clients in great numbers, and the largest volume of art trade occurred in this context. Fairs operated at various sites across Europe—at Geneva, in Savoy, Frankfurt in Germany, Medina del Campo in Castile—but the Antwerp fairs appear to have been most extensive. Medici agents in Flanders regularly attended them to procure objects for themselves and their employers. Fairs, moreover, offered not only a wide variety of merchandise at prices lower than custom-ordered works but also the opportunity to buy in quantity for resale abroad: numerous Brabantine carved wooden altarpieces, for example, were acquired by merchants and ship captains for export to Italy, Spain, Scandinavia, and elsewhere.

Patronage could elevate the standing of not only the patron but also the artist, particularly if he served an illustrious employer. While Raphael, for example, was undoubtedly a great master, he benefited immeasurably from the patronage of mighty popes, bankers, and cardinals in Rome. Doubtless a skillful politician also, Raphael was able to rise well above his station as a craftsman. When he died at age thirty-seven, he owned a handsome palazzo in Rome, and his fortune was reckoned at 16,000 ducats, 1,500 of which he ordered to be spent on the embellishment of a funerary chapel in the Pantheon, consisting of an altar surmounted by a statue of the Virgin by Lorenzetto and a grave for himself and his betrothed, Maria Bibbiena. He assigned 600 ducats for the upkeep of the chapel and for the masses to be said for his soul.

See also biographies of artists and patrons mentioned in this entry.

BIBLIOGRAPHY

Anderson, Jaynie. "Rewriting the History of Art Patronage." *Renaissance Studies* 10, no. 2 (1996): 129–138.

Armstrong, Charles Arthur John. "The Golden Age of Burgundy." In *The Courts of Europe: Politics, Patronage, and Royalty, 1400–1800.* Edited by A. G. Dickens. London, 1977. Pages 54–75.

Baxandall, Michael. *Painting and Experience in Fifteenth Century Italy.* Oxford, 1974.

Blair, Claude. "Ci-gît Richard Beauchamp." *Connaissance des Arts* 333 (November 1979): 72–79.

Blunt, Anthony. *Art and Architecture in France, 1500 to 1700.* 1953. Rev. ed., London, 1988.

Brown, Patricia Fortini. "Honor and Necessity: The Dynamics of Patronage in the Confraternities of Renaissance Venice." *Studi veneziani,* n.s., 14 (1987): 179–212.

Campbell, Lorne. "The Art Market in the Southern Netherlands in the Fifteenth Century." *Burlington Magazine* 118 (April 1976): 188–198.

Cox-Rearick, Janet. *The Collection of Francis I: Royal Treasures.* New York, 1996.

De Winter, Patrick M. "A Book of Hours of Queen Isabel la Católica." *Bulletin of the Cleveland Museum of Art* 68 (December 1981): 342–427.

Ewing, Dan. "Marketing Art in Antwerp, 1460–1560: Our Lady's Pand." *Art Bulletin* 72 (December 1990): 558–584.

Goldthwaite, Richard. *The Building of Renaissance Florence: An Economic and Social History.* Baltimore, 1980.

Goldthwaite, Richard. *Wealth and the Demand for Art in Italy, 1300–1600.* Baltimore, 1993.

Haskell, Francis. *Patrons and Painters: A Study in the Relations between Italian Art and Society in the Age of the Baroque.* London, 1963.

Henry VIII: A European Court in England. Edited by David Starkey. New York, 1991.

Hollingsworth, Mary. *Patronage in Renaissance Italy: From 1400 to the Early Sixteenth Century.* Baltimore, 1994.

Hollingsworth, Mary. *Patronage in Sixteenth-Century Italy.* London, 1996.

Iongh, Jane de. *Margaret of Austria, Regent of the Netherlands.* Translated by M. D. Herter Norton. New York, 1953.

Kempers, Bram. *Painting, Power, and Patronage: The Rise of the Professional Artist in the Italian Renaissance.* London, 1992.

Kent, F. W., and Simons, Patricia, eds. *Patronage, Art, and Society in Renaissance Italy.* Oxford, 1987.

King, Catherine. *Renaissance Women Patrons: Wives and Widows in Italy, c. 1300–1550.* Manchester, U.K., 1998.

Lytle, Guy Fitch, and Stephen Orgel, eds. *Patronage in the Renaissance.* Princeton, N.J., 1981.

Martens, Maximilian Pieter. "*Artistic Patronage in Bruges Institutions, ca. 1440–1482.*" Ph.D. diss., University of California at Santa Barbara, 1992.

Paravicini, Werner. "The Court of the Dukes of Burgundy: A Model for Europe?" In *Princes, Patronage, and the Nobility: The Court at the Beginning of the Modern Age, c. 1450–1650.* Edited by Ronald G. Asch and Adolf M. Birke. Oxford, 1991. Pages 69–102.

Reyes y mecenas: Los reyes católicos, Maximiliano I, y los inicios de la casa de Austria en España. (Kings and patrons: The Catholic kings, Maximilian I, and the beginnings of the Austro-Spanish royal house). Toledo, Spain, 1992.

San Juan, Rose Marie. "The Court Lady's Dilemma: Isabella d'Este and Art Collecting in the Renaissance." *Oxford Art Journal* 14, no. 1 (1991): 67–78.

Smith, Jeffrey Chipps. "The Artistic Patronage of Philip the Good, Duke of Burgundy (1419–1467)." Ph.D. diss., Columbia University, 1979.

Thurley, Simon. *The Royal Palaces of Tudor England: Architecture and Court Life, 1460–1547.* New Haven, Conn., 1993.

MARINA BELOZERSKAYA

Literary Patronage in England

English bookseller-publishers during the Renaissance paid very small sums to the authors of the works they published; consequently, most writers of the period who were not independently wealthy were forced to seek patronage to support themselves as they pursued their literary careers. Although often complex in its details, such patronage may be divided roughly into three, sometimes overlapping, forms.

First, there is the patronage of the theater. Because of the frequent hostility of the London authorities toward plays, as well as several penal statutes declaring unattached actors to be rogues and vagabonds, theatrical companies were forced to seek the patronage of powerful nobles and even monarchs to protect themselves. In addition to protecting and occasionally subsidizing the acting companies, these royal and noble patrons often employed playwrights directly to provide entertainments for public occasions. This practice found its fullest expression in the elaborate court masques of the early Stuart period.

Some writers were employed as secretaries, stewards, or chaplains by wealthy, most often noble, patrons—or by the government itself—and allowed to pursue their literary endeavors as part of their official duties or as adjuncts to them. Indeed, throughout the Tudor and early Stuart periods, a major way in which ambitious young men could command the attention of the great was through a display of their cleverness in writing, especially in poetry; and many officials in both state and church seemed to have used the evidence of such skill as a kind of test for bureaucratic appointment.

Still other writers, however, were not fortunate enough to obtain such full-time employment from patrons and were forced to write occasional verse or prose now and then at the behest of wealthy clients or to dedicate works to prospective patrons in the hope of being financially rewarded for them.

Chief among these patrons were the sitting monarchs, most notably Elizabeth and James I, and members of the royal family, including James's queen, elder son, and daughter. In addition to patronizing drama, they had from four to twenty-five books of prose and poetry a year dedicated to them. Royal favorites, having the ear of the monarch, were also popular dedicatees, as were many aristocrats, especially those who held positions of power or influence in the government. Also notable patrons during the period were several noblewomen.

The careers of three major writers of the Tudor and early Stuart periods illustrate both the scope and the complexity of the patronage system. One of the authors most successful in employing patronage to his advantage was Edmund Spenser (1552?–1599). After completing his education at Cambridge, he was successively employed as secretary by John Young, bishop of Rochester; Robert Dudley, earl of Leicester and a favorite of Queen Elizabeth; and Lord Grey of Wilton, the lord deputy of Ireland. In Ireland he was awarded several important and remunerative posts, which allowed him to pursue his literary endeavors. Finally, at least in part as a reward for dedicating the first three books of *The Faerie Queene* to Queen Elizabeth in 1590, he was granted an annual pension of fifty pounds for life. In *Amoretti* 74, he paid tribute to the queen "most kind/That honour and large richesse to me lent."

The fortunes of John Donne (1572–1631) were much less steady and unbroken. After an education at Oxford and the Inns of Court, Donne was successively employed as secretary by Robert Devereux, second earl of Essex and a favorite of Queen Elizabeth, and Thomas Egerton, Elizabeth's lord keeper of the great seal. While in their employ, Donne wrote his five satires, several verse letters, and many of his elegies and love lyrics. As a result of his impolitic marriage in 1601, however, he was dismissed from Egerton's service. For the next fourteen years, he was thwarted in an attempt to obtain regular employment and was forced to eke out an existence for himself and his growing family by writing individual poems to or for various patrons and prospective patrons, who rewarded him for his efforts, though not always to his satisfaction. Most notable among his patrons were Lucy Russell, countess of Bedford, for whom he wrote several funeral poems and to whom he wrote several verse letters; Sir Robert Drury, for whom he wrote the *Anniversaries;* and a favorite of James I, Robert Ker, earl of Somerset, for whose scandalous marriage he wrote an epithalamion. The king refused to consider Donne for secular preferment, but through Somerset, he urged him to take holy orders and put his literary talents to the service of the church. Entering the priesthood in 1615, Donne turned to the writing of sermons and devotional pieces, and in 1621 he was appointed dean of Saint Paul's Cathedral in London.

Both a playwright and a poet, Ben Jonson (1573?–1637) was thoroughly enmeshed in the patronage culture. As a result of the early plays he wrote for the Admiral's Men, the Lord Chamberlain's Men, and the Children of Queen Elizabeth's Chapel, he was commissioned on several occasions by King James and members of his court to write entertainments and masques. When he was granted a royal pension in 1616, he in effect became the first poet laureate of England. In addition, he was patronized by the Sidney family, for whose members he wrote several poems in *The Forest,* and especially by William Herbert, third earl of Pembroke, to whom he dedicated his *Epigrams* and *Catiline,* and who rewarded him with an annual stipend of twenty pounds to buy books. Moreover, Pembroke seems to have helped Jonson during such periods of difficulty as those occasioned by allegations of slander in *Eastward Ho* and *Sejanus.*

The patronage system is among the most important material factors affecting literary production in England during the Renaissance. It influenced writers in numerous ways, most obviously in the proliferation of epideictic poetry and prose (works of praise), but also less obviously in the determination of genres, as in the exaltation of epic, an aristocratic form; in the shaping of authorial visions of society, as in the celebration of the patriarchal hierarchy that was the wellspring of the patronage system itself; and in the often fierce competitiveness that it fostered among the writers. The patronage system not only helped make possible the profession of authorship, but it also helped shape the contours of that profession.

BIBLIOGRAPHY

Evans, Robert C. *Ben Jonson and the Poetics of Patronage.* Lewisburg, Pa., 1989.

Lytle, Guy Fitch, and Stephen Orgel, eds. *Patronage in the Renaissance.* Princeton, N.J., 1981.

Schoenfeldt, Michael. "Courts and Patronage." In *The Cambridge History of Literary Criticism.* Edited by Glyn P. Norton. Cambridge, U.K., 1999.

Williams, Franklin B. *Index of Dedications and Commendatory Verses in English Books before 1641.* London, 1962.

TED-LARRY PEBWORTH and CLAUDE J. SUMMERS

PAUL III (Alessandro Farnese; 1468–1549), pope (1534–1549). Alessandro Farnese was from an old and important family in the Papal State. His mother, born a Caetani, belonged to a prominent Roman noble family that boasted many cardinals and one pope. Alessandro received an extensive education at several universities, including Pisa, and at the age of fifteen embarked upon an ecclesiastical career. During his stay in Florence from 1486 to 1489 he was part of the circle of humanists, poets, and artists around Lorenzo de' Medici, and he became steeped in Renaissance culture. His rise in the church was rapid, beginning with the office of apostolic protonotary in 1491. Pope Alexander VI, who had a liaison with Giulia Orsini, Alessandro's sister, became the young prelate's patron, made him a cardinal in 1493, and granted him numerous benefices, including the bishopric of Parma. His diplomatic skills enabled Alessandro to remain one of the key figures at the papal court under subsequent popes as well, and to reach the position of dean of the college of cardinals in 1524.

Before his ordination to the priesthood in 1519, Alessandro fathered several children. His nepotism was extraordinary even for his times. His children were acknowledged, legitimized, and granted possessions, riches, and offices, especially his first-born son Pier Luigi.

After a brief conclave Cardinal Farnese, who had carefully cultivated a reputation for political neutrality, was elected pope on 13 October 1534, much to the delight of Romans, who considered him one of their own. Like a Renaissance prince, he elevated his family by appointing two grandsons, aged fourteen and sixteen, to the cardinalate, but a few months later, in May 1535, he signaled his support for church reform by giving the red hat to several of its advo-

Pope Paul III. Copy of the portrait by Titian. GALLERIA SPADA, ROME/ALINARI/ART RESOURCE

cates. Pope Paul III's long reign was defined by elements that coexisted uneasily, giving it an ambiguous character: boundless nepotism; political shrewdness, even ruthlessness; patronage of art and artists; and prudential concern with reforming the church.

The pope alienated part of the church state to form the duchy of Parma and Piacenza for the Farnese and made Pier Luigi the first duke. His grandson Cardinal Alessandro Farnese, an able politician, was the richest prince of the church at the time thanks to untold benefices he held. His grandson Ottavio was married to Margaret, the illegitimate daughter of Emperor Charles V, thus allying the Farnese and the Habsburgs. Another grandson, Orazio, married the illegitimate daughter of the French king. Thus the Farnese became a dynasty.

In politics Paul III steered a careful course between the two great enemies, King Francis I of France and Emperor Charles V. Repeatedly the pope attempted to bring about peace in Europe and urged common defense measures against the Ottoman Turks. In the Papal State he put down rebellions by the city of Perugia and the Roman noble Ascanio Colonna, and tightened administrative and fiscal control. Among the artists active under his patronage

were Michelangelo, active both as a painter and architect, and Antonio di Sangallo. During his pontificate the magnificent Palazzo Farnese was begun; it remains one of the grandest of Roman palaces.

One of the most important achievements of Paul III was the meeting of the Council of Trent. From the beginning of his pontificate he had worked tirelessly toward the convocation of a council that would deal with the Lutheran challenge to the Catholic Church. Already in 1536 he appointed a commission of reform-minded prelates under the leadership of Cardinal Gasparo Contarini to make suggestions for reform in preparation for the council. Nine years later, despite the enormous obstacles caused by wars between France and the Holy Roman Empire and Protestant unwillingness to participate, the council opened. Its decree on justification was the most important achievement of the first meeting period that lasted in Trent from 1545 to 1547.

Paul III was a transitional figure. Very much a Renaissance pope in his Italian power politics and the aggrandizement of his family, and in his building projects in Perugia, Rome, and other towns of the Papal States, he was also an intelligent churchman who supported innovative religious orders, above all the Jesuits, and efforts to tighten church discipline. In some ways he was a Counter-Reformation pope. Under him the Roman Inquisition was founded to safeguard Catholic orthodoxy. His reign was a mixture of the old and the new, of wisdom and limitation. But he clearly understood that a new age had dawned for Europe with the irreparable split of the Christian church, and with Protestantism as a religious and political force.

See also **Farnese, House of.**

BIBLIOGRAPHY

Capasso, Carlo. *Paolo III.* 2 vols. Messina, Italy, 1923–1924. Rich documentation, with an emphasis on political history.

Pastor, Ludwig von. *The History of the Popes from the Close of the Middle Ages.* 3d ed. Vols. 11–12. Edited by Ralph Francis Kerr. St. Louis, Mo., 1950. Despite its age still indispensable.

Zapperi, Roberto. *Tiziano, Paolo III, e i suoi nipoti.* Turin, Italy, 1990. Emphasis on patronage of art, with a bibliography of recent works.

ELISABETH G. GLEASON

PAUL IV (Gian Pietro Carafa; 1476–1559), pope (1555–1559). Gian Pietro Carafa was born in Capriglia to a noble Neapolitan family. As a young man he went to live with his uncle, Cardinal Oliviero Carafa, in Rome, where he continued his humanistic and theological studies and was introduced to the court of Pope Alexander VI. His ecclesiastic career pro-grooved rapidly: from protonotary apostolic, to bishop of Chieti (1504), to papal nuncio to Naples (1506). He attended the Fifth Lateran Council, was papal legate to England (1513), and finally nuncio to Spain (1515), where Charles V proposed his nomination as bishop of Brindisi (1519). When he returned to Rome (1520), Adrian VI entrusted him with the disciplinary reform of the clergy (1523). A member of the Roman Oratory of Divine Love, a confraternity dedicated to personal sanctification through works of charity, he developed a rigoristic concept of ecclesiastic reform, previously evident in the provisions adopted in the diocese of Chieti and later in the creation, along with St. Cajetan of Thiene, of the Order of Clerics Regular (1524), called Theatines. He escaped the Sack of Rome (1527) and settled in Venice.

Called to Rome by Paul III and promoted to cardinal (1536), he was one of the leaders of the reform of the Curia. He was also one of the principal drafters of the *Consilium de emendanda ecclesia* (Advice for mending the church; 1537), a document that is emblematic of the attempts to renew the sixteenth-century church. During this period he took an anti-Habsburg stance, which he tied to the struggle against those who favored doctrinal compromise with the Reformation, whose positions often coincided with imperial interests. With the failure of the religious meetings between Catholics and Protestants in Regensburg (1541), Carafa gradually won others to his intransigent views, promoting the creation of the Roman Inquisition (1542), of which he remained undisputed leader until his death. Carafa used this institution to repress Italian heterodox circles inspired by the doctrines of Juan de Valdés.

Elected pope on 23 May 1555, he immediately began a rigid program of reforms, one of which was the establishment of the Jewish ghetto in Rome. He allied himself with France and waged war against Spain (1556). He brought charges of heresy against Giovanni Morone and Reginald Pole, both of whom were pro-Habsburg, although he ignored the heterodox sympathies of his own political allies. The unscrupulous personal goals of his nephews, particularly Cardinal Carlo Carafa, played a significant role in this war, and while they initially enjoyed papal support, they were later punished with exile. The pope held the Habsburgs responsible for the spread of the Reformation and political oppression of Italy. Defeated by the Spanish in 1557, Paul IV resumed his reformist activities, which he entrusted in large measure to the Inquisition, the jurisdiction and membership of which he expanded. In 1559 he issued the

Pope Paul IV. Funeral monument by Pirro Ligorio (c. 1510–1583) in the Caraffa Chapel, church of Sta. Maria sopra Minerva, Rome. ALINARI/ART RESOURCE

first Roman Index of Prohibited Books. He died later that year, and his funeral was interrupted by popular uprisings, during which the prisons of the Roman Inquisition were set afire and the prisoners freed.

BIBLIOGRAPHY

Aubert, Alberto. *Paolo IV: Politica, inquisitione, e storiografia.* Florence, 1999.

Pastor, Ludwig von. *The History of the Popes from the Close of the Middle Ages.* Edited by Ralph Francis Kerr. Vol. 14. St. Louis, Mo., 1936. Pages 56–494.

ALBERTO AUBERT

Translated from Italian by Marguerite Shore

PAUL V (Camillo Borghese; 1552–1621), pope (1605–1621). Camillo Borghese was born in Rome, where his father, Marcantonio Borghese, of a distinguished Sienese family, had emigrated in the mid-sixteenth century. The son followed in the footsteps of his father, who became a prominent jurist at the papal court. After taking his doctorate in Perugia, Camillo returned to Rome, was ordained priest, and rose rapidly in the curia. For five years he served in the papal government as vice legate for Bologna. In 1593 he undertook a special mission to Spain for Clement VIII (1592–1605) and upon his return received in 1596 the red hat. Two years as bishop of Jesi (1597–1599) followed, and in 1603 he was named vicar general of Rome. A man of unusual dignity of appearance and manner, he displayed a firm moral character, celebrated mass daily, and participated in Roman devotional observances.

Borghese emerged from the conclave on 16 May 1605 as pope. He was to keep the direction of government firmly in his own hands. His determination to uphold the rights of the church against the claims of the emerging European states met with little success. Immediately he faced a challenge from Venice, which prohibited construction of buildings or purchase of land by the church without the state's approval, and violated clerical privilege by imprisoning two unworthy clerics. After first protesting, Paul threatened excommunication and interdict in April 1606. When the Venetian Senate did not back down, these took effect, the last time in history that a pope imposed an interdict on a whole state. A war of polemics ensued that engaged writers across Europe, and a real war threatened to break out. Through the mediation of France a compromise was reached by April 1607, whereby the pope was the greater loser in that the Venetians did not yield on principle. Paul also denounced the Oath of Allegiance required by James I (1603–1625) after the Gunpowder Plot (1605) as an infringement on church rights and prohibited English Catholics from taking it.

Paul V observed a policy of neutrality with respect to Spain and France and generally did not encourage war with Protestant powers, although as the Thirty Years' War (1618–1648) began he granted significant subsidies to the Catholic League and Emperor Ferdinand II (1619–1637) and supported them diplomatically.

In 1607 the pope ended the long conflict over grace and free will between the Dominicans and the Jesuits without any decision, thus conceding legitimacy to both positions. The first stage of the Galileo affair concluded with the condemnation of Copernicanism in 1616. Early in Paul's pontificate the decision was made to depart from Michelangelo's plan for a centralized church and to add an extensive nave to Saint Peter's. The construction of the church was essentially completed in 1617 under the direction of Carlo Maderno with the name Borghese emblazoned directly in the center of the facade.

Paul V was a lavish nepotist, and he succeeded in establishing the Borghese firmly in Roman aristocratic society. The principal vehicle for this was his nephew, Scipione Caffarelli (1576–1633), who became a cardinal in 1605 shortly after Paul's consecration and received enormous sums from his uncle. The Villa Borghese with its landscaped park was above all his project. Bernini has preserved the likenesses of the pope and the cardinal in magnificent busts.

BIBLIOGRAPHY

Magnuson, Torgil. *Rome in the Age of Bernini*. Vol. 1, *From the Election of Sixtus V to the Death of Urban VIII*. Translated by Nancy Adler. Stockholm, Sweden, and Atlantic Highlands, N.J., 1982. Provides an overview of Paul V's papacy with an emphasis on art and architecture.

Pastor, Ludwig von. *History of the Popes, from the Close of the Middle Ages*. Vols. 25–26, *Leo XI and Paul V (1605–1621)*. Translated and edited by Dom Ernest Graf. London, 1937.

Reinhard, Wolfgang. "Papal Power and Family Strategy in the Sixteenth and Seventeenth Centuries." In *Princes, Patronage, and the Nobility: The Court at the Beginning of the Modern Age, c. 1450–1650*. Edited by Ronald G. Asch and Adolf M. Birke. London, 1991. Pages 329–356. Contains considerable material on the Borghese family.

ROBERT BIRELEY

PAVIA, BATTLE OF (24 February 1525). The most important battle of the Wars of Italy (1494–1559), waged by France and the Habsburgs for hegemony in Europe, the Battle of Pavia was a decisive victory for the forces of Spain and the Holy Roman Empire.

In the second half of 1524, Charles de Bourbon-Montpensier (1490–1527), who had switched his loyalty from France to the Holy Roman Empire, convinced Emperor Charles V (ruled 1519–1556) to attempt a combined operation against France, an attack from Spain, Picardy, Burgundy, and Italy. The plan failed because of stubborn French resistance at Marseille. Bourbon was forced to withdraw to Italy with the French in pursuit. King Francis I of France (ruled 1515–1547) moved toward Lombardy, as the imperial forces seemed defeated. In their search for refuge, the imperialists split their army into three forces, each of which sought refuge in a Lombard city. One group went to Pavia, an important center on the route to Genoa and France, nineteen miles (thirty-one kilometers) south of Milan. The French pursued, laying siege to the city, which was defended by five thousand *Landsknechten* (German mercenary soldiers) and one thousand Spanish troops. The town's seven thousand inhabitants also favored Spain.

France seemed to be winning, but the French king made three substantial errors. He did not pursue his early advantage decisively; wishing to conquer Pavia, the rest of Lombardy, and Naples simultaneously, he dispersed his forces, sending seven thousand troops toward Naples; and he misjudged the determination of the enemy at Pavia. Meanwhile, the imperial forces regrouped. They were boosted by the arrival in early 1525 of between eight and nine thousand more *Landsknechten* under the famous mercenary leader Georg Frundsberg.

The imperialists had a difficult task before them. The French army, camped in front of Pavia, held an impressive defensive position, with a large river at the side and the high, strong wall of a park around them. The imperial commanders Charles de Lannoy (c. 1487–1527) and the marquis of Pescara, Ferdinando Francesco d'Avalos (c. 1489–1525), were reluctant to attack but were forced to do so because their mercenaries threatened to leave. The forces were roughly equal in number: the French had between twenty-four and twenty-six thousand foot soldiers and six thousand horsemen; the imperialists had twenty-two thousand foot soldiers and twenty-five hundred horsemen.

During the night of 23 February 1525, Pescara and Lannoy breached the park's wall in three places and surprised the enemy with an attack in the misty dawn of 24 February. The French army stopped the first assault but was eventually routed. Francis I was taken prisoner.

The French lost for several reasons. In addition to being surprised, they were unable to coordinate their attacks. They deployed their forces in a piece-meal fashion, and they did not use their superior field artillery effectively. Finally, the Spanish used their firearms (muskets and harquebuses) with deadly offensive power. Encumbered by the rough terrain, targeted by the imperialist firearms, and threatened by pikemen on their flanks, the French heavy cavalry became easy targets. Not since the battle of Agincourt (1415) had so many French knights fallen on the battlefield. The French lost between six and twelve thousand, while the imperialists' casualties numbered only five to six hundred.

The Battle of Pavia crowned Spanish success in the most important phase of the Wars of Italy. Thereafter, Italy was controlled by Spain, as French influence waned.

See also **Wars of Italy**.

BIBLIOGRAPHY

The most extensive secondary account is Jean Giono, *The Battle of Pavia,* translated by A. E. Murdi (London, 1963). Short but well done analyses are in Bert S. Hall, *Weapons and Warfare in Renaissance Europe* (Baltimore, 1997), pp. 179–183, and especially Piero Pieri, *Il Rinascimento e la crisi militare italiana* (Turin, Italy, 1952), pp. 554–566. Two popular accounts are Luigi Casali, *La battaglia di Pavia: 24 Febbraio 1525* (Pavia, Italy, 1984), and Angus Konstam, *Pavia 1525: The Climax of the Italian Wars* (London, 1996).

ANTONIO SANTOSUOSSO

PAVIA, UNIVERSITY OF. The University of Pavia was third in importance, after Padua and Bologna, among Italian universities in the Renaissance. It educated students from Lombardy and attracted an international clientele of students, especially from Germany, France, and Spain.

Foundation to 1500. Pavia was one of many new universities founded across Europe in the early Renaissance. Galeazzo II Visconti (duke of Milan, 1354–1378) established the university of his state in the modest town of Pavia, thirty-five kilometers south of the capital of Milan. He may have chosen Pavia because of its tradition of legal scholarship beginning in the eleventh century. On 13 April 1361 he obtained a charter from the emperor Charles IV, and the university opened its doors in the autumn of 1361 with at least four professors of law. By the 1390s Pavia had a faculty of about fifty professors: twenty-nine for canon and civil law, twenty for arts and medicine, and one for theology. Plague and a financial dispute between the ruling duke and the city government of Pavia caused the university to move to nearby Piacenza in 1398. It returned to Pavia in May 1402.

After some difficult years in the early fifteenth century, the University of Pavia grew in size to about eighty-five professors by the middle of the century, shrinking to between sixty and seventy later in the century. Pavia had the second largest faculty (after Bologna and ahead of Padua) among Italian universities in the fifteenth century. Classes met in a Dominican convent and other rented rooms. Pavia had six to seven hundred students in 1480, of whom about two-thirds studied law, the rest arts and medicine. About one-fourth were non-Italians, especially Germans. The university awarded thirty to fifty doctorates annually in the last quarter of the century, about two-thirds in law, one-third in arts and medicine, and a handful in theology. Like other Italian universities, Pavia did not award bachelor's degrees.

The Sixteenth Century. The Italian wars of the first half of the sixteenth century severely dis-

A Lecturer at the University of Pavia. Funeral monument of Francesco Corti the Elder, professor of canon law, who died in 1495. Bas-relief at Certosa di Pavia, Italy.

rupted the University of Pavia because the town was in the path of the armies that crisscrossed northern Italy. From 1500 to 1540 the university often functioned with only a few professors and students or was closed completely. The number and duration of university closures are not known for certain because few records survive for this period. Despite the difficulties, the university continued to appoint and train distinguished legal scholars. Although Milan and Lombardy became part of the Spanish Empire in 1535, nothing changed for the university, since the Senate of Milan oversaw it.

In 1533 the senate authorized the construction of a large building in the center of the city to house all the teaching of the university. Construction began the following year, with many additions over the centuries. This building still houses the central administration and lecture rooms. Benefactors also endowed several residences for students. The Collegio Ghislieri (founded 1567) and Collegio Borromeo (founded 1581) still serve as student residences. In 1723 Carlo Goldoni, the future playwright, was expelled from the Collegio Ghislieri for composing a satirical poem that described the private parts of some women of Pavia.

After the difficulties of the first half of the century, the University of Pavia revived in the second half. It maintained a faculty of about twenty professors for law, twenty-seven for arts and medicine, and three for theology and sacred scripture. Like other Italian universities, Pavia established a professorship to study the medicinal properties of plants in 1546 and a botanical garden in 1559.

But the university declined in intellectual importance in the second half of the sixteenth century. Previously the dukes and the Senate of Milan had appointed distinguished scholars drawn from Lombardy and beyond. Now local men from Pavia, Milan, and Lombardy dominated the faculty. When a major professorial vacancy occurred, the university did not seek a distinguished outsider but promoted a junior professor, who cost less. Nevertheless, the number of students probably remained at five to six hundred. By the last third of the century, Pavia awarded up to eighty doctorates annually. The distribution of doctorates had altered slightly from the fifteenth century: about 52 percent were in law, 34 percent in arts and medicine, and 14 percent in theology. Fewer non-Italian students obtained doctorates than in the fifteenth century.

Pavia's Reputation. Pavia had a number of famous professors, especially in law. Giason del Maino (1435–1519) taught civil law there from 1467 to 1485 and from 1497 to 1519. Andrea Alciato (1492–1550), who pioneered the application of a humanistic historical approach to the study of Roman law, studied at Pavia, probably from 1507 to 1511, then taught at Pavia from 1533 to 1537 and from 1546 to 1550. The polymath Girolamo Cardano (1501–1576), known for original speculation, mathematics, natural science, hydrodynamics, geology, and medicine, taught at Pavia from 1543 to 1551 and the 1559–1560 academic year.

The most important teaching function of the University of Pavia was educating men from Lombardy and elsewhere in northern Italy. Consequently, the university enrolled many students from upper-class families of Lombardy. Probably the most famous graduate was Carlo Borromeo (1538–1584), the future saint and archbishop of Milan, who took a doctorate in law at Pavia in 1559. His cousin, Federico Borromeo (1564–1631), also a future cardinal and archbishop of Milan, took a doctorate of theology at Pavia in 1585.

The University of Pavia specialized in law. Its most famous professors taught that subject; the majority of students, including many non-Italians, came to study it. Pavia competed well with Bologna and Padua in law through much of the Renaissance but was less important in medicine, philosophy, and the humanities.

See also **Universities**.

BIBLIOGRAPHY

Maiocchi, Rodolpho, ed. *Codice diplomatico dell'Università di Pavia.* 2 vols. Pavia, Italy, 1905–1915. Reprint, Bologna, Italy, 1971. Fundamental collection of documents for the years 1361–1450.

Rizzo, Mario. "University, Administration, Taxation, and Society in Italy in the Sixteenth Century: The Case of Fiscal Exemptions for the University of Pavia." *History of Universities* 8 (1989): 75–116. Deals with the withdrawal of fiscal privileges and the decline of the university. It is the only English work on Pavia.

Sottili, Agostino. *Università e cultura: Studi sui rapporti italotedeschi nell'età dell'Umanesimo.* Goldbach, Germany, 1993. Contains the author's fundamental articles on the University of Pavia during the fifteenth century and on Italian-German university relations.

Vaccari, Pietro. *Storia della Università di Pavia.* 2d ed., revised. Pavia, Italy, 1957. First published in 1940, this is the only study of the university in its entirety.

PAUL F. GRENDLER

PAZZI CONSPIRACY (26 April 1478). The Pazzi Conspiracy attempted to eliminate the de facto lead-

The Pazzi Conspiracy. Medal cast by Bertoldo di Giovanni (c. 1420–1491) commemorating the murdered Giuliano de' Medici. © THE BRITISH MUSEUM, LONDON

ers of the Florentine government, Lorenzo and Giuliano de' Medici, and bring about a change of regime. It represented a combination of internal, Florentine opposition to Medici ascendancy and wider, Italian hostility to Florentine policies. The former centered on the Pazzi family, who by the early 1470s had emerged as political as well as commercial rivals of the Medici. During the pontificate of Sixtus IV (Francesco della Rovere, reigned 1471–1484), the Pazzi became linked with similar anti-Medici sentiment developing in Rome. Relations between Lorenzo de' Medici and Sixtus IV, though initially friendly, degenerated as Sixtus attempted to increase his control over the Papal States by promoting his own relatives to powerful positions there. This objective was hindered by Lorenzo, who pursued his city's traditional policy of maintaining Florentine influence in the area.

The first serious conflict arose in 1473, when Sixtus undertook to procure the town of Imola for his nephew, Girolamo Riario. As the official papal bankers, the Medici were asked to contribute part of the money for this purchase, but Lorenzo, hoping to acquire Imola for Florence, refused. The money was consequently acquired from other sources, especially the Pazzi bank, which subsequently enjoyed papal favor while the Medici were punished by the loss of their position as official papal bankers and by the disappointment of their ecclesiastic ambitions. In particular, in 1474, the vacant archbishopric of Pisa was granted to Francesco Salviati, who had close relations with both the Riario and the Pazzi. Lorenzo's refusal for a full year to allow Salviati to take possession of his diocese contributed to the deterioration of his relations with the Holy See.

By 1474, the triple alliance of Naples, Florence, and Milan, formed in 1467, had foundered on growing hostility between King Ferrante of Naples and Duke Galeazzo Sforza of Milan. Lorenzo's determination to maintain his family's traditional link with the Sforza led in 1474 to both powers' abandoning Naples for an alliance with Venice. To reduce his isolation, Ferrante subsequently attempted to break up this new league and to find alternative allies. Hence his rapprochement with the pope and, after the assassination of Galeazzo Sforza late in 1476, his effort to restore good relations with Milan. The fact that Lorenzo thwarted his aims meant growing hostility toward the Medici in Naples and in Urbino, where the military commander, Federigo da Montefeltro, made himself a spokesman for both Ferrante's and papal interests.

The plot to assassinate Lorenzo and Giuliano de' Medici, hatched in circles around the Riario, thus possessed much wider support. Discussed as early as 1475, it was put into effect only in 1478, during a visit to Florence by Cardinal Raffaele Sansoni Riario. The attack was carried out during mass in the Florentine cathedral but proved unsuccessful, for, although Giuliano was killed, Lorenzo was merely wounded, and the archbishop of Pisa's effort to seize control of the Florentine government failed. The conspirators had also failed to establish contacts with other anti-Medici currents in Florence and their effort to arouse the populace with a call to liberty received no response. Rather, the Florentines turned their fury against the conspirators, most of whom were captured and summarily executed.

Subsequently, Sixtus used the Florentines' treatment of the ecclesiastics involved in the conspiracy as another reason for undertaking war against the "tyrant" Lorenzo. In this he was joined by Ferrante of Naples and their joint military captain, Federigo of Urbino. The war, however, like the conspiracy itself, served ultimately to strengthen the Medici position in Florence. Lorenzo succeeded in personally reaching an accord with Ferrante (which included the reestablishment of the Naples-Florence-Milan alliance), while internal measures taken in 1480 concentrated political power yet further in pro-Medici hands. Therefore, the final results of the conflict

were a still closer identification of the Medici with the government of Florence and, on Lorenzo's part, less aggressive policies giving greater attention to conciliating the king of Naples and the papacy.

See also **Medici, House of.**

BIBLIOGRAPHY

Capponi, Gino. *Storia della repubblica di Firenze.* 3 vols. Florence, 1876. See volume 2 for the confession of Giovanbattista da Montesecco.

Fubini, Riccardo. "La congiura dei Pazzi: radici politico-sociali e ragioni di un fallimento" and "Federigo da Montefeltro e la congiura dei Pazzi: immagine propagandistica e realtà politica," now in his *Italia quattrocentesca: Politica e diplomazia nell'età di Lorenzo il Magnifico.* Milan, 1994.

Medici, Lorenzo de'. *Lettere.* vols. 1 and 2 edited by Riccardo Fubini and vol. 3 edited by Nicolai Rubinstein. Florence, 1977.

Poliziano, Angelo. *Della congiura de' Pazzi.* Edited by Alessandro Perosa. Padua, Italy, 1958. Translated by Elizabeth Welles in *The Earthly Republic: Italian Humanists on Government and Society.* Edited by Benjamin Kohl and Ronald Witt. Philadelphia, 1978.

PAULA C. CLARKE

PEASANTRY. Before the industrial revolution, agricultural production was by far the most important economic activity in all European countries and occupied the enormous bulk of the population. Historians commonly refer to medieval and early modern Europeans who planted crops and tended animals as "peasants," and to their class as "the peasantry"—terms derived from French words meaning rural or country people. Social scientists have refined the definition of the peasantry to mean rural people who possess (even if they do not own) the means of agricultural production; are integrated into the structures of the state and surrounding society; and are partially engaged in the marketplace. When rural people produce primarily for the market rather than for subsistence, they may be called farmers, instead of peasants.

Renaissance Europe was overwhelmingly rural, with less than 5 percent of its people living in "cities" of more than twenty thousand inhabitants. The rest lived in smaller towns, or in peasant villages. There was considerable regional variation, but the peasantry probably constituted around 90 percent of the total population of Renaissance Europe. These rural people produced the surpluses that fed and clothed Europe's urban elites.

Serfdom. During the Middle Ages most European peasants were legally bound to the land as serfs, who owed numerous obligations to their lord.

Peasant Holiday. Woodblock print by Barthel Beham (1502–1540). FOTO MARBURG/ART RESOURCE, NY

The nature of serfdom varied greatly from region to region, and there were some areas where serfdom never developed. In western Europe serfdom began to decline in the 1300s, becoming virtually extinct by the end of the 1500s. But in central and eastern Europe, the institution persisted many centuries longer.

Peasant Villages. These rural communities comprised the demographic, economic, and political foundation of Renaissance society. Villages were governed by semiautonomous local assemblies who elected their own officials and drew up their own local ordinances. The outside political authorities, whether ecclesiastical, noble, or municipal, tolerated a substantial degree of village self-rule because they realized that local people needed to make certain local decisions. Typically, the village assembly met in the local church, under a large tree, or in some other public place. The elected officials often displayed remarkable political astuteness, both within the village and in dealing with external authorities. In theory, participation in the government was open to all local citizens on equal terms, but with the passage of time, village councils throughout Renaissance Europe tended to fall under the domination of wealthy local landowners or merchants.

Peasant villagers through their local assemblies and governing councils regulated the use of local resources such as forests, pastures, and arable lands, with the aim of protecting and guaranteeing equitable access to them. The local community also took charge of building and maintaining roads, wells, ovens, and other projects of common benefit. And almost everywhere, the peasant communities established some form of agrarian communitarianism. For example, villagers in many parts of Europe practiced the periodic distribution of communal lands. But in most places, community ownership coexisted with private property, the latter gradually ascendant.

The collective values and administrative structure of the village gave it a leadership role in the defense of peasant rights. Village governments were often active in the hundreds of peasant rebellions of Renaissance Europe; many of these uprisings became quite violent. However, the uprisings nearly always began as conservative rebellions aimed at defending rural society against what the peasants regarded as violations of their time-honored rights. Typically, the peasant revolts were provoked by the growing power of the nation-state, which demanded higher taxes. In the end, the political state's superior military usually crushed peasant armies. But the victorious state subsequently often introduced reforms that satisfied some of the major peasant grievances.

Peasant Types. The peasantry was by no means a homogeneous rural proletariat. On the contrary, rural society was highly stratified, with rich, middling, and poor peasants of infinite variety. Moreover, rural communities all over Europe included many "peasants" who practiced trades and crafts in addition to their agro-pastoral activities. Village censuses therefore included shopkeepers, artisans, traders, carters (those who transported goods), and others who catered to local and outside customers. Furthermore, the boundaries between rural and urban society were often quite hazy. All towns and cities had residents who went out to work in the surrounding fields and pastures, and who therefore could be called "peasants" although they were citizens of large urban communities. And there was considerable social, economic, and administrative interaction between villages and cities, making it all the more difficult to distinguish between "rural" and "urban."

During the fifteenth and sixteenth centuries, many peasants abandoned the traditional quasi-subsistence lifestyle and dedicated themselves largely to producing cash crops for the emerging market economy. A minority of these peasants became wealthy, often buying up the lands of their neighbors. Others moved into mercantile or other entrepreneurial activities, leading to increasing differences between members of the rural community. When the rich peasants or other powerful local parties gained control of the local government, they often usurped the village commons, undermining the old village communities. Royal governments further weakened the villages by finding pretexts to seize and sell communal lands.

Peasant Mobility. There is an enduring myth that preindustrial peasant villages were stagnant, unchanging, immobile places. But this myth has been repeatedly disproven by historical research. Although peasants valued stability and self-sufficiency, in reality peasant society was economically and demographically dynamic, featuring regular exchanges with the outside world. Peasants were highly mobile, often migrating to other villages, other regions, or to towns and cities to take advantage of economic opportunities or to seek marriage partners. Those most likely to migrate were the landless and the young. Throughout Europe, a substantial proportion of peasant boys and girls went through a period of domestic service as a phase in their lives before settling down as adults. These adolescent "life-cycle servants" usually found jobs with families in neighboring villages, but sometimes they ended up in regions far from their birthplace. Adult peasants frequently became seasonal migrants, working in harvests of far-flung parts of their own (or even a foreign) country. Other peasants during slack periods of the agricultural calendar became muleteers or carters, occupations that often took them to distant locations and sometimes enabled them to discover opportunities for advantageous permanent moves.

The peasantry of Renaissance Europe was a complex group defying easy generalizations. But most peasants were free to move (and often did), and many became quite wealthy by exploiting market opportunities. Peasant villages were not isolated communities but were well-integrated into larger social and economic frameworks.

[Pieter Brueghel the Elder's *Harvesters,* an artist's view of peasants in the fields, appears in the color plates in this volume.]

See also **Agriculture; Popular Revolts; Protest.**

BIBLIOGRAPHY

Le Roy Ladurie, Emmanuel. *The French Peasantry, 1450–1660.* Translated by Alan Sheridan. Aldershot, U.K., 1987. Includes translation of part of *Histoire économique et sociale de la France* (1970–1982).

Rösener, Werner. *The Peasantry of Europe.* Translated by Thomas M. Barker. Oxford and Cambridge, Mass., 1994.

Vassberg, David E. *The Village and the Outside World in Golden Age Castile: Mobility and Migration in Everyday Rural Life.* Cambridge, U.K., and New York, 1996.

Watts, Sheldon J. *A Social History of Western Europe, 1450–1720: Tensions and Solidarities among Rural People.* London and Dover, N.H., 1984.

DAVID E. VASSBERG

PEASANTS' WAR. The greatest popular uprising of early modern German history, the Peasants' War involved most of south Germany and parts of central Germany. Its high point was from January to June 1525, but, including preliminaries and aftershocks, it extended from May 1524 to July 1526. Traditionally the movement is said to have had 300,000 participants and to have claimed 100,000 lives. Its major published manifestos, the Twelve Articles and the Federal Ordinance, originated in Upper Swabia in March 1525; the Federal Ordinance, however, was also significant in the Upper Rhine regions, while the Twelve Articles served as a model for the uprising in all affected territories except for northern Switzerland and the Alpine territories of Tirol and Salzburg. The rebels were not only rural tillers of the soil and village artisans but also unprivileged townsmen and miners; hence the movement was supported by diverse social groups of commoners, and its characterization as a "peasants' war" was a disparaging label applied by its adversaries.

Until April 1525 the rebellion was not primarily of a military character. It involved large assemblages and marches of commoners in support of an armed boycott of clerical and lay lords. In accord with the traditions of the medieval feud the subjects sought to force justice from their overlords.

The military phase of the Peasants' War, from April 1525 onward, saw the suppression of the uprising by mercenary armies, above all in the service of the Swabian League, but also by the princes of Lorraine, the Palatinate, Hesse, and Saxony. In this

Peasants in Arms. Sixteenth-century German engraving.
COLLECTION, VISUAL CONNECTION

gional and supraregional markets. Since c. 1450, Western Europe had been experiencing a demographic and economic upswing that accentuated inequalities of wealth and status among its agricultural population. Landholding peasants controlled village self-government, dominating cottagers, landless laborers, and servants, but their incomes were skimmed by aristocratic landlords, governmental officials, and churchmen to whom they owed rents, taxes, and tithes. The complaints of the peasant landholders appeared in the many regional lists of grievances presented during the 1525 uprising. Deeply resented were the efforts of landlords and rulers to debase the peasantry from free to servile status, although these efforts were applied only to some regions.

Far more common were complaints about attempts of the lords to exclude the peasantry from using the products of forests, waterways, and meadows, including game and fish. These traditional sources of supplemental income were being wrested from the peasantry. Other objects of protest were labor services owed to landlords and rulers, rents that seemed excessive, and arbitrary penalties that departed from customary law. Very small market towns dominated by agricultural occupations had common interests with the villages, while middling craft towns (for example, Freiburg im Breisgau) had a long-developed tradition of hostility toward their rural hinterlands. In 1525 the market towns tended to side with the rebels, and the craft towns tended to oppose them.

Political Goals. Modern scholarship has shown that the rebels of 1525 had no ambition to reform the constitution of the Empire. Their goals were regional ones informed by sixteenth-century political realities. The Federal Ordinance, in its various versions in Upper Swabia and the Black Forest, envisaged self-governing confederations of local communes ("towns, villages, and rural regions") patterned on the neighboring Swiss Confederation, which had grown in the past by absorbing smaller confederations on its borders (for example, Graubünden in 1500). One well-known pamphlet in support of the peasantry even alluded to becoming part of an expanding Switzerland. In larger territorial principalities like Württemberg or Tirol the rebels aspired to have a peasant estate join nobles and townsmen in already established representative assemblies. It was unusual but by no means unheard of in early modern Europe for peasants to participate in representative assemblies. The relative moderation

phase the rebels were successful in confiscating the stores of monasteries and in dismantling aristocratic fortresses and castles, often in an organized and orderly manner, sometimes amid carnival rowdiness. Some towns, such as Freiburg im Breisgau and Heilbronn, were forcibly occupied, but more common was the extortion of cannon from towns that the rebel bands did not enter. Violence against persons, like the execution of captured nobles at Weinsberg on 16 April 1525, was relatively rare. The battles were usually one-sided slaughters of the commoners, like those in May 1525 at Frankenhausen, Thuringia, where 6,000 were slain, and Saverne, Alsace, where 18,000 perished.

Contrary to earlier historiography, the suppression of the Peasants' War did not establish princely absolutism in Germany. A dualist government of princes and estates continued throughout the sixteenth century with some participation by peasant estates. Regionally limited peasant uprisings continued in sixteenth- and seventeenth-century Germany.

Socioeconomic Context. The Peasants' War occurred in the most urbanized region of the Holy Roman Empire. Although its farms produced the bulk of their own necessities, they were significantly integrated into the monetary economy of re-of rebel objectives in 1525 makes it misleading to call the Peasants' War a political revolution.

The Peasants' War and the Reformation.

The fact that in the Black Forest, Upper Swabia, and Alsace the rising began with attacks on monastic landlords points to economic anticlericalism as the factor that connected the Reformation with the Peasants' War. Widespread spontaneous resistance to tithes occurred in 1523 and 1524. Rejection of the ecclesiastical tithe was an important part of the message of the Memmingen pastor, Christoph Schappeler, who annotated the Twelve Articles with scriptural citations. Reformation pamphlets attacked the tithe and demanded that parishes have the right to choose and dismiss pastors and to insist that they preach the "unadulterated" gospel.

These same ideas were subsumed unchanged into the programs of the rebels. The prologue to the Twelve Articles made the same point that Luther had made earlier, that any disorder occasioned by the preaching of the gospel should properly be blamed on those who resisted the gospel, not on those who preached it. The "divine law" of the scriptures was the rebels' norm for the reorganization of human society; the Federal Ordinance appealed to fourteen leading Reformation theologians to determine the content of this law. The list contained such theological notables as Martin Luther, Philipp Melanchthon, Ulrich Zwingli, Andreas Osiander, and Johannes Brenz. Thomas Müntzer was the only prominent Reformation theologian to side with the rebels, while Luther denounced them with particular vehemence. Nevertheless, despite Luther's statement that the rebels had a mistaken, "fleshly" interpretation of the gospel, the German princes, both Romanist and Lutheran, connected the Peasants' War to the religiously inspired upheaval that had been sweeping over Germany since 1520. Opponents of Luther had characterized his appeal to princes and nobility against clerical authority as anarchic, and predicted that it would imperil temporal authority as well. The apparent fulfillment of these predictions in the 1525 uprising led German princes of all parties to assume firm control of the practice of religion. As a direct result of the Peasants' War the Reformation lost the undisciplined spontaneity that it had enjoyed in the years 1520–1525.

See also **Peasantry**; **Protest**.

BIBLIOGRAPHY

Primary Work

Scott, Tom, and R. W. Scribner, eds. and trans. *The German Peasants' War: A History in Documents*. Atlantic Highlands, N.J., 1991. The best documentary collection in English, containing a long introduction that is the best narrative account in English.

Secondary Works

Blickle, Peter. *The Revolution of 1525: The German Peasants' War from a New Perspective*. Translated by Thomas A. Brady Jr. and H. C. Erik Midelfort. Baltimore, 1981. A multicausal but unified presentation that connects the Peasants' War and the Reformation.

Scott, Tom. *Freiburg and the Breisgau: Town-Country Relations in the Age of Reformation and Peasants' War*. Oxford, 1986. Views the structural hostilities between town and country as the Achilles' heel of the peasant rebellion.

Scribner, R. W., and Gerhard Benecke, eds. *The German Peasant War 1525: New Viewpoints*. London, 1979. A representative collection of previously published interpretive essays.

Stayer, James M. *The German Peasants' War and Anabaptist Community of Goods*. Montreal, 1991. Argues for a connection between the Peasants' War and later religious nonconformity in the German Reformation.

JAMES M. STAYER

PÉREZ, ANTONIO

PÉREZ, ANTONIO (1540–1611), Spanish statesman and aphorist. Pérez was raised as the illegitimate son of Gonzalo Pérez, a priest and royal secretary; some contemporaries believed that his true father was Ruy Gómez de Silva, the favorite of Philip II. Pérez enjoyed patronage from both men, and after a thorough education culminating at Padua and Salamanca, he became royal secretary for Italian affairs in 1566. A masterful bureaucrat and ingratiating personality, Pérez became Philip II's chief aide in the 1570s. He traded upon his influence to maintain a lavish style of life and was embroiled in several murky intrigues.

Pérez's most notorious intrigue involved the murder of Juan de Escobedo, secretary to Don John of Austria while the latter governed the Spanish Netherlands in 1576–1578. Fearing exposure of his double-dealing with Don John (Philip's half brother), Pérez somehow secured the king's approval for the assassination, which was carried out in Madrid in 1578.

Although the king had Pérez arrested in 1579, no serious proceedings were begun until 1585. Even then, the inquiry moved slowly; not until 1590 was Pérez's full confession extracted under torture. Fearing a death sentence, Pérez escaped from prison and fled into the kingdom of Aragon, where he claimed asylum. The king's attempts to use the Inquisition to recapture the fugitive provoked serious unrest in Aragon; royal authority was restored by Castilian armed force.

Meanwhile, Pérez escaped to France in late 1591, fleeing to the court of Catherine of Navarre in Pau.

In exile he published a series of writings damaging to Philip II, rendered credible by his intimate knowledge of the king's affairs and by state papers that remained in his possession. Pérez also published volumes of letters and aphorisms offering political wisdom reminiscent of Tacitus. Pérez's attempts to negotiate a return to Spain after the death of Philip II failed, and the exile died in Paris.

BIBLIOGRAPHY

Primary Work

Pérez, Antonio. *Relaciones y cartas.* 2 vols. Edited by Alfredo Alvar Ezquerra. Madrid, 1986. Good modern edition of the principal works, with a useful biographical introduction.

Secondary Work

Marañón, Gregorio. *Antonio Pérez (el hombre, el drama, la época).* 8th ed. 2 vols. Madrid, 1969. The standard biography. There is an English abridgement: *Antonio Pérez, "Spanish Traitor."* Translated by C. D. Ley. New York, 1955.

JAMES M. BOYDEN

PERSPECTIVE. *See* Optics; Space and Perspective.

PERU, CONQUEST OF. *See* Americas; Pizarro, Francisco.

PERUGIA.

In the middle of the fourteenth century, Perugia was the preeminent city-state in the central Italian region of Umbria. With approximately 28,500 inhabitants in the city and 47,900 in its surrounding territory, Perugia had reached the height of its premodern demographic expansion. Its location on the trade route between Ancona, Florence, and Pisa and its wool and leather production had formed the economic basis for the triumph in 1303 of a *popolo* (popular) party, the exclusion of the feudal nobles and their allies from political power, and the establishment of a guild republic. The university was enjoying its golden age with prominent faculty such as the legist Bartolo da Sassaferrato (1314–1357).

By 1360, however, the city suffered from repeated disasters of plague and famine and had entered a period of demographic decline, political upheaval, and gradual erosion of its independence. Perugia had been under the overlordship of the pope since 1198 but actually remained fiercely independent until 1371, when the papacy militarily defeated the Perugians and imposed the brief lordship of a papal legate. Although the guild structure and communal councils remained intact, the trend for the next century would be an ever-increasing aristocratization of politics and society, punctuated by interludes of

lordship under Biordo Michelotti (1393–1398), Giangaleazzo Visconti, duke of Milan (1400–1403), Ladislao, king of Naples (1408–1414), and Braccio Fortebraccio (1416–1424).

Fortebraccio's lordship marked the triumph of the nobility and their dominance over guilds and public offices. Moreover, in 1424 the papacy transformed its nominal overlordship into a dyarchy of shared government consisting of papal representatives and communal councils. The Baglioni, the most prominent of the noble families, tried several times to establish themselves as lords of the city between 1488 and 1540. Baglioni attempts to limit their rivals' participation in public office led to increasing papal intervention in Perugian affairs, and after the Salt War in 1540 papal control of Perugia became absolute. The collapse of political independence paralleled a deterioration of artisan industries, especially wool and leather. Although Perugia's population recovered significantly during the fifteenth century, the city suffered heavy losses in the plagues of the 1520s and had only 12,000 inhabitants in 1529. By 1551, however, the population had recovered to about 19,900.

Perugia. The griffin, symbol of the city, suckles two native sons, the condottieri Braccio da Montone and Niccolò Piccinino.

Despite these catastrophes, Perugia retained into the sixteenth century the cultural vitality it had achieved in the fifteenth century, when Agostino di Duccio had sculpted the facade of the San Bernardino Oratory (1457–1461), and when, for the first time in its history, Perugia produced local artists whose reputations extended beyond Umbria, the most celebrated of whom was Pietro Vannucci, known as Perugino (c. 1445–1523). In the sixteenth century Galeazzo Alessi brought mannerist urban planning to Perugia, and many new churches and palaces were built. Still culturally vibrant but politically and economically transformed, Perugia had declined by the end of the century from its role as capital city of Umbria to that of obscure provincial center within the papal state.

BIBLIOGRAPHY

Primary Work

Matarazzo, Francesco. *Chronicles of the City of Perugia, 1492–1503*. Translated by E. S. Morgan. Reprint, New York, 1969. Translation of *Cronaca della città di Perugia dal 1492 al 1503* (1488–1506).

Secondary Works

Black, C. F. "The Baglioni as Tyrants of Perugia (1488–1540)." *English Historical Review* 85 (1970): 245–281.

Blanshei, Sarah Rubin. "Population, Wealth, and Patronage in Medieval and Renaissance Perugia." *Journal of Interdisciplinary History* 9 (1979): 597–619.

Grohmann, Alberto. *Città e territorio tra medioevo ed età moderna*. 2 Vols. Perugia, Italy, 1981.

Heywood, William. *A History of Perugia*. New York and London, 1910.

SARAH RUBIN BLANSHEI

PERUGINO (Pietro Vannucci; c. 1450–1523), Umbrian painter and draftsman. Perugino is one of the supreme exponents of Renaissance painting and drawing in Perugia, a somewhat conservative school that came into its own by the mid-fifteenth century. Perugino's considerable, and relatively well-documented, work is lyrical in nature, eliciting a response of peaceful contemplativeness. His art is distinguished by gentle, sweet-faced figures gracefully posed and schematically deployed in a frieze-like manner, often before a far-extending landscape dotted with delicately rendered trees and rolling hills. Perugino worked almost exclusively in oil, the first painter to do so. His drawings are among the finest of the early Renaissance, exhibiting a freshness of realistic observation suggestive of Raphael.

Although today renowned above all as the probable teacher of Raphael (1483–1520), he was much praised by contemporaries and enjoyed considerable

Perugino. *Self-Portrait.* Formerly thought to be a portrait of Andrea del Verrocchio by Lorenzo di Credi. GALLERIA DEGLI UFFIZI, FLORENCE/ALINARI/ART RESOURCE

success. There persists, nonetheless, a tendency, possibly earliest evinced in Giorgio Vasari's *Le vite de' più eccelenti architetti, pittori, et sculteri italiani* (1550, 1568; trans. *Lives of the Artists*), to portray Perugino as victim of his popularity, as an artist without bold or innovative instinct, and as drawing upon, ever more flagrantly during the course of his long career, an established (and lucrative) body of figural and compositional formulae in his oversight of large workshops in Perugia and Florence.

Origins and Early Career. While born almost certainly in Città della Pieve, a town long controlled by Perugia, he is known as "the one from Perugia" (Il Perugino). Reconstruction of his training and first activity is difficult, and is based chiefly on Vasari's assertions that he was taught by an obscure Peruginan master before arriving in Florence (c. 1470?) to work in the shop of Andrea del Verrocchio, this position putatively coming before or after yet further apprenticeship to Piero della Francesca. A documented foundation of his first Florentine years records Perugino's membership, in 1472, in the

Perugino. **Triptych**. *The Virgin and Child with an Angel, the Archangel Michael, and the Archangel Raphael with Tobias.* Oil, with some tempera, on poplar; late 1490s; side panels 126 × 58 cm (49.5 × 23 in.); center panel 127 × 64 cm (50 × 23 in.). NATIONAL GALLERY, LONDON/ANDERSON/ALINARI/ART RESOURCE

Company of Saint Luke, a religious confraternity composed mainly of painters.

The visual evidence afforded by the early works points unquestionably to an affinity with Verrocchio and Piero. The early move from Perugia to Florence, and very soon back to Perugia (1472), establishes a pattern followed through much of his career of work alternating in the two cities, his talent being highly valued in both. Perugino's style has, inevitably, been described as a compound of Umbrian spaciousness and Florentine perspectival and figural structure.

The first attributed works (dating from the early to mid-1470s) exhibit a density of detail, coloristic brilliance, and concentrated groupings of foreground figures (note, for example, *Adoration of the Magi,* Galleria Nazionale dell'Umbria, Perugia, 1475). His art quickly moved toward a cohesiveness, an all-encompassing harmony of effect and an openness of space.

Major Works. Within Perugino's still relatively early production, these last traits are most clearly evidenced in the work for which he is best known, *Christ Giving the Keys to Saint Peter* (Rome, Sistine Chapel; c. 1480–1482; see the color plates in volume 5). The iconographic cornerstone of the imposing ensemble of grand murals executed for Pope Sixtus IV in the newly constructed papal chapel (Luca Signorelli and Sandro Botticelli, among other distinguished painters, also contributed to this undertaking probably overseen by Perugino himself), the fresco reveals Perugino's particular consideration of space and bespeaks, more broadly, an extraordinary preeminence for one so newly established as an independent master. Thus was launched a period, some two-and-a-half decades in duration, that saw Perugino become one of the most sought-after (and mobile) artists in central and northern Italy.

The magnitude of Perugino's achievement is suggested by a listing of several high points of a career as artist-on-the-go during this time: work in Florence throughout the 1480s and 1490s, for Lorenzo de' Medici, among others; continued papal patronage in

Rome (as an instance, in 1492 he was among those who prepared the decoration for the coronation of Alexander VI) and first employment by Cardinal Giuliano della Rovere (1491), soon to be Pope Julius II; a contract for a mural, never actually undertaken, in the Doge's Palace, Venice (1494); pursuit of Perugino, through the last years of the century, by Duke Ludovico Sforza of Milan and Isabella d'Este of Mantua, two of the commanding patrons of the day; and engagement of the painter by Orvieto and Perugia, to mention but two other cities where he was active.

Of the many works that direct attention to these decades following the Sistine Chapel, three may be singled out: *Portrait of Francesco delle Opere* (Florence, Uffizi; 1494), *Lamentation over the Dead Christ* (Florence, Palazzo Pitti; 1495), and the frescoes in the Audience Chamber of the Guild of the Exchange in Perugia (Sala dell' Udienza del Collegio del Cambio, 1496–1500).

The perfect balance achieved between the contours of the figure of Francesco delle Opere and the background is one reason the portrait is recognized as a significant early Renaissance example of the genre. Interest in Netherlandish art is disclosed in the composition and technique of the painting.

The *Lamentation* exemplifies the restrained emotionalism of Perugino, a control expressed through the tentative manner in which the pious, even angelic, figures interact, and, too, through the structural geometry of the composition.

In collaboration with a humanist scholar, Perugino created one of the most ambitious concordances of pagan and Christian thought during the early Renaissance in the Cambio. Even Vasari, Perugino's severest critic, was impressed by the murals. Clearly Perugino was able to make the transition from the hallmark refined lyricism of the Madonna altarpieces to a work of notable intellectual range.

While the last decades of Perugino's life began with the promise of continued success—the completion of the *Combat between Love and Chastity* (Paris, Louvre; 1505) for Isabella d'Este, and the painting of a ceiling in the Vatican apartments of Pope Julius II (1508)—this promise went unfulfilled. An epoch of nearly unqualified triumph had come to an end. The *Combat between Love and Chastity* displeased Isabella, and Julius's Vatican project, at least that brief phase of which Perugino was a part, abruptly concluded with Raphael's assumption of work for the pope.

Influence. His pupil and assistant, Raphael, eclipsed the master in the Vatican, and although Perugino remained active until his death (in 1523), he was no longer in wide demand. His last labors were, for the most part, confined to Perugia, and his work became increasingly formulaic. Yet, toward the end of his life, Perugino began to employ a range of complementary pastel colors, and his figures became utterly weightless in aspect, tendencies that influenced a new generation of so-called mannerist painters.

Perugino's impact, however, is most decisively felt in Raphael's early assimilation of his style. And if Perugino himself cannot be considered a principal figure of the high Renaissance, through Raphael, in chief measure, his art became a springboard for that idealizing manner marked by a controlling geometry, a refinement of expression, and an expansiveness of space—foundations of Perugino's own vast output.

BIBLIOGRAPHY

Becherer, Joseph A., ed. *Pietro Perugino: Master of the Italian Renaissance.* Exhibition catalog, Grand Rapids Art Museum. New York and Grand Rapids, Mich., 1997.

Bombe, Walter. *Geschichte der Perugeiner Malerei bis zu Perugino und Pinturicchio.* Berlin, 1912.

Ferino Pagden, Sylvia, ed. *Disegni umbri del Rinascimento da Perugino a Raffaello.* Exhibition catalog, Uffizi. Florence, 1982.

Scarpellini, Pietro. *Perugino.* Milan, 1984.

JONATHAN B. RIESS

PERUZZI, BALDASSARE (1481–1536), Italian painter and architect. Peruzzi was baptized on 15 January, the son of the weaver Giovanni di Salvatore Peruzzi from Volterra in Ancaiano at Siena. It is said that he was apprenticed to a goldsmith and was a student of Francesco di Giorgio.

About 1505 to 1511 he built the Farnese Palace in Rome. It follows an antique type of wall system similar to that of the Cancelleria, also in Rome. So far the first decoration of the Farnesina and some works for Julius II (1443–1513; pope, 1503–1513) are the earliest certain evidence of his work as a painter. In the paintings he did from 1507 to 1515, he combines Francesco di Giorgio's figurative style with a detailed knowledge of Luca Signorelli (1441–1523) and of mythological sarcophagi. But Peruzzi emerged again as an architect, taking Donato Bramante (1444–1514) as a model, only after Count Alberto Pio commissioned him (1514 to 1516) to construct the new cathedral, the facade of the old cathedral, and the nave of San Niccolò in Carpi.

In Rome Peruzzi was still primarily active as a figurative designer until 1520, from early on leaving parts of the material realization to others. This was particularly true for the frescos of the Sala delle Prospettive of the Farnesina (1518–1519), of the Cancelleria (1519–1520), the Villa Stati (1519–1520), or for the Casina Vagnuzzi (c. 1521). With the figurative style and the decorative system of these frescos, he follows the tradition of Raphael's loggias and the Sala dei Palafrenieri. At the same time Peruzzi also proves his ever more sovereign knowledge of antique prototypes such as the Domus Aurea (Nero's Golden House). In the Sala delle Prospettive of the Farnesina, he combines painting, feigned architecture, and feigned sculpture to create the illusion of a *Gesamtkunstwerk* (total work of art). In 1519 he began constructing a palace of monumental simplicity in Bomarzo for Giovanni Corrado Orsini.

But his breakthrough as the leading architect comes with his nomination to be second architect of St. Peter's in the summer of 1520. In his plan, he opted for a central construction with Raphael's circular passages. From 1520 to 1524 he constructed the Tribuna (later changed) for the confraternity of San Rocco in Rome, where he was a member from 1508 until his death and in which he kept several honorary posts. After Leo's death in 1521 he followed a call to the stonemasons' lodge of San Petronio in Bologna in 1522. There he produced designs for the completion of the choir as well as the facade, thereby subordinating gothic vocabulary to Bramante's principles.

With his cartoon *Adoration of the Magi* (London, British Museum) he made an even bigger impression on Bolognese art. Presumably belonging to the same period are the tables with *Apollo and the Muses,* inspired by Andrea Mantegna (1431–1506) (Palazzo Pitti, Florence), as well as the representatives of antique music (Louvre, Paris). The latter were obviously designed for a musical instrument. Back in Rome in 1523/24, in the "temple corridor" of Santa Maria della Pace, he combines the style of classical statuary of these years with the style of Giulio Romano's frescos in the Sala di Constantino. The designs for the ovals of the right vault in the garden loggia of the Villa Madama are also considered to be done about 1523, the designs for the middle cupola presumably completed by 1521.

After all the prominent sculptors had left Rome, Peruzzi also designed burial places for celebrities like Pope Adrian VI (1459–1523; pope 1522–23) and various cardinals and other figures, as well as the Madonna above the portal of Santa Maria in Porta Paradisi. About 1523 he approached Romano's style as an architect as well, most distinctively in the abstract arrangement of the Villa Trivulzi at the Salone.

Only a short time later he found his own style in the design of the triglyph corbels of the Palazzo Fusconi. In the same years before the Sack of Rome (1527) he rebuilt the Theater of Marcellus with volute windows for Savelli and executed other architectural commissions.

But his career as an architect reached its zenith when he moved to Siena after the Sack of Rome. He lived there until 1534 and worked mostly as architect of the cathedral and architect to the republic. He left behind masterly constructed buildings: the Palazzo Pollini—with its monumental facade arising from the sloped town wall—the unfinished Palazzo Francesconi, as well as his own house and the house in Via Fusari. The fortress of the Rocca Sinibalda is considered one of his most original inventions; he developed the ground plan based on the heraldic eagle of his client, Cardinal Alessandro Cesarini. His innovative designs for the cathedral choir and the rebuilding of San Domenico (1532) paved the way for the late classicist style which should culminate in the vestibule of the Palazzo Massimo (1532). There he achieved an utterly distinctive mastery, never surpassed in the Renaissance, by creating tensions between the low ground floor with its double columns and the second floor lifted by two mezzanines, as well as between the symmetrical curvature of the facade and the asymmetrical yard.

At the end of 1534, Paul III (1468–1549; pope 1534–1549) put him in a position equivalent to Sangallo's as architect of St. Peter's. The series of magnificent designs for St. Peter's culminates in the perspective drawings in the Uffizi (Florence, Uffizi U2A), where he placed an enormous atrium, also supported by groups of columns, before the central building with its Raphaelesque arcades. He also worked on the Cortile del Belvedere and designed the apartment of Cardinal von Schomberg in the Vatican as well as the corridor leading to the Torre Paolina on the Capitol (both destroyed). His stage scene for the play *Bacchides* (1531) by Plautus and his designs for the triumphal procession (1535–1536) of Charles V (1500–1558; Holy Roman Emperor 1519–1556; Charles I of Spain 1516–1556) demonstrate that even in the field of ephemera he held a leading position until the end.

Peruzzi's inexhaustible inventive power covering almost all visual media also lives on in at least six-hundred drawings, known in originals or in copies. These are considered among the most beautiful of the Renaissance and they prove him to be a sensitive master of *disegno:* He was able to use to utmost effect not only the art of antiquity but also that of the leading artists of his time. Especially with his late architectural projects he was to have a significant influence on the architects of the second third of the sixteenth century, including Sebastiano Serlio, Sangallo, Michele Sanmicheli, Michelangelo, Giacomo Barozzi da Vignola, and Andrea Palladio.

See also **Architecture; Rome.**

BIBLIOGRAPHY

Adams, Nicholas. "Baldassare Peruzzi: Architect to the Republic of Siena, 1527–1535." Ph.D. dissertation, New York University, 1977.

Frommel, Christoph L. *Baldassare Peruzzi als Maler und Zeichner.* Beiheft zum römischen Jahrbuch für Kunstgeschichte, no. 11. Vienna, 1967–1968.

Frommel, Christoph L. *Die Farnesina und Peruzzis architectonisches Frühwerk.* Berlin, 1961.

Frommel, Christoph L. *Der römische Palastbau der Hochrenaissance.* 3 vols. Tübingen, 1973.

Millon, Henry A., and Vittorio Magnago, eds. *The Renaissance from Brunelleschi to Michelangelo: The Representation of Architecture.* New York, 1997.

Stollhans, Cynthia Jeanne. "Baldassare Peruzzi and His Patrons: Religious Paintings in Rome, 1503–1527." Ph.D. dissertation, Northwestern University, 1988.

CHRISTOPH LUITPOLD FROMMEL

Translated from German by Christin Merkel

PETRARCH (1304–1374), Italian poet and scholar. Late in his life Francesco Petrarca addressed a letter to "Posterity" (the Latin title is *Ad posteros* or *Posteritati*), to those who at some future time might be curious to learn more about his life. Petrarch's intent is to speak about himself, his interests, his outlook—his personality. We are struck by the egotism evident in the letter, by the radical departure from the more humble attitude generally adopted by medieval authors, who were less likely to display themselves and their accomplishments in so self-centered and self-serving a way. Idealized, conventional portraits are, of course, common in works of medieval literature, but the authorial "I" and the empirical "I" remain distinctly separate persons. With Petrarch, however, we witness a dramatic change in the attitude toward autobiography, with this different result: we know more about this fourteenth-century author than about virtually any other person of his age because the author himself wanted us to know it. He left large collections of letters, copious annotations on his manuscripts, and other pieces of evidence that open, quite self-consciously, a window on his life, at least as he wanted it to be recorded and remembered. Thus the well-known *Letter to Posterity* perfectly represents Petrarch's desire to fashion his own identity, to create his own historical persona, and to empha-size the role that he specifically had in the events of his time. Petrarch was a master of self-promotion, and he was acutely aware of his particular place in his times and in history generally. In this regard he anticipates the emphasis on humanism and the individual that would emerge in the next centuries.

In the *Letter to Posterity* Petrarch depicts himself as modest and even-tempered. He prefers sacred literature to vernacular poetry, the greatness of antiquity to the miserable quality of his own age, the tranquil life of the country to the hectic pace of urban society. He admits that in his youth he had been overwhelmed by a powerful love but asserts that this is a thing of the past. Of his prodigious literary production in Latin and Italian he mentions only works in the former category: his epic poem *Africa,* his treatise on the solitary life—*De vita solitaria*—and his pastoral poems, the *Bucolicum carmen.* After all, it was for his Latin works that he received an invitation to Rome, to be crowned poet laureate atop the Capitoline Hill—a "triumph" that he hoped would help to restore the ancient glory of the Eternal City.

In the *Letter* he also speaks about his family and friends, his personal habits, his travels, the cities in which he resided, and the benefits—for work and mind—of his "transalpine solitude." In the last few sentences of the *Letter* Petrarch speaks of the affection he felt for Jacopo da Carrara the Younger, ruler of Padua. While the happiness he experienced in Padua made him seriously consider residing in that city permanently, he was foiled in his plans by Jacopo's untimely death in December 1350. "I could stay no longer [in Padua], and I returned to France, not so much from a desire to see again what I had already seen a thousand times as, like a sick man, to be rid of distress by shifting position." This last sentence perfectly comprehends the carefully constructed persona of Petrarch the restless traveler and seeker, hunting down old manuscripts and haunting ancient sites in the attempt to recapture something of their past glory. We are made to see, too, the drama of his own internal conflict as one caught between earthly attractions and spiritual aspirations, one who, profoundly discontented with his own age but powerless to change it, dreams of a past grandeur and of a better future time. His confessional work, *Secretum,* deals much with this same problem; and the final verse of canzone 264 in the *Canzoniere* is a direct and sympathetic translation from Ovid: "Veggio 'l meglio et al peggior m'appiglio" (I see the better, but I cling to the worse).

Early Years. Francesco Petrarca was born in Arezzo on 20 July 1304 to Pietro di Parenzo and

Petrarch. The poet in his study. Miniature (detail), mid-fourteenth century. BIBLIOTECA TRIVULZIANA, MILAN/SCALA/ ART RESOURCE

Eletta Canigiani. His father, usually called Ser Petracco, was a notary who had migrated from his hometown of Incisa in the Arno River valley to Florence. In the tumultuous early years of the fourteenth century he made some political enemies in Florence and was exiled on false charges of corruption in public office in October 1302—some nine months, coincidentally, after the expulsion of Dante Alighieri on similar grounds. Early in 1305 Petrarch and his mother moved to Incisa, where they remained for

six years. His brother Gherardo was born there in 1307. In 1311 the family moved to Pisa, where perhaps Petrarch saw Dante for the first and only time. After one year in Pisa the family settled anew at Carpentras in southern France, where Ser Petracco was associated with the papal court of Clement V in Avignon. In Carpentras Petrarch began his study of grammar and rhetoric with Convenevole da Prato and struck up a friendship with Guido Sette, a boy his own age whose family had moved to France from Genoa. In 1316, when Petrarch was twelve years old, his father decided that he should train for the law and sent him to the University of Montpellier. During this couple of years his mother died. To mark the sorrowful occasion Petrarch composed an elegiac poem in thirty-eight Latin hexameters—the earliest of his works to survive. In 1320 he went, together with his brother and Guido Sette, to Bologna, the seat of the oldest university in Europe, to continue his legal studies. Although he excelled academically, he came to realize that the legal profession was not for him. The years in Bologna were not, however, unimportant for his literary and cultural formation. He made friends with a number of other students and became familiar with the Italian lyric tradition. Upon the death of his father in April of 1326, he returned to Avignon.

Finding a Vocation. On 6 April 1327 in the Church of Saint Clare in Avignon, Petrarch first saw and fell immediately in love with the woman whom he would call Laura. This passion would fuel his poetic imagination for the rest of his life. A great number of poems contained in the evolving collection known as the *Canzoniere* speak of his love for her and what she symbolized. Her name, Laura—like that of Dante's Beatrice ("one who gives blessedness or salvation")—had significance for him, suggesting as it did the evergreen laurel tree, sacred to Apollo, and thus the laurel crown of poetic glory. Throughout the *Canzoniere* he engages in wordplay based on "Laura," using such puns as "l'aura" ("the breeze") or "aureo/a" ("golden") to reiterate her importance.

In 1330 Petrarch and his brother Gherardo found themselves rapidly running through their inheritance. Because he scorned both law and medicine as professions, Petrarch had to find other employment. Fortunately, the bishop of Lombez, Giacomo Colonna, with whom Petrarch had become friends, recommended him to his brother Cardinal Giovanni Colonna, who offered him a position as personal chaplain in his household. It was during the summer of 1330 at Giacomo Colonna's residence that Petrarch made fast friendships with two other young men: Lello di Pietro Stefano dei Tosetti from Rome (whom Petrarch nicknamed "Laelius") and Ludwig van Kempen ("Socrates") from Flanders, who served as chanter in Cardinal Colonna's chapel. These and other close friends would be very important to him throughout his life.

As a member of the cardinal's staff, Petrarch had the opportunity to travel and to meet many people. In 1333 he traveled to Paris and, from there, to Ghent, Liège, Aix-la-Chapelle, Cologne, and Lyon. It was during these travels that he began his lifelong pursuit of manuscripts containing works by classical authors. At Liège, for example, he discovered some of Cicero's orations (*Pro Archia*). In this same year, in Avignon, he became acquainted with Dionigi da Borgo San Sepolcro, a monk who introduced him to the richness of the early Christian writers, especially St. Augustine. It was Dionigi who gave Petrarch his pocket-sized copy of the *Confessions,* which he carried with him for the rest of his life. In January 1335, on the recommendation of Cardinal Colonna, Pope Benedict XII named Petrarch to a canonry in the cathedral of Lombez, an appointment that provided him with income without requiring him to be at the place.

Vaucluse, Solitude, and the Laurel Crown. Some time before that appointment, Petrarch had written a long letter in Latin verse to Pope Benedict XII in which he strongly encouraged the pontiff to return to Rome. This is the first indication we have of Petrarch's abiding belief in the preeminence of Rome as the rightful seat both of the papacy and of the Holy Roman Empire. Petrarch's first journey to Rome, as a guest of the Colonna family, began late in 1336. That visit was a determining factor in his attitude toward the classical past. In a letter to Cardinal Giovanni Colonna, dated 15 March 1337, he speaks of his first impressions of the Eternal City:

> No doubt I have accumulated a lot of matter to write about later, but at present I am so overwhelmed and stunned by the abundant marvels that I shouldn't dare to begin. . . . Rome was greater than I thought, and so are its remains. Now I wonder not that the world was ruled by this city but that the rule came so late.

In line with his enthusiasm for Rome is his patriotism for Italy in general, as expressed, for example, in canzone 128 of the *Canzoniere,* "Italia mia, benché 'l parlar sia indarno" (My Italy, although words may be little), in which he decries his country's abject, strife-torn state and calls it to duty: "vertù contra furore / prenderà l'arme; e fia 'l combatter corto, / ché

l'antiquo valore / ne l'italici cor non è ancor morto" (virtue against brute rage will take up arms; and the combat will be short, for the ancient valor in the Italian hearts is not yet dead; lines 93–96). He concludes the poem with a heartfelt plea for peace: "i' vo gridando: Pace, pace, pace" (I go about crying: "Peace, peace, peace"; line 122).

Shortly after his return to Avignon, he purchased a house in Vaucluse along the river Sorgue, and this became his resort of peace and solitude: "Transalpina solitudo mea jocundissima" (My most delightful transalpine solitary refuge). Here he could find the time to read, meditate, write, and entertain close friends. For Petrarch Vaucluse represented the Ciceronian ideal of *otium,* the leisure to pursue one's interests without having to attend to the cares of the everyday world. One of his new acquaintances in Vaucluse was Philippe de Cabassoles, the bishop of Cavaillon, to whom he would later dedicate his Latin treatise *De vita solitaria* (On the solitary life).

During this period Petrarch began a number of his works, many of which were of classical inspiration: the treatise on the lives of famous men, *De viris illustribus;* his epic poem on the deeds of Scipio Africanus, *Africa;* his collection of Italian poems, *Canzoniere* or *Rerum vulgarium fragmenta* (Fragments of vernacular matters); and *Triumphus cupidinis* (Triumph of love), the first of the *Trionfi*—allegorical poems in terza rima, based on the descriptions of ancient triumphal pageants. Petrarch would continue to revise most of these works for the rest of his life. How the *Canzoniere* evolved, for example, we may observe through extant manuscripts, some in his own hand, that disclose the successive forms of the collection that would culminate in the version contained in the Vatican Library. At Vaucluse Petrarch divided his interests between Latin and Italian works and clearly indicated his preference for the former.

On 1 September 1340 Petrarch received two invitations to be crowned poet laureate; one letter came from the University of Paris and the other from the Roman Senate. Given that Petrarch had carefully orchestrated the sequence of events that would lead to the proffering of these invitations, we recognize the coyness with which he reports his careful weighing of these offers, his asking advice from Cardinal Colonna, and his eventual decision to accept the invitation from Rome—as though there were any real choice. Petrarch was well aware of the coronation of poets in antiquity and of the more recent revivals of that tradition, as in Padua, for example, with the coronation of Albertino Mussato in 1315. He was keen to receive this signal honor, which, he thought, would ensure his fame for posterity and, just as importantly, reestablish Rome as the locus for culture in the world. To be satisfied as to his worthiness for this honor, he voluntarily underwent a rigorous examination by his sponsor, Robert of Anjou, king of Naples. On 8 April 1341, in the Palace of the Senate on the Capitoline, Petrarch was crowned poet laureate and delivered an oration, in which he set forth the task and rewards of the poet as well as the nature of the poetic profession. The *Oration* is a marvelous combination of medieval homily and classical rhetoric. Petrarch begins by citing a passage from Virgil's *Georgics;* interrupts it with a recitation of the *Ave Maria,* and then immediately returns to the Virgilian passage. The rest of the oration features numerous citations from Virgil, Ovid, Cicero, Horace, and other classical authors.

The fame that Petrarch had achieved in this single event was immeasurable; indeed, he was now a celebrity, in demand as the honored guest in cities throughout Europe and cheered wherever he went. This was, in many ways, the beginning of what we might call the cult of personality that Petrarch cultivated and shaped for himself. After Rome, Petrarch spent time in Parma as a guest of the Correggio family and finished a draft of *Africa.* Upon his return to Provence he began his study of Greek with the Calabrian monk Barlaam, but his knowledge remained at a very elementary level.

1343: Crisis and Beyond.
The year 1343 was a momentous one for Petrarch. He met Cola di Rienzo, who would later become the Roman tribune of the people, at the papal court in Avignon. In January 1343, Robert of Anjou, his royal sponsor, died. Petrarch's brother Gherardo became a Carthusian monk, causing him to reexamine his own life and goals. In 1343 his illegitimate daughter, Francesca, was born. Out of these troubles arose his soul-searching imaginary dialogue with St. Augustine, *Secretum,* as well as his seven penitential psalms and his treatise on the cardinal virtues, *Rerum memorandarum libri* (Books of memorable things). In terms of its form and subject matter, *Secretum* is based on classical and early Christian models, especially St. Augustine's *Confessions.* But whereas the saint achieves a relative peace, Petrarch is constantly besieged by the unresolved conflict between spiritual aspirations and worldly cares. Despite the sound Christian advice imparted by the character Augustinus to Franciscus and the constant plea to meditate on death in order to prepare one's soul for the af-

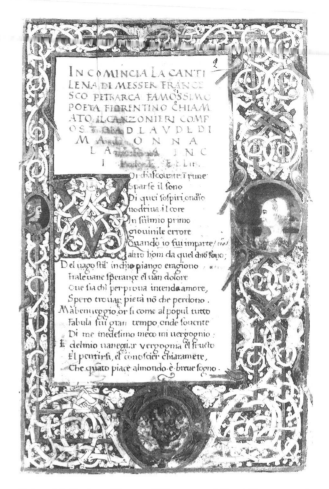

Petrarch's Praise of Laura. Title page of *Sonetti e canzoni* with portraits of Petrarch and Laura. Miniature by Petrus van Middelbourg, 1470. BIBLIOTHÈQUE INGUIBERTINE, CARPENTRAS, FRANCE/GIRAUDON/ART RESOURCE, NY

terlife, the latter cannot easily abandon his earthly pursuits, nor does he really wish to. The lack of resolution at the end of the three-day dialogue suggests not so much the lack of faith on the part of Petrarch as the very human resistance to give up one's immediate worldly pursuits in favor of less immediate eternal rewards.

Over the next several years Petrarch would travel frequently: to Naples in 1343; to Parma in 1344–1345; and to Verona in 1345, where, in the cathedral library, he discovered and copied the manuscript of Cicero's letters to Atticus, which encouraged him to begin his own collection of letters addressed to classical authors. In 1346, back in Vaucluse, he began work on his treatise on the solitary life, *De vita solitaria,* which he would dedicate to Philippe de Cabassoles. In 1347 Petrarch learned of the revolution in Rome and the elevation of Cola di Rienzo to the position of tribune and, essentially, dictator—glad news to Petrarch, who saw in it some glimmerings of the old Roman grandeur. Petrarch wrote to Cola and the Roman people, encouraging them in their battle for liberty. However, Cola's excesses and megalomania would gradually undermine his position and destroy Petrarch's faith in him. Indeed, after imprisonment in Avignon on charges of heresy, Cola returned to Rome as a senator, only to meet his death at the hands of the Roman people in 1354.

The Black Death and the Jubilee of 1350.
At the time of the Black Death in 1347–1348 Petrarch was in Verona at the behest of the pope, as well as in Parma. It was in the latter city that news of Laura's death (on 6 April 1348) came to him by means of a letter from his old friend Socrates. This date and that of his first encounter with Laura exactly twenty-one years before in 1327 would provide a sort of special chronology for the so-called "anniversary" poems in the *Canzoniere*. The grim circumstances surrounding the plague year and the deaths of several friends (such as Cardinal Colonna and Franceschino degli Albizzi) led him to write the *Triumph of Death* (*Triumphus mortis*).

As mentioned above, Petrarch's discovery of Cicero's letters in Verona in 1345 gave him the idea of collecting his own letters, and by 1350 he was actively engaged in this project, which would eventually result in the formation of the *Epistolae familiares* (Letters on familiar matters; 24 books), the *Seniles* (Letters of riper years; 17 books), the *Sine nomine* (Book without a name; 19 letters), and the *Epistolae metricae* (Metrical letters; 3 books). The year 1350 had been proclaimed a jubilee year, and Petrarch journeyed to Rome, stopping in Florence on the way. It was there that he and Giovanni Boccaccio met for the first time. Petrarch had many admirers in Florence in addition to Boccaccio: Zanobi da Strada, Francesco Nelli, and Lapo da Castiglionchio, in the library of the last of whom he found a copy of Quintilian's *Institutes* and some orations by Cicero. In the years following his Roman pilgrimage, Petrarch spent time in Parma and Padua. He also received an offer from the Florentine Republic to teach at the university there, as well as a summons from the pope for him to return to Avignon. In 1351–1352 Petrarch once again was in Vaucluse, where he continued to work on *De viris illustribus* and the *Canzoniere*. During his last months in Vaucluse, in 1353, he engaged one of the pope's doctors in an extended and heated debate over the relative values of medicine and poetry—the result being the *Invective contra medicum*. In this work Petrarch defends the liberal arts against accusations by the lower mechanical arts and praises poetry as the highest form of wisdom.

The Years in Milan.
For the next eight years, from 1353 to 1361, Petrarch lived primarily in Milan, where he was supported by the Visconti family and by the archbishop Giovanni Visconti in particular. Although many of his friends criticized him for living under an autocracy, Petrarch was very satisfied with his situation, which allowed him to do virtually anything he pleased. One of the projects he began in Milan turned into his longest work, the moral treatise in two books, *De remediis utriusque fortune* (Remedies for good and bad fortune), which treats first the perils of good fortune and, next, the opposite dangers of adverse fortune. The work is constructed as a series of dialogues between personified attributes: in book 1 Joy and Hope, the children of Prosperity, argue against Reason; in book 2 Reason's opponents are Sorrow and Fear, the offspring of Adversity. It was also during his Milanese residence that he had extensive dealings with Emperor Charles IV, whom he was encouraging to reestablish Rome as the capital of the Empire. These dealings, on behalf of the Visconti, involved a trip to Basel and Prague. In 1361 he was also sent by the Visconti to Paris, where he delivered an oration, in Latin, in the presence of King John of France and his court. The eight years that Petrarch spent in Milan represent the longest period of near continuous residence that he had at any time in his life. And they were productive years: he completed the *De remediis* and made good progress in his compilation of the *Canzoniere* and the *Familiares*.

The Years in Padua and Venice.
In the summer of 1361, after his move to Padua, Petrarch was saddened by the deaths of his illegitimate son Giovanni of the plague in Milan and of his old friends Socrates and Philippe de Vitry. His correspondence and meetings with Boccaccio were frequent, the latter often providing copies of rare manuscripts (e.g., Augustine's *Expositions on the Psalms,* Varro's *De lingua latina* [On the Latin language], and the life of Peter Damian). In May 1362 Petrarch had occasion to provide Boccaccio with good advice. Acting as the representative of the late Pietro Petroni of Siena, a fanatical monk informed Boccaccio that he did not have long to live and that he should renounce the study of poetry. Boccaccio was initially persuaded to dispose of all his books, but Petrarch successfully prevented such a disastrous decision. (It is interesting to note that, although encouraging Boccaccio to

elfercominuade tien falla Simeftra
P trignaleon collaftia doma uiua
e mille che caftaha, et aghanipe
ut Giramtar pluna, etaltra ruia
eum uomo be ffata alfin ei fine

Petrarch's Triumph of Love. Illustration from *I trionfi* showing Cupid shooting arrows from atop a triumphal chariot. BIBLIOTECA LAURENZIANA, FLORENCE/SCALA/ART RESOURCE

continue with his studies, Petrarch also made sure that his friend was aware of his keen interest in buying his collection of books, should he choose not to follow his advice.) Through his assiduous collecting habits, Petrarch had amassed what was then perhaps the largest private library in Europe. He reached a formal agreement with the government of Venice which would give his library to the city in exchange for a suitable house there and a guarantee besides that his books would not be dispersed. During his residence in Venice he received visits from numerous friends, including Boccaccio, and had both the happiness of the births of his grandchildren (Eletta and Francesco) and the sadness of the deaths of his friends Laelius and Francesco Nelli.

In 1364 Petrarch employed Giovanni Malpaghini for the tedious task of copying the *Familiares* and the *Canzoniere*. In 1367, on the occasion of a trip to Pavia by canal barge, Petrarch had the opportunity to write a response to the accusations lodged against him a year previously by four Aristotelian philosophers (Leonardo Dandolo, Tommaso Talenti, Zac-

caria Contarini, and Guido da Bagnolo), who claimed that he was "a good man, but uneducated." This response took the form of an invective, *De sui ipsius et multorum ignorantia* (On his own ignorance and that of many others), in which he signals the passage from the outmoded ideas of scholastic philosophy to the new humanism; in particular, he locates the source of knowledge not in pseudoscientific syllogistic arguments but rather in a profound intuitive awareness of the self.

The Final Years: Padua and Arquà. In 1368 Petrarch was given some land in the community of Arquà, some ten miles to the southwest of Padua, and a house was finished in 1370. Among his possessions were a lute and a painting of the Madonna by Giotto, both of which have disappeared. Failing health prevented him from undertaking some very desirable trips to Rome and Avignon. Among his last works are the translation into Latin of Boccaccio's story of Griselda (*Decameron* 10.10) and the invective against the man who maligned Italy (*Invectiva contra eum qui maledixit Italie*). Petrarch's provocation to write the latter work was an anonymous letter written by a Frenchman (Jean de Hesdin) that praised the French and spoke ill of Italy. As for the tale of patient Griselda, Petrarch was so taken by its value as a moral example that he wanted to make it available to readers who did not know Italian. Chaucer used Petrarch's translation as his model for "The Clerk's Tale." The last years of Petrarch's life were spent carrying out some diplomatic missions for Francesco da Carrara, writing letters, and working on the definitive versions of the *Canzoniere, Trionfi,* and *De viris illustribus,* as well as the compilations of his letters. In the night between 18 and 19 July 1374, Petrarch died. He was buried on 24 July in a marble tomb in the parish church at Arquà.

The Vernacular Works. Despite the virtual silence in the *Letter to Posterity* about his Italian works, Petrarch obviously considered them to be of great importance, for he continuously revised them up to the very end of his life. If we take what he says in the *Letter* to be truly indicative of how he wanted to be remembered, then it is ironic that his fame today rests primarily on his Italian poetry, which proved so influential afterward in the Renaissance, particularly in France, Spain, and England. He took enormous care in the composition of the *Canzoniere,* whose 366 poems are divided into two major sections—"In vita di madonna Laura" and "In morte di madonna Laura"—beginning with the secular sonnet "Voi ch'ascoltate in rime sparse il suono"

(You who hear the sound in scattered rhymes) and ending with the religious ode to the Virgin, "Vergine bella, che di sol vestita" (Beautiful Virgin, clothed with the sun). Amorous, political, artistic, moral, and religious themes are all treated; nevertheless, it is the obsessive attention to the presentation of his own persona that is usually most remarkable. The stylized, conventional attitudes toward love and the presentation of the pensive, introspective lover that characterize many of the poems in the *Canzoniere* became the basis for the wholesale imitations in the Renaissance. This combination of psychological and poetic conceits would come to constitute what we generally refer to as "Petrarchism." Although not the inventor of the sonnet, he did perfect it to such a degree that this fourteen-line metrical form has become known as the "Petrarchan sonnet." Also very influential on Renaissance literature, art, and pageantry were the six allegorical *Triumphs* (*Trionfi*) marking the progress of the soul in relation to Love, Chastity, Death, Fame, Time, and Eternity.

The Latin Works.   Petrarch's literary production in Latin touches on a number of major themes that highlight his pivotal place in the history of Western civilization. On the one hand, his treatises on Fortune, *De remediis utriusque fortune,* and on the monastic life, *De otio religioso* (On monastic freedom), are distinctly medieval in flavor and intent. On the other hand, there is a definite Renaissance cast to many of the Latin works. He consciously attempted to revive classical genres and patterns in the epic poem *Africa* and in the series of famous lives (*De viris illustribus*) and famous events (*Rerum memorandarum libri*). His treatise on the solitary life, *De vita solitaria,* is a well-reasoned defense of the classical ideal of studious leisure (*otium*) which he tried to imitate. He followed classical examples in his collections of letters, in his invectives, in his pastoral poems (*Bucolicum carmen*), and in his dialogue with Augustine (*Secretum*).

See also **Biography and Autobiography,** *subentry on* **Europe; Boccaccio, Giovanni; Classical Antiquity, Discovery of; Humanism,** *subentries on* **The Origins of Humanism** *and* **Italy; Petrarchism.**

BIBLIOGRAPHY

Primary Works
Collections
Petrarch. *Petrarch: A Humanist among Princes; An Anthology of Petrarch's Letters and of Selections from His Other Works.* Edited by David Thompson. New York, 1971.
Petrarch. *Prose.* Edited by Guido Martellotti et al. Milan, 1955. Contains editions and Italian translations of the following works either in their entirety or in representative selections: *Posteritati, Secretum, De viris illustribus, Rerum memorandum libri, De vita solitaria, De remediis utriusque fortune, Invectiva contra medicum, Invectiva contra quendam magni status hominem sed nullius scientie aut virtutis, De sui ipsius et multorum ignorantia, Invective contra eum qui maledixit Italie, Familiarium rerum libri,* and *Senilium rerum libri.*
Petrarch. *Rime, Trionfi, e Poesie Latine.* Edited by Ferdinand Neri et al. Milan, 1951.
The Renaissance Philosophy of Man. Edited by Ernst Cassirer, Paul Oskar Kristeller, and John Herman Randall Jr. Chicago, 1948. Contains translations of the following works by Petrarch: *A Self-portrait, The Ascent of Mont Ventoux, On His Own Ignorance and That of Many Others, A Disapproval of an Unreasonable Use of the Discipline of Dialectic, An Averroist Visits Petrarca. Petrarca's Aversion to Arab Science,* and *A Request to Take up the Fight against Averroës.*

Works in Italian
Petrarch. *Canzoniere.* 2 vols. Edited by Ugo Dotti. Rome, 1996.
Petrarch. *Canzoniere.* Edited by Gianfranco Contini. Turin, Italy, 1968.
Petrarch. *The* Canzoniere *or* Rerum vulgarium fragmenta. Translated by Mark Musa. Bloomington, Ind., 1996.
Petrarch. *Petrarch's Songbook:* Rerum vulgarium fragmenta: *A Verse Translation.* Translated by James Wyatt Cook. Binghamton, N.Y., 1995.
Petrarch. *Petrarch's Lyric Poems: The* Rime Sparse *and Other Lyrics.* Edited and translated by Robert M. Durling. Cambridge, Mass., 1976.
Petrarch. *Rime disperse.* Edited by Angelo Solerti. Florence, 1909.
Petrarch. *Rime disperse.* Edited and translated by Joseph A. Barber. New York, 1991.
Petrarch. *Trionfi, Rime estravaganti, Codice degli abbozzi.* Edited by Vinicio Pacca and Laura Paolino. Milan, 1996.
Petrarch. *Triumphs.* Translated by Ernest Hatch Wilkins. Chicago, 1962.
Petrarch. *Lord Morley's* Tryumphes of Fraunces Petrarcke: *The First English Translation of the* Trionfi. Edited by D. D. Carnicelli. Cambridge, Mass., 1971.

Works in Latin
Petrarch. *Petrarch's* Africa. Translated and annotated by Thomas G. Bergin and Alice S. Wilson. New Haven, Conn., 1977.
Petrarch. *Petrarch's* Bucolicum Carmen. Translated by Thomas G. Bergin. New Haven, Conn., 1974.
Petrarch. *Il Bucolicum carmen e i suoi commenti inediti.* Edited by Antonio Avena. 1906. Reprint, Bologna, Italy, 1969.
Petrarch. *Il De otio religioso* (On monastic freedom). Edited by Giuseppe Rotondi. Vatican City, Italy, 1958.
Petrarch. *Petrarch's Remedies for Fortune Fair and Foul.* 5 vols. Translated by Conrad H. Rawski. Bloomington, Ind., 1991. Translation of *De remediis utriusque fortune.*
Petrarch. *De viris illustribus* (Concerning famous men). Edited by Guido Martellotti. Florence, 1964.
Petrarch. *The Life of Solitude.* Translated by Jacob Zeitlin. Urbana, Ill., 1924. Translation of *De vita solitaria.*
Petrarch. *De vita solitaria, Buch 1: Kritische Textausgabe und Ideengeschichtlicher Kommentar.* Edited by K. A. E. Enenkel. Leiden, Netherlands, 1990.

Petrarch, *Rerum familiarium: libri I–VIII*. Translated by Aldo S. Bernardo. Albany, N.Y.,1975.

Petrarch. *Rerum familiarum libri, IX–XVI: Letters on Familiar Matters*. Translated by Aldo S. Bernardo. Baltimore and London, 1982.

Petrarch. *Rerum familiarum libri, XVII–XXIV: Letters on Familiar Matters*. Translated by Aldo S. Bernardo. Baltimore and London, 1985.

Petrarch. *Letters of Old Age: Rerum senilium libri, XVIII*. 2 vols. Translated by Aldo S. Bernardo, Saul Levin, and Reta A. Bernardo. Baltimore, 1992.

Petrarch. *Letters from Petrarch*. Translated by Morris Bishop. Bloomington, Ind., 1966.

Petrarch. *Sine nomine: Lettere polemiche e politiche*. Edited by Ugo Dotti. Bari, Italy, 1974.

Petrarch. *Petrarch's Book Without a Name: A Translation of the Liber sine nomine*. Translated by Norman P. Zacour. Toronto, 1973.

Petrarch. *Epistolae de rebus familiaribus et varie*. 3 vols. Edited by Giuseppe Fracassetti. Florence, 1859.

Petrarch. *Petrarch's Letters to Classical Authors*. Translated by Mario Cosenza. Chicago, 1910.

Petrarch. *Petrarch at Vaucluse: Letters in Verse and Prose*. Translated by Ernest Hatch Wilkins. Chicago, 1958.

Petrarch. *Invective contra medicum* (Invective against the doctor). Edited by Pier Giorgio Ricci. Rome, 1950.

Petrarch. *Rerum memorandarum libri* (Books of memorable things). Edited by Giuseppe Billanovich. Florence, 1945.

Petrarch. *Secretum*. Edited by Ugo Dotti. Rome, 1993.

Petrarch. *Petrarch's Secretum: With Introduction, Notes, and Critical Anthology*. Translated by Davy A. Carozza and H. James Shey. New York, 1989.

Petrarch. *Testament*. Edited and translated by Theodor E. Mommsen. Ithaca, N.Y., 1957.

Petrarch. *Salmi penitenziali* (Penitential psalms). Edited by Roberto Gigliucci. Rome, 1997.

Secondary Works

Baron, Hans. *Petrarch's* Secretum: *Its Making and Its Meaning*. Cambridge, Mass., 1985.

Bernardo, Aldo S., ed. *Francesco Petrarca, Citizen of the World*. Padua, Italy, and Albany, N.Y., 1980.

Bernardo, Aldo S. *Petrarch, Scipio and the Africa: The Birth of Humanism's Dream*. Baltimore, 1962.

Bishop, Morris. *Petrarch and His World*. Bloomington, Ind., 1963.

Foster, Kenelm. *Petrarch: Poet and Humanist*. Edinburgh, 1984.

Hainsworth, Peter. *Petrarch the Poet: An Introduction to the Rerum Vulgarium Fragmenta*. New York and London, 1988.

Jones, Frederic J. *The Structure of Petrarch's Canzoniere: A Chronological, Psychological, and Stylistic Analysis*. Cambridge, U.K., 1995.

Kennedy, William J. *Authorizing Petrarch*. Ithaca, N.Y., 1994.

Mazzotta, Giuseppe. *The Worlds of Petrarch*. Durham, N.C., 1993.

Petrarch's Triumphs: *Allegory and Spectacle*. Edited by Konrad Eisenbichler and Amilcare A. Iannucci. Ottawa, Canada, 1990.

Scaglione, Aldo, ed. *Francis Petrarch, Six Centuries Later: A Symposium*. Chapel Hill, N.C., and Chicago, 1975.

Shapiro, Marianne. *Hieroglyph of Time: The Petrarchan Sestina*. Minneapolis, Minn., 1980.

Sturm-Maddox, Sara. *Petrarch's Laurels*. University Park, Pa., 1992.

Trinkaus, Charles. *The Poet as Philosopher: Petrarch and the Formation of Renaissance Consciousness*. New Haven, Conn., 1979.

Whitfield, J. H. *Petrarch and the Renascence*. 1943. Reprint, New York, 1966.

Wilkins, Ernest Hatch. *Life of Petrarch*. Chicago, 1961.

CHRISTOPHER KLEINHENZ

PETRARCHISM. Petrarchism is the imitation or emulation of the lyric works of the Italian poet Petrarch and his disciples. Its primary source is the fourteenth-century collection of poems generally known as *Canzoniere* (Songbook), or *Rime sparse* (Scattered rhymes), which is loosely ordered to form a psychological diary. Petrarch and this work had astonishing literary importance for more than three centuries throughout Europe. In Italy poets used Petrarch as an exemplary model during the second half of the fifteenth century. His verse provided a repertory of metaphors, situations, and themes and furnished techniques, meters, and rhyme schemes to versifiers composing in Italian and Latin. For poets like Angelo Poliziano and Jacopo Sannazaro, Petrarch represented the continuity of a vernacular tradition that also included Dante and the exponents of the Dolce Stil Nuovo (Sweet New Style). Others, notably the court poets Serafino Aquilano and Cariteo, experimented with the language of *Canzoniere*, drawn to its potential for rhetorical artifice. However, it was Pietro Bembo's discussions that launched Petrarch as a paragon of good taste rather than of artifice.

Bembo's Influence. Bembo dictated the literary tastes of sixteenth-century Italians. Although humanist admiration for antiquity had fostered the creation of a literary tradition founded in the past, with Latin providing a linguistic continuum, the vernacular asserted itself ever more strongly. In his treatise *Prose della volgar lingua* (Prose of the vernacular language; 1525), Bembo synthesized the contrasting viewpoints in the heated debate surrounding the emergence of the vernacular as an appropriate language for written communication and offered a solution. The treatise urged the creation of a superior language not forged on current speech but derived from the application of classical standards to the vernacular. In his linguistic theories Bembo sought to standardize the vernacular through the imitation of perfect models. Petrarch was chosen as the ideal author for poets to emulate. This choice influenced generations of versifiers and promoted a national addiction to composing imitative verse—much of it bad—among the upper classes.

Petrarch's work perfectly absorbed the literary tradition that had influenced his poetry. In his work readers could discover the classical world, Provençal and Sicilian poets, and the Dolce Stil Nuovo. Thus, his poetry combined the present with choice elements of the cultural past. Bembo's own poetry, published in 1530 as *Rime,* was proposed as a secondary model (Bembism) for later imitators, initiating the long tradition of Petrarchan imitation in Italy. Bembo borrowed stylistically and lexically from Petrarch's *Canzoniere* and fostered the use of specific meters and genres, notably the sonnet but also the madrigal, ballad, sestina, and canzone. In being reworked, the original was altered and renewed, producing an imitation that could be unique and beautiful. Fidelity to the master was reflected in the themes and imagery of the imitators, such as the use of verbal antithesis to capture the conflictual nature of love or the conceit of a storm-tossed ship to represent psychological chaos in search of spiritual harmony. Originality lay in the personalized manipulation of such commonplaces. In the sixteenth century a hedonistic note infused such typically Petrarchan motifs as the transient nature of life.

Bembo had also implicitly acknowledged the connection between Petrarch's lyric universe and Neoplatonism in his earlier treatise on love, *Gli asolani* (The wedding feast at Asola; 1505), merging two threads that would be interwoven throughout Renaissance popular culture. In Bembo's treatise Petrarch's persona functions as a mirror of behavior for contemporary lovers, who could see themselves reflected in the psychological and emotional complexities described. In the same text a sinner could see the path of temptation rejected in favor of mournful contrition and pleas to heaven. Thus, Petrarch was used as an example on two levels: the aesthetic and the moral. Besides Petrarch the writer, there was Petrarch the archetypal man: both were to be emulated. For Renaissance readers and imitators, there was a clear association between the poet's existential condition and its literary manifestation.

The Petrarchan Model. Petrarch was infinitely more than a literary fad. His artistic world was assimilated into the core of Renaissance cultural life, concurrently mirroring it, synthesizing it, and typifying its ideals. Petrarch's personal discourse, not current usage, became the universal vocabulary for generations of poets, from the emulating Baldassare Castiglione to the inventive Michelangelo Buonarroti. However, there was an inherent risk in the propagation of one model. Imitation allowed for a secure grasp of the mechanics of prosody, but in many disciples it led to mediocrity and repetition rather than authenticity and originality. Art often gave way to parroting, psychological insight to clichés. Nevertheless, Petrarch's verse framed the nature of lyric poetry for centuries. If reworkings of the *Canzoniere's* ideal love story dominated the first half of the sixteenth century, readers in Counter-Reformation Italy were moved by its religious elements. Others found inspiration in the master's meditations on suffering, sin, and death.

The convergence of printing, broader education, and the vernacular also gave women an entrée into the literary world, where female poets were greatly influenced by both Petrarchism and Neoplatonism. Throughout Renaissance Europe women writers of quality emerged. In Italy aristocrats, merchants' wives, and courtesans found a voice by borrowing from Bembo's proposed paragon. Like all sixteenth-century versifiers, women had to confront the power of tradition, which was both written by and directed to men. The better poets developed strategies to overcome the exclusion of women authors from literary tradition without overturning the Petrarchan model that indirectly validated their work. Some, like Gaspara Stampa and Vittoria Colonna, stayed close to the model while using its language and imagery to propose feminine variants and interpretations. Other female practitioners, however, were unable to escape the masculine worldview inherent to Petrarchism and lost their sexual identity and individual voice to the dominant style.

The diffusion of Petrarchism throughout western Europe was achieved not only through the reading of Petrarch's opus but also through his Italian interpreters, such as the court poets and Giovanni Della Casa, who generated an international way of writing love poetry utilized throughout Europe in the late sixteenth century by poets such as Thomas Wyatt, Pierre de Ronsard, and Juan Boscán. Linking the Petrarchan tradition to their own cultural heritage, English, French, and Spanish poets adopted the *Canzoniere's* format to their own meters, creating highly individualized sequences of love poetry, from the *dizains* of Maurice Scève's *Délie* (1544) to the sonnets—tinged with anti-Petrarchism—of Philip Sidney's *Astrophel and Stella* (1591). Few Renaissance poets were immune to the long-reaching influence of the Petrarchan model, although a lyric backlash did develop in Italy and abroad. But well into the seventeenth century and beyond, Petrarchism continued to filter into the lyric idiom, a presence in the verse of both minor versifiers and such

such exceptional poets as Edmund Spenser and William Shakespeare.

See also **Poetics** *and biographies of figures mentioned in this entry.*

BIBLIOGRAPHY

Cabello Porras, Gregorio. *Ensayos sobre tradición clásica y petrarquismo en el siglo de oro.* Alméria, Spain, 1995.

Dubrow, Heather. *Echoes of Desire: English Petrarchism and Its Counterdiscourses.* Ithaca, N.Y., 1995.

Forster, Leonard Wilson. *The Icy Fire: Five Studies in European Petrarchism.* Cambridge, U.K., 1969.

Greene, Thomas M. *The Light in Troy: Imitation and Discovery in Renaissance Poetry.* New Haven, Conn., 1982.

Jones, Ann Rosalind. *The Currency of Eros: Women's Love Lyric in Europe, 1540–1620.* Bloomington, Ind., 1990.

Kennedy, William J. *Authorizing Petrarch.* Ithaca, N.Y., 1994.

Minta, Stephen. *Petrarch and Petrarchism: The English and French Traditions.* Manchester, U.K., and New York, 1980.

Navarrete, Ignacio Enrique. *Orphans of Petrarch: Poetry and Theory in the Spanish Renaissance.* Berkeley, Calif., 1994.

Roche, Thomas P. *Petrarch and the English Sonnet Sequences.* New York, 1989.

Waller, Marguerite R. *Petrarch's Poetics and Literary History.* Amherst, Mass., 1980.

FIORA A. BASSANESE